CASES AND MATERIALS ON
CRIMINAL PROCEDURE

Third Edition

By

Phillip E. Johnson
Professor of Law
University of California, Berkeley

AMERICAN CASEBOOK SERIES®

WEST GROUP

ST. PAUL, MINN., 2000

American Casebook Series and the WP symbol are
registered trademarks used herein under license.

COPYRIGHT © 1994 WEST PUBLISHING CO.

COPYRIGHT © 2000 By WEST GROUP
                610 Opperman Drive
                P.O. Box 64526
                St. Paul, MN 55164–0526
                1–800–328–9352

ISBN 0–314–24119–1

TEXT IS PRINTED ON 10% POST
CONSUMER RECYCLED PAPER

Preface

This book is for use in law school courses in Criminal Procedure of two, three or four semester units. It has the following distinctive features;

1. It covers the field in just over 900 pages, with no double columns. Despite the relatively limited number of pages, the coverage is broad. All the major subjects are included: search and seizure, the right to counsel, interrogation, self-incrimination, identification, plea bargaining, prosecutorial discretion, the grand jury, the preliminary hearing, pretrial motions, bail and detention, extradition, jury trial, jury selection and double jeopardy. Subjects such as retroactivity, habeas corpus, and appeals are not given separate chapters, but are explained in connection with other topics. There is also a fair amount of historical material, and comparative material dealing with practice in other countries.

2. In order to combine all this coverage with a strict page limitation that permits classroom assignments of realistic length, I have prepared "commentaries" of varying length to accompany the cases and other materials. These commentaries provide students with background material and analysis to supplement the cases and statutory materials, so that the student can come to class with many of the preliminary questions answered, permitting class discussion to focus on the most important areas of controversy or uncertainty.

3. One of the major goals of this book is to keep the students' attention focused on the forest rather than the trees. Criminal Procedure is such a detailed subject, with such an enormous amount of case law, that it is very easy to become lost in the minutiae. The best way to prevent that is to introduce students to the "big picture" at the beginning, and then to show them continually how each detailed issue relates to the major themes that were introduced at the start. For example, I begin Part One (Search and Seizure) with a detailed analysis of New Jersey v. T.L.O., a case ordinarily used only for its specific holding that there is a limited Fourth Amendment protection for public school students. The T.L.O. opinions debate nearly all of the major issues of search and seizure, and can be used to present students at the very beginning of their studies with a sense of how everything fits together. Some of the discussion may be obscure to students at first, but the point is that the introductory section sets a framework for understanding to which the students can refer again as they gain a more detailed understanding of the Fourth Amendment.

*

Summary of Contents

*

Table of Contents

The Bill of Rights

Amendment I

Congress shall make no law respecting an establishment of religion, or prohibiting the free exercise thereof; or abridging the freedom of speech, or of the press; or the right of the people peaceably to assemble, and to petition the Government for a redress of grievances.

Amendment II

A well regulated Militia, being necessary to the security of a free State, the right of the people to keep and bear Arms, shall not be infringed.

Amendment III

No Soldier shall, in time of peace be quartered in any house, without the consent of the Owner, nor in time of war, but in a manner to be prescribed by law.

Amendment IV

The right of the people to be secure in their persons, houses, papers, and effects, against unreasonable searches and seizures, shall not be violated, and no Warrants shall issue, but upon probable cause, supported by Oath or affirmation, and particularly describing the place to be searched, and the persons or things to be seized.

Amendment V

No person shall be held to answer for a capital, or otherwise infamous crime, unless on a presentment or indictment of a Grand Jury, except in cases arising in the land or naval forces, or in the Militia, when in actual service in time of War or public danger; nor shall any person be subject for the same offence to be twice put in jeopardy of life or limb; nor shall be compelled in any criminal case to be a witness against himself, nor be deprived of life, liberty, or property, without due process of law; nor shall private property be taken for public use, without just compensation.

Amendment VI

In all criminal prosecutions, the accused shall enjoy the right to a speedy and public trial, by an impartial jury of the State and district wherein the crime shall have been committed, which district shall have been previously ascertained by law, and to be informed of the nature and cause of the accusation; to be confronted with the witnesses against him; to have compulsory process for obtaining witnesses in his favor, and to have the Assistance of Counsel for his defence.

Amendment VII

In Suits at common law, where the value in controversy shall exceed twenty dollars, the right of trial by jury shall be preserved, and no fact tried by jury, shall be otherwise re-examined in any Court of the United States, than according to the rules of the common law.

Amendment VIII

Excessive bail shall not be required, nor excessive fines imposed, nor cruel and unusual punishments inflicted.

Amendment IX

The enumeration in the Constitution, of certain rights, shall not be construed to deny or disparage others retained by the people.

*   *   *

Amendment XIV

Section 1.   All persons born or naturalized in the United States, and subject to the jurisdiction thereof, are citizens of the United States and of the State wherein they reside.   No State shall make or enforce any law which shall abridge the privileges or immunities of citizens of the United States; nor shall any State deprive any person of life, liberty, or property, without due process of law; nor deny to any person within its jurisdiction the equal protection of the laws.

*   *   *

Section 5.   The Congress shall have power to enforce, by appropriate legislation, the provisions of this article.

Table of Cases

The principal cases are in bold type. Cases cited or discussed in the text are roman type. References are to pages. Cases cited in principal cases and within other quoted materials are not included.

CASES AND MATERIALS ON
CRIMINAL PROCEDURE

Third Edition

*

Part One

SEARCH AND SEIZURE

Chapter 1

AN OVERVIEW OF THE FOURTH AMENDMENT

NEW JERSEY v. T.L.O.

Supreme Court of the United States, 1985.
469 U.S. 325, 105 S.Ct. 733, 83 L.Ed.2d 720.

JUSTICE WHITE delivered the opinion of the Court.

We granted certiorari in this case to examine the appropriateness of the exclusionary rule as a remedy for searches carried out in violation of the Fourth Amendment by public school authorities. Our consideration of the proper application of the Fourth Amendment to the public schools, however, has led us to conclude that the search that gave rise to the case now before us did not violate the Fourth Amendment. Accordingly, we here address only the questions of the proper standard for assessing the legality of searches conducted by public school officials and the application of that standard to the facts of this case.

I

On March 7, 1980, a teacher at Piscataway High School in Middlesex County, N.J., discovered two girls smoking in a lavatory. One of the two girls was the respondent T.L.O., who at that time was a 14–year-old high school freshman. Because smoking in the lavatory was a violation of a school rule, the teacher took the two girls to the Principal's office, where they met with Assistant Vice Principal Theodore Choplick. In response to questioning by Mr. Choplick, T.L.O.'s companion admitted that she had violated the rule. T.L.O., however, denied that she had been smoking in the lavatory and claimed that she did not smoke at all.

Mr. Choplick asked T.L.O. to come into his private office and demanded to see her purse. Opening the purse, he found a pack of cigarettes, which he removed from the purse and held before T.L.O. as he accused her of having lied to him. As he reached into the purse for the cigarettes, Mr. Choplick also noticed a package of cigarette rolling papers. In his experience, possession of rolling papers by high school students was closely associated with the use of marihuana. Suspecting that a closer examination of the purse might yield further evidence of

2

drug use, Mr. Choplick proceeded to search the purse thoroughly. The search revealed a small amount of marihuana, a pipe, a number of empty plastic bags, a substantial quantity of money in one-dollar bills, an index card that appeared to be a list of students who owed T.L.O. money, and two letters that implicated T.L.O. in marihuana dealing.

Mr. Choplick notified T.L.O.'s mother and the police, and turned the evidence of drug dealing over to the police. At the request of the police, T.L.O.'s mother took her daughter to police headquarters, where T.L.O. confessed that she had been selling marihuana at the high school. On the basis of the confession and the evidence seized by Mr. Choplick, the State brought delinquency charges against T.L.O. in the Juvenile and Domestic Relations Court of Middlesex County.[3] Contending that Mr. Choplick's search of her purse violated the Fourth Amendment, T.L.O. moved to suppress the evidence found in her purse as well as her confession, which, she argued, was tainted by the allegedly unlawful search.

[The juvenile court held that school searches are subject to Fourth Amendment requirements but that the search in this case was reasonable because Mr. Choplick had a well-founded suspicion that T.L.O. had violated the smoking rule. Once the purse was open, evidence of drug violations was in plain view, and Mr. Choplick was entitled to conduct a thorough search to determine the nature and extent of T.L.O.'s drug-related activities. Denying the motion to suppress, the juvenile court found T.L.O. to be a delinquent and sentenced her to a year's probation.

The New Jersey Supreme Court held that the search was unreasonable because mere possession of cigarettes did not violate a school rule, because Mr. Choplick had no specific information that there were cigarettes in the purse, and because the slight evidence of drug use that he initially saw did not justify the extensive "rummaging" through T.L.O.'s papers and effects that followed.]

Although we originally granted certiorari to decide the issue of the appropriate remedy in juvenile court proceedings for unlawful school searches, our doubts regarding the wisdom of deciding that question in isolation from the broader question of what limits, if any, the Fourth Amendment places on the activities of school authorities prompted us to order reargument on that question. Having heard argument on the legality of the search of T.L.O.'s purse, we are satisfied that the search did not violate the Fourth Amendment.[4]

---

3. T.L.O. also received a 3–day suspension from school for smoking cigarettes in a nonsmoking area and a 7–day suspension for possession of marihuana. On T.L.O.'s motion, the Superior Court of New Jersey, Chancery Division, set aside the 7–day suspension on the ground that it was based on evidence seized in violation of the Fourth Amendment. The Board of Education apparently did not appeal the decision of the Chancery Division.

4. In holding that the search of T.L.O.'s purse did not violate the Fourth Amendment, we do not implicitly determine that the exclusionary rule applies to the fruits of unlawful searches conducted by school authorities. The question whether evidence should be excluded from a criminal proceeding involves two discrete inquiries: whether the evidence was seized in violation of the Fourth Amendment, and whether the exclusionary rule is the appropriate remedy for

II

In determining whether the search at issue in this case violated the Fourth Amendment, we are faced initially with the question whether that Amendment's prohibition on unreasonable searches and seizures applies to searches conducted by public school officials. We hold that it does. * * *

It may well be true that the evil toward which the Fourth Amendment was primarily directed was the resurrection of the pre-Revolutionary practice of using general warrants or "writs of assistance" to authorize searches for contraband by officers of the Crown. But this Court has never limited the Amendment's prohibition on unreasonable searches and seizures to operations conducted by the police. * * * Accordingly, we have held the Fourth Amendment applicable to the activities of civil as well as criminal authorities: building inspectors, and even firemen entering privately owned premises to battle a fire, are all subject to the restraints imposed by the Fourth Amendment. [Citations omitted.] Because the individual's interest in privacy and personal security suffers whether the government's motivation is to investigate violations of criminal laws or breaches of other statutory or regulatory standards, it would be anomalous to say that the individual and his private property are fully protected by the Fourth Amendment only when the individual is suspected of criminal behavior.

Notwithstanding the general applicability of the Fourth Amendment to the activities of civil authorities, a few courts have concluded that school officials are exempt from the dictates of the Fourth Amendment by virtue of the special nature of their authority over schoolchildren. Teachers and school administrators, it is said, act *in loco parentis* in their dealings with students: their authority is that of the parent, not the State, and is therefore not subject to the limits of the Fourth Amendment.

Such reasoning is in tension with contemporary reality and the teachings of this Court. We have held school officials subject to the commands of the First Amendment, and the Due Process Clause of the Fourteenth Amendment. If school authorities are state actors for purposes of the constitutional guarantees of freedom of expression and due process, it is difficult to understand why they should be deemed to be exercising parental rather than public authority when conducting searches of their students. More generally, the Court has recognized that the concept of parental delegation as a source of school authority is not entirely consonant with compulsory education laws. [Citations omitted.] Today's public school officials do not merely exercise authority voluntarily conferred on them by individual parents; rather, they act in furtherance of publicly mandated educational and disciplinary policies. In carrying out searches and other disciplinary functions pursuant to such

the violation. Neither question is logically antecedent to the other, for a negative answer to either question is sufficient to dispose of the case. Thus, our determination that the search at issue in this case did not violate the Fourth Amendment implies no particular resolution of the question of the applicability of the exclusionary rule.

policies, school officials act as representatives of the State, not merely as surrogates for the parents, and they cannot claim the parents' immunity from the strictures of the Fourth Amendment.

III

To hold that the Fourth Amendment applies to searches conducted by school authorities is only to begin the inquiry into the standards governing such searches. Although the underlying command of the Fourth Amendment is always that searches and seizures be reasonable, what is reasonable depends on the context within which a search takes place. The determination of the standard of reasonableness governing any specific class of searches requires balancing the need to search against the invasion which the search entails. On one side of the balance are arrayed the individual's legitimate expectations of privacy and personal security; on the other, the government's need for effective methods to deal with breaches of public order.

We have recognized that even a limited search of the person is a substantial invasion of privacy. *Terry v. Ohio*, [p. 224, infra.] We have also recognized that searches of closed items of personal luggage are intrusions on protected privacy interests, for "the Fourth Amendment provides protection to the owner of every container that conceals its contents from plain view." *United States v. Ross*, [p. 147, infra.] A search of a child's person or of a closed purse or other bag carried on her person,[5] no less than a similar search carried out on an adult, is undoubtedly a severe violation of subjective expectations of privacy.

Of course, the Fourth Amendment does not protect subjective expectations of privacy that are unreasonable or otherwise "illegitimate." To receive the protection of the Fourth Amendment, an expectation of privacy must be one that society is prepared to recognize as legitimate. The State of New Jersey has argued that because of the pervasive supervision to which children in the schools are necessarily subject, a child has virtually no legitimate expectation of privacy in articles of personal property "unnecessarily" carried into a school. This argument has two factual premises: (1) the fundamental incompatibility of expectations of privacy with the maintenance of a sound educational environment; and (2) the minimal interest of the child in bringing any items of personal property into the school. Both premises are severely flawed.

Although this Court may take notice of the difficulty of maintaining discipline in the public schools today, the situation is not so dire that students in the schools may claim no legitimate expectations of privacy. We have recently recognized that the need to maintain order in a prison is such that prisoners retain no legitimate expectations of privacy in their cells, but it goes almost without saying that "[t]he prisoner and the

---

5. We do not address the question, not presented by this case, whether a schoolchild has a legitimate expectation of privacy in lockers, desks, or other school property provided for the storage of school supplies. Nor do we express any opinion on the standards (if any) governing searches of such areas by school officials or by other public authorities acting at the request of school officials.

schoolchild stand in wholly different circumstances, separated by the harsh facts of criminal conviction and incarceration." *Ingraham v. Wright*, 430 U.S., at 669. We are not yet ready to hold that the schools and the prisons need be equated for purposes of the Fourth Amendment.

Nor does the State's suggestion that children have no legitimate need to bring personal property into the schools seem well anchored in reality. Students at a minimum must bring to school not only the supplies needed for their studies, but also keys, money, and the necessaries of personal hygiene and grooming. In addition, students may carry on their persons or in purses or wallets such nondisruptive yet highly personal items as photographs, letters, and diaries. Finally, students may have perfectly legitimate reasons to carry with them articles of property needed in connection with extracurricular or recreational activities. In short, schoolchildren may find it necessary to carry with them a variety of legitimate, noncontraband items, and there is no reason to conclude that they have necessarily waived all rights to privacy in such items merely by bringing them onto school grounds.

Against the child's interest in privacy must be set the substantial interest of teachers and administrators in maintaining discipline in the classroom and on school grounds. Maintaining order in the classroom has never been easy, but in recent years, school disorder has often taken particularly ugly forms: drug use and violent crime in the schools have become major social problems. Even in schools that have been spared the most severe disciplinary problems, the preservation of order and a proper educational environment requires close supervision of schoolchildren, as well as the enforcement of rules against conduct that would be perfectly permissible if undertaken by an adult. Events calling for discipline are frequent occurrences and sometimes require immediate, effective action. Accordingly, we have recognized that maintaining security and order in the schools requires a certain degree of flexibility in school disciplinary procedures, and we have respected the value of preserving the informality of the student-teacher relationship.

How, then, should we strike the balance between the schoolchild's legitimate expectations of privacy and the school's equally legitimate need to maintain an environment in which learning can take place? It is evident that the school setting requires some easing of the restrictions to which searches by public authorities are ordinarily subject. The warrant requirement, in particular, is unsuited to the school environment: requiring a teacher to obtain a warrant before searching a child suspected of an infraction of school rules (or of the criminal law) would unduly interfere with the maintenance of the swift and informal disciplinary procedures needed in the schools. Just as we have in other cases dispensed with the warrant requirement when the burden of obtaining a warrant is likely to frustrate the governmental purpose behind the search, we hold today that school officials need not obtain a warrant before searching a student who is under their authority.

The school setting also requires some modification of the level of suspicion of illicit activity needed to justify a search. Ordinarily, a search—even one that may permissibly be carried out without a warrant—must be based upon "probable cause" to believe that a violation of the law has occurred. However, "probable cause" is not an irreducible requirement of a valid search. * * * Thus, we have in a number of cases recognized the legality of searches and seizures based on suspicions that, although "reasonable," do not rise to the level of probable cause. [Citations omitted.] Where a careful balancing of governmental and private interests suggests that the public interest is best served by a Fourth Amendment standard of reasonableness that stops short of probable cause, we have not hesitated to adopt such a standard.

We join the majority of courts that have examined this issue in concluding that the accommodation of the privacy interests of schoolchildren with the substantial need of teachers and administrators for freedom to maintain order in the schools does not require strict adherence to the requirement that searches be based on probable cause to believe that the subject of the search has violated or is violating the law. Rather, the legality of a search of a student should depend simply on the reasonableness, under all the circumstances, of the search. Determining the reasonableness of any search involves a twofold inquiry: first, one must consider whether the action was justified at its inception; second, one must determine whether the search as actually conducted was reasonably related in scope to the circumstances which justified the interference in the first place. Under ordinary circumstances, a search of a student by a teacher or other school official[6] will be "justified at its inception" when there are reasonable grounds for suspecting that the search will turn up evidence that the student has violated or is violating either the law or the rules of the school.[7] Such a search will be permissible in its scope when the measures adopted are reasonably related to the objectives of the search and not excessively intrusive in light of the age and sex of the student and the nature of the infraction.[8]

This standard will, we trust, neither unduly burden the efforts of school authorities to maintain order in their schools nor authorize unrestrained intrusions upon the privacy of schoolchildren. By focusing

6. We here consider only searches carried out by school authorities acting alone and on their own authority. This case does not present the question of the appropriate standard for assessing the legality of searches conducted by school officials in conjunction with or at the behest of law enforcement agencies, and we express no opinion on that question.

7. We do not decide whether individualized suspicion is an essential element of the reasonableness standard we adopt for searches by school authorities. * * * Because the search of T.L.O.'s purse was based upon an individualized suspicion that she had violated school rules, we need not consider the circumstances that might justify school authorities in conducting searches unsupported by individualized suspicion.

8. Our reference to the nature of the infraction is not intended as an endorsement of Justice Stevens' suggestion that some rules regarding student conduct are by nature too "trivial" to justify a search based upon reasonable suspicion. We are unwilling to adopt a standard under which the legality of a search is dependent upon a judge's evaluation of the relative importance of various school rules.

* * *

attention on the question of reasonableness, the standard will spare teachers and school administrators the necessity of schooling themselves in the niceties of probable cause and permit them to regulate their conduct according to the dictates of reason and common sense. At the same time, the reasonableness standard should ensure that the interests of students will be invaded no more than is necessary to achieve the legitimate end of preserving order in the schools.

IV

There remains the question of the legality of the search in this case. We recognize that the "reasonable grounds" standard applied by the New Jersey Supreme Court in its consideration of this question is not substantially different from the standard that we have adopted today. Nonetheless, we believe that the New Jersey court's application of that standard to strike down the search of T.L.O.'s purse reflects a somewhat crabbed notion of reasonableness. Our review of the facts surrounding the search leads us to conclude that the search was in no sense unreasonable for Fourth Amendment purposes.[9]

The incident that gave rise to this case actually involved two separate searches, with the first—the search for cigarettes—providing the suspicion that gave rise to the second—the search for marihuana. Although it is the fruits of the second search that are at issue here, the validity of the search for marihuana must depend on the reasonableness of the initial search for cigarettes, as there would have been no reason to suspect that T.L.O. possessed marihuana had the first search not taken place. Accordingly, it is to the search for cigarettes that we first turn our attention.

The New Jersey Supreme Court pointed to two grounds for its holding that the search for cigarettes was unreasonable. First, the court observed that possession of cigarettes was not in itself illegal or a violation of school rules. Because the contents of T.L.O.'s purse would therefore have "no direct bearing on the infraction" of which she was accused (smoking in a lavatory where smoking was prohibited), there was no reason to search her purse. Second, even assuming that a search of T.L.O.'s purse might under some circumstances be reasonable in light of the accusation made against T.L.O., the New Jersey court concluded that Mr. Choplick in this particular case had no reasonable grounds to suspect that T.L.O. had cigarettes in her purse. At best, according to the court, Mr. Choplick had "a good hunch."

Both these conclusions are implausible. T.L.O. had been accused of smoking, and had denied the accusation in the strongest possible terms when she stated that she did not smoke at all. Surely it cannot be said that under these circumstances, T.L.O.'s possession of cigarettes would be irrelevant to the charges against her or to her response to those charges. T.L.O.'s possession of cigarettes, once it was discovered, would

9. Of course, New Jersey may insist on a more demanding standard under its own Constitution or statutes. In that case, its courts would not purport to be applying the Fourth Amendment when they invalidate a search.

both corroborate the report that she had been smoking and undermine the credibility of her defense to the charge of smoking. * * *

Of course, the New Jersey Supreme Court also held that Mr. Choplick had no reasonable suspicion that the purse would contain cigarettes. This conclusion is puzzling. A teacher had reported that T.L.O. was smoking in the lavatory. Certainly this report gave Mr. Choplick reason to suspect that T.L.O. was carrying cigarettes with her; and if she did have cigarettes, her purse was the obvious place in which to find them. * * * Because the hypothesis that T.L.O. was carrying cigarettes in her purse was itself not unreasonable, it is irrelevant that other hypotheses were also consistent with the teacher's accusation. Accordingly, it cannot be said that Mr. Choplick acted unreasonably when he examined T.L.O.'s purse to see if it contained cigarettes.

Our conclusion that Mr. Choplick's decision to open T.L.O.'s purse was reasonable brings us to the question of the further search for marihuana once the pack of cigarettes was located. The suspicion upon which the search for marihuana was founded was provided when Mr. Choplick observed a package of rolling papers in the purse as he removed the pack of cigarettes. Although T.L.O. does not dispute the reasonableness of Mr. Choplick's belief that the rolling papers indicated the presence of marihuana, she does contend that the scope of the search Mr. Choplick conducted exceeded permissible bounds when he seized and read certain letters that implicated T.L.O. in drug dealing. This argument, too, is unpersuasive. The discovery of the rolling papers concededly gave rise to a reasonable suspicion that T.L.O. was carrying marihuana as well as cigarettes in her purse. This suspicion justified further exploration of T.L.O.'s purse, which turned up more evidence of drug-related activities: a pipe, a number of plastic bags of the type commonly used to store marihuana, a small quantity of marihuana, and a fairly substantial amount of money. Under these circumstances, it was not unreasonable to extend the search to a separate zippered compartment of the purse; and when a search of that compartment revealed an index card containing a list of "people who owe me money" as well as two letters, the inference that T.L.O. was involved in marihuana trafficking was substantial enough to justify Mr. Choplick in examining the letters to determine whether they contained any further evidence. In short, we cannot conclude that the search for marihuana was unreasonable in any respect.

Because the search resulting in the discovery of the evidence of marihuana dealing by T.L.O. was reasonable, the New Jersey Supreme Court's decision to exclude that evidence from T.L.O.'s juvenile delinquency proceedings on Fourth Amendment grounds was erroneous. Accordingly, the judgment of the Supreme Court of New Jersey is reversed.

JUSTICE POWELL, with whom JUSTICE O'CONNOR joins, concurring.

I agree with the Court's decision, and generally with its opinion. I would place greater emphasis, however, on the special characteristics of elementary and secondary schools that make it unnecessary to afford students the same constitutional protections granted adults and juveniles in a nonschool setting.

In any realistic sense, students within the school environment have a lesser expectation of privacy than members of the population generally. They spend the school hours in close association with each other, both in the classroom and during recreation periods. The students in a particular class often know each other and their teachers quite well. Of necessity, teachers have a degree of familiarity with, and authority over, their students that is unparalleled except perhaps in the relationship between parent and child. It is simply unrealistic to think that students have the same subjective expectation of privacy as the population generally. * * *

The special relationship between teacher and student also distinguishes the setting within which school children operate. Law enforcement officers function as adversaries of criminal suspects. These officers have the responsibility to investigate criminal activity, to locate and arrest those who violate our laws, and to facilitate the charging and bringing of such persons to trial. Rarely does this type of adversarial relationship exist between school authorities and pupils. Instead, there is a commonality of interests between teachers and their pupils. The attitude of the typical teacher is one of personal responsibility for the student's welfare as well as for his education.

The primary duty of school officials and teachers, as the Court states, is the education and training of young people. A state has a compelling interest in assuring that the schools meet this responsibility. Without first establishing discipline and maintaining order, teachers cannot begin to educate their students. And apart from education, the school has the obligation to protect pupils from mistreatment by other children, and also to protect teachers themselves from violence by the few students whose conduct in recent years has prompted national concern. For me, it would be unreasonable and at odds with history to argue that the full panoply of constitutional rules applies with the same force and effect in the schoolhouse as it does in the enforcement of criminal laws.

In sum, although I join the Court's opinion and its holding, my emphasis is somewhat different.

JUSTICE BLACKMUN, concurring in the judgment.

I join the judgment of the Court and agree with much that is said in its opinion. I write separately, however, because I believe the Court omits a crucial step in its analysis of whether a school search must be based upon probable cause. The Court correctly states that we have recognized limited exceptions to the probable cause requirement "[w]here a careful balancing of governmental and private interests suggests that the public interest is best served" by a lesser standard. I believe that we have used such a balancing test, rather than strictly applying the Fourth Amendment's Warrant and Probable Cause Clause, only when we were confronted with "a special law enforcement need for greater flexibility." * * *

The Court's implication that the balancing test is the rule rather than the exception is troubling for me because it is unnecessary in this case. The elementary and secondary school setting presents a special need for flexibility justifying a departure from the balance struck by the Framers. * * * The special need for an immediate response to behavior that threatens either the safety of school children and teachers or the educational process itself justifies the Court in excepting school searches from the warrant and probable cause requirement, and in applying a standard determined by balancing the relevant interests. I agree with the standard the Court has announced, and with its application of the standard to the facts of this case. I therefore concur in its judgment.

JUSTICE BRENNAN, with whom JUSTICE MARSHALL joins, concurring in part and dissenting in part.

I fully agree with Part II of the Court's opinion. Teachers, like all other government officials, must conform their conduct to the Fourth Amendment's protections of personal privacy and personal security. As Justice Stevens points out, this principle is of particular importance when applied to schoolteachers, for children learn as much by example as by exposition. It would be incongruous and futile to charge teachers with the task of imbuing their students with an understanding of our system of constitutional democracy, while at the same time immunizing those same teachers from the need to respect constitutional protections.

I do not, however, otherwise join the Court's opinion. Today's decision sanctions school officials to conduct full-scale searches on a "reasonableness" standard whose only definite content is that it is *not* the same test as the "probable cause" standard found in the text of the Fourth Amendment. In adopting this unclear, unprecedented, and unnecessary departure from generally applicable Fourth Amendment standards, the Court carves out a broad exception to standards that this Court has developed over years of considering Fourth Amendment problems. Its decision is supported neither by precedent nor even by a fair application of the "balancing test" it proclaims in this very opinion.

I

Three basic principles underly this Court's Fourth Amendment jurisprudence. First, warrantless searches are *per se* unreasonable, subject only to a few specifically delineated and well-recognized exceptions. [Citations omitted.] Second, full-scale searches—whether conducted in accordance with the warrant requirement or pursuant to one of its exceptions—are "reasonable" in Fourth Amendment terms only on a showing of probable cause to believe that a crime has been committed and that evidence of the crime will be found in the place to be searched. [Citations omitted.] Third, categories of intrusions that are substantially less intrusive than full-scale searches or seizures may be justifiable in accordance with a balancing test even absent a warrant or probable cause, provided that the balancing test used gives sufficient weight to the privacy interests that will be infringed. [Citations omitted.]

Vice Principal Choplick's thorough excavation of T.L.O.'s purse was undoubtedly a serious intrusion on her privacy. Unlike the search in *Terry v. Ohio*, [see p. 224], the search at issue here encompassed a detailed and minute examination of respondent's pocketbook, in which the contents of private papers and letters were thoroughly scrutinized. Wisely, neither petitioner nor the Court today attempt to justify the search of T.L.O.'s pocketbook as a minimally intrusive search in the *Terry* line. To be faithful to the Court's settled doctrine, the inquiry therefore must focus on the warrant and probable-cause requirements.

A

I agree that schoolteachers or principals, when not acting as agents of law enforcement authorities, generally may conduct a search of their students' belongings without first obtaining a warrant. To agree with the Court on this point is to say that school searches may justifiably be held to that extent to constitute an exception to the Fourth Amendment's warrant requirement. Such an exception, however, is not to be justified, as the Court apparently holds, by assessing net social value through application of an unguided "balancing test" in which "the individual's legitimate expectations of privacy and personal security" are weighed against "the government's need for effective methods to deal with breaches of public order." The Warrant Clause is something more than an exhortation to this Court to maximize social welfare as *we* see fit. It requires that the authorities must obtain a warrant before conducting a full-scale search. The undifferentiated governmental interest in law enforcement is insufficient to justify an exception to the warrant requirement. Rather, some *special* governmental interest beyond the need merely to apprehend lawbreakers is necessary to justify a categorical exception to the warrant requirement. * * *

In this case, such extraordinary governmental interests do exist and are sufficient to justify an exception to the warrant requirement. Students are necessarily confined for most of the school day in close proximity to each other and to the school staff. I agree with the Court that we can take judicial notice of the serious problems of drugs and violence that plague our schools. As Justice Blackmun notes, teachers must not merely "maintain an environment conducive to learning" among children who "are inclined to test the outer boundaries of acceptable conduct," but must also "protect the very safety of students and school personnel." A teacher or principal could neither carry out essential teaching functions nor adequately protect students' safety if required to wait for a warrant before conducting a necessary search.

B

I emphatically disagree with the Court's decision to cast aside the constitutional probable-cause standard when assessing the constitutional validity of a schoolhouse search. The Court's decision jettisons the probable-cause standard—the only standard that finds support in the text of the Fourth Amendment—on the basis of its Rohrschach-like "balancing test." Use of such a "balancing test" to determine the standard for evaluating the validity of a full-scale search represents a sizable innovation in Fourth Amendment analysis. This innovation finds support neither in precedent nor policy and portends a dangerous weakening of the purpose of the Fourth Amendment to protect the privacy and security of our citizens. Moreover, even if this Court's historic understanding of the Fourth Amendment were mistaken and a balancing test of some kind were appropriate, any such test that gave adequate weight to the privacy and security interests protected by the Fourth Amendment would not reach the preordained result the Court's conclusory analysis reaches today. Therefore, because I believe that the balancing test used by the Court today is flawed both in its inception and in its execution, I respectfully dissent.

1

An unbroken line of cases in this Court have held that probable cause is a prerequisite for a full-scale search. * * *

Our holdings that probable cause is a prerequisite to a full-scale search are based on the relationship between the two clauses of the Fourth Amendment. The first clause ("The right of the people to be secure in their persons, houses, papers and effects, against unreasonable searches and seizures, shall not be violated * * *.") states the purpose of the amendment and its coverage. The second clause (" * * * and no Warrants shall issue but upon probable cause * * *") gives content to the word "unreasonable" in the first clause. "For all but * * * narrowly defined intrusions, the requisite 'balancing' has been performed in centuries of precedent and is embodied in the principle that seizures are 'reasonable' only if supported by probable cause." [Citation omitted]

I therefore fully agree with the Court that "the underlying command of the Fourth Amendment is always that searches and seizures be reasonable." But this "underlying command" is not directly interpreted in each category of cases by some amorphous "balancing test." Rather, the provisions of the warrant clause—a warrant and probable cause—provide the yardstick against which official searches and seizures are to be measured. The Fourth Amendment neither requires nor authorizes the conceptual free-for-all that ensues when an unguided balancing test is used to assess specific categories of searches. If the search in question is more than a minimally intrusive *Terry*-stop, the constitutional probable-cause standard determines its validity. * * *

2

I thus do not accept the majority's premise that "[t]o hold that the Fourth Amendment applies to searches conducted by school authorities is only to begin the inquiry into the standards governing such searches." For me, the finding that the Fourth Amendment applies, coupled with the observation that what is at issue is a full-scale search, is the end of the inquiry. But even if I believed that a "balancing test" appropriately replaces the judgment of the Framers of the Fourth Amendment, I would nonetheless object to the cursory and short-sighted "test" that the Court employs to justify its predictable weakening of Fourth Amendment protections. In particular, the test employed by the Court vastly overstates the social costs that a probable-cause standard entails and, though it plausibly articulates the serious privacy interests at stake, inexplicably fails to accord them adequate weight in striking the balance.

The Court begins to articulate its "balancing test" by observing that "the government's need for effective methods to deal with breaches of public order" is to be weighed on one side of the balance. Of course, this is not correct. It is not the government's need for effective enforcement methods that should weigh in the balance, for ordinary Fourth Amendment standards—including probable cause—may well permit methods for maintaining the public order that are perfectly effective. If that were the case, the governmental interest in having effective standards would carry no weight at all as a justification for *departing* from the probable-cause standard. Rather, it is the costs of applying probable cause as opposed to applying some lesser standard that should be weighed on the government's side.[10]

In order to tote up the costs of applying the probable-cause standard, it is thus necessary first to take into account the nature and content of that standard, and the likelihood that it would hamper achievement of the goal—vital not just to teachers and administrators, of maintaining an effective educational setting in the public schools. The seminal statement concerning the nature of the probable-cause standard is found in *Carroll v. United States*, 267 U.S. 132 (1925). *Carroll* held that law enforcement authorities have probable cause to search where "the facts and circumstances within their knowledge and of which they had reasonably trustworthy information [are] sufficient in themselves to warrant a man of reasonable caution in the belief" that a criminal offense had occurred. In *Brinegar v. United States*, 338 U.S. 160 (1949), the Court amplified this requirement, holding that probable cause depends upon "the factual and practical considerations of everyday life on which reasonable and prudent men, not legal technicians, act."

Two Terms ago, in *Illinois v. Gates* [infra, p. 200], this Court expounded at some length its view of the probable-cause standard. Among the adjectives used to describe the standard were "practical," "fluid," "flexible," "easily applied," and "nontechnical." The probable-cause standard was to be seen as a "common-sense" test whose application depended on an evaluation of the "totality of the circumstances."

10. I speak of the "government's side" only because it is the terminology used by the Court. In my view, this terminology itself is seriously misleading. The government is charged with protecting the privacy and security of the citizen, just as it is charged with apprehending those who violate the criminal law. Consequently, the government has *no* legitimate interest in conducting a search that unduly intrudes on the privacy and security of the citizen. The balance is not between the rights of the government and the rights of the citizen, but between opposing conceptions of the constitutionally legitimate means of carrying out the government's varied responsibilities.

Ignoring what *Gates* took such great pains to emphasize, the Court today holds that a new "reasonableness" standard is appropriate because it "will spare teachers and school administrators the necessity of schooling themselves in the niceties of probable cause and permit them to regulate their conduct according to the dictates of reason and common sense." I had never thought that our pre-*Gates* understanding of probable cause defied either reason or common sense. But after *Gates*, I would have thought that there could be no doubt that this "nontechnical," "practical," and "easily applied" concept was eminently serviceable in a context like a school, where teachers require the flexibility to respond quickly and decisively to emergencies.

A consideration of the likely operation of the probable-cause standard reinforces this conclusion. Discussing the issue of school searches, Professor LaFave has noted that the cases that have reached the appellate courts "strongly suggest that in most instances the evidence of wrongdoing prompting teachers or principals to conduct searches is sufficiently detailed and specific to meet the traditional probable cause test." 3 W. LaFave, Search and Seizure § 10.11, pp. 459–460 (1978). * * *

As compared with the relative ease with which teachers can apply the probable-cause standard, the amorphous "reasonableness under all the circumstances" standard freshly coined by the Court today will likely spawn increased litigation and greater uncertainty among teachers and administrators. Of course, as this Court should know, an essential purpose of developing and articulating legal norms is to enable individuals to conform their conduct to those norms. A school system conscientiously attempting to obey the Fourth Amendment's dictates under a probable-cause standard could, for example, consult decisions and other legal materials and prepare a booklet expounding the rough outlines of the concept. Such a booklet could be distributed to teachers to provide them with guidance as to when a search may be lawfully conducted. I cannot but believe that the same school system faced with interpreting what is permitted under the Court's new "reasonableness" standard would be hopelessly adrift as to when a search may be permissible. The sad result of this uncertainty may well be that some teachers will be reluctant to conduct searches that are fully permissible and even necessary under the constitutional probable-cause standard, while others may intrude arbitrarily and unjustifiably on the privacy of students. * * *

II

Applying the constitutional probable-cause standard to the facts of this case, I would find that Mr. Choplick's search violated T.L.O.'s Fourth Amendment rights. After escorting T.L.O. into his private office, Mr. Choplick demanded to see her purse. He then opened the purse to find evidence whether she had been smoking in the bathroom. When he opened the purse, he discovered the pack of cigarettes. At this point, his search for evidence of the smoking violation was complete.

Mr. Choplick then noticed, below the cigarettes, a pack of cigarette rolling papers. Believing that such papers were "associated" with the use of marihuana, he proceeded to conduct a detailed examination of the contents of her purse, in which he found some marihuana, a pipe, some money, an index card, and some private letters indicating that T.L.O. had sold marihuana to other students. The State sought to introduce this latter material in evidence at a criminal proceeding, and the issue before the Court is whether it should have been suppressed.

On my view of the case, we need not decide whether the initial search conducted by Mr. Choplick—the search for evidence of the smoking violation that was completed when Mr. Choplick found the pack of cigarettes—was valid. For Mr. Choplick at that point did not have probable cause to continue to rummage through T.L.O.'s purse. Mr. Choplick's suspicion of marihuana possession at this time was based *solely* on the presence of the package of cigarette papers. The mere presence without more of such a staple item of commerce is insufficient to warrant a person of reasonable caution in inferring both that T.L.O. had violated the law by possessing marihuana and that evidence of that violation would be found in her purse. Just as a police officer could not obtain a warrant to search a home based solely on his claim that he had seen a package of cigarette papers in that home, Mr. Choplick was not entitled to search possibly the most private possessions of T.L.O. based on the mere presence of a package of cigarette papers. Therefore, the fruits of this illegal search must be excluded and the judgment of the New Jersey Supreme Court affirmed. * * *

JUSTICE STEVENS, with whom JUSTICE MARSHALL joins, and with whom JUSTICE BRENNAN joins as to Part I, concurring in part and dissenting in part.

Assistant Principal Choplick searched T.L.O.'s purse for evidence that she was smoking in the girls' restroom. Because T.L.O.'s suspected misconduct was not illegal and did not pose a serious threat to school discipline, the New Jersey Supreme Court held that Choplick's search of her purse was an unreasonable invasion of her privacy and that the evidence which he seized could not be used against her in criminal proceedings. The New Jersey court's holding was a careful response to the case it was required to decide. * * *

The majority holds that "a search of a student by a teacher or other school official will be 'justified at its inception' when there are reasonable grounds for suspecting that the search will turn up evidence *that the student has violated or is violating* either the law or *the rules of the school.*" This standard will permit teachers and school administrators to search students when they suspect that the search will reveal evidence of even the most trivial school regulation or precatory guideline for student behavior. The Court's standard for deciding whether a search is justified "at its inception" treats all violations of the rules of the school as though they were fungible. For the Court, a search for curlers and sunglasses in order to enforce the school dress code is apparently just as important as a search for evidence of heroin addiction or violent gang activity.

The majority, however, does not contend that school administrators have a compelling need to search students in order to achieve optimum enforcement of minor school regulations. To the contrary, when minor violations are involved, there is every indication that the informal school disciplinary process, with only minimum requirements of due process, can function effectively without the power to search for enough evidence to prove a criminal case. In arguing that teachers and school administrators need the power to search students based on a lessened standard, the United States as *amicus curiae* relies heavily on empirical evidence of a contemporary crisis of violence and unlawful behavior that is seriously undermining the process of education in American schools. A standard better attuned to this concern would permit teachers and school administrators to search a student when they have reason to believe that the search will uncover *evidence that the student is violating the law or engaging in conduct that is seriously disruptive of school order, or the educational process.* * * * There is a quite obvious, and material difference between a search for evidence relating to violent or disruptive activity, and a search for evidence of a smoking rule violation. This distinction does not imply that a no smoking rule is a matter of minor importance. Rather, like a rule that prohibits a student from being tardy, its occasional violation in a context that poses no threat of disrupting school order and discipline offers no reason to believe that an immediate search is necessary to avoid unlawful conduct, violence, or a serious impairment of the educational process. * * *

The schoolroom is the first opportunity most citizens have to experience the power of government. Through it passes every citizen and public official, from schoolteachers to policemen and prison guards. The values they learn there, they take with them in life. One of our most cherished ideals is the one contained in the Fourth Amendment: that the Government may not intrude on the personal privacy of its citizens without a warrant or compelling circumstance. The Court's decision today is a curious moral for the Nation's youth. Although the search of T.L.O.'s purse does not trouble today's majority, I submit that we are not dealing with "matters relatively trivial to the welfare of the Nation. There are village tyrants as well as village Hampdens, but none who acts under color of law is beyond the reach of the Constitution." *West Virginia State Board of Education v. Barnette,* 319 U.S. 624, 638 (1943).

I respectfully dissent.

Commentary

The opinions in *New Jersey v. T.L.O.* are assigned here not because of the specific holding, but because the case raises many of the major disputed issues in Fourth Amendment law. The specific case law on each of these issues will be covered in the succeeding chapters. The Supreme Court has developed Fourth Amendment law in such excruciating detail, however, in the course of innumerable confusing and even contradictory holdings, that it is easy to lose sight of the garden due to the profusion of monstrous weeds. This book proceeds on the theory that students will best understand the mass of case law if they first have an introductory view of the major issues through close discussion of a single case. After reading the opinions in *New Jersey v. T.L.O.*, consider the following questions:

1. *Does the Fourth Amendment apply at all to searches of students by school officials?* On the one hand, previous decisions had made clear that the Amendment applies not only to police officers who are making arrests or searching for violations of the criminal law, but also to civil regulatory officials like building and environmental inspectors. On the other hand, it is equally clear that the Amendment does not restrict the authority that parents have over minor children living at home. This is not only because parents are considered private citizens rather than public officials, but also because parents have a supervisory authority over their own children which is far broader than whatever authority police have to supervise adult citizens. The Fourth Amendment also does not protect prisoners from searches by guards, in this case because the Supreme Court has concluded that the requirements of prison security make it unreasonable for prisoners to expect protection for their privacy. See Hudson v. Palmer, 468 U.S. 517 (1984). All these conclusions reflect value judgments which, of course, could have been made differently.

Is a public school teacher or principal more like a policeman or building inspector on the one hand, or a parent or prison warden on the other? Ironically, one could argue that the Fourth Amendment does not apply in schools *either* because teachers and students have a "commonality of interests" rather than an "adversarial relationship," *or* because the public schools in some areas have such serious problems with drugs and violence that they are analogous to prisons.

Supreme Court Justices seem to find it difficult to avoid circular reasoning in explaining why the Fourth Amendment is applicable to a particular situation. They have a tendency to assert that the Fourth Amendment applies because it ought to apply, and it ought to apply because otherwise Fourth Amendment rights will not be respected. For example, Justice Brennan's dissent in *T.L.O.* remarks that it would be "incongruous and futile to charge teachers with the task of imbuing their students with an understanding of our system of constitutional democracy, while at the same time immunizing those same teachers from the need to respect constitutional protections." The incongruity would vanish if we made the contrary assumption that the particular protections of the Fourth Amendment are not fully applicable to the teacher-student relationship. Then, teachers who search would be demonstrating to students that "our system of constitutional democracy" places a higher value on keeping the schools free of drugs than it does on protecting the right of students to privacy in their belongings. We might say that it would be incongruous and futile to charge teachers with the task of imbuing their students with an understanding of the unacceptability of drug use in our society while immunizing student drug pushers like T.L.O. from prompt and certain punishment.

The formulation of the issue in Part III of the majority opinion also fails to avoid circularity. The majority asks two questions: (a) Does the student have a subjective expectation of privacy from teacher searches (doesn't *this* depend in part upon what the rule of law is?); and (b) Is this expectation one which "society is prepared to recognize as legitimate?", unlike the "illegitimate" expectation of privacy that a prisoner might have in his cell. But the Supreme Court itself decides for "society" what is legitimate and what is not. When the Court refers to society's judgment, it is looking in a mirror.

The problem with any formulation based on "societal" values is that American society is not a single collective entity with a unified point of view, but a cacophony of competing opinions. Even if we assume that most people would agree that public school students have a legitimate expectation of privacy in their personal belongings, it does not follow that these same people would necessarily agree that judges rather than school administrators ought to set the limits of that privacy interest. Justices Brennan and Stevens make the point that applying the Fourth Amendment strictly in the school context teaches students to regard themselves as rights-bearing citizens, who are not subject to the arbitrary power of public officials. This may be true, but one could also argue that under contemporary conditions it is more important to remind students of their social obligations than their individual rights. Majority opinion in many communities might favor giving priority to the message "drug use in the schools is totally unacceptable," over the message "students have rights of privacy which teachers and school administrators must respect." It is tempting to avoid the question of priorities by stating that the Fourth Amendment itself gives priority to individual privacy, but this move is unavailable if the Fourth Amendment refers us back to "society's" views about the extent to which expectations of privacy are legitimate.

2. *Assuming that the Fourth Amendment applies to school searches, must evidence obtained through a violation of the Amendment be excluded from: (a) juvenile criminal proceedings; or (b) school disciplinary hearings that might lead to suspension or expulsion?* This set of questions has to do with the appropriate remedy, rather than the existence of a right to privacy. If an exclusionary rule does not apply, some other remedy (such as civil lawsuits for damages) may at least theoretically be available.

The Supreme Court at one time held that exclusion is required not only in criminal trials, but in other proceedings which are "quasi-criminal" in nature. More recently, there has been a marked trend toward restricting the kind of proceedings where exclusion is required, as several Supreme Court Justices have become doubtful whether excluding reliable evidence is a good way of enforcing constitutional rights. If there is to be any remedy at all for Fourth Amendment violations, however, exclusion of evidence may be less damaging to the morale of teachers and principals than tort lawsuits.

At one time, juvenile proceedings were generally thought to be in the nature of a substitute for parental discipline, sincerely aimed at furthering the child's true long-term interests, and so the procedural protections common to adult criminal trials did not apply. Today, it is generally recognized that juvenile proceedings that may impose confinement or probation as sanctions are essentially punitive in nature, and most constitutional protections other than the right to jury trial are applicable. Juvenile courts also hear matters that are not essentially criminal in nature, and in such cases the rule of exclusion may not apply. For example, few courts would be willing to send a sexually abused child back to the custody of the abusing parent merely because the evidence of abuse had been obtained in violation of the Fourth Amendment. Even though the authorities would not have discovered the evidence if they had obeyed the Constitution, as they ought to have done, granting this kind of remedy would pay too high a price in other values.

Note that the New Jersey trial court assumed (footnote 1) that the exclusionary rule applied to the suspension from school as well as to the delinquency proceeding. See also, Justice Stevens' reference to "the informal school disciplinary process, with only minimum requirements of due process, [that] can function effectively without the power to search for enough evidence to prove a criminal case." It is unclear whether Stevens would include an exclusionary rule as within "minimum requirements of due process" if the school administrator *did* make a search on the basis of suspicion of a minor violation of school regulations. The school disciplinary process may be informal, but shouldn't the principal have pretty solid evidence that the student is guilty before imposing a suspension or dismissal?

3. *Assuming that the Fourth Amendment is applicable to school searches, what constitutes a "search" or a "seizure?"* (a) A teacher inspected a lavatory (a toilet stall?) to look for rule violations. Was this a search? Some cases have held that police engage in a search if they look into toilet stalls from a concealed observation point to observe unlawful homosexual activity. (b) The teacher then ordered the girls to come to the principal's office. If police officers did something like this to an adult, it would constitute a temporary detention and perhaps a full arrest, which would have to be justified by probable cause. (See e.g. *Florida v. Royer, infra* p. 244.) The analogy is a poor one, of course, and the point is merely that it is not easy to compare the situations of school children and adult citizens for Fourth Amendment purposes. (c) Next, there was the brief inspection of the contents of the purse, in which Mr. Choplick found the pack of cigarettes. This was a relatively limited intrusion, but if done to an adult by a police officer it would probably be a search, requiring probable cause. Even Justice Brennan's dissent implies (Part II) that this search might have been constitutionally permissible, presumably because Mr. Choplick had probable cause to look for cigarettes. (d) Finally, there was the extensive search of the entire contents of the purse following the discovery of cigarette papers, which involved the reading of personal letters. This was a far greater invasion of privacy than the limited search for cigarettes, and arguably should require much greater justification in the form of probable cause or even a search warrant. Indeed, some early authorities which are no longer followed had suggested that a search and seizure of "private papers" would be unreasonable even if pursuant to a warrant issued upon probable cause. Some investigative activities (e.g. electronic eavesdropping) are so intrusive that it is arguable that they should never be allowed, or at least should be allowed only on a special showing of necessity, for the investigation of exceptionally serious crimes.

4. *Given that it is the extensive search of the purse that concerns the court, was a warrant (i.e. advance judicial authorization) required for this search?* Note the language of the Fourth Amendment, which says that warrants shall not issue except upon probable cause, but which does not say

when the absence of a warrant makes a search "unreasonable." Justice Brennan, for all his spirited denunciation of the majority for employing a "Rohrschach-like balancing test," employs just such a test himself to decide that "the serious problems of drugs and violence that plague our schools" require an exception to the warrant requirement. But there would be an exception to the warrant requirement in any case if there was a genuine emergency situation that required prompt action; Brennan's proposition is that there should be a general exception to the warrant requirement for school searches, regardless of whether there is a need for hasty action in the circumstances of the individual case.

Although T.L.O. was not literally under arrest when she was taken to Mr. Choplick's office for the smoking violation, her situation was closely analogous to that of an adult under arrest for a minor offense. Police may search the person of an arrestee for weapons and for evidence of a crime, even if the arrest is for a traffic offense like driving with a suspended license. Police may also search an automobile without first obtaining a warrant, if they have probable cause to believe the vehicle contains contraband or evidence. The existence of these and other very broad exceptions to the warrant requirement is probably best explained by the fact that obtaining a warrant takes time, effort, and a certain amount of professional skill in drafting the papers correctly. Put yourself in vice-principal Choplick's position. If you were told that the law does not permit you to examine a student's purse, locker or pockets for drugs without getting a search warrant, would you be inclined to try to get a warrant when you have evidence of drug activity or would you just wash your hands of the problem?

5. *Assuming that no warrant was required, does a school official need "probable cause," or only "individualized suspicion," to make the extensive search of the purse?* Although many Supreme Court opinions contain a great deal of argument about which of these tests is appropriate for various kinds of searches and seizures, the Court has given very little guidance as to exactly how to define and differentiate these terms. If probable cause exists only "when the facts and circumstances within the officerS' knowledge and of which they have reasonably trustworthy information are sufficient in themselves to warrant a person of reasonable caution in the belief that a crime has occurred," then what lesser degree of information would suffice to generate "reasonable grounds for suspecting" that a search will turn up incriminating evidence? Obviously, "reasonable suspicion" is meant to be a less exacting standard than "probable cause," but it is hard to determine the absolute meaning of either term. After all, the Supreme Court of New Jersey found a lack of grounds for reasonable suspicion on the same facts.

These verbal formulations conceal some mysterious policy decisions concerning the degree of certainty that is required before a particular search can be justified. For example, consider Justice Brennan's statement that the mere presence in the purse of such a "staple item of commerce" as cigarette papers would not warrant a person of reasonable caution in inferring that evidence of marijuana possession could be found in the purse. On the other hand, Mr. Choplick's experience had led him to believe that possession of cigarette rolling papers by high school students is "closely associated with the use of marijuana." Is Justice Brennan implying that he knows better, and that high school students generally use cigarette rolling papers for lawful purposes? If about half of the students who possess cigarette papers also possess marijuana, is this correlation sufficient to justify a search or do we demand a greater degree of certainty than that? Should a greater degree of probable cause be required to read letters than to look inside a purse or paper bag? Would Justice Brennan have upheld this search if Mr. Choplick had found a hypodermic needle in his initial inspection? As you can see, application of the "probable cause" or "reasonable suspicion" tests leaves room for a great deal of interest balancing.

Many commentators have been critical of the decision in *T.L.O.* because it applies a "watered down" version of the Fourth Amendment to school searches. From this point of view "reasonable suspicion" is so vague a concept that it both fails to protect students from arbitrary searches and fails to inform school officials of what they may and may not do. The Supreme Court has frequently held the Fourth Amendment applicable in borderline situations while substantially modifying the Amendment's specific requirements of a warrant, probable cause, and specific description. The advantage and disadvantage of this approach is *flexibility*: the Court is able to compromise between applying the Amendment in its entirety and not providing any constitutional protection at all. The question is whether this "half-way" approach provides substantial protection for privacy, or whether it creates the illusion and nuisance of regulation without substantially affecting official behavior.

6. *Finally, New Jersey v. T.L.O. provides an introduction to the deep and sometimes bitter ideological division on the Supreme Court over Fourth Amendment issues.* The current majority considers the operative language in the Fourth Amendment to be the prohibition of "unreasonable" searches and seizures, and it employs a balancing test to determine whether the warrant and probable cause requirements apply to a particular type of search or seizure. The minority position, most forcefully articulated by Justice Brennan, starts with the warrant clause, and asserts that searches are presumptively unlawful unless authorized in advance by a warrant issued upon probable cause. The minority test permits some balancing, as Justice Brennan's opinion in *T.L.O.* illustrates, but it seeks to confine any exceptions to the warrant and probable cause requirements as narrowly as possible. The minority accuses the majority of undermining constitutional protections on the basis of perceived (and generally *mis*perceived) necessities of law enforcement, while the majority considers the minority to be much more inflexible than the language of the Fourth Amendment requires.

In the opinion of this writer, the battle over the Fourth Amendment reflects differing ideological perspectives on the role of law enforcement generally, and especially on the effectiveness of intrusive investigatory procedures in controlling crime. How important is it to curtail marijuana use in the schools, or in society generally? How much will drug use in the schools be reduced if school officials are allowed to search without probable cause? If a Justice thinks that the amount of drug use in the schools is likely to be about the same whether or not a probable cause requirement is enforced, then there is not much of a case for allowing searches on mere suspicion even under a balancing test. If a Justice thinks that stringent enforcement measures can create a relatively drug-free school environment, or at least thinks that local authorities are permitted to make that judgment in our constitutional system, then the rights of those who want a drug free environment have to be considered as well as the rights of those who want to protect privacy.

Note

In People v. Dilworth, 169 Ill.2d 195, 214 Ill.Dec. 456, 661 N.E.2d 310 (1996), a divided Illinois Supreme Court faced a difficult application of the conflict between the principle that "drug use in the schools is totally unacceptable," and the countervailing principle that "students have privacy rights which teachers, administrators and police officers must respect." Police officer Ruettiger was assigned full-time to prevent criminal activity at the Joliet Alternate School, a special public high school for students with behavior disorders. Two teachers asked Ruettiger to search a student named Weeks, because they had heard Weeks telling other students that he had sold drugs and would bring more drugs to school the next day.

The next day Ruettiger did search Weeks and, after finding nothing, escorted Weeks to his locker, which was next to that of Dilworth. According to Ruettiger, Weeks and Dilworth began talking and giggling "like they put one over on [him]." Ruettiger further testified that they turned toward him and they were "looking, laughing at [him] like [he] was played for a fool." Ruettiger noticed a flashlight in Dilworth's hand and immediately thought that it might contain drugs. He grabbed the flashlight, unscrewed the top, and observed a bag containing a white chunky substance underneath the flashlight batteries. The substance later tested positive for the presence of cocaine. Dilworth ran from the scene, but was captured by Ruettiger and transported to the police station. While there, Dilworth gave a statement admitting that he intended to sell the cocaine because he was tired of being poor. The 15–year-old Dilworth was tried as an adult for "unlawful possession of cocaine with intent to deliver on school property," and sentenced to the minimum four-year term of imprisonment.

The majority of the Illinois Supreme Court held that, because Ruettiger was a liaison police officer on staff at the school, only a reasonable individualized suspicion was required to justify the search of the flashlight. The majority held that "the totality of these circumstances (related above) would lead a reasonable person to suspect that defendant was carrying drugs in his flashlight." The dissenting judges argued that, because Ruettiger was not a teacher or principal but a police officer assigned to prevent and investigate criminal activity, the search could only be justified by probable cause—which was clearly absent. The dissent observed that the majority opinion allowed officers to search students at school on the ground that they are children, and then to sentence them to prison as adults with the evidence so obtained. "The majority's conclusion is a threat to the rights of all children in school to be free from unreasonable searches and seizures and from overzealous and aggressive police conduct. Children do not learn respect for their basic constitutional rights, or the rights of others, in such a setting. Instead, such a negative environment only fosters cynicism as well as suspicion of, and contempt for, all police activity."

Compare the dissent's viewpoint with the police officer's testimony that the students were "looking, laughing at [him] like [he] was played for a fool." In the setting of an alternative (disciplinary) school, is it more important to assure the students that the police will respect their privacy rights or that the authorities (including the courts) will not tolerate drug selling? Is it possible to do both?

In Vernonia School District 47J v. Acton, 515 U.S. 646 (1995) (infra, p. 75), the Supreme Court upheld a program of random drug testing (urinalysis) of student athletes in a public school district. The majority opinion by Justice Scalia reasoned that the program was adopted in response to a drug problem of "epidemic proportions," that student athletes are role models for students generally, that student athletes routinely submit to physical examinations (which include a urine sample), and that the invasion of privacy is minimal. The majority opinion also observed that only one student's parents objected to the drug testing program, although a public meeting was held to obtain the views of parents. How important is it whether few or many parents (or students) object?

Chapter 2

THE DEVELOPMENT OF THE EX-CLUSIONARY RULE FROM *WEEKS* TO *MAPP*

WEEKS v. UNITED STATES

Supreme Court of the United States, 1914.
232 U.S. 383, 34 S.Ct. 341, 58 L.Ed. 652.

MR. JUSTICE DAY delivered the opinion of the court.

An indictment was returned against the plaintiff in error, defendant below, and herein so designated, in the District Court of the United States for the Western District of Missouri, containing nine counts. The seventh count, upon which a conviction was had, charged the use of the mails for the purpose of transporting certain coupons or tickets representing chances or shares in a lottery or gift enterprise, in violation of § 213 of the Criminal Code. Sentence of fine and imprisonment was imposed. This writ of error is to review that judgment.

The defendant was arrested by a police officer, so far as the record shows, without warrant, at the Union Station in Kansas City, Missouri, where he was employed by an express company. Other police officers had gone to the house of the defendant and being told by a neighbor where the key was kept, found it and entered the house. They searched the defendant's room and took possession of various papers and articles found there, which were afterwards turned over to the United States Marshal. Later in the same day police officers returned with the Marshal, who thought he might find additional evidence, and, being admitted by someone in the house, probably a boarder, in response to a rap, the Marshal searched the defendant's room and carried away certain letters and envelopes found in the drawer of a chiffonier. Neither the Marshal nor the police officers had a search warrant. * * *

After the jury had been sworn and before any evidence had been given, the defendant again urged his petition for the return of his property, which was denied by the court. Upon the introduction of such papers during the trial, the defendant objected on the ground that the papers had been obtained without a search warrant and by breaking

25

open his home, in violation of the Fourth and Fifth Amendments to the Constitution of the United States, which objection was overruled by the court. Among the papers retained and put in evidence were a number of lottery tickets and statements with reference to the lottery, taken at the first visit of the police to the defendant's room, and a number of letters written to the defendant in respect to the lottery, taken by the Marshal upon his search of defendant's room.

The defendant assigns error, among other things, in the court's refusal to grant his petition for the return of his property and in permitting the papers to be used at the trial. * * *

The effect of the Fourth Amendment is to put the courts of the United States and Federal officials, in the exercise of their power and authority, under limitations and restraints as to the exercise of such power and authority, and to forever secure the people, their persons, houses, papers and effects against all unreasonable searches and seizures under the guise of law. This protection reaches all alike, whether accused of crime or not, and the duty of giving to it force and effect is obligatory upon all entrusted under our Federal system with the enforcement of the laws. The tendency of those who execute the criminal laws of the country to obtain conviction by means of unlawful seizures and enforced confessions, the latter often obtained after subjecting accused persons to unwarranted practices destructive of rights secured by the Federal Constitution, should find no sanction in the judgments of the courts which are charged at all times with the support of the Constitution and to which people of all conditions have a right to appeal for the maintenance of such fundamental rights. * * * The United States Marshal could only have invaded the house of the accused when armed with a warrant issued as required by the Constitution, upon sworn information and describing with reasonable particularity the thing for which the search was to be made. Instead, he acted without sanction of law, doubtless prompted by the desire to bring further proof to the aid of the Government, and under color of his office undertook to make a seizure of private papers in direct violation of the constitutional prohibition against such action. Under such circumstances, without sworn information and particular description, not even an order of court would have justified such procedure, much less was it within the authority of the United States Marshal to thus invade the house and privacy of the accused. * * *

We therefore reach the conclusion that the letters in question were taken from the house of the accused by an official of the United States acting under color of his office in direct violation of the constitutional rights of the defendant; that having made a seasonable application for their return, which was heard and passed upon by the court, there was involved in the order refusing the application a denial of the constitutional rights of the accused, and that the court should have restored these letters to the accused. In holding them and permitting their use upon the trial, we think prejudicial error was committed. As to the papers and property seized by the policemen, it does not appear that they acted under any claim of Federal authority such as would make the Amendment applicable to such unauthorized seizures. The record shows that what they did by way of arrest and search and seizure was done before the finding of the indictment in the Federal court, under what supposed right or authority does not appear. What remedies the defendant may have against them we need not inquire, as the Fourth Amendment is not directed to individual misconduct of such officials. Its limitations reach the Federal Government and its agencies.

It results that the judgment of the court below must be reversed, and the case remanded for further proceedings in accordance with this opinion.

Reversed.

SILVERTHORNE LUMBER CO. v. UNITED STATES

Supreme Court of the United States, 1920.
251 U.S. 385, 40 S.Ct. 182, 64 L.Ed. 319.

MR. JUSTICE HOLMES delivered the opinion of the court.

This is a writ of error brought to reverse a judgment of the District Court fining the Silverthorne Lumber Company two hundred and fifty dollars for contempt of court and ordering Frederick W. Silverthorne to be imprisoned until he should purge himself of a similar contempt. The contempt in question was a refusal to obey subpœnas and an order of Court to produce books and documents of the company before the grand jury to be used in regard to alleged violation of the statutes of the United States by the said Silverthorne and his father. One ground of the refusal was that the order of the Court infringed the rights of the parties under the Fourth Amendment of the Constitution of the United States.

The facts are simple. An indictment upon a single specific charge having been brought against the two Silverthornes mentioned, they both were arrested at their homes early in the morning of February 25, 1919, and were detained in custody a number of hours. While they were thus detained representatives of the Department of Justice and the United States marshal without a shadow of authority went to the office of their company and made a clean sweep of all the books, papers and documents found there. All the employees were taken or directed to go to the office of the District Attorney of the United States to which also the books, & c., were taken at once. An application was made as soon as might be to the District Court for a return of what thus had been taken unlawfully. It was opposed by the District Attorney so far as he had found evidence against the plaintiffs in error, and it was stated that the evidence so obtained was before the grand jury. Color had been given by the District Attorney to the approach of those concerned in the act by an invalid subpœna for certain documents relating to the charge in the indictment then on file. Thus the case is not that of knowledge acquired through the wrongful act of a stranger, but it must be assumed that the Government planned or at all events ratified the whole performance. Photographs and copies of material papers were made and a new indictment was framed based upon the knowledge thus obtained. The District Court ordered a return of the originals but impounded the photographs and copies. Subpœnas to produce the originals then were served and on the refusal of the plaintiffs in error to produce them the Court made an order that the subpœnas should be complied with, although it had found that all the papers had been seized in violation of the parties' constitutional rights. The refusal to obey this order is the contempt alleged. The Government now, while in form repudiating and condemning the illegal seizure, seeks to maintain its right to avail itself of the knowledge obtained by that means which otherwise it would not have had.

The proposition could not be presented more nakedly. It is that although of course its seizure was an outrage which the Government now regrets, it may study the papers before it returns them, copy them, and then may use the knowledge that it has gained to call upon the owners in a more regular form to produce them; that the protection of the Constitution covers the physical possession but not any advantages that the Government can gain over the object of its pursuit by doing the forbidden act. *Weeks v. United States*, 232 U.S. 383, to be sure, had established that laying the papers directly before the grand jury was unwarranted, but it is taken to mean only that two steps are required instead of one. In our opinion such is not the law. It reduces the Fourth Amendment to a form of words. The essence of a provision forbidding the acquisition of evidence in a certain way is that not merely evidence so acquired shall not be used before the Court but that it shall not be used at all. Of course this does not mean that the facts thus obtained become sacred and inaccessible. If knowledge of them is gained from an independent source they may be proved like any others, but the knowledge gained by the Government's own wrong cannot be used by it in the way proposed. * * *

Judgment reversed.

The Chief Justice and Mr. Justice Pitney dissent.

WOLF v. PEOPLE OF THE STATE OF COLORADO

Supreme Court of the United States, 1949.
338 U.S. 25, 69 S.Ct. 1359, 93 L.Ed. 1782.

Mr. Justice Frankfurter delivered the opinion of the Court.

The precise question for consideration is this: Does a conviction by a State court for a State offense deny the "due process of law" required by the Fourteenth Amendment, solely because evidence that was admitted at the trial was obtained under circumstances which would have rendered it inadmissible in a prosecution for violation of a federal law in a court of the United States because there deemed to be an infraction of the Fourth Amendment as applied in *Weeks v. United States*, 232 U.S. 383? The Supreme Court of Colorado has sustained convictions in which such evidence was admitted, and we brought the cases here.

Unlike the specific requirements and restrictions placed by the Bill of Rights (Amendments I to VIII) upon the administration of criminal justice by federal authority, the Fourteenth Amendment did not subject criminal justice in the States to specific limitations. The notion that the "due process of law" guaranteed by the Fourteenth Amendment is shorthand for the first eight amendments of the Constitution and thereby incorporates them has been rejected by this Court again and again, after impressive consideration. * * *

For purposes of ascertaining the restrictions which the Due Process Clause imposed upon the States in the enforcement of their criminal law, we adhere to the views expressed in *Palko v. Connecticut*, 302 U.S. 319. That decision speaks to us with the great weight of the authority, particularly in matters of civil liberty, of a court that included Mr. Chief Justice Hughes, Mr. Justice Brandeis, Mr. Justice Stone and Mr. Justice Cardozo, to name only the dead. In rejecting the suggestion that the Due Process Clause incorporated the original Bill of Rights, Mr. Justice Cardozo reaffirmed on behalf of that Court a different but deeper and more pervasive conception of the Due Process Clause. This Clause exacts from the States for the lowliest and the most outcast all that is "implicit in the concept of ordered liberty." 302 U.S. at 325.

Due process of law thus conveys neither formal nor fixed nor narrow requirements. It is the compendious expression for all those rights which the courts must enforce because they are basic to our free society. But basic rights do not become petrified as of any one time, even though, as a matter of human experience, some may not too rhetorically be called eternal verities. It is of the very nature of a free society to advance in its standards of what is deemed reasonable and right. Representing as it does a living principle, due process is not confined within a permanent catalogue of what may at a given time be deemed the limits or the essentials of fundamental rights. * * *

The security of one's privacy against arbitrary intrusion by the police—which is at the core of the Fourth Amendment—is basic to a free society. It is therefore implicit in "the concept of ordered liberty" and as such enforceable against the States through the Due Process Clause. The knock at the door, whether by day or by night, as a prelude to a search, without authority of law but solely on the authority of the police, did not need the commentary of recent history to be condemned as inconsistent with the conception of human rights enshrined in the history and the basic constitutional documents of English-speaking peoples.

Accordingly, we have no hesitation in saying that were a State affirmatively to sanction such police incursion into privacy it would run counter to the guaranty of the Fourteenth Amendment. But the ways of enforcing such a basic right raise questions of a different order. How such arbitrary conduct should be checked, what remedies against it should be afforded, the means by which the right should be made effective, are all questions that are not to be so dogmatically answered as to preclude the varying solutions which spring from an allowable range of judgment on issues not susceptible of quantitative solution.

In *Weeks v. United States, supra,* this Court held that in a federal prosecution the Fourth Amendment barred the use of evidence secured through an illegal search and seizure. This ruling was made for the first time in 1914. It was not derived from the explicit requirements of the Fourth Amendment; it was not based on legislation expressing Congressional policy in the enforcement of the Constitution. The decision was a matter of judicial implication. Since then it has been frequently applied and we stoutly adhere to it. But the immediate question is whether the basic right to protection against arbitrary intrusion by the police demands the exclusion of logically relevant evidence obtained by an unreasonable search and seizure because, in a federal prosecution for a federal crime, it would be excluded. As a matter of inherent reason, one would suppose this to be an issue as to which men with complete devotion to the protection of the right of privacy might give different answers. When we find that in fact most of the English-speaking world does not regard as vital to such protection the exclusion of evidence thus obtained, we must hesitate to treat this remedy as an essential ingredient of the right. The contrariety of views of the States is particularly impressive in view of the careful reconsideration which they have given the problem in the light of the *Weeks* decision. * * * As of today 31 States reject the *Weeks* doctrine, 16 States are in agreement with it. Of 10 jurisdictions within the United Kingdom and the British Commonwealth of Nations which have passed on the question, none has held evidence obtained by illegal search and seizure inadmissible.

The jurisdictions which have rejected the *Weeks* doctrine have not left the right to privacy without other means of protection. Indeed, the exclusion of evidence is a remedy which directly serves only to protect those upon whose person or premises something incriminating has been found. We cannot, therefore, regard it as a departure from basic standards to remand such persons, together with those who emerge scatheless from a search, to the remedies of private action and such protection as the internal discipline of the police, under the eyes of an alert public opinion, may afford. Granting that in practice the exclusion of evidence may be an effective way of deterring unreasonable searches, it is not for this Court to condemn as falling below the minimal standards assured by the Due Process Clause a State's reliance upon other methods which, if consistently enforced, would be equally effective. Weighty testimony against such an insistence on our own view is furnished by the opinion of Mr. Justice (then Judge) Cardozo in *People v. Defore,* 150 N.E. 585. We cannot brush aside the experience of States which deem the incidence of such conduct by the police too slight to call for a deterrent remedy not by way of disciplinary measures but by overriding the relevant rules of evidence. There are, moreover, reasons for excluding evidence unreasonably obtained by the federal police which are less compelling in the case of police under State or local authority. The public opinion of a community can far more effectively be exerted against oppressive conduct on the part of police directly responsible to the community itself than can local opinion, sporadically aroused, be brought to bear upon remote authority pervasively exerted throughout the country.

We hold, therefore, that in a prosecution in a State court for a State crime the Fourteenth Amendment does not forbid the admission of evidence obtained by an unreasonable search and seizure. And though we have interpreted the Fourth Amendment to forbid the admission of such evidence, a different question would be presented if Congress under its legislative powers were to pass a statute purporting to negate the *Weeks* doctrine. We would then be faced with the problem of the respect to be accorded the legislative judgment on an issue as to which, in default of that judgment, we have been forced to depend upon our own. Problems of a converse character, also not before us, would be presented should Congress under § 5 of the Fourteenth Amendment undertake to enforce the rights there guaranteed by attempting to make the *Weeks* doctrine binding upon the States.

Affirmed.

[The concurring opinion of JUSTICE BLACK, and the dissenting opinion of JUSTICE DOUGLAS, are omitted.]

MR. JUSTICE MURPHY, with whom MR. JUSTICE RUTLEDGE joins, dissenting.

It is disheartening to find so much that is right in an opinion which seems to me so fundamentally wrong. Of course I agree with the Court that the Fourteenth Amendment prohibits activities which are proscribed by the search and seizure clause of the Fourth Amendment. See my dissenting views, and those of MR. JUSTICE BLACK, in *Adamson v. California*, 332 U.S. 46, 68, 123. Quite apart from the blanket application of the Bill of Rights to the States, a devotee of democracy would ill suit his name were he to suggest that his home's protection against unlicensed governmental invasion was not "of the very essence of a scheme of ordered liberty." It is difficult for me to understand how the Court can go this far and yet be unwilling to make the step which can give some meaning to the pronouncements it utters.

Imagination and zeal may invent a dozen methods to give content to the commands of the Fourth Amendment. But this Court is limited to the remedies currently available. It cannot legislate the ideal system. If we would attempt the enforcement of the search and seizure clause in the ordinary case today, we are limited to three devices: judicial exclusion of the illegally obtained evidence; criminal prosecution of violators; and civil action against violators in the action of trespass.

Alternatives are deceptive. Their very statement conveys the impression that one possibility is as effective as the next. In this case their statement is blinding. For there is but one alternative to the rule of exclusion. That is no sanction at all.

* * *

Little need be said concerning the possibilities of criminal prosecution. Self-scrutiny is a lofty ideal, but its exaltation reaches new heights if we expect a District Attorney to prosecute himself or his associates for well-meaning violations of the search and seizure clause during a raid the District Attorney or his associates have ordered. But there is an appealing ring in another alternative. A trespass action for damages is a venerable means of securing reparation for unauthorized invasion of the home. Why not put the old writ to a new use? When the Court cites cases permitting the action, the remedy seems complete.

But what an illusory remedy this is, if by "remedy" we mean a positive deterrent to police and prosecutors tempted to violate the Fourth Amendment. The appealing ring softens when we recall that in a trespass action the measure of damages is simply the extent of the injury to physical property. If the officer searches with care, he can avoid all but nominal damages—a penny, or a dollar. Are punitive damages possible? Perhaps. But a few states permit none, whatever the circumstances. In those that do, the plaintiff must show the real ill will or malice of the defendant, and surely it is not unreasonable to assume that one in honest pursuit of crime bears no malice toward the search victim. If that burden is carried, recovery may yet be defeated by the rule that there must be physical damages before punitive damages may be awarded. In addition, some states limit punitive damages to the actual expenses of litigation. Others demand some arbitrary ratio between actual and punitive damages before a verdict may stand. Even assuming the ill will of the officer, his reasonable grounds for belief that the home he searched harbored evidence of crime is admissible in mitigation of punitive damages. The bad reputation of the plaintiff is likewise admissible. If the evidence seized was actually used at a trial, that fact has been held a complete justification of the search, and a defense against the trespass action. *Elias v. Pasmore* [1934] 2 K.B. 164. And even if the plaintiff hurdles all these obstacles, and gains a substantial verdict, the individual officer's finances may well make the judgment useless—for the municipality, of course, is not liable without its consent. Is it surprising that there is so little in the books concerning trespass actions for violation of the search and seizure clause?

The conclusion is inescapable that but one remedy exists to deter violations of the search and seizure clause. That is the rule which excludes illegally obtained evidence. Only by exclusion can we impress upon the zealous prosecutor that violation of the Constitution will do him no good. And only when that point is driven home can the prosecutor be expected to emphasize the importance of observing constitutional demands in his instructions to the police. * * *

I cannot believe that we should decide due process questions by simply taking a poll of the rules in various jurisdictions, even if we follow the *Palko* "test." Today's decision will do inestimable harm to the cause of fair police methods in our cities and states. Even more important, perhaps, it must have tragic effect upon public respect for our judiciary.

For the Court now allows what is indeed shabby business: lawlessness by officers of the law.

Since the evidence admitted was secured in violation of the Fourth Amendment, the judgment should be reversed.

ROCHIN v. PEOPLE OF CALIFORNIA

Supreme Court of the United States, 1952.
342 U.S. 165, 72 S.Ct. 205, 96 L.Ed. 183.

MR. JUSTICE FRANKFURTER delivered the opinion of the Court.

Having "some information that [the petitioner here] was selling narcotics," three deputy sheriffs of the County of Los Angeles, on the morning of July 1, 1949, made for the two-story dwelling house in which Rochin lived with his mother, common-law wife, brothers and sisters. Finding the outside door open, they entered and then forced open the door to Rochin's room on the second floor. Inside they found petitioner sitting partly dressed on the side of the bed, upon which his wife was lying. On a "night stand" beside the bed the deputies spied two capsules. When asked "Whose stuff is this?" Rochin seized the capsules and put them in his mouth. A struggle ensued, in the course of which the three officers "jumped upon him" and attempted to extract the capsules. The force they applied proved unavailing against Rochin's resistance. He was handcuffed and taken to a hospital. At the direction of one of the officers a doctor forced an emetic solution through a tube into Rochin's stomach against his will. This "stomach pumping" produced vomiting. In the vomited matter were found two capsules which proved to contain morphine.

Rochin was brought to trial before a California Superior Court, sitting without a jury, on the charge of possessing "a preparation of morphine" in violation of the California Health and Safety Code, 1947, § 11,500. Rochin was convicted and sentenced to sixty days' imprisonment. The chief evidence against him was the two capsules. They were admitted over petitioner's objection, although the means of obtaining them was frankly set forth in the testimony by one of the deputies, substantially as here narrated.

On appeal, the District Court of Appeal affirmed the conviction, despite the finding that the officers "were guilty of unlawfully breaking into and entering defendant's room and were guilty of unlawfully assaulting and battering defendant while in the room," and "were guilty of unlawfully assaulting, battering, torturing and falsely imprisoning the defendant at the alleged hospital." One of the three judges, while finding that "the record in this case reveals a shocking series of violations of constitutional rights," concurred only because he felt bound by decisions of his Supreme Court. These, he asserted, "have been looked upon by law enforcement officers as an encouragement, if not an invitation, to the commission of such lawless acts." The Supreme Court of California denied without opinion Rochin's petition for a hearing. * * *

Regard for the requirements of the Due Process Clause "inescapably imposes upon this Court an exercise of judgment upon the whole course of the proceedings [resulting in a conviction] in order to ascertain whether they offend those canons of decency and fairness which express the notions of justice of English-speaking peoples even toward those charged with the most heinous offenses." *Malinski v. New York*, 324 U.S. at 416–417. These standards of justice are not authoritatively formulated anywhere as though they were specifics. Due process of law is a summarized constitutional guarantee of respect for those personal immunities which, as Mr. Justice Cardozo twice wrote for the Court, are "so rooted in the traditions and conscience of our people as to be ranked as fundamental," or are "implicit in the concept of ordered liberty."

The vague contours of the Due Process Clause do not leave judges at large. We may not draw on our merely personal and private notions and disregard the limits that bind judges in their judicial function. Even though the concept of due process of law is not final and fixed, these limits are derived from considerations that are fused in the whole nature of our judicial process. See Cardozo, The Nature of the Judicial Process; The Growth of the Law; The Paradoxes of Legal Science. These are considerations deeply rooted in reason and in the compelling traditions of the legal profession. The Due Process Clause places upon this Court the duty of exercising a judgment, within the narrow confines of judicial power in reviewing State convictions, upon interests of society pushing in opposite directions. * * * The faculties of the Due Process Clause may be indefinite and vague, but the mode of their ascertainment is not self-willed. In each case "due process of law" requires an evaluation based on a disinterested inquiry pursued in the spirit of science, on a balanced order of facts exactly and fairly stated, on the detached consideration of conflicting claims, on a judgment not *ad hoc* and episodic but duly mindful of reconciling the needs both of continuity and of change in a progressive society.

Applying these general considerations to the circumstances of the present case, we are compelled to conclude that the proceedings by which this conviction was obtained do more than offend some fastidious squeamishness or private sentimentalism about combatting crime too energetically. This is conduct that shocks the conscience. Illegally breaking into the privacy of the petitioner, the struggle to open his mouth and remove what was there, the forcible extraction of his stomach's contents—this course of proceeding by agents of government to obtain evidence is bound to offend even hardened sensibilities. They are methods too close to the rack and the screw to permit of constitutional differentiation.

It has long since ceased to be true that due process of law is heedless of the means by which otherwise relevant and credible evidence is obtained. This was not true even before the series of recent cases enforced the constitutional principle that the States may not base convictions upon confessions, however much verified, obtained by coercion. These decisions are not arbitrary exceptions to the comprehensive right of States to fashion their own rules of evidence for criminal trials. They are not sports in our constitutional law but applications of a general principle. They are only instances of the general requirement that States in their prosecutions respect certain decencies of civilized conduct. Due process of law, as a historic and generative principle, precludes defining, and thereby confining, these standards of conduct more precisely than to say that convictions cannot be brought about by methods that offend "sense of justice." It would be a stultification of the responsibility which the course of constitutional history has cast upon this Court to hold that in order to convict a man the police cannot extract by force what is in his mind but can extract what is in his stomach.

To attempt in this case to distinguish what lawyers call "real evidence" from verbal evidence is to ignore the reasons for excluding coerced confessions. Use of involuntary verbal confessions in State criminal trials is constitutionally obnoxious not only because of their unreliability. They are inadmissible under the Due Process Clause even though statements contained in them may be independently established as true. Coerced confessions offend the community's sense of fair play and decency. So here, to sanction the brutal conduct which naturally enough was condemned by the court whose judgment is before us, would be to afford brutality the cloak of law. Nothing would be more calculated to discredit law and thereby to brutalize the temper of a society.

Reversed.

[Concurring opinions omitted.]

PEOPLE v. CAHAN

Supreme Court of California, 1955.
44 Cal.2d 434, 282 P.2d 905.

TRAYNOR, J.—Defendant and 15 other persons were [convicted of] conspiring to engage in horse-race bookmaking and related offenses * * *. Gerald Wooters, an officer attached to the intelligence unit of that department testified that after securing the permission of the chief of police to make microphone installations* at two places occupied by defendants, he, Sergeant Keeler, and Officer Phillips one night at about 8:45 entered one "house through the side window of the first floor," and that he "directed the officers to place a listening device under a chest of drawers." Another officer made recordings and transcriptions of the conversations that came over wires from the listening device to receiving

---

* Section 653h of the Penal Code provides: "Any person who, without consent of the owner, lessee, or occupant, installs or attempts to install or use a dictograph in any house, room, apartment, tenement, office, shop, warehouse, store, mill, barn, stable, or other building, tent, vessel, railroad car, vehicle, mine or any underground portion thereof, is guilty of a misdemeanor; provided, that nothing herein shall prevent the use and installation of dictographs by a regular salaried police officer expressly authorized thereto by the head of his office or department or by a district attorney when such use and installation are necessary in the performance of their duties in detecting crime and in the apprehension of criminals."

equipment installed in a nearby garage. About a month later, at Officer Wooters' direction, a similar device was surreptitiously installed in another house and receiving equipment was also set up in a nearby garage. Such methods of getting evidence have been caustically censured by the United States Supreme Court: "That officers of the law would break and enter a home, secrete such a device, even in a bedroom, and listen to the conversations of the occupants for over a month would be almost incredible if it were not admitted. Few police measures have come to our attention that more flagrantly, deliberately and persistently violate the fundamental principle declared by the Fourth Amendment. * * *" (*Irvine v. California*, 347 U.S. 128, 132.) Section 653h of the Penal Code does not and could not authorize violations of the Constitution, and the proviso under which the officers purported to act at most prevents their conduct from constituting a violation of that section itself.

The evidence obtained from the microphones was not the only unconstitutionally obtained evidence introduced at the trial over defendants' objection. In addition there was a mass of evidence obtained by numerous forcible entries and seizures without search warrants.

The forcible entries and seizures were candidly admitted by the various officers. * * *

Thus, without fear of criminal punishment or other discipline, law enforcement officers, sworn to support the Constitution of the United States and the Constitution of California, frankly admit their deliberate, flagrant acts in violation of both Constitutions and the laws enacted thereunder. It is clearly apparent from their testimony that they casually regard such acts as nothing more than the performance of their ordinary duties for which the city employs and pays them. * * *

[Justice Traynor reviewed the opinions in Wolf v. Colorado and Irvine v. California, supra, which had declined to impose the federal exclusionary rule on the states. These decisions appeared to establish by a narrow margin that the federal exclusionary rule is not an essential ingredient of the Fourth Amendment, but a judicially created rule of evidence which Congress could negate, Justice Jackson's opinion for the Supreme Court in *Irvine*—on facts similar to the facts in *Cahan*—had invited the states to reconsider their evidentiary rules in light of *Wolf's* holding that the Fourth Amendment applies to the states through the Fourteenth.]

Meanwhile, pursuant to the suggestion of the United States Supreme Court, we have reconsidered the rule we have heretofore followed that the unconstitutional methods by which evidence is obtained does not affect its admissibility and have carefully weighed the various arguments that have been advanced for and against that rule. It bears emphasis that in the absence of a holding by the United States Supreme Court that the due process clause requires exclusion of unconstitutionally obtained evidence, whatever rule we adopt, whether it excludes or admits the evidence, will be a judicially declared rule of evidence.

The rule admitting the evidence has been strongly supported by both scholars and judges. Their arguments may be briefly summarized as follows:

The rules of evidence are designed to enable courts to reach the truth and, in criminal cases, to secure a fair trial to those accused of crime. Evidence obtained by an illegal search and seizure is ordinarily just as true and reliable as evidence lawfully obtained. The court needs all reliable evidence material to the issue before it, the guilt or innocence of the accused, and how such evidence is obtained is immaterial to that issue. It should not be excluded unless strong considerations of public policy demand it. There are no such considerations.

Exclusion of the evidence cannot be justified as affording protection or recompense to the defendant or punishment to the officers for the illegal search and seizure. It does not protect the defendant from the search and seizure, since that illegal act has already occurred. If he is innocent or if there is ample evidence to convict him without the illegally obtained evidence, exclusion of the evidence gives him no remedy at all. Thus the only defendants who benefit by the exclusionary rule are those criminals who could not be convicted without the illegally obtained evidence. Allowing such criminals to escape punishment is not appropriate recompense for the invasion of their constitutional rights; it does not punish the officers who violated the constitutional provisions; and it fails to protect society from known criminals who should not be left at large. For his crime the defendant should be punished. For his violation of the constitutional provisions the offending officer should be punished. As the exclusionary rule operates, however, the defendant's crime and the officer's flouting of constitutional guarantees both go unpunished. "The criminal is to go free because the constable has blundered" (Cardozo, J., in *People v. Defore, supra*, 242 N.Y. 13, 21), and "Society is deprived of its remedy against one lawbreaker, because he has been pursued by another." (Jackson, J., in *Irvine v. California, supra*, 347 U.S. 128, at 136; see also 8 Wigmore on Evidence [3d ed.] § 2184, p. 40.)

Opponents of the exclusionary rule also point out that it is inconsistent with the rule allowing private litigants to use illegally obtained evidence, and that as applied in the federal courts, it is capricious in its operation, either going too far or not far enough. "[S]o many exceptions to [the exclusionary] rule have been granted the judicial blessing as largely to destroy any value it might otherwise have had. Instead of adding to the security of legitimate individual rights, its principal contribution has been to add further technicalities to the law of criminal procedure. A district attorney who is willing to pay the price may easily circumvent its limitations. And the price to be paid is by no means high." (Grant, *Circumventing the Fourth Amendment*, 14 So.Cal.L.Rev. 359.) Thus, the rule as applied in the federal courts has been held to protect only defendants whose own rights have been invaded by federal officers. If the illegal search and seizure have been conducted by a state officer or a private person not acting in cooperation with federal officers, or if the property seized is not defendant's the rule does not apply.

Finally, it has been pointed out that there is no convincing evidence that the exclusionary rule actually tends to prevent unreasonable searches and seizures and that the disciplinary or educational effect of the court's releasing the defendant for police misbehavior is so indirect as to be no more than a mild deterrent at best.

Despite the persuasive force of the foregoing arguments, we have concluded that evidence obtained in violation of the constitutional guarantees is inadmissible. * * * We have been compelled to reach that conclusion because other remedies have completely failed to secure compliance with the constitutional provisions on the part of police officers with the attendant result that the courts under the old rule have been constantly required to participate in, and in effect condone, the lawless activities of law enforcement officers.

When, as in the present case, the very purpose of an illegal search and seizure is to get evidence to introduce at a trial, the success of the lawless venture depends entirely on the court's lending its aid by allowing the evidence to be introduced. * * * It is morally incongruous for the state to flout constitutional rights and at the same time demand that its citizens observe the law. The end that the state seeks may be a laudable one, but it no more justifies unlawful acts than a laudable end justifies unlawful action by any member of the public. Moreover, any process of law that sanctions the imposition of penalties upon an individual through the use of the fruits of official lawlessness tends to the destruction of the whole system of restraints on the exercise of the public force that are inherent in the "concept of ordered liberty." (See Allen, *The Wolf Case*, 45 Ill.L.Rev. 1, 20.) "Decency, security, and liberty alike demand that government officials shall be subjected to the same rules of conduct that are commands to the citizen. In a government of laws, existence of the government will be imperilled if it fails to observe the law scrupulously. Our Government is the potent, the omnipresent teacher. For good or for ill, it teaches the whole people by its example. Crime is contagious. If the Government becomes a law-breaker, it breeds contempt for law, it invites every man to become a law unto himself; it invites anarchy. To declare that in the administration of the criminal law the end justifies the means—to declare that the Government may commit crimes in order to secure the conviction of a private criminal— would bring terrible retribution. Against that pernicious doctrine this Court should resolutely set its face." Brandeis, J., dissenting in *Olmstead v. United States*, 277 U.S. 438, 485. * * *

If the unconstitutional guarantees against unreasonable searches and seizures are to have significance they must be enforced, and if courts are to discharge their duty to support the state and federal Constitutions they must be willing to aid in their enforcement. If those guarantees were being effectively enforced by other means than excluding evidence obtained by their violation, a different problem would be presented. If such were the case there would be more force to the argument that a particular criminal should not be redressed for a past violation of his rights by excluding the evidence against him. Experience has demonstrated, however, that neither administrative, criminal nor civil remedies are effective in suppressing lawless searches and seizures. The innocent suffer with the guilty, and we cannot close our eyes to the effect the rule we adopt will have on the rights of those not before the court. * * *

Granted that the adoption of the exclusionary rule will not prevent all illegal searches and seizures, it will discourage them. Police officers and prosecuting officials are primarily interested in convicting criminals. Given the exclusionary rule and a choice between securing evidence by legal rather than illegal means, officers will be impelled to obey the law themselves since not to do so will jeopardize their objectives. Moreover, the same considerations that justify the privilege against self-incrimination are not irrelevant here. As Wigmore pointed out, that privilege, just as the prohibition against unreasonable searches and seizures, is primarily for the protection of the innocent. "The real objection is that *any system of administration which permits the prosecution to trust habitually to compulsory self-disclosure as a source of proof must itself morally suffer thereby.* The inclination develops to rely mainly upon such evidence, and to be satisfied with an incomplete investigation of the other sources. The exercise of the power to extract answers begets a forgetfulness of the just limitations of that power. Similarly, a system that permits the prosecution to trust habitually to the use of illegally obtained evidence cannot help but encourage violations of the Constitution at the expense of lawful means of enforcing the law. (See Frankfurter, J., dissenting in *Harris v. United States, supra*, 331 U.S. 145, 172.) On the other hand, if courts respect the constitutional provisions by refusing to sanction their violation, they will not only command the respect of law-abiding citizens for themselves adhering to the law, they will also arouse public opinion as a deterrent to lawless enforcement of the law by bringing just criticism to bear on law enforcement officers who allow criminals to escape by pursuing them in lawless ways.

It is contended, however, that the police do not always have a choice of securing evidence by legal means and that in many cases the criminal will escape if illegally obtained evidence cannot be used against him. This contention is not properly directed at the exclusionary rule, but at the constitutional provisions themselves. It was rejected when those provisions were adopted. In such cases had the Constitution been obeyed, the criminal could in no event be convicted. He does not go free because the constable blundered, but because the Constitutions prohibit securing the evidence against him. * * *

We are not unmindful of the contention that the federal exclusionary rule has been arbitrary in its application and has introduced needless confusion into the law of criminal procedure. The validity of this contention need not be considered now. Even if it is assumed that it is meritorious, it does not follow that the exclusionary rule should be rejected.

In developing a rule of evidence applicable in the state courts, this court is not bound by the decisions that have applied the federal rule, and if it appears that those decisions have developed needless refinements and distinctions, this court need not follow them. Similarly, if the federal cases indicate needless limitations on the right to conduct reasonable searches and seizures or to secure warrants, this court is free to reject them. Under these circumstances the adoption of the exclusionary rule need not introduce confusion into the law of criminal procedure. Instead it opens the door to the development of workable rules governing searches and seizures and the issuance of warrants that will protect both the rights guaranteed by the constitutional provisions and the interest of society in the suppression of crime.

The orders are reversed.

[Dissenting opinion omitted.]

JONES v. UNITED STATES

Supreme Court of the United States, 1960.
362 U.S. 257, 80 S.Ct. 725, 4 L.Ed.2d 697.

Mr. Justice Frankfurter delivered the opinion of the Court.

This is a prosecution for violation of federal narcotics laws. * * * Possession was the basis of the Government's case against petitioner. The evidence against him may be briefly summarized. He was arrested in an apartment in the District of Columbia by federal narcotics officers, who were executing a warrant to search for narcotics. Those officers found narcotics, without appropriate stamps, and narcotics paraphernalia in a bird's nest in an awning just outside a window in the apartment. Another officer, stationed outside the building, had a short time before seen petitioner put his hand on the awning. Upon the discovery of the narcotics and the paraphernalia petitioner had admitted to the officers that some of these were his and that he was living in the apartment.

Prior to trial petitioner duly moved to suppress the evidence obtained through the execution of the search warrant on the ground that the warrant had been issued without a showing of probable cause. The Government challenged petitioner's standing to make this motion because petitioner alleged neither ownership of the seized articles nor an interest in the apartment greater than that of an "invitee or guest." The District Court agreed to take evidence on the issue of petitioner's standing. Only petitioner gave evidence. On direct examination he testified that the apartment belonged to a friend, Evans, who had given him the use of it, and a key, with which petitioner had admitted himself on the day of the arrest. On cross-examination petitioner testified that he had a suit and shirt at the apartment, that his home was elsewhere, that he paid nothing for the use of the apartment, that Evans had let him use it "as a friend," that he had slept there "maybe a night," and that at the time of the search Evans had been away in Philadelphia for about five days.

Solely on the basis of petitioner's lack of standing to make it, the district judge denied petitioner's motion to suppress. When the case came on for trial before a different judge, the motion to suppress was renewed and was denied on the basis of the prior ruling. An unsuccessful objection was made when the seized items were offered in evidence at the trial. * * *

The issue of petitioner's standing is to be decided with reference to Rule 41(e) of the Federal Rules of Criminal Procedure. This is a statutory direction governing the suppression of evidence acquired in violation of the conditions validating a search. It is desirable to set forth the Rule.

> "A person aggrieved by an unlawful search and seizure may move the district court for the district in which the property was seized for the return of the property and to suppress for use as evidence anything so obtained on the ground that (1) the property was illegally seized without warrant, or (2) the warrant is insufficient on its face, or (3) the property seized is not that described in the warrant, or (4) there was not probable cause for believing the existence of the grounds on which the warrant was issued, or (5) the warrant was illegally executed. The judge shall receive evidence on any issue of fact necessary to the decision of the motion. If the motion is granted the property shall be restored unless otherwise subject to lawful detention and it shall not be admissible in evidence at any hearing or trial. The motion to suppress evidence may also be made in the district where the trial is to be had. The motion shall be made before trial or hearing unless opportunity therefor did not exist or the defendant was not aware of the grounds for the motion, but the court in its discretion may entertain the motion at the trial or hearing."

In order to qualify as a "person aggrieved by an unlawful search and seizure" one must have been a victim of a search or seizure, one against whom the search was directed, as distinguished from one who claims prejudice only through the use of evidence gathered as a consequence of a search or seizure directed at someone else. Rule 41(e) applies the general principle that a party will not be heard to claim a constitutional protection unless he "belongs to the class for whose sake the constitutional protection is given." *Hatch v. Reardon*, 204 U.S. 152, 160. The restrictions upon searches and seizures were obviously designed for protection against official invasion of privacy and the security of property. They are not exclusionary provisions against the admission of kinds of evidence deemed inherently unreliable or prejudicial. The exclusion in federal trials of evidence otherwise competent but gathered by federal officials in violation of the Fourth Amendment is a means for making effective the protection of privacy.

Ordinarily, then, it is entirely proper to require of one who seeks to challenge the legality of a search as the basis for suppressing relevant evidence that he allege, and if the allegation be disputed that he establish, that he himself was the victim of an invasion of privacy. But prosecutions like this one have presented a special problem. To establish "standing," Courts of Appeals have generally required that the movant claim either to have owned or possessed the seized property or to have had a substantial possessory interest in the premises searched. Since narcotics charges like those in the present indictment may be established through proof solely of possession of narcotics, a defendant seeking to comply with what has been the conventional standing requirement has been forced to allege facts the proof of which would tend, if indeed not be sufficient, to convict him. At the least, such a defendant has been placed in the criminally tendentious position of explaining his possession of the premises. He has been faced, not only with the chance that the allegations made on the motion to suppress may be used against him at the trial, although that they may is by no means an inevitable holding, but also with the encouragement that he perjure himself if he seeks to establish "standing" while maintaining a defense to the charge of possession.

The dilemma that has thus been created for defendants in cases like this has been pointedly put by Judge Learned Hand:

"Men may wince at admitting that they were the owners, or in possession, of contraband property; may wish at once to secure the remedies of a possessor, and avoid the perils of the part; but equivocation will not serve. If they come as victims, they must take on that role, with enough detail to cast them without question. The petitioners at bar shrank from that predicament; but they were obliged to choose one horn of the dilemma." *Connolly v. Medalie*, 58 F.2d 629, 630. * * *

Judge Hand's dilemma is not inescapable. It presupposes requirements of "standing" which we do not find compelling. Two separate lines of thought effectively sustain defendant's standing in this case. (1) The same element in this prosecution which has caused a dilemma, *i.e.*, that possession both convicts and confers standing, eliminates any necessity for a preliminary showing of an interest in the premises searched or the property seized, which ordinarily is required when standing is challenged. (2) Even were this not a prosecution turning on illicit possession, the legally requisite interest in the premises was here satisfied, for it need not be as extensive a property interest as was required by the courts below.

As to the first ground, we are persuaded by this consideration: to hold to the contrary, that is, to hold that petitioner's failure to acknowledge interest in the narcotics or the premises prevented his attack upon the search, would be to permit the Government to have the advantage of contradictory positions as a basis for conviction. Petitioner's conviction flows from his possession of the narcotics at the time of the search. Yet the fruits of that search, upon which the conviction depends, were admitted into evidence on the ground that petitioner did not have possession of the narcotics at that time. The prosecution here thus subjected the defendant to the penalties meted out to one in lawless possession while refusing him the remedies designed for one in that situation. It is not consonant with the amenities, to put it mildly, of the administration of criminal justice to sanction such squarely contradictory assertions of power by the Government. The possession on the basis of which petitioner is to be and was convicted suffices to give him standing under any fair and rational conception of the requirements of Rule 41(e). * * *

As a second ground sustaining "standing" here we hold that petitioner's testimony on the motion to suppress made out a sufficient interest in the premises to establish him as a "person aggrieved" by their search. That testimony established that at the time of the search petitioner was present in the apartment with the permission of Evans, whose apartment it was. The Government asserts that such an interest is insufficient to give standing. The Government does not contend that only ownership of the premises may confer standing. It would draw distinctions among various classes of possessors, deeming some, such as "guests" and "invitees" with only the "use" of the premises, to have too "tenuous" an interest although concededly having "some measure of control" through their "temporary presence," while conceding that others, who in a "realistic sense, have dominion of the apartment" or who are "domiciled" there, have standing. Petitioner, it is insisted, by his own testimony falls in the former class.

While this Court has never passed upon the interest in the searched premises necessary to maintain a motion to suppress, the Government's argument closely follows the prevailing view in the lower courts. * * *

We do not lightly depart from this course of decisions by the lower courts. We are persuaded, however, that it is unnecessary and ill-advised to import into the law surrounding the constitutional right to be free from unreasonable searches and seizures subtle distinctions, developed and refined by the common law in evolving the body of private property law which, more than almost any. other branch of law, has been shaped by distinctions whose validity is largely historical.* Even in the area from which they derive, due consideration has led to the discarding of these distinctions in the homeland of the common law. Distinctions such as those between "lessee," "licensee," "invitee" and "guest," often only of gossamer strength, ought not to be determinative in fashioning procedures ultimately referable to constitutional safeguards. * * *

[The Court held that the search warrant was valid, but vacated the judgment and remanded the case to the trial court for a hearing on petitioner's claim that the officers executed the warrant in an unlawful manner.]

MAPP v. OHIO

Supreme Court of the United States, 1961.
367 U.S. 643, 81 S.Ct. 1684, 6 L.Ed.2d 1081.

Mr. Justice Clark delivered the opinion of the Court.

* The Supreme Court held in Minnesota v. Olson, 495 U.S. 91 (1990), that an overnight guest staying in a home with the permission of the owner has a reasonable expectation of privacy in the home, and may obtain suppression of any evidence obtained by an unlawful entry into the premises. Officers had entered the home unlawfully without a warrant to arrest Olson, and an inculpatory statement he made to them was therefore excluded as obtained in violation of his Fourth Amendment rights.

Appellant stands convicted of knowingly [possessing obscene books and photographs]. * * *

On May 23, 1957, three Cleveland police officers arrived at appellant's residence in that city pursuant to information that "a person [was] hiding out in the home, who was wanted for questioning in connection with a recent bombing, and that there was a large amount of policy paraphernalia being hidden in the home." Miss Mapp and her daughter by a former marriage lived on the top floor of the two-family dwelling. Upon their arrival at that house, the officers knocked on the door and demanded entrance but appellant, after telephoning her attorney, refused to admit them without a search warrant. They advised their headquarters of the situation and undertook a surveillance of the house.

The officers again sought entrance some three hours later when four or more additional officers arrived on the scene. When Miss Mapp did not come to the door immediately, at least one of the several doors to the house was forcibly opened and the policemen gained admittance. Meanwhile Miss Mapp's attorney arrived, but the officers, having secured their own entry, and continuing in their defiance of the law, would permit him neither to see Miss Mapp nor to enter the house. It appears that Miss Mapp was halfway down the stairs from the upper floor to the front door when the officers, in this highhanded manner, broke into the hall. She demanded to see the search warrant. A paper, claimed to be a warrant, was held up by one of the officers. She grabbed the "warrant" and placed it in her bosom. A struggle ensued in which the officers recovered the piece of paper and as a result of which they handcuffed appellant because she had been "belligerent" in resisting their official rescue of the "warrant" from her person. Running roughshod over appellant, a policeman "grabbed" her, "twisted [her] hand," and she "yelled [and] pleaded with him" because "it was hurting." Appellant, in handcuffs, was then forcibly taken upstairs to her bedroom where the officers searched a dresser, a chest of drawers, a closet and some suitcases. They also looked into a photo album and through personal papers belonging to the appellant. The search spread to the rest of the second floor including the child's bedroom, the living room, the kitchen and a dinette. The basement of the building and a trunk found therein were also searched. The obscene materials for possession of which she was ultimately convicted were discovered in the course of that widespread search.

At the trial no search warrant was produced by the prosecution, nor was the failure to produce one explained or accounted for. * * *

The State says that even if the search were made without authority, or otherwise unreasonably, it is not prevented from using the unconstitutionally seized evidence at trial, citing *Wolf v. Colorado*, 338 U.S. 25 (1949), in which this Court did indeed hold "that in a prosecution in a

State court for a State crime the Fourteenth Amendment does not forbid the admission of evidence obtained by an unreasonable search and seizure." On this appeal, * * * it is urged once again that we review that holding.[1] * * * While in 1949, prior to the *Wolf* case, almost two-thirds of the States were opposed to the use of the exclusionary rule, now, despite the *Wolf* case, more than half of those since passing upon it, by their own legislative or judicial decision, have wholly or partly adopted or adhered to the *Weeks* rule. Significantly, among those now following the rule is California, which, according to its highest court, was "compelled to reach that conclusion because other remedies have completely failed to secure compliance with the constitutional provisions * * *." *People v. Cahan* [p. 33, supra.] In connection with this California case, we note that the second basis elaborated in *Wolf* in support of its failure to enforce the exclusionary doctrine against the States was that "other means of protection" have been afforded "the right to privacy." The experience of California that such other remedies have been worthless and futile is buttressed by the experience of other States. The obvious futility of relegating the Fourth Amendment to the protection of other remedies has, moreover, been recognized by this Court since *Wolf*. See *Irvine v. California*, 347 U.S. 128, 137 (1954).

Likewise, time has set its face against what *Wolf* called the "weighty testimony" of *People v. Defore*, 242 N.Y. 13, 150 N.E. 585 (1926). There Justice (then Judge) Cardozo, rejecting adoption of the *Weeks* exclusionary rule in New York, had said that "[t]he Federal rule as it stands is either too strict or too lax." However, the force of that reasoning has been largely vitiated by later decisions of this Court. These include the recent discarding of the "silver platter" doctrine which allowed federal judicial use of evidence seized in violation of the Constitution by state agents, *Elkins v. United States*, 364 U.S. 206 (1960); the relaxation of the formerly strict requirements as to standing to challenge the use of evidence thus seized, so that now the procedure of exclusion, "ultimately referable to constitutional safeguards," is available to anyone even "legitimately on [the] premises" unlawfully searched, *Jones v. United States*, 362 U.S. 257, 266–267 (1960); and, finally, the formulation of a method to prevent state use of evidence unconstitutionally seized by federal agents, *Rea v. United States*, 350 U.S. 214 (1956). Because there can be no fixed formula, we are admittedly met with "recurring questions of the reasonableness of searches," but less is not to be expected when dealing with a Constitution, and, at any rate, "[r]easonableness is in the first instance for the [trial court] * * * to determine." *United States v. Rabinowitz*, 339 U.S. 56, 63 (1950).

It, therefore, plainly appears that the factual considerations supporting the failure of the *Wolf* Court to include the *Weeks* exclusionary rule

---

1. Other issues have been raised on this appeal but, in the view we have taken of the case, they need not be decided. Although appellant chose to urge what may have appeared to be the surer ground for favorable disposition and did not insist that *Wolf* be overruled, the *amicus curiae*, who was also permitted to participate in the oral argument, did urge the Court to overrule *Wolf*.

when it recognized the enforceability of the right to privacy against the States in 1949, while not basically relevant to the constitutional consideration, could not, in any analysis, now be deemed controlling. * * *

Since the Fourth Amendment's right of privacy has been declared enforceable against the States through the Due Process Clause of the Fourteenth, it is enforceable against them by the same sanction of exclusion as is used against the Federal Government. Were it otherwise, then just as without the *Weeks* rule the assurance against unreasonable federal searches and seizures would be "a form of words," valueless and undeserving of mention in a perpetual charter of inestimable human liberties, so too, without that rule the freedom from state invasions of privacy would be so ephemeral and so neatly severed from its conceptual nexus with the freedom from all brutish means of coercing evidence as not to merit this Court's high regard as a freedom "implicit in the concept of ordered liberty." At the time that the Court held in *Wolf* that the Amendment was applicable to the States through the Due Process Clause, the cases of this Court, as we have seen, had steadfastly held that as to federal officers the Fourth Amendment included the exclusion of the evidence seized in violation of its provisions. Even *Wolf* "stoutly adhered" to that proposition. The right to privacy, when conceded operatively enforceable against the States, was not susceptible of destruction by avulsion of the sanction upon which its protection and enjoyment had always been deemed dependent under the *Boyd, Weeks* and *Silverthorne* cases. Therefore, in extending the substantive protections of due process to all constitutionally unreasonable searches—state or federal—it was logically and constitutionally necessary that the exclusion doctrine—an essential part of the right to privacy—be also insisted upon as an essential ingredient of the right newly recognized by the *Wolf* case. In short, the admission of the new constitutional right by *Wolf* could not consistently tolerate denial of its most important constitutional privilege, namely, the exclusion of the evidence which an accused had been forced to give by reason of the unlawful seizure. To hold otherwise is to grant the right but in reality to withhold its privilege and enjoyment. Only last year the Court itself recognized that the purpose of the exclusionary rule "is to deter—to compel respect for the constitutional guaranty in the only effectively available way—by removing the incentive to disregard it." *Elkins v. United States, supra,* at 217.

Indeed, we are aware of no restraint, similar to that rejected today, conditioning the enforcement of any other basic constitutional right. The right to privacy, no less important than any other right carefully and particularly reserved to the people, would stand in marked contrast to all other rights declared as "basic to a free society." This Court has not hesitated to enforce as strictly against the States as it does against the Federal Government the rights of free speech and of a free press, the rights to notice and to a fair, public trial, including, as it does, the right not to be convicted by use of a coerced confession, however logically relevant it be, and without regard to its reliability. *Rogers v. Richmond,* 365 U.S. 534 (1961). And nothing could be more certain than that when a coerced confession is involved, "the relevant rules of evidence" are overridden without regard to "the incidence of such conduct by the police," slight or frequent. Why should not the same rule apply to what is tantamount to coerced testimony by way of unconstitutional seizure of goods, papers, effects, documents, etc.? We find that, as to the Federal Government, the Fourth and Fifth Amendments and, as to the States, the freedom from unconscionable invasions of privacy and the freedom from convictions based upon coerced confessions do enjoy an "intimate relation" in their perpetuation of "principles of humanity and civil liberty [secured] * * * only after years of struggle," *Bram v. United States*, 168 U.S. 532, 543–544 (1897). They express "supplementing phases of the same constitutional purpose—to maintain inviolate large areas of personal privacy." *Feldman v. United States*, 322 U.S. 487, 489–490 (1944). The philosophy of each Amendment and of each freedom is complementary to, although not dependent upon, that of the other in its sphere of influence—the very least that together they assure in either sphere is that no man is to be convicted on unconstitutional evidence.

V.

Moreover, our holding that the exclusionary rule is an essential part of both the Fourth and Fourteenth Amendments is not only the logical dictate of prior cases, but it also makes very good sense. There is no war between the Constitution and common sense. Presently, a federal prosecutor may make no use of evidence illegally seized, but a State's attorney across the street may, although he supposedly is operating under the enforceable prohibitions of the same Amendment. Thus the State, by admitting evidence unlawfully seized, serves to encourage disobedience to the Federal Constitution which it is bound to uphold. Moreover, as was said in *Elkins*, "[t]he very essence of a healthy federalism depends upon the avoidance of needless conflict between state and federal courts." 364 U.S., at 221. Such a conflict, hereafter needless, arose this very Term, in *Wilson v. Schnettler*, 365 U.S. 381 (1961), in which, and in spite of the promise made by *Rea*, we gave full recognition to our practice in this regard by refusing to restrain a federal officer from testifying in a state court as to evidence unconstitutionally seized by him in the performance of his duties. Yet the double standard recognized until today hardly put such a thesis into practice. In non-exclusionary States, federal officers, being human, were by it invited to and did, as our cases indicate, step across the street to the State's attorney with their unconstitutionally seized evidence. Prosecution on the basis of that evidence was then had in a state court in utter disregard of the enforceable Fourth Amendment. If the fruits of an unconstitutional search had been inadmissible in both state and federal courts, this inducement to evasion would have been sooner eliminated. There would be no need to reconcile such cases as *Rea* and *Schnettler*, each pointing up the hazardous uncertainties of our heretofore ambivalent approach.
* * *

There are those who say, as did Justice (then Judge) Cardozo, that under our constitutional exclusionary doctrine "[t]he criminal is to go free because the constable has blundered." *People v. Defore*, 242 N.Y., at 21, 150 N.E., at 587. In some cases this will undoubtedly be the result. But, as was said in *Elkins*, "there is another consideration—the imperative of judicial integrity." The criminal goes free, if he must, but it is the law that sets him free. Nothing can destroy a government more quickly than its failure to observe its own laws, or worse, its disregard of the charter of its own existence. As Mr. Justice Brandeis, dissenting, said in *Olmstead v. United States*, 277 U.S. 438, 485 (1928): "Our Government is the potent, the omnipresent teacher. For good or for ill, it teaches the whole people by its example. * * * If the Government becomes a lawbreaker, it breeds contempt for law; it invites every man to become a law unto himself; it invites anarchy." Nor can it lightly be assumed that, as a practical matter, adoption of the exclusionary rule fetters law enforcement. Only last year this Court expressly considered that contention and found that "pragmatic evidence of a sort" to the contrary was not wanting. *Elkins v. United States, supra*, at 218. The Court noted that

> "The federal courts themselves have operated under the exclusionary rule of *Weeks* for almost half a century; yet it has not been suggested either that the Federal Bureau of Investigation has thereby been rendered ineffective, or that the administration of criminal justice in the federal courts has thereby been disrupted. Moreover, the experience of the states is impressive. * * * The movement towards the rule of exclusion has been halting but seemingly inexorable." *Id.*, at 218–219.

The ignoble shortcut to conviction left open to the State tends to destroy the entire system of constitutional restraints on which the liberties of the people rest. Having once recognized that the right to privacy embodied in the Fourth Amendment is enforceable against the States, and that the right to be secure against rule invasions of privacy by state officers is, therefore, constitutional in origin, we can no longer permit that right to remain an empty promise. Because it is enforceable in the same manner and to like effect as other basic rights secured by the Due Process Clause, we can no longer permit it to be revocable at the whim of any police officer who, in the name of law enforcement itself, chooses to suspend its enjoyment. Our decision, founded on reason and truth, gives to the individual no more than that which the Constitution guarantees him, to the police officer no less than that to which honest law enforcement is entitled, and, to the courts, that judicial integrity so necessary in the true administration of justice.

Reversed and Remanded.

[Concurring and dissenting opinions omitted.]

Commentary

A Closely Divided Court

The Supreme Court was very closely divided in *Mapp*. Justice Black provided the crucial fifth vote for the majority opinion, but he also wrote a separate opinion taking a different line of reasoning. Black had concurred in the holding in *Wolf v. Colorado, supra* page 28, and he continued to be troubled by the fact that the Fourth Amendment does not expressly forbid the use of evidence obtained by an unreasonable search or seizure. In the meantime, however, he had become convinced by some reasoning advanced in the Supreme Court's venerable decision in Boyd v. United States, 116 U.S. 616 (1886). The opinion in *Boyd* had theorized that there is a "close interrelationship" between the Fourth and Fifth Amendments, and reflection upon that relationship persuaded Black that "when the Fourth Amendment's ban against unreasonable searches and seizures is considered together with the Fifth Amendment's ban against compelled self-incrimination, a constitutional basis emerges which not only justifies but actually requires the exclusionary rule." Mapp v. Ohio, 367 U.S. at 662 (Black, J. concurring). Most commentators have found this reasoning somewhat murky, especially when applied to evidence other than private papers which contain incriminating statements, and the theory today is primarily of historical interest.

Justice Harlan wrote a dissenting opinion, in which Justices Frankfurter and Whittaker joined, which began by pointing out that the Supreme Court had granted review in *Mapp* to decide the constitutionality of the Ohio statute punishing the mere possession of obscene materials, and not to decide whether the exclusionary rule should be imposed upon the states. The five Justices in the majority had thus reached out to decide a question not presented by the parties. The dissent did not question the continuing vitality of the *Weeks* doctrine in the federal courts, but argued that the various states should remain free to adopt or reject the exclusionary rule for state criminal prosecutions.

Justice Stewart concurred in the judgment on the ground that the obscenity statute violated the First Amendment. As a result, the majority opinion had only five votes, and its fifth adherent seemed to join the opinion while rejecting its rationale.

The Retroactivity of Mapp

Before the mid–1960s, the Supreme Court routinely applied newly-announced constitutional rules to past cases. According to orthodox theories, the Court was merely interpreting the Constitution and not changing it, and appellate opinions are necessarily retroactive in that they affirm or reverse a judgment already in existence. The Warren Court's "due process revolution" strained this theory to the breaking point, as the Court interpreted the Constitution to require overruling settled doctrines on which state and local authorities had come to rely. The Court automatically applied the *Mapp* doctrine to reverse Mapp's conviction and other cases pending on direct appeal, but it balked at overturning the convictions of prisoners whose appeals had already been exhausted.

Federal law permits state prisoners who have exhausted their state remedies to file a petition for habeas corpus in a federal district court, alleging that their convictions were obtained by unconstitutional means. In a series of decisions culminating in Fay v. Noia, 372 U.S. 391 (1963), the Supreme Court had substantially modified the concept of finality for criminal convictions where constitutional error was alleged. A state prisoner whose appeals have been exhausted, or even one who has chosen not to appeal, can sometimes obtain a hearing years later in federal court on a constitutional claim. For example, the Supreme Court voided a murder conviction in *Fay v. Noia, supra,* 21 years after the trial, because the prosecution had used coerced confession. In 1986 the Supreme Court granted the writ to void a murder conviction obtained in 1962, because of racial discrimination in the selection of the state grand jury that returned the indictment. Vasquez v. Hillery, 474 U.S. 254 (1986).

In Linkletter v. Walker, 381 U.S. 618 (1965), the Supreme Court held that the exclusionary rule would not be applied to overturn convictions which became final on appeal before the date of the Supreme Court's decision in *Mapp.* (Ironically, the search and conviction in the *Mapp* case occurred *before* the search and conviction in *Linkletter,* although the *Linkletter* judgment became final earlier.) The majority opinion by Justice Clark acknowledged that earlier decisions had applied the coerced confession and right to counsel doctrines with full retroactivity, but distinguished those decisions because there "the principle that we applied went to the fairness of the trial—the very integrity of the fact-finding process. Here * * * the fairness of the trial is not under attack. All that petitioner attacks is the admissibility of evidence, the reliability and relevancy of which is not questioned, and which may well have had no effect on the outcome." 381 U.S. at 639.

Almost immediately after the decision in *Mapp,* the Supreme Court thus gave notice that the Fourth Amendment exclusionary rule was a kind of second-class constitutional principle. Although "an essential part of both the Fourth and Fourteenth Amendments," the exclusionary rule was described as irrelevant to the integrity of the fact-finding process and the fairness of the trial. This reasoning, announced while the Supreme Court was at the height of its "liberal activist" period under the leadership of Chief Justice Earl Warren, set the stage for later decisions that restricted the scope of the exclusionary rule. Only Justices Black and Douglas dissented.

ONE 1958 PLYMOUTH SEDAN v. COMMONWEALTH OF PENNSYLVANIA

Supreme Court of the United States, 1965.
380 U.S. 693, 85 S.Ct. 1246, 14 L.Ed.2d 170.

Mr. Justice Goldberg delivered the opinion of the Court.

At approximately 6:30 a.m. on December 16, 1960, two law enforcement officers of the Pennsylvania Liquor Control Board stationed near Camden, New Jersey, at the approach to the Benjamin Franklin Bridge, observed a 1958 Plymouth sedan bearing Pennsylvania license plates proceeding toward the bridge in the direction of Philadelphia, Pennsylvania. The officers, noting that "[t]he car was low in the rear, quite low," followed it across the bridge into Philadelphia. They stopped the automobile a short distance within the city, identified themselves and questioned the owner, George McGonigle. The officers then searched the car and, in the rear and the trunk, found 31 cases of liquor not bearing Pennsylvania tax seals. The car and liquor were seized and McGonigle was arrested and charged with violation of Pennsylvania law. The officers did not have either a search or arrest warrant.

Pursuant to a Pennsylvania statute the Commonwealth filed a petition for forfeiture of the automobile. At the hearing, McGonigle, by timely objection, sought dismissal of the forfeiture petition on the ground that the forfeiture of the automobile depended upon the admission of evidence illegally obtained in violation of the Fourth Amendment to the Constitution as applied to the States by the Fourteenth Amendment. The trial court sustained this position and dismissed the forfeiture petition. In doing so, the trial judge made a specific finding that "[t]he seizure was founded upon evidence illegally obtained, since under the particular circumstances the officers acted without probable cause."

[The state Supreme Court reversed, taking the view that the exclusionary rule does not apply to civil forfeitures.]

As this Court has acknowledged, "[t]he leading case on the subject of search and seizure is Boyd v. United States, [noted on p. 47, supra. *Boyd*] itself was not a criminal case but was a proceeding by the United States to forfeit 35 cases of plate glass which had allegedly been imported without payment of the customs duty. The District Judge in the case entered an order compelling the owners of the plate glass to produce certain records which would aid the United States in proving its case for forfeiture. The question before the Court in Boyd was whether the compulsory production of a man's private papers for their evidentiary use against him in a proceeding to forfeit his property for alleged fraud against the revenue laws constituted an unreasonable search and seizure within the meaning of the Fourth Amendment of the Constitution. In holding that the Fourth Amendment applied and barred such attempted seizure, Mr. Justice Bradley, for the Court stated:

"We are also clearly of opinion that proceedings instituted for the purpose of declaring the forfeiture of a man's property by reason of offenses committed by him, though they may be civil in form, are in their nature criminal." * * * 116 U.S. at 633.

The Commonwealth further argues that Boyd's unequivocal statement that the Fourth Amendment applies to forfeiture proceedings as well as criminal prosecutions has been undermined by the statements of this Court in United States v. Jeffers, 342 U.S. 48, 54, and Trupiano v. United States, 334 U.S. 699, 710. Jeffers and Trupiano, unlike Boyd, were not forfeiture cases. They were federal criminal prosecutions. In both cases the Court held that evidence seized in violation of the Fourth Amendment was not admissible notwithstanding the fact that the evidence involved was contraband. By way of dictum, however, since the point was not before it, the Court stated in these cases that its ruling that the contraband was excludable as illegally seized did not mean that the Government was required to return the illegally imported narcotics to Jeffers or the unregistered still, alcohol and mash to Trupiano.

The nature of the contraband involved in these cases clearly explains these statements of the Court. Both Trupiano and Jeffers concerned objects the possession of which, without more, constitutes a crime. The repossession of such *per se* contraband by Jeffers and

Trupiano would have subjected them to criminal penalties. The return of the contraband would clearly have frustrated the express public policy against the possession of such objects.

It is apparent that the nature of the property here, though termed contraband by Pennsylvania, is quite different. There is nothing even remotely criminal in possessing an automobile. It is only the alleged use to which this particular automobile was put that subjects Mr. McGonigle to its possible loss. And it is conceded here that the Commonwealth could not establish an illegal use without using the evidence resulting from the search which is challenged as having been in violation of the Constitution. Furthermore, the return of the automobile to the owner would not subject him to any possible criminal penalties for possession or frustrate any public policy concerning automobiles, as automobiles. This distinction between what has been described as contraband per se and only derivative contraband has indeed been recognized by Pennsylvania itself in its requirement of mandatory forfeiture of illegal liquor, and stills, and only discretionary forfeiture of such things as automobiles illegally used. * * *

Finally as Mr. Justice Bradley aptly pointed out in Boyd, a forfeiture proceeding is quasi-criminal in character. Its object, like a criminal proceeding, is to penalize for the commission of an offense against the law. * * *

In sum, we conclude that the nature of a forfeiture proceeding, so well described by Mr. Justice Bradley in Boyd, and the reasons which led the Court to hold that the exclusionary rule of Weeks v. United States, supra, is obligatory upon the States under the Fourteenth Amendment, so well articulated by Mr. Justice Clark in Mapp, support the conclusion that the exclusionary rule is applicable to forfeiture proceedings such as the one involved here. This being the case, the judgment of the Pennsylvania Supreme Court must be reversed. Our holding frees the Pennsylvania court on remand to review the trial court's finding that the officials did not in this case have probable cause for the search involved, a question which it previously did not consider necessary to decide.

The judgment of the Supreme Court of Pennsylvania is reversed and the cause is remanded for proceedings not inconsistent with this opinion.

BIVENS v. SIX UNKNOWN NAMED AGENTS OF THE FEDERAL BUREAU OF NARCOTICS

Supreme Court of the United States, 1971.
403 U.S. 388, 91 S.Ct. 1999, 29 L.Ed.2d 619.

MR. JUSTICE BRENNAN delivered the opinion of the Court. * * *

This case has its origin in an arrest and search carried out on the morning of November 26, 1965. Petitioner's complaint alleged that on that day respondents, agents of the Federal Bureau of Narcotics acting under claim of federal authority, entered his apartment and arrested him for alleged narcotics violations. The agents manacled petitioner in front of his wife and children, and threatened to arrest the entire family. They searched the apartment from stem to stern. Thereafter, petitioner was taken to the federal courthouse in Brooklyn, where he was interrogated, booked, and subjected to a visual strip search.

On July 7, 1967, petitioner brought suit in Federal District Court. In addition to the allegations above, his complaint asserted that the arrest and search were effected without a warrant, and that unreasonable force was employed in making the arrest; fairly read, it alleges as well that the arrest was made without probable cause. Petitioner claimed to have suffered great humiliation, embarrassment, and mental suffering as a result of the agents' unlawful conduct, and sought $15,000 damages from each of them. * * *

[The lower federal courts dismissed the case on the ground that federal law provides no damage remedy for Fourth Amendment violations by federal officers. Petitioner would have to sue the officers in state court under ordinary tort doctrines. The Supreme Court reversed, holding that the complaint stated a cause of action under the Fourth Amendment directly. The Court then remanded the case for further proceedings on other issues, including the claim that the agents were immune by virtue of their official position.]*

Mr. Chief Justice Burger, dissenting.

I dissent from today's holding which judicially creates a damage remedy not provided for by the Constitution and not enacted by Congress. We would more surely preserve the important values of the doctrine of separation of powers—and perhaps get a better result—by recommending a solution to the Congress as the branch of government in which the Constitution has vested the legislative power. Legislation is the business of the Congress, and it has the facilities and competence for that task—as we do not. * * *

This case has significance far beyond its facts and its holding. For more than 55 years this Court has enforced a rule under which evidence of undoubted reliability and probative value has been suppressed and excluded from criminal cases whenever it was obtained in violation of the Fourth Amendment. The rule has rested on a theory that suppression of evidence in these circumstances was imperative to deter law enforcement authorities from using improper methods to obtain evidence. * * *

From time to time members of the Court, recognizing the validity of these protests, have articulated varying alternative justifications for the suppression of important evidence in a criminal trial. Under one of these alternative theories the rule's foundation is shifted to the "sporting contest" thesis that the government must "play the game fairly" and cannot be allowed to profit from its own illegal acts. But the exclusionary rule does not ineluctably flow from a desire to ensure that government

---

* On remand, the Court of Appeals held that the officers did not have complete immunity, but they would have a valid defense if they acted in good faith and with a reasonable belief that their actions were lawful. 456 F.2d 1339 (2d Cir.1972). ed.

plays the "game" according to the rules. If an effective alternative remedy is available, concern for official observance of the law does not require adherence to the exclusionary rule. Nor is it easy to understand how a court can be thought to endorse a violation of the Fourth Amendment by allowing illegally seized evidence to be introduced against a defendant if an effective remedy is provided against the government.

The exclusionary rule has also been justified on the theory that the relationship between the Self–Incrimination Clause of the Fifth Amendment and the Fourth Amendment requires the suppression of evidence seized in violation of the latter. * * *

It is clear, however, that neither of these theories undergirds the decided cases in this Court. Rather the exclusionary rule has rested on the deterrent rationale—the hope that law enforcement officials would be deterred from unlawful searches and seizures if the illegally seized, albeit trustworthy, evidence was suppressed often enough and the courts persistently enough deprived them of any benefits they might have gained from their illegal conduct.

This evidentiary rule is unique to American jurisprudence. Although the English and Canadian legal systems are highly regarded, neither has adopted our rule.

I do not question the need for some remedy to give meaning and teeth to the constitutional guarantees against unlawful conduct by government officials. Without some effective sanction, these protections would constitute little more than rhetoric. Beyond doubt the conduct of some officials requires sanctions as cases like *Irvine* indicate. But the hope that this objective could be accomplished by the exclusion of reliable evidence from criminal trials was hardly more than a wistful dream. Although I would hesitate to abandon it until some meaningful substitute is developed, the history of the suppression doctrine demonstrates that it is both conceptually sterile and practically ineffective in accomplishing its stated objective. This is illustrated by the paradox that an unlawful act against a totally innocent person—such as petitioner claims to be—has been left without an effective remedy, and hence the Court finds it necessary now—55 years later—to construct a remedy of its own.

Some clear demonstration of the benefits and effectiveness of the exclusionary rule is required to justify it in view of the high price it extracts from society—the release of countless guilty criminals. But there is no empirical evidence to support the claim that the rule actually deters illegal conduct of law enforcement officials. Oaks, Studying the Exclusionary Rule in Search and Seizure, 37 U.Chi.L.Rev. 665, 667 (1970).

There are several reasons for this failure. The rule does not apply any direct sanction to the individual official whose illegal conduct results in the exclusion of evidence in a criminal trial. With rare exceptions law enforcement agencies do not impose direct sanctions on the individual officer responsible for a particular judicial application of the suppression doctrine. Thus there is virtually nothing done to bring about a change in his practices. The immediate sanction triggered by the application of the rule is visited upon the prosecutor whose case against a criminal is either weakened or destroyed. The doctrine deprives the police in no real sense; except that apprehending wrongdoers is their business, police have no more stake in successful prosecutions than prosecutors or the public.

The suppression doctrine vaguely assumes that law enforcement is a monolithic governmental enterprise. * * * But the prosecutor who loses his case because of police misconduct is not an official in the police department; he can rarely set in motion any corrective action or administrative penalties. Moreover, he does not have control or direction over police procedures or police actions that lead to the exclusion of evidence. It is the rare exception when a prosecutor takes part in arrests, searches, or seizures so that he can guide police action.

Whatever educational effect the rule conceivably might have in theory is greatly diminished in fact by the realities of law enforcement work. Policemen do not have the time, inclination, or training to read and grasp the nuances of the appellate opinions that ultimately define the standards of conduct they are to follow. The issues that these decisions resolve often admit of neither easy nor obvious answers, as sharply divided courts on what is or is not "reasonable" amply demonstrate. Nor can judges, in all candor, forget that opinions sometimes lack helpful clarity.

The presumed educational effect of judicial opinions is also reduced by the long time lapse—often several years—between the original police action and its final judicial evaluation. Given a policeman's pressing responsibilities, it would be surprising if he ever becomes aware of the final result after such a delay. Finally, the exclusionary rule's deterrent impact is diluted by the fact that there are large areas of police activity that do not result in criminal prosecutions—hence the rule has virtually no applicability and no effect in such situations. Oaks, *supra*, at 720–724. * * *

Although unfortunately ineffective, the exclusionary rule has increasingly been characterized by a single, monolithic, and drastic judicial response to all official violations of legal norms. Inadvertent errors of judgment that do not work any grave injustice will inevitably occur under the pressure of police work. These honest mistakes have been treated in the same way as deliberate and flagrant *Irvine*-type violations of the Fourth Amendment. For example, in Miller v. United States, 357 U.S. 301, 309–310 (1958), reliable evidence was suppressed because of a police officer's failure to say a "few more words" during the arrest and search of a known narcotics peddler.

This Court's decision announced today in Coolidge v. New Hampshire,* dramatically illustrates the extent to which the doctrine repre-

---

* In *Coolidge v. New Hampshire*, 403 U.S. 443 (1971), the Court by a narrow majority overturned a murder conviction because crucial evidence had been seized under an

sents a mechanically inflexible response to widely varying degrees of police error and the resulting high price that society pays. I dissented in *Coolidge* primarily because I do not believe the Fourth Amendment had been violated. Even on the Court's contrary premise, however, whatever violation occurred was surely insufficient in nature and extent to justify the drastic result dictated by the suppression doctrine. A fair trial by jury has resolved doubts as to Coolidge's guilt. But now his conviction on retrial is placed in serious question by the remand for a new trial—years after the crime—in which evidence that the New Hampshire courts found relevant and reliable will be withheld from the jury's consideration. It is hardly surprising that such results are viewed with incomprehension by nonlawyers in this country and lawyers, judges, and legal scholars the world over.

Freeing either a tiger or a mouse in a schoolroom is an illegal act, but no rational person would suggest that these two acts should be punished in the same way. From time to time judges have occasion to pass on regulations governing police procedures. I wonder what would be the judicial response to a police order authorizing "shoot to kill" with respect to every fugitive. It is easy to predict our collective wrath and outrage. We, in common with all rational minds, would say that the police response must relate to the gravity and need; that a "shoot" order might conceivably be tolerable to prevent the escape of a convicted killer but surely not for a car thief, a pickpocket or a shoplifter.

I submit that society has at least as much right to expect rationally graded responses from judges in place of the universal "capital punishment" we inflict on all evidence when police error is shown in its acquisition. * * *

I do not propose, however, that we abandon the suppression doctrine until some meaningful alternative can be developed. In a sense our legal system has become the captive of its own creation. To overrule *Weeks* and *Mapp*, even assuming the Court was now prepared to take that step, could raise yet new problems. Obviously the public interest would be poorly served if law enforcement officials were suddenly to gain the impression, however erroneous, that all constitutional restraints on police had somehow been removed—that an open season on "criminals" had been declared. I am concerned lest some such mistaken impression might be fostered by a flat overruling of the suppression doctrine cases. For years we have relied upon it as the exclusive remedy for unlawful official conduct; in a sense we are in a situation akin to the narcotics addict whose dependence on drugs precludes any drastic or immediate withdrawal of the supposed prop, regardless of how futile its continued use may be.

Reasonable and effective substitutes can be formulated if Congress would take the lead, as it did for example in 1946 in the Federal Tort

invalid search warrant. The warrant was invalid because it was issued by a prosecutor (the state Attorney–General, in his ca- pacity as a Justice of the Peace), rather than by a neutral and disinterested magistrate.

Claims Act. I see no insuperable obstacle to the elimination of the suppression doctrine if Congress would provide some meaningful and effective remedy against unlawful conduct by government officials.

The problems of both error and deliberate misconduct by law enforcement officials call for a workable remedy. Private damage actions against individual police officers concededly have not adequately met this requirement, and it would be fallacious to assume today's work of the Court in creating a remedy will really accomplish its stated objective. There is some validity to the claims that juries will not return verdicts against individual officers except in those unusual cases where the violation has been flagrant or where the error has been complete, as in the arrest of the wrong person or the search of the wrong house. There is surely serious doubt, for example, that a drug peddler caught packing his wares will be able to arouse much sympathy in a jury on the ground that the police officer did not announce his identity and purpose fully or because he failed to utter a "few more words." See Miller v. United States, *supra*. Jurors may well refuse to penalize a police officer at the behest of a person they believe to be a "criminal" and probably will not punish an officer for honest errors of judgment. In any event an actual recovery depends on finding non-exempt assets of the police officer from which a judgment can be satisfied.

I conclude, therefore, that an entirely different remedy is necessary but it is one that in my view is as much beyond judicial power as the step the Court takes today. Congress should develop an administrative or quasi-judicial remedy against the government itself to afford compensation and restitution for persons whose Fourth Amendment rights have been violated. The venerable doctrine of *respondeat superior* in our tort law provides an entirely appropriate conceptual basis for this remedy. If, for example, a security guard privately employed by a department store commits an assault or other tort on a customer such as an improper search, the victim has a simple and obvious remedy—an action for money damages against the guard's employer, the department store. W. Prosser, The Law of Torts § 68, pp. 470–480 (3d ed., 1964).[2] Such a statutory scheme would have the added advantage of providing some remedy to the completely innocent persons who are sometimes the victims of illegal police conduct—something that the suppression doctrine, of course, can never accomplish.

A simple structure would suffice. For example, Congress could enact a statute along the following lines:

(a) a waiver of sovereign immunity as to the illegal acts of law enforcement officials committed in the performance of assigned duties;

(b) the creation of a cause of action for damages sustained by any person aggrieved by conduct of governmental agents in violation of the Fourth Amendment or statutes regulating official conduct;

2. Damage verdicts for such acts are often sufficient in size to provide an effective deterrent and stimulate employers to corrective action.

(c) the creation of a tribunal, quasi-judicial in nature or perhaps patterned after the United States Court of Claims to adjudicate all claims under the statute;

(d) a provision that this statutory remedy is in lieu of the exclusion of evidence secured for use in criminal cases in violation of the Fourth Amendment; and

(e) a provision directing that no evidence, otherwise admissible, shall be excluded from any criminal proceeding because of violation of the Fourth Amendment.

I doubt that lawyers serving on such a tribunal would be swayed either by undue sympathy for officers or by the prejudice against "criminals" that has sometimes moved lay jurors to deny claims. In addition to awarding damages, the record of the police conduct that is condemned would undoubtedly become a relevant part of an officer's personnel file so that the need for additional training or disciplinary action could be identified or his future usefulness as a public official evaluated. Finally, appellate judicial review could be made available on much the same basis that it is now provided as to district courts and regulatory agencies. This would leave to the courts the ultimate responsibility for determining and articulating standards.

Once the constitutional validity of such a statute is established,[3] it can reasonably be assumed that the States would develop their own remedial systems on the federal model. Indeed there is nothing to prevent a State from enacting a comparable statutory scheme without waiting for the Congress. Steps along these lines would move our system toward more responsible law enforcement on the one hand and away from the irrational and drastic results of the suppression doctrine on the other. Independent of the alternative embraced in this dissenting opinion, I believe the time has come to re-examine the scope of the exclusionary rule and consider at least some narrowing of its thrust so as to eliminate the anomalies it has produced.

In a country that prides itself on innovation, inventive genius, and willingness to experiment, it is a paradox that we should cling for more than a half century to a legal mechanism that was poorly designed and never really worked. I can only hope now that the Congress will manifest a willingness to view realistically the hard evidence of the half-century history of the suppression doctrine revealing thousands of cases in which the criminal was set free because the constable blundered and virtually no evidence that innocent victims of police error—such as petitioner claims to be—have been afforded meaningful redress.

Commentary

There are three distinct theories which support the exclusionary rule. They are not mutually exclusive, and so one could support the rule on a single theory or on a combination of the three theories.

3. Any such legislation should emphasize the interdependence between the waiver of sovereign immunity and the elimination of the judicially created exclusionary rule so that if the legislative determination to repudiate the exclusionary rule falls, the entire statutory scheme would fall.

1. *The personal right theory.* A remedy for any violation of the law should seek to restore the victim to the position he would have been in if the law had not been violated. When we exclude illegally obtained evidence from a criminal trial, we are doing no more than restoring the situation that would have existed if the illegal search or seizure had never occurred. We exclude the evidence not because doing so is likely to have an effect on police activity in other situations, but because it is an appropriate partial remedy for the violation in this particular case. There is no need, if the personal right theory is accepted, for justifying the exclusionary rule on the basis of its supposed "deterrent effect" on police activity. Any such effect is desirable but basically beside the point, because the primary object is to correct the wrong done to this particular victim of unlawful police activity, not to protect the rights of other people.

Of course, this remedy like many others is not carried through to its logical conclusion. We exclude evidence, but we do not return narcotics or stolen goods to the suspect even if they were discovered in an illegal search. It is also well established that the mere fact of an illegal arrest, or even a kidnapping to bring an accused across a state or international border to avoid extradition formalities, does not deprive the court before which the accused has been brought of jurisdiction. [See *I.N.S. v. Lopez–Mendoza,* page 333, *infra.*] The principle that the courts should protect suspects from suffering losses caused by illegal police activities, like many other legal principles, is subject to certain limitations based on public policy. The existence of such limitations does not necessarily call into question the fundamental soundness of the principle itself.

Certain exceptions to the exclusionary rule which are controversial under other theories are readily explained under the personal right theory. In particular, the "standing" limitation discussed in *Jones v. United States, supra* page 38, follows logically from the premise that it is the violation of a defendant's personal right that justifies the remedy. Where the personal rights of the defendant have not been violated, there is no reason to grant a remedy. Similarly, by excluding evidence we are only trying to restore the *status quo ante,* not to give the defendant a windfall. If it is likely that the police would have found the evidence lawfully absent the illegal search, then the evidence should be admitted. This consideration explains what the courts call the "inevitable discovery" exception.

2. *The "judicial integrity" theory.* This theory finds its earliest support in the frequently-quoted dissenting opinions by Justices Holmes and Brandeis in Olmstead v. United States, 277 U.S. 438 (1928). The emphasis here is on the responsibilities of the judiciary, rather than the rights of the accused. When the courts allow law enforcement officers to make use of evidence which has been seized in violation of constitutional rights, they encourage the police to believe that such violations are tacitly condoned. They are roughly like purchasers of stolen goods, who deplore the theft but willingly profit from it. By strictly enforcing an exclusionary rule, on the other hand, the courts acquit themselves of hypocrisy and demonstrate that they take constitutional rights seriously.

The judicial integrity rationale has merit, but it is also subject to objections. First, it is often stated that courts in other countries reject the exclusionary rule as a remedy for search and seizure violations, although they do exclude coerced statements. The highest courts of England and Canada have been particularly adamant in rejecting the rule,[a] and these are countries whose legal traditions are comparable to our own. On the other hand, judges in a number of other countries have the discretion to exclude illegally obtained evidence regardless of its reliability, and the trend seems to be towards increasing use of this remedy. For descriptions of the exclusionary rule in other countries, see Polyviou, *Search and Seizure* 319–340 (Duckworth 1982); Bradley, "The Exclusionary Rule in Germany," 96 Harv. L.Rev. 1032, (1983); Pakter, "Exclusionary Rules in France, Germany and Italy," 9 Hastings, Int. & Comp.L.Rev. 1 (1985); Weigand, "Criminal Procedure: Comparative Aspects," in *Encyclopedia of Crime and Justice* (Kadish ed. 1983). West German practice is particularly interesting because comparative law scholars have frequently admired the German criminal justice system, and because, according to Professor Bradley:

> Contrary to the traditional view, Germany in fact has a well-developed system of exclusionary rules founded on constitutional principles and statutory provisions. The German and the American exclusionary rules both reflect the fundamental principle that relevant evidence must occasionally be excluded to safeguard constitutional rights, but the rules sometimes differ significantly in the scope of protection that they afford. The German rule, for example, is less stringent than the American rule in excluding evidence derived from improper searches of the home, and the failure to give *Miranda*-type warnings to suspects generally will not result in exclusion in Germany. On the other hand, in comparison to their American counterparts, the German courts afford significantly greater protection to witnesses with personal or professional ties to the defendant and are stricter in suppressing evidence obtained in violation of wiretapping statutes. The German courts have also defined a doctrine of personal privacy that will cause certain private material, such as diaries, to be excluded even when such material has been obtained legally. The two systems converge, however, in their treatment of coerced confessions and evidence obtained through brutality or deceit.

The mechanics of the German and American systems also reflect both similarities and differences. Germany's statutory exclusionary rules operate automatically, much like the American rule: if the police have violated the law, any resulting evidence will be excluded without regard to other considerations. In cases in which general constitutional principles are the basis for exclusion, however, the only police conduct that leads to automatic exclusion in Germany is a seizure that violates the *Rechtsstaatsprinzip*[b] through brutality or deceit. In all other situations, in dramatic contrast to the American system, the fact that evidence was legally or illegally obtained is not dispositive. The decision to admit or suppress will be determined by balancing the relative importance of the defendant's privacy rights against the seriousness of the offense charged. Bradley, *supra*, at 1064–65.

Do the judges in England and Canada lack judicial integrity because they refuse to follow the American model? Possibly the answer depends upon whether police illegality in those countries is as pervasive a problem as it was in the United States in 1961. The judicial integrity rationale only requires that the courts not be seen as condoning police illegality; it does not necessarily require that they exclude evidence if the obligation of the police to obey the law is otherwise solidly established. If the police generally have the confidence of the public, and if police misconduct is ordinarily adequately checked by disciplinary procedures or remedied by lawsuits, then a judicial policy of refusing to inquire into the legality of police action in individual criminal prosecutions might be justifiable. Another distinction might be that the United States Constitution is a unique document, which places an extraordinary degree of importance upon protecting the individual from governmental overreaching, and which therefore places special obligations on the courts. In any event, the evidence from comparative law studies is inconclusive. Although the precise form the exclusionary rule takes in the United States is unique, the principle that reliable evidence should sometimes be excluded because it was illegally obtained is widely acknowledged.

A second line of objection to the judicial integrity rationale takes the form of asserting that "judicial integrity" is a double-edged sword. The courts must demonstrate that they take Fourth Amendment violations seriously, of course, but they ought to be taking the laws against murder, rape, and narcotics selling equally seriously. Many of the cases in this Chapter involve both egregiously unlawful police activity and fairly marginal or controversial law enforcement interests. When the police ransack a house to find lottery tickets or pornographic photographs, they commit substantial violations of constitutional rights in the pursuit of relatively trivial law enforcement interests. But the exclusionary rule also has the potential of permitting a murderer to go free because of some relatively technical default of the police in obtaining the evidence. However infrequently such cases occur in practice, they raise the question whether "judicial integrity" includes a sense of proportion. When courts insist on excluding evidence no matter how serious the crime, and no matter how technical the violation, important critics like Chief Justices Burger and Rehnquist may accuse them of demonstrating a misguided sense of priorities rather than integrity.[c]

3. *The "deterrent theory."* This theory argues that we exclude evidence not to remedy a violation in this case, but to have an effect on police conduct in *other* cases. The deterrent theory of the exclusionary rule is linked to a *substantive* theory of the Fourth Amendment, which argues that the purpose of the Amendment is to protect the "innocent," i.e. persons who are not in possession of the contraband or evidence that the police are looking for.

---

c. "[W]hile it is quite true that courts are not to be participants in 'dirty business,' neither are they to be ethereal vestal virgins of another world, so determined to be like Caesar's wife, Calpurnia, that they cease to be effective forums in which both those charged with committing criminal acts and the society which makes the charge may have a fair trial in which relevant competent evidence is received in order to determine whether or not the charge is true." California v. Minjares, 443 U.S. 916, 925 (1979) (Rehnquist, J. dissenting from denial of stay).

According to this approach, we permit searches only upon probable cause (and require a judicial warrant for the most intrusive searches) because we want to minimize the number of occasions in which officers disturb the peace and privacy of persons who are not involved in criminal activity. We are *not* trying to give the narcotics possessors, for example, a reasonable chance of avoiding arrest and conviction provided that they are sufficiently discrete in their activities. Ideally, we would like every hidden supply of contraband to be discovered, but we also want to protect innocent citizens from police searches based on inaccurate information. To accomplish this we allow the police to search only when they have reliable indications that seizable items are present, and require in many situations that a disinterested magistrate review the decision in advanced. The sole purpose of excluding evidence is to enforce these rules. The guilty defendant receives a windfall so that the police will not have an incentive to violate rules that protect innocent people. For a more complete development of this theory, see Loewy, "The Fourth Amendment as a Device for Protecting the Innocent," 81 Mich.L.Rev. 1229 (1983).

In recent years, the deterrent theory has had the support of a majority of the Supreme Court, to the exclusion of other theories. Cases establishing this point are included in Chapter 7, *infra*. In reality, excluding evidence is not a deterrent: a better word would be "disincentive." Suppression of evidence does not punish the police in the way that imprisonment punishes a burglar. It merely prevents them from profiting from their illegal conduct in a certain manner. The police still have plenty of reasons for making illegal searches and seizures, because they often have purposes other than conviction. For example, narcotics officers are interested in seizing narcotics, whether or not the seizure leads to a conviction. If they can make the seizure lawfully and obtain a conviction as well, they will attempt to do so. When the alternative to an unlawful seizure is no seizure at all, the existence of an exclusionary rule will not deter them from seizing unlawfully.

If the purpose of the exclusionary rule is to deprive the police of an incentive for violating the law, then the existence of a "standing" limitation is difficult to justify. Any such limitation permits the police to make at least some use of illegally obtained evidence, and thus provides an incentive to violate the law. For this reason, the California courts following the *Cahan* decision decided to exclude all illegally obtained evidence from criminal cases, regardless of whether the privacy rights of the defendant personally were violated.[d] On the other hand, the United States Supreme Court has recently been expanding the standing limitation, in spite of its adherence to the deterrent theory for the exclusionary rule generally. For an explanation and defense of this questionable practice, see *Rakas v. Illinois, infra* page 307.

The exclusionary rule is inherently a debatable idea if the deterrent theory is assumed to be its sole basis. It requires the courts to be continually committing an "injustice" in the present case (giving a guilty defendant a windfall), in order to provide a highly speculative benefit in other cases. It is always more obvious that exclusion prevents or hinders the conviction of a

---

d. By virtue of a state constitutional amendment, California now follows the Federal rule on standing and other search and seizure questions. See In re Lance W, 37 Cal.3d 873, 210 Cal.Rptr. 631, 694 P.2d 744 (1985).

guilty person in *this* case than that it has positive effect on police conduct in *other* cases. It is therefore not surprising that the Supreme Court Justices who adhere to the deterrent theory tend to be inclined to cut back on the exclusionary rule. Further consideration of how the rule has been cut back will be postponed until the concluding Chapter of this section of the book.

4. *Alternatives to the Exclusionary Rule.* Although the *Bivens* case, page 52, is a post-*Mapp* decision, it is included in this Chapter because Chief Justice Burger's dissenting opinion demonstrates that the decision in *Mapp v. Ohio* did not put an end to the controversy. It is significant that neither the federal government nor any of the states took up Chief Justice Burger's invitation to provide a special tort remedy as a substitute for the exclusion of evidence. It may be that, upon reflection, legislators concerned with budgetary priorities saw the prospect of expanded tort remedies as vastly more unwelcome than the exclusion of evidence in a limited number of criminal cases. If it seems unreasonable to reverse the conviction of a "known narcotics peddler" because a police officer failed to say a few more words during his arrest, would it seem any more reasonable to give that same narcotics peddler a substantial award of damages? Some of Chief Justice Burger's complaints seem directed at the substance of the rules governing police activity, rather than the particular remedy employed for violations of those rules.

The principal problem with a tort remedy is not sovereign immunity or jury prejudice. Very little is left of the doctrine of sovereign immunity in most states, and local communities and even individual police officers typically carry liability insurance. Jury verdicts have been sufficiently generous that this insurance is increasingly expensive and even difficult to obtain, and plaintiffs' lawyers consider the jury to be an asset rather than a liability. Where the victim of police illegality has suffered substantial injuries, the contingent fee system is likely to produce a dedicated lawyer to press the claim for damages. Victims of unconstitutional activity can sue state and local police officers in Federal Court under the Civil Rights Act, 42 U.S.C.A. § 1983, and can also recover damages from a local government if the officers acted pursuant to official policy. See Monell v. New York City Dept. of Social Services, 436 U.S. 658 (1978). The Federal Tort Claims Act was amended in 1974 to permit claims against the government for a variety of unlawful acts by federal law enforcement officers. [28 U.S.C.A. 2680 Ch.]

Monetary damages are appropriate where there has been substantial property damage or personal injury, but they are much less easy to calculate where the only damage is to dignity or privacy. If the police stop people at random, and detain them for a few minutes while searching their pockets, purses and automobile trunks, what is the appropriate measure of damages? If contingent fee lawsuits are to be brought, the anticipated award must be large enough to cover the costs of litigation and the lawyer's fee, as well as compensation for the plaintiff. Any system of awards which is generous enough to encourage lawsuits is apt to seem far too generous when put into practice.

The federal statute governing wiretapping and electronic surveillance, 18 U.S.C.A. § 2510–2520, provides an unusual combination of remedies for unlawful electronic eavesdropping and wiretapping. Section 2515 of the Act prohibits the use as evidence of the fruits of unlawful surveillance, and this exclusionary rule is broader than the constitutionally mandated exclusionary rule of *Mapp v. Ohio*. For example, it specifically applies to grand jury proceedings, where the Supreme Court has held that the Fourth Amendment exclusionary rule does not apply. The Act also provides for criminal penalties and civil damages, including punitive damages and an award for attorney fees and other litigation costs. Because the injury from invasions of privacy is frequently intangible and impossible to quantify, the Act provides for "actual damages but not less than liquidated damages computed at the rate of $100 a day for each day of violation or $1000, whichever is higher." 18 U.S.C.A. § 2520. The existence of all these remedies is explained by the fact that electronic surveillance is an extremely controversial practice, and it was necessary to provide extensive protection against abuses in order to get the legislation through Congress.

The Supreme Court declined an opportunity to experiment with an innovative method of remedying pervasive police misconduct in Rizzo v. Goode, 423 U.S. 362 (1976). The plaintiffs brought class actions under the Civil Rights Act against the Mayor and Police Commissioner of Philadelphia, alleging a pervasive pattern of unconstitutional police conduct which was either supported or tolerated by the city government. The Federal District Court ordered the city to adopt an effective method of dealing with citizen complaints against police officers, and set out guidelines that such a process must follow. (In a number of cases, federal district courts have taken similar action against unconstitutional conditions in state prisons and hospitals, in some cases virtually taking over the operation of these institutions to the extent necessary to bring them into line with constitutional standards.) The Supreme Court reversed the District Court order in *Rizzo*, however, holding that the court's order constituted an unwarranted federal intrusion into the autonomy provided for state and local governments under our federal system. The opinion distinguished cases which had upheld federal injunctions against more specific instances of local law enforcement misconduct, where the individual plaintiffs were more directly threatened by the activity in question.

Note

The purpose of this chapter has been to trace the development of the exclusionary rule from its beginning in Weeks v. United States through Chief Justice's Burger's unsuccessful attempt to enlist Congress in a campaign against the rule. Students should be aware that some of the rules discussed in this chapter were altered during the 1970s and 1980s, as a more conservative Supreme Court sought to cut back the rule without eliminating it. In particular, the approach to "standing" announced in Jones v. United States (*supra*, p. 40) was significantly changed by cases such as Rakas v. Illinois, 439 U.S. 128 (1978), and United States v. Salvucci, 448 U.S. 83 (1980)(which abolished the "automatic standing" rule for defendants charged with possession of seized property). The theory of the exclusionary rule itself took a new turn with the recognition of a "reasonable good faith" exception in United States v. Leon, 468 U.S. 897 (1984). These more recent developments are included in Chapter Seven. At this point, we turn to the substantive content of the law of search and seizure.

Chapter 3

PROTECTED PLACES
AND INTERESTS

COMMONWEALTH v. OGLIALORO

Supreme Court of Pennsylvania, 1990.
525 Pa. 250, 579 A.2d 1288.

PAPADAKOS, JUSTICE.

[Defendant was convicted of unlawfully possessing a quantity of marijuana plants.]

On October 11, 1985, Pennsylvania State Police at the Trevose Barracks received an anonymous telephone tip, allegedly from a private aircraft pilot reporting the presence of marijuana in the defendant's pole-barn. Acting on the tip, three police officers flew over the premises in a state police helicopter on October 16. The day was bright and sunny. The helicopter initially flew over the property at a height of approximately 500 feet above the barn; however, the police were unable to ascertain the barn's contents at that altitude and therefore reduced their altitude to approximately 50 feet over the barn. The police were not using any visual aids to assist their observations. While hovering at 50 feet, police observed the tops of plants which were pressed up against the barn's roof, and which clearly matched the color, size, and configuration of marijuana. The police helicopter hovered at a height of 50 feet for approximately 15 seconds and made a total of three or more passes over the property, lasting approximately five minutes. Defendant's wife was present in the home at the time. She experienced various sensations caused by the helicopters proximity, such as loud noise, and vibration of the house and windows.

After clearly identifying the marijuana from an altitude of 50 feet over the barn the helicopter returned to the State Police Barracks. On the basis of the officers' aerial observations, the local police chief proceeded to obtain a search warrant, while other officers drove to the site to secure the property in the interim. The officers participating in the aerial viewing had significant training and experience in the detection of marijuana. Marijuana has a precise growing configuration, and grows in a distinctive color, distinguishable from other vegetation growing in Pennsylvania. From an altitude of 500 feet it was possible to observe through the barn roof a color identical to the color of growing marijuana plants. At 50 feet, it was possible to identify, clearly as marijuana, the leaves of a plant which were pressed against the barn roof. In general, it was possible to observe objects inside the barn through the roof, especially if the object was positioned close to the roof.

When the search warrant arrived, the police forcibly entered the barn and observed 91 very large marijuana plants. The plants appear to have ranged in height between 12 to 18 feet tall, and some were stopped over and pressed against the barn's roof * * *.

To prevail successfully on a claim of governmental invasion of privacy, a person is required first to show that a subjective expectation of privacy exists as to the area being searched. An expectation of privacy is present when the individual, by his conduct, "exhibits an actual (subjective) expectation of privacy" and that the subjective expectation "is one that society is prepared to recognize as 'reasonable.'" Katz v. United States, 389 U.S. 347, 361 (1967). The controlling consideration is whether the individual contesting the search and seizure entertains a legitimate expectation of privacy in the premises or area searched.

Defendant contends that he exhibited an expectation of privacy in the pole-barn because of the manner of its construction and its location in a rural area. This structure stood approximately 18 feet tall. The sides of the barn were completely opaque and the roof consisted of transparent plastic sheets. He assembled his pole-barn entirely upon his property: approximately 446 feet from the road, and 251 feet from his residence. The building and placement of this structure appear to be such that he successfully denied anyone adjacent to this structure, or parallel to this structure, a view of the goings on inside of it.

However, while this expectation may be adequate to persons attempting to view the contents from ground level, the question is whether defendant's expectation extended to aerial observations of the roof. His use of a transparent roof created an unobstructed window to the sky. People in the barn could gaze through the opening skyward and overhead spectators, with equal ease, could peer into the barn because of the transparent roof. Since the construction of the roof made it like an open or uncovered window, it would be most instructive to review the case law as to whether an expectation of privacy is present where one opens his windows.

The mere looking at that which is open to view is not a search. [Citations] In Commonwealth v. Hernley, 216 Pa.Superior Ct. 177, 263 A.2d 904 (1970), cert. denied, 401 U.S. 914 (1971), a Federal Bureau of Investigation Agent, standing on a ladder and using binoculars, observed gambling records through a window on the third floor of a print shop. The Superior Court accepted the Commonwealth's argument that the defendant left his activities open to view; therefore, there was no violation of the Fourth Amendment. The court stated that "it was incumbent on the suspect to preserve his privacy from visual observation.''

Failure of a defendant, or those with him, to close the window shades negates defendant's argument that he was deprived of his privacy. Commonwealth v. Johnson, 247 Pa.Superior Ct. 208, 372 A.2d 11, 13 (1977). In Johnson, the defendant and his accomplice were observed as they left the scene of a robbery. A witness spotted their getaway vehicle in front of an apartment building five blocks from the scene of the crime, and subsequently informed police that he watched three men run into the apartment building. Investigating officers stationed themselves upon a common area patio attached to the rear of the apartment building where they could peer into the apartment through a four inch gap between curtains on a kitchen window. In effect, the Johnson court found that the opening in the window negated any expectation of privacy from the eyes of the world or of the police.

We agree with our Superior Court that there can be no expectation of privacy when one leaves his windows open or uncovered so that any passerby might peer into one's dwelling with impunity, and we have little trouble in concluding that the same result should apply regardless of where the window or opening is placed in the dwelling.

By installing a transparent, or at most translucent, roof, Appellee readily allowed exposure of the contents of the structure to the sunlight outside and also knowingly exposed his activities therein to persons lawfully operating aircraft over his property who might decide to take a look. We reject the suggestion that any expectation of privacy attaches in such situations.

Nor is our answer different if we consider that the barn was in close proximity to Appellee's home * * *. As long as the police have the right to be where they are, and the activity is clear and visible, the fact they are peering into curtilage is of no significance. Here, there is little question that a transparent roof of a barn presents a clear and visible view of the activities going on in the barn from any height above the barn, and the question becomes whether the police have the right to fly above Appellee's property.

In California v. Ciraolo, 476 U.S. 207 (1986), the United States Supreme Court recognized that police have a right to be present in public navigable airspace and to make non-intrusive observations from aircraft over property, including curtilage, consistent with the strictures of the Fourth Amendment.

The facts in *Ciraolo* reveal that the Santa Clara Police received an anonymous tip that Ciraolo was growing marijuana in his backyard. Police were unable to observe the contents of Ciraolo's backyard because a 6 foot outer fence and a 10 foot inner fence completely enclosed the yard. The investigating officer then secured a private plane and flew over Ciraolo's house at an altitude of 1,000 feet—within "navigable airspace". ["Navigable airspace" is defined as that altitude above the minimum prescribed by the Civil Aeronautics Board.] A search warrant was issued on the basis of an affidavit describing the anonymous tip and the officer's observations from the air.

The Court concluded the fact that the observation took place within the curtilage was not by itself a bar to all police observation. Since any member of the public flying in the airspace above Ciraolo's yard, or a power company repair mechanic on the pole overlooking the yard, who glanced down could have seen everything the officers observed, there was no Fourth Amendment violation.

Defendant in this case, however, argues, that because the observation was made in "non-navigable airspace", at an altitude of 50 feet above the structure, the observation of his pole-barn amounted to an illegal search and subsequent seizure. This distinction fails to account for the fact that helicopters are permitted to fly at any altitude if the operation is conducted without hazard to persons or property on the surface. Since helicopters are permitted to fly at any altitude, all airspace is navigable, in the technical sense, and police, like the rest of the public, are permitted to travel in this space.

One final question remains. While the police had a right to fly above Appellee's property and he had no reasonable expectation of privacy that they would not peer into his barn, it remains to be decided whether the conduct of the police in flying at 50 feet above the barn was hazardous to persons or property on the surface. If so, the search would be unreasonable and violative of constitutional requirements prohibiting unreasonable searches and seizures. When weighing the issue of whether or not a helicopter surveillance is intrusive to the point of being hazardous, or non-intrusive, a trial court should ask whether or not a risk of harm or danger exists in regards to the person(s) present or property being observed, whether or not a danger, or threat of injury exists, in regards to persons present within the area being searched.

A similar argument was made in the case of Florida v. Riley, 488 U.S. 445 (1989). Both *Riley* and the case at bar deal with aerial investigations conducted by police authorities after they received anonymous tips that the defendants were cultivating marijuana within the confines of their property. Further, both investigations were conducted from a helicopter which was below the altitude of 500 feet. In *Riley,* a Florida county sheriff received an anonymous tip that marijuana was being grown on Riley's property. A plurality of the United States Supreme Court in *Riley* held [that the observation from a helicopter flying lawfully at 400 feet was not an intrusion regulated by the Fourth Amendment].

At the suppression hearing in this case, the police testified that when they could not make a positive identification of the barn's contents from an altitude of 500 feet, they reduced their altitude to 50 feet, where they hovered over the property for 15 seconds and then made 3 passes over the property over a five minute period. Defendant's wife testified that she was home during this time and that she experienced sensations caused by the helicopter's proximity, including loud noise and vibration of the house and windows.

We believe that such evidence is sufficient to establish that the helicopter's presence at 50 feet above the barn represented a hazard to persons and property on the ground and that the conduct of the police in flying at this level was unreasonable. We perceive in the testimony of the wife that the surveillance was, in fact, intrusive and that flying the helicopter at this low level created a risk of harm to her and her property during the search. Finally, there is no evidence to rebut the wife's testimony, nor is there testimony from the police to explain that their positive observation could only be made from this dangerously low altitude.

The order of the Superior Court [reversing the conviction on the ground that the defendant's motion to suppress evidence should have been granted] is affirmed.

McDERMOTT, JUSTICE, dissenting.

The majority, with the faintful solicitude of maiden aunts, would not ruffle the sensibilities of a deliberate, careful, business-like "pot" farmer, because his windows shook when the cops came by helicopter and caught him out. The poor dears were all a-tremble and just about scared out of their conniving wits because a helicopter hovered over their barn 150 yards from the road and 100 yards from their peaceful, rural home where they counted their money and prayed for the success of their crop. It may well be that some occasions are a danger larger than the offense sought. Under the facts here, this was not one. I dissent.

CALIFORNIA v. GREENWOOD

Supreme Court of the United States, 1988.
486 U.S. 35, 108 S.Ct. 1625, 100 L.Ed.2d 30.

JUSTICE WHITE delivered the opinion of the Court.

The issue here is whether the Fourth Amendment prohibits the warrantless search and seizure of garbage left for collection outside the curtilage of a home. We conclude, in accordance with the vast majority of lower courts that have addressed the issue, that it does not.

I

In early 1984, Investigator Jenny Stracner of the Laguna Beach Police Department received information indicating that respondent Greenwood might be engaged in narcotics trafficking. Stracner learned that a criminal suspect had informed a federal drug-enforcement agent in February 1984 that a truck filled with illegal drugs was en route to the Laguna Beach address at which Greenwood resided. In addition, a neighbor complained of heavy vehicular traffic late at night in front of Greenwood's single-family home. The neighbor reported that the vehicles remained at Greenwood's house for only a few minutes.

Stracner sought to investigate this information by conducting a surveillance of Greenwood's home. She observed several vehicles make brief stops at the house during the late-night and early-morning hours, and she followed a truck from the house to a residence that had previously been under investigation as a narcotics trafficking location.

On April 6, 1984, Stracner asked the neighborhood's regular trash collector to pick up the plastic garbage bags that Greenwood had left on the curb in front of his house and to turn the bags over to her without mixing their contents with garbage from other houses. The trash collector cleaned his truck bin of other refuse, collected the garbage bags from the street in front of Greenwood's house, and turned the bags over to Stracner. The officer searched through the rubbish and found items indicative of narcotics use. She recited the information that she had gleaned from the trash search in an affidavit in support of a warrant to search Greenwood's home.

Police officers encountered both respondents at the house later that day when they arrived to execute the warrant. The police discovered quantities of cocaine and hashish during their search of the house. Respondents were arrested on felony narcotics charges. They subsequently posted bail.

The police continued to receive reports of many late-night visitors to the Greenwood house. On May 4, Investigator Robert Rahaeuser obtained Greenwood's garbage from the regular trash collector in the same manner as had Stracner. The garbage again contained evidence of narcotics use.

Rahaeuser secured another search warrant for Greenwood's home based on the information from the second trash search. The police found more narcotics and evidence of narcotics trafficking when they executed the warrant. Greenwood was again arrested.

[The state courts dismissed the charges on the ground that the warrantless trash searches violated the Fourth Amendment.]

II

The warrantless search and seizure of the garbage bags left at the curb outside the Greenwood house would violate the Fourth Amendment only if respondents manifested a subjective expectation of privacy in their garbage that society accepts as objectively reasonable. [Citations.] Respondents do not disagree with this standard.

They assert, however, that they had, and exhibited, an expectation of privacy with respect to the trash that was searched by the police: The trash, which was placed on the street for collection at a fixed time, was contained in opaque plastic bags, which the garbage collector was expected to pick up, mingle with the trash of others, and deposit at the garbage dump. The trash was only temporarily on the street, and there was little likelihood that it would be inspected by anyone.

It may well be that respondents did not expect that the contents of their garbage bags would become known to the police or other members of the public. An expectation of privacy does not give rise to Fourth Amendment protection, however, unless society is prepared to accept that expectation as objectively reasonable.

Here, we conclude that respondents exposed their garbage to the public sufficiently to defeat their claim to Fourth Amendment protection. It is common knowledge that plastic garbage bags left on or at the side of a public street are readily accessible to animals, children, scavengers, snoops, and other members of the public. Moreover, respondents placed their refuse at the curb for the express purpose of conveying it to a third party, the trash collector, who might himself have sorted through respondents' trash or permitted others, such as the police, to do so. Accordingly, having deposited their garbage in an area particularly suited for public inspection and, in a manner of speaking, public consumption, for the express purpose of having strangers take it, respondents could have had no reasonable expectation of privacy in the inculpatory items that they discarded.

Our conclusion that society would not accept as reasonable respondents' claim to an expectation of privacy in trash left for collection in an area accessible to the public is reinforced by the unanimous rejection of similar claims by the Federal Courts of Appeals. [Citations] * * *

The judgment of the California Court of Appeal is therefore reversed, and this case is remanded for further proceedings not inconsistent with this opinion.

*It is so ordered.**

JUSTICE BRENNAN, with whom JUSTICE MARSHALL joins, dissenting.

[The dissent reviewed Supreme Court decisions which had established that portable containers such as the plastic bags involved here are protected from warrantless searches when used to store or transport personal possessions.]

Respondents deserve no less protection just because Greenwood used the bags to discard rather than to transport his personal effects. Their contents are not inherently any less private, and Greenwood's decision to discard them, at least in the manner in which he did, does not diminish his expectation of privacy. * * * A single bag of trash testifies eloquently to the eating, reading, and recreational habits of the person who produced it. A search of trash, like a search of the bedroom, can relate intimate details about sexual practices, health, and personal hygiene. Like rifling through desk drawers or intercepting phone calls, rummaging through trash can divulge the target's financial and professional status, political affiliations and inclinations, private thoughts, personal relationships, and romantic interests. * * * When a tabloid

---

* In United States v. Scott, 975 F.2d 927 (1st Cir.1992), the Court of Appeals applied *Greenwood* to hold that no Fourth Amendment intrusion occurred where IRS agents painstaking pieced together shredded documents they found in garbage bags outside his house, to make a case of tax fraud. The court observed that defendant "is in no better position than the citizen who merely tears up a document by hand and discards the pieces into the sidewalk."

reporter examined then-Secretary of State Henry Kissinger's trash and published his findings, Kissinger was "really revolted" by the intrusion and his wife suffered "grave anguish." N.Y. Times, July 9, 1975, p. A1, col. 8. The public response roundly condemning the reporter demonstrates that society not only recognized those reactions as reasonable, but shared them as well. Commentators variously characterized his conduct as "a disgusting invasion of personal privacy," Flieger, Investigative Trash, U.S. News & World Report, July 28, 1975, p. 72 (editor's page); "indefensible * * * as civilized behavior," Washington Post, July 10, 1975, p. A18, col. 1 (editorial); and contrary to "the way decent people behave in relation to each other," *ibid.* * * *

Had Greenwood flaunted his intimate activity by strewing his trash all over the curb for all to see, or had some nongovernmental intruder invaded his privacy and done the same, I could accept the Court's conclusion that an expectation of privacy would have been unreasonable. Similarly, had police searching the city dump run across incriminating evidence that, despite commingling with the trash of others, still retained its identity as Greenwood's, we would have a different case. But all that Greenwood exposed to the public, were the exteriors of several opaque, sealed containers. Until the bags were opened by police, they hid their contents from the public's view every bit as much as did Chadwick's double-locked footlocker and Robbins' green, plastic wrapping. Faithful application of the warrant requirement does not require police to avert their eyes from evidence of criminal activity that could have been observed by any member of the public. Rather, it only requires them to adhere to norms of privacy that members of the public plainly acknowledge. * * *

I dissent.

Commentary

There is no violation of the Fourth Amendment if officers enter farmlands or other "open fields" to examine crops or other outside objects, even though the entry is a trespass and the farmer has tried to conceal the area from public view. The Supreme Court reaffirmed the open fields doctrine in Oliver v. United States, 466 U.S. 170 (1984). A search for Fourth Amendment purposes occurs only if the officers intrude into some structure within the "curtilage" of the dwelling. This has been defined as an area of domestic use immediately surrounding the dwelling, and determining the precise extent of the curtilage requires the courts to make some fine distinctions.

The Supreme Court discussed the extent of the curtilage in United States v. Dunn, 480 U.S. 294 (1987). DEA agents, having discovered that one Carpenter had bought large quantities of chemicals and equipment used to make drugs, followed Carpenter's truck to Dunn's ranch. Aerial photographs of the ranch showed the truck backed up to a barn behind the ranch house. The ranch was completely encircled by a perimeter fence, and contained several interior barbed wire fences, including one around the residence approximately 50 yards from the barn. There was also a wooden fence enclosing the front of the barn, which had an open overhang and locked, waist-high gates. Without a warrant, the agents crossed the perimeter fence, several interior barbed wire fences, and the wooden fence in front of the barn. They were led there by the smell of chemicals and could hear a motor running inside. They did not enter the barn but stopped at the locked gate and shined a flashlight inside, observing a drug laboratory. They subsequently obtained a search warrant and executed it, seizing the chemicals and equipment as well as bags of amphetamines that they found in the residence. A federal Court of Appeals held that the barn lay within the curtilage of the residence, and affirmed the district court's order suppressing the evidence seized pursuant to the warrant that was obtained as a result of the agents' intrusion onto the area immediately surrounding the barn.

The Supreme Court reversed, holding that the agents did not penetrate the curtilage. The majority opinion by Justice White reasoned that "curtilage questions should be resolved with particular reference to four factors: the proximity of the area claimed to be curtilage to the home, whether the area is included within an enclosure surrounding the home, the nature of the uses to which the area is put, and the steps taken by the resident to protect the area from observation by people passing by." 480 U.S. at 300. Because the barn was located 50 yards from the fence surrounding the house, because the agents "possessed objective data indicating that the barn was not being used for intimate activities of the home," and because Dunn "did little to protect the barn area from observation by those standing in the open fields," the barn was not within the curtilage. The majority also held that the agents did not violate any reasonable expectation of privacy which Dunn may have had in the barn itself. The majority accepted *arguendo* that the agents could not enter the barn without a warrant, but held that no Fourth Amendment violation occurred when the agents merely peered into the barn from outside.

In United States v. Hall, 47 F.3d 1091 (11th Cir.1995), Special Agent Parks of the United States Customs Service was investigating allegations that Bet–Air Corporation was supplying restricted military parts to Iran. Parks and an Assistant United States Attorney met with two attorneys representing Bet–Air. At the meeting, Bet–Air agreed to supply the government with certain requested corporate minutes within ten days.

On July 3 Agent Parks entered Bet–Air's property and removed a bag of paper shreddings from a garbage dumpster located near the Bet–Air offices in a parking area reserved for Bet–Air employees. In order to get to the dumpster, Parks had to travel forty yards on a private paved road. No signs indicated that the road was private, and Parks testified that at the time he traveled on the road, he did not know he was on private property. Thus, notwithstanding its location on Bet–Air's private property, the dumpster was readily accessible to the public. One of the reconstructed shredded documents was titled "British Airways—Bet–Air, Inc., Minutes of Meeting." On July 5, 1989, Parks met with Bet–Air's new attorney who provided Parks with the Bet–Air corporate minutes previously requested. Those documents did not include the minutes from the British Airways–Bet–Air meeting. Parks used the shredded documents as the basis for obtaining a search warrant of the Bet–Air premises. Pursuant to the search warrant, Parks and other law enforcement officers seized numerous documents and other records from Bet–Air's premises. These were used to convict Hall, CEO of Bet–Air, of various federal charges.

On appeal Hall argued the warrant was invalid as based upon a prior illegal search of the dumpster. His theory was that Bet–Air had a reasonable expectation of privacy in the shredded documents because it took at least four affirmative measures to safeguard its privacy interest: the documents were shredded; the documents were sealed inside a green garbage bag; the green garbage bag was placed inside an enclosed garbage dumpster; and the garbage dumpster was within the "commercial curtilage" adjacent to Bet–Air offices forty yards from public property. Parks's entry onto Bet–Air's premises therefore constituted unauthorized entry onto private property.

The Court of Appeals doubted whether the "curtilage" concept applies to business property, but held in any case that Bet–Air's subjective expectation of privacy was not objectively reasonable because the company did not take steps to limit the public's access to the dumpster via the private road.

Some difficult curtilage questions arise when an officer peers into a dwelling or other protected structure from outside. At one extreme it is clear that no Fourth Amendment violation occurs if an officer looks into a window from a sidewalk or other area commonly frequented by members of the public. At the other extreme, there is clearly a search if an officer climbs a tree to be able to see, peeping-Tom style, into an upper bedroom window. The outcome is more doubtful where the officer leaves the public way to look into a ground floor window from a yard. The California Supreme Court found a violation of the Fourth Amendment in these circumstances in Lorenzana v. Superior Court of Los Angeles County, 9 Cal.3d 626, 108 Cal.Rptr. 585, 511 P.2d 33 (1973). The balance tipped the other way in the 1990s. See United States v. Fields, 113 F.3d 313 (2d Cir.1997). The federal court held that no search occurred where officers stood in the fenced-in side yard of a 3–family apartment house and peered into a ground floor bedroom window whose shade was partly raised. Defendants were using the room to bag crack cocaine. Although the officers were trespassing, they were in a place where other tenants might reasonably be expected to be, and the defendants did not take readily available steps to protect their privacy by lowering the shade.

In State v. Sarantopoulos, 604 So.2d 551 (Fla.App. 2d Dist.1992), a detective learned that an unidentified informer had told police that the defendant had marijuana in his home and marijuana plants growing in his backyard. The yard was surrounded by a six-foot opaque board fence. The detective entered a neighbor's unfenced yard without asking permission, and said that he stood on his tiptoes to look over the fence. He saw marijuana plants growing, and used this information to obtain a search warrant for the yard and house. The court held that the detective committed no fourth amendment intrusion in looking over the fence from the neighbor's yard. The court also indicated, contrary to another Florida appellate decision, that it would have held the same even if the detective had stood on a ladder to look over the fence. The opinion reasoned that "for people who can see over the fence from adjoining yards, be they roof repairmen, tree trimmers, power company pole climbers, or seven-foot basketball players, there is no zone of privacy within a backyard surrounded by a six-foot fence that society is prepared to recognize." The Florida Supreme Court upheld this decision and its reasoning in Sarantopoulos v. State, 629 So.2d 121 (Fla.1993).

A manner of observation that does not inherently violate the defendant's Fourth Amendment rights may be prohibited or regulated if it is conducted in such a manner as to amount to harassment. For example, see National Organization for Reform of Marijuana Laws (NORML) v. Mullen, 608 F.Supp. 945 (N.D.Cal.1985), involving the extensive use of airplanes and helicopters to identify suspected marijuana growers in rural areas of Northern California. The continual aerial surveillance was conducted in a manner that frequently disturbed the peace and quiet of residents, and also created safety hazards. The district court ordered the officials to conduct the flights in a manner less disturbing to inhabitants of the area. The Court of Appeals affirmed the order in principle but remanded for certain modifications in light of the intervening *Ciraolo* decision. NORML v. Mullen, 796 F.2d 276 (9th Cir.1986).

Another interesting decision involved reputed Mafia boss Sam Giancana, who brought a civil rights action to enjoin extensive and intrusive FBI surveillance. The FBI made a practice of keeping Giancana under constant observation, with agents following him everywhere he went and even playing immediately behind him on the golf course. A district judge ordered certain modifications in the surveillance procedures, but the Court of Appeals reversed on the highly technical ground that the complaint failed to establish the existence of a controversy involving a sum in excess of $10,000, necessary to confer federal jurisdiction. Giancana v. Johnson, 335 F.2d 366 (7th Cir.1964).

VERNONIA SCHOOL DISTRICT 47J v. ACTON

Supreme Court of the United States, 1995.
515 U.S. 646, 115 S.Ct. 2386, 132 L.Ed.2d 564.

JUSTICE SCALIA delivered the opinion of the Court.

The Student Athlete Drug Policy adopted by School District 47J in the town of Vernonia, Oregon, authorizes random urinalysis drug testing of students who participate in the District's school athletics programs. We granted certiorari to decide whether this violates the Fourth and Fourteenth Amendments to the United States Constitution.

I

Petitioner Vernonia School District 47J (District) operates one high school and three grade schools in the logging community of Vernonia, Oregon. As elsewhere in small-town America, school sports play a prominent role in the town's life, and student athletes are admired in their schools and in the community.

Drugs had not been a major problem in Vernonia schools. In the mid-to-late 1980's, however, teachers and administrators observed a sharp increase in drug use. Students began to speak out about their attraction to the drug culture, and to boast that there was nothing the school could do about it. Along with more drugs came more disciplinary problems. Between 1988 and 1989 the number of disciplinary referrals in

Vernonia schools rose to more than twice the number reported in the early 1980's, and several students were suspended. Students became increasingly rude during class; outbursts of profane language became common.

Not only were student athletes included among the drug users but, as the District Court found, athletes were the leaders of the drug culture. 796 F.Supp. 1354, 1357 (D.Or.1992). This caused the District's administrators particular concern, since drug use increases the risk of sports-related injury. Expert testimony at the trial confirmed the deleterious effects of drugs on motivation, memory, judgment, reaction, coordination, and performance. The high school football and wrestling coach witnessed a severe sternum injury suffered by a wrestler, and various omissions of safety procedures and misexecutions by football players, all attributable in his belief to the effects of drug use.

Initially, the District responded to the drug problem by offering special classes, speakers, and presentations designed to deter drug use. It even brought in a specially trained dog to detect drugs, but the drug problem persisted. According to the District Court: "The administration was at its wits end and * * * a large segment of the student body, particularly those involved in interscholastic athletics, was in a state of rebellion. Disciplinary problems had reached 'epidemic proportions.' The coincidence of an almost three-fold increase in classroom disruptions and disciplinary reports along with the staff's direct observations of students using drugs or glamorizing drug and alcohol use led the administration to the inescapable conclusion that the rebellion was being fueled by alcohol and drug abuse as well as the student's misperceptions about the drug culture."

At that point, District officials began considering a drug-testing program. They held a parent "input night" to discuss the proposed Student Athlete Drug Policy (Policy), and the parents in attendance gave their unanimous approval. The school board approved the Policy for implementation in the fall of 1989. Its expressed purpose is to prevent student athletes from using drugs, to protect their health and safety, and to provide drug users with assistance programs.

The Policy applies to all students participating in interscholastic athletics. Students wishing to play sports must sign a form consenting to the testing and must obtain the written consent of their parents. Athletes are tested at the beginning of the season for their sport. In addition, once each week of the season the names of the athletes are placed in a "pool" from which a student, with the supervision of two adults, blindly draws the names of 10% of the athletes for random testing. Those selected are notified and tested that same day, if possible.

The student to be tested completes a specimen control form which bears an assigned number. Prescription medications that the student is taking must be identified by providing a copy of the prescription or a doctor's authorization. The student then enters an empty locker room accompanied by an adult monitor of the same sex. Each boy selected produces a sample at a urinal, remaining fully clothed with his back to the monitor, who stands approximately 12 to 15 feet behind the student. Monitors may (though do not always) watch the student while he produces the sample, and they listen for normal sounds of urination. Girls produce samples in an enclosed bathroom stall, so that they can be heard but not observed. After the sample is produced, it is given to the monitor, who checks it for temperature and tampering and then transfers it to a vial.

The samples are sent to an independent laboratory, which routinely tests them for amphetamines, cocaine, and marijuana. Other drugs, such as LSD, may be screened at the request of the District, but the identity of a particular student does not determine which drugs will be tested. The laboratory's procedures are 99.94% accurate. The District follows strict procedures regarding the chain of custody and access to test results. The laboratory does not know the identity of the students whose samples it tests. It is authorized to mail written test reports only to the superintendent and to provide test results to District personnel by telephone only after the requesting official recites a code confirming his authority. Only the superintendent, principals, vice-principals, and athletic directors have access to test results, and the results are not kept for more than one year.

If a sample tests positive, a second test is administered as soon as possible to confirm the result. If the second test is negative, no further action is taken. If the second test is positive, the athlete's parents are notified, and the school principal convenes a meeting with the student and his parents, at which the student is given the option of (1) participating for six weeks in an assistance program that includes weekly urinalysis, or (2) suffering suspension from athletics for the remainder of the current season and the next athletic season. The student is then retested prior to the start of the next athletic season for which he or she is eligible. The Policy states that a second offense results in automatic imposition of option (2); a third offense in suspension for the remainder of the current season and the next two athletic seasons.

In the fall of 1991, respondent James Acton, then a seventh-grader, signed up to play football at one of the District's grade schools. He was denied participation, however, because he and his parents refused to sign the testing consent forms. The Actons filed suit, seeking declaratory and injunctive relief from enforcement of the Policy on the grounds that it violated the Fourth and Fourteenth Amendments to the United States Constitution and Article I, § 9, of the Oregon Constitution. After a bench trial, the District Court entered an order denying the claims on the merits and dismissing the action. 796 F.Supp. at 1355. The United States Court of Appeals for the Ninth Circuit reversed, holding that the Policy violated both the Fourth and Fourteenth Amendments and Article I, § 9, of the Oregon Constitution. 23 F.3d 1514 (1994). We granted certiorari.

II

The Fourth Amendment to the United States Constitution provides that the Federal Government shall not violate "the right of the people to be secure in their persons, houses, papers, and effects, against unreasonable searches and seizures, ... " We have held that the Fourteenth Amendment extends this constitutional guarantee to searches and seizures by state officers, including public school officials, New Jersey v. T. L. O., 469 U.S. 325, 336–337 (1985). In Skinner v. Railway Labor Executives' Assn., 489 U.S. 602, 617 (1989), we held that state-compelled collection and testing of urine, such as that required by the Student Athlete Drug Policy, constitutes a "search" subject to the demands of the Fourth Amendment. See also National Treasury Employees Union v. Von Raab, 489 U.S. 656, 665 (1989).

As the text of the Fourth Amendment indicates, the ultimate measure of the constitutionality of a governmental search is "reasonableness." At least in a case such as this, where there was no clear practice, either approving or disapproving the type of search at issue, at the time the constitutional provision was enacted, whether a particular search meets the reasonableness standard is judged by balancing its intrusion on the individual's Fourth Amendment interests against its promotion of legitimate governmental interests. Where a search is undertaken by law enforcement officials to discover evidence of criminal wrongdoing, this Court has said that reasonableness generally requires the obtaining of a judicial warrant. Warrants cannot be issued, of course, without the showing of probable cause required by the Warrant Clause. But a warrant is not required to establish the reasonableness of all government searches; and when a warrant is not required (and the Warrant Clause therefore not applicable), probable cause is not invariably required either. A search unsupported by probable cause can be constitutional, we have said, "when special needs, beyond the normal need for law enforcement, make the warrant and probable-cause requirement impracticable." Griffin v. Wisconsin, 483 U.S. 868, 873 (1987)

We have found such "special needs" to exist in the public-school context. There, the warrant requirement "would unduly interfere with the maintenance of the swift and informal disciplinary procedures [that are] needed," and "strict adherence to the requirement that searches be based upon probable cause" would undercut "the substantial need of teachers and administrators for freedom to maintain order in the schools." T. L. O., supra, at 340, 341. The school search we approved in T. L. O., while not based on probable cause, was based on individualized suspicion of wrongdoing. As we explicitly acknowledged, however, the Fourth Amendment imposes no irreducible requirement of such suspicion. We have upheld suspicionless searches and seizures to conduct drug testing of railroad personnel involved in train accidents, see *Skinner*, supra; to conduct random drug testing of federal customs officers who carry arms or are involved in drug interdiction, see *Von Raab*, supra; and to maintain automobile checkpoints looking for illegal immigrants and contraband, and drunk drivers, Michigan Dept. of State Police v. Sitz, 496 U.S. 444 (1990).

III

The first factor to be considered is the nature of the privacy interest upon which the search here at issue intrudes. The Fourth Amendment does not protect all subjective expectations of privacy, but only those that society recognizes as "legitimate." What expectations are legitimate varies, of course, with context, depending, for example, upon whether the individual asserting the privacy interest is at home, at work, in a car, or in a public park. In addition, the legitimacy of certain privacy expectations vis-a-vis the State may depend upon the individual's legal relationship with the State. For example, in *Griffin*, supra, we held that, although a "probationer's home, like anyone else's, is protected by the Fourth Amendment," the supervisory relationship between probationer and State justifies "a degree of impingement upon [a probationer's] privacy that would not be constitutional if applied to the public at large." 483 U.S. at 873, 875. Central, in our view, to the present case is the fact that the subjects of the Policy are (1) children, who (2) have been committed to the temporary custody of the State as schoolmaster.

Traditionally at common law, and still today, unemancipated minors lack some of the most fundamental rights of self-determination—including even the right of liberty in its narrow sense, i.e., the right to come and go at will. They are subject, even as to their physical freedom, to the control of their parents or guardians. When parents place minor children in private schools for their education, the teachers and administrators of those schools stand in loco parentis over the children entrusted to them. In fact, the tutor or schoolmaster is the very prototype of that status. As Blackstone describes it, a parent "may * * * delegate part of his parental authority, during his life, to the tutor or schoolmaster of his child; who is then in loco parentis, and has such a portion of the power of the parent committed to his charge, viz. that of restraint and correction, as may be necessary to answer the purposes for which he is employed." 1 W. Blackstone, Commentaries on the Laws of England 441 (1769).

In T. L. O. we rejected the notion that public schools, like private schools, exercise only parental power over their students, which of course is not subject to constitutional constraints. Such a view of things, we said, "is not entirely consonant with compulsory education laws," and is inconsistent with our prior decisions treating school officials as state actors for purposes of the Due Process and Free Speech Clauses, But while denying that the State's power over schoolchildren is formally no more than the delegated power of their parents, T. L. O. did not deny, but indeed emphasized, that the nature of that power is custodial and tutelary, permitting a degree of supervision and control that could not be exercised over free adults. * * *

Fourth Amendment rights, no less than First and Fourteenth Amendment rights, are different in public schools than elsewhere; the "reasonableness" inquiry cannot disregard the schools' custodial and tutelary responsibility for children. For their own good and that of their classmates, public school children are routinely required to submit to various physical examinations, and to be vaccinated against various diseases. * * *

Legitimate privacy expectations are even less with regard to student athletes. School sports are not for the bashful. They require "suiting up" before each practice or event, and showering and changing afterwards. Public school locker rooms, the usual sites for these activities, are not notable for the privacy they afford. The locker rooms in Vernonia are typical: no individual dressing rooms are provided; shower heads are lined up along a wall, unseparated by any sort of partition or curtain; not even all the toilet stalls have doors. * * *

There is an additional respect in which school athletes have a reduced expectation of privacy. By choosing to "go out for the team," they voluntarily subject themselves to a degree of regulation even higher than that imposed on students generally. In Vernonia's public schools, they must submit to a preseason physical exam (James testified that his included the giving of a urine sample), they must acquire adequate insurance coverage or sign an insurance waiver, maintain a minimum grade point average, and comply with any "rules of conduct, dress, training hours and related matters as may be established for each sport by the head coach and athletic director with the principal's approval." Record, Exh. 2, p. 30, P8. Somewhat like adults who choose to participate in a "closely regulated industry," students who voluntarily participate in school athletics have reason to expect intrusions upon normal rights and privileges, including privacy.

IV

Having considered the scope of the legitimate expectation of privacy at issue here, we turn next to the character of the intrusion that is complained of. We recognized in *Skinner* that collecting the samples for urinalysis intrudes upon "an excretory function traditionally shielded by great privacy." We noted, however, that the degree of intrusion depends upon the manner in which production of the urine sample is monitored. Under the District's Policy, male students produce samples at a urinal along a wall. They remain fully clothed and are only observed from behind, if at all. Female students produce samples in an enclosed stall, with a female monitor standing outside listening only for sounds of tampering. These conditions are nearly identical to those typically encountered in public restrooms, which men, women, and especially school children use daily. Under such conditions, the privacy interests compromised by the process of obtaining the urine sample are in our view negligible. The other privacy-invasive aspect of urinalysis is, of course, the information it discloses concerning the state of the subject's body, and the materials he has ingested. In this regard it is significant that the tests at issue here look only for drugs, and not for whether the student is, for example, epileptic, pregnant, or diabetic. Moreover, the drugs for which the samples are screened are standard, and do not vary according to the identity of the student. And finally, the results of the tests are disclosed only to a limited class of school personnel who have a need to know; and they are not turned over to law enforcement authorities or used for any internal disciplinary function.

Respondents argue, however, that the District's Policy is in fact more intrusive than this suggests, because it requires the students, if they are to avoid sanctions for a falsely positive test, to identify in advance prescription medications they are taking. We agree that this raises some cause for concern. In *Von Raab*, we flagged as one of the salutary features of the Customs Service drug-testing program the fact that employees were not required to disclose medical information unless they tested positive, and, even then, the information was supplied to a licensed physician rather than to the Government employer. On the other hand, we have never indicated that requiring advance disclosure of medications is per se unreasonable. Indeed, in *Skinner* we held that it was not "a significant invasion of privacy." It can be argued that, in *Skinner*, the disclosure went only to the medical personnel taking the sample, and the Government personnel analyzing it, and that disclosure to teachers and coaches—to persons who personally know the student— is a greater invasion of privacy. Assuming for the sake of argument that both those propositions are true, we do not believe they establish a difference that respondents are entitled to rely on here.

The General Authorization Form that respondents refused to sign, which refusal was the basis for James's exclusion from the sports program, said only (in relevant part): "I * * * authorize the Vernonia School District to conduct a test on a urine specimen which I provide to test for drugs and/or alcohol use. I also authorize the release of information concerning the results of such a test to the Vernonia School District and to the parents and/or guardians of the student." While the practice of the District seems to have been to have a school official take medication information from the student at the time of the test, that practice is not set forth in, or required by, the Policy, which says simply: "Student athletes who * * * are or have been taking prescription medication must provide verification (either by a copy of the prescription or by doctor's authorization) prior to being tested." It may well be that, if and when James was selected for random testing at a time that he was taking medication, the School District would have permitted him to provide the requested information in a confidential manner—for example, in a sealed envelope delivered to the testing lab. Nothing in the Policy contradicts that, and when respondents choose, in effect, to challenge the Policy on its face, we will not assume the worst. Accordingly, we reach the same conclusion as in *Skinner*: that the invasion of privacy was not significant.

V

Finally, we turn to consider the nature and immediacy of the governmental concern at issue here, and the efficacy of this means for meeting it. In both *Skinner* and *Von Raab*, we characterized the government interest motivating the search as "compelling." *Skinner*, supra, at 628 (interest in preventing railway accidents); *Von Raab*, supra, at 670 (interest in insuring fitness of customs officials to interdict drugs and handle firearms). Relying on these cases, the District Court held that because the District's program also called for drug testing in the absence of individualized suspicion, the District "must demonstrate a 'compelling need' for the program." 796 F.Supp. at 1363. The Court of Appeals appears to have agreed with this view. See 23 F.3d at 1526. It is a mistake, however, to think that the phrase "compelling state interest," in the Fourth Amendment context, describes a fixed, minimum quantum of governmental concern, so that one can dispose of a case by answering in isolation the question: Is there a compelling state interest here? Rather, the phrase describes an interest which appears important enough to justify the particular search at hand, in light of other factors which show the search to be relatively intrusive upon a genuine expectation of privacy. Whether that relatively high degree of government concern is necessary in this case or not, we think it is met.

That the nature of the concern is important—indeed, perhaps compelling—can hardly be doubted. Deterring drug use by our Nation's schoolchildren is at least as important as enhancing efficient enforcement of the Nation's laws against the importation of drugs, which was the governmental concern in *Von Raab*, or deterring drug use by engineers and trainmen, which was the governmental concern in *Skinner*. School years are the time when the physical, psychological, and addictive effects of drugs are most severe. [Citations] And of course the effects of a drug-infested school are visited not just upon the users, but upon the entire student body and faculty, as the educational process is disrupted. In the present case, moreover, the necessity for the State to act is magnified by the fact that this evil is being visited not just upon individuals at large, but upon children for whom it has undertaken a special responsibility of care and direction. Finally, it must not be lost sight of that this program is directed more narrowly to drug use by school athletes, where the risk of immediate physical harm to the drug user or those with whom he is playing his sport is particularly high. Apart from psychological effects, which include impairment of judgment, slow reaction time, and a lessening of the perception of pain, the particular drugs screened by the District's Policy have been demonstrated to pose substantial physical risks to athletes. * * *

As for the immediacy of the District's concerns: We are not inclined to question—indeed, we could not possibly find clearly erroneous—the District Court's conclusion that "a large segment of the student body, particularly those involved in interscholastic athletics, was in a state of rebellion," that "disciplinary actions had reached 'epidemic proportions,'" and that "the rebellion was being fueled by alcohol and drug abuse as well as by the student's misperceptions about the drug culture." 796 F.Supp. at 1357. That is an immediate crisis of greater proportions than existed in *Skinner*, where we upheld the Government's drug testing program based on findings of drug use by railroad employees nationwide, without proof that a problem existed on the particular railroads whose employees were subject to the test. And of much greater proportions than existed in *Von Raab*, where there was no documented history of drug use by any customs officials. See Von Raab, 489 U.S. at 673; id., at 683 (Scalia, J., dissenting).

As to the efficacy of this means for addressing the problem: It seems to us self-evident that a drug problem largely fueled by the "role model" effect of athletes' drug use, and of particular danger to athletes, is effectively addressed by making sure that athletes do not use drugs. Respondents argue that a "less intrusive means to the same end" was available, namely, "drug testing on suspicion of drug use." We have repeatedly refused to declare that only the "least intrusive" search practicable can be reasonable under the Fourth Amendment. *Skinner*, supra, at 629, n. 9 (collecting cases). Respondents' alternative entails substantial difficulties—if it is indeed practicable at all. It may be impracticable, for one thing, simply because the parents who are willing to accept random drug testing for athletes are not willing to accept accusatory drug testing for all students, which transforms the process into a badge of shame. Respondents' proposal brings the risk that teachers will impose testing arbitrarily upon troublesome but not drug-likely students. It generates the expense of defending lawsuits that charge such arbitrary imposition, or that simply demand greater process before accusatory drug testing is imposed. And not least of all, it adds to the ever-expanding diversionary duties of schoolteachers the new function of spotting and bringing to account drug abuse, a task for which they are ill prepared, and which is not readily compatible with their vocation.

VI

Taking into account all the factors we have considered above—the decreased expectation of privacy, the relative unobtrusiveness of the search, and the severity of the need met by the search—we conclude Vernonia's Policy is reasonable and hence constitutional.

We caution against the assumption that suspicionless drug testing will readily pass constitutional muster in other contexts. The most significant element in this case is the first we discussed: that the Policy was undertaken in furtherance of the government's responsibilities, under a public school system, as guardian and tutor of children entrusted to its care. Just as when the government conducts a search in its capacity as employer (a warrantless search of an absent employee's desk to obtain an urgently needed file, for example), the relevant question is whether that intrusion upon privacy is one that a reasonable employer might engage in, see O'Connor v. Ortega, 480 U.S. 709, (1987); so also when the government acts as guardian and tutor the relevant question is whether the search is one that a reasonable guardian and tutor might undertake. Given the findings of need made by the District Court, we conclude that in the present case it is.

We may note that the primary guardians of Vernonia's schoolchildren appear to agree. The record shows no objection to this districtwide program by any parents other than the couple before us here—even though, as we have described, a public meeting was held to obtain parents' views. We find insufficient basis to contradict the judgment of Vernonia's parents, its school board, and the District Court, as to what was reasonably in the interest of these children under the circumstances.

* * *

The Ninth Circuit held that Vernonia's Policy not only violated the Fourth Amendment, but also, by reason of that violation, contravened Article I, § 9 of the Oregon Constitution. Our conclusion that the former holding was in error means that the latter holding rested on a flawed premise. We therefore vacate the judgment, and remand the case to the Court of Appeals for further proceedings consistent with this opinion.

JUSTICE GINSBURG, concurring.

The Court constantly observes that the School District's drug-testing policy applies only to students who voluntarily participate in interscholastic athletics. Correspondingly, the most severe sanction allowed under the District's policy is suspension from extracurricular athletic programs. I comprehend the Court's opinion as reserving the question whether the District, on no more than the showing made here, constitutionally could impose routine drug testing not only on those seeking to engage with others in team sports, but on all students required to attend school.

JUSTICE O'CONNOR, with whom JUSTICE STEVENS and JUSTICE SOUTER join, dissenting.

The population of our Nation's public schools, grades 7 through 12, numbers around 18 million. By the reasoning of today's decision, the millions of these students who participate in interscholastic sports, an overwhelming majority of whom have given school officials no reason whatsoever to suspect they use drugs at school, are open to an intrusive bodily search.

In justifying this result, the Court dispenses with a requirement of individualized suspicion on considered policy grounds. First, it explains that precisely because every student athlete is being tested, there is no concern that school officials might act arbitrarily in choosing who to test. Second, a broad-based search regime, the Court reasons, dilutes the accusatory nature of the search. In making these policy arguments, of course, the Court sidesteps powerful, countervailing privacy concerns. Blanket searches, because they can involve "thousands or millions" of searches, "pose a greater threat to liberty" than do suspicion-based ones, which "affect one person at a time," Illinois v. Krull, 480 U.S. 340, 365 (1987)(O'Connor, J., dissenting). Searches based on individualized suspicion also afford potential targets considerable control over whether they will, in fact, be searched because a person can avoid such a search by not acting in an objectively suspicious way. And given that the surest way to avoid acting suspiciously is to avoid the underlying wrongdoing, the costs of such a regime, one would think, are minimal.

But whether a blanket search is "better," than a regime based on individualized suspicion is not a debate in which we should engage. In my view, it is not open to judges or government officials to decide on policy grounds which is better and which is worse. For most of our constitutional history, mass, suspicionless searches have been generally considered per se unreasonable within the meaning of the Fourth Amendment. And we have allowed exceptions in recent years only where it has been clear that a suspicion-based regime would be ineffectual. Because that is not the case here, I dissent.

* * *

[On remand following the Supreme Court's decision, the Court of Appeals for the Ninth Circuit affirmed the District Court, after denying plaintiffs' motion to certify the case to the Oregon Supreme Court for a ruling on the state constitutional questions. The majority of the panel was "of the opinion that the Oregon Supreme Court would not offer greater protection under the provisions of the Oregon Constitution in this case." Judge Reinhart dissented, arguing that "I am not prepared to say that the Oregon Supreme Court will decide that the rights of its school children must be shaped by the national frenzy over the war-on-drugs. To the contrary, given its history of rugged individualism and its concern for constitutional rights, Oregon might well opt for a more generous and enlightened reading of its constitution." Acton v. Vernonia School Dist., 66 F.3d 217 (9th Cir.1995).]

Note

The Supreme Court limited the scope of *Vernonia* in Chandler v. Miller, 520 U.S. 305 (1997). A Georgia law provided that candidates for election to certain state offices must certify that they tested negative (by urinalysis) for drugs within 30 days prior to qualifying for nomination. Justice Ginsberg's opinion for the majority applied the reasoning of *Vernonia* and its predecessors to hold that a suspicionless search is constitutional unless it is based on "special needs" beyond the general need for effective law enforcement. The majority opinion rejected the State's argument that unlawful drug use calls into question a public official's judgment and integrity, and thus jeopardizes the discharge of public functions. The majority reasoned that "nothing in the record hints that the hazards respondents broadly describe are real and not simply hypothetical for Georgia's polity." Only Chief Justice Rehnquist dissented, arguing that the Georgia statutory policy was as compelling as the interest asserted by the federal government in National Treasury Employees Union v. Von Raab, 489 U.S. 656 (1989). In *Von Raab*, the Supreme Court upheld (5–4) a U.S. Treasury Department regulation requiring mandatory urine testing for employees involved in drug law enforcement, the carrying or firearms, or handling of classified material.

Commentary

When the courts have determined that a particular investigative activity is within the scope of the Fourth Amendment, they next have to determine what level of regulation is appropriate for the particular kind of search or seizure which is under consideration. Among the possibilities are these:

1. The search is lawful only if the police first obtain a judicial warrant issued upon probable cause. The Supreme Court has often said that the warrant requirement is the general rule, subject only to certain well-defined exceptions, but in fact the exceptions are very broad and only a minority of searches are conducted pursuant to judicial warrants. As we saw in the introductory case of *New Jersey v. T.L.O.,* the Supreme Court does not require a judicial warrant in circumstances where it would be "impracticable" to require the investigators to obtain one. Chapter 4 of this book deals with the warrant requirement and its exceptions.

2. When the warrant clause is inapplicable the Fourth Amendment's probable cause requirement may still be enforced, but in some circumstances the Court has held that searches may be made under the more permissive standard of "individualized suspicion." Chapters 5 and 6 of this book discuss what these terms mean and how they have been applied in the cases.

3. Cases such as *Vernonia* illustrate that, in some circumstances, a Fourth Amendment search may be made in the absence of a warrant, probable cause, or individualized suspicion. In that case, what protection *does* the Fourth Amendment provide? The answer seems to be that the regulations providing for the search in question must themselves be "reasonable." The Court evaluates the reasonableness of regulations under a balancing test which considers the urgency of the governmental interest, the degree to which the required inspection or testing is necessary to further that governmental interest, and the degree to which the procedures in question invade legitimate expectations of privacy.

National Treasury Employees Union v. Von Raab, 489 U.S. 656 (1989) was a companion case to Skinner v. Railway Labor Executives' Association, 489 U.S. 602 (1989). In *Von Raab* the Supreme Court upheld by a narrower margin the drug testing program of the United States Customs Service. The Customs Service had announced a program of mandatory urine testing for persons appointed or promoted to positions involving drug law enforcement, the carrying of firearms, or the handling of classified material. By a 5–4 majority, the Supreme Court held that, at least with respect to persons directly involved in the interdiction of illegal drugs or in carrying firearms, "The Government's compelling interests in preventing the promotion of drug users to positions where they might endanger the integrity of our Nation's borders or the life of the citizenry outweigh the privacy interests of those who seek promotion to these positions, who enjoy a diminished expectation of privacy by virtue of the special, and obvious physical and ethical demands of these positions." Justice Scalia in dissent thought that the only real reason for imposing the drug testing was to "set a good example" for the rest of the country by having the Government's law enforcement personnel submit to the testing. Justice Scalia did not think that making this symbolic point was sufficient justification for the invasion of privacy.

The New York Court of Appeals upheld the New York City Police Department's plan to conduct random urinalysis drug testing of members of a special elite voluntary unit within the Department, the Organized Crime Control Bureau. The New York court distinguished an earlier case, in which it had held unconstitutional a public school authority's declared policy of requiring urinalysis drug testing of all probationary teachers as a condition to qualifying for tenure. The Court thought that members of an elite police unit have a lesser privacy interest than public employees generally because of the intensive character investigations that their employment entails, and because of the special dangers of drug involvement by organized crime investigators. See Caruso v. Ward, 72 N.Y.2d 432, 534 N.Y.S.2d 142, 530 N.E.2d 850 (1988). See also Shoemaker v. Handel, 795 F.2d 1136 (3d Cir.1986), which upheld mandatory breathalyzer and urine testing for jockeys.

The mandatory drug testing programs reviewed in these cases arose within a work place environment, where the inspection was not primarily for purposes of criminal prosecution and where it was expected that violations would lead ordinarily to suspension or dismissal from employment rather than prosecution. An employment relationship does not make the Fourth Amendment inapplicable, but it does affect the balance of interests. Obviously, an employer can impose a variety of obligations upon employees (such as the obligation to show up for work) which might constitute invasion of Fourth Amendment rights if imposed by the police upon the general public. A private employer is not subject to Fourth Amendment regulation at all, but employees of a government agency have certain limited Fourth Amendment rights against their governmental employer. In O'Connor v. Ortega, 480 U.S. 709 (1987), investigators working for the Director of a state psychiatric hospital searched the office of a staff doctor for evidence of misconduct. The Supreme Court Justices all agreed that the doctor had a reasonable expectation of privacy in his office, but they disagreed about how much protection this gave him. The four dissenting Justices thought that the Director's investigators could only have made the search pursuant to a judicial warrant issued upon probable cause, but the other five Justices thought that the warrant and probable cause requirements were not applicable and remanded the case to the trial court for a determination of the lawfulness of the search under a more general standard of reasonableness. There was no majority opinion.

UNITED STATES v. COHEN

United States Court of Appeals, Second Circuit, 1986.
796 F.2d 20.

CARDAMONE, CIRCUIT JUDGE:

Appellants Barr, Winchester and Cohen challenge the evidentiary and constitutional bases for their convictions in this multi-defendant drug conspiracy case. Except for one issue Barr raises, these challenges are without merit and do not warrant discussion. Therefore, the judgments of conviction of appellants Winchester and Cohen are affirmed.
* * *

On July 5, 1984 MCC corrections officer, Lt. William Chevere, conducted a so-called "contraband" search of Barr's cell. The search lasted approximately half an hour and consisted entirely of an examination of Barr's papers. A short time later, Lt. Chevere returned and examined Barr's papers for an additional hour. Assistant United States Attorney Michael R. Bromwich later admitted in his affidavit that he initiated the July 5 "contraband" search by Lt. Chevere. He directed MCC prison authorities to enter Barr's cell "to look for certain types of documents that may have contained the names and phone numbers of other of Barr's co-conspirators and witnesses who Barr had already contacted and was still in the process of trying to contact."

In order to establish the requisite probable cause to obtain a search warrant for Barr's cell the next day, Det. Rocco R. Sanfillippo relied primarily on the information found by Lt. Chevere during the July 5 warrantless search of Barr's papers. Based on this information, a magistrate issued a search warrant on July 6 authorizing the seizure of all "written, non-legal materials belonging to Harold Barr." Pursuant to the warrant, Det. Sanfillippo and Lt. Chevere seized numerous sheets of paper from Barr's cell which included witness lists, notes on specific charges, personal matters, notes on conversations between Barr and his attorneys, and a sheet of paper on which the government contended Barr was practicing to disguise his handwriting.

Upon Barr's motion to suppress this evidence, the district court suppressed some of the material on Sixth Amendment grounds because they related to Barr's right to counsel. But the trial court refused to suppress the remaining papers or to declare the search unlawful on Fourth Amendment grounds.

On appeal Barr challenges the July 5th search of his prison cell as a warrantless search conducted in violation of the Fourth Amendment. If he succeeds on this claim the evidence seized on July 6th will be suppressed since the information establishing probable cause for that search was the fruit of an unlawful search. Barr further argues that the district court should have conducted a taint hearing to determine what fruits, if any, were obtained as a result of information derived from the warrantless search. The government relies on *Hudson v. Palmer*, 468 U.S. 517 (1984), for the proposition that the Fourth Amendment provides no protection for a prisoner's claim of a privacy right in his prison cell. * * *

In [Hudson] a convicted inmate filed an action against a prison official under 42 U.S.C. § 1983 (1982) claiming that an unreasonable "shake down" search of his prison locker and cell violated his Fourth Amendment rights. The Court restated the now self-evident truth that prisoners retain rights as prisoners that are not "fundamentally inconsistent with imprisonment itself or incompatible with the objectives of incarceration." Yet, because the interest of society in the security of its penal institutions outweighs the interest of the prisoner in privacy within his cell, it held that the traditional Fourth Amendment privacy right is "fundamentally incompatible with the close and continual surveillance of inmates and their cells required to ensure institutional security and internal order." Such a conclusion is bottomed on common sense because if drugs, weapons, and contraband are to be ferreted out of jail cells, then prison officials must have unrestricted access to those places to accomplish that objective. Concededly, isolated instances of unreasonable searches by prison officials may occur, but overall considerations of institutional security outweigh a prisoner's claim to privacy in particular cases. * * * In determining whether pre-trial detainees had superior rights to convicted prisoners, the Supreme Court stated in *Bell v. Wolfish*, 441 U.S. at 546, that the *fact* of confinement and the legitimate objectives of the penal institution curtail the constitutional rights of any prisoner, whether convicted or not. Although pretrial detainees have not been adjudicated guilty of the crimes for which they have been charged, the Court believed that in terms of prison security there was no basis to conclude that pre-trial detainees pose a lesser risk to security than convicted inmates. * * *

In this case it is plain that no institutional need is being served. Were it a prison official that initiated the search of Barr's cell, established decisional law holds that the search would not be subject to constitutional challenge, regardless of whether security needs could justify it. But here the search was initiated by the prosecution solely to obtain information for a superseding indictment. In our view, this kind of warrantless search of a prisoner's cell falls well outside the rationale of the decided cases. Barr retains a Fourth Amendment right—though much diminished in scope—tangible enough to mount the attack on this warrantless search. * * *

Thus, the district court's refusal to suppress all of the evidence obtained in Barr's cell search is reversed. Nevertheless, we remand the case to that court for it to decide whether—in light of the overwhelming evidence of Barr's guilt—the failure to suppress this material was harmless error. The trial court should hold a taint hearing to consider what fruits, if any, were obtained from information seized in the warrantless search of July 5th.

Affirmed in part, reversed and remanded in part.

Comment

The weight of authority holds that there is no search (and hence no need for a warrant or probable cause) where: (1) officers use a thermal imaging device to measure heat emissions from a dwelling or other building to confirm that marijuana-growing technology is being employed; or (2) a trained dog sniffs luggage or similar movable containers to detect the presence of unlawful drugs. Such measures are held not to intrude into protected privacy interests, since they involve no trespass and do not threaten the privacy of persons who are not possessing or growing unlawful drugs. See United States v. Place, 462 U.S. 696 (1983); United States v. Kyllo, 190 F.3d 1041 (9th Cir.1999). Such measure are therefore similar to airplane overflights or garbage inspections. Motions to suppress evidence in such cases must therefore depend upon finding some illegality that proceeded the lawful inspection.

UNITED STATES v. GWINN

United States Court of Appeals for the Eighth Circuit, 1999.
191 F.3d 874.

BEAM, CIRCUIT JUDGE.

On the morning of September 27, 1998, drug interdiction detectives Robert Delameter and Larry Ealy of the Kansas City, Missouri, Police Department, dressed in plain clothes, boarded the "Southwest Chief," an Amtrak train en route from Los Angeles to Chicago, during its regularly scheduled stop in Kansas City. They were assigned to look for narcotics on the train's coach section. Delameter testified that the train frequently transported narcotics from the Southwest to the Midwest and that he had interdicted drugs on that train on numerous occasions in the past.

On board, the passengers' luggage was stored in open overhead racks located above the seat rows. As Delameter made his way through one of the coach cars, he spotted a soft-sided black Nike bag next to a gray bag in the overhead compartment. The black bag had no name tag or other identification. [Delameter testified that in performing interdiction duties, he had been trained to look for people with new luggage, over-stuffed luggage, heavy luggage, luggage with no name tags, people who are very possessive of their luggage, and people acting in a suspicious manner.] To obtain a better look, Delameter stepped up on the back of a foot rest and the arm rest of one of the seats. He reached up, lifted the black bag, and felt its sides. As he did so, Delameter felt what he thought were bundles of narcotics. Delameter then pushed on the sides of the bag to expel air from inside, at which time he smelled the odor of marijuana. He then slid the bag back in its original location.

Delameter and Ealy then waited at the rear of the car while passengers reboarded to see if anyone would pick up the bag or in some way claim it. When no one did so, they decided to move the bag to see if anyone would claim ownership. With Ealy remaining at the rear of the car, Delameter picked up the bag and took a few steps with it, whereupon he heard someone say, "Hey, that's my bag." As Delameter turned around with the bag in his arms, he saw Gwinn stand up. Gwinn again stated, "That's my bag." Delameter asked him, "This is your bag?" Gwinn replied, "Yes, that's my bag." Delameter then walked towards Gwinn, handed him the bag, and identified himself as a police officer. Delameter testified that Gwinn looked frightened and shocked, and began eyeing the stairs leading to the lower portion of the car. Thinking that Gwinn might attempt to flee, Delameter motioned to Ealy, who came up behind Gwinn, grabbed his arms, and handcuffed him. The bag fell onto a seat. Delameter then asked Gwinn if he had any other luggage. Gwinn answered that the gray bag belonged to him. Delameter then asked Gwinn if those were the only two bags he had. Gwinn responded that he had only one bag, the gray bag. Delameter testified that he twice asked Gwinn again if the black bag was his, and Gwinn denied ownership of it each time.

Detective Ealy took Gwinn and the black bag off the train and onto the platform area where a police dog sniffed the bag for drugs. The dog alerted to the bag. * * * Delameter then opened the bag and searched it. He found three bundles of marijuana and a bundle of cocaine. Gwinn was charged with knowingly and intentionally possessing with intent to distribute cocaine, in an amount of 500 grams or more. After a hearing, the magistrate judge recommended suppression of the evidence, concluding that Delameter's manipulation of the black bag, as well as the subsequent detention of the bag for the dog sniff, violated Gwinn's Fourth Amendment rights. The magistrate judge rejected the government's contention that Gwinn had no standing to challenge the search because he had abandoned the bag. The district court adopted the report and recommendation and granted Gwinn's motion to suppress. The government appeals.

Gwinn argues that Delameter's manipulation of the exterior of his bag while in the overhead compartment constitutes a search within the meaning of the Fourth Amendment and that the search was unlawful because it was conducted without a warrant, consent, probable cause, or even reasonable suspicion. The government claims that feeling the exterior of Gwinn's bag is not a search for Fourth Amendment purposes because passengers have no reasonable expectation that bags placed in an overhead compartment will not be subject to such touching. Alternatively, the government argues that Gwinn lacks standing to assert any Fourth Amendment violation because he voluntarily abandoned the bag when he twice denied its ownership. [The Court held that Gwinn denied ownership of the bag only after the officers had seized it.]

Because we find Gwinn's abandonment of the black bag was not voluntary, we must address the constitutionality of Delameter's manipulation of the bag's exterior. * * * Individuals possess a privacy interest in the contents of their personal luggage that is protected by the Fourth Amendment. Of course, not every intrusion with an individual's luggage constitutes a search within the meaning of the Fourth Amendment. For example, a canine sniff of an individual's luggage does not constitute a search. United States v. Place, 462 U.S. 696 (1983). Similarly, no search occurs when an officer briefly moves luggage from the overhead compartment of a bus to the aisle in order to facilitate a canine sniff, because it is not uncommon for other passengers or the bus driver to move baggage in order to rearrange and maximize use of compartment space.

We think, however, that Delameter's contact with Gwinn's bag, went beyond the limited intrusiveness of a canine sniff or the incidental touching of luggage which took place in *Harvey*. Just recently, we stated that we had "grave doubts about the constitutional propriety" of an officer's conduct when he lifted, manipulated, and felt along the bottom of a bag in the overhead compartment of a Greyhound bus. * * * While a passenger can expect that others will perhaps push aside or briefly touch his bag in an attempt to accommodate their own luggage or to maximize storage space, we think that the majority of the traveling public would not expect their luggage, even those pieces placed in an overhead compartment, to be subject to a calculated and thorough squeezing and manipulation of their exteriors. Unlike a canine sniff or the incidental touching that accompanies the moving of luggage from the overhead, the feeling and manipulation of a bag's exterior involves a much more intrusive and prolonged contact with the piece. Indeed, we can envision situations where the extensive tactile examination of a soft-sided bag's exterior by an officer may reveal almost as much information as opening the bag itself, such as information about the number, shape, and character of items, perhaps very personal items, inside the bag. * * * We conclude that Delameter's feeling of Gwinn's bag while it was on the overhead rack constitutes a search within the meaning of the Fourth Amendment and because the officers had neither a warrant, probable cause, reasonable suspicion, nor consent, the search was unlawful.

STATE v. ORTIZ

Supreme Court of Nebraska, 1999.
257 Neb. 784, 600 N.W.2d 805.

MILLER-LERMAN, J.

Sometime during the early evening of August 7, 1997, Omaha police received a telephone call from a concerned citizen (C/C) who told police that she or he "knew of" Ortiz and alleged that Ortiz "has been active in distributing cocaine from his apartment within the past year." Police were given Ortiz' address and a general physical description of Ortiz by C/C. The record indicates that at the time the call was received, Ortiz was not a suspect.

Police verified that Ortiz had lived at the address given by the caller for about 2 years. The police checked their internal records, which showed that Ortiz had a prior conviction in 1991 for possession of a controlled substance, for which he had been sentenced to a 6–month term of imprisonment, and that a concurrent charge had been dismissed. The police records also showed that Ortiz was charged in early 1994 with possession of marijuana and hashish with intent to deliver but that the charges were dropped.

At about 8:45 p.m. on the same evening, police officers took Pogo, a police dog specially trained to detect the scents of marijuana, cocaine, cocaine base, methamphetamine, amphetamine, and heroin into the hallway outside Ortiz' apartment to perform a canine sniff of the area. The officers ran Pogo in the hallway outside Ortiz' apartment, and Pogo "alerted" by the door to Ortiz' apartment.

On August 8, 1997, officers applied for and obtained a "no-knock" daytime search warrant which entitled them to search the interior of Ortiz' apartment. * * * Shortly thereafter, the police officers executed the warrant. Within Ortiz' apartment, the officers found one-quarter of an ounce of cocaine and $6,300 in a kitchen drawer, 4 ounces of marijuana and $11,000 in a freezer, and a notebook containing records of suspected drug transactions. [Ortiz objected to the admission of this evidence on the ground that the warrant was tainted by the prior canine sniff.] * * *

The leading case regarding canine sniffs is United States v. Place, 462 U.S. 696 (1983), in which it was concluded that the evidence of cocaine involved therein should be suppressed. In *Place*, the U.S. Supreme Court considered the federal Fourth Amendment implications of the use of a drug detection dog to sniff luggage in an airport. After Place arrived at a New York airport, he refused to voluntarily allow police to search his two suitcases. The officers allowed Place to leave, but took his luggage to a separate location for a drug detection dog to sniff. The dog alerted aggressively to one of Place's suitcases. At this point, approximately 90 minutes had elapsed from the officers' initial contact with Place. It was a Friday afternoon, and rather than immediately seeking a search warrant, the officers held Place's suitcases over the weekend and applied for a search warrant the following Monday morning. When police executed the warrant and searched Place's suitcases, they found 1,125 grams of cocaine.

The Court in *Place* observed that a canine sniff is sui generis in that the canine alert is limited to the existence of contraband and that the sniff is not highly intrusive. The *Place* Court determined that the canine sniff of the luggage did not, by itself, violate the Fourth Amendment. The *Place* Court concluded, however, that because the police detained the luggage for a lengthy period and failed to diligently pursue the investigation, the cocaine discovered in Place's luggage pursuant to the search warrant should have been suppressed. * * *

With respect to canine sniffs in hallways adjoining residential quarters, the type of sniff which is the subject of the instant case, numerous courts have held that a canine sniff intrudes into an area where an individual has a reasonable expectation of privacy and that a canine sniff in a residential hallway must be supported by at least a reasonable suspicion based on articulable facts. * * * For the sake of completeness, we note that some courts have held that there is no legitimate privacy expectation in a residential apartment hallway and that thus, canine sniffs do not implicate the Fourth Amendment. See, e.g., Brown v. U.S., 627 A.2d 499 (D.C.1993); State v. Taylor, 763 S.W.2d 756 (Tenn.Crim. App.1988). At the other end of the spectrum, some courts have stated that there is a heightened expectation of privacy in a residential apartment hallway, United States v. Thomas, 757 F.2d 1359 (2d Cir.1985); and thus a canine sniff may not proceed in the absence of probable cause. See, similarly, State v. Dearman, 962 P.2d 850 (Wash.App.1998) (holding that probable cause is required prior to canine sniff outside residential garage).

We agree with the courts which conclude an individual's Fourth Amendment privacy interests may extend in a limited manner beyond the four walls of the home, depending on the facts, including some expectation of privacy to be free from police canine sniffs for illegal drugs in the hallway outside an apartment or at the threshold of a residence, and that a canine sniff under these circumstances must be based on no less than reasonable, articulable suspicion. * * * [The court held that the anonymous tip, minimally corroborated, was insufficient to establish reasonable suspicion; the search warrant was therefore invalid because the probable cause was obtained by an unlawful canine sniff search.]

UNITED STATES v. WHITE

Supreme Court of the United States, 1971.
401 U.S. 745, 91 S.Ct. 1122, 28 L.Ed.2d 453.

MR. JUSTICE WHITE announced the judgment of the Court and an opinion in which THE CHIEF JUSTICE, MR. JUSTICE STEWART, and MR. JUSTICE BLACKMUN join.

In 1966, respondent James A. White was tried and convicted under two consolidated indictments charging various illegal transactions in narcotics. He was fined and sentenced as a second offender to 25–year concurrent sentences. The issue before us is whether the Fourth Amendment bars from evidence the testimony of governmental agents who related certain conversations which had occurred between defendant White and a government informant, Harvey Jackson, and which the agents overheard by monitoring the frequency of a radio transmitter carried by Jackson and concealed on his person. On four occasions the conversations took place in Jackson's home; each of these conversations was overheard by an agent concealed in a kitchen closet with Jackson's consent and by a second agent outside the house using a radio receiver. Four other conversations—one in respondent's home, one in a restaurant, and two in Jackson's car—were overheard by the use of radio equipment. The prosecution was unable to locate and produce Jackson at the trial and the trial court overruled objections to the testimony of the agents who conducted the electronic surveillance. The jury returned a guilty verdict and defendant appealed.

The Court of Appeals read *Katz v. United States*, 389 U.S. 347 (1967), as overruling *On Lee v. United States*, 343 U.S. 747 (1952), and interpreting the Fourth Amendment to forbid the introduction of the agents' testimony in the circumstances of this case. Accordingly, the court reversed but without adverting to the fact that the transactions at issue here had occurred before *Katz* was decided in this Court. In our view, the Court of Appeals misinterpreted both the *Katz* case and the Fourth Amendment and in any event erred in applying the *Katz* case to events that occurred before that decision was rendered by this Court.

I

Until *Katz v. United States*, neither wiretapping nor electronic eavesdropping violated a defendant's Fourth Amendment rights "unless there has been an official search and seizure of his person, or such a seizure of his papers or his tangible material effects, or an actual physical invasion of his house 'or curtilage' for the purpose of making a seizure." *Olmstead v. United States*, 277 U.S. 438, 466 (1928); *Goldman v. United States*, 316 U.S. 129, 135–136 (1942). But where "eavesdropping was accomplished by means of an unauthorized physical penetration into the premises occupied" by the defendant, although falling short of a "technical trespass under the local property law," the Fourth Amendment was violated and any evidence of what was seen and heard, as well as tangible objects seized, was considered the inadmissible fruit of an unlawful invasion. [Citations]

Katz v. United States, however, finally swept away doctrines that electronic eavesdropping is permissible under the Fourth Amendment unless physical invasion of a constitutionally protected area produced the challenged evidence. In that case government agents, without petitioner's consent or knowledge, attached a listening device to the outside of a public telephone booth and recorded the defendant's end of his telephone conversations. In declaring the recordings inadmissible in evidence in the absence of a warrant authorizing the surveillance, the Court overruled *Olmstead* and *Goldman* and held that the absence of physical intrusion into the telephone booth did not justify using electronic devices in listening to and recording Katz' words, thereby violating the privacy on which he justifiably relied while using the telephone in those circumstances.

The Court of Appeals understood *Katz* to render inadmissible against White the agents' testimony concerning conversations that Jackson broadcast to them. We cannot agree. *Katz* involved no revelation to the Government by a party to conversations with the defendant nor did the Court indicate in any way that a defendant has a justifiable and constitutionally protected expectation that a person with whom he is conversing will not then or later reveal the conversation to the police.

Hoffa v. United States, 385 U.S. 293 (1966), which was left undisturbed by *Katz*, held that however strongly a defendant may trust an apparent colleague, his expectations in this respect are not protected by the Fourth Amendment when it turns out that the colleague is a government agent regularly communicating with the authorities. In these circumstances, "no interest legitimately protected by the Fourth Amendment is involved," for that amendment affords no protection to "a wrongdoer's misplaced belief that a person to whom he voluntarily confides his wrongdoing will not reveal it." *Hoffa v. United States*, at 302. No warrant to "search and seize" is required in such circumstances, nor is it when the Government sends to defendant's home a secret agent who conceals his identity and makes a purchase of narcotics from the accused, *Lewis v. United States*, 385 U.S. 206 (1966), or when the same agent, unbeknown to the defendant, carries electronic equipment to record the defendant's words and the evidence so gathered is later offered in evidence. *Lopez v. United States*, 373 U.S. 427 (1963).

Conceding that *Hoffa, Lewis*, and *Lopez* remained unaffected by *Katz*, the Court of Appeals nevertheless read both *Katz* and the Fourth Amendment to require a different result if the agent not only records his conversations with the defendant but instantaneously transmits them electronically to other agents equipped with radio receivers. Where this occurs, the Court of Appeals held, the Fourth Amendment is violated and the testimony of the listening agents must be excluded from evidence.

To reach this result it was necessary for the Court of Appeals to hold that *On Lee v. United States* was no longer good law. In that case, which involved facts very similar to the case before us, the Court first rejected claims of a Fourth Amendment violation because the informer had not trespassed when he entered the defendant's premises and conversed with him. To this extent the Court's rationale cannot survive *Katz*. But the Court announced a second and independent ground for its decision; for it went on to say that overruling *Olmstead* and *Goldman* would be of no aid to On Lee since he "was talking confidentially and indiscreetly with one he trusted, and he was overheard. * * * It would be a dubious service to the genuine liberties protected by the Fourth Amendment to make them bedfellows with spurious liberties improvised by farfetched analogies which would liken eavesdropping on a conversation, with the connivance of one of the parties, to an unreasonable search or seizure. We find no violation of the Fourth Amendment here." 343 U.S., at 753–754. We see no indication in *Katz* that the Court meant to disturb that understanding of the Fourth Amendment or to disturb the result reached in the *On Lee* case, nor are we now inclined to overturn this view of the Fourth Amendment. * * *

Our problem is not what the privacy expectations of particular defendants in particular situations may be or the extent to which they may in fact have relied on the discretion of their companions. Very probably, individual defendants neither know nor suspect that their colleagues have gone or will go to the police or are carrying recorders or transmitters. Otherwise, conversation would cease and our problem with these encounters would be nonexistent or far different from those now before us. Our problem, in terms of the principles announced in *Katz*, is what expectations of privacy are constitutionally "justifiable"—what expectations the Fourth Amendment will protect in the absence of a warrant. So far, the law permits the frustration of actual expectations of privacy by permitting authorities to use the testimony of those associates who for one reason or another have determined to turn to the police, as well as by authorizing the use of informants in the manner exemplified by *Hoffa* and *Lewis*. If the law gives no protection to the wrongdoer whose trusted accomplice is or becomes a police agent, neither should it protect him when that same agent has recorded or transmitted the conversations which are later offered in evidence to prove the State's case. * * * An electronic recording will many times produce a more reliable rendition of what a defendant has said than will the unaided memory of a police agent. It may also be that with the recording in existence it is less likely that the informant will change his mind, less chance that threat or injury will suppress unfavorable evidence and less chance that cross-examination will confound the testimony. Considerations like these obviously do not favor the defendant, but we are not prepared to hold that a defendant who has no constitutional right to exclude the informer's unaided testimony nevertheless has a Fourth Amendment privilege against a more accurate version of the events in question.

It is thus untenable to consider the activities and reports of the police agent himself, though acting without a warrant, to be a "reasonable" investigative effort and lawful under the Fourth Amendment but to view the same agent with a recorder or transmitter as conducting an "unreasonable" and unconstitutional search and seizure. * * *

No different result should obtain where, as in *On Lee* and the instant case, the informer disappears and is unavailable at trial; for the issue of whether specified events on a certain day violate the Fourth Amendment should not be determined by what later happens to the informer. His unavailability at trial and proffering the testimony of other agents may raise evidentiary problems or pose issues of prosecutorial misconduct with respect to the informer's disappearance, but they do not appear critical to deciding whether prior events invaded the defendant's Fourth Amendment rights.

II

The Court of Appeals was in error for another reason. In *Desist v. United States*, 394 U.S. 244 (1969), we held that our decision in *Katz v. United States* applied only to those electronic surveillances that occurred subsequent to the date of that decision. Here the events in question took place in late 1965 and early 1966, long prior to *Katz*. * * * The court should have judged this case by the pre-*Katz* law and under that law, as *On Lee* clearly holds, the electronic surveillance here involved did not violate White's rights to be free from unreasonable searches and seizures.

The judgment of the Court of Appeals is reversed.

[JUSTICE BLACK wrote a brief concurring opinion citing his dissenting opinion in *Katz*. That opinion had argued that electronic surveillance (consensual or otherwise) was not a "search" within the meaning of the Fourth Amendment. Black thus provided the crucial fifth vote for the holding that consensual surveillance (*i.e.* electronic transmitting or recording with the consent of one party to the conversation) is not limited by the Fourth Amendment.]

[JUSTICE BRENNAN, concurring in the result, agreed that the overheard conversations were admissible under pre-*Katz* definitions of "search" that required a physical trespass. He argued, however, *Katz* had undercut the doctrinal basis for both *On Lee* and *Lopez*, and that a warrant should henceforth be required for any surreptitious electronic monitoring, even if the suspect is aware he is speaking to a government agent (as in *Lopez*).]

Mr. Justice Douglas, dissenting. * * *

Now that the discredited decisions in *On Lee* and *Lopez* are resuscitated and revived, must everyone live in fear that every word he speaks may be transmitted or recorded and later repeated to the entire world? I can imagine nothing that has a more chilling effect on people speaking their minds and expressing their views on important matters. The advocates of that regime should spend some time in totalitarian countries and learn first-hand the kind of regime they are creating here. * * *

Mr. Justice Harlan, dissenting.

* * * The analysis must, in my view, transcend the search for subjective expectations or legal attribution of assumptions of risk. Our expectations, and the risks we assume, are in large part reflections of laws that translate into rules the customs and values of the past and present.

Since it is the task of the law to form and project, as well as mirror and reflect, we should not, as judges, merely recite the expectations and risks without examining the desirability of saddling them upon society. The critical question, therefore, is whether under our system of government, as reflected in the Constitution, we should impose on our citizens the risks of the electronic listener or observer without at least the protection of a warrant requirement. * * *

The impact of the practice of third-party bugging, must, I think, be considered such as to undermine that confidence and sense of security in dealing with one another that is characteristic of individual relationships between citizens in a free society. It goes beyond the impact on privacy occasioned by the ordinary type of "informer" investigation upheld in *Lewis* and *Hoffa*. The argument of the plurality opinion, to the effect that it is irrelevant whether secrets are revealed by the mere tattletale or the transistor, ignores the differences occasioned by third-party monitoring and recording which insures full and accurate disclosure of all that is said, free of the possibility of error and oversight that inheres in human reporting.

Authority is hardly required to support the proposition that words would be measured a good deal more carefully and communication inhibited if one suspected his conversations were being transmitted and transcribed. Were third-party bugging a prevalent practice, it might well smother that spontaneity—reflected in frivolous, impetuous, sacrilegious, and defiant discourse—that liberates daily life. Much off-hand exchange is easily forgotten and one may count on the obscurity of his remarks, protected by the very fact of a limited audience, and the likelihood that the listener will either overlook or forget what is said, as well as the listener's inability to reformulate a conversation without having to contend with a documented record. All these values are sacrificed by a rule of law that permits official monitoring of private discourse limited only by the need to locate a willing assistant. * * *

Finally, it is too easy to forget—and, hence, too often forgotten—that the issue here is whether to interpose a search warrant procedure between law enforcement agencies engaging in electronic eavesdropping and the public generally. By casting its "risk analysis" solely in terms of the expectations and risks that "wrongdoers" or "one contemplating illegal activities" ought to bear, the plurality opinion, I think, misses the mark entirely. *On Lee* does not simply mandate that criminals must daily run the risk of unknown eavesdroppers prying into their private affairs; it subjects each and every law-abiding member of society to that risk. The very purpose of interposing the Fourth Amendment warrant requirement is to redistribute the privacy risks throughout society in a way that produces the results the plurality opinion ascribes to the *On Lee* rule. Abolition of *On Lee* would not end electronic eavesdropping. It would prevent public officials from engaging in that practice unless they first had probable cause to suspect an individual of involvement in illegal activities and had tested their version of the facts before a detached judicial officer. The interest *On Lee* fails to protect is the expectation of the ordinary citizen, who has never engaged in illegal conduct in his life, that he may carry on his private discourse freely, openly, and spontaneously without measuring his every word against the connotations it might carry when instantaneously heard by others unknown to him and unfamiliar with his situation or analyzed in a cold, formal record played days, months, or years after the conversation. Interposition of a warrant requirement is designed not to shield "wrongdoers," but to secure a measure of privacy and a sense of personal security throughout our society.

The Fourth Amendment does, of course, leave room for the employment of modern technology in criminal law enforcement, but in the stream of current developments in Fourth Amendment law I think it must be held that third-party electronic monitoring, subject only to the self-restraint of law enforcement officials, has no place in our society.

Commentary

The Massachusetts Supreme Judicial Court rejected the reasoning of the plurality opinion in *United States v. White* when it interpreted the state constitution's prohibition of unreasonable searches. The Massachusetts court concluded that "society" would think it "objectively reasonable to expect that conversational interchange in a private home will not be invaded surreptitiously by warrantless electronic transmission," and that consent of one party "only affords the State a person willing to transport the invisible instruments of eavesdropping into 'earshot.' " Commonwealth v. Blood, 400 Mass. 61, 507 N.E.2d 1029, 1034 (Mass.1987). The court therefore held unconstitutional a state statute which authorized warrantless consensual electronic surveillance. The dissenting opinion argued that the statute itself is the best guide to determining what expectations of privacy society would regard as reasonable. The point is a troublesome one. Is "society" something distinct from a majority of the voters? If reliable public opinion polls indicated that two-thirds of the citizens believe that the police should be allowed to tap telephone lines at will because "the innocent have nothing to fear," would this establish that society does not consider it reasonable to have an expectation of privacy in telephone conversations?

In Commonwealth v. Eason, 427 Mass. 595, 694 N.E.2d 1264 (Mass. 1998), the Massachusetts Supreme Judicial Court limited its decision in *Blood.* State troopers investigating a crime persuaded a witness named Disorbo to make two telephone calls to defendant Eason at his home. Without the defendant's knowledge, but with Disorbo's consent, the troopers listened to these calls on an extension telephone. They testified at trial to admissions that they heard the defendant make during those telephone conversations. The court held that in these circumstances admitting the testimony did not violate the state constitution. It distinguished *Blood* because that case involved a challenge to the admissibility of statements obtained by means of a concealed transmitter worn by a cooperating confederate of the defendant during meetings in private homes. In contrast defendant Eason knew, when speaking on the telephone, that his words were being transmitted electronically beyond his home. A defendant who speaks incriminating words over the telephone runs the risk that the conversation . . . may be overheard on an extension telephone"—i.e., with the consent of the other party to the conversation.

The 1967 decision in *Katz v. United States,* 389 U.S. 347 which is discussed in the preceding opinions, made it clear that *nonconsensual* electronic eavesdropping or wiretapping constitutes a "search" whether or not a physical trespass is employed to install the equipment. Congress responded to this development in the Omnibus Crime Control and Safe Streets Act of 1968, codified as 18 U.S.C.A. §§ 2510–2520. In summary, the Act permits federal law enforcement officers to engage in nonconsensual wiretapping and electronic eavesdropping pursuant to court order. An application for such an order must be authorized by the Attorney General or a specially designated Assistant Attorney General, an important requirement which ensures that top-level Justice Department officials will take personal responsibility for these activities. The affidavit in support of the application must show not only probable cause for belief that "particular communications" concerning a serious crime will be intercepted, but also that other investigative procedures are unlikely to be successful.

The judge receiving the application may approve the surveillance for a particular location for a definite period of time up to a maximum of 30 days, although this period is renewable. The order is supposed to contain a provision requiring that the interception be conducted in such a manner as to minimize the interception of communications other than those described in the order, but a failure to minimize the number of irrelevant conversations overheard does not ordinarily lead to suppression of conversations that were properly overheard. All intercepted conversations are to be recorded, and the recordings are to be turned over to the court at the termination of the period of surveillance. The judge thereafter gives the suspect named in the application notice that surveillance occurred during the period. This provision for notice is extremely important, because it ensures that persons who are the subject of surveillance will find out about it even if no criminal prosecution is brought.

When the surveillance does not involve the overhearing of confidential conversations, the intrusion on privacy is much less and the surveillance may not be governed by the Fourth Amendment at all. For example, the Supreme Court has held that it is not a search for the police to utilize a "pen register," which records all telephone numbers dialed from a particular telephone. A telephone user necessarily conveys this numerical information to the telephone company which records it for use in its business, and the majority opinion concluded that the user therefore "assumes the risk" that the company would reveal the information to the police. Smith v. Maryland, 442 U.S. 735 (1979).* The reasoning is similar to that employed by the Supreme Court in holding that law enforcement officers violate no Fourth Amendment rights of a defendant when they obtain a subpoena directed at his bank to produce financial records concerning the defendant and his company in the bank's possession. The majority found the analogy to the "false friend" cases persuasive; one who entrusts information to a bank, a telephone company, or a friend assumes the risk that the information will also be conveyed to the government. United States v. Miller, 425 U.S. 435 (1976); contra, Burrows v. Superior Court of San Bernardino County, 13 Cal.3d 238, 118 Cal.Rptr. 166, 529 P.2d 590 (1974).

All these holdings are controversial, of course, and dissenting justices made powerful arguments for giving more protection to privacy. It is important to remember that granting Fourth Amendment protection would not prevent the government from obtaining the information pursuant to a search warrant issued upon probable cause. In the absence of a warrant requirement the authorities can engage in a "fishing expedition," in the hope that something incriminating may turn up.

The Supreme Court has also decided cases involving the use of electronic tracking devices (beepers) to assist agents in following movements of a car, an airplane, or a container. The Fourth Amendment issue might be raised either with respect to the installation of the beeper, or with respect to the subsequent activities of the police in following the container with the aid of the beeper.

In United States v. Knotts, 460 U.S. 276 (1983), the police obtained the consent of a chemical company to install a beeper into a container of chloroform (used to make illegal drugs) which was subsequently sold to a suspect. With the assistance of the beeper, the police were then able to follow the suspect to the location of an illicit drug laboratory in a remote area. Given that merely following the suspect's automobile raises no Fourth Amendment issue, the Supreme Court majority held that nothing in the Fourth Amendment prohibits the police from making use of this kind of scientific assistance to augment their senses.

In a second "beeper" case, the Court decided two questions left unresolved in *Knotts*: (1) Whether installation of a beeper in a container of chemicals with the consent of its original owner constitutes a search or seizure when the container is subsequently delivered to a buyer having no knowledge of its presence; and (2) whether monitoring of a beeper constitutes a Fourth Amendment search when it reveals information that could

---

* Similar to the pen register is the "mail cover," whereby postal authorities record addresses, postmarks, etc. on the outside of envelopes received by a suspect. United States v. Choate, 576 F.2d 165 (9th Cir. 1978) held that mail covers do not violate the Fourth Amendment.

not have been obtained through unaided visual surveillance (the movements of the container inside a building, which police could not see but could follow electronically). The majority opinion held that the installation violated no Fourth Amendment right of the ultimate recipient, but that the subsequent monitoring required prior judicial authorization to the extent that the police continue to monitor the beeper when the container has been taken inside private premises. The Court observed that it would be obviously desirable for police to obtain warrants for the installation and monitoring of beepers in all cases, because it would often be important to continue monitoring to determine precisely where the container is located in a place not open to visual surveillance. The majority left open the possibility that warrants might be obtainable on a showing of reasonable suspicion rather than probable cause, given that the invasion of privacy in such cases is not as great as it is with a traditional search. United States v. Karo, 468 U.S. 705 (1984).

Why should the police object when surveillance activities of this nature are classified as "searches" and therefore regulated by the Fourth Amendment? One answer might be that they wish to engage in fishing expeditions, *i.e.* surveillance where there is only a general suspicion of criminal activity. But the kind of extensive surveillance involved in the "beeper" cases is expensive and time-consuming, and it is therefore unlikely that the authorities would proceed without fairly strong grounds for believing that the suspects are engaged in criminal activity. In that case, can't they easily get a warrant?

This question anticipates subjects that will be considered in the next two chapters, and so only preliminary thoughts will be suggested at this point. Remember that the Fourth Amendment requires that search warrants contain a particular description of the place to be searched, and the persons or things to be seized. If this requirement were enforced strictly and literally, it would be difficult to get a warrant to "search" the unpredictable movements of a container, or to "seize" the contents of a conversation that has not yet occurred.

In fact, however, these difficulties have been overcome. In the *Karo* case, for example, the majority opinion reassured the government that a description of the object into which the beeper is to be placed, the circumstances that led agents to wish to install it, and the length of time of the anticipated surveillance would be sufficient to obtain a warrant. Similarly, the federal statute governing electronic eavesdropping requires only "a particular description of the *type* of communications sought to be intercepted." In other words, the law has required only as much specificity as the practical circumstances permit.

Nonetheless, law enforcement officers often regard the warrant requirement as a meaningless paperwork obstacle which impedes and delays their legitimate activities to no useful purpose. We will not attempt to investigate the extent to which this perception is or is not justifiable at this point, except to note that opinions about the value of the warrant requirement are bound to affect one's viewpoint about how broadly the requirement ought to be applied. If there is nothing particularly burdensome about requiring warrants, and if they serve an important purpose in protecting citizens from abuse of police power, then the warrant requirement ought to be construed broadly. If requiring a warrant means requiring burdensome paperwork without any substantial benefit in terms of protecting legitimate expectations of privacy, then the requirement should be construed more narrowly.

Of course, holding that an activity is not a search or seizure means not only that it is not regulated by the warrant requirement, but also that it is not regulated by the Fourth Amendment at all. It would be possible to say that, for example, surreptitious recording of conversations as occurred in United States v. White is a search, but may be conducted with probable cause (or reasonable suspicion) under an exception to the warrant requirement. (Recall that this was done in *New Jersey v. T.L.O., supra* page 2.) The significance or utility of such a requirement would depend upon whether arbitrary recording of conversations by law enforcement agencies occurs with any frequency, and whether it is enough of a danger to privacy that after-the-fact judicial review is desirable. Conceivably, bringing consensual electronic surveillance within the scope of the Fourth Amendment would curtail excessive employment of the practice. On the other hand, it might merely add another issue to be litigated in criminal trials without substantially affecting law enforcement practice.

A famous West German decision illustrates the different approach which the courts of that country employ in determining the admissibility of recordings of private conversations. The defendant purchased some property, arranging to understate the sale price on the contract so that he could value it at a lower figure for tax purposes. The seller secretly tape-recorded some of the conversations relating to the tax fraud, and turned the tapes over to the police. In American terms, there was thus not only no search but also no law enforcement activity. Nonetheless, the German court excluded the evidence. It held that the taped conversations fell within a private sphere which could be invaded only if justified by an overriding public interest. The Court concluded that the state interest in this case was not sufficiently strong to permit use of the tapes, but indicated that the result might have been different if the defendant had been charged with a crime of violence rather than tax fraud. The decision seems curious from an American point of view because the police did nothing wrong, and it is not clear that the seller did anything wrong either. The German court was concerned not with regulating the conduct of police officers or other persons who secretly record conversations, but rather with regulating the use of those recordings in court. The decision is described in Bradley, "The Exclusionary Rule in Germany," 96 Harv.L.Rev. 1032, 1044–46 (1983).

UNITED STATES v. JACOBSEN

Supreme Court of the United States, 1984.
466 U.S. 109, 104 S.Ct. 1652, 80 L.Ed.2d 85.

JUSTICE STEVENS delivered the opinion of the Court.

During their examination of a damaged package, the employees of a private freight carrier observed a white powdery substance, originally concealed within eight layers of wrappings. They summoned a federal agent, who removed a trace of the powder, subjected it to a chemical test and determined that it was cocaine. The question presented is whether the Fourth Amendment required the agent to obtain a warrant before he did so.

The relevant facts are not in dispute. Early in the morning of May 1, 1981, a supervisor at the Minneapolis–St. Paul airport Federal Express office asked the office manager to look at a package that had been damaged and torn by a forklift. They then opened the package in order to examine its contents pursuant to a written company policy regarding insurance claims.

The container was an ordinary cardboard box wrapped in brown paper. Inside the box five or six pieces of crumpled newspaper covered a tube about 10 inches long; the tube was made of the silver tape used on basement ducts. The supervisor and office manager cut open the tube, and found a series of four zip-lock plastic bags, the outermost enclosing the other three and the innermost containing about six and a half ounces of white powder. When they observed the white powder in the innermost bag, they notified the Drug Enforcement Administration. Before the first DEA agent arrived, they replaced the plastic bags in the tube and put the tube and the newspapers back into the box.

When the first federal agent arrived, the box, still wrapped in brown paper, but with a hole punched in its side and the top open, was placed on a desk. The agent saw that one end of the tube had been slit open; he removed the four plastic bags from the tube and saw the white powder. He then opened each of the four bags and removed a trace of the white substance with a knife blade. A field test made on the spot identified the substance as cocaine.[1]

In due course, other agents arrived, made a second field test, rewrapped the package, obtained a warrant to search the place to which it was addressed, executed the warrant, and arrested respondents. After they were indicted for the crime of possessing an illegal substance with intent to distribute, their motion to suppress the evidence on the ground that the warrant was the product of an illegal search and seizure was denied; they were tried and convicted, and appealed. The Court of Appeals reversed. It held that the validity of the search warrant depended on the validity of the agents' warrantless test of the white powder, that the testing constituted a significant expansion of the earlier private search, and that a warrant was required. * * *

I

The first clause of the Fourth Amendment provides that the "right of the people to be secure in their persons, houses, papers and effects, against unreasonable searches and seizures, shall not be violated * * *." This text protects two types of expectations, one involving "searches," the other "seizures." A "search" occurs when an expectation of privacy

---

1. As the test is described in the evidence, it involved the use of three test tubes. When a substance containing cocaine is placed in one test tube after another, it will cause liquids to take on a certain sequence of colors. Such a test discloses whether or not the substance is cocaine, but there is no evidence that it would identify any other substances.

that society is prepared to consider reasonable is infringed. A "seizure" of property occurs when there is some meaningful interference with an individual's possessory interests in that property. This Court has also consistently construed this protection as proscribing only governmental action; it is wholly inapplicable to a search or seizure, even an unreasonable one, effected by a private individual not acting as an agent of the Government or with the participation or knowledge of any governmental official.

When the wrapped parcel involved in this case was delivered to the private freight carrier, it was unquestionably an "effect" within the meaning of the Fourth Amendment. Letters and other sealed packages are in the general class of effects in which the public at large has a legitimate expectation of privacy; warrantless searches of such effects are presumptively unreasonable. Even when government agents may lawfully seize such a package to prevent loss or destruction of suspected contraband, the Fourth Amendment requires that they obtain a warrant before examining the contents of such a package.[8] Such a warrantless search could not be characterized as reasonable simply because, after the official invasion of privacy occurred, contraband is discovered. Conversely, in this case the fact that agents of the private carrier independently opened the package and made an examination that might have been impermissible for a government agent cannot render otherwise reasonable official conduct unreasonable. The reasonableness of an official invasion of the citizen's privacy must be appraised on the basis of the facts as they existed at the time that invasion occurred.

The initial invasions of respondents' package were occasioned by private action. Those invasions revealed that the package contained only one significant item, a suspicious looking tape tube. Cutting the end of the tube and extracting its contents revealed a suspicious looking plastic bag of white powder. Whether those invasions were accidental or deliberate,[10] and whether they were reasonable or unreasonable, they did not violate the Fourth Amendment because of their private character.

The additional invasions of respondents' privacy by the government agent must be tested by the degree to which they exceeded the scope of the private search. * * *

II

When the first federal agent on the scene initially saw the package, he knew it contained nothing of significance except a tube containing plastic bags and, ultimately, white powder. It is not entirely clear that

8. [Citations.] There is, of course, a well recognized exception for customs searches; but that exception is not involved in this case.

10. A post-trial affidavit indicates that an agent of Federal Express may have opened the package because he was suspicious about its contents, and not because of damage from a forklift. However, the lower courts found no governmental involvement in the private search, a finding not challenged by respondents. The affidavit thus is of no relevance to the issue we decide. [Subsequent cases have established that Federal Express has a (lawful) corporate policy of opening packages that may contain drugs. See United States v. Young, 153 F.3d 1079 (9th Cir. 1998.—editor] the powder was visible to him before he removed the tube from the box. Even if the white powder was not itself in "plain view" because it was still enclosed in so many containers and covered with papers, there was a virtual certainty that nothing else of significance was in the package and that a manual inspection of the tube and its contents would not tell him anything more than he already had been told. Respondents do not dispute that the Government could utilize the Federal Express employees' testimony concerning the contents of the package. If that is the case, it hardly infringed respondents' privacy for the agents to reexamine the contents of the open package by brushing aside a crumpled newspaper and picking up the tube. The advantage the Government gained thereby was merely avoiding the risk of a flaw in the employees' recollection, rather than in further infringing respondents' privacy. Protecting the risk of misdescription hardly enhances any legitimate privacy interest, and is not protected by the Fourth Amendment. * * *

Similarly, the removal of the plastic bags from the tube and the agent's visual inspection of their contents enabled the agent to learn nothing that had not previously been learned during the private search. It infringed no legitimate expectation of privacy and hence was not a "search" within the meaning of the Fourth Amendment.

While the agents' assertion of dominion and control over the package and its contents did constitute a "seizure," that seizure was not unreasonable. * * *

III

The question remains whether the additional intrusion occasioned by the field test, which had not been conducted by the Federal Express agents and therefore exceeded the scope of the private search, was an unlawful "search" or "seizure" within the meaning of the Fourth Amendment.

The field test at issue could disclose only one fact previously unknown to the agent—whether or not a suspicious white powder was cocaine. It could tell him nothing more, not even whether the substance was sugar or talcum powder. We must first determine whether this can be considered a "search" subject to the Fourth Amendment—did it infringe an expectation of privacy that society is prepared to consider reasonable?

The concept of an interest in privacy that society is prepared to recognize as reasonable is, by its very nature, critically different from the mere expectation, however well justified, that certain facts will not come to the attention of the authorities. Indeed, this distinction underlies the rule that Government may utilize information voluntarily disclosed to a governmental informant, despite the criminal's reasonable expectation that his associates would not disclose confidential information to the authorities. See *United States v. White*, [p. 94 of this book].

A chemical test that merely discloses whether or not a particular substance is cocaine does not compromise any legitimate interest in privacy. * * * Congress has decided—and there is no question about its power to do so—to treat the interest in "privately" possessing cocaine as illegitimate; thus governmental conduct that can reveal whether a substance is cocaine, and no other arguably "private" fact, compromises no legitimate privacy interest.

This conclusion is dictated by *United States v. Place*, 462 U.S. 696 (1983), in which the Court held that subjecting luggage to a "sniff test" by a trained narcotics detection dog was not a "search" within the meaning of the Fourth Amendment.

* * *

[The majority also held that the fact that the field test necessarily destroyed a minute trace of the powder did not make the seizure unreasonable.]

In sum, the federal agents did not infringe any constitutionally protected privacy interest that had not already been frustrated as the result of private conduct. To the extent that a protected possessory interest was infringed, the infringement was *de minimis* and constitutionally reasonable. The judgment of the Court of Appeals is reversed.

JUSTICE WHITE, concurring in part and concurring in the judgment.

It is relatively easy for me to concur in the judgment in this case, since in my view the case should be judged on the basis of the Magistrate's finding that, when the first DEA agent arrived, the tube was in plain view in the box and the bags of white powder were visible from the end of the tube. Although this finding was challenged before the District Court, that court found it unnecessary to pass on the issue. As I understand its opinion, however, the Court of Appeals accepted the Magistrate's finding * * *

If this case must be judged on the basis that the plastic bags and their contents were concealed when the first agent arrived, I disagree with the Court's conclusion that the agent could, without a warrant, uncover or unwrap the tube and remove its contents simply because a private party had previously done so. * * *

The majority opinion is particularly troubling when one considers its logical implications. I would be hard-pressed to distinguish this case, which involves a private search, from (1) one in which the private party's knowledge, later communicated to the government, that a particular container concealed contraband and nothing else arose from his presence at the time the container was sealed; (2) one in which the private party learned that a container concealed contraband and nothing else when it was previously opened in his presence; or (3) one in which the private party knew to a certainty that a container concealed contraband and nothing else as a result of conversations with its owner. In each of these cases, the approach adopted by the Court today would seem to suggest that the owner of the container has no legitimate expectation of privacy in its contents and that government agents opening that container without a warrant on the strength of information provided by the private party would not violate the Fourth Amendment.*

Because I cannot accept the majority's novel extension of the private-search doctrine and its implications for the entire concept of legitimate expectations of privacy, I concur only in Part III of its opinion and in the judgment.

JUSTICE BRENNAN, with whom JUSTICE MARSHALL joins, dissenting. * * *

[For the reasons given by Justice White], I am not persuaded that the DEA officer actually came upon respondents' cocaine without violating the Fourth Amendment and accordingly, I need not address the legality of the chemical field test. Since the Court has done so, however, I too will address the question, assuming, *arguendo*, that the officer committed neither an unconstitutional search nor an unconstitutional seizure prior to the point at which he took the sample of cocaine out of the plastic bags to conduct the test.

I agree that, under the hypothesized circumstances, the field test in this case was not a search within the meaning of the Fourth Amendment for the following reasons: *First*, the officer came upon the white powder innocently; *second*, under the hypothesized circumstances, respondents could not have had a reasonable expectation of privacy in the chemical identity of the powder because the DEA agents were already able to identify it as contraband with virtual certainty, and *third*, the test required the destruction of only a minute quantity of the powder. The Court, however, has reached this conclusion on a much broader ground, relying on two factors alone to support the proposition that the field test was not a search; *first*, the fact that the test revealed only whether or not the substance was cocaine, without providing any further information; and *second*, the assumption that an individual does not have a reasonable expectation of privacy in such a fact. * * *

It is certainly true that a surveillance technique that identifies only the presence or absence of contraband is less intrusive than a technique that reveals the precise nature of an item regardless of whether it is contraband. But by seizing upon this distinction alone to conclude that the first type of technique, as a general matter, is not a search, the Court

* The majority responded to this argument in a footnote:

"We reject Justice White's suggestion that this case is indistinguishable from one in which the police simply learn from a private party that a container contains contraband, seize it from its owner, and conduct a warrantless search which, as Justice White properly observes, would be unconstitutional. Here, the Federal Express employees who were lawfully in possession of the package invited the agent to examine its contents; the governmental conduct was made possible only because private parties had compromised the integrity of this container. Justice White would have this case turn on the fortuity of whether the Federal Express agents placed the tube back into the box. But in the context of their previous examination of the package, their communication of what they had learned to the agent, and their offer to have the agent inspect it, that act surely could not create any privacy interest with respect to the package that would not otherwise exist." * * * [Footnote 17 of the majority opinion.]

has foreclosed any consideration of the circumstances under which the technique is used, and may very well have paved the way for technology to override the limits of law in the area of criminal investigation.

For example, under the Court's analysis in these cases, law enforcement officers could release a trained cocaine-sensitive dog to roam the streets at random, alerting the officers to people carrying cocaine. Or, if a device were developed that, when aimed at a person, would detect instantaneously whether the person is carrying cocaine, there would be no Fourth Amendment bar, under the Court's approach, to the police setting up such a device on a street corner and scanning all passersby. In fact, the Court's analysis is so unbounded that if a device were developed that could detect, from the outside of a building, the presence of cocaine inside, there would be no constitutional obstacle to the police cruising through a residential neighborhood and using the device to identify all homes in which the drug is present. In short, under the interpretation of the Fourth Amendment first suggested in *Place* and first applied in this case, these surveillance techniques would not constitute searches and therefore could be freely pursued whenever and wherever law enforcement officers desire. Hence, at some point in the future, if the Court stands by the theory it has adopted today, search warrants, probable cause, and even "reasonable suspicion" may very well become notions of the past. Fortunately, we know from precedents such as *Katz v. United States, supra,* that this Court ultimately stands ready to prevent this Orwellian world from coming to pass. * * *

Commentary

It is settled that the Fourth Amendment applies only to agents of the government, and not to private parties acting on their own initiative. The weight of authority is that even private security guards and store detectives are not covered by the Amendment, although such persons and their employers can of course be sued for damages for false arrest and other torts under state law. Footnote 10 in the majority opinion in *Jacobsen* is therefore orthodox in stating that, absent governmental involvement in the private search, it is irrelevant whether the Federal Express employee opened the package accidentally or because he suspected it contained contraband. Can you think of arguments for extending Fourth Amendment protection to this kind of private search?

Subsequent police activities that go beyond the scope of the private search may invade privacy interests protected by the Fourth Amendment. In Walter v. United States, 447 U.S. 649 (1980), a package containing apparently pornographic films was mistakenly delivered to the wrong person, and this individual opened the package and turned the contents over to FBI agents. The agents screened the films, thus determining that they were pornographic, and brought a prosecution against the sender. The Supreme Court held that the screening of the films by the agents was a governmental search, which was unlawful in the absence of a warrant. Obscenity cases have frequently provided the occasion for courts to take an expansive view of Fourth Amendment protections. But see New York v. P.J. Video, Inc., 475 U.S. 868 (1986) in which the Supreme Court rejected the argument that there is a higher standard of probable cause for warrants authorizing the seizure of books or photographs than for warrants aimed at materials like weapons or drugs.

Many commentators would agree with the view, expressed by Justice White in his concurring opinion, that the agents committed a "search" if they opened the package, regardless of whether a private party had previously opened it. The observations by the private person could, of course, give them probable cause to conduct this search, and so on this view their activities would still be lawful if they could come within an exception to the warrant requirement. That is precisely the problem, however; absent an emergency justification, agents must obtain a search warrant before opening a closed container of this type. The scope of the warrant requirement is the subject of the next chapter.

The most interesting aspect of the majority opinion in *Jacobsen* is its holding that a chemical test which merely discloses whether a particular substance is contraband does not compromise any legitimate interest in privacy.* It is not only criminals who object to having their telephones tapped, or their houses searched, or their mail opened by police agents; citizens with "nothing to hide" would also be expected to resent such intrusions on their privacy. If the police set a trained dog to sniff for marijuana at random through the baggage area of an airport, however, the privacy interests of people who do not have marijuana in their luggage are not threatened (unless the dog sometimes makes mistakes). Consider the "parade of horribles" listed in the final paragraph of the dissenting opinion. What is so "Orwellian" about a world in which the police employ an infallible technique for locating cocaine?

The majority's holding on this point seems closely linked to the general theory, discussed in the note at the end of the preceding chapter, that the purpose of the Fourth Amendment is to protect the innocent from invasions of privacy that would occur if the police searched without probable cause. If this theory is correct, then the Amendment is not concerned with investigative techniques that by their nature threaten only the interests that narcotics possessors have in avoiding detection. At this point, it might be useful to try to articulate and defend a contrary theory of the Fourth Amendment, one that asserts that its purpose is to protect the guilty as well as the innocent. Why might we want to limit or prohibit extremely effective law enforcement techniques of the type imagined in Justice Brennan's dissent?

SCHNECKLOTH v. BUSTAMONTE

Supreme Court of the United States, 1973.
412 U.S. 218, 93 S.Ct. 2041, 36 L.Ed.2d 854.

MR. JUSTICE STEWART delivered the opinion of the Court. * * *

* * *

While on routine patrol in Sunnyvale, California, at approximately 2:40 in the morning, Police Officer James Rand stopped an automobile

---

* Compare, State v. von Bulow, 475 A.2d 995 (R.I.1984), which distinguished *Jacobsen* in holding that extensive chemical testing of a variety of drugs (which had been unlawfully obtained by a private detective) was unlawful in the absence of a warrant. See also, United States v. Mulder, 808 F.2d 1346 (9th Cir.1987) (Agents who came into possession of pills after private search should have obtained a warrant before subjecting them to extensive chemical tests in a laboratory.)

when he observed that one headlight and its license plate light were burned out. Six men were in the vehicle. Joe Alcala and the respondent, Robert Bustamonte, were in the front seat with Joe Gonzales, the driver. Three older men were seated in the rear. When, in response to the policeman's question, Gonzales could not produce a driver's license, Officer Rand asked if any of the other five had any evidence of identification. Only Alcala produced a license, and he explained that the car was his brother's. After the six occupants had stepped out of the car at the officer's request and after two additional policemen had arrived, Officer Rand asked Alcala if he could search the car. Alcala replied, "Sure, go ahead." Prior to the search no one was threatened with arrest and, according to Officer Rand's uncontradicted testimony, it "was all very congenial at this time." Gonzales testified that Alcala actually helped in the search of the car, by opening the trunk and glove compartment. In Gonzales' words: "[T]he police officer asked Joe [Alcala], he goes, 'Does the trunk open?' And Joe said, 'Yes.' He went to the car and got the keys and opened up the trunk." Wadded up under the left rear seat, the police officers found three checks that had previously been stolen from a car wash.

The trial judge denied the motion to suppress, and the checks in question were admitted in evidence at Bustamonte's trial. On the basis of this and other evidence he was convicted, and the [state appellate courts affirmed.]

Thereafter, the respondent sought a writ of habeas corpus in a federal district court. It was denied. On appeal, the Court of Appeals for the Ninth Circuit * * * reasoned that a consent was a waiver of a person's Fourth and Fourteenth Amendment rights, and that the State was under an obligation to demonstrate, not only that the consent had been uncoerced, but that it had been given with an understanding that it could be freely and effectively withheld. Consent could not be found, the court held, solely from the absence of coercion and a verbal expression of assent. Since the District Court had not determined that Alcala had *known* that his consent could have been withheld and that he could have refused to have his vehicle searched, the Court of Appeals vacated the order denying the writ and remanded the case for further proceedings.

The precise question in this case, then, is what must the prosecution prove to demonstrate that a consent was "voluntarily" given. * * *

[The majority opinion went on to discuss the meaning of "voluntary" as the Court had used the term in the pre-*Miranda* coerced confession cases which are described in Chapter 11, in Part Two of this book. The voluntariness test in the coerced confession cases sought to balance "the acknowledged need for police questioning as a tool for the effective enforcement of criminal laws" against the "deeply felt belief that the criminal law cannot be used as an instrument of unfairness."

None of these pre-*Miranda* confession cases relied on a single controlling criterion to determine voluntariness, and none of them required the prosecution to prove as part of its initial burden that the defendant knew he had a right to refuse to answer questions.]

Similar considerations lead us to agree with the courts of California that the question whether a consent to a search was in fact "voluntary" or was the product of duress or coercion, express or implied, is a question of fact to be determined from the totality of all the circumstances. While knowledge of the right to refuse consent is one factor to be taken into account, the government need not establish such knowledge as the *sine qua non* of an effective consent. As with police questioning, two competing concerns must be accommodated in determining the meaning of a "voluntary" consent—the legitimate need for such searches and the equally important requirement of assuring the absence of coercion.

In situations where the police have some evidence of illicit activity, but lack probable cause to arrest or search, a search authorized by a valid consent may be the only means of obtaining important and reliable evidence. In the present case for example, while the police had reason to stop the car for traffic violations, the State does not contend that there was probable cause to search the vehicle or that the search was incident to a valid arrest of any of the occupants. Yet, the search yielded tangible evidence that served as a basis for a prosecution, and provided some assurance that others, wholly innocent of the crime, were not mistakenly brought to trial. And in those cases where there is probable cause to arrest or search, but where the police lack a warrant, a consent search may still be valuable. If the search is conducted and proves fruitless, that in itself may convince the police that an arrest with its possible stigma and embarrassment is unnecessary, or that a far more extensive search pursuant to a warrant is not justified. In short, a search pursuant to consent may result in considerably less inconvenience for the subject of the search, and, properly conducted, is a constitutionally permissible and wholly legitimate aspect of effective police activity. * * *

The problem of reconciling the recognized legitimacy of consent searches with the requirement that they be free from any aspect of official coercion cannot be resolved by any infallible touchstone. To approve such searches without the most careful scrutiny would sanction the possibility of official coercion; to place artificial restrictions upon such searches would jeopardize their basic validity.

One alternative that would go far toward proving that the subject of a search did know he had a right to refuse consent would be to advise him of that right before eliciting his consent. That, however, is a suggestion that has been almost universally repudiated by both federal and state courts, and, we think, rightly so. For it would be thoroughly impractical to impose on the normal consent search the detailed requirements of an effective warning. Consent searches are part of the standard investigatory techniques of law enforcement agencies. They normally occur on the highway, or in a person's home or office, and under informal and unstructured conditions. The circumstances that prompt the initial request to search may develop quickly or be a logical extension of investigative police questioning. The police may seek to investigate further suspicious circumstances or to follow up leads developed in questioning persons at the scene of a crime. These situations are a far cry from the structured atmosphere of a trial where, assisted by counsel if he chooses, a defendant is informed of his trial rights. And, while surely a closer question, these situations are still immeasurably, far removed from "custodial interrogation" where, in Miranda v. Arizona, [p. 445 of this book], we found that the Constitution required certain now familiar warnings as a prerequisite to police interrogation. * * *

C

It is said, however, that a "consent" is a "waiver" of a person's rights under the Fourth and Fourteenth Amendments. The argument is that by allowing the police to conduct a search, a person "waives" whatever right he had to prevent the police from searching. It is argued that under the doctrine of Johnson v. Zerbst, 304 U.S. 458, 464 (1938), to establish such a "waiver" the State must demonstrate "an intentional relinquishment or abandonment of a known right or privilege."

But these standards were enunciated in *Johnson* in the context of the safeguards of a fair criminal trial. Our cases do not reflect an uncritical demand for a knowing and intelligent waiver in every situation where a person has failed to invoke a constitutional protection. * * *

A strict standard of waiver has been applied to those rights guaranteed to a criminal defendant to insure that he will be accorded the greatest possible opportunity to utilize every facet of the constitutional model of a fair criminal trial. Any trial conducted in derogation of that model leaves open the possibility that the trial reached an unfair result precisely because all the protections specified in the Constitution were not provided. A prime example is the right to counsel. For without that right, a wholly innocent accused faces the real and substantial danger that simply because of his lack of legal expertise he may be convicted. * * *

The protections of the Fourth Amendment are of a wholly different order, and have nothing whatever to do with promoting the fair ascertainment of truth at a criminal trial. * * * Nor can it even be said that a search, as opposed to an eventual trial, is somehow "unfair" if a person consents to a search. While the Fourth and Fourteenth Amendments limit the circumstances under which the police can conduct a search, there is nothing constitutionally suspect in a person's voluntarily allowing a search. The actual conduct of the search may be precisely the same as if the police had obtained a warrant. And, unlike those constitutional guarantees that protect a defendant at trial, it cannot be said every reasonable presumption ought to be indulged against voluntary relinquishment. * * * Rather, the community has a real interest in encouraging consent, for the resulting search may yield necessary evidence for the solution and prosecution of crime, evidence that may insure that a wholly innocent person is not wrongly charged with a criminal offense. * * *

Judgment of Court of Appeals reversed.

[Concurring and dissenting opinions omitted.]

ILLINOIS v. RODRIGUEZ

Supreme Court of the United States, 1990.
497 U.S. 177, 110 S.Ct. 2793, 111 L.Ed.2d 148.

JUSTICE SCALIA delivered the opinion of the Court.

* * * Police were summoned to the residence of Dorothy Jackson in Chicago. They were met by Ms. Jackson's daughter, Gail Fischer, who showed signs of a severe beating. She told the officers that she had been assaulted by respondent Rodriguez earlier that day in an apartment on South California. Fischer stated that Rodriguez was then asleep in the apartment, and she consented to travel there with the police in order to unlock the door with her key so that the officers could enter and arrest him. During this conversation, Fischer several times referred to the apartment on South California as "our" apartment, and said that she had clothes and furniture there. It is unclear whether she indicated that she currently lived at the apartment, or only that she used to live there.

The police officers drove to the apartment on South California, accompanied by Fischer. They did not obtain an arrest warrant for Rodriguez, nor did they seek a search warrant for the apartment. At the apartment, Fischer unlocked the door with her key and gave the officers permission to enter. They moved through the door into the living room, where they observed in plain view drug paraphernalia and containers filled with white powder that they believed (correctly, as later analysis showed) to be cocaine. They proceeded to the bedroom, where they found Rodriguez asleep and discovered additional containers of white powder in two open attache cases. The officers arrested Rodriguez and seized the drugs and related paraphernalia.

[The state courts suppressed the evidence on the ground that Gail Fischer did not have common authority over the apartment. The trial court concluded that Fischer was not a "usual resident" but rather an "infrequent visitor" at the apartment, based upon its findings that Fischer's name was not on the lease, that she did not contribute to the rent, that she was not allowed to invite others to the apartment on her own, that she did not have access to the apartment when respondent was away, and that she had moved some of her possessions from the apartment. The state courts rejected the prosecution's argument that the search would be lawful if the officers reasonably but erroneously believed that Fischer possessed the authority to consent to a search.]

The Fourth Amendment generally prohibits the warrantless entry of a person's home, whether to make an arrest or to search for specific objects. The prohibition does not apply, however, to situations in which voluntary consent has been obtained, either from the individual whose property is searched, or from a third party who possesses common authority over the premises. The burden of establishing that common authority rests upon the State, [and] it is clear that burden was not sustained. The evidence showed that although Fischer, with her two small children, had lived with Rodriguez beginning in December 1984, she had moved out on July 1, 1985, almost a month before the search at issue here, and had gone to live with her mother. She took her and her children's clothing with her, though leaving behind some furniture and household effects. During the period after July 1 she sometimes spent the night at Rodriguez's apartment, but never invited her friends there, and never went there herself when he was not home. Her name was not on the lease nor did she contribute to the rent. She had a key to the apartment, which she said at trial she had taken without Rodriguez's knowledge (though she testified at the preliminary hearing that Rodriguez had given her the key). On these facts the State has not established that, with respect to the South California apartment, Fischer had "joint access or control for most purposes."

The State contends that, even if Fischer did not in fact have authority to give consent, it suffices to validate the entry that the law enforcement officers reasonably believed she did. * * * Respondent asserts that permitting a reasonable belief of common authority to validate an entry would cause a defendant's Fourth Amendment rights to be "vicariously waived." We disagree.

We have been unyielding in our insistence that a defendant's waiver of his trial rights cannot be given effect unless it is "knowing" and "intelligent." [Citations] We would assuredly not permit, therefore, evidence seized in violation of the Fourth Amendment to be introduced on the basis of a trial court's mere "reasonable belief"—derived from statements by unauthorized persons—that the defendant has waived his objection. But one must make a distinction between, on the one hand, trial rights that derive from the violation of constitutional guarantees and, on the other hand, the nature of those constitutional guarantees themselves. * * *

What Rodriguez is assured by the trial right of the exclusionary rule, where it applies, is that no evidence seized in violation of the Fourth Amendment will be introduced at his trial unless he consents. What he is assured by the Fourth Amendment itself, however, is not that no government search of his house will occur unless he consents; but that no such search will occur that is "unreasonable." There are various elements, of course, that can make a search of a person's house "reasonable"—one of which is the consent of the person or his cotenant. The essence of respondent's argument is that we should impose upon this element a requirement that we have not imposed upon other elements that regularly compel government officers to exercise judgment regarding the facts: namely, the requirement that their judgment be not only responsible but correct. * * *

The fundamental objective that alone validates all unconsented government searches is, of course, the seizure of persons who have committed or are about to commit crimes, or of evidence related to crimes. But "reasonableness," with respect to this necessary element, does not demand that the government be factually correct in its assessment that that is what a search will produce. Warrants need only be supported by "probable cause," which demands no more than a proper "assessment of probabilities in particular factual contexts * * *." Illinois v. Gates, 462 U.S. 213, 232 (1983). If a magistrate, based upon seemingly reliable but factually inaccurate information, issues a warrant for the search of a house in which the sought-after felon is not present, has never been present, and was never likely to have been present, the owner of that house suffers one of the inconveniences we all expose ourselves to as the cost of living in a safe society; he does not suffer a violation of the Fourth Amendment. * * *

In Hill v. California, 401 U.S. 797 (1971), we upheld a search incident to an arrest, even though the arrest was made of the wrong person. We said: "The upshot was that the officers in good faith believed Miller was Hill and arrested him. They were quite wrong as it turned out, and subjective good-faith belief would not in itself justify either the arrest or the subsequent search. But sufficient probability, not certainty, is the touchstone of reasonableness under the Fourth Amendment and on the record before us the officers' mistake was understandable and the arrest a reasonable response to the situation facing them at the time." * * *

The Constitution is no more violated when officers enter without a warrant because they reasonably (though erroneously) believe that the person who has consented to their entry is a resident of the premises, than it is violated when they enter without a warrant because they reasonably (though erroneously) believe they are in pursuit of a violent felon who is about to escape. * * *

What we hold today does not suggest that law enforcement officers may always accept a person's invitation to enter premises. Even when the invitation is accompanied by an explicit assertion that the person lives there, the surrounding circumstances could conceivably be such that a reasonable person would doubt its truth and not act upon it without further inquiry. * * * In the present case, the [state] Appellate Court found it unnecessary to determine whether the officers reasonably believed that Fischer had the authority to consent, because it ruled as a matter of law that a reasonable belief could not validate the entry. Since we find that ruling to be in error, we remand for consideration of that question. * * *

Justice Marshall, with whom Justice Brennan and Justice Stevens join, dissenting.

The baseline for the reasonableness of a search or seizure in the home is the presence of a warrant. Indeed, "searches and seizures inside a home without a warrant are presumptively unreasonable." Payton v.

New York, 445 U.S. 573, 586 (1980). Exceptions to the warrant requirement must therefore serve "compelling" law enforcement goals. * * *

Unlike searches conducted pursuant to the recognized exceptions to the warrant requirement, third-party consent searches are not based on an exigency and therefore serve no compelling social goal. Police officers, when faced with the choice of relying on consent by a third party or securing a warrant, should secure a warrant, and must therefore accept the risk of error should they instead choose to rely on consent. * * *

Our prior cases discussing searches based on third-party consent have never suggested that such searches are "reasonable." In United States v. Matlock, this Court upheld a warrantless search conducted pursuant to the consent of a third party who was living with the defendant. The Court rejected the defendant's challenge to the search, stating that a person who permits others to have "joint access or control for most purposes * * * assume[s] the risk that [such persons] might permit the common area to be searched." As the Court's assumption-of-risk analysis makes clear, third-party consent limits a person's ability to challenge the reasonableness of the search only because that person voluntarily has relinquished some of his expectation of privacy by sharing access or control over his property with another person. A search conducted pursuant to an officer's reasonable but mistaken belief that a third party had authority to consent is thus on an entirely different constitutional footing from one based on the consent of a third party who in fact has such authority. Even if the officers reasonably believed that Fischer had authority to consent, she did not, and Rodriguez's expectation of privacy was therefore undiminished. * * *

That a person who allows another joint access over his property thereby limits his expectation of privacy does not justify trampling the rights of a person who has not similarly relinquished any of his privacy expectation. * * * Where this free-floating creation of "reasonable" exceptions to the warrant requirement will end, now that the Court has departed from the balancing approach that has long been part of our Fourth Amendment jurisprudence, is unclear. But by allowing a person to be subjected to a warrantless search in his home without his consent and without exigency, the majority has taken away some of the liberty that the Fourth Amendment was designed to protect.

IN THE MATTER OF THE WELFARE OF D.A.G.

Supreme Court of Minnesota, 1992.
484 N.W.2d 787.

YETKA, JUSTICE.

The state appeals from a court of appeals' decision affirming a trial court order which suppressed evidence on the basis of an unreasonable, warrantless search and seizure. We affirm the decisions of the courts below.

At about 3:45 p.m. on August 30, 1990, Deputy Brian Nielson of the Douglas County Sheriff's Department contacted Officer Larry Dailey of the Alexandria Police Department regarding information about a large quantity of marijuana at 1002 Hawthorne in Alexandria. Nielson [had] received the information from Thomas Charles Howard, who had appeared at the sheriff's department on his own initiative. Officer Dailey agreed to go to the Alexandria Police Department to interview Howard about the drugs.

During the interview with Officers Dailey and Nielson, Howard told the officers that he had recently moved into 1002 Hawthorne with D.A.G. and another individual. Howard stated that, in the early morning hours of August 30, 1990, Michael Ray Erickson came to the house and asked Howard's friend, Cory Keller, if he could use Keller's vehicle to pick up a package located at a rest area near Alexandria. Keller lent his car to Dat Quang, who drove Erickson to the rest area. After Erickson and Quang left, D.A.G. informed Howard that Erickson was going to pick up approximately 2 pounds of marijuana. Howard stated that Erickson was a "known drug dealer."

Erickson and Quang returned to 1002 Hawthorne at about 4:00 a.m. on August 30. Howard stated that Erickson had a large amount of marijuana when he returned to the house. Howard knew it was marijuana because, as a former user, he recognized the drug by sight and smell.

Howard expressed to Erickson and D.A.G. his extreme displeasure with Erickson's having brought the drugs into the house, then left the residence. When he returned to the house later in the morning, Howard found Erickson still present. By this time, however, Erickson had apportioned the marijuana in clear plastic baggies and stuffed them in his "black leather, motorcycle type jacket."

Based on Howard's status as a cotenant and the foregoing information, the officers "decided to obtain permission to search" the residence at 1002 Hawthorne. Howard signed a standard "Permission to Search" form at 4:54 p.m. on August 30. Three Alexandria police officers and two Douglas County deputy sheriffs conducted the "raid" shortly after Howard signed the consent form. Howard did not accompany the officers on the raid.

The officers did not obtain a search warrant because they believed Howard's consent authorized a warrantless search of the residence. Officer Dailey testified that he believed he had probable cause to search the house for drugs based on the information Howard had given him. The officers did not knock and announce their purpose and authority when they entered the residence; rather, they "walked in" with their guns drawn. Finally, although D.A.G. was present when the officers entered the house, they did not ask D.A.G. for permission to search the house.

During the search of the residence, the officers found a black leather jacket like the one Howard had described to them. In it, the officers found several baggies of marijuana. Michael Ray Erickson identified the jacket and its contents as his. The police also found some marijuana in a canister in the kitchen. In total, the police found approximately 1/2 pound of marijuana.

Finally, the officers recovered an illegal sawed-off 20–gauge shotgun, the evidence at issue in this case. The shotgun was in plain view in the living room of the residence. In a statement to the police after the raid, D.A.G. admitted that he owned the gun and knew its length was unlawful. On September 21, 1990, D.A.G. was charged, by way of delinquency petition, with [possession of a short-barreled shotgun and delinquency]. * * *

The court of appeals correctly concluded that this case does not involve the question of whether Howard had authority to consent. Without question, as a cotenant with "common authority" over the premises, Howard had actual authority to consent to a search of the common areas of the apartment. Likewise, this case does not present the question of what should happen when police are confronted with the consent of one present joint occupant and the objection of another present joint occupant. Rather, we agree that this case involves the competing rights of an absent, consenting cotenant and those of a present, objecting cotenant.

Both the trial court and the court of appeals relied on Justice Traynor's analysis in Tompkins v. Superior Court, 59 Cal.2d 65 (Cal. 1963) to support their holdings:

> One joint occupant who is away from the premises may not authorize police officers to enter and search the premises over the objection of another joint occupant who is present at the time, at least where * * * no prior warning is given, no emergency exists, and the officer fails even to disclose his purpose to the occupant who is present or to inform him that he has the consent of the absent occupant to enter. [Citations]

"The *Tompkins* case, however, does not stand solely for the proposition that a present joint occupant's right to refuse consent is superior to or otherwise overrides an absent joint occupant's right to consent to a search; rather, the most critical fact [in *Tompkins*] is not that the present tenant objected, but rather that the consent was by an absent tenant and that the officer never made this known to the other occupant. * * * The basis of Tompkins, then, is that one joint occupant cannot give a consent which will have the effect of permitting an intrusion upon that part of another occupant's privacy which entitles him to be free of unannounced intrusion and its attendant dangers." W. LaFave, Search and Seizure, § 8.3(d) at 250–51 (2d ed. 1987). Under this analysis, the inquiry in the instant case must focus on whether, in the absence of exigent circumstances, the police must knock and announce their authority and purpose prior to entry when conducting a search pursuant to an absent third party's consent. However, we do not reach the issue of whether the police were required to knock and announce their authority and purpose in this case because we think the search cannot be upheld on either consent or exigent-circumstances grounds.

The reasons often given to support searches conducted pursuant to a third-party's consent when the defendant is absent or unavailable (and the third party is present) are that (1) the third party is waiving his own rights and not those of the defendant, and (2) the defendant has assumed the risk that the third person will waive his constitutional rights.

The "waiver" and "assumption of risk" rationales, however, are not compelling in a case such as this, where the person against whom the search is directed is present and the consenting joint occupant is not. First, an absent third-party's consent should not be used to "waive" another individual's constitutional rights when that individual is present at the search to give or withhold consent in his or her own right. Similarly, the risk that one co-inhabitant might permit the common area of a jointly occupied premises to be searched in the absence of another is qualitatively different from the risk that a warrantless search will be conducted over the objection of a present joint occupant: A present, objecting joint occupant cannot be said to have assumed the risk that an absent third party will vicariously waive his or her constitutional rights. We agree that "the risk assumed by joint occupancy is merely an inability to control access to the premises during one's absence." 3 W. LaFave, Search and Seizure § 8.3(d) at 252 (2d ed. 1987). We do not, however, decide what the result would be where both consenting and non-consenting joint occupants are present when the police request permission to search a premises. * * *

Nor do we believe the search can be upheld on exigent-circumstances grounds. If there had been "exigent circumstances," then the police would not have needed Howard's consent to search without a warrant. * * * We agree with the trial court that "no reason, except inconvenience of the officers and delay in preparing papers and getting before a magistrate, appears for the failure to seek a search warrant. But those reasons are no justification for by-passing the constitutional requirement * * *." McDonald v. United States, 335 U.S. 451, 455 (1948).

The decisions of the trial court and the court of appeals are affirmed.

DAVIS v. STATE

Supreme Court of Georgia, 1992.
262 Ga. 578, 422 S.E.2d 546.

SEARS-COLLINS, JUSTICE.

THE FACTS

[Appellant Davis was charged with drug possession] after his 10–year–old stepson, Darrin Davis ("Darrin") called for emergency assistance (911) to report the presence of drugs in the house. * * * We granted a writ of certiorari for the limited purpose of considering whether the consent to search given by the child in this case was valid.

At the time of the search, Darrin Davis was routinely left at home alone after school until his mother returned from work around 4:30 p.m. He had a key to the house, and was required to call his mother immediately upon getting home each day so that she would know he arrived safely. During the time he was home alone on weekday afternoons, approximately one and one-half hours, the child was not allowed to invite anyone to the house or to play outside. Darrin's mother had instructed him, however, to call 911 if he needed help. On January 28, 1991, Darrin arrived home from school and called his mother. While in his parents' bedroom, the child found what he believed to be drugs. Acting on advice he had received in drug abuse classes at school, Darrin called 911. Darrin spoke with Deputy Greg Kirby in the Douglas County Sheriff's Department and reported that drugs belonging to his mother and step-father were in his house. Darrin stated that he "would like to get them some help." Deputy Kirby dispatched Deputy Cheryl Smith to the house. Before Deputy Smith arrived, Deputy Kirby called Darrin back and told him to wait outside the house so that Deputy Smith would recognize the house when she arrived. When Deputy Smith arrived, Darrin was waiting outside the house. Darrin walked over to the driveway when the deputy drove up. Deputy Smith followed the child into the house and into the appellant's bedroom, where Darrin retrieved a mirror with white powder and a razor blade on it. Darrin also opened a nightstand drawer and pulled out a bag of marijuana and some rolling papers. Deputy Smith observed a "marijuana joint" in an ashtray next to the bed. Deputy Smith seized all of the drugs and took them to her patrol car. Another officer arrived, and all present then waited in the house for the arrival of Darrin's mother. When the mother arrived, she consented to the search of her handbag, containing additional drugs, precipitating her arrest. When the appellant arrived home, he was also arrested. Both Darrin's mother and the appellant refused to consent to a search of their home. * * *

The appellant now contends that the Court of Appeals erred in failing to find that the appellant's rights under the Fourth Amendment to the United States Constitution were violated when the officers entered his home and his bedroom without a warrant, without probable cause, and without his consent. The appellant argues that his 10–year-old step-son lacked sufficient authority to provide the necessary consent.

THE LAW

1. It is well established "that searches conducted outside the judicial process, without prior approval by judge or magistrate, are per se unreasonable under the Fourth Amendment—subject only to a few specifically established and well-delineated exceptions." Katz v. United States, 389 U.S. 347, 357 (1967). One such exception is when consent to search is "obtained from a third party who possessed common authority over or other sufficient relationship to the premises or effects sought to be inspected." Atkins v. State, 254 Ga. 641, 642, 331 S.E.2d 597 (1985) quoting United States v. Matlock, 415 U.S. 164 (1974). In *Atkins,* the Court of Appeals set forth the following factors which have been exam-

ined by courts to determine if a minor's consent to search was valid: "whether the minor lived on the premises; whether the minor had a right of access to the premises and the right to invite others thereto; whether the minor was of an age at which he or she could be expected to exercise at least minimal discretion; and whether officers acted reasonably in believing that the minor had sufficient control over the premises to give a valid consent to search." * * *

We now find, applying the foregoing criteria to the facts of this case, that Darrin Davis did not have sufficient authority to validly consent to the search of his parents' home. Considering the *Atkins* criteria, the child lived at the same address as the appellant, and had access to the house to the extent that he was allowed to come home there every afternoon by himself. There is no evidence, however, that the fact that the child was allowed to stay at home for one and one-half hours in the afternoon gave the child access and control of the house equal to that of the appellant, and we do not believe that the appellant assumed the risk that the child would compromise the appellant's constitutional rights by allowing the house to be searched. Also, although the child's mother had given him permission to call for emergency assistance if he needed help, the child had no right, absent an emergency, to invite anyone into the house while he was alone there, much less into his parents' bedroom.

Most compelling, however, is Darrin's youth. The younger a child the less likely that he or she can be said to have the minimal discretion required to validly consent to a search, much less waive important constitutional rights. Judicial vigilance is especially merited when, as here, the child is quite young. Most 10–year–old children are incapable of understanding and waiving their own rights, much less those of their parents. In this case both the trial court and the Court of Appeals evaluated Darrin Davis' mental age and found that he possessed sufficient maturity to consent to the search.* However, it appears to us that Darrin believed that by calling the police and reporting that his parents had drugs in the house he would achieve familial harmony, not disharmony, disruption, and the burden of the state's enforcement powers. While it can be hoped that some good does come from this episode in the form of rehabilitation, such a level of immaturity and naivety in the child leads us to the inescapable conclusion that Darrin lacked that degree of mental discretion necessary for a minor to give valid consent to the search of his, and his parents', home. This child simply did not know or completely understand what the consequences of his consent would be. We cannot allow such an unknowing and uninformed surrender of constitutional rights.

* According to its brief filed after this Court granted certiorari, the state has "reevaluated its position" on this issue. The state asserts that "in good conscience [it] cannot now ethically and honorably represent to this Court under the facts of this case, [that] it would be appropriate to rule that this ten year old child could give a valid consent to search his home in the absence of his parents within the meaning of the Fourth Amendment."

2. The state argues that while the child may not have had the authority to consent to a general search of his home, what occurred at Darrin's home was not a search. Hence, the state contends, no consent was necessary. The state reasons that Darrin did have the authority to call 911 if he needed help, and to invite the responding officer into his home. After having done so in this instance, the state argues, Darrin's action of leading the officer into the appellant's bedroom to retrieve and turn over the drugs which he had already searched for and discovered privately did not constitute a search. We agree that the child possessed the power to call for police assistance if necessary, and concomitant with that power, possessed the power to "invite" the responding officer to the house, to the extent required by the emergency. We do not question the right of law enforcement officers to respond in emergency situations. In this case, however, the officer arrived at the house and met Darrin outside of the house, in the driveway. The officer testified that it was apparent to her then that Darrin was not in any present danger, and that she did not suspect that there was anyone else in the house. At the point that the officer realized, based on her maturity and training, that there was no emergency imminently threatening Darrin's welfare in the driveway, it became incumbent upon the officer not to exceed the scope of the child's limited right of invitation. The officer's further intrusion onto the appellant's property and into the appellant's bedroom was an invasion of a reasonable expectation of privacy in an attempt to locate illegal drugs, and as such constituted a search for which either valid consent or a warrant was required.

3. Next, the state contends that even if there was no valid consent to search, warrantless entry was necessitated by exigent circumstances. First, the state argues that exigent circumstances were created by the fact that the child was in the house with drugs, which are inherently dangerous. * * * The state further argues that exigent circumstances existed because, if the officer had left to try to secure a warrant, the appellant could have destroyed the drugs after arriving home and learning that the police had been notified. It is true that had the appellant or the child's mother been at home at the time the search was conducted, the prospective loss of evidence may have excused the warrantless search. In this case, however, the officer testified that she did not even suspect that there was anyone in the home when she arrived and met the child in the driveway. Therefore, at the time Deputy Smith entered the house, there was no threat, actual or perceived, of the drugs being destroyed if a search was not commenced right away, and the possibility that the drugs might be destroyed does not excuse the deputy's warrantless entry. * * *

Our decision is intended to imply no criticism of Darrin Davis or of the police, and certainly no praise for the appellant. By this opinion we simply acknowledge the right of privacy in one's home, and, under the facts present, we refuse to entrust that precious right to the judgment of the 10–year–old child in this case.

Judgment reversed.

Commentary

The Supreme Court has dealt with only a few issues pertaining to consent, but the subject has generated a fair amount of interesting case law in the lower federal and state courts. Following are some of the recurrent problems:

1. *Voluntariness of consent.* Some federal court decisions have listed six factors which are relevant to determining whether the "totality of circumstances" indicate that a consent was voluntary: (1) the voluntariness of the defendant's custodial status; (2) the presence of coercive police procedures; (3) the extent and level of the defendant's cooperation with the police; (4) the defendant's awareness of his right to refuse to consent; (5) the defendant's education and intelligence; and (6) the defendant's belief that no incriminating evidence will be found. See United States v. Jenkins, 46 F.3d 447, 451 (5th Cir.1995). The court in *Jenkins* stated that "although all of the above factors are highly relevant, no one of the six factors is dispositive or controlling of the voluntariness issue."

2. *Vicarious consent.* In Owens v. State, 322 Md. 616, 589 A.2d 59 (Md.1991), defendant Owen left a nylon bag with a zipper closure with his friend Mrs. Gardin, intending to pick it up at some time in the future. The bag was closed, and had an attached luggage tag bearing his name and address. Defendant gave Gardin no authority to open the bag. Police officers arrived later in the day, told Gardin that they had information there were drugs in the apartment, and asked for permission to search. Gardin signed a consent-to-search form, pointed to some luggage belonging to Owens and other persons, and stated that "they had just brought it here this morning and if there's any drugs it would be in there." The officers searched the bags and found a large amount of crack cocaine in the bag belonging to Owens. The Maryland Supreme Court held that "Gardin did not possess common authority over Owens' bag and had no other sufficient relationship to its contents to validate any consent by her to search the bag." The dissent argued that Gardin might have been suspected as an accomplice in the possession of the crack cocaine, and so she "should be able to demonstrate her innocence by authorizing the police to ascertain whether, in fact, there were drugs in her apartment and, if so, to remove them." See also, U.S. v. Fultz, 146 F.3d 1102 (9th Cir.1998). After he was evicted from his apartment, Fultz stored his belongings in closed containers in the garage of a friend. Police investigating Fultz for a burglary obtained consent from the friend to search the containers. The federal court held that she had authority over the garage, but no actual or apparent authority to consent to a search of the containers belonging to Fultz.

In United States v. Evans, 27 F.3d 1219 (7th Cir.1994), defendant Evans was convicted of operating a "chop shop" for stolen automobiles out of his father's garage. FBI agents came to the garage to make arrests. In a discussion with Evans's father, the agents learned that the father owned the garage and paid the utility bills. The son's auto business was in a separate, enclosed part of the building, but the father had access to it. The Court of Appeals held that the father had common authority over the property, and that his voluntary consent to search was therefore valid. Compare, State v. Kieffer, 217 Wis.2d 531, 577 N.W.2d 352 (Wis.1998). The Wisconsin Supreme

Court held that the defendant's father-in-law did not have either actual or apparent authority to consent to entry into a renovated garage loft where defendant Kieffer and his wife were living. The young couple had renovated the loft themselves and had the only keys to it (although they left the door unlocked on the day of the search). They had no formal lease but made some payment for utilities, sleeping in the loft but using the main house for bathroom purposes and telephone calls. The Wisconsin court held that in these circumstances there were insufficient indicia of joint control over the loft for the officers to reasonably believe that the wife's father had authority to consent to a search of the premises. See also, State v. Benson, 133 Idaho 152, 983 P.2d 225 (Idaho App.1999).

In United States v. Rith, 164 F.3d 1323 (10th Cir.1999), defendant Rith's parents telephone police from a neighbors home and reported that they had seen their 18–year-old son bringing firearms into the family home. Fearful of guns and afraid that their son was involved in a gang, the parents requested that police check the home and ascertain if the guns were stolen. Fearing confrontation with his son, the father declined to go to the home with the officers. Instead, he gave them a house key so that no damage would be done to the house in the event they were not otherwise allowed entry. During his discussion with the officers, the father told the officers that his son Mesa Rith was eighteen years of age and was not paying rent. When the officers arrived at the Rith home, they encountered Mesa on the porch talking to two officers from another Utah town who were conducting an unrelated investigation. Detective Chen indicated Mesa's father had informed them that he had brought guns into the house and that they were there to search for the guns. Mesa told the officers that they could not search the house and he asked them for a search warrant. When Chen showed Mesa the house key Mesa said, "Okay, come in." The officers then searched Mesa's bedroom and found a loaded sawed-off shotgun underneath the mattress. The federal Court of Appeals held that the shotgun was admissible. The parents had authority to consent to a search of the bedroom even over their son's objection, because he was not paying rent, and there was no lock on the bedroom door or evidence of any agreement that they would not enter without his consent. This case was decided before the infamous massacre at Columbine High School in Littleton, Colorado. In the wake of that tragedy, it is likely that courts will take a generous view of the right of parents to consent to a police search for weapons in the room of a teenager living at home.

In United States v. Brown, 961 F.2d 1039 (2d Cir.1992), defendant occupied a basement apartment in the home of Mrs. Davis. Frequently his use of electrical appliances would cause a short circuit. If Brown was not at home, Davis would then use her key to enter his apartment to turn off appliances so that she could restore power to the house. On one such occasion she saw two guns in plain view and notified police. When they arrived she directed them to the guns (one of which was an UZI machine gun), which they seized. At the suppression hearing, an officer explained that "the way it seemed to me, the fuse always blew, and she was always going in and out of this apartment. It was like she was able to go any time she wanted." The District Court held that, although the landlady did not have authority to authorize a "general search of the apartment," she could consent to "a limited entry for the purpose of retrieving a firearm." The Court of Appeals reversed, holding that consent to entry for a limited purpose (turning off the appliances) did not authorize the landlady to consent to a police search even of limited scope. The officers may have believed that she had authority to consent, but this erroneous belief was founded on a misunderstanding of law and not a misapprehension of fact, and hence did not authorize them to search without first obtaining a warrant.

(3) *Actual versus apparent consent.* The voluntariness of an alleged consent is judged by the "totality of circumstances," but are these the actual circumstances or the circumstances as they reasonably appear to the officer? If the officer *knows* that a defendant is drunk, or mentally retarded, then it may be unreasonable for the officer to think she is obtaining a voluntary consent. One leading decision held that mental incompetence would invalidate a consent even if unknown to the officer, because waiver of a constitutional protection requires actual, not merely apparent, consent. See United States v. Elrod, 441 F.2d 353 (5th Cir.1971).

In *Illinois v. Rodriguez, supra,* p. 114, the Supreme Court rejected this "waiver" theory of consent in favor of the view that officers may act upon reasonable appearances in determining whether they have either probably cause or a valid consent. The waiver theory is still attractive to judges who think that exceptions to the warrant requirement should be strictly limited, however, and hence may continue to be employed in the interpretation of state constitutional provisions.

(4) *Problems involving minors.* As a rule, a parent has authority to consent to a search of a minor child's room, although this would not necessarily be the case for an older child who was (for example) paying rent. Children do not have comparable authority (real or apparent) to consent to a search of the parents' quarters, or even to the common areas of the house. It is not easy to say when children reach the age of consent. See People v. Jacobs, 43 Cal.3d 472, 233 Cal.Rptr. 323, 729 P.2d 757 (1987), holding that an 11–year–old girl could not give valid consent to police to enter the family home to look for her (absent) stepfather (4–3 decision). Compare, Pesterfield v. Commissioner of Public Safety, 399 N.W.2d 605 (Minn.App.1987), upholding a consent to police entry into the family home given by a 17–year–old.

(5) *Scope of consent.* In Florida v. Jimeno, 500 U.S. 248 (1991), the Supreme Court held that a suspect's consent to search the interior of a suspect's automobile also authorizes the opening of some closed containers found inside the car. An officer stopped a suspected drug dealer, and obtained a valid consent to search the car. He found a folded brown paper bag on the floorboard, opened it, and found a kilogram of cocaine. The Florida Supreme Court affirmed the suppression of the cocaine on the basis of an earlier Florida decision holding that consent to search an automobile's trunk did not authorize breaking open a locked briefcase found therein.

The Supreme Court upheld the search of the paper bag in a 7–2 opinion by Chief Justice Rehnquist. The majority opinion held that "the standard for measuring the scope of a suspect's consent under the Fourth Amendment is that of 'objective' reasonableness—what would the typical reasonable person have understood by the exchange between the officer and the suspect?"

Because narcotics are generally stored in some kind of container rather than strewn across the trunk or floor of a car, the officer could reasonably have understood the consent to extend to the paper bag. The opinion acknowledged that "It is very likely unreasonable to think that a suspect, by consenting to the search of his trunk, has agreed to the breaking open of a locked briefcase within the trunk, but it is otherwise with respect to a closed paper bag."

In United States v. Maldonado, 38 F.3d 936 (7th Cir.1994), the defendant disembarked from an Amtrak train at Chicago. DEA agents looking for drug couriers approached and asked to speak with him. Upon request, Maldonado showed them a one-way train ticket that had been purchased with cash. The agents then asked for permission to search his luggage for drugs. He consented. While searching the bag, an agent came across two boxes marked "juicer," purportedly contained juice machines. Maldonado testified that the agents asked him to open the juicer boxes, which were taped shut, but he replied that he did not want to do that because the items inside were gift wrapped. One of the agents then offered to open the boxes without disturbing the wrapping, and did so. Inside he found, instead of gift-wrapped juice machines, several kilogram-sized packages of cocaine. The issue on appeal was whether the search of the juicer boxes exceeded the scope of the consent to search the luggage. The federal Court of Appeals held that consent to search the luggage for drugs implied consent to search included containers that might contain drugs. The Court recognized that "a suspect may of course delimit as he chooses the scope of the search to which he consents." Defendant's expressed reluctance to disturb the gift wrapping did not constitute a withdrawal or limiting of the consent previously given.

(6) *Hotel rooms* are a fertile source of third party consent problems. The Supreme Court has held that a hotel clerk has neither actual nor apparent authority to consent to a search of a guest's room. Stoner v. California, 376 U.S. 483 (1964). The general rule is subject to exceptions and borderline qualifications. The hotel management is entitled to retake possession of the room after check-out time, or in the event of extraordinary circumstances like a fire hazard. Although a maid who sees contraband while cleaning the room may not consent to a police entry into the room, she may tell what she knows to the police and they can use the information to obtain a warrant.

(7) *Assertions of official authority.* Sometimes officers obtain consent after falsely claiming to have a warrant or other legal authority to make the search, or after saying that they can get a warrant. In the former situation, the "consent" is merely an acquiescence in the inevitable, and thus invalid. See Bumper v. North Carolina, 391 U.S. 543 (1968). The statement "we will get a warrant if you do not consent" presents a more subtle problem. In some cases, it may amount to a misrepresentation of legal authority, *i.e.* a bluff. In other cases, it may be a plain statement of fact; the officers have probable cause and can get a warrant, and they are merely hoping that the defendant will agree to save them unnecessary trouble.

(8) *Consent as a condition of probation.* In some jurisdictions it is common to require a person placed on probation to agree in advance to waive certain Fourth Amendment rights as a condition of probation. For example, an Idaho case involved a term of probation that provided: "That probationer does hereby agree and consent to the search of his person,

automobile, real property, and any other property at any time and at any place by any law enforcement officer, peace officer, probation officers, and does waive his constitutional right to be free from such searches." When officers obtained information that the probationer was involved in burglaries, they went to his home and searched it without a warrant while he was away, finding stolen goods. The Idaho Supreme Court held that the probation condition was valid, and that by signing it the defendant had consented in advance to the search. A dissent discussed authorities from other jurisdictions which had held similar probation conditions invalid. The dissent pointed out that such broadly worded probation conditions could lead to invasions of the privacy of innocent third parties who lived with or were otherwise associated with the probationer. State v. Gawron, 112 Idaho 841, 736 P.2d 1295 (Idaho 1987). Without invoking any concept of consent, a search of a probationer by a probation officer can also be upheld as a "regulatory search" justified by the special needs of effective probation supervision. See *Griffin v. Wisconsin* [p. 174 of this book].

(9) *The use of deception* invalidates consent in some cases, but not in others. Many cases have held that there is no illegal entry when a police officer poses as a drug purchaser to gain consensual entry to the premises of a drug seller. See Lewis v. United States, 385 U.S. 206 (1966). In other words, concealment of one's status as a law enforcement officer does not invalidate the consent, at least in the case of a transaction understood to be illegal. Probably the result would be different if the policeman obtained entry pretending to be a gas meter reader, and in any case the consent is limited by its scope. If the policeman pretending to be a drug buyer took the opportunity while the defendant was in the bathroom to look into closed drawers and envelopes, he could not justify these additional intrusions on the basis of consent.

An additional variation involves officers who disclose their identity but misrepresent their purpose. In State v. Johnson, 253 Kan. 356, 856 P.2d 134 (1993), the defendant (Johnson) had murdered a drug informer (Boyce). Police, who had become concerned about Boyce's safety and were looking for him, went to Johnson's house. They gained entry by falsely telling Johnson that they had a warrant to arrest Boyce, and that they had a tip that he was inside. While pretending to look for Boyce, the officers observed items in plain view that were later used to connect Johnson to the murder. The Kansas Supreme Court adopted "the reasoning of other courts that have interpreted [*Bumper v. North Carolina, supra*] narrowly, upholding the voluntariness of consent despite deceptive practices by government agents." The court reasoned that, because the officers' behavior was not threatening or coercive, Johnson was willing to let them enter and knew Boyce would not be found, and the officers did not exceed the scope of the consent, the evidence was admissible.

(10) *Judicial attitudes.* How one resolves the many ambiguities inherent in the concept of "consent" depends in large part on the attitude one brings to the problem. According to one view, the police ought to be encouraged to obtain probable cause and a warrant before they search, and the consent exception should be very narrowly construed to avoid creating a huge loophole in Fourth Amendment requirements. Those holding this view also

insist that it is hypocritical to grant broad constitutional rights in theory while encouraging citizens to abdicate those rights due to unawareness.

The opposing view is illustrated by Justice Stewart's majority opinion in *Schneckloth v. Bustamonte.* When the majority argues that a broad consent exception is necessary because otherwise the police will not be able to obtain important and reliable evidence when they lack probable cause to arrest or search, is it in effect saying that Fourth Amendment standards are unrealistic and ought to be generally relaxed? After all, other countries (including democratic countries like England, Canada, and West Germany) grant police broad authority to make discretionary searches and do not very often enforce search and seizure rules by excluding evidence from criminal trials.

Our own tradition is ambivalent. Although we have had the Fourth Amendment for nearly 200 years, it had practically no impact upon our local law enforcement before the decision in *Mapp v. Ohio,* in 1961. (Note that Justice Stewart, a moderate who was on the Court in 1961, did not join the majority opinion in *Mapp.*) The majority opinion in *Schneckloth* stands as evidence that there remains substantial doubt on the Supreme Court about the desirability of regulating routine police-citizen encounters through the warrant and probable cause requirements of the Fourth Amendment.

Chapter 4

THE WARRANT REQUIREMENT

CHIMEL v. CALIFORNIA

Supreme Court of the United States, 1969.
395 U.S. 752, 89 S.Ct. 2034, 23 L.Ed.2d 685.

MR. JUSTICE STEWART delivered the opinion of the Court.

This case raises basic questions concerning the permissible scope under the Fourth Amendment of a search incident to a lawful arrest.

The relevant facts are essentially undisputed. Late in the afternoon of September 13, 1965, three police officers arrived at the Santa Ana, California, home of the petitioner with a warrant authorizing his arrest for the burglary of a coin shop. The officers knocked on the door, identified themselves to the petitioner's wife, and asked if they might come inside. She ushered them into the house, where they waited 10 or 15 minutes until the petitioner returned home from work. When the petitioner entered the house, one of the officers handed him the arrest warrant and asked for permission to "look around." The petitioner objected, but was advised that "on the basis of the lawful arrest," the officers would nonetheless conduct a search. No search warrant had been issued.

Accompanied by the petitioner's wife, the officers then looked through the entire three-bedroom house, including the attic, the garage, and a small workshop. In some rooms the search was relatively cursory. In the master bedroom and sewing room, however, the officers directed the petitioner's wife to open drawers and "to physically move contents of the drawers from side to side so that [they] might view any items that would have come from [the] burglary." After completing the search, they seized numerous items—primarily coins, but also several medals, tokens, and a few other objects. The entire search took between 45 minutes and an hour.

At the petitioner's subsequent state trial on two charges of burglary, the items taken from his house were admitted into evidence against him, over his objection that they had been unconstitutionally seized. * * *

[The opinion reviewed pre-World War II cases in which a limited right to search the premises of an arrestee incident to an arrest had been established.]

The limiting views expressed in [earlier cases] were thrown to the winds, however, in *Harris v. United States*, 331 U.S. 145, decided in 1947. In that case, officers had obtained a warrant for Harris' arrest on the basis of his alleged involvement with the cashing and interstate transportation of a forged check. He was arrested in the living room of his four-room apartment, and in an attempt to recover two canceled checks thought to have been used in effecting the forgery, the officers undertook a thorough search of the entire apartment. Inside a desk drawer they found a sealed envelope marked "George Harris, personal papers." The envelope, which was then torn open, was found to contain altered Selective Service documents, and those documents were used to secure Harris' conviction for violating the Selective Training and Service Act of 1940. The Court rejected Harris' Fourth Amendment claim, sustaining the search as "incident to arrest."

Only a year after *Harris*, however, the pendulum swung again. In *Trupiano v. United States*, 334 U.S. 699, agents raided the site of an illicit distillery, saw one of several conspirators operating the still, and arrested him, contemporaneously "seiz[ing] the illicit distillery." The Court held that the arrest and others made subsequently had been valid, but that the unexplained failure of the agents to procure a search warrant—in spite of the fact that they had had more than enough time before the raid to do so—rendered the search unlawful. * * *

In 1950, two years after *Trupiano*, came *United States v. Rabinowitz*, 339 U.S. 56, the decision upon which California primarily relies in the case now before us. In *Rabinowitz*, federal authorities had been informed that the defendant was dealing in stamps bearing forged overprints. On the basis of that information they secured a warrant for his arrest, which they executed at his one-room business office. At the time of the arrest, the officers "searched the desk, safe, and file cabinets in the office for about an hour and a half," and seized 573 stamps with forged overprints. The stamps were admitted into evidence at the defendant's trial, and this Court affirmed his conviction, rejecting the contention that the warrantless search had been unlawful. The Court held that the search in its entirety fell within the principle giving law enforcement authorities "[t]he right 'to search the place where the arrest is made in order to find and seize things connected with the crime * * *.' " *Id.*, at 61. *Harris* was regarded as "ample authority" for that conclusion. *Id.*, at 63. The opinion rejected the rule of *Trupiano* that "in seizing goods and articles, law enforcement agents must secure and use search warrants wherever reasonably practicable." The test, said the Court, "is not whether it is reasonable to procure a search warrant, but whether the search was reasonable."

Rabinowitz has come to stand for the proposition, *inter alia*, that a warrantless search "incident to a lawful arrest" may generally extend to the area that is considered to be in the "possession" or under the "control" of the person arrested. And it was on the basis of that proposition that the California courts upheld the search of the petitioner's entire house in this case. That doctrine, however, at least in the broad sense in which it was applied by the California courts in this case, can withstand neither historical nor rational analysis. * * * When an arrest is made, it is reasonable for the arresting officer to search the person arrested in order to remove any weapons that the latter might seek to use in order to resist arrest or effect his escape. Otherwise, the officer's safety might well be endangered, and the arrest itself frustrated. In addition, it is entirely reasonable for the arresting officer to search for and seize any evidence on the arrestee's person in order to prevent its concealment or destruction. And the area into which an arrestee might reach in order to grab a weapon or evidentiary items must, of course, be governed by a like rule. A gun on a table or in a drawer in front of one who is arrested can be as dangerous to the arresting officer as one concealed in the clothing of the person arrested. There is ample justification, therefore, for a search of the arrestee's person and the area "within his immediate control"—construing that phrase to mean the area from within which he might gain possession of a weapon or destructible evidence.

There is no comparable justification, however, for routinely searching any room other than that in which an arrest occurs—or, for that matter, for searching through all the desk drawers or other closed or concealed areas in that room itself. Such searches, in the absence of well-recognized exceptions, may be made only under the authority of a search warrant. The "adherence to judicial processes" mandated by the Fourth Amendment requires no less. * * *

The petitioner correctly points out that one result of decisions such as *Rabinowitz* and *Harris* is to give law enforcement officials the opportunity to engage in searches not justified by probable cause, by the simple expedient of arranging to arrest suspects at home rather than elsewhere. We do not suggest that the petitioner is necessarily correct in his assertion that such a strategy was utilized here,[13] but the fact remains that had he been arrested earlier in the day, at his place of employment rather than at home, no search of his house could have been made without a search warrant. * * *

Rabinowitz and *Harris* have been the subject of critical commentary for many years, and have been relied upon less and less in our own decisions. It is time, for the reasons we have stated, to hold that on their own facts, and insofar as the principles they stand for are inconsistent

13. Although the warrant was issued at 10:39 a.m. and the arrest was not made until late in the afternoon, the State suggests that the delay is accounted for by normal police procedures and by the heavy workload of the officer in charge. In addition, that officer testified that he and his colleagues went to the petitioner's house "to keep from approaching him at his place of business to cause him any problem there."

with those that we have endorsed today, they are no longer to be followed.

Application of sound Fourth Amendment principles to the facts of this case produces a clear result. The search here went far beyond the petitioner's person and the area from within which he might have obtained either a weapon or something that could have been used as evidence against him. There was no constitutional justification, in the absence of a search warrant, for extending the search beyond that area. The scope of the search was, therefore, "unreasonable" under the Fourth and Fourteenth Amendments, and the petitioner's conviction cannot stand.

Reversed.

MR. JUSTICE WHITE, with whom MR. JUSTICE BLACK joins, dissenting. * * *

The rule which has prevailed, but for very brief or doubtful periods of aberration, is that a search incident to an arrest may extend to those areas under the control of the defendant and where items subject to constitutional seizure may be found. The justification for this rule must, under the language of the Fourth Amendment, lie in the reasonableness of the rule. * * * The Amendment does not proscribe "warrantless searches" but instead it proscribes "unreasonable searches" and this Court has never held nor does the majority today assert that warrantless searches are necessarily unreasonable.

Applying this reasonableness test to the area of searches incident to arrests, one thing is clear at the outset. Search of an arrested man and of the items within his immediate reach must in almost every case be reasonable. There is always a danger that the suspect will try to escape, seizing concealed weapons with which to overpower and injure the arresting officers, and there is a danger that he may destroy evidence vital to the prosecution. Circumstances in which these justifications would not apply are sufficiently rare that inquiry is not made into searches of this scope, which have been considered reasonable throughout.

The justifications which make such a search reasonable obviously do not apply to the search of areas to which the accused does not have ready physical access. This is not enough, however, to prove such searches unconstitutional. The Court has always held, and does not today deny, that when there is probable cause to search and it is "impracticable" for one reason or another to get a search warrant, then a warrantless search may be reasonable. This is the case whether an arrest was made at the time of the search or not.

This is not to say that a search can be reasonable without regard to the probable cause to believe that seizable items are on the premises. But when there are exigent circumstances, and probable cause, then the search may be made without a warrant, reasonably. An arrest itself may often create an emergency situation making it impracticable to obtain a warrant before embarking on a related search. Again assuming that there is probable cause to search premises at the spot where a suspect is arrested, it seems to me unreasonable to require the police to leave the scene in order to obtain a search warrant when they are already legally there to make a valid arrest, and when there must almost always be a strong possibility that confederates of the arrested man will in the meanwhile remove the items for which the police have probable cause to search. This must so often be the case that it seems to me as unreasonable to require a warrant for a search of the premises as to require a warrant for search of the person and his very immediate surroundings.

This case provides a good illustration of my point that it is unreasonable to require police to leave the scene of an arrest in order to obtain a search warrant when they already have probable cause to search and there is a clear danger that the items for which they may reasonably search will be removed before they return with a warrant. Petitioner was arrested in his home after an arrest whose validity will be explored below, but which I will now assume was valid. There was doubtless probable cause not only to arrest petitioner, but also to search his house. He had obliquely admitted, both to a neighbor and to the owner of the burglarized store, that he had committed the burglary. In light of this, and the fact that the neighbor had seen other admittedly stolen property in petitioner's house, there was surely probable cause on which a warrant could have issued to search the house for the stolen coins. Moreover, had the police simply arrested petitioner, taken him off to the station house, and later returned with a warrant, it seems very likely that petitioner's wife, who in view of petitioner's generally garrulous nature must have known of the robbery, would have removed the coins. For the police to search the house while the evidence they had probable cause to search out and seize was still there cannot be considered unreasonable.

This line of analysis, supported by the precedents of this Court, hinges on two assumptions. One is that the arrest of petitioner without a valid warrant[7] was constitutional as the majority assumes; the other is that the police were not required to obtain a search warrant in advance, even though they knew that the effect of the arrest might well be to alert petitioner's wife that the coins had better be removed soon. Thus it is necessary to examine the constitutionality of the arrest since if it was illegal, the exigent circumstances which it created may not, as the consequences of a lawless act, be used to justify the contemporaneous warrantless search. But for the arrest, the warrantless search may not be justified. And if circumstances can justify the warrantless arrest, it would be strange to say that the Fourth Amendment bars the warrantless search, regardless of the circumstances, since the invasion and disruption of a man's life and privacy which stem from his arrest are

7. An arrest warrant was in fact issued, but it was issued on an inadequate supporting affidavit and was therefore invalid, so that the case must be considered as though no warrant had been issued.

ordinarily far greater than the relatively minor intrusions attending a search of his premises.

Congress has expressly authorized a wide range of officials to make arrests without any warrant in criminal cases. United States Marshals have long had this power, which is also vested in the agents of the Federal Bureau of Investigation, and in the Secret Service and the narcotics law enforcement agency. That warrantless arrest power may apply even when there is time to get a warrant without fear that the suspect may escape is made perfectly clear by the legislative history of the statute granting arrest power to the FBI. * * *

In light of the uniformity of judgment of the Congress, past judicial decisions, and common practice rejecting the proposition that arrest warrants are essential wherever it is practicable to get them, the conclusion is inevitable that such arrests and accompanying searches are reasonable, at least until experience teaches the contrary. It must very often be the case that by the time probable cause to arrest a man is accumulated, the man is aware of police interest in him or for other good reasons is on the verge of flight. Moreover, it will likely be very difficult to determine the probability of his flight. Given this situation, it may be best in all cases simply to allow the arrest if there is probable cause, especially since that issue can be determined very shortly after the arrest. * * *

If circumstances so often require the warrantless arrest that the law generally permits it, the typical situation will find the arresting officers lawfully on the premises without arrest or search warrant. Like the majority, I would permit the police to search the person of a suspect and the area under his immediate control either to assure the safety of the officers or to prevent the destruction of evidence. And like the majority, I see nothing in the arrest alone furnishing probable cause for a search of any broader scope. However, where as here the existence of probable cause is independently established and would justify a warrant for a broader search for evidence, I would follow past cases and permit such a search to be carried out without a warrant, since the fact of arrest supplies an exigent circumstance justifying police action before the evidence can be removed, and also alerts the suspect to the fact of the search so that he can immediately seek judicial determination of probable cause in an adversary proceeding, and appropriate redress. * * *

STEAGALD v. UNITED STATES

Supreme Court of the United States, 1981.
451 U.S. 204, 101 S.Ct. 1642, 68 L.Ed.2d 38.

Justice Marshall delivered the opinion of the Court.

The issue in this case is whether, under the Fourth Amendment, a law enforcement officer may legally search for the subject of an arrest warrant in the home of a third party without first obtaining a search warrant. Concluding that a search warrant must be obtained absent exigent circumstances or consent, we reverse the judgment of the United States Court of Appeals for the Fifth Circuit affirming petitioner's conviction.

In early January 1978, an agent of the Drug Enforcement Administration (DEA) was contacted in Detroit, Mich., by a confidential informant who suggested that he might be able to locate Ricky Lyons, a federal fugitive wanted on drug charges. On January 14, 1978, the informant called the agent again, and gave him a telephone number in the Atlanta, Ga., area where, according to the informant, Ricky Lyons could be reached during the next 24 hours. On January 16, 1978, the agent called fellow DEA Agent Kelly Goodowens in Atlanta and relayed the information he had obtained from the informant. Goodowens contacted Southern Bell Telephone Co., and secured the address corresponding to the telephone number obtained by the informant. Goodowens also discovered that Lyons was the subject of a 6–month-old arrest warrant.

Two days later, Goodowens and 11 other officers drove to the address supplied by the telephone company to search for Lyons. The officers observed two men standing outside the house to be searched. These men were Hoyt Gaultney and petitioner Gary Steagald. The officers approached with guns drawn, frisked both men, and, after demanding identification, determined that neither man was Lyons. Several agents proceeded to the house. Gaultney's wife answered the door, and informed the agents that she was alone in the house. She was told to place her hands against the wall and was guarded in that position while one agent searched the house. Ricky Lyons was not found, but during the search of the house the agent observed what he believed to be cocaine. Upon being informed of this discovery, Agent Goodowens sent an officer to obtain a search warrant and in the meantime conducted a second search of the house, which uncovered additional incriminating evidence. During a third search conducted pursuant to a search warrant, the agents uncovered 43 pounds of cocaine. Petitioner was arrested and indicted on federal drug charges.

Prior to trial, petitioner moved to suppress all evidence uncovered during the various searches on the ground that it was illegally obtained because the agents had failed to secure a search warrant before entering the house. Agent Goodowens testified at the suppression hearing that there had been no "physical hinderance" preventing him from obtaining a search warrant and that he did not do so because he believed that the arrest warrant for Ricky Lyons was sufficient to justify the entry and search. The District Court agreed with this view, and denied the suppression motion. * * *

The question before us is a narrow one.[6] The search at issue here took place in the absence of consent or exigent circumstances. Except in such special situations, we have consistently held that the entry into a

6. Initially, we assume without deciding that the information relayed to Agent Goodowens concerning the whereabouts of Ricky Lyons would have been sufficient to establish probable cause to believe that Lyons was at the house searched by the agents.

home to conduct a search or make an arrest is unreasonable under the Fourth Amendment unless done pursuant to a warrant. See *Payton v. New York*, 445 U.S. 573 (1980); *Johnson v. United States*, 333 U.S. 10, 13–15 (1948). * * * Here, of course, the agents had a warrant—one authorizing the arrest of Ricky Lyons. However, the Fourth Amendment claim here is not being raised by Ricky Lyons. Instead, the challenge to the search is asserted by a person not named in the warrant who was convicted on the basis of evidence uncovered during a search of his residence for Ricky Lyons. * * *

[W]hile an arrest warrant and a search warrant both serve to subject the probable-cause determination of the police to judicial review, the interests protected by the two warrants differ. An arrest warrant is issued by a magistrate upon a showing that probable cause exists to believe that the subject of the warrant has committed an offense and thus the warrant primarily serves to protect an individual from an unreasonable seizure. A search warrant, in contrast is issued upon a showing of probable cause to believe that the legitimate object of a search is located in a particular place, and therefore safeguards an individual's interest in the privacy of his home and possessions against the unjustified intrusion of the police.

Thus, whether the arrest warrant issued in this case adequately safeguarded the interests protected by the Fourth Amendment depends upon what the warrant authorized the agents to do. To be sure, the warrant embodied a judicial finding that there was probable cause to believe that Ricky Lyons had committed a felony, and the warrant therefore authorized the officers to seize Lyons. However, the agents sought to do more than use the warrant to arrest Lyons in a public place or in his home; instead, they relied on the warrant as legal authority to enter the home of a third person based on their belief that Ricky Lyons might be a guest there. Regardless of how reasonable this belief might have been, it was never subject to the detached scrutiny of a judicial officer. Thus, while the warrant in this case may have protected Lyons from an unreasonable seizure, it did absolutely nothing to protect petitioner's privacy interest in being free from an unreasonable invasion and search of his home. Instead, petitioner's only protection from an illegal entry and search was the agent's personal determination of probable cause. In the absence of exigent circumstances, we have consistently held that such judicially untested determinations are not reliable enough to justify an entry into a person's home to arrest him without a warrant, or a search of a home for objects in the absence of a search warrant. * * *

A contrary conclusion—that the police, acting alone and in the absence of exigent circumstances, may decide when there is sufficient justification for searching the home of a third party for the subject of an arrest warrant—would create a significant potential for abuse. Armed solely with an arrest warrant for a single person, the police could search all the homes of that individual's friends and acquaintances. See, *e.g., Lankford v. Gelston*, 364 F.2d 197 (C.A.4 1966) (enjoining police practice under which 300 homes were searched pursuant to arrest warrants for two fugitives). Moreover, an arrest warrant may serve as the pretext for entering a home in which the police have a suspicion, but not probable cause to believe, that illegal activity is taking place. * * *

The Government also suggests that practical problems might arise if law enforcement officers are required to obtain a search warrant before entering the home of a third party to make an arrest. The basis of this concern is that persons, as opposed to objects, are inherently mobile, and thus officers seeking to effect an arrest may be forced to return to the magistrate several times as the subject of the arrest warrant moves from place to place. We are convinced, however, that a search warrant requirement will not significantly impede effective law enforcement efforts.

First, the situations in which a search warrant will be necessary are few. As noted in *Payton v. New York, supra*, an arrest warrant alone will suffice to enter a suspect's own residence to effect his arrest. Furthermore, if probable cause exists, no warrant is required to apprehend a suspected felon in a public place. *United States v. Watson*, 423 U.S. 411 (1976). Thus, the subject of an arrest warrant can be readily seized before entering or after leaving the home of a third party.[14] Finally, the exigent-circumstances doctrine significantly limits the situations in which a search warrant would be needed. For example, a warrantless entry of a home would be justified if the police were in "hot pursuit" of a fugitive. See *United States v. Santana*, 427 U.S. 38, 42–43 (1976); *Warden v. Hayden*, 387 U.S. 294 (1967). Thus, to the extent that searches for persons pose special problems, we believe that the exigent-circumstances doctrine is adequate to accommodate legitimate law enforcement needs.

Moreover, in those situations in which a search warrant is necessary, the inconvenience incurred by the police is simply not that significant. First, if the police know of the location of the felon when they obtain an arrest warrant, the additional burden of obtaining a search warrant at the same time is miniscule. The inconvenience of obtaining such a warrant does not increase significantly when an outstanding arrest warrant already exists. In this case, for example, Agent Goodowens knew the address of the house to be searched two days in advance, and planned the raid from the federal courthouse in Atlanta where, we are informed, three full-time magistrates were on duty. In routine search cases such as this, the short time required to obtain a search warrant from a magistrate will seldom hinder efforts to apprehend a felon. Finally, if a magistrate is not nearby, a telephonic search warrant can usually be obtained. See Fed.Rule Crim.Proc. 41(c)(1), (2).

Whatever practical problems remain, however, cannot outweigh the constitutional interests at stake. Any warrant requirement impedes to

---

14. Indeed, the "inherent mobility" of persons noted by the Government suggests that in most situations the police may avoid altogether the need to obtain a search warrant simply by waiting for a suspect to leave the third person's home before attempting to arrest that suspect.

some extent the vigor with which the Government can seek to enforce its laws, yet the Fourth Amendment recognizes that this restraint is necessary in some cases to protect against unreasonable searches and seizures. We conclude that this is such a case. The additional burden imposed on the police by a warrant requirement is minimal. In contrast, the right protected—that of presumptively innocent people to be secure in their homes from unjustified, forcible intrusions by the Government—is weighty. Thus, in order to render the instant search reasonable under the Fourth Amendment, a search warrant was required.

Accordingly, the judgment of the Court of Appeals is reversed, and the case is remanded to that court for further proceedings consistent with this opinion.

So ordered.

THE CHIEF JUSTICE concurs in the judgment.

JUSTICE REHNQUIST, with whom JUSTICE WHITE joins, dissenting. * * *

The government's interests in the warrantless entry of a third-party dwelling to execute an arrest warrant are compelling. The basic problem confronting police in such situations is the inherent mobility of the fugitive. By definition, the police have probable cause to believe that the fugitive is in a dwelling which is not his home. He may stay there for a week, a day, or 10 minutes. Fugitives from justice tend to be mobile, and police officers will generally have no way of knowing whether the subject of an arrest warrant will be at the dwelling when they return from seeking a search warrant. Imposition of a search warrant requirement in such circumstances will frustrate the compelling interests of the government and indeed the public in the apprehension of those subject to outstanding arrest warrants.

The Court's responses to these very real concerns are singularly unpersuasive. It first downplays them by stating that "the situations in which a search warrant will be necessary are few," because no search warrant is necessary to arrest a suspect at his home and, if the suspect is at another's home, the police need only wait until he leaves, since no search warrant is needed to arrest him in a public place. These beguilingly simple answers to a serious law enforcement problem simply will not wash. Criminals who know or suspect they are subject to arrest warrants would not be likely to return to their homes, and while the police could reduce the likelihood of escape by staking out all possible exits the costs of such a stakeout seems excessive in an era of rising crime and scarce police resources. The Court's ivory tower misconception of the realities of the apprehension of fugitives from justice reaches its apogee when it states: "In routine search cases such as this, the short time required to obtain a search warrant from a magistrate will seldom hinder efforts to apprehend a felon." The cases we are considering are *not* "routine search cases." They are cases of attempted arrest, pursuant to a warrant, when the object of the arrest may flee at any time—including the "short time" during which the police are endeavoring to obtain a search warrant.

At the same time the interference with the Fourth Amendment privacy interests of those whose homes are entered to apprehend the felon is not nearly as significant as suggested by the Court. The arrest warrant serves some of the functions a separate search warrant would. It assures the occupants that the police officer is present on official business. The arrest warrant also limits the scope of the search, specifying what the police may search for—*i.e.*, the subject of the arrest warrant. No general search is permitted, but only a search of those areas in which the object of the search might hide. Indeed there may be no intrusion on the occupant's privacy at all, since if present the suspect will have the opportunity to voluntarily surrender at the door. Even if the suspect does not surrender but secretes himself within the house, the occupant can limit the search by pointing him out to the police. It is important to remember that the contraband discovered during the entry and search for Lyons was in plain view, and was discovered during a "sweep search" for Lyons, not a probing of drawers or cabinets for contraband.

Because the burden on law enforcement officers to obtain a separate search warrant before entering the dwelling of a third party to execute a concededly valid arrest warrant is great, and carries with it a high possibility that the fugitive named in the arrest warrant will escape apprehension, I would conclude that the application of the traditional "reasonableness" standard of the Fourth Amendment does not require a separate search warrant in a case such as this. * * *

While I cannot subscribe to the Court's decision today, I will not falsely cry "wolf" in this dissent. The decision rests on a very special set of facts, and with a change in one or more of them it is clear that no separate search warrant would be required even under the reasoning of the Court.

On the one side *Payton* makes clear that an arrest warrant is all that is needed to enter the suspect's "home" to effect the arrest. If a suspect has been living in a particular dwelling for any significant period, say a few days, it can certainly be considered his "home" for Fourth Amendment purposes, even if the premises are owned by a third party and others are living there, and even if the suspect concurrently maintains a residence elsewhere as well. In such a case the police could enter the premises with only an arrest warrant. On the other side, the more fleeting a suspect's connection with the premises, such as when he is a mere visitor, the more likely that exigent circumstances will exist justifying immediate police action without departing to obtain a search warrant. The practical damage done to effective law enforcement by today's decision, without any basis in the Constitution, may well be minimal if courts carefully consider the various congeries of facts in the actual case before them.

The genuinely unfortunate aspect of today's ruling is not that fewer fugitives will be brought to book, or fewer criminals apprehended, though both of these consequences will undoubtedly occur; the greater misfortune is the increased uncertainty imposed on police officers in the field, committing magistrates, and trial judges, who must confront variations and permutations of this factual situation on a day-to-day basis. They will, in their various capacities, have to weigh the time during which a suspect for whom there is an outstanding arrest warrant has been in the building, whether the dwelling is the suspect's home, how long he has lived there, whether he is likely to leave immediately, and a number of related and equally imponderable questions. Certainty and repose, as Justice Holmes said, may not be the destiny of man, but one might have hoped for a higher degree of certainty in this one narrow but important area of the law than is offered by today's decision.

Commentary

The Supreme Court's decision in *Payton v. New York*, cited in the *Steagald* opinions, established that "an arrest warrant founded on probable cause implicitly carries with it the limited authority to enter a dwelling in which the suspect lives when there is reason to believe the suspect is within." The majority opinion explained this holding by stating that "if there is sufficient evidence of a citizen's participation in a felony to persuade a judicial officer that his arrest is justified, it is constitutionally reasonable to require him to open his doors to the officers of the law." 445 U.S. at 602–03. But when the suspect is not home, a fruitless search of the residence may invade the privacy of other persons who are living or visiting there. Arguably, the police should be required to demonstrate to a judicial officer not only that they have probable cause to arrest the suspect, but also that they have probable cause to believe that he will be at home when they serve the warrant.

It is not clear how much protection such a requirement would provide. Some courts might issue search warrants routinely along with arrest warrants on the theory that it is inherently likely that a suspect will be at his residence, absent evidence to the contrary. Others might require the police to "stake out" the residence and obtain confirmation of the suspect's presence before applying for the warrant. If the suspect left the residence before the warrant could be obtained, the officers could arrest him upon leaving. The cost in police resources in proceeding this way might be substantial.

Does an arrest warrant also suffice for authority to enter the suspect's place of employment during business hours? The plaintiff in Pembaur v. Cincinnati, 475 U.S. 469 (1986) was a physician who had been suspected of fraudulently obtaining payments from state welfare agencies for services not actually provided to patients. Two of his employees failed to respond to grand jury subpoenas, and the authorities obtained writs of "capias" commanding the police to bring the witnesses to court. When the police attempted to serve the writs at Pembaur's clinic, he barred the door. After consulting with the County Prosecutor, the police broke down the door and went in to look for the witnesses (who were not there). Pembaur subsequently sued for damages under the Federal Civil Rights Act (42 U.S.C.A. § 1983).

When the case came to the Supreme Court, the principal issue was whether the County was liable for the conduct of the officers. A city or county is liable for damages under the statute only for deprivations of federally protected rights caused by action taken "pursuant to official municipal policy." See Monell v. Dept. of Social Services of New York, 436 U.S. 658 (1978). The Supreme Court majority held that the County Prosecutor had the authority to establish governmental policy in the situation, and the County was therefore liable for the activity he had authorized. The Court assumed that the officers violated Pembaur's rights under *Steagald*, because they had forcibly entered the premises of a third party to execute something roughly equivalent to an arrest warrant in the absence of exigent circumstances or other extraordinary justification.

The majority opinion noted that the County conceded that the officers' activity violated *Steagald* and no one seems to have suggested that *Payton* rather than *Steagald* might be the governing precedent. The likelihood that a suspect will be at his or her place of employment during ordinary business hours would seem to be at least as great as the likelihood that the suspect would be at home at other times, however. If a warrant to search the clinic during office hours could issue merely on the basis of the writ of capias and the employment relationship, it is not easy to see how the *Steagald* rule protects an individual in Pembaur's situation, or how the failure to obtain a search warrant caused him substantial damages.

Execution of the Warrant

Assuming that the police have obtained a valid search or arrest warrant, they must execute it in a manner consistent with legal requirements. Among the issues that sometimes arise are the following:

1. *Description of the Premises.* Occasionally there are discrepancies or ambiguities in the designation of the place to be searched, particularly when an apartment building or other structure containing multiple units is involved. In Maryland v. Garrison, 480 U.S. 79 (1987), the officers obtained and executed a warrant to search the person of Lawrence McWebb and "the premises known as 2036 Park Avenue third floor apartment." When the police obtained the warrant they reasonably believed that there was only one apartment on the third floor. In fact, the floor was divided into two apartments, one occupied by McWebb and one by Garrison. Before the officers executing the warrant became aware that there were two apartments, they had entered Garrison's apartment and found contraband there. The majority opinion by Justice Stevens held that the warrant was valid because it was based on a reasonable belief that there was only one apartment on the third floor, and the search pursuant to that warrant was lawful because all the officers reasonably believed that they were searching McWebb's apartment at the time they discovered the contraband. The majority opinion relied heavily on Hill v. California, 401 U.S. 797 (1971), which upheld the lawfulness of an arrest that turned out to be a case of mistaken identity. The lawfulness of police action depends on what the police at the time reasonably believed to be the circumstances, even if this reasonable belief happens to be mistaken.

2. *Time considerations.* Arrest warrants may remain valid indefinitely, or as long as prosecution for the underlying offense is possible, but in some jurisdictions unreasonable delay may make an arrest unlawful. Statutes and court rules normally require that search warrants be executed within a

definite time after issuance, typically ten days, and tardiness in execution will result in exclusion of the evidence. Even if the statutory requirements are met, a substantial period of delay might make the search unreasonable under the Fourth Amendment, because the information on which the warrant was based has become stale. Many states require that search warrants be executed in daytime hours unless there is authorization upon sufficient cause for a night time search. It is not clear whether there is any constitutional doctrine to this effect; see Gooding v. United States, 416 U.S. 430 (1974).

3. *Knock-Notice requirements.* Most jurisdictions have some requirement that police give notice of their authority and purpose prior to entering a building to execute a search warrant or to make an arrest. When police unnecessarily break through a door or window to gain entry, this action is often very frightening to persons inside and may lead to violence. On the other hand, police are not required to wait helplessly outside while the suspects inside the dwelling destroy the evidence, nor are they required to give notice of their authority and purpose when to do so would be perilous. If the officers know that the suspects are armed and dangerous, or have a specific indication that they will destroy evidence if given the opportunity to do so, then the officers may enter without giving advance notice of their authority and purpose.

In Wilson v. Arkansas, 514 U.S. 927 (1995), the Supreme Court unanimously held that the common law "knock and announce" requirement is incorporated into the Fourth Amendment's concept of reasonableness. The requirement is to be flexibly interpreted, however, and countervailing law enforcement interest may justify an unannounced entry if (for example) there is a threat of physical harm to police, or an officer is in hot pursuit of a fugitive, or there is a likelihood that persons inside the premises may destroy evidence.

Many cases deal with whether the officers can make a forcible entry immediately after announcing their authority and purpose, on the ground that a defendant's delay in admitting them amounts to a refusal. In United States v. Hromada, 49 F.3d 685 (11th Cir.1995) officers had a warrant to arrest the defendant for selling marijuana which he grew in his home. They came to his door, knocked loudly, and shouted "Sheriff's Office, arrest warrant." Several seconds later a man (later identified as Hromada) appeared at the large picture window next to the front door. The officer shouted at him to open the door, but Hromada did not respond to this demand but continued to stand at the window. The officers then broke the front door open and entered the house, finding marijuana plants in plain view in a "protective sweep." Although there was no evidence that Hormada had any guns or had been involved in violence, the Court of Appeals observed that "guns and violence go hand-in-hand with illegal drug operations." The court upheld the entry and search because "any further delay [in entering] might well have involved great risk to the officers undertaking the arrest."

The Supreme Court returned to the knock-notice rule in Richards v. Wisconsin, 520 U.S. 385 (1997). The Court held unanimously that it is unconstitutional for a state to create a blanket exception to the "knock and announce" rule for warrant-authorized searches in all felony drug cases. A no-knock entry is reasonable only where information known to officers at the time of entry gives rise to a reasonable suspicion that complying with the knock-and-announce rule would be dangerous or futile, or risk the destruction of evidence. The unanimous opinion by Justice Stevens upheld the search and affirmed the conviction, however, because the officers who executed the warrant had reason to believe that the defendant knew of their presence and purpose, and could have destroyed the drug evidence if they had not entered immediately. The circumstances at the time of entry justified their action even though the issuing magistrate had refused to include authorization for a no-knock entry in the warrant itself—on the basis of the information available at that time.

4. *Detention and Search of Persons on the Premises.* Authorization to search certain premises does not necessarily imply authorization to search persons on those premises. For example, in Ybarra v. Illinois, 444 U.S. 85 (1979), the police executed a warrant to search a bar for drugs and incidentally searched customers who were present at the time. The Supreme Court ruled that the search of customers was unlawful, absent probable cause to arrest them, although a "frisk" for weapons would have been reasonable to protect the safety of the officers. On the other hand, the Supreme Court has ruled that officers executing a warrant to search for contraband may temporarily detain any occupants of the premises while the search is going on. Michigan v. Summers, 452 U.S. 692 (1981). The majority thought that such detention would prevent flight in case grounds for arrest are found in the search, would minimize the risk of harm to the officers, and would facilitate the orderly completion of the search.

5. *Scope of the Search and Plain View.* The scope of the search is as broad as reasonably authorized in the warrant, and may be as intensive as necessary to find the objects whose seizure is authorized. Officers ordinarily may search through drawers and other containers on the premises that are capable of containing items whose seizure is authorized. Frequently, the officers come upon additional contraband or evidence while searching for the items specified in the warrant, and the "plain view" doctrine permits them to seize such items if they come upon them inadvertently without exceeding the scope of the authorized search. The plain view doctrine is discussed in the plurality opinion in Coolidge v. New Hampshire, 403 U.S. 443 (1971). This opinion stated that the plain view doctrine would not apply to evidence of which the police had advance knowledge, because in that event they could have included the object in the warrant application. It is uncertain whether the Supreme Court would enforce the "inadvertence" requirement today. See Texas v. Brown, 460 U.S. 730 (1983).

The Supreme Court strictly limited the plain view doctrine in Arizona v. Hicks, 480 U.S. 321 (1987). After a bullet fired through the floor of Hick's apartment wounded a man in the apartment below, police officers lawfully entered the apartment without a warrant to search for the shooter, for other victims, and for weapons. They found and seized three weapons and a stocking-cap mask. One of the officers also noticed two sets of expensive stereo components, which seemed out of place in the otherwise ill-furnished apartment. Suspecting that the components were stolen, he read and recorded their serial numbers—moving some of the components in order to do so. On being advised by telephone that one of the items had been taken in an armed robbery, he seized it. Officers later determined that some of the other serial numbers matched those on other stereo equipment taken in the same armed robbery, and a warrant was obtained and executed to seize these other items.

In an opinion by Justice Scalia, the Supreme Court held that, although recording the serial numbers did not constitute a "seizure," moving the equipment to view the numbers was a "search" separate and apart from the lawful search that brought the officers to the apartment. Although the plain view doctrine would permit the officer to seize the stereo component without a warrant if he had probable cause to believe it stolen, even so limited a search as a slight movement to view serial numbers violated the Fourth Amendment in the absence of probable cause. (The state conceded that the presence of expensive equipment in an otherwise squalid apartment provided only a basis for reasonable suspicion, and not probable cause.) Responding to Justice O'Connor's suggestion in dissent that a "cursory inspection" could be undertaken on reasonable suspicion, the majority announced that it was "unwilling to send police and judges into a new thicket of Fourth Amendment law, to seek a creature of uncertain description that is neither a plain-view inspection nor yet a 'full-blown search.' "

6. *Protective Sweeps.* When officers lawfully enter a home to make an arrest, they may make a "protective sweep" of the premises to look for any confederates of the arrested person who might endanger their safety. According to the majority opinion by Justice White in Maryland v. Buie, 494 U.S. 325 (1990), the arresting officers do not need either probable cause or reasonable suspicion to "look in closets and other spaces immediately adjoining the place of arrest from which an attack could immediately be launched. Beyond that, however, * * * there must be articulable facts which * * * would warrant a reasonably prudent officer in believing that the area to be swept harbors an individual posing a danger to those on the arrest scene." If the officers are making a lawful protective sweep, they may seize any contraband or evidence which they happen to see under the plain view doctrine, as interpreted in *Arizona v. Hicks.*

In Horton v. California, 496 U.S. 128 (1990), the Supreme Court held by a 7–2 majority that evidence need not be discovered "inadvertently" for the plain view description to apply. An officer applied for a warrant to search for weapons and stolen property, but the warrant as signed by the magistrate authorized only a search for stolen property. The officers executing the warrant did not find the property but found the weapons in plain view. The Court held that the fact that the officers knew about the weapons and hoped to find them did not invalidate the search.

7. *Notice, Receipt and Return.* Statutes and court rules normally require officers to exhibit a copy of the warrant at the place searched to demonstrate their authority, to give the occupant a receipt for anything seized, and to return the executed warrant promptly to the court together with an inventory of the items seized. Courts have generally held that failure to comply with these requirements does not require exclusion of evidence found in an otherwise valid search.

FEDERAL RULES OF CRIMINAL PROCEDURE

Rule 41. Search and Seizure

(a) Authority to Issue Warrant. A search warrant authorized by this rule may be issued by a federal magistrate or a judge of a state court of record within the district wherein the property or person sought is located, upon request of a federal law enforcement officer or an attorney for the government.

(b) Property or Persons Which May Be Seized With a Warrant. A warrant may be issued under this rule to search for and seize any (1) property that constitutes evidence of the commission of a criminal offense; or (2) contraband, the fruits of crime, or things otherwise criminally possessed; or (3) property designed or intended for use or which is or has been used as the means of committing a criminal offense; or (4) person for whose arrest there is probable cause, or who is unlawfully restrained.

(c) Issuance and Contents.

(1) Warrant Upon Affidavit. A warrant other than a warrant upon oral testimony under paragraph (2) of this subdivision shall issue only on an affidavit or affidavits sworn to before the federal magistrate or state judge and establishing the grounds for issuing the warrant. If the federal magistrate or state judge is satisfied that grounds for the application exist or that there is probable cause to believe that they exist, that magistrate or state judge shall issue a warrant identifying the property or person to be seized and naming or describing the person or place to be searched. The finding of probable cause may be based upon hearsay evidence in whole or in part. Before ruling on a request for a warrant the federal magistrate or state judge may require the affiant to appear personally and may examine under oath the affiant and any witnesses the affiant may produce, provided that such proceeding shall be taken down by a court reporter or recording equipment and made part of the affidavit. The warrant shall be directed to a civil officer of the United States authorized to enforce or assist in enforcing any law thereof or to a person so authorized by the President of the United States. It shall command the officer to search, within a specified period of time not to exceed 10 days, the person or place named for the property or person specified. The warrant shall be served in the daytime, unless the issuing authority, by appropriate provision in the warrant, and for reasonable cause shown, authorizes its execution at times other than daytime. It shall designate a federal magistrate to whom it shall be returned.

(2) Warrant Upon Oral Testimony.*

(A) General Rule. If the circumstances make it reasonable to dispense with a written affidavit, a Federal magistrate may issue a warrant based upon sworn oral testimony communicated by telephone or other appropriate means.

(B) Application. The person who is requesting the warrant shall prepare a document to be known as a duplicate original warrant and shall read such duplicate original warrant, verbatim, to the Federal magistrate. The Federal magistrate shall enter, verbatim, what is so read to such magistrate on a document to be known as the original warrant. The Federal magistrate may direct that the warrant be modified.

(C) Issuance. If the Federal magistrate is satisfied that the circumstances are such as to make it reasonable to dispense with a written affidavit and that grounds for the application exist or that there is probable cause to believe that they exist, the Federal magistrate shall order the issuance of a warrant by directing the person requesting the warrant to sign the Federal magistrate's name on the duplicate original warrant. The Federal magistrate shall immediately sign the original warrant and enter on the face of the original warrant the exact time when the warrant was ordered to be issued. The finding of probable cause for a warrant upon oral testimony may be based on the same kind of evidence as is sufficient for a warrant upon affidavit.

(D) Recording and Certification of Testimony. When a caller informs the Federal magistrate that the purpose of the call is to request a warrant, the Federal magistrate shall immediately place under oath each person whose testimony forms a basis of the application and each person applying for that warrant. If a voice recording device is available, the Federal magistrate shall record by means of such device all of the call after the caller informs the Federal magistrate that the purpose of the call is to request a warrant. Otherwise a stenographic or longhand verbatim record shall be made. If a voice recording device is used or a stenographic record made, the Federal magistrate shall have the record transcribed, shall certify the accuracy of the transcription, and shall file a copy of the original record and the transcription with the court. If a longhand verbatim record is made, the Federal magistrate shall file a signed copy with the court.

(E) Contents. The contents of a warrant upon oral testimony shall be the same as the contents of a warrant upon affidavit.

---

* For a discussion of the requirements for issuance of a telephonic warrant, see United States v. Rome, 809 F.2d 665 (10th Cir. 1987), which held that procedural errors committed by the investigating officer and the magistrate while attempting in good faith to comply with Rule 41 did not invalidate the warrant.

(F) Additional Rule for Execution. The person who executes the warrant shall enter the exact time of execution on the face of the duplicate original warrant.

(G) Motion to Suppress Precluded. Absent a finding of bad faith, evidence obtained pursuant to a warrant issued under this paragraph is not subject to a motion to suppress on the ground that the circumstances were not such as to make it reasonable to dispense with a written affidavit.

(d) Execution and Return with Inventory. The officer taking property under the warrant shall give to the person from whom or from whose premises the property was taken a copy of the warrant and a receipt for the property taken or shall leave the copy and receipt at the place from which the property was taken. The return shall be made promptly and shall be accompanied by a written inventory of any property taken. The inventory shall be made in the presence of the applicant for the warrant and the person from whose possession or premises the property was taken, if they are present, or in the presence of at least one credible person other than the applicant for the warrant or the person from whose possession or premises the property was taken, and shall be verified by the officer. The federal magistrate shall upon request deliver a copy of the inventory to the person from whom or from whose premises the property was taken and to the applicant for the warrant.

(e) Motion for Return of Property. A person aggrieved by an unlawful search and seizure may move the district court for the district in which the property was seized for the return of the property on the ground that such person is entitled to lawful possession of the property which was illegally seized. The judge shall receive evidence on any issue of fact necessary to the decision of the motion. If the motion is granted the property shall be restored and it shall not be admissible in evidence at any hearing or trial. If a motion for return of property is made or comes on for hearing in the district of trial after an indictment or information is filed, it shall be treated also as a motion to suppress under Rule 12.

(f) Motion to Suppress. A motion to suppress evidence may be made in the court of the district of trial as provided in Rule 12.

(g) Return of Papers to Clerk. The federal magistrate before whom the warrant is returned shall attach to the warrant a copy of the return, inventory and all other papers in connection therewith and shall file them with the clerk of the district court for the district in which the property was seized.

(h) Scope and Definition. This rule does not modify any act, inconsistent with it, regulating search, seizure and the issuance and execution of search warrants in circumstances for which special provision is made. The term "property" is used in this rule to include documents, books, papers and any other tangible objects. The term "daytime" is used in this rule to mean the hours from 6:00 a.m. to 10:00

p.m. according to local time. The phrase "federal law enforcement officer" is used in this rule to mean any government agent, other than an attorney for the government as defined in Rule 54(c), who is engaged in the enforcement of the criminal laws and is within any category of officers authorized by the Attorney General to request the issuance of a search warrant.

UNITED STATES v. SALGADO

United States Court of Appeals, Seventh Circuit, 1986.
807 F.2d 603.

POSNER, CIRCUIT JUDGE.

A jury convicted Salgado of federal narcotics offenses, and he was sentenced to 20 years in prison, fined $500,000, and ordered to serve a special parole term for life.

The charges against Salgado arose out of a transaction in which he sold an ounce of cocaine to a Chicago police officer, Lett, for $1,500. The transaction was arranged by a confidential government informant named Alan, and the sale took place in Alan's home and in his presence. * * * When Salgado left Alan's home after selling the ounce of cocaine to officer Lett, federal agents followed him and after a half hour arrested him on the street, searched him, and found several keys, a portable telephone, and a receipt from a lock company. The receipt revealed that the company had, a few days earlier, rekeyed the door lock to an apartment at 2580 West Golf Road in a suburb of Chicago (the sale of cocaine and the arrest had occurred in Chicago), for a customer named "Salgado."

During the negotiations with Lett, Salgado had used his portable telephone to summon an associate, Bernal—who, as a security precaution, was driving around with the cocaine for the deal—to Alan's home to complete the deal. After Bernal arrived, Salgado was called on the portable phone, had a conversation in Spanish, and then told Lett, "You see, I'm a busy man. That was an order for five kilos."

When Bernal left, the agents followed him too, arrested him, and found in his car what appeared to be additional cocaine that Bernal had brought to Alan's residence but had not sold to Lett. Bernal told the agents that the cocaine had come from 2600 West Golf Road, and they went there, and encountered the agents who had arrested Salgado and who had then proceeded with Salgado's keys to 2580. 2580 West Golf Road and 2600 West Golf Road are two apartment buildings, under common management, located about 100 yards apart. The janitor told the agents that Salgado had moved recently to 2580. Bridges, a Chicago police officer who (like Lett) was working with the federal drug agents, used the keys taken from Salgado to open Salgado's apartment. The apartment was unfurnished and there was no one in it. Bridges, accompanied by federal agents, glanced in each room. They touched nothing and opened no closets or other closed areas. Bridges saw a white plastic box, a balance scale, and a money-counting machine. He and the agents sealed the apartment, then waited in the hallway.

About four hours later another group of agents appeared with a search warrant and made a thorough search. They seized the items that Bridges had seen, plus much else besides, including a large amount of cocaine. The warrant was based on an affidavit by officer Lett describing the circumstances in which Salgado and Bernal had been arrested and establishing that the apartment to be searched was indeed Salgado's and was probably the place where Bernal had gotten the cocaine. The warrant authorized the seizure of cocaine, currency, scales, packaging materials, etc., but did not mention anything that officer Bridges (or the agents accompanying him) had seen. Nor had Lett's affidavit, on the basis of which the warrant was issued, referred to anything that Bridges' group had seen. Another warrant was obtained later and executed but it need not be discussed separately.

Salgado argues that the initial search of the apartment by Bridges and others (but we shall ignore the others to simplify exposition) violated the Fourth Amendment. The government argues that, even if this were so, it would not help Salgado. The only remedy against an unlawful search, in a criminal proceeding, is the suppression of its fruits; and since the evidence used against Salgado was obtained not from the initial search but from the execution of a warrant that had been issued without any reliance on what Bridges had seen, there were no fruits. Bridges' search was immaterial.

The matter is more complicated than this, in two respects. The first and lesser is that the absence of any causal connection between Bridges' search and the issuance of the warrant is not so clear as the government asserts. Granted, neither the warrant itself, nor Lett's affidavit on which the warrant was based, refers to anything Bridges saw. But Lett and his associates might not have sought a warrant had they not known from Bridges' search that executing such a warrant would yield valuable evidence for trial. This assumes of course that whoever participated in the decision to seek the warrant had spoken to Bridges, but that is entirely possible. The government says its *prosecutors* who applied for the warrant didn't know about Bridges' search, and in support it cites to a page in the appendix. The cited page does not support the statement, and in any event the government does not claim that the *drug agents* who advised the prosecutors to seek a search warrant did not know about the search and did not give them information obtained from it, without disclosing the source.

Despite this, we think it reasonably plain that the search warrant would have been applied for, issued, and executed even if Bridges had never conducted the allegedly unlawful search. The arrest of Bernal with cocaine—Salgado's cocaine—in his possession, coupled with Bernal's statement that it came from 2600 West Golf Road and the janitor's that Salgado had moved recently from 2600 to 2580, made it more than likely that a search of Salgado's apartment at 2580, which the arresting agents knew Salgado had recently had rekeyed, would turn up contraband or other evidence of Salgado's drug dealings. Thus, information in the agents' possession that owed nothing to Bridges' search abundantly established probable cause for obtaining a warrant—so much so that the agents would have been derelict in their duty had they failed to apply for a warrant based just on what they knew, independently of what Bridges learned and may or may not have told them. Since the warrant would have been obtained and executed even if Bridges had never made his search, Salgado was not hurt by the search, at least in this criminal proceeding. *Segura v. United States*, 468 U.S. 796 (1984), a factually similar case, is controlling on this point.

Our conclusion that the warrant was not "tainted" by the earlier search might seem to end the case, but it merely brings on the second and bigger complication. Salgado argues that even if Bridges' search did not taint the evidence obtained *only* by virtue of the warrant—that is, the evidence that Bridges had never laid eyes on and therefore could not have been thought to have seized before the execution of the warrant—the evidence that Bridges did see was seized in the moment when Bridges saw it (during what Salgado contends is an illegal search) and thus could not have been seized later by the execution of the warrant. And that evidence, he contends, must be suppressed regardless of the sufficiency of Lett's affidavit.

The idea that when Bridges saw something he "seized" it, so that when a different group of officers came along later and carted it off pursuant to their search warrant they were not "seizing" it, is semantically intriguing but is unrelated to the policies that animate and limit the exclusionary rule that has been grafted onto the Fourth Amendment. The legal issue is whether the fruits of a search and seizure made pursuant to a valid warrant, amply supported by probable cause obtained without violating anybody's rights, should be excluded from a criminal proceeding because another officer made an illegal search, assuming it *was* illegal. We think the answer is "no." The exclusionary rule is a sanction, and sanctions are supposed to be proportioned to the wrongdoing that they punish. The exclusionary rule punishes the government for obtaining evidence by unconstitutional means. It does this by forbidding the government to use such evidence to convict the person whose constitutional rights it violated. It does not go further and forbid the government to convict him on the basis of lawfully obtained evidence. It thus does not seek to make the person whose rights have been violated better off than he would have been if no violation had occurred. We conclude that the exclusionary rule does not require the exclusion of evidence that would have been obtained lawfully, just in order to punish a search that did not harm the defendant in any sense relevant to a criminal proceeding, because the search was not a necessary step in obtaining evidence used to convict him. Since the evidence would have been obtained anyway, the alleged violation of Salgado's rights was not a cause, in the legal sense, of his conviction. Maybe Salgado's privacy was invaded, though in rather an ethereal sense, by the fact that Bridges laid eyes on his drug paraphernalia. But for such invasions the only remedy is a tort remedy unless evidence that would not otherwise have been obtained is used in a criminal proceeding against the owner of the paraphernalia.

Salgado argues, however, that the Supreme Court's decision in *Segura* requires the exclusion of the things Bridges saw. Segura was arrested in the lobby of his apartment building. The arresting officers took him to his apartment and entered it without his permission or that of the other occupants, conducted a cursory "glance around" search similar to Bridges' search in this case, and then secured the premises for 19 hours while a search warrant was obtained and executed. The court of appeals held that the initial search was illegal, because there wasn't the kind of emergency ("exigent circumstances," in legalese) that would justify searching a residence without a warrant (or consent); so the items seen during that search had to be suppressed. The government did not seek further review of this part of the court of appeals' decision. The court of appeals also held, however, that the search warrant, not having been based on the initial (and in the court's view unlawful) search, was valid; hence the items seized pursuant to it, other than the items seen in the initial search, were admissible. The only issue considered by the Supreme Court was the admissibility of these other items. Our case involves the admissibility of the items first seen, then seized. Salgado argues that even if the warrant was not tainted by the search, items seen in that search and thereby (he argues) "seized" could not be "reseized" later, however valid the warrant pursuant to which they were seized.

We disagree that the Supreme Court's decision supports Salgado. The issue of the admissibility of the "seen" items was not before the Supreme Court, those items having been held inadmissible in a part of the court of appeals' decision that the government did not seek further review of. The closest the Supreme Court came to saying that the initial search required exclusion of the items seen in it was in the statement, "As the Court of Appeals held, absent exigent circumstances, the entry may have constituted an illegal *search*, or interference with petitioners' privacy interests, requiring suppression of all evidence observed during the entry." *Id.* at 811, (emphasis in original). This passage not only is dictum (i.e., removable without damage to the rest of the opinion), but it appears in a part of the opinion that only two members of the Court joined, see *id.* at 797.

Thus *Segura* does not answer the question whether illegally seized evidence (if sight is seizure) can ever be cured of its taint by being "reseized" under a lawful warrant—that is, a warrant not dependent on information obtained from the illegal seizure. Suppose one team of officers seizes a piece of evidence illegally for which another team has already obtained, but not yet executed, a lawful search warrant—which is one way to describe the present case. Then even if the initial search and seizure had never taken place the evidence would still have come into the hands of the government lawfully and could have been used in the defendant's trial. There would be no closer causal relationship between the initial search and the introduction of evidence at trial than in a case where the police have two independent sources of information regarding the location of a corpse, one source having been coerced illegally, the other being lawful; evidence of the location, having an independent untainted source, would be admissible. *Silverthorne Lumber Co. v. United States*, 251 U.S. 385, 392 (1920) (Holmes, J.); *Nix v. Williams*, 467 U.S. 431, 441–44 (1984) (dictum); *United States v. Palumbo*, 742 F.2d 656, 659–60 (1st Cir.1984). This principle, which underlies our earlier holding that the seizure of the items not seen by Bridges was not tainted by his search, applies equally to the issue whether the search made it impossible for the items he did see to be seized later pursuant to a valid warrant, on the theory that what is seen is seized and cannot be reseized. The considerations are the same. For constitutional violations that do not increase the victim's risk of being convicted of a crime, because they do not produce evidence that would not have been obtained without a violation, the victim's remedy is a tort suit rather than to have his conviction set aside.

Our conclusion is that whether there is an interim illegal seizure of evidence is irrelevant to the issue of exclusion, provided there is (as there is here) very great confidence that the evidence would have been obtained for use at trial even if there had not been that seizure. This conclusion agrees with that reached by the other courts of appeals in similar cases. See *United States v. Silvestri*, 787 F.2d 736 (1st Cir.1986), and cases cited there. It is also strongly supported by the Supreme Court's recent endorsement, in the *Nix*, case, of the "inevitable discovery" exception to the exclusionary rule, and by the Court's rationale: the police should not be put "in a *worse* position than they would have been in if no unlawful conduct had transpired," 467 U.S. at 445 (emphasis in original). Yet that would be the result if because of Bridges' search the government were forbidden to introduce evidence that would have been obtained if that search had never taken place. A contrary result was reached in *United States v. Griffin*, 502 F.2d 959, 961 (6th Cir.1974) (per curiam), but that was before *Nix* was decided.

We do not suggest that in cases where a warrant is necessary for a lawful search, the government can use evidence seized without a warrant if it can show that it would have gotten a warrant if it had asked for one. That would defeat the purpose of requiring a warrant, which is to interpose a neutral judicial officer between the police and its quarry and also (and maybe more important) to require that the grounds for probable cause be set forth before rather than after the search—after is too easy. To excuse getting a warrant on such grounds would be like saying that lynching a man is okay provided you have a well-grounded belief that if tried he would have been convicted and sentenced to death and the sentence carried out. But in this case the government did obtain a warrant. The only question is whether the warrant should be treated as a nullity regarding those items that Bridges had seen (and maybe should not have seen) earlier. We hold that the items that Bridges saw and that later were seized pursuant to a valid warrant were admissible at Salgado's criminal trial even if Bridges can be said to have "seized" them by seeing them in the course of his search.

We therefore need not consider, and do not decide, whether the search Bridges conducted was lawful. On the rather similar facts of *Segura* the Second Circuit, in the part of its decision not reviewed by the Supreme Court, held that the initial search had been illegal. See *United States v. Segura*, 663 F.2d 411, 414–15 (2d Cir.1981). The Second Circuit was unwilling to embrace the proposition that any time you arrest a drug dealer you can enter his home without a search warrant in order to prevent any confederates who may be lurking there from destroying evidence. Courts take a very hard line against the search of a person's home without a warrant (or consent, but that is not a factor here), and therefore demand a genuine showing of emergency before they will excuse the failure of the police to get a warrant. See, e.g., *Walsh v. Wisconsin*, 466 U.S. 740, 748–54 (1984); *Llaguno v. Mingey*, 763 F.2d 1560, 1564 (7th Cir.1985) (en banc) (plurality opinion). A mere possibility that evidence will be destroyed—a possibility that exists any time a drug dealer is arrested outside of his home or other place of (illicit) business—is not enough. Otherwise the requirement of a warrant would have little meaning in the investigation of drug crimes. A man who lived in New York might be arrested on a trip to Florida, and the police would argue that they could search his home in New York; maybe he had an arrangement with confederates there whereby if he didn't call in at stated intervals they should clear out with all the evidence.

The present case is not quite so stark. The police knew that Salgado had at least one confederate (Bernal), that Salgado's apartment almost certainly was the center of the drug operation and the place where the drugs were stored for distribution, and that Salgado was carrying around a portable telephone, implying that he was in continuous telephonic contact—with Bernal certainly but possibly with someone else as well, someone at the apartment who might become alarmed either if Salgado did not call in or if he did not answer his portable phone when called on it. The person who called Salgado may not have been the customer for the five kilos but an associate of Salgado's, relaying an order received at the apartment. The size of the "order" (assuming Salgado wasn't just puffing) was indicative of a large operation, not a two-man (Salgado and Bernal) operation. Maybe the situation presented an emergency justifying the agents in securing Salgado's apartment while they got a warrant. Some decisions have upheld quick security checks in comparable circumstances. See, e.g., *United States v. Vasquez*, 638 F.2d 507, 531–32 (2d Cir.1980); *United States v. Webster*, 750 F.2d 307, 326–28 (5th Cir.1984). Others, however, have condemned them, see, e.g., *United States v. Veillette*, 778 F.2d 899, 902–03 (1st Cir.1985); *United States v. Kolodziej*, 706 F.2d 590, 595–97 (5th Cir.1983), and maybe this circuit must be ranged on the side of the condemnors on the strength of *United States v. Gamble*, 473 F.2d 1274, 1277 (7th Cir.1973), and *United States v. Cooks*, 493 F.2d 668, 672 (7th Cir.1974). One can argue that the officers in this case should have taken additional steps to find out whether there really was anyone in Salgado's apartment, by asking the janitor or neighbors or simply by listening at the door for signs of activity inside. The counterargument is that judges have no competence to evaluate the minutiae of police practice and the relative effectiveness of alternative tactics for securing potential evidence from destruction.

We need not weigh these arguments in this case. We hold that the items seen by officer Bridges were lawfully seized later pursuant to a valid warrant, even if the initial search was (though we do not decide whether it was) unlawful.

Affirmed.

CALIFORNIA v. ACEVEDO

Supreme Court of the United States, 1991.
500 U.S. 565, 111 S.Ct. 1982, 114 L.Ed.2d 619.

JUSTICE BLACKMUN delivered the opinion of the Court.

This case requires us once again to consider the so-called "automobile exception" to the warrant requirement of the Fourth Amendment and its application to the search of a closed container in the trunk of a car.

I

On October 28, 1987, Officer Coleman of the Santa Ana, Cal., Police Department received a telephone call from a federal drug enforcement agent in Hawaii. The agent informed Coleman that he had seized a package containing marijuana which was to have been delivered to the Federal Express Office in Santa Ana and which was addressed to J.R. Daza at 805 West Stevens Avenue in that city. The agent arranged to send the package to Coleman instead. Coleman then was to take the package to the Federal Express office and arrest the person who arrived to claim it.

Coleman received the package on October 29, verified its contents, and took it to the Senior Operations Manager at the Federal Express office. At about 10:30 a.m. on October 30, a man, who identified himself as Jamie Daza, arrived to claim the package. He accepted it and drove to his apartment on West Stevens. He carried the package into the apartment.

At 11:45 a.m., officers observed Daza leave the apartment and drop the box and paper that had contained the marijuana into a trash bin. Coleman at that point left the scene to get a search warrant. About 12:05 p.m., the officers saw Richard St. George leave the apartment carrying a blue knapsack which appeared to be half full. The officers stopped him as he was driving off, searched the knapsack, and found 1½ pounds of marijuana.

At 12:30 p.m., respondent Charles Steven Acevedo arrived. He entered Daza's apartment, stayed for about 10 minutes, and reappeared carrying a brown paper bag that looked full. The officers noticed that the bag was the size of one of the wrapped marijuana packages sent from Hawaii. Acevedo walked to a silver Honda in the parking lot. He placed the bag in the trunk of the car and started to drive away. Fearing the loss of evidence, officers in a marked police car stopped him. They opened the trunk and the bag, and found marijuana.[1]

Respondent was charged in state court with possession of marijuana for sale. He moved to suppress the marijuana found in the car. The motion was denied. He then pleaded guilty but appealed the denial of the suppression motion.

The California Court of Appeal, Fourth District, concluded that the marijuana found in the paper bag in the car's trunk should have been suppressed. People v. Acevedo, 216 Cal.App.3d 586, 265 Cal.Rptr. 23 (1989). The court concluded that the officers had probable cause to believe that the paper bag contained drugs but lacked probable cause to suspect that Acevedo's car, itself, otherwise contained contraband. Because the officers' probable cause was directed specifically at the bag, the court held that the case was controlled by United States v. Chadwick, 433 U.S. 1 (1977), rather than by United States v. Ross, 456 U.S. 798 (1982). Although the court agreed that the officers could seize the paper bag, it held that, under *Chadwick,* they could not open the bag without first obtaining a warrant for that purpose. The court then recognized "the anomalous nature" of the dichotomy between the rule in *Chadwick* and the rule in *Ross.* That dichotomy dictates that if there is probable cause to search a car, then the entire car—including any closed container found therein—may be searched without a warrant, but if there is probable cause only as to a container in the car, the container may be held but not searched until a warrant is obtained. * * *

We granted certiorari to reexamine the law applicable to a closed container in an automobile, a subject that has troubled courts and law enforcement officers since it was first considered in *Chadwick.*

II

* * * Contemporaneously with the adoption of the Fourth Amendment, the First Congress, and, later, the Second and Fourth Congresses, distinguished between the need for a warrant to search for contraband concealed in "a dwelling house or similar place" and the need for a warrant to search for contraband concealed in a movable vessel. See Carroll v. United States, 267 U.S. 132, 151 (1925). See also Boyd v. United States, 116 U.S. 616, 623–624 (1886). In *Carroll,* this Court established an exception to the warrant requirement for moving vehicles, for it recognized [that a vehicle can be quickly moved out of the locality or jurisdiction in which the warrant must be sought.]

The Court refined the exigency requirement in Chambers v. Maroney, 399 U.S. 42 (1970), when it held that the existence of exigent circumstances was to be determined at the time the automobile is seized.

---

1. When Officer Coleman returned with a warrant, the apartment was searched and bags of marijuana were found there. We are here concerned, of course, only with what was discovered in the automobile.

The car search at issue in *Chambers* took place at the police station, where the vehicle was immobilized, some time after the driver had been arrested. Given probable cause and exigent circumstances at the time the vehicle was first stopped, the Court held that the later warrantless search at the station passed constitutional muster. The validity of the later search derived from the ruling in *Carroll* that an immediate search without a warrant at the moment of seizure would have been permissible. The Court reasoned in *Chambers* that the police could search later whenever they could have searched earlier, had they so chosen. Following *Chambers,* if the police have probable cause to justify a warrantless seizure of an automobile on a public roadway, they may conduct either an immediate or a delayed search of the vehicle.

In United States v. Ross, 456 U.S. 798, decided in 1982, we held that a warrantless search of an automobile under the *Carroll* doctrine could include a search of a container or package found inside the car when such a search was supported by probable cause. The warrantless search of Ross' car occurred after an informant told the police that he had seen Ross complete a drug transaction using drugs stored in the trunk of his car. The police stopped the car, searched it, and discovered in the trunk a brown paper bag containing drugs. * * * In *Ross,* therefore, we clarified the scope of the *Carroll* doctrine as properly including a "probing search" of compartments and containers within the automobile so long as the search is supported by probable cause.

In addition to this clarification, *Ross* distinguished the *Carroll* doctrine from the separate rule that governed the search of closed containers. The Court had announced this separate rule, unique to luggage and other closed packages, bags, and containers, in United States v. Chadwick, 433 U.S. 1 (1977). In *Chadwick,* federal narcotics agents had probable cause to believe that a 200–pound double-locked footlocker contained marijuana. The agents tracked the locker as the defendants removed it from a train and carried it through the station to a waiting car. As soon as the defendants lifted the locker into the trunk of the car, the agents arrested them, seized the locker, and searched it. In this Court, the United States did not contend that the locker's brief contact with the automobile's trunk sufficed to make the *Carroll* doctrine applicable. Rather, the United States urged that the search of movable luggage could be considered analogous to the search of an automobile. 433 U.S., at 11–12.

The Court rejected this argument because, it reasoned, a person expects more privacy in his luggage and personal effects than he does in his automobile. Moreover, it concluded that as "may often not be the case when automobiles are seized," secure storage facilities are usually available when the police seize luggage.

In Arkansas v. Sanders, 442 U.S. 753 (1979), the Court extended *Chadwick's* rule to apply to a suitcase actually being transported in the trunk of a car. In *Sanders,* the police had probable cause to believe a suitcase contained marijuana. They watched as the defendant placed the suitcase in the trunk of a taxi and was driven away. The police pursued the taxi for several blocks, stopped it, found the suitcase in the trunk, and searched it. Although the Court had applied the *Carroll* doctrine to searches of integral parts of the automobile itself (indeed, in *Carroll,* contraband whiskey was in the upholstery of the seats), it did not extend the doctrine to the warrantless search of personal luggage "merely because it was located in an automobile lawfully stopped by the police." Again, the *Sanders* majority stressed the heightened privacy expectation in personal luggage and concluded that the presence of luggage in an automobile did not diminish the owner's expectation of privacy in his personal items. Cf., California v. Carney, 471 U.S. 386 (1985).

In *Ross,* the Court endeavored to distinguish between *Carroll,* which governed the *Ross* automobile search, and *Chadwick,* which governed the *Sanders* automobile search. It held that the *Carroll* doctrine covered searches of automobiles when the police had probable cause to search an entire vehicle but that the *Chadwick* doctrine governed searches of luggage when the officers had probable cause to search only a container within the vehicle. Thus, in a *Ross* situation, the police could conduct a reasonable search under the Fourth Amendment without obtaining a warrant, whereas in a *Sanders* situation, the police had to obtain a warrant before they searched. * * *

Dissenters in *Ross* asked why the suitcase in *Sanders* was "more private, less difficult for police to seize and store, or in any other relevant respect more properly subject to the warrant requirement, than a container that police discover in a probable-cause search of an entire automobile?" We now agree that a container found after a general search of the automobile and a container found in a car after a limited search for the container are equally easy for the police to store and for the suspect to hide or destroy. In fact, we see no principled distinction in terms of either the privacy expectation or the exigent circumstances between the paper bag found by the police in *Ross* and the paper bag found by the police here. Furthermore, by attempting to distinguish between a container for which the police are specifically searching and a container which they come across in a car, we have provided only minimal protection for privacy and have impeded effective law enforcement.

The line between probable cause to search a vehicle and probable cause to search a package in that vehicle is not always clear, and separate rules that govern the two objects to be searched may enable the police to broaden their power to make warrantless searches and disserve privacy interests. * * * At the moment when officers stop an automobile, it may be less than clear whether they suspect with a high degree of certainty that the vehicle contains drugs in a bag or simply contains drugs. If the police know that they may open a bag only if they are actually searching the entire car, they may search more extensively than they otherwise would in order to establish the general probable cause required by Ross.

Such a situation is not far fetched. In United States v. Johns, 469 U.S. 478 (1985), customs agents saw two trucks drive to a private airstrip and approach two small planes. The agents drew near the trucks, smelled marijuana, and then saw in the backs of the trucks packages wrapped in a manner that marijuana smugglers customarily employed. The agents took the trucks to headquarters and searched the packages without a warrant. Relying on *Chadwick,* the defendants argued that the search was unlawful. The defendants contended that *Ross* was inapplicable because the agents lacked probable cause to search anything but the packages themselves and supported this contention by noting that a search of the entire vehicle never occurred. We rejected that argument and found *Chadwick* and *Sanders* inapposite because the agents had probable cause to search the entire body of each truck, although they had chosen not to do so. We cannot see the benefit of a rule that requires law enforcement officers to conduct a more intrusive search in order to justify a less intrusive one.

To the extent that the *Chadwick–Sanders* rule protects privacy, its protection is minimal. Law enforcement officers may seize a container and hold it until they obtain a search warrant. Since the police, by hypothesis, have probable cause to seize the property, we can assume that a warrant will be routinely forthcoming in the overwhelming majority of cases. And the police often will be able to search containers without a warrant, despite the *Chadwick–Sanders* rule, as a search incident to a lawful arrest. * * *

Finally, the search of a paper bag intrudes far less on individual privacy than does the incursion sanctioned long ago in *Carroll.* * * *

Until today, this Court has drawn a curious line between the search of an automobile that coincidentally turns up a container and the search of a container that coincidentally turns up in an automobile. The protections of the Fourth Amendment must not turn on such coincidences. We therefore interpret *Carroll* as providing one rule to govern all automobile searches. The police may search an automobile and the containers within it where they have probable cause to believe contraband or evidence is contained.

The judgment of the California Court of Appeal is reversed and the case is remanded to that court for further proceedings not inconsistent with this opinion.

Justice Scalia, concurring in the judgment.

I agree with the dissent that it is anomalous for a briefcase to be protected by the "general requirement" of a prior warrant when it is being carried along the street, but for that same briefcase to become unprotected as soon as it is carried into an automobile. On the other hand, I agree with the Court that it would be anomalous for a locked compartment in an automobile to be unprotected by the "general requirement" of a prior warrant, but for an unlocked briefcase within the automobile to be protected. * * *

I would reverse the judgment in the present case, not because a closed container carried inside a car becomes subject to the "automobile" exception to the general warrant requirement, but because the search of a closed container, outside a privately owned building, with probable cause to believe that the container contains contraband, and when it in fact does contain contraband, is not one of those searches whose Fourth Amendment reasonableness depends upon a warrant. For that reason I concur in the judgment of the Court.

JUSTICE STEVENS, with whom JUSTICE MARSHALL joins, dissenting.

* * * To the extent there was any "anomaly" in our prior jurisprudence, the Court has "cured" it at the expense of creating a more serious paradox. For, surely it is anomalous to prohibit a search of a briefcase while the owner is carrying it exposed on a public street yet to permit a search once the owner has placed the briefcase in the locked trunk of his car. One's privacy interest in one's luggage can certainly not be diminished by one's removing it from a public thoroughfare and placing it— out of sight—in a privately owned vehicle. Nor is the danger that evidence will escape increased if the luggage is in a car rather than on the street. In either location, if the police have probable cause, they are authorized to seize the luggage and to detain it until they obtain judicial approval for a search. Any line demarking an exception to the warrant requirement will appear blurred at the edges, but the Court has certainly erred if it believes that, by erasing one line and drawing another, it has drawn a clearer boundary. * * *

The Court's statement that *Chadwick* and *Sanders* provide only "minimal protection to privacy," is also unpersuasive. Every citizen clearly has an interest in the privacy of the contents of his or her luggage, briefcase, handbag or any other container that conceals private papers and effects from public scrutiny. That privacy interest has been recognized repeatedly in cases spanning more than a century.

Under the Court's holding today, the privacy interest that protects the contents of a suitcase or a briefcase from a warrantless search when it is in public view simply vanishes when its owner climbs into a taxicab. Unquestionably, the rejection of the *Sanders* line of cases by today's decision will result in a significant loss of individual privacy. * * *

It is too early to know how much freedom America has lost today. The magnitude of the loss is, however, not nearly as significant as the Court's willingness to inflict it without even a colorable basis for its rejection of prior law.

I respectfully dissent.

COLORADO v. BERTINE

Supreme Court of the United States, 1987.
479 U.S. 367, 107 S.Ct. 738, 93 L.Ed.2d 739.

CHIEF JUSTICE REHNQUIST delivered the opinion of the Court.

On February 10, 1984, a police officer in Boulder, Colorado arrested respondent Steven Lee Bertine for driving while under the influence of alcohol. After Bertine was taken into custody and before the arrival of a tow truck to take Bertine's van to an impoundment lot, a backup officer inventoried the contents of the van. The officer opened a closed backpack in which he found controlled substances, cocaine paraphernalia, and a large amount of cash. Bertine was subsequently charged with driving while under the influence of alcohol, unlawful possession of cocaine with intent to dispense, sell, and distribute, and unlawful possession of methaqualone. We are asked to decide whether the Fourth Amendment prohibits the State from proving these charges with the evidence discovered during the inventory of Bertine's van. We hold that it does not.

The backup officer inventoried the van in accordance with local police procedures, which require a detailed inspection and inventory of impounded vehicles. He found the backpack directly behind the front seat of the van. Inside the pack, the officer observed a nylon bag containing metal canisters. Opening the canisters, the officer discovered that they contained cocaine, methaqualone tablets, cocaine paraphernalia, and $700 in cash. In an outside zippered pouch of the backpack, he also found $210 in cash in a sealed envelope. After completing the inventory of the van, the officer had the van towed to an impound lot and brought the backpack, money, and contraband to the police station.

After Bertine was charged with the offenses described above, he moved to suppress the evidence found during the inventory search on the ground, *inter alia*, that the search of the closed backpack and containers exceeded the permissible scope of such a search under the Fourth Amendment. The Colorado trial court ruled that probable cause supported Bertine's arrest and that the police officers had made the decisions to impound the vehicle and to conduct a thorough inventory search in good faith. Although noting that the inventory of the vehicle was performed in a "somewhat slipshod" manner, the District Court concluded that "the search of the backpack was done for the purpose of protecting the owner's property, protection of the police from subsequent claims of loss or stolen property, and the protection of the police from dangerous instrumentalities." The court observed that the standard procedures for impounding vehicles mandated a "detailed inventory involving the opening of containers and the listing of [their] contents." Based on these findings, the court determined that the inventory search did not violate Bertine's rights under Fourth Amendment of the United States Constitution. The court, nevertheless, granted Bertine's motion to suppress, holding that the inventory search violated the Colorado Constitution.

On the State's interlocutory appeal, the Supreme Court of Colorado affirmed. *People v. Bertine*, 706 P.2d 411 (1985). In contrast to the District Court, however, the Colorado Supreme Court premised its ruling on the United States Constitution. The court recognized that in *South Dakota v. Opperman*, 428 U.S. 364 (1976), we had held inventory searches of automobiles to be consistent with the Fourth Amendment, and that in *Illinois v. Lafayette*, 462 U.S. 640 (1983), we had held that the inventory search of personal effects of an arrestee at a police station was also permissible under that Amendment. The Supreme Court of Colorado felt, however, that our decisions in *Arkansas v. Sanders*, 442 U.S. 753 (1979), and *United States v. Chadwick*, 433 U.S. 1 (1977), holding searches of closed trunks and suitcases to violate the Fourth Amendment, meant that *Opperman* and *Lafayette* did not govern this case.

* * *

* * * Colorado Supreme Court's reliance on *Arkansas v. Sanders* and *United States v. Chadwick* was incorrect. Both of these cases concerned searches solely for the purpose of investigating criminal conduct, with the validity of the searches therefore dependent on the application of the probable cause and warrant requirements of the Fourth Amendment.

By contrast, an inventory search may be "reasonable" under the Fourth Amendment even though it is not conducted pursuant to warrant based upon probable cause. In *Opperman*, this Court assessed the reasonableness of an inventory search of the glove compartment in an abandoned automobile impounded by the police. We found that inventory procedures serve to protect an owner's property while it is in the custody of the police, to insure against claims of lost, stolen, or vandalized property, and to guard the police from danger. In light of these strong governmental interests and the diminished expectation of privacy in an automobile, we upheld the search. In reaching this decision, we observed that our cases accorded deference to police caretaking procedures designed to secure and protect vehicles and their contents within police custody.

In our more recent decision, *Lafayette*, a police officer conducted an inventory search of the contents of a shoulder bag in the possession of an individual being taken into custody. In deciding whether this search was reasonable, we recognized that the search served legitimate governmental interests similar to those identified in *Opperman*. We determined that those interests outweighed the individual's Fourth Amendment interests and upheld the search.

In the present case, as in *Opperman* and *Lafayette*, there was no showing that the police, who were following standardized procedures, acted in bad faith or for the sole purpose of investigation. In addition, the governmental interests justifying the inventory searches in *Opperman* and *Lafayette* are nearly the same as those which obtain here. In each case, the police were potentially responsible for the property taken into their custody. By securing the property, the police protected the property from unauthorized interference. Knowledge of the precise nature of the property helped guard against claims of theft, vandalism, or negligence. Such knowledge also helped to avert any danger to police or others that may have been posed by the property.

The Supreme Court of Colorado opined that *Lafayette* was not controlling here because there was no danger of introducing contraband or weapons into a jail facility. Our opinion in *Lafayette*, however, did not suggest that the station-house setting of the inventory search was critical to our holding in that case. Both in the present case and in *Lafayette*, the common governmental interests described above were served by the inventory searches.

The Supreme Court of Colorado also expressed the view that the search in this case was unreasonable because Bertine's van was towed to a secure, lighted facility and because Bertine himself could have been offered the opportunity to make other arrangements for the safekeeping of his property. But the security of the storage facility does not completely eliminate the need for inventorying; the police may still wish to protect themselves or the owners of the lot against false claims of theft or dangerous instrumentalities. And while giving Bertine an opportunity to make alternate arrangements would undoubtedly have been possible, we said in *Lafayette*:

> "[t]he real question is not what 'could have been achieved,' but whether the Fourth Amendment *requires* such steps * * * The reasonableness of any particular governmental activity does not necessarily or invariably turn on the existence of alternative 'less intrusive' means." *Lafayette*, 462 U.S. at 647.

We conclude that here, as in *Lafayette*, reasonable police regulations relating to inventory procedures administered in good faith satisfy the Fourth Amendment, even though courts might as a matter of hindsight be able to devise equally reasonable rules requiring a different procedure.[2]

* * *

Bertine finally argues that the inventory search of his van was unconstitutional because departmental regulations gave the police officers discretion to choose between impounding his van and parking and locking it in a public parking place. The Supreme Court of Colorado did not rely on this argument in reaching its conclusion, and we reject it. Nothing in *Opperman* or *Lafayette* prohibits the exercise of police discretion so long as that discretion is exercised according to standard criteria and on the basis of something other than suspicion of evidence of criminal activity. Here, the discretion afforded the Boulder police was exercised in light of standardized criteria, related to the feasibility and appropriateness of parking and locking a vehicle rather than impounding

2. We emphasize that, in this case, the trial court found that the police department's procedures mandated the opening of closed containers and the listing of their contents. Our decisions have always adhered to the requirement that inventories be conducted according to standardized criteria.

By quoting a portion of the Colorado Supreme Court's decision out of context, the dissent suggests that the inventory here was not authorized by the standard procedures of the Boulder Police Department. Yet that court specifically stated that the procedure followed here was "officially authorized." *People v. Bertine*, 706 P.2d 411, 413, n. 2 (1985). In addition, the court did not disturb the trial court's finding that the police procedures for impounding vehicles required a detailed inventory of Bertine's van.

it. There was no showing that the police chose to impound Bertine's van in order to investigate suspected criminal activity.

While both *Opperman* and *Lafayette* are distinguishable from the present case on their facts, we think that the principles enunciated in those cases govern the present one. The judgment of the Supreme Court of Colorado is therefore *Reversed*.

JUSTICE BLACKMUN, with whom JUSTICE POWELL and JUSTICE O'CONNOR join, concurring.

The Court today holds that police officers may open closed containers while conducting a routine inventory search of an impounded vehicle. I join the Court's opinion, but write separately to underscore the importance of having such inventories conducted only pursuant to standardized police procedures. The underlying rationale for allowing an inventory exception to the Fourth Amendment warrant rule is that police officers are not vested with discretion to determine the scope of the inventory search. This absence of discretion ensures that inventory searches will not be used as a purposeful and general means of discovering evidence of crime. Thus, it is permissible for police officers to open closed containers in an inventory search only if they are following standard police procedures that mandate the opening of such containers in every impounded vehicle. As the Court emphasizes, the trial court in this case found that the police department's standard procedures did mandate the opening of closed containers and the listing of their contents. See *ante*, n. 6.

JUSTICE MARSHALL, with whom JUSTICE BRENNAN joins, dissenting.
* * *

As the Court acknowledges, inventory searches are reasonable only if conducted according to standardized procedures. In both *Opperman* and *Lafayette*, the Court relied on the absence of police discretion in determining that the inventory searches in question were reasonable.
* * *

The Court today attempts to evade these clear prohibitions on unfettered police discretion by declaring that "the discretion afforded the Boulder police was exercised in light of standardized criteria, related to the feasibility and appropriateness of parking and locking a vehicle rather than impounding it." This vital assertion is flatly contradicted by the record in this case. The officer who conducted the inventory, Officer Reichenbach, testified at the suppression hearing that the decision not to "park and lock" respondent's vehicle was his "own individual discretionary decision." Indeed, application of these supposedly standardized "criteria" upon which the Court so heavily relies would have yielded a different result in this case. Since there was ample public parking adjacent to the intersection where respondent was stopped, consideration of "feasibility" would certainly have militated in favor of the "park and lock" option, not against it. I do not comprehend how consideration of "appropriateness" serves to channel a field officer's discretion; nonetheless, the "park and lock" option would seem particularly appropriate in this case, where respondent was stopped for a traffic offense and was not likely to be in custody for a significant length of time.

Indeed, the record indicates that *no* standardized criteria limit a Boulder police officer's discretion. According to a departmental directive, after placing a driver under arrest, an officer has three options for disposing of the vehicle. First, he can allow a third party to take custody. Second, the officer or the driver (depending on the nature of the arrest) may take the car to the nearest public parking facility, lock it, and take the keys. Finally, the officer can do what was done in this case: impound the vehicle, and search and inventory its contents, including closed containers.

Under the first option, the police have no occasion to search the automobile. Under the "park and lock" option, "[c]losed containers that give no indication of containing either valuables or a weapon *may not be opened and the contents searched* (i.e., inventoried)." Only if the police choose the third option are they entitled to search closed containers in the vehicle. Where the vehicle is not itself evidence of a crime, as in this case, the police apparently have totally unbridled discretion as to which procedure to use. * * *

Once a Boulder police officer has made this initial completely discretionary decision to impound a vehicle, he is given little guidance as to which areas to search and what sort of items to inventory. The arresting officer, Officer Toporek, testified at the suppression hearing as to what items would be inventoried: "That would I think be very individualistic as far as what an officer may or may not go into. I think whatever arouses his suspicious [*sic*] as far as what may be contained in any type of article in the car." * * *

Officer Reichenbach's inventory in this case would not have protected the police against claims lodged by respondent, false or otherwise. Indeed, the trial court's characterization of the inventory as "slipshod" is the height of understatement. For example, Officer Reichenbach failed to list $150 in cash found in respondent's wallet or the contents of a sealed envelope marked "rent," $210, in the relevant section of the property form. His reports make no reference to other items of value, including respondent's credit cards, and a converter, a hydraulic jack, and a set of tire chains, worth a total of $125. The $700 in cash found in respondent's backpack, along with the contraband, appeared only on a property form completed later by someone other than Officer Reichenbach. The interior of the vehicle was left in disarray, and the officer "inadvertently" retained respondent's keys—including his house keys— for two days following his arrest.

* * *

In *Lafayette*, we upheld a station house inventory search of an arrestee's shoulder bag. Notwithstanding the Court's assertions to the contrary, the inventory in that case *was* justified primarily by compelling governmental interests unique to the station house, preincarceration context. There is a powerful interest in preventing the introduction of contraband or weapons into a jail. "Arrested persons have also been known to injure themselves—or others—with belts, knives, drugs, or other items on their person while being detained. Dangerous instrumentalities—such as razor blades, bombs, or weapons—can be concealed in innocent-looking articles taken from the arrestee's possession." 462 U.S., at 646. Removing such items from persons about to be incarcerated is necessary to reasonable jail security; once these items have been identified and removed, "inventorying them is an entirely reasonable administrative procedure." *Id.*, at 646. Although *Lafayette* also involved the property justifications relied on in *Opperman*, I do not believe it can fairly be read to expand the scope of inventory searches where the pressing security concerns of the station house are absent.

Not only are the government's interests weaker here than in *Opperman* and *Lafayette*, but respondent's privacy interest is greater. In upholding the search in *Opperman*, the Court emphasized the fact that the defendant had a diminished expectation of privacy in his automobile, due to "pervasive and continuing governmental regulation and controls, including periodic inspection and licensing requirements" and "the obviously public nature of automobile travel." 428 U.S., at 368. Similarly, in *Lafayette*, the Court emphasized the fact that the defendant was in custody at the time the inventory took place.

Here the Court completely ignores respondent's expectation of privacy in his backpack. Whatever his expectation of privacy in his automobile generally, our prior decisions clearly establish that he retained a reasonable expectation of privacy in the backpack and its contents. [Citations] Thus, even if the governmental interests in this case were the same as those in *Opperman*, they would nonetheless be outweighed by respondent's comparatively greater expectation of privacy in his luggage.

In *Coolidge v. New Hampshire*, 403 U.S. 443, 461–462 (1971), a plurality of this Court stated: "The word 'automobile' is not a talisman in whose presence the Fourth Amendment fades away and disappears." By upholding the search in this case, the Court not only ignores that principle, but creates another talisman to overcome the requirements of the Fourth Amendment—the term "inventory." Accordingly, I dissent.

Note

In Florida v. Wells, 495 U.S. 1 (1990), the defendant was arrested for drunk driving and gave Florida Highway Patrol officers consent to open the trunk of his impounded car. An inventory search of the car turned up two marijuana cigarette butts in an ashtray and a locked suitcase in the trunk. Officers forced open the suitcase and found inside a garbage bag containing a considerable amount of marijuana. (The evidence at the suppression hearing suggested that the purpose of this "inventory" search was to look for drugs rather than to safeguard property.) The Florida Supreme Court held that the marijuana should have been suppressed because the Highway Patrol had no policy concerning the opening of closed containers found in inventory searches. The Florida court interpreted *Colorado v. Bertine* as requiring police to mandate either that all containers be opened during inventory searches or that no containers be opened, thus leaving no discretion to individual officers.

The Supreme Court affirmed because the police agency had no policy whatever governing the opening of containers in inventory searches, but the 5–4 majority opinion by Justice Rehnquist denied that *Bertine* imposed an "all or nothing" rule. The majority thought that "it would be equally permissible, for example, to allow the opening of closed containers whose contents officers determine they are unable to ascertain from examining the containers' exteriors." The four concurring Justices objected to giving officers such a degree of discretion.

MICHIGAN v. CLIFFORD

Supreme Court of the United States, 1984.
464 U.S. 287, 104 S.Ct. 641, 78 L.Ed.2d 477.

JUSTICE POWELL announced the judgment of the Court and delivered an opinion in which JUSTICES BRENNAN, WHITE, and MARSHALL joined.

This case presents questions as to the authority of arson investigators, in the absence of exigent circumstances or consent, to enter a private residence without a warrant to investigate the cause of a recent fire. * * *

II

In the early morning hours of October 18, 1980, a fire erupted at the Clifford home. The Cliffords were out of town on a camping trip at the time. The fire was reported to the Detroit Fire Department, and fire units arrived on the scene at about 5:42 a.m. The fire was extinguished and all fire officials and police left the premises at 7:04 a.m.

At 8:00 a.m. on the morning of the fire, Lieutenant Beyer, a fire investigator with the arson section of the Detroit Fire Department, received instructions to investigate the Clifford fire. He was informed that the Fire Department suspected arson. Because he had other assignments, Lieutenant Beyer did not proceed immediately to the Clifford residence. He and his partner finally arrived at the scene of the fire about 1:00 p.m. on October 18.

When they arrived, they found a work crew on the scene. The crew was boarding up the house and pumping some six inches of water out of the basement. A neighbor told the investigators that he had called Clifford and had been instructed to request the Cliffords' insurance agent to send a boarding crew out to secure the house. The neighbor also advised that the Cliffords did not plan to return that day. While the investigators waited for the water to be pumped out, they found a Coleman fuel can in the driveway that was seized and marked as evidence.[1]

---

1. The can had been found in the basement by the fire officials who had fought   the blaze. The firemen removed the can and

By 1:30 p.m., the water had been pumped out of the basement and Lieutenant Beyer and his partner, without obtaining consent or an administrative warrant, entered the Clifford residence and began their investigation into the cause of the fire. Their search began in the basement and they quickly confirmed that the fire had originated there beneath the basement stairway. They detected a strong odor of fuel throughout the basement, and found two more Coleman fuel cans beneath the stairway. As they dug through the debris, the investigators also found a crock pot with attached wires leading to an electrical timer that was plugged into an outlet a few feet away. The timer was set to turn on at approximately 3:45 a.m. and to turn back off at approximately 9:00 a.m. It had stopped somewhere between 4:00 and 4:30 a.m. All of this evidence was seized and marked.

After determining that the fire had originated in the basement, Lieutenant Beyer and his partner searched the remainder of the house. The warrantless search that followed was extensive and thorough. The investigators called in a photographer to take pictures throughout the house. They searched through drawers and closets and found them full of old clothes. They inspected the rooms and noted that there were nails on the walls but no pictures. They found wiring and cassettes for a video tape machine but no machine.

Respondents moved to exclude all exhibits and testimony based on the basement and upstairs searches on the ground that they were searches to gather evidence of arson, that they were conducted without a warrant, consent, or exigent circumstances, and that they therefore were *per se* unreasonable under the Fourth and Fourteenth Amendments. Petitioner, on the other hand, argues that the entire search was reasonable and should be exempt from the warrant requirement.

III

In its petition for certiorari, the State does not challenge the state court's finding that there were no exigent circumstances justifying the search of the Clifford home. Instead, it asks us to exempt from the warrant requirement all administrative investigations into the cause and origin of a fire. We decline to do so.

In *Michigan v. Tyler*, 436 U.S. 499 (1978), we restated the Court's position that administrative searches generally require warrants. We reaffirm that view again today. Except in certain carefully defined classes of cases,[2] the nonconsensual entry and search of property is governed by the warrant requirement of the Fourth and Fourteenth Amendments. The constitutionality of warrantless and nonconsensual entries onto fire-damaged premises, therefore, normally turns on several factors: whether there are legitimate privacy interests in the fire-dam-

---

put it by the side door where Lieutenant Beyer discovered it on his arrival.

2. See *e.g. Donovan v. Dewey*, 452 U.S. 594 (1981) (heavily regulated business); *United States v. Biswell*, 406 U.S. 311 (1972) (same); *Colonnade v. United States*, 397 U.S. 72 (1970) (same). The exceptions to the warrant requirement recognized in these cases are not applicable to the warrantless search in this case.

aged property that are protected by the Fourth Amendment; whether exigent circumstances justify the government intrusion regardless of any reasonable expectations of privacy; and, whether the object of the search is to determine the cause of the fire or to gather evidence of criminal activity.

A

We observed in *Tyler* that reasonable privacy expectations may remain in fire-damaged premises. * * * Privacy expectations will vary with the type of property, the amount of fire damage, the prior and continued use of the premises, and in some cases the owner's efforts to secure it against intruders. Some fires may be so devastating that no reasonable privacy interests remain in the ash and ruins, regardless of the owner's subjective expectations. * * * If reasonable privacy interests remain in the fire-damaged property, the warrant requirement applies, and any official entry must be made pursuant to a warrant in the absence of consent or exigent circumstances.

B

A burning building of course creates an exigency that justifies a warrantless entry by fire officials to fight the blaze. Moreover, in *Tyler* we held that once in the building, officials need no warrant to *remain* for a reasonable time to investigate the cause of the blaze after it has been extinguished. Where, however, reasonable expectations of privacy remain in the fire-damaged property, additional investigations begun after the fire has been extinguished and fire and police officials have left the scene, generally must be made pursuant to a warrant or the identification of some new exigency.

The aftermath of a fire often presents exigencies that will not tolerate the delay necessary to obtain a warrant or to secure the owner's consent to inspect fire-damaged premises.[4] Because determining the cause and origin of a fire serves a compelling public interest, the warrant requirement does not apply in such cases.

C

If a warrant is necessary, the object of the search determines the type of warrant required. If the primary object is to determine the cause and origin of a recent fire, an administrative warrant will suffice.[5] To obtain such a warrant, fire officials need show only that a fire of undetermined origin has occurred on the premises, that the scope of the proposed search is reasonable and will not intrude unnecessarily on the fire victim's privacy, and that the search will be executed at a reasonable and convenient time.

---

4. For example, an immediate threat that the blaze might rekindle presents an exigency that would justify a warrantless and nonconsensual post-fire investigation. Immediate investigation may also be necessary to preserve evidence from intentional or accidental destruction.

5. Probable cause to issue an administrative warrant exists if reasonable legislative, administrative, or judicially prescribed standards for conducting an inspection are satisfied with respect to a particular dwelling.

If the primary object of the search is to gather evidence of criminal activity, a criminal search warrant may be obtained only on a showing of probable cause to believe that relevant evidence will be found in the place to be searched. If evidence of criminal activity is discovered during the course of a valid administrative search, it may be seized under the "plain view" doctrine. *Coolidge v. New Hampshire*, 403 U.S. 443, 465–466 (1971). This evidence then may be used to establish probable cause to obtain a criminal search warrant. Fire officials may not, however, rely on this evidence to expand the scope of their administrative search without first making a successful showing of probable cause to an independent judicial officer.

The object of the search is important even if exigent circumstances exist. Circumstances that justify a warrantless search for the cause of a fire may not justify a search to gather evidence of criminal activity once that cause has been determined. If, for example, the administrative search is justified by the immediate need to ensure against rekindling, the scope of the search may be no broader than reasonably necessary to achieve its end. A search to gather evidence of criminal activity not in plain view must be made pursuant to a criminal warrant upon a traditional showing of probable cause.

The searches of the Clifford home, at least arguably, can be viewed as two separate ones: the delayed search of the basement area, followed by the extensive search of the residential portion of the house. We now apply the principles outlined above to each of these searches.

[The plurality held (1) that the Cliffords retained reasonable privacy interests in their fire-damaged home; (2) that the post-fire search of the basement was not a mere continuation of the earlier entry to extinguish the blaze; (3) that the arson investigator therefore should have obtained an administrative warrant before entering; and (4) that the search of the upper portion of the house (after the cause of the fire was known) was for the purpose of gathering evidence of arson and thus required a criminal search warrant. Accordingly, all the challenged evidence was inadmissible except the single fuel can found in the driveway.]

JUSTICE STEVENS, concurring in the judgment. * * *

There is unanimity within the Court on three general propositions regarding the scope of Fourth Amendment protection afforded to the owner of a fire-damaged building. No one questions the right of the firefighters to make a forceful, unannounced, nonconsensual, warrantless entry into a burning building. The reasonableness of such an entry is too plain to require explanation. Nor is there any disagreement concerning the firemen's right to remain on the premises, not only until the fire has been extinguished and they are satisfied that there is no danger of rekindling, but also while they continue to investigate the cause of the fire. We are also unanimous in our opinion that after investigators have determined the cause of the fire and located the place it originated, a search of other portions of the premises may be conducted only pursuant to a warrant, issued upon probable cause that a crime has been committed, and specifically describing the places to be searched and the items to be seized. The issues that divide us in this case are (1) whether the entry by Lieutenant Beyer and his partner at 1:30 p.m. should be regarded as a continuation of the original entry or a separate post-fire search, and (2) whether a warrantless entry to make a post-fire investigation into the cause of a fire without the owner's consent is constitutional. * * *

[I] would require the fire investigator to obtain a traditional criminal search warrant in order to make an unannounced entry, but would characterize a warrantless entry as reasonable whenever the inspector had either given the owner sufficient advance notice to enable him or an agent to be present, or had made a reasonable effort to do so. * * * Advance notice of the search is the best safeguard of the owner's legitimate interests in the privacy of his premises, allowing him to place certain possessions he would legitimately prefer strangers not to see out of sight, and permitting him to be present during the search to assure that it does not exceed reasonable bounds. Moreover, the risk of unexplained harm or loss to the owner's personal effects would be minimized and the owner would have an opportunity to respond to questions about the premises or to volunteer relevant information that might assist the investigators. It is true, of course, that advance notice would increase somewhat the likelihood that a guilty owner would conceal or destroy relevant evidence, but it seems fair to assume that the criminal will diligently attempt to cover his traces in all events. In any event, if probable cause to believe that the owner committed arson is lacking, and if the justifications for a general policy of unannounced spot inspections that obtain in some regulatory contexts are also lacking, a mere suspicion that an individual has engaged in criminal activity is insufficient to justify the intrusion on an individual's privacy that an unannounced, potentially forceful entry entails. * * *

In this case, an argument may be made that the notice requirement is inapplicable because the owners were out of town. But no attempt whatever was made to provide them with notice, or even to prove that it would have been futile to do so. The record does not foreclose the possibility that an effort to advise them, possibly through the same party that notified the representatives of the insurance company to board up the building, might well have resulted in a request that a friend or neighbor be present in the house while the search was carried out and thus might have avoided the plainly improper search of the entire premises after the cause of the fire had already been identified.

I therefore conclude that the search in this case was unreasonable in contravention of the Fourth Amendment because the investigators made no effort to provide fair notice of the inspection to the owners of the premises. Accordingly, I concur in the Court's judgment.

JUSTICE REHNQUIST, with whom THE CHIEF JUSTICE, JUSTICE BLACKMUN, and JUSTICE O'CONNOR join, dissenting.

* * * I would hold that the "exigent circumstances" doctrine enunciated in *Tyler* authorized the search of the basement of the Clifford home, although the remaining parts of the house could not have been searched without the issuance of a warrant issued upon probable cause. * * *

* * * Under the emergency doctrine, it is beyond dispute that fire fighters may enter a building in order to extinguish the flames. In their efforts to control the blaze fire fighters may knock in doors and windows, chop holes in roofs and walls, and generally take full control of a structure to extinguish a fire. In the aftermath of a fire an individual is unlikely to have much concern over the limited intrusion of a fire inspector coming into his premises to learn why there had been a fire. Fire victims, unlike occupants at ordinary times, generally expect and welcome the intrusions of fire, police, and medical officials in the period following a fire. Likewise, as here, relative strangers such as insurance agents will frequently have authority to enter the structure. In these circumstances, the intrusion of the fire inspector is hardly a new or substantially different intrusion from that which occurred when the fire fighters first arrived to extinguish the flames. Instead, it is analogous to intrusions of medical officials and insurance investigators who may arrive at the scene of the fire shortly after its origin.

Ample justification exists for a state or municipality to authorize a fire inspection program that would permit fire inspectors to enter premises to determine the cause and origin of the fire. But in no real sense can the investigation of the Cliffords' home be considered the result of the unbridled discretion of the city fire investigators who came to the Cliffords' home. No justification existed to inspect the Cliffords' home until there was a fire. The fire investigators were not authorized to enter the Cliffords' home until the happening of some fortuitous or exigent event over which they had no control. Thus, if the warrant requirement exists to prevent individuals from being subjected to an unfettered power of government officials to initiate a search, a warrant is simply not required in these circumstances to limit the authority of a fire investigator, so long as his authority to inspect is contingent upon the happening of an event over which he has no control.

In my view, the utility of requiring a magistrate to evaluate the grounds for a search following a fire is so limited that the incidental protection of an individual's privacy interests simply does not justify imposing a warrant requirement. Here the inspection was conducted within a short time of extinguishing of the flames, while the owners were away from the premises, and before the premises had been fully secured from trespass. In these circumstances the search of the basement to determine the cause and origin of the fire was reasonable.[6]

6. There may be some justification for requiring the inspectors to contact or attempt to contact the building's owners of the inspection. But where, as here, the owners were out of town, it does not appear unreasonable to have conducted the inspection without prior notice to the owners.

THOMPSON v. LOUISIANA

Supreme Court of the United States, 1984.
469 U.S. 17, 105 S.Ct. 409, 83 L.Ed.2d 246.

PER CURIAM.

[Petitioner Thompson's daughter called police to report a homicide at the family home. When the deputies arrived, they found petitioner's husband dead of a gunshot wound in a bedroom and petitioner lying unconscious in another bedroom due to an apparent drug overdose. According to the daughter, Thompson had shot her husband, taken pills in a suicide attempt, and then changed her mind and called for help. Upon arrival the deputies immediately transported Thompson to a hospital and secured the premises. Thirty-five minutes later two homicide investigators arrived and began what they later described as "a general exploratory search for evidence of a crime." The search lasted about two hours, and covered every room of the house.

Indicted for murder, Thompson moved to suppress three items discovered during the search: (1) a pistol found inside a chest of drawers in the same room as her husband's body; (2) a torn up note found in a wastepaper basket in an adjoining bathroom; and (3) an apparent suicide note found inside an envelope on the top of a chest of drawers. A divided Louisiana Supreme Court held all this evidence to be admissible.]

Although the homicide investigators in this case may well have had probable cause to search the premises, it is undisputed that they did not obtain a warrant. Therefore, for the search to be valid, it must fall within one of the narrow and specifically delineated exceptions to the warrant requirement. In *Mincey v. Arizona*, 437 U.S. 385 (1978), we unanimously rejected the contention that one of the exceptions to the warrant clause is a "murder scene exception." Although we noted that police may make warrantless entries on premises where "they reasonably believe that a person within is in need of immediate aid," and that "they may make a prompt warrantless search of the area to see if there are other victims or if a killer is still on the premises," we held that "the 'murder scene exception' * * * is inconsistent with the Fourth and Fourteenth Amendments—that the warrantless search of Mincey's apartment was not constitutionally permissible simply because a homicide had recently occurred there." *Mincey* is squarely on point in the instant case.

The Louisiana Supreme Court attempted to distinguish *Mincey* in several ways. The court noted that *Mincey* involved a four-day search of the premises, while the search in this case took only two hours and was conducted on the same day as the murder. Although we agree that the scope of the intrusion was certainly greater in *Mincey* than here, nothing in *Mincey* turned on the length of time taken in the search or the date on which it was conducted. A two-hour general search remains a significant intrusion on petitioner's privacy and therefore may only be conducted subject to the constraints—including the warrant requirement—of the Fourth Amendment.

The Louisiana Court also believed that petitioner had a "diminished" expectation of privacy in her home, thus validating a search that otherwise would have been unconstitutional. The court noted that petitioner telephoned her daughter to request assistance. The daughter then called the police and let them in to the residence. These facts, according to the court, demonstrated a diminished expectation of privacy in petitioner's dwelling and therefore legitimated the warrantless search.

Petitioner's attempt to get medical assistance does not evidence a diminished expectation of privacy on her part. To be sure, this action would have justified the authorities in seizing evidence under the plain view doctrine while they were in petitioner's house to offer her assistance. In addition, the same doctrine may justify seizure of evidence obtained in the limited "victim-or-suspect" search discussed in *Mincey*. However, the evidence at issue here was not discovered in plain view while the police were assisting petitioner to the hospital, nor was it discovered during the "victim-or-suspect" search that had been completed by the time the homicide investigators arrived. Petitioner's call for help can hardly be seen as an invitation to the general public that would have converted her home into the sort of public place for which no warrant to search would be necessary. Therefore, the Louisiana Supreme Court's diminished expectation of privacy argument fails to distinguish this case from *Mincey*.

The State contends that there was a sufficient element of consent in this case to distinguish it from the facts of *Mincey*. The Louisiana Supreme Court's decision does not attempt to validate the search as consensual, although it attempts to support its diminished expectation of privacy argument by reference to the daughter's "apparent authority" over the premises when she originally permitted the police to enter. Because the issue of consent is ordinarily a factual issue unsuitable for our consideration in the first instance, we express no opinion as to whether the search at issue here might be justified as consensual. However, we note that both homicide investigators explicitly testified that they had received no consent to search. * * *

[Reversed.]

GRIFFIN v. WISCONSIN

Supreme Court of the United States, 1987.
483 U.S. 868, 107 S.Ct. 3164, 97 L.Ed.2d 709.

JUSTICE SCALIA delivered the opinion of the Court.

* * *

On September 4, 1980, Griffin, who had previously been convicted of a felony, was convicted in Wisconsin state court of resisting arrest, disorderly conduct, and obstructing an officer. He was placed on probation.

Wisconsin law puts probationers in the legal custody of the State Department of Health and Social Services and renders them "subject * * * to * * * conditions set by the court and rules and regulations established by the department." One of the Department's regulations permits any probation officer to search a probationer's home without a warrant as long as his supervisor approves and as long as there are "reasonable grounds" to believe the presence of contraband—including any item that the probationer cannot possess under the probation conditions. The rule provides that an officer should consider a variety of factors in determining whether "reasonable grounds" exist, among which are information provided by an informant, the reliability and specificity of that information, the reliability of the informant (including whether the informant has any incentive to supply inaccurate information), the officer's own experience with the probationer, and the "need to verify compliance with rules of supervision and state and federal law." Another regulation makes it a violation of the terms of probation to refuse to consent to a home search. And still another forbids a probationer to possess a firearm without advance approval from a probation officer.

On April 5, 1983, while Griffin was still on probation, Michael Lew, the supervisor of Griffin's probation officer, received information from a detective on the Beloit Police Department that there were or might be guns in Griffin's apartment. Unable to secure the assistance of Griffin's own probation officer, Lew, accompanied by another probation officer and three plainclothes policemen, went to the apartment. When Griffin answered the door, Lew told him who they were and informed him that they were going to search his home. During the subsequent search—carried out entirely by the probation officers under the authority of Wisconsin's probation regulation—they found a handgun.

Griffin was charged with possession of a firearm by a convicted felon, which is itself a felony. [The Wisconsin Supreme Court upheld the search and affirmed the conviction.] * * *

We think the Wisconsin Supreme Court correctly concluded that this warrantless search did not violate the Fourth Amendment. To reach that result, however, we find it unnecessary to embrace a new principle of law, as the Wisconsin court evidently did, that any search of a probationer's home by a probation officer satisfies the Fourth Amendment as long as the information possessed by the officer satisfies a federal "reasonable grounds" standard. As his sentence for the commission of a crime, Griffin was committed to the legal custody of the Wisconsin State Department of Health and Social Services, and thereby made subject to that department's rules and regulations. The search of Griffin's home satisfied the demands of the Fourth Amendment because it was carried out pursuant to a regulation that itself satisfies the Fourth Amendment's reasonableness requirement under well established principles. * * *

A warrant requirement would interfere to an appreciable degree with the probation system, setting up a magistrate rather than the probation officer as the judge of how close a supervision the probationer requires. Moreover, the delay inherent in obtaining a warrant would make it more difficult for probation officials to respond quickly to evidence of misconduct, and would reduce the deterrent effect that the possibility of expeditious searches would otherwise create. By way of analogy, one might contemplate how parental custodial authority would be impaired by requiring judicial approval for search of a minor child's room. And on the other side of the equation—the effect of dispensing with a warrant upon the probationer: Although a probation officer is not an impartial magistrate, neither is he the police officer who normally conducts searches against the ordinary citizen. He is an employee of the State Department of Health and Social Services who, while assuredly charged with protecting the public interest, is also supposed to have in mind the welfare of the probationer (who in the regulations is called a "client.") * * * In such a setting, we think it reasonable to dispense with the warrant requirement.

JUSTICE BLACKMUN's dissent would retain a judicial warrant requirement, though agreeing with our subsequent conclusion that reasonableness of the search does not require probable cause. This, however, is a combination that neither the text of the Constitution nor any of our prior decisions permits. While it is possible to say that Fourth Amendment reasonableness demands probable cause without a judicial warrant, the reverse runs up against the constitutional provision that "no Warrants shall issue, but upon probable cause." The Constitution prescribes, in other words, that where the matter is of such a nature as to require a judicial warrant, it is also of such a nature as to require probable cause. Although we have arguably come to permit an exception to that prescription for administrative search warrants,[7] which may but do not necessarily have to be issued by courts, we have never done so for constitutionally mandated judicial warrants. There it remains true that "[i]f a search warrant be constitutionally required, the requirement cannot be flexibly interpreted to dispense with the rigorous constitutional restrictions for its issue." *Frank v. Maryland*, 359 U.S. 360, 373 (1959). JUSTICE BLACKMUN neither gives a justification for departure from that principle nor considers its implications for the body of Fourth Amendment law.

We think that the probation regime would also be unduly disrupted by a requirement of probable cause. * * * In some cases—especially those involving drugs or illegal weapons—the probation agency must be able to act based upon a lesser degree of certainty than the Fourth Amendment would otherwise require in order to intervene before a probationer does damage to himself or society. The agency, moreover, must be able to proceed on the basis of its entire experience with the

7. In the administrative search context, we formally require that administrative warrants be supported by "probable cause," because in that context we use that term as referring not to a quantum of evidence, but merely to a requirement of reasonableness. * * *

probationer, and to assess probabilities in the light of its knowledge of his life, character and circumstances.

To allow adequate play for such factors, we think it reasonable to permit information provided by a police officer, whether or not on the basis of first-hand knowledge, to support a probationer search. The same conclusion is suggested by the fact that the police may be unwilling to disclose their confidential sources to probation personnel. For the same reason, and also because it is the very assumption of the institution of probation that the probationer is in need of rehabilitation and is more likely than the ordinary citizen to violate the law, we think it enough if the information provided indicates, as it did here, only the likelihood ("had or might have guns") of facts justifying the search. * * *

[The dissenting opinion of Justice Blackmun, joined in part by Justices Marshall, Brennan, and Stevens, is omitted. Justice Blackmun conceded that searches of probationers may be based on reasonable suspicion rather than probable cause, but he saw no need for an exception to the warrant requirement. He observed that "This case provides an excellent illustration of the need for neutral review of a probation officer's decision to conduct a search, for it is obvious that the search was not justified even by a reduced standard of reasonable suspicion."]

JUSTICE STEVENS, with whom JUSTICE MARSHALL joins, dissenting.

Mere speculation by a police officer that a probationer "may have had" contraband in his possession is not a constitutionally sufficient basis for a warrantless, non-consensual search of a private home. I simply do not understand how five Members of this Court can reach a contrary conclusion. Accordingly, I respectfully dissent.

FRAZIER v. STATE OF FLORIDA

Florida District Court of Appeal, Third District, 1989.
537 So.2d 662.

PER CURIAM.

George Frazier was convicted of first-degree murder and related offenses arising out of an armed home invasion which resulted in the death of one of the occupants. His only point on appeal which merits discussion is that his convictions were obtained through the admission, over his objection, of a highly incriminating cloth ski mask which, he contended, had been illegally seized from his apartment. We affirm upon a holding that the evidence was lawfully seized and properly admitted.

The search of the defendant's apartment and seizure of the evidence was pursuant to a search warrant. The following are the facts leading up to the procurement of the warrant.

Michael Fisten, a homicide detective, believing that Frazier was involved in a home invasion robbery-killing and anxious to search Frazier's apartment for physical evidence linking Frazier to the crime, called Richard Fandry, a narcotics detective. Fisten, convinced that he did not know of facts sufficient to justify the issuance of a warrant to search Frazier's apartment,[1] told Fandry of his situation. He did not tell Fandry to get a warrant for Frazier's apartment, but did say that if Fandry got one, he would like to come along when it was executed.

Fandry was aware of the comings and goings at Frazier's apartment, having received many complaints that drug sales were occurring there. He was not, however, in the process of seeking a warrant to search the apartment when his colleague from homicide called. However, two or three days after Fisten expressed interest in Apartment 133, Fandry sent a confidential informant to make a controlled buy in the apartment. This controlled buy established the necessary probable cause to search the apartment for narcotics, and Fandry obtained a search warrant. Notwithstanding that he had already decided that Fisten would accompany him when the search took place, Fandry said nothing to the issuing judge about Fisten's interest or role in the matter.

Fisten did, of course, go with Fandry to search Frazier's apartment. During the search, in which cocaine as well as the ski masks were found, Fisten played an active role in seeking out and confiscating the evidence used to establish Frazier's complicity in the homicide.

The defendant contends that the search was invalid because Fisten "used a narcotics search warrant to accomplish by subterfuge what he could not have done otherwise." He makes no other attack upon the warrant.

What support there is for the defendant's contention is found in a body of search and seizure law that has been outdated for some ten years and, although quite possibly meriting our attention as historical fact, no longer merits our attention as precedent. To be sure, cases such as *United States v. Sanchez,* 509 F.2d 886 (6th Cir.1975), *United States v. Tranquillo,* 330 F.Supp. 871 (M.D.Fla.1971), and *State v. Watkins,* 89 S.D. 661, 237 N.W.2d 14 (1975), condemn activity like that engaged in by Fisten in the present case and order the suppression of evidence obtained by piggybacking law enforcement agents. For example, in *Sanchez,* it was held that a valid warrant authorizing federal narcotics agents to search for narcotics "could not be used to validate the entrance of a federal officer [of the Alcohol, Tobacco and Firearms Bureau] having both probable cause and the opportunity to obtain a separate warrant to search for different items of property." 509 F.2d at 889.[2] In *Tranquillo,* a warrant authorizing a search of the defendant's home for items of stolen

---

1. Fisten had been told that the perpetrators of the home invasion wore dark clothing, dark gloves, ski masks, and hand guns; that Frazier lived in and sold cocaine from Apartment 133 at 2575 Northwest 207th Street; and that, based on two identifications of Frazier's voice, Frazier was one of the individuals involved in the murder.

2. In *United States v. Hare,* 589 F.2d 1291 (6th Cir.1979), the court distinguished

Sanchez and upheld a piggyback search where the piggybacking Drug Enforcement agents lacked probable cause to search for narcotics. Because in *Sanchez* the piggybacking ATF agents had probable cause to get their own warrant to search for explosives, it could not there be said that their discovery of explosives during the search for narcotics was inadvertent.

clothing was held not to authorize narcotics agents, invited to come along, to search for and seize narcotics during the course of the authorized search. Similarly, in *Watkins,* a search for items stolen in burglaries was held not to support a search for drugs by accompanying narcotics agents.

These cases essentially announce a rule that items which are not the objects of a search warrant should be suppressed as being obtained in violation of the fourth amendment where, although the police enter a home pursuant to a valid search warrant, some of their number are admittedly far more interested in searching for and seizing items not listed on the warrant. The announced basis of the rule is that the otherwise valid warrant was obtained in bad faith or as a subterfuge for a search for different items.[3]

However, contrary to the defendant's contention, cases such as *Sanchez, Tranquillo,* and *Watkins* can no longer be considered as reliable authority in light of the United States Supreme Court's declaration in *Scott v. United States,* 436 U.S. 128 (1978),[a] that searches and seizures are to be examined under a standard of objective reasonableness without regard to the good faith or bad faith, or the underlying intent or motivation of the officers involved. And, as might be expected, various courts have upheld piggyback searches since *Scott.* * * * Therefore, because Article I, Section 12 of the Florida Constitution requires that we follow *Scott,* and because *Scott* makes irrelevant that Fisten intended to search for evidence of the murder and robbery while his colleague searched for narcotics, the search and seizure was entirely lawful. Accordingly, the convictions under review are

AFFIRMED.

Commentary

The first clause of the Fourth Amendment states that the people should be protected from "unreasonable searches and seizures," and the second clause states that warrants shall issue only on the basis of "probable cause."

3. Cases such as *Purcell v. State,* 325 So.2d 83 (Fla. 1st DCA 1976); *Harding v. State,* 301 So.2d 513 (Fla. 2d DCA 1974); and *Stanley v. State,* 189 So.2d 898 (Fla. 1st DCA 1966), are entirely inapposite, involving, as they do, scenarios very different than the present case.

The activity condemned in *Purcell* was that the officers continued to search the premises after having found precisely what the search warrant authorized them to look for and seize. The fruits of this continuing search were properly suppressed as deriving from an unconstitutional general search.

The activity condemned in *Stanley* and *Harding* was the use of an arrest warrant to gain entrance into the defendant's home for the primary purpose of searching it. The

courts in *Stanley* and *Harding* quite correctly foresaw the United States Supreme Court's decision in *Payton v. New York,* 445 U.S. 573 (1980). Thus, these decisions remain as good law despite the amendment of Article I, Section 12, of the Florida Constitution. *Stanley, Harding,* and *Payton,* unlike the present case, are cases in which the authority of the police to enter the premises is to arrest, not search.

a. In *Scott* the Supreme Court upheld a conviction based upon wiretap evidence, even though the investigating agents did not make a good faith effort to minimize the interception of conversations not related to the crime under investigation. The Court concluded that, whatever their intent, the agents actually did nothing unreasonable.—ed.

The connection between these two clauses is somewhat mysterious. Are warrantless searches and seizures inherently unreasonable, unless some carefully limited emergency exception applies? Or is the absence of a warrant only one of the circumstances to be taken into account in determining after the fact whether the search or seizure was reasonable? The perennial Supreme Court debate on these questions reflects an underlying controversy over the purpose of the warrant requirement and the desirability of enforcing it through the exclusionary rule.

Arguably, the real protection of a suspect's rights is provided by the probable cause requirement, and the absence of prior judicial authorization certifying the existence of probable cause is merely a formal defect if probable cause in fact existed. Various answers can be given to this contention:

1.   The Supreme Court has frequently explained that the purpose of the warrant requirement is to ensure that the facts allegedly giving rise to probable cause are evaluated by a "neutral and detached" magistrate instead of being judged by officers whose natural professional emphasis is on solving crimes rather than protecting the rights of suspects. The policy of placing a disinterested judicial officer between the possibly over-zealous policeman and the suspect is praiseworthy, but there is some question as to whether it is realistic. Warrant applications are necessarily *ex parte* so there is no one to point out flaws in the affidavit to the magistrate. In some jurisdictions magistrates may be non-lawyers, and therefore poorly equipped to challenge professional law enforcement officers on technical grounds.* In any urban jurisdiction, the officers are likely to have some freedom to select the magistrate to whom they will make the application, and they can therefore bypass any magistrate whom they consider uncooperative. Even the most conscientious magistrate would find it difficult to give detailed advance scrutiny to applications for arrest warrants, because of the quantity of such warrants that have to be issued. Because of all these factors careful advance review of searches and seizures by a judicial officer is more an ideal than a practical reality in most jurisdictions.

2.   Even if the magistrate does not exercise meaningful discretion, enforcement of the warrant requirement has value because it requires the police to commit themselves on the issue of probable cause and specificity *before* they make the search. After the search, when they know exactly what they have found and where they found it, they may be tempted to reconstruct the information that led to the search in light of what they now know to be the case. The information in the warrant application may provide the victim of the search with valuable information for preparing either a suppression motion or a civil lawsuit for damages. We have already observed (see page 93, supra) that the existence of such a record may be particularly valuable where the "search" involves telephone wire tapping or electronic "bugging" of private conversations. If there is a warrant requirement, and if

* In Shadwick v. Tampa, 407 U.S. 345 (1972), the Court unanimously upheld a city charter provision authorizing court clerks to issue arrest warrants for city ordinance violations. Compare, Connally v. Georgia, 429 U.S. 245 (1977), holding that an unsalaried justice of the peace who was paid a fee of $5 if he issued a warrant and nothing if he did not was not the "neutral and detached magistrate" contemplated by the Fourth Amendment. See also, Coolidge v. New Hampshire, 403 U.S. 443 (1971) (State Attorney General acting as justice of the peace may not issue search warrant).

the law provides the suspect with notice of the fact that a warrant was applied for, then the existence of the electronic eavesdropping will be known even if the investigators overhear nothing incriminating. The potential for lawsuits or bad publicity may deter some abuses of the power to conduct electronic surveillance.

3. The search or arrest warrant gives notice to the suspect and to others whose cooperation might be solicited that the officers are acting pursuant to legal authority, and it also specifies the limits on that authority. The homeowner or apartment renter who sees such a document may be more willing to cooperate. Third parties such as custodians of bank records or telephone companies have assurance that in cooperating with the investigators they are acting within the law.

4. The very fact that the warrant requirement imposes a certain burden and inconvenience upon the police can be seen as either an advantage or a disadvantage. Searches and seizures are always an invasion of individual privacy and liberty, and particularly intrusive practices such as searches of dwelling places and electronic eavesdropping should be employed sparingly. The fact that officers have to go to the trouble of preparing fairly elaborate papers justifying what they propose to do imposes a cost upon these activities which libertarians might think desirable. The ceremonial aspect of the warrant procedure also should not be ignored. When we require the police to seek advance judicial approval before acting to invade individual privacy, we are requiring them to engage in a ritual which emphasizes the authority of the judiciary and de-emphasizes the authority of the police. (That very fact may help to explain why the warrant requirement tends to be popular with judges and unpopular with police officers.) Symbolically, the warrant requirement affirms that the police have only so much power as the law—or the judiciary—chooses to give them.

Limitations on the Warrant Requirement

1. *Arrest warrants.* The search incident to a lawful arrest has historically been the most important exception to the *search* warrant requirement. For the arrest to be lawful, however, an *arrest* warrant is sometimes required. Payton v. New York, 445 U.S. 573 (1980) established the rule that (absent exigent circumstances) police officers possessing probable cause must obtain an arrest warrant before entering a suspect's home to make the arrest. On the other hand, officers with probable cause may arrest a suspect in a public place without a warrant, even if there was plenty of time to obtain one. See United States v. Santana, 427 U.S. 38 (1976). In *Santana,* officers came to arrest the defendant at her house on the basis of information that she possessed marked money used to make a heroin "buy" arranged by an undercover agent. Santana was standing in the doorway holding a paper bag, but as the officers approached she retreated into the vestibule of her house where they caught her. When she tried to escape, envelopes containing what was later determined to be heroin fell to the floor from the paper bag, and she was found to have been carrying some of the marked money on her person. The Supreme Court held that Santana was in a "public place" while in the doorway, and that officers "in hot pursuit" were permitted to pursue her into the vestibule to prevent the destruction of evidence.

The Ninth Circuit illustrated how to draw the line between a public place and a private residence in United States v. Vaneaton, 49 F.3d 1423 (9th Cir.1995). Officers with probably cause but without a warrant came to arrest Vaneaton at his motel room. They knocked on the door, but said nothing. Defendant opened the curtains of a window, saw the officers, and then opened the door. They asked him if he was Jack Veneaton. Upon being told that he was, they arrested him while he was standing just inside the threshold of the doorway. The majority of the panel accepted the government's argument that "a warrantless arrest at the doorway of a suspect's dwelling is constitutionally proper, provided that law enforcement has not misidentified itself, has not used coercion, and the suspect acquiesces to the encounter." The majority distinguished United States v. Johnson, 626 F.2d 753 (9th Cir.1980). "In *Johnson*, * * * the agents had used a subterfuge to get Johnson to open the door, and because of their use of that subterfuge— they misrepresented their identities—we held that 'Johnson's initial exposure to the view and the physical control of the agents was not consensual on his part.'"

The dissent in *Vaneaton* argued that "The majority's opinion is also bad policy. It will have the effect of discouraging private citizens from answering knocks on the door by uniformed police officers, by subjecting citizens to warrantless arrests inside their own homes, stemming from nothing more than the exercise of common courtesy in answering a police officer's knock on the door. Indeed, it provides a justification for refusing to answer a police officer's knock. The result is bound to make routine police investigation more difficult and further to strain relations between the citizenry and police."

Officers possessing probable cause are not required to obtain a warrant if there are "exigent circumstances" to pursue a defendant into her home. In City of Orem v. Henrie, 868 P.2d 1384 (Utah App.1994), officers obtained the description and license plate number of a car which had fled from the scene of an accident. They soon located a car matching the description at a fourplex apartment near the scene of the accident. The car had front-end damage consistent with the accident. In addition, it was parked at an extreme angle, and the door on the driver's side was ajar. A strong odor of alcohol emanated from the car. As an officer approached the fourplex, he noticed that "the door on the bottom left apartment that had the lights out was closing slowly." He then went upstairs to an illuminated apartment, where he learned from its occupant that defendant Henrie owned the car and lived in the darkened apartment where he had seen the door closing. He knocked several times on the outer screen door of defendant's apartment but received no response. As he was turning away from the door, Officer Steele found defendant's purse on the stairs. The officers found that the keys were still in the door of Henrie's apartment, and so they entered to arrest her. Subsequent field sobriety tests, interrogation, and Henrie's inability to complete an "intoxilyzer" breath test produced additional evidence that she was highly intoxicated.

Henrie moved to suppress the tests and other evidence obtained subsequent to her arrest on the ground that the entry violated the *Payton* rule. The prosecution justified the warrantless entry on the ground of exigent circumstances, specifically, the need to preserve blood alcohol evidence.

Henrie relied upon the Supreme Court's decision in Welsh v. Wisconsin, 466 U.S. 740 (1984). The defendant in *Welsh* was observed driving his car erratically, eventually swerving off the road but causing no injury or damage. He left his car and walked away. The driver who had observed him told the police that the defendant looked either very drunk or very ill. The police went to the defendant's house, entered without a warrant, and arrested him. The Court held the warrantless entry unlawful, in part because Wisconsin characterized driving under the influence as a "noncriminal, civil forfeiture offense for which no imprisonment [was] possible." The Supreme Court reasoned that "Before agents of the government may invade the sanctity of the home, the burden is on the government to demonstrate exigent circumstances that overcome the presumption of unreasonableness that attaches to all warrantless home entries. When the government's interest is only to arrest for a minor offense, that presumption of unreasonableness is difficult to rebut, and the government usually should be allowed to make such arrests only with a warrant issued upon probable cause by a neutral and detached magistrate."

The Utah appellate court held that the suppression motion was properly denied, distinguishing *Welsh* on the ground that "In Utah, driving under the influence of alcohol is a misdemeanor punishable by imprisonment and a monetary fine." The Utah Court addressed defendant's argument that "the police could have obtained a telephonic warrant in minutes" (once they located a judge) and answered that "the availability of a telephonic warrant is only one of the several factors relevant to the exigency determination." The Court found decisive that the officers "conducted a model investigation, quickly locating the vehicle involved in the accident, identifying defendant as its owner, and locating defendant." Besides, the defendant should not benefit from her criminal act in fleeing the scene of the accident to seek the protection of her home.

According to the *Payton* opinion, even the possession of a valid arrest warrant does not justify the entry unless the officers also have "reason to believe" that the suspect is present. 445 U.S. at 603. Does "reason to believe" mean the same thing as "probable cause," or some lesser standard? In United States v. Magluta, 44 F.3d 1530 (11th Cir.1995), federal marshals with arrest warrants received a tip about the location of a home belonging to Magluta, who was a fugitive on major drug trafficking charges. They had information placing Magluta's confederate Lorenzo at the home, but Magluta had not been seen there "for at least a month." There was disputed testimony as to whether Magluta had been seen in an automobile parked near the home. A raid on the home led to the arrest of Lorenzo and Magluta, and the discovery of evidence. The district court suppressed the evidence because "the marshals did not have probable cause or reason to believe that Magluta was at the residence at the time the search took place." The Court of Appeals reversed. Its opinion did not clearly decide whether "reason to believe" is a lesser standard than "probable cause." It held that, under a "common sense approach," considering that Magluta was a fugitive and might be expected to be hiding, the officers had reason to believe that he was at home.

2. *Scope of search incident to arrest.* Although some early decisions allowed a search of the entire premises on which the arrest occurred, the

scope of the permissible search incident to an arrest was subsequently narrowed to the room in which the arrest was made, and in the 1969 decision in *Chimel* to the person of the arrestee and the "grabbing area" into which he might reach. (Of course, once a person is arrested, his ability to grab is usually restricted by the use of handcuffs.) The pendulum swung back in the other direction in New York v. Belton, 453 U.S. 454 (1981), where the Supreme Court held that the entire passenger compartment of an automobile (including the glove compartment but excluding the trunk) could be searched incident to the arrest of the driver and passengers, even though the arrestees had been removed from the vehicle before the search. The approach seems to be roughly similar to that taken in 1950 in the *Rabinowitz* case (discussed in the *Chimel* opinion at page 131, supra), which allowed the search of the room in which the arrest occurred.

After the decision in *Steagald v. United States* (supra, page 135), the police must obtain an arrest warrant (absent exigent circumstances) to make an arrest of the suspect at home, and a search warrant if they have probable cause to believe him to be on the premises of another. If they do so and are on the premises lawfully to make an arrest, the "plain view" doctrine permits them to seize anything incriminating that is open to view, and the *Chimel-Belton* rule seemingly permits them to look into purses, briefcases, drawers, and similar containers that are reasonably near to the arrested person. For their own safety, the officers may also check the premises for other persons, and this may lead to the discovery of additional items "in plain view." In short, a pretty fair amount of exploratory searching may still be conducted incident to a lawful arrest.

3. *Automobile searches.* The second most important exception to the warrant requirement is the "automobile search" exception described in California v. Acevedo (page 155). If the police have probable cause to believe that an automobile contains contraband or evidence, they may search it without obtaining a warrant, even if there is no need to act immediately. Earlier decisions justified this decision somewhat unconvincingly on the theory that the automobile is inherently mobile, but of course the vehicle is not going anywhere until the police choose to release it. Holding the automobile in custody for hours while the police go about obtaining a warrant would in many cases be a greater burden on the owner than searching immediately, but the (presumably innocent) owner could always consent to a warrantless search to avoid the delay.

More recently, the opinions have tended to emphasize the supposedly "diminished" expectation of privacy that one has in an automobile as opposed to a dwelling, and the assertedly "relatively minor protection" that enforcement of the warrant requirement would provide for privacy interests. [An "automobile" for this purpose includes a small motor home temporarily resting in a city parking lot. See California v. Carney, 471 U.S. 386 (1985).] It seemed at one time as if the Court were moving towards extending the automobile exception to all "movable containers," or even towards holding that the search warrant requirement applies only to such extremely intrusive activities as searches of dwellings or offices and non-consensual electronic eavesdropping. In that event, the warrant requirement would become the exception rather than the rule. The Government argued for this position in the *Chadwick* case (discussed in the *Acevedo* opinion at page 157), but the

Court rejected that argument with surprising vigor. As a consequence, the Court has had to try to reconcile the *Chadwick* line of cases (police may not search a suitcase or closed package without a warrant) with the automobile search exception (authority to make warrantless search of automobile includes authority to open containers found within the automobile).

For example, in Wyoming v. Houghton, 526 U.S. 295 (1999), the Supreme Court held that probable cause to search a vehicle justifies the search of the purse of a passenger who is not herself under suspicion. During a routine traffic stop, a Wyoming Highway Patrol officer noticed a hypodermic syringe in the driver's shirt pocket, which the driver admitted using to take drugs. The officer then searched the passenger compartment for contraband, removing and searching what respondent, a passenger in the car, identified as her purse. The Supreme Court held that she was properly convicted of possession of the drug paraphernalia found in the purse, because the officer had probable cause to search the car for contraband, including any containers therein that could hold such contraband.

Under the "wingspan" doctrine of New York v. Belton, 453 U.S. 454 (1981), officers who have probable cause to arrest a driver or passenger in an automobile may search the entire passenger compartment "incident to the arrest"—even though the arrestee is handcuffed outside the car when the search actually occurs. If the officers have probable cause to search an automobile (not necessarily the same thing as probable cause to arrest the occupants) they may search the entire vehicle, including luggage and closed containers found within, under the rule of the *Acevedo* case and its ancestors (casebook, pp. 145–151). If the officers have custody of the automobile for any reason (usually to store it because they have arrested the driver), they make make an "inventory search" within the limitations of the Supreme Court's decision in Colorado v. Bertine [p. 160, supra]. Recent decisions have illustrated the broad sweep of these principles.

In United States v. Doward, 41 F.3d 789 (1st Cir.1994), the federal court of appeals upheld the admissibility under *Belton* of a firearm found in a search of "partially zipped suitcases" in the hatchback area of a Ford Mustang. The driver, who was arrested on outstanding felony warrants after a traffic stop, was handcuffed in a patrol car when the gun was found shortly after the arrest.

In State v. Johnson, 128 Wash.2d 431, 909 P.2d 293 (1996) a state Trooper arrested the driver of a tractor-trailer rig on a bench warrant for failing to appear on a charge of driving with a suspended license. The Trooper searched the sleeping compartment behind the seating area of the cab, and found there a pouch containing unlawful drugs. The Washington Supreme Court held that the sleeping compartment of a tractor-trailer rig is subject to search under the *Belton* doctrine. The Washington court noted that "The law regarding whether to apply to motor homes the established search and seizure principles applicable to motor vehicles, or those applicable to fixed places of residence has not been developed." United States v. Adams, 46 F.3d 1080, 1081 (11th Cir.1995).

The automobile "inventory search" exception continues to be controversial, because it allows searches that seem to go far beyond its official justification of protecting property. In Autran v. State, 887 S.W.2d 31

(Tex.Crim.App.1994), a closely divided Texas Court of Criminal Appeals refused to follow Colorado v. Bertine. The plurality opinion held that Texas Constitution's equivalent to the Fourth Amendment "provides a privacy interest in closed containers which is not overcome by the general policy considerations underlying an inventory." The defendant in *Autran* was arrested on a traffic charge for failure to "drive as nearly as practical entirely within a single lane." A subsequent inventory search, which the Texas court found acceptable under federal standards, uncovered cocaine and cash inside a closed container within the automobile. The Texas court concluded that "The officer's interest in the protection of appellant's property, as well as the protection of the agency from claims of theft, can be satisfied by recording the existence of and describing and/or photographing the closed or locked container."

4. *Packages.* In some circumstances, police may open a package without a warrant even though the automobile exception is not involved. For example, see *United States v. Jacobsen*, page 103 of this book, where the Court held that federal agents who reopened a package previously opened by a private party did not infringe any privacy interests that had not already been frustrated by the conduct of the private party. The same result would follow if the reopening was preceded by a legitimate inspection by a law enforcement officer. In Illinois v. Andreas, 463 U.S. 765 (1983) customs agents found marijuana inside a table being shipped into the country. They repackaged the table and had police officers posing as delivery men take it to the defendant's residence. Police saw the defendant pull the container into his apartment, and when he re-emerged with it 30 to 45 minutes later they arrested him and searched the package without a warrant. The Supreme Court upheld this search, holding that "absent a substantial likelihood that the contents have been changed, there is no legitimate expectation of privacy in the contents of a container previously opened under lawful authority."

Despite the Supreme Court's refusal to distinguish between "worthy" and "unworthy" containers in *Ross*, there may be a category of containers that does not merit constitutional protection. For example, suppose that officers lawfully come upon a balloon or condom that apparently contains narcotics. Apparently, they may open the item and test the substance inside without first obtaining a warrant either because the invasion of privacy is so minimal, or because the balloon is "one of those rare single-purpose containers which by their very nature cannot support any reasonable expectation of privacy because their contents can be inferred from their outward appearance." Texas v. Brown, 460 U.S. 730, 750–51 (1983) (opinion of Justice Stevens, concurring).

5. *Exigent circumstances.* The exception to the warrant requirement which is least controversial in principle is the "exigent circumstances" exception. There is a great deal of controversy, however, over how strictly or generously the exception is to be interpreted. In Brimage v. State, 918 S.W.2d 466 (Tex.Crim.App.1994) defendant had murdered a young woman whom he had lured to his home. After the victim was missing for two days, officers obtained information implicating defendant, including some bloodstained clothing found in a suitcase he had abandoned. The officers searched defendant's home without a warrant, finding the victim's body in an automobile trunk on the premises. The Texas Court of Criminal Appeals initially

held the search unlawful, but on rehearing reversed itself and affirmed defendant's conviction. The very slight chance that the victim might be injured and alive inside the residence created the necessary exigent circumstances to excuse the failure to obtain a search warrant.

The ability to obtain a search warrant by telephone should in theory make it much more difficult for officers to justify a need to proceed without judicial authorization, but there are indications in the case law that the telephonic procedure has not been frequently used. In United States v. Alvarez, 810 F.2d 879 (9th Cir.1987), federal agents lawfully arrested a suspect in an automobile with 42 pounds of recently imported pure cocaine. The suspect told the agents that he was to deliver the cocaine to defendant Alvarez at a nearby hotel, and the agents arrested Alvarez and searched his room about an hour later. Although the agents obtained approval of their actions from an Assistant U.S. Attorney, they made no effort to obtain a telephonic warrant and there was no showing that they could not have done so in the time available to them. A majority of the Court of Appeals held that the search at the hotel was unlawful in the absence of a good-faith effort to obtain a telephonic warrant or an explanation as to why such an effort could not have been made. Judge Noonan dissented, arguing that there was a legitimate need for haste in rounding up all the participants in a rapidly-developing major drug smuggling case, and that the officers properly used the time at their disposal to plan their tactics rather than to seek judicial approval.

With respect to the call to the prosecutor, Judge Noonan observed that "A quick check with a lawyer is different from submission of sworn facts to a magistrate who will make an independent evaluation of their sufficiency. Unless it is assumed that a magistrate would have instantly issued a warrant after a pro-forma recital, the time to get even a telephonic warrant would have taken precious moments from the pursuit." 810 F.2d at 889. Judge Noonan's dissent also argued more generally that some federal courts are too willing to exclude evidence on marginal Fourth Amendment grounds, especially in view of the enormous damage done by cocaine and the extreme difficulty of enforcing the laws against drug trafficking.

Officers frequently make an entry before obtaining a warrant in order to secure the premises, or simply in order to make sure that their information is accurate before they go to the trouble of preparing an affidavit and presenting it to a magistrate. If this initial entry is not justified by exigent circumstances, then the question becomes whether the illegality is cured by the subsequent seizure of the evidence pursuant to a lawful search warrant. If the officer has to rely on observations made during the unlawful entry to establish probable cause, then the warrant itself is a fruit of the poisonous tree. Ordinarily, however, the affidavit makes no reference to the entry and information previously available is adequate for probable cause. In that case the unlawful entry arguably had no effect on the issuance of the warrant and the ultimate seizure, although exclusion of the evidence could nonetheless arguably be justified as a means of deterring officers from making such warrantless entries.

In Murray v. United States, 487 U.S. 533 (1988), a closely divided Supreme Court held that in such a case the independent source doctrine allows the admission of the evidence viewed during the illegal entry if the officers can demonstrate that no information gained from the illegal entry affected either the officers' decision to seek a warrant or the magistrate's decision to grant it.

6. *Entry of a building for caretaking.* In United States v. Bute, 43 F.3d 531 (10th Cir.1994), a Sheriff's Deputy on routine night patrol noticed an open garage door at an old manufacturing plant. He suspected that the building might have been burglarized or vandalized earlier, and entered to inspect the premises. No one was present but he discovered a makeshift chemical laboratory, and called narcotics officers and a hazardous materials team. After two brief further inspections, the officers obtained a search warrant for what turned out to be a methamphetamine manufacturing operation. The majority opinion of the Court of Appeals held the search unlawful because "observing an open an unsecured building, without more" does not provide grounds for "an objectively reasonable belief that an emergency exists requiring immediate entry to render assistance or prevent harm to persons or property within." The dissenting judge argued that the entry was to protect property and not to search for evidence, that the entries were brief and involved "no rummaging," and that "the average citizen will be dumbfounded at the notion that this officer was prohibited by the Federal Constitution from checking on the safe condition of these premises."

The "community caretaking" exception has been invoked in a variety of circumstances. In United States v. Rohrig, 98 F.3d 1506 (6th Cir.1996), local officers approached defendant's home in the early morning hours because neighbors were complaining about loud music coming from the house. No one answered their knocking, and the officers eventually entered through an open rear door to find the source of the noise and resolve the problem. Inside they found evidence of a marijuana-growing enterprise, unlawful firearms, and the defendant asleep in a bedroom. In the ensuing federal prosecution, the district judge granted a motion to suppress, ruling that "regardless of whether anyone appeared to be at home or whether the door was unlocked, the officers could not lawfully enter Defendant's home in order to turn down the loud music without first securing a warrant." The Court of Appeals reversed (2–1) and upheld the warrantless entry as justified by the need to abate a nuisance, observing that

> The officers testified that they arrived at Defendant's residence in the middle of the night in response to complaints from neighbors, and that they could hear loud music at least a block away from the home. Upon their arrival at the scene, they were confronted by an irate group of pajama-clad neighbors. Had the officers attempted to secure a warrant, it is clear that the aural assault emanating from Defendant's home would have continued unabated for a significant period of time. Thus, if we insist on holding to the warrant requirement under these circumstances, we in effect tell Defendant's neighbors that "mere" loud and disruptive noise in the middle of the night does not pose "enough" of an emergency to warrant an immediate response, perhaps because such a situation "only" threatens the neighbors' tranquility rather than their lives or property. We doubt that this result would comport with the neighbors' understanding of "reasonableness." Further, because nothing in the Fourth Amendment requires us to set aside our common sense, we decline to read that Amendment's "reasonableness" and

warrant requirements as authorizing timely governmental responses only in cases involving life-threatening danger.

The dissent argued that "When mere nuisance abatement rises to the level of an 'exigent circumstance,' and the propriety of a search is judged by a post facto determination of the reasonableness of the search, the warrant requirement becomes a virtual nullity and the privacy interest in our homes exists only to the extent that our neighbors do not cry too loudly."

In Wood v. Commonwealth, 24 Va.App. 654, 484 S.E.2d 627 (1997), defendant's wife complained to police that her husband had assaulted her. Previously, defendant's teenage stepson had been reported missing. Officers proceeded to the home, arrested the defendant, and waited until a social welfare worker had taken charge of defendant's two small children. They had seen a light from an upper window and, noticing a foul smell from somewhere, went upstairs "to secure the residence, make sure there was nobody else there." In an upstairs room they saw in plain view some of the evidence later used to convict defendant of unlawful possession of drugs and firearms. The defendant subsequently consented to a further search. The majority opinion held that the inspection of the upper room was justified under the community caretaking doctrine because "the officers were guided by their concern for the child they believed to be missing, their investigation was limited to those places where they could reasonably expect to find a person; they did not open any cabinets or containers. And, the record is devoid of evidence that the officers' entry of the second floor was a pretext for the investigation of criminal conduct."

Police were less successful in invoking the community caretaking doctrine in a Wisconsin case, State v. Dull, 211 Wis.2d 652, 565 N.W.2d 575 (Wis.App.1997). Responding to a noise complaint, police found 15–year old Matthew in front of his home, and arrested him for underage drinking. An officer asked Matthew if there were a responsible adult at home with whom he could leave him. Matthew replied that only his 21–year-old brother Gregory was at home sleeping, and that the officers could not enter without a warrant. Matthew offered to go inside and wake Gregory, but the officers were reluctant to give him a chance to flee or to lock the door. The officers then entered the home with Matthew, and opened Gregory's bedroom door, finding Gregory in bed with an underage girl. The Wisconsin appellate court ordered the suppression of their testimony in the subsequent prosecution of Gregory on sex charges. The court reasoned that the community caretaking exception was inapplicable because the officers were engaged in enforcing a criminal statute, and because "we do not know why the deputy did not first try ringing the doorbell to awake Gregory or tell the dispatcher to phone the residence to tell Gregory that the police were outside."

7. *Administrative Warrants.* The Fourth Amendment is not specific about when warrants are required, but one thing it is quite specific about is that warrants shall not issue except upon probable cause to believe that specified items are present. Nonetheless, the Supreme Court has held that there is a category of "regulatory searches," which are governed by the warrant requirement but not by the ordinary probable cause requirement. Before 1967, "non-criminal" inspections of businesses or residences by investigators working for fire, health or housing departments were not considered to be within the Fourth Amendment at all. The Supreme Court's

decisions in Camara v. Municipal Court of City and County of San Francisco, 387 U.S. 523 (1967) and See v. Seattle, 387 U.S. 541 (1967), decided that these inspections were sufficiently invasive of privacy that Fourth Amendment protection is desirable, but that the public interest requires greater flexibility in authorizing such inspections than the law has provided for searches aimed at criminal prosecution. Such regulatory searches are reasonable if pursuant to a reasonable plan for inspecting an entire area, and therefore " 'probable cause' to issue a warrant to inspect must exist if reasonable legislative or administrative standards for conducting an area inspection are satisfied with respect to a particular dwelling." [See p. 160, n. 5.] In other words, there does not have to be evidence that any particular set of premises contains code violations.

The category of regulatory or administrative searches is an expansive one, and in some cases even the relatively easily obtained administrative warrant is not required. For example, in United States v. Biswell, 406 U.S. 311 (1972), the Supreme Court upheld the warrantless inspection of a licensed gun dealer's storeroom by a federal agent looking for violations of the reporting and record-keeping requirements of the Federal Gun Control Act. The opinion observed that surprise inspections are essential to enforcement of the Act, and enforcement of a warrant requirement would impede the inspections without granting any substantial protection to a dealer engaged in such a "pervasively regulated business." On the other hand, the Court held unconstitutional a provision in the Occupational Safety and Health Act which allowed federal agents to inspect factories and other employment facilities for safety hazards without a warrant. Marshall v. Barlow's, Inc., 436 U.S. 307 (1978).

The Supreme Court has held that an automobile junkyard is a "pervasively regulated business," so that a state statute may constitutionally authorize a warrantless inspection of the premises by police for stolen vehicles and parts. New York v. Burger, 482 U.S. 691 (1987). The dissenting opinion by Justice Brennan argued that: (1) vehicle-dismantling is no more closely regulated than most other businesses; (2) the statute authorized warrantless inspections at the unguided discretion of police officers; (3) the searches in question had essentially no other purpose than to uncover evidence of crime; and (4) requiring the police to obtain a criminal search warrant would not thwart legitimate law enforcement goals. In *Burger*, the police made a warrantless search after the junkyard owner told them that he did not have the records regarding automobiles and vehicle parts in his possession which he was required by law to keep. The dissent indicated that this refusal to produce required records could have been used to establish probable cause for a criminal search warrant, and "several of the officers might have stayed on the premises to assure that this unlicensed dismantler did no further business, while the others obtained a warrant." The majority permitted the officers to make the search without having to go to the trouble to obtain a warrant.

The most important category of regulatory searches involves the activities of customs and immigration officials at or near international borders who are looking for contraband and illegal entrants. The special problems presented by these "border searches" are considered in Chapter 6.

ZURCHER v. STANFORD DAILY

Supreme Court of the United States, 1978.
436 U.S. 547, 98 S.Ct. 1970, 56 L.Ed.2d 525.

MR. JUSTICE WHITE delivered the opinion of the Court.

* * *

[Demonstrators at Stanford University in 1971 attacked a group of police officers with clubs, injuring several. The officers were unable to identify most of their assailants, but they did see someone photographing the incident. Subsequently, a special edition of the Stanford Daily (student newspaper) carried photographs of the clash. The county prosecutor's office secured a warrant to search the Daily's offices for negatives and pictures relating to the demonstration. The affidavit made a showing of probable cause to believe that such photographic evidence could be found, but it did not allege that members of the newspaper staff were in any way involved in the unlawful acts.

Pursuant to the warrant, four officers thoroughly searched the newspaper premises, without finding any relevant photographs other than those already published. Thereafter, the Daily and members of its staff brought a civil action challenging the legality of the search.

A federal district judge granted a declaratory judgment, ruling that the Fourth and Fourteenth Amendments forbid the issuance of a warrant to search for materials in possession of one who is not suspected of crime, unless there is a showing that a subpoena *duces tecum* would be ineffective. The district court further held that, where the innocent object of the search is a newspaper, First Amendment interests are also involved and therefore such a search is constitutionally permissible only on the basis of a clear showing that important materials will be destroyed or removed from the jurisdiction and that a restraining order would be futile. Since these preconditions had not been satisfied, the warrant was invalid and the search illegal. The Court of Appeals affirmed, and the Supreme Court granted certiorari.]

It is an understatement to say that there is no direct authority in this or any other federal court for the District Court's sweeping revision of the Fourth Amendment. Under existing law, valid warrants may be issued to search *any* property, whether or not occupied by a third party, at which there is probable cause to believe that fruits, instrumentalities, or evidence of a crime will be found. Nothing on the face of the Amendment suggests that a third-party search warrant should not normally issue. The Warrant Clause speaks of search warrants issued on "probable cause" and "particularly describing the place to be searched, and the persons or things to be seized." In situations where the State does not seek to seize "persons" but only those "things" which there is probable cause to believe are located on the place to be searched, there is no apparent basis in the language of the Amendment for also imposing the requirements for a valid arrest—probable cause to believe that the third party is implicated in the crime. * * * Because of the fundamental public interest in implementing the criminal law, the search warrant, a heretofore effective and constitutionally acceptable enforcement tool, should not be suppressed on the basis of surmise and without solid evidence supporting the change. As the District Court understands it, denying third-party search warrants would not have substantial adverse effects on criminal investigations because the nonsuspect third party, once served with a subpoena, will preserve the evidence and ultimately lawfully respond. The difficulty with this assumption is that search warrants are often employed early in an investigation, perhaps before the identity of any likely criminal and certainly before all the perpetrators are or could be known. The seemingly blameless third party in possession of the fruits or evidence may not be innocent at all; and if he is, he may nevertheless be so related to or so sympathetic with the culpable that he cannot be relied upon to retain and preserve the articles that may implicate his friends, or at least not to notify those who would be damaged by the evidence that the authorities are aware of its location. In any event, it is likely that the real culprits will have access to the property, and the delay involved in employing the subpoena *duces tecum*, offering as it does the opportunity to litigate its validity, could easily result in the disappearance of the evidence, whatever the good faith of the third party.

Forbidding the warrant and insisting on the subpoena instead when the custodian of the object of the search is not then suspected of crime, involves hazards to criminal investigation much more serious than the District Court believed; and the record is barren of anything but the District Court's assumptions to support its conclusions. At the very least, the burden of justifying a major revision of the Fourth Amendment has not been carried.

We are also not convinced that the net gain to privacy interests by the District Court's new rule would be worth the candle. In the normal course of events, search warrants are more difficult to obtain than subpoenas, since the latter do not involve the judiciary and do not require proof of probable cause. Where, in the real world, subpoenas would suffice, it can be expected that they will be employed by the rational prosecutor. On the other hand, when choice is available under local law and the prosecutor chooses to use the search warrant, it is unlikely that he has needlessly selected the more difficult course. His choice is more likely to be based on the solid belief, arrived at through experience but difficult, if not impossible, to sustain a specific case, that the warranted search is necessary to secure and to avoid the destruction of evidence.

The District Court held, and respondents assert here, that whatever may be true of third-party searches generally, where the third party is a newspaper, there are additional factors derived from the First Amendment that justify a nearly *per se* rule forbidding the search warrant and permitting only the subpoena *duces tecum*. The general submission is that searches of newspaper offices for evidence of crime reasonably believed to be on the premises will seriously threaten the ability of the press to gather, analyze, and disseminate news. This is said to be true for several reasons: First, searches will be physically disruptive to such an extent that timely publication will be impeded. Second, confidential sources of information will dry up, and the press will also lose opportunities to cover various events because of fears of the participants that press files will be readily available to the authorities. Third, reporters will be deterred from recording and preserving their recollections for future use if such information is subject to seizure. Fourth, the processing of news and its dissemination will be chilled by the prospects that searches will disclose internal editorial deliberations. Fifth, the press will resort to self-censorship to conceal its possession of information of potential interest to the police. * * *

Neither the Fourth Amendment nor the cases requiring consideration of First Amendment values in issuing search warrants, however, call for imposing the regime ordered by the District Court. Aware of the long struggle between Crown and press and desiring to curb unjustified official intrusions, the Framers took the enormously important step of subjecting searches to the test of reasonableness and to the general rule requiring search warrants issued by neutral magistrates. They nevertheless did not forbid warrants where the press was involved, did not require special showings that subpoenas would be impractical, and did not insist that the owner of the place to be searched, if connected with the press, must be shown to be implicated in the offense being investigated. Further, the prior cases do no more than insist that the courts apply the warrant requirements with particular exactitude when First Amendment interests would be endangered by the search. As we see it, no more than this is required where the warrant requested is for the seizure of criminal evidence reasonably believed to be on the premises occupied by a newspaper. Properly administered, the preconditions for a warrant—probable cause, specificity with respect to the place to be searched and the things to be seized, and overall reasonableness—should afford sufficient protection against the harms that are assertedly threatened by warrants for searching newspaper offices.

Reversed.

[The concurring opinion of JUSTICE POWELL, and the dissenting opinion of JUSTICE STEWART, joined by JUSTICE MARSHALL, are omitted.]

MR. JUSTICE STEVENS, dissenting.

The novel problem presented by this case is an outgrowth of the profound change in Fourth Amendment law that occurred in 1967, when *Warden v. Hayden*, 387 U.S. 294, was decided. The question is what kind of "probable cause" must be established in order to obtain a warrant to conduct an unannounced search for documentary evidence in the private files of a person not suspected of involvement in any criminal activity. The Court holds that a reasonable belief that the files contain relevant evidence is a sufficient justification. This holding rests on a misconstruction of history and of the Fourth Amendment's purposely broad language.

The Amendment contains two Clauses, one protecting "persons, houses, papers, and effects, against unreasonable searches and seizures," the other regulating the issuance of warrants: "no Warrants shall issue, but upon probable cause, supported by Oath or affirmation, and particularly describing the place to be searched, and the persons or things to be seized." When these words were written, the procedures of the Warrant Clause were not the primary protection against oppressive searches. It is unlikely that the authors expected private papers ever to be among the "things" that could be seized with a warrant, for only a few years earlier, in 1765, Lord Camden had delivered his famous opinion denying that any magistrate had power to authorize the seizure of private papers.* Because all such seizures were considered unreasonable, the Warrant Clause was not framed to protect against them. * * *

In the pre-*Hayden* era warrants were used to search for contraband, weapons, and plunder, but not for "mere evidence." The practical effect of the rule prohibiting the issuance of warrants to search for mere evidence was to narrowly limit not only the category of objects, but also the category of persons and the character of the privacy interests that might be affected by an unannounced police search.

Just as the witnesses who participate in an investigation or a trial far outnumber the defendants, the persons who possess evidence that may help to identify an offender, or explain an aspect of a criminal transaction, far outnumber those who have custody of weapons or plunder. Countless law-abiding citizens—doctors, lawyers, merchants, customers, bystanders—may have documents in their possession that relate to an ongoing criminal investigation. The consequences of subjecting this large category of persons to unannounced police searches are extremely serious. The *ex parte* warrant procedure enables the prosecutor to obtain access to privileged documents that could not be examined if advance notice gave the custodian an opportunity to object. The search for the documents described in a warrant may involve the inspection of files containing other private matter. The dramatic character of a sudden search may cause an entirely unjustified injury to the reputation of the persons searched. * * *

A showing of probable cause that was adequate to justify the issuance of a warrant to search for stolen goods in the 18th century does not automatically satisfy the new dimensions of the Fourth Amendment in the post-*Hayden* era. In *Hayden* itself, the Court recognized that the

---

* "Papers are the owner's goods and chattels: they are his dearest property; and are so far from enduring a seizure, that they will hardly bear an inspection; and though the eye cannot by the laws of England be guilty of a trespass, yet where private papers are removed and carried away, the secret nature of those goods will be an aggravation of the trespass, and demand more considerable damages in that respect. Where is the written law that gives any magistrate such a power? I can safely answer, there is none; and therefore it is too much for us without such authority to pronounce a practice legal, which would be subversive of all the comforts of society." *Entick v. Carrington*, 19 How.St.Tr. 1029, 1066 (1765).

meaning of probable cause should be reconsidered in the light of the new authority it conferred on the police. The only conceivable justification for an unannounced search of an innocent citizen is the fear that, if notice were given, he would conceal or destroy the object of the search. Probable cause to believe that the custodian is a criminal, or that he holds a criminal's weapons, spoils, or the like, justifies that fear, and therefore such a showing complies with the Clause. But if nothing said under oath in the warrant application demonstrates the need for an unannounced search by force, the probable-cause requirement is not satisfied. In the absence of some other showing of reasonableness, the ensuing search violates the Fourth Amendment. * * *

UNITED STATES v. TORRES

United States Court of Appeals, Seventh Circuit, 1984.
751 F.2d 875.

Posner, Circuit Judge.

This appeal by the United States raises two novel and important questions: whether the federal government may ever secretly televise the interior of a private building as part of a criminal investigation and use the videotapes in a criminal trial, and if so whether the warrants under which television surveillance was conducted in this case complied with constitutional requirements. A federal grand jury indicted the four defendants, who are members of the FALN (Fuerzas Armadas de Liberacion Nacional Puertorriquena), on charges of seditious conspiracy (18 U.S.C. § 2384) and related weapons and explosives violations. On the eve of trial, the district judge ordered the suppression of videotapes that the FBI had made as part of its surveillance of two FALN safe houses. The government appeals this order under 18 U.S.C. § 3731. The videotapes had no sound track; but at the same time that the FBI was televising the interior of the safe houses it was recording the sounds on different equipment. The judge refused to order suppression of the sound tapes, and they are not in issue in this appeal.

The FALN is a secret organization of Puerto Rican separatists that has been trying to win independence for Puerto Rico by tactics that include bombing buildings in New York, Chicago, and Washington. The bombs are assembled and stored, and members of the organization meet, in safe houses rented under false names. The bombings have killed several people, injured many others, and caused millions of dollars of property damage. * * *

The background to the present case is the arrest in 1980 in a Chicago suburb of several members of the FALN, one of whom agreed to help the FBI's investigation of the organization. He identified as members two of the people later charged in this case. FBI agents followed one, who unwittingly led the agents to an apartment in Chicago that was being used as an FALN safe house. The U.S. Attorney obtained from Chief Judge McGarr of the Northern District of Illinois an order authorizing the FBI to make surreptitious entries into the apartment to install electronic "bugs" and television cameras in every room. The FBI wanted to see as well as hear because it had reason to believe that the people using the safe houses, concerned they might be bugged, would play the radio loudly when they were speaking to each other and also would speak in code, and that the actual assembly of bombs would be carried on in silence. The television surveillance of the first apartment paid off: the FBI televised two of the defendants assembling bombs. On the basis of these observations the FBI obtained a search warrant for the apartment and found dynamite, blasting caps, guns, and maps showing the location of prisons. Tailing the same two defendants led to the second safe house involved in this appeal. Again a warrant was obtained to conduct electronic, including television, surveillance; and it was by televising meetings in this safe house that the other two defendants in this case were identified.

The trial judge held that there was no statutory or other basis for Chief Judge McGarr's order authorizing television surveillance of the safe houses and that therefore the fruits of the surveillance, including the videotapes, would be inadmissible in the defendants' forthcoming trial. The defendants and amici curiae advance the following additional grounds for this result: television surveillance in criminal investigations (other than of foreign agents) is forbidden by federal statute; it is in any event so intrusive—so reminiscent of the "telescreens" by which "Big Brother" in George Orwell's *1984* maintained visual surveillance of the entire population of "Oceania," the miserable country depicted in that anti-utopian novel—that it can in no circumstances be authorized (least of all, one imagines, in the year 1984) without violating both the Fourth Amendment and the Fifth Amendment's due process clause; and even if all this is wrong, still the particular orders ("warrants," as we shall call them) in this case did not satisfy the requirements of the Fourth Amendment's warrant clause.

The trial judge appears, however, to have overlooked *United States v. New York Tel. Co.*, 434 U.S. 159, 168–70 (1977), where the Supreme Court held that Rule 41 of the Federal Rules of Criminal Procedure, which authorizes the issuance of search warrants, embraces orders to install "pen registers" (devices that record the phone numbers that a telephone subscriber is dialing). Although the language of Rule 41 is that of conventional searches (see especially subsection (b)), the Court in the *New York Telephone* case read the rule flexibly and concluded that it covers "electronic intrusions" as well—including bugging. We cannot think of any basis on which the rule might be thought sufficiently flexible to authorize a pen register, bug, or wiretap, but not a camera. It is true that secretly televising people (or taking still or moving pictures of them) while they are in what they think is a private place is an even greater intrusion on privacy than secretly recording their conversations. But the fact that electronic eavesdropping is more intrusive than conventional searching did not prevent the Supreme Court in the *New York Telephone* case from reading Rule 41—very broadly in view of its language—to embrace electronic eavesdropping. The next step, to television surveillance, is smaller than the one the Court took.

There is another basis, besides Rule 41, for the issuance of warrants for television surveillance. Like the power to prescribe or regulate procedure, to punish for contempts of court, and to issue writs in aid of the court's jurisdiction, the power to issue a search warrant was historically, and is still today, an inherent (by which we mean simply a nonstatutory, or common law) power of a court of general jurisdiction. Indeed, it is an aspect of the court's power to regulate procedure. A search warrant is often used to obtain evidence for use in a criminal proceeding, and is thus a form of (or at least an analogue to) pretrial discovery. Although Congress can limit the procedural authority of the federal courts—if nothing else, Congress's power to create lower federal courts (Art. I, § 8, cl. 9) so implies—until it does so with respect to a particular subject the courts retain their traditional powers. Rule 57(b) of the Federal Rules of Criminal Procedure virtually so states. And much of federal criminal procedure, especially in the early days of the federal courts, was judge-made. * * *

But a conclusion that neither Rule 41 nor the inherent common law powers of the federal courts allow warrants for television surveillance would have a most curious implication that in combination with all else we have said persuades us to reject it. A search without a warrant certainly is permissible in an emergency, and a situation in which the FBI had strong reason to believe that an organization was operating a bomb factory but the FBI could not obtain a warrant to conduct the only type of search that would be effective in obtaining necessary evidence of this, because no court had been given authority to issue such a warrant, could fairly be described as an emergency. Therefore the government would have an argument that the fruits of such a search, though it had been conducted without a warrant, would be admissible in the criminal proceeding, provided the search was otherwise reasonable (an important qualification, as we shall see). A holding that federal courts have no power to issue warrants authorizing television surveillance might, therefore, simply validate the conducting of such surveillance without warrants. This would be a Pyrrhic victory for those who view the search warrant as a protection of the values in the Fourth Amendment.

The defendants argue, however, that Title III of the Omnibus Crime Control and Safe Streets Act of 1968, 18 U.S.C. §§ 2510–2520, as amended by the Foreign Intelligence Surveillance Act of 1978, 50 U.S.C. §§ 1801 *et seq.*, deprives the federal courts of the power they would otherwise have to issue a warrant for television surveillance. Title III authorizes federal judges to issue warrants (called "orders") for wiretapping and bugging, and establishes elaborate requirements for such warrants. But it does not authorize warrants for television surveillance. The statute regulates only the "interception of wire or oral communications." A man televised while silently making a bomb is not engaged in any form of communication, let alone "wire or oral communication." * * *

It does not follow, however, that because Title III does not authorize warrants for television surveillance, it forbids them. The motto of the Prussian state—that everything which is not permitted is forbidden—is not a helpful guide to statutory interpretation. Television surveillance (with no soundtrack) just is not within the statute's domain. The legislative history does not refer to it, probably because television cameras in 1968 were too bulky and noisy to be installed and operated surreptitiously. It would be illogical to infer from Congress's quite natural omission to deal with a nonproblem that it meant to tie the federal courts' hands when and if the problem arose. * * *

The Foreign Intelligence Surveillance Act establishes procedures for electronic surveillance of foreign agents. Reflecting changes in technology in the decade that had passed since the enactment of Title III, the Act defines electronic surveillance broadly enough to cover television, by including in the definition the use of "an electronic, mechanical, or other surveillance device * * * for monitoring to acquire information, other than from a wire or radio communication." 50 U.S.C. § 1801(f)(4). Although the procedures in the Act have no direct application to this case—these defendants are not agents of a foreign power, and the government does not argue that the Act authorized television surveillance of them—the Act also amended Title III as follows: "procedures in [Title III] and the Foreign Intelligence Surveillance Act of 1978 shall be the exclusive means by which electronic surveillance, as defined [in the Foreign Intelligence Surveillance Act], and the interception of domestic wire and oral communications may be conducted." 18 U.S.C. § 2511(2)(f). The defendants read this to mean that television surveillance, a form of electronic surveillance that does not involve the interception of wire or oral communications, may be conducted only in accordance with the Foreign Intelligence Surveillance Act; since that Act did not authorize the surveillance in this case, section 2511(2)(f) forbids it.

All this section means to us, however, is that the Foreign Intelligence Surveillance Act is intended to be exclusive in its domain and Title III in its. The powers that the Act gives the government to keep tabs on agents of foreign countries are not to be used for purely domestic investigations, and conversely the limitations that Title III places on wiretapping and bugging are not to be used to hobble the government's activities against foreign agents. To read the Foreign Intelligence Surveillance Act as the defendants would have us do would give a statute designed to regularize the government's broad powers to deal with the special menace posed by agents of foreign powers the side effect of curtailing the government's powers in domestic law enforcement. * * *

The fact is that Congress has never addressed the issue of judicial authorization of television surveillance in federal criminal investigations. But of course that observation cannot be the end of our analysis. It is too late in the day to argue that the Fourth Amendment regulates only the types of search that were technically feasible in the eighteenth century. The government therefore quite properly does not argue that television surveillance is outside the scope of the Fourth Amendment. We think it also unarguable that television surveillance is exceedingly intrusive, especially in combination (as here) with audio surveillance, and inherently indiscriminate, and that it could be grossly abused—to eliminate personal privacy as understood in modern Western nations.

The precise application of the Fourth Amendment to television surveillance has, therefore, now to be considered. The usual way in which judges interpreting the Fourth Amendment take account of the fact that searches vary in the degree to which they invade personal privacy is by requiring a higher degree of probable cause (to believe that the search will yield incriminating evidence), and by being more insistent that a warrant be obtained if at all feasible, the more intrusive the search is. But maybe in dealing with *so* intrusive a technique as television surveillance, other methods of control as well, such as banning the technique outright from use in the home in connection with minor crimes, will be required, in order to strike a proper balance between public safety and personal privacy. That question is not before us, but we mention it to make clear that in declining to hold television surveillance unconstitutional per se we do not suggest that the Constitution must be interpreted to allow it to be used as generally as less intrusive techniques can be used. * * *

But we do not think there can never be a case where secretly televising people in private places is reasonable. The facts of the present case argue against so absolute an approach. The FALN has the plans, the materials, and the know-how to kill in gross. A sophisticated as well as lethal practitioner of urban terrorism, it meets to plan its operations and assemble bombs in safe houses leased under false names. Alert to the possibility that its safe houses might be bugged by the FBI, it takes effective steps to defeat this form of electronic surveillance, making it highly resistant to conventional methods of law enforcement even as enhanced by modern techniques for overhearing conversations. We do not think the Fourth Amendment prevents the government from coping with the menace of this organization by installing and operating secret television cameras in the organization's safe houses. The benefits to the public safety are great, and the costs to personal privacy are modest. A safe house is not a home. No one lives in these apartments, amidst the bombs and other paraphernalia of terrorism. They are places dedicated exclusively to illicit business; and though the Fourth Amendment protects business premises as well as homes, the invasion of privacy caused by secretly televising the interior of business premises is less than that caused by secretly televising the interior of a home, while the social benefit of the invasion is greater when the organization under investigation runs a bomb factory than it would be if it ran a chop shop or a numbers parlor. There is no right to be let alone while assembling bombs in safe houses.

Having concluded that the district court could validly authorize television surveillance in this case, we come to the question whether the two warrants complied with the requirements of the Fourth Amendment's warrant clause. On this aspect of the case the defendants do not argue that the warrants were not issued on the basis of an oath and probable cause, but that they are not particular enough to satisfy the requirements of the Fourth Amendment. * * *

The government asked for the warrants in its applications for Title III warrants—applications the government had to make because it wanted to record the sounds in the apartments at the same time that it was televising the interiors—and the warrants it got covered both methods of surveillance. Title III imposes many restrictions on intercept warrants. Those related to the constitutional requirement of particularity are that the judge must certify that "normal investigative procedures have been tried and have failed or reasonably appear to be unlikely to succeed if tried or to be too dangerous," 18 U.S.C. § 2518(3)(c), and that the warrant must contain "a particular description of the type of communication sought to be intercepted, and a statement of the particular offense to which it relates," § 2518(4)(c), must not allow the period of interception to be "longer than is necessary to achieve the objective of the authorization, nor in any event longer than thirty days" (though renewals are possible), § 2518(5), and must require that the interception "be conducted in such a way as to minimize the interception of communications not otherwise subject to interception under [Title III]," *id.* Each of these four requirements is a safeguard against electronic surveillance that picks up more information than is strictly necessary and so violates the Fourth Amendment's requirement of particular description.

After stating that there was probable cause to believe both that the individuals named in the warrant were using the specified premises (the safe house) in connection with specified federal crimes and that intercepts of oral and wire communications at this address would yield evidence concerning these crimes, after stating that normal investigative methods had been tried and had failed, and after authorizing intercepts at the address, each of the original warrants in this case went on to authorize the FBI "to install [at the address] devices that will visually monitor and record the activity taking place in furtherance of the above-described [illegal] purposes." Each warrant then specified the number of surreptitious entries that the FBI was authorized to make to install, adjust, and remove both the audio and video equipment (a total of 34 separate entries were authorized), required progress reports to be made to the court every five days, required that the electronic surveillance cease "upon the attainment of the authorized objective," and put a deadline of 30 days on both the audio and video surveillance. One of the warrants was renewed a total of four times, so that it authorized a total of 150 days of surveillance, and the other was renewed twice; and in all, 130 hours of videotape were made. The renewal warrants were essentially identical to the original ones, but were supported by even more compelling showings of probable cause, based on information yielded by the execution of the original warrants.

In short, the warrants complied with all four of the requirements of Title III that implement the constitutional requirement of particularity.

In fact, the only requirement of Title III that the government may not have complied with in its television surveillance was the requirement that the application be authorized by the Attorney General or an Assistant Attorney General specially designated by him. See 18 U.S.C. § 2516(1). Actually, the authorization *was* obtained; it just was not communicated to the district judge. We need not decide whether this was a failure to comply with the statute, (nothing in the statute suggests it is); it is in any event not relevant to the Fourth Amendment's requirement of particularity.

A warrant for video surveillance that complies with those provisions that Congress put into Title III in order to implement the Fourth Amendment ought to satisfy the Fourth Amendment's requirement of particularity as applied to such surveillance. Title III was Congress's carefully thought out, and constitutionally valid effort to implement the requirements of the Fourth Amendment with regard to the necessarily unconventional type of warrant that is used to authorize electronic eavesdropping. In a conventional search the police go through a home or an office looking for contraband or evidence of a crime, and they either find what they are looking for or not, and then they leave. By rummaging through a person's possessions in search of what they came for they invade the person's privacy, and much of what they examine may be at once personal and irrelevant to the objective of the search, but the search is usually brief. Electronic interception, being by nature a continuing rather than one-shot invasion, is even less discriminating than a physical search, because it picks up private conversations (most of which will usually have nothing to do with any illegal activity) over a long period of time. Whether because it is more indiscriminate, or because people regard their conversations as more private than their possessions, or for both reasons, electronic interception is thought to pose a greater potential threat to personal privacy than physical searches, and Congress therefore pitched the requirements for a valid intercept warrant higher than those for a conventional Rule 41 warrant: except for probable cause, the requirements in 18 U.S.C. § 2518 are not found in Rule 41. Television surveillance is identical *in its indiscriminate character* to wiretapping and bugging. It is even more invasive of privacy, just as a strip search is more invasive than a pat-down search, but it is not more indiscriminate: the microphone is as "dumb" as the television camera; both devices pick up anything within their electronic reach, however irrelevant to the investigation. If the government conducts television surveillance in conformity with the requirements of particularity that Title III imposes on electronic eavesdropping (not literal conformity, of course, since words such as "communications" and "intercept" in Title III do not fit television surveillance), the government has also conformed to the requirement of particularity in the Fourth Amendment's warrant clause.

Since the government did this here, we need not, strictly speaking, decide what would happen if it had not done so. But because television surveillance is potentially so menacing to personal privacy, we want to make clear our view that a warrant for television surveillance that did not satisfy the four provisions of Title III that implement the Fourth Amendment's requirement of particularity would violate the Fourth Amendment. Invoking our common law power to interpret the Constitution in a novel context, we borrow the warrant procedure of Title III, a careful legislative attempt to solve a very similar problem, and hold that it provides the measure of the government's constitutional obligation of particular description in using television surveillance to investigate crime. We doubt that the government will resist this view, for there will be few if any cases where it does not try anyway to conform its application for a television-surveillance warrant to Title III. It wants the sounds as well as the sights, and it can get a warrant for the former only by complying with Title III; the soundtrack of a videotape, no less than a free-standing tape recording, is within the scope of Title III.

But we are unwilling to go further and hold that warrants for television surveillance are subject to Title III, as warrants for bugging and wiretapping are, so that if for example a television-surveillance warrant was destroyed without an order by the issuing judge, the person destroying it could be punished for contempt under 18 U.S.C. § 2518(8)(c), a provision of Title III that punishes unauthorized destruction of intercept warrants. It is only the requirements (listed earlier) of Title III that implement the constitutional requirement of particularity in the novel setting of electronic surveillance that we have borrowed to give content to the Fourth Amendment as applied to television surveillance. Of course it is anomalous to have detailed statutory regulation of bugging and wiretapping but not of television surveillance, in Title III, and detailed statutory regulation of television surveillance of foreign agents but not of domestic criminal suspects, in the Foreign Intelligence Surveillance Act; and we would think it a very good thing if Congress responded to the issues discussed in this opinion by amending Title III to bring television surveillance within its scope. But judges are not authorized to amend statutes even to bring them up to date. * * * To read the words of this statute—intercept, aural, communication—as if they encompassed silent visual surveillance would be to say to Congress that there is no form of words that it can use to mark off the limits of a statute that will prevent aggressive, imaginative judges from disregarding those limits. And we naturally shrink from saying any such thing. * * *

The order of suppression is reversed and the case remanded for trial.

Reversed and Remanded.

CUDAHY, CIRCUIT JUDGE, concurring in the result.

I am in complete accord with the majority's conclusion that "[t]here is no right to be let alone while assembling bombs in safe houses." It is hard to imagine facts stronger than those before us to justify means of surveillance necessary to protect the public. No society may be lightly presumed to have denied itself the means necessary to defend itself against this kind of assault.

If there were no Title III of the Omnibus Crime Control and Safe Streets Act of 1968, and no Foreign Intelligence Surveillance Act of 1978 ("FISA"), I would have no great difficulty in this case in following the majority down the path of inherent powers (fortified by Rule 41 of the Federal Rules of Criminal Procedure). That route has considerable appeal where, as here, we are apparently responding to the threat of a war to be waged randomly against the populace. But given the existing statutory scheme, that route is, I think, neither necessary nor justifiable.

I believe that, if Title III and FISA are construed together, it is possible and desirable to find in them not only the authority to conduct video surveillance in appropriate circumstances but a procedure which brings authorization of, and responsibility for, such surveillance under centralized and high-level control. * * * By leaving an extraordinarily intrusive form of domestic electronic surveillance uncontrolled by statute, the majority acts contrary to the purposes of both statutes and produces a highly improbable result.

This most improbable result may be described in the following way. Based on the definition of "electronic surveillance" in FISA, 50 U.S.C. § 1801(f)(4), any attempt to employ video surveillance in a foreign intelligence case would be subject to FISA's restrictions. In these highly sensitive cases of perhaps extraordinary importance to the nation, video surveillance may be employed only with the approval of officials at the highest levels of the federal government and of a special court established for this purpose in 50 U.S.C. § 1803. To be more precise, the application must be approved by the Attorney General or Deputy Attorney General of the United States, 50 U.S.C. § 1804(a); and the need for using such intrusive surveillance measures must be certified by the President's national security affairs adviser or a national security official whose appointment is subject to Senate confirmation, 50 U.S.C. § 1804(a)(7). Only then may the government apply to the special court for a warrant. And FISA imposes numerous other requirements designed to ensure that highly intrusive surveillance measures are used only when and to the extent necessary. * * * The surveillance must be carried out subject to court order and supervision, and the court is a special one selected by the Chief Justice of the United States, § 1803(a), to develop expertise in the subject matter and to impose some controls on the executive branch in conducting this type of surveillance. The court operates in secret but it is still an Article III court with the authority to deny permission for surveillance.

Congress was so concerned about potential abuses of these investigative techniques in foreign intelligence cases that it imposed these numerous requirements—checks and balances affecting officials at the highest levels of government. It imposed those requirements in cases of utmost importance and sensitivity to national security. I am unpersuaded by the suggestion that Congress could have subjected these techniques to such tight controls in those cases and still left open the use of the same techniques for every local police department in every minor investigation. The majority's interpretation would presumably give the power to engage in this intrusive video surveillance to virtually any officer with a badge and to any official with a robe and gavel. In fact, the majority runs the risk of leaving open the use of video surveillance with such relatively loose controls in every case *except* those of greatest importance. According to the majority, Congress entrusted powers to a deputy sheriff and half-time magistrate on a local gambling investigation that it expressly denied the director of the Federal Bureau of Investigation and a special expert court in foreign intelligence cases of the utmost sensitivity and importance. This result is irrational and contrary to Congressional intent. If statutory language must be bent, as the majority must bend the language of 18 U.S.C. § 2511(2)(f) and 50 U.S.C. § 1809, we should at least bend it in the general direction of Congressional purpose and method.

The defendants make a plausible argument, based on the statutory language, for a third interpretation of FISA and Title III, under which video surveillance is prohibited except in foreign intelligence cases. * * *

The inclusion of video surveillance in FISA's definition of electronic surveillance is relatively obscure and becomes explicit only in a few sentences buried in the committee reports. Congress' attention was clearly elsewhere with regard to FISA. And it seems evident to me that the potential problems of either the majority position or the defendants' position were simply not recognized in the development of one complicated statute and its integration with another complicated statute. Either result—the exemption of video surveillance from any statutory regulation or the prohibition of video surveillance—is extreme enough to persuade me that Congress, if it had noticed the possibility, would at least have commented on it somewhere. Instead, there is silence.

In view of the language of both Title III and FISA, the purposes of both statutes, the practical connections between audio and video surveillance methods and the silence in the legislative history on the subject, it is most sensible to view the statutory dilemma as the result of inadvertence rather than design. FISA's "conforming amendments" simply did not mesh the gears of the statutes quite as smoothly as Congress had intended.

There is a further difficulty with the defendants' argument. If Congress chose to prohibit video surveillance, it chose a remarkably roundabout and subtle way to do it, and it never indicated clearly any intention to do so. In fact, neither Title III nor FISA *prohibits any* specific surveillance method. Instead, both statutes are designed to *control* intrusive methods of electronic surveillance by regulating their use. There is no indication in the language or legislative history of either statute that Congress meant to outlaw *any* form of surveillance, and I think it quite implausible that Congress—faced with a situation such as confronts us—would have prohibited surveillance in almost any form.

Although the defendants' argument is certainly not frivolous, and, indeed, tracks the statutory language more closely than the interpretations offered in this and the majority opinions, we should, in order to avoid absurd results, construe Title III to apply to video surveillance for domestic law enforcement investigations where the targets of the surveillance have a reasonable expectation of privacy, as in this case.* * * *

---

* Congress has still not amended the statutes to clarify the status of video surveillance in "domestic" cases. In United States v. Koyomejian, 970 F.2d 536 (9th Cir.1992), the Ninth Circuit *en banc* reviewed the case law to date, and came to basically the same position taken by Judge Posner's opinion in *Torres*.

Chapter 5

PROBABLE CAUSE AND PARTICULARITY

AGUILAR v. TEXAS

Supreme Court of the United States, 1964.
378 U.S. 108, 84 S.Ct. 1509, 12 L.Ed.2d 723.

MR. JUSTICE GOLDBERG delivered the opinion of the Court.

This case presents questions concerning the constitutional requirements for obtaining a state search warrant.

Two Houston police officers applied to a local Justice of the Peace for a warrant to search for narcotics in petitioner's home. In support of their application, the officers submitted an affidavit which, in relevant part, recited that:

> "Affiants have received reliable information from a credible person and do believe that heroin, marijuana, barbiturates and other narcotics and narcotic paraphernalia are being kept at the above described premises for the purpose of sale and use contrary to the provisions of the law."[1]

The search warrant was issued.

In executing the warrant, the local police, along with federal officers, announced at petitioner's door that they were police with a warrant. Upon hearing a commotion within the house, the officers forced their way into the house and seized petitioner in the act of attempting to dispose of a packet of narcotics.

At his trial in the state court, petitioner, through his attorney, objected to the introduction of evidence obtained as a result of the

---

1. The record does not reveal, nor is it claimed, that any other information was brought to the attention of the Justice of the Peace. * * * The fact that the police may have kept petitioner's house under surveillance is thus completely irrelevant in this case, for, in applying for the warrant, the police did not mention any surveillance. Moreover, there is no evidence in the record that a surveillance was actually set up on petitioner's house. Officer Strickland merely testified that "we *wanted* to set up surveillance on the house." If the fact and results of such a surveillance had been appropriately presented to the magistrate, this would, of course, present an entirely different case.

206

execution of the warrant. The objections were overruled and the evidence admitted. Petitioner was convicted of illegal possession of heroin and sentenced to serve 20 years in the state penitentiary. * * *

In *Ker v. California*, 374 U.S. 23, we held that the Fourth "Amendment's proscriptions are enforced against the States through the Fourteenth Amendment," and that "the standard of reasonableness is the same under the Fourth and Fourteenth Amendments." * * *

In *Nathanson v. United States*, 290 U.S. 41, a warrant was issued upon the sworn allegation that the affiant "has cause to suspect and does believe" that certain merchandise was in a specified location. The Court, noting that the affidavit "went upon a mere affirmation of suspicion and belief *without any statement of adequate supporting facts*," announced the following rule:

> "Under the Fourth Amendment, an officer may not properly issue a warrant to search a private dwelling unless he can find probable cause therefor from *facts or circumstances* presented to him under oath or affirmation. Mere affirmance of belief or suspicion is not enough." *Id.*, at 47. (Emphasis added.)

The Court, in *Giordenello* v. *United States*, 357 U.S. 480, applied this rule to an affidavit similar to that relied upon here. Affiant in that case swore that petitioner "did receive, conceal, etc., narcotic drugs * * * with knowledge of unlawful importation * * *." The Court announced the guiding principles to be:

> "that the inferences from the facts which lead to the complaint '[must] be drawn by a neutral and detached magistrate instead of being judged by the officer engaged in the often competitive enterprise of ferreting out crime.' *Johnson v. United States*, 333 U.S. 10, 14. The purpose of the complaint, then, is to enable the appropriate magistrate * * * to determine whether the 'probable cause' required to support a warrant exists. The Commissioner must judge for himself the persuasiveness of the facts relied on by a complaining officer to show probable cause. He should not accept without question the complainant's mere conclusion * * *." 357 U.S., at 486.

The Court, applying these principles to the complaint in that case, stated that:

> "it is clear that it does not pass muster because it does not provide any basis for the Commissioner's determination * * * that probable cause existed. The complaint contains no affirmative allegation that the affiant spoke with personal knowledge of the matters contained therein; it does not indicate any sources for the complainant's belief; and it does not set forth any other sufficient basis upon which a finding of probable cause could be made." *Ibid.*

The vice in the present affidavit is at least as great as in *Nathanson* and *Giordenello*. Here the "mere conclusion" that petitioner possessed narcotics was not even that of the affiant himself; it was that of an unidentified informant. The affidavit here not only "contains no affirmative allegation that the affiant spoke with personal knowledge of the matters contained therein," it does not even contain an "affirmative allegation" that the affiant's unidentified source "spoke with personal knowledge." For all that appears, the source here merely suspected, believed or concluded that there were narcotics in petitioner's possession.[2] The magistrate here certainly could not "judge for himself the persuasiveness of the facts relied on * * * to show probable cause." He necessarily accepted "without question" the informant's "suspicion," "belief" or "mere conclusion."

Although an affidavit may be based on hearsay information and need not reflect the direct personal observations of the affiant, the magistrate must be informed of some of the underlying circumstances from which the informant concluded that the narcotics were where he claimed they were, and some of the underlying circumstances from which the officer concluded that the informant, whose identity need not be disclosed, was "credible" or his information "reliable."[3] Otherwise, "the inferences from the facts which lead to the complaint" will be drawn not "by a neutral and detached magistrate," as the Constitution requires, but instead, by a police officer "engaged in the often competi-

---

2. To approve this affidavit would open the door to easy circumvention of the rule announced in *Nathanson* and *Giordenello*. A police officer who arrived at the "suspicion," "belief" or "mere conclusion" that narcotics were in someone's possession could not obtain a warrant. But he could convey this conclusion to another police officer, who could then secure the warrant by swearing that he had "received reliable information from a credible person" that the narcotics were in someone's possession.

3. Such an affidavit was sustained by this Court in *Jones v. United States*, 362 U.S. 257. The affidavit in that case reads as follows:

"Affidavit in Support of a U.S. Commissioners Search Warrant for Premises 1436 Meridian Place, N.W., Washington, D.C., apartment 36, including window spaces of said apartment. Occupied by Cecil Jones and Earline Richardson.

"In the late afternoon of Tuesday, August 20, 1957, I, Detective Thomas Didone, Jr. received information that Cecil Jones and Earline Richardson were involved in the illicit narcotic traffic and that they kept a ready supply of heroin on hand in the above mentioned apartment. The source of information also relates that the two aforementioned persons kept these same narcotics either on their person, under a pillow, on a dresser or on a window ledge in said apartment. The source of information goes on to relate that on many occasions the source of information has gone to said apartment

and purchased narcotic drugs from the above mentioned persons and that the narcotics were secreated [*sic*] in the above mentioned places. The last time being August 20, 1957.

"Both the aforementioned persons are familiar to the undersigned and other members of the Narcotic Squad. Both have admitted to the use of narcotic drugs and display needle marks as evidence of same.

"This same information, regarding the illicit narcotic traffic, conducted by Cecil Jones and Earline Richardson, has been given to the undersigned and to other officers of the narcotic squad by other sources of information.

"Because the source of information mentioned in the opening paragraph has given information to the undersigned on previous occasion and which was correct, and because this same information is given by other sources does believe that there is now illicit narcotic drugs being secreated [*sic*] in the above apartment by Cecil Jones and Earline Richardson.

"Det. Thomas Didone, Jr., Narcotic

Squad, MPDC.

"Subscribed and sworn to before me this

21 day of August, 1957.

"James F. Splain, U.S. Commissioner, D.C."

tive enterprise of ferreting out crime," or, as in this case, by an unidentified informant.

We conclude, therefore, that the search warrant should not have been issued because the affidavit did not provide a sufficient basis for a finding of probable cause and that the evidence obtained as a result of the search warrant was inadmissible in petitioner's trial.

The judgment of the Texas Court of Criminal Appeals is reversed and the case remanded for proceedings not inconsistent with this opinion.

Reversed and remanded.

Mr. Justice Harlan, concurring.

But for *Ker v. California*, 374 U.S. 23, I would have voted to affirm the judgment of the Texas court. Given *Ker*, I cannot escape the conclusion that to do so would tend to relax Fourth Amendment standards in derogation of law enforcement standards in the *federal* system. * * * Being unwilling to relax those standards for federal prosecutions, I concur in the opinion of the Court.

Mr. Justice Clark, whom Mr. Justice Black and Mr. Justice Stewart join, dissenting. * * *

The Court seems to hold that what the informer says is the test of his reliability. I submit that this has nothing to do with it. The officer's experience with the informer is the test and here the two officers swore that the informer was credible and the information reliable. At the hearing on the motion to suppress Officer Strickland testified that he delayed getting the search warrant for a week in order to "set up surveillance on the house." The informant's statement, Officer Strickland said, was "the first information" received and was only "some of" that which supported the application for the warrant. The totality of the circumstances upon which the officer relied is certainly pertinent to the validity of the warrant. * * * And, * * * there is nothing in the record here to show what the officers verbally told the magistrate. The surveillance of Aguilar's house, which is confirmed by the State's brief, apparently gave the officers further evidence upon which they based their personal belief. Hence the affidavit here is a far cry from "suspicion" or "affirmance of belief." It was based on reliable information from a credible informant plus personal surveillance by the officers. * * *

Believing that the Court has substituted a rigid, academic formula for the unrigid standards of reasonableness and "probable cause" laid down by the Fourth Amendment itself—a substitution of technicality for practicality—and believing that the Court's holding will tend to obstruct the administration of criminal justice throughout the country, I respectfully dissent.

Commentary

The Fourth Amendment states that "no Warrants shall issue, but upon probable cause, supported by Oath or affirmation." Therefore, the officers must disclose the circumstances supporting the finding of probable cause to the magistrate under oath. A written affidavit is not necessary: for example, a statute or rule may provide for the officer to make an oral declaration under oath in a recorded telephone conversation. The important point is that the validity of the warrant depends upon what was stated to the magistrate under "oath or affirmation," and any other information which the officers happened to possess cannot be used to support the warrant.

On the other hand, the information only has to be sufficient to establish probable cause; it does not necessarily have to be *true*. If an informant gives apparently reliable information, the officers and the magistrate may rely upon it and the validity of a warrant so obtained is unaffected if the information later turns out to be erroneous. Similarly, an officer who makes an arrest without a warrant, necessarily acts on the basis of the information available at the time and the arrest may be reasonable even if mistaken. If the officer arrests an individual who happens to resemble closely a wanted fugitive, and searches the individual incident to that arrest, the arrest and search will be valid even if the resemblance was coincidental. See Hill v. California, 401 U.S. 797 (1971).* The following cases help to explain what is meant by "probable cause:"

1.   McCray v. Illinois, 386 U.S. 300 (1967), held that the identity of the informant does not necessarily have to be disclosed to establish reliability. *McCray* involved a warrantless search incident to an arrest. At the suppression hearing, the arresting officers testified that an informant who had supplied reliable information in about 20 previous cases had told them that he had observed McCray selling narcotics. Taking note of the well known fact that informers desire anonymity because they fear retaliation, a narrow majority of the Supreme Court held that the search was valid even though the officers refused to disclose the identity of the informer. The four dissenters argued that the police should at least be required to identify the informer to the magistrate, to establish that such an individual in fact existed and gave information. Despite the holding in *McCray*, the defense will be entitled to disclosure of the identity of the informant if it can establish that this individual may be a material witness on the issue of guilt. See Roviaro v. United States, 353 U.S. 53 (1957).

Some states interpret the *Roviaro* exception to the *McCray* doctrine more expansively than the federal courts do, with the consequence that the identity of the informer frequently has to be disclosed to the defense. In State v. Petrina, 73 Wash.App. 779, 871 P.2d 637 (1994), an informant told police that Theron Petrina's son Tony was receiving marijuana for sale and

---

* Justice Blackmun questioned whether Hill v. California stands for the broad proposition stated in the text above, in his dissenting opinion in Maryland v. Garrison, 480 U.S. 79, 94–96 (1987). He pointed out that the officers in that case went to Hill's apartment with probable cause to arrest Hill, and found Miller there. Mistaking Miller for Hill, the officers arrested him and conducted a contemporaneous search which led to the discovery of evidence later used to convict Hill. The Court upheld the arrest and search because the mistake of identity was reasonable, but the case did not involve any evidence that was used against Miller. According to Justice Blackmun, "It may make some sense to excuse a reasonable mistake by police that produces evidence against the intended target of an investigation or warrant if the officers had probable cause for arresting that individual or searching his residence. Similar reasoning does *not* apply with respect to one whom probable cause has not singled out and who is the victim of the officers' error."

storing it in the basement of the Petrina home, and that Theron had full knowledge of the marijuana distributing activities of his son. The informant, who met with police, said that he/she wished to remain anonymous due to fear of reprisals from the Petrinas or their associates. The informant had smoked marijuana, had a criminal record, and had an intimate knowledge of Tony Petrina's illegal operations. A search pursuant to a warrant based on this information resulted in the seizure of a quantity of marijuana and related items in the Petrina basement. Police charged Theron separately with possession of the marijuana with intent to distribute. Theron, claiming lack of knowledge of the marijuana, moved for disclosure of the informant's identity. The State opposed the motion, and in the alternative asked the trial judge to examine the informant *in camera* before deciding upon disclosure. The judge declined to hold the *in camera* proceeding and ordered disclosure. When the State declined to comply, the judge dismissed the charges. The Washington Court of Appeals affirmed the dismissal, explaining that the *Roviaro* exception requires disclosure of the informant's identity whenever such disclosure "is relevant and helpful to the defense of an accused, or is essential to a fair determination of a cause." The opinion concluded that the informer's extensive personal knowledge of Tony's operation was potentially helpful to Theron's claim of non-involvement.

Judging from the affidavit, the informant probably would have testified that Theron *did* know of the drug activity, and hence helped the prosecution rather than the defense. Apparently the police had unreservedly promised to protect the informant's identity, however, and felt bound to keep the promise even at the cost of losing the case. What the defense frequently wants from a *Roviaro* disclosure motion is not the informant's testimony, but the dismissal that follows a prosecutor's refusal to disclose. Accordingly, many courts are reluctant to grant disclosure on the basis of speculation about how the informant might be helpful.

The District Court decision in United States v. Mangum, 871 F.Supp. 1486 (D.D.C.1995) illustrates the reluctance of many judges to apply the *Roviaro* exception broadly. A confidential informant whose past reliability was established told police that Mangum (a convicted felon) carried a gun to work in his backpack, and would have the gun on his person or in his backpack when he left work. Officers watched defendant place the backpack in the trunk of an automobile after work, and then stopped the car and searched the backpack pursuant to the automobile exception. Defendant argued that the informant's identity should be disclosed because he might have planted the loaded gun in the backpack to curry favor with the police. The District Court cited *Roviaro* and United States v. Skeens, 449 F.2d 1066 (D.C.Cir.1971) as establishing that "speculation [that the informer might possibly be of some assistance] is not sufficient to meet the heavy burden which rests on an accused to establish that the identity of the informant is necessary to his defense." If the need for disclosure could be established solely from "the fertile imagination of counsel, * * * all would be revealed and the informer privilege, deemed essential for the public interest, for all practical purposes would be no more."

2. Spinelli v. United States, 393 U.S. 410 (1969), applied the "two-pronged test" for determining probable cause that came to be known as the "*Aguilar-Spinelli*" rule. Spinelli was convicted of conducting gambling activ-

ities at his apartment on the basis of evidence discovered in a search pursuant to a warrant. The affidavit stated that Spinelli frequently used the apartment, that there were two telephones at the apartment, that Spinelli was known to the FBI as a bookmaker and gambler, and that the FBI had been informed by a "confidential reliable informant" that Spinelli was using the telephones at the apartment for bookmaking. The Supreme Court held that this information failed to establish either: (1) that the informer obtained the information in a reliable manner; or (2) that the informer himself was a reliable person.[a] Such corroboration as there was only established that Spinelli used the apartment, not that he was engaged in any unlawful business. The test applied in *Spinelli* is discussed in the opinions in *Illinois v. Gates*, immediately following this commentary.

3.   In United States v. Harris, 403 U.S. 573 (1971), the Supreme Court upheld a search warrant under circumstances which many observers found difficult to distinguish from *Spinelli*. In *Harris*, a federal investigator obtained a search warrant on the basis of an affidavit which said that Harris was known to be a seller of bootleg liquor, and that a "prudent person" who feared for his life had told of purchasing bootleg whiskey from Harris at his residence. The opinion by Chief Justice Burger upheld the warrant because the undisclosed informant purported to speak from personal knowledge, because his reliability was supported by the use of the adjective "prudent," and because he was admitting his own complicity in illegal conduct. This last point is particularly unconvincing, because informants typically give information to the police in anticipation of favorable treatment, and for obvious reasons they do not expect to be prosecuted on the basis of the information that they provide. Criminal informants are not to be relied upon because they are inherently truthful people, but because they are seeking favors from the police and know that they will not get them unless they provide truthful information. Nonetheless, officers typically establish the reliability of the informant by reciting the number of previous occasions on which he has given allegedly truthful information, rather than by explaining that the informant is seeking leniency by identifying other guilty parties.

4.   Franks v. Delaware, 438 U.S. 154 (1978), dealt with the problem of the officer who prepares an affidavit which is sufficient on its face but which contains untruthful information. As a theoretical matter, one could argue that even outright police perjury is irrelevant to the validity of the warrant, if the issuing magistrate had no reason to question the accuracy of the affidavit. The dissenters in *Franks* took just this position, but the majority held that "where the defendant makes a substantial preliminary showing that a false statement knowingly and intentionally, or with reckless disregard for the truth, was included by the affiant in the warrant affidavit, and if the allegedly false statement is necessary to the finding of probable cause," then the defendant is entitled to a hearing and the search will be unlawful if the knowingly or recklessly false statements were necessary to the determination of probable cause. The California Supreme Court has gone further and held that suppression is in order if officers negligently made false

---

a.   In fact, it is possible that the informant was fictitious: the FBI at this time often employed illegal wiretaps and concealed their existence by attributing the information thus obtained to a "confidential reliable informant."

statements to establish probable cause. See Theodor v. Superior Court of Orange County, 8 Cal.3d 77, 104 Cal.Rptr. 226, 501 P.2d 234 (1972).

Recently, the emphasis in warrant cases has shifted from concern about the correctness of the decision by the issuing magistrate to concern about the conduct by the officers who obtain or serve the warrant. Since the decision in *United States v. Leon, infra* page 311, a search pursuant to a warrant is lawful if the officers acted in "reasonable good faith" reliance upon a search warrant, even if the magistrate erred in issuing the warrant because the probable cause was insufficient. Under this approach, a suppression motion will be successful only where the officers acted unreasonably or in bad faith; the sufficiency of the affidavit on its face will no longer be the primary issue. It is important to keep in mind, however, that some state courts reject the *Leon* doctrine.

5. Whiteley v. Warden, 401 U.S. 560 (1971), involved the situation where the arresting officers rely on information obtained from other officers, or from another police department. In *Whiteley*, officers arrested two suspects on the basis of a police radio bulletin which had announced that a warrant had been issued for their arrest. The affidavit on which the warrant had been obtained was insufficient, but of course the arresting officers had no way of knowing this. The particular officers who made the arrest thus acted properly, but the police department which obtained the arrest warrant acted unreasonably. The Supreme Court held the arrest unlawful, remarking that "an otherwise illegal arrest cannot be insulated from challenge by the decision of the instigating officer to rely on fellow officers to make the arrest."

6. Most of the Supreme Court decisions dealing with probable cause involve the evaluation of information provided by informers. There are relatively few decisions dealing with the sufficiency of observations made personally by the arresting officer. Such cases tend to turn on their particular facts, and it is difficult to set out rules of general application. One recurrent problem is the weight to be given to furtive or evasive conduct, as when a person walks quickly away upon observing a police officer or when a driver stopped for a traffic violation bends over as if to conceal something under the seat. If probable cause can be established by such ambiguous movements, then officers will find it relatively easy to justify arrests and searches. For an opinion holding such furtive gestures insufficient, see People v. Superior Court of Yolo County, 3 Cal.3d 807, 91 Cal.Rptr. 729, 478 P.2d 449 (1970).

In Peters v. New York, 392 U.S. 40 (1968), a police officer had been at home taking a shower when he heard a noise at his door. He looked through a peephole and saw two men tiptoeing down the hall of the apartment building. Believing that the two men were attempting a burglary, he took his service revolver, opened the door, stepped into the hallway, and slammed the door loudly behind him. The two men ran away, and the officer pursued. He caught one of the men and searched him, finding burglar's tools. The majority opinion by Chief Justice Warren concluded that the suspicious circumstances combined with flight gave the officer probable cause to search incident to an arrest. Justice Harlan's concurring opinion argued that flight at the appearance of a gun-carrying stranger is not indicative of guilt.

ILLINOIS v. GATES

Supreme Court of the United States, 1983.
462 U.S. 213, 103 S.Ct. 2317, 76 L.Ed.2d 527.

JUSTICE REHNQUIST delivered the opinion of the Court.

Respondents Lance and Susan Gates were indicted for violation of state drug laws after police officers, executing a search warrant, discovered marihuana and other contraband in their automobile and home. Prior to trial the Gateses moved to suppress evidence seized during this search. The Illinois Supreme Court affirmed the decisions of lower state courts granting the motion. It held that the affidavit submitted in support of the State's application for a warrant to search the Gateses' property was inadequate under this Court's decisions in [*Aguilar* and *Spinelli*.] * * * Bloomingdale, Ill., is a suburb of Chicago located in Du Page County. On May 3, 1978, the Bloomingdale Police Department received by mail an anonymous handwritten letter which read as follows:

> "This letter is to inform you that you have a couple in your town who strictly make their living on selling drugs. They are Sue and Lance Gates, they live on Greenway, off Bloomingdale Rd. in the condominiums. Most of their buys are done in Florida. Sue his wife drives their car to Florida, where she leaves it to be loaded up with drugs, then Lance flys down and drives it back. Sue flys back after she drops the car off in Florida. May 3 she is driving down there again and Lance will be flying down in a few days to drive it back. At the time Lance drives the car back he has the trunk loaded with over $100,000.00 in drugs. Presently they have over $100,000.00 worth of drugs in their basement.

> "They brag about the fact they never have to work, and make their entire living on pushers.

> "I guarantee if you watch them carefully you will make a big catch. They are friends with some big drugs dealers, who visit their house often.

> "Lance & Susan Gates" Greenway "in Condominiums"

The letter was referred by the Chief of Police of the Bloomingdale Police Department to Detective Mader, who decided to pursue the tip. Mader learned, from the office of the Illinois Secretary of State, that an Illinois driver's license had been issued to one Lance Gates, residing at a stated address in Bloomingdale. He contacted a confidential informant, whose examination of certain financial records revealed a more recent address for the Gateses, and he also learned from a police officer assigned to O'Hare Airport that "L. Gates" had made a reservation on Eastern Airlines Flight 245 to West Palm Beach, Fla., scheduled to depart from Chicago on May 5 at 4:15 p.m.

Mader then made arrangements with an agent of the Drug Enforcement Administration for surveillance of the May 5 Eastern Airlines flight. The agent later reported to Mader that Gates had boarded the flight, and that federal agents in Florida had observed him arrive in West Palm Beach and take a taxi to the nearby Holiday Inn. They also reported that Gates went to a room registered to one Susan Gates and that, at 7 o'clock the next morning, Gates and an unidentified woman left the motel in a Mercury bearing Illinois license plates and drove northbound on an interstate highway frequently used by travelers to the Chicago area. In addition, the DEA agent informed Mader that the license plate number on the Mercury was registered to a Hornet station wagon owned by Gates. The agent also advised Mader that the driving time between West Palm Beach and Bloomingdale was approximately 22 to 24 hours.

Mader signed an affidavit setting forth the foregoing facts, and submitted it to a judge of the Circuit Court of Du Page County, together with a copy of the anonymous letter. The judge of that court thereupon issued a search warrant for the Gateses' residence and for their automobile. The judge, in deciding to issue the warrant, could have determined that the *modus operandi* of the Gateses had been substantially corroborated. As the anonymous letter predicted, Lance Gates had flown from Chicago to West Palm Beach late in the afternoon of May 5th, had checked into a hotel room registered in the name of his wife, and, at 7 o'clock the following morning, had headed north, accompanied by an unidentified woman, out of West Palm Beach on an interstate highway used by travelers from South Florida to Chicago in an automobile bearing a license plate issued to him.

At 5:15 a.m. on March 7, only 36 hours after he had flown out of Chicago, Lance Gates, and his wife, returned to their home in Bloomingdale, driving the car in which they had left West Palm Beach some 22 hours earlier. The Bloomingdale police were awaiting them, searched the trunk of the Mercury, and uncovered approximately 350 pounds of marihuana. A search of the Gateses' home revealed marihuana, weapons, and other contraband. * * *

[The state courts ordered the evidence suppressed because the affidavit failed to establish probable cause.]

The Illinois Supreme Court concluded—and we are inclined to agree—that, standing alone, the anonymous letter sent to the Bloomingdale Police Department would not provide the basis for a magistrate's determination that there was probable cause to believe contraband would be found in the Gateses' car and home. The letter provides virtually nothing from which one might conclude that its author is either honest or his information reliable; likewise, the letter gives absolutely no indication of the basis for the writer's predictions regarding the Gateses' criminal activities. Something more was required, then, before a magistrate could conclude that there was probable cause to believe that contraband would be found in the Gateses' home and car.

The Illinois Supreme Court also properly recognized that Detective Mader's affidavit might be capable of supplementing the anonymous letter with information sufficient to permit a determination of probable cause. In holding that the affidavit in fact did not contain sufficient additional information to sustain a determination of probable cause, the Illinois court applied a "two-pronged test," derived from our decision in *Spinelli*. The Illinois Supreme Court, like some others, apparently understood *Spinelli* as requiring that the anonymous letter satisfy each of two independent requirements before it could be relied on. According to this view, the letter, as supplemented by Mader's affidavit, first had to adequately reveal the "basis of knowledge" of the letterwriter—the particular means by which he came by the information given in his report. Second, it had to provide facts sufficiently establishing either the "veracity" of the affiant's informant, or, alternatively, the "reliability" of the informant's report in this particular case.

The Illinois court, alluding to an elaborate set of legal rules that have developed among various lower courts to enforce the "two-pronged test," found that the test had not been satisfied. First, the "veracity" prong was not satisfied because, "[t]here was simply no basis [for] conclud[ing] that the anonymous person [who wrote the letter to the Bloomingdale Police Department] was credible." The court indicated that corroboration by police of details contained in the letter might never satisfy the "veracity" prong, and in any event, could not do so if, as in the present case, only "innocent" details are corroborated. In addition, the letter gave no indication of the basis of its writer's knowledge of the Gateses' activities. The Illinois court understood *Spinelli* as permitting the detail contained in a tip to be used to infer that the informant had a reliable basis for his statements, but it thought that the anonymous letter failed to provide sufficient detail to permit such an inference. Thus, it concluded that no showing of probable cause had been made.

We agree with the Illinois Supreme Court that an informant's "veracity," "reliability," and "basis of knowledge" are all highly relevant in determining the value of his report. We do not agree, however, that these elements should be understood as entirely separate and independent requirements to be rigidly exacted in every case, which the opinion of the Supreme Court of Illinois would imply. Rather, as detailed below, they should be understood simply as closely intertwined issues that may usefully illuminate the common-sense, practical question whether there is "probable cause" to believe that contraband or evidence is located in a particular place. * * * Unlike a totality-of-the-circumstances analysis, which permits a balanced assessment of the relative weights of all the various indicia of reliability (and unreliability) attending an informant's tip, the "two-pronged test" has encouraged an excessively technical dissection of informants' tips,[4] with undue atten-

---

4. Some lower court decisions, brought to our attention by the State, reflect a rigid application of such rules. In *Bridger v. State*, 503 S.W.2d 801 (Tex.Crim.App.1974), the affiant had received a confession of armed robbery from one of two suspects in the robbery; in addition, the suspect had given the officer $800 in cash stolen during the robbery. The suspect also told the officer that the gun used in the robbery was hidden in the other suspect's apartment. A warrant issued on the basis of this was

tion being focused on isolated issues that cannot sensibly be divorced from the other facts presented to the magistrate.

* * *

We also have recognized that affidavits "are normally drafted by nonlawyers in the midst and haste of a criminal investigation. Technical requirements of elaborate specificity once exacted under common law pleadings have no proper place in this area." *United States v. Ventresca*, 380 U.S. 102, 108 (1965). Likewise, search and arrest warrants long have been issued by persons who are neither lawyers nor judges, and who certainly do not remain abreast of each judicial refinement of the nature of "probable cause." The rigorous inquiry into the *Spinelli* prongs and the complex superstructure of evidentiary and analytical rules that some have seen implicit in our *Spinelli* decision, cannot be reconciled with the fact that many warrants are—quite properly—issued on the basis of nontechnical, common-sense judgments of laymen applying a standard less demanding than those used in more formal legal proceedings.

If the affidavits submitted by police officers are subjected to the type of scrutiny some courts have deemed appropriate, police might well resort to warrantless searches, with the hope of relying on consent or some other exception to the Warrant Clause that might develop at the time of the search. In addition, the possession of a warrant by officers conducting an arrest or search greatly reduces the perception of unlawful or intrusive police conduct, by assuring the individual whose property is searched or seized of the lawful authority of the executing officer, his need to search, and the limits of his power to search. Reflecting this preference for the warrant process, the traditional standard for review of an issuing magistrate's probable-cause determination has been that so long as the magistrate had a "substantial basis for * * * conclud[ing]" that a search would uncover evidence of wrongdoing, the Fourth Amendment requires no more. *Jones v. United States*, 362 U.S. 257, 271 (1960). We think reaffirmation of this standard better serves the purpose of encouraging recourse to the warrant procedure and is more consistent

---

invalidated on the ground that the affidavit did not satisfactorily describe how the accomplice had obtained his information regarding the gun.

Likewise, in *People v. Palanza*, 55 Ill. App.3d 1028, 371 N.E.2d 687 (1978), the affidavit submitted in support of an application for a search warrant stated that an informant of proven and uncontested reliability had seen, in specifically described premises, "a quantity of a white crystalline substance which was represented to the informant by a white male occupant of the premises to be cocaine. Informant has observed cocaine on numerous occasions in the past and is thoroughly familiar with its appearance. The informant states that the white crystalline powder he observed in the

above described premises appeared to him to be cocaine." The warrant issued on the basis of the affidavit was invalidated because "[t]here is no indication as to how the informant or for that matter any other person could tell whether a white substance was cocaine and not some other substance such as sugar or salt."

Finally, in *People v. Brethauer*, 482 P.2d 369 (Colo.1971), an informant, stated to have supplied reliable information in the past, claimed that L. S. D. and marihuana were located on certain premises. The informant supplied police with drugs, which were tested by police and confirmed to be illegal substances. The affidavit setting forth these, and other, facts was found defective under both prongs of *Spinelli*.

with our traditional deference to the probable-cause determinations of magistrates than is the "two-pronged test."

Finally, the direction taken by decisions following *Spinelli* poorly serves "[t]he most basic function of any government": "to provide for the security of the individual and of his property." *Miranda v. Arizona*, 384 U.S. 436, 539 (1966) (White, J., dissenting). The strictures that inevitably accompany the "two-pronged test" cannot avoid seriously impeding the task of law enforcement, see, *e.g.*, n. 9, *supra*. If, as the Illinois Supreme Court apparently thought, that test must be rigorously applied in every case, anonymous tips would be of greatly diminished value in police work. Ordinary citizens, like ordinary witnesses, generally do not provide extensive recitations of the basis of their everyday observations. Likewise, as the Illinois Supreme Court observed in this case, the veracity of persons supplying anonymous tips is by hypothesis largely unknown, and unknowable. As a result, anonymous tips seldom could survive a rigorous application of either of the *Spinelli* prongs. Yet, such tips, particularly when supplemented by independent police investigation, frequently contribute to the solution of otherwise "perfect crimes." While a conscientious assessment of the basis for crediting such tips is required by the Fourth Amendment, a standard that leaves virtually no place for anonymous citizen informants is not.

For all these reasons, we conclude that it is wiser to abandon the "two-pronged test" established by our decisions in *Aguilar* and *Spinelli*. In its place we reaffirm the totality-of-the-circumstances analysis that traditionally has informed probable-cause determinations. The task of the issuing magistrate is simply to make a practical, common-sense decision whether, given all the circumstances set forth in the affidavit before him, including the "veracity" and "basis of knowledge" of persons supplying hearsay information, there is a fair probability that contraband or evidence of a crime will be found in a particular place. And the duty of a reviewing court is simply to ensure that the magistrate had a "substantial basis for * * * conclud[ing]" that probable cause existed. We are convinced that this flexible, easily applied standard will better achieve the accommodation of public and private interests that the Fourth Amendment requires than does the approach that has developed from *Aguilar* and *Spinelli*.

Our earlier cases illustrate the limits beyond which a magistrate may not venture in issuing a warrant. A sworn statement of an affiant that "he has cause to suspect and does believe" that liquor illegally brought into the United States is located on certain premises will not do. *Nathanson v. United States*, 290 U.S. 41 (1933). An affidavit must provide the magistrate with a substantial basis for determining the existence of probable cause, and the wholly conclusory statement at issue in *Nathanson* failed to meet this requirement. An officer's statement that "[a]ffiants have received reliable information from a credible person and do believe" that heroin is stored in a home, is likewise inadequate. *Aguilar v. Texas*, 378 U.S. 108 (1964). As in *Nathanson*, this is a mere conclusory statement that gives the magistrate virtually no basis at all for making a judgment regarding probable cause. Sufficient information must be presented to the magistrate to allow that official to determine probable cause; his action cannot be a mere ratification of the bare conclusions of others. In order to ensure that such an abdication of the magistrate's duty does not occur, courts must continue to conscientiously review the sufficiency of affidavits on which warrants are issued. But when we move beyond the "bare bones" affidavits present in cases such as *Nathanson* and *Aguilar*, this area simply does not lend itself to a prescribed set of rules, like that which had developed from *Spinelli*. * * *

IV

Our decisions applying the totality-of-the-circumstances analysis outlined above have consistently recognized the value of corroboration of details of an informant's tip by independent police work. * * *

Our decision in *Draper v. United States*, 358 U.S. 307 (1959), however, is the classic case on the value of corroborative efforts of police officials. There, an informant named Hereford reported that Draper would arrive in Denver on a train from Chicago on one of two days, and that he would be carrying a quantity of heroin. The informant also supplied a fairly detailed physical description of Draper, and predicted that he would be wearing a light colored raincoat, brown slacks, and black shoes, and would be walking "real fast." Hereford gave no indication of the basis for his information.[5]

On one of the stated dates police officers observed a man matching this description exit a train arriving from Chicago; his attire and luggage matched Hereford's report and he was walking rapidly. We explained in *Draper* that, by this point in his investigation, the arresting officer "had personally verified every facet of the information given him by Hereford except whether petitioner had accomplished his mission and had the three ounces of heroin on his person or in his bag. And surely, with every other bit of Hereford's information being thus personally verified, [the officer] had 'reasonable grounds' to believe that the remaining unverified bit of Hereford's information—that Draper would have the heroin with him—was likewise true," *id.*, at 313.

The showing of probable cause in the present case was fully as compelling as that in *Draper*. Even standing alone, the facts obtained through the independent investigation of Mader and the DEA at least suggested that the Gateses were involved in drug trafficking. In addition to being a popular vacation site, Florida is well known as a source of

---

5. The tip in *Draper* might well not have survived the rigid application of the "two-pronged test" that developed following *Spinelli*. The only reference to Hereford's reliability was that he had "been engaged as a 'special employee' of the Bureau of Narcotics at Denver for about six months, and from time to time gave information to [the police for] small sums of money, and that [the officer] had always found the information given by Hereford to be accurate and reliable." 358 U.S., at 309. Likewise, the tip gave no indication of how Hereford came by his information. At most, the detailed and accurate predictions in the tip indicated that, however Hereford obtained his information, it was reliable.

narcotics and other illegal drugs. Lance Gates' flight to Palm Beach, his brief, overnight stay in a motel, and apparent immediate return north to Chicago in the family car, conveniently awaiting him in West Palm Beach, is as suggestive of a prearranged drug run, as it is of an ordinary vacation trip.

In addition, the judge could rely on the anonymous letter, which had been corroborated in major part by Mader's efforts—just as had occurred in *Draper*.[6] The Supreme Court of Illinois reasoned that *Draper* involved an informant who had given reliable information on previous occasions, while the honesty and reliability of the anonymous informant in this case were unknown to the Bloomingdale police. While this distinction might be an apt one at the time the Police Department received the anonymous letter, it became far less significant after Mader's independent investigative work occurred. The corroboration of the letter's predictions that the Gateses' car would be in Florida, that Lance Gates would fly to Florida in the next day or so, and that he would drive the car north toward Bloomingdale all indicated, albeit not with certainty, that the informant's other assertions also were true. * * *

Finally, the anonymous letter contained a range of details relating not just to easily obtained facts and conditions existing at the time of the tip, but to future actions of third parties ordinarily not easily predicted. The letterwriter's accurate information as to the travel plans of each of the Gateses was of a character likely obtained only from the Gateses themselves, or from someone familiar with their not entirely ordinary travel plans. If the informant had access to accurate information of this type a magistrate could properly conclude that it was not unlikely that he also had access to reliable information of the Gateses' alleged illegal activities.[7] Of course, the Gateses' travel plans might have been learned from a talkative neighbor or travel agent; under the "two-pronged test" developed from *Spinelli*, the character of the details in the anonymous letter might well not permit a sufficiently clear inference regarding the letterwriter's "basis of knowledge." But, as discussed previously, probable cause does not demand the certainty we associate with formal trials. It is enough that there was a fair probability that the writer of the anonymous letter had obtained his entire story either from the Gateses or someone they trusted. And corroboration of major portions of the letter's predictions provides just this probability. It is apparent, there-

---

6. The Illinois Supreme Court thought that the verification of details contained in the anonymous letter in this case amounted only to "[t]he corroboration of innocent activity," and that this was insufficient to support a finding of probable cause. We are inclined to agree, however, with the observation of Justice Moran in his dissenting opinion that "[i]n this case, just as in *Draper*, seemingly innocent activity became suspicious in light of the initial tip." And it bears noting that *all* of the corroborating detail established in *Draper* was of entirely innocent activity. * * *

7. Justice Stevens' dissent seizes on one inaccuracy in the anonymous informant's letter—its statement that Sue Gates would fly from Florida to Illinois, when in fact she drove—and argues that the probative value of the entire tip was undermined by this allegedly "material mistake." We have never required that informants used by the police be infallible, and can see no reason to impose such a requirement in this case. Probable cause, particularly when police have obtained a warrant, simply does not require the perfection the dissent finds necessary. * * *

fore, that the judge issuing the warrant had a "substantial basis for * * * conclud[ing]" that probable cause to search the Gateses' home and car existed. The judgment of the Supreme Court of Illinois therefore must be reversed.

Justice White, concurring in the judgment.

* * * Although I agree that the warrant should be upheld, I reach this conclusion in accordance with the *Aguilar-Spinelli* framework. * * *

* * *

As in *Draper*, the police investigation in the present case satisfactorily demonstrated that the informant's tip was as trustworthy as one that would alone satisfy the *Aguilar* tests. The tip predicted that Sue Gates would drive to Florida, that Lance Gates would fly there a few days after May 3, and that Lance would then drive the car back. After the police corroborated these facts, the judge could reasonably have inferred, as he apparently did, that the informant, who had specific knowledge of these unusual travel plans, did not make up his story and that he obtained his information in a reliable way. It is theoretically possible, as respondents insist, that the tip could have been supplied by a "vindictive travel agent" and that the Gateses' activities, although unusual, might not have been unlawful. But *Aguilar* and *Spinelli*, like our other cases, do not require that certain guilt be established before a warrant may properly be issued. "[O]nly the probability, and not a prima facie showing, of criminal activity is the standard of probable cause." *Spinelli, supra*, at 419 (citing *Beck v. Ohio*, 379 U.S. 89, 96 (1964)). I therefore conclude that the judgment of the Illinois Supreme Court invalidating the warrant must be reversed. * * *

Justice Brennan, with whom Justice Marshall joins, dissenting.

Although I join Justice Stevens' dissenting opinion and agree with him that the warrant is invalid even under the Court's newly announced "totality of the circumstances" test, I write separately to dissent from the Court's unjustified and ill-advised rejection of the two-prong test for evaluating the validity of a warrant based on hearsay announced in *Aguilar* and *Spinelli*. * * *

* * * Findings of probable cause, and attendant intrusions, should not be authorized unless there is some assurance that the information on which they are based has been obtained in a reliable way by an honest or credible person. As applied to police officers, the rules focus on the way in which the information was acquired. As applied to informants, the rules focus both on the honesty or credibility of the informant and on the reliability of the way in which the information was acquired. Insofar as it is more complicated, an evaluation of affidavits based on hearsay involves a more difficult inquiry. This suggests a need to structure the inquiry in an effort to insure greater accuracy. The standards announced in *Aguilar*, as refined by *Spinelli*, fulfill that need. The standards inform the police of what information they have to provide and magistrates of what information they should demand. The standards also inform magis-

trates of the subsidiary findings they must make in order to arrive at an ultimate finding of probable cause. *Spinelli*, properly understood, directs the magistrate's attention to the possibility that the presence of self-verifying detail might satisfy *Aguilar*'s basis of knowledge prong and that corroboration of the details of a tip might satisfy *Aguilar*'s veracity prong. By requiring police to provide certain crucial information to magistrates and by structuring magistrates' probable-cause inquiries, *Aguilar* and *Spinelli* assure the magistrate's role as an independent arbiter of probable cause, insure greater accuracy in probable-cause determinations, and advance the substantive value identified above.
* * *

By replacing *Aguilar* and *Spinelli* with a test that provides no assurance that magistrates, rather than the police, or informants, will make determinations of probable cause; imposes no structure on magistrates' probable-cause inquiries; and invites the possibility that intrusions may be justified on less than reliable information from an honest or credible person, today's decision threatens to "obliterate one of the most fundamental distinctions between our form of government, where officers are under the law, and the police-state where they are the law." *Johnson v. United States*, 333 U.S., at 17.

JUSTICE STEVENS, with whom JUSTICE BRENNAN joins, dissenting.

The fact that Lance and Sue Gates made a 22–hour nonstop drive from West Palm Beach, Florida, to Bloomingdale, Illinois, only a few hours after Lance had flown to Florida provided persuasive evidence that they were engaged in illicit activity. That fact, however, was not known to the judge when he issued the warrant to search their home.

What the judge did know at that time was that the anonymous informant had not been completely accurate in his or her predictions. The informant had indicated that "Sue * * * drives their car to Florida *where she leaves it to be loaded up with drugs* * * *. *Sue fl[ies] back after she drops the car off in Florida*." Yet Detective Mader's affidavit reported that she "left the West Palm Beach area driving the Mercury northbound."

The discrepancy between the informant's predictions and the facts known to Detective Mader is significant for three reasons. First, it cast doubt on the informant's hypothesis that the Gates already had "over [$100,000] worth of drugs in their basement." The informant had predicted an itinerary that always kept one spouse in Bloomingdale, suggesting that the Gates did not want to leave their home unguarded because something valuable was hidden within. That inference obviously could not be drawn when it was known that the pair was actually together over a thousand miles from home.

Second, the discrepancy made the Gates' conduct seem substantially less unusual than the informant had predicted it would be. It would have been odd if, as predicted, Sue had driven down to Florida on Wednesday, left the car, and flown right back to Illinois. But the mere facts that Sue was in West Palm Beach with the car, that she was joined by her husband at the Holiday Inn on Friday, and that the couple drove north together the next morning are neither unusual nor probative of criminal activity.

Third, the fact that the anonymous letter contained a material mistake undermines the reasonableness of relying on it as a basis for making a forcible entry into a private home.

Of course, the activities in this case did not stop when the judge issued the warrant. The Gates drove all night to Bloomingdale, the officers searched the car and found 400 pounds of marihuana, and then they searched the house. However, none of these subsequent events may be considered in evaluating the warrant, and the search of the house was legal only if the warrant was valid. I cannot accept the Court's casual conclusion that, *before the Gates arrived in Bloomingdale*, there was probable cause to justify a valid entry and search of a private home. No one knows who the informant in this case was, or what motivated him or her to write the note. Given that the note's predictions were faulty in one significant respect, and were corroborated by nothing except ordinary innocent activity, I must surmise that the Court's evaluation of the warrant's validity has been colored by subsequent events.[8]

Although the foregoing analysis is determinative as to the house search, the car search raises additional issues because there is a constitutional difference between houses and cars. An officer who has probable cause to suspect that a highly movable automobile contains contraband does not need a valid warrant in order to search it. This point was developed in our opinion in *United States v. Ross* [p. 147 of this book], which was not decided until after the Illinois Supreme Court rendered its decision in this case. Under *Ross*, the car search may have been valid if the officers had probable cause *after* the Gates arrived. * * * I would simply vacate the judgment of the Illinois Supreme Court and remand the case for reconsideration in the light of our intervening decision in *United States v. Ross*.

Commentary

1. *Analysis*. The issue presented in *Gates* is substantially different from the issues presented in *Aguilar* and *Spinelli*. In those cases the police may well have been in possession of information amounting to probable cause, but the conclusory affidavits did not communicate enough of the background information for a magistrate to make an informed judgment. The Supreme Court's holdings were intended to require the police to supply sufficiently detailed information to permit the magistrate to make an independent determination of probable cause.

8. *Draper v. United States*, 358 U.S. 307 (1959), affords no support for today's holding. That case did not involve an anonymous informant. On the contrary, as the Court twice noted, Mr. Hereford was "employed for that purpose and [his] information had always been found accurate and reliable." In this case, the police had no prior experience with the informant, and some of his or her information in this case was unreliable and inaccurate.

In *Gates*, on the other hand, the police *did* provide the magistrate in the affidavit with the relevant background information which they had obtained. The problem is not that the police held back information and communicated only conclusions; the problem is that the essential corroborating detail was inconclusive. But what degree of certainty is required to establish probable cause? The essential point in the majority opinion in *Gates* is not the abandonment of the two-prong analysis but the insistence that only a "fair probability" is required. If we require only that the information be sufficient to indicate that there is a fairly good chance that the search will uncover contraband, then we accept a risk that innocent people suspected of criminal activity may be searched. If we require virtual certainty, then we protect possibly innocent persons from searches but pay a price in law enforcement effectiveness.

There is confirmation in the other opinions that whether or not one uses the two-prong analysis is not what determines the outcome in cases like *Gates*. Justice White is able to conclude that the affidavit satisfies the *Aguilar-Spinelli* test because of the relatively generous way in which he evaluates the corroboration. The dissenters conclude that the affidavit fails even the flexible "totality of the circumstances" test because of the importance they attach to the acknowledged discrepancy in the corroborating circumstances. Is the Stevens dissent arguing that the information in the affidavit fails to establish even a fair probability that the couple was engaged in drug trafficking? Suppose that Detective Mader had met you at the time the warrant was issued and offered to bet a large sum of money that the *Gates* couple were coming back from Florida with a load of marijuana. Would you have been willing to take the bet at even money? What odds would you think were fair?

Another way to approach the case is to ask what (if anything) the officers should have done differently. Should they have ignored the anonymous letter on the theory that it was insufficiently reliable to justify the expenditure of substantial police resources in obtaining corroboration? Should Detective Mader have anticipated the importance which reviewing courts would attach to the discrepancy in the travel arrangements, and obtained a warrant authorizing a search only if the suspects returned home within 24 hours? Should Mader have ignored the warrant procedure, waited until the *Gates* couple arrived at home, and then searched their car with probable cause under the automobile exception to the warrant requirement? (After being caught in possession of 350 pounds of marijuana, one or both of the suspects might well have consented to a search of the house, considering that little would be gained by a refusal.) How do you think the dissenters would prefer the police to have acted?

Commentators were mostly critical of *Gates*. See e.g. Kamisar, "Gates, 'Probable Cause,' 'Good Faith,' and Beyond," 69 Iowa L.Rev. 557 (1984); Wasserstrom, "The Incredible Shrinking Fourth Amendment," 21 Am.Crim. L.Rev. 257 (1984); 1 LaFave & Israel Criminal Procedure 192–203 (1984). Professor Grano defends the decision in his article "Probable Cause and Common Sense: A Reply to the Critics of Illinois v. Gates," 17 U.Mich. J.L.Ref. 465 (1984).

2. *Some state courts went in a different direction.* The Supreme Court applied the *Gates* standard in Massachusetts v. Upton, 466 U.S. 727 (1984).

A Lt. Beland had participated in a search of a motel room reserved by one Richard Kelleher, in the course of which the police recovered some items stolen from two recently burglarized homes. Later than day, he received a telephone call from an unidentified woman who told him that there was "a motor home full of stolen stuff" parked behind the home of one George Upton. She said that the stolen items included jewelry, silver and gold (similar items had been taken in the two burglaries previously mentioned). She further told Lt. Beland that Upton was going to move the motor home soon because he had learned of the raid on Kelleher's motel room and he had purchased the stolen items from Kelleher. She said she had seen the stolen items but refused to identify herself because Upton would kill her. Lt. Beland responded that he knew that the caller was Upton's girlfriend Lynn Alberico, whom he had previously met. The caller admitted that she was that person, and said that she had "broken up" with Upton and wanted to "burn him."

Following the telephone call, Beland went to the Upton house to verify that a motor home was parked on the property. Then, while other officers watched the premises, he prepared an affidavit setting out the information related above. He also attached the police reports on the two prior burglaries, along with lists of the stolen property. A magistrate issued the search warrant, and a subsequent search of the motor home produced the items described by the caller and other stolen property.

The Massachusetts Supreme Court held the warrant invalid, explaining that probable cause was lacking for the following reasons: (1) The basis of the informant's knowledge was not "forcefully apparent.... Although she said that she had seen the stolen property, she did not say that she had seen it in the motor home or when she had seen it." (2) The informer's reliability was not sufficiently demonstrated. She was essentially anonymous, despite her unverified assent to the proposition that she was Lynn Alberico. Beland did not state that he really did know who she was, and she may have been covering up her true identity. (3) The corroboration was insufficient to cure the preceding deficiencies. Commonwealth v. Upton, 390 Mass. 562, 458 N.E.2d 717 (Mass. 1983).

The Supreme Court reversed per curiam, emphasizing that *Gates* had abandoned the two-pronged test, and that the information in the affidavit taken as a whole satisfied the new standard announced in *Gates*. After the remand, the Massachusetts Supreme Court held the warrant invalid under the search and seizure provision of the *state* constitution. Commonwealth v. Upton, 394 Mass. 363, 476 N.E.2d 548 (1985). The Massachusetts court observed that the *Gates* standard was "unacceptably shapeless and permissive," and announced that it would continue to apply the two-pronged test of the *Aguilar* and *Spinelli* cases in interpreting the state constitution. Several other states courts have also declined to follow *Gates* when interpreting their state constitutions.

The New York Court of Appeals also declined to follow *Gates* in interpreting its state constitutional search and seizure provision, in People v. Griminger, 71 N.Y.2d 635, 529 N.Y.S.2d 55, 524 N.E.2d 409 (1988). In that case a counterfeiting suspect gave U.S. Secret Service agents a detailed statement describing drugs which he had observed in Griminger's bedroom. One of the agents then obtained a warrant to search Griminger's home.

According to the affidavit this agent prepared, a confidential informant known as "Source A" had observed the drugs in the bedroom and attic and had observed the defendant selling drugs as recently as seven days ago. The affidavit also stated that, pursuant to a consent search, about four pounds of marijuana were found in a garbage can at the same residence. Although the agent did not personally know the counterfeiting suspect, his affidavit identified the informer as "a person known to your deponent." The agent did not say that the informer was under arrest when he provided the information, and gave no other information pertaining to reliability. The New York court affirmed findings by lower courts that this information failed to establish the reliability prong, and defended the *Aguilar–Spinelli* test against charges that it is excessively technical. The New York court also held that the state constitutional standard would apply even though the warrant was issued by a federal judge at the request of a federal officer.

3.   *Anticipatory warrants*. Should Detective Mader have obtained an "anticipatory search warrant," allowing a search of the Gates residence only if the automobile arrived from Florida on schedule? At the time such warrants were highly unusual, but after *Gates* they became common. The United States Court of Appeals for the Seventh Circuit discussed anticipatory warrants in United States v. Leidner, 99 F.3d 1423 (7th Cir.1996). In that case Missouri police found 200 pounds of marijuana in a car driven by Sapp. Sapp said that he was transporting the marijuana to Leidner's home in Illinois, and agreed to make a controlled delivery to Leidner. On the basis of those facts Illinois police obtained a warrant to search Leidner's residence. The issuing magistrate orally told them that they should not execute the warrant until the delivery occurred, but the warrant itself did not contain this limitation. Sapp made the delivery and the police then made the search.

A federal district judge held the ASW invalid because it did not state that the search was to be made only if the delivery occurred. The Court of Appeals reversed this holding, reasoning that it was implicit in all the circumstances that the controlled delivery would precede the search. A more difficult issue was that there was no independent evidence, other than the word of the informer, that the marijuana really had been intended for Leidner. Leidner's counsel argued that Sapp could have named anyone he knew in an effort to transfer the blame from himself after being caught with the contraband, in hope of getting a better deal from the authorities. The Court of Appeals held that Sapp's information was sufficiently detailed and credible to meet the probable cause standard of *Gates*.

The Ninth Circuit took a different view of the anticipatory warrant in United States v. Hotal, 143 F.3d 1223 (9th Cir.1998). The defendant had ordered videotapes containing child pornography from a mailed offer which was part of a government sting operation. A postal inspector obtained a warrant authorizing a search of the defendant's home "forthwith." The warrant also incorporated by reference the inspector's affidavit, which said that the search would be conducted only after the defendant received the tapes and took them into his home. Case law in the Ninth Circuit does not permit the government to cure a defective warrant by using information contained in the affidavit unless there is proof that the affidavit accompanied the warrant at the time of the search. There was no such proof in this case, and so the Ninth Circuit panel, in an opinion by the frequently reversed

Judge Stephen Reinhardt, held that the warrant was invalid even though the search was actually conducted only after the triggering event.

See also, United States v. Gendron, 18 F.3d 955, 965 (1st Cir.1994), where Chief Judge Breyer, now Justice Breyer, wrote that "the simple fact that a warrant is 'anticipatory'—i.e., that it takes effect, not upon issuance, but at a specified future time—does not invalidate a warrant or make it somehow suspect or legally disfavored."

UNITED STATES v. CELIO

United States Court of Appeals, Seventh Circuit, 1991.
945 F.2d 180.

CUDAHY, CIRCUIT JUDGE

* * * Lino Celio was a passenger in a large truck travelling through Illinois on February 14, 1985, when the vehicle was stopped by the Illinois State Police. After the vehicle was towed to the police station and then to a garage, a search revealed that Celio's suitcase contained approximately one pound of heroin. Defendant claims the police had no probable cause to conduct this search. But his argument disregards the rather important sequence of events that took place just prior to the vehicle's search.

Toward the end of 1984, several law enforcement agencies including the DEA and the FBI conducted an investigation of a suspected large-scale drug operation smuggling heroin and other drugs from Mexico into the United States. The organization, allegedly run by one Jaime Herrera–Nevarez, maintained ties to California, Chicago, Detroit, parts of Indiana and, most directly, Texas. Pursuant to a judicial order, the FBI installed a pen register on the telephone of Jesus Herrera, a suspected collaborator, in Calumet City outside Chicago, and also began intercepting the phone calls of putative coconspirator Luis Armando Villela–Jurado. During the relevant time period, persons at these two numbers repeatedly contacted each other, two other residences in Chicago and a motel in Alsip, Illinois. We refer to those involved in this crisscrossing network as the Chicago group.

Between November 30, 1984, and the date Celio was stopped, there was likewise a flurry of activity centered around two motels in the El Paso, Texas area. In most instances, Ubaldo Esparza–Corral would register for a room at one of the motels, keep the room anywhere from four to eight days and check out. The rooms Esparza–Corral occupied would always be the source and recipient of numerous long-distance phone calls, most of them to or from members of the Chicago group. Those conversations that agents actually intercepted were frequently carried on in language recognized as drug-code. Esparza–Corral was usually accompanied in the rooms by one or more of the same group of persons, including the defendant on several occasions. One member of this El Paso group, Rodolfo Esparza–Corral, even showed up in the motel room in Alsip in late December, at about the time that room was receiving phone calls from other Chicago group members. In the same general time period, an older, five-ton white truck was first spotted on December 6, and continually appeared at or near the El Paso motels at which Esparza–Corral was staying.

The phone conversations began sounding more urgent, and by the beginning of February 1985 it became clear from the drug-code being used that a major shipment was on its way into the Chicago area. In a February 5 phone call to his motel room, Esparza–Corral reported in code that the cake had arrived, would be ready tomorrow and was being cut for the fiesta. On February 13 agents noticed three persons unloading plastic-wrapped packages and a triple-beam scale from a car into Esparza–Corral's room at one motel. Later that night, officers observed Esparza–Corral and Celio driving away from that same motel and out of the city in the identical five-ton white truck often spotted with the El Paso group. The truck headed north and was kept under surveillance until it was inside Illinois. At that point the DEA requested that the Illinois State Police stop and search the truck in connection with suspected drug smuggling. The police found the truck speeding illegally on an interstate highway and stopped the vehicle.

The state police towed the truck to a garage, where they searched it for a number of hours. According to the government's argument, this search was based strictly on the message from the DEA agents (and not at all on the truck's illegal speed or any apparent, suspicious activity). The officers found the heroin in the defendant's suitcase (alongside his passport) almost immediately, but only later were they able to discover the hidden compartment in the truck which contained 812 pounds of marijuana. Defendant was tried and convicted of possession with intent to distribute heroin.

Defendant first challenges the district court's denial of his motion to suppress the heroin for fourth amendment violations. This challenge has two prongs: no probable cause existed to permit the warrantless search of the truck, or alternatively, even if the federal agents had sufficient suspicion of the transportation of contraband, their conclusory statements to the state police could not supply the arresting officers with probable cause to search. We can dispose of the first point briefly. Assuming for the moment that we may treat the state officers as if they possessed the information obtained by the federal surveillance, we affirm the finding of probable cause. * * *

In response to our conclusion that the federal authorities had probable cause to search the truck, defendant protests that this probable cause was never at the disposal of the state officials making the arrest. If the state police possessed probable cause, they acquired it on February 14, when the DEA contacted the state police and requested that the truck be stopped and searched on suspicion of drug smuggling. The agents relayed none of the facts forming the basis of that conclusion. The state conducted its search on the bald assertion by the federal agents that they suspected drug trafficking.

The government could point us to no precedent directly supporting the search in this case. Still, we believe the district court's decision involved a logical extension of precedent. In United States v. Hensley, 469 U.S. 221 (1985) [infra this casebook, p. 250], the Supreme Court recognized the validity of inter-sovereign transference of suspicion of crimes. A flyer issued by a foreign sovereign (Ohio), seeking Hensley for investigation of a completed robbery, prompted a Kentucky police officer to conduct a *Terry* stop of the suspect. During the brief questioning that ensued, a fellow officer spied a gun protruding from beneath the passenger seat of the car Hensley was driving. The car was subsequently searched and the defendant was later arrested for possession of a weapon by a felon. Hensley challenged the stop itself, based as it was on a foreign state's unelaborated belief that probable cause existed to stop the suspect for questioning. The Supreme Court upheld the admission of the weapon at trial nonetheless, reasoning that the relevant question was whether the officers who issued the flyer possessed probable cause for the *Terry* stop. * * *

The case before us parallels *Hensley* in two respects. The police action was based entirely on a request from a different jurisdiction that the subject be apprehended, and the representation involved only a generalized statement without the factual details in which the suspicion was rooted. If this search can be defended at all, it must be justified, like the search in *Hensley,* on the "collective knowledge" of the various authorities involved. But this case is at once both a harder and easier case than *Hensley* and other cases relying on that decision. The case is harder because the police action in this case was far more intrusive than a mere investigatory *Terry* stop. Without any first-hand knowledge giving rise to a suspicion, the state officers interrupted the defendant's trip, towed his vehicle to the station and then to a garage and searched the truck along with its contents for four hours.

The case is easier, however, due to the more specific information available to the Illinois police before they conducted the search. Though the DEA did not inform the state officers of the intricate details of its surveillance, it did provide them with the location and direction of a specific vehicle and its suspected contents. * * * The case is easier still because the request described a continuing crime rather than one already completed or still in the future. The increased specificity and the more exigent circumstances permit the more intrusive search based on "collective knowledge" alone.

In upholding this particular search, we do not take lightly the general requirement that the apprehending officer must have probable cause before making a warrantless stop or search. And we broaden "collective knowledge" searches with the understanding that one or both governmental entities involved stand to incur any resulting civil liability should the suspicion on which the request was based prove insufficient or the action taken in reliance on it prove excessive. See Capone v. Marinelli, 868 F.2d 102, 105 (3d Cir.1989) (officer arresting on basis of different jurisdiction's bulletin will have good faith defense to civil suit only if "objective reading of the bulletin" allows officer to reasonably rely on it); Donta v. Hooper, 774 F.2d 716 (6th Cir.1985) (officers of arresting department potentially liable for illegal arrest founded on bulletin from sheriff's office in neighboring state), cert. denied, 483 U.S. 1019 (1987); cf. Hensley, 469 U.S. at 232–33 ("The officers making the stop may have a good-faith defense to any civil suit * * *. It is the objective reading of the flyer or bulletin that determines whether other police officers can defensibly act in reliance on it.").

Nevertheless, we recognize the importance of coordinated law enforcement activities in this day of international drug cartels and interstate contraband delivery networks.

In an era when criminal suspects are increasingly mobile and increasingly likely to flee across jurisdictional boundaries, this rule is a matter of common sense: it minimizes the volume of information concerning suspects that must be transmitted to other jurisdictions and enables police in one jurisdiction to act promptly in reliance on information from another jurisdiction. * * * The conviction is AFFIRMED.

ANDRESEN v. MARYLAND

Supreme Court of the United States, 1976.
427 U.S. 463, 96 S.Ct. 2737, 49 L.Ed.2d 627.

MR. JUSTICE BLACKMUN delivered the opinion of the Court.

[State investigators obtained substantial evidence that Andresen, a lawyer specializing in real estate settlements, had committed fraud in connection with the sale of property described as "Lot 13T." A judge found that there was probable cause and issued a warrant to search Andresen's offices and seize documents pertaining to the sale of Lot 13T. The investigators seized the described documents and many others as well. Following a hearing on Andresen's suppression motion, the state trial court ordered the return of a number of files not related to the charges concerning Lot 13T. Some of the remaining documents were used to convict Andresen of fraud.

The Supreme Court first considered whether the seizure of business records violated Andresen's Fifth Amendment privilege not to be a witness against himself. The majority held that the seizure did not violate the privilege because Andresen was not compelled to say or do anything. He was not compelled to make the records, and the seizure was by law enforcement officers without his assistance. A handwriting expert authenticated the documents at trial, and so Andresen was not required to do anything to assist in his own conviction. The Court thus repudiated a frequently quoted statement from the opinion in Boyd v. United States, 116 U.S. 616, 633 (1886), where the Court had said: "We have been unable to perceive that the seizure of a man's private books and papers to be used in evidence against him is substantially different from compelling him to be a witness against himself."]

We turn next to petitioner's contention that rights guaranteed him by the Fourth Amendment were violated because the descriptive terms of the search warrants were so broad as to make them impermissible "general" warrants, and because certain items were seized in violation of the principles of *Warden v. Hayden*, 387 U.S. 294 (1967).

The specificity of the search warrants. Although petitioner concedes that the warrants for the most part were models of particularity, he contends that they were rendered fatally "general" by the addition, in each warrant, to the exhaustive list of particularly described documents, of the phrase "together with other fruits, instrumentalities and evidence of crime at this [time] unknown." The quoted language, it is argued, must be read in isolation and without reference to the rest of the long sentence at the end of which it appears. When read "properly," petitioner contends, it permits the search for and seizure of any evidence of any crime.

General warrants, of course, are prohibited by the Fourth Amendment. "[T]he problem [posed by the general warrant] is not that of intrusion *per se*, but of a general, exploratory rummaging in a person's belongings. * * * [The Fourth Amendment addresses the problem] by requiring a 'particular description' of the things to be seized." *Coolidge v. New Hampshire*, 403 U.S. 443, 467 (1971). This requirement " 'makes general searches * * * impossible and prevents the seizure of one thing under a warrant describing another. As to what is to be taken, nothing is left to the discretion of the officer executing the warrant.' " *Stanford v. Texas*, 379 U.S. 476, 485 (1965), quoting *Marron v. United States*, 275 U.S., at 196.

In this case we agree with the determination of the Court of Special Appeals of Maryland that the challenged phrase must be read as authorizing only the search for and seizure of evidence relating to "the crime of false pretenses with respect to Lot 13T." The challenged phrase is not a separate sentence. Instead, it appears in each warrant at the end of a sentence containing a lengthy list of specified and particular items to be seized, all pertaining to Lot 13T. We think it clear from the context that the term "crime" in the warrants refers only to the crime of false pretenses with respect to the sale of Lot 13T. The "other fruits" clause is one of a series that follows the colon after the word "Maryland." All clauses in the series are limited by what precedes that colon, namely, "items pertaining to * * * lot 13, block T." The warrants, accordingly, did not authorize the executing officers to conduct a search for evidence of other crimes but only to search for and seize evidence relevant to the crime of false pretenses and Lot 13T.

The admissibility of certain items of evidence in light of Warden v. Hayden. Petitioner charges that the seizure of documents pertaining to a lot other than Lot 13T violated the principles of *Warden v. Hayden* and therefore should have been suppressed. His objection appears to be that these papers were not relevant to the Lot 13T charge and were admissible only to prove another crime with which he was charged after the search. The fact that these documents were used to help form the evidentiary basis for another charge, it is argued, shows that the documents were seized solely for that purpose. * * *

In *Warden v. Hayden*, 387 U.S., at 307, the Court stated that when the police seize " 'mere evidence,' probable cause must be examined in terms of cause to believe that the evidence sought will aid in a particular apprehension or conviction. In so doing, consideration of police purposes will be required." In this case, we conclude that the trained special investigators reasonably could have believed that the evidence specifically dealing with another lot in the Potomac Woods subdivision could be used to show petitioner's intent with respect to the Lot 13T transaction. * * * Although these records subsequently were used to secure additional charges against petitioner, suppression of this evidence in this case was not required. The fact that the records could be used to show intent to defraud with respect to Lot 13T permitted the seizure and satisfied the requirements of *Warden v. Hayden*.

The judgment of the Court of Special Appeals of Maryland is affirmed.

It is so ordered.

Mr. Justice Brennan, dissenting. * * *

Even if a Fifth Amendment violation is not to be recognized in the seizure of petitioner's papers, a violation of Fourth Amendment protections clearly should be, for the warrants under which those papers were seized were impermissibly general. General warrants are especially prohibited by the Fourth Amendment. * * * After a lengthy and admittedly detailed listing of items to be seized, the warrants in this case further authorized the seizure of "other fruits, instrumentalities and evidence of crime at this [time] unknown." The Court construes this sweeping authorization to be limited to evidence pertaining to the crime of false pretenses with respect to the sale of Lot 13T. However, neither this Court's construction of the warrants nor the similar construction by the Court of Special Appeals of Maryland was available to the investigators at the time they executed the warrants. The question is not how those warrants are to be viewed in hindsight, but how they were in fact viewed by those executing them. The overwhelming quantity of seized material that was either suppressed or returned to petitioner is irrefutable testimony to the unlawful generality of the warrants. The Court's attempt to cure this defect by *post hoc* judicial construction evades principles settled in this Court's Fourth Amendment decisions. "The scheme of the Fourth Amendment becomes meaningful only when it is assured that at some point the conduct of those charged with enforcing the laws can be subjected to the more detached, neutral scrutiny of a judge * * *." *Terry v. Ohio*, 392 U.S. 1, 21 (1968). It is not the function of a detached and neutral review to give effect to warrants whose terms unassailably authorize the far-reaching search and seizure of a person's papers, especially where that has in fact been the result of executing those warrants.

Commentary

When the police have probable cause to obtain a warrant to search a home or place of business for something, they rarely find the "particularity" requirement of the Fourth Amendment to be troublesome. The typical warrant authorizes the seizure of narcotics or stolen property, and a search of the entire premises under the suspect's control can ordinarily be justified in pursuit of these items. Whatever else turns up will be admissible under the "plain view" doctrine. Warrants also frequently authorize the seizure of additional items that are relevant to proving possession, ownership or intent with respect to the contraband or stolen property named in the warrant. When the officers go too far and seize unrelated material, the courts simply order them to return the excess.

The only Supreme Court case to give any content to the particularity requirement is Stanford v. Texas, 379 U.S. 476 (1965). The officers in that case were enforcing a Texas statute which outlawed the Communist Party. In that effort they obtained a warrant authorizing the search and seizure of "books, records, pamphlets, cards, receipts, lists, memoranda, pictures, recordings and other written instruments concerning the Communist Party of Texas." Pursuant to that warrant they seized from petitioner's home and place of business some two thousand books and pamphlets including works by "such diverse writers as Karl Marx, Jean Paul Sartre, Theodore Draper, Fidel Castro, Earl Browder, Pope John XXIII, and Mr. Justice Hugo L. Black." The Supreme Court unanimously and with a straight face held that "this warrant was of a kind which it was the purpose of the Fourth Amendment to forbid—a general warrant." Hence, all the seized property had to be returned.

Fourth Amendment theory suggests that a general warrant is altogether invalid, so that even items that could legitimately be seized under a narrowly-drawn warrant will be inadmissible. In United States v. Foster, 100 F.3d 846 (10th Cir.1996), Oklahoma deputy sheriffs obtained a valid warrant to search Foster's residence for marijuana and for 3 specified firearms. They actually seized some 35 items, including VCR's, television sets, tools, and videotapes showing the defendant engaged in sexual acts with his stepdaughter. At the suppression hearing, the supervising deputy candidly admitted that it was standard policy in his department, when executing a search warrant, to seize everything of value on the premises to investigate whether some items might be stolen goods. The Court of Appeals affirmed the District Court's finding that the officers had acted in flagrant disregard of the terms of the warrant, and held that the appropriate remedy was to suppress all items seized in the search, including the items that were actually named in the warrant. The Court cited United States v. Medlin, 842 F.2d 1194 (10th Cir.1988) for the proposition that "when law enforcement officers grossly exceed the scope of a search warrant in seizing property, the particularity requirement is undermined and a valid warrant is transformed into a general warrant thereby requiring suppression of all evidence seized under that warrant." (842 F.2d at 1199). Compare United States v. Matias, 836 F.2d 744, 747–48 (2d Cir.1988) (refusing to employ the "drastic remedy" of suppression of all evidence seized because the "normal remedy" of suppressing and returning only the items seized outside the scope of the warrant was more appropriate).

In some high/profile, violent/crime cases, Fourth Amendment concerns collide with other public values. The California Supreme Court dealt with a "particularity" issue under its state constitutional prohibition of unreasonable searches in People v. Frank, 38 Cal.3d 711, 214 Cal.Rptr. 801, 700 P.2d 415 (1985). There the defendant abducted, sexually molested, tortured and murdered a two-year-old girl. Suspicion immediately focused upon Frank because he was known to be a recidivist child molester recently released from a mental institution, and because he had been seen in the child's neighborhood at the time of the disappearance. On the basis of this circumstantial evidence, the police obtained a warrant to search his residence for items such as bits of the victim's skin and hair and the locking pliers used to torture her. The warrant also contained three broad "boilerplate" clauses authorizing the police to search for and seize any papers or documentary evidence that might conceivably link Frank to the murder.[a]

The police made a very through search of the entire residence pursuant to the warrant. Among the many items seized were the vise-grip pliers (identified scientifically as the instrument used to torture the child), and two notebooks in which the defendant had detailed his extensive experience in abducting and sexually abusing children. The prosecution made some use of these notebooks to bolster its circumstantial case of murder, and quoted from them repeatedly at the penalty phase of the trial to obtain a death sentence.

The California Supreme Court upheld the conviction but reversed the death sentence. The plurality opinion held that the search warrant was valid insofar as it authorized a search for specified items of physical evidence, but concluded that there was no probable cause to search for incriminating papers. The plurality also held that the extensive exploratory search of papers authorized by the warrant violated the particularity requirement of the search and seizure provision of the California Constitution, which is identical in wording to the Fourth Amendment. The plurality did not hold that this defect invalidated the warrant in its entirety; it ruled merely that the notebooks should have been suppressed. The plurality went on to hold that the admission of the notebooks was harmless error on the issue of guilt, but prejudicial on the issue of penalty.

A dissenting opinion in *Frank* conceded that the warrant was overbroad, but advanced the argument that the seizure of the notebooks could nonetheless be justified if the officers discovered them in the course of a search for the items of physical evidence that were properly specified in the warrant.

a. The clauses were:

"1. Evidence tending to establish the identities of the occupants, users or owners of the residence, including, but not limited to utility bills or receipts, envelopes, traffic tickets, insurance papers or vehicle registration;

"2. Documentary evidence tending to show the whereabouts of Theodore Frank during March 14 and 15, 1978, including, but not limited to credit card receipts, receipts from businesses, records of telephone toll calls made during that period of time; cancelled checks made out or cashed on those dates, ledgers or personal diary notations which would indicate the whereabouts of Theodore Frank on those dates; * * *

"8. Scrapbooks, newspaper clippings, photographs (developed or undeveloped), tape recordings or writings which could relate to the death of Amy [S.] and would indicate either participation and/or an interest in that death by Theodore Frank; * * *"

For example, locks of the victim's hair could have been hidden in the pages of the notebooks, and the police might have discovered the incriminating admissions while leafing through the books in search of the hair. The dissent went on to suggest that the prosecution may not have presented evidence on this "plain view" theory because the defense made only a vague and general suppression motion which did not alert the prosecution to the importance of the particularity issue. This suggestion helps to illustrate why the particularity requirement is so rarely an obstacle to a resourceful officer.

Very strict enforcement of the particularity requirement would be a substantial obstacle to the effective prosecution of fraud and other white collar crimes, where proof may depend upon documents whose precise nature cannot be known in advance. In the majority opinion in *Andresen*, for example, the Supreme Court noted that "under investigation was a complex real estate scheme whose existence could be proved only by piecing together many bits of evidence," and announced that "the complexity of an illegal scheme may not be used as a shield to avoid detection." The implication seems to be that the particularity requirement is satisfied when the investigators describe the general nature of what they are looking for, if they cannot reasonably be expected to do more.

Many searches are based on tips by informers who claim to have seen narcotics, stolen property or the like on the premises. In other cases, such as People v. Frank, the police have probable cause to believe the defendant committed the crime but can only speculate as to what if any evidence might be on the premises. People v. Frank is also extraordinary in that it involved a horrible murder, where the public interest in identifying the guilty person was especially great. Another court might have held that it was reasonable in the circumstances to issue a warrant authorizing a broad search for evidence relating to the particular murder under investigation. From time to time there have even been suggestions that the exclusionary rule should be inapplicable to some narrow category of extremely serious crimes, where the release of a highly dangerous individual may be too high a price to pay for enforcing the Fourth Amendment. See Kaplan, "The Limits of the Exclusionary Rule," 26 Stan.L.Rev. 1027 (1974). The suggestion has never been adopted, but probably the courts are more likely to uphold a search or find harmless error in a borderline case when the crime is particularly serious.

Documentary searches are particularly troublesome when they involve news gathering organizations (see *Zurcher v. Stanford Daily, supra,* p. 191), or law offices. The potential for invasion of privacy is enormous if investigators look through a large number of files as they often must to determine relevance, and there is a substantial danger that the authorities may abuse the warrant procedure to harass troublesome lawyers or their clients. California has adopted an interesting procedure for controlling potential abuses of this type. California Penal Code § 1524 provides special protections where a warrant authorizes a search for documentary evidence in the possession of a professional person who is not reasonably suspected of having engaged in criminal activity relating to that evidence. When the warrant is issued the Court appoints a special master (selected from a list of qualified attorneys maintained by the State Bar) who accompanies the officers. This special master informs the party served of the specific items being sought and gives that person an opportunity to provide the items requested. If the person does not do so, or cannot be located, then the special master conducts the search. Documents which are arguably privileged are taken to the court under seal for determination of whether they should be disclosed.

It is important to remember that documents and other evidence may be protected by a privilege, even if Fourth and Fifth Amendment concerns are set aside. For example, confidential communications between lawyer and client or husband and wife are likely to be privileged, regardless of whether they are obtained by methods that comply with the Fourth Amendment. Detailed consideration of the applicable privileges and their scope and limitations is left to the course in Evidence.

Chapter 6

DETENTION AND SEARCH
OF THE PERSON

Introductory Commentary

We have already seen that the police may make an arrest if they have probable cause, and that they frequently may do so without a warrant.[1] We have also seen that, incident to a lawful arrest, officers may search the person of the arrestee and a rather vaguely defined "grabbing area" in the immediate vicinity.

The Supreme Court has often said that the purpose of the search incident to arrest is to permit the officer to search for dangerous weapons, or for evidence which the arrestee might try to conceal or destroy. That rationale is easy to understand when the suspect is apprehended fleeing from a robbery, but the police may search an arrestee even if the circumstances do not suggest any likelihood that evidence or weapons will be found. In United States v. Robinson, 414 U.S. 218 (1973), police arrested the defendant for operating a motor vehicle after his driver's license had been revoked. The arresting officer made an initial "pat-down" search, then removed a crumpled up cigarette package from the defendant's pocket, and looked inside. The package contained heroin. The Supreme Court's majority opinion by Justice Rehnquist held the search lawful, stating that "the authority to search the person incident to a lawful custodial arrest, while based upon the need to disarm and to discover evidence, does not depend on what a court may later decide was the probability in a particular arrest situation that weapons or evidence would in fact be found upon the person of the suspect." See also, Gustafson v. Florida, 414 U.S. 260 (1973).

The *Robinson* decision was controversial, and a number of state supreme courts have refused to follow it in interpreting the search and seizure provisions of their state constitutions. In any event, the opinions in both *Robinson* and *Gustafson* stress that the officers were justified in each case in making a full custodial arrest. State laws often restrict the authority of

---

1. This statement is subject to the qualification in some jurisdictions that the arrest must be for a felony. State laws frequently provide that an officer may make an arrest for a misdemeanor only if the crime occurred in his or her presence. If a reliable informant tells the officer that someone has committed a misdemeanor, the officer must obtain a warrant before making the arrest.

237

officers to make such arrests for traffic violations and other minor offenses. Persons stopped for relatively serious offenses like drunk driving or driving with a suspended license are arrested, but persons stopped for less serious violations who present proper identification may be released with a citation to appear in court at a later date. In a state having a system of citation release, a full arrest for a minor traffic offense might not be lawful. Where the officer has discretionary authority either to issue a citation or to make an arrest for a traffic violation, a search for evidence is lawful only if he actually chooses to make the arrest. Knowles v. Iowa, 525 U.S. 113 (1998).

After a full custodial arrest, the arrestee is ordinarily subject to a second "booking search" to prevent the introduction of weapons or contraband into the jail. At this time the jail officers may also make an inventory search of the arrestee's clothing and personal property on the same rationale that permits an inventory search of an automobile in police custody. (See *Colorado v. Bertine, supra*, p. ___.) As in the case of the automobile inventory search, the principal contested issue is whether the police may open purses, briefcases and other containers to inventory the contents. In Illinois v. Lafayette, 462 U.S. 640 (1983), the Supreme Court upheld the admissibility of drugs found in the arrestee's shoulder bag following his arrest for disturbing the peace. Conceding that the defendant's property might have been adequately protected by sealing it in a locker without opening it, the majority refused to "second-guess police departments as to what practical administrative method will best deter theft by and false claims against its employees and preserve the security of the station house."

Before 1968, Supreme Court decisions treated any seizure of the person as an arrest, requiring probable cause. Searches of the person usually had to be justified as incident to a lawful arrest, and their legality turned upon whether the officer had probable cause before acting.[2] The underlying theory seemed to be that officers should not subject an individual to a search or seizure—however limited in time, scope and intrusiveness—unless they can meet the probable cause standard.

The difficulty with this "all or nothing" approach is that it theoretically requires the same justification for police actions that invade privacy and dignity interests only slightly as for full custodial arrests and thorough searches of the person. Why should an officer need to have the same justification for detaining an individual for a few minutes on the street as for subjecting him to the extensive inconvenience, humiliation, and even danger involved in a full-scale arrest and booking?

Proponents of a more flexible approach argued that officers in a modern urban police department cannot simply wait passively for probable cause to

2. A search may be justified as incident to an arrest even if the search preceded the officer's decision to take the suspect into custody. For example, suppose that a reliable informant tells an officer that he has personal knowledge that an individual is carrying narcotics in his pockets. The officer has probable cause to make the arrest, but in fact he will let the suspect go if he does not find the narcotics (or other incriminating material) in the search. Ordinarily, he will not tell the suspect that he is under arrest until he has found the incriminating evidence. Courts generally classify this type of search as incident to an arrest, and uphold it if the officer had probable cause before he searched. It might be more accurate to say that the officer has probable cause to search, under an "exigent circumstances" exception to the warrant requirement, and that this lawful search produces the grounds for the arrest.

appear so that they can arrest individuals for prosecution. The police are expected to prevent crime as well as to make arrests when crimes have already occurred, and this task often requires them to stop individuals for investigation on the basis of suspicious circumstances that do not amount to probable cause for arrest. To protect his own safety, an officer will often "frisk" such an individual by patting down his clothing to make sure that he is not carrying a gun or a knife. A holding that such essential law enforcement activities are inherently unconstitutional would be unrealistic and unenforceable, or so the argument went. The courts would eventually have to relax probable cause standards across the board to permit "stop and frisk" patrolling, or they would have to declare that these activities are not regulated by the Fourth Amendment at all. A better alternative, proponents of the flexible approach argued, would be to seek to regulate stops and frisks by subjecting them to a standard less rigorous than probable cause.

There were important arguments on the other side as well. A rigid "all or nothing" approach to searches and seizures has its disadvantages, but so does a flexible approach which balances the degree of the intrusion and the law enforcement need against the privacy interests of the suspect in every case. There is no way for the Supreme Court to promulgate rules for the guidance of police officers if every situation turns on its individual facts and requires the balancing of a variety of legitimate considerations. As one commentator put it, a general balancing approach "converts the Fourth Amendment into one immense Rorschach blot."[3] Moreover, what a police chief calls "preventive patrolling" may seem more like harassment and discrimination to the residents of high crime areas whose appearance or activities are of the kind that arouse the suspicions of the police. It is difficult enough to define and enforce a standard of probable cause. To permit intrusive police practices on less than probable cause is little different from abandoning the attempt to regulate them all together, or so this side of the argument went.

The Supreme Court settled the argument in Terry v. Ohio, 392 U.S. 1 (1968), a case which may be cited as evidence that the Supreme Court remained highly sensitive to the practical needs of law enforcement even at the height of its reforming period under the leadership of Chief Justice Earl Warren. In *Terry*, an experienced plainclothes detective observed three suspects peering repeatedly into a store window, walking on, and then returning to peer again. The detective suspected that these individuals were "casing a stickup," and proceeded to confront them. He identified himself and asked the suspects for their names, receiving only a mumbled reply. He then "spun Terry around," patted his breast pocket, and removed a pistol which formed the basis of a concealed weapons charge.

The majority opinion by Chief Justice Warren emphatically rejected the notion that stops and frisks are outside the purview of the Fourth Amendment altogether, announcing that "there can be no question [that the officer] 'seized' petitioner and subjected him to a 'search' when he took hold of him and patted down the outer surfaces of his clothing." The action was therefore subject to the "reasonableness" requirement of the Fourth Amend-

3. Amsterdam, "Perspectives on the Fourth Amendment," 58 Minn.L.Rev. 349, 393 (1974).

ment, but not to the probable cause standard. It was reasonable for the officer to investigate the suspicious behavior, and in the circumstances reasonable to protect his own safety by the limited search for weapons. In explaining this holding, Chief Justice Warren reasoned that "an arrest is a wholly different type of intrusion upon individual freedom from a limited search for weapons," and that "there must be a narrowly drawn authority to permit a reasonable search for weapons for the protection of the police officer, where he has reason to believe that he is dealing with an armed and dangerous individual, regardless of whether he has probable cause to arrest the individual for a crime." *Id.*, at 27.[4]

Only Justice Douglas dissented from the principle that temporary detentions and frisks may be justifiable on less than probable cause. According to his dissenting opinion, "The infringement on personal liberty of any 'seizure' of a person can only be 'reasonable' under the Fourth Amendment if we require the police to possess 'probable cause' before they seize him. Only that line draws a meaningful distinction between an officer's mere inkling and the presence of facts within the officer's personal knowledge which would convince a reasonable man that the person seized has committed, is committing, or is about to commit a particular crime." *Id.* at 38.

The Supreme Court decided two companion cases along with *Terry*, which involved applications of New York's "stop-and-frisk" law. This statute provided that a police officer may stop any person in a public place whom he reasonably suspects to be involved in a felony, may demand of him his name, address and an explanation of his actions, and may "search such person for a dangerous weapon" if he "reasonably suspects that he is in danger of life or limb." The statute also authorized the seizure of any "weapon or any other thing the possession of which may constitute a crime." The Supreme Court declined to rule on the constitutionality of this statute in the abstract, and instead simply applied constitutional principles directly to the facts of the cases.

In Sibron v. New York, 392 U.S. 40 (1968), a uniformed officer observed Sibron over a period of eight hours on his beat engaging in conversations with six or eight persons whom the officer knew to be narcotics addicts. Eventually Sibron entered a restaurant and spoke with three more known addicts inside. At no time did the officer overhear any of the conversations, nor did he see anything pass between Sibron and the addicts. As Sibron sat down to eat, the officer approached him and told him to come outside. Once outside, the officer said "You know what I am after." Sibron mumbled something and reached into his pocket, at which time the officer put his hand into the same pocket and discovered several glassine envelopes which contained heroin. As in *Terry*, the Supreme Court declined to decide whether a seizure occurred before the officer reached into the pocket. The Court found the search unlawful because there was no indication that Sibron was armed or dangerous, the officer made it clear that he was looking for

4. The majority opinion in *Terry* focused upon the frisk as the activity requiring justification under the Fourth Amendment; it expressly refrained from deciding whether any "seizure" for Fourth Amendment purposes took place prior to the frisk. The case therefore decided nothing "concerning the constitutional propriety of an investigative 'seizure' upon less than probable cause for purposes of 'detention' and/or interrogation." *Id.*, at 19, note 16.

narcotics and not weapons, and the intrusion into the pocket was not preceded by a patting of the outer clothing.

Peters v. New York, the second companion case, was decided in the same opinion with *Sibron*. In *Peters* a police officer, at home in the apartment where he had lived for twelve years, heard a noise at the door. Through the peephole he saw two strangers tiptoeing about the hallway. He telephoned the police station, dressed, and took his revolver. Returning to the peephole, he again saw the two men tiptoeing toward the stairway. Believing he was witnessing an attempted burglary, he opened his door, entered the hallway and slammed the door loudly behind him. The two men fled down the stairs and the officer gave chase. He apprehended one of them (Peters) who claimed that he was visiting a girlfriend but refused to reveal her name on the ground that she was a married woman. The officer made a pat-down search for weapons, and discovered a hard object in Peters' pocket. He stated at the suppression hearing that the object did not feel like a gun, but that it might have been a knife. Removing the object, he found that it was "an opaque plastic envelope, containing burglar's tools." 392 U.S. at 49. *Peters* therefore involved difficult questions regarding the scope of the frisk permitted by *Terry*, and the admissibility of items other than weapons. The Supreme Court avoided these questions, however, by holding that the officer had probable cause to make an arrest and therefore could also make the more extensive search permitted incident to a lawful arrest. Justice Harlan, concurring in the result, doubted that the tip-toeing plus flight at the approach of a gun-carrying stranger amounted to probable cause, but he concluded that the officer had sufficient reasonable suspicion to justify a limited stop and frisk. Although the frisk turned up burglar's tools rather than a weapon, when the frisk "is lawful the State is of course entitled to the use of any other contraband that appears." 392 U.S. at 79 (Harlan, J., concurring).

The *Terry* principle was extended in Adams v. Williams, 407 U.S. 143 (1972). An officer on patrol in a high crime area was approached at 2:15 a.m. by a person known to him and informed that an individual in a nearby car was carrying narcotics and had a gun at his waist. The officer approached the vehicle to investigate and asked the occupant (Williams) to open the door. Williams instead rolled down the window, and the officer immediately reached into the car and removed a loaded revolver from his waistband. The officer then arrested Williams for unlawful possession of the gun, and a search incident to that arrest uncovered heroin. The Supreme Court affirmed the convictions for narcotics and weapons possession, ruling that reasonable cause for a stop and frisk may be based on an informant's tip as well as the officer's personal observation. "While properly investigating the activity of a person who was reported to be carrying narcotics and a concealed weapon and who was sitting alone in a car in a high-crime area at 2:15 in the morning," the majority opinion by Justice Rehnquist reasoned, the officer had reason to fear for his safety and his action in reaching to the spot where the gun was thought to be hidden constituted a "limited intrusion" which was reasonable in the circumstances. Dissenting Justices (Douglas, Marshall and Brennan) protested the extension of the *Terry* principle to investigation of narcotics possession, emphasized the conclusory nature of the unsubstantiated tip, and pointed out that the officer did not know whether the possession of the pistol was unlawful (because Williams might have had a permit).

Adams v. Williams was extended in Alabama v. White, 496 U.S. 325 (1990). Police received an anonymous tip that White would be leaving a particular address at a specified time in a brown Plymouth station wagon with a broken right taillight, that she would be going to Dobey's Motel, and that she would be in possession of about an ounce of cocaine inside a brown attache case. Officers went to the address, where they saw White leave the apartment carrying nothing in her hands, enter the described brown Plymouth, and drive directly to Dobey's Motel. There they stopped her, obtained consent to search, and found marijuana in a locked attache case in the car. They arrested her, and in a subsequent booking search found 3 milligrams of cocaine in her purse.

The state appellate court held that the officers did not have the reasonable suspicion required by *Terry,* so that the stop was unlawful. The Supreme Court majority opinion by Justice White likened the anonymous tip to the one in *Illinois v. Gates,* supra, p. ___, and said that by itself it did not furnish either probable cause or reasonable suspicion. The Court held, however, that by the time of the stop the officers had corroborated the tip in sufficient detail to furnish a reasonable suspicion that White was engaged in criminal activity. Justice Stevens dissented, joined by Justices Marshall and Brennan. He complained that "under the Court's holding, every citizen is subject to being seized and questioned by any officer who is prepared to testify that the warrantless stop was based on an anonymous tip predicting whatever conduct the officer just observed."

The "stop and frisk" rationale has also been used to uphold an inspection of the passenger compartment of an automobile. In Michigan v. Long, 463 U.S. 1032 (1983), two officers saw a car swerve into a ditch and stopped to investigate. Long, the only occupant of the car, got out to meet the deputies and supplied his driver's license upon demand. When asked for the vehicle registration, he started toward the open automobile door. The officer saw a large hunting knife on the floorboard, so they frisked Long and one officer entered the vehicle to look for a weapon. He found an open pouch of marijuana under an armrest, and Long's conviction for possessing this drug was affirmed. The Supreme Court majority opinion by Justice O'Connor held that a limited search of the passenger compartment of an automobile may be made where the officer possesses a reasonable belief based on specific and articulable facts that the suspect may be dangerous and may have a weapon in the vehicle. *Long* was distinguished in United States v. Lott, 870 F.2d 778 (1st Cir.1989). The officers in *Lott* had not frisked the suspects before looking into the vehicle, were not fearful of their own safety, and were admittedly looking for contraband, not weapons.

The Supreme Court clarified the scope of the frisk permitted in a *"Terry* stop" in Minnesota v. Dickerson, 508 U.S. 366 (1993). An officer observed Dickerson emerge from a notorious "crack house" and then turn abruptly to walk away when he became aware that police were watching him. The officer stopped Dickerson and administered a pat-down search. He found no weapons but felt a small lump in Dickerson's jacket pocket. He testified that "I examined it with my fingers and it slid and it felt to be a lump of crack cocaine in cellophane." The Minnesota Supreme Court held that the stop and frisk were both lawful, but the state court refused "to extend the plain view doctrine to the sense of touch." The Supreme Court affirmed on a different rationale. The majority opinion by Justice White reasoned that the logic of "plain view" extends to "plain feel"—if the officer feels an object and immediately recognizes it as contraband. In this case, however, the officer never thought the object was a weapon and did not immediately recognize it as crack cocaine until after "he squeezed, slid, and otherwise manipulated the pocket's contents." Because this further tactile manipulation was justified neither by the *Terry* rationale nor by probable cause, the contraband was inadmissible.

In State v. Jones, 103 Md.App. 548, 653 A.2d 1040 (Md.App.1995), the majority opinion by Justice Moylan observed that, although the prosecution lost the battle in Minnesota v. Dickerson, it won the "war" because the Supreme Court accepted in principle the concept of "plain feel." Thereafter, an officer could legitimate an arrest and seizure of drugs in similar circumstances by testifying credibly that his expertise enabled him to determine *immediately* that "rock-like substances" felt during a frisk were crack cocaine. In *Jones* the officer testified that the suspect consented to a frisk, and withdrew the consent only after the officer had felt the "rock-like" packages which (in a location notorious for drug dealing) the officer could identify at once as probably crack cocaine.

A *Terry* stop is ordinarily based upon a suspicion that the subject of the stop is involved in criminal activity. In a New York state case, officers looking for a suspect saw one of the suspect's friends in an automobile and stopped his car to ask if he knew the whereabouts of the suspect. The officers shined their flashlights into the stopped car, and saw a clear plastic bag containing marijuana in plain view. The New York Court of Appeals (split 4–3) held that the stop was unlawful because "If motorists could be pulled over at an individual officer's discretion based upon the mere right to request information, a pandora's box of pretextual police stops would be opened." The dissent argued that "the objective, factual basis for an informational stop is fully capable of assessment in order to insure that the police are not acting from pure whim or caprice, no less than in the case of an investigative stop of a vehicle whose occupants are suspected of criminal activity." People v. Spencer, 84 N.Y.2d 749, 622 N.Y.S.2d 483, 646 N.E.2d 785 (1995).

The following cases illustrate the current state of the law regarding detention and search of the person.

DUNAWAY v. NEW YORK

Supreme Court of the United States, 1979.
442 U.S. 200, 99 S.Ct. 2248, 60 L.Ed.2d 824.

MR. JUSTICE BRENNAN delivered the opinion of the Court. * * *

I

On March 26, 1971, the proprietor of a pizza parlor in Rochester, N.Y., was killed during an attempted robbery. On August 10, 1971, Detective Anthony Fantigrossi of the Rochester Police was told by another officer that an informant had supplied a possible lead implicating petitioner in the crime. Fantigrossi questioned the supposed source of the lead—a jail inmate awaiting trial for burglary—but learned nothing that supplied "enough information to get a warrant" for petitioner's arrest. Nevertheless, Fantigrossi ordered other detectives to "pick up" petitioner and "bring him in." Three detectives located petitioner at a neighbor's house on the morning of August 11. Petitioner was taken into custody; although he was not told he was under arrest, he would have been physically restrained if he had attempted to leave. He was driven to police headquarters in a police car and placed in an interrogation room, where he was questioned by officers after being given the [*Miranda*] warnings. Petitioner waived counsel and eventually made statements and drew sketches that incriminated him in the crime.

At petitioner's jury trial for attempted robbery and felony murder, his motions to suppress the statements and sketches were denied, and he was convicted. * * *

II

We first consider whether the Rochester police violated the Fourth and Fourteenth Amendments when, without probable cause to arrest, they took petitioner into custody, transported him to the police station, and detained him there for interrogation.

* * *

Before *Terry v. Ohio*, 392 U.S. 1 (1968), the Fourth Amendment's guarantee against unreasonable seizures of persons was analyzed in terms of arrest, probable cause for arrest, and warrants based on such probable cause. The basic principles were relatively simple and straightforward: The term "arrest" was synonymous with those seizures governed by the Fourth Amendment. While warrants were not required in all circumstances, the requirement of probable cause, as elaborated in numerous precedents, was treated as absolute. * * *

Terry for the first time recognized an exception to the requirement that Fourth Amendment seizures of persons must be based on probable cause. That case involved a brief, on-the-spot stop on the street and a frisk for weapons, a situation that did not fit comfortably within the traditional concept of an "arrest." * * *

Because *Terry* involved an exception to the general rule requiring probable cause, this Court has been careful to maintain its narrow scope. *Terry* itself involved a limited, on-the-street frisk for weapons. Two subsequent cases which applied *Terry* also involved limited weapons frisks. See *Adams v. Williams*, 407 U.S. 143 (1972) (frisk for weapons on basis of reasonable suspicion); *Pennsylvania v. Mimms*, 434 U.S. 106 (1977) (order to get out of car is permissible "*de minimis*" intrusion after car is lawfully detained for traffic violations; frisk for weapons justified after "bulge" observed in jacket). *United States v. Brignoni–Ponce*, 422 U.S. 873 (1975), applied *Terry* in the special context of roving border patrols stopping automobiles to check for illegal immigrants. The investigative stops usually consumed less than a minute and involved "a brief question or two." The Court stated that "[b]ecause of the limited nature of the intrusion, stops of this sort may be justified on facts that do not amount to the probable cause required for an arrest." See also *United States v. Martinez–Fuerte*, 428 U.S. 543 (1976) (fixed checkpoint to stop and check vehicles for aliens); *Delaware v. Prouse*, 440 U.S. 648 (1979) (random checks for drivers' licenses and proper vehicle registration not permitted on less than articulable reasonable suspicion).

Respondent State now urges the Court to apply a balancing test, rather than the general rule, to custodial interrogations, and to hold that "seizures" such as that in this case may be justified by mere "reasonable suspicion." *Terry* and its progeny clearly do not support such a result. * * *

In contrast to the brief and narrowly circumscribed intrusions involved in those cases, the detention of petitioner was in important respects indistinguishable from a traditional arrest. Petitioner was not questioned briefly where he was found. Instead, he was taken from a neighbor's home to a police car, transported to a police station, and placed in an interrogation room. He was never informed that he was "free to go"; indeed, he would have been physically restrained if he had refused to accompany the officers or had tried to escape their custody. The application of the Fourth Amendment's requirement of probable cause does not depend on whether an intrusion of this magnitude is termed an "arrest" under state law. The mere facts that petitioner was not told he was under arrest, was not "booked," and would not have had an arrest record if the interrogation had proved fruitless, while not insignificant for all purposes, obviously do not make petitioner's seizure even roughly analogous to the narrowly defined intrusions involved in *Terry* and its progeny. Indeed, any "exception" that could cover a seizure as intrusive as that in this case would threaten to swallow the general rule that Fourth Amendment seizures are "reasonable" only if based on probable cause. * * *

Moreover, two important decisions since *Terry* confirm the conclusion that the treatment of petitioner, whether or not it is technically characterized as an arrest, must be supported by probable cause. *Davis v. Mississippi*, 394 U.S. 721 (1969), decided the Term after *Terry*, considered whether fingerprints taken from a suspect detained without probable cause must be excluded from evidence. The State argued that the detention "was of a type which does not require probable cause," because it occurred during an investigative, rather than accusatory, stage, and because it was for the sole purpose of taking fingerprints. * * * In *Davis*, however, the Court found it unnecessary to decide the validity of a "narrowly circumscribed procedure for obtaining" the fingerprints of suspects without probable cause—in part because, as the Court emphasized, "petitioner was not merely fingerprinted during the * * * detention but *also subjected to interrogation*." *Id.*, at 728. The detention therefore violated the Fourth Amendment.

Brown v. Illinois, 422 U.S. 590 (1975), similarly disapproved arrests made for "investigatory" purposes on less than probable cause. * * *

These passages from *Davis* and *Brown* reflect the conclusion that detention for custodial interrogation—regardless of its label—intrudes so severely on interests protected by the Fourth Amendment as necessarily to trigger the traditional safeguards against illegal arrest. We accordingly hold that the Rochester police violated the Fourth and Fourteenth Amendments when, without probable cause, they seized petitioner and transported him to the police station for interrogation.

[The majority went on to hold that the giving of the *Miranda* warnings did not sufficiently "attenuate the taint" of the illegal arrest to permit the use of the incriminating statements and sketches.]

Reversed.

[Concurring and dissenting opinions omitted.]

Note

A statement obtained from a suspect following an unlawful arrest may have to be excluded as the fruit of a Fourth Amendment violation even if the statement satisfied Fifth Amendment requirements because it was voluntary and the *Miranda* warnings were given. In New York v. Harris, 495 U.S. 14 (1990), police entered the defendant's home without a warrant to arrest him on probable cause for murder, gave the *Miranda* warnings, and obtained an admission of guilt. Subsequently the defendant signed a written confession at the police station. The trial court suppressed the first statement because the arrest was unlawful under the warrant requirement of *Payton v. New York* (supra, p. 181), but the written statement was used to convict Harris of murder. The New York Court of Appeals reversed the conviction, ruling that the written statement should also have been excluded because the connection between it and the unlawful arrest was not sufficiently attenuated.

The Supreme Court reinstated the conviction in a 5–4 opinion by Justice White. Conceding that the entry into defendant's dwelling was unlawful under *Payton,* the majority reasoned that defendant was nonetheless lawfully in custody when he made the written statement because the arrest was based upon probable cause. The purpose of the warrant requirement is to protect the home, and any violation would be adequately remedied by excluding evidence found in the home incident to the arrest. The majority therefore held that the subsequent statement at the police station "was not an exploitation of the illegal entry into Harris' home."

UNITED STATES v. SOKOLOW

Supreme Court of the United States, 1989.
490 U.S. 1, 109 S.Ct. 1581, 104 L.Ed.2d 1.

CHIEF JUSTICE REHNQUIST delivered the opinion of the Court. * * *

This case involves a typical attempt to smuggle drugs through one of the Nation's airports. On a Sunday in July 1984, respondent went to the United Airlines ticket counter at Honolulu Airport, where he purchased two round-trip tickets for a flight to Miami leaving later that day. The tickets were purchased in the names of "Andrew Kray" and "Janet Norian," and had open return dates. Respondent paid $2,100 for the tickets from a large roll of $20 bills, which appeared to contain a total of $4,000. He also gave the ticket agent his home telephone number. The ticket agent noticed that respondent seemed nervous; he was about 25 years old; he was dressed in a black jumpsuit and wore gold jewelry; and he was accompanied by a woman, who turned out to be Janet Norian. Neither respondent nor his companion checked any of their four pieces of luggage.

After the couple left for their flight, the ticket agent informed Officer John McCarthy of the Honolulu Police Department of respondent's cash purchase of tickets to Miami. Officer McCarthy determined that the telephone number respondent gave to the ticket agent was subscribed to a "Karl Herman," who resided at 348–A Royal Hawaiian Avenue in Honolulu. Unbeknownst to McCarthy (and later to the DEA agents), respondent was Herman's roommate. The ticket agent identified respondent's voice on the answering machine at Herman's number. Officer McCarthy was unable to find any listing under the name "Andrew Kray" in Hawaii. McCarthy subsequently learned that return reservations from Miami to Honolulu had been made in the names of Kray and Norian, with their arrival scheduled for July 25, three days after respondent and his companion had left. He also learned that Kray and Norian were scheduled to make stopovers in Denver and Los Angeles.

On July 25, during the stopover in Los Angeles, DEA agents identified respondent. He "appeared to be very nervous and was looking all around the waiting area." Later that day, at 6:30 p.m., respondent and Norian arrived in Honolulu. As before, they had not checked their luggage. Respondent was still wearing a black jumpsuit and gold jewelry. The couple proceeded directly to the street and tried to hail a cab, where Agent Richard Kempshall and three other DEA agents approached them. Kempshall displayed his credentials, grabbed respondent by the arm and moved him back onto the sidewalk. Kempshall asked respondent for his airline ticket and identification; respondent said that he had neither. He told the agents that his name was "Sokolow," but that he was traveling under his mother's maiden name, "Kray."

Respondent and Norian were escorted to the DEA office at the airport. There, the couple's luggage was examined by "Donker," a narcotics detector dog, which alerted to respondent's brown shoulder bag. The agents arrested respondent. He was advised of his constitutional rights and declined to make any statements. The agents obtained a warrant to search the shoulder bag. They found no illicit drugs, but the bag did contain several suspicious documents indicating respondent's involvement in drug trafficking. The agents had Donker reexamine the remaining luggage, and this time the dog alerted to a medium sized Louis Vuitton bag. By now, it was 9:30 p.m., too late for the agents to obtain a second warrant. They allowed respondent to leave for the night, but kept his luggage. The next morning, after a second dog confirmed Donker's alert, the agents obtained a warrant and found 1,063 grams of cocaine inside the bag. * * *

The United States Court of Appeals for the Ninth Circuit reversed respondent's conviction by a divided vote, holding that the DEA agents did not have a reasonable suspicion to justify the stop. The majority divided the facts bearing on reasonable suspicion into two categories. In the first category, the majority placed facts describing "ongoing criminal activity," such as the use of an alias or evasive movement through an airport; the majority believed that at least one such factor was always needed to support a finding of reasonable suspicion. In the second category, it placed facts describing "personal characteristics" of drug couriers, such as the cash payment for tickets, a short trip to a major source city for drugs, nervousness, type of attire, and unchecked luggage. The majority believed that such facts, "shared by drug couriers and the public at large," were only relevant if there was evidence of ongoing criminal behavior and the Government offered "[e]mpirical documentation" that the combination of facts at issue did not describe the behavior of "significant numbers of innocent persons." Applying this two-part test to the facts of this case, the majority found that there was no evidence of ongoing criminal behavior, and thus that the agents' stop was impermissible. The dissenting judge took the view that the majority's approach was "overly mechanistic" and "contrary to the case-by-case determination of reasonable articulable suspicion based on *all* the facts."

The rule enunciated by the Court of Appeals, in which evidence available to an officer is divided into evidence of "ongoing criminal behavior," on the one hand, and "probabilistic" evidence, on the other, * * * seems to us to draw a sharp line between types of evidence, the probative value of which varies only in degree. The Court of Appeals classified evidence of traveling under an alias, or evidence that the suspect took an evasive or erratic path through an airport, as meeting the test for showing "ongoing criminal activity." But certainly instances are conceivable in which traveling under an alias would not reflect ongoing criminal activity: for example, a person who wished to travel to a hospital or clinic for an operation and wished to conceal that fact. One taking an evasive path through an airport might be seeking to avoid a confrontation with an angry acquaintance or with a creditor. This is not to say that each of these types of evidence is not highly probative, but they do not have the sort of ironclad significance attributed to them by the Court of Appeals.

On the other hand, the factors in this case that the Court of Appeals treated as merely "probabilistic" also have probative significance. Paying $2,100 in cash for two airplane tickets is out of the ordinary, and it is even more out of the ordinary to pay that sum from a roll of $20 bills containing nearly twice that amount of cash. Most business travelers, we feel confident, purchase airline tickets by credit card or check so as to have a record for tax or business purposes, and few vacationers carry with them thousands of dollars in $20 bills. We also think the agents had a reasonable ground to believe that respondent was traveling under an alias; the evidence was by no means conclusive, but it was sufficient to warrant consideration. While a trip from Honolulu to Miami, standing alone, is not a cause for any sort of suspicion, here there was more: surely few residents of Honolulu travel from that city for 20 hours to spend 48 hours in Miami during the month of July.

Any one of these factors is not by itself proof of any illegal conduct and is quite consistent with innocent travel. But we think taken together they amount to reasonable suspicion.

* * *

We do not agree with respondent that our analysis is somehow changed by the agents' belief that his behavior was consistent with one of the DEA's "drug courier profiles." A court sitting to determine the existence of reasonable suspicion must require the agent to articulate the factors leading to that conclusion, but the fact that these factors may be set forth in a "profile" does not somehow detract from their evidentiary significance as seen by a trained agent. * * * The judgment of the Court of Appeals is therefore reversed and the case remanded for further proceedings consistent with our decision.

JUSTICE MARSHALL, with whom JUSTICE BRENNAN joins, dissenting. * * * It is highly significant that the DEA agents stopped Sokolow because he matched one of the DEA's "profiles" of a paradigmatic drug courier. In my view, a law enforcement officer's mechanistic application of a formula of personal and behavioral traits in deciding whom to detain can only dull the officer's ability and determination to make sensitive and fact-specific inferences in light of his experience, particularly in ambiguous or borderline cases. Reflexive reliance on a profile of drug courier characteristics runs a far greater risk than does ordinary, case-by-case police work, of subjecting innocent individuals to unwarranted police harassment and detention. * * * In asserting that it is not "somehow" relevant that the agents who stopped Sokolow did so in reliance on a prefabricated profile of criminal characteristics, the majority thus ducks serious issues relating to a questionable law enforcement practice * * *.

The remaining circumstantial facts known about Sokolow, considered either singly or together, are scarcely indicative of criminal activity. * * * The fact that Sokolow took a brief trip to a resort city for which he brought only carry-on luggage also describes a very large category of presumably innocent travelers. That Sokolow embarked from Miami, "a source city for illicit drugs," is no more suggestive of illegality; thousands of innocent persons travel from "source cities" every day and, judging from the DEA's testimony in past cases, nearly every major city in the country may be characterized as a source or distribution city. That Sokolow had his phone listed in another person's name also does not support the majority's assertion that the DEA agents reasonably believed Sokolow was using an alias; it is commonplace to have one's phone registered in the name of a roommate, which, it later turned out, was precisely what Sokolow had done. That Sokolow was dressed in a black jumpsuit and wore gold jewelry also provides no grounds for suspecting wrongdoing, the majority's repeated and unexplained allusions to Sokolow's style of dress notwithstanding. For law enforcement officers to base a search, even in part, on a pop guess that persons dressed in a particular fashion are likely to commit crimes not only stretches the concept of reasonable suspicion beyond recognition, but also is inimical to the self-expression which the choice of wardrobe may provide.

Finally, that Sokolow paid for his tickets in cash indicates no imminent or ongoing criminal activity. The majority "feel[s] confident" that "[m]ost business travelers * * * purchase airline tickets by credit card or check." Why the majority confines its focus only to "business travelers" I do not know, but I would not so lightly infer ongoing crime from the use of legal tender. Making major cash purchases, while surely less common today, may simply reflect the traveler's aversion to, or inability to obtain, plastic money. Conceivably, a person who spends large amounts of cash may be trying to launder his proceeds from *past* criminal enterprises by converting them into goods and services. But, as I have noted, investigating completed episodes of crime goes beyond the appropriately limited purview of the brief, *Terry*-style seizure. Moreover, it is unreasonable to suggest that, had Sokolow left the airport, he would have been gone forever and thus immune from subsequent investigation. Sokolow, after all, had given the airline his phone number, and the DEA, having ascertained that it was indeed Sokolow's voice on the answering machine at that number, could have learned from that information where Sokolow resided.

Note

Because airline passengers are now required to present a "photo ID," use of false identification would be an offense in itself rather than merely cause for suspicion. For a typical illustration of an invalid drug courier stop, see United States v. Lambert, 46 F.3d 1064 (10th Cir.1995). Lambert purchased for $360 cash a one-way air ticket to Wichita at the Los Angeles Airport. DEA agents relayed this fact and the tag number of Lambert's checked suitcase to agents in Wichita, who met Lambert at the Wichita Airport's baggage carousel. The agents, who noted that Lambert appeared nervous, identified themselves and asked Lambert for his ticket and driver's license, which they retained for the next 25 minutes while questioning him and making a computer check for outstanding warrants (there were none). Lambert's answers were not incriminating and he refused to consent to a search of his suitcase. The agents then allowed Lambert to leave but retained the suitcase until a dog could be obtained to sniff it. After two dogs alerted, the agents obtained a warrant to search the suitcase and found unlawful drugs. The Court of Appeals held that the initial approach to talk to Lambert was consensual, but "what began as a consensual encounter quickly became an investigative detention once the agents received Mr. Lambert's driver's license and did not return it to him."

The Court held that the detention was unlawful because "The only information known to the agents prior to their seizure was Mr. Lambert: (1)

was flying alone; (2) had a one-way ticket he had purchased with cash shortly before departure from a drug-source city; (3) had checked one piece of luggage; and (4) appeared nervous and left the airport quickly after retrieving his suitcase. All of this is perfectly consistent with innocent behavior and thus, raises very little suspicion. Mr. Lambert's nervous appearance and quick departure from the airport are of little significance because none of the agents had any prior contact with Mr. Lambert with which to compare his behavior in the airport. Given the risks and time pressures associated with air travel, it is not uncommon to see nervous people in airports. It is also a common experience to see people who, for whatever reason, desire to leave airport terminals as quickly as they can. Thus, Mr. Lambert's demeanor could have created nothing more than a 'hunch' on the part of the agents that something was suspicious. Finally, it is important to note that Mr. Lambert was not traveling under an alias but, in fact, had made his plane reservations in his name and identified his luggage with his correct name and address. In short, there were no objectively suspicious facts known to the agents prior to their seizure of Mr. Lambert, but only information entirely consistent with innocent travel. As such, the agents did not have the reasonable suspicion necessary to justifiably seize Mr. Lambert. The circumstances were all consistent with innocent behaviour." 46 F.3d at 1070–71.

FLORIDA v. BOSTICK

Supreme Court of the United States, 1991.
501 U.S. 429, 111 S.Ct. 2382, 115 L.Ed.2d 389.

JUSTICE O'CONNOR delivered the opinion of the Court.

* * *

I

Drug interdiction efforts have led to the use of police surveillance at airports, train stations, and bus depots. Law enforcement officers stationed at such locations routinely approach individuals, either randomly or because they suspect in some vague way that the individuals may be engaged in criminal activity, and ask them potentially incriminating questions. Broward County has adopted such a program. County Sheriff's Department officers routinely board buses at scheduled stops and ask passengers for permission to search their luggage.

In this case, two officers discovered cocaine when they searched a suitcase belonging to Bostick. The underlying facts of the search are in dispute, but the Florida Supreme Court, whose decision we review here, stated explicitly the factual premise for its decision:

> "Two officers, complete with badges, insignia and one of them holding a recognizable zipper pouch containing a pistol, boarded a bus bound from Miami to Atlanta during a stopover in Fort Lauderdale. Eyeing the passengers, the officers admittedly without articulable suspicion, picked out the defendant passenger and asked to inspect his ticket and identification. The ticket, from Miami to Atlanta, matched the defendant's identification and both were im-

mediately returned to him as unremarkable. However, the two police officers persisted and explained their presence as narcotics agents on the lookout for illegal drugs. In pursuit of that aim, they then requested the defendant's consent to search his luggage. Needless to say, there is a conflict in the evidence about whether the defendant consented to the search of the second bag in which the contraband was found and as to whether he was informed of his right to refuse consent. However, any conflict must be resolved in favor of the state, it being a question of fact decided by the trial judge."

Two facts are particularly worth noting. First, the police specifically advised Bostick that he had the right to refuse consent. Bostick appears to have disputed the point, but, as the Florida Supreme Court noted explicitly, the trial court resolved this evidentiary conflict in the State's favor. Second, at no time did the officers threaten Bostick with a gun. The Florida Supreme Court indicated that one officer carried a zipper pouch containing a pistol—the equivalent of carrying a gun in a holster—but the court did not suggest that the gun was ever removed from its pouch, pointed at Bostick, or otherwise used in a threatening manner. The dissent's characterization of the officers as "gun-wielding inquisitors," is colorful, but lacks any basis in fact.

Bostick was arrested and charged with trafficking in cocaine. [The Florida Supreme Court held that "an impermissible seizure results when police mount a drug search on buses during scheduled stops and question boarded passengers without articulable reasons for doing so, thereby obtaining consent to search the passengers' luggage."] The Florida Supreme Court thus adopted a per se rule that the Broward County Sheriff's practice of "working the buses" is unconstitutional. * * *

II

* * * Our cases make it clear that a seizure does not occur simply because a police officer approaches an individual and asks a few questions. So long as a reasonable person would feel free "to disregard the police and go about his business," the encounter is consensual and no reasonable suspicion is required. * * * There is no doubt that if this same encounter had taken place before Bostick boarded the bus or in the lobby of the bus terminal, it would not rise to the level of a seizure. The Court has dealt with similar encounters in airports and has found them to be the sort of consensual encounters that implicate no Fourth Amendment interest. We have stated that even when officers have no basis for suspecting a particular individual, they may generally ask questions of that individual, ask to examine the individual's identification, and request consent to search his or her luggage—as long as the police do not convey a message that compliance with their requests is required. [Citations omitted]

Bostick insists that this case is different because it took place in the cramped confines of a bus. A police encounter is much more intimidating in this setting, he argues, because police tower over a seated passenger and there is little room to move around. Bostick claims to find support in language from Michigan v. Chesternut, 486 U.S. 567 (1988), and other cases, indicating that a seizure occurs when a reasonable person would believe that he or she is not "free to leave." Bostick maintains that a reasonable bus passenger would not have felt free to leave under the circumstances of this case because there is nowhere to go on a bus. Also, the bus was about to depart. Had Bostick disembarked, he would have risked being stranded and losing whatever baggage he had locked away in the luggage compartment.

The Florida Supreme Court found this argument persuasive, so much so that it adopted a per se rule prohibiting the police from randomly boarding buses as a means of drug interdiction. The state court erred, however, in focusing on whether Bostick was "free to leave" rather than on the principle that those words were intended to capture. When police attempt to question a person who is walking down the street or through an airport lobby, it makes sense to inquire whether a reasonable person would feel free to continue walking. But when the person is seated on a bus and has no desire to leave, the degree to which a reasonable person would feel that he or she could leave is not an accurate measure of the coercive effect of the encounter.

Here, for example, the mere fact that Bostick did not feel free to leave the bus does not mean that the police seized him. Bostick was a passenger on a bus that was scheduled to depart. He would not have felt free to leave the bus even if the police had not been present. Bostick's movements were "confined" in a sense, but this was the natural result of his decision to take the bus; it says nothing about whether or not the police conduct at issue was coercive. * * * In such a situation, the appropriate inquiry is whether a reasonable person would feel free to decline the officers' requests or otherwise terminate the encounter. * * * Where the encounter takes place is one factor, but it is not the only one. And, as the Solicitor General correctly observes, an individual may decline an officer's request without fearing prosecution. We have consistently held that a refusal to cooperate, without more, does not furnish the minimal level of objective justification needed for a detention or seizure. [Citations]

The facts of this case, as described by the Florida Supreme Court, leave some doubt whether a seizure occurred. Two officers walked up to Bostick on the bus, asked him a few questions, and asked if they could search his bags. As we have explained, no seizure occurs when police ask questions of an individual, ask to examine the individual's identification, and request consent to search his or her luggage—so long as the officers do not convey a message that compliance with their requests is required. Here, the facts recited by the Florida Supreme Court indicate that the officers did not point guns at Bostick or otherwise threaten him and that they specifically advised Bostick that he could refuse consent.

Nevertheless, we refrain from deciding whether or not a seizure occurred in this case. The trial court made no express findings of fact, and the Florida Supreme Court rested its decision on a single fact—that the encounter took place on a bus—rather than on the totality of the circumstances. We remand so that the Florida courts may evaluate the seizure question under the correct legal standard. We do reject, however, Bostick's argument that he must have been seized because no reasonable person would freely consent to a search of luggage that he or she knows contains drugs. This argument cannot prevail because the "reasonable person" test presupposes an innocent person. * * *

The dissent characterizes our decision as holding that police may board buses and by an "intimidating show of authority," demand of passengers their "voluntary" cooperation. That characterization is incorrect. Clearly, a bus passenger's decision to cooperate with law enforcement officers authorizes the police to conduct a search without first obtaining a warrant only if the cooperation is voluntary. "Consent" that is the product of official intimidation or harassment is not consent at all. Citizens do not forfeit their constitutional rights when they are coerced to comply with a request that they would prefer to refuse. The question to be decided by the Florida courts on remand is whether Bostick chose to permit the search of his luggage.

The dissent also attempts to characterize our decision as applying a lesser degree of constitutional protection to those individuals who travel by bus, rather than by other forms of transportation. This, too, is an erroneous characterization. Our Fourth Amendment inquiry in this case—whether a reasonable person would have felt free to decline the officers' requests or otherwise terminate the encounter—applies equally to police encounters that take place on trains, planes, and city streets. It is the dissent that would single out this particular mode of travel for differential treatment by adopting a per se rule that random bus searches are unconstitutional.

The dissent reserves its strongest criticism for the proposition that police officers can approach individuals as to whom they have no reasonable suspicion and ask them potentially incriminating questions. But this proposition is by no means novel; it has been endorsed by the Court any number of times. * * * Unless the dissent advocates overruling a long, unbroken line of decisions dating back more than 20 years, its criticism is not well taken.

This Court, as the dissent correctly observes, is not empowered to suspend constitutional guarantees so that the Government may more effectively wage a "war on drugs." If that war is to be fought, those who fight it must respect the rights of individuals, whether or not those individuals are suspected of having committed a crime. By the same token, this Court is not empowered to forbid law enforcement practices simply because it considers them distasteful. The Fourth Amendment proscribes unreasonable searches and seizures; it does not proscribe voluntary cooperation. The cramped confines of a bus are one relevant factor that should be considered in evaluating whether a passenger's consent is voluntary. We cannot agree, however, with the Florida Supreme Court that this single factor will be dispositive in every case.

We adhere to the rule that, in order to determine whether a particular encounter constitutes a seizure, a court must consider all the circumstances surrounding the encounter to determine whether the police conduct would have communicated to a reasonable person that the person was not free to decline the officers' requests or otherwise terminate the encounter. That rule applies to encounters that take place on a city street or in an airport lobby, and it applies equally to encounters on a bus. The Florida Supreme Court erred in adopting a per se rule.

The judgment of the Florida Supreme Court is reversed, and the case remanded for further proceedings not inconsistent with this opinion.

JUSTICE MARSHALL, with whom JUSTICE BLACKMUN and JUSTICE STEVENS join, dissenting. * * *

At issue in this case is a new and increasingly common tactic in the war on drugs: the suspicionless police sweep of buses in interstate or intrastate travel. [Citations] Typically under this technique, a group of state or federal officers will board a bus while it is stopped at an intermediate point on its route. Often displaying badges, weapons or other indicia of authority, the officers identify themselves and announce their purpose to intercept drug traffickers. They proceed to approach individual passengers, requesting them to show identification, produce their tickets, and explain the purpose of their travels. Never do the officers advise the passengers that they are free not to speak with the officers. An "interview" of this type ordinarily culminates in a request for consent to search the passenger's luggage.

These sweeps are conducted in "dragnet" style. The police admittedly act without an "articulable suspicion" in deciding which buses to board and which passengers to approach for interviewing. By proceeding systematically in this fashion, the police are able to engage in a tremendously high volume of searches. See, e.g., Florida v. Kerwick, 512 So.2d 347, 348–349 (Fla.App.1987) (single officer employing sweep technique able to search over 3,000 bags in nine-month period). The percentage of successful drug interdictions is low. See United States v. Flowers, 912 F.2d 707, 710 (C.A.4 1990) at 710 (sweep of 100 buses in Charlotte, North Carolina, resulted in seven arrests).

To put it mildly, these sweeps are inconvenient, intrusive, and intimidating. They occur within cramped confines, with officers typically placing themselves in between the passenger selected for an interview and the exit of the bus. Because the bus is only temporarily stationed at a point short of its destination, the passengers are in no position to leave as a means of evading the officers' questioning. Undoubtedly, such a sweep holds up the progress of the bus. Thus, this new and increasingly common tactic, burdens the experience of traveling by bus with a degree of governmental interference to which, until now, our society has been proudly unaccustomed. * * * This aspect of the suspicionless sweep has not been lost on many of the lower courts called upon to review the constitutionality of this practice. Remarkably, the courts located at the heart of the "drug war" have been the most adamant in condemning this technique. * * *

I have no objection to the manner in which the majority frames the test for determining whether a suspicionless bus sweep amounts to a Fourth Amendment "seizure." I agree that the appropriate question is whether a passenger who is approached during such a sweep "would feel free to decline the officers' requests or otherwise terminate the encounter." What I cannot understand is how the majority can possibly suggest an affirmative answer to this question.

* * * Inexplicably, the majority repeatedly stresses the trial court's implicit finding that the police officers advised respondent that he was free to refuse permission to search his travel bag. This aspect of the exchange between respondent and the police is completely irrelevant to the issue before us. For as the State concedes, and as the majority purports to "accept," if respondent was unlawfully seized when the officers approached him and initiated questioning, the resulting search was likewise unlawful no matter how well advised respondent was of his right to refuse it. Consequently, the issue is not whether a passenger in respondent's position would have felt free to deny consent to the search of his bag, but whether such a passenger—without being apprised of his rights—would have felt free to terminate the antecedent encounter with the police.

Unlike the majority, I have no doubt that the answer to this question is no. Apart from trying to accommodate the officers, respondent had only two options. First, he could have remained seated while obstinately refusing to respond to the officers' questioning. But in light of the intimidating show of authority that the officers made upon boarding the bus, respondent reasonably could have believed that such behavior would only arouse the officers' suspicions and intensify their interrogation. Indeed, officers who carry out bus sweeps like the one at issue here frequently admit that this is the effect of a passenger's refusal to cooperate. [Citations] The majority's observation that a mere refusal to answer questions, "without more," does not give rise to a reasonable basis for seizing a passenger, ante, is utterly beside the point, because a passenger unadvised of his rights and otherwise unversed in constitutional law has no reason to know that the police cannot hold his refusal to cooperate against him.

Second, respondent could have tried to escape the officers' presence by leaving the bus altogether. But because doing so would have required respondent to squeeze past the gunwielding inquisitor who was blocking the aisle of the bus, this hardly seems like a course that respondent reasonably would have viewed as available to him. The majority lamely protests that nothing in the stipulated facts shows that the questioning officer pointed his gun at respondent or otherwise threatened him with the weapon. Our decisions recognize the obvious point, however, that the choice of the police to "display" their weapons during an encounter exerts significant coercive pressure on the confronted citizen. [Citations] We have never suggested that the police must go so far as to put a citizen in immediate apprehension of being shot before a court can take account of the intimidating effect of being questioned by an officer with weapon in hand.

Even if respondent had perceived that the officers would let him leave the bus, moreover, he could not reasonably have been expected to resort to this means of evading their intrusive questioning. For so far as respondent knew, the bus' departure from the terminal was imminent. Unlike a person approached by the police on the street, or at a bus or airport terminal after reaching his destination, a passenger approached by the police at an intermediate point in a long bus journey cannot simply leave the scene and repair to a safe haven to avoid unwanted probing by law enforcement officials. The vulnerability that an intrastate or interstate traveler experiences when confronted by the police outside of his "own familiar territory" surely aggravates the coercive quality of such an encounter. * * *

Withdrawing this particular weapon from the government's drug-war arsenal would hardly leave the police without any means of combatting the use of buses as instrumentalities of the drug trade. The police would remain free, for example, to approach passengers whom they have a reasonable, articulable basis to suspect of criminal wrongdoing. Alternatively, they could continue to confront passengers without suspicion so long as they took simple steps, like advising the passengers confronted of their right to decline to be questioned, to dispel the aura of coercion and intimidation that pervades such encounters. There is no reason to expect that such requirements would render the Nation's buses law enforcement-free zones. * * *

Note

In Florida v. Bostick the Supreme Court held only that the bus search cases should be decided on their particular facts, rather than on a *per se* rule. The Court remanded for a determination on whether a "seizure" occurred before consent was given. On remand, the Florida Supreme Court upheld the search (per curiam, 4–3) in Bostick v. Florida, 593 So.2d 494 (Fl.1992). Federal Courts of Appeal have tended to find in the bus search cases, on facts similar to those in *Bostick*, that the consent was involuntary, or preceded by an illegal detention. See United States v. Guapi, 144 F.3d 1393 (11th Cir.1998); United States v. Washington, 151 F.3d 1354 (11th Cir.1998). Probably a high percentage of judges ruling on these cases disagree with the Supreme Court and believe that the bus searches are coercive *per se*.

WHREN v. UNITED STATES

Supreme Court of the United States, 1996.
517 U.S. 806, 116 S.Ct. 1769, 135 L.Ed.2d 89.

JUSTICE SCALIA delivered the opinion of the Court.

In this case we decide whether the temporary detention of a motorist who the police have probable cause to believe has committed a civil traffic violation is inconsistent with the Fourth Amendment's prohibition against unreasonable seizures unless a reasonable officer would have been motivated to stop the car by desire to enforce the traffic laws.

I

On the evening of June 10, 1993, plainclothes vice-squad officers of the District of Columbia Metropolitan Police Department were patrolling a "high drug area" of the city in an unmarked car. Their suspicions were aroused when they passed a dark Pathfinder truck with temporary license plates and youthful occupants waiting at a stop sign, the driver looking down into the lap of the passenger at his right. The truck remained stopped at the intersection for what seemed an unusually long time-more than 20 seconds. When the police car executed a U-turn in order to head back toward the truck, the Pathfinder turned suddenly to its right, without signalling, and sped off at an "unreasonable" speed. The policemen followed, and in a short while overtook the Pathfinder when it stopped behind other traffic at a red light. They pulled up alongside, and Officer Ephraim Soto stepped out and approached the driver's door, identifying himself as a police officer and directing the driver, petitioner Brown, to put the vehicle in park. When Soto drew up to the driver's window, he immediately observed two large plastic bags of what appeared to be crack cocaine in petitioner Whren's hands. Petitioners were arrested, and quantities of several types of illegal drugs were retrieved from the vehicle.

Petitioners were charged in a four-count indictment with violating various federal drug laws. At a pretrial suppression hearing, they challenged the legality of the stop and the resulting seizure of the drugs. They argued that the stop had not been justified by probable cause to believe, or even reasonable suspicion, that petitioners were engaged in illegal drug-dealing activity; and that Officer Soto's asserted ground for approaching the vehicle-to give the driver a warning concerning traffic violations-was pretextual. The District Court denied the suppression motion, concluding that "the facts of the stop were not controverted," and "there was nothing to really demonstrate that the actions of the officers were contrary to a normal traffic stop." [The Court of Appeals affirmed.]

II

* * * Petitioners accept that Officer Soto had probable cause to believe that various provisions of the District of Columbia traffic code had been violated. They argue, however, that "in the unique context of civil traffic regulations" probable cause is not enough. Since, they contend, the use of automobiles is so heavily and minutely regulated that total compliance with traffic and safety rules is nearly impossible, a police officer will almost invariably be able to catch any given motorist in a technical violation. This creates the temptation to use traffic stops as a means of investigating other law violations, as to which no probable cause or even articulable suspicion exists. Petitioners, who are both black, further contend that police officers might decide which motorists to stop based on decidedly impermissible factors, such as the race of the car's occupants. To avoid this danger, they say, the Fourth Amendment test for traffic stops should be, not the normal one (applied by the Court of Appeals) of whether probable cause existed to justify the stop; but rather, whether a police officer, acting reasonably, would have made the stop for the reason given.

A

Petitioners contend that the standard they propose is consistent with our past cases' disapproval of police attempts to use valid bases of action against citizens as pretexts for pursuing other investigatory agendas. We are reminded that in Florida v. Wells, 495 U.S. 1, 4 (1990), we stated that "an inventory search must not be used as a ruse for a general rummaging in order to discover incriminating evidence"; that in Colorado v. Bertine, 479 U.S. 367, 372 (1987), in approving an inventory search, we apparently thought it significant that there had been "no showing that the police, who were following standard procedures, acted in bad faith or for the sole purpose of investigation"; and that in New York v. Burger, 482 U.S. 691, 716–717, n. 27 (1987), we observed, in upholding the constitutionality of a warrantless administrative inspection, that the search did not appear to be "a 'pretext' for obtaining evidence of * * * violation of * * * penal laws." But only an undiscerning reader would regard these cases as endorsing the principle that ulterior motives can invalidate police conduct that is justifiable on the basis of probable cause to believe that a violation of law has occurred. In each case we were addressing the validity of a search conducted in the absence of probable cause. Our quoted statements simply explain that the exemption from the need for probable cause (and warrant), which is accorded to searches made for the purpose of inventory or administrative regulation, is not accorded to searches that are not made for those purposes. * * *

Not only have we never held, outside the context of inventory search or administrative inspection (discussed above), that an officer's motive invalidates objectively justifiable behavior under the Fourth Amendment; but we have repeatedly held and asserted the contrary. In United States v. Villamonte–Marquez, 462 U.S. 579, 584, n. 3 (1983), we held that an otherwise valid warrantless boarding of a vessel by customs officials was not rendered invalid "because the customs officers were accompanied by a Louisiana state policeman, and were following an informant's tip that a vessel in the ship channel was thought to be carrying marihuana." We flatly dismissed the idea that an ulterior motive might serve to strip the agents of their legal justification. In United States v. Robinson, 414 U.S. 218 (1973), we held that a traffic-violation arrest (of the sort here) would not be rendered invalid by the fact that it was "a mere pretext for a narcotics search," id., at 221, n. 1; and that a lawful postarrest search of the person would not be rendered invalid by the fact that it was not motivated by the officer-safety concern that justifies such searches, see id., at 236. See also Gustafson v. Florida, 414 U.S. 260, 266 (1973). And in Scott v. United States, 436 U.S. 128, 138 (1978), in rejecting the contention that wiretap evidence was subject to exclusion because the agents conducting the tap had failed to make any effort to comply with the statutory requirement that unauthorized acquisitions be minimized, we said that "subjective intent alone * * * does not make otherwise lawful conduct illegal or unconstitutional." We described *Robinson* as having established that "the fact that the officer does not have the state of mind which is hypothecated by the reasons which provide the legal justification for the officer's action does not invalidate the action taken as long as the circumstances, viewed objectively, justify that action." 436 U.S. at 138.

We think these cases foreclose any argument that the constitutional reasonableness of traffic stops depends on the actual motivations of the individual officers involved. We of course agree with petitioners that the Constitution prohibits selective enforcement of the law based on considerations such as race. But the constitutional basis for objecting to intentionally discriminatory application of laws is the Equal Protection Clause, not the Fourth Amendment. Subjective intentions play no role in ordinary, probable-cause Fourth Amendment analysis.

B

Recognizing that we have been unwilling to entertain Fourth Amendment challenges based on the actual motivations of individual officers, petitioners disavow any intention to make the individual officer's subjective good faith the touchstone of "reasonableness." They insist that the standard they have put forward-whether the officer's conduct deviated materially from usual police practices, so that a reasonable officer in the same circumstances would not have made the stop for the reasons given-is an "objective" one.

But although framed in empirical terms, this approach is plainly and indisputably driven by subjective considerations. Its whole purpose is to prevent the police from doing under the guise of enforcing the traffic code what they would like to do for different reasons. Petitioners' proposed standard may not use the word "pretext," but it is designed to combat nothing other than the perceived "danger" of the pretextual stop, albeit only indirectly and over the run of cases. Instead of asking whether the individual officer had the proper state of mind, the petitioners would have us ask, in effect, whether (based on general police practices) it is plausible to believe that the officer had the proper state of mind.

Why one would frame a test designed to combat pretext in such fashion that the court cannot take into account actual and admitted pretext is a curiosity that can only be explained by the fact that our cases have foreclosed the more sensible option. If those cases were based only upon the evidentiary difficulty of establishing subjective intent, petitioners' attempt to root out subjective vices through objective means might make sense. But they were not based only upon that, or indeed even principally upon that. Their principal basis-which applies equally to attempts to reach subjective intent through ostensibly objective means-is simply that the Fourth Amendment's concern with "reasonableness" allows certain actions to be taken in certain circumstances, whatever the subjective intent. * * * But even if our concern had been only an evidentiary one, petitioners' proposal would by no means assuage it. Indeed, it seems to us somewhat easier to figure out the intent of an individual officer than to plumb the collective consciousness of law enforcement in order to determine whether a "reasonable officer" would have been moved to act upon the traffic violation. While police manuals and standard procedures may sometimes provide objective assistance, ordinarily one would be reduced to speculating about the hypothetical reaction of a hypothetical constable-an exercise that might be called virtual subjectivity.

Moreover, police enforcement practices, even if they could be practicably assessed by a judge, vary from place to place and from time to time. We cannot accept that the search and seizure protections of the Fourth Amendment are so variable, and can be made to turn upon such trivialities. The difficulty is illustrated by petitioners' arguments in this case. Their claim that a reasonable officer would not have made this stop is based largely on District of Columbia police regulations which permit plainclothes officers in unmarked vehicles to enforce traffic laws "only in the case of a violation that is so grave as to pose an immediate threat to the safety of others." Metropolitan Police Department–Washington, D.C., General Order 303.1, pt. 1, Objectives and Policies (A)(2)(4) (Apr. 30, 1992), reprinted as Addendum to Brief for Petitioners. This basis of invalidation would not apply in jurisdictions that had a different practice. And it would not have applied even in the District of Columbia, if Officer Soto had been wearing a uniform or patrolling in a marked police cruiser. * * *

III

In what would appear to be an elaboration on the "reasonable officer" test, petitioners argue that the balancing inherent in any Fourth Amendment inquiry requires us to weigh the governmental and individual interests implicated in a traffic stop such as we have here. That balancing, petitioners claim, does not support investigation of minor traffic infractions by plainclothes police in unmarked vehicles; such investigation only minimally advances the government's interest in traffic safety, and may indeed retard it by producing motorist confusion and alarm-a view said to be supported by the Metropolitan Police Department's own regulations generally prohibiting this practice. And as for the Fourth Amendment interests of the individuals concerned, petitioners point out that our cases acknowledge that even ordinary traffic stops entail "a possibly unsettling show of authority"; that they at best "interfere with freedom of movement, are inconvenient, and consume time" and at worst "may create substantial anxiety," Prouse, 440 U.S. at 657. That anxiety is likely to be even more pronounced when the stop is conducted by plainclothes officers in unmarked cars.

It is of course true that in principle every Fourth Amendment case, since it turns upon a "reasonableness" determination, involves a balancing of all relevant factors. With rare exceptions not applicable here, however, the result of that balancing is not in doubt where the search or seizure is based upon probable cause. That is why petitioners must rely upon cases like *Prouse* to provide examples of actual "balancing" analysis. There, the police action in question was a random traffic stop for the purpose of checking a motorist's license and vehicle registration, a practice that-like the practices at issue in the inventory search and administrative inspection cases upon which petitioners rely in making their "pretext" claim-involves police intrusion without the probable cause that is its traditional justification. * * *

Where probable cause has existed, the only cases in which we have found it necessary actually to perform the "balancing" analysis involved searches or seizures conducted in an extraordinary manner, unusually harmful to an individual's privacy or even physical interests-such as, for example, seizure by means of deadly force, see Tennessee v. Garner, 471 U.S. 1 (1985), unannounced entry into a home, see Wilson v. Arkansas, 514 U.S. 927 (1995), entry into a home without a warrant, see Welsh v. Wisconsin, 466 U.S. 740 (1984), or physical penetration of the body, see Winston v. Lee, 470 U.S. 753 (1985). The making of a traffic stop out-of-uniform does not remotely qualify as such an extreme practice, and so is governed by the usual rule that probable cause to believe the law has been broken "outbalances" private interest in avoiding police contact.

Petitioners urge as an extraordinary factor in this case that the "multitude of applicable traffic and equipment regulations" is so large and so difficult to obey perfectly that virtually everyone is guilty of violation, permitting the police to single out almost whomever they wish for a stop. But we are aware of no principle that would allow us to decide at what point a code of law becomes so expansive and so commonly violated that infraction itself can no longer be the ordinary measure of the lawfulness of enforcement. And even if we could identify such exorbitant codes, we do not know by what standard (or what right) we would decide, as petitioners would have us do, which particular provisions are sufficiently important to merit enforcement.

For the run-of-the-mine case, which this surely is, we think there is no realistic alternative to the traditional common-law rule that probable cause justifies a search and seizure.

* * *

Here the District Court found that the officers had probable cause to believe that petitioners had violated the traffic code. That rendered the stop reasonable under the Fourth Amendment, the evidence thereby discovered admissible, and the upholding of the convictions by the Court of Appeals for the District of Columbia Circuit correct.

Judgment affirmed.

Commentary

The preceding cases illustrate stops and searches that grow out of the nationwide "war on drugs." The general pattern is that the officers approach a person and engage in questioning, hoping either to obtain consent to a search or to uncover facts sufficient to constitute probable cause. The cases recognize three levels or tiers of police-citizen contact in these situations:

1. *No Fourth Amendment intrusion.* Mere communications or conversation between the officer and the citizen that involve no element of coercion or detention do not implicate the Fourth Amendment at all. Officers do not need to have reasonable suspicion to observe citizens closely, or follow them about an airport, or even to engage them in conversation. According to Florida v. Royer, 460 U.S. 491 (1983), "there is no Constitutional infringement when an officer merely approaches and speaks to an individual in a public place."

2. *Temporary detention.* According to the oft-cited standard of United States v. Mendenhall, 446 U.S. 544 (1980), a seizure of this type has occurred if "in view of all the circumstances surrounding the incident, a reasonable person would have believed he was not free to leave." The moment at which a mere conversation becomes a detention may turn on a subjective assessment, because the officer rarely says in so many words that the citizen may not leave. A detention will ordinarily be found where the officer retains the citizen's travel ticket or identification, or asks the citizen to accompany him to another location, or otherwise signals he is exercising authority. In *United States v. Sokolow, supra,* the District Court originally found that the initial encounter on the street was not a detention, citing *Florida v. Royer, supra.* Subsequently, the District Court added the finding that Agent Kempshall "grabbed respondent by the arm and moved him back onto the sidewalk." The Court of Appeals found that the grabbing made the encounter a clear instance of detention.

3. *Full-scale arrest.* In *Florida v. Royer, supra,* the suspect gave consent to search his luggage after being removed to an interrogation room at the airport. The Supreme Court opinion by Justice White held that at that point the encounter had escalated beyond a detention into an arrest, and that the fact that the suspect was travelling under an assumed name and had paid cash for a one-way ticket did not amount to probable cause. The consent was thus invalid as the product of an unlawful arrest. The opinion in *Royer* suggested that the officers should have used trained dogs to check the suitcases for drugs instead of trying to get consent, in which case "Royer and his luggage could have been momentarily detained which this investigative procedure was carried out." In *Sokolow,* the officers complied with this suggestion. As a result the detention apparently did not become an arrest until after the dog alerted, and then they had probable cause.

Aggressive drug interdiction efforts of the type involved in the preceding cases may not be desirable on policy grounds even if Fourth Amendment standards can be satisfied in individual cases. Whether the marginal effect on the narcotics traffic achieved by such efforts justifies subjecting many innocent travellers to police investigations that may be humiliating and frightening is a subject that ought to be addressed by policymaking bodies such as the Congress, rather than merely by the narcotics police themselves. If the courts had ruled that such detentions on less than probable cause are permitted only where specifically authorized by statute, then legislative hearings on practices such as the bus investigations involved in *Florida v. Bostick, supra,* might have given opponents of these practices an opportunity to make their case. The courts in suppression hearings deal only with travellers who were in fact carrying drugs; the legislatures ought to hear from the innocent travellers who were stopped, delayed, and questioned.

4. *Traffic stops for drug enforcement.* Police officers in some departments routinely ask drivers stopped for traffic offenses for consent to search their vehicles for drugs or weapons. Continuing its opposition to "bright line" rules restricting the police, the Supreme Court has held that the officer is not required to advise the motorist that he or she is free to leave before requesting consent to search the automobile. Ohio v. Robinette, 519 U.S. 33 (1996). If the driver refuses to consent, the officer may send for a narcotics detection dog to "sniff" the vehicle. Assuming that the "sniff" is not itself a search which must be justified by prior probable cause or reasonable suspicion, the detention itself may be unlawful if it was prolonged beyond the period necessary to complete the traffic investigation and citation. See United States v. Holloman,113 F.3d 192 (11th Cir.1997). When an officer makes a lawful traffic stop, he or she may routinely order both the driver and any passengers to exit the vehicle—and presumably, to frisk them for weapons. See Pennsylvania v. Mimms, 434 U.S. 106 (1977); Maryland v. Wilson, 519 U.S. 408 (1997). In *Wilson* the Supreme Court observed in a footnote: "Respondent argues that, because we have generally eschewed bright-line rules in the Fourth Amendment context, see, e.g., Ohio v. Robinette, 519 U.S. 33(1996), we should not here conclude that passengers may constitutionally be ordered out of lawfully stopped vehicles. But, that we typically avoid per se rules concerning searches and seizures does not mean that we have always done so; *Mimms* itself drew a bright line, and we believe the principles that underlay that decision apply to passengers as well."

UNITED STATES v. HENSLEY

Supreme Court of the United States, 1985.
469 U.S. 221, 105 S.Ct. 675, 83 L.Ed.2d 604.

Justice O'Connor delivered the opinion of the Court.

We granted certiorari in this case to determine whether police officers may stop and briefly detain a person who is the subject of a "wanted flyer" while they attempt to find out whether an arrest warrant has been issued. We conclude that such stops are consistent with the Fourth Amendment under appropriate circumstances.

I

On December 4, 1981, two armed men robbed a tavern in the Cincinnati suburb of St. Bernard, Ohio. Six days later, a St. Bernard police officer, Kenneth Davis, interviewed an informant who passed along information that respondent Thomas Hensley had driven the getaway car during the armed robbery. Officer Davis obtained a written statement from the informant and immediately issued a "wanted flyer" to other police departments in the Cincinnati metropolitan area.

The flyer twice stated that Hensley was wanted for investigation of an aggravated robbery. It described both Hensley and the date and location of the alleged robbery, and asked other departments to pick up and hold Hensley for the St. Bernard police in the event he were located. The flyer also warned other departments to use caution and to consider Hensley armed and dangerous.

The St. Bernard Police Department's "wanted flyer" was received by teletype in the headquarters of the Covington Police Department on December 10, 1981. Covington is a Kentucky suburb of Cincinnati that is approximately five miles from St. Bernard. The flyer was read aloud at each change of shift in the Covington Police Department between December 10 and December 16, 1981. Some of the Covington officers were acquainted with Hensley, and after December 10 they periodically looked for him at places in Covington he was known to frequent.

On December 16, 1981, Covington Officer Terence Eger saw a white Cadillac convertible stopped in the middle of a Covington street. Officer Eger saw Hensley in the driver's seat and asked him to move on. As Hensley drove away, Eger inquired by radio whether there was a warrant outstanding for Hensley's arrest. Before the dispatcher could answer, two other Covington officers who were in separate cars on patrol interrupted to say that there might be an Ohio robbery warrant outstanding on Hensley. The officers, Daniel Cope and David Rassache, subsequently testified that they had heard or read the St. Bernard flyer on several occasions, that they recalled that the flyer sought a stop for investigation only, and that in their experience the issuance of such a flyer was usually followed by the issuance of an arrest warrant. While the dispatcher checked to see whether a warrant had been issued, Officer Cope drove to a Holman Street address where Hensley occasionally stayed, and Officer Rassache went to check a second location.

The dispatcher had difficulty in confirming whether a warrant had been issued. Unable to locate the flyer, she called the Cincinnati Police Department on the mistaken belief that the flyer had originated in Cincinnati. The Cincinnati Police Department transferred the call to its records department, which placed the dispatcher on hold. In the meantime, Officer Cope reported that he had sighted a white Cadillac approaching him on Holman Street. Cope turned on his flashing lights and Hensley pulled over to the curb. Before Cope left his patrol car, the dispatcher advised him that she had "Cincinnati hunting for the warrant," but that she had not yet confirmed it. Cope approached Hensley's car with his service revolver drawn and pointed into the air. He had Hensley and a passenger seated next to him step out of the car.

Moments later, Officer Rassache arrived in his separate car. He recognized the passenger, Albert Green, a convicted felon. Rassache stepped up to the open passenger door of Hensley's car and observed the butt of a revolver protruding from underneath the passenger's seat. Green was then arrested. A search of the car uncovered a second handgun wrapped in a jacket in the middle of the front seat and a third handgun in a bag in the back seat. After the discovery of these weapons, Hensley was also arrested.

[Hensley was convicted in federal court on a charge of being a convicted felon in possession of firearms.]

The United States Court of Appeals for the Sixth Circuit reversed the conviction. 713 F.2d 220 (1983). The panel noted that the Covington police could not justifiably conclude from the St. Bernard flyer that a warrant had been issued for Hensley's arrest; nor could the Covington police stop the respondent while they attempted to find out whether a warrant had in fact been issued. Reviewing this Court's decisions applying *Terry*, the Sixth Circuit concluded that investigative stops remain a narrow exception to the probable-cause requirement, and that this Court has manifested a "clear intention to restrict investigative stops to settings involving the investigation of ongoing crimes." Since Covington police encountered Hensley almost two weeks after the armed robbery in St. Bernard, they had no reason to believe they were investigating an ongoing crime. Because the Covington police were familiar only with the St. Bernard flyer, and not with the specific information which led the St. Bernard police to issue the flyer, the Court of Appeals held they lacked a reasonable suspicion sufficient to justify an investigative stop. The Court of Appeals concluded that Hensley's conviction rested on evidence obtained through an illegal arrest, and therefore had to be reversed. We disagree, and now reverse.

II. A

* * *

[W]here police have been unable to locate a person suspected of involvement in a past crime, the ability to briefly stop that person, ask questions, or check identification in the absence of probable cause promotes the strong government interest in solving crimes and bringing offenders to justice. Restraining police action until after probable cause is obtained would not only hinder the investigation, but might also enable the suspect to flee in the interim and to remain at large. Particularly in the context of felonies or crimes involving a threat to public safety, it is in the public interest that the crime be solved and the suspect detained as promptly as possible. The law enforcement interests at stake in these circumstances outweigh the individual's interest to be free of a stop and detention that is no more extensive than permissible in the investigation of imminent or ongoing crimes.

We need not and do not decide today whether *Terry* stops to investigate all past crimes, however serious, are permitted. It is enough to say that, if police have a reasonable suspicion, grounded in specific and articulable facts, that a person they encounter was involved in or is wanted in connection with a completed felony, then a *Terry* stop may be made to investigate that suspicion. The automatic barrier to such stops erected by the Court of Appeals accordingly cannot stand.

B

At issue in this case is a stop of a person by officers of one police department in reliance on a flyer issued by another department indicating that the person is wanted for investigation of a felony. * * *

This Court discussed a related issue in *Whiteley v. Warden*, 401 U.S. 560 (1971). In *Whiteley*, a county sheriff in Wyoming obtained an arrest warrant for a person suspected of burglary. The sheriff then issued a message through a statewide law enforcement radio network describing the suspect, his car, and the property taken. At least one version of the message also indicated that a warrant had been issued. The message did not specify the evidence that gave the sheriff probable cause to believe the suspect had committed the breaking and entering. In reliance on the radio message, police in Laramie stopped the suspect and searched his car. The Supreme Court, in an opinion by Justice Harlan, ultimately concluded that the sheriff had lacked probable cause to obtain the warrant and that the evidence obtained during the search by the police in Laramie had to be excluded. * * *

This language in *Whiteley* suggests that, had the sheriff who issued the radio bulletin possessed probable cause for arrest, then the Laramie police could have properly arrested the defendant even though they were unaware of the specific facts that established probable cause. Thus *Whiteley* supports the proposition that, when evidence is uncovered during a search incident to an arrest in reliance merely on a flyer or bulletin, its admissibility turns on whether the officers who *issued* the flyer possessed probable cause to make the arrest. It does not turn on whether those relying on the flyer were themselves aware of the specific facts which led their colleagues to seek their assistance. In an era when criminal suspects are increasingly mobile and increasingly likely to flee across jurisdictional boundaries, this rule is a matter of common sense: it minimizes the volume of information concerning suspects that must be transmitted to other jurisdictions and enables police in one jurisdiction to act promptly in reliance on information from another jurisdiction. * * *

It could be argued that police can more justifiably rely on a report that a magistrate has issued a warrant than on a report that another law enforcement agency has simply concluded that it has a reasonable suspicion sufficient to authorize an investigatory stop. We do not find this distinction significant. The law enforcement interests promoted by allowing one department to make investigatory stops based upon another department's bulletins or flyers are considerable, while the intrusion on personal security is minimal. The same interests that weigh in favor of permitting police to make a *Terry* stop to investigate a past crime, support permitting police in other jurisdictions to rely on flyers or bulletins in making stops to investigate past crimes. * * *

III

It remains to apply the two sets of principles described above to the stop and subsequent arrest of respondent Hensley.

At the outset, we assume, *arguendo*, that the St. Bernard police who issued the "wanted flyer" on Hensley lacked probable cause for his arrest. * * *

We agree with the District Court that the St. Bernard police possessed a reasonable suspicion, based on specific and articulable facts, that Hensley was involved in an armed robbery. The District Judge heard testimony from the St. Bernard officer who interviewed the informer. On the strength of the evidence, the District Court concluded that the wealth of detail concerning the robbery revealed by the informer, coupled with her admission of tangential participation in the robbery, established that the informer was sufficiently reliable and credible "to arouse a reasonable suspicion of criminal activity by [Hensley] and to constitute the specific and articulable facts needed to underly a stop." * * *

Turning to the flyer issued by the St. Bernard police, we believe it satisfies the objective test announced today. An objective reading of the entire flyer would lead an experienced officer to conclude that Thomas Hensley was at least wanted for questioning and investigation in St. Bernard. Since the flyer was issued on the basis of articulable facts supporting a reasonable suspicion, this objective reading would justify a brief stop to check Hensley's identification, pose questions, and inform the suspect that the St. Bernard police wished to question him. As an experienced officer could well assume that a warrant might have been obtained in the period after the flyer was issued, we think the flyer would further justify a brief detention at the scene of the stop while officers checked whether a warrant had in fact been issued. It is irrelevant whether the Covington officers intended to detain Hensley only long enough to confirm the existence of a warrant, or for some longer period; what matters is that the stop and detention that occurred were in fact no more intrusive than would have been permitted an experienced officer on an objective reading of the flyer.

To be sure, the St. Bernard flyer at issue did not request that other police departments briefly detain Hensley merely to check his identification or confirm the existence of a warrant. Instead, it asked other departments to pick up and hold Hensley for St. Bernard. Our decision today does not suggest that such a detention, whether at the scene or at the Covington police headquarters, would have been justified. Given the distance involved and the time required to identify and communicate with the department that issued the flyer, such a detention might well be so lengthy or intrusive as to exceed the permissible limits of a *Terry* stop. Nor do we mean to endorse St. Bernard's request in its flyer for actions that could forseeably violate the Fourth Amendment. We hold only that this flyer, objectively read and supported by a reasonable suspicion on the part of the issuing department, justified the length and intrusiveness of the stop and detention that actually occurred.

When the Covington officers stopped Hensley, they were authorized to take such steps as were reasonably necessary to protect their personal safety and to maintain the status quo during the course of the stop. The Covington officers' conduct was well within the permissible range in the context of suspects who are reported to be armed and dangerous. See *Michigan v. Long*, 463 U.S. 1032, 1049–1050 (1983); *Pennsylvania v. Mimms*, 434 U.S. 106, 110–111 (1977) (*per curiam*). Having stopped Hensley, the Covington police were entitled to seize evidence revealed in plain view in the course of the lawful stop, to arrest Hensley's passenger when evidence discovered in plain view gave probable cause to believe the passenger had committed a crime, and subsequently to search the passenger compartment of the car because it was within the passenger's immediate control. Finally, having discovered additional weapons in Hensley's car during the course of a lawful search, the Covington officers had probable cause to arrest Hensley himself for possession of firearms.

* * *

The judgment of the Court of Appeals is reversed, and the case is remanded for proceedings consistent with this opinion.

[The concurring opinion of Justice Brennan, who also joined the majority opinion, is omitted.]

ILLINOIS v. WARDLOW

Supreme Court of the United States, 2000.
___ U.S. ___, 120 S.Ct. 673, 145 L.Ed.2d 570

Chief Justice Rehnquist delivered the opinion of the Court.

On September 9, 1995, Officers Nolan and Harvey were working as uniformed officers in the special operations section of the Chicago Police Department. The officers were driving the last car of a four car caravan converging on an area known for heavy narcotics trafficking in order to investigate drug transactions. The officers were traveling together because they expected to find a crowd of people in the area, including lookouts and customers.

As the caravan passed 4035 West Van Buren, Officer Nolan observed respondent Wardlow standing next to the building holding an opaque bag. Respondent looked in the direction of the officers and fled. Nolan and Harvey turned their car southbound, watched him as he ran through the gangway and an alley, and eventually cornered him on the street. Nolan then exited his car and stopped respondent. He immediately conducted a protective pat-down search for weapons because in his experience it was common for there to be weapons in the near vicinity of narcotics transactions. During the frisk, Officer Nolan squeezed the bag respondent was carrying and felt a heavy, hard object similar to the shape of a gun. The officer then opened the bag and discovered a .38–

caliber handgun with five live rounds of ammunition. The officers arrested Wardlow.

The Illinois trial court denied respondent's motion to suppress, finding the gun was recovered during a lawful stop and frisk. [The Illinois Supreme Court reversed the conviction, concluding that the gun should have been suppressed because Officer Nolan did not have reasonable suspicion sufficient to justify an investigative stop pursuant to Terry v. Ohio, 392 U.S. 1 (1968).]

* * * Nolan and Harvey were among eight officers in a four car caravan that was converging on an area known for heavy narcotics trafficking, and the officers anticipated encountering a large number of people in the area, including drug customers and individuals serving as lookouts. It was in this context that Officer Nolan decided to investigate Wardlow after observing him flee. An individual's presence in an area of expected criminal activity, standing alone, is not enough to support a reasonable, particularized suspicion that the person is committing a crime. But officers are not required to ignore the relevant characteristics of a location in determining whether the circumstances are sufficiently suspicious to warrant further investigation. Accordingly, we have previously noted the fact that the stop occurred in a "high crime area" among the relevant contextual considerations in a Terry analysis. Adams v. Williams, 407 U.S. 143, 144 (1972).

In this case, moreover, it was not merely respondent's presence in an area of heavy narcotics trafficking that aroused the officers' suspicion but his unprovoked flight upon noticing the police. Our cases have also recognized that nervous, evasive behavior is a pertinent factor in determining reasonable suspicion. [citations] Headlong flight—wherever it occurs—is the consummate act of evasion: it is not necessarily indicative of wrongdoing, but it is certainly suggestive of such. In reviewing the propriety of an officer's conduct, courts do not have available empirical studies dealing with inferences drawn from suspicious behavior, and we cannot reasonably demand scientific certainty from judges or law enforcement officers where none exists. Thus, the determination of reasonable suspicion must be based on commonsense judgments and inferences about human behavior. We conclude Officer Nolan was justified in suspecting that Wardlow was involved in criminal activity, and, therefore, in investigating further.

Such a holding is entirely consistent with our decision in Florida v. Royer, 460 U.S. 491 (1983), where we held that when an officer, without reasonable suspicion or probable cause, approaches an individual, the individual has a right to ignore the police and go about his business. And any "refusal to cooperate, without more, does not furnish the minimal level of objective justification needed for a detention or seizure." Florida v. Bostick, 501 U.S. 429, 437,(1991). But unprovoked flight is simply not a mere refusal to cooperate. Flight, by its very nature, is not "going about one's business"; in fact, it is just the opposite. Allowing officers confronted with such flight to stop the fugitive and investigate further is quite consistent with the individual's right to go about his business or to stay put and remain silent in the face of police questioning.

Respondent and amici also argue that there are innocent reasons for flight from police and that, therefore, flight is not necessarily indicative of ongoing criminal activity. This fact is undoubtedly true, but does not establish a violation of the Fourth Amendment. Even in *Terry*, the conduct justifying the stop was ambiguous and susceptible of an innocent explanation. The officer observed two individuals pacing back and forth in front of a store, peering into the window and periodically conferring. All of this conduct was by itself lawful, but it also suggested that the individuals were casing the store for a planned robbery. *Terry* recognized that the officers could detain the individuals to resolve the ambiguity.

In allowing such detentions, *Terry* accepts the risk that officers may stop innocent people. Indeed, the Fourth Amendment accepts that risk in connection with more drastic police action; persons arrested and detained on probable cause to believe they have committed a crime may turn out to be innocent. The *Terry* stop is a far more minimal intrusion, simply allowing the officer to briefly investigate further. If the officer does not learn facts rising to the level of probable cause, the individual must be allowed to go on his way. But in this case the officers found respondent in possession of a handgun, and arrested him for violation of an Illinois firearms statute. No question of the propriety of the arrest itself is before us.

The judgment of the Supreme Court of Illinois is reversed, and the cause is remanded for further proceedings not inconsistent with this opinion.

Justice Stevens, with whom Justice Souter, Justice Ginsburg, and Justice Breyer join, concurring in part and dissenting in part.

The State of Illinois asks this Court to announce a "bright-line rule" authorizing the temporary detention of anyone who flees at the mere sight of a police officer. Respondent counters by asking us to adopt the opposite per se rule—that the fact that a person flees upon seeing the police can never, by itself, be sufficient to justify a temporary investigative stop of the kind authorized by *Terry*.

The Court today wisely endorses neither per se rule. * * * Although I agree with the Court's rejection of the per se rules proffered by the parties, unlike the Court, I am persuaded that in this case the brief testimony of the officer who seized respondent does not justify the conclusion that he had reasonable suspicion to make the stop. * * *

The question in this case concerns "the degree of suspicion that attaches to" a person's flight—or, more precisely, what "commonsense conclusions" can be drawn respecting the motives behind that flight. A pedestrian may break into a run for a variety of reasons—to catch up with a friend a block or two away, to seek shelter from an impending storm, to arrive at a bus stop before the bus leaves, to get home in time for dinner, to resume jogging after a pause for rest, to avoid contact with a bore or a bully, or simply to answer the call of nature—any of which might coincide with the arrival of an officer in the vicinity. A pedestrian might also run because he or she has just sighted one or more police officers. In the latter instance, the State properly points out "that the fleeing person may be, inter alia, (1) an escapee from jail; (2) wanted on a warrant, (3) in possession of contraband, (i.e. drugs, weapons, stolen goods, etc.); or (4) someone who has just committed another type of crime." In short, there are unquestionably circumstances in which a person's flight is suspicious, and undeniably instances in which a person runs for entirely innocent reasons. Compare, e.g., Proverbs 28:1 ("The wicked flee when no man pursueth: but the righteous are as bold as a lion") with Proverbs 22:3 ("A shrewd man sees trouble coming and lies low; the simple walk into it and pay the penalty").

I have rejected reliance on the former proverb in the past, because its "ivory-towered analysis of the real world" fails to account for the experiences of many citizens of this country, particularly those who are minorities. That this pithy expression fails to capture the total reality of our world, however, does not mean it is inaccurate in all instances.

Given the diversity and frequency of possible motivations for flight, it would be profoundly unwise to endorse either per se rule. The inference we can reasonably draw about the motivation for a person's flight, rather, will depend on a number of different circumstances. Factors such as the time of day, the number of people in the area, the character of the neighborhood, whether the officer was in uniform, the way the runner was dressed, the direction and speed of the flight, and whether the person's behavior was otherwise unusual might be relevant in specific cases. This number of variables is surely sufficient to preclude either a bright-line rule that always justifies, or that never justifies, an investigative stop based on the sole fact that flight began after a police officer appeared nearby. * * *

Guided by that totality-of-the-circumstances test, the Court concludes that Officer Nolan had reasonable suspicion to stop respondent. In this respect, my view differs from the Court's. The entire justification for the stop is articulated in the brief testimony of Officer Nolan. Some facts are perfectly clear; others are not. This factual insufficiency leads me to conclude that the Court's judgment is mistaken.

Respondent Wardlow was arrested a few minutes after noon on September 9, 1995. Nolan was part of an eight-officer, four-car caravan patrol team. The officers were headed for "one of the areas in the 11th District [of Chicago] that's high [in] narcotics traffic." The reason why four cars were in the caravan was that "normally in these different areas there's an enormous amount of people, sometimes lookouts, customers." Officer Nolan testified that he was in uniform on that day, but he did not recall whether he was driving a marked or an unmarked car. This terse testimony is most noticeable for what it fails to reveal. Though asked whether he was in a marked or an unmarked car, Officer Nolan could not recall the answer. He was not asked whether any of the other three cars in the caravan were marked, or whether any of the other seven officers were in uniform. Though he explained that the size of the caravan was because "normally in these different areas there's an enormous amount of people, sometimes lookouts, customers," Officer Nolan did not testify as to whether anyone besides Wardlow was nearby 4035 West Van Buren. Nor is it clear that that address was the intended destination of the caravan. As the Appellate Court of Illinois interpreted the record, "it appears that the officers were simply driving by, on their way to some unidentified location, when they noticed defendant standing at 4035 West Van Buren." Officer Nolan's testimony also does not reveal how fast the officers were driving. It does not indicate whether he saw respondent notice the other patrol cars. And it does not say whether the caravan, or any part of it, had already passed Wardlow by before he began to run. * * *

It is the State's burden to articulate facts sufficient to support reasonable suspicion. In my judgment, Illinois has failed to discharge that burden. I am not persuaded that the mere fact that someone standing on a sidewalk looked in the direction of a passing car before starting to run is sufficient to justify a forcible stop and frisk.

I therefore respectfully dissent from the Court's judgment to reverse the court below.

FLORIDA v. J.L.

Supreme Court of the United States, 2000.
——— U.S. ———, 120 S.Ct. 1375, ——— L.Ed.2d ———.

JUSTICE GINSBERG, delivered the opinion of the Court.

The question presented in this case is whether an anonymous tip that a person is carrying a gun is, without more, sufficient to justify a police officer's stop and frisk of that person. We hold that it is not.

I

On October 13, 1995, an anonymous caller reported to the Miami-Dade Police that a young black male standing at a particular bus stop and wearing a plaid shirt was carrying a gun. So far as the record reveals, there is no audio recording of the tip, and nothing is known about the informant. Sometime after the police received the tip—the record does not say how long—two officers were instructed to respond. They arrived at the bus stop about six minutes later and saw three black males "just hanging out [there]." One of the three, respondent J.L., was wearing a plaid shirt. Apart from the tip, the officers had no reason to suspect any of the three of illegal conduct. The officers did not see a firearm, and J.L. made no threatening or otherwise unusual movements. One of the officers approached J.L., told him to put his hands up on the bus stop, frisked him, and seized a gun from J.L.'s pocket. The second officer frisked the other two individuals, against whom no allegations had been made, and found nothing.

J.L., who was at the time of the frisk "10 days shy of his 16th birthday," was charged under state law with carrying a concealed firearm without a license and possessing a firearm while under the age of 18. He moved to suppress the gun as the fruit of an unlawful search, and the trial court granted the motion. The intermediate appellate court reversed, but the Supreme Court of Florida quashed that decision and held the search invalid under the Fourth Amendment. 727 So.2d 204 (1998).

Anonymous tips, the Florida Supreme Court stated, are generally less reliable than tips from known informants and can form the basis for reasonable suspicion only if accompanied by specific indicia of reliability, for example, the correct forecast of a subject's "not easily predicted" movements (quoting Alabama v. White, 496 U.S. 325, 332 (1990)). The tip leading to the frisk of J.L., the court observed, provided no such predictions, nor did it contain any other qualifying indicia of reliability. Two justices dissented. The safety of the police and the public, they maintained, justifies a "firearm exception" to the general rule barring investigatory stops and frisks on the basis of bare-boned anonymous tips.

Seeking review in this Court, the State of Florida noted that the decision of the State's Supreme Court conflicts with decisions of other courts declaring similar searches compatible with the Fourth Amendment. We granted certiorari, and now affirm the judgment of the Florida Supreme Court.

II

Our "stop and frisk" decisions begin with Terry v. Ohio, 392 U.S. 1 (1968). This Court held in *Terry*

> "Where a police officer observes unusual conduct which leads him reasonably to conclude in light of his experience that criminal activity may be afoot and that the persons with whom he is dealing may be armed and presently dangerous, where in the course of investigating this behavior he identifies himself as a policeman and makes reasonable inquiries, and where nothing in the initial stages of the encounter serves to dispel his reasonable fear for his own safety, he is entitled for the protection of himself and others in the area to conduct a carefully limited search of the outer clothing of such persons in an attempt to discover weapons which might be used to assault him." Id., at 30.

In the instant case, the officers' suspicion that J.L. was carrying a weapon arose not from any observations of their own but solely from a call made from an unknown location by an unknown caller. Unlike a tip from a known informant whose reputation can be assessed and who can be held responsible if her allegations turn out to be fabricated, an anonymous tip alone seldom demonstrates the informant's basis of knowledge or veracity. As we have recognized, however, there are situations in which an anonymous tip, suitably corroborated, exhibits sufficient indicia of reliability to provide reasonable suspicion to make the investigatory stop." The question we here confront is whether the tip pointing to J.L. had those indicia of reliability.

In Alabama v. White, 496 U.S. 325 (1990) the police received an anonymous tip asserting that a woman was carrying cocaine and predicting that she would leave an apartment building at a specified time, get into a car matching a particular description, and drive to a named motel. Standing alone, the tip would not have justified a *Terry* stop. Only after police observation showed that the informant had accurately predicted the woman's movements, we explained, did it become reasonable to think the tipster had inside knowledge about the suspect and therefore to credit his assertion about the cocaine. Although the court held that the suspicion in *White* became reasonable after police surveillance, we regarded the case as borderline. Knowledge about a person's future movements indicates some familiarity with that person's affairs, but having such knowledge does not necessarily imply that the informant knows, in particular, whether that person is carrying hidden contraband. We accordingly classified *White* as a "closed case."

The tip in the instant case lacked the moderate indicia of reliability present in *White* and essential to the Court's decision in that case. The anonymous call concerning J.L. provided no predictive information and therefore left the police without means to test the informant's knowledge or credibility. That the allegation about the gun turned out to be correct does not suggest that the officers, prior to the frisks, had a reasonable basis for suspecting J.L. of engaging in unlawful conduct: The reasonableness of official suspicion must be measured by what the officers knew before they conducted their search. All the police had to go on in this case was the bare report of an unknown, unaccountable informant who neither explained how he knew of the gun nor supplied any basis for believing he had inside information about J.L. If *White* was a close case on the reliability of anonymous tips, this one surely falls on the other side of the line.

Florida contends that the tip was reliable because its description of the suspect's visible attributes proved accurate: There really was a young black male wearing a plaid shirt at the bus stop. The United States as amicus curiae makes a similar argument, proposing that a stop and frisk should be permitted "when (1) an anonymous tip provides a description of a particular person at a particular location illegally carrying a concealed firearm, (2) police promptly verify the pertinent details of the tip except the existence of the firearm, and (3) there are no factors that cast doubt on the reliability of the tip. . . ." Brief for United States 16. These contentions misapprehend the reliability needed for a tip to justify *Terry* stop.

An accurate description of a subject's readily observable location and appearance is of course reliable in this limited sense: It will help the police correctly identify the person whom the tipster means to accuse. Such a tip, however, does not show that the tipster has knowledge of concealed criminal activity. The reasonable suspicion here at issue requires that a tip be reliable in its assertion of illegality, not just in its tendency to identify a determinate person. Cf. 4 W. LaFave, *Search and Seizure* § 9.4(h), p. 213 (3d ed. 1996) (distinguishing reliability as to identification, which is often important in other criminal law contexts, from reliability as to the likelihood of criminal activity, which is central in anonymous-tip cases).

A second major argument advanced by Florida and the United States as amicus is, in essence, that the standard *Terry* analysis should be modified to license a "firearm exception." Under such an exception, a tip alleging an illegal gun would justify a stop and frisk even if the accusation would fail standard pre-search reliability testing. We decline to adopt this position.

Firearms are dangerous, and extraordinary dangers sometimes justify unusual precautions. Our decisions recognize the serious threat that armed criminals pose to public safety; *Terry*'s rule, which permits protective police searches on the basis of reasonable suspicion rather than demanding that officers meet the higher standard of probable cause, responds to this very concern. But an automatic firearm exception to our established reliability analysis would rove too far. Such an exception would enable any person seeking to harass another to set in motion an intrusive, embarrassing police search of the targeted person simply by placing an anonymous call falsely reporting the target's unlawful carriage of a gun. Nor could one securely confine such an exception to allegations involving firearms. Several Courts of Appeals have held it per se foreseeable for people carrying significant amounts of illegal drugs to be carrying guns as well. [citations] If police officers may properly conduct *Terry* frisks on the basis of bare-boned tips about guns, it would be reasonable to maintain under the above-cited decisions that the police should similarly have discretion to frisk based on bare-boned tips about narcotics. As we clarified when we made indicia of reliability critical in *Adams* and *White*, the Fourth Amendment is not so easily satisfied. Cf. Richards v. Wisconsin, 520 U.S. 385, 393–394 (1997) (rejecting a per se exception to the "knock and announce" rule for narcotics cases partly because "the reasons for creating an exception in one category [of Fourth Amendment cases] can, relatively easily, be applied to others," thus allowing the exception to swallow the rule).

Finally, the requirement that an anonymous tip bear standard indicia of reliability in order to justify a stop in no way diminishes a police officer's prerogative, in accord with *Terry*, to conduct a protective search of a person who has already been legitimately stopped. We speak in today's decision only of cases in which the officer's authority to make the initial stop is at issue. In that context, we hold that an anonymous tip lacking indicia of reliability of the kind contemplated in *Adams* and *White* does not justify a stop and frisk whenever and however it alleges the illegal possession of a firearm.

The judgment of the Florida Supreme Court is affirmed.

Justice Kennedy, with whom The Chief Justice joins, concurring.

On the record created at the suppression hearing, the Court's decision is correct. The Court says all that is necessary to resolve this case, and I join the opinion in all respects. It might be noted, however, that there are many indicia of reliability respecting anonymous tips that we have yet to explore in our cases.

When a police officer testifies that a suspect aroused the officer's suspicion, and so justifies a stop and frisk, the courts can weigh the officer's credibility and admit evidence seized pursuant to the frisk even if no one, aside from the officer and defendant themselves, was present or observed the seizure. An anonymous telephone tip without more is different, however; for even if the officer's testimony about receipt of the tip is found credible, there is a second layer of inquiry respecting the reliability of the informant that cannot be pursued. If the telephone call is truly anonymous, the informant has not placed his credibility at risk and can lie with impunity. The reviewing court cannot judge the credibility of the informant and the risk of fabrication becomes unacceptable.

On this record, then, the Court is correct in holding that the telephone tip did not justify the arresting officer's immediate stop and frisk of respondent. There was testimony that an anonymous tip came in by a telephone call and nothing more. The record does not show whether some notation or other documentation of the call was either by a voice recording or tracing the call to a telephone number. The prosecution recounted just the tip itself and the later verification of the presence of the three young men in the circumstances the Court describes.

It seems appropriate to observe that a tip might be anonymous in some sense yet have certain other features, either supporting reliability or narrowing the likely class of informants, so that the tip does provide the lawful basis for some police action. One such feature, as the Court recognizes, is that the tip predicts future conduct of the alleged criminal. There may be others. For example, if an unnamed caller with a voice which sounds the same each time tells police on two successive nights about criminal activity which in fact occurs each night, a similar call on the third night ought not be treated automatically like the tip in the case now before us. In the instance supposed, there would be a plausible argument that experience cures some of the uncertainty surrounding the anonymity, justifying a proportionate police response. In today's case, however, the State provides us no data about the reliability of anonymous tips. Nor do we know whether the dispatcher or arresting officer had any objective reason to believe that this tip had some particular indicia of reliability.

If an informant places his anonymity at risk, a court can consider this factor in weighing the reliability of the tip. An instance where a tip might be considered anonymous but nevertheless sufficiently reliable to justify a proportionate police response may be when an unnamed person driving a car the police officer later describes stops for a moment and, face to face, informs the police that criminal activity is occurring. This too seems different from the tip in the present case. See United States v. Sierra-Hernandez, 581 F.2d 760 (C.A.9 1978).

Instant caller identification is widely available to police, and, if anonymous tips are proving unreliable and distracting to police, squad cars can be sent within seconds to the location of the telephone used by the informant. Voice recording of telephone tips might, in appropriate cases, be used by police to locate the caller. It is unlawful to make false reports to the police, e.g., Fla.Stat.Ann. § 365.171(16) (Supp.2000); Fla. Stat.Ann. § 817.49 (1994), and the ability of the police to trace the identity of anonymous telephone informants may be a factor which lends reliability to what, years earlier, might have been considered unreliable anonymous tips.

These matters, of course, must await discussion in other cases, where the issues are presented by the record.

UNITED STATES v. MONTOYA DE HERNANDEZ

Supreme Court of the United States, 1985.
473 U.S. 531, 105 S.Ct. 3304, 87 L.Ed.2d 381.

JUSTICE REHNQUIST delivered the opinion of the Court.

Respondent Rosa Elvira Montoya de Hernandez was detained by customs officials upon her arrival at the Los Angeles airport on a flight from Bogota, Colombia. She was found to be smuggling 88 cocaine-filled balloons in her alimentary canal, and was convicted after a bench trial of various federal narcotics offenses. A divided panel of the United States Court of Appeals for the Ninth Circuit reversed her convictions, holding that her detention violated the Fourth Amendment to the United States Constitution because the customs inspectors did not have a "clear indication" of alimentary canal smuggling at the time she was detained. * * *

Respondent arrived at Los Angeles International Airport shortly after midnight, March 5, 1983, on Avianca Flight 080, a direct 10–hour flight from Bogota, Colombia. Her visa was in order so she was passed through Immigration and proceeded to the customs desk. At the customs desk she encountered Customs Inspector Talamantes, who reviewed her documents and noticed from her passport that she had made at least eight recent trips to either Miami or Los Angeles. Talamantes referred respondent to a secondary customs' desk for further questioning. At this desk Talamantes and another inspector asked respondent general questions concerning herself and the purpose of her trip. Respondent revealed that she spoke no English and had no family or friends in the United States. She explained in Spanish that she had come to the United States to purchase goods for her husband's store in Bogota. The customs inspectors recognized Bogota as a "source city" for narcotics. Respondent possessed $5,000 in cash, mostly $50 bills, but had no billfold. She indicated to the inspectors that she had no appointments with merchandise vendors, but planned to ride around Los Angeles in taxicabs visiting retail stores such as J. C. Penney and K–Mart in order to buy goods for her husband's store with the $5,000.

Respondent admitted that she had no hotel reservations, but stated that she planned to stay at a Holiday Inn. Respondent could not recall how her airline ticket was purchased. When the inspectors opened respondent's one small valise they found about four changes of "cold weather" clothing. Respondent had no shoes other than the high-heeled pair she was wearing. Although respondent possessed no checks, waybills, credit cards, or letters of credit, she did produce a Colombian business card and a number of old receipts, waybills, and fabric swatches displayed in a photo album.

At this point Talamantes and the other inspector suspected that respondent was a "balloon swallower," one who attempts to smuggle narcotics into this country hidden in her alimentary canal. Over the years Inspector Talamantes had apprehended dozens of alimentary canal smugglers arriving on Avianca Flight 080.

The inspectors requested a female customs inspector to take respondent to a private area and conduct a patdown and strip search. During the search the female inspector felt respondent's abdomen area and noticed a firm fullness, as if respondent were wearing a girdle. The search revealed no contraband but the inspector noticed that respondent was wearing two pair of elastic underpants with a paper towel lining the crotch area.

When respondent returned to the customs area and the female inspector reported her discoveries, the inspector in charge told respondent that he suspected she was smuggling drugs in her alimentary canal. Respondent agreed to the inspector's request that she be x rayed at a hospital but in answer to the inspector's query stated that she was pregnant. She agreed to a pregnancy test before the x ray. Respondent withdrew the consent for an x ray when she learned that she would have to be handcuffed en route to the hospital. The inspector then gave respondent the option of returning to Colombia on the next available flight, agreeing to an x ray, or remaining in detention until she produced a monitored bowel movement that would confirm or rebut the inspectors' suspicions. Respondent chose the first option and was placed in a customs' office under observation. She was told that if she went to the toilet she would have to use a wastebasket in the women's restroom, in order that female customs inspectors could inspect her stool for balloons or capsules carrying narcotics. The inspectors refused respondent's request to place a telephone call.

Respondent sat in the customs office, under observation, for the remainder of the night. During the night customs officials attempted to place respondent on a Mexican airline that was flying to Bogota via Mexico City in the morning. The airline refused to transport respondent because she lacked a Mexican visa necessary to land in Mexico City. Respondent was not permitted to leave, and was informed that she would be detained until she agreed to an x ray or her bowels moved. She remained detained in the customs office under observation, for most of the time curled up in a chair leaning to one side. She refused all offers of food and drink, and refused to use the toilet facilities. The Court of Appeals noted that she exhibited symptoms of discomfort consistent with "heroic efforts to resist the usual calls of nature."

At the shift change at 4:00 p.m. the next afternoon, almost 16 hours after her flight had landed, respondent still had not defecated or urinated or partaken of food or drink. At that time customs officials sought a court order authorizing a pregnancy test, an x ray, and a rectal examination. The Federal Magistrate issued an order just before midnight that evening, which authorized a rectal examination and involuntary x ray, provided that the physician in charge considered respondent's claim of pregnancy. Respondent was taken to a hospital and given a pregnancy test, which later turned out to be negative. Before the results of the pregnancy test were known, a physician conducted a rectal examination and removed from respondent's rectum a balloon containing a foreign substance. Respondent was then placed formally under arrest. By 4:10 a.m. respondent had passed 6 similar balloons; over the next 4 days she passed 88 balloons containing a total of 528 grams of 80% pure cocaine hydrochloride. * * *

Here the seizure of respondent took place at the international border. Since the founding of our Republic, Congress has granted the Executive plenary authority to conduct routine searches and seizures at the border, without probable cause or a warrant, in order to regulate the collection of duties and to prevent the introduction of contraband into this country. * * *

Consistently, therefore, with Congress' power to protect the Nation by stopping and examining persons entering this country, the Fourth Amendment's balance of reasonableness is qualitatively different at the international border than in the interior. Routine searches of the persons and effects of entrants are not subject to any requirement of reasonable suspicion, probable cause, or warrant, and first-class mail may be opened without a warrant on less than probable cause. *United States v. Ramsey*, 431 U.S. 606 (1977). Automotive travelers may be stopped at fixed check points near the border without individualized suspicion even if the stop is based largely on ethnicity, *United States v. Martinez–Fuerte*, 428 U.S. 543, 562–563 (1976), and boats on inland waters with ready access to the sea may be hailed and boarded with no suspicion whatever. *United States v. Villamonte–Marquez*, 462 U.S. 579 (1983).

These cases reflect longstanding concern for the protection of the integrity of the border. This concern is, if anything, heightened by the veritable national crisis in law enforcement caused by smuggling of illicit narcotics, and in particular by the increasing utilization of alimentary canal smuggling. This desperate practice appears to be a relatively recent addition to the smugglers' repertoire of deceptive practices, and it also appears to be exceedingly difficult to detect. * * *

We have not previously decided what level of suspicion would justify a seizure of an incoming traveler for purposes other than a routine border search. The Court of Appeals held that the initial detention of respondent was permissible only if the inspectors possessed a "clear indication" of alimentary canal smuggling. This "clear indication" language comes from our opinion in *Schmerber v. California*, 384 U.S. 757 (1966), but we think that the Court of Appeals misapprehended the significance of that phrase in the context in which it was used in *Schmerber*.[7] The Court of Appeals for the Ninth Circuit viewed "clear indication" as an intermediate standard between "reasonable suspicion" and "probable cause." But we think that the words in *Schmerber* were used to indicate the necessity for particularized suspicion that the evidence sought might be found within the body of the individual, rather than as enunciating still a third Fourth Amendment threshold between "reasonable suspicion" and "probable cause." * * *

We hold that the detention of a traveler at the border, beyond the scope of a routine customs search and inspection, is justified at its inception if customs agents, considering all the facts surrounding the traveler and her trip, reasonably suspect that the traveler is smuggling contraband in her alimentary canal.[8]

The facts, and their rational inferences, known to customs inspectors in this case clearly supported a reasonable suspicion that respondent was an alimentary canal smuggler. * * *

The final issue in this case is whether the detention of respondent was reasonably related in scope to the circumstances which justified it initially. In this regard we have cautioned that courts should not indulge in unrealistic second-guessing, and we have noted that creative judges, engaged in *post hoc* evaluations of police conduct can almost always imagine some alternative means by which the objectives of the police might have been accomplished. [Citations]. * * *

The rudimentary knowledge of the human body which judges possess in common with the rest of humankind tells us that alimentary canal smuggling cannot be detected in the amount of time in which other illegal activity may be investigated through brief *Terry*-type stops. It presents few, if any external signs; a quick frisk will not do, nor will even a strip search. In the case of respondent the inspectors had available, as an alternative to simply awaiting her bowel movement, an x ray. They

7. In that case we stated:
"The interests in human dignity and privacy which the Fourth Amendment protects forbid any such intrusion [beyond the body's surface] on the mere chance that desired evidence might be obtained. In the absence of a clear indication that in fact such evidence will be found, these fundamental human interests require law officers to suffer the risk that such evidence may disappear unless there is an immediate search." 384 U.S., at 769.

8. It is also important to note what we do *not* hold. Because the issues are not presented today we suggest no view on what level of suspicion, if any, is required for nonroutine border searches such as strip, body cavity, or involuntary x-ray searches. Both parties would have us decide the issue of whether aliens possess lesser Fourth Amendment rights at the border; that question was not raised in either court below and we do not consider it today.

offered her the alternative of submitting herself to that procedure. But when she refused that alternative, the customs inspectors were left with only two practical alternatives: detain her for such time as necessary to confirm their suspicions, a detention which would last much longer than the typical *"Terry"* stop, or turn her loose into the interior carrying the reasonably suspected contraband drugs.

The inspectors in this case followed this former procedure. They no doubt expected that respondent, having recently disembarked from a 10–hour direct flight with a full and stiff abdomen, would produce a bowel movement without extended delay. But her visible efforts to resist the call of nature, which the court below labeled "heroic," disappointed this expectation and in turn caused her humiliation and discomfort. Our prior cases have refused to charge police with delays in investigatory detention attributable to the suspect's evasive actions, and that principle applies here as well. Respondent alone was responsible for much of the duration and discomfort of the seizure. * * *

Under these circumstances, we conclude that the detention in this case was not unreasonably long. * * * The judgment of the Court of Appeals is therefore reversed.

JUSTICE STEVENS, concurring in the judgment.

If a seizure and a search of the person of the kind disclosed by this record may be made on the basis of reasonable suspicion, we must assume that a significant number of innocent persons will be required to undergo similar procedures. The rule announced in this case cannot, therefore, be supported on the ground that respondent's prolonged and humiliating detention resulted solely from the method by which she chose to smuggle illicit drugs into this country.

The prolonged detention of respondent was, however, justified by a different choice that respondent made; she withdrew her consent to an X-ray examination that would have easily determined whether the reasonable suspicion that she was concealing contraband was justified. I believe that Customs agents may require that a non-pregnant person reasonably suspected of this kind of smuggling submit to an X-ray examination as an incident to a border search. I therefore concur in the judgment.

JUSTICE BRENNAN, with whom JUSTICE MARSHALL joins, dissenting. * * *

I

Travelers at the national border are routinely subjected to questioning, pat-downs, and thorough searches of their belongings. These measures, which involve relatively limited invasions of privacy and which typically are conducted on all incoming travelers, do not violate the Fourth Amendment given the interests of "national self-protection reasonably requiring one entering the country to identify himself as entitled to come in, and his belongings as effects which may lawfully be brought in." *Carroll v. United States*, 267 U.S. 132, 154 (1925). Individual travelers also may be singled out on "reasonable suspicion" and briefly held for further investigation. At some point, however, further investigation involves such severe intrusions on the values the Fourth Amendment protects that more stringent safeguards are required. For example, the length and nature of a detention may, at least when conducted for criminal-investigative purposes, ripen into something approximating a full-scale custodial arrest—indeed, the arrestee, unlike the detainee in cases such as this, is at least given such basic rights as a telephone call, *Miranda* warnings, a bed, a prompt hearing before the nearest federal magistrate, an appointed attorney, and consideration of bail. In addition, border detentions may involve the use of such highly intrusive investigative techniques as body-cavity searches, x-ray searches, and stomach-pumping.

I believe that detentions and searches falling into these more intrusive categories are presumptively "reasonable" within the meaning of the Fourth Amendment only if authorized by a judicial officer. * * *

Something has gone fundamentally awry in our constitutional jurisprudence when a neutral and detached magistrate's authorization is required before the authorities may inspect the plumbing, heating, ventilation, gas, and electrical systems in a person's home, investigate the back rooms of his workplace, or poke through the charred remains of his gutted garage, but *not* before they may hold him in indefinite involuntary isolation at the nation's border to investigate whether he might be engaged in criminal wrongdoing. * * * Although the Court previously has declined to require a warrant for border searches involving minor interference with privacy resulting from the mere stop for questioning, surely there is no parallel between such "minor" intrusions and the extreme invasion of personal privacy and dignity that occurs in detentions and searches such as that before us today.

Moreover, the available evidence suggests that the number of highly intrusive border searches of suspicious-looking but ultimately innocent travelers may be very high. One physician who at the request of customs officials conducted many "internal searches"—rectal and vaginal examinations and stomach-pumping—estimated that he had found contraband in only 15 to 20 percent of the persons he had examined. It has similarly been estimated that only 16 percent of women subjected to body-cavity searches at the border were in fact found to be carrying contraband.[9] It is precisely to minimize the risk of harassing so many innocent people

9. *United States v. Holtz*, 479 F.2d, at 94 (Ely, J., dissenting) (citing testimony from congressional hearings in 1972). It was suggested at oral argument that "with all the experience the government has had in the intervening years with increasing drug traffic" there might be "a little more skill in detection today." There are, however, no published statistics more recent than the information discussed in text. It is of course the Government's burden to muster facts demonstrating the reasonableness of its investigative practices. The Government advised the Court at argument that it has more recent statistical evidence respecting the number of innocent travelers who are subjected to x-ray searches, but did not disclose that evidence because "it's not in the record and it's not public."

that the Fourth Amendment requires the intervention of a judicial officer. * * *

Finally, I disagree with Justice Stevens that de Hernandez' alternative "choice" of submitting to abdominal x-irradiation at the discretion of customs officials made this detention "justified." Medical x-rays are of course a common diagnostic technique; that is exactly why there is such a sharp debate among the medical community concerning the cellular and chromosomal effects of routine reliance on x-rays, both from the perspective of individual health (it having been estimated that a routine medical x-ray takes about 6 days off a person's life-expectancy) and from the perspective of successive generations. The "additivity" factor—the cumulative effect of x-rays on an individual's biological and genetic well-being—has been the subject of particularly disturbing debate.

But these dangers are not the gravamen of my dispute with Justice Stevens; the Court has concluded that medical practices far more immediately intrusive than this may in carefully limited circumstances be employed as a tool of criminal investigation. Cf. *Winston v. Lee*, 470 U.S. 753 (1985). Rather, the crux of my disagreement is this: We have learned in our lifetimes, time and again, the inherent dangers that result from coupling unchecked "law enforcement" discretion with the tools of medical technology. Accordingly, in this country at least, "[t]he importance of informed, detached and deliberate [judicial] determinations of the issue whether or not to invade another's body in search of evidence of guilt is indisputable and great." *Schmerber v. California*, 384 U.S. 757, 770 (1966). Because "[s]earch warrants are ordinarily required for searches of dwellings, * * * *absent an emergency*, no less could be required where intrusions into the human body are concerned." *Ibid.* (emphasis added). This should be so whether the intrusion is by incision, by stomach-pumping, or by exposure to x-irradiation. Because no exigent circumstances prevented the authorities from seeking a magistrate's authorization so to probe de Hernandez' abdominal cavity, the proffered alternative "choice" of a warrantless x-ray was just as impermissible as the 27–hour detention that actually occurred.

II

I believe that de Hernandez' detention violated the Fourth Amendment for an additional reason: it was not supported by probable cause. In the domestic context, a detention of the sort that occurred here would be permissible only if there were probable cause at the outset. * * *

To be sure, it is commonly asserted that as a result of the Fourth Amendment's "border exception" there is no requirement of probable cause for such investigations. But the justifications for the border exception necessarily limit its breadth. * * * As a condition of entry, the traveler may be subjected to exhaustive processing and examinations, and his belongings may be scrutinized with exacting care. I have no doubt as well that, *as a condition of entry*, travelers in appropriate circumstances may be required to excrete their bodily wastes for further scrutiny and to submit to diagnostic x-rays.

Contrary to the Court's reasoning, however, the Government in carrying out such immigration and customs functions does not simply have the two stark alternatives of either forcing a traveler to submit to such procedures or allowing him to pass into the interior. There is a third alternative: to instruct the traveler who refuses to submit to burdensome but reasonable conditions of entry that he is free to turn around and leave the country. In fact, I believe that the "reasonableness" of any burdensome requirement for entry is necessarily conditioned on the potential entrant's freedom to leave the country if he objects to that requirement. Surely the Government's manifest interest in preventing potentially excludable individuals carrying potential contraband from crossing our borders is fully vindicated if those individuals voluntarily decided not to cross the borders.

This does not, of course, mean that such individuals are not fully subject to the criminal laws while on American soil. If there is probable cause to believe they have violated the law, they may be arrested just like any other person within our borders. And if there is "reasonable suspicion" to believe they may be engaged in such violations, they may briefly be detained pursuant to *Terry* for further investigation, subject to the same limitations and conditions governing *Terry* stops anywhere else in the country. But if such *Terry* suspicion does not promptly ripen into probable cause, such travelers must be given a meaningful choice: either agree to further detention as a condition of eventual entry, or leave the country.

The Government disagrees. We were advised at oral argument that it "definitely" is the policy of customs authorities "not to allow such people, if they're reasonably suspected of drug smuggling, to return before that suspicion can be checked out" and that, whether citizen, resident alien, or alien, "[w]e would not simply let them go back." Tr. of Oral Arg. 5, 48.[10] The result is to sanction an authoritarian twilight zone on the border. The suspicious-looking traveler may not enter the country. Nor may he leave. Instead, he is trapped on the border. * * * But notwithstanding that he is on American soil, he is *not* fully protected by the guarantees of the Bill of Rights applicable everywhere else in the country. To be sure, a watered-down "reasonableness" requirement will

---

10. Although the Government now disavows those actions, the customs authorities apparently sought to arrange to have de Hernandez flown either to Mexico or back to Colombia, but concluded that she would not be able to secure a flight for at least two days. Even if the Government had not repudiated these efforts, it is clear that, as the District Court found, de Hernandez was subjected to exacting surveillance during this time for purposes of criminal investigation and possible arrest.

The Government argues that giving a traveler the option of leaving the country rather than being forced to undergo lengthy custodial criminal investigations based on mere suspicion "is an unsatisfactory alternative because it would allow the suspect to escape apprehension and return to repeat his smuggling efforts another day. In addition, this approach would remove a disincentive to smuggling activity by materially reducing the risk of apprehension and prosecution." This is exactly the same argument made whenever courts enforce the safeguards of the Fourth Amendment, and we have consistently stressed that if constitutionally permissible investigative stops do not promptly uncover sufficient evidence to support an arrest, the detainee must be released as a necessary consequence of constitutional liberty.

technically govern such detentions, but it will accommodate itself to assaults on privacy and personal autonomy that would not for one moment pass constitutional muster anywhere else in the country and that would surely provide grounds for an open-and-shut damages action for violations of basic civil rights if conducted anywhere but on the border. * * *

Commentary

Strip searches and body cavity searches are frequently performed upon prison inmates, and also upon arrested persons who are booked into local jails. The practice has led to many civil lawsuits under the federal Civil Rights Act. Where the searches are conducted as part of a regular security program at a prison housing convicted felons, the weight of authority is to uphold the searches without requiring particularized suspicion or other cause. According to the opinion in Goff v. Nix, 803 F.2d 358 (8th Cir.1986), there is no appellate case holding routine body cavity searches in prisons unconstitutional, although a few district court decisions have placed restrictions upon the practice.

The divided panel in *Goff* reversed a district court decision that had ordered prison authorities to discontinue the practice of subjecting inmates to body cavity searches before and after every inmate contact visit with persons such as attorneys, clergy, and the prison ombudsman. The majority stressed the extreme difficulty of preventing the introduction of weapons and drugs into a maximum security prison, and concluded that "Given the serious problems that accompany contact visitation, we do not believe that we have any constitutional authority selectively to disapprove of VBC searches of prisoners in this context based on the identity or occupation of their visitors." The dissent countered that "these searches are dehumanizing to the prisoners and must be revolting to the guards," and defended the district court order as carefully designed to protect the prisoners without adversely affecting prison security. 803 F.2d at 368–69, 372.

A number of cases have upheld civil actions against routine body cavity searches of arrested persons, however. Despite the constitutional presumption of innocence, the decisions generally uphold such searches on a routine basis in the case of detainees awaiting trial on serious felony charges. When routine body cavity searches are conducted upon misdemeanants and traffic offenders, however, the decisions generally hold the searches unlawful and allow suits for damages. For example, see Weber v. Dell, 804 F.2d 796 (2d Cir.1986), and the many cases cited in that opinion. The Court in *Weber* held that "the Fourth Amendment precludes prison officials from performing strip/body cavity searches of arrestees charged with misdemeanors or other minor offenses unless the officials have a reasonable suspicion that the arrestee is concealing weapons or other contraband based on the crime charged, the particular characteristics of the arrestee, and/or the circumstances of the arrest." The Court also held that the illegality of routine body cavity searches of minor offenders was sufficiently clear at the time that the sheriff could be held personally liable.

See also, Fuller v. M.G. Jewelry, 950 F.2d 1437 (9th Cir.1991). In that case female defendants were arrested for felony theft of a ring, and were subjected to strip and visual body cavity searches pursuant to an unconstitutional Los Angeles Police Department practice of performing such searches on all felony arrestees without regard to the seriousness of the felony or the circumstances of the particular case. The court held that such searches may be performed for jail security purposes if the officers have "reasonable suspicion" that the arrestee may be in possession of dangerous contraband such as weapons or drugs. If a body cavity search is directed only at finding evidence (such as the stolen ring in this case), the search is subject to the probable cause and warrant requirements of the Fourth Amendment.

EDMOND v. GOLDSMITH

United States Court of Appeals, 7th Circuit, 1999.
183 F.3d 659, cert. granted, _____ U.S. _____,
120 S.Ct. 1156, 145 L.Ed.2d 1068 (2000).

POSNER, CHIEF JUDGE.

A class action has been brought to enjoin the City of Indianapolis from setting up roadblocks to catch drug offenders, a practice that the plaintiffs claim violates the Fourth Amendment. The plaintiffs' motion for a preliminary injunction was denied on the ground that the City's practice is lawful, precipitating this interlocutory appeal under 28 U.S.C. § 1292(a)(1). The legality of drug roadblocks has divided the other courts that have been asked to decide the issue. [Citations] This is our first case. Because it was decided by the district court on a very skimpy stipulation of facts, our ruling on the legality of the City's program is necessarily tentative.

Six times between August and November of last year, the City's police department set up roadblocks on Indianapolis streets to catch drug offenders. A total of 1,161 cars were stopped at these roadblocks—for how long is unclear but the police endeavor to operate the checkpoints in such a manner that the stop does not exceed five minutes. During the stop, the police demand the driver's license and car registration, peer through the car's windows into its interior, and lead a drug-sniffing dog around the car. The stopping of the 1,161 vehicles resulted in 55 drug-related arrests, meaning that 5 percent of the total number of stops resulted in successful drug "hits," and 49 arrests for conduct unrelated to drugs, such as driving with an expired driver's license, for an overall hit rate of 9 percent. The City is continuing the program.

Stopping a car at a roadblock is a seizure within the meaning of the Fourth Amendment, even though the sequel—the peering into the car windows and the sniffing of the car by the dog outside—does not rise to the level of a search as that term of the amendment has been interpreted by the Supreme Court. [Citations] Whether the seizures effected by Indianapolis's drug roadblocks are reasonable may depend on whether reasonableness is to be assessed at the level of the entire program or of the individual stop. If the former, these roadblocks probably are legal, given the high "hit" rate and the only modestly intrusive character of the stops. In many Fourth Amendment contexts, the reasonableness of a practice is held to depend on the balance between its benefits (usually nonpecuniary) and its costs (ditto). [Citations] The benefits of a random system of searches or seizures, such as vehicle stops pursuant to a roadblock system, are a function of, first, the probability that the stop will result in an arrest or a seizure of contraband or evidence of crime, and, second, the gain to the achievement of a lawful governmental goal that such an arrest or seizure will produce. The costs are a function of the harm that the stop will cause to the property or privacy of the people whose cars are stopped. In the case of Indianapolis's drug-roadblock program, the probability of a "hit" is high (vastly higher than, for example, the probability of a hit as a result of the screening of embarking passengers and their luggage at airports, and the deterrence of drug offenses produced by these hits advances the strong national, state, and local policy of discouraging the illegal use of controlled substances. The cost—in delay, anxiety, and invasion of privacy—to the drivers and passengers stopped for five minutes at a roadblock and subjected to a visual inspection of the interior and a sniff by a dog is small, though it is greater than the cost of the normal airport screening and (like that screening) is incurred in all stops while the benefit from the program is obtained only when there is a hit.

But courts do not usually assess reasonableness at the program level when they are dealing with searches related to general criminal law enforcement, rather than to primarily civil regulatory programs for the protection of health, safety, and the integrity of our borders. Because it is infeasible to quantify the benefits and costs of most law enforcement programs, the program approach might well permit deep inroads into privacy. In high-crime areas of America's cities it might justify methods of policing that are associated with totalitarian nations. One can imagine an argument that it would be reasonable in a drug-infested neighborhood to administer drug tests randomly to drivers and pedestrians. Although there is nothing in the text of the Fourth Amendment to prevent dragnet searches (read literally, the text requires only that searches and seizures be "reasonable" and confines the requirement of "probable cause" to searches or seizures made pursuant to warrant), the Supreme Court has insisted that "to be reasonable under the Fourth Amendment, a search ordinarily must be based on individualized suspicion of wrongdoing," save in cases of "special need" based on "concerns other than crime detection." Chandler v. Miller, 520 U.S. 305 (1997; see also Vernonia School District 47J v. Acton, 515 U.S. 646, 653(1995). Program-level justifications for searches in support of specific regulatory programs do not carry over to general criminal law enforcement.

The qualification in "ordinarily" must not be overlooked. When the police establish a roadblock on a route that they know or strongly suspect is being used by a dangerous criminal to escape, the probability is high not only of apprehending the criminal but also of preventing him from engaging in further criminal, or otherwise hazardous, activity incidental to his escape. So the roadblock is allowed even though it is likely to "seize" some individuals who are not suspected of wrongdoing.

But here the roadblock is meant to intercept a completely random sample of drivers; there is neither probable cause nor articulable suspicion to stop any given driver. Even so, we can imagine cases in which, although the police do not suspect anyone, a roadblock or other dragnet method of criminal law enforcement would be reasonable. We may assume that if the Indianapolis police had a credible tip that a car loaded with dynamite and driven by an unidentified terrorist was en route to downtown Indianapolis, they would not be violating the Constitution if they blocked all the roads to the downtown area even though this would amount to stopping thousands of drivers without suspecting any one of them of criminal activity. When urgent considerations of the public safety require compromise with the normal principles constraining law enforcement, the normal principles may have to bend. The Constitution is not a suicide pact. But no such urgency has been shown here.

The Supreme Court has upheld the validity of roadblocks in less extreme cases, however, and it is on these that the City pitches its defense of its program. The Court upheld sobriety checkpoints—roadblocks at which drivers are checked for being under the influence of alcohol or (other) mind-altering drugs—in Michigan Dept. of State Police v. Sitz, 496 U.S. 444 (1990), and roadblocks designed to intercept illegal immigrants, in United States v. Martinez–Fuerte, 428 U.S. 543 (1976). The Court has not, however, ever held or stated that all roadblock programs (even those not vulnerable to a charge of delegating too much discretion to individual police officers) are consistent with the Fourth Amendment. On the contrary, the amendment would be violated if "the roadblock was a pretext whereby evidence of narcotics violation might be uncovered in 'plain view' in the course of a check for driver's licenses." Texas v. Brown, 460 U.S. 730, 743 (1983) (plurality opinion).

Randomized search programs have been upheld that involved the compelled provision of urine samples for drug testing of law enforcement officers, jockeys, railroad workers, and other classes of employee, as well as administrative searches conducted without any basis to suspect any particular individual of wrongdoing, but rather pursuant to a program of inspections incidental to a general scheme of licensing or other regulation. But again the Court has not granted carte blanche.

Many of the cases we have cited do involve criminal prosecutions, however, and we must consider how they can be squared with the principle that the requirement of individualized suspicion is to be relaxed only on the basis of (as the Supreme Court said in the *Chandler* case, an example of a systematic search program that did not pass constitutional muster) "concerns other than crime detection." The answer is that the concern which lies behind the randomized or comprehensive systems of inspections or searches that have survived challenge under the Fourth Amendment is not primarily with catching crooks, but rather with securing the safety or efficiency of the activity in which the people who are searched are engaged. Consider employment drug tests for transport workers, as in Skinner v. Railway Labor Executives' Ass'n, 489 U.S. 602 (1989). The employee who uses drugs will perform badly in his work, to the detriment of fellow employees or the general public; and the most effective preventive measure may be to test all or a random selection of applicants or employees. Similar are sobriety checkpoints, which are designed to protect other users of the road from the dangers posed by drunk drivers; administrative searches that are ancillary to concededly lawful systems of inspection; and the use of metal detectors and x-ray machines to screen entrants to government buildings and embarking air travelers. These cases rest on the commonsense principle that employers and other proprietors (such as the state as the owner of public roads), including the quasi-proprietor that is the government in heavily regulated industries, have a right to take reasonable measures to protect the safety and efficiency of their operations. These measures, moreover, usually make only limited inroads into privacy, because a person can avoid being searched or seized by avoiding the regulated activity, though we hesitate to put much weight on this point; people are unlikely to feel they can afford to "ground" themselves in order to avoid airport searches.

Indianapolis does not claim to be concerned with protecting highway safety against drivers high on drugs. Its program of drug roadblocks belongs to the genre of general programs of surveillance which invade privacy wholesale in order to discover evidence of crime. Imagine if the government set up a metal detector outside each person's home and required the person to step through it whenever he entered or left, in order to determine whether he was carrying a gun for which he lacked a permit. A principle that justified a drug roadblock would justify such surveillance.

We mentioned cases that allow the police or the Border Patrol to set up roadblocks to intercept illegal immigrants, a form of "contraband" to which illegal drugs might be analogized. Other cases allow custom searches of the luggage of people entering the United States. But such cases depend ultimately on sovereign powers over foreign relations, foreign commerce, citizenship, and immigration that states and cities do not possess. *Martinez-Fuerte* involved searches well inland from the border, but the Court emphasized the infeasibility of preventing illegal immigration by border checks alone. 428 U.S. at 552.

We are mindful of the paradoxical implication that the Fourth Amendment, though originally limited to federal law enforcement, may pinch the states more tightly. But the paradox need not detain us. Indianapolis makes no attempt to defend its roadblocks on the basis that it is trying to exclude a harmful substance or dangerous persons. Though that may be the ultimate aim, the City concedes that its proximate goal is to catch drug offenders in the hope of incapacitating them, and deterring others, by criminal prosecution. The program has no regulatory purpose that might be compared to that of the immigration laws, which seek to exclude and deport illegal immigrants rather than just to prosecute them for criminal violations of the immigration laws.

It is true that in the course of looking for drugs in vehicles stopped at its drug roadblocks, the Indianapolis police often discover violations of the traffic laws. If the purpose of the roadblock program were to discover such violations, and if a program having such a purpose could be justified under the cases that allow searches and seizures without individualized suspicion of wrongdoing, then the seizure, in the course of such searches, of drugs that were in plain view would be lawful. But the first "if" has not been shown. It is necessary in this regard to distinguish between two kinds of purpose, that of the program's designers and that of the police officers manning the roadblocks. The test for the lawfulness of a particular search or seizure is an objective one; the motives of the officer carrying out the search or seizure are irrelevant. But the purpose behind the program is critical to its legality. The program must be a bona fide effort to implement an authorized regulatory policy rather than a pretext for a dragnet search for criminals. Leading a drug-sniffing dog around a car cannot be justified by reference to a desire to detect traffic violations, and so the use of the dog at the City's roadblocks shows—what is anyway not contested—that the purpose of the roadblocks is to catch drug offenders. We are not asked to decide whether, if the primary purpose were to detect drunken drivers, the dog could be added to the roadblock scenario on the theory that since a sniff is not a search, the incremental invasion of privacy would be negligible, or at least would not violate the Fourth Amendment.

It can be objected that requiring consideration of purpose injects too large an element of uncertainty into the interpretation of the amendment, and that purpose may be difficult to determine when it is corporate in nature. But law like politics is the art of the possible and often requires imperfect compromises. Inquiry into purpose is one method of identifying and banning the most flagrantly abusive governmental conduct without handcuffing government altogether. The alternative would be to rule that either all roadblocks are illegal or none are, which would be akin to punishing all killings identically because the "objective" fact is that someone has died.

To summarize, we have identified four exceptions to the principle that a search or seizure is forbidden by the Fourth Amendment unless there is a basis for believing that a particular search or seizure, as distinct from a program of universal or randomized searches or seizures, will yield evidence or fruits or instrumentalities of crime. The first exception, illustrated by the roadblock set up to catch a fleeing criminal, is where there is a suspect—the police have identified the criminal and have only to find him—but it is infeasible to avoid an indiscriminate search or seizure of other persons, persons not suspected of crime, as well. The second exception, illustrated by the hypothetical dynamite case, is where no specific person is under suspicion but the circumstances make it impossible to prevent a crime without an indiscriminate search. The third exception is the regulatory search, the objective of which is to protect a specific activity rather than to operate as an adjunct to general criminal law enforcement. The last exception is the prevention of illegal importation whether of persons (a power limited to the federal government, On the basis of the record compiled in the preliminary-injunction proceedings—a record essentially limited to the parties' stipulation of facts—the Indianapolis roadblock program has not been shown to fit any of these exceptions, and thus the lawfulness of the program has not, as the district judge believed, been established. As that was the only ground on which she denied the preliminary injunction, her order cannot stand.

Whether there may be other grounds for denying the preliminary injunction, or whether on a fuller record the Indianapolis program might pass Fourth Amendment muster, are issues for the district court to decide in the first instance. We are not enthusiastic about the use of the Constitution to squelch experiments in dealing with serious social problems. The high hit rate of Indianapolis's roadblock scheme suggests that Indianapolis has placed the roadblocks in areas of the city in which drug use approaches epidemic proportions; and if so the roadblocks might be justified by reference to the second exception, as illustrated by such cases as Maxwell v. City of New York, 102 F.3d 664 (2d Cir.1996)(involving a flurry of drive-by shootings); Norwood v. Bain, 143 F.3d 843 (4th Cir.1998);(threat of violence at a rally of motorcycle gangs), and United States v. Williams, 372 F.Supp. 65 (D.S.D.1974) (Indian insurrection). But this is not argued either.

REVERSED.

EASTERBROOK, CIRCUIT JUDGE, dissenting.

Roadblocks in Indianapolis check for both driving and drug offenses. Someone driving a car without a license, or with drugs, can expect arrest. The program is spectacularly successful as roadblocks go; 9.4% of those stopped are arrested, with the reason equally divided between driving and drug crimes. Roadblocks with much lower rates of success have been held consistent with the fourth amendment. United States v. Martinez–Fuerte, 428 U.S. 543(1976) (0.12% success rate); Michigan Department of State Police v. Sitz, 496 U.S. 444(1990) (1.6% success rate). Yet my colleagues declare that the fourth amendment forbids what Indianapolis has done, because its primary purpose is to enforce the criminal laws. *Martinez-Fuerte* approved a roadblock to search for alien smuggling, a violation of a criminal law; *Sitz* approved a roadblock to search for drunk driving, a violation of a criminal law. So how can the fact that possessing drugs violates the criminal laws doom this program? One would suppose that our case is *a fortiori* from *Sitz*, because alcohol, marijuana, and cocaine all are drugs, any of which can impair a driver's performance. If the Constitution allows a roadblock to intercept alcohol users, how can it condemn a roadblock to intercept marijuana and cocaine users?

My colleagues' answer is that everything depends on the "primary" or "real" motive for the roadblock. Thus if Indianapolis set out to find people driving without licenses and only later added a dog to sniff for drugs (a step that does not entail a search or seizure of any kind, see

United States v. Place, 462 U.S. 696 (1983)) in cars that already were stopped, then the program would pass constitutional muster. But if the City first decides to search for drugs, then adds license checks to make better use of the time while the dog does its work, then the program is invalid. If a city starts a license + drug program, then its validity depends on the primary motivation: if to search for people not legally entitled to drive, the program is valid; if to search for people not legally entitled to carry drugs, invalid. If a program is designed primarily to search for people using drugs in the car, and only secondarily to locate drugs in the trunk, then it is valid; if it is designed primarily to search for carried drugs, and only secondarily for ingested drugs, then it is invalid.

Why should the constitutionality of a roadblock program turn on what its promoters think (or the order in which its components were approved), rather than on what happens to the citizenry? Over and over, the Supreme Court says that the reasonableness inquiry under the fourth amendment is objective; it depends on what the police do, not on what they want or think. Whren v. United States, 517 U.S. 806, 811–13 (1996); Graham v. Connor, 490 U.S. 386, 397 (1989); Maryland v. Macon, 472 U.S. 463, 470–71(1985); Scott v. United States, 436 U.S. 128, 136–38 (1978). The majority believes that things are otherwise when a program's design is in issue: "the *purpose* behind the program is critical to its legality. The program must be a bona fide effort to implement an authorized regulatory policy rather than a pretext for a dragnet search for criminals." 183 F.3d at 665 (emphasis in original). Where does "purpose" come into the fourth amendment? Not from its text; reasonableness fairly screams an objective inquiry. Not from its history; my colleagues do not mention the amendment's genesis. Not from the Supreme Court's cases. None of the opinions my colleagues cites requires a tour through the heads of the programs' sponsors. None suggests that the Constitution blesses a program in which a criminal-investigation component is added to a regulatory-enforcement one, while condemning an identical program in which the criminal-investigation component comes first. When the Supreme Court speaks of "regulatory" programs, such as the searches of business premises in New York v. Burger, 482 U.S. 691 (1987), or Marshall v. Barlow's, Inc., 436 U.S. 307(1978), it asks what the programs do, not what the sponsors of the programs had in mind. So far as the fourth amendment is concerned, there is no difference between a roadblock originally designed to catch drug peddlers and also used to catch drunk drivers, and a roadblock originally designed to catch drunk drivers and also used to catch drug peddlers. Only observable differences in police behavior enter into the calculus of "reasonableness."

To be consistent, therefore, my colleagues should say that the fourth amendment would not permit the Michigan Department of State Police to add a drug-detection dog to the roadblock program sustained in *Sitz*. That conclusion would be so jarring, given received doctrine that a dog's sense of smell is not a search and requires no justification, that it could not be sustained. Yet if a dog may be added to the program sustained in *Sitz*, it can't matter to "reasonableness" whether some of the program's sponsors thought the dog more important than the breathalyzer. The trial envisaged by my colleagues—one at which officials of Indianapolis will testify about their motivations in approving the roadblock program, and the district judge must make credibility findings to resolve the fourth amendment objection—has no relation to the objective standard that a "reasonableness" benchmark demands. * * *

One glory of a federal society is that the people may choose for themselves not only laws but also law-enforcement methods. State A may employ extra police to follow a high-probability-of-detection and low-sentence approach; State B may choose fewer police, fewer intrusions on privacy, but higher sentences for those who are caught. Each may be reasonable. Indianapolis selected a roadblock system, one that may catch any of its drivers. If this strikes the wrong balance, the people may throw out of office those who adopted it. Given the modest intrusion that roadblocks create for personal privacy, this is a legitimate choice for the public to make. The real threat to civil liberties comes from the national government, not from law-enforcement variations that can be avoided by driving a few miles to the east or west. Local governments should have more, not less, leeway than does the national government to decide how the tradeoff between privacy and effective law enforcement shall be handled.

Chapter 7

THE RETREAT FROM THE EXCLUSIONARY RULE

STONE v. POWELL

Supreme Court of the United States, 1976.
428 U.S. 465, 96 S.Ct. 3037, 49 L.Ed.2d 1067.

Mr. Justice Powell delivered the opinion of the Court. * * *

I

We summarize first the relevant facts and procedural history of these cases.

A

Respondent Lloyd Powell was convicted of murder in June 1968 after trial in a California state court. At about midnight on February 17, 1968, he and three companions entered the Bonanza Liquor Store in San Bernardino, Cal., where Powell became involved in an altercation with Gerald Parsons, the store manager, over the theft of a bottle of wine. In the scuffling that followed Powell shot and killed Parsons' wife. Ten hours later an officer of the Henderson, Nev., Police Department arrested Powell for violation of the Henderson vagrancy ordinance,[1] and in the search incident to the arrest discovered a .38–caliber revolver with six expended cartridges in the cylinder.

Powell was extradited to California and convicted of second-degree murder in the Superior Court of San Bernardino County. Parsons and Powell's accomplices at the liquor store testified against him. A criminologist testified that the revolver found on Powell was the gun that killed Parsons' wife. The trial court rejected Powell's contention that testimony by the Henderson police officer as to the search and the discovery of the revolver should have been excluded because the vagrancy ordinance

---

1. The ordinance provides:

"Every person is a vagrant who:

"[1] Loiters or wanders upon the streets or from place to place without apparent reason or business and [2] who refuses to identify himself and to account for his presence when asked by a police officer to do so [3] if surrounding circumstances are such as to indicate to a reasonable man that the public safety demands such identification."

was unconstitutional. In October 1969, the conviction was affirmed by a California District Court of Appeal. Although the issue was duly presented, that court found it unnecessary to pass upon the legality of the arrest and search because it concluded that the error, if any, in admitting the testimony of the Henderson officer was harmless beyond a reasonable doubt under *Chapman v. California*, 386 U.S. 18 (1967). [Powell's federal habeas corpus petition was denied by the District Court, but the Court of Appeals for the Ninth Circuit reversed.] The court concluded that the vagrancy ordinance was unconstitutionally vague, that Powell's arrest was therefore illegal, and that although exclusion of the evidence would serve no deterrent purpose with regard to police officers who were enforcing statutes in good faith, exclusion would serve the public interest by deterring legislators from enacting unconstitutional statutes. After an independent review of the evidence the court concluded that the admission of the evidence was not harmless error since it supported the testimony of Parsons and Powell's accomplices.

B

Respondent David Rice was convicted of murder in April 1971 after trial in a Nebraska state court. At 2:05 a.m. on August 17, 1970, Omaha police received a telephone call that a woman had been heard screaming at 2867 Ohio Street. As one of the officers sent to that address examined a suitcase lying in the doorway, it exploded, killing him instantly. By August 22 the investigation of the murder centered on Duane Peak, a 15–year-old member of the National Committee to Combat Fascism (NCCF), and that afternoon a warrant was issued for Peak's arrest. The investigation also focused on other known members of the NCCF, including Rice, some of whom were believed to be planning to kill Peak before he could incriminate them. In their search for Peak, the police went to Rice's home at 10:30 that night and found lights and a television on, but there was no response to their repeated knocking. While some officers remained to watch the premises, a warrant was obtained to search for explosives and illegal weapons believed to be in Rice's possession. Peak was not in the house, but upon entering the police discovered, in plain view, dynamite, blasting caps, and other materials useful in the construction of explosive devices. Peak subsequently was arrested, and on August 27, Rice voluntarily surrendered. The clothes Rice was wearing at that time were subjected to chemical analysis, disclosing dynamite particles.

Rice was tried for first-degree murder in the District Court of Douglas County. At trial Peak admitted planting the suitcase and making the telephone call, and implicated Rice in the bombing plot. As corroborative evidence the State introduced items seized during the search, as well as the results of the chemical analysis of Rice's clothing. The court denied Rice's motion to suppress this evidence. On appeal the Supreme Court of Nebraska affirmed the conviction, holding that the search of Rice's home had been pursuant to a valid search warrant.

[Rice petitioned for federal habeas corpus. The District Court held that the search warrant affidavit was defective under the *Aguilar-Spinelli* test. The affidavit had stated that police believed that explosives and illegal weapons were in the Rice home because: (1) Rice was an official of the NCCF, (2) it appeared that the NCCF was involved in the violent killing of a police officer, and (3) police had received information in the past that Rice possessed weapons and explosives, which he said should be used against the police. The police had additional information relating to probable cause at the time of the search, but the District Court did not consider it because it was not included in the affidavit.]

The court also rejected the State's contention that even if the warrant was invalid the search was justified because of the valid arrest warrant for Peak and because of the exigent circumstances of the situation—danger to Peak and search for bombs and explosives believed in possession of the NCCF. The court reasoned that the arrest warrant did not justify the entry as the police lacked probable cause to believe Peak was in the house, and further concluded that the circumstances were not sufficiently exigent to justify an immediate warrantless search. The Court of Appeals for the Eighth Circuit affirmed. * * *

II

[This section of the majority opinion reviewed the history of the writ of habeas corpus, and its gradual expansion through Supreme Court decisions.]

III

* * *

The exclusionary rule was a judicially created means of effectuating the rights secured by the Fourth Amendment. * * * The *Mapp* majority justified the application of the rule to the States on several grounds, but relied principally upon the belief that exclusion would deter future unlawful police conduct. Although our decisions often have alluded to the "imperative of judicial integrity," they demonstrate the limited role of this justification in the determination whether to apply the rule in a particular context. [The opinion noted that there are many recognized exceptions to the exclusionary rule which would be disallowed by a rigid application of the judicial integrity rationale, *e.g.* the "standing" limitation.]

While courts, of course, must ever be concerned with preserving the integrity of the judicial process, this concern has limited force as a justification for the exclusion of highly probative evidence. The force of this justification becomes minimal where federal habeas corpus relief is sought by a prisoner who previously has been afforded the opportunity for full and fair consideration of his search-and-seizure claim at trial and on direct review.

The primary justification for the exclusionary rule then is the deterrence of police conduct that violates Fourth Amendment rights. Post-*Mapp* decisions have established that the rule is not a personal constitutional right. It is not calculated to redress the injury to the privacy of the victim of the search or seizure, for any "[r]eparation comes too late." *Linkletter v. Walker*, 381 U.S. 618, 637 (1965). Instead,

> "the rule is a judicially created remedy designed to safeguard Fourth Amendment rights generally through its deterrent effect * * *." *United States v. Calandra*, 414 U.S. at 348 (1974) (holding that illegally seized evidence may be used in grand jury proceedings).[2]
> * * *

IV

We turn now to the specific question presented by these cases. Respondents allege violations of Fourth Amendment rights guaranteed them through the Fourteenth Amendment. The question is whether state prisoners—who have been afforded the opportunity for full and fair consideration of their reliance upon the exclusionary rule with respect to seized evidence by the state courts at trial and on direct review—may invoke their claim again on federal habeas corpus review. The answer is to be found by weighing the utility of the exclusionary rule against the costs of extending it to collateral review of Fourth Amendment claims.

The costs of applying the exclusionary rule even at trial and on direct review are well known: the focus of the trial, and the attention of the participants therein, are diverted from the ultimate question of guilt or innocence that should be the central concern in a criminal proceeding. Moreover, the physical evidence sought to be excluded is typically reliable and often the most probative information bearing on the guilt or innocence of the defendant. * * * Application of the rule thus deflects the truthfinding process and often frees the guilty. The disparity in particular cases between the error committed by the police officer and the windfall afforded a guilty defendant by application of the rule is contrary to the idea of proportionality that is essential to the concept of justice. Thus, although the rule is thought to deter unlawful police activity in part through the nurturing of respect for Fourth Amendment values, if applied indiscriminately it may well have the opposite effect of generating disrespect for the law and administration of justice. These long-recognized costs of the rule persist when a criminal conviction is sought to be overturned on collateral review on the ground that a search-and-seizure claim was erroneously rejected by two or more tiers of state courts.

2. As Professor Amsterdam has observed:

> "The rule is unsupportable as reparation or compensatory dispensation to the injured criminal; its sole rational justification is the experience of its indispensability in 'exert[ing] general legal pressures to secure obedience to the Fourth Amendment on the part of * * * law-enforcing officers.' As it serves this function, the rule is a needed, but grud[g]ingly taken, medicament; no more should be swallowed than is needed to combat the disease. Granted that so many criminals must go free as will deter the constables from blundering, pursuance of this policy of liberation beyond the confines of necessity inflicts gratuitous harm on the public interest * * *." Search, Seizure, and Section 2255: A Comment, 112 U.Pa.L.Rev. 378, 388–389 (1964) (footnotes omitted).

Evidence obtained by police officers in violation of the Fourth Amendment is excluded at trial in the hope that the frequency of future violations will decrease. Despite the absence of supportive empirical evidence,[3] we have assumed that the immediate effect of exclusion will be to discourage law enforcement officials from violating the Fourth Amendment by removing the incentive to disregard it. More importantly, over the long term, this demonstration that our society attaches serious consequences to violation of constitutional rights is thought to encourage those who formulate law enforcement policies, and the officers who implement them, to incorporate Fourth Amendment ideals into their value system.

We adhere to the view that these considerations support the implementation of the exclusionary rule at trial and its enforcement on direct appeal of state-court convictions. But the additional contribution, if any, of the consideration of search-and-seizure claims of state prisoners on collateral review is small in relation to the costs. * * * The view that the deterrence of Fourth Amendment violations would be furthered rests on the dubious assumption that law enforcement authorities would fear that federal habeas review might reveal flaws in a search or seizure that went undetected at trial and on appeal. Even if one rationally could assume that some additional incremental deterrent effect would be presented in isolated cases, the resulting advance of the legitimate goal of furthering Fourth Amendment rights would be outweighed by the acknowledged costs to other values vital to a rational system of criminal justice.

In sum, we conclude that where the State has provided an opportunity for full and fair litigation of a Fourth Amendment claim, a state prisoner may not be granted federal habeas corpus relief on the ground that evidence obtained in an unconstitutional search or seizure was introduced at his trial.

Reversed.

MR. CHIEF JUSTICE BURGER, concurring.

* * *

In *Bivens* [p. 52 of this book], I suggested that, despite its grave shortcomings, the [exclusionary] rule need not be totally abandoned until some meaningful alternative could be developed to protect innocent persons aggrieved by police misconduct. With the passage of time, it now

---

3. The efficacy of the exclusionary rule has long been the subject of sharp debate. Until recently, scholarly empirical research was unavailable. And, the evidence derived from recent empirical research is still inconclusive. Compare, *e.g.*, Oaks, Studying the Exclusionary Rule in Search and Seizure, 37 U.Chi.L.Rev. 665, 736–754 (1970); Spiotto, Search and Seizure: An Empirical Study of the Exclusionary Rule and Its Alternatives, 2 J. Legal Studies 243 (1973), with,

e.g., Canon, Is the Exclusionary Rule in Failing Health?, Some New Data and a Plea Against a Precipitous Conclusion, 62 Ky. L.J. 681 (1974). See also, Amsterdam, Perspectives on the Fourth Amendment, 58 Minn.L.Rev. 349, 475 n. 593 (1974); Comment, On the Limitations of Empirical Evaluations of the Exclusionary Rule: A Critique of the Spiotto Research and United States v. Calandra, 69 Nw.U.L.Rev. 740 (1974).

appears that the continued existence of the rule, as presently implemented, inhibits the development of rational alternatives. The reason is quite
simple: Incentives for developing new procedures or remedies will remain minimal or nonexistent so long as the exclusionary rule is retained
in its present form.

It can no longer be assumed that other branches of government will
act while judges cling to this Draconian, discredited device in its present
absolutist form. Legislatures are unlikely to create statutory alternatives, or impose direct sanctions on errant police officers or on the public
treasury by way of tort actions so long as persons who commit serious
crimes continue to reap the enormous and undeserved benefits of the
exclusionary rule. * * * And even if legislatures were inclined to experiment with alternative remedies, they have no assurance that the judicially created rule will be abolished or even modified in response to such
legislative innovations. The unhappy result, as I see it, is that alternatives will inevitably be stymied by rigid adherence on our part to the
exclusionary rule. I venture to predict that overruling this judicially
contrived doctrine—or limiting its scope to egregious, bad-faith conduct—would inspire a surge of activity toward providing some kind of
statutory remedy for persons injured by police mistakes or misconduct.
* * *

MR. JUSTICE BRENNAN, with whom MR. JUSTICE MARSHALL concurs,
dissenting.

[After arguing at length that the majority's holding was inconsistent
with the language of the habeas corpus statute,* Justice Brennan
commented on the specific cases before the Court:]

If proof of the necessity of the federal habeas jurisdiction were
required, the disposition by the state courts of the underlying Fourth
Amendment issues presented by these cases supplies it. In *Powell*,
respondent was arrested pursuant to a statute which obviously is unconstitutional under *Papachristou v. City of Jacksonville*, 405 U.S. 156
(1972). Even apart from its vagueness and concomitant potential for
arbitrary and discriminatory enforcement, the statute purports to crimi-
nalize the presence of one unable to account for his presence in a
situation where a reasonable person might believe that public safety
demands identification. It is no crime in a free society not to have
"identification papers" on one's person, and the statute is a palpable
effort to enable police to arrest individuals on the basis of mere suspicion
and to facilitate detention even when there is no probable cause to
believe a crime has been or is likely to be committed. Without elaborating on the various arguments buttressing this result, including the self-
incrimination aspects of the ordinance and its attempt to circumvent

---

* Title 28 U.S.C. § 2254 provides:

§ 2254. State custody; remedies in Federal courts.

(a) The Supreme Court, a Justice thereof, a circuit judge, or a district court shall
entertain an application for a writ of habeas
corpus in behalf of a person in custody
pursuant to the judgment of a State court
only on the ground that he is in custody in
violation of the Constitution or laws or
treaties of the United States. * * *

Fourth Amendment safeguards in a situation that, under *Terry v. Ohio* [p. 224 of this book], would at most permit law enforcement officials to conduct a protective search for weapons, I would note only that the ordinance, due to the Court's failure to address its constitutionality today, remains in full force and effect, thereby affirmatively encouraging further Fourth Amendment violations. Moreover, the fact that only a single state judge ever addressed the validity of the ordinance, and the lack of record evidence as to why or how he rejected respondent's claim, gives me pause as to whether there is any real content to the Court's "exception" for bringing Fourth Amendment claims on habeas in situations in which state prisoners were not accorded an opportunity for a full and fair state-court resolution of those claims; that fact also makes irrelevant the Court's presumption that deterrence is not furthered when there is federal habeas review of a search-and-seizure claim that was erroneously rejected by "two or more tiers of state courts."

Even more violative of constitutional safeguards is the manner in which the Nebraska courts dealt with the merits in respondent Rice's case. Indeed, the manner in which Fourth Amendment principles were applied in the Nebraska Supreme Court is paradigmatic of Congress' concern respecting attempts by state courts to structure Fourth Amendment jurisprudence so as not to upset convictions of the "guilty" or the "unworthy." As Judge Urbom fully detailed in two thorough and thoughtful opinions in the District Court on Rice's petition for habeas, the affidavit upon which the Omaha police obtained a warrant and thereby searched Rice's apartment was clearly deficient under prevailing constitutional standards, and no extant exception to the warrant requirement justified the search absent a valid warrant. Yet the Nebraska Supreme Court upheld the search on the alternative and patently untenable ground that there is no Fourth Amendment violation if a defective warrant is supplemented *at a suppression hearing* by facts that theoretically could have been, but were not, presented to the issuing magistrate. Such a construction of the Fourth Amendment would obviously abrogate the warrant requirement of the Fourth Amendment * * *

[The dissenting opinion of Justice White, who urged consideration of a "reasonable good faith" exception to the exclusionary rule, is omitted.]

Commentary

A state prisoner who has exhausted available state remedies may file a petition for federal habeas corpus under 28 U.S.C.A. § 2254, in the federal district court which has jurisdiction over the place of confinement. If the federal court determines that the custody is pursuant to a state court judgment obtained in violation of the Constitution or other provisions of federal law, the court may order appropriate relief. Frequently, the state is ordered in the alternative either to release the prisoner or grant a new trial. Federal prisoners who have exhausted their regular appellate remedies may attack their convictions by filing a motion under 28 U.S.C.A. § 2255. This motion is filed in the district where the trial was conducted, rather than the district having jurisdiction over the place of confinement. (Federal prisoners are often confined at a location distant from the place of conviction.)

In Kaufman v. United States, 394 U.S. 217 (1969), the Supreme Court had held that federal prisoners may raise search and seizure claims under Section 2255. The majority opinion by Justice Brennan started from the premise that there is no doubt that the federal habeas remedy extends to state prisoners who allege that unconstitutionally obtained evidence was submitted against them at trial. A major argument for keeping federal courts open to such claims by state prisoners is that state court judges may be unsympathetic to federally created rights that impede the enforcement of state criminal laws. The same reasoning does not apply in the case of federal prisoners, who have already had an opportunity to present their constitutional claims in federal court. Conceding the distinction, the majority opinion reasoned that the more fundamental reason for providing collateral review of state and federal convictions rests upon a recognition that adequate protection of constitutional rights in the criminal process requires the continuing availability of a mechanism for relief. This consideration is applicable to both state and federal prisoners equally.

In other words, the case for granting a collateral remedy for state prisoners is stronger than the case for granting similar remedies to federal prisoners, if we make the key assumption that some state courts are insufficiently protective of federal constitutional rights. As the Supreme Court has become more doubtful about the desirability of the Fourth Amendment exclusionary rule, it has become correspondingly less concerned about the possibility that state courts may be insufficiently vigorous in enforcing the rule. In fact, many state supreme courts are now invoking "independent state grounds" to extend the rights of defendants beyond what the Federal Constitution requires.

In Kimmelman v. Morrison, 477 U.S. 365 (1986), the state prisoner was convicted of rape in part on the basis of a bedsheet (which contained stains and hair) that was taken in a search of his apartment. Trial counsel objected to the introduction of the bedsheet on Fourth Amendment grounds, but the trial judge refused to reach the merits of the claim because counsel had not filed a pretrial suppression motion as required by state court rules. Counsel was unaware of the seizure until the trial began, but he would have been aware of it in advance if he had filed appropriate discovery motions and obtained the police reports.

After an unsuccessful appeal, Morrison sought federal habeas corpus relief. The district court found that direct consideration of the Fourth Amendment claim was barred by *Stone v. Powell*, but that Morrison could nonetheless challenge the conviction on the ground that counsel's negligence in failing to seek discovery, combined with the likelihood that a suppression motion would succeed if it had been made in timely fashion, constituted ineffective assistance of counsel. After the district court made its decision, the Supreme Court handed down its decision in *Strickland v. Washington*, reprinted on page 412 of this book. Reviewing the district court's ruling under *Strickland*, the Court of Appeals agreed that trial counsel had been "grossly ineffective," but vacated the order and remanded for the district court to determine whether Morrison had been "prejudiced" by the negligence under the *Strickland* standard.

The Supreme Court affirmed the Court of Appeals. The majority opinion by Justice Brennan held that counsel's total failure to request discovery or investigate the case established ineffective performance under the *Strickland* standard. The majority also affirmed the remand to the district court for a determination of prejudice. The State would have an opportunity on remand to establish either that the search was lawful, or that there was no reasonable probability that the verdict would have been different if the bedsheet had been excluded. Justice Powell, concurring, addressed an issue not argued by the parties or considered by the Court of Appeals. He argued that the "prejudice" prong of the *Strickland* test would not be satisfied if the only effect of counsel's negligence was to lead to the admission of illegally seized but reliable evidence.

The evidence in *Stone v. Powell* was in fact admissible under the subsequent holding in Michigan v. DeFillippo, 443 U.S. 31 (1979). There the defendant was convicted in state court of drug possession on the basis of evidence found in a search incident to an arrest under a loitering ordinance roughly similar to the Nevada statute involved in *Stone v. Powell*. The state Court of Appeals reversed the conviction on the ground that the arrest was invalid because the statute was unconstitutionally vague. The Supreme Court reversed and reinstated the conviction, reasoning that police officers act properly if they enforce statutes until and unless they are declared unconstitutional. An additional argument for refusing to apply the exclusionary rule in *Stone v. Powell* could be that California was not responsible for the unconstitutionality of the Nevada ordinance. Excluding evidence from a California trial is a questionable remedy for a wrong committed by the Nevada legislature. In the companion *Rice* case, the search was pursuant to a warrant and may have been lawful under the "reasonable good faith" doctrine of *United States v. Leon*, reprinted at page 311 of this book. Assuming that the Supreme Court was determined to reverse the lower federal courts and reinstate the convictions, would it have been better to do so by a ruling that the particular searches in question were lawful?

In Withrow v. Williams, 507 U.S. 680 (1993), the Supreme Court held that *Stone v. Powell's* exclusion of Fourth Amendment claims from federal habeas corpus proceedings does not extend to a petitioner's claim that his conviction rests on statements obtained in violation of the *Miranda* doctrine (see Chapter Eleven, *infra*).

UNITED STATES v. CECCOLINI

Supreme Court of the United States, 1978.
435 U.S. 268, 98 S.Ct. 1054, 55 L.Ed.2d 268.

Mr. Justice Rehnquist delivered the opinion of the Court.

In December 1974, Ronald Biro, a uniformed police officer on assignment to patrol school crossings, entered respondent's place of business, the Sleepy Hollow Flower Shop, in North Tarrytown, N.Y. He went behind the customer counter and, in the words of Ichabod Crane, one of Tarrytown's more illustrious inhabitants of days gone past, "tarried," spending his short break engaged in conversation with his friend Lois Hennessey, an employee of the shop. During the course of the conversation he noticed an envelope with money sticking out of it lying on the drawer of the cash register behind the counter. Biro picked up the envelope and, upon examining its contents, discovered that it contained not only money but policy slips. He placed the envelope back on the register and, without telling Hennessey what he had seen, asked her to whom the envelope belonged. She replied that the envelope belonged to respondent Ceccolini, and that he had instructed her to give it to someone.

The next day, Officer Biro mentioned his discovery to North Tarrytown detectives who in turn told Lance Emory, an FBI agent. [Four months later, Emory interviewed Hennessey and obtained her cooperation in the FBI investigation of gambling at Ceccolini's flower shop. In May, 1975, respondent Ceccolini was summoned before a federal grand jury, where he denied taking policy bets at the flower shop. Hennessey testified to the contrary, and this led to respondent's indictment for perjury.] Respondent was found guilty after a bench trial in the United States District Court for the Southern District of New York, but immediately after the finding of guilt the District Court granted respondent's motion to "suppress" the testimony of Hennessey because the court concluded that the testimony was a "fruit of the poisonous tree"; assuming respondent's motion for a directed verdict included a motion to set aside the verdict of guilty, the District Court granted the motion because it concluded that without Hennessey's testimony there was insufficient evidence of respondent's guilt. The Government appealed these rulings to the Court of Appeals for the Second Circuit.

That court rightly concluded that the Government was entitled to appeal both the order granting the motion to suppress and the order setting aside the verdict of guilty, since further proceedings if the Government were successful on the appeal would not be barred by the Double Jeopardy Clause. The District Court had sensibly first made its finding on the factual question of guilt or innocence, and then ruled on the motion to suppress; a reversal of these rulings would require no further proceedings in the District Court, but merely a reinstatement of the finding of guilt.

The Government, however, was not successful on the merits of its appeal; the Court of Appeals by a divided vote affirmed the District Court's suppression ruling, * * * reasoning that "the road to Miss Henness[e]y's testimony from Officer Biro's concededly unconstitutional search is both straight and uninterrupted." The Court of Appeals also concluded that there was support in the record for the District Court's finding that the ongoing investigation would not have inevitably led to the evidence in question without Biro's discovery of the two policy slips. Because of our traditional deference to the "two court rule," and the fact that the Government has not sought review of this latter ruling, we leave undisturbed this part of the Court of Appeals' decision. Because we decide that the Court of Appeals was wrong in concluding that there was insufficient attenuation between Officer Biro's search and Hennessey's testimony at the trial, we also do not reach the Government's contention that the exclusionary rule should not be applied when the evidence derived from the search is being used to prove a subsequent crime such as perjury.

II

[The majority opinion briefly reviewed two major cases which stated the rule that exclusion is not required where "the connection between the lawless conduct of the police and the discovery of the challenged evidence has become so attenuated as to dissipate the taint." *Wong Sun v. United States*, 371 U.S. 471 (1963); *Nardone v. United States*, 308 U.S. 338, 341 (1939).] Our cases subsequent to *Nardone* have laid out the fundamental tenets of the exclusionary rule, from which the elements that are relevant to the causal inquiry can be divined.

An examination of these cases leads us to reject the Government's suggestion that we adopt what would in practice amount to a *per se* rule that the testimony of a live witness should not be excluded at trial no matter how close and proximate the connection between it and a violation of the Fourth Amendment. We also reaffirm the holding of *Wong Sun*, that "verbal evidence which derives so immediately from an unlawful entry and an unauthorized arrest as the officers' action in the present case is no less the 'fruit' of official illegality than the more common tangible fruits of the unwarranted intrusion." We are of the view, however, that cases decided since *Wong Sun* significantly qualify its further observation that "the policies underlying the exclusionary rule [do not] invite any logical distinction between physical and verbal evidence." Rather, at least in a case such as this, where not only was the alleged "fruit of the poisonous tree" the testimony of a live witness, but unlike *Wong Sun* the witness was not a putative defendant, an examination of our cases persuades us that the Court of Appeals was simply wrong in concluding that if the road were uninterrupted, its length was immaterial. * * *

[The opinion discussed *Stone v. Powell* and other decisions which had established "deterrence" as the purpose of the exclusionary rule, and which used a balancing test to determine its scope.]

III

Viewing this case in the light of the principles just discussed, we hold that the Court of Appeals erred in holding that the degree of attenuation was not sufficient to dissipate the connection between the illegality and the testimony. The evidence indicates overwhelmingly that the testimony given by the witness was an act of her own free will in no way coerced or even induced by official authority as a result of Biro's discovery of the policy slips. Nor were the slips themselves used in questioning Hennessey. Substantial periods of time elapsed between the time of the illegal search and the initial contact with the witness, on the one hand, and between the latter and the testimony at trial on the other. While the particular knowledge to which Hennessey testified at trial can be logically traced back to Biro's discovery of the policy slips both the identity of Hennessey and her relationship with the respondent were well known to those investigating the case. There is, in addition, not the slightest evidence to suggest that Biro entered the shop or picked up the envelope with the intent of finding tangible evidence bearing on an illicit gambling operation, much less any suggestion that he entered the shop and searched with the intent of finding a willing and knowledgeable witness to testify against respondent. Application of the exclusionary rule in this situation could not have the slightest deterrent effect on the behavior of an officer such as Biro. The cost of permanently silencing Hennessey is too great for an evenhanded system of law enforcement to bear in order to secure such a speculative and very likely negligible deterrent effect.

Obviously no mathematical weight can be assigned to any of the factors which we have discussed, but just as obviously they all point to the conclusion that the exclusionary rule should be invoked with much greater reluctance where the claim is based on a causal relationship between a constitutional violation and the discovery of a live witness than when a similar claim is advanced to support suppression of an inanimate object. The judgment of the Court of Appeals is accordingly reversed.

Mr. Chief Justice Burger, concurring in the judgment.

I agree with the Court's ultimate conclusion that there is a fundamental difference, for purposes of the exclusionary rule, between live-witness testimony and other types of evidence. I perceive this distinction to be so fundamental, however, that I would not prevent a factfinder from hearing and considering the relevant statements of any witness, except perhaps under the most remarkable of circumstances—although none such have ever been postulated that would lead me to exclude the testimony of a live witness. * * *

Mr. Justice Marshall, with whom Mr. Justice Brennan joins, dissenting.

* * *

Both the independent-source and inevitable-discovery rules can apply to physical evidence as well as to verbal evidence. The police may show, for example, that they learned from an independent source, or would inevitably have discovered through legal means, the location of an object that they also knew about as a result of illegal police activity. It may be that verbal evidence is more likely to have an independent source, because live witnesses can indeed come forward of their own volition, but this simply underscores the degree to which the Court's approach involves a form of judicial "double counting." The Court would apparently first determine whether the evidence stemmed from an independent source or would inevitably have been discovered; if neither of these rules was found to apply, as here, the Court would still somehow take into account the fact that, as a general proposition (but not in the particular case), witnesses sometimes do come forward of their own volition. * * *

I would affirm the judgment of the Court of Appeals.

RAKAS v. ILLINOIS

Supreme Court of the United States, 1978.
439 U.S. 128, 99 S.Ct. 421, 58 L.Ed.2d 387.

MR. JUSTICE REHNQUIST delivered the opinion of the Court.

Petitioners were convicted of armed robbery in the Circuit Court of Kankakee County, Ill., and their convictions were affirmed on appeal. * * *

I

Because we are not here concerned with the issue of probable cause, a brief description of the events leading to the search of the automobile will suffice. A police officer on a routine patrol received a radio call notifying him of a robbery of a clothing store in Bourbonnais, Ill., and describing the getaway car. Shortly thereafter, the officer spotted an automobile which he thought might be the getaway car. After following the car for some time and after the arrival of assistance, he and several other officers stopped the vehicle. The occupants of the automobile, petitioners and two female companions, were ordered out of the car and, after the occupants had left the car, two officers searched the interior of the vehicle. They discovered a box of rifle shells in the glove compartment, which had been locked, and a sawed-off rifle under the front passenger seat. After discovering the rifle and the shells, the officers took petitioners to the station and placed them under arrest.

Before trial petitioners moved to suppress the rifle and shells seized from the car on the ground that the search violated the Fourth and Fourteenth Amendments. They conceded that they did not own the automobile and were simply passengers; the owner of the car had been the driver of the vehicle at the time of the search. Nor did they assert that they owned the rifle or the shells seized. The prosecutor challenged petitioners' standing to object to the lawfulness of the search of the car because neither the car, the shells nor the rifle belonged to them. The trial court agreed that petitioners lacked standing and denied the motion to suppress the evidence.

[The state appellate courts affirmed this ruling.]

II

Petitioners first urge us to relax or broaden the rule of standing enunciated in *Jones v. United States*, [reprinted at p. 38 of this casebook] so that any criminal defendant at whom a search was "directed" would have standing to contest the legality of that search and object to the admission at trial of evidence obtained as a result of the search. Alternatively, petitioners argue that they have standing to object to the search under *Jones* because they were "legitimately on [the] premises" at the time of the search. * * *

A

We decline to extend the rule of standing in Fourth Amendment cases in the manner suggested by petitioners. As we stated in *Alderman v. United States*, 394 U.S. 165, 174 (1969), "Fourth Amendment rights are personal rights which, like some other constitutional rights, may not be vicariously asserted." * * * And since the exclusionary rule is an attempt to effectuate the guarantees of the Fourth Amendment, it is proper to permit only defendants whose Fourth Amendment rights have been violated to benefit from the rule's protections. * * *

In *Alderman v. United States*, Mr. Justice Fortas, in a concurring and dissenting opinion, argued that the Court should "include within the category of those who may object to the introduction of illegal evidence 'one against whom the search was directed.' " The Court did not directly comment on Mr. Justice Fortas' suggestion, but it left no doubt that it rejected this theory by holding that persons who were not parties to unlawfully overheard conversations or who did not own the premises on which such conversations took place did not have standing to contest the legality of the surveillance, regardless of whether or not they were the "targets" of the surveillance. Mr. Justice Harlan, concurring and dissenting, did squarely address Mr. Justice Fortas' arguments and declined to accept them. *Id.*, at 188–189, n. 1. He identified administrative problems posed by the target theory:

> "[T]he [target] rule would entail very substantial administrative difficulties. In the majority of cases, I would imagine that the police plant a bug with the expectation that it may well produce leads to a large number of crimes. A lengthy hearing would, then, appear to be necessary in order to determine whether the police knew of an accused's criminal activity at the time the bug was planted and whether the police decision to plant a bug was motivated by an effort to obtain information against the accused or some other individual. I do not believe that this administrative burden is justified in any substantial degree by the hypothesized marginal increase in Fourth Amendment protection." *Ibid.*

When we are urged to grant standing to a criminal defendant to assert a violation, not of his own constitutional rights but of someone else's, we cannot but give weight to practical difficulties such as those foreseen by Mr. Justice Harlan in the quoted language.

Conferring standing to raise vicarious Fourth Amendment claims would necessarily mean a more widespread invocation of the exclusionary rule during criminal trials. The Court's opinion in *Alderman* counseled against such an extension of the exclusionary rule:

> "The deterrent values of preventing the incrimination of those whose rights the police have violated have been considered sufficient to justify the suppression of probative evidence even though the case against the defendant is weakened or destroyed. We adhere to that judgment. But we are not convinced that the additional benefits of extending the exclusionary rule to other defendants would justify

further encroachment upon the public interest in prosecuting those accused of crime and having them acquitted or convicted on the basis of all the evidence which exposes the truth." *Id.*, at 174–175.

Each time the exclusionary rule is applied it exacts a substantial social cost for the vindication of Fourth Amendment rights. Relevant and reliable evidence is kept from the trier of fact and the search for truth at trial is deflected. Since our cases generally have held that one whose Fourth Amendment rights are violated may successfully suppress evidence obtained in the course of an illegal search and seizure, misgivings as to the benefit of enlarging the class of persons who may invoke that rule are properly considered when deciding whether to expand standing to assert Fourth Amendment violations.

B

Had we accepted petitioners' request to allow persons other than those whose own Fourth Amendment rights were violated by a challenged search and seizure to suppress evidence obtained in the course of such police activity, it would be appropriate to retain *Jones'* use of standing in Fourth Amendment analysis. Under petitioners' target theory, a court could determine that a defendant had standing to invoke the exclusionary rule without having to inquire into the substantive question of whether the challenged search or seizure violated the Fourth Amendment rights of that particular defendant. However, having rejected petitioners' target theory and reaffirmed the principle that the "rights assured by the Fourth Amendment are personal rights, [which] * * * may be enforced by exclusion of evidence only at the instance of one whose own protection was infringed by the search and seizure," *Simmons v. United States*, 390 U.S., at 389, the question necessarily arises whether it serves any useful analytical purpose to consider this principle a matter of standing, distinct from the merits of a defendant's Fourth Amendment claim. We can think of no decided cases of this Court that would have come out differently had we concluded, as we do now, that the type of standing requirement discussed in *Jones* and reaffirmed today is more properly subsumed under substantive Fourth Amendment doctrine. Rigorous application of the principle that the rights secured by this Amendment are personal, in place of a notion of "standing," will produce no additional situations in which evidence must be excluded. The inquiry under either approach is the same. But we think the better analysis forthrightly focuses on the extent of a particular defendant's rights under the Fourth Amendment, rather than on any theoretically separate, but invariably intertwined concept of standing. * * *

C

Here petitioners, who were passengers occupying a car which they neither owned nor leased, seek to analogize their position to that of the defendant in *Jones v. United States*. In *Jones*, petitioner was present at the time of the search of an apartment which was owned by a friend. The friend had given Jones permission to use the apartment and a key to it, with which Jones had admitted himself on the day of the search. He had a suit and shirt at the apartment and had slept there "maybe a night," but his home was elsewhere. At the time of the search, Jones was the only occupant of the apartment because the lessee was away for a period of several days. * * *

We do not question the conclusion in *Jones* that the defendant in that case suffered a violation of his personal Fourth Amendment rights if the search in question was unlawful. Nonetheless, we believe that the phrase "legitimately on premises" coined in *Jones* creates too broad a gauge for measurement of Fourth Amendment rights. For example, applied literally, this statement would permit a casual visitor who has never seen, or been permitted to visit, the basement of another's house to object to a search of the basement if the visitor happened to be in the kitchen of the house at the time of the search. Likewise, a casual visitor who walks into a house one minute before a search of the house commences and leaves one minute after the search ends would be able to contest the legality of the search. The first visitor would have absolutely no interest or legitimate expectation of privacy in the basement, the second would have none in the house, and it advances no purpose served by the Fourth Amendment to permit either of them to object to the lawfulness of the search.

We think that *Jones* on its facts merely stands for the unremarkable proposition that a person can have a legally sufficient interest in a place other than his own home so that the Fourth Amendment protects him from unreasonable governmental intrusion into that place. * * * Viewed in this manner, the holding in *Jones* can best be explained by the fact that Jones had a legitimate expectation of privacy in the premises he was using and therefore could claim the protection of the Fourth Amendment with respect to a governmental invasion of those premises, even though his "interest" in those premises might not have been a recognized property interest at common law. * * *

D

Judged by the foregoing analysis, petitioners' claims must fail. They asserted neither a property nor a possessory interest in the automobile, nor an interest in the property seized. And as we have previously indicated, the fact that they were "legitimately on [the] premises" in the sense that they were in the car with the permission of its owner is not determinative of whether they had a legitimate expectation of privacy in the particular areas of the automobile searched. It is unnecessary for us to decide here whether the same expectations of privacy are warranted in a car as would be justified in a dwelling place in analogous circumstances. We have on numerous occasions pointed out that cars are not to be treated identically with houses or Apartments for Fourth Amendment purposes. But here petitioners' claim is one which would fail even in an analogous situation in a dwelling place, since they made no showing that they had any legitimate expectation of privacy in the glove compartment or area under the seat of the car in which they were merely passengers. Like the trunk of an automobile, these are areas in which a passenger *qua* passenger simply would not normally have a legitimate expectation of privacy. * * *4

Affirmed.

Mr. Justice Powell, with whom The Chief Justice joins, concurring.

I concur in the opinion of the Court, and add these thoughts. I do not believe my dissenting Brethren correctly characterize the rationale of the Court's opinion when they assert that it ties "the application of the Fourth Amendment * * * to property law concepts." On the contrary, I read the Court's opinion as focusing on whether there was a *legitimate* expectation of privacy protected by the Fourth Amendment.

The petitioners do not challenge the constitutionality of the police action in stopping the automobile in which they were riding; nor do they complain of being made to get out of the vehicle. Rather, petitioners assert that their constitutionally protected interest in privacy was violated when the police, after stopping the automobile and making them get out, searched the vehicle's interior, where they discovered a sawed-off rifle under the front seat and rifle shells in the locked glove compartment. The question before the Court, therefore, is a narrow one: Did the search of their friend's automobile after they had left it violate any Fourth Amendment right of the petitioners?

The ultimate question, therefore, is whether one's claim to privacy from government intrusion is reasonable in light of all the surrounding circumstances. As the dissenting opinion states, this standard "will not provide law enforcement officials with a bright line between the protected and the unprotected." Whatever the application of this standard may lack in ready administration, it is more faithful to the purposes of the Fourth Amendment than a test focusing solely or primarily on whether the defendant was legitimately present during the search.

We are concerned here with an automobile search. Nothing is better established in Fourth Amendment jurisprudence than the distinction between one's expectation of privacy in an automobile and one's expectation when in other locations. * * * Here there were three passengers and a driver in the automobile searched. None of the passengers is said to have had control of the vehicle or the keys. It is unrealistic—as the

4. For reasons which they do not explain, our dissenting Brethren repeatedly criticize our "holding" that unless one has a common-law property interest in the premises searched, one cannot object to the search. We have rendered no such "holding," however. To the contrary, we have taken pains to reaffirm the statements in *Jones* and *Katz* that "arcane distinctions developed in property * * * law * * * ought not to control." In a similar vein, the dissenters repeatedly state or imply that we now "hold" that a passenger lawfully in an automobile "may not invoke the exclusionary rule and challenge a search of that vehicle unless he happens to own or have a possessory interest in it." It is not without significance that these statements of today's "holding" come from the dissenting opinion, and not from the Court's opinion. The case before us involves the search of and seizure of property from the glove compartment and area under the seat of a car in which petitioners were riding as passengers. Petitioners claimed only that they were "legitimately on [the] premises" and did not claim that they had any legitimate expectation of privacy in the areas of the car which were searched. We cannot, therefore, agree with the dissenters' insistence that our decision will encourage the police to violate the Fourth Amendment.

shared experience of us all bears witness—to suggest that these passengers had any reasonable expectation that the car in which they had been riding would not be searched after they were lawfully stopped and made to get out. The minimal privacy that existed simply is not comparable to that, for example, of an individual in his place of abode, of one who secludes himself in a telephone booth, or of the traveler who secures his belongings in a locked suitcase or footlocker.

MR. JUSTICE WHITE, with whom MR. JUSTICE BRENNAN, MR. JUSTICE MARSHALL, and MR. JUSTICE STEVENS join, dissenting.

* * *

The Court's holding is contrary not only to our past decisions and the logic of the Fourth Amendment but also to the everyday expectations of privacy that we all share. Because of that, it is unworkable in all the various situations that arise in real life. If the owner of the car had not only invited petitioners to join her but had said to them, "I give you a temporary possessory interest in my vehicle so that you will share the right to privacy that the Supreme Court says that I own," then apparently the majority would reverse. But people seldom say such things, though they may mean their invitation to encompass them if only they had thought of the problem. If the nonowner were the spouse or child of the owner, would the Court recognize a sufficient interest? If so, would distant relatives somehow have more of an expectation of privacy than close friends? What if the nonowner were driving with the owner's permission? Would nonowning drivers have more of an expectation of privacy than mere passengers? What about a passenger in a taxicab? *Katz* expressly recognized protection for such passengers. Why should Fourth Amendment rights be present when one pays a cabdriver for a ride but be absent when one is given a ride by a friend?*

The distinctions the Court would draw are based on relationships between private parties, but the Fourth Amendment is concerned with the relationship of one of those parties to the government. Divorced as it is from the purpose of the Fourth Amendment, the Court's essentially property-based rationale can satisfactorily answer none of the questions posed above. That is reason enough to reject it. The *Jones* rule is relatively easily applied by police and courts; the rule announced today will not provide law enforcement officials with a bright line between the protected and the unprotected. Only rarely will police know whether one private party has or has not been granted a sufficient possessory or other interest by another private party. Surely in this case the officers had no such knowledge. The Court's rule will ensnare defendants and police in

---

* The taxicab passenger question divided the Texas Court of Criminal Appeals in Chapa v. State, 729 S.W.2d 723 (Tex.1987). The majority held that a taxicab passenger has a legitimate expectation of privacy in the passenger compartment, including the area under the front seat where police found narcotics. Presiding Judge Onion, who described the majority opinion as "hogwash," insisted in his dissent that defendant made no specific claim to a privacy interest in the area under the seat, whatever may have been his interest in the passenger compartment generally.—ed.

needless litigation over factors that should not be determinative of Fourth Amendment rights.

More importantly, the ruling today undercuts the force of the exclusionary rule in the one area in which its use is most certainly justified—the deterrence of bad-faith violations of the Fourth Amendment. This decision invites police to engage in patently unreasonable searches every time an automobile contains more than one occupant.
* * *

Of course, most police officers will decline the Court's invitation and will continue to do their jobs as best they can in accord with the Fourth Amendment. But the very purpose of the Bill of Rights was to answer the justified fear that governmental agents cannot be left totally to their own devices, and the Bill of Rights is enforceable in the courts because human experience teaches that not all such officials will otherwise adhere to the stated precepts. Some policemen simply do act in bad faith, even if for understandable ends, and some deterrent is needed. In the rush to limit the applicability of the exclusionary rule somewhere, anywhere, the Court ignores precedent, logic, and common sense to exclude the rule's operation from situations in which, paradoxically, it is justified and needed.

Commentary

Most commentators have been critical of the Supreme Court's standing doctrine, particularly in the expanded form it has assumed following the *Rakas* decision.[5] The possibility that the standing limitation may blunt the effectiveness of the exclusionary rule as a deterrent or disincentive for unlawful police activity is only one objection. The doctrine also adds an additional layer of complexity to Fourth Amendment decisionmaking. When evidence from a single search is admitted against some participants in a common criminal enterprise and excluded against others, the results are apt to appear capricious and to bring the exclusionary rule into further disrepute. In the years preceding the Supreme Court's decision in *Mapp v. Ohio*, a major argument against adopting the exclusionary rule was that, as applied in the federal courts, it had been "capricious in its operation," largely because of the standing limitation. See the opinion in *People v. Cahan, supra* page 35.

There has never been much support on the United States Supreme Court for abolishing the standing limitation altogether, but decisions like *Jones v. United States*, reprinted *supra* at page 38, took such a generous view of the interests that can confer standing that the doctrine was relatively unimportant. In particular, the "automatic standing" rule of *Jones* permitted anyone charged with possessing seized property to object to the

5. This commentary disregards Justice Rehnquist's suggestion in *Rakas* that the standing requirement "is more properly subsumed under substantive Fourth Amendment doctrine." While it is possible to dispense with the term "standing" and proceed directly to the question of whether there was a violation of "a particular defen- dant's rights under the Fourth Amendment," proceeding in this way obscures the fact that two distinct questions are involved. One issue is whether the police conduct was lawful; the other issue is whether the conduct invaded a recognized interest of the defendant.

legality of its search or seizure. *Jones* also rejected the practice of drawing "subtle distinctions" among categories of possessors or occupiers of property. The result was that the standing limitation was only a minor impediment to the enforcement of the Fourth Amendment.

In recent years, the situation has become quite different. The Supreme Court abolished the automatic standing rule in United States v. Salvucci, 448 U.S. 83 (1980). The majority opinion by Justice Rehnquist reasoned that the principal basis for the rule was that the defendant should not have to give evidence that would incriminate him on the merits in order to establish standing to object to the search. Subsequent to *Jones*, however, the Supreme Court had held that testimony given by a defendant to establish his standing may not be used against him at trial on the issue of guilt. See Simmons v. United States, 390 U.S. 377 (1968). Since the defendant's dilemma no longer existed, the automatic standing doctrine was no longer necessary. The dissenting opinion pointed out that the defendant's testimony on the search issue can still be used for impeachment if he later takes the stand and testifies to the contrary. To that extent, the dilemma continues to exist.

The opinion in *Jones* had also said that it was contradictory for the prosecution to charge the defendant with possession of seized property, but then also to claim that he lacked a sufficient possessory interest to object to its seizure. The *Salvucci* opinion explained that there is no necessary contradiction, because a defendant may be in criminal possession of seized property without having a legitimate expectation of privacy in the area in which it was discovered.

This point was important to the controversial decision in Rawlings v. Kentucky, 448 U.S. 98 (1980). Rawlings and a Ms. Cox were visitors at the home of one Marquess. Shortly before police officers arrived with a warrant to arrest Marquess, Rawlings dumped a large quantity of drugs which he had been carrying into the purse of Cox. The police later ordered Cox to empty her purse onto a table, after which Rawlings claimed ownership of the drugs. The majority opinion by Justice Rehnquist held that the fact that Rawlings owned the drugs did not give him a legitimate expectation of privacy in his companion's purse.[6] The opinion noted that Rawlings had known Cox only for a few days, that he had never sought or received access to her purse previously, that he had no right to exclude other persons from her purse, and that he had admitted that he had no subjective expectation that the purse would remain free from police intrusion. The search of the purse, therefore, was not a violation of his own Fourth Amendment rights.[7]

6. Presumably Rawlings had standing to object to the seizure of the drugs. Once contraband is discovered, however, its seizure is ordinarily lawful.

7. Compare with *Rawlings* the decision in United States v. McKennon, 814 F.2d 1539 (11th Cir.1987). McKennon gave his traveling companion (Lee) cocaine to carry in her carry-on luggage. He told Lee that he would pretend not to know her and would walk away if she were detained or searched. A suspicious drug agent at the airport detained Lee, and searched the bag unlawfully. The Court of Appeals held that McKennon had no standing to object to the search, because his efforts to disassociate himself from Lee were inconsistent with asserting a personal privacy interest in her bag. The irony of this holding is that McKennon had Lee carry the drugs so that she would be the one to take the blame if anything went wrong. As a result of the standing doctrine, she turned out to be the only one with a defense.

Leading commentators have been scathingly critical of the *Rawlings* decision. Professor LaFave attributes the decision to "certain undercurrents in the case" rather than to the reasoning in the opinion. Although Rawlings testified that Cox agreed to take the drugs, and none of the lower courts specifically found to the contrary, the trial court seemed to think that Rawlings had thrust the drugs upon Cox over her objection, after he saw the police approaching. On that assumption, it would be more reasonable to deny him a legitimate expectation of privacy in the purse. See LaFave, Search and Seizure § 11.3 (1986 Supp.). The suggestion in the opinion that Rawlings' belief that the police *would* search the purse is relevant to his standing is particularly troublesome. Surely the police cannot deprive someone of a reasonable expectation of privacy by making clear that they are going to search.

United States v. Payner, 447 U.S. 727 (1980), has also been the target of vigorous criticism. In that case Internal Revenue Service investigators stole the briefcase of an officer of a Bahamian bank to photograph documents. The Government then used the documents to convict depositors such as Payner of tax fraud. Because this type of prosecution was precisely what the agents had in mind when they egregiously violated the bank official's Fourth Amendment rights, the case dramatically illustrates how the standing limitation can encourage unconstitutional police activity. The federal district court conceded that Payner lacked standing to complain of the search under the applicable precedents, but invoked its "supervisory power" to exclude the evidence anyway. The Supreme Court reversed, holding that an extension of the supervisory power concept could not be used to avoid the standing limitation. The holding is particularly controversial because the government conduct was so flagrantly lawless, and so plainly encouraged by the ability to use the evidence against third parties.

So much for criticism of the current standing doctrine. It is also necessary to consider how the doctrine is to be applied. The majority opinion in *Rakas* emphasized that petitioners "asserted neither a property nor a possessory interest in the automobile, nor an interest in the property seized." After *Rawlings*, would it make a difference if they claimed ownership of the rifle and shells? Does footnote 17 of the majority opinion help to answer the questions asked in Justice White's dissenting opinion?

The concurring opinion of Justice Powell suggests that the result would be different if petitioners had established that the stop (as opposed to the search of the car) was unlawful. In the circumstances, the stop was probably lawful as based on reasonable suspicion. The point is of general significance, however, because a casual visitor or passenger may have standing to object to some parts of the police activity but not to others. For example, Professor LaFave has suggested that a guest at a dinner party would have standing to object to an unlawful police entry that disturbed his peace and privacy, even though he might lack a reasonable expectation of privacy in the areas of the house subsequently searched for evidence. LaFave, Search and Seizure § 11.3(b) (1986 Supp.). If the further search is the product of the unlawful entry, just as the search of an automobile might be the product of an unlawful stop, then the dinner guest might have standing to contest the admissibility of evidence found in, say, the basement. LaFave concedes, however, that several lower court decisions have ignored the distinction and held that casual visitors in a residence lack standing to object to an unconstitutional entry as well as to an unconstitutional search of the premises.

It is extremely difficult to determine the precise extent of the standing doctrine because the doctrine is not anchored in any coherent policy. As has frequently been noted, the doctrine conflicts with the "deterrent" theory of the exclusionary rule, a theory repeatedly endorsed by the Supreme Court majority. The doctrine has been maintained and extended solely because to abolish or limit it "would necessarily mean a more widespread invocation of the exclusionary rule during criminal trials." If the purpose of the doctrine is to limit the occasions on which evidence is excluded, then the doctrine will more effectively achieve its purpose if more and more defendants are denied standing to complain of Fourth Amendment violations. On that basis the category of possessors and occupiers denied standing should expand continually, with the result that exclusion of evidence in the remaining cases will seem increasingly pointless. Eventually, the Supreme Court majority may conclude that there is no point in maintaining an exclusionary rule whose deterrent effect has been riddled by so many arbitrary exceptions.

Supplemental Note

Coconspirator standing. In United States v. Padilla, 508 U.S. 77 (1993), the Supreme Court held that there is no such thing as "coconspirator standing." Officers unlawfully stopped and searched a vehicle driven by Arcinega, finding 560 pounds of cocaine in the trunk. Arcinega agreed to make a controlled delivery, which led to the arrest of the owners of the vehicle and several other persons involved in the drug smuggling conspiracy. The Court of Appeals for the Ninth Circuit held that all the defendants had standing to contest the legality of the search because they were involved in "a joint venture for transportation * * * that had control of the contraband." It thus did not distinguish between the automobile's owners and other persons involved in the transportation of the cocaine.

The Supreme Court observed in a Per Curiam opinion that only the Ninth Circuit recognized coconspirator standing under the Rakas doctrine. Standing turns upon "expectations of privacy and property interests" rather than participation in a criminal conspiracy. The Court remanded the case for the Court of Appeals to consider "whether each respondent had either a property interest protected by the Fourth Amendment that was interfered with by the stop of the automobile driven by Arcinega, or a reasonable expectation of privacy that was invaded by the search thereof."

Standing to challenge the stop as opposed to the search. In a factual situation such as that involved in *Rakas*, where several persons are in an automobile which is stopped and searched, the occupants frequently have standing to complain of an illegal stop, even though they do not have a reasonable expectation of privacy in the part of the automobile in which the evidence was found. In United States v. Roberson, 6 F.3d 1088, 1091 (5th Cir.1993), contraband was found in the spare tire of a vehicle after a dubious traffic stop that was a pretext for a drug investigation. The Court of Appeals explained that "Typically, a passenger without a possessory interest in an automobile lacks standing to complain of its search because his privacy expectation is not infringed. Whereas the search of an automobile does not implicate a passenger's fourth amendment rights, a stop results in the seizure of the passenger and driver alike. Thus, a passenger of a stopped automobile does have standing to challenge the seizure as unconstitutional."

In Mayes v. United States, 653 A.2d 856 (D.C.App.1995), officers approached a double-parked vehicle because they had a vague suspicion that it might have been involved in gang activity. They ordered one passenger (Mayes) to come out, frisked him, and found a pistol. Then they frisked the other passengers, finding another gun on the person of Graves. The District of Columbia Court of Appeals held that the frisk of Mayes was unlawful-but Graves had no standing to complain of it. After the pistol was found on Mayes, a frisk of the other passengers was reasonable. Was Graves illegally detained? The Court explained that "We assume, without deciding, that the actions of the police in ordering Mayes out of the car and frisking him would have conveyed to a reasonable person in Graves' position the message that he was not free to leave the vehicle; upon that assumption, Graves was seized. * * * The detention of Graves became legitimate at the latest, however, when Sergeant Ferguson frisked Mayes and discovered a pistol on his person; that discovery legitimated a seizure of the others in the car. Graves has not argued, either to the trial court or on appeal, that aside from the seizure of Mayes, he (Graves) was unlawfully detained for the brief period-apparently a matter of seconds-between the arrival of the police and the discovery of Mayes' weapon. The government thus has not had the occasion to respond to such a contention in either court, and we therefore decline to address the issue." The Court therefore affirmed the conviction of Graves for unlawful weapons possession, but reversed the conviction of Mayes on the same charge.

The Supreme Court discussed the standing of social and business visitors in Minnesota v. Carter, 525 U.S. 83 (1998). An officer investigating a tip went to a grassy area outside a ground floor apartment window, looked inside through a gap in a closed venetian blind, and saw Carter, Johns, and Thompson inside bagging cocaine. The Supreme Court assumed, without deciding, that this observation constituted a search. Thompson was the lessor of the building and she, presumably having standing to complain of a search of her premises, was not involved in the prosecution. Carter and Johns had never been to the apartment before, and occupied it on this occasion for approximately 2/12 hours for the sole purpose of bagging cocaine, giving Thompson a small amount of the drug for its use. The majority opinion by Chief Justice Rehnquist recognized that in Minnesota v. Olson, 495 U.S. 91 (1990), the Court had held that an overnight guest has a legitimate interest in the privacy of the home, so that an unlawful search violates his or her rights, whereas a person merely legitimately on the premises (such as a short-term business visitor) does not. "[T]he purely commercial nature of the transaction engaged in here, the relatively short period of time on the premises, and the lack of any previous connection between respondents and the householder, all lead us to conclude that respondents' situation is closer to that of one simply permitted on the premises. We therefore hold that any search which may have occurred did not violate their Fourth Amendment rights." Justice Breyer concurred in the judgment on the ground that the officer's observation was made from a public area outside the curtilage and hence did not violate anyone's Fourth

Amendment rights. Justices Ginsburg, Stevens, and Souter dissented. Their opinion argued that "when a homeowner or lessor personally invites a guest into her home to share in a common endeavor, whether it be for conversation, to engage in leisure activities, or for business purposes licit or illicit, that guest should share his host's shelter against unreasonable searches and seizures."

UNITED STATES v. HAVENS

Supreme Court of the United States, 1980.
446 U.S. 620, 100 S.Ct. 1912, 64 L.Ed.2d 559.

Mr. Justice White delivered the opinion of the Court. * * *

I

Respondent was convicted of importing, conspiring to import, and intentionally possessing a controlled substance, cocaine. According to the evidence at his trial, Havens and John McLeroth, both attorneys from Ft. Wayne, Ind., boarded a flight from Lima, Peru, to Miami, Fla. In Miami, a customs officer searched McLeroth and found cocaine sewed into makeshift pockets in a T-shirt he was wearing under his outer clothing. McLeroth implicated respondent, who had previously cleared customs and who was then arrested. His luggage was seized and searched without a warrant. The officers found no drugs but seized a T-shirt from which pieces had been cut that matched the pieces that had been sewn to McLeroth's T-shirt. The T-shirt and other evidence seized in the course of the search were suppressed on motion prior to trial.

Both men were charged in a three-count indictment, but McLeroth pleaded guilty to one count and testified against Havens. Among other things, he asserted that Havens had supplied him with the altered T-shirt and had sewed the makeshift pockets shut. Havens took the stand in his own defense and denied involvement in smuggling cocaine. His direct testimony included the following:

"Q. And you heard Mr. McLeroth testify earlier as to something to the effect that this material was taped or draped around his body and so on, you heard that testimony?

"A. Yes, I did.

"Q. Did you ever engage in that kind of activity with Mr. McLeroth and Augusto or Mr. McLeroth and anyone else on that fourth visit to Lima, Peru?

"A. I did not."

On cross-examination, Havens testified as follows:

"Q. Now, on direct examination, sir, you testified that on the fourth trip you had absolutely nothing to do with the wrapping of any bandages or tee shirts or anything involving Mr. McLeroth; is that correct?

"A. I don't—I said I had nothing to do with any wrapping or bandages or anything, yes. I had nothing to do with anything with McLeroth in connection with this cocaine matter.

* * *

"Q. And your testimony is that you had nothing to do with the sewing of the cotton swatches to make pockets on that tee shirt?

"A. Absolutely not.

"Q. Sir, when you came through Customs, the Miami International Airport, on October 2, 1977, did you have in your suitcase Size 38–40 medium tee shirts?"

An objection to the latter question was overruled and questioning continued:

"Q. On that day, sir, did you have in your luggage a Size 38–40 medium man's tee shirt with swatches of clothing missing from the tail of that tee shirt?

"A. Not to my knowledge.

* * *

"Q. Mr. Havens, I'm going to hand you what is Government's Exhibit 9 for identification and ask you if this tee shirt was in your luggage on October 2nd, 1975 [*sic*]?

"A. Not to my knowledge. No."

Respondent Havens also denied having told a Government agent that the T-shirts found in his luggage belonged to McLeroth.

On rebuttal, a Government agent testified that Exhibit 9 had been found in respondent's suitcase and that Havens claimed the T-shirts found in his bag, including Exhibit 9, belonged to McLeroth. Over objection, the T-shirt was then admitted into evidence, the jury being instructed that the rebuttal evidence should be considered only for impeaching Havens' credibility.

The Court of Appeals reversed, relying on *Agnello v. United States*, 269 U.S. 20 (1925), and *Walder v. United States*, 347 U.S. 62 (1954). The court held that illegally seized evidence may be used for impeachment only if the evidence contradicts a particular statement made by a defendant in the course of his direct examination. We reverse.

II

In *Agnello v. United States, supra,* a defendant charged with conspiracy to sell a package of cocaine testified on direct examination that he had possessed the packages involved but did not know what was in them. On cross-examination, he denied ever having seen narcotics and ever having seen a can of cocaine which was exhibited to him and which had been illegally seized from his apartment. The can of cocaine was permitted into evidence on rebuttal. Agnello was convicted and his conviction was affirmed by the Court of Appeals. This Court reversed, holding that the Fourth Amendment required exclusion of the evidence. The Court pointed out that "[i]n his direct examination, Agnello was not asked and did not testify concerning the can of cocaine" and "did nothing to waive his constitutional protection or to justify cross-examination in respect of the evidence claimed to have been obtained by the search." The Court also said, quoting from *Silverthorne Lumber Co. v. United States* [p. 26 of this book] that the exclusionary rule not only commands that illegally seized evidence "shall not be used before the Court but that it shall not be used at all."

The latter statement has been rejected in our later cases, however, and *Agnello* otherwise limited. In *Walder v. United States, supra*, the use of evidence obtained in an illegal search and inadmissible in the Government's case in chief was admitted to impeach the direct testimony of the defendant. This Court approved, saying that it would pervert the rule of *Weeks v. United States*, to hold otherwise. Similarly, in *Harris v. New York*, 401 U.S. 222 (1971), and *Oregon v. Hass*, 420 U.S. 714 (1975), statements taken in violation of [the Miranda rule], and unusable by the prosecution as part of its own case, were held admissible to impeach statements made by the defendant in the course of his direct testimony. *Harris* also made clear that the permitted impeachment by otherwise inadmissible evidence is not limited to collateral matters.

These cases were understood by the Court of Appeals to hold that tainted evidence, inadmissible when offered as part of the Government's main case, may not be used as rebuttal evidence to impeach a defendant's credibility unless the evidence is offered to contradict a particular statement made by a defendant during his direct examination; a statement made for the first time on cross-examination may not be so impeached. This approach required the exclusion of the T-shirt taken from Havens' luggage because, as the Court of Appeals read the record, Havens was asked nothing on his direct testimony about the incriminating T-shirt or about the contents of his luggage; the testimony about the T-shirt, which the Government desired to impeach first appeared on cross-examination, not on direct.

It is true that *Agnello* involved the impeachment of testimony first brought out on cross-examination and that in *Walder, Harris*, and *Hass*, the testimony impeached was given by the defendant while testifying on direct examination. In our view, however, a flat rule permitting only statements on direct examination to be impeached misapprehends the underlying rationale of *Walder, Harris* and *Hass*. These cases repudiated the statement in *Agnello* that no use at all may be made of illegally obtained evidence. Furthermore, in *Walder*, the Court said that in *Agnello*, the Government had "smuggled in" the impeaching opportunity in the course of cross-examination. In terms of impeaching a defendant's seemingly false statements with his prior inconsistent utterances or with other reliable evidence available to the government, we see no difference of constitutional magnitude between the defendant's statements on direct examination and his answers to questions put to him on cross-examination that are plainly within the scope of the defendant's direct examination. Without this opportunity, the normal function of cross-examination would be severely impeded.

We also think that the policies of the exclusionary rule no more bar impeachment here than they did in *Walder, Harris,* and *Hass.* In those cases, the ends of the exclusionary rules were thought adequately implemented by denying the government the use of the challenged evidence to make out its case in chief. The incremental furthering of those ends by forbidding impeachment of the defendant who testifies was deemed insufficient to permit or require that false testimony go unchallenged, with the resulting impairment of the integrity of the factfinding goals of the criminal trial. We reaffirm this assessment of the competing interests, and hold that a defendant's statements made in response to proper cross-examination reasonably suggested by the defendant's direct examination are subject to otherwise proper impeachment by the government, albeit by evidence that has been illegally obtained and that is inadmissible on the government's direct case, or otherwise, as substantive evidence of guilt. * * *

MR. JUSTICE BRENNAN, joined by MR. JUSTICE MARSHALL and joined in Part I by MR. JUSTICE STEWART and MR. JUSTICE STEVENS, dissenting.

* * *

The question before us is not of first impression. The identical issue was confronted in *Agnello v. United States,* which determined—contrary to the instant decision—that it was constitutionally impermissible to admit evidence obtained in violation of the Fourth Amendment to rebut a defendant's response to a matter first raised during the Government's cross-examination. Subsequently, *Walder v. United States,* affirmed the introduction of unlawfully acquired evidence to impeach an accused's false assertions about previous conduct that had been offered during *direct* testimony. But *Walder* took pains to draw the distinction between its own holding and *Agnello,* noting that "the defendant [Walder] went beyond a mere denial of complicity in the crimes of which he was charged and made the sweeping [and untrue] claim that he had never dealt in or possessed any narcotics." * * *

In fact, the Court's current interpretation of *Agnello* and *Walder* simply trivializes those decisions by transforming their Fourth Amendment holdings into nothing more than a constitutional reflection of the common-law evidentiary rule of relevance.

Finally, the rationale of *Harris v. New York* and *Oregon v. Hass* does not impel the decision at hand. The exclusionary rule exception established by *Harris* and *Hass* may be fairly easily cabined by defense counsel's willingness to forgo certain areas of questioning. But the rule prescribed by the Court in this case passes control of the exception to the Government, since the prosecutor can lay the predicate for admitting otherwise suppressible evidence with his own questioning. To be sure, the Court requires that cross-examination be "proper"; however, traditional evidentiary principles accord parties fairly considerable latitude in cross-examining opposing witnesses. In practical terms, therefore, to-day's holding allows even the moderately talented prosecutor to "work in * * * evidence on cross-examination [as it would] in its case in chief * * *." *Walder v. United States*, 347 U.S., at 66. To avoid this consequence, a defendant will be compelled to forgo testifying on his own behalf. * * *

In James v. Illinois, 493 U.S. 307 (1990) the Supreme Court held that rule permitting prosecutors to use unlawfully obtained evidence to impeach the defendant's testimony should not be extended to permit impeachment of defense witnesses other than the defendant. Defendant James was arrested for murder, and admitted to police that he had had reddish brown, straight hair on the day of the crime but had since dyed his hair black and curled it. This statement was excluded as the fruit of an unlawful arrest. At the trial several witnesses testified for the prosecution that the killer had had reddish hair worn shoulder length in a slicked-back style, and that they had previously seen James with hair that color and style. James did not testify, but called a witness named Henderson who said that James' hair was black on the day of the killing. The prosecution was permitted to introduce the unlawfully obtained statement to impeach this testimony.

The Illinois Supreme Court affirmed, reasoning that the impeachment exception needed to be extended to prevent the defendant from committing "perjury by proxy." The Supreme Court reversed in a 5–4 opinion by Justice Brennan. The opinion observed that the threat of a perjury prosecution is a more effective deterrent to perjury by defense witnesses than the prospect of impeachment, and argued that expanding the impeachment exception would unacceptably weaken the deterrent effect of the exclusionary rule.

UNITED STATES v. LEON

Supreme Court of the United States, 1984.
468 U.S. 897, 104 S.Ct. 3405, 82 L.Ed.2d 677.

JUSTICE WHITE delivered the opinion of the Court.

This case presents the question whether the Fourth Amendment exclusionary rule should be modified so as not to bar the use in the prosecution's case-in-chief of evidence obtained by officers acting in reasonable reliance on a search warrant issued by a detached and neutral magistrate but ultimately found to be unsupported by probable cause. * * *

I

In August 1981, a confidential informant of unproven reliability informed an officer of the Burbank Police Department that two persons known to him as "Armando" and "Patsy" were selling large quantities of cocaine and methaqualone from their residence at 620 Price Drive in Burbank, Cal. The informant also indicated that he had witnessed a sale of methaqualone by "Patsy" at the residence approximately five months earlier and had observed at that time a shoebox containing a large amount of cash that belonged to "Patsy." He further declared that "Armando" and "Patsy" generally kept only small quantities of drugs at their residence and stored the remainder at another location in Burbank.

On the basis of this information, the Burbank police initiated an extensive investigation focusing first on the Price Drive residence and later on two other residences as well. Cars parked at the Price Drive residence were determined to belong to respondents Armando Sanchez, who had previously been arrested for possession of marihuana, and Patsy Stewart, who had no criminal record. During the course of the investigation, officers observed an automobile belonging to respondent Ricardo Del Castillo, who had previously been arrested for possession of 50 pounds of marihuana, arrive at the Price Drive residence. The driver of that car entered the house, exited shortly thereafter carrying a small paper sack, and drove away. A check of Del Castillo's probation records led the officers to respondent Alberto Leon, whose telephone number Del Castillo had listed as his employer's. Leon had been arrested in 1980 on drug charges, and a companion had informed the police at that time that Leon was heavily involved in the importation of drugs into this country. Before the current investigation began, the Burbank officers had learned that an informant had told a Glendale police officer that Leon stored a large quantity of methaqualone at his residence in Glendale. During the course of this investigation, the Burbank officers learned that Leon was living at 716 South Sunset Canyon in Burbank.

Subsequently, the officers observed several persons, at least one of whom had prior drug involvement, arriving at the Price Drive residence and leaving with small packages; observed a variety of other material activity at the two residences as well as at a condominium at 7902 Via Magdalena; and witnessed a variety of relevant activity involving respondents' automobiles. The officers also observed respondents Sanchez and Stewart board separate flights for Miami. The pair later returned to Los Angeles together, consented to a search of their luggage that revealed only a small amount of marihuana, and left the airport. Based on these and other observations summarized in the affidavit, Officer Cyril Rombach of the Burbank Police Department, an experienced and well-trained narcotics investigator, prepared an application for a warrant to search 620 Price Drive, 716 South Sunset Canyon, 7902 Via Magdalena, and automobiles registered to each of the respondents for an extensive list of items believed to be related to respondents' drug-trafficking activities. Officer Rombach's extensive application was reviewed by several Deputy District Attorneys.

A facially valid search warrant was issued in September 1981 by a state superior court judge. The ensuing searches produced large quantities of drugs at the Via Magdalena and Sunset Canyon addresses and a small quantity at the Price Drive residence. Other evidence was discovered at each of the residences and in Stewart's and Del Castillo's automobiles. Respondents were indicted by a grand jury in the District Court for the Central District of California and charged with conspiracy to possess and distribute cocaine and a variety of substantive counts.

The respondents then filed motions to suppress the evidence seized pursuant to the warrant. The District Court held an evidentiary hearing and, while recognizing that the case was a close one, granted the motions to suppress in part. It concluded that the affidavit was insufficient to establish probable cause, but did not suppress all of the evidence as to all of the respondents because none of the respondents had standing to challenge all of the searches.[8] In response to a request from the Government, the court made clear that Officer Rombach had acted in good faith, but it rejected the Government's suggestion that the Fourth Amendment exclusionary rule should not apply where evidence is seized in reasonable, good-faith reliance on a search warrant.

[The Court of Appeals affirmed the suppression order. Subsequently, the Supreme Court announced its decision in Illinois v. Gates (p. 200 of this book). The government, wishing to obtain a decision on the "good faith exception" issue, declined to seek review of the holding that the affidavit did not establish probable cause.]

II

A

The Fourth Amendment contains no provision expressly precluding the use of evidence obtained in violation of its commands, and an examination of its origin and purposes makes clear that the use of fruits of a past unlawful search or seizure "work[s] no new Fourth Amendment wrong." *United States v. Calandra*, 414 U.S. 338, 354 (1974). The wrong condemned by the Amendment is "fully accomplished" by the unlawful search or seizure itself, *ibid.*, and the exclusionary rule is neither intended nor able to cure the invasion of the defendant's rights which he has already suffered. The rule thus operates as a judicially created remedy designed to safeguard Fourth Amendment rights generally through its deterrent effect, rather than a personal constitutional right of the person aggrieved. * * *

The substantial social costs exacted by the exclusionary rule for the vindication of Fourth Amendment rights have long been a source of concern. * * * An objectionable collateral consequence of this interference with the criminal justice system's truth-finding function is that some guilty defendants may go free or receive reduced sentences as a result of favorable plea bargains.[9] Particularly when law enforcement

8. The District Court concluded that Sanchez and Stewart had standing to challenge the search of 620 Price Drive; that Leon had standing to contest the legality of the search of 716 South Sunset Canyon; that none of the respondents had established a legitimate expectation of privacy in the condominium at 7902 Via Magdalena; and that Stewart and Del Castillo each had standing to challenge the searches of their automobiles. * * *

9. Researchers have only recently begun to study extensively the effects of the exclusionary rule on the disposition of felony arrests. One study suggests that the rule results in the nonprosecution or nonconviction of between 0.6% and 2.35% of individuals arrested for felonies. Davies, A Hard Look at What We Know (and Still Need to

officers have acted in objective good faith or their transgressions have been minor, the magnitude of the benefit conferred on such guilty defendants offends basic concepts of the criminal justice system. Indiscriminate application of the exclusionary rule, therefore, may well generate disrespect for the law and the administration of justice. * * *

B

Close attention to those remedial objectives has characterized our recent decisions concerning the scope of the Fourth Amendment exclusionary rule. The Court has, to be sure, not seriously questioned, "in the absence of a more efficacious sanction, the continued application of the rule to suppress evidence from the [prosecution's] case where a Fourth Amendment violation has been substantial and deliberate * * *." *Franks v. Delaware*, 438 U.S. 154, 171 (1978). Nevertheless, the balancing approach that has evolved in various contexts—including criminal trials—forcefully suggests that the exclusionary rule be more generally modified to permit the introduction of evidence obtained in the reasonable good-faith belief that a search or seizure was in accord with the Fourth Amendment.

In *Stone v. Powell, supra*, the Court emphasized the costs of the exclusionary rule, expressed its view that limiting the circumstances under which Fourth Amendment claims could be raised in federal habeas corpus proceedings would not reduce the rule's deterrent effect, and held that a state prisoner who has been afforded a full and fair opportunity to litigate a Fourth Amendment claim may not obtain federal habeas relief on the ground that unlawfully obtained evidence had been introduced at his trial. * * * Proposed extensions of the exclusionary rule to proceedings other than the criminal trial itself have been evaluated and rejected under the same analytic approach. In *United States v. Calandra, supra*, for example, we declined to allow grand jury witnesses to refuse to

Learn) About the "Costs" of the Exclusionary Rule: The NIJ Study and Other Studies of "Lost" Arrests, 1983 A.B.F.Res.J. 611, 621. The estimates are higher for particular crimes the prosecution of which depends heavily on physical evidence. Thus, the cumulative loss due to nonprosecution or nonconviction of individuals arrested on felony drug charges is probably in the range of 2.8% to 7.1%. *Id.*, at 680. Davies' analysis of California data suggests that screening by police and prosecutors results in the release because of illegal searches or seizures of as many as 1.4% of all felony arrestees, *id.*, at 650, that 0.9% of felony arrestees are released because of illegal searches or seizures at the preliminary hearing or after trial, *id.*, at 653, and that roughly 0.05% of all felony arrestees benefit from reversals on appeal because of illegal searches. *Id.*, at 654. See also K. Brosi, A Cross–City Comparison of Felony Case Processing 16, 18–19 (1979); Report of the Comptroller General of the

United States, Impact of the Exclusionary Rule on Federal Criminal Prosecutions 10–11, 14 (1979); F. Feeney, F. Dill & A. Weir, Arrests Without Convictions: How Often They Occur and Why 203–206 (1983); National Institute of Justice, The Effects of the Exclusionary Rule: A Study in California 1–2 (1982); Nardulli, The Societal Cost of the Exclusionary Rule: An Empirical Assessment, 1983 A.B.F.Res.J. 585, 600. The exclusionary rule also has been found to affect the plea-bargaining process. S. Schlesinger, Exclusionary Injustice: The Problem of Illegally Obtained Evidence 63 (1977). But see Davies, *supra*, at 668–669; Nardulli, *supra*, at 604–606.

Many of these researchers have concluded that the impact of the exclusionary rule is insubstantial, but the small percentages with which they deal mask a large absolute number of felons who are released because the cases against them were based in part on illegal searches or seizures. * * *

answer questions based on evidence obtained from an unlawful search or seizure since "[a]ny incremental deterrent effect which might be achieved by extending the rule to grand jury proceedings is uncertain at best." 414 U.S., at 348. Similarly, in *United States v. Janis*, 428 U.S. 433 (1976), we permitted the use in federal civil proceedings of evidence illegally seized by state officials since the likelihood of deterring police misconduct through such an extension of the exclusionary rule was insufficient to outweigh its substantial social costs. * * *

[The opinion reviewed the importance of the "standing" limitation, especially after Rakas v. Illinois, p. 297 of this book, as restricting the scope of the exclusionary rule. The opinion then went on to point out that unlawfully seized evidence may be used for impeachment (see U.S. v. Havens, p. 318 of this book); and that the "fruit of the poisonous tree" rule is limited by the attenuation doctrine (see U.S. v. Ceccolini, p. 293).]

The same attention to the purposes underlying the exclusionary rule also has characterized decisions not involving the scope of the rule itself. We have not required suppression of the fruits of a search incident to an arrest made in good-faith reliance on a substantive criminal statute that subsequently is declared unconstitutional. *Michigan v. DeFillippo*, 443 U.S. 31 (1979). Similarly, although the Court has been unwilling to conclude that new Fourth Amendment principles are always to have only prospective effect,[10] no Fourth Amendment decision marking a "clear break with the past" has been applied retroactively. See *United States v. Peltier*, 422 U.S. 531 (1975); *Desist v. United States*, 394 U.S. 244 (1969); *Linkletter v. Walker*, 381 U.S. 618 (1965). The propriety of retroactive application of a newly announced Fourth Amendment principle, moreover, has been assessed largely in terms of the contribution retroactivity might make to the deterrence of police misconduct.

As yet, we have not recognized any form of good-faith exception to the Fourth Amendment exclusionary rule. But the balancing approach that has evolved during the years of experience with the rule provides strong support for the modification currently urged upon us. As we discuss below, our evaluation of the costs and benefits of suppressing reliable physical evidence seized by officers reasonably relying on a warrant issued by a detached and neutral magistrate leads to the conclusion that such evidence should be admissible in the prosecution's case-in-chief.

10. The Court held in *United States v. Johnson*, 457 U.S. 537 (1982), that a construction of the Fourth Amendment that did not constitute a "clear break with the past" is to be applied to all convictions not yet final when the decision was handed down. The limited holding, turned in part on the Court's judgment that "[f]ailure to accord *any* retroactive effect to Fourth Amendment rulings would 'encourage police or other courts to disregard the plain purport of our decisions and to adopt a let's-wait-until-it's-decided approach.'" Contrary to respondents' assertions, nothing in *Johnson* precludes adoption of a good-faith exception tailored to situations in which the police have reasonably relied on a warrant issued by a detached and neutral magistrate but later found to be defective.

III

A

Because a search warrant "provides the detached scrutiny of a neutral magistrate, which is a more reliable safeguard against improper searches than the hurried judgment of a law enforcement officer 'engaged in the often competitive enterprise of ferreting out crime,' '' we have expressed a strong preference for warrants and declared that "in a doubtful or marginal case a search under a warrant may be sustainable where without one it would fail." * * *

Deference to the magistrate, however, is not boundless. It is clear, first, that the deference accorded to a magistrate's finding of probable cause does not preclude inquiry into the knowing or reckless falsity of the affidavit on which that determination was based. *Franks v. Delaware*, 438 U.S. 154 (1978). Second, the courts must also insist that the magistrate purport to perform his "neutral and detached" function and not serve merely as a rubber stamp for the police. A magistrate failing to "manifest that neutrality and detachment demanded of a judicial officer when presented with a warrant application" and who acts instead as "an adjunct law enforcement officer" cannot provide valid authorization for an otherwise unconstitutional search. *Lo-Ji Sales, Inc. v. New York*, 442 U.S. 319, 326–327 (1979).

Third, reviewing courts will not defer to a warrant based on an affidavit that does not "provide the magistrate with a substantial basis for determining the existence of probable cause." * * *

Only in the first of these three situations, however, has the Court set forth a rationale for suppressing evidence obtained pursuant to a search warrant; in the other areas, it has simply excluded such evidence without considering whether Fourth Amendment interests will be advanced. To the extent that proponents of exclusion rely on its behavioral effects on judges and magistrates in these areas, their reliance is misplaced. First, the exclusionary rule is designed to deter police misconduct rather than to punish the errors of judges and magistrates. Second, there exists no evidence suggesting that judges and magistrates are inclined to ignore or subvert the Fourth Amendment or that lawlessness among these actors requires application of the extreme sanction of exclusion.

Third, and most important, we discern no basis, and are offered none, for believing that exclusion of evidence seized pursuant to a warrant will have a significant deterrent effect on the issuing judge or magistrate. Many of the factors that indicate that the exclusionary rule cannot provide an effective "special" or "general" deterrent for individual offending law enforcement officers apply as well to judges or magistrates. And, to the extent that the rule is thought to operate as a "systemic" deterrent on a wider audience, it clearly can have no such effect on individuals empowered to issue search warrants. Judges and magistrates are not adjuncts to the law enforcement team; as neutral judicial officers, they have no stake in the outcome of particular criminal prosecutions. The threat of exclusion thus cannot be expected significantly to deter them. Imposition of the exclusionary sanction is not necessary meaningfully to inform judicial officers of their errors, and we cannot conclude that admitting evidence obtained pursuant to a warrant while at the same time declaring that the warrant was somehow defective will in any way reduce judicial officers' professional incentives to comply with the Fourth Amendment, encourage them to repeat their mistakes, or lead to the granting of all colorable warrant requests.[11]

B

If exclusion of evidence obtained pursuant to a subsequently invalidated warrant is to have any deterrent effect, therefore, it must alter the behavior of individual law enforcement officers or the policies of their departments. One could argue that applying the exclusionary rule in cases where the police failed to demonstrate probable cause in the warrant application deters future inadequate presentations or "magistrate shopping" and thus promotes the ends of the Fourth Amendment. Suppressing evidence obtained pursuant to a technically defective warrant supported by probable cause also might encourage officers to scrutinize more closely the form of the warrant and to point out suspected judicial errors. We find such arguments speculative and conclude that suppression of evidence obtained pursuant to a warrant should be ordered only on a case-by-case basis and only in those unusual cases in which exclusion will further the purposes of the exclusionary rule.[12]

We have frequently questioned whether the exclusionary rule can have any deterrent effect when the offending officers acted in the objectively reasonable belief that their conduct did not violate the Fourth Amendment. * * * But even assuming that the rule effectively deters some police misconduct and provides incentives for the law enforcement profession as a whole to conduct itself in accord with the Fourth Amendment, it cannot be expected, and should not be applied, to deter objectively reasonable law enforcement activity. * * *[13]

This is particularly true, we believe, when an officer acting with objective good faith has obtained a search warrant from a judge or

---

11. Limiting the application of the exclusionary sanction may well increase the care with which magistrates scrutinize warrant applications. We doubt that magistrates are more desirous of avoiding the exclusion of evidence obtained pursuant to warrants they have issued than of avoiding invasions of privacy.

Federal magistrates, moreover, are subject to the direct supervision of district courts. They may be removed for "incompetency, misconduct, neglect of duty, or physical or mental disability." 28 U.S.C. § 631(i). If a magistrate serves merely as a "rubber stamp" for the police or is unable to exercise mature judgment, closer supervision or removal provides a more effective remedy than the exclusionary rule.

12. Our discussion of the deterrent effect of excluding evidence obtained in reasonable reliance on a subsequently invalidated warrant assumes, of course, that the officers properly executed the warrant and searched only those places and for those objects that it was reasonable to believe were covered by the warrant. * * *

13. We emphasize that the standard of reasonableness we adopt is an objective one. Many objections to a good-faith exception assume that the exception will turn on the subjective good faith of individual officers. * * * The objective standard we adopt, moreover, requires officers to have a reasonable knowledge of what the law prohibits.

magistrate and acted within its scope. In most such cases, there is no police illegality and thus nothing to deter. It is the magistrate's responsibility to determine whether the officer's allegations establish probable cause and, if so, to issue a warrant comporting in form with the requirements of the Fourth Amendment. In the ordinary case, an officer cannot be expected to question the magistrate's probable-cause determination or his judgment that the form of the warrant is technically sufficient. * * *

C

We conclude that the marginal or nonexistent benefits produced by suppressing evidence obtained in objectively reasonable reliance on a subsequently invalidated search warrant cannot justify the substantial costs of exclusion. We do not suggest, however, that exclusion is always inappropriate in cases where an officer has obtained a warrant and abided by its terms. * * * Suppression therefore remains an appropriate remedy if the magistrate or judge in issuing a warrant was misled by information in an affidavit that the affiant knew was false or would have known was false except for his reckless disregard of the truth. The exception we recognize today will also not apply in cases where the issuing magistrate wholly abandoned his judicial role in the manner condemned in *Lo-Ji Sales, Inc. v. New York*, 442 U.S. 319 (1979); in such circumstances, no reasonably well-trained officer should rely on the warrant. Nor would an officer manifest objective good faith in relying on a warrant based on an affidavit so lacking in indicia of probable cause as to render official belief in its existence entirely unreasonable. Finally, depending on the circumstances of the particular case, a warrant may be so facially deficient—*i.e.*, in failing to particularize the place to be searched or the things to be seized—that the executing officers cannot reasonably presume it to be valid.

In so limiting the suppression remedy, we leave untouched the probable-cause standard and the various requirements for a valid warrant. Other objections to the modification of the Fourth Amendment exclusionary rule we consider to be insubstantial. The good-faith exception for searches conducted pursuant to warrants is not intended to signal our unwillingness strictly to enforce the requirements of the Fourth Amendment, and we do not believe that it will have this effect. As we have already suggested, the good-faith exception, turning as it does on objective reasonableness, should not be difficult to apply in practice. When officers have acted pursuant to a warrant, the prosecution should ordinarily be able to establish objective good faith without a substantial expenditure of judicial time.

Nor are we persuaded that application of a good-faith exception to searches conducted pursuant to warrants will preclude review of the constitutionality of the search or seizure, deny needed guidance from the courts, or freeze Fourth Amendment law in its present state. There is no need for courts to adopt the inflexible practice of always deciding whether the officers' conduct manifested objective good faith before turning to the question whether the Fourth Amendment has been violated. * * *

Accordingly, the judgment of the Court of Appeals is reversed.

* * *

MASSACHUSETTS v. SHEPPARD

Supreme Court of the United States, 1984.
468 U.S. 981, 104 S.Ct. 3424, 82 L.Ed.2d 737.

JUSTICE WHITE delivered the opinion of the Court.

This case involves the application of the rules articulated today in *United States v. Leon*, to a situation in which police officers seize items pursuant to a warrant subsequently invalidated because of a technical error on the part of the issuing judge.

I

The badly burned body of Sandra Boulware was discovered in a vacant lot in the Roxbury section of Boston at approximately 5 a.m., Saturday, May 5, 1979. An autopsy revealed that Boulware had died of multiple compound skull fractures caused by blows to the head. After a brief investigation, the police decided to question one of the victim's boyfriends, Osborne Sheppard. Sheppard told the police that he had last seen the victim on Tuesday night and that he had been at a local gaming house (where card games were played) from 9 p.m. Friday until 5 a.m. Saturday. He identified several people who would be willing to substantiate the latter claim.

By interviewing the people Sheppard had said were at the gaming house on Friday night, the police learned that although Sheppard was at the gaming house that night, he had borrowed an automobile at about 3 a.m. Saturday morning in order to give two men a ride home. Even though the trip normally took only fifteen minutes, Sheppard did not return with the car until nearly 5 a.m.

On Sunday morning, police officers visited the owner of the car Sheppard had borrowed. He consented to an inspection of the vehicle. Bloodstains and pieces of hair were found on the rear bumper and within the trunk compartment. In addition, the officers noticed strands of wire in the trunk similar to wire strands found on and near the body of the victim. The owner of the car told the officers that when he last used the car on Friday night, shortly before Sheppard borrowed it, he had placed articles in the trunk and had not noticed any stains on the bumper or in the trunk.

On the basis of the evidence gathered thus far in the investigation, Detective Peter O'Malley drafted an affidavit designed to support an application for an arrest warrant and a search warrant authorizing a search of Sheppard's residence. The affidavit set forth the results of the investigation and stated that the police wished to search for "[a] fifth bottle of amaretto liquor, 2 nickel bags of marijuana, a woman's jacket that has been described as black-grey (charcoal), any possessions of Sandra D. Boulware, similar type wire and rope that match those on the body of Sandra D. Boulware, or in the above Thunderbird. A blunt instrument that might have been used on the victim, men's or women's clothing that may have blood, gasoline burns on them. Items that may have fingerprints of the victim."[14]

Detective O'Malley showed the affidavit to the district attorney, the district attorney's first assistant, and a sergeant, who all concluded that it set forth probable cause for the search and the arrest.

Because it was Sunday, the local court was closed, and the police had a difficult time finding a warrant application form. Detective O'Malley finally found a warrant form previously in use in the Dorchester District. The form was entitled "Search Warrant—Controlled Substance G.L. c. 276 §§ 1 through 3A." Realizing that some changes had to be made before the form could be used to authorize the search requested in the affidavit, Detective O'Malley deleted the subtitle "controlled substance" with a typewriter. He also substituted "Roxbury" for the printed "Dorchester" and typed Sheppard's name and address into blank spaces provided for that information. However, the reference to "controlled substance" was not deleted in the portion of the form that constituted the warrant application and that, when signed, would constitute the warrant itself.

Detective O'Malley then took the affidavit and the warrant form to the residence of a judge who had consented to consider the warrant application. The judge examined the affidavit and stated that he would authorize the search as requested. Detective O'Malley offered the warrant form and stated that he knew the form as presented dealt with controlled substances. He showed the judge where he had crossed out the subtitles. After unsuccessfully searching for a more suitable form, the judge informed O'Malley that he would make the necessary changes so as to provide a proper search warrant. The judge then took the form, made some changes on it, and dated and signed the warrant. However, he did not change the substantive portion of the warrant, which continued to authorize a search for controlled substances;[15] nor did he alter the form so as to incorporate the affidavit. The judge returned the affidavit and the warrant to O'Malley, informing him that the warrant was sufficient authority in form and content to carry out the search as requested. O'Malley took the two documents and, accompanied by other officers, proceeded to Sheppard's residence. The scope of the ensuing search was limited to the items listed in the affidavit, and several

14. The liquor and marihuana were included in the request because Sheppard had told the officers that when he was last with the victim, the two had purchased two bags of marihuana and a fifth of amaretto before going to his residence.

15. The warrant directed the officers to "search for any controlled substance, article, implement or other paraphernalia used in, for, or in connection with the unlawful possession or use of any controlled substance, and to seize and securely keep the same until final action * * *."

incriminating pieces of evidence were discovered. Sheppard was then charged with first degree murder.

* * *

II

Having already decided that the exclusionary rule should not be applied when the officer conducting the search acted in objectively reasonable reliance on a warrant issued by a detached and neutral magistrate that subsequently is determined to be invalid, the sole issue before us in this case is whether the officers reasonably believed that the search they conducted was authorized by a valid warrant. * * *

The officers in this case took every step that could reasonably be expected of them. Detective O'Malley prepared an affidavit which was reviewed and approved by the District Attorney. He presented that affidavit to a neutral judge. The judge concluded that the affidavit established probable cause to search Sheppard's residence, and informed O'Malley that he would authorize the search as requested. O'Malley then produced the warrant form and informed the judge that it might need to be changed. He was told by the judge that the necessary changes would be made. He then observed the judge make some changes and received the warrant and the affidavit. At this point, a reasonable police officer would have concluded, as O'Malley did, that the warrant authorized a search for the materials outlined in the affidavit. * * * Suppressing evidence because the judge failed to make all the necessary clerical corrections despite his assurances that such changes would be made will not serve the deterrent function that the exclusionary rule was designed to achieve. Accordingly, federal law does not require the exclusion of the disputed evidence in this case. The judgment of the Supreme Judicial Court is therefore reversed, and the case is remanded for further proceedings not inconsistent with this opinion.

JUSTICE BRENNAN, with whom JUSTICE MARSHALL joins, dissenting. * * *

I

A

At bottom, the Court's decision turns on the proposition that the exclusionary rule is merely a " 'judicially created remedy designed to safeguard Fourth Amendment rights generally through its deterrent effect, rather than a personal constitutional right.' " * * * Because seizures are executed principally to secure evidence, and because such evidence generally has utility in our legal system only in the context of a trial supervised by a judge, it is apparent that the admission of illegally obtained evidence implicates the same constitutional concerns as the initial seizure of that evidence. Indeed, by admitting unlawfully seized evidence, the judiciary becomes a part of what is in fact a single governmental action prohibited by the terms of the Amendment. Once that connection between the evidence-gathering role of the police and the evidence-admitting function of the courts is acknowledged, the plausibility of the Court's interpretation becomes more suspect. Certainly nothing in the language or history of the Fourth Amendment suggests that a recognition of this evidentiary link between the police and the courts was meant to be foreclosed. It is difficult to give any meaning at all to the limitations imposed by the Amendment if they are read to proscribe only certain conduct by the police but to allow other agents of the same government to take advantage of evidence secured by the police in violation of its requirements. The Amendment therefore must be read to condemn not only the initial unconstitutional invasion of privacy—which is done, after all, for the purpose of securing evidence—but also the subsequent use of any evidence so obtained. * * *

Such a conception of the rights secured by the Fourth Amendment was unquestionably the original basis of what has come to be called the exclusionary rule when it was first formulated in *Weeks v. United States.* * * *

[Despite the clear pronouncement of *Weeks* and *Mapp,* however, the Court in the last 10 years has gradually pressed the deterrence rationale for the exclusionary rule back to center stage.]

The various arguments advanced by the Court in this campaign have only strengthened my conviction that the deterrence theory is both misguided and unworkable. First, the Court has frequently bewailed the "cost" of excluding reliable evidence. In large part, this criticism rests upon a refusal to acknowledge the function of the Fourth Amendment itself. If nothing else, the Amendment plainly operates to disable the government from gathering information and securing evidence in certain ways. In practical terms, of course, this restriction of official power means that some incriminating evidence inevitably will go undetected if the government obeys these constitutional restraints. It is the loss of that evidence that is the "price" our society pays for enjoying the freedom and privacy safeguarded by the Fourth Amendment. Thus, some criminals will go free *not*, in Justice (then Judge) Cardozo's misleading epigram, "because the constable has blundered," but rather because official compliance with Fourth Amendment requirements makes it more difficult to catch criminals. Understood in this way, the Amendment directly contemplates that some reliable and incriminating evidence will be lost to the government; therefore, it is not the exclusionary rule, but the Amendment itself that has imposed this cost.

In addition, the Court's decisions over the past decade have made plain that the entire enterprise of attempting to assess the benefits and costs of the exclusionary rule in various contexts is a virtually impossible task for the judiciary to perform honestly or accurately. Although the Court's language in those cases suggests that some specific empirical basis may support its analyses, the reality is that the Court's opinions represent inherently unstable compounds of intuition, hunches, and occasional pieces of partial and often inconclusive data. * * *

By remaining within its redoubt of empiricism and by basing the rule solely on the deterrence rationale, the Court has robbed the rule of legitimacy. A doctrine that is explained as if it were an empirical proposition but for which there is only limited empirical support is both inherently unstable and an easy mark for critics. * * *

II

Application of that principle clearly requires affirmance in the two cases decided today. * * * [The dissent noted that the government would still be able to prosecute the defendants in *Leon*, because most of the seized drugs were found in the Via Magdalena condominium, and none of the defendants had established standing to object to the search of this condominium.] Since the indictment focused upon a conspiracy among all respondents to use the Via Magdalena condominium as a storage area for controlled substances, and since the bulk of the evidence seized was from that condominium and was plainly admissible under the District Court's order, the Government would clearly still be able to present a strong case to the jury following the court's suppression order. I emphasize these details not to suggest how the Government's case would fare before the jury but rather to clarify a point that is lost in the Court's rhetorical excesses over the costs of the exclusionary rule—namely, that the suppression of evidence will certainly tend to weaken the Government's position but it will rarely force the Government to abandon a prosecution. In my view, a doctrine that preserves intact the constitutional rights of the accused, and, at the same time, is sufficiently limited to permit society's legitimate and pressing interest in criminal law enforcement to be served should not be so recklessly discarded. * * *

In the second case before the Court, *Massachusetts v. Sheppard*, the State concedes and the Court accepts that the warrant issued to search respondent's home completely failed to state with particularity the things to be seized. * * *

Although the Court's opinion tends to overlook this fact, the requirement of particularity is not a mere "technicality," it is an express constitutional command. * * * The purpose of that requirement is to prevent precisely the kind of governmental conduct that the faulty warrant at issue here created a grave risk of permitting—namely, a search that was not narrowly and particularly limited to the things that a neutral and detached magistrate had reason to believe might be found at respondent's home. Although it is true, as Justice Stevens observes, that the affidavit submitted by the police set forth with particularity those items that they sought authority to search for, it is nevertheless clear that the warrant itself—the document which actually gave the officers legal authority to invade respondent's privacy—made no mention of these items. And, although it is true that the particular officers who applied for the warrant also happened to execute it and did so in accordance with the limits proposed in their affidavit, this happenstance should have no bearing on the central question whether these officers secured that prior judicial authority to conduct their search required by the Fourth Amendment. * * * Had the warrant actually been enforced by officers other than those who prepared the affidavit, the same result might not have occurred; indeed, the wholly erroneous nature of the warrant might have led such officers to feel at liberty to roam throughout respondent's home in search of drugs. * * * I am convinced that it is not too much to ask that an attentive magistrate take those minimum steps necessary to ensure that every warrant he issues describes with particularity the things that his independent review of the warrant application convinces him are likely to be found in the premises. And I am equally convinced that it is not too much to ask that well-trained and experienced police officers take a moment to check that the warrant they have been issued at least describes those things for which they have sought leave to search. These convictions spring not from my own view of sound criminal law enforcement policy, but are instead compelled by the language of the Fourth Amendment and the history that led to its adoption.

III

Even if I were to accept the Court's general approach to the exclusionary rule, I could not agree with today's result. * * *

At the outset, the Court suggests that society has been asked to pay a high price—in terms either of setting guilty persons free or of impeding the proper functioning of trials—as a result of excluding relevant physical evidence in cases where the police, in conducting searches and seizing evidence, have made only an "objectively reasonable" mistake concerning the constitutionality of their actions. But what evidence is there to support such a claim?

Significantly, the Court points to none, and, indeed, as the Court acknowledges, see *ante*, n. 6, recent studies have demonstrated that the "costs" of the exclusionary rule—calculated in terms of dropped prosecutions and lost convictions—are quite low. Contrary to the claims of the rule's critics, * * * these studies have demonstrated that federal and state prosecutors very rarely drop cases because of potential search and seizure problems. * * *

What then supports the Court's insistence that this evidence be admitted? Apparently, the Court's only answer is that even though the costs of exclusion are not very substantial, the potential deterrent effect in these circumstances is so marginal that exclusion cannot be justified. The key to the Court's conclusion in this respect is its belief that the prospective deterrent effect of the exclusionary rule operates only in those situations in which police officers, when deciding whether to go forward with some particular search, have reason to know that their planned conduct will violate the requirements of the Fourth Amendment. * * *

At first blush, there is some logic to this position. Undoubtedly, in the situation hypothesized by the Court, the existence of the exclusionary rule cannot be expected to have any deterrent effect on the particular officers at the moment they are deciding whether to go forward with the search. Indeed, the subsequent exclusion of any evidence seized under such circumstances appears somehow "unfair" to the particular officers involved. * * *

If the overall educational effect of the exclusionary rule is considered, application of the rule to even those situations in which individual police officers have acted on the basis of a reasonable but mistaken belief that their conduct was authorized can still be expected to have a considerable long-term deterrent effect. If evidence is consistently excluded in these circumstances, police departments will surely be prompted to instruct their officers to devote greater care and attention to providing sufficient information to establish probable cause when applying for a warrant, and to review with some attention the form of the warrant that they have been issued, rather than automatically assuming that whatever document the magistrate has signed will necessarily comport with Fourth Amendment requirements.

After today's decision, however, that institutional incentive will be lost. Indeed, the Court's "reasonable mistake" exception to the exclusionary rule will tend to put a premium on police ignorance of the law. Armed with the assurance provided by today's decision that evidence will always be admissible whenever an officer has "reasonably" relied upon a warrant, police departments will be encouraged to train officers that if a warrant has simply been signed, it is reasonable, without more, to rely on it. * * *

Although the Court brushes these concerns aside, a host of grave consequences can be expected to result from its decision to carve this new exception out of the exclusionary rule. A chief consequence of today's decision will be to convey a clear and unambiguous message to magistrates that their decisions to issue warrants are now insulated from subsequent judicial review. Creation of this new exception for good faith reliance upon a warrant implicitly tells magistrates that they need not take much care in reviewing warrant applications, since their mistakes will from now on have virtually no consequence: If their decision to issue a warrant was correct, the evidence will be admitted; if their decision was incorrect but the police relied in good faith on the warrant, the evidence will also be admitted. Inevitably, the care and attention devoted to such an inconsequential chore will dwindle. * * *

Moreover, the good faith exception will encourage police to provide only the bare minimum of information in future warrant applications. * * *

The clear incentive that operated in the past to establish probable cause adequately because reviewing courts would examine the magistrate's judgment carefully, * * * has now been so completely vitiated that the police need only show that it was not "entirely unreasonable" under the circumstances of a particular case for them to believe that the warrant they were issued was valid. The long-run effect unquestionably will be to undermine the integrity of the warrant process.

Finally, even if one were to believe, as the Court apparently does, that police are hobbled by inflexible and hypertechnical warrant procedures, today's decision cannot be justified. This is because, given the relaxed standard for assessing probable cause established just last Term in *Illinois v. Gates* [p. 200 of this book], the Court's newly fashioned good faith exception, when applied in the warrant context, will rarely, if ever, offer any greater flexibility for police than the *Gates* standard already supplies. In *Gates*, the Court held that "the task of an issuing magistrate is simply to make a practical, common-sense decision whether, given all the circumstances set forth in the affidavit before him, * * * there is a fair probability that contraband or evidence of a crime will be found in a particular place." The task of a reviewing court is confined to determining whether "the magistrate had a 'substantial basis' for concluding that probable cause existed." Given such a relaxed standard, it is virtually inconceivable that a reviewing court, when faced with a defendant's motion to suppress, could first find that a warrant was invalid under the new *Gates* standard, but then, at the same time, find that a police officer's reliance on such an invalid warrant was nevertheless "objectively reasonable" under the test announced today. Because the two standards overlap so completely, it is unlikely that a warrant could be found invalid under *Gates* and yet the police reliance upon it could be seen as objectively reasonable; otherwise, we would have to entertain the mind-boggling concept of objectively reasonable reliance upon an objectively unreasonable warrant.

This paradox, as Justice Stevens suggests, perhaps explains the Court's unwillingness to remand [*Leon*] for reconsideration in light of *Gates*, for it is quite likely that on remand the Court of Appeals would find no violation of the Fourth Amendment, thereby demonstrating that the supposed need for the good faith exception in this context is more apparent than real. Therefore, although the Court's decisions are clearly limited to the situation in which police officers reasonably rely upon an apparently valid warrant in conducting a search, I am not at all confident that the exception unleashed today will remain so confined. Indeed, the full impact of the Court's regrettable decision will not be felt until the Court attempts to extend this rule to situations in which the police have conducted a warrantless search solely on the basis of their own judgment about the existence of probable cause and exigent circumstances. When that question is finally posed, I for one will not be surprised if my colleagues decide once again that we simply cannot afford to protect Fourth Amendment rights. * * *

[The separate opinion of Justice Stevens is omitted. He would have remanded *Leon* to the Court of Appeals for reconsideration in the light of *Gates*. He would have upheld the warrant in *Sheppard v. Maxwell* because, in light of all the circumstances including the affidavit, the magistrate and the officers knew precisely what the officers were entitled to search for.]

Commentary

Justice Brennan's dissenting opinion in *Leon* and *Sheppard* relies on two lines of argument that are somewhat at odds with each other. First, the dissent warns of the "host of grave consequences" that can be expected to follow from the new doctrine. Second, it concludes that "it is virtually inconceivable" that a police officer could be objectively justified in relying upon a warrant that was invalid under the *Gates* standard. If *Leon* does not make any substantial change in the law, how can it have grave consequences? The explanation for the paradox is presumably that Justice Brennan is more concerned with the use that the majority is likely to make of the good faith exception in the future than with its application to borderline situations involving search warrants.

It is not easy to understand precisely how "objectively reasonable good faith" differs from "probable cause," in light of what the majority opinions in *Leon* and *Gates* say about the two standards. Perhaps the major difference in warrant cases is a shift in the direction of the inquiry. Instead of inquiring into the reasonableness of the magistrate's decision to issue the warrant, we should be concerned with how reasonable it was for the police officers to conclude that they had grounds to obtain a valid warrant. If this is correct, then the Supreme Court may eventually discard the requirement that reviewing courts insist that the magistrate be "neutral and detached" and not merely serve as a rubber stamp for the police. For example, suppose that police officers properly prepare an affidavit establishing probable cause, take it to a magistrate, and obtain an apparently valid search warrant. Should it matter if the magistrate signed the warrant without reading the affidavit, and the officers were aware of this? Should the police be expected to lecture magistrates on the proper performance of their duties, or to postpone the search until they can find another magistrate who is more conscientious?

An issue of this type arose in McCommon v. State, 467 So.2d 940 (Miss.1985), cert. denied 474 U.S. 984 (1985). State narcotics officers who had ample probable cause to search an automobile for marijuana obtained a search warrant from a nonlawyer Justice Court judge. The judge frankly admitted at the suppression hearing that he relied on the judgment of the law enforcement officers and made no independent determination because he thought it was his duty to help the police. The state courts ruled the search lawful and the Supreme Court denied certiorari, with Justices Brennan and Marshall dissenting. The case is a curious one because the officers could have searched without a warrant under the automobile exception. Apparently, neither the police nor the prosecutor was aware of the exception. It is difficult to fault the conduct of the officers, but the magistrate clearly was not neutral and detached. Holding the search invalid might have had the salutary effect of encouraging the state to initiate a training program for magistrates, but it would be odd to "punish" the officers for doing more than the Fourth Amendment requires.

The Supreme Court applied the good faith exception in a non-warrant context in Illinois v. Krull, 480 U.S. 340 (1987). An Illinois statute required licensed motor vehicle and vehicular parts sellers to permit officers to inspect certain required records without probable cause or a warrant. A Chicago police detective inspected an automobile wrecking yard pursuant to this statutory authority, and discovered evidence that some of the vehicles at the yard were stolen. The following day, a federal court held the inspection statute unconstitutional on the basis of the Supreme Court's ruling in Donovan v. Dewey, 452 U.S. 594 (1981). [But see, *New York v. Burger*, p. 177

of this book] The state trial court then granted a motion to suppress the evidence obtained from the inspection, and the Illinois Supreme Court affirmed. The state court rejected the prosecution's argument that the search should be upheld despite the unconstitutionality of the statute because the detective had acted in good faith reliance on a statute not yet held unconstitutional. The opinion distinguished Michigan v. DeFillippo, 443 U.S. 31 (1979), where the Supreme Court had upheld an arrest and search made pursuant to a city ordinance, where the ordinance was subsequently held unconstitutional. *DeFillippo* had involved a statute defining a substantive criminal offense,[a] whereas the statute in *Krull* was a procedural enactment directly authorizing warrantless searches. The Illinois Supreme Court concluded that good faith reliance upon such a statute could not be used to justify the admission of evidence.

The Supreme Court reversed this holding, reasoning that where an apparently valid "statute is subsequently declared unconstitutional, excluding evidence obtained pursuant to it prior to such a judicial declaration will not deter future Fourth Amendment violations by an officer who has simply fulfilled his responsibility to enforce the statute as written." The detective reasonably relied on the legislative judgment, just as the officers in *Leon* were justified in relying upon the magistrate's determination that probable cause existed.

In response to the defendant's argument that application of a good faith exception would discourage defendants from contesting the validity of statutes if they are unable to benefit directly by the subsequent exclusion of evidence, the *Krull* majority pointed out that affected businesses or persons could bring a declaratory judgment action against an inspection statute without waiting for criminal prosecutions. Indeed, the federal court decision which held the Illinois statute unconstitutional was the product of just such a declaratory judgment action. Justice O'Connor (joined by Brennan, Marshall and Stevens) dissented. She relied upon history and precedent, and also argued that "providing legislatures a grace period during which the police may freely perform unreasonable searches in order to convict those who might have otherwise escaped creates a positive incentive to promulgate unconstitutional laws."

ARIZONA v. EVANS

Supreme Court of the United States, 1995.
514 U.S. 1, 115 S.Ct. 1185, 131 L.Ed.2d 34.

CHIEF JUSTICE REHNQUIST delivered the opinion of the Court.

This case presents the question whether evidence seized in violation of the Fourth Amendment by an officer who acted in reliance on a police record indicating the existence of an outstanding arrest warrant—a record that is later determined to be erroneous—must be suppressed by virtue of the exclusionary rule regardless of the source of the error. The Supreme Court of Arizona held that the exclusionary rule required

---

a. The ordinance made it a crime for a person lawfully stopped by police to refuse to provide evidence of his or her identity. A search incident to the arrest for violating this ordinance led to the discovery of unlawful drugs.

suppression of evidence even if the erroneous information resulted from an error committed by an employee of the office of the Clerk of Court. We disagree.

In January 1991, Phoenix police officer Bryan Sargent observed respondent Evans driving the wrong way on a one-way street in front of the police station. The officer stopped respondent and asked to see his driver's license. After respondent told him that his license had been suspended, the officer entered respondent's name into a computer data terminal located in his patrol car.* The computer inquiry confirmed that respondent's license had been suspended and also indicated that there was an outstanding misdemeanor warrant for his arrest. Based upon the outstanding warrant, Officer Sargent placed respondent under arrest. While being handcuffed, respondent dropped a hand-rolled cigarette that the officers determined smelled of marijuana. Officers proceeded to search his car and discovered a bag of marijuana under the passenger's seat.

The State charged respondent with possession of marijuana. When the police notified the Justice Court that they had arrested him, the Justice Court discovered that the arrest warrant previously had been quashed and so advised the police. Respondent argued that because his arrest was based on a warrant that had been quashed 17 days prior to his arrest, the marijuana seized incident to the arrest should be suppressed as the fruit of an unlawful arrest. Respondent also argued that "the 'good faith' exception to the exclusionary rule [was] inapplicable * * * because it was police error, not judicial error, which caused the invalid arrest."

At the suppression hearing, the Chief Clerk of the Justice Court testified that a Justice of the Peace had issued the arrest warrant on December 13, 1990, because respondent had failed to appear to answer for several traffic violations. On December 19, 1990, respondent appeared before a pro tem Justice of the Peace who entered a notation in respondent's file to "quash warrant."

The Chief Clerk also testified regarding the standard court procedure for quashing a warrant. Under that procedure a justice court clerk calls and informs the warrant section of the Sheriff's Office when a warrant has been quashed. The Sheriff's Office then removes the warrant from its computer records. After calling the Sheriff's Office, the clerk makes a note in the individual's file indicating the clerk who made the phone call and the person at the Sheriff's Office to whom the clerk spoke. The Chief Clerk testified that there was no indication in respondent's file that a clerk had called and notified the Sheriff's Office that his arrest warrant had been quashed. A records clerk from the Sheriff's Office also testified that the Sheriff's Office had no record of a telephone call informing it that respondent's arrest warrant had been quashed.

---

* Alert students will realize that the officer had probable cause to arrest upon learning that the suspect had a suspended driver's license. It seems that the officer testified that he would not have made the arrest absent the warrant.–editor.

At the close of testimony, respondent argued that the evidence obtained as a result of the arrest should be suppressed because "the purposes of the exclusionary rule would be served here by making the clerks for the court, or the clerk for the Sheriff's office, whoever is responsible for this mistake, to be more careful about making sure that warrants are removed from the records." The trial court granted the motion to suppress because it concluded that the State had been at fault for failing to quash the warrant. Presumably because it could find no "distinction between State action, whether it happens to be the police department or not," the trial court made no factual finding as to whether the Justice Court or Sheriff's Office was responsible for the continued presence of the quashed warrant in the police records. [The Arizona Supreme Court affirmed.]

We granted certiorari to determine whether the exclusionary rule requires suppression of evidence seized incident to an arrest resulting from an inaccurate computer record, regardless of whether police personnel or court personnel were responsible for the record's continued presence in the police computer. We now reverse.

* * * [The majority held that the Supreme Court had jurisdiction to review the decision of the Arizona Supreme Court even though the Arizona court's opinion was interpreting a state "good faith" statute. In Michigan v. Long, 463 U.S. 1032 (1983), the Supreme Court held that when "a state court decision fairly appears to rest primarily on federal law, or to be interwoven with the federal law, and when the adequacy and independence of any possible state law ground is not clear from the face of the opinion, we will accept as the most reasonable explanation that the state court decided the case the way it did because it believed that federal law required it to do so."]

Applying that standard here, we conclude that we have jurisdiction. In reversing the Court of Appeals, the Arizona Supreme Court stated that "while it may be inappropriate to invoke the exclusionary rule where a magistrate has issued a facially valid warrant (a discretionary judicial function) based on an erroneous evaluation of the facts, the law, or both, Leon, 468 U.S. 897 (1984), it is useful and proper to do so where negligent record keeping (a purely clerical function) results in an unlawful arrest." Thus, the Arizona Supreme Court's decision to suppress the evidence was based squarely upon its interpretation of federal law. * * *

Respondent relies on United States v. Hensley, 469 U.S. 221 (1985), and argues that the evidence seized incident to his arrest should be suppressed because he was the victim of a Fourth Amendment violation. In *Hensley* [casebook, p. 250], the Court determined that evidence uncovered as a result of a *Terry* stop was admissible because the officers who made the stop acted in objectively reasonable reliance on a flyer that had been issued by officers of another police department who possessed a reasonable suspicion to justify a *Terry* stop. Because the *Hensley* Court determined that there had been no Fourth Amendment violation, the Court never considered whether the seized evidence should have been excluded. *Hensley* does not contradict our earlier pronouncements that "the question whether the exclusionary rule's remedy is appropriate in a particular context has long been regarded as an issue separate from the question whether the Fourth Amendment rights of the party seeking to invoke the rule were violated by police conduct." [citations]

Respondent also argues that Whiteley v. Warden, Wyoming State Penitentiary, 401 U.S. 560 (1971), compels exclusion of the evidence. In *Whiteley*, the Court determined that the Fourth Amendment had been violated when police officers arrested Whiteley and recovered inculpatory evidence based upon a radio report that two suspects had been involved in two robberies. Although the "police were entitled to act on the strength of the radio bulletin," the Court determined that there had been a Fourth Amendment violation because the initial complaint, upon which the arrest warrant and subsequent radio bulletin were based, was insufficient to support an independent judicial assessment of probable cause. The Court concluded that "an otherwise illegal arrest cannot be insulated from challenge by the decision of the instigating officer to rely on fellow officers to make the arrest." Because the "arrest violated [Whiteley's] constitutional rights under the Fourth and Fourteenth Amendments; the evidence secured as an incident thereto should have been excluded from his trial." *Whiteley*, supra at 568–569.

Although *Whiteley* clearly retains relevance in determining whether police officers have violated the Fourth Amendment, its precedential value regarding application of the exclusionary rule is dubious. In *Whiteley*, the Court treated identification of a Fourth Amendment violation as synonymous with application of the exclusionary rule to evidence secured incident to that violation. Subsequent case law has rejected this reflexive application of the exclusionary rule. Cf. Illinois v. Krull, 480 U.S. 340 (1987); Massachusetts v. Sheppard, 468 U.S. 981 (1984); United States v. Leon, 468 U.S. 897 (1984); United States v. Calandra, 414 U.S. 338 (1974). These later cases have emphasized that the issue of exclusion is separate from whether the Fourth Amendment has been violated, and exclusion is appropriate only if the remedial objectives of the rule are thought most efficaciously served.

Our approach is consistent with the dissenting Justices' position in Illinois v. Krull, supra, our only major case since *Leon* and *Sheppard* involving the good-faith exception to the exclusionary rule. In that case, the Court found that the good-faith exception applies when an officer conducts a search in objectively reasonable reliance on the constitutionality of a statute that subsequently is declared unconstitutional. Even the dissenting Justices in *Krull* agreed that *Leon* provided the proper framework for analyzing whether the exclusionary rule applied; they simply thought that "application of Leon's stated rationales led to a contrary result." 480 U.S. at 362 (O'Connor, J., dissenting). In sum, respondent does not persuade us to abandon the *Leon* framework.

Applying the reasoning of *Leon* to the facts of this case, we conclude that the decision of the Arizona Supreme Court must be reversed. The

Arizona Supreme Court determined that it could not "support the distinction drawn * * * between clerical errors committed by law enforcement personnel and similar mistakes by court employees," 866 P.2d at 871, and that "even assuming * * * that responsibility for the error rested with the justice court, it does not follow that the exclusionary rule should be inapplicable to these facts."

This holding is contrary to the reasoning of *Leon*, supra; Massachusetts v. Sheppard, 468 U.S. 981 (1984); and, *Krull*, supra. If court employees were responsible for the erroneous computer record, the exclusion of evidence at trial would not sufficiently deter future errors so as to warrant such a severe sanction. First, as we noted in *Leon*, the exclusionary rule was historically designed as a means of deterring police misconduct, not mistakes by court employees. Second, respondent offers no evidence that court employees are inclined to ignore or subvert the Fourth Amendment or that lawlessness among these actors requires application of the extreme sanction of exclusion. To the contrary, the Chief Clerk of the Justice Court testified at the suppression hearing that this type of error occurred once every three or four years.

Finally, and most important, there is no basis for believing that application of the exclusionary rule in these circumstances will have a significant effect on court employees responsible for informing the police that a warrant has been quashed. Because court clerks are not adjuncts to the law enforcement team engaged in the often competitive enterprise of ferreting out crime, they have no stake in the outcome of particular criminal prosecutions. The threat of exclusion of evidence could not be expected to deter such individuals from failing to inform police officials that a warrant had been quashed.

If it were indeed a court clerk who was responsible for the erroneous entry on the police computer, application of the exclusionary rule also could not be expected to alter the behavior of the arresting officer. * * * There is no indication that the arresting officer was not acting objectively reasonably when he relied upon the police computer record. Application of the *Leon* framework supports a categorical exception to the exclusionary rule for clerical errors of court employees.*

The judgment of the Supreme Court of Arizona is therefore reversed, and the case is remanded to that court for proceedings not inconsistent with this opinion.

It is so ordered.

JUSTICE O'CONNOR, with whom JUSTICE SOUTER and JUSTICE BREYER join, concurring.

---

* The Solicitor General, as amicus curiae, argues that an analysis similar to that we apply here to court personnel also would apply in order to determine whether the evidence should be suppressed if police personnel were responsible for the error. As the State has not made any such argument here, we agree that "the record in this case * * * does not adequately present that issue for the Court's consideration." Brief for United States as Amicus Curiae 13. Accordingly, we decline to address that question.

The evidence in this case strongly suggests that it was a court employee's departure from established record-keeping procedures that caused the record of respondent's arrest warrant to remain in the computer system after the warrant had been quashed. Prudently, then, the Court limits itself to the question whether a court employee's departure from such established procedures is the kind of error to which the exclusionary rule should apply. The Court holds that it is not such an error, and I agree with that conclusion and join the Court's opinion. The Court's holding reaffirms that the exclusionary rule imposes significant costs on society's law enforcement interests and thus should apply only where its deterrence purposes are "most efficaciously served."

In limiting itself to that single question, however, the Court does not hold that the court employee's mistake in this case was necessarily the only error that may have occurred and to which the exclusionary rule might apply. While the police were innocent of the court employee's mistake, they may or may not have acted reasonably in their reliance on the recordkeeping system itself. Surely it would not be reasonable for the police to rely, say, on a recordkeeping system, their own or some other agency's, that has no mechanism to ensure its accuracy over time and that routinely leads to false arrests, even years after the probable cause for any such arrest has ceased to exist (if it ever existed).

This is saying nothing new. We have said the same with respect to other information sources police use, informants being an obvious example. * * * Certainly the reliability of recordkeeping systems deserves no less scrutiny than that of informants. Of course, the comparison to informants may be instructive the opposite way as well. So long as an informant's reliability does pass constitutional muster, a finding of probable cause may not be defeated by an after-the-fact showing that the information the informant provided was mistaken.

In recent years, we have witnessed the advent of powerful, computer-based recordkeeping systems that facilitate arrests in ways that have never before been possible. The police, of course, are entitled to enjoy the substantial advantages this technology confers. They may not, however, rely on it blindly. With the benefits of more efficient law enforcement mechanisms comes the burden of corresponding constitutional responsibilities.

JUSTICE SOUTER, with whom JUSTICE BREYER joins, concurring.

In joining the Court's opinion, I share Justice O'Connor's understanding of the narrow scope of what we hold today. To her concurrence, which I join as well, I add only that we do not answer another question that may reach us in due course, that is, how far, in dealing with fruits of computerized error, our very concept of deterrence by exclusion of evidence should extend to the government as a whole, not merely the police, on the ground that there would otherwise be no reasonable expectation of keeping the number of resulting false arrests within an acceptable minimum limit.

JUSTICE STEVENS, dissenting.

* * * The Court seems to assume that the Fourth Amendment—and particularly the exclusionary rule, which effectuates the Amendment's commands—has the limited purpose of deterring police misconduct. Both the constitutional text and the history of its adoption and interpretation identify a more majestic conception. The Amendment protects the fundamental "right of the people to be secure in their persons, houses, papers, and effects," against all official searches and seizures that are unreasonable. The Amendment is a constraint on the power of the sovereign, not merely on some of its agents. The remedy for its violation imposes costs on that sovereign, motivating it to train all of its personnel to avoid future violations.

* * * Even if one accepts deterrence as the sole rationale for the exclusionary rule, the Arizona Supreme Court's decision is correct on the merits. * * * The Phoenix Police Department was part of the chain of information that resulted in petitioner's unlawful, warrantless arrest. We should reasonably presume that law enforcement officials, who stand in the best position to monitor such errors as occurred here, can influence mundane communication procedures in order to prevent those errors. That presumption comports with the notion that the exclusionary rule exists to deter future police misconduct systemically. The deterrent purpose extends to law enforcement as a whole, not merely to "the arresting officer." Consequently, the Phoenix officers' good faith does not diminish the deterrent value of invalidating their arrest of petitioner. * * *

I respectfully dissent.

[The dissenting opinion of Justice Ginsburg, with whom Justice Stevens joined, is omitted. Justice Ginsburg would have abolished the jurisdictional presumption established in Michigan v. Long, 463 U.S. 1032 (1983), and dismissed the writ of certiorari on the ground that the Arizona Supreme Court rested upon an adequate state ground.]

Commentary

Compare the decision of the Supreme Court of Illinois in People v. Turnage, 162 Ill.2d 299, 205 Ill.Dec. 118, 642 N.E.2d 1235 (1994). Turnage was arrested on a warrant for a drug offense and released on bond after a preliminary hearing. Subsequently, a grand jury returned an indictment on the same charge and a different judge issued a new arrest warrant. Police arrested Turner on this repetitive warrant, and found drugs in a search incident to the arrest. The officer (Podschweit) who made the arrest and search acted in reasonable reliance on the warrant, but the second warrant should not have been issued when defendant had posted bond on the same charge. The Illinois Supreme Court upheld a suppression order, and explained that the good faith exception of *Leon* did not apply because of the still-valid principle of Whiteley v. Warden [casebook p. 199]:

Officer Podschweit was entitled to "assume" that the information he received was correct and that he was executing a valid warrant. However, an otherwise illegal arrest is not insulated from challenge by the ignorance of the executing officer of the circumstances surrounding the issuance of the warrant. Therefore, the appropriate focus for determining whether to suppress the evidence is at the source of the warrant. As we have already determined, the warrant was invalid when issued. Therefore, under *Whiteley* defendant's arrest based on this invalid warrant was illegal and Officer Podschweit's good faith inapposite.

We do not imply that the good-faith analysis of *Leon* could have no application to the present facts. The appropriate focus for such an inquiry, however, is not on the conduct of the arresting officer, but on the conduct of those who obtained the warrant and informed the arresting officer of its continued vitality. The record is entirely silent in this regard. For this reason, we have no ability to determine whether the State's Attorney who sought issuance of the warrant or the sheriff's department that signaled its vitality harbored an objectively reasonable belief that the warrant was valid. Obviously, if either office was aware or should have been aware of the repetitive nature of the warrant, then such a belief could not be reasonably held.

We also note that suppression of the evidence in such a case would further the deterrent purposes of the exclusionary rule. Specifically, exclusion of evidence where the State's Attorney or the sheriff's department may be charged with knowledge of the repetitive nature of a warrant will deter fishing expeditions and provide an incentive to keep accurate records.

Without any facts from which we can determine whether those obtaining the warrant possessed an objectively reasonable belief in the warrant's validity, we are forced to decide application of the good-faith exception on the basis of the burden of proof. As the defendant has satisfied his burden of proving a violation of his fourth amendment rights, the burden shifts to the prosecution to prove that exclusion of the evidence is not necessary because of the good-faith exception.

The State * * * erroneously limited its inquiry to the good faith of the arresting officer. The State failed to argue that the State's Attorney and the sheriff's department had an objectively reasonable belief in the validity of the warrant. Therefore, the State has failed to carry its burden of establishing good faith in the present case.

Plainly, the good faith of the officer who actually makes an arrest can not be the sole test. When a police chief orders a subordinate officer to arrest a particular person, the subordinate will properly make the arrest without asking the chief to demonstrate that he has probable cause. The subordinate acts in reasonable good faith, but the arrest is unlawful if the law enforcement agency as a whole lacks probable cause. (Similarly, the arrest would be valid if the chief had probable cause even though the subordinate did not know anything except that he had been directed to make an arrest.) As the *Whiteley* opinion put it, "an otherwise illegal arrest cannot be insulated from challenge by the decision of the instigating officer to rely on fellow officers to make the arrest." On the other hand, the arrest may be valid if it is based upon erroneous information that comes from a source outside the law enforcement chain of command, such as a magistrate finding probable cause or a court clerk reporting the existence of a warrant.

For another application of the same principle, see United States v. Medina–Reyes, 877 F.Supp. 468 (S.D.Iowa 1995). An officer (Leighter) obtained a search warrant, relying upon information from another officer (Frampton), who received it from an informer (Flores), who made various false statements. The District Judge found that Frampton acted in reckless disregard of the falsity of the informer's statements. Officer Leighter was the sole applicant for the warrant, and he had no knowledge that the information was not reliable. However, "The *Franks* doctrine [see Franks v. Delaware, casebook, p. 198] cannot be circumvented by an officer with full information selectively providing just some information to another officer who, left ignorant of the falsity of some of the information he has been provided, or ignorant of relevant information he has not been provided, or both, then becomes the affiant-applicant for the search warrant." 877 F.Supp. at 474.

I.N.S. v. LOPEZ–MENDOZA

Supreme Court of the United States, 1984.
468 U.S. 1032, 104 S.Ct. 3479, 82 L.Ed.2d 778.

JUSTICE O'CONNOR delivered the opinion of the Court.

This litigation requires us to decide whether an admission of unlawful presence in this country made subsequent to an allegedly unlawful arrest must be excluded as evidence in a civil deportation hearing. We hold that the exclusionary rule need not be applied in such a proceeding.

[Respondents are Mexican nationals who were arrested on suspicion in the course of "factory sweeps" at their places of employment. They subsequently admitted under questioning that they were unlawfully in the country.]

In *United States v. Janis*, 428 U.S. 433 (1976), this Court set forth a framework for deciding in what types of proceeding application of the exclusionary rule is appropriate. Imprecise as the exercise may be, the Court recognized in *Janis* that there is no choice but to weigh the likely social benefits of excluding unlawfully seized evidence against the likely costs. On the benefit side of the balance "the 'prime purpose' of the [exclusionary] rule, if not the sole one, 'is to deter future unlawful police conduct.' " *Id.*, at 446. On the cost side there is the loss of often probative evidence and all of the secondary costs that flow from the less accurate or more cumbersome adjudication that therefore occurs.

At stake in *Janis* was application of the exclusionary rule in a federal civil tax assessment proceeding following the unlawful seizure of evidence by state, not federal, officials. The Court noted at the outset that "[i]n the complex and turbulent history of the rule, the Court never has applied it to exclude evidence from a civil proceeding, federal or state." 428 U.S., at 447. Two factors in *Janis* suggested that the deterrence value of the exclusionary rule in the context of that case was slight. First, the state law enforcement officials were already "punished" by the exclusion of the evidence in the state criminal trial as a result of the same conduct. Second, the evidence was also excludable in any federal criminal trial that might be held. Both factors suggested that further application of the exclusionary rule in the federal civil proceeding would contribute little more to the deterrence of unlawful conduct by state officials. On the cost side of the balance, *Janis* focused simply on the loss of concededly relevant and reliable evidence. The Court concluded that, on balance, this cost outweighed the likely social benefits achievable through application of the exclusionary rule in the federal civil proceeding.

While it seems likely that the deterrence value of applying the exclusionary rule in deportation proceedings would be higher than it was in *Janis*, it is also quite clear that the social costs would be very much greater as well. Applying the *Janis* balancing test to the benefits and costs of excluding concededly reliable evidence from a deportation proceeding, we therefore reach the same conclusion as in *Janis*.

The likely deterrence value of the exclusionary rule in deportation proceedings is difficult to assess. On the one hand, a civil deportation proceeding is a civil complement to a possible criminal prosecution, and to this extent it resembles the civil proceeding under review in *Janis*. The INS does not suggest that the exclusionary rule should not continue to apply in criminal proceedings against an alien who unlawfully enters or remains in this country, and the prospect of losing evidence that might otherwise be used in a criminal prosecution undoubtedly supplies some residual deterrent to unlawful conduct by INS officials. But it must be acknowledged that only a very small percentage of arrests of aliens are intended or expected to lead to criminal prosecutions. Thus the arresting officer's primary objective, in practice, will be to use evidence in the civil deportation proceeding. Moreover, here, in contrast to *Janis*, the agency officials who effect the unlawful arrest are the same officials who subsequently bring the deportation action. As recognized in *Janis*, the exclusionary rule is likely to be most effective when applied to such "intrasovereign" violations.

Nonetheless, several other factors significantly reduce the likely deterrent value of the exclusionary rule in a civil deportation proceeding. First, regardless of how the arrest is effected, deportation will still be possible when evidence not derived directly from the arrest is sufficient to support deportation. [Since the I.N.S. needs to prove only that respondent is an alien, and then the burden is upon the alien to establish lawful entry, suppression of evidence would frequently have no effect on the outcome.] * * *

The second factor is a practical one. In the course of a year the average INS agent arrests almost 500 illegal aliens. Over 97.5% apparently agree to voluntary deportation without a formal hearing. Among the remainder who do request a formal hearing (apparently a dozen or so in all, per officer, per year) very few challenge the circumstances of their arrests. As noted by the Court of Appeals, "the BIA was able to find only two reported immigration cases since 1899 in which the [exclusionary] rule was applied to bar unlawfully seized evidence, only one other case in which the rule's application was specifically addressed, and fewer than fifty BIA proceedings since 1952 in which a Fourth Amendment challenge to the introduction of evidence was even raised." Every INS agent knows, therefore, that it is highly unlikely that any particular arrestee will end up challenging the lawfulness of his arrest in a formal deportation proceeding. When an occasional challenge is brought, the consequences from the point of view of the officer's overall arrest and deportation record will be trivial. In these circumstances, the arresting officer is most unlikely to shape his conduct in anticipation of the exclusion of evidence at a formal deportation hearing.

Third, and perhaps most important, the INS has its own comprehensive scheme for deterring Fourth Amendment violations by its officers. Most arrests of illegal aliens away from the border occur during farm, factory, or other workplace surveys. Large numbers of illegal aliens are often arrested at one time, and conditions are understandably chaotic. To safeguard the rights of those who are lawfully present at inspected workplaces the INS has developed rules restricting stop, interrogation, and arrest practices. These regulations require that no one be detained without reasonable suspicion of illegal alienage, and that no one be arrested unless there is an admission of illegal alienage or other strong evidence thereof. New immigration officers receive instruction and examination in Fourth Amendment law, and others receive periodic refresher courses in law. Evidence seized through intentionally unlawful conduct is excluded by Department of Justice policy from the proceeding for which it was obtained. The INS also has in place a procedure for investigating and punishing immigration officers who commit Fourth Amendment violations. The INS's attention to Fourth Amendment interests cannot guarantee that constitutional violations will not occur, but it does reduce the likely deterrent value of the exclusionary rule. Deterrence must be measured at the margin.

Finally, the deterrent value of the exclusionary rule in deportation proceedings is undermined by the availability of alternative remedies for institutional practices by the INS that might violate Fourth Amendment rights. The INS is a single agency, under central federal control, and engaged in operations of broad scope but highly repetitive character. The possibility of declaratory relief against the agency thus offers a means for challenging the validity of INS practices, when standing requirements for bringing such an action can be met.

Respondents contend that retention of the exclusionary rule is necessary to safeguard the Fourth Amendment rights of ethnic Americans, particularly the Hispanic–Americans lawfully in this country. We recognize that respondents raise here legitimate and important concerns. But application of the exclusionary rule to civil deportation proceedings can be justified only if the rule is likely to add significant protection to these Fourth Amendment rights. The exclusionary rule provides no remedy for completed wrongs; those lawfully in this country can be interested in its application only insofar as it may serve as an effective deterrent to future INS misconduct. * * * Important as it is to protect the Fourth Amendment rights of all persons, there is no convincing indication that application of the exclusionary rule in civil deportation proceedings will contribute materially to that end.

On the other side of the scale, the social costs of applying the exclusionary rule in deportation proceedings are both unusual and significant. The first cost is one that is unique to continuing violations of the law. Applying the exclusionary rule in proceedings that are intended not to punish past transgressions but to prevent their continuance or renewal would require the courts to close their eyes to ongoing violations of the law. This Court has never before accepted costs of this character in applying the exclusionary rule.

Presumably no one would argue that the exclusionary rule should be invoked to prevent an agency from ordering corrective action at a leaking hazardous waste dump if the evidence underlying the order had been improperly obtained, or to compel police to return contraband explosives or drugs to their owner if the contraband had been unlawfully seized. On the rare occasions that it has considered costs of this type the Court has firmly indicated that the exclusionary rule does not extend this far.

Other factors also weigh against applying the exclusionary rule in deportation proceedings. The INS currently operates a deliberately simple deportation hearing system, streamlined to permit the quick resolution of very large numbers of deportation actions, and it is against this backdrop that the costs of the exclusionary must be assessed. The costs of applying the exclusionary rule, like the benefits, must be measured at the margin.

The average immigration judge handles about six deportation hearings per day. Neither the hearing officers nor the attorneys participating in those hearings are likely to be well versed in the intricacies of Fourth Amendment law. The prospect of even occasional invocation of the exclusionary rule might significantly change and complicate the character of these proceedings. * * * Immigration officers apprehend over one million deportable aliens in this country every year. A single agent may arrest many illegal aliens every day. Although the investigatory burden does not justify the commission of constitutional violations, the officers cannot be expected to compile elaborate, contemporaneous, written reports detailing the circumstances of every arrest. At present an officer simply completes a "Record of Deportable Alien" that is introduced to prove the INS's case at the deportation hearing; the officer rarely must attend the hearing. Fourth Amendment suppression hearings would undoubtedly require considerably more, and the likely burden on the administration of the immigration laws would be correspondingly severe.

Finally, the INS advances the credible argument that applying the exclusionary rule to deportation proceedings might well result in the suppression of large amounts of information that had been obtained entirely lawfully. INS arrests occur in crowded and confused circumstances. Though the INS agents are instructed to follow procedures that adequately protect Fourth Amendment interests, agents will usually be able to testify only to the fact that they followed INS rules. The demand for a precise account of exactly what happened in each particular arrest would plainly preclude mass arrests, even when the INS is confronted, as it often is, with massed numbers of ascertainably illegal aliens, and even when the arrests can be and are conducted in full compliance with all Fourth Amendment requirements. * * *

V

We do not condone any violations of the Fourth Amendment that may have occurred in the arrests of respondents Lopez or Sandoval. Moreover, no challenge is raised here to the INS's own internal regulations. Our conclusions concerning the exclusionary rule's value might change, if there developed good reason to believe that Fourth Amendment violations by INS officers were widespread. Finally, we do not deal here with egregious violations of Fourth Amendment or other liberties that might transgress notions of fundamental fairness and undermine the probative value of the evidence obtained.* At issue here is the exclusion of credible evidence gathered in connection with peaceful arrests by INS officers. We hold that evidence derived from such arrests need not be suppressed in an INS civil deportation hearing.

The judgment of the Court of Appeals is therefore reversed.

JUSTICE WHITE, dissenting.

The Court today holds that the exclusionary rule does not apply in civil deportation proceedings. Because I believe that the conclusion of the majority is based upon an incorrect assessment of the costs and benefits of applying the rule in such proceedings, I respectfully dissent. * * *

The majority believes "perhaps most important" the fact that the INS has a "comprehensive scheme" in place for deterring Fourth Amendment violations by punishing agents who commit such violations, but it points to not a single instance in which that scheme has been invoked.** Also, immigration officers are instructed and examined in Fourth Amendment law, and it is suggested that this education is another reason why the exclusionary rule is unnecessary. A contrary lesson could be discerned from the existence of these programs, however, when it is recalled that they were instituted during "a legal regime in which the cases and commentators uniformly sanctioned the invocation of the rule in deportation proceedings." *Lopez-Mendoza v. INS*, 705 F.2d 1059, 1071 (C.A.9 1983). Thus, rather than supporting a conclusion that

---

* We note that subsequent to its decision in *Matter of Sandoval*, 17 I. & N. Dec. 70 (1979), the BIA held that evidence will be excluded if the circumstances surrounding a particular arrest and interrogation would render use of the evidence obtained thereby "fundamentally unfair" and in violation of due process requirements of the fifth amendment.

** The Government suggests that INS disciplinary rules are "not mere paper procedures" and that over a period of four years 20 officers were suspended or terminated for misconduct toward aliens. The Government does not assert, however, that any of these officers were disciplined for Fourth Amendment violations, and it appears that the 11 officers who were terminated were terminated for rape or assault.

the exclusionary rule is unnecessary, the existence of these programs instead suggests that the exclusionary rule has created incentives for the agency to ensure that its officers follow the dictates of the Constitution. * * *

It is also my belief that the majority exaggerates the costs associated with applying the exclusionary rule in this context. Evidence obtained through violation of the Fourth Amendment is not automatically suppressed, and any inquiry into the burdens associated with application of the exclusionary rule must take that fact into account. In *United States v. Leon*, we have held that the exclusionary rule is not applicable when officers are acting in objective good faith. Thus, if the agents neither knew nor should have known that they were acting contrary to the dictates of the Fourth Amendment, evidence will not be suppressed even if it is held that their conduct was illegal.

As the majority notes, the BIA has already held that evidence will be suppressed if it results from egregious violations of constitutional standards. Thus, the mechanism for dealing with suppression motions exists and is utilized, significantly decreasing the force of the majority's predictions of dire consequences flowing from "even occasional invocation of the exclusionary rule." Although the standard currently utilized by the BIA may not be precisely coextensive with the good-faith exception, any incremental increase in the amount of evidence that is suppressed through application of *Leon* is unlikely to be significant. Likewise, any difference that may exist between the two standards is unlikely to increase significantly the number of suppression motions filed.

* * *

* * * The simple fact is that prior to 1979 the exclusionary rule was available in civil deportation proceedings and there is no indication that it significantly interfered with the ability of the INS to function.

Finally, the majority suggests that application of the exclusionary rule might well result in the suppression of large amounts of information legally obtained because of the "crowded and confused circumstances" surrounding mass arrests. The result would be that INS agents would have to keep a "precise account of exactly what happened in each particular arrest," which would be impractical considering the "massed numbers of ascertainably illegal aliens." Rather than constituting a rejection of the application of the exclusionary rule in civil deportation proceedings, however, this argument amounts to a rejection of the application of the Fourth Amendment to the activities of INS agents. If the pandemonium attending immigration arrests is so great that violations of the Fourth Amendment cannot be ascertained for the purpose of applying the exclusionary rule, there is no reason to think that such violations can be ascertained for purposes of civil suits or internal disciplinary proceedings, both of which are proceedings that the majority suggests provide adequate deterrence against Fourth Amendment violations. The Court may be willing to throw up its hands in dismay because it is administratively inconvenient to determine whether constitutional rights have been violated, but we neglect our duty when we subordinate constitutional rights to expediency in such a manner. Particularly is this so when, as here, there is but a weak showing that administrative efficiency will be seriously compromised.

In sum, I believe that the costs and benefits of applying the exclusionary rule in civil deportation proceedings do not differ in any significant way from the costs and benefits of applying the rule in ordinary criminal proceedings. Unless the exclusionary rule is to be wholly done away with and the Court's belief that it has deterrent effects abandoned, it should be applied in deportation proceedings when evidence has been obtained by deliberate violations of the Fourth Amendment or by conduct a reasonably competent officer would know is contrary to the Constitution. Accordingly, I dissent.

JUSTICE STEVENS, dissenting.

Because the Court has not yet held that the rule of *United States v. Leon* has any application to warrantless searches, I do not join the portion of Justice White's opinion that relies on that case. I do, however, agree with the remainder of his dissenting opinion.

[The separate dissenting opinions of Justices Brennan and Marshall are omitted.]

UNITED STATES v. TEJADA

United States Court of Appeals, Second Circuit, 1992.
956 F.2d 1256.

MESKILL, CIRCUIT JUDGE:

These are consolidated appeals from judgments of conviction entered in the United States District Court for the Southern District of New York. * * * Because both cases arise out of the same transaction and raise the same issue regarding the use of illegally seized evidence at sentencing, we granted the government's motion to consolidate the appeals. * * * We hold that a sentencing judge should consider illegally obtained evidence where it was not seized expressly to enhance the sentence. Thus, we also remand for a determination of whether suppressed evidence was seized expressly to enhance Cabrera's sentence.

BACKGROUND

On November 13, 1989, Detective Miguel Monge of the New York Drug Enforcement Task Force (NYDETF) [made a controlled buy of narcotics from a Cabrera, who was assisted by Tejada and Pumerol]. * * * Acting on a prearranged signal, other NYDETF officers then moved in and arrested Cabrera, Tejada and Pumerol and seized the 1.989 kilograms of cocaine that the flowered box contained. On Tejada's person, the detectives found, among other papers, a money order and a receipt for rent for apartment 3k at 2800 Jerome Avenue (although neither was in Tejada's name) and business cards inscribed with [another drug dealer's] beeper number. What occurred next between Detective

O'Flaherty and Tejada gave rise to the Fourth Amendment issue in this case.

Detective O'Flaherty testified at the evidentiary hearing on Tejada's motion to suppress as follows. Cabrera waived his Miranda rights and told O'Flaherty that he had retrieved the cocaine from apartment 3k at 2800 Jerome Avenue. Cabrera also disclosed to Detective O'Flaherty that no one was in apartment 3k, but that cocaine and a gun remained there in a closet. When O'Flaherty asked Cabrera if he had keys to apartment 3k, Cabrera gave them to the detective. O'Flaherty testified further that Cabrera willingly signed a DEA consent-to-search form and hand wrote his consent to a search of the apartment.

Detective O'Flaherty also testified that after leaving Cabrera in custody outside 2800 Jerome Avenue he joined other NYDETF officers in the third floor hallway of 2800 Jerome Avenue. After showing his supervisor the consent-to-search forms and testing Cabrera's keys in apartment 3k's doorlock, Detective O'Flaherty heard voices that he believed emanated from inside the apartment. Another officer then used a battering ram to open the door. Inside, the detectives found additional cocaine and a loaded gun, but no people.

In June 1990, the government filed a three count indictment charging that Cabrera and Tejada had conspired to distribute and possess with intent to distribute * * * cocaine, that they had distributed and possessed the cocaine and that they had used a firearm during and in relation to drug trafficking in violation of federal law.

Prior to trial, Tejada moved to suppress various items, including the narcotics and loaded firearm found during the search of apartment 3k. Judge Martin granted Tejada's motion in a memorandum order. Finding that Cabrera did not consent to the search, he expressed disbelief that an officer with keys to an apartment would have employed a battering ram. Responding to Judge Martin's ruling, the government dropped the firearms charge.

Soon thereafter, Tejada's case was transferred for trial before Judge Walker. The trial lasted five days, concluding with a jury verdict convicting Tejada on both remaining counts of the indictment.

At sentencing, Judge Walker considered the suppressed evidence and increased defendant Tejada's sentence in accordance with the Guidelines, stating that "I must consider the gun." Conversely, at Cabrera's sentencing [after a guilty plea to one count], Judge Martin refused to consider the gun, holding that, as a matter of law, a court may not consider illegally seized evidence in calculating a Guidelines sentence. In his view, pre-Guidelines precedent no longer applied. * * *

DISCUSSION

Although it remains clear that illegally seized evidence may not be used in the prosecution's case-in-chief, societal interests have led the Supreme Court narrowly to cabin the reach of the exclusionary rule. The issue before us now is whether the exclusionary rule prevents judges from considering illegally obtained evidence at sentencing.

Prior to the Guidelines, we answered this question in the negative. See United States v. Schipani, 435 F.2d 26, 28 (2d Cir.1970), cert. denied, 401 U.S. 983 (1971). In *Schipani*, we stated that "where illegally seized evidence is reliable and it is clear, as here, that it was not gathered for the express purpose of improperly influencing the sentencing judge, there is no error in using it in connection with fixing sentence." [Citations] Because the Guidelines remove a great deal of judicial discretion and the consideration of illegally seized evidence at sentencing is likely to result in increased penalties, the consideration of such evidence at sentencing now takes on greater significance. Accordingly, we now will examine whether under the Guidelines sentencing judges may consider illegally seized evidence.

A search that violates the Fourth Amendment does not confer on its victim a personal right to suppression of the illegally seized evidence. * * * Although a victim of an illegal search benefits from the exclusion of evidence that links him to an illegal act, the admission of the evidence does not itself invade the privacy of the search victim, which is a fait accompli. We suppress evidence only because doing so will deter future violations of the Fourth Amendment. [Citations]

Moreover, the Supreme Court has instructed us not to suppress evidence solely because doing so might deter illegal searches. Rather, the likelihood of increased deterrence must be balanced against the considerable cost of excluding reliable information. [Citations] * * *

The defendants and amici argue that allowing sentencing judges to consider illegally seized evidence will give police an incentive to violate the Fourth Amendment. They posit that police and prosecutors with enough lawfully obtained evidence for a conviction of a relatively minor offense that has a broad sentencing range could guarantee a heavier sentence by seizing other evidence illegally and introducing it at sentencing. They argue that as a result nothing will deter police from making illegal searches, especially in those situations where a conviction of a greater crime would lead to a similar sentence.

Defendants and amici do not explain why this supposed incentive to violate the Fourth Amendment will prove incrementally stronger than the rewards that already exist. * * *

The argument also has been put before us that requiring the consideration of previously suppressed evidence at sentencing is the last step in wholly gutting the exclusionary rule, the other steps having been taken by the Supreme Court in its more recent Fourth Amendment opinions. We do not agree that this case "is the straw that breaks the camel's back" where Fourth Amendment concerns are at stake.

Great rewards still exist for following accepted police procedures. Here, for example, the government could have brought a more concrete case, supported by all the evidence, had the officers searched apartment

3k pursuant to a search warrant. Instead, suppression of the evidence found in apartment 3k forced the government to drop the firearms count of its indictment and the additional sentence that it could have carried. Having had the firearms charge would have allowed the prosecution to have made a strong case based on concrete evidence; instead, it had to proceed on the more circumstantial conspiracy case. * * *

We must determine whether consideration of illegally seized evidence is mandatory, discretionary or prohibited. Obviously, we reject the latter. Instead of compelling the consideration of all evidence at sentencing, we could leave the decision to the judgment of the district courts. The argument supporting this position asserts that district judges would gain greater discretion if we were to allow them to disregard illegally seized evidence. By not considering suppressed items, a judge could impose a more lenient sentence.

We have given this argument serious consideration and, while we do not disagree with its underlying premise, we conclude that it represents a fundamental misunderstanding of our task. The Guidelines evince a clear desire for uniformity, and ad hoc determinations would create disparities in sentences in the absence of differences in conduct. To allow judges to decide whether to consider illegally seized evidence at sentencing without factoring in the Fourth Amendment—by excluding evidence only where a systemic remedy of substantial deterrence will ensue— would sidestep Congress and violate Separation of Powers principles. We will not overstep the proper bounds of our judicial role.

We conclude that the benefits of providing sentencing judges with reliable information about the defendant outweigh the likelihood that allowing consideration of illegally seized evidence will encourage unlawful police conduct. Absent a showing that officers obtained evidence expressly to enhance a sentence, a district judge may not refuse to consider relevant evidence at sentencing, even if that evidence has been seized in violation of the Fourth Amendment. Consistent with our holding are the recent decisions of the District of Columbia Circuit, the Eleventh Circuit and the Third Circuit holding that district judges may consider illegally seized evidence at sentencing. [Citations]

Tejada argues that even if *Schipani* remains good law, Judge Walker acted mistakenly when he stated that he had to consider the gun at sentencing. The argument is premised on the assumption that Judge Walker ignored *Schipani's* exception for cases where evidence was seized expressly for the improper purpose of influencing the sentencing judge. We disagree with the foundation of this argument. Although Judge Walker did state that "I must consider the gun under *Schipani,*" we interpret his statement as evincing his compulsion to consider the evidence in light of the circumstances. The record makes clear that Judge Walker properly familiarized himself with *Schipani.*

Judge Martin, on the other hand, made it clear that he did not consider *Schipani* valid in light of the Guidelines. On remand, he should consider whether the [officers] acted with the intent of enhancing sentencing rather than under the misinformed assumption that Cabrera had consented to the search. If the illegal search was not motivated by a desire to enhance sentencing, then Judge Martin must consider the gun at sentencing. * * *

We affirm defendant Tejada's sentence and judgment of conviction. * * * We vacate Cabrera's judgment of conviction as to the sentence only and remand to the district court for resentencing.

Chapter 8

ENTRAPMENT AND OUTRAGEOUS INDUCEMENT

UNITED STATES v. RUSSELL

Supreme Court of the United States, 1973.
411 U.S. 423, 93 S.Ct. 1637, 36 L.Ed.2d 366.

MR. JUSTICE REHNQUIST delivered the opinion of the Court.

Respondent Richard Russell was charged in three counts of a five count indictment returned against him and codefendants John and Patrick Connolly. After a jury trial in the District Court, in which his sole defense was entrapment, respondent was convicted on all three counts of having unlawfully manufactured and processed methamphetamine ("speed") and of having unlawfully sold and delivered that drug * * *.

There is little dispute concerning the essential facts in this case. On December 7, 1969, Joe Shapiro, an undercover agent for the Federal Bureau of Narcotics and Dangerous Drugs, went to respondent's home on Whidbey Island in the State of Washington where he met with respondent and his two codefendants, John and Patrick Connolly. Shapiro's assignment was to locate a laboratory where it was believed that methamphetamine was being manufactured illicitly. He told the respondent and the Connollys that he represented an organization in the Pacific Northwest that was interested in controlling the manufacture and distribution of methamphetamine. He then made an offer to supply the defendants with the chemical phenyl–2–propanone, an essential ingredient in the manufacture of methamphetamine, in return for one-half of the drug produced. This offer was made on the condition that Agent Shapiro be shown a sample of the drug which they were making and the laboratory where it was being produced.

During the conversation Patrick Connolly revealed that he had been making the drug since May 1969 and since then had produced three pounds of it.[2] John Connolly gave the agent a bag containing a quantity

---

2. At trial Patrick Connolly admitted making this statement to Agent Shapiro but asserted that the statement was not true. .

of methamphetamine that he represented as being from "the last batch that we made". Shortly thereafter, Shapiro and Patrick Connolly left respondent's house to view the laboratory which was located in the Connolly house on Whidbey Island. At the house Shapiro observed an empty bottle bearing the chemical label phenyl–2–propanone.

By prearrangement Shapiro returned to the Connolly house on December 9, 1969, to supply 100 grams of propanone and observe the chemical reaction. When he arrived he observed Patrick Connolly and the respondent cutting up pieces of aluminum foil and placing them in a large flask. There was testimony that some of the foil pieces accidentally fell on the floor and were picked up by the respondent and Shapiro and put into the flask.[3] Thereafter Patrick Connolly added all of the necessary chemicals, including the propanone brought by Shapiro, to make two batches of methamphetamine. The manufacturing process having been completed the following morning, Shapiro was given one-half of the drug and respondent kept the remainder. Shapiro offered to buy, and the respondent agreed to sell, part of the remainder for $60.

About a month later Shapiro returned to the Connolly house and met with Patrick Connolly to ask if he was still interested in their "business arrangement." Connolly replied that he was interested but that he had recently obtained two additional bottles of phenyl–2–propanone and would not be finished with them for a couple of days. He provided some additional methamphetamine to Shapiro at that time. Three days later Shapiro returned to the Connolly house with a search warrant and, among other items, seized an empty 500–gram bottle of propanone and a 100–gram bottle, not the one he had provided, that was partially filled with the chemical.

There was testimony at the trial of respondent and Patrick Connolly that phenyl–2–propanone was generally difficult to obtain. At the request of the Bureau of Narcotics and Dangerous Drugs, some chemical supply firms had voluntarily ceased selling the chemical.

At the close of the evidence, and after receiving the District Judge's standard entrapment instruction,[4] the jury found the respondent guilty on all counts charged. On appeal the respondent conceded that the jury could have found him predisposed to commit the offenses, but argued that on the facts presented there was entrapment as a matter of law. The Court of Appeals agreed, although it did not find the District Court had misconstrued or misapplied the traditional standards governing the entrapment defense. Rather, the court in effect expanded the traditional notion of entrapment, which focuses on the predisposition of the defen-

3. Agent Shapiro did not otherwise participate in the manufacture of the drug or direct any of the work.

4. The District Judge stated the governing law on entrapment as follows: "Where a person already has the willingness and the readiness to break the law, the mere fact that the government agent provides what appears to be a favorable opportunity is not entrapment." He then instructed the jury to acquit respondent if it had a "reasonable doubt whether the defendant had the previous intent or purpose to commit the offense * * * and did so only because he was induced or persuaded by some officer or agent of the government." No exception was taken by respondent to this instruction.

dant, to mandate dismissal of a criminal prosecution whenever the court determines that there has been "an intolerable degree of governmental participation in the criminal enterprise." In this case the court decided that the conduct of the agent in supplying a scarce ingredient essential for the manufacture of a controlled substance established that defense.

This new defense was held to rest on either of two alternative theories. One theory is based on two lower court decisions which have found entrapment, regardless of predisposition, whenever the government supplies contraband to the defendants. United States v. Bueno, 447 F.2d 903 (C.A.5 1971); United States v. Chisum, 312 F.Supp. 1307 (C.D.Cal.1970).[a] The second theory, a nonentrapment rationale, is based on a recent Ninth Circuit decision that reversed a conviction because a government investigator was so enmeshed in the criminal activity that the prosecution of the defendants was held to be repugnant to the American criminal justice system. Greene v. United States, 454 F.2d 783 (C.A.9 1971).[b] The court below held that these two rationales constitute the same defense, and that only the label distinguishes them. In any event, it held that "[b]oth theories are premised on fundamental concepts of due process and evince the reluctance of the judiciary to countenance 'overzealous law enforcement.'"

This Court first recognized and applied the entrapment defense in Sorrells v. United States, 287 U.S. 435 (1932). In Sorrells a federal prohibition agent visited the defendant while posing as a tourist and engaged him in conversation about their common war experiences. After gaining the defendant's confidence the agent asked for some liquor, was twice refused, but upon asking a third time the defendant finally capitulated, and was subsequently prosecuted for violating the National Prohibition Act.

Chief Justice Hughes, speaking for the Court, held that as a matter of statutory construction the defense of entrapment should have been available to the defendant. Under the theory propounded by the Chief Justice, the entrapment defense prohibits law enforcement officers from instigating criminal acts by persons "otherwise innocent in order to lure them to its commission and to punish them." Thus, the thrust of the

a. In *Bueno*, an informer in the pay of the government furnished narcotics to defendant, who was charged with selling the same narcotics to a federal agent. The defendant in *Chisum* approached a man named Metzger, whom he knew to be under indictment for counterfeiting, and offered to buy counterfeit money. Metzger introduced him to Larry, who was in fact a Secret Service Agent. Larry supplied defendant with counterfeit money and then arrested him for receiving it.—ed.

b. The defendants in *Greene* had been convicted of selling bootleg whiskey and sentenced to prison. Being incredibly stupid, they did not realize that the man to whom they had sold the whiskey, an undercover federal agent named Courtney, was responsible for their arrest and conviction. Upon their release from prison, they reestablished contact with Courtney and offered to sell him more whiskey. He urged them to go back into bootlegging, bought whiskey, and helped in numerous ways to maintain them in business for over two years. Then he arrested them. The Court of Appeals held that the defense of entrapment was inapplicable because of the defendants' obvious predisposition to commit the offense, but that the Government's involvement with the criminal activity was so pervasive that prosecution should not be allowed.—ed.

entrapment defense was held to focus on the intent or predisposition of the defendant to commit the crime. "[I]f the defendant seeks acquittal by reason of entrapment he cannot complain of an appropriate and searching inquiry into his own conduct and predisposition as bearing upon that issue."

Justice Roberts concurred in the result but was of the view "that courts must be closed to the trial of a crime instigated by the government's own agents." The difference in the view of the majority and the concurring opinions is that in the former the inquiry focuses on the predisposition of the defendant, whereas in the latter the inquiry focuses on whether the government "instigated the crime."

In 1958 the Court again considered the theory underlying the entrapment defense and expressly reaffirmed the view expressed by the *Sorrells* majority. Sherman v. United States, 356 U.S. 369 (1958). In *Sherman* the defendant was convicted of selling narcotics to a government informer. As in *Sorrells* it appears that the government agent gained the confidence of the defendant and, despite initial reluctance, the defendant finally acceded to the repeated importunings of the agent to commit the criminal act. On the basis of *Sorrells*, this Court reversed the affirmance of the defendant's conviction.

In affirming the theory underlying *Sorrells*, Chief Justice Warren for the Court, held that "[t]o determine whether entrapment has been established, a line must be drawn between the trap for the unwary innocent and the trap for the unwary criminal." Justice Frankfurter stated in a concurring opinion that he believed Justice Roberts had the better view in *Sorrells* and would have framed the question to be asked in an entrapment defense in terms of "whether the police conduct revealed in the particular case falls below standards * * * for the proper use of governmental power."

In the instant case respondent asks us to reconsider the theory of the entrapment defense as it is set forth in the majority opinions in *Sorrells* and *Sherman*. His principal contention is that the defense should rest on constitutional grounds. He argues that the level of Shapiro's involvement in the manufacture of the methamphetamine was so high that a criminal prosecution for the drug's manufacture violates the fundamental principles of due process. The respondent contends that the same factors that led this Court to apply the exclusionary rule to illegal searches and seizures and confessions should be considered here. But he would have the Court go further in deterring undesirable official conduct by requiring that any prosecution be barred absolutely because of the police involvement in criminal activity. The analogy is imperfect in any event, for the principal reason behind the adoption of the exclusionary rule was the government's "failure to observe its own laws." Unlike the situations giving rise to the holdings in *Mapp* and *Miranda*, the government's conduct here violated no independent constitutional right of the respondent. Nor did Shapiro violate any federal statute or rule or commit any crime in infiltrating the respondent's drug enterprise.

Respondent would overcome this basic weakness in his analogy to the exclusionary rule cases by having the Court adopt a rigid constitutional rule that would preclude any prosecution when it is shown that the criminal conduct would not have been possible had not an undercover agent "supplied an indispensable means to the commission of the crime that could not have been obtained otherwise, through legal or illegal channels." Even if we were to surmount the difficulties attending the notion that due process of law can be embodied in fixed rules, and those attending respondent's particular formulation, the rule he proposes would not appear to be of significant benefit to him. For on the record presented it appears that he cannot fit within the terms of the very rule he proposes.

The record discloses that although the propanone was difficult to obtain it was by no means impossible. The defendants admitted making the drug both before and after those batches made with the propanone supplied by Shapiro. Shapiro testified that he saw an empty bottle labeled phenyl–2–propanone on his first visit to the laboratory on December 7, 1969. And when the laboratory was searched pursuant to a search warrant on January 10, 1970, two additional bottles labeled phenyl–2–propanone were seized. Thus, the facts in the record amply demonstrate that the propanone used in the illicit manufacture of methamphetamine not only *could* have been obtained without the intervention of Shapiro but was in fact obtained by these defendants.

While we may some day be presented with a situation in which the conduct of law enforcement agents is so outrageous that due process principles would absolutely bar the government from invoking judicial processes to obtain a conviction, cf. Rochin v. California, 342 U.S. 165 (1952), the instant case is distinctly not of that breed. Shapiro's contribution of propanone to the criminal enterprise already in process was scarcely objectionable. The chemical is by itself a harmless substance and its possession is legal. While the government may have been seeking to make it more difficult for drug rings, such as that of which respondent was a member, to obtain the chemical, the evidence described above shows that it nonetheless was obtainable. The law enforcement conduct here stops far short of violating that "fundamental fairness, shocking to the universal sense of justice," mandated by the Due Process Clause of the Fifth Amendment. Kinsella v. United States ex rel. Singleton, 361 U.S. 234, 246 (1960).

The illicit manufacture of drugs is not a sporadic, isolated criminal incident, but a continuing, though illegal, business enterprise. In order to obtain convictions for illegally manufacturing drugs, the gathering of evidence of past unlawful conduct frequently proves to be an all but impossible task. Thus in drug-related offenses law enforcement personnel have turned to one of the only practicable means of detection: the infiltration of drug rings and a limited participation in their unlawful present practices. Such infiltration is a recognized and permissible means of apprehension; if that be so, then the supply of some item of value that the drug ring requires must, as a general rule, also be permissible. For an agent will not be taken into the confidence of the illegal entrepreneurs unless he has something of value to offer them. Law enforcement tactics such as this can hardly be said to violate "fundamental fairness" or "shocking to the universal sense of justice."

Respondent also urges, as an alternative to his constitutional argument, that we broaden the nonconstitutional defense of entrapment in order to sustain the judgment of the Court of Appeals. This Court's opinions in Sorrells v. United States, supra, and Sherman v. United States, supra, held that the principal element in the defense of entrapment was the defendant's predisposition to commit the crime. Respondent conceded in the Court of Appeals, as well he might, "that he may have harbored a predisposition to commit the charged offenses." Yet he argues that the jury's refusal to find entrapment under the charge submitted to it by the trial court should be overturned and the views of Justices Roberts and Frankfurter, concurring in Sorrells and Sherman, respectively, which make the essential element of the defense turn on the type and degree of governmental conduct, be adopted as the law.

We decline to overrule these cases. Sorrells is a precedent of long standing that has already been once reexamined in Sherman and implicitly there reaffirmed. Since the defense is not of a constitutional dimension, Congress may address itself to the question and adopt any substantive definition of the defense that it may find desirable.

Critics of the rule laid down in Sorrells and Sherman have suggested that its basis in the implied content of Congress is largely fictitious, and have pointed to what they conceive to be the anomalous difference between the treatment of a defendant who is solicited by a private individual and one who is entrapped by a government agent. Questions have been likewise raised as to whether "predisposition" can be factually established with the requisite degree of certainty. Arguments such as these, while not devoid of appeal, have been twice previously made to this Court, and twice rejected by it, first in Sorrells and then in Sherman.

We believe that at least equally cogent criticism has been made of the concurring views in these cases. Commenting in Sherman on Justice Roberts' position in Sorrells that "although the defendant could claim that the Government had induced him to commit the crime, the Government could not reply by showing that the defendant's criminal conduct was due to his own readiness and not to the persuasion of government agents," Chief Justice Warren quoted the observation of Judge Learned Hand in an earlier stage of that proceeding:

> "Indeed, it would seem probable that, if there were no reply [to the claim of inducement], it would be impossible ever to secure convictions of any offences which consist of transactions that are carried on in secret."

Nor does it seem particularly desirable for the law to grant complete immunity from prosecution to one who himself planned to commit a crime, and then committed it, simply because government undercover agents subjected him to inducements which might have seduced a hypothetical individual who was not so predisposed. * * *

Sorrells and *Sherman* both recognize "that the fact that officers or employees of the government merely afford opportunities or facilities for the commission of the offense does not defeat the prosecution." Nor will the mere fact of deceit defeat a prosecution, for there are circumstances when the use of deceit is the only practicable law enforcement technique available. It is only when the government's deception actually implants the criminal design in the mind of the defendant that the defense of entrapment comes into play.

Respondent's concession in the Court of Appeals that the jury finding as to predisposition was supported by the evidence is, therefore, fatal to his claim of entrapment. He was an active participant in an illegal drug manufacturing enterprise which began before the government agent appeared on the scene, and continued after the government agent had left the scene. He was, in the words of *Sherman*, not an "unwary innocent" but an "unwary criminal." The Court of Appeals was wrong, we believe, when it sought to broaden the principle laid down in *Sorrells* and *Sherman*. Its judgment is therefore reversed.

Reversed.

Mr. Justice Stewart, with whom Mr. Justice Brennan and Mr. Justice Marshall join, dissenting. * * *

In my view, this objective approach to entrapment advanced by the concurring opinions in *Sorrells* and *Sherman* is the only one truly consistent with the underlying rationale of the defense. Indeed, the very basis of the entrapment defense itself demands adherence to an approach that focuses on the conduct of the governmental agents, rather than on whether the defendant was "predisposed" or "otherwise innocent." I find it impossible to believe that the purpose of the defense is to effectuate some unexpressed congressional intent to exclude from its criminal statutes persons who committed a prohibited act, but would not have done so except for the Government's inducements. For, as Mr. Justice Frankfurter put it, "the only legislative intention that can with any show of reason be extracted from the statute is the intention to make criminal precisely the conduct in which the defendant has engaged." Sherman v. United States, supra, at 379. Since, by definition, the entrapment defense cannot arise unless the defendant actually committed the proscribed act, that defendant is manifestly covered by the terms of the criminal statute involved.*

* The notion that "the entrapment defense cannot arise unless the defendant actually committed the proscribed act" implies that it is inconsistent for a defendant to claim both that he did not commit the crime and that he was entrapped into committing it. Accordingly, some federal courts have refused to give entrapment instructions where the defendant denied any element of the crime. In Mathews v. United States, 485 U.S. 58 (1988), the Supreme Court held that even if the defendant in a federal criminal case denies one or more elements of the crime, he is entitled to an entrapment instruction whenever there is sufficient evidence from which a reasonable jury could find entrapment.—ed.

Furthermore, to say that such a defendant is "otherwise innocent" or not "predisposed" to commit the crime is misleading, at best. The very fact that he has committed an act that Congress has determined to be illegal demonstrates conclusively that he is not innocent of the offense. He may not have originated the precise plan or the precise details, but he was "predisposed" in the sense that he has proved to be quite capable of committing the crime. That he was induced, provoked, or tempted to do so by government agents does not make him any more innocent or any less predisposed than he would be if he had been induced, provoked, or tempted by a private person—which, of course, would not entitle him to cry "entrapment." Since the only difference between these situations is the identity of the temptor, it follows that the significant focus must be on the conduct of the government agents, and not on the predisposition of the defendant.

The purpose of the entrapment defense, then, cannot be to protect persons who are "otherwise innocent." Rather, it must be to prohibit unlawful governmental activity in instigating crime. * * *

[W]hether the particular defendant was "predisposed" or "otherwise innocent" is irrelevant; and the important question becomes whether the Government's conduct in inducing the crime was beyond judicial toleration.

Moreover, a test that makes the entrapment defense depend on whether the defendant had the requisite predisposition permits the introduction into evidence of all kinds of hearsay, suspicion, and rumor—all of which would be inadmissible in any other context—in order to prove the defendant's predisposition. It allows the prosecution, in offering such proof, to rely on the defendant's bad reputation or past criminal activities, including even rumored activities of which the prosecution may have insufficient evidence to obtain an indictment, and to present the agent's suspicions as to why they chose to tempt this defendant. This sort of evidence is not only unreliable, as the hearsay rule recognizes; but it is also highly prejudicial, especially if the matter is submitted to the jury, for, despite instructions to the contrary, the jury may well consider such evidence as probative not simply of the defendant's predisposition, but of his guilt of the offense with which he stands charged.

More fundamentally, focusing on the defendant's innocence or predisposition has the direct effect of making what is permissible or impermissible police conduct depend upon the past record and propensities of the particular defendant involved. Stated another way, this subjective test means that the Government is permitted to entrap a person with a criminal record or bad reputation, and then to prosecute him for the manufactured crime, confident that his record or reputation itself will be enough to show that he was predisposed to commit the offense anyway. * * * In my view, a person's alleged "predisposition" to crime should not open him to government participation in the criminal transaction that would be otherwise unlawful.

This does not mean, of course, that the Government's use of undercover activity, strategy, or deception is necessarily unlawful. Indeed, many crimes, especially so-called victimless crimes, could not otherwise be detected. Thus, government agents may engage in conduct that is likely, when objectively considered, to afford a person ready and willing to commit the crime an opportunity to do so.

But when the agents' involvement in criminal activities goes beyond the mere offering of such an opportunity and when their conduct is of a kind that could induce or instigate the commission of a crime by one not ready and willing to commit it, then—regardless of the character or propensities of the particular person induced—I think entrapment has occurred. For in that situation, the Government has engaged in the impermissible manufacturing of crime, and the federal courts should bar the prosecution in order to preserve the institutional integrity of the system of federal criminal justice. * * *

It cannot be doubted that if phenyl–2–propanone had been wholly unobtainable from other sources, the agent's undercover offer to supply it to the respondent in return for part of the illicit methamphetamine produced therewith—an offer initiated and carried out by the agent for the purpose of prosecuting the respondent for producing methamphetamine—would be precisely the type of governmental conduct that constitutes entrapment under any definition. For the agent's conduct in that situation would make possible the commission of an otherwise totally impossible crime, and, I should suppose, would thus be a textbook example of instigating the commission of a criminal offense in order to prosecute someone for committing it.

But assuming in this case that the phenyl–2–propanone was obtainable through independent sources, the fact remains that that used for the particular batch of methamphetamine involved in all three counts of the indictment with which the respondent was charged—i.e., that produced on December 10, 1969—was supplied by the Government. This essential ingredient was indisputably difficult to obtain, and yet that used in committing the offenses of which the respondent was convicted was offered to the respondent by the government agent on the agent's own initiative, and was readily supplied to the respondent in needed amounts. If the chemical was so easily available elsewhere, then why did not the agent simply wait until the respondent had himself obtained the ingredients and produced the drug, and then buy it from him? The very fact that the agent felt it incumbent upon him to offer to supply phenyl–2–propanone in return for the drug casts considerable doubt on the theory that the chemical could easily have been procured without the agent's intervention, and that therefore the agent merely afforded an opportunity for the commission of a criminal offense.

In this case, the chemical ingredient was available only to licensed persons, and the Government itself had requested suppliers not to sell that ingredient even to people with a license. Yet the government agent readily offered and supplied that ingredient to an unlicensed person and asked him to make a certain illegal drug with it. The Government then prosecuted that person for making the drug produced *with the very ingredient* which its agent had so helpfully supplied. This strikes me as the very pattern of conduct that should be held to constitute entrapment as a matter of law.

It is the Government's duty to prevent crime, not to promote it. Here, the Government's agent asked that the illegal drug be produced for him, solved his quarry's practical problems with the assurance that he could provide the one essential ingredient that was difficult to obtain, furnished that element as he had promised, and bought the finished product from the respondent—all so that the respondent could be prosecuted for producing and selling the very drug for which the agent had asked and for which he had provided the necessary component. Under the objective approach that I would follow, this respondent was entrapped, regardless of his predisposition or "innocence." * * *

STATE v. POWELL

Supreme Court of Hawaii, 1986.
68 Hawaii 635, 726 P.2d 266.

PER CURIAM.

* * *

The incidence of thefts and robberies in the vicinity of the intersection of Wilikina Drive and Kamehameha Highway in Wahiawa prompted a police decision to institute a series of "drunk decoy" operations in the area of the reported crimes. And between November of 1984 and March of 1985 officers of the Honolulu Police Department organized such operations on eleven occasions and arrested nineteen individuals. Laverne Powell was arrested on March 21, 1985 when she pilfered a wallet containing nine dollars.

The victim on this occasion was a police officer feigning drunkenness. As he lay on his side in a fetal position with a paper bag containing a beer bottle in his hand, a wallet protruded from a rear pocket of his jeans. That the wallet contained money was rendered obvious by the partial exposure of currency. Several other officers stationed themselves at nearby vantage points and awaited possible criminal activity. Shortly after 11:00 p.m., Laverne Powell walked by the officer posing as a helpless drunkard. She then turned back, approached the apparently vulnerable victim, and stole the wallet planted on his person. Two officers who witnessed the theft sprang from cover and apprehended Ms. Powell as she left the scene.

The Grand Jury returned an indictment charging Laverne Powell with Theft in the First Degree. Averring she had been induced by the police to commit the offense, the defendant moved for dismissal of the charge. The circuit court conducted an evidentiary hearing in which the only testimony offered was that of the police sergeant who supervised the "drunk decoy" operation. The court found the dispositive facts were not in dispute, concluded the police conduct in question constituted entrapment as a matter of law, and dismissed the indictment with prejudice.

II.

A.

"Since the defense is not of a constitutional dimension, [the legislature] may address itself to the question and adopt any substantive definition of [entrapment] that it may find desirable." *United States v. Russell*, [supra. p. 349] (footnote omitted). "The rationale for providing a defense based on entrapment," in the legislature's view, "does not reside in the fact that entrapped defendants are less culpable or dangerous than those who formulate their intent without outside inducement. * * * The real basis for the defense * * * is a purpose to deter improper conduct on the part of law enforcement officials." HRS § 702–237 (1976), Commentary. The Hawaii Penal Code's definition of "entrapment" therefore focuses "not on the [propensities and] predisposition of the defendant to commit the crime charged, but rather * * * on the conduct of * * * law enforcement officials." *State v. Anderson*, 572 P.2d 159, 162 (1977). And by virtue of HRS § 702–237

> [i]n any prosecution, it is an affirmative defense that the defendant engaged in the prohibited conduct or caused the prohibited result because he was induced or encouraged to do so by a law enforcement officer, or by a person acting in cooperation with a law enforcement officer, who, for the purpose of obtaining evidence of the commission of an offense. * * *

> * * *

> (b) Employed methods of persuasion or inducement which created a substantial risk that the offense would be committed by persons other than those who are ready to commit it.

Whether the defendant was entrapped or not ordinarily is a matter for the jury to decide. But when "the evidence is undisputed and * * * clear" entrapment may be established as a matter of law. Here, the circuit court was neither compelled to choose between conflicting witnesses nor judge their credibility. It ruled on the basis of undisputed testimony elicited from the officer who organized the operation in question. Moreover, the findings rendered by the circuit court are not challenged by the State.

B.

The State nonetheless argues a reversal of the court's ruling is in order because the police were "looking to interrupt ongoing criminal activity" and employed means "reasonably tailored to apprehend those involved in stealing from intoxicated persons." But we are convinced from a review of the record that the police "[e]mployed methods of * * * inducement which created a substantial risk that [theft] would be committed by persons other than those who [were] ready to commit it." HRS § 702–237(1)(b).

That the police were concerned with reports of "thefts and robberies in the area" is not to be disputed. Nor can the decision to organize covert operations be faulted. "Criminal activity is such that stealth and strategy are necessary weapons in the arsenal of the police officer." *Sherman v. United States*, 356 U.S. at 372. Yet as the circuit court found, the reported thefts and robberies did not "involve[ ] 'sleeping drunks' or thefts of the same nature as the instant case." We would be hard put to contradict the court's further finding that the "drunk decoy" operations were expressly designed to ensnare anyone who would commit theft when "bait money" is placed in plain view and within easy reach.

The stealth and strategy employed here resulted in the apprehension of nineteen persons, including Laverne Powell, for "rolling drunks." Undeniably, "[t]he function of law enforcement is the prevention of crime and the apprehension of criminals." *Id*. Yet, what was reported previously as happening in the vicinity were thefts of a different nature, including robberies. "Manifestly, [the law enforcement] function does not include the manufacturing of crime." *Id*. Under the circumstances, we would have to agree with the circuit court that the "drunk decoy" operation "created a substantial risk that [theft] would be committed by persons other than those who [were] ready to commit it." HRS § 702–237(1)(b).

Affirmed.

Commentary

A substantial majority of commentators have favored the "objective" or minority approach to entrapment, essentially for the reasons advanced in the dissenting opinion by Justice Stewart in United States v. Russell. The authorities and arguments are thoroughly reviewed in LaFave and Scott, Criminal Law 420–32 (2d Ed. 1986). Is is clear, however, that use of the objective test would lead to a finding of entrapment on the facts of *Russell*? Would a person not otherwise "ready and willing" to manufacture illegal drugs be likely to do so if offered a supply of an essential but difficult-to-obtain chemical? The fact that it may have been difficult or even impossible for the defendants to manufacture methamphetamine at this time without a supply of the chemical does not mean that a hypothetical law-abiding person can be seduced into drug manufacturing merely by an offer to make the chemical available.

This reasoning suggests that "predisposition" should not be the only factor considered, whether we are talking about the predisposition of the actual defendant or of the hypothetical person who is the concern of the objective test. Justice Stewart is surely right in arguing that, if phenyl–2–propanone had been wholly unobtainable from other sources, it would be irrational and outrageous for the government to make supplies of the chemicals available so that they could prosecute persons for drug offenses that would be otherwise impossible to commit. The wrong here is not necessarily the seduction of the innocent, however. The inducement may be attractive only to those who are otherwise predisposed, but their predisposition would not lead to criminal activity if the government did not make it possible. For example, the prisons are full of individuals who are predisposed to use drugs. The government could produce any number of cases for prosecution by introducing marijuana into a prison, but the activity would be pointless.

One difficulty with the objective formulation is that the persuasion or inducement may look more or less reprehensible depending upon to whom it is addressed. Regardless of the methods employed, it would be reprehensible for the government to seek out recovering drug addicts in the hope of inducing them to return to drug use. For example, the California Supreme Court adopted the objective test in People v. Barraza, 23 Cal.3d 675, 153 Cal.Rptr. 459, 591 P.2d 947 (1979). In applying that test to the facts before it, however, the opinion emphasized that the defendant was "a man who, after a long history of drug addiction and criminal behavior, was making a sincere effort to gain control of his life and function responsibly in the community." According to his testimony he was "a past offender trying desperately to reform himself but was prevented from doing so by an overzealous law enforcement agent who importuned him relentlessly until his resistance was worn down and overcome." Of course, the particular defendant's predisposition and resistance is supposed to be irrelevant under the objective test. Nevertheless, the Court might have viewed the governmental conduct quite differently if it had been directed against a wary professional criminal who was trying to test the agent's sincerity.

The last point suggests another difficulty with objective or definite standards of government conduct in inducement cases. If the professional criminals learn about these standards, they may be able to exploit them by insisting that prospective drug buyers, etc., engage in conduct which, objectively considered, constitutes entrapment. Drawing the line between legitimate "undercover activity, strategy or deception," and unlawful inducement or furtherance, may be difficult without some consideration of the character and motives of the individual against whom the deception is aimed.

Another consideration is that inducements offered to persons in particularly sensitive positions may seem less reprehensible than similar inducements offered to members of the public generally. For example, United States v. Myers, 692 F.2d 823 (2d Cir.1982), involved a bribery conviction growing out of the "Abscam" scandal. The court there rejected an argument that it was excessive for undercover agents to offer members of Congress cash bribes of $50,000 together with offers of financing multi-million dollar projects in their districts. The inducements insidiously appealed to the recipients' legitimate interests in furthering the economic health of their districts, as well as their personal greed. See also, United States v. Kelly, 707 F.2d 1460 (D.C.Cir.1983), reversing a district court's order dismissing an indictment in an Abscam case where the F.B.I.'s pursuit of the initially reluctant Congressman was particularly relentless. Should public officials be expected to have an extraordinary resistance to temptation, or is it outrageous for government agents to offer them enormous bribes without prior suspicion? The district judge in the Kelly case made the following important point:

When improper proposals are rejected in these virtue-testing ventures, the guinea pig should be left alone. In ordinary real life situations, anyone who would seek to corrupt a Congressman would certainly not continue to press in the face of a rejection for fear of being reported and arrested. The FBI of course had no such restraints in this case. 539 F.Supp. at 373–74.

Supplemental Commentary

In State v. Beddoes, 890 P.2d 1 (Utah App.1995), the Utah Court of Appeals interpreted Utah's "objective" statutory entrapment defense, similar to the Hawaii statute, which "focuses solely on the actions of the government, and not on the defendant's predisposition, to determine whether entrapment has occurred." The Court explained that, under the objective standard, the pivotal questions are: (1) "Does the conduct of the government comport with a fair and honorable administration of justice;" and (2) "Did the government conduct create a substantial risk that an average person would be induced to commit the crime defendant committed?" The *Beddoes* case involved a "reverse sting" in which the informer took the initiative in approaching the defendant and selling him $1600 worth of marijuana on credit. The jury found that the defendant was not entrapped, and the Utah Court of Appeals affirmed the conviction.

"Sentencing entrapment" occurs when government agents induce a defendant to engage in some additional conduct that he is not predisposed to commit in order to increase his sentence. For example, in United States v. Cannon, 886 F.Supp. 705 (D.N.D.1995), the jury found defendants guilty of using a machine gun in the course of a drug transaction, an enhancement which called for a mandatory 30–year prison term. The defendants had offered to buy ordinary guns from undercover officers posing as drug buyers, and one of the officers took it upon himself to offer them a machine gun. The district judge held that the machine gun count should not be considered in sentencing, because "It is simply wrong and a violation of any concept of fair play that the machine gun was voluntarily injected [into the transaction] for the sole purpose of sentence enhancement." The Court of Appeals reversed the convictions on another ground. United States v. Cannon, 88 F.3d 1495 (8th Cir.1996).

Evidence of inducement short of entrapment may also justify a "downward departure" from mandatory sentence guidelines. In United States v. McClelland, 72 F.3d 717 (9th Cir.1995), defendant attempted to hire Russell to murder his estranged wife for $10,000. Russell informed the FBI, and some of the subsequent conversations between Russell and defendant about the planned murder were recorded. Defendant from time to time attempted to back out of the plan which he had initiated, but on each such occasion Russell would cajole him to go ahead. After being convicted on a federal charge of "use of interstate commerce facilities in the commission of murder-for-hire," defendant appealed on grounds of entrapment. The Court of Appeals affirmed the verdict of guilty, but also affirmed the district judge's decision to depart substantially from the sentence otherwise required by the sentencing guidelines on the ground of "imperfect entrapment."

JACOBSON v. UNITED STATES

Supreme Court of the United States, 1992.
503 U.S. 540, 112 S.Ct. 1535, 118 L.Ed.2d 174.

JUSTICE WHITE delivered the opinion of the Court.

[Jacobson was indicted for violating the Child Protection Act of 1984, which criminalizes the knowing receipt through the mails of a visual depiction [that] involves the use of a minor engaging in sexually explicit conduct. He defended unsuccessfully on the ground that the Government entrapped him into committing the crime through a series of communications from undercover agents that spanned the 26 months preceding his arrest.[5] The jury found him guilty, and the Court of Appeals affirmed.]

I

In February 1984, petitioner, a 56–year–old veteran-turned-farmer who supported his elderly father in Nebraska, ordered two magazines and a brochure from a California adult bookstore. The magazines, entitled Bare Boys I and Bare Boys II, contained photographs of nude preteen and teenage boys. The contents of the magazines startled petitioner, who testified that he had expected to receive photographs of "young men 18 years or older." * * * The young men depicted in the magazines were not engaged in sexual activity, and petitioner's receipt of the magazines was legal under both federal and Nebraska law. Within three months, the law with respect to child pornography changed; Congress passed the Act illegalizing the receipt through the mails of sexually explicit depictions of children. In the very month that the new provision became law, postal inspectors found petitioner's name on the mailing list of the California bookstore that had mailed him Bare Boys I and II. There followed over the next 2½ years, repeated efforts by two Government agencies, through five fictitious organizations and a bogus pen pal, to explore petitioner's willingness to break the new law by ordering sexually explicit photographs of children through the mail.

The Government began its efforts in January 1985 when a postal inspector sent petitioner a letter supposedly from the American Hedonist Society, which in fact was a fictitious organization. The letter included a membership application and stated the Society's doctrine: that members

---

5. The district judge instructed the jury on entrapment as follows: "As mentioned, one of the issues in this case is whether the defendant was entrapped. If the defendant was entrapped he must be found not guilty. The government has the burden of proving beyond a reasonable doubt that the defendant was not entrapped.

"If the defendant before contact with law-enforcement officers or their agents did not have any intent or disposition to commit the crime charged and was induced or persuaded by law-enforcement officers or their agents to commit that crime, then he was entrapped. On the other hand, if the defendant before contact with law-enforcement officers or their agents did have an intent or disposition to commit the crime charged, then he was not entrapped even though law-enforcement officers or their agents provided a favorable opportunity to commit the crime or made committing the crime easier or even participated in acts essential to the crime."

had the "right to read what we desire, the right to discuss similar interests with those who share our philosophy, and finally that we have the right to seek pleasure without restrictions being placed on us by outdated puritan morality." Petitioner enrolled in the organization and returned a sexual attitude questionnaire that asked him to rank on a scale of one to four his enjoyment of various sexual materials, with one being "really enjoy," two being "enjoy," three being "somewhat enjoy," and four being "do not enjoy." Petitioner ranked the entry "preteen sex" as a two, but indicated that he was opposed to pedophilia.

For a time, the Government left petitioner alone. But then a new "prohibited mail specialist" in the Postal Service found petitioner's name in a file, and in May 1986, petitioner received a solicitation from a second fictitious consumer research company, "Midlands Data Research," seeking a response from those who "believe in the joys of sex and the complete awareness of those lusty and youthful lads and lasses of the neophite [sic] age." The letter never explained whether "neophite" referred to minors or young adults. Petitioner responded: "Please feel free to send me more information, I am interested in teenage sexuality. Please keep my name confidential."

Petitioner then heard from yet another Government creation, "Heartland Institute for a New Tomorrow" (HINT), which proclaimed that it was an organization founded to protect and promote sexual freedom and freedom of choice. "We believe that arbitrarily imposed legislative sanctions restricting your sexual freedom should be rescinded through the legislative process." The letter also enclosed a second survey. Petitioner indicated that his interest in "preteen sex-homosexual" material was above average, but not high. In response to another question, petitioner wrote: "Not only sexual expression but freedom of the press is under attack. We must be ever vigilant to counter attack right wing fundamentalists who are determined to curtail our freedoms."

"HINT" replied, portraying itself as a lobbying organization seeking to repeal all statutes which regulate sexual activities, except those laws which deal with violent behavior, such as rape. "HINT is also lobbying to eliminate any legal definition of the 'age of consent'." These lobbying efforts were to be funded by sales from a catalog to be published in the future "offering the sale of various items which we believe you will find to be both interesting and stimulating." HINT also provided computer matching of group members with similar survey responses; and, although petitioner was supplied with a list of potential "pen pals," he did not initiate any correspondence.

Nevertheless, the Government's "prohibited mail specialist" began writing to petitioner, using the pseudonym "Carl Long." The letters employed a tactic known as "mirroring," which the inspector described as "reflecting whatever the interests are of the person we are writing to." Petitioner responded at first, indicating that his interest was primarily in "male-male items." Inspector "Long" wrote back: "My interests too are primarily male-male items. Are you satisfied with the type of VCR tapes available? Personally, I like the amateur stuff better if its [sic] well produced as it can get more kinky and also seems more real. I think the actors enjoy it more."

Petitioner responded: "As far as my likes are concerned, I like good looking young guys (in their late teens and early 20's) doing their thing together." Petitioner's letters to "Long" made no reference to child pornography. After writing two letters, petitioner discontinued the correspondence.

By March 1987, 34 months had passed since the Government obtained petitioner's name from the mailing list of the California bookstore, and 26 months had passed since the Postal Service had commenced its mailings to petitioner. Although petitioner had responded to surveys and letters, the Government had no evidence that petitioner had ever intentionally possessed or been exposed to child pornography. The Postal Service had not checked petitioner's mail to determine whether he was receiving questionable mailings from persons—other than the Government—involved in the child pornography industry.

At this point, a second Government agency, the Customs Service, included petitioner in its own child pornography sting, "Operation Borderline," after receiving his name on lists submitted by the Postal Service. Using the name of a fictitious Canadian company called "Produit Outaouais," the Customs Service mailed petitioner a brochure advertising photographs of young boys engaging in sex. Petitioner placed an order that was never filled.

The Postal Service also continued its efforts in the Jacobson case, writing to petitioner as the "Far Eastern Trading Company Ltd." The letter began: "As many of you know, much hysterical nonsense has appeared in the American media concerning 'pornography' and what must be done to stop it from coming across your borders. This brief letter does not allow us to give much comments; however, why is your government spending millions of dollars to exercise international censorship while tons of drugs, which makes yours the world's most crime ridden country are passed through easily."

The letter went on to say: "We have devised a method of getting these to you without prying eyes of U.S. Customs seizing your mail. * * * After consultations with American solicitors, we have been advised that once we have posted our material through your system, it cannot be opened for any inspection without authorization of a judge." The letter invited petitioner to send for more information. It also asked petitioner to sign an affirmation that he was "not a law enforcement officer or agent of the U.S. Government acting in an undercover capacity for the purpose of entrapping Far Eastern Trading Company, its agents or customers." Petitioner responded. A catalogue was sent, and petitioner ordered "Boys Who Love Boys," a pornographic magazine depicting young boys engaged in various sexual activities. Petitioner was arrested after a controlled delivery of a photocopy of the magazine.

When petitioner was asked at trial why he placed such an order, he explained that the Government had succeeded in piquing his curiosity: "Well, the statement was made of all the trouble and the hysteria over pornography and I wanted to see what the material was. It didn't describe the—I didn't know for sure what kind of sexual action they were referring to in the Canadian letter."

In petitioner's home, the Government found the Bare Boys magazines and materials that the Government had sent to him in the course of its protracted investigation, but no other materials that would indicate that petitioner collected or was actively interested in child pornography. * * *

II

There can be no dispute about the evils of child pornography or the difficulties that laws and law enforcement have encountered in eliminating it. Likewise, there can be no dispute that the Government may use undercover agents to enforce the law. "It is well settled that the fact that officers or employees of the Government merely afford opportunities or facilities for the commission of the offense does not defeat the prosecution. Artifice and stratagem may be employed to catch those engaged in criminal enterprises." Sorrells v. United States, 287 U.S. 435, 441 (1932); Sherman v. United States, 356 U.S., at 372; United States v. Russell, 411 U.S. 423, 435–436 (1973).

In their zeal to enforce the law, however, Government agents may not originate a criminal design, implant in an innocent person's mind the disposition to commit a criminal act, and then induce commission of the crime so that the Government may prosecute. Where the Government has induced an individual to break the law and the defense of entrapment is at issue, as it was in this case, the prosecution must prove beyond reasonable doubt that the defendant was disposed to commit the criminal act prior to first being approached by Government agents.[6]

---

6. * * * The Government does not dispute that it induced petitioner to commit the crime. The sole issue is whether the Government carried its burden of proving that petitioner was predisposed to violate the law before the Government intervened. The dissent is mistaken in claiming that this is an innovation in entrapment law and in suggesting that the Government's conduct prior to the moment of solicitation is irrelevant. The Court rejected these arguments five decades ago in *Sorrells,* when the Court wrote that the Government may not punish an individual for an alleged offense which is the product of the creative activity of its own officials "and that in such a case the Government is in no position to object to evidence of the activities of its representatives in relation to the accused * * *." 287 U.S., at 451. Indeed, the proposition that the accused must be predisposed prior to contact with law enforcement officers is so firmly established that the Government conceded the point at oral argument, submitting that the evidence it developed during the course of its investigation was probative because it indicated petitioner's state of mind prior to the commencement of the Government's investigation.

This long-established standard in no way encroaches upon Government investigatory activities. Indeed, the Government's internal guidelines for undercover operations provide that an inducement to commit a crime should not be offered unless:

"(a) there is a reasonable indication, based on information developed through informants or other means, that the subject is engaging, has engaged, or is likely to engage in illegal activity of a similar type; or

Thus, an agent deployed to stop the traffic in illegal drugs may offer the opportunity to buy or sell drugs, and, if the offer is accepted, make an arrest on the spot or later. In such a typical case, or in a more elaborate "sting" operation involving government-sponsored fencing where the defendant is simply provided with the opportunity to commit a crime, the entrapment defense is of little use because the ready commission of the criminal act amply demonstrates the defendant's predisposition. Had the agents in this case simply offered petitioner the opportunity to order child pornography through the mails, and petitioner—who must be presumed to know the law—had promptly availed himself of this criminal opportunity, it is unlikely that his entrapment defense would have warranted a jury instruction.

But that is not what happened here. By the time petitioner finally placed his order, he had already been the target of 26 months of repeated mailings and communications from Government agents and fictitious organizations. Therefore, although he had become predisposed to break the law by May 1987, it is our view that the Government did not prove that this predisposition was independent and not the product of the attention that the Government had directed at petitioner since January 1985.

The prosecution's evidence of predisposition falls into two categories: evidence developed prior to the Postal Service's mail campaign, and that developed during the course of the investigation. The sole piece of preinvestigation evidence is petitioner's 1984 order and receipt of the Bare Boys magazines. But this is scant if any proof of petitioner's predisposition to commit an illegal act, the criminal character of which a defendant is presumed to know. It may indicate a predisposition to view sexually-oriented photographs that are responsive to his sexual tastes; but evidence that merely indicates a generic inclination to act within a broad range, not all of which is criminal, is of little probative value in establishing predisposition.

Furthermore, petitioner was acting within the law at the time he received these magazines. Receipt through the mails of sexually explicit depictions of children for noncommercial use did not become illegal under federal law until May 1984, and Nebraska had no law that forbade petitioner's possession of such material until 1988. Evidence of predisposition to do what once was lawful is not, by itself, sufficient to show predisposition to do what is now illegal, for there is a common understanding that most people obey the law even when they disapprove of it. This obedience may reflect a generalized respect for legality or the fear of prosecution, but for whatever reason, the law's prohibitions are matters of consequence. Hence, the fact that petitioner legally ordered and received the Bare Boys magazines does little to further the Govern-

"(b) The opportunity for illegal activity has been structured so that there is reason for believing that persons drawn to the opportunity, or brought to it, are predisposed to engage in the contemplat- ed illegal activity." Attorney General's Guidelines on FBI Undercover Operations (Dec. 31, 1980), reprinted in S.Rep. No. 97–682, p. 551 (1982).

ment's burden of proving that petitioner was predisposed to commit a criminal act. This is particularly true given petitioner's unchallenged testimony was that he did not know until they arrived that the magazines would depict minors.

The prosecution's evidence gathered during the investigation also fails to carry the Government's burden. Petitioner's responses to the many communications prior to the ultimate criminal act were at most indicative of certain personal inclinations, including a predisposition to view photographs of preteen sex and a willingness to promote a given agenda by supporting lobbying organizations. Even so, petitioner's responses hardly support an inference that he would commit the crime of receiving child pornography through the mails. * * *

On the other hand, the strong arguable inference is that, by waving the banner of individual rights and disparaging the legitimacy and constitutionality of efforts to restrict the availability of sexually explicit materials, the Government not only excited petitioner's interest in sexually explicit materials banned by law but also exerted substantial pressure on petitioner to obtain and read such material as part of a fight against censorship and the infringement of individual rights. * * *

Petitioner's ready response to these solicitations cannot be enough to establish beyond reasonable doubt that he was predisposed, prior to the Government acts intended to create predisposition, to commit the crime of receiving child pornography through the mails. The evidence that petitioner was ready and willing to commit the offense came only after the Government had devoted 2½ years to convincing him that he had or should have the right to engage in the very behavior proscribed by law. Rational jurors could not say beyond a reasonable doubt that petitioner possessed the requisite predisposition prior to the Government's investigation and that it existed independent of the Government's many and varied approaches to petitioner. * * * When the Government's quest for convictions leads to the apprehension of an otherwise law-abiding citizen who, if left to his own devices, likely would have never run afoul of the law, the courts should intervene.

Because we conclude that this is such a case and that the prosecution failed, as a matter of law, to adduce evidence to support the jury verdict that petitioner was predisposed, independent of the Government's acts and beyond a reasonable doubt, to violate the law by receiving child pornography through the mails, we reverse the Court of Appeals' judgment affirming the conviction of Keith Jacobson.

JUSTICE O'CONNOR, with whom THE CHIEF JUSTICE and JUSTICE KENNEDY join, and with whom JUSTICE SCALIA joins except as to Part II, dissenting.

Keith Jacobson was offered only two opportunities to buy child pornography through the mail. Both times, he ordered. Both times, he asked for opportunities to buy more. He needed no Government agent to coax, threaten, or persuade him; no one played on his sympathies, friendship, or suggested that his committing the crime would further a greater good. In fact, no Government agent even contacted him face-to-face. The Government contends that from the enthusiasm with which Mr. Jacobson responded to the chance to commit a crime, a reasonable jury could permissibly infer beyond a reasonable doubt that he was predisposed to commit the crime. I agree. * * *

The first time the Government sent Mr. Jacobson a catalog of illegal materials, he ordered a set of photographs advertised as picturing "young boys in sex action fun." He enclosed the following note with his order: "I received your brochure and decided to place an order. If I like your product, I will order more later." For reasons undisclosed in the record, Mr. Jacobson's order was never delivered.

The second time the Government sent a catalog of illegal materials, Mr. Jacobson ordered a magazine called "Boys Who Love Boys," described as: "11 year old and 14 year old boys get it on in every way possible. Oral, anal sex and heavy masturbation. If you love boys, you will be delighted with this." Along with his order, Mr. Jacobson sent the following note: "Will order other items later. I want to be discreet in order to protect you and me."

Government agents admittedly did not offer Mr. Jacobson the chance to buy child pornography right away. Instead, they first sent questionnaires in order to make sure that he was generally interested in the subject matter. Indeed, a "cold call" in such a business would not only risk rebuff and suspicion, but might also shock and offend the uninitiated, or expose minors to suggestive materials. Mr. Jacobson's responses to the questionnaires gave the investigators reason to think he would be interested in photographs depicting preteen sex. * * *

I

* * * Today, the Court holds that Government conduct may be considered to create a predisposition to commit a crime, even before any Government action to induce the commission of the crime. In my view, this holding changes entrapment doctrine. Generally, the inquiry is whether a suspect is predisposed before the Government induces the commission of the crime, not before the Government makes initial contact with him. There is no dispute here that the Government's questionnaires and letters were not sufficient to establish inducement; they did not even suggest that Mr. Jacobson should engage in any illegal activity. If all the Government had done was to send these materials, Mr. Jacobson's entrapment defense would fail. Yet the Court holds that the Government must prove not only that a suspect was predisposed to commit the crime before the opportunity to commit it arose, but also before the Government came on the scene.

The rule that preliminary Government contact can create a predisposition has the potential to be misread by lower courts as well as criminal investigators as requiring that the Government must have sufficient evidence of a defendant's predisposition before it ever seeks to contact him. Surely the Court cannot intend to impose such a requirement, for it would mean that the Government must have a reasonable suspicion of criminal activity before it begins an investigation, a condition that we have never before imposed. The Court denies that its new rule will affect run-of-the-mill sting operations, and one hopes that it means what it says. Nonetheless, after this case, every defendant will claim that something the Government agent did before soliciting the crime "created" a predisposition that was not there before. For example, a bribe taker will claim that the description of the amount of money available was so enticing that it implanted a disposition to accept the bribe later offered. A drug buyer will claim that the description of the drug's purity and effects was so tempting that it created the urge to try it for the first time. In short, the Court's opinion could be read to prohibit the Government from advertising the seductions of criminal activity as part of its sting operation, for fear of creating a predisposition in its suspects. That limitation would be especially likely to hamper sting operations such as this one, which mimic the advertising done by genuine purveyors of pornography. No doubt the Court would protest that its opinion does not stand for so broad a proposition, but the apparent lack of a principled basis for distinguishing these scenarios exposes a flaw in the more limited rule the Court today adopts.

The Court's rule is all the more troubling because it does not distinguish between Government conduct that merely highlights the temptation of the crime itself, and Government conduct that threatens, coerces, or leads a suspect to commit a crime in order to fulfill some other obligation. For example, in *Sorrells*, the Government agent repeatedly asked for illegal liquor, coaxing the defendant to accede on the ground that "one former war buddy would get liquor for another." In *Sherman*, the Government agent played on the defendant's sympathies, pretending to be going through drug withdrawal and begging the defendant to relieve his distress by helping him buy drugs.

The Government conduct in this case is not comparable. While the Court states that the Government "exerted substantial pressure on petitioner to obtain and read such material as part of a fight against censorship and the infringement of individual rights," one looks at the record in vain for evidence of such "substantial pressure." The most one finds is letters advocating legislative action to liberalize obscenity laws, letters which could easily be ignored or thrown away. Much later, the Government sent separate mailings of catalogs of illegal materials. Nowhere did the Government suggest that the proceeds of the sale of the illegal materials would be used to support legislative reforms. While one of the HINT letters suggested that lobbying efforts would be funded by sales from a catalog, the catalogs actually sent, nearly a year later, were from different fictitious entities (Produit Outaouais and Far Eastern Trading Company), and gave no suggestion that money would be used for any political purposes. Nor did the Government claim to be organizing a civil disobedience movement, which would protest the pornography laws by breaking them. Contrary to the gloss given the evidence by the Court, the Government's suggestions of illegality may also have made buyers beware, and increased the mystique of the materials offered: "for those of you who have enjoyed youthful material * * * we have devised a method of getting these to you without prying eyes of U.S. Customs seizing your mail." Mr. Jacobson's curiosity to see what "all the trouble and the hysteria" was about, is certainly susceptible of more than one interpretation. And it is the jury that is charged with the obligation of interpreting it. In sum, the Court fails to construe the evidence in the light most favorable to the Government, and fails to draw all reasonable inferences in the Government's favor. It was surely reasonable for the jury to infer that Mr. Jacobson was predisposed beyond a reasonable doubt, even if other inferences from the evidence were also possible.

II

The second puzzling thing about the Court's opinion is its redefinition of predisposition. * * * The Court seems to add something new to the burden of proving predisposition. Not only must the Government show that a defendant was predisposed to engage in the illegal conduct, here, receiving photographs of minors engaged in sex, but also that the defendant was predisposed to break the law knowingly in order to do so. The statute violated here, however, does not require proof of specific intent to break the law; it requires only knowing receipt of visual depictions produced by using minors engaged in sexually explicit conduct. Under the Court's analysis, however, the Government must prove more to show predisposition than it need prove in order to convict.

The Court ignores the judgment of Congress that specific intent is not an element of the crime of receiving sexually explicit photographs of minors. The elements of predisposition should track the elements of the crime. The predisposition requirement is meant to eliminate the entrapment defense for those defendants who would have committed the crime anyway, even absent Government inducement. Because a defendant might very well be convicted of the crime here absent Government inducement even though he did not know his conduct was illegal, a specific intent requirement does little to distinguish between those who would commit the crime without the inducement and those who would not. In sum, although the fact that Mr. Jacobson's purchases of Bare Boys I and Bare Boys II were legal at the time may have some relevance to the question of predisposition, it is not, as the Court suggests, dispositive. * * *

There is no dispute that the jury in this case was fully and accurately instructed on the law of entrapment, and nonetheless found Mr. Jacobson guilty. Because I believe there was sufficient evidence to uphold the jury's verdict, I respectfully dissent.

UNITED STATES v. KNOX

United States Court of Appeals for the Fifth Circuit, 1997.
112 F.3d 802.

DeMoss, Circuit Judge:

A preacher and his financial advisor were caught in a government sting designed to snare money launderers. Both raised entrapment at trial, but the jury rejected the defense and they were convicted of laundering drug proceeds. Because the government failed to prove that the preacher was likely to engage in money laundering absent the government's conduct, we hold that he was entrapped as a matter of law.

BACKGROUND

Defendant/Appellant Reverend David Brace was pastor of the Faith Metro Church in Wichita, Kansas. Faith Metro had financial difficulties and, by late 1993, was heavily in debt. The church had to pay over $60,000 per month in debt service and needed to raise $10 million to pay its bondholders and other creditors. In an effort to raise money, Brace hired a Houston financial consulting firm First Diversified Financial Services, in early 1994. Brace met with Mike Clark, the president of First Diversified, and Clark's assistant, 24–year-old Defendant/Appellant Shannon Knox. Brace paid First Diversified $75,000 to prepare a prospectus for a $10.8 million limited private offering by Faith Metro. [This attempt to raise money by a private offering was unsuccessful.] * * *

In October or November 1994, Knox met Roy Clarkston, who worked for the Brazos Valley Small Business Development Center. Clarkston had several clients in the Bryan–College Station area interested in private placements, so Clark, who was also at the meeting, gave Clarkston a copy of the Faith Metro prospectus. In mid to late February 1995, Clarkston told Knox that he had several potential investors in San Antonio. Clarkston told Knox that he knew them through his business dealings in South and Central America. Brace was not present at any of these meetings and did not meet Clarkston until March 24, 1995.

At the same time Clark and Knox were seeking financing for Faith Metro, undercover federal agents were running an elaborate sting operation in San Antonio designed to catch money launderers. Beginning in October 1994, undercover agents from the United States Drug Enforcement Agency, the Internal Revenue Service, and United States Customs were involved in the operation. As part of the sting operation, undercover agents investigated Clarkston, who they suspected was a money launderer. The undercover agents told Clarkston that they were seeking to launder cocaine proceeds and requested his assistance. Clarkston suggested several long-term laundering schemes, including investing in a cattle business and a sports bar, but the undercover agents rejected the ideas, saying they were interested in short-term investments.

In early March 1995, Clarkston told the undercover agents that he had a "major big time guy," a church group, anxious to do business. At this time the undercover agents had no knowledge of Brace or Knox. On March 17, 1995, Clarkston met with the undercover agents in San Antonio and explained that he knew a minister who was interested in laundering cocaine funds, and that the preacher's representative, his financial advisor, was in town and anxious to meet with them. The undercover agents explained to Clarkston that they did not want innocent people involved in the business, and asked him if the minister knew they were cocaine traffickers and that the money would be cocaine proceeds. Clarkston replied that the preacher and the other person knew and did not care.

Later that day, Knox met with Clarkston and the undercover agents. Knox said that he was representing Brace and that he was there to negotiate a deal. Early in the conversation, the undercover agents told Knox that the money was from drug proceeds; Knox said that this was not a problem. Knox showed the prospectus to the undercover agents, who indicated that they might be able to lend Brace $3 million.

On March 24, the undercover agents met Brace for the first time at a meeting also attended by Knox and Clarkston. The undercover agents told Brace that they would be able to loan him the entire $10 million, not just the $3 million previously discussed. To make sure that Brace and Knox could handle such a large sum, the undercover agents told them that they would have a practice transfer of $100,000, a condition to which Brace readily agreed. The undercover agents then informed Brace that the money came from the sale of cocaine, and that he was being asked to launder it. Brace stated that he was not troubled by the money's source. At the end of the meeting, Brace said he was ready to start the test money, but the undercover agents told him to have patience.

Brace and Clarkston met with the undercover agents on April 26. Before the meeting, Knox told the undercover agents that he and Brace had already "contrived a system" to quickly deposit and transfer the first $100,000. At the meeting, the undercover agents gave Brace an account number for an undercover account in a London bank where Brace was to wire the $100,000 in the first test. Brace was given $100,000 in cash, which he wired to the English bank the next week.

On May 5, the undercover agents again met with Brace in San Antonio. The undercover agents suggested another $100,000 test, this time to a domestic account controlled by the undercover agents. Brace agreed to this, stating that to conceal the source of the money, he would carry it on his books as a loan. The undercover agents again gave Brace $100,000 in cash. As he counted it, he commented, "I have a feeling that neither one of you, have ever come across a pastor like me." Brace took the money and wired it the account. * * *

On May 12, the undercover agents met with Brace, Clarkston and Knox, and delivered the cash for another test, this time $150,000. Four days later Brace and Knox wired the money to the English bank. The undercover agents told Brace and Knox that they would soon be ready to transfer the entire $10 million.

On June 21, the final meeting took place. The undercover agents met Brace and Knox in a San Antonio parking lot and gave them three canvas bags purportedly containing $10 million. The bags actually contained an amount of newspaper clippings approximating the weight of $10 million in cash. Brace and Knox were arrested as they left the parking lot.

Brace and Knox were charged with money laundering in a four count indictment. [Clarkson was also charged but pleaded guilty.] * * * After a jury trial, Brace and Knox were convicted on all counts and sentenced to 175 and 97 month imprisonment, respectively.

DISCUSSION: Entrapment as a Matter of Law

Brace argues that, as a matter of law, he was entrapped. [Knox did not argue that he was entrapped as a matter of law and hence waived the issue.] "Where the Government has induced an individual to break the law, and the defense of entrapment is at issue, ... the prosecution must prove beyond reasonable doubt that the defendant was disposed to commit the criminal act prior to first being approached by Government agents." Jacobson v. United States, 503 U.S. 540, 548–49 (1992). The government concedes that Brace was induced; therefore, the evidence must prove beyond reasonable doubt that Brace was predisposed to launder money. Because this is a sufficiency review, we will reverse only if no rational juror could have found predisposition beyond a reasonable doubt. * * *

The en banc Seventh Circuit recently wrestled with the meaning of Jacobson in United States v. Hollingsworth, 27 F.3d 1196 (7th Cir.1994) (en banc). Writing for the majority, Chief Judge Posner stated that in examining predisposition, we must ask ourselves what the defendant would have done, had the government not been involved. To properly answer that question, we must look to more than the defendant's mental state; we must also consider the defendant's skills, background and contacts. As Chief Judge Posner explained, predisposition "has positional as well as dispositional force. The defendant must be so situated by reason of previous training or experience or occupation or acquaintances that it is likely that if the government had not induced him to commit the crime some criminal would have done so...." Id. at 1200. A defendant may have the desire to commit the crime, but may be without any ability to do so. The defendant is able to commit the crime only when the government steps in and provides the means to do so. In those cases, we cannot say that, absent government involvement, the defendant would likely have committed the crime.

The facts of *Hollingsworth* illustrate the Seventh Circuit's point. The *Hollingsworth* defendants were an orthodontist and a farmer, both from Arkansas. The pair, who had attempted and failed at many business ventures, decided to become international financiers, "a vocation for which neither had any training, contacts, aptitude, or experience." They secured two foreign banking licenses, one from Grenada, and attempted to make money. Unfortunately, they had no customers and were rapidly going broke. The orthodontist, deciding to raise capital by selling the Grenadan banking license, placed an ad in *USA Today* offering the license for $29,950.

A Customs agent saw the ad and, "knowing that foreign banks are sometimes used for money laundering, ... assumed that someone who wanted to sell one would possibly be interested in money laundering."

The agent, acting undercover, contacted the orthodontist and, ultimately, persuaded him to launder money. The orthodontist and farmer were convicted of money laundering.

The en banc Seventh Circuit reversed, stating that, "had the government left [him] to his own devices . . . in all likelihood [the orthodontist], a middle-aged man who so far as anyone knows had never before committed any crime, would never have committed a money-laundering or related offense." The government "turned two harmless, though weak, foolish, . . . and greedy, men into felons." Chief Judge Posner made clear that "whatever it takes to become an international money launderer, they did not have it." "Even if they had wanted to go into money laundering before they met [the agent,] . . . the likelihood that they could have done so was remote. They were objectively harmless." It was "highly unlikely that if [the agent] had not providentially appeared someone else would have guided them into money laundering. No real criminal would do business with such [novices]."

We recognize that the Seventh Circuit's reading of *Jacobson* has not been universally embraced. The Ninth Circuit has rejected the Seventh Circuit's positional predisposition requirement and the First Circuit has adopted a different test. See United States v. Thickstun, 1997 WL 152744, * 4 (9th Cir. April 3, 1997); United States v. Gendron, 18 F.3d 955, 962–63 (1st Cir.1994); see also *Hollingsworth*, 27 F.3d at 1211 (Easterbrook, J., dissenting) (criticizing positional predisposition requirement). In *Gendron*, then Chief Judge (now Justice) Breyer held that *Jacobson* stands for the proposition that in trying to induce the target of a sting to commit a crime, the government may not confront him with circumstances that are different from the ordinary circumstances a real criminal would use in inducing one to engage in wrongdoing. * * * Nonetheless, we are persuaded that the Seventh Circuit's Hollingsworth decision is correct. See Paul Marcus, Presenting Back From the [Almost] Dead, the Entrapment Defense, 47 Fla. L. Rev. 205, 233–34 (1995) (arguing Hollingsworth is proper approach to entrapment law). The Supreme Court instructs that in determining predisposition we are to ask what the defendant would have done absent government involvement. To give effect to that command, we must look not only to the defendant's mental state (his "disposition"), but also to whether the defendant was able and likely, based on experience, training, and contacts, to actually commit the crime (his "position").

In this case, the result would not differ under the First Circuit's *Gendron* test. The government failed to prove that real drug dealers would provide the same, or even similar, terms to a launderer as the undercover agents offered Brace. Thus, the government failed to offer any evidence that Brace would accept an "ordinary opportunity" to launder money.

Under the deal worked out between Brace and the undercover agents, Brace would have the use of $10 million for four years. He would pay back $50,000 a month for the first two years, and then $100,000 for the last two. At the end of four years, a balloon payment of $6.4 million would be due. The money would be paid back without interest. With the undercover agents' approval, Brace would use the money to pay the church's debts. This arrangement was similar to Brace's proposal in the prospectus, except the payments were lower and there was no interest.

This structuring was necessary to Brace's participation. Brace had pressing financial needs and needed to restructure his debts. He needed the use of $10 million for several years. Had the laundering of the $10 million been structured the same as the test amounts, the scheme would have offered no benefit to Brace. Under the tests, Brace had to immediately wire the money, and thus could not use it. Without use of the money for several years, Brace had no incentive to launder money. Therefore, without the deal being structured as it was, Brace would not have laundered money.

The government presented no evidence as to what is involved in an ordinary opportunity to launder money. Perhaps real drug dealers regularly give launderers the interest free use of millions of dollars for several years, with low monthly payments and a large balloon payment. If that is the case, then we can infer that Brace would accept an ordinary opportunity to launder drug proceeds. But, it seems just as likely that real drug dealers would not want their money tied up for years, with only token payments coming back at first. It also seems just as likely that real drug dealers would not allow a launderer to use $10 million in to-be-laundered cash to pay off current debts, hoping that an income stream was available to pay them back. Instead, real drug dealers might only give the cash as needed, and ask that it be laundered immediately, so that the launderer receives no benefit from the use of the money, as in the tests. If the latter scenario is how real drug dealers operate, then Brace would likely not have accepted an ordinary opportunity to launder money.

The fact is that we do not know what constitutes an ordinary opportunity to launder money. This is a subject on which the record is silent. Because the record does not show what is an ordinary opportunity to launder money, it follows that it provides no support for the proposition that Brace would accept an ordinary opportunity to launder money. Because predisposition is an issue on which the government bears the burden of proof, we would hold that, under the First Circuit's test, the evidence is insufficient to conclude that Brace was predisposed to launder money. * * *

After examining the record, we must conclude that the government failed to prove that Brace was in a position to launder money. When we ask the question of what Brace would have done if he had never met the undercover agents, we cannot answer "launder money for real drug dealers." In all likelihood, Brace never would have laundered money, but instead would have missed his bond payments and been forced into bankruptcy, as ultimately happened. Because the government failed to establish that Brace would have laundered money absent government involvement, the evidence is insufficient to prove predisposition.

Accordingly, we hold that Brace was entrapped as a matter of law, and his convictions must be reversed.

*

Part Two

SELF–INCRIMINATION AND THE RIGHT TO COUNSEL

Chapter 9

THE "ACCUSATORIAL" SYSTEM OF JUSTICE

MORAN v. BURBINE

Supreme Court of the United States, 1986.
475 U.S. 412, 106 S.Ct. 1135, 89 L.Ed.2d 410.

Justice O'Connor delivered the opinion of the Court. * * *

On the morning of March 3, 1977, Mary Jo Hickey was found unconscious in a factory parking lot in Providence, Rhode Island. Suffering from injuries to her skull apparently inflicted by a metal pipe found at the scene, she was rushed to a nearby hospital. Three weeks later she died from her wounds.

Several months after her death, the Cranston, Rhode Island police arrested respondent and two others in connection with a local burglary. Shortly before the arrest, Detective Ferranti of the Cranston police force had learned from a confidential informant that the man responsible for Ms. Hickey's death lived at a certain address and went by the name of "Butch." Upon discovering that respondent lived at that address and was known by that name, Detective Ferranti informed respondent of his *Miranda* rights. When respondent refused to execute a written waiver, Detective Ferranti spoke separately with the two other suspects arrested on the breaking and entering charge and obtained statements further implicating respondent in Ms. Hickey's murder. At approximately 6:00 p.m., Detective Ferranti telephoned the police in Providence to convey the information he had uncovered. An hour later, three officers from that department arrived at the Cranston headquarters for the purpose of questioning respondent about the murder.

That same evening, at about 7:45 p.m., respondent's sister telephoned the Public Defender's Office to obtain legal assistance for her brother. Her sole concern was the breaking and entering charge, as she was unaware that respondent was then under suspicion for murder. She asked for Richard Casparian who had been scheduled to meet with respondent earlier that afternoon to discuss another charge unrelated to either the break-in or the murder. As soon as the conversation ended, the attorney who took the call attempted to reach Mr. Casparian. When those efforts were unsuccessful, she telephoned Allegra Munson, another Assistant Public Defender, and told her about respondent's arrest and his sister's subsequent request that the office represent him.

At 8:15 p.m., Ms. Munson telephoned the Cranston police station and asked that her call be transferred to the detective division. In the words of the Supreme Court of Rhode Island, whose factual findings we treat as presumptively correct, 28 U.S.C. § 2254(d), the conversation proceeded as follows:

> "A male voice responded with the word 'Detectives.' Ms. Munson identified herself and asked if Brian Burbine was being held; the person responded affirmatively. Ms. Munson explained to the person that Burbine was represented by attorney Casparian who was not available; she further stated that she would act as Burbine's legal counsel in the event that the police intended to place him in a lineup or question him. The unidentified person told Ms. Munson that the police would not be questioning Burbine or putting him in a lineup and that they were through with him for the night. Ms. Munson was not informed that the Providence Police were at the Cranston police station or that Burbine was a suspect in Mary's murder."

At all relevant times, respondent was unaware of his sister's efforts to retain counsel and of the fact and contents of Ms. Munson's telephone conversation.

Less than an hour later, the police brought respondent to an interrogation room and conducted the first of a series of interviews concerning the murder. Prior to each session, respondent was informed of his *Miranda* rights, and on three separate occasions he signed a written form acknowledging that he understood his right to the presence of an attorney and explicitly indicating that he "[did] not want an attorney called or appointed for [him]" before he gave a statement. Uncontradicted evidence at the suppression hearing indicated that at least twice during the course of the evening, respondent was left in a room where he had access to a telephone, which he apparently declined to use. Eventually, respondent signed three written statements fully admitting to the murder.

[The statements were admitted into evidence at Burbine's trial, and the state Supreme Court affirmed the conviction for murder.]

After unsuccessfully petitioning the United States District Court for the District of Rhode Island for a writ of habeas corpus, respondent appealed to the Court of Appeals for the First Circuit. That court reversed. 753 F.2d 178 (1985). Finding it unnecessary to reach any arguments under the Sixth and Fourteenth Amendments, the court held that the police's conduct had fatally tainted respondent's "otherwise valid" waiver of his Fifth Amendment privilege against self incrimination and right to counsel. The court reasoned that by failing to inform respondent that an attorney had called and that she had been assured that no questioning would take place until the next day, the police had deprived respondent of information crucial to his ability to waive his rights knowingly and intelligently. The court also found that the record would support "no other explanation for the refusal to tell Burbine of Attorney Munson's call than * * * deliberate or reckless irresponsibility." This kind of "blameworthy action by the police," the court concluded, together with respondent's ignorance of the telephone call, "vitiate[d] any claim that [the] waiver of counsel was knowing and voluntary."

We granted certiorari to decide whether a pre-arraignment confession preceded by an otherwise valid waiver must be suppressed either because the police misinformed an inquiring attorney about their plans concerning the suspect or because they failed to inform the suspect of the attorney's efforts to reach him.

We now reverse.

II

In *Miranda v. Arizona*, the Court recognized that custodial interrogations, by their very nature, generate "compelling pressures which work to undermine the individual's will to resist and to compel him to speak where he would not otherwise do so freely." To combat this inherent compulsion, and thereby protect the Fifth Amendment privilege against self incrimination, *Miranda* imposed on the police an obligation to follow certain procedures in their dealings with the accused. In particular, prior to the initiation of questioning, they must fully apprise the suspect of the state's intention to use his statements to secure a conviction, and must inform him of his rights to remain silent and to "have counsel present * * * if [he] so desires." Beyond this duty to inform, *Miranda* requires that the police respect the accused's decision to exercise the rights outlined in the warnings. "If the individual indicates in any manner, at any time prior to or during questioning, that he wishes to remain silent, [or if he] states that he wants an attorney, the interrogation must cease."

Respondent does not dispute that the Providence police followed these procedures with precision. The record amply supports the state-court findings that the police administered the required warnings, sought to assure that respondent understood his rights, and obtained an express written waiver prior to eliciting each of the three statements. Nor does respondent contest the Rhode Island courts' determination that he at no point requested the presence of a lawyer. He contends instead that the confessions must be suppressed because the police's failure to inform him of the attorney's telephone call deprived him of information essential to his ability to knowingly waive his Fifth Amendment rights. In the alternative, he suggests that to fully protect the Fifth Amendment values served by *Miranda*, we should extend that decision to condemn the conduct of the Providence police. We address each contention in turn.

A

Echoing the standard first articulated in *Johnson v. Zerbst*, 304 U.S. 458, 464 (1938), *Miranda* holds that "[t]he defendant may waive effectuation" of the rights conveyed in the warnings "provided the waiver is made voluntarily, knowingly and intelligently." The inquiry has two distinct dimensions. First the relinquishment of the right must have been voluntary in the sense that it was the product of a free and deliberate choice rather than intimidation, coercion or deception. Second, the waiver must have been made with a full awareness both of the nature of the right being abandoned and the consequences of the decision to abandon it. Only if the "totality of the circumstances surrounding the interrogation" reveal both an uncoerced choice and the requisite level of comprehension may a court properly conclude that the *Miranda* rights have been waived.

Under this standard, we have no doubt that respondent validly waived his right to remain silent and to the presence of counsel. The voluntariness of the waiver is not at issue. As the Court of Appeals correctly acknowledged, the record is devoid of any suggestion that police resorted to physical or psychological pressure to elicit the statements. Indeed it appears that it was respondent, and not the police, who spontaneously initiated the conversation that led to the first and most damaging confession. Nor is there any question about respondent's comprehension of the full panoply of rights set out in the *Miranda* warnings and of the potential consequences of a decision to relinquish them. Nonetheless, the Court of Appeals believed that the "[d]eliberate or reckless" conduct of the police, in particular their failure to inform respondent of the telephone call, fatally undermined the validity of the otherwise proper waiver. We find this conclusion untenable as a matter of both logic and precedent.

Events occurring outside of the presence of the suspect and entirely unknown to him surely can have no bearing on the capacity to comprehend and knowingly relinquish a constitutional right. Under the analysis of the Court of Appeals, the same defendant, armed with the same information and confronted with precisely the same police conduct, would have knowingly waived his *Miranda* rights had a lawyer not telephoned the police station to inquire about his status. Nothing in any of our waiver decisions or in our understanding of the essential components of a valid waiver requires so incongruous a result. No doubt the additional information would have been useful to respondent; perhaps even it might have affected his decision to confess. But we have never read the Constitution to require that the police supply a suspect with a flow of information to help him calibrate his self interest in deciding whether to speak or stand by his rights. * * * Nor do we believe that the level of the police's culpability in failing to inform respondent of the telephone call has any bearing on the validity of the waiver. In light of the state-court findings that there was no "conspiracy or collusion" on the part of the police, we have serious doubts about whether the Court of Appeals was free to conclude that their conduct constituted "deliberate or reckless irresponsibility." But whether intentional or inadvertent, the state of mind of the police is irrelevant to the question of the intelligence and voluntariness of respondent's election to abandon his rights. Although highly inappropriate, even deliberate deception of an attorney could not possibly affect a suspect's decision to waive his *Miranda* rights unless he were at least aware of the incident. * * *

B

* * * [R]eading *Miranda* to require the police in each instance to inform a suspect of an attorney's efforts to reach him would work a substantial and, we think, inappropriate shift in the subtle balance struck in that decision. Custodial interrogations implicate two competing concerns. On the one hand, "the need for police questioning as a tool for effective enforcement of criminal laws" cannot be doubted. Admissions of guilt are more than merely "desirable;" they are essential to society's compelling interest in finding, convicting and punishing those who violate the law. On the other hand, the Court has recognized that the interrogation process is "inherently coercive" and that, as a consequence, there exists a substantial risk that the police will inadvertently traverse the fine line between legitimate efforts to elicit admissions and constitutionally impermissible compulsion. *Miranda* attempted to reconcile these opposing concerns by giving the *defendant* the power to exert some control over the course of the interrogation. Declining to adopt the more extreme position that the actual presence of a lawyer was necessary to dispel the coercion inherent in custodial interrogation, the Court found that the suspect's Fifth Amendment rights could be adequately protected by less intrusive means. Police questioning, often an essential part of the investigatory process, could continue in its traditional form, the Court held, but only if the suspect clearly understood that, at any time, he could bring the proceeding to a halt or, short of that, call in an attorney to give advice and monitor the conduct of his interrogators.

The position urged by respondent would upset this carefully drawn approach in a manner that is both unnecessary for the protection of the Fifth Amendment privilege and injurious to legitimate law enforcement. Because, as *Miranda* holds, full comprehension of the rights to remain silent and request an attorney are sufficient to dispel whatever coercion is inherent in the interrogation process, a rule requiring the police to inform the suspect of an attorney's efforts to contact him would contribute to the protection of the Fifth Amendment privilege only incidentally, if at all. This minimal benefit, however, would come at a substantial cost to society's legitimate and substantial interest in securing admissions of guilt. Indeed, the very premise of the Court of Appeals was not that awareness of Ms. Munson's phone call would have dissipated the coercion of the interrogation room, but that it might have convinced respondent not to speak at all. Because neither the letter nor purposes of *Miranda* require this additional handicap on otherwise permissible investigatory efforts, we are unwilling to expand the *Miranda* rules to require the police to keep the suspect abreast of the status of his legal representation. * * *

We hold therefore that the Court of Appeals erred in finding that the Federal Constitution required the exclusion of the three inculpatory statements. Accordingly, we reverse and remand for proceedings consistent with this opinion.

So ordered.

JUSTICE STEVENS, with whom JUSTICE BRENNAN and JUSTICE MARSHALL join, dissenting.

This case poses fundamental questions about our system of justice. As this Court has long recognized, and reaffirmed only weeks ago, "ours is an accusatorial and not an inquisitorial system." *Miller v. Fenton*, 106 S.Ct. 445, 449 (1985).[1] The Court's opinion today represents a startling departure from that basic insight. * * *

The murder of Mary Jo Hickey was a vicious crime, fully meriting a sense of outrage and a desire to find and prosecute the perpetrator swiftly and effectively. Indeed, by the time Burbine was arrested on an unrelated breaking and entering charge, the Hickey murder had been the subject of a local television special. Not surprisingly, Detective Ferranti, the Cranston Detective who "broke" the case, was rewarded with a special commendation for his efforts.

The recognition that ours is an accusatorial, and not an inquisitorial system nevertheless requires that the government's actions, even in responding to this brutal crime, respect those liberties and rights that distinguish this society from most others. As Justice Jackson observed shortly after his return from Nuremberg, cases of this kind present "a real dilemma in a free society * * * for the defendant is shielded by such safeguards as no system of law except the Anglo–American concedes to him."[2] Justice Frankfurter similarly emphasized that it is "a fair sum-

1. Justice Frankfurter succinctly explained the character of that distinction in his opinion in *Watts v. Indiana*, 338 U.S. 49, 54 (1949):

"Ours is the accusatorial as opposed to the inquisitorial system. Such has been the characteristic of Anglo–American criminal justice since it freed itself from practices borrowed by the Star Chamber from the Continent whereby an accused was interrogated in secret for hours on end. Under our system society carries the burden of proving its charge against the accused not out of his own mouth. It must establish its case, not by interrogation of the accused even under judicial safeguards, but by evidence independently secured through skillful investigation. 'The law will not suffer a prisoner to be made the deluded instrument of his own conviction.' 2 Hawkins, Pleas of the Crown, c. 46, § 34 (8th ed. 1924). The requirement of specific charges, their proof beyond a reasonable doubt, the protection of the accused from confessions

extorted through whatever form of police pressures, the right to a prompt hearing before a magistrate, the right to assistance of counsel, to be supplied by government when circumstances make it necessary, the duty to advise an accused of his constitutional rights—these are all characteristics of the accusatorial system and manifestations of its demands. Protracted, systematic and uncontrolled subjection of an accused to interrogation by the police for the purpose of eliciting disclosures or confession is subversive of the accusatorial system."

2. "Amid much that is irrelevant or trivial, one serious situation seems to me to stand out in these cases. The suspect neither had nor was advised of his right to get counsel. This presents a real dilemma in a free society. To subject one without counsel to questioning which may and is intended to convict him is a real peril to individual freedom. To bring in a lawyer means a real peril to solution of the crime, because, under our adversary system, he deems that his

mary of history to say that the safeguards of liberty have been forged in controversies involving not very nice people." And, almost a century and a half ago, Macaulay observed that the guilt of Titus Oates could not justify his conviction by improper methods: "That Oates was a bad man is not a sufficient excuse; for the guilty are almost always the first to suffer those hardships which are afterwards used as precedents against the innocent."

The Court's holding focuses on the period after a suspect has been taken into custody and before he has been charged with an offense. The core of the Court's holding is that police interference with an attorney's access to her client during that period is not unconstitutional. The Court reasons that a State has a compelling interest, not simply in custodial interrogation, but in lawyer-free, incommunicado custodial interrogation. Such incommunicado interrogation is so important that a lawyer may be given false information that prevents her presence and representation; it is so important that police may refuse to inform a suspect of his attorney's communications and immediate availability. This conclusion flies in the face of this Court's repeated expressions of deep concern about incommunicado questioning. Until today, incommunicado questioning has been viewed with the strictest scrutiny by this Court; today, incommunicado questioning is embraced as a societal goal of the highest order that justifies police deception of the shabbiest kind.

It is not only the Court's ultimate conclusion that is deeply disturbing; it is also its manner of reaching that conclusion. The Court completely rejects an entire body of law on the subject—the many carefully reasoned state decisions that have come to precisely the opposite conclusion.* The Court similarly dismisses the fact that the police deception which it sanctions quite clearly violates the American Bar Association's Standards for Criminal Justice[3]—Standards which The Chief Justice has

sole duty is to protect his client—guilty or innocent—and that in such a capacity he owes no duty whatever to help society solve its crime problem. Under this conception of criminal procedure, any lawyer worth his salt will tell the suspect in no uncertain terms to make no statement to police under any circumstances.

"If the State may arrest on suspicion and interrogate without counsel, there is no denying the fact that it largely negates the benefits of the constitutional guaranty of the right to assistance of counsel. Any lawyer who has ever been called into a case after his client has 'told all' and turned any evidence he has over to the Government, knows how helpless he is to protect his client against the facts thus disclosed.

"I suppose the view one takes will turn on what one thinks should be the right of an accused person against the State. Is it his right to have the judgment on the facts? Or is it his right to have a judgment based on only such evidence as he

cannot conceal from the authorities, who cannot compel him to testify in court and also cannot question him before? Our system comes close to the latter by any interpretation, for the defendant is shielded by such safeguards as no system of law except the Anglo–American concedes to him." *Watts v. Indiana*, 338 U.S. 49, 59 (1949) (Jackson, J., concurring in result).

* The state court decisions are reviewed in People v. Houston, 42 Cal.3d 595, 230 Cal.Rptr. 141, 724 P.2d 1166 (1986). The California Supreme Court found the majority opinion in *Moran* unpersuasive, and held a voluntary confession inadmissible on state grounds where police deliberately kept the defendant ignorant that a lawyer retained by friends was at the police station attempting to consult with him.

3. See ABA Standards for Criminal Justice 5–5.1 (2d ed. 1980) ("Counsel should be provided to the accused as soon as feasible after custody begins"); ABA Standards for

described as "the single most comprehensive and probably the most monumental undertaking in the field of criminal justice ever attempted by the American legal profession in our national history," and which this Court frequently finds helpful. And, of course, the Court dismisses the fact that the American Bar Association has emphatically endorsed the prevailing state court position and expressed its serious concern about the effect that a contrary view—a view, such as the Court's, that exalts incommunicado interrogation, sanctions police deception, and demeans the right to consult with an attorney—will have in police stations and courtrooms throughout this Nation. Of greatest importance, the Court misapprehends or rejects the central principles that have, for several decades, animated this Court's decisions concerning incommunicado interrogation.

Police interference with communications between an attorney and his client is a recurrent problem. The factual variations in the many state court opinions condemning this interference as a violation of the federal Constitution suggest the variety of contexts in which the problem emerges. In Oklahoma, police led a lawyer to several different locations while they interrogated the suspect; in Oregon, police moved a suspect to a new location when they learned that his lawyer was on his way; in Illinois, authorities failed to tell a suspect that his lawyer had arrived at the jail and asked to see him; in Massachusetts, police did not tell suspects that their lawyers were at or near the police station. In all these cases, the police not only failed to inform the suspect, but also misled the attorneys. The scenarios vary, but the core problem of police interference remains. * * *

The Court makes the argument that requiring police to inform a suspect of his attorney's communications to and about him is not required because it would upset the careful "balance" of *Miranda*. * * *

The Court's balancing approach is profoundly misguided. The cost of suppressing evidence of guilt will always make the value of a procedural safeguard appear "minimal," "marginal," or "incremental." Indeed, the value of any trial at all seems like a "procedural technicality" when balanced against the interest in administering prompt justice to a murderer or a rapist caught redhanded. The individual interest in procedural safeguards that minimize the risk of error is easily discounted when the fact of guilt appears certain beyond doubt.

What is the cost of requiring the police to inform a suspect of his attorney's call? It would decrease the likelihood that custodial interrogation will enable the police to obtain a confession. This is certainly a real cost, but it is the same cost that this Court has repeatedly found necessary to preserve the character of our free society and our rejection of an inquisitorial system. * * * The "cost" that concerns the Court amounts to nothing more than an acknowledgment that the law enforcement interest in obtaining convictions suffers whenever a suspect exer-

Criminal Justice 5–7.1 (2d ed. 1980) ("At the earliest opportunity, a person in custo- dy should be effectively placed in communi- cation with a lawyer").

cises the rights that are afforded by our system of criminal justice. In other words, it is the fear that an individual may exercise his rights that tips the scales of justice for the Court today. The principle that ours is an accusatorial, not an inquisitorial, system, however, has repeatedly led the Court to reject that fear as a valid reason for inhibiting the invocation of rights.

If the Court's cost benefit analysis were sound, it would justify a repudiation of the right to a warning about counsel itself. There is only a difference in degree between a presumption that advice about the immediate availability of a lawyer would not affect the voluntariness of a decision to confess, and a presumption that every citizen knows that he has a right to remain silent and therefore no warnings of any kind are needed. In either case, the withholding of information serves precisely the same law enforcement interests. And in both cases, the cost can be described as nothing more than an incremental increase in the risk that an individual will make an unintelligent waiver of his rights. * * *[4]

The possible reach of the Court's opinion is stunning. For the majority seems to suggest that police may deny counsel all access to a client who is being held. At least since *Escobedo v. Illinois* [infra, p. 442], it has been widely accepted that police may not simply deny attorneys access to their clients who are in custody. That this prevailing view is shared *by the police* can be seen in the state court opinions detailing various forms of police deception of attorneys. For, if there were no obligation to give attorneys access, there would be no need to take elaborate steps to avoid access, such as shuttling the suspect to a different location, or taking the lawyer to different locations; police could simply refuse to allow the attorneys to see the suspects. But the law enforcement profession has apparently believed, quite rightly in my view, that denying lawyers access to their clients is impermissible. The Court today seems to assume that this view was error—that, from the federal constitutional perspective, the lawyer's access is, as a question from the Court put it in oral argument, merely "a matter of prosecutorial grace." Certainly, nothing in the Court's Fifth and Sixth Amendments analysis acknowledges that there is *any* federal constitutional bar to an absolute denial of lawyer access to a suspect who is in police custody. * * *

This case turns on a proper appraisal of the role of the lawyer in our society. If a lawyer is seen as a nettlesome obstacle to the pursuit of wrongdoers—as in an inquisitorial society—then the Court's decision today makes a good deal of sense. If a lawyer is seen as an aid to the

---

4. * * *

In his argument as *amicus curiae*, the Solicitor General advanced the remarkable suggestion that *Miranda*'s requirement that an individual be told that he has a right to consult with counsel while in custody is "a sort of a white lie" that is "harmless" and "useful." Tr. of Oral Arg. 21. He contended that "police do not have to pro-

vide a lawyer if he asks for a lawyer. They need simply terminate the interrogation." *Ibid.* I find this view completely untenable, and I take it that the Court's opinion, in today's sanctioning of police deception, does not in any way accept the suggestion that this Court's required warnings are themselves a constitutionally compelled form of deception, or "white lie."

understanding and protection of constitutional rights—as in an accusatorial society—then today's decision makes no sense at all.

Like the conduct of the police in the Cranston station on the evening of June 29, 1977, the Court's opinion today serves the goal of insuring that the perpetrator of a vile crime is punished. Like the police on that June night as well, however, the Court has trampled on well-established legal principles and flouted the spirit of our accusatorial system of justice.

I respectfully dissent.

Commentary

"Ours is an accusatorial and not an inquisitorial system." This is the constantly repeated refrain of Justice Stevens' dissenting opinion, quoting one of the most familiar maxims about American criminal procedure. But what is an inquisitorial system of criminal justice, and what is so bad about it? What is an accusatorial system, and why do "we" prefer it? When did we become committed to an accusatorial system, and who made the commitment?

The term "inquisitorial" is used in American judicial opinions with a distinctly pejorative connotation, bringing immediately to mind the Spanish Inquisition and the English Court of Star Chamber, both of which employed torture and other abusive procedures to suppress religious dissent. But the modern judicial systems of continental Europe are also classified as "inquisitorial," and many comparative law scholars think that these systems are superior to the American system, not inferior. The essential characteristic of an inquisitorial system is not that it burns heretics at the stake, or employs torture to obtain confessions, but that it regards orderly questioning of the accused person as a legitimate means of getting at the truth.

For example, a (West) German criminal trial begins with a questioning of the accused person concerning his or her "personal circumstances," and then the presiding judge asks for a response to the accusation. Both the presiding judge and the defendant take a much more active role in a German trial than in an American trial, and the prosecutor and defense counsel take a correspondingly less active role. According to Professor John Langbein:

"German procedure is significantly 'delawyerized' by comparison with ours, not only because the judge performs functions that we leave to counsel but because the accused does too. In the usual Anglo-American trial the accused is a strangely awkward bystander. His lawyer does the talking. Even if the accused elects to testify, his role is assimilated to that of other witnesses: he is examined and cross-examined, then he relapses into silence. By contrast, German law takes a sharp distinction between the accused and the witnesses. The accused and the court engage in a direct and continuing dialogue, without the intermediation of counsel. The accused is not labelled as a witness. He is neither required nor permitted to be sworn, hence he never risks perjury for the conduct of his defense.

"From start to finish in a German trial the accused is encouraged to talk directly to the court that is inquiring into his conduct and that will decide his fate. The trial begins with the judge's examination of the accused. Thereafter, the accused may be invited to respond to witness testimony and must be permitted to put questions to the witnesses. The last word is also his. StPO § 258(III) provides: 'Even if defense counsel has spoken for him, the accused shall be asked whether he himself has anything to add to his defense.' He seldom does, but the symbolism of the offer is consistent with the whole of the trial procedure." Langbein, *Comparative Criminal Procedure: Germany*, p. 65, (West Publishing Company, 1977).

German criminal procedure does recognize a privilege against self-incrimination. The accused is not required to respond to questions, and the law forbids the tribunal to draw adverse inferences from his failure to respond to questions at trial. Nevertheless, German defendants almost always choose to speak. Another distinguished comparative law scholar, Professor Mirjan Damaska, has explained why:

"In contrast to the common law concept of the privilege, the continental defendant is not free to decide whether to take the stand and submit to the interrogation process. Questions can always be asked of him. He only has the right to refuse to answer at all, or refuse to respond to particular questions. Although, as a matter of formal doctrine, the trier of fact is usually not permitted to draw unfavorable inferences from his silence, the defendant's quite realistic concern that such inferences will, consciously or unconsciously, in fact be drawn, acts in a typical case as a psychological pressure to speak and respond to questions. Thus, it should occasion no surprise that almost all continental defendants choose to testify. The pressure to speak is, I believe, somewhat stronger than the parallel pressure in the common law trial on the defendant to take the stand, as more immediate inferences can be drawn from refusal to answer specific questions than from the general refusal to submit to the questioning process." Damaska, Evidentiary Barriers to Conviction and Two Models of Criminal Procedure: A Comparative Study, 121 U.Pa.L.Rev. 506, 527 (1973) (footnotes omitted).

The essential element in inquisitorial procedure, then, is not the questioning of the accused by the police in incommunicado detention (although some inquisitorial systems may employ such questioning). The following elements are characteristic of inquisitorial procedure: (1) the presiding judge takes an active role in questioning the defendant and the witnesses, while the prosecutor and defense counsel play a subordinate and supplementary role; (2) the accused has to answer or refuse to answer questions in front of the tribunal that will decide on guilt or innocence; and (3) the accused has to give his story before all the other evidence is taken, and therefore has less opportunity to fabricate a false account. Americans routinely employ inquisitorial procedures in contexts other than the criminal law. For example, Congressional investigating committees frequently begin their hearings with aggressive questioning of officials suspected of wrongdoing or incompetence.

In the past, Anglo–American criminal procedure was much more like its continental counterpart than it is today. A great lawyer and historian of the English common law once described the criminal trial of the Sixteenth Century as "a long argument between the prisoner and the counsel for the Crown, in which they questioned each other and grappled with each other's arguments with the utmost eagerness and closeness of reasoning." 1 Stephen, *History of the Criminal Law of England*, 326 (1883). At that time the accused was neither allowed to call witnesses in his behalf nor permitted the assistance of counsel. Later, when the defense was allowed to present witnesses, a distinction was drawn between these witnesses and the accused: they gave evidence but he did not. Common law judges excluded the testimony of all witnesses with an interest in the outcome, and of course the defendant was the outstanding example of an interested witness. The disqualification did not mean that he could not tell his story, but whatever he said was unsworn and not subject to ordinary cross-examination. Because many defendants (especially indigents) had to act as their own lawyers, they could hardly remain silent.

Disqualification of defendants as witnesses persisted until the middle of the Nineteenth Century: Maine was the first American state to permit the criminal defendant to testify as a witness, in 1859. A remnant of the common law disqualification persisted in Georgia until 1961, when it was declared unconstitutional. See Ferguson v. Georgia, 365 U.S. 570 (1961). In Rock v. Arkansas, 483 U.S. 44 (1987), the Supreme Court held it unconstitutional for a state to apply a rule barring hypnotically refreshed testimony to exclude testimony by the defendant. The opinion stated that the defendant's right to testify is grounded in the Due Process Clause, the Compulsory Process Clause, and the Fifth Amendment privilege.

Today, we take it for granted that our "accusatorial" system requires that the accused be completely free of any courtroom questioning until and unless he chooses to take the stand as a witness after the prosecution has presented its case-in-chief. The Supreme Court has held that it is unconstitutional for a state to require a defendant who intends to take the stand to testify at the beginning of the defense case, before other defense witnesses have testified. Brooks v. Tennessee, 406 U.S. 605 (1972). Except when testifying most defendants have little to do: counsel does the talking and makes most of the decisions.

Observers have generally agreed that American defendants have a better chance of acquittal than defendants in continental inquisitorial trials. The defense advantages inherent in the accusatorial system have been the subject of many eloquent tributes, such as those by Justices Frankfurter and Jackson in the two footnotes reproduced on pages 377–378, supra. There is a heavy irony in Justice Stevens' use of these quotations to bolster his position on the right to counsel at pre-trial *police* interrogation, however. In fact, both of these famous Justices favored a "totality of the circumstances" approach which balanced the need for effective interrogation against the rights of the defendant, much like the approach in Justice O'Connor's opinion for the majority in *Moran v. Burbine*. Both Frankfurter and Jackson were troubled by the practice of incommunicado police interrogation of uncounseled suspects, but on balance both thought the practice had to be allowed, precisely *because* the defendant is so thoroughly protected by the right to counsel and the privilege against self-incrimination when he gets to court. See Culombe v. Connecticut, 367 U.S. 568 (1961) (opinion of Frankfurter, J.); Watts v. Indiana, 338 U.S. 49, 61–62 (1949) (opinion of Jackson, J.).

It seemed as if the "dilemma" of how to balance the need for interrogation against the defense rights implied by the accusatorial system was firmly resolved in favor of the defendant by the Supreme Court's famous decision in Miranda v. Arizona, 384 U.S. 436 (1966). As we see from the opinions in *Moran v. Burbine*, however, the resolution was at most temporary. Behind the dispute over the particular holding, however, there is actually a broad agreement among the Justices upon principles. Both opinions agree, at least for purposes of the present argument, upon the following principles:

1.   Under the *Miranda* decision, the police must warn the accused of his constitutional rights and may not question him unless he makes a voluntary and understanding waiver. Once he makes an initial refusal to waive, any statements the police obtain thereafter by interrogation may not be used against him.

2.   It is obviously in the suspect's interest to have counsel present at the interrogation, just as it is obviously in his interest not to confess to the murder. If the lawyer were present at the interrogation, she would strenuously advise her client not to talk to the police, knowing that he would later regret any admissions he might make.

3.   If the *suspect* had become a *defendant* by appearing in court on this charge (for example, at an arraignment on a complaint or arrest warrant), any statement obtained by subsequent questioning in the absence of counsel could not have been used against him. In a portion of the majority opinion omitted for the sake of brevity from the edited version reprinted in this book, the majority conceded that "the defendant has the right to the presence of an attorney during any interrogation occurring after the first formal charging proceeding," and that thereafter "the police may not interfere with the efforts of a defendant's attorney to act as a medium between the suspect and the State during the interrogation." 475 U.S. at 412. This doctrine, which prevents the police from employing stratagems to circumvent the protective efforts of counsel once the formal adversary process has begun, is discussed in detail later in this part of the book. For now, it is enough to note that the majority conceded that the police would lose their opportunity for questioning once the defendant made a formal appearance in court.

4.   On the other hand, the dissent concedes that the police may question a suspect in custody if he knowingly waives his constitutional rights, provided that counsel is not already in the picture. This "waiver" principle is stated in the *Miranda* opinion itself, but isn't it a little odd in view of what is stated in paragraph 2, above? When the police obtain a waiver from an uncounseled defendant, knowing full well that "any lawyer worth his salt will tell the suspect in no uncertain terms to make no statement to police under any circumstances," aren't they taking advantage of the suspect's ignorance or vulnerability? If we are willing to tolerate *that*, then what is so bad about allowing the police a fair opportunity to question every suspect without counsel? Or does the logic of the accusatorial system require that we exclude all statements unless the defendant ratifies them at some later date after consulting with counsel?

The penultimate paragraph of Justice Stevens' dissent points out the ambivalence with which courts and law enforcement officials regard criminal defense lawyers. Perhaps a defense lawyer is *both* "a nettlesome obstacle to the pursuit of wrongdoers" and "an aid to the understanding and protection of constitutional rights." From the point of view of a detective trying to solve a murder, a defense lawyer is an obstacle to the ascertainment of truth and the pursuit of justice. From the standpoint of a constitutional lawyer, a defense lawyer is absolutely essential to the enforcement of constitutional rights. As a Supreme Court opinion once put it, "no system of criminal justice can, or should, survive if it comes to depend for its continued effectiveness on the citizens' abdication through unawareness of their constitutional rights." Escobedo v. Illinois, 378 U.S. 478, 490 (1964). On the opposing side, one can quote the concluding words of Justice Jackson's previously cited opinion in *Watts v. Indiana*:

> "I doubt very much if [precedent] requires us to hold that the State may not take into custody and question one suspected reasonably of unwitnessed murder. If it does, the people of this country must discipline themselves to seeing their police stand by helplessly while those suspected of murder prowl about unmolested. Is it a necessary price to pay for the fairness which we know as 'due process of law'? And if not a necessary one, should it be demanded by this Court? I do not know the ultimate answer to these questions; but for the present, I should not increase the handicap on society." 338 U.S. at 61–62.

In short, there is a tension between our high constitutional ideals and our desire to see criminals brought to justice, which leads to a certain amount of equivocation, ambivalence, and even downright hypocrisy. The remaining chapters in this Part of the book will illustrate how our courts have tried to resolve the tension in developing the right to counsel and the privilege against self-incrimination within the context of an accusatorial system of justice.

Chapter 10

THE RIGHT TO COUNSEL AND EQUAL TREATMENT

GIDEON v. WAINWRIGHT

Supreme Court of the United States, 1963.
372 U.S. 335, 83 S.Ct. 792, 9 L.Ed.2d 799.

MR. JUSTICE BLACK delivered the opinion of the Court.

Petitioner was charged in a Florida state court with having broken and entered a poolroom with intent to commit a misdemeanor. This offense is a felony under Florida law. Appearing in court without funds and without a lawyer, petitioner asked the court to appoint counsel for him, whereupon the following colloquy took place:

The COURT: Mr. Gideon, I am sorry, but I cannot appoint Counsel to represent you in this case. Under the laws of the State of Florida, the only time the Court can appoint Counsel to represent a Defendant is when that person is charged with a capital offense. I am sorry, but I will have to deny your request to appoint Counsel to defend you in this case.

The DEFENDANT: The United States Supreme Court says I am entitled to be represented by Counsel.

Put to trial before a jury, Gideon conducted his defense about as well as could be expected from a layman. He made an opening statement to the jury, cross-examined the State's witnesses, presented witnesses in his own defense, declined to testify himself, and made a short argument "emphasizing his innocence to the charge contained in the Information filed in this case." The jury returned a verdict of guilty, and petitioner was sentenced to serve five years in the state prison. Later, petitioner filed in the Florida Supreme Court this habeas corpus petition attacking his conviction and sentence on the ground that the trial court's refusal to appoint counsel for him denied him rights "guaranteed by the Constitution and the Bill of Rights by the United States Government." Treating the petition for habeas corpus as properly before it, the State Supreme Court, "upon consideration thereof" but without an opinion, denied all relief. Since 1942, when Betts v. Brady, 316 U.S. 455, was decided by a divided Court, the problem of a defendant's federal constitutional right to counsel in a state court has been a continuing source of controversy and litigation in both state and federal courts. To give this problem another review here, we granted certiorari. * * *

The Sixth Amendment provides, "In all criminal prosecutions, the accused shall enjoy the right * * * to have the Assistance of Counsel for his defence." We have construed this to mean that in federal courts counsel must be provided for defendants unable to employ counsel unless the right is competently and intelligently waived. Betts argued that this right is extended to indigent defendants in state courts by the Fourteenth Amendment. In response the Court stated that, while the Sixth Amendment laid down "no rule for the conduct of the states, the question recurs whether the constraint laid by the amendment upon the national courts expresses a rule so fundamental and essential to a fair trial, and so, to due process of law, that it is made obligatory upon the states by the Fourteenth Amendment." In order to decide whether the Sixth Amendment's guarantee of counsel is of this fundamental nature, the Court in Betts set out and considered "[r]elevant data on the subject * * * afforded by constitutional and statutory provisions subsisting in the colonies and the states prior to the inclusion of the Bill of Rights in the national Constitution, and in the constitutional, legislative, and judicial history of the states to the present date." On the basis of this historical data the Court concluded that "appointment of counsel is not a fundamental right essential to a fair trial." It was for this reason the Betts Court refused to accept the contention that the Sixth Amendment's guarantee of counsel for indigent federal defendants was extended to or, in the words of that Court, "made obligatory upon the states by the Fourteenth Amendment". Plainly, had the Court concluded that appointment of counsel for an indigent criminal defendant was "a fundamental right, essential to a fair trial," it would have held that the Fourteenth Amendment requires appointment of counsel in a state court, just as the Sixth Amendment requires in a federal court. * * *

We accept Betts v. Brady's assumption, based as it was on our prior cases, that a provision of the Bill of Rights which is "fundamental and essential to a fair trial" is made obligatory upon the States by the Fourteenth Amendment. We think the Court in Betts was wrong, however, in concluding that the Sixth Amendment's guarantee of counsel is not one of these fundamental rights. * * *

Governments, both state and federal, quite properly spend vast sums of money to establish machinery to try defendants accused of crime. Lawyers to prosecute are everywhere deemed essential to protect the public's interest in an orderly society. Similarly, there are few defendants charged with crime, few indeed, who fail to hire the best lawyers they can get to prepare and present their defenses. That government hires lawyers to prosecute and defendants who have the money hire lawyers to defend are the strongest indications of the widespread belief that lawyers in criminal courts are necessities, not luxuries. The right of one charged with crime to counsel may not be deemed fundamental and essential to fair trials in some countries, but it is in ours. From the very beginning, our state and national constitutions and laws have laid great emphasis on procedural and substantive safeguards designed to assure fair trials before impartial tribunals in which every defendant stands equal before the law. This noble ideal cannot be realized if the poor man charged with crime has to face his accusers without a lawyer to assist him. A defendant's need for a lawyer is nowhere better stated than in the moving words of Mr. Justice Sutherland in Powell v. Alabama:

> The right to be heard would be, in many cases, of little avail if it did not comprehend the right to be heard by counsel. Even the intelligent and educated layman has small and sometimes no skill in the science of law. If charged with crime, he is incapable, generally, of determining for himself whether the indictment is good or bad. He is unfamiliar with the rules of evidence. Left without the aid of counsel he may be put on trial without a proper charge, and convicted upon incompetent evidence, or evidence irrelevant to the issue or otherwise inadmissible. He lacks both the skill and knowledge adequately to prepare his defense, even though he have a perfect one. He requires the guiding hand of counsel at every step in the proceedings against him. Without it, though he be not guilty, he faces the danger of conviction because he does not know how to establish his innocence. 287 U.S., at 68–69.

The Court in Betts v. Brady departed from the sound wisdom upon which the Court's holding in Powell v. Alabama rested. Florida, supported by two other States, has asked that Betts v. Brady by left intact. Twenty-two States, as friends of the Court, argue that Betts was "an anachronism when handed down" and that it should now be overruled. We agree.

The judgment is reversed and the cause is remanded to the Supreme Court of Florida for further action not inconsistent with this opinion.

Reversed.

DOUGLAS v. CALIFORNIA

Supreme Court of the United States, 1963.
372 U.S. 353, 83 S.Ct. 814, 9 L.Ed.2d 811.

MR. JUSTICE DOUGLAS delivered the opinion of the Court. * * *

Although several questions are presented in the petition for certiorari, we address ourselves to only one of them. The record shows that petitioners requested, and were denied, the assistance of counsel on appeal, even though it plainly appeared they were indigents. In denying petitioners' requests, the California District Court of Appeal stated that it had "gone through" the record and had come to the conclusion that "no good whatever could be served by appointment of counsel." The District Court of Appeal was acting in accordance with a California rule of criminal procedure which provides that state appellate courts, upon the request of an indigent for counsel, may make "an independent investigation of the record and determine whether it would be of advantage to the defendant or helpful to the appellate court to have counsel appointed. * * * After such investigation, appellate courts should appoint counsel if in their opinion it would be helpful to the defendant or the court, and should deny the appointment of counsel only if in their judgment such appointment would be of no value to either the defendant or the court." People v. Hyde, 51 Cal.2d 152, 154.

We agree, however, with Justice Traynor of the California Supreme Court, who said that the "[d]enial of counsel on appeal [to an indigent] would seem to be a discrimination at least as invidious as that condemned in Griffin v. People of State of Illinois * * *." In Griffin v. Illinois, 351 U.S. 12, we held that a State may not grant appellate review in such a way as to discriminate against some convicted defendants on account of their poverty. There, as in Draper v. Washington, 372 U.S. 487, the right to a free transcript on appeal was in issue. Here the issue is whether or not an indigent shall be denied the assistance of counsel on appeal. In either case the evil is the same: discrimination against the indigent. For there can be no equal justice where the kind of an appeal a man enjoys "depends on the amount of money he has." Griffin v. Illinois, supra.

In spite of California's forward treatment of indigents, under its present practice the type of an appeal a person is afforded in the District Court of Appeal hinges upon whether or not he can pay for the assistance of counsel. If he can the appellate court passes on the merits of this case only after having the full benefit of written briefs and oral argument by counsel. If he cannot the appellate court is forced to prejudge the merits before it can even determine whether counsel should be provided. At this stage in the proceedings only the barren record speaks for the indigent, and, unless the printed pages show that an injustice has been committed, he is forced to go without a champion on appeal. Any real chance he may have had of showing that his appeal has hidden merit is deprived him when the court decides on an *ex parte* examination of the record that the assistance of counsel is not required.

We are not here concerned with problems that might arise from the denial of counsel for the preparation of a petition for discretionary or mandatory review beyond the stage in the appellate process at which the claims have once been presented by a lawyer and passed upon by an appellate court. We are dealing only with the first appeal, granted as a matter of right to rich and poor alike, from a criminal conviction. We need not now decide whether California would have to provide counsel for an indigent seeking a discretionary hearing from the California Supreme Court after the District Court of Appeal had sustained his conviction or whether counsel must be appointed for an indigent seeking review of an appellate affirmance of his conviction in this Court by appeal as of right or by petition for a writ of certiorari which lies within the Court's discretion. But it is appropriate to observe that a State can, consistently with the Fourteenth Amendment, provide for differences so long as the result does not amount to a denial of due process or an invidious discrimination. Absolute equality is not required; lines can be and are drawn and we often sustain them. But where the merits of the one and only appeal an indigent has as of right are decided without benefit of counsel, we think an unconstitutional line has been drawn between rich and poor.

* * *

[Judgment vacated and case remanded.]

Mr. Justice Harlan, whom Mr. Justice Stewart joins, dissenting.
* * *

To approach the present problem in terms of the Equal Protection Clause is, I submit, but to substitute resounding phrases for analysis. I dissented from this approach in Griffin v. Illinois, and I am constrained to dissent from the implicit extension of the equal protection approach here—to a case in which the State denies no one an appeal, but seeks only to keep within reasonable bounds the instances in which appellate counsel will be assigned to indigents.

The States, of course, are prohibited by the Equal Protection Clause from discriminating between "rich" and "poor" *as such* in the formulation and application of their laws. But it is a far different thing to suggest that this provision prevents the State from adopting a law of general applicability that may affect the poor more harshly than it does the rich, or, on the other hand, from making some effort to redress economic imbalances while not eliminating them entirely.

Every financial exaction which the State imposes on a uniform basis is more easily satisfied by the well-to-do than by the indigent. Yet I take it that no one would dispute the constitutional power of the State to levy a uniform sales tax, to charge tuition at a state university, to fix rates for the purchase of water from a municipal corporation, to impose a standard fine for criminal violations, or to establish minimum bail for various categories of offenses. Nor could it be contended that the State may not classify as crimes acts which the poor are more likely to commit than are the rich. And surely, there would be no basis for attacking a state law which provided benefits for the needy simply because those benefits fell short of the goods or services that others could purchase for themselves.

Laws such as these do not deny equal protection to the less fortunate for one essential reason: the Equal Protection Clause does not impose on the States "an affirmative duty to lift the handicaps flowing from differences in economic circumstances." To so construe it would be to read into the Constitution a philosophy of leveling that would be foreign to many of our basic concepts of the proper relations between government and society. The State may have a moral obligation to eliminate the evils of poverty, but it is not required by the Equal Protection Clause to give to some whatever others can afford. * * *

ANDERS v. CALIFORNIA

Supreme Court of the United States, 1967.
386 U.S. 738, 87 S.Ct. 1396, 18 L.Ed.2d 493.

Mr. Justice Clark delivered the opinion of the Court.

We are here concerned with the extent of the duty of a court-appointed appellate counsel to prosecute a first appeal from a criminal conviction, after that attorney has conscientiously determined that there is no merit to the indigent's appeal.

After he was convicted of the felony of possession of marijuana, petitioner sought to appeal and moved that the California District Court of Appeal appoint counsel for him. Such motion was granted; however, after a study of the record and consultation with petitioner, the appointed counsel concluded that there was no merit to the appeal. He so advised the court by letter and, at the same time, informed the court that petitioner wished to file a brief in his own behalf. At this juncture, petitioner requested the appointment of another attorney. This request was denied and petitioner proceeded to file his own brief *pro se*. The State responded and petitioner filed a reply brief. On January 9, 1959, the District Court of Appeal unanimously affirmed the conviction. * * *

The constitutional requirement of substantial equality and fair process can only be attained where counsel acts in the role of an active advocate in behalf of his client, as opposed to that of *amicus curiae*. The no-merit letter and the procedure it triggers do not reach that dignity. Counsel should, and can with honor and without conflict, be of more assistance to his client and to the court. His role as advocate requires that he support his client's appeal to the best of his ability. Of course, if counsel finds his case to be wholly frivolous, after a conscientious examination of it, he should so advise the court and request permission to withdraw. That request must, however, be accompanied by a brief referring to anything in the record that might arguably support the appeal. A copy of counsel's brief should be furnished the indigent and time allowed him to raise any points that he chooses; the court—not counsel—then proceeds, after a full examination of all the proceedings, to decide whether the case is wholly frivolous. If it so finds it may grant counsel's request to withdraw and dismiss the appeal insofar as federal requirements are concerned, or proceed to a decision on the merits, if state law so requires. On the other hand, if it finds any of the legal points arguable on their merits (and therefore not frivolous) it must, prior to decision, afford the indigent the assistance of counsel to argue the appeal.

This requirement would not force appointed counsel to brief his case against his client but would merely afford the latter that advocacy which a nonindigent defendant is able to obtain. It would also induce the court to pursue all the more vigorously its own review because of the ready references not only to the record, but also to the legal authorities as furnished it by counsel. The no-merit letter, on the other hand, affords neither the client nor the court any aid. The former must shift entirely for himself while the court has only the cold record which it must review without the help of an advocate. Moreover, such handling would tend to protect counsel from the constantly increasing charge that he was ineffective and had not handled the case with that diligence to which an indigent defendant is entitled. This procedure will assure penniless defendants the same rights and opportunities on appeal—as nearly as is practicable—as are enjoyed by those persons who are in a similar situation but who are able to afford the retention of private counsel.

* * *

[Judgment reversed and case remanded]

MR. JUSTICE STEWART, whom MR. JUSTICE BLACK and MR. JUSTICE HARLAN join, dissenting.

The system used by California for handling indigent appeals was described by the California Supreme Court in In re Nash, 61 Cal.2d 491, 495:

> We believe that the requirement of the *Douglas* case is met * * * when, as in this case, counsel is appointed to represent the defendant on appeal, thoroughly studies the record, consults with the defendant and trial counsel, and conscientiously concludes that there are no meritorious grounds of appeal. If thereafter the appellate court is satisfied *from its own review* of the record in the light of any points raised by the defendant personally that counsel's assessment of the record is correct, it need not appoint another counsel to represent the defendant on appeal and may properly decide the appeal without oral argument. (Emphasis added.)

The Court today holds this procedure unconstitutional, and imposes upon appointed counsel who wishes to withdraw from a case he deems "wholly frivolous" the requirement of filing "a brief referring to anything in the record that might arguably support the appeal." But if the record did present any such "arguable" issues, the appeal would not be frivolous and counsel would not have filed a "no-merit" letter in the first place.

The quixotic requirement imposed by the Court can be explained, I think, only upon the cynical assumption that an appointed lawyer's professional representation to an appellate court in a "no-merit" letter is not to be trusted. That is an assumption to which I cannot subscribe. I cannot believe that lawyers appointed to represent indigents are so likely to be lacking in diligence, competence, or professional honesty. Certainly there was no suggestion in the present case that the petitioner's counsel was either incompetent or unethical.

But even if I could join in this degrading appraisal of the *in forma pauperis* bar, it escapes me how the procedure that the Court commands is constitutionally superior to the system now followed in California. The fundamental error in the Court's opinion, it seems to me, is its implicit assertion that there can be but a single inflexible answer to the difficult problem of how to accord equal protection to indigent appellants in each of the 50 States.

Believing that the procedure under which Anders' appeal was considered was free of constitutional error, I would affirm the judgment.

Note

A Wisconsin rule of Appellate Procedure requires appointed counsel who have conscientiously determined that an indigent's appeal is wholly frivolous to submit with the request to withdraw not only "a brief referring to anything in the record that might arguably support the appeal," but also "a discussion of why the issue lacks merit." This last requirement was challenged as inconsistent with *Anders* because it requires counsel to argue the case *against* the client. A closely divided Supreme Court upheld the Wisconsin rule in McCoy v. Court of Appeals of Wisconsin, District 1, 486 U.S. 429 (1988). The majority reasoned that requiring the explanation assists the court to determine that counsel has been diligent and that the appeal is indeed frivolous, and furnishing the explanation does not burden the right to effective representation on appeal any more than does stating the bald conclusion that the appeal is frivolous.

UNITED STATES v. ELY

United States Court of Appeals, Seventh Circuit, 1983.
719 F.2d 902.

POSNER, CIRCUIT JUDGE.

* * *

Ely was apprehended in 1982 and at the arraignment the district judge, after ascertaining that Ely was indigent and wanted counsel, appointed a lawyer named Brady to represent him. Ely requested the judge to appoint another lawyer instead, Bartley, who at Ely's request was in the courtroom. (Both Brady and Bartley are lawyers in private practice.) Ely stated, "Mr. Bartley had represented business of mine at one time and I have—I feel a more closer relationship with Mr. Bartley in understanding what is before me * * *." Although Bartley was willing to accept the appointment and had represented other indigent criminal defendants before the district judge, the judge refused to appoint him to represent Ely: "the Court appoints an attorney for you under the program that this Court has of attorneys on its list and in some relative degree of sequence and frequency. * * * I know that Mr. Brady is [a] thoroughly competent and experienced attorney in this Court. I don't have anything different to say about Mr. Bartley, but we cannot start the practice of allowing defendants to select attorneys to be appointed." * * *

Ely argues that in denying him the counsel of his choice the judge violated the Sixth Amendment. Enacted against the background of the much criticized common law rule that forbade felony defendants to be represented by counsel, the Sixth Amendment removed that bar for federal trials and thus allowed federal criminal defendants to hire counsel—counsel of their choice, see, e.g., *United States v. Agosto*, 675 F.2d 965, 969 (8th Cir.1982). But as originally understood, the Sixth Amendment did not require the government to provide a lawyer to a criminal defendant too poor to be able to hire one. Although the Sixth Amendment has, of course, been reinterpreted in modern times to impose such a requirement, the government's constitutional obligation is exhausted "when 'the court appoints competent counsel who is uncommitted to any position or interest which would conflict with providing an effective defense.'" United States v. Davis, 604 F.2d 474, 479 (7th Cir.1979).

Ely does not argue that Brady was incompetent or had a conflict of interest. Brady was a natural choice to represent Ely, having been his counsel when he was first charged in 1979. Although he preferred Bartley, Ely expressed no dissatisfaction with Brady. It was not that Brady was not good but that Bartley was, in Ely's opinion, better. Our decision in *Davis* approved the district judge's refusal to allow the indigent defendant to choose his own court-appointed counsel. True, Davis had expressed dissatisfaction with four lawyers offered him in lieu of the one he wanted, but as Ely expressed no dissatisfaction with his substitute counsel we do not think *Davis* is a stronger case than this one for denying the indigent the counsel of his choice.

In relation to indigent criminal defendants, the Sixth Amendment seeks not to maximize free choice of counsel but to prevent anyone from being unjustly convicted or illegally sentenced. These are distinct goals. Not only is there no indication that Ely would have fared better with Bartley at his side than with Brady; even if Bartley is the better lawyer, some other indigent criminal defendant might have been denied his assistance had he been appointed in Brady's place.

There are practical reasons for not giving indigent criminal defendants their choice of counsel. Appointed counsel are not paid at munificent rates under the Criminal Justice Act, 18 U.S.C. § 3006A(d); in the Central District of Illinois, in the most recent year for which data are available (1980), the average fee per case under the Act was only $426.31. The best criminal lawyers who accept appointments therefore limit the amount of time they are willing to devote to this relatively unremunerative type of work; some criminal lawyers, indeed, only reluctantly agree to serve as appointed counsel, under pressure by district judges to whom they feel a sense of professional obligation. The services of the criminal defense bar cannot be auctioned to the highest bidder among the indigent accused—by definition, indigents are not bidders. But these services must be allocated somehow; indigent defendants cannot be allowed to paralyze the system by all flocking to one lawyer. The district judge in this case could not, realistically, be required to arbitrate a dispute between Ely and another indigent criminal defendant who wanted to be represented by Bartley.

Neither party presented any evidence regarding the list of attorneys available for appointment that this district judge uses, or, more generally, the supply of lawyers for indigents in the Central District relative to demand. The transcript of the hearing on appointment of counsel for Ely indicates that this judge uses a rotation system for handling the appointment of counsel for indigents. If Ely wanted to show that the judge's refusal to appoint Bartley to represent him nevertheless was unreasonable, he would have to produce evidence to this effect; he failed to produce any. Ely argues, no doubt correctly, that if he were rich he could have hired Bartley. But the government is not responsible for Ely's poverty, and could not, under any reasonable system for the appointment of counsel, rectify all the consequences of the inequality of wealth among criminal defendants. In general, the best criminal lawyers are retained by the most affluent defendants, who pay them on a much more generous scale than under the Criminal Justice Act. The government cannot eliminate the consequences of poverty; it can only limit them, as it did in this case by supplying Ely with the services of competent and experienced legal counsel. * * *

[Conviction affirmed.]*

Commentary

There are two distinct constitutional principles at work in these cases: (1) The "due process" principle that the state must provide an indigent defendant with a lawyer and whatever other resources are absolutely necessary to a fair trial; and (2) the "equal protection" principle, which requires the state to take affirmative steps to narrow the gap between the resources available to rich and poor criminal defendants. The second principle is plainly the more far-reaching, and indeed it appears to promise more than the courts and the rest of society are prepared to deliver. Fees for appointed defense counsel are typically quite low in comparison to the fees private litigants pay their lawyers. The problem is not only one of unwillingness to provide resources, however. As long as rich defendants are allowed to use all the resources at their command to retain the best lawyers and supporting services, it is difficult to see how any realistic program of public assistance could achieve anything like "equality." If we were truly dedicated to achieving this elusive goal, then we would probably have to consider "leveling down," by imposing a ceiling on what the rich can spend or by assigning defense counsel to rich and poor alike by random selection. The measures necessary to achieve equality might in themselves be unconstitutional.

The Supreme Court apparently felt it necessary to invoke the equal protection principle in the cases involving transcripts and counsel on appeal because the Constitution contains no explicit guarantee of a right to appeal. At common law there was no appeal in criminal cases, and the only remedy a convicted defendant had was executive clemency. The Supreme Court has said in *dicta* that the states are under no constitutional obligation to provide

---

* Compare, Harris v. Superior Court, 19 Cal.3d 786, 140 Cal.Rptr. 318, 567 P.2d 750 (1977), which held that the state trial court should have appointed the lawyers requested by the indigent defendants where defendants had previously established a close relationship with the requested lawyers.

for appeal in criminal cases, although all states do. See McKane v. Durston, 153 U.S. 684 (1894). If there is no constitutional right to appeal, then it would seem that there can be no constitutional right to a transcript and a lawyer on appeal. Rather than declare that modern notions of "due process" require that there be a right to appeal in criminal cases, the Supreme Court chose to invoke the expansive equal protection principle. One wonders what the Court would do if a state actually chose to abolish all criminal appeals.

Given the proviso that "absolute equality is not required," what must a state do beyond providing free counsel to indigents at trial and on the first appeal to satisfy the Supreme Court's ban on invidious discrimination against the poor? The Supreme Court has held that a state is not required to provide counsel for an indigent defendant to seek discretionary review in the state supreme court or in the United States Supreme Court, after his conviction has been initially affirmed in the state's intermediate court of appeals. Ross v. Moffitt, 417 U.S. 600 (1974). In its opinion, the Supreme Court observed that denial of appointed counsel at this stage would not deprive the indigent defendant of meaningful access to the state supreme court, because that court could determine whether or not to hear the case on the basis of the brief filed by appointed counsel in the intermediate court, together with the intermediate court's opinion and any supplemental materials that the defendant wished to submit *pro se*. The Court concluded that "The duty of the State under our cases is not to duplicate the legal arsenal that may be privately retained by a criminal defendant in a continuing effort to reverse his conviction, but only to assure the indigent defendant an adequate opportunity to present his claims fairly in the context of the State's appellate process." In dissent Mr. Justice Douglas noted that it would be a relatively easy matter for the attorney who had argued the first appeal to prepare a petition for further discretionary review, and repeated the admonition that "there can be no equal justice where the kind of appeal a man enjoys 'depends upon the amount of money he has.' "

The Sixth Amendment right to counsel extends to all "criminal prosecutions." This language does not suggest any exception for misdemeanors or "petty offenses," but there is a long tradition in many jurisdictions of providing lesser protections for defendants accused of minor offenses. In addition, the Supreme Court had previously held the Sixth Amendment right to jury trial inapplicable to petty offenses, defined as crimes where the penalty is no greater than six months in jail. See Baldwin v. New York, 399 U.S. 66 (1970). The Court gave a broader scope to the right to counsel, however, holding that it extends to any case in which the defendant is actually sentenced to jail for any time whatsoever. Argersinger v. Hamlin, 407 U.S. 25 (1972). On the other hand, a state may refuse to appoint counsel for a defendant charged with a crime punishable by jail, provided that a jail sentence is not actually imposed after conviction. Scott v. Illinois, 440 U.S. 367 (1979). Of course, misdemeanors like petty theft and indecent exposure may carry a substantial moral stigma and collateral consequences, apart from any question of confinement.

Although the Constitution specifically provides for a right to counsel in all criminal trials but says nothing about a right to an appeal or a transcript, the Court has nonetheless given a broader scope to the equality-based right to a transcript than it has to the due process-based right to trial counsel. In

Mayer v. Chicago, 404 U.S. 189 (1971), the Court unanimously held that an indigent defendant cannot be denied a record of sufficient completeness to permit proper consideration of his claims on appeal merely because he was convicted of ordinance violations punishable by a fine only. The opinion noted that a fine may bear as heavily on an indigent defendant as a jail sentence, and that the collateral consequences of a conviction may be substantial even in the absence of a jail term. These considerations are, of course, equally pertinent to the issue of a right to counsel at trial.

The absolute right to counsel extends to sentencing procedures, but not to probation or parole revocation hearings. See Gagnon v. Scarpelli, 411 U.S. 778 (1973); compare, Mempa v. Rhay, 389 U.S. 128 (1967). In such proceedings the probationer or parolee must be advised that he has a right to request counsel, but counsel is actually appointed only where the hearing officer makes a preliminary determination that the case involves issues which indicate a need for the assistance of counsel. In other words, the *Betts v. Brady* approach continues to be used for revocation hearings, with all its well-known disadvantages. A person who is unable to make a proper defense without counsel will often be unable to make a proper showing as to precisely why counsel is needed. In the opinion of most commentators, it is easier and more efficient simply to provide a lawyer upon request rather than to attempt to make a determination of whether counsel would be helpful.

Appointment of counsel to assist an inmate in collateral proceedings such as federal habeas corpus is also discretionary, although counsel is generally provided if the petition has sufficient merit to call for an evidentiary hearing. Prisoners generally have to prepare their own petitions in the first instance, relying on whatever legal materials are available to them and the assistance of fellow inmates. The Supreme Court has held that states may not arbitrarily prohibit such inmate "writ-writers" from providing assistance to other prisoners. Johnson v. Avery, 393 U.S. 483 (1969). States also have an obligation to provide minimally adequate law libraries or other legal assistance to allow prisoners to have meaningful access to the courts. See Bounds v. Smith, 430 U.S. 817 (1977); Hooks v. Wainwright, 716 F.2d 913 (11th Cir.1983). The need for post-appeal assistance of counsel is particularly acute for defendants sentenced to death, who may file petitions for stays of execution and other relief right up to the moment of execution.

Effective defense representation requires not only a lawyer and a transcript, but also in some cases resources like investigators or expert witnesses. The federal Criminal Justice Act, 18 U.S.C.A. Section 3006A (as amended, 1982), grants the courts discretion to provide such services at government expense upon defense request. State laws also ordinarily provide some such discretionary authority, although of course they do not guarantee that defendants will receive fully adequate resources, especially in comparison to the resources available to the very rich. Free lawyers and other resources are ordinarily provided only to indigents; middle class defendants must pay for their own defense. The State does not pay these costs even if the defendant is found not guilty, and so a defendant may be ruined by a criminal prosecution regardless of the outcome. In this respect, indigents actually have an advantage over individuals with modest means, who may be deterred from pursuing all available remedies by cost considerations.

CAPLIN & DRYSDALE, CHARTERED
v. UNITED STATES

Supreme Court of the United States, 1989.
491 U.S. 617, 109 S.Ct. 2646, 105 L.Ed.2d 528.

JUSTICE WHITE delivered the opinion of the Court.

We are called on to determine whether the federal drug forfeiture statute includes an exemption for assets that a defendant wishes to use to pay an attorney who conducted his defense in the criminal case where forfeiture was sought. Because we determine that no such exemption exists, we must decide whether that statute, so interpreted, is consistent with the Fifth and Sixth Amendments. We hold that it is.

I

In January 1985, Christopher Reckmeyer was charged in a multi-count indictment with running a massive drug importation and distribution scheme. The scheme was alleged to be a continuing criminal enterprise (CCE), in violation of 21 U.S.C. section 848. Relying on a portion of the CCE statute that authorizes forfeiture to the government of "property constitution, or derived from * * * proceeds * * * obtained" from drug-law violations, 21 U.S.C. section 853(a), the indictment sought forfeiture of specified assets in Reckmeyer's possession. At this time, the District Court entered a restraining order forbidding Reckmeyer to transfer any of the listed assets that were potentially forfeitable. Sometime earlier, Reckmeyer had retained petitioner, a law firm, to represent him in the ongoing grand jury investigation which resulted in the January 1985 indictments. Notwithstanding the restraining order, Reckmeyer paid the firm $25,000 for preindictment legal services a few days after the indictment was handed down; this sum was placed by petitioner in an escrow account. Petitioner continued to represent Reckmeyer following the indictment. On March 7, 1985, Reckmeyer moved to modify the District Court's earlier restraining order to permit him to use some of the restrained assets to pay petitioner's fees; Reckmeyer also sought to exempt from any postconviction forfeiture order the assets that he intended to use to pay petitioner. However, one week later, before the District Court could conduct a hearing on this motion, Reckmeyer entered a plea agreement with the Government. Under the agreement, Reckmeyer pleaded guilty to the drug-related CCE charge, and agreed to forfeit all of the specified assets listed in the indictment. The day after the Reckmeyer's plea was entered, the District Court denied his earlier motion to modify the restraining order, concluding that the plea and forfeiture agreement rendered irrelevant any further consideration of the propriety of the court's pretrial restraints. Subsequently, an order forfeiting virtually all of the assets in Reckmeyer's possession was entered by the District Court in conjunction with his sentencing. After this order was entered petitioner filed a petition under 21 U.S.C. section 853(n), which permits third parties with an interest in forfeited property to ask the sentencing court for an adjudication of their rights to that property; specifically section 853(n)(6)(B) gives a third party who entered into a bona fide transaction with a defendant a right to make claims against forfeited property, if that third party was 'at the time of [the transaction] reasonably without cause to believe that the [defendant's assets were] subject to forfeiture.' Petitioner claimed an interest in $170,000 of Reckmeyer's assets, for services it had provided Reckmeyer in conducting his defense; petitioner also sought the $25,000 being held in the escrow account, as payment for preindictment legal services. Petitioner argued alternatively that assets used to pay an attorney were exempt from forfeiture under section 853, and if not, the failure of the statute to provide such an exemption rendered it unconstitutional. The District Court granted petitioner's claim for a share of the forfeited assets.

[The Court of Appeals reversed, en banc.] All the judges of the Fourth Circuit agreed that the language of the CCE statute acknowledged no exception to its forfeiture requirement that would recognize petitioner's claim to the forfeited assets. A majority found this statutory scheme constitutional; four dissenting judges, however, agreed with the panel's view that the statute so-construed violated the Sixth Amendment. * * *

II

Petitioner's first submission is that the statutory provision that authorizes pretrial restraining orders on potentially forfeitable assets in a defendant's possession, 21 U.S.C. section 853(e), grants district courts equitable discretion to determine when such orders should be imposed. This discretion should be exercised under "traditional equitable standards," petitioner urges, including a "weigh[ing] of the equities and competing hardships on the parties"; under this approach, a court "must invariably strike the balance so as to allow a defendant [to pay] * * * for bona fide attorneys fees," petitioner argues. Petitioner further submits that once a district court so exercises its discretion, and fails to freeze assets that a defendant then uses to pay an attorney, the statute's provision for recapture of forfeitable assets transferred to third parties, 21 U.S.C. section 853(c), may not operate on such sums.

Petitioner's argument, as it acknowledges, is based on the view of the statute expounded by Judge Winter of the Second Circuit in his concurring opinion in that Court of Appeals' en banc decision, United States v. Monsanto, 852 F.2d 1400, 1405–1411 (1988). We reject this interpretation of the statute today in our decision in United States v. Monsanto, which reverses the Second Circuit's holding in that case. As we explain in our Monsanto decision, whatever discretion section 853(e) provides district court judges to refuse to enter pretrial restraining orders, it does not extend as far as petitioner urges—nor does the exercise of that discretion "immunize" nonrestrained assets from subsequent forfeiture under section 853(c), if they are transferred to an attorney to pay legal fees. Thus, for the reasons provided in our opinion in Monsanto, we reject petitioner's statutory claim.

III

We therefore address petitioner's constitutional challenges to the forfeiture law. Petitioner contends that the statute infringes on criminal defendants' Sixth Amendment right to counsel of choice, and upsets the "balance of power" between the government and the accused in a manner contrary to the Due Process Clause of the Fifth Amendment. We consider these contentions in turn.

A

Petitioner's first claim is that the forfeiture law makes impossible, or at least impermissibly burdens, a defendant's right to select and be represented by one's preferred attorney. Petitioner does not, nor could it defensibly do so, assert that impecunious defendants have a Sixth Amendment right to choose their counsel. The amendment guarantees defendants in criminal cases the right to adequate representation, but those who do not have the means to hire their own lawyers have no cognizable complaint so long as they are adequately represented by attorneys appointed by the courts. * * *

The forfeiture statute does not prevent a defendant who has nonforfeitable assets from retaining any attorney of his choosing. Nor is it necessarily the case that a defendant who possesses nothing but assets the Government seeks to have forfeited will be prevented from retaining counsel of choice. Defendants like Reckmeyer may be able to find lawyers willing to represent them, hoping that their fees will be paid in the event of acquittal, or via some other means that a defendant might come by in the future. The burden placed on defendants by the forfeiture law is therefore a limited one. * * *

A defendant has no Sixth Amendment right to spend another person's money for services rendered by an attorney, even if those funds are the only way that that defendant will be able to retain the attorney of his choice. A robbery suspect for example, has no Sixth Amendment right to use funds he has stolen from a bank to retain an attorney to defend him if he is apprehended. The money, though in his possession, is not rightfully his; the government does not violate the Sixth Amendment if it seizes the robbery proceeds, and refuses to permit the defendant to use them to pay for his defense. * * * Petitioner seeks to distinguish such cases for Sixth Amendment purposes by arguing that the bank's claim to robbery proceeds rests on "pre-existing property rights," while the Government's claim to forfeitable assets rests on a "penal statute" which embodies the "fictive property-law concept of * * * relation-back" and is merely "a mechanism for preventing fraudulent conveyances of the defendant's assets, not * * * a device for determining true title to property." In light of this, petitioner contends, the burden placed on defendant's Sixth Amendment rights by the forfeiture statute outweighs the Government's interest in forfeiture. * * *

Petitioner's "balancing analysis" rests substantially on the view that the Government has only a modest interest in forfeitable assets that may be used to retain an attorney. Petitioner takes the position that, in large part, once assets have been paid over from client to attorney, the principal ends of forfeiture have been achieved: dispossessing a drug dealer or racketeer of the proceeds of his wrongdoing. We think that this view misses the mark for three reasons. First, the Government has a pecuniary interest in forfeiture that goes beyond merely separating a criminal from his ill-gotten gains; that legitimate interest extends to recovering ALL forfeitable assets, for such assets are deposited in a Fund that supports law-enforcement efforts in a variety of important and useful ways. See 28 U.S.C. section 524(c), which establishes the Department of Justice Assets Forfeiture Fund. The sums of money that can be raised for law-enforcement activities this way are substantial, and the Government's interest in using the profits of crime to fund these activities should not be discounted.

Second, the statute permits "rightful owners" of forfeited assets to make claims for forfeited assets before they are retained by the government. The Government's interest in winning undiminished forfeiture thus includes the objective of returning property, in full, to those wrongfully deprived or defrauded of it. Where the Government pursues this restitutionary end, the government's interest in forfeiture is virtually indistinguishable from its interest in returning to a bank the proceeds of a bank robbery; and a forfeiture-defendant's claim of right to use such assets to hire an attorney, instead of having them returned to their rightful owners, is no more persuasive than a bank robber's similar claim.

Finally, as we have recognized previously, a major purpose motivating congressional adoption and continued refinement of the RICO and CCE forfeiture provisions has been the desire to lessen the economic power of organized crime and drug enterprises. This includes the use of such economic power to retain private counsel. As the Court of Appeals put it: "Congress has already underscored the compelling public interest in stripping criminals such as Reckmeyer of their undeserved economic power, and part of that undeserved power may be the ability to command high-priced legal talent." The notion that the government has a legitimate interest in depriving criminals of economic power, even insofar as that power is used to retain counsel of choice, may be somewhat unsettling. But when a defendant claims that he has suffered some substantial impairment of his Sixth Amendment rights by virtue of the seizure or forfeiture of assets in his possession, such a complaint is no more than the reflection of "the harsh reality that the quality of a criminal defendant's representation frequently may turn on his ability to retain the best counsel money can buy." Morris v. Slappy, 461 U.S. 1, 23 (1983) (BRENNAN, J., concurring in result). Again, the Court of Appeals put it aptly: "The modern day Jean Valjean must be satisfied with appointed counsel. Yet the drug merchant claims that his possession of huge sums of money * * * entitles him to something more. We reject this contention, and any notion of a constitutional right to use the proceeds of crime to finance an expensive defense." 837 F.2d, at 649.

It is our view that there is a strong governmental interest in obtaining full recovery of all forfeitable assets, and interest that overrides any Sixth Amendment interest in permitting criminals to use assets adjudged forfeitable to pay for their defense. Otherwise, there would be an interference with a defendant's Sixth Amendment rights whenever the government freezes or takes some property in a defendant's possession before, during or after a criminal trial. So-called "jeopardy assessments"—IRS seizures of assets to secure potential tax liabilities—may impair a defendant's ability to retain counsel in a way similar to that complained of here. Yet these assessments have been upheld against constitutional attack, and we note that the respondent in Monsanto concedes their constitutionality. Moreover, petitioner's claim to a share of the forfeited assets postconviction would suggest that the government could never impose a burden on assets within a defendant's control that could be used to pay a lawyer. Criminal defendants, however, are not exempted from federal, state, and local taxation simply because these financial levies may deprive them of resources that could be used to hire an attorney. * * *

B

Petitioner's second constitutional claim is that the forfeiture statute is invalid under the Due Process Clause of the Fifth Amendment because it permits the Government to upset the balance of forces between the accused and his accuser. * * *

Forfeiture provisions are powerful weapons in the war on crime; like any such weapons, their impact can be devastating when used unjustly. But due process claims alleging such abuses are cognizable only in specific cases of prosecutorial misconduct (and petitioner has made no such allegation here) or when directed to a rule that is inherently unconstitutional. * * *

We rejected a claim similar to petitioner's last Term, in Wheat v. United States, 486 U.S. 153 (1988). In Wheat, the petitioner argued that permitting a court to disqualify a defendant's chosen counsel because of conflicts of interest—over that defendant's objection to the disqualification—would encourage the government to "manufacture" such conflicts to deprive a defendant of his chosen attorney. While acknowledging that this was possible, we declined to fashion the per se constitutional rule petitioner sought in Wheat, instead observing that "trial courts are undoubtedly aware of [the] possibility" of abuse, and would have to "take it into consideration," when dealing with disqualification motions. A similar approach should be taken here. The Constitution does not forbid the imposition of an otherwise permissible criminal sanction, such as forfeiture, merely because in some cases prosecutors may abuse the processes available to them, e.g., by attempting to impose them on persons who should not be subjected to that punishment. Cases involving particular abuses can be dealt with individually by the lower courts, when (and if) any such cases arise.

IV

For the reasons given above, we find that petitioner's statutory and constitutional challenges to the forfeiture imposed here are without merit. The judgment of the Court of Appeals is therefore

Affirmed.

JUSTICE BLACKMUN, with whom JUSTICE BRENNAN, JUSTICE MARSHALL, and JUSTICE STEVENS join, dissenting.

Those jurists who have held forth against the result the majority reaches in these cases have been guided by one core insight: that it is unseemly and unjust for the Government to beggar those it prosecutes in order to disable their defense at trial. The majority trivializes the burden the forfeiture law imposes on a criminal defendant. Instead, it should heed the warnings of our district court judges, whose day-to-day exposure to the criminal-trial process enables them to understand, perhaps far better than we, the devastating consequences of attorney's fee forfeiture for the integrity of our adversarial system of justice.

[The dissent endorsed the argument of Judge Winter's opinion in the *Monsanto* case, reasoning that Congress did not explicitly consider the attorney's fee issue and the statute could be construed to allow otherwise forfeitable assets to be used to the reasonable fees of privately retained counsel.]

The majority has decided otherwise, however, and for that reason is compelled to reach the constitutional issue it could have avoided. But the majority pauses hardly long enough to acknowledge the Sixth Amendment's protection of one's right to retain counsel of his choosing, let alone to explore its "full extent." Instead, it moves rapidly from the observation that "a defendant may not insist on representation by an attorney he cannot afford," to the conclusion that the Government is free to deem the defendant indigent by declaring his assets "tainted" by criminal activity the Government has yet to prove. * * * The majority's decision in this case reveals that it has lost track of the distinct role of the right to counsel of choice in protecting the integrity of the judicial process, a role that makes "the right to be represented by privately retained counsel * * * the primary, preferred component of the basic right" protected by the Sixth Amendment. The right to retain private counsel serves to foster the trust between attorney and client that is necessary for the attorney to be a truly effective advocate. Not only are decisions crucial to the defendant's liberty placed in counsel's hands, but the defendant's perception of the fairness of the process, and his willingness to acquiesce in its results, depend upon his confidence in his counsel's dedication, loyalty, and ability. * * *

The right to privately chosen and compensated counsel also serves broader institutional interests. The "virtual socialization of criminal defense work in this country" that would be the result of a widespread abandonment of the right to retain chosen counsel, too readily would standardize the provision of criminal-defense services and diminish de-

fense counsel's independence. There is a place in our system of criminal justice for the maverick and the risk-taker, for approaches that might not fit into the structured environment of a public defender's office, or that might displease a judge whose preference for nonconfrontational styles of advocacy might influence the judge's appointment decisions.
* * *

Had it been Congress' express aim to undermine the adversary system as we know it, it could hardly have found a better engine of destruction that attorney's-fee forfeiture. The main effect of forfeitures under the Act, of course, will be to deny the defendant the right to retain counsel, and therefore the right to have his defense designed and presented by an attorney he has chosen and trusts. If the Government restrains the defendant's assets before trial, private counsel will be unwilling to continue or to take on the defense. Even if no restraining order is entered, the possibility of forfeiture after conviction will itself substantially diminish the likelihood that private counsel will agree to take the case. The message to private counsel is "Do not represent this defendant or you will lose your fee." That being the kind of message lawyers are likely to take seriously, the defendant will find it difficult or impossible to secure representation.

The resulting relationship between the defendant and his court-appointed counsel will likely begin in distrust, and be exacerbated to the extent that the defendant perceives his new-found "indigency" as a form of punishment imposed by the Government in order to weaken his defense. If the defendant had been represented by private counsel earlier in the proceedings, the defendant's sense that the Government has stripped him of his defenses will be sharpened by the concreteness of his loss. Appointed counsel may be inexperienced and undercompensated and, for that reason, may not have adequate opportunity or resources to deal with the special problems presented by what is likely to be a complex trial. The already scarce resources of a public defender's office will be stretched to the limit. Facing a lengthy trial against a better-armed adversary, the temptation to recommend a guilty plea will be great. The result, if the defendant is convicted, will be a sense, often well grounded, that justice was not done.

Even if the defendant finds a private attorney who is "so foolish, ignorant, beholden or idealistic as to take the business," the attorney-client relationship will be undermined by the forfeiture statute. Perhaps the attorney will be willing to violate ethical norms by working on a contingent fee basis in a criminal case. But if he is not—and we should question the integrity of any criminal-defense attorney who would violate the ethical norms of the profession by doing so—the attorney's own interests will dictate that he remain ignorant of the source of the assets from which he is paid. Under section 853(c), a third-party transferee may keep assets if "the transferee establishes * * * that he is a bona fide purchaser for value of such property who at the time of purchase was reasonably without cause to believe that the property was subject to forfeiture under this section." The less an attorney knows, the greater the likelihood that he can claim to have been an "innocent" third party. The attorney's interest in knowing nothing is directly adverse to his client's interest in full disclosure. The result of the conflict may be a less vigorous investigation of the defendant's circumstances, leading in turn to a failure to recognize or pursue avenues of inquiry necessary to the defense. Other conflicts of interest are also likely to develop. The attorney who fears for his fee will be tempted to make the Government's waiver of fee-forfeiture the sine qua non for any plea agreement, a position which conflicts with his client's best interests. Perhaps most troubling is the fact that forfeiture statutes place the Government in the position to exercise an intolerable degree of power over any private attorney who takes on the task of representing a defendant in a forfeiture case. The decision whether to seek a restraining order rests with the prosecution, as does the decision whether to waive forfeiture upon a plea of guilty or a conviction at trial. The Government will be ever tempted to use the forfeiture weapon against a defense attorney who is particularly talented or aggressive on the client's behalf—the attorney who is better than what, in the Government's view, the defendant deserves. The spectre of the Government's selectively excluding only the most talented defense counsel is a serious threat to the equality of forces necessary for the adversarial system to perform at its best. An attorney whose fees are potentially subject to forfeiture will be forced to operate in an environment in which the Government is not only the defendant's adversary, but also his own. The long-term effects of the fee-forfeiture practice will be to decimate the private criminal-defense bar. As the use of the forfeiture mechanism expands to new categories of federal crimes and spreads to the States, only one class of defendants will be free routinely to retain private counsel: the affluent defendant accused of a crime that generates no economic gain. As the number of private clients diminishes, only the most idealistic and the least skilled of young lawyers will be attracted to the field, while the remainder seek greener pastures elsewhere.

In short, attorney's fee-forfeiture substantially undermines every interest served by the Sixth Amendment right to chosen counsel, on the individual and institutional levels, over the short term and the long haul.
* * *

In my view, the Act as interpreted by the majority is inconsistent with the intent of Congress, and seriously undermines the basic fairness of our criminal-justice system. That a majority of this Court has upheld the constitutionality of the Act as so interpreted will not deter Congress, I hope, from amending the Act to make clear that Congress did not intend this result. This Court has the power to declare the Act constitutional, but it cannot thereby make it wise.

I dissent.

DE FREECE v. STATE

Court of Criminal Appeals of Texas, 1993.
848 S.W.2d 150.

CLINTON, JUDGE

Appellant was convicted by a jury of the offense of murder and his punishment assessed by the trial court at 60 years confinement in the penitentiary. On appeal he argued that the trial court erred in failing to appoint an expert to assist him in evaluation, preparation, and presentation of his insanity defense, in violation of his constitutional rights to due process, equal protection, effective assistance of counsel and compulsory process * * *.

I.

Appellant and the deceased, Juanita Rodriguez, had a five-month-old son. On the morning of February 17, 1989, appellant went to the home of Juanita's parents in Eagle Pass, where she and the baby were staying. Appellant was told by Juanita's sister that Juanita and her parents and brother had left that morning to drive to Pecos. Based upon statements he claimed Juanita's mother had made on prior occasions, appellant decided that the group intended to sell the baby in Pecos, and set out after them. He caught up with them on Highway 90 between Dryden and Sanderson, and ran them off the road. According to his testimony, at this time appellant heard voices he "couldn't overcome" which commanded him to "kill, kill." He forced Juanita into his car, where he stabbed her numerous times in the chest and abdomen, and then cut her throat. Texas Rangers apprehended him the next day a mile from the scene, and he readily confessed * * *.

On June 23, 1989, the State filed a motion requesting that appellant be examined both for competency to stand trial and sanity at the time of the offense. Pursuant to [statutes], the trial court ordered appellant sent to Vernon State Hospital "for observation, examination and treatment." There, Dr. D.F. Martinez, a psychiatrist, diagnosed him as suffering from "Schizophrenia, Chronic, Undifferentiated Type." Dr. F.E. Heynen, a clinical psychologist, opined that appellant was incompetent to stand trial, but that at the time of the offense he "had substantial capacity to appreciate the wrongfulness of his behavior and understood that his behavior was unlawful." On September 11, 1989, a jury found appellant presently incompetent, but capable of attaining competency in the foreseeable future; judgment to that effect was entered on September 13, 1989. Accordingly, appellant was returned to Vernon State Hospital, where he was re-evaluated every ninety days. On December 7, 1989, and again on March 12, 1990, the hospital reported that appellant had not yet attained competency, apparently on recommendations from Dr. Martinez. Finally, on June 1, 1990, the trial court was notified that appellant was competent to stand trial, although Dr. Martinez advised that "he should continue his present medications consisting of neuroleptics and antidepressants."

On August 20, 1990, counsel for appellant filed a motion requesting the appointment of a psychiatric expert to assist in preparing and presenting his insanity defense * * *. Counsel clarified that he sought no particular expert, but simply any competent psychiatrist who: "would be a member of the defense team, would be available for helping preparation of the case, preparation for cross examination, deciding which tests were needed, range and form, that sort of thing, as well as being present during trial to help the defendant."

The trial court stated, inter alia, that "I've already appointed a psychiatrist to conduct an evaluation, and I don't feel I have to appoint another one." Instead, the court assured appellant's counsel that he would be afforded an opportunity to interview Dr. Heynen, who was scheduled to testify for the State, prior to cross-examining her. Counsel for appellant complained that he "did not believe the ability to speak to this one doctor solves the problem, because number one, she's already on record in writing as supporting the State's position, and number two, she will give no assistance in how to cross-examine her * * *. We think that we still need the expert on the defense team." The trial court denied both appellant's motions.

Trial commenced that same day. Other than his testimony that he had heard voices commanding him to "kill, kill," appellant presented no direct evidence to show he was insane at the time of the offense. In rebuttal the State put Dr. Heynen on the witness stand to testify that any voices appellant may have heard would not be "sufficiently compelling to cause him to forget that this was a wrongful thing to do." After reading a number of reports from other clinics, conducting a battery of tests, and consulting with other staff members at Vernon State Hospital, she concluded that appellant had known the difference between right and wrong when he committed the offense. After this testimony the trial court adjourned for the day, and Dr. Heynen assured the court that she would be available to consult with appellant's counsel.

The next morning counsel took Dr. Heynen on cross-examination. She agreed that appellant's records from his stay at Vernon State Hospital "weigh several pounds." Out of the presence of the jury appellant then renewed his motion for expert assistance to help him interpret those voluminous records with a view to cross-examining Dr. Heynen * * *. The trial court again denied the motion.

As cross-examination continued, Dr. Heynen verified that Dr. Martinez had diagnosed appellant as suffering from undifferentiated schizophrenia, organic brain syndrome, and extreme psychosocial stressors. Dr. Heynen admitted that she herself had found that appellant had "diffuse organic brain damage." She believed his earlier history of commitment to mental hospitals, however, was "generally because of drug abuse." Disagreeing with Dr. Martinez' evaluation of appellant as schizophrenic, Dr. Heynen opined that her own diagnostic skills "far exceed those of

Dr. Martinez." She acknowledged that another doctor had earlier found in appellant "the capacity * * * to decompensate and to be a danger to himself and others." She pointed out, however, that this doctor did not "give any reason why he thought he had decompensated." On redirect examination Dr. Heynen noted several typical characteristics of schizophrenia (e.g., incoherence, impaired personal hygiene, "flat affect") that appellant did not manifest.

During final argument appellant's counsel conceded that the evidence showed appellant caused the death of Rodriguez. Emphasizing appellant's history of mental health commitments and his apparently delusional belief that Rodriguez' family intended to sell his baby, counsel argued that the jury should find that when appellant killed Rodriguez, he did not appreciate the wrongfulness of his conduct. In rebuttal, the State stressed Dr. Heynen's testimony that appellant could distinguish right from wrong when he committed the offense. After deliberating for five hours, the jury returned a guilty verdict * * *.

We confront the question whether examination by "disinterested experts" at Vernon State Hospital, and testimony from at least one of those experts at trial about conclusions she drew from that examination, were sufficient to meet the due process minimum announced in Ake v. Oklahoma, 470 U.S. 68 (1985). Appellant does not claim he was deprived of the opportunity to be examined by a competent expert on the question of sanity, as was Ake. He does claim, however, that, having shown his sanity would be a significant factor at his trial, he should have been provided an expert of the court's choosing to help him evaluate and prepare his insanity defense, and meaningfully confront expert testimony adduced by the State. We agree, and hold that the trial court erred in denying him that assistance * * *.

Ake v. Oklahoma

Accused of capital murder, Glen Burton Ake displayed such odd behavior at his arraignment that the trial court ordered an examination to decide whether he should be observed to determine his competency to stand trial. The psychiatrist who examined Ake concluded he was a paranoid schizophrenic, and he was committed to a state hospital, where he was found incompetent. Six weeks later he was found to have regained competency, subject to continued treatment with an antipsychotic drug, Thorazine. Prior to trial his attorney indicated he would raise the defense of insanity, and requested psychiatric assistance, since Ake was indigent. Even though the state hospital had made no determination of Ake's sanity at the time of the offense, the trial court denied his request. "As a result there was no expert testimony for either side on Ake's sanity at the time of the offense." Ake v. Oklahoma, 470 U.S. at 72. The Oklahoma Court of Criminal Appeals affirmed Ake's conviction, holding that the State had no obligation to provide psychiatric services to indigents in capital cases.

The United States Supreme Court reversed Ake's conviction. In its opinion the Court began by reaffirming the principle that due process requires that the indigent accused in a criminal trial must be equipped with the "basic tools" to ensure "a proper functioning of the adversary process." Deciding whether a psychiatric expert was necessary to that end, the Court considered three factors borrowed from cases involving questions of procedural due process, viz:

> "The first is the private interest that will be affected by the action of the State. The second is the governmental interest that will be affected if the safeguard is to be provided. The third is the probable value of the additional or substitute procedural safeguards that are sought, and the risk of an erroneous deprivation of the affected interest if those safeguards are not provided."

The accused's interest in maintaining the institutional presumption of innocence, the Court observed, "is obvious." The State, on the other hand, has more than the ordinary adversarial interest in prevailing; it has a concomitant interest in the fairness of the proceeding and the accuracy of the result. Moreover, because most states already provide some level of psychiatric assistance to the accused, that burden cannot be prohibitive. In these lights the Court concluded that the State's interest "is not substantial."

Assessing the third factor, the Court began "by considering the pivotal role that psychiatry has come to play in criminal proceedings." "In this role, psychiatrists gather facts, through professional examination, interviews, and elsewhere, that they will share with the judge and jury; they analyze the information gathered and from it draw plausible conclusions about the defendant's mental condition, and about the effects of any disorder on behavior; and they offer opinions about how the defendant's mental condition might have affected his behavior at the time in question. They know the probative questions to ask of the opposing party's psychiatrists and how to interpret their answers." Id., U.S. at 80.

Thus, psychiatric experts may assist lay judges and jurors to make an informed decision about the sanity of the accused at the time of the offense. Because psychiatry is not "an exact science," however, juries remain the "primary factfinders," and, the Court suggested, it is important that the jury hear "the psychiatrists for each party" to equip it to make as informed a decision as possible. To avoid the risk of an inaccurate verdict, the Court concluded, an indigent accused must be provided an expert "to conduct a professional examination on issues relevant to the defense, to help determine whether the insanity defense is viable, to present testimony, and to assist in preparing the cross-examination of a State's psychiatric witnesses." Id., U.S. at 82.

The Court concluded: "We therefore hold that when a defendant demonstrates to the trial judge that his sanity at the time of the offense is to be a significant factor at trial, the State must, at a minimum, assure the defendant access to a competent psychiatrist who will conduct an appropriate examination and assist in evaluation, preparation, and presentation of the defense. That is not to say, of course, that the indigent defendant has a constitutional right to choose a psychiatrist of his personal liking or to receive funds to hire his own. Our concern is that the indigent defendant have access to a competent psychiatrist for the purpose we have discussed, and as in the case of the provision of counsel we leave to the State the decision on how to implement this right." 470 U.S. at 83.[1]

Commentators have noted an "ambiguity" in *Ake,* a seeming internal contradiction between the express right to a single competent psychiatric expert not of the accused's choosing, on the one hand, and indications throughout the opinion, on the other, that the accused is entitled to an expert who will participate with him as a partisan in the case. Some courts have targeted the first aspect of *Ake* to hold that a single "neutral" expert is all the State need supply to ensure proper adversarial functioning. Thus, many courts have denied *Ake* claims where the accused has received an examination in a state mental institution pursuant to court order, holding that the state-sponsored examination met all due process requirements. [Citations] In each of these cases, however, the state institution had found no reason to doubt the defendant's sanity, and therefore the court also found the defendant had not shown insanity would be a significant factor at trial in any event. Many other courts have held similarly that, where a state-sponsored examination reveals no likelihood of insanity at the time of the offense, a defendant has not met the threshold requirements for relief under *Ake.* [Citations] [Almost every] court that has found the defendant did make an adequate showing that insanity would be a significant factor, however, has also held that *Ake* entitled him to more than an examination and testimony, if favorable, from a neutral psychiatric expert.

Thus, it is true that some jurisdictions have said, essentially in dicta, that the statutory provision of a single neutral psychiatrist to service both parties and the court is sufficient to meet the due process minimum of *Ake.* However, it appears that * * * the greater weight of authority holds otherwise. And, in our view, with good reason.

Ours is an adversarial system of criminal justice, not an inquisitorial one. Either mode of inquiry is aimed at assessing the truth. However, the adversarial model rests on the assumption that each party to a dispute, motivated by self-interest, will develop his position to the greatest extent possible within the boundaries of the rules of evidence and procedure, thus providing the factfinder an optimal vantage from which to gauge all relevant facts and make an informed decision on the merits. In Ake the Supreme Court reiterated that where the defendant is indigent, due process requires that the State guarantee he be at least minimally equipped to participate meaningfully in this adversarial process.

Where sanity of the indigent accused will be a significant factor at trial, psychiatry has come to play a "pivotal role." But since psychiatry

---

1. This Court does not understand the holding of Ake to be limited to the context of capital offenses. See McBride v. State, 838 S.W.2d 248 (Tex.Cr.App.1992).

"is not * * * an exact science," equally competent practitioners confronted with the same raw data often disagree in their diagnoses in an area that is "inevitably complex and foreign" to lawyers and juries alike. Ake, 470 U.S. at 81. Although psychiatric testimony is undoubtedly useful in the resolution of many issues in the adversary trial context, including sanity at the time of the offense: "none of these issues * * * can be addressed by a psychiatrist with absolute certainty. Thus, to expect the 'objective' opinion of an amicus expert to yield 'the answer' in a particular case is unrealistic. Unless the choices made by the psychiatrist in the establishment and proof of his or her hypothesis are open to informed scrutiny, the psychiatrist's conclusions are of limited value. And, unless each party has access to psychiatric assistance in preparing and directing this scrutiny, it cannot be expected that the scrutiny will be adequately informed. Indeed, each party must have the opportunity to explore and explain the relevant psychiatric data in a case if the conclusions drawn from these data are properly to be understood by the judge or the jury and the 'truth' is to be most closely approximated. This is the teaching of Ake v. Oklahoma." Showalter & Fitch, Objectivity and Advocacy in "Forensic Psychiatry After Ake v. Oklahoma," 15 J. Psychiatry & L., 177, at 186 (1987).

Because psychiatric evidence is at once esoteric and uncertain, the indigent accused needs a psychiatrist, inter alia, "to help determine whether the insanity defense is viable, to present testimony, and to assist in preparing the cross-examination of a State's psychiatric witness," if he is to present the factfinder with a perspective broad enough to ensure an informed resolution of the sanity question. 470 U.S. at 82. Otherwise the risk of error is intolerably high, and due process will be offended * * *.

The State does not contest that in this cause appellant demonstrated to the trial court that insanity would be a significant factor at trial, as indeed it turned out to be * * *. Counsel for appellant did not ask for anything more than he was minimally entitled to under *Ake.* He did not request a particular psychiatrist, but only a single competent one. Nor did he seek a psychiatrist who would necessarily testify that his client was insane at the time of the offense. He simply sought expert guidance in evaluating the strength of appellant's defense, presenting it in the best possible light to the jury, and, in particular, in scrutinizing the testimony of Dr. Heynen, the only expert opinion then available that directly addressed the question of appellant's ability to distinguish right from wrong. Even a neutral "court's expert" cannot effectively prepare counsel to cross-examine herself. We hold that the trial court erred in denying appellant's request for the appointment of a psychiatrist to aid in the preparation and presentation of his insanity defense.

We therefore reverse the judgment and remand the cause for a new trial.

STRICKLAND v. WASHINGTON

Supreme Court of the United States, 1984.
466 U.S. 668, 104 S.Ct. 2052, 80 L.Ed.2d 674.

JUSTICE O'CONNOR delivered the opinion of the Court.

This case requires us to consider the proper standards for judging a criminal defendant's contention that the Constitution requires a conviction or death sentence to be set aside because counsel's assistance at the trial or sentencing was ineffective.

I

A

During a ten-day period in September 1976, respondent planned and committed three groups of crimes, which included three brutal stabbing murders, torture, kidnapping, severe assaults, attempted murders, attempted extortion, and theft. After his two accomplices were arrested, respondent surrendered to police and voluntarily gave a lengthy statement confessing to the third of the criminal episodes. The State of Florida indicted respondent for kidnapping and murder and appointed an experienced criminal lawyer to represent him.

Counsel actively pursued pretrial motions and discovery. He cut his efforts short, however, and he experienced a sense of hopelessness about the case, when he learned that, against his specific advice, respondent had also confessed to the first two murders. By the date set for trial, respondent was subject to indictment for three counts of first degree murder and multiple counts of robbery, kidnapping for ransom, breaking and entering and assault, attempted murder, and conspiracy to commit robbery. Respondent waived his right to a jury trial, again acting against counsel's advice, and pleaded guilty to all charges, including the three capital murder charges.

In the plea colloquy, respondent told the trial judge that, although he had committed a string of burglaries, he had no significant prior criminal record and that at the time of his criminal spree he was under extreme stress caused by his inability to support his family. He also stated, however, that he accepted responsibility for the crimes. The trial judge told respondent that he had "a great deal of respect for people who are willing to step forward and admit their responsibility" but that he was making no statement at all about his likely sentencing decision. App. 62.

Counsel advised respondent to invoke his right under Florida law to an advisory jury at his capital sentencing hearing. Respondent rejected the advice and waived the right. He chose instead to be sentenced by the trial judge without a jury recommendation.

In preparing for the sentencing hearing, counsel spoke with respondent about his background. He also spoke on the telephone with respondent's wife and mother, though he did not follow up on the one unsuccessful effort to meet with them. He did not otherwise seek out character witnesses for respondent. Nor did he request a psychiatric examination, since his conversations with his client gave no indication that respondent had psychological problems.

Counsel decided not to present and hence not to look further for evidence concerning respondent's character and emotional state. That decision reflected trial counsel's sense of hopelessness about overcoming the evidentiary effect of respondent's confessions to the gruesome crimes. It also reflected the judgment that it was advisable to rely on the plea colloquy for evidence about respondent's background and about his claim of emotional stress: the plea colloquy communicated sufficient information about these subjects, and by foregoing the opportunity to present new evidence on these subjects, counsel prevented the State from cross-examining respondent on his claim and from putting on psychiatric evidence of its own.

Counsel also excluded from the sentencing hearing other evidence he thought was potentially damaging. He successfully moved to exclude respondent's "rap sheet." Because he judged that a presentence report might prove more detrimental than helpful, as it would have included respondent's criminal history and thereby undermined the claim of no significant history of criminal activity, he did not request that one be prepared.

At the sentencing hearing, counsel's strategy was based primarily on the trial judge's remarks at the plea colloquy as well as on his reputation as a sentencing judge who thought it important for a convicted defendant to own up to his crime. Counsel argued that respondent's remorse and acceptance of responsibility justified sparing him from the death penalty. Counsel also argued that respondent had no history of criminal activity and that respondent committed the crimes under extreme mental or emotional disturbance, thus coming within the statutory list of mitigating circumstances. He further argued that respondent should be spared death because he had surrendered, confessed, and offered to testify against a co-defendant and because respondent was fundamentally a good person who had briefly gone badly wrong in extremely stressful circumstances. The State put on evidence and witnesses largely for the purpose of describing the details of the crimes. Counsel did not cross-examine the medical experts who testified about the manner of death of respondent's victims.

The trial judge found several aggravating circumstances with respect to each of the three murders. He found that all three murders were especially heinous, atrocious, and cruel, all involving repeated stabbings. All three murders were committed in the course of at least one other dangerous and violent felony, and since all involved robbery, the murders were for pecuniary gain. All three murders were committed to avoid arrest for the accompanying crimes and to hinder law enforcement. In the course of one of the murders, respondent knowingly subjected numerous persons to a grave risk of death by deliberately stabbing and shooting the murder victim's sisters-in-law, who sustained severe—in one case, ultimately fatal—injuries.

With respect to mitigating circumstances, the trial judge made the same findings for all three capital murders. First, although there was no admitted evidence of prior convictions, respondent had stated that he had engaged in a course of stealing. In any case, even if respondent had no significant history of criminal activity, the aggravating circumstances "would still clearly far outweigh" that mitigating factor. Second, the judge found that, during all three crimes, respondent was not suffering from extreme mental or emotional disturbance and could appreciate the criminality of his acts. Third, none of the victims was a participant in, or consented to, respondent's conduct. Fourth, respondent's participation in the crimes was neither minor nor the result of duress or domination by an accomplice. Finally, respondent's age (26) could not be considered a factor in mitigation, especially when viewed in light of respondent's planning of the crimes and disposition of the proceeds of the various accompanying thefts.

In short, the trial judge found numerous aggravating circumstances and no (or a single comparatively insignificant) mitigating circumstance. * * * He therefore sentenced respondent to death on each of the three counts of murder and to prison terms for the other crimes. The Florida Supreme Court upheld the convictions and sentences on direct appeal.

B

Respondent subsequently sought collateral relief in state court on numerous grounds, among them that counsel had rendered ineffective assistance at the sentencing proceeding. Respondent challenged counsel's assistance in six respects. He asserted that counsel was ineffective because he failed to move for a continuance to prepare for sentencing, to request a psychiatric report, to investigate and present character witnesses, to seek a presentence investigation report, to present meaningful arguments to the sentencing judge, and to investigate the medical examiner's reports or cross-examine the medical experts. In support of the claim, respondent submitted fourteen affidavits from friends, neighbors, and relatives stating that they would have testified if asked to do so. He also submitted one psychiatric report and one psychological report stating that respondent, though not under the influence of extreme mental or emotional disturbance, was "chronically frustrated and depressed because of his economic dilemma" at the time of his crimes. * * *

[After the state courts denied relief, respondent brought this action for federal habeas corpus. The federal district court denied the petition, but the Court of Appeals ordered further hearings on the ineffective assistance of counsel claim. The Supreme Court granted the State's petition for certiorari

> "to consider the standards by which to judge a contention that the Constitution requires that a criminal judgment be overturned because of the actual ineffective assistance of counsel." * * *

II

Court has recognized that "the right to counsel is the right to the effective assistance of counsel." *McMann v. Richardson*, 397 U.S. 759, 771 (1970). Government violates the right to effective assistance when it interferes in certain ways with the ability of counsel to make independent decisions about how to conduct the defense. See, *e.g., Geders v. United States*, 425 U.S. 80 (1976) (bar on attorney-client consultation during overnight recess); *Herring v. New York*, 422 U.S. 853 (bar on summation at bench trial); *Brooks v. Tennessee*, 406 U.S. 605 (requirement that defendant be first defense witness); *Ferguson v. Georgia*, 365 U.S. 570 (bar on direct examination of defendant). Counsel, however, can also deprive a defendant of the right to effective assistance, simply by failing to render "adequate legal assistance," *Cuyler v. Sullivan* [p. 422 of this book] (actual conflict of interest adversely affecting lawyer's performance renders assistance ineffective).

The Court has not elaborated on the meaning of the constitutional requirement of effective assistance in the latter class of cases—that is, those presenting claims of "actual ineffectiveness." In giving meaning to the requirement, however, we must take its purpose—to ensure a fair trial—as the guide. The benchmark for judging any claim of ineffectiveness must be whether counsel's conduct so undermined the proper functioning of the adversarial process that the trial cannot be relied on as having produced a just result.

The same principle applies to a capital sentencing proceeding such as that provided by Florida law. We need not consider the role of counsel in an ordinary sentencing, which may involve informal proceedings and standardless discretion in the sentencer, and hence may require a different approach to the definition of constitutionally effective assistance. A capital sentencing proceeding like the one involved in this case, however, is sufficiently like a trial in its adversarial format and in the existence of standards for decision, that counsel's role in the proceeding is comparable to counsel's role at trial—to ensure that the adversarial testing process works to produce a just result under the standards governing decision. For purposes of describing counsel's duties, therefore, Florida's capital sentencing proceeding need not be distinguished from an ordinary trial.

III

A convicted defendant's claim that counsel's assistance was so defective as to require reversal of a conviction or death sentence has two components. First, the defendant must show that counsel's performance was deficient. This requires showing that counsel made errors so serious that counsel was not functioning as the "counsel" guaranteed the defendant by the Sixth Amendment. Second, the defendant must show that the deficient performance prejudiced the defense. This requires showing that counsel's errors were so serious as to deprive the defendant of a fair trial, a trial whose result is reliable. Unless a defendant makes both showings, it cannot be said that the conviction or death sentence resulted from a breakdown in the adversary process that renders the result unreliable.

A

As all the Federal Courts of Appeals have now held, the proper standard for attorney performance is that of reasonably effective assistance. * * * Representation of a criminal defendant entails certain basic duties. Counsel's function is to assist the defendant, and hence counsel owes the client a duty of loyalty, a duty to avoid conflicts of interest. From counsel's function as assistant to the defendant derive the overarching duty to advocate the defendant's cause and the more particular duties to consult with the defendant on important decisions and to keep the defendant informed of important developments in the course of the prosecution. Counsel also has a duty to bring to bear such skill and knowledge as will render the trial a reliable adversarial testing process. * * *

Judicial scrutiny of counsel's performance must be highly deferential. It is all too tempting for a defendant to second-guess counsel's assistance after conviction or adverse sentence, and it is all too easy for a court, examining counsel's defense after it has proved unsuccessful, to conclude that a particular act or omission of counsel was unreasonable. * * *

These standards require no special amplification in order to define counsel's duty to investigate, the duty at issue in this case. As the Court of Appeals concluded, strategic choices made after thorough investigation of law and facts relevant to plausible options are virtually unchallengeable; and strategic choices made after less than complete investigation are reasonable precisely to the extent that reasonable professional judgments support the limitations on investigation. In other words, counsel has a duty to make reasonable investigations or to make a reasonable decision that makes particular investigations unnecessary. In any ineffectiveness case, a particular decision not to investigate must be directly assessed for reasonableness in all the circumstances, applying a heavy measure of deference to counsel's judgments. * * *

B

An error by counsel, even if professionally unreasonable, does not warrant setting aside the judgment of a criminal proceeding if the error had no effect on the judgment. The purpose of the Sixth Amendment guarantee of counsel is to ensure that a defendant has the assistance necessary to justify reliance on the outcome of the proceeding. Accordingly, any deficiencies in counsel's performance must be prejudicial to the defense in order to constitute ineffective assistance under the Constitution.

In certain Sixth Amendment contexts, prejudice is presumed. Actual or constructive denial of the assistance of counsel altogether is legally presumed to result in prejudice. So are various kinds of state interference with counsel's assistance. Prejudice in these circumstances is so likely that case by case inquiry into prejudice is not worth the cost. Moreover, such circumstances involve impairments of the Sixth Amendment right that are easy to identify and, for that reason and because the prosecution is directly responsible, easy for the government to prevent.

One type of actual ineffectiveness claim warrants a similar, though more limited, presumption of prejudice. In *Cuyler v. Sullivan*, the Court held that prejudice is presumed when counsel is burdened by an actual conflict of interest. In those circumstances, counsel breaches the duty of loyalty, perhaps the most basic of counsel's duties. Moreover, it is difficult to measure the precise effect on the defense of representation corrupted by conflicting interests. Given the obligation of counsel to avoid conflicts of interest and the ability of trial courts to make early inquiry in certain situations likely to give rise to conflicts, see, *e.g.*, Fed.Rule Crim.Proc. 44(c), it is reasonable for the criminal justice system to maintain a fairly rigid rule of presumed prejudice for conflicts of interest. Even so, the rule is not quite the *per se* rule of prejudice that exists for the Sixth Amendment claims mentioned above. Prejudice is presumed only if the defendant demonstrates that counsel "actively represented conflicting interests" and "that an actual conflict of interest adversely affected his lawyer's performance."

Conflict of interest claims aside, actual ineffectiveness claims alleging a deficiency in attorney performance are subject to a general requirement that the defendant affirmatively prove prejudice. * * *

On the other hand, we believe that a defendant need not show that counsel's deficient conduct more likely than not altered the outcome in the case. This outcome-determinative standard has several strengths. It defines the relevant inquiry in a way familiar to courts, though the inquiry, as is inevitable, is anything but precise. The standard also reflects the profound importance of finality in criminal proceedings. Moreover, it comports with the widely used standard for assessing motions for new trial based on newly discovered evidence. Nevertheless, the standard is not quite appropriate.

Even when the specified attorney error results in the omission of certain evidence, the newly discovered evidence standard is not an apt source from which to draw a prejudice standard for ineffectiveness claims. The high standard for newly discovered evidence claims presupposes that all the essential elements of a presumptively accurate and fair proceeding were present in the proceeding whose result is challenged. An ineffective assistance claim asserts the absence of one of the crucial assurances that the result of the proceeding is reliable, so finality concerns are somewhat weaker and the appropriate standard of prejudice should be somewhat lower. The result of a proceeding can be rendered unreliable, and hence the proceeding itself unfair, even if the errors of counsel cannot be shown by a preponderance of the evidence to have determined the outcome.

Accordingly, the appropriate test for prejudice finds its roots in the test for materiality of exculpatory information not disclosed to the defense by the prosecution, *United States v. Agurs*, [p. 685 of this book], and in the test for materiality of testimony made unavailable to the defense by Government deportation of a witness, *United States v. Valenzuela–Bernal*, 458 U.S., at 872–874. The defendant must show that there is a reasonable probability that, but for counsel's unprofessional errors, the result of the proceeding would have been different. A reasonable probability is a probability sufficient to undermine confidence in the outcome. * * *

V

Application of the governing principles is not difficult in this case. The facts as described above, make clear that the conduct of respondent's counsel at and before respondent's sentencing proceeding cannot be found unreasonable. They also make clear that, even assuming the challenged conduct of counsel was unreasonable, respondent suffered insufficient prejudice to warrant setting aside his death sentence.

With respect to the performance component, the record shows that respondent's counsel made a strategic choice to argue for the extreme emotional distress mitigating circumstance and to rely as fully as possible on respondent's acceptance of responsibility for his crimes. Although counsel understandably felt hopeless about respondent's prospects, nothing in the record indicates, that counsel's sense of hopelessness distorted his professional judgment. Counsel's strategy choice was well within the range of professionally reasonable judgments, and the decision not to seek more character or psychological evidence than was already in hand was likewise reasonable.

The trial judge's views on the importance of owning up to one's crimes were well known to counsel. The aggravating circumstances were utterly overwhelming. Trial counsel could reasonably surmise from his conversations with respondent that character and psychological evidence would be of little help. Respondent had already been able to mention at the plea colloquy the substance of what there was to know about his financial and emotional troubles. Restricting testimony on respondent's character to what had come in at the plea colloquy ensured that contrary character and psychological evidence and respondent's criminal history, which counsel had successfully moved to exclude, would not come in. On these facts, there can be little question, even without application of the presumption of adequate performance, that trial counsel's defense, though unsuccessful, was the result of reasonable professional judgment.

With respect to the prejudice component, the lack of merit of respondent's claim is even more stark. The evidence that respondent says his trial counsel should have offered at the sentencing hearing would barely have altered the sentencing profile presented to the sentencing judge. As the state courts and District Court found, at most this evidence shows that numerous people who knew respondent thought he was generally a good person and that a psychiatrist and a psychologist believed he was under considerable emotional stress that did not rise to the level of extreme disturbance. Given the overwhelming aggravating factors, there is no reasonable probability that the omitted evidence would have changed the conclusion that the aggravating circumstances outweighed the mitigating circumstances and, hence, the sentence imposed. Indeed, admission of the evidence respondent now offers might even have been harmful to his case: his "rap sheet" would probably have been admitted into evidence, and the psychological reports would have directly contradicted respondent's claim that the mitigating circumstance of extreme emotional disturbance applied to his case. * * *

We conclude, therefore, that the District Court properly declined to issue a writ of habeas corpus. The judgment of the Court of Appeals is accordingly reversed.

Justice Brennan, concurring in part and dissenting in part.

I join the Court's opinion but dissent from its judgment. Adhering to my view that the death penalty is in all circumstances cruel and unusual punishment forbidden by the Eighth and Fourteenth Amendments, I would vacate respondent's death sentence and remand the case for further proceedings.

I join the Court's opinion because I believe that the standards it sets out today will both provide helpful guidance to courts considering claims of actual ineffectiveness of counsel and also permit those courts to continue their efforts to achieve progressive development of this area of the law. * * *

Justice Marshall, dissenting.

* * *

It is undisputed that respondent's trial counsel made virtually no investigation of the possibility of obtaining testimony from respondent's relatives, friends, or former employers pertaining to respondent's character or background. Had counsel done so, he would have found several persons willing and able to testify that, in their experience, respondent was a responsible, nonviolent man, devoted to his family, and active in the affairs of his church. Respondent contends that his lawyer could have and should have used that testimony to "humanize" respondent, to counteract the impression conveyed by the trial that he was little more than a cold-blooded killer. Had this evidence been admitted, respondent argues, his chances of obtaining a life sentence would have been significantly better. * * * The State makes a colorable—though in my view not compelling—argument that defense counsel in this case might have made a reasonable "strategic" decision not to present such evidence at the sentencing hearing on the assumption that an unadorned acknowledgement of respondent's responsibility for his crimes would be more likely to appeal to the trial judge, who was reputed to respect persons who accepted responsibility for their actions. But however justifiable such a choice might have been after counsel had fairly assessed the potential strength of the mitigating evidence available to him, counsel's failure to make any significant effort to find out what evidence might be garnered from respondent's relatives and acquaintances surely cannot be described as "reasonable." Counsel's failure to investigate is particularly suspicious in light of his candid admission that respondent's confessions and conduct in the course of the trial gave him a feeling of "hopelessness" regarding the possibility of saving respondent's life.

That the aggravating circumstances implicated by respondent's criminal conduct were substantial does not vitiate respondent's constitutional claim; judges and juries in cases involving behavior at least as egregious have shown mercy, particularly when afforded an opportunity to see other facets of the defendant's personality and life. Nor is respondent's contention defeated by the possibility that the material his counsel turned up might not have been sufficient to establish a statutory mitigating circumstance under Florida law; Florida sentencing judges and the Florida Supreme Court sometimes refuse to impose death sentences in cases in which, even though *statutory* mitigating circumstances do not outweigh statutory aggravating circumstances, the addition of nonstatutory mitigating circumstances tips the scales in favor of life imprisonment.

If counsel had investigated the availability of mitigating evidence, he might well have decided to present some such material at the hearing. If he had done so, there is a significant chance that respondent would have been given a life sentence. In my view, those possibilities, conjoined with the unreasonableness of counsel's failure to investigate, are more than sufficient to establish a violation of the Sixth Amendment and to entitle respondent to a new sentencing proceeding.

I respectfully dissent.

Commentary

There are two basically different approaches which may be used to resolve claims of ineffective assistance of counsel. First, there is the approach employed by the Supreme Court in *Strickland*. This approach requires the defendant to demonstrate that counsel made very serious errors or inexcusable omissions, and that there is a reasonable probability that these errors or omissions affected the outcome. The fact that counsel was lazy, or inexperienced, or unprepared would not in itself indicate ineffective assistance unless specific errors of judgment or tactics resulted from these defects and caused prejudice to the defendant. Moreover, the reviewing court is careful to grant all reasonable deference to counsel's judgment, and to avoid second-guessing in the light of hindsight. Where this approach is taken, convicted defendants seldom obtain relief on the ground of ineffective assistance of counsel.

The alternative approach is more effective in protecting badly represented defendants, perhaps *too* effective. A court favoring this "categorical" approach looks to see if counsel did all the things which a well-prepared and diligent defense lawyer ought to have done. Did counsel interview and advise the defendant, make appropriate discovery motions, study the reports obtained, interview potential witnesses, and in general prepare all reasonable defense issues to the extent necessary to make informed tactical judgments? If the lawyer did not do all these things then the defendant did not have the effective assistance of counsel, however guilty he may have been and however richly he deserved the punishment imposed. Prejudice ought to be presumed, unless the *prosecution* can show beyond a reasonable doubt that counsel's inadequate performance could not have affected the outcome. Such a showing ought to be extremely difficult to make, because it is so inherently difficult to know for certain whether a better lawyer could have achieved a better result. The case for the categorical approach is argued in Judge Bazelon's dissenting opinion in United States v. Decoster, 624 F.2d 196 (D.C.Cir.1976) (en banc). The Supreme Court decisively rejected this approach in Strickland and in United States v. Cronic, 466 U.S. 648 (1984).

The categorical approach has some obvious advantages. An inquiry into whether a better lawyer could have won the case is not a satisfactory substitute for having the better lawyer in the first place. It may be difficult to provide every defendant with a dedicated and competent lawyer, but this is not a fully satisfactory response to the claim that due process of law requires no less. Even so, leading courts have found sufficient difficulties with the categorical approach to justify their consistent refusal to adopt it. The prospect that the defense attorney can cause a new trial by failing to perform some duty of preparation invites "extensive supervision by the trial judge through a pretrial 'checklist' to ensure that counsel has met his duties of preparation, and oversight of the conduct of the trial." United States v. Decoster, 624 F.2d 196, 216 (D.C.Cir.1976) (opinion of Judge Leventhal). According to Judge Leventhal, "the manifest consequence would be inevitable and increasing intrusion into the development and presentation of the defense case by the trial judge, and (out of self-protection) by the prosecution." The result might be a "reordering of the adversary system" in the direction of "the inquisitorial system of the Continent." *Id.* at 216–217.

Whether a reordering of the adversary system would be altogether a bad thing is a matter of opinion. The adversary system at its best has great virtues, but there may be grounds to question whether it can be expected to operate effectively in the conditions of contemporary urban American society, with our enormous crime rates, overburdened courts, and poverty-impaired defendants. Lack of sufficient resources is not the only problem. The "sense of hopelessness" described by defense counsel in *Strickland* is not uncommon among attorneys who regularly defend persons who seem obviously guilty of serious crimes. On the other hand, if by some miracle we actually did succeed in providing every defendant with the kind of representation that an intelligent millionaire might purchase, the adversary system might have to be modified to protect the courts from the resulting profusion of motions and hearings.

The Supreme Court has said that ineffective assistance of counsel claims are judged by the same standard regardless of whether counsel is retained and chosen by the defendant or appointed by the court. According to an opinion for the Court by Justice Powell:

> A proper respect for the Sixth Amendment disarms petitioner's contention that defendants who retain their own lawyers are entitled to less protection than defendants for whom the State appoints counsel. We may assume with confidence that most counsel, whether retained or appointed, will protect the rights of an accused. But experience teaches that, in some cases, retained counsel will not provide adequate represen-

tation. The vital guarantee of the Sixth Amendment would stand for little if the often uninformed decision to retain a particular lawyer could reduce or forfeit the defendant's entitlement to constitutional protection. Since the State's conduct of a criminal trial itself implicates the State in the defendant's conviction, we see no basis for drawing a distinction between retained and appointed counsel that would deny equal justice to defendants who must choose their own lawyers. Cuyler v. Sullivan, 446 U.S. 335, 344–45 (1980).

The defendant in *Cuyler v. Sullivan* was charged with two other persons (Carchidi and DiPasquale) in a double murder. Originally represented by his own counsel, defendant Sullivan eventually accepted representation from two privately retained lawyers (DiBona and Peruto) who were paid by friends of the three defendants and represented all three throughout the proceedings. The three defendants were tried separately: Sullivan was convicted, and the other two were acquitted. The prosecution's circumstantial case was based entirely on the testimony of a janitor, who saw the three defendants in the building just before he heard sounds that must have been the fatal shots. Before the shooting the defendants had urged him to do his work another day, and after the shooting defendant Carchidi told the janitor to leave the building and say nothing. At the close of the prosecution's case in the Sullivan trial, the defense rested without presenting any evidence.

In subsequent federal habeas corpus proceedings, the constitutional question turned on whether the failure to present any defense evidence was a reasonable tactical decision in view of the circumstantial nature of the prosecution's case, or whether it was affected by counsel's concern to protect the interests of Carchidi and DiPasquale in their upcoming trials. Carchidi later claimed that he would have testified at Sullivan's trial to deny that he had directed the janitor to leave the building immediately after the shooting. The two lawyers gave conflicting testimony on whether the decision not to call Carchidi or present other evidence had been influenced by a desire to protect the other defendants (who of course could have refused to testify in any event). The federal Court of Appeals held that resting at the close of the prosecutor's case "would have been a legitimate tactical decision if made by independent counsel," but that in the circumstances the action provided sufficient indication of a conflict of interest to require a new trial.

The Supreme Court vacated and remanded. The opinion by Justice Powell first distinguished Holloway v. Arkansas, 435 U.S. 475 (1978). In *Holloway*, a single public defender represented three defendants at the same trial, and the state trial judge refused to consider the appointment of separate counsel despite the defense lawyer's timely and repeated assertions that the interests of the clients conflicted. The Supreme Court found that this failure to inquire into the need for separate representation unconstitutionally endangered the right to counsel, and required reversal of the resulting convictions without further determination of prejudice.

In *Cuyler v. Sullivan*, by way of contrast, no one had objected to the multiple representation and nothing in the circumstances indicated that there would be conflicting defenses. The trial court therefore had no constitutional duty to inquire into any possible conflict of interest. If, however, an *actual* conflict of interest adversely affected the defense lawyer's performance, the defendant should have a new trial without having to demonstrate further prejudice. In other words, if the failure to call defense witnesses was motivated by a desire to protect other clients, then Sullivan should have a new trial without the need to show that the defense might have been successful. On remand, the Court of Appeals found that counsel's performance had been adversely affected, and ordered a new trial despite the argument that Carchidi probably would have invoked the Fifth Amendment if he had been represented by independent counsel and called as a witness at Sullivan's trial. Sullivan v. Cuyler, 723 F.2d 1077 (3d Cir.1983).

Sometimes, two or more defendants desire to be represented by the same lawyer despite the existence of an apparent conflict of interest. The right to waive the conflict and proceed to trial with joint representation is not absolute, however. In Wheat v. United States, 486 U.S. 153 (1988), a closely divided Supreme Court held that trial courts have an independent responsibility to ensure compliance with the appropriate standards of professional responsibility for attorneys, and upheld a conviction where a federal district judge had exercised his discretion not to allow a defendant to substitute as trial counsel an attorney who was also representing co-defendants in the same prosecution. In *Wheat* it was the prosecution that objected to the substitution, and the defendant claimed that the prosecutor was imagining implausible possibilities for conflict of interest when its real motive was to deny this defendant the services of a particularly effective lawyer. Apart from the question of effectiveness, prosecutors may benefit when each defendant in a conspiracy is represented by separate counsel, because this arrangement increases the likelihood that each individual will be motivated to bargain for leniency and agree to testify against the others. See United States v. Dempsey, 724 F.Supp. 573 (N.D.Ill.1989).

Counsel is an officer of the court as well as an advocate for a client, and this dual role may also give rise to conflicting loyalties. In the leading Supreme Court Case, the defendant announced that he would embellish his testimony with a claim the lawyer knew to be a lie. The lawyer replied, according to his later testimony, that:

> "we could not allow him to [testify falsely] because that would be perjury, and as officers of the court we would be suborning perjury if we allowed him to do it; * * * I advised him that if he did so that it would be my duty to advise the Court of what he was going and that I felt he was committing perjury; also, that I probably would be allowed to attempt to impeach that particular testimony."

The defendant did testify without the proposed embellishment.

A federal Court of Appeals on habeas corpus held that this statement amounted to a threat to reveal confidential attorney-client communications, and created a conflict between the attorney's perceived ethical duty and his duty of loyalty to the client. This "actual conflict" affected his performance and thus eliminated the need to show further prejudice under *Cuyler*. Whiteside v. Scurr, 750 F.2d 713 (8th Cir.1984) (en banc).

The Supreme Court unanimously reversed, holding that the attorney's ethical scruples created neither the kind of conflict of interest contemplated by the opinion in *Cuyler*, nor ineffective assistance as defined in *Strickland*. Nix v. Whiteside, 475 U.S. 157 (1986).

A defendant is not deprived of effective assistance because counsel refused to do something illegal or unethical, even though a defendant with sufficient resources could probably find a "mouthpiece" willing to take the risk. Further consideration of the ethical dimensions of the attorney's role is left to the course on Professional Responsibility.

FARETTA v. CALIFORNIA

Supreme Court of the United States, 1975.
422 U.S. 806, 95 S.Ct. 2525, 45 L.Ed.2d 562.

MR. JUSTICE STEWART delivered the opinion of the Court.

The Sixth and Fourteenth Amendments of our Constitution guarantee that a person brought to trial in any state or federal court must be afforded the right to the assistance of counsel before he can be validly convicted and punished by imprisonment. This clear constitutional rule has emerged from a series of cases decided here over the last 50 years. The question before us now is whether a defendant in a state criminal trial has a constitutional right to proceed *without* counsel when he voluntarily and intelligently elects to do so. Stated another way, the question is whether a State may constitutionally hale a person into its criminal courts and there force a lawyer upon him, even when he insists that he wants to conduct his own defense. It is not an easy question, but we have concluded that a State may not constitutionally do so.

I

Anthony Faretta was charged with grand theft in an information filed in the Superior Court of Los Angeles County, California. At the arraignment, the Superior Court Judge assigned to preside at the trial appointed the public defender to represent Faretta. Well before the date of trial, however, Faretta requested that he be permitted to represent himself. Questioning by the judge revealed that Faretta had once represented himself in a criminal prosecution, that he had a high school education, and that he did not want to be represented by the public defender because he believed that that office was "very loaded down with * * * a heavy case load." The judge responded that he believed Faretta was "making a mistake" and emphasized that in further proceedings Faretta would receive no special favors.[2] Nevertheless, after establishing that Faretta wanted to represent himself and did not want a lawyer, the judge, in a "preliminary ruling," accepted Faretta's waiver of the assistance of counsel. The judge indicated, however, that he might reverse this ruling if it later appeared that Faretta was unable adequately to represent himself.

2. The judge informed Faretta:

"You are going to follow the procedure. You are going to have to ask the questions right. If there is an objection to the form of the question and it is properly taken, it is going to be sustained. We are going to treat you like a gentleman. We are going to respect you. We are going to give you every chance, but you are going to play with the same ground rules that anybody plays. And you don't know those ground rules. You wouldn't know those ground rules any more than any other lawyer will know those ground rules until he gets out and tries a lot of cases. And you haven't done it."

Several weeks thereafter, but still prior to trial the judge *sua sponte* held a hearing to inquire into Faretta's ability to conduct his own defense, and questioned him specifically about both the hearsay rule and the state law governing the challenge of potential jurors.* After consideration of Faretta's answers, and observation of his demeanor, the judge ruled that Faretta had not made an intelligent and knowing waiver of his right to the assistance of counsel, and also ruled that Faretta had no constitutional right to conduct his own defense. The judge accordingly reversed his earlier ruling permitting self-representation and again appointed the public defender to represent Faretta. Faretta's subsequent request for leave to act as co-counsel was rejected, as were his efforts to make certain motions on his own behalf. Throughout the subsequent trial, the judge required that Faretta's defense be conducted only through the appointed lawyer from the public defender's office. At the conclusion of the trial, the jury found Faretta guilty as charged, and the judge sentenced him to prison. [The conviction was affirmed on appeal, and the Supreme Court granted certiorari.]

There can be no blinking the fact that the right of an accused to conduct his own defense seems to cut against the grain of this Court's decisions holding that the Constitution requires that no accused can be convicted and imprisoned unless he has been accorded the right to the assistance of counsel. For it is surely true that the basic thesis of those decisions is that the help of a lawyer is essential to assure the defendant a fair trial. And a strong argument can surely be made that the whole thrust of those decisions most inevitably lead to the conclusion that a State may constitutionally impose a lawyer upon even an unwilling defendant.

But it is one thing to hold that every defendant, rich or poor, has the right to the assistance of counsel, and quite another to say that a State may compel a defendant to accept a lawyer he does not want. The value of state-appointed counsel was not unappreciated by the Founders, yet the notion of compulsory counsel was utterly foreign to them. And whatever else may be said of those who wrote the Bill of Rights, surely there can be no doubt that they understood the inestimable worth of free choice.

It is undeniable that in most criminal prosecutions defendants could better defend with counsel's guidance than by their own unskilled efforts. But where the defendant will not voluntarily accept representation by counsel, the potential advantage of a lawyer's training and experience can be realized, if at all, only imperfectly. To force a lawyer on a defendant can only lead him to believe that the law contrives against him. Moreover, it is not inconceivable that in some rare instances, the defendant might in fact present his case more effectively by

* The trial judge decided to re-open the self-representation question after the California Supreme Court issued an opinion holding that there is no constitutional right to self-representation. The questions asked at this hearing appear to have been designed to support a finding that Faretta lacked sufficient legal knowledge to represent himself competently.—ed.

conducting his own defense. Personal liberties are not rooted in the law of averages. The right to defend is personal. The defendant, and not his lawyer or the State, will bear the personal consequences of a conviction. It is the defendant, therefore, who must be free personally to decide whether in his particular case counsel is to his advantage. And although he may conduct his own defense ultimately to his own detriment, his choice must be honored out of that respect for the individual which is the lifeblood of the law.

When an accused manages his own defense, he relinquishes, as a purely factual matter, many of the traditional benefits associated with the right to counsel. For this reason, in order to represent himself, the accused must "knowingly and intelligently" forego those relinquished benefits. * * * Although a defendant need not himself have the skill and experience of a lawyer in order competently and intelligently to choose self-representation, he should be made aware of the dangers and disadvantages of self-representation, so that the record will establish that he knows what he is doing and his choice is made with eyes open.

Here, weeks before trial, Faretta clearly and unequivocally declared to the trial judge that he wanted to represent himself and did not want counsel. The record affirmatively shows that Faretta was literate, competent, and understanding and that he was voluntarily exercising his informed free will. The trial judge had warned Faretta that he thought it was a mistake not to accept the assistance of counsel, and that Faretta would be required to follow all the "ground rules" of trial procedure. We need make no assessment of how well or poorly Faretta had mastered the intricacies of the hearsay rule and the California code provisions that govern challenges of potential jurors on *voir dire*. For his technical legal knowledge, as such, was not relevant to an assessment of his knowing exercise of the right to defend himself.[3]

In forcing Faretta, under these circumstances, to accept against his will a state-appointed public defender, the California courts deprived him of his constitutional right to conduct his own defense. Accordingly, the judgment before us is vacated, and the case is remanded for further proceedings not inconsistent with this opinion.

It is so ordered.

3. We are told that many criminal defendants representing themselves may use the courtroom for deliberate disruption of their trials. But the right of self-representation has been recognized from our beginnings by federal law and by most of the States, and no such result has thereby occurred. Moreover, the trial judge may terminate self-representation by a defendant who deliberately engages in serious and obstructionist misconduct. See Illinois v. Allen, 397 U.S. 337. Of course, a State may— even over objection by the accused—appoint a "standby counsel" to aid the accused if and when the accused requests help, and to be available to represent the accused in the event that termination of the defendant's self-representation is necessary.

The right of self-representation is not a license to abuse the dignity of the courtroom. Neither is it a license not to comply with relevant rules of procedural and substantive law. Thus, whatever else may or may not be open to him on appeal, a defendant who elects to represent himself cannot thereafter complain that the quality of his own defense amounted to a denial of "effective assistance of counsel."

Judgment vacated and case remanded.

Mr. Justice Blackmun, with whom The Chief Justice and Mr. Justice Rehnquist join, dissenting.

* * *

I note briefly the procedural problems that, I suspect, today's decision will visit upon trial courts in the future. Although the Court indicates that a *pro se* defendant necessarily waives any claim he might otherwise make on ineffective assistance of counsel, the opinion leaves open a host of other procedural questions. Must every defendant be advised of his right to proceed *pro se*? If so, when must that notice be given? Since the right to assistance of counsel and the right to self-representation are mutually exclusive, how is the waiver of each right to be measured? If a defendant has elected to exercise his right to proceed *pro se*, does he still have a constitutional right to assistance of standby counsel? How soon in the criminal proceeding must a defendant decide between proceeding by counsel or *pro se*? Must he be allowed to switch in mid-trial? May a violation of the right to self-representation ever be harmless error? Must the trial court treat the *pro se* defendant differently than it would professional counsel? I assume that many of these questions will be answered with finality in due course. Many of them, however, such as the standards of waiver and the treatment of the *pro se* defendant, will haunt the trial of every defendant who elects to exercise his right to self-representation. The procedural problems spawned by an absolute right to self-representation will far outweigh whatever tactical advantage the defendant may feel he has gained by electing to represent himself.

If there is any truth to the old proverb that "one who is his own lawyer has a fool for a client," the Court by its opinion today now bestows a *constitutional* right on one to make a fool of himself.

Commentary

The problems in administering the *Faretta* doctrine do not seem to have been as great as predicted by Justice Blackmun's dissenting opinion. Most appellate courts have had little difficulty deciding that there is no requirement that the defendant be advised of the right to self-representation, and they do not require trial courts to make special efforts to protect the *pro se* defendant from the consequences of a lack of professional skill. Defendants are ordinarily not allowed to "switch in mid-trial," or otherwise to manipulate the exercise of the right in a manner likely to disrupt the proceedings. Trial courts occasionally but rarely allow a defendant to "have it both ways" by acting as co-counsel along with a defense attorney who also participates in the proceedings. In many cases attorneys are unwilling to participate in such an arrangement, because it deprives the lawyer of the traditional prerogative of exercising independent professional judgment in managing the proceedings. Where the lawyer has no objection, courts are often unwilling to allow the defendant to give what amounts to unsworn testimony in the form of an opening or closing statement, and thus to avoid cross-examination by the prosecutor. See generally, 2 LaFave & Israel, Criminal Procedure 42–62 (1984).

On the other hand, courts do frequently appoint "standby" counsel, to give the defendant advice and information on legal matters without directly participating in the trial. Although there is no right to the appointment of such counsel, at least one decision reversed a conviction for capital murder because the trial judge erroneously ruled that he did not have the discretionary authority to appoint standby counsel. People v. Bigelow, 37 Cal.3d 731, 209 Cal.Rptr. 328, 691 P.2d 994 (1984). The California Supreme Court indicated that, considering the intricate rules governing the administration of the death penalty in California, failure to appoint standby counsel for defendant who insisted on representing himself would be an abuse of discretion.

Standby counsel may also be appointed even over the defendant's objection, and this has sometimes led to claims that counsel's activities interfered with the defendant's right to self-representation. See *McKaskle v. Wiggins*, 465 U.S. 168 (1984).

Some of the most interesting problems raised by *Faretta* involve the allocation of authority between the defendant and counsel when the defendant does *not* elect to proceed *pro se*. If defendants should be allowed to control their own destiny, and to be assisted rather than dominated by counsel, then should the defendant rather than the lawyer have the final say about tactical decisions? The American Bar Association's Standards Relating to the Administration of Criminal Justice, reflecting the weight of professional opinion, allocate certain basic decisions to the defendant but give final authority over other matters to counsel. The accused decides (after consultation with counsel) what plea to enter, whether to waive jury trial, and whether to testify. The lawyer decides (after consultation with the client) what witnesses to call, whether and how to conduct cross-examination, what jurors to accept or strike, what motions to make, and "all other strategic and tactical decisions." ABA Standards for Criminal Justice 4–5.2 (2d ed. 1980); See also, ABA Model Rules of Professional Conduct, Rule 1.2(a).

Although standards promulgated by the American Bar Association are not conclusive on questions of constitutional law, most courts would probably uphold this division of authority. The Supreme Court has held that appointed counsel on *appeal* may exercise professional judgment over which points to argue, and need not raise every non-frivolous issue urged by the client (who was permitted to file his own *pro se* brief in addition to the brief submitted by counsel). Jones v. Barnes, 463 U.S. 745 (1983). The majority opinion by Chief Justice Burger pointed out that effective advocacy requires concentrating on the strongest points, and that raising every colorable issue runs the risk of distracting the court from the most promising ones. Justice Brennan's dissent reasoned that "from the standpoint of effective administration of justice, the need to confer decisive authority on the attorney is paramount with regard to the hundreds of decisions that must be made quickly in the course of a trial. Decisions regarding which issues to press on appeal, in contrast, can and should be made more deliberately, in the course of deciding whether to appeal at all." 463 U.S. at 760. Although counsel should try to persuade the client to defer to the lawyer's judgment on what issues to argue, the dissent reasoned that "the role of the defense lawyer should be above all to function as the instrument and defender of the client's autonomy and dignity in all phases of the criminal process." Id. at 763.

Delicate problems arise when the defendant in a capital case wishes to plead guilty, or to introduce no mitigating evidence at the penalty phase, or to abandon an appeal. For example, see People v. Chadd, 28 Cal.3d 739, 170 Cal.Rptr. 798, 621 P.2d 837 (1981). The defendant, charged with capital murder, announced his intention to plead guilty over counsel's objection. He explained that he had tried to commit suicide, and that after giving serious consideration to his situation he felt that the death penalty would be best for him. A section of the California Penal Code specifically provides that a court may not receive a plea of guilty to a crime punishable by death "without the consent of the defendant's counsel." The California court reasoned that the defendant has no absolute right to plead guilty to a capital charge, because the state has an independent interest in the accuracy and fairness of the proceeding. Accordingly, the court reversed the judgment based on the guilty plea. See also, People v. Massie, 40 Cal.3d 620, 221 Cal.Rptr. 140, 709 P.2d 1309 (1985); People v. Deere, 41 Cal.3d 353, 222 Cal.Rptr. 13, 710 P.2d 925 (1985). In *Deere*, the California court held that defense counsel has the authority and duty to present mitigating evidence at the penalty phase of a capital case, notwithstanding the defendant's wish to the contrary.

On the other hand, the United States Supreme Court terminated a stay of execution and refused to consider further appeals when Gary Gilmore directed his attorneys not to appeal or otherwise challenge his Utah death sentence. The majority ruled that Gilmore had knowingly and intelligently waived all his rights, and refused to consider an application for a stay filed by his mother as "next friend." Justice White, joined in dissent by Justices Marshall and Brennan, stated that there were substantial doubts as to the constitutionality of the Utah death penalty statute, and argued that "the consent of a convicted defendant in a criminal case does not privilege a State to impose a punishment otherwise forbidden by the Eighth Amendment." Gilmore v. Utah, 429 U.S. 1012, 1018 (1976).

Finally, the *Faretta* opinion leaves open the possibility that a mentally ill defendant might be competent to stand trial, but insufficiently "literate, competent, and understanding" to waive his right to counsel. The Supreme Court of Washington closed the gap between the two standards in State v. Hahn, 106 Wash.2d 885, 726 P.2d 25 (Wash. 1986). Charged with second degree murder, Hahn was initially found incompetent to stand trial due to his psychotic, paranoid delusions. After a few weeks of treatment the psychiatrists concluded that, although he continued to be delusional and paranoid in many areas of his thinking, he could understand the nature of the proceedings against him and assist an attorney in preparing a defense. After Hahn was found competent to stand trial, the prosecutor sought to enter an insanity plea over his objection. The trial court conducted a lengthy and careful examination of Hahn, and then allowed him to withdraw the insanity plea, to waive counsel, and to represent himself at the jury trial with the assistance of a legal advisor. The jury returned a verdict of guilty and the judge sentenced Hahn to life in prison. Affirming the conviction, the Washington Supreme Court concluded that "Hahn was fully informed of the alternatives available, comprehended the consequences of representing himself, and freely chose to proceed. If the trial court had denied Hahn's request, it would have been subject to reversal under the *Faretta* standards." 726 P.2d at 34.

The question of whether a defendant is competent to waive counsel can become entangled with the determination on the merits when the defendant's sanity is at issue. For example, the defendant in a California case had been found not guilty by reason of insanity on various criminal charges, and was committed to a mental institution. He filed a petition for release on the ground that he had recovered his sanity, and elected to represent himself at the trial on this issue. The trial judge inquired into his knowledge of legal principles and advised him on the hazards of self-representation, but did not obtain expert testimony before allowing him to represent himself. The trial court subsequently granted the state's motion for a directed verdict after the petitioner had presented only a single witness who had no knowledge of his mental capacity. The California Court of Appeals held that in these circumstances the trial judge should not have accepted a waiver of counsel without obtaining expert testimony establishing the petitioner's competence to waive his right to counsel. State v. Burnett, 188 Cal.App.3d 1314, 234 Cal.Rptr. 67 (1987). But if the Court found that the petitioner was not competent to waive counsel, would it not also be finding that his sanity had not been restored?

Chapter 11

CONFESSIONS FROM *BROWN* TO *MIRANDA*

Commentary

The Coerced Confession Cases, 1936–1963

Before the mid–1960s, the admissibility of confessions in *state* criminal cases was evaluated under the "Due Process" clause of the Fourteenth Amendment. The Supreme Court looked at the "totality of circumstances," to determine whether the suspect's "will was overborne," on the one hand, or whether the confession was "free and voluntary," on the other. In practice, this meant that the Court tried to draw a line between those pressures to confess which were tolerable and those which were not. Following are brief summaries of some of the most important pre-*Miranda* cases applying the due process approach:

(1) Brown v. Mississippi, 297 U.S. 278 (1936), was the first state criminal conviction to be reversed because of a coerced confession. The case involved the virtual lynching of three black tenant farmers by sheriff's deputies who were "investigating" the murder of a white planter. The deputies freely admitted hanging one of the defendants from a tree and severely whipping all three with a leather strap with buckles on it. The defendants were virtually cut to pieces by this torture, and were made to understand that the whipping would be continued unless and until they confessed in every detail to the satisfaction of their torturers. In a particularly chilling comment, one deputy remarked that he had whipped one of the defendants "Not too much for a Negro; not as much as I would have done if it were left to me." Although the confessions so obtained were the only evidence implicating the defendants in the murder, the Mississippi Supreme Court affirmed their convictions and death sentences. The United States Supreme Court unanimously reversed, holding that a conviction on such a basis violated due process of law. For a background history of this case see Cortner, a *"Scottsboro" Case in Mississippi* (1986).

(2) In Ashcraft v. Tennessee, 322 U.S. 143 (1944), the officers took the defendant (who was suspected of hiring another man to murder his wife) into custody at 7:00 o'clock p.m. on a Saturday evening and interrogated him in relays without allowing him any rest until 9:30 Monday morning. Al-

though the details of what occurred during this marathon interrogation were disputed, the Supreme Court held that the admitted relay questioning for thirty-six hours without rest was in itself sufficient to establish that the confession was involuntary. Justice Jackson dissented, arguing that the length of the questioning was only one circumstance to be considered in evaluating the voluntariness of a confession, and that apart from the defendant's testimony, which the state courts were entitled to disbelieve, there was evidence that "the confession when made was deliberate, free and voluntary in the sense in which that term is used in criminal law." 322 U.S. at 164.

(3) Malinski v. People of State of New York, 324 U.S. 401 (1945), shows that use of the "third degree" was by no means restricted to the southern and border states. After arresting Malinski early on a Friday morning for a robbery in which a policeman was killed, New York Police officers took him not to the police station but to a room in a hotel. There he was immediately stripped and kept naked for about three hours, after which he was given underwear and a blanket. He remained that way during questioning until about 6:00 o'clock p.m., when he made his first confession. After that he was allowed to dress, but he was kept at the hotel that night and the next three days. He was questioned on several occasions, taken out to identify places having a relationship to the crime, and questioned further. He made a final, detailed confession to a stenographer at 2:00 o'clock a.m. the following Tuesday, after which he was finally taken to the jail and booked. The most remarkable aspect of *Malinski* is the candid defense of the police conduct which the prosecutor offered in his final argument. He told the jury:

> "Why this talk about being undressed? Of course, they had a right to undress him to look for bullet scars, and keep the clothes off him. That was quite proper police procedure. That is some more psychology— let him sit around with a blanket on him, humiliate him there for a while; let him sit in the corner, let him think he is going to get a shellacking."

Although most of the evidence of coercion related to the first confession given on Friday, and the prosecution relied primarily on the complete confession dictated the following Tuesday, there were some references at the trial to the first confession. Accordingly, the Supreme Court majority held that "the judgment before us rests in part on a confession obtained as a result of coercion," and did not reach the question of whether the subsequent confessions were free from the constitutional infirmities of the first one.

(4) Leyra v. Denno, 347 U.S. 556 (1954) involved a defendant who was charged with beating his aged parents to death with a hammer. After interrogating him for several days without success, the police promised to provide a physician to treat him for a painful sinus attack. The doctor whom they produced, however, was a police psychiatrist who used his professional skills to continue the interrogation. According to the Supreme Court opinion, "Time and time and time again the psychiatrist told petitioner how much he wanted to and could help him, how bad it would be for petitioner if he did not confess, and how much better he would feel, and how much lighter and easier it would be on him if he would just unbosom himself to the doctor." Eventually the defendant, "encouraged by the doctor's assurances that he

had done no wrong and would be let off easily," called for the police captain and gave a confession. He subsequently confessed to other persons as well.

The New York Court of Appeals held that the first admissions made to the psychiatrist were the product of "mental coercion," but that the subsequent confessions, including the one made immediately afterward to the captain, were properly admitted at the murder trial. Under the New York procedure prevailing at the time, a confession whose voluntariness was in dispute was submitted to the jury, which was told not to consider the confession if it found it to be involuntary. [This procedure was later held unconstitutional in Jackson v. Denno, 378 U.S. 368 (1964).] A majority of the United States Supreme Court held that all the confessions were "parts of one continuous process," and that their use violated due process. Three Justices dissented, arguing that it was not unfair to allow the jury to pass on whether the subsequent confessions were "completely under the influence of the first confession." The transcript of the interrogation by the psychiatrist, which was secretly recorded by the police, is attached to the majority opinion and makes interesting reading.

(5) Crooker v. California, 357 U.S. 433 (1958), involved a defendant who was a 31–year-old college graduate who had attended the first year of law school and studied criminal law. While going to law school he had been a "houseboy" in the home of a woman with whom he had had an affair, and whom he was accused of murdering. He confessed after about 14 hours of sporadic questioning, with the usual conflict in the testimony about just how coercive that questioning was. The police conceded, however, that he had asked for an opportunity to consult a specific lawyer at the beginning of the questioning, but was told that "after the investigation was concluded he could call an attorney." 357 U.S. at 436. The Supreme Court majority held that the refusal to allow a suspect to contact counsel is only one of the circumstances to be considered in evaluating the voluntariness of a confession, and that, taking into account the defendant's age, intelligence and education, including his apparent awareness that he had a right to be silent, the confession in these circumstances was voluntary. Four Justices dissented.

(6) Cicenia v. LaGay, 357 U.S. 504 (1958), was decided on the same day as *Crooker*. The defendant, who was wanted for a robbery murder, surrendered at the police station at 9:00 o'clock a.m. on the advice of his lawyer. He was questioned throughout the day, and his lawyer's requests to see him were refused, as were his own requests to see the lawyer. The lawyer and client were not permitted to confer until 9:30 p.m., by which time the defendant had made and signed a written confession. The Supreme Court majority opinion by Justice Harlan expressed "strong distaste" both for the refusal to allow the suspect to consult with his lawyer, and for the delay in bringing him to court after arrest for arraignment, but observed that "the States should have the widest latitude in the administration of their own systems of criminal justice." 357 U.S. at 510. The majority concluded that "the contention that petitioner had a constitutional right to confer with counsel is disposed of by *Crooker v. California* decided today." In other words, the holding in *Crooker* did not depend upon the relative legal sophistication of the defendant in that case. Three Justices dissented, and another who would have dissented did not participate in the case.

(7) Spano v. People of State of New York, 360 U.S. 315 (1959), is perhaps the most interesting and significant of the coerced confession cases. The defendant, a 25–year-old immigrant working man, had been severely beaten by a bully in a bar. He walked home to his apartment, obtained a gun, and returned to shoot the bully dead in front of several witnesses. He then disappeared, and authorities obtained an indictment for murder and an arrest warrant. Subsequently, Spano telephoned his friend Bruno, who was a police recruit, to say he would get a lawyer and give himself up. The following day Spano appeared at the police station with a lawyer, who had told him not to answer any questions. He succeeded in maintaining silence throughout approximately six hours of incommunicado interrogation, until the questioners decided to try a sympathy ploy, using Bruno. Bruno was told to tell Spano that the telephone call had put his job in jeopardy, and to try to play upon Spano's sympathy for Bruno's pregnant wife and three children. This ploy was tried twice without success, but after the third trial Spano succumbed and agreed to make a statement. He subsequently took the officers to find the gun, and told them that the victim was always "on his back," and that he was "not sorry" he had shot him. These statements were used to obtain a conviction for first degree murder, and a death sentence.

The Supreme Court reversed unanimously. The majority opinion by Chief Justice Warren concluded that "petitioner's will was overborne by official pressure, fatigue and sympathy falsely aroused after considering all the facts in their post-indictment setting." Four concurring Justices took the view that interrogating the defendant in the absence of counsel after indictment violated his Sixth Amendment right to counsel, whether or not the interrogation was otherwise coercive. This became the majority position in *Massiah v. United States, infra* p. 438.

(8) Rogers v. Richmond, 365 U.S. 534 (1961), is noteworthy for its emphatic statement that the purpose of the coerced confession doctrine is not merely to guard against conviction of the innocent. The defendant had refused to confess to a robbery murder despite interrogation for about six hours by a team of police officers. The police chief then threatened to bring in the defendant's wife for questioning, and this threat induced the defendant to confess. The state courts found that the confessions were admissible because they were not obtained by any artifice or deception "calculated to procure an untrue statement." The Supreme Court majority opinion by Justice Frankfurter reversed the conviction, explaining that involuntary confessions are excluded not because they "are unlikely to be true but because the methods used to extract them offend an underlying principle in the enforcement of our criminal law: that ours is an accusatorial and not an inquisitorial system—a system in which the State must establish guilt by evidence independently and freely secured and may not by coercion prove its charge against an accused out of his own mouth." 365 U.S. at 540–41.

(9) In Lynumn v. Illinois, 372 U.S. 528 (1963), Chicago police officers had arrested one Zeno for unlawful possession of narcotics, and had told him that if he "would set somebody up for them, they would go light on him." He agreed to cooperate and telephoned Mrs. Lynumn, telling her he was coming to her apartment. The officers watched him enter Lynumn's apartment building, and about 20 minutes later he emerged from her apartment with a package containing a substance later determined to be marijuana. Upon

arrest, she denied at first selling the marijuana to Zeno, insisting that he had merely repaid her a loan. The police told her that an arrest would lead to a cut-off of her welfare payments, and that she would probably lose custody of her children to strangers and receive a prison term. If she were to cooperate, on the other hand, "it would go light on her." Facing this apparently hopeless situation, she provided the confession and received a prison sentence of from 10 to 11 years. The Supreme Court unanimously held that the confession was coerced, and that the error in admitting it required reversal regardless of the strength of the other evidence.

(10) Haynes v. Washington, 373 U.S. 503 (1963), involved a suspect who was held incommunicado and questioned over a 16–hour period. From the standpoint of the Supreme Court, the crucial circumstance was that the police acknowledged that he had repeatedly asked police to allow him to call an attorney and to call his wife. They had refused permission, indicating that he would not be allowed to contact other persons until he cooperated. A narrow majority of the Supreme Court found this circumstance sufficiently coercive to make the resulting confessions involuntary *per se*. The four dissenting Justices observed that Haynes made an initial confession only one hour and 20 minutes after surrendering, and that he was a mature adult familiar with police procedures. For such a person, the dissenters thought, the fact of incommunicado detention in itself was not sufficient to subvert his rationality and free will.

The Federal Cases

Before 1964, the Fifth Amendment's privilege against self-incrimination was thought to be applicable only against the federal government, and not against the states. In addition, the United States Supreme Court has no "supervisory power" over the administration of criminal justice in the state courts, but can only decide whether some convictions are consistent with the "due process of law" required by the Fourteenth Amendment. In federal cases, however, the Supreme Court could make use of both the Fifth Amendment and the supervisory power. Three federal cases were particularly significant:

(1) Bram v. United States, 168 U.S. 532 (1897) established that, in federal cases, the voluntariness of a confession is to be determined by the Fifth Amendment's privilege against self-incrimination. Bram was the first officer of an American ship who was suspected of murdering the captain and two other persons while the ship was on the high seas. A seaman named Brown, who was at first suspected of the crime, said that he saw Bram kill the captain. Crewmembers then put Bram in irons and took the ship to Halifax, Nova Scotia. There a police detective questioned Bram, after stripping him to examine his clothing. He first told Bram that Brown had said that he saw Bram commit the murder, to which Bram replied that Brown could not have "seen me" from where he was at the wheel. The detective then said that he was satisfied that Bram had committed the crime, but that "If you had an accomplice, you should say so, and not have the blame of this horrible crime on your own shoulders." Bram replied, "Well, I think, and many others on board the ship think, that Brown is the murderer; but I don't know anything about it."

The Supreme Court majority opinion by Justice White held that these statements were involuntary under the Fifth Amendment standard. The very broad holding suggested that the mere fact that the accused was told that someone else had seen him commit the murder gave him the impression that silence would be taken as an admission of guilt, and made his resulting statement involuntary. Additionally, the suggestion that the blame for the horrible crime could somehow be removed from his shoulders implied "a suggestion of some benefit as to the crime and its punishment as arising from making a statement." Finally, although the statement weakly denied guilt and was thus (in contemporary terminology) at most an admission rather than a confession, the majority held that there could be no question of harmless error. The majority also ignored the fact that the alleged coercion was committed by an officer of a foreign government. In short, the *Bram* opinion was substantially more protective of the rights of defendants than any of the "due process" cases summarized above. Three Justices dissented.

(2) In McNabb v. United States, 318 U.S. 332 (1943), the defendants were members of a clan of Tennessee mountaineer "moonshiners" who were involved in the shooting of a federal revenue agent. After arrest, they were interrogated separately and collectively over a period of two days, under circumstances which might have made a borderline case of coercion under the due process standard applied in state cases. The majority opinion by Justice Frankfurter held, however, that the due process standard is supplemented in federal cases by statutes, and by rules formulated by the Supreme Court in the exercise of its supervisory authority over the administration of criminal justice in the federal courts. The opinion went on to observe that a statute commands a federal officer who arrests a person "to take the defendant before the nearest United States commissioner or the nearest judicial officer having jurisdiction under existing laws for a hearing, commitment, or taking bail for trial." The agents violated this statute by taking the defendants instead to a jail for interrogation, and "a conviction resting on evidence secured through such a flagrant disregard of the procedure which Congress has commanded cannot be allowed to stand without making the courts themselves accomplices in willful disobedience of law." 332 U.S. at 345. Only one Justice dissented from the reversal of the convictions.

(3) Mallory v. United States, 354 U.S. 449 (1957), solidified what has come to be known as the *"McNabb-Mallory"* rule. The defendant and two of his nephews were arrested as suspects in a rape case at about 2:30 p.m. All three agreed to take a "lie detector" test at about 4:00 p.m., but the test was delayed until just after 8:00 p.m. After almost 90 minutes of steady questioning on the polygraph, Mallory began to make admissions, and he made a full confession at about 10:00 p.m. Following this, the officers for the first time attempted to reach a United States Commissioner for the purpose of arraignment. The Supreme Court unanimously reversed the resulting conviction, citing Rule 5(a) of the Federal Rules of Criminal Procedure, which provides that "An officer making an arrest * * * shall take the arrested person *without unnecessary delay* before the nearest available commissioner * * *." The majority held that delay "to give opportunity for the extraction of a confession" was unnecessary delay, and required exclusion of the resulting confession.

MALLOY v. HOGAN

Supreme Court of the United States, 1964.
378 U.S. 1, 84 S.Ct. 1489, 12 L.Ed.2d 653.

MR. JUSTICE BRENNAN delivered the opinion of the Court.

In this case we are asked to reconsider prior decisions holding that the privilege against self-incrimination is not safeguarded against state action by the Fourteenth Amendment. Twining v. New Jersey, 211 U.S. 78; Adamson v. California, 332 U.S. 46.

The petitioner was arrested during a gambling raid in 1959 by Hartford, Connecticut, police. He pleaded guilty to the crime of pool selling, a misdemeanor, and was sentenced to one year in jail and fined $500. The sentence was ordered to be suspended after 90 days, at which time he was to be placed on probation for two years. About 16 months after his guilty plea, petitioner was ordered to testify before a referee appointed by the Superior Court of Hartford County to conduct an inquiry into alleged gambling and other criminal activities in the county. The petitioner was asked a number of questions related to events surrounding his arrest and conviction. He refused to answer any question "on the grounds it may tend to incriminate me." The Superior Court adjudged him in contempt, and committed him to prison until he was willing to answer the questions. * * *

[The Connecticut Supreme Court of Errors upheld the contempt citation, ruling that the Fifth Amendment's privilege against self-incrimination was not applicable in state proceedings, and that petitioner had not properly invoked the privilege available under the Connecticut Constitution. The Supreme Court granted certiorari.]

We hold today that the Fifth Amendment's exception from compulsory self-incrimination is also protected by the Fourteenth Amendment against abridgment by the States. Decisions of the Court since Twining and Adamson have departed from the contrary view expressed in those cases. We discuss first the decisions which forbid the use of coerced confessions in state criminal prosecutions.

Brown v. Mississippi [see p. 447, supra] was the first case in which the Court held that the Due Process Clause prohibited the States from using the accused's coerced confessions against him. The Court in Brown felt impelled, in light of Twining, to say that its conclusion did not involve the privilege against self-incrimination. "Compulsion by torture to extort a confession is a different matter." But this distinction was soon abandoned, and today the admissibility of a confession in a state criminal prosecution is tested by the same standard applied in federal prosecutions since 1897, when, in Bram v. United States, [see p. 435, supra] the Court held that "[i]n criminal trials, in the courts of the United States, wherever a question arises whether a confession is incompetent because not voluntary, the issue is controlled by that portion of the Fifth Amendment to the constitution of the United States commanding that no person 'shall be compelled in any criminal case to be a witness against himself.' " Under this test, the constitutional inquiry is not whether the conduct of state officers in obtaining the confession was shocking, but whether the confession was "free and voluntary; that is, [it] must not be extracted by any sort of threats or violence, nor obtained by any direct or implied promises, however slight, nor by the exertion of any improper influence. * * * " Id., 168 U.S. at 542–543. In other words the person must not have been compelled to incriminate himself. We have held inadmissible even a confession secured by so mild a whip as the refusal, under certain circumstances, to allow a suspect to call his wife until he confessed. Haynes v. Washington, [see p. 451, supra.]

The marked shift to the federal standard in state cases began with Lisenba v. California, 314 U.S. 219, where the Court spoke of the accused's "free choice to admit, to deny, or to refuse to answer." The shift reflects recognition that the American system of criminal prosecution is accusatorial, not inquisitorial, and that the Fifth Amendment privilege is its essential mainstay. Rogers v. Richmond, [see p. 434, supra.] Governments, state and federal, are thus constitutionally compelled to establish guilt by evidence independently and freely secured, and may not by coercion prove a charge against an accused out of his own mouth. Since the Fourteenth Amendment prohibits the States from inducing a person to confess through "sympathy falsely aroused," or other like inducement far short of "compulsion by torture," Haynes v. Washington, supra, it follows *a fortiori* that it also forbids the States to resort to imprisonment, as here, to compel him to answer questions that might incriminate him. The Fourteenth Amendment secures against state invasion the same privilege that the Fifth Amendment guarantees against federal infringement—the right of a person to remain silent unless he chooses to speak in the unfettered exercise of his own will, and to suffer no penalty, as held in Twining, for such silence. * * *

[The majority went on to hold that the contempt order violated petitioner's privilege because truthful answers about his prior gambling activities might have helped the authorities to link him to more recent crimes for which he could still be prosecuted.]

Reversed.

[Dissenting opinions omitted.]

MASSIAH v. UNITED STATES

Supreme Court of the United States, 1964.
377 U.S. 201, 84 S.Ct. 1199, 12 L.E.2d 246.

Mr. Justice Stewart delivered the opinion of the Court. * * *

[Federal agents found a quantity of cocaine on a ship in New York harbor, and indicted petitioner Massiah and one Colson for conspiring with others to import it. Massiah retained a lawyer, pleaded not guilty, and was released on bail to await trial. Subsequently, Colson secretly agreed to cooperate with the continuing government investigation of the smuggling operation. He arranged to meet with Massiah to discuss their situation, and the two held a lengthy conversation one evening while sitting in Colson's automobile parked on a city street. Colson was wearing a radio transmitter, and by this means the entire conversation was overhead by a federal agent. This agent testified at Massiah's trial on a variety of narcotics charges, relating various incriminating statements that Massiah made in the conversation with Colson.]

The petitioner argues that it was an error of constitutional dimensions to permit the agent Murphy at the trial to testify to the petitioner's incriminating statements which Murphy had overheard under the circumstances disclosed by this record. This argument is based upon two distinct and independent grounds. First, we are told that Murphy's use of the radio equipment violated the petitioner's rights under the Fourth Amendment * * * Secondly, it is said that the Fifth and Sixth Amendment rights were violated by the use in evidence against him of incriminating statements which government agents had deliberately elicited from him after he had been indicted and in the absence of his retained counsel. Because of the way we dispose of the case, we do not reach the Fourth Amendment issue.

In Spano v. New York, this Court reversed a state criminal conviction because a confession had been wrongly admitted into evidence against the defendant at his trial. * * * While the Court's opinion relied upon the totality of the circumstances under which the confession had been obtained, four concurring Justices pointed out that the Constitution required reversal of the conviction upon the sole and specific ground that the confession had been deliberately elicited by the police after the defendant had been indicted, and therefore at a time when he was clearly entitled to a lawyer's help. * * *

Here we deal not with a state court conviction, but with a federal case, where the specific guarantee of the Sixth Amendment directly applies.

We hold that the petitioner was denied the basic protections of that guarantee when there was used against him at his trial evidence of his own incriminating words, which federal agents had deliberately elicited from him after he had been indicted and in the absence of his counsel. It is true that in the Spano case the defendant was interrogated in a police station, while here the damaging testimony was elicited from the defendant without his knowledge while he was free on bail. But, as Judge Hays pointed out in his dissent in the Court of Appeals, "if such a rule is to have any efficacy it must apply to indirect and surreptitious interrogations as well as those conducted in the jailhouse. In this case, Massiah was more seriously imposed upon * * * because he did not even know that he was under interrogation by a government agent."

The Solicitor General, in his brief and oral argument, has strenuously contended that the federal law enforcement agents had the right, if not indeed the duty, to continue their investigation of the petitioner and his alleged criminal associates even though the petitioner had been indicted. He points out that the Government was continuing its investigation in order to uncover not only the source of narcotics found on the S.S. *Santa Maria*, but also their intended buyer. He says that the quantity of narcotics involved was such as to suggest that the petitioner was part of a large and well-organized ring, and indeed that the continuing investigation confirmed this suspicion, since it resulted in criminal charges against many defendants. Under these circumstances the Solicitor General concludes that the government agents were completely "justified in making use of Colson's cooperation by having Colson continue his normal associations and by surveilling them."

We may accept and, at least for present purposes, completely approve all that this argument implies, Fourth Amendment problems to one side. We do not question that in this case, as in many cases, it was entirely proper to continue an investigation of the suspected criminal activities of the defendant and his alleged confederates, even though the defendant had already been indicted. All that we hold is that the defendant's own incriminating statements, obtained by federal agents under the circumstances here disclosed, could not constitutionally be used by the prosecution as evidence against *him* at his trial.

Reversed.

[Dissenting opinion omitted.]

Commentary

Given the division of the Court in *Spano v. New York*, summarized on page 450, *supra*, a holding that post-indictment questioning of a defendant outside the presence of his lawyer violates the Sixth Amendment was not unexpected. What *was* a little surprising was that the Court equated the use of a "wired informer" with police interrogation. The majority may have been attracted to this theory because it was unable to decide the Fourth Amendment issue in the case. Recall that, at this period, the Court was about equally divided on whether this kind of electronic monitoring was a search requiring advance judicial authorization. See *United States v. White, supra,* p. 94. It was easier to obtain a majority to decide the case on Sixth Amendment grounds.

The other interesting feature of the *Massiah* opinion is that it separates the Sixth Amendment issue from any finding of police misconduct. The final paragraph concedes that it may have been lawful for the federal authorities to do exactly what they did, if their purpose was to obtain evidence of criminal involvement by other persons. It seems to follow that the Sixth Amendment would not prevent use of evidence so obtained (or its fruits) against those other persons, or even against *Massiah* himself if he told Colson about ongoing narcotics smuggling independent of the charge for which he was currently under indictment.

This understanding of *Massiah* was confirmed by the Supreme Court's decision more than 20 years later in Maine v. Moulton, 474 U.S. 159 (1985). The police had reason to suspect that Moulton, who was under indictment for charges relating to an auto theft ring, might be planning to murder a prosecution witness. They obtained the cooperation of his co-defendant Colson [by coincidence bearing the same surname as the informer in *Massiah*], and thereby recorded conversations in which Moulton made admissions relating to the original auto theft charges. The state claimed that the recorded conversations were admissible on the original charges, because the police had a legitimate reason for listening to Moulton's conversations with Colson: to investigate the alleged plan to kill the prosecution witness and to protect Colson's safety in case Moulton threatened *him*.

The majority opinion by Justice Brennan held that the recorded conversations were inadmissible against Moulton on the original charges, in an opinion which included the following paragraph:

> The police have an interest in the thorough investigation of crimes for which formal charges have already been filed. They also have an interest in investigating new or additional crimes. Investigations of either type of crime may require surveillance of individuals already under indictment. Moreover, law enforcement officials investigating an individual suspected of committing one crime and formally charged with having committed another crime obviously seek to discover evidence useful at a trial of either crime. In seeking evidence pertaining to pending charges, however, the Government's investigative powers are limited by the Sixth Amendment rights of the accused. To allow the admission of evidence obtained from the accused in violation of his Sixth Amendment rights whenever the police assert an alternative, legitimate reason for their surveillance invites abuse by law enforcement personnel in the form of fabricated investigations and risks the evisceration of the Sixth Amendment right recognized in *Massiah*. On the other hand, to exclude evidence pertaining to charges as to which the Sixth Amendment right to counsel had not attached at the time the evidence was obtained, simply because other charges were pending at that time, would unnecessarily frustrate the public's interest in the investigation of criminal activities. Consequently, incriminating statements pertaining to pending charges are inadmissible at the trial of those charges, notwithstanding the fact that the police were also investigating other crimes, if, in obtaining this evidence, the State violated the Sixth Amendment by knowingly circumventing the accused's right to the assistance of counsel. 474 U.S. at 179–180.

In a footnote added at the end of this excerpt, Brennan's opinion stated that "Incriminating statements pertaining to other crimes, as to which the Sixth Amendment right has not attached, are, of course, admissible at a trial of those offenses."

When a *Fourth* Amendment issue is involved, evidence is excluded only if it was obtained as a result of identifiable police misconduct. The focus is not on whether the defendant's privacy rights were violated, but on whether the police acted unreasonably in the circumstances known to them. For example, if police have probable cause and obtain a warrant to search a residence for a murder weapon, narcotics found "in plain view" during this search are admissible even though the police had no probable cause to search for narcotics and even though the apparently reliable information concerning the murder weapon was entirely mistaken.

Commentators have occasionally suggested that evidence should some-times be excluded even in the absence of provable police misconduct, to reduce the temptation for officers to use a limited authority as a pretext for a wider search. For example, narcotics are occasionally discovered in routine airport security searches aimed at discovering weapons or explosives. Exclud-ing the narcotics in such cases would reduce the temptation for officers to search for narcotics while pretending to search for weapons. Although lower court opinions have occasionally been attracted by this kind of reasoning, the Supreme Court has consistently restricted the Fourth Amendment exclusion-ary rule to instances of demonstrable police misconduct. The recently-promulgated "reasonable good faith reliance" doctrine in search warrant cases is a particularly far-reaching example of this principle. See *United States v. Leon*, reprinted *supra*, p. 311.

ESCOBEDO v. ILLINOIS

Supreme Court of the United States, 1964.
378 U.S. 478, 84 S.Ct. 1758, 12 L.Ed.2d 977.

Mr. Justice Goldberg delivered the opinion of the Court. * * *

On the night of January 19, 1960, petitioner's brother-in-law was fatally shot. In the early hours of the next morning, at 2:30 a.m., petitioner was arrested without a warrant and interrogated. Petitioner made no statement to the police and was released at 5 that afternoon pursuant to a state court writ of habeas corpus obtained by Mr. Warren Wolfson, a lawyer who had been retained by petitioner.

On January 30, Benedict DiGerlando, who was then in police custo-dy and who was later indicted for the murder along with petitioner, told the police that petitioner had fired the fatal shots. Between 8 and 9 that evening, petitioner and his sister, the widow of the deceased, were arrested and taken to police headquarters. En route to the police station, the police "had handcuffed the defendant behind his back," and "one of the arresting officers told defendant that DiGerlando had named him as the one who shot" the deceased. Petitioner testified, without contra-diction, that the "detectives said they had us pretty well, up pretty tight, and we might as well admit to this crime," and that he replied, "I am sorry but I would like to have advice from my lawyer." A police officer testified that although petitioner was not formally charged "he was in custody" and "couldn't walk out the door."

Shortly after petitioner reached police headquarters, his retained lawyer arrived. [The lawyer testified that the police refused to allow him to talk to his client. He did catch a glimpse of Escobedo through an open door and they exchanged waves.]

Petitioner testified that during the course of the interrogation he repeatedly asked to speak to his lawyer and that the police said that his lawyer "didn't want to see" him. The testimony of the police officers confirmed these accounts in substantial detail.

Notwithstanding repeated requests by each, petitioner and his re-tained lawyer were afforded no opportunity to consult during the course of the entire interrogation. At one point, as previously noted, petitioner and his attorney came into each other's view for a few moments but the attorney was quickly ushered away. Petitioner testified "that he heard a detective telling the attorney the latter would not be allowed to talk to [him] 'until they were done'" and that he heard the attorney being refused permission to remain in the adjoining room. A police officer testified that he had told the lawyer that he could not see petitioner until "we were through interrogating" him.

There is testimony by the police that during the interrogation, petitioner, a 22–year-old of Mexican extraction with no record of previous experience with the police, "was handcuffed" in a standing position and that he "was nervous, he had circles under his eyes and he was upset" and was "agitated" because "he had not slept well in over a week."

It is undisputed that during the course of the interrogation Officer Montejano, who "grew up" in petitioner's neighborhood, who knew his family, and who uses "Spanish language in [his] police work," conferred alone with petitioner "for about a quarter of an hour * * *." Petitioner testified that the officer said to him "in Spanish that my sister and I could go home if I pinned it on Benedict DiGerlando," that "he would see to it that we would go home and be held only as witnesses, if anything, if we had made a statement against DiGerlando * * *, that we would be able to go home that night." Petitioner testified that he made the statement in issue because of this assurance. Officer Montejano denied offering any such assurance.

A police officer testified that during the interrogation the following occurred:

> "I informed him of what DiGerlando told me and when I did, he told me that DiGerlando was [lying] and I said, 'Would you care to tell DiGerlando that?' and he said, 'Yes, I will.' So, I brought * * * Escobedo in and he confronted DiGerlando and he told him that he was lying and said, 'I didn't shoot Manuel, you did it.'"

In this way, petitioner, for the first time admitted to some knowledge of the crime. After that he made additional statements further implicating himself in the murder plot. At this point an Assistant State's Attorney, Theodore J. Cooper, was summoned "to take" a statement. Mr. Cooper, an experienced lawyer who was assigned to the Homicide Division to take "statements from some defendants and some prisoners that they had in custody," "took" petitioner's statement by asking carefully framed questions apparently designed to assure the admissibility into evidence of the resulting answers. Mr. Cooper testified that he did not advise petitioner of his constitutional rights, and it is undisputed that no one during the course of the interrogation so advised him.

Petitioner moved both before and during trial to suppress the incriminating statement, but the motions were denied. Petitioner was convicted of murder and he appealed the conviction.

[The majority discussed its then-recent opinion in *Massiah*, supra p. 438.]

The interrogation here was conducted before petitioner was formally indicted. But in the context of this case,[6] that fact should make no difference. When petitioner requested, and was denied, an opportunity to consult with his lawyer, the investigation had ceased to be a general investigation of an unsolved crime. Petitioner had become the accused, and the purpose of the interrogation was to "get him" to confess his guilt despite his constitutional right not to do so. At the time of his arrest and throughout the course of the interrogation, the police told petitioner that they had convincing evidence that he had fired the fatal shots. Without informing him of his absolute right to remain silent in the face of this accusation, the police urged him to make a statement. * * *

In Gideon v. Wainwright, we held that every person accused of a crime, whether state or federal, is entitled to a lawyer at trial. The rule sought by the State here, however, would make the trial no more than an appeal from the interrogation; and the "right to use counsel at the formal trial [would be] a very hollow thing [if], for all practical purposes, the conviction is already assured by pretrial examination." In re Groban, 352 U.S. 330, 344 (Black, J., dissenting). "One can imagine a cynical prosecutor saying: 'Let them have the most illustrious counsel, now. They can't escape the noose. There is nothing that counsel can do for them at the trial.'" Ex parte Sullivan, D.C., 107 F.Supp. 514, 517–518.

It is argued that if the right to counsel is afforded prior to indictment, the number of confessions obtained by the police will diminish significantly, because most confessions are obtained during the period between arrest and indictment, and "any lawyer worth his salt will tell the suspect in no uncertain terms to make no statement to police under any circumstances." Watts v. Indiana, 338 U.S. 49, 59 (Jackson, J., concurring in part and dissenting in part). This argument, of course, cuts two ways. The fact that many confessions are obtained during this period points up its critical nature as a stage when legal aid and advice are surely needed. The right to counsel would indeed be hollow if it began at a period when few confessions were obtained. There is necessarily a direct relationship between the importance of a stage to the police in their quest for a confession and the criticalness of that stage to the accused in his need for legal advice. Our Constitution, unlike some others, strikes the balance in favor of the right of the accused to be advised by his lawyer of his privilege against self-incrimination.

6. The English Judges' Rules also recognize that a functional rather than a formal test must be applied and that, under circumstances such as those here, no special significance should be attached to formal indictment. The applicable Rule does not permit the police to question an accused, except in certain extremely limited situations not relevant here, at any time after the defendant "has been charged *or informed that he may be prosecuted.*" [1964] Crim.L.Rev. 166–170 (emphasis supplied). Although voluntary statements obtained in violation of these rules are not automatically excluded from evidence the judge may, in the exercise of his discretion, exclude them.

We have learned the lesson of history, ancient and modern, that a system of criminal law enforcement which comes to depend on the "confession" will, in the long run, be less reliable and more subject to abuses than a system which depends on extrinsic evidence independently secured through skillful investigation. * * * We have also learned the companion lesson of history that no system of criminal justice can, or should, survive if it comes to depend for its continued effectiveness on the citizens' abdication through unawareness of their constitutional rights. No system worth preserving should have to *fear* that if an accused is permitted to consult with a lawyer, he will become aware of, and exercise, these rights. If the exercise of constitutional rights will thwart the effectiveness of a system of law enforcement, then there is something very wrong with that system.[7]

We hold, therefore, that where, as here, the investigation is no longer a general inquiry into an unsolved crime but has begun to focus on a particular suspect, the suspect has been taken into police custody, the police carry out a process of interrogations that lends itself to eliciting incriminating statements, the suspect has requested and been denied an opportunity to consult with his lawyer, and the police have not effectively warned him of his absolute constitutional right to remain silent, the accused has been denied "the Assistance of Counsel" in violation of the Sixth Amendment to the Constitution as made obligatory upon the States by the Fourteenth Amendment, and that no statement elicited by the police during the interrogation may be used against him at a criminal trial. * * *

Reversed and remanded.

[Dissenting opinions omitted.]

MIRANDA v. ARIZONA

Supreme Court of the United States, 1966.
384 U.S. 436, 86 S.Ct. 1602, 16 L.Ed.2d 694.

MR. CHIEF JUSTICE WARREN delivered the opinion of the Court.

* * *

I.

The constitutional issue we decide in each of these cases is the admissibility of statements obtained from a defendant questioned while in custody or otherwise deprived of his freedom of action in any significant way. In each, the defendant was questioned by police officers, detectives, or a prosecuting attorney in a room in which he was cut off from the outside world. In none of these cases was the defendant given a

---

7. The accused may, of course, intelligently and knowingly waive his privilege against self-incrimination and his right to counsel either at a pretrial stage or at the trial. See Johnson v. Zerbst, 304 U.S. 458. But no knowing and intelligent waiver of any constitutional right can be said to have occurred under the circumstances of this case.

full and effective warning of his rights at the outset of the interrogation process. In all the cases, the questioning elicited oral admissions, and in three of them, signed statements as well which were admitted at their trials. They all thus share salient features—incommunicado interrogation of individuals in a police-dominated atmosphere, resulting in self-incriminating statements without full warnings of constitutional rights.

An understanding of the nature and setting of this in-custody interrogation is essential to our decisions today. The difficulty in depicting what transpires at such interrogations stems from the fact that in this country they have largely taken place incommunicado. From extensive factual studies undertaken in the early 1930's, including the famous Wickersham Report to Congress by a Presidential Commission, it is clear that police violence and the "third degree" flourished at that time. In a series of cases decided by this Court long after these studies, the police resorted to physical brutality—beatings, hanging, whipping—and to sustained and protracted questioning incommunicado in order to extort confessions. The Commission on Civil Rights in 1961 found much evidence to indicate that "some policemen still resort to physical force to obtain confessions." The use of physical brutality and violence is not, unfortunately, relegated to the past or to any part of the country. Only recently in Kings County, New York, the police brutally beat, kicked and placed lighted cigarette butts on the back of a potential witness under interrogation for the purpose of securing a statement incriminating a third party. People v. Portelli, 205 N.E.2d 857 (1965).

The examples given above are undoubtedly the exception now, but they are sufficiently widespread to be the object of concern. Unless a proper limitation upon custodial interrogation is achieved—such as these decisions will advance—there can be no assurance that practices of this nature will be eradicated in the foreseeable future. * * * Interrogation still takes place in privacy. Privacy results in secrecy and this in turn results in a gap in our knowledge as to what in fact goes on in the interrogation rooms. A valuable source of information about present police practices, however, may be found in various police manuals and texts which document procedures employed with success in the past, and which recommend various other effective tactics. These texts are used by law enforcement agencies themselves as guides.[a] It should be noted that these texts professedly present the most enlightened and effective means presently used to obtain statements through custodial interrogation. By considering these texts and other data, it is possible to describe procedures observed and noted around the country.

The officers are told by the manuals that the "principal psychological factor contributing to a successful interrogation is privacy—being alone with the person under interrogation." The efficacy of this tactic has been explained as follows:

a. The texts to which the Court refers are Inbau & Reid, *Criminal Interrogation and Confessions* (1962), and O'Hara, *Fun-* *damentals of Criminal Investigation* (1956). The quotations which follow are from those two books.—ed.

"If at all practicable, the interrogation should take place in the investigator's office or at least in a room of his own choice. The subject should be deprived of every psychological advantage. In his own home he may be confident, indignant, or recalcitrant. He is more keenly aware of his rights and more reluctant to tell of his indiscretions or criminal behavior within the walls of his home. Moreover his family and other friends are nearby, their presence lending moral support. In his office, the investigator possesses all the advantages. The atmosphere suggests the invincibility of the forces of the law."

To highlight the isolation and unfamiliar surroundings, the manuals instruct the police to display an air of confidence in the suspect's guilt and from outward appearance to maintain only an interest in confirming certain details. The guilt of the subject is to be posited as a fact. The interrogator should direct his comments toward the reasons why the subject committed the act, rather than court failure by asking the subject whether he did it. Like other men, perhaps the subject has had a bad family life, had an unhappy childhood, had too much to drink, had an unrequited desire for women. The officers are instructed to minimize the moral seriousness of the offense, to cast blame on the victim or on society. These tactics are designed to put the subject in a psychological state where his story is but an elaboration of what the police purport to know already—that he is guilty. Explanations to the contrary are dismissed and discouraged.

The texts thus stress that the major qualities an interrogator should possess are patience and perseverance. One writer describes the efficacy of these characteristics in this manner:

"In the preceding paragraphs emphasis has been placed on kindness and stratagems. The investigator will, however, encounter many situations where the sheer weight of his personality will be the deciding factor. Where emotional appeals and tricks are employed to no avail, he must rely on an oppressive atmosphere of dogged persistence. He must interrogate steadily and without relent, leaving the subject no prospect of surcease. He must dominate his subject and overwhelm him with his inexorable will to obtain the truth. He should interrogate for a spell of several hours pausing only for the subject's necessities in acknowledgement of the need to avoid a charge of duress that can be technically substantiated. In a serious case, the interrogation may continue for days, with the required intervals for food and sleep, but with no respite from the atmosphere of domination. It is possible in this way to induce the subject to talk without resorting to duress or coercion. The method should be used only when the guilt of the subject appears highly probable."

The manuals suggest that the suspect be offered legal excuses for his actions in order to obtain an initial admission of guilt. Where there is a suspected revenge-killing, for example, the interrogator may say:

"Joe, you probably didn't go out looking for this fellow with the purpose of shooting him. My guess is, however, that you expected something from him and that's why you carried a gun—for your own protection. You knew him for what he was, no good. Then when you met him he probably started using foul, abusive language and he gave some indication that he was about to pull a gun on you, and that's when you had to act to save your own life. That's about it, isn't it, Joe?"

Having then obtained the admission of shooting, the interrogator is advised to refer to circumstantial evidence which negates the self-defense explanation. This should enable him to secure the entire story. One text notes that "Even if he fails to do so, the inconsistency between the subject's original denial of the shooting and his present admission of at least doing the shooting will serve to deprive him of a self-defense 'out' at the time of trial."

When the techniques described above prove unavailing, the texts recommend they be alternated with a show of some hostility. One ploy often used has been termed the "friendly-unfriendly" or the "Mutt and Jeff" act:

"* * * In this technique, two agents are employed. Mutt, the relentless investigator, who knows the subject is guilty and is not going to waste any time. He's sent a dozen men away for this crime and he's going to send the subject away for the full term. Jeff, on the other hand, is obviously a kindhearted man. He has a family himself. He has a brother who was involved in a little scrape like this. He disapproves of Mutt and his tactics and will arrange to get him off the case if the subject will cooperate. He can't hold Mutt off for very long. The subject would be wise to make a quick decision. The technique is applied by having both investigators present while Mutt acts out his role. Jeff may stand by quietly and demur at some of Mutt's tactics. When Jeff makes his plea for cooperation, Mutt is not present in the room."

The interrogators sometimes are instructed to induce a confession out of trickery. The technique here is quite effective in crimes which require identification or which run in series. In the identification situation, the interrogator may take a break in his questioning to place the subject among a group of men in a line-up. "The witness or complainant (previously coached, if necessary) studies the line-up and confidently points out the subject as the guilty party." Then the questioning resumes "as though there were now no doubt about the guilt of the subject." A variation on this technique is called the "reverse line-up":

"The accused is placed in a line-up, but this time he is identified by several fictitious witnesses or victims who associated him with different offenses. It is expected that the subject will become desperate and confess to the offense under investigation in order to escape from the false accusations."

The manuals also contain instructions for police on how to handle the individual who refuses to discuss the matter entirely, or who asks for an attorney or relatives. The examiner is to concede him the right to remain silent. "This usually has a very undermining effect. First of all, he is disappointed in his expectation of an unfavorable reaction on the part of the interrogator. Secondly, a concession of this right to remain silent impresses the subject with the apparent fairness of his interrogator." After this psychological conditioning, however, the officer is told to point out the incriminating significance of the suspect's refusal to talk:

> "Joe, you have a right to remain silent. That's your privilege and I'm the last person in the world who'll try to take it away from you. If that's the way you want to leave this, O.K. But let me ask you this. Suppose you were in my shoes and I were in yours and you called me in to ask me about this and I told you, 'I don't want to answer any of your questions.' You'd think I had something to hide, and you'd probably be right in thinking that. That's exactly what I'll have to think about you, and so will everybody else. So let's sit here and talk this whole thing over."

Few will persist in their initial refusal to talk, it is said, if this monologue is employed correctly. * * *

It is obvious that such an interrogation environment is created for no purpose other than to subjugate the individual to the will of his examiner. This atmosphere carries its own badge of intimidation. To be sure, this is not physical intimidation, but it is equally destructive of human dignity.[8] The current practice of incommunicado interrogation is at odds with one of our Nation's most cherished principles—that the individual may not be compelled to incriminate himself. Unless adequate protective devices are employed to dispel the compulsion inherent in custodial surroundings, no statement obtained from the defendant can truly be the product of his free choice.

From the foregoing, we can readily perceive an intimate connection between the privilege against self-incrimination and police custodial questioning. It is fitting to turn to history and precedent underlying the Self–Incrimination Clause to determine its applicability in this situation.

---

8. The absurdity of denying that a confession obtained under these circumstances is compelled is aptly portrayed by an example in Professor Sutherland's recent article, Crime and Confession, 79 Harv.L.Rev. 21, 37 (1965):

> "Suppose a well-to-do testatrix says she intends to will her property to Elizabeth. John and James want her to bequeath it to them instead. They capture the testatrix, put her in a carefully designed room, out of touch with everyone but themselves and their convenient 'witnesses,' keep her secluded there for hours while they make insistent demands, weary her with contradictions of her assertions that she wants to leave her money to Elizabeth, and finally induce her to execute the will in their favor. Assume that John and James are deeply and correctly convinced that Elizabeth is unworthy and will make base use of the property if she gets her hands on it, whereas John and James have the noblest and most righteous intentions. Would any judge of probate accept the will so procured as the 'voluntary' act of the testatrix?"

II.

* * * [T]he privilege against self-incrimination—the essential main-stay of our adversary system—is founded on a complex of values. All these policies point to one overriding thought: the constitutional foundation underlying the privilege is the respect a government—state or federal—must accord to the dignity and integrity of its citizens. To maintain a "fair state-individual balance," to require the government "to shoulder the entire load," 8 Wigmore, Evidence 317 (McNaughton rev. 1961), to respect the inviolability of the human personality, our accusatory system of criminal justice demands that the government seeking to punish an individual produce the evidence against him by its own independent labors, rather than by the cruel, simple expedient of compelling it from his own mouth. In sum, the privilege is fulfilled only when the person is guaranteed the right to remain silent unless he chooses to speak in the unfettered exercise of his own will.

The question in these cases is whether the privilege is fully applicable during a period of custodial interrogation. * * * We are satisfied that all the principles embodied in the privilege apply to informal compulsion exerted by law-enforcement officers during in-custody questioning. An individual swept from familiar surroundings into police custody, surrounded by antagonistic forces, and subjected to the techniques of persuasion described above cannot be otherwise than under compulsion to speak. As a practical matter, the compulsion to speak in the isolated setting of the police station may well be greater than in courts or other official investigations, where there are often impartial observers to guard against intimidation or trickery. * * *

III.

Today, then, there can be no doubt that the Fifth Amendment privilege is available outside of criminal court proceedings and serves to protect persons in all settings in which their freedom of action is curtailed in any significant way from being compelled to incriminate themselves. We have concluded that without proper safeguards the process of in-custody interrogation of persons suspected or accused of crime contains inherently compelling pressures which work to undermine the individual's will to resist and to compel him to speak where he would not otherwise do so freely. In order to combat these pressures and to permit a full opportunity to exercise the privilege against self-incrimination, the accused must be adequately and effectively apprised of his rights and the exercise of those rights must be fully honored.

It is impossible for us to foresee the potential alternatives for protecting the privilege which might be devised by Congress or the States in the exercise of their creative rule-making capacities. Therefore we cannot say that the Constitution necessarily requires adherence to any particular solution for the inherent compulsions of the interrogation process as it is presently conducted. Our decision in no way creates a constitutional straitjacket which will handicap sound efforts at reform, nor is it intended to have this effect. We encourage Congress and the

States to continue their laudable search for increasingly effective ways of protecting the rights of the individual while promoting efficient enforcement of our criminal laws. However, unless we are shown other procedures which are at least as effective in apprising accused persons of their right of silence and in assuring a continuous opportunity to exercise it, the following safeguards must be observed.

At the outset, if a person in custody is to be subjected to interrogation, he must first be informed in clear and unequivocal terms that he has the right to remain silent. For those unaware of the privilege, the warning is needed simply to make them aware of it—the threshold requirement for an intelligent decision as to its exercise. More important, such a warning is an absolute prerequisite in overcoming the inherent pressures of the interrogation atmosphere. It is not just the subnormal or woefully ignorant who succumb to an interrogator's imprecations, whether implied or expressly stated, that the interrogation will continue until a confession is obtained or that silence in the face of accusation is itself damning and will bode ill when presented to a jury. Further, the warning will show the individual that his interrogators are prepared to recognize his privilege should he choose to exercise it. * * *

The warning of the right to remain silent must be accompanied by the explanation that anything said can and will be used against the individual in court. This warning is needed in order to make him aware not only of the privilege, but also of the consequences of forgoing it. It is only through an awareness of these consequences that there can be any assurance of real understanding and intelligent exercise of the privilege. Moreover, this warning may serve to make the individual more acutely aware that he is faced with a phase of the adversary system—that he is not in the presence of persons acting solely in his interest.

The circumstances surrounding in-custody interrogation can operate very quickly to overbear the will of one merely made aware of his privilege by his interrogators. Therefore, the right to have counsel present at the interrogation is indispensable to the protection of the Fifth Amendment privilege under the system we delineate today. Our aim is to assure that the individual's right to choose between silence and speech remains unfettered throughout the interrogation process. A once-stated warning, delivered by those who will conduct the interrogation, cannot itself suffice to that end among those who most require knowledge of their rights. A mere warning given by the interrogators is not alone sufficient to accomplish that end. Prosecutors themselves claim that the admonishment of the right to remain silent without more "will benefit only the recidivist and the professional." Brief for the National District Attorneys Association as *amicus curiae*, p. 14. Even preliminary advice given to the accused by his own attorney can be swiftly overcome by the secret interrogation process. * * *

Accordingly we hold that an individual held for interrogation must be clearly informed that he has the right to consult with a lawyer and to have the lawyer with him during interrogation under the system for protecting the privilege we delineate today. As with the warnings of the right to remain silent and that anything stated can be used in evidence against him, this warning is an absolute prerequisite to interrogation. No amount of circumstantial evidence that the person may have been aware of this right will suffice to stand in its stead. Only through such a warning is there ascertainable assurance that the accused was aware of this right.

If an individual indicates that he wishes the assistance of counsel before any interrogation occurs, the authorities cannot rationally ignore or deny his request on the basis that the individual does not have or cannot afford a retained attorney. The financial ability of the individual has no relationship to the scope of the rights involved here. * * *

In order fully to apprise a person interrogated of the extent of his rights under this system then, it is necessary to warn him not only that he has the right to consult with an attorney, but also that if he is indigent a lawyer will be appointed to represent him. Without this additional warning, the admonition of the right to consult with counsel would often be understood as meaning only that he can consult with a lawyer if he has one or has the funds to obtain one. The warning of a right to counsel would be hollow if not couched in terms that would convey to the indigent—the person most often subjected to interrogation—the knowledge that he too has a right to have counsel present. As with the warnings of the right to remain silent and of the general right to counsel, only by effective and express explanation to the indigent of this right can there be assurance that he was truly in a position to exercise it.

Once warnings have been given, the subsequent procedure is clear. If the individual indicates in any manner, at any time prior to or during questioning, that he wishes to remain silent, the interrogation must cease. At this point he has shown that he intends to exercise his Fifth Amendment privilege; any statement taken after the person invokes his privilege cannot be other than the product of compulsion, subtle or otherwise. Without the right to cut off questioning, the setting of in-custody interrogation operates on the individual to overcome free choice in producing a statement after the privilege has been once invoked. If the individual states that he wants an attorney, the interrogation must cease until an attorney is present. At that time, the individual must have an opportunity to confer with the attorney and to have him present during any subsequent questioning. If the individual cannot obtain an attorney and he indicates that he wants one before speaking to police, they must respect his decision to remain silent.

This does not mean, as some have suggested, that each police station must have a "station house lawyer" present at all times to advise prisoners. It does mean, however, that if police propose to interrogate a person they must make known to him that he is entitled to a lawyer and that if he cannot afford one, a lawyer will be provided for him prior to any interrogation. If authorities conclude that they will not provide counsel during a reasonable period of time in which investigation in the field is carried out, they may refrain from doing so without violating the person's Fifth Amendment privilege so long as they do not question him during that time.

If the interrogation continues without the presence of an attorney and a statement is taken, a heavy burden rests on the government to demonstrate that the defendant knowingly and intelligently waived his privilege against self-incrimination and his right to retained or appointed counsel. This Court has always set high standards of proof for the waiver of constitutional rights, and we reassert these standards as applied to in-custody interrogation. Since the State is responsible for establishing the isolated circumstances under which the interrogation takes place and has the only means of making available corroborated evidence of warnings given during incommunicado interrogation, the burden is rightly on its shoulders.

An express statement that the individual is willing to make a statement and does not want an attorney followed closely by a statement could constitute a waiver. But a valid waiver will not be presumed simply from the silence of the accused after warnings are given or simply from the fact that a confession was in fact eventually obtained. * * *

Whatever the testimony of the authorities as to waiver of rights by an accused, the fact of lengthy interrogation or incommunicado incarceration before a statement is made is strong evidence that the accused did not validly waive his rights. In these circumstances the fact that the individual eventually made a statement is consistent with the conclusion that the compelling influence of the interrogation finally forced him to do so. It is inconsistent with any notion of a voluntary relinquishment of the privilege. Moreover, any evidence that the accused was threatened, tricked, or cajoled into a waiver will, of course, show that the defendant did not voluntarily waive his privilege. The requirement of warnings and waiver of rights is a fundamental with respect to the Fifth Amendment privilege and not simply a preliminary ritual to existing methods of interrogation.

The warnings required and the waiver necessary in accordance with our opinion today are, in the absence of a fully effective equivalent, prerequisites to the admissibility of any statement made by a defendant. No distinction can be drawn between statements which are direct confessions and statements which amount to "admissions" of part or all of an offense. The privilege against self-incrimination protects the individual from being compelled to incriminate himself in any manner; it does not distinguish degrees of incrimination. Similarly, for precisely the same reason, no distinction may be drawn between inculpatory statements and statements alleged to be merely "exculpatory." If a statement made were in fact truly exculpatory it would, of course, never be used by the prosecution. In fact, statements merely intended to be exculpatory by the defendant are often used to impeach his testimony at trial or to demonstrate untruths in the statement given under interrogation and thus to prove guilt by implication. These statements are incriminating in any meaningful sense of the word and may not be used without the full warnings and effective waiver required for any other statement. * * *

The principles announced today deal with the protection which must be given to the privilege against self-incrimination when the individual is first subjected to police interrogation while in custody at the station or otherwise deprived of his freedom of action in any significant way. It is at this point that our adversary system of criminal proceedings commences, distinguishing itself at the outset from the inquisitorial system recognized in some countries. Under the system of warnings we delineate today or under any other system which may be devised and found effective, the safeguards to be erected about the privilege must come into play at this point.

Our decision is not intended to hamper the traditional function of police officers in investigating crime. When an individual is in custody on probable cause, the police may, of course, seek out evidence in the field to be used at trial against him. Such investigation may include inquiry of persons not under restraint. General on-the-scene questioning as to facts surrounding a crime or other general questioning of citizens in the fact-finding process is not affected by our holding. It is an act of responsible citizenship for individuals to give whatever information they may have to aid in law enforcement. In such situations the compelling atmosphere inherent in the process of in-custody interrogation is not necessarily present.

In dealing with statements obtained through interrogation, we do not purport to find all confessions inadmissible. Confessions remain a proper element in law enforcement. Any statement given freely and voluntarily without any compelling influences is, of course, admissible in evidence. The fundamental import of the privilege while an individual is in custody is not whether he is allowed to talk to the police without the benefit of warnings and counsel, but whether he can be interrogated. There is no requirement that police stop a person who enters a police station and states that he wishes to confess to a crime, or a person who calls the police to offer a confession or any other statement he desires to make. Volunteered statements of any kind are not barred by the Fifth Amendment and their admissibility is not affected by our holding today. * * * [Reversed]

MR. JUSTICE HARLAN, whom MR. JUSTICE STEWART and MR. JUSTICE WHITE join, dissenting. * * *

Without at all subscribing to the generally black picture of police conduct painted by the Court, I think it must be frankly recognized at the outset that police questioning allowable under due process precedents may inherently entail some pressure on the suspect and may seek advantage in his ignorance or weaknesses. The atmosphere and questioning techniques, proper and fair though they be, can in themselves exert a tug on the suspect to confess, and in this light "[t]o speak of any confessions of crime made after arrest as being 'voluntary' or 'uncoerced' is somewhat inaccurate, although traditional. A confession is wholly and incontestably voluntary only if a guilty person gives himself up to the law and becomes his own accuser." Ashcraft v. State of Tennessee, 322 U.S. 143, 161 (Jackson, J., dissenting). Until today, the role of the Constitution has been only to sift out *undue* pressure, not to assure spontaneous confessions.

The Court's new rules aim to offset these minor pressures and disadvantages intrinsic to any kind of police interrogation. The rules do not serve due process interests in preventing blatant coercion since * * * they do nothing to contain the policeman who is prepared to lie from the start. The rules work for reliability in confessions almost only in the Pickwickian sense that they can prevent some from being given at all. * * *

What the Court largely ignores is that its rules impair, if they will not eventually serve wholly to frustrate, an instrument of law enforcement that has long and quite reasonably been thought worth the price paid for it.[9] There can be little doubt that the Court's new code would markedly decrease the number of confessions. To warn the suspect that he may remain silent and remind him that his confession may be used in court are minor obstructions. To require also an express waiver by the suspect and an end to questioning whenever he demurs must heavily handicap questioning. And to suggest or provide counsel for the suspect simply invites the end of the interrogation.

How much harm this decision will inflict on law enforcement cannot fairly be predicted with accuracy. * * * We do know that some crimes cannot be solved without confessions, that ample expert testimony attests to their importance in crime control, and that the Court is taking a real risk with society's welfare in imposing its new regime on the country. The social costs of crime are too great to call the new rules anything but a hazardous experimentation.

While passing over the costs and risks of its experiment, the Court portrays the evils of normal police questioning in terms which I think are exaggerated. Albeit stringently confined by the due process standards interrogation is no doubt often inconvenient and unpleasant for the suspect. However, it is no less so for a man to be arrested and jailed, to have his house searched, or to stand trial in court, yet all this may properly happen to the most innocent given probable cause, a warrant, or an indictment. Society has always paid a stiff price for law and order, and peaceful interrogation is not one of the dark moments of the law.

This brief statement of the competing considerations seems to me ample proof that the Court's preference is highly debatable at best and therefore not to be read into the Constitution. However, it may make the

---

9. This need is, of course, what makes so misleading the Court's comparison of a probate judge readily setting aside as involuntary the will of an old lady badgered and beleaguered by the new heirs. Ante, n. 26. With wills, there is no public interest save in a totally free choice; with confessions, the solution of crime is a countervailing gain, however the balance is resolved.

analysis more graphic to consider the actual facts of one of the four cases reversed by the Court. Miranda v. Arizona serves best, being neither the hardest nor easiest of the four under the Court's standards.

On March 3, 1963, an 18–year-old girl was kidnapped and forcibly raped near Phoenix, Arizona. Ten days later, on the morning of March 13, petitioner Miranda was arrested and taken to the police station. At this time Miranda was 23 years old, indigent, and educated to the extent of completing half the ninth grade. He had "an emotional illness" of the schizophrenic type, according to the doctor who eventually examined him; the doctor's report also stated that Miranda was "alert and oriented as to time, place, and person," intelligent within normal limits, competent to stand trial, and sane within the legal definition. At the police station the victim picked Miranda out of a lineup, and two officers then took him into a separate room to interrogate him, starting about 11:30 a.m. Though at first denying his guilt, within a short time Miranda gave a detailed oral confession and then wrote out in his own hand and signed a brief statement admitting and describing the crime. All this was accomplished in two hours or less without any force, threats or promises and—I will assume this though the record is uncertain, without any effective warnings at all.

Miranda's oral and written confessions are now held inadmissible under the Court's new rules. One is entitled to feel astonished that the Constitution can be read to produce this result. These confessions were obtained during brief, daytime questioning conducted by two officers and unmarked by any of the traditional indicia of coercion. They assured a conviction for a brutal and unsettling crime, for which the police had and quite possibly could obtain little evidence other than the victim's identifications, evidence which is frequently unreliable. There was, in sum, a legitimate purpose, no perceptible unfairness, and certainly little risk of injustice in the interrogation. Yet the resulting confessions, and the responsible course of police practice they represent, are to be sacrificed to the Court's own finespun conception of fairness which I seriously doubt is shared by many thinking citizens in this country. * * *

Mr. Justice White, with whom Mr. Justice Harlan and Mr. Justice Stewart join, dissenting.

* * *

Although in the Court's view in-custody interrogation is inherently coercive, the Court says that the spontaneous product of the coercion of arrest and detention is still to be deemed voluntary. An accused, arrested on probable cause, may blurt out a confession which will be admissible despite the fact that he is alone and in custody, without any showing that he had any notion of his right to remain silent or of the consequences of his admission. Yet, under the Court's rule, if the police ask him a single question such as "Do you have anything to say?" or "Did you kill your wife?" his response, if there is one, has somehow been compelled, even if the accused has been clearly warned of his right to remain silent. Common sense informs us to the contrary. While one may say that the response was "involuntary" in the sense the question provoked or was the occasion for the response and thus the defendant was induced to speak out when he might have remained silent if not arrested and not questioned, it is patently unsound to say the response is compelled. * * *

* * * Even if one were to postulate that the Court's concern is not that all confessions induced by police interrogation are coerced but rather that some such confessions are coerced and present judicial procedures are believed to be inadequate to identify the confessions that are coerced and those that are not, it would still not be essential to impose the rule that the Court has now fashioned. Transcripts or observers could be required, specific time limits, tailored to fit the cause, could be imposed, or other devices could be utilized to reduce the chances that otherwise indiscernible coercion will produce an inadmissible confession.

On the other hand, even if one assumed that there was an adequate factual basis for the conclusion that all confessions obtained during in-custody interrogation are the product of compulsion, the rule propounded by the Court will still be irrational, for, apparently, it is only if the accused is also warned of his right to counsel and waives both that right and the right against self-incrimination that the inherent compulsiveness of interrogation disappears. But if the defendant may not answer without a warning a question such as "Where were you last night?" without having his answer be a compelled one, how can the Court ever accept his negative answer to the question of whether he wants to consult his retained counsel or counsel whom the court will appoint? And why if counsel is present and the accused nevertheless confesses, or counsel tells the accused to tell the truth, and that is what the accused does, is the situation any less coercive insofar as the accused is concerned? The Court apparently realizes its dilemma of foreclosing questioning without the necessary warnings but at the same time permitting the accused, sitting in the same chair in front of the same policemen, to waive his right to consult an attorney. It expects, however, that the accused will not often waive the right; and if it is claimed that he has, the State faces a severe, if not impossible burden of proof.

All of this makes very little sense in terms of the compulsion which the Fifth Amendment proscribes. That amendment deals with compelling the accused himself. It is his free will that is involved. Confessions and incriminating admissions, as such, are not forbidden evidence; only those which are compelled are banned. I doubt that the Court observes these distinctions today. By considering any answers to any interrogation to be compelled regardless of the content and course of examination and by escalating the requirements to prove waiver, the Court not only prevents the use of compelled confessions but for all practical purposes forbids interrogation except in the presence of counsel. That is, instead of confining itself to protection of the right against compelled self-incrimination the Court has created a limited Fifth Amendment right to counsel—or, as the Court expresses it, a "need for counsel to protect the

Fifth Amendment privilege * * *.'' The focus then is not on the will of the accused but on the will of counsel and how much influence he can have on the accused. Obviously there is no warrant in the Fifth Amendment for thus installing counsel as the arbiter of the privilege.

In sum, for all the Court's expounding on the menacing atmosphere of police interrogation procedures, it has failed to supply any foundation for the conclusions it draws or the measures it adopts.

Commentary

Chief Justice Warren's majority opinion in *Miranda* stated that "the experience in some other countries * * * suggests that the danger to law enforcement in curbs on interrogation is overplayed.'' The majority then went on to explain:

> The English procedure since 1912 under the Judge's Rules is significant. As recently strengthened, the Rules require that a cautionary warning be given an accused by a police officer as soon as he has evidence that affords reasonable grounds for suspicion; they also require that any statement must be given by the accused without questioning by the police. The right of the individual to consult with an attorney during this period is expressly recognized. 384 U.S. at 487–88.

Justice Harlan's dissenting opinion agreed that the English experience was relevant, but described it quite differently:

> In [England], a caution as to silence but not counsel has long been mandated by the "Judges' Rules,'' which also place other somewhat imprecise limits on police cross-examination of suspects. However, in the court's discretion confessions can be and apparently quite frequently are admitted in evidence despite disregard of the Judges' Rules, so long as they are found voluntary under the common-law test. Moreover, the check that exists on the use of pretrial statements is counter-balanced by the evident admissibility of fruits of an illegal confession and by the judge's often-used authority to comment adversely on the defendant's failure to testify. 384 U.S. at 522.

Professor Gordon Van Kessel has provided an illuminating analysis of English practice and its history in his article "The Suspect as a Source of Testimonial Evidence: A Comparison of the English and American Approaches,'' 38 Hastings L.J. 1 (1986). According to this article, the Judges' Rules as promulgated in 1912 by the judges of the Queen's Bench Division of the High Court could be summarized as follows:

> (1) when a police officer decides to charge a person with a crime, he should caution him, explaining that he is not obligated to say anything unless he wishes and that whatever he does say will be taken down in writing and may be used in evidence; (2) persons in custody should not be questioned without the usual caution being first administered; and (3) a prisoner making a voluntary statement must not be cross-examined, and no questions may be put to him about the statement except for the purpose of removing ambiguity in what he has actually said. Id. at 35.

These rules were controversial and difficult to interpret, and the judges gradually gave up the effort to enforce them. In 1961 the leading English criminal law scholar Glanville Williams concluded that "The Rules have been abandoned, by tacit consent, just because they are an unreasonable restriction upon activities of the police in bringing criminals to book." Id. at 36.

The Queen's Bench judges amended the rules in 1964 to give the police greater freedom to question suspects in custody, and the rules existed in this less restrictive form for the next 20 years. The requirement of cautioning suspects was retained, and also a limited right to access to a solicitor following arrest. Officers were not required to cease interrogating if the suspect initially claimed a right to silence or to the assistance of counsel, however, and they were not required to wait for a solicitor to arrive before going on with the questioning. They could and did attempt to persuade the suspect to respond to their questions despite any initial refusal. In any event, violations of the Rules did not lead to exclusion of a confession that was otherwise "voluntary." In short, the Judges' Rules as of the time of the *Miranda* decision were not an effective barrier to police interrogation, and were not regarded as such by the police themselves.

In 1981 a Royal Commission on Criminal Procedure declared the Judges' Rules to be unsatisfactory and proposed a detailed Code of Practice to replace them. The interrogation practices of English police are now governed by the Police and Criminal Evidence Act of 1984, and by administrative regulations (called Codes of Practice) enacted pursuant to the Act and subsequently approved by Parliament. The Act expressly provides that senior police officers may detain a suspect lawfully arrested for a serious offense for up to 36 hours on their own authority, and for a longer period pursuant to court order, if they have reasonable grounds for believing that detention is necessary in order to obtain evidence by questioning the suspect about the charge for which he has been arrested. In other words, there is explicit authorization for detaining suspects for a substantial period of time in order to persuade them to confess.

On the other hand, the Act does provide substantial protections for suspects under investigation. First, there is requirement that they be cautioned that they need not answer questions and that answers that they do give may be used in evidence. Second, the suspect is entitled, upon request, to have a solicitor or other person told of the arrest and place of detention, and also "to consult a solicitor privately at any time." Moreover, the Act provides for the establishment of "duty solicitor" arrangements which are designed to make legal advice available as a practical matter. Advice about the right to consult with a solicitor is not part of the caution which investigating officers are required to give before questioning, but rather is part of the information which the "custody officer" provides the arrestee upon arrival at the police station. Even where the suspect has requested legal assistance, police may commence questioning at once in the absence of the solicitor if the suspect agrees "in writing or on tape." Id. at 58.

The majority opinion in *Miranda* seemed to imply that the presence of a defense attorney can protect suspects from abuse without making the interrogation itself impossible. At one point in the opinion, the majority remarked that "The presence of an attorney, and the warnings delivered to the individual, enable the defendant under otherwise compelling circumstances to tell his story without fear, effectively, and in a way that eliminates the evils in the interrogation process." 384 U.S. at 466. In fact, invocation of the right to counsel simply puts an end to the interrogation, because the police know very well that a lawyer will order the suspect not to answer questions. In the oral argument in *Moran v. Burbine, supra,* p. 372, the Solicitor General of the United States candidly told the court that the requirement that an individual be told that he has a right to consult with counsel while in custody is "a sort of white lie" because the police do not actually provide a lawyer but simply terminate the interrogation when counsel is requested. See p. 380, supra.

English lawyers are not always so insistent upon preventing their clients from talking to the police. In part, this is because English law permits the jury to be told that the accused declined to answer questions after receiving the caution. A lawyer advising a client in custody has to take into account the possibility that the jury will consider silence to be incriminating despite the fact that the judge instructs them not to draw this inference. In addition, English police have considerable authority to grant pre-trial release from custody and other favors, an authority they may use on behalf of a defendant who is cooperative. Statements obtained in response to this type of inducement are not necessarily regarded as involuntary by the courts. Finally, English criminal law practice has a generally less adversarial style than its American counterpart, and Professor Van Kessel observes that English lawyers are "more willing to settle for a fair and just determination rather than to object and enforce each and every rule in the hope of frustrating the prosecution." Id. at 140. For all these reasons, the presence of a solicitor does not automatically put an end to effective questioning in England as it does in America.

English law continues to disfavor excluding reliable evidence, including confessions, as a sanction for violations of the rules regulating police conduct. The 1984 Act requires exclusion of a confession only if it was obtained by "oppression" (defined as including torture, inhuman or degrading treatment, and the use or threat of violence") or by means that were likely "to render unreliable" any confession made in response. Id. at 20. Courts have an additional discretionary authority to exclude evidence if admitting it would have a sufficiently "adverse effect on the fairness of the proceedings," but on the basis of past experience it is highly unlikely that English courts will use this authority to exclude confessions which are voluntary and reliable even if obtained through methods which violate the law. The "fruit of the poisonous tree" doctrine has never been a part of English law, and presumably reliable physical evidence found as a result of even an involuntary confession will continue to be admitted.

The new English Act contains an important provision which directs the Home Secretary to prepare regulations leading to a national system of tape recording of police interviews of suspects at police stations. In the past this innovation had been resisted by the police themselves, but more recently the police have been persuaded that they will benefit from accurate recording of the interrogation, any admissions made by the suspect, or even the suspect's silence under questioning. As Professor Van Kessel puts it: "Since evidence of silence of the accused in the face of accusation may be heard by the trier of fact, a tape recording of a suspect's prolonged refusal to answer forceful questioning or dramatic accusations by the police may be powerful evidence in the hands of the prosecution." Id. at 78. Preliminary field trials of the new recording system "have not demonstrated any significant loss of suspect statements or information-gathering opportunities, even in the few interviews at which solicitors have been present." Id. at 79. Of course, recording can also protect the police from false accusations of coercion.

English experience and practice is of particular relevance to Americans because the two countries share a common legal tradition, because English legal traditions place a high value on fairness, and because the specific rules that ought to govern interrogation have received sustained consideration over a period of many decades from judges, legal experts and political leaders, including the Royal Commission that reported in 1981. On the other hand, many would probably distinguish the English situation on the ground that police misconduct in general and racial discrimination in particular have been far more prevalent in America than in England. In recent years, however, England has begun to experience American-style problems as its population has become more racially pluralistic and its crime rate has risen steadily. During this period, the law has steadily moved in the direction of supporting police interrogation as a legitimate and necessary method of solving crimes and obtaining evidence for conviction, under a system of regulation aimed at protecting suspects from abuse but not at preventing police efforts to encourage confessions.

Supplementary Note

After the preceding note was written, the criminal justice system in England has been rocked by a series of scandals. These scandals involve the convictions of persons now conceded to be innocent, who had been serving long prison terms for serious offenses as a result of coerced confessions. Many of the crimes were terrorist acts of violence, but a number were more routine armed robberies and similar offenses investigated by an elite squad of Birmingham police. All the convictions occurred in the 1970s, before the enactment of the Police and Criminal Evidence Act (PACE) in 1984. The protections of the PACE Act would have had no effect in the terrorism cases in any event, because such cases are treated as exceptional. Suspected terrorists may be detained in some instances for up to 96 hours without being brought before a magistrate; they may be denied access to a lawyer for up to 36 hours; and the provisions relating to the tape recording of interviews do not apply to them.

The shocking miscarriages of justice led to the appointment in 1991 of a Royal Commission on Criminal Justice to determine whether further reforms of police and judicial practices are necessary. Meanwhile, the use of audio tape recordings (and to some extent video recordings) has become routine in ordinary criminal cases. John Baldwin, Director of the Institute for Criminal Justice at Birmingham University (England), described current English practice in his paper "Rethinking Police Interrogation in England and Wales," published in 1992 by the Center for Research in Crime and Justice at New York University School of Law.

Professor Baldwin reviewed several hundred audio and video tape recordings of interrogations for crimes ranging from minor theft to murder. He found that police questioning in most cases is amateurish and far from aggressive. Suspects who do not want to confess rarely do. "Of the six hundred interviews included in the study, only twenty were cases in which suspects completely changed their story in the course of an interview and admitted their guilt." The general picture is of suspects who are compliant and willing to talk and interrogators who are unprepared and rarely press them with penetrating questions.

Although recording of interrogations has become commonplace, the resulting tapes are rarely used as evidence. Prosecutors continue to present summaries of the interrogation prepared by an officer, and Professor Baldwin observes that these summaries are often incomplete or misleading. He concludes that "defense lawyers in England and Wales, by not bothering to play the tapes, take on trust what police officers state has happened in an interview to a dangerous extent."

The 1984 PACE Act provides that a suspect may consult with a solicitor, and the actual presence of solicitors at interrogations is much more common than it used to be. However, it is still rare for solicitors to advise their clients to remain silent or to intervene in the questioning. Baldwin notes that this is in stark contrast to American practice, where the presence of a defense attorney almost always means that the interrogation is at an end. English solicitors may advise their clients to remain silent, but this does not stop the police from continuing to ask questions and solicitors may actually be expelled from interview rooms if their conduct disrupts the questioning. Given the fact that many offenders are seeking favors from the police, and given the English practice of permitting the defendant's refusal to answer questions to be disclosed to the jury, solicitors apparently feel that their clients are best advised to cooperate in answering questions.

Chapter 12

THE IDENTIFICATION CASES

UNITED STATES v. WADE

Supreme Court of the United States, 1967.
388 U.S. 218, 87 S.Ct. 1926, 18 L.Ed.2d 1149.

Mr. Justice Brennan delivered the opinion of the Court.

The question here is whether courtroom identifications of an accused at trial are to be excluded from evidence because the accused was exhibited to the witness before trial at a post-indictment lineup conducted for identification purposes without notice to and in the absence of the accused's appointed counsel.

The federally insured bank in Eustace, Texas, was robbed on September 21, 1964. A man with a small strip of tape on each side of his face entered the bank, pointed a pistol at the female cashier and the vice president, the only persons in the bank at the time, and forced them to fill a pillowcase with the bank's money. The man then drove away with an accomplice who had been waiting in a stolen car outside the bank. On March 23, 1965, an indictment was returned against respondent, Wade, and two others for conspiring to rob the bank, and against Wade and the accomplice for the robbery itself. Wade was arrested on April 2, and counsel was appointed to represent him on April 26. Fifteen days later an FBI agent, without notice to Wade's lawyer, arranged to have the two bank employees observe a lineup made up of Wade and five or six other prisoners and conducted in a courtroom of the local county courthouse. Each person in the line wore strips of tape such as allegedly worn by the robber and upon direction each said something like "put the money in the bag," the words allegedly uttered by the robber. Both bank employees identified Wade in the lineup as the bank robber.

At trial the two employees, when asked on direct examination if the robber was in the courtroom, pointed to Wade. The prior lineup identification was then elicited from both employees on cross-examination. At the close of testimony, Wade's counsel moved for a judgment of acquittal or, alternatively, to strike the bank officials' courtroom identifications on the ground that conduct of the lineup, without notice to and in the absence of his appointed counsel, violated his Fifth Amendment privilege against self-incrimination and his Sixth Amendment right to the assistance of counsel. The motion was denied, and Wade was convicted. * * *

I.

Neither the lineup itself nor anything shown by this record that Wade was required to do in the lineup violated his privilege against self-incrimination. We have only recently reaffirmed that the privilege "protects an accused only from being compelled to testify against himself, or otherwise provide the State with evidence of a testimonial or communicative nature * * *." Schmerber v. State of California, 384 U.S. 757, 761 (1966). We there held that compelling a suspect to submit to a withdrawal of a sample of his blood for analysis for alcohol content and the admission in evidence of the analysis report were not compulsion to those ends. * * *

We have no doubt that compelling the accused merely to exhibit his person for observation by a prosecution witness prior to trial involves no compulsion of the accused to give evidence having testimonial significance. It is compulsion of the accused to exhibit his physical characteristics, not compulsion to disclose any knowledge he might have. It is no different from compelling Schmerber to provide a blood sample or Holt to wear the blouse, and, as in those instances, is not within the cover of the privilege. Similarly, compelling Wade to speak within hearing distance of the witnesses, even to utter words purportedly uttered by the robber, was not compulsion to utter statements of a "testimonial" nature; he was required to use his voice as an identifying physical characteristic, not to speak his guilt. * * *

II.

The fact that the lineup involved no violation of Wade's privilege against self-incrimination does not, however, dispose of his contention that the courtroom identifications should have been excluded because the lineup was conducted without notice to and in the absence of his counsel. * * * [The opinion discussed the development of the right to counsel from *Powell v. Alabama* to *Miranda*.]

Of course, nothing decided or said in the opinions in the cited cases links the right to counsel only to protection of Fifth Amendment rights. Rather those decisions "no more than [reflect] a constitutional principle established as long ago as Powell v. Alabama * * *." Massiah v. United States, supra, [p. 454]. It is central to that principle that in addition to counsel's presence at trial, the accused is guaranteed that he need not stand alone against the State at any stage of the prosecution, formal or informal, in court or out, where counsel's absence might derogate from the accused's right to a fair trial. The presence of counsel at such critical confrontations, as at the trial itself, operates to assure that the accused's interests will be protected consistently with our adversary theory of criminal prosecution. * * *

III.

The Government characterizes the lineup as a mere preparatory step in the gathering of the prosecution's evidence, not different—for Sixth Amendment purposes—from various other preparatory steps, such as systematized or scientific analyzing of the accused's fingerprints, blood sample, clothing, hair, and the like. We think there are differences which preclude such stages being characterized as critical stages at which the accused has the right to the presence of his counsel. Knowledge of the techniques of science and technology is sufficiently available, and the variables in techniques few enough, that the accused has the opportunity for a meaningful confrontation of the Government's case at trial through the ordinary processes of cross-examination of the Government's expert witnesses and the presentation of the evidence of his own experts. The denial of a right to have his counsel present at such analyses does not therefore violate the Sixth Amendment; they are not critical stages since there is minimal risk that his counsel's absence at such stages might derogate from his right to a fair trial.

IV.

But the confrontation compelled by the State between the accused and the victim or witnesses to a crime to elicit identification evidence is peculiarly riddled with innumerable dangers and variable factors which might seriously, even crucially, derogate from a fair trial. The vagaries of eyewitness identification are well-known; the annals of criminal law are rife with instances of mistaken identification. * * * A major factor contributing to the high incidence of miscarriage of justice from mistaken identification has been the degree of suggestion inherent in the manner in which the prosecution presents the suspect to witnesses for pretrial identification. * * * As is the case with secret interrogations, there is serious difficulty in depicting what transpires at lineups and other forms of identification confrontations. The defense can seldom reconstruct the manner and mode of lineup identification for judge or jury at trial. Those participating in a lineup with the accused may often be police officers; in any event, the participants' names are rarely recorded or divulged at trial. The impediments to an objective observation are increased when the victim is the witness. Lineups are prevalent in rape and robbery prosecutions and present a particular hazard that a victim's understandable outrage may excite vengeful or spiteful motives. In any event, neither witnesses nor lineup participants are apt to be alert for conditions prejudicial to the suspect. And if they were, it would likely be of scant benefit to the suspect since neither witnesses nor lineup participants are likely to be schooled in the detection of suggestive influences. Improper influences may go undetected by a suspect, guilty or not, who experiences the emotional tension which we might expect in one being confronted with potential accusers. Even when he does observe abuse, if he has a criminal record he may be reluctant to take the stand and open up the admission of prior convictions. Moreover any protestations by the suspect of the fairness of the lineup made at trial are likely to be in vain; the jury's choice is between the accused's unsupported version and that of the police officers present. In short, the accused's inability effectively to reconstruct at trial any unfairness that occurred at the lineup may deprive him of his only opportunity meaningfully to attack the credibility of the witness' courtroom identification.

What facts have been disclosed in specific cases about the conduct of pretrial confrontations for identification illustrate both the potential for substantial prejudice to the accused at that stage and the need for its revelation at trial. A commentator provides some striking examples:

> "In a Canadian case * * * the defendant had been picked out of a lineup of six men, of which he was the only Oriental. In other cases, a black-haired suspect was placed among a group of light-haired persons, tall suspects have been made to stand with short non-suspected, and, in a case where the perpetrator of the crime was known to be a youth, a suspect under twenty was placed in a lineup with five other persons, all of whom were forty or over."

Similarly state reports, in the course of describing prior identifications admitted as evidence of guilt, reveal numerous instances of suggestive procedures, for example, that all in the lineup but the suspect were known to the identifying witness, that the other participants in a lineup were grossly dissimilar in appearance to the suspect, that only the suspect was required to wear distinctive clothing which the culprit allegedly wore, that the witness is told by the police that they have caught the culprit after which the defendant is brought before the witness alone or is viewed in jail, that the suspect is pointed out before or during a lineup, and that the participants in the lineup are asked to try on an article of clothing which fits only the suspect.

The potential for improper influence is illustrated by the circumstances, insofar as they appear, surrounding the prior identifications in the three cases we decide today. In the present case, the testimony of the identifying witnesses elicited on cross-examination revealed that those witnesses were taken to the courthouse and seated in the courtroom to await assembly of the lineup. The courtroom faced on a hallway observable to the witnesses through an open door. The cashier testified that she saw Wade "standing in the hall" within sight of an FBI agent. Five or six other prisoners later appeared in the hall. The vice president testified that he saw a person in the hall in the custody of the agent who "resembled the person that we identified as the one that had entered the bank." * * * Since it appears that there is grave potential for prejudice, intentional or not, in the pretrial lineup, which may not be capable of reconstruction at trial, and since presence of counsel itself can often avert prejudice and assure a meaningful confrontation at trial, there can be little doubt that for Wade the post-indictment lineup was a critical stage of the prosecution at which he was "as much entitled to such aid [of counsel] * * * as at the trial itself." Powell v. State of Alabama, 287 U.S. 45, at 57. Thus both Wade and his counsel should have been notified of the impending lineup, and counsel's presence should have been a requisite to conduct of the lineup, absent an intelligent waiver.

No substantial countervailing policy considerations have been advanced against the requirement of the presence of counsel. Concern is expressed that the requirement will forestall prompt identifications and result in obstruction of the confrontations. As for the first, we note that in the two cases in which the right to counsel is today held to apply, counsel had already been appointed and no argument is made in either case that notice to counsel would have prejudicially delayed the confrontations. Moreover, we leave open the question whether the presence of substitute counsel might not suffice where notification and presence of the suspect's own counsel would result in prejudicial delay. And to refuse to recognize the right to counsel for fear that counsel will obstruct the course of justice is contrary to the basic assumptions upon which this Court has operated in Sixth Amendment cases. * * * In our view counsel can hardly impede legitimate law enforcement; on the contrary, for the reasons expressed, law enforcement may be assisted by preventing the infiltration of taint in the prosecution's identification evidence. That result cannot help the guilty avoid conviction but can only help assure that the right man has been brought to justice.

Legislative or other regulations, such as those of local police departments, which eliminate the risks of abuse and unintentional suggestion at lineup proceedings and the impediments to meaningful confrontation at trial may also remove the basis for regarding the stage as "critical." But neither Congress nor the federal authorities have seen fit to provide a solution. What we hold today "in no way creates a constitutional straitjacket which will handicap sound efforts at reform, nor is it intended to have this effect." Miranda v. State of Arizona, supra, at 467.

V.

We come now to the question whether the denial of Wade's motion to strike the courtroom identification by the bank witnesses at trial because of the absence of his counsel at the lineup required, as the Court of Appeals held, the grant of a new trial at which such evidence is to be excluded. We do not think this disposition can be justified without first giving the Government the opportunity to establish by clear and convincing evidence that the in-court identifications were based upon observations of the suspect other than the lineup identification. Where, as here, the admissibility of evidence of the lineup identification itself is not involved, a per se rule of exclusion of courtroom identification would be unjustified. A rule limited solely to the exclusion of testimony concerning identification at the lineup itself, without regard to admissibility of the courtroom identification, would render the right to counsel an empty one. The lineup is most often used, as in the present case, to crystallize the witnesses' identification of the defendant for future reference. We have already noted that the lineup identification will have that effect. The State may then rest upon the witnesses' unequivocal courtroom identification, and not mention the pretrial identification as part of the State's case at trial. Counsel is then in the predicament in which Wade's counsel found himself—realizing that possible unfairness at the lineup may be the sole means of attack upon the unequivocal courtroom

identification, and having to probe in the dark in an attempt to discover
and reveal unfairness, while bolstering the government witness' courtroom identification by bringing out and dwelling upon his prior identification. Since counsel's presence at the lineup would equip him to attack
not only the lineup identification but the courtroom identification as
well, limiting the impact of violation of the right to counsel to exclusion
of evidence only of identification at the lineup itself disregards a critical
element of that right.

We think it follows that the proper test to be applied in these
situations is that quoted in Wong Sun v. United States, 371 U.S. 471,
488, " '[W]hether, granting establishment of the primary illegality, the
evidence to which instant objection is made has been come at by
exploitation of that illegality or instead by means sufficiently distinguishable to be purged of the primary taint.' Maguire, Evidence of Guilt,
221 (1959)."

Application of this test in the present context requires consideration
of various factors; for example, the prior opportunity to observe the
alleged criminal act, the existence of any discrepancy between any pre-
lineup description and the defendant's actual description, any identification prior to lineup of another person, the identification by picture of the
defendant prior to the lineup, failure to identify the defendant on a prior
occasion, and the lapse of time between the alleged act and the lineup
identification. It is also relevant to consider those facts which, despite
the absence of counsel, are disclosed concerning the conduct of the
lineup. * * *

The judgment of the Court of Appeals is vacated and the case is
remanded to that court with direction to enter a new judgment vacating
the conviction and remanding the case to the District Court for further
proceedings consistent with this opinion. It is so ordered.

MR. JUSTICE BLACK, dissenting in part and concurring in part. * * *

I.

In rejecting Wade's claim that his privilege against self-incrimination was violated by compelling him to appear in the lineup wearing the
tape and uttering the words given him by the police, the Court relies on
the recent holding in *Schmerber*. In that case the Court held that taking
blood from a man's body against his will in order to convict him of a
crime did not compel him to be a witness against himself. I dissented
from that holding, and still dissent. The Court's reason for its holding
was that the sample of Schmerber's blood taken in order to convict him
of crime was neither "testimonial" nor "communicative" evidence. I
think it was both. It seems quite plain to me that the Fifth Amendment's Self-incrimination Clause was designed to bar the Government
from forcing any person to supply proof of his own crime, precisely what
Schmerber was forced to do when he was forced to supply his blood. The
Government simply took his blood against his will and over his counsel's
protest for the purpose of convicting him of crime. So here, having Wade
in its custody awaiting trial to see if he could or would be convicted of

crime, the Government forced him to stand in a lineup, wear strips on his face, and speak certain words, in order to make it possible for government witnesses to identify him as a criminal. Had Wade been compelled to utter these or any other words in open court, it is plain that he would have been entitled to a new trial because of having been compelled to be a witness against himself. Being forced by the Government to help convict himself and to supply evidence against himself by talking outside the courtroom is equally violative of his constitutional right not to be compelled to be a witness against himself. Consequently, because of this violation of the Fifth Amendment, and not because of my own personal view that the Government's conduct was "unfair," "prejudicial," or "improper," I would prohibit the prosecution's use of lineup identification at trial.

II.

I agree with the Court, in large part because of the reasons it gives, that failure to notify Wade's counsel that Wade was to be put in a lineup by government officers and to be forced to talk and wear tape on his face denied Wade the right to counsel in violation of the Sixth Amendment. * * *

III.

I would reverse Wade's conviction without further ado had the prosecution at trial made use of his lineup identification either in place of courtroom identification or to bolster in a harmful manner crucial courtroom identification. But the prosecution here did neither of these things. After prosecution witnesses under oath identified Wade in the courtroom, it was the defense, and not the prosecution, which brought out the prior lineup identification. While stating that "a *per se* rule of exclusion of courtroom identification would be unjustified," the Court, nevertheless remands this case for "a hearing to determine whether the in-court identifications had an independent source," or were the tainted fruits of the invalidly conducted lineup. From this holding I dissent.

In the first place, even if this Court has power to establish such a rule of evidence, I think the rule fashioned by the Court is unsound. The "tainted fruit" determination required by the Court involves more than considerable difficulty. I think it is practically impossible. How is a witness capable of probing the recesses of his mind to draw a sharp line between a courtroom identification due exclusively to an earlier lineup and a courtroom identification due to memory not based on the lineup? What kind of "clear and convincing evidence" can the prosecution offer to prove upon what particular events memories resulting in an in-court identification rest? How long will trials be delayed while judges turn psychologists to probe the subconscious minds of witnesses? All these questions are posed but not answered by the Court's opinion. In my view, the Fifth and Sixth Amendments are satisfied if the prosecution is precluded from using lineup identification as either an alternative to or corroboration of courtroom identification. If the prosecution does neither and its witnesses under oath identify the defendant in the courtroom, then I can find no justification for stopping the trial in midstream to hold a lengthy "tainted fruit" hearing. The fact of and circumstances surrounding a prior lineup identification might be used by the defense to impeach the credibility of the in-court identifications, but not to exclude them completely.

But more important, there is no constitutional provision upon which I can rely that directly or by implication gives this Court power to establish what amounts to a constitutional rule of evidence to govern, not only the Federal Government, but the States in their trial of state crimes under state laws in state courts. * * *

I would affirm Wade's conviction.

Mr. Justice White, whom Mr. Justice Harlan and Mr. Justice Stewart join, dissenting in part and concurring in part. * * *

I share the Court's view that the criminal trial, at the very least, should aim at truthful factfinding, including accurate eyewitness identifications. I doubt, however, on the basis of our present information, that the tragic mistakes which have occurred in criminal trials are as much the product of improper police conduct as they are the consequence of the difficulties inherent in eyewitness testimony and in resolving evidentiary conflicts by court or jury. I doubt that the Court's new rule will obviate these difficulties, or that the situation will be measurably improved by inserting defense counsel into the investigative processes of police departments everywhere.

But, it may be asked, what possible state interest militates against requiring the presence of defense counsel at lineups? After all, the argument goes, he *may* do some good, he *may* upgrade the quality of identification evidence in state courts and he can scarcely do any harm. Even if true, this is a feeble foundation for fastening an ironclad constitutional rule upon state criminal procedures. Absent some reliably established constitutional violation, the processes by which the States enforce their criminal laws are their own prerogative. The States *do* have an interest in conducting their own affairs, an interest which cannot be displaced simply by saying that there are no valid arguments with respect to the merits of a federal rule emanating from this Court.

Beyond this, however, requiring counsel at pretrial identifications as an invariable rule trenches on other valid state interests. One of them is its concern with the prompt and efficient enforcement of its criminal laws. Identifications frequently take place after arrest but before an indictment is returned or an information is filed. The police may have arrested a suspect on probable cause but may still have the wrong man. Both the suspect and the State have every interest in a prompt identification at that stage, the suspect in order to secure his immediate release and the State because prompt and early identification enhances *accurate* identification and because it must know whether it is on the right investigative track. Unavoidably, however, the absolute rule requiring the presence of counsel will cause significant delay and it may very well result in no pretrial identification at all. Counsel must be appointed and a time arranged convenient for him and the witnesses. Meanwhile, it may be necessary to file charges against the suspect who may then be released on bail, in the federal system very often on his own recognizance, with neither the State nor the defendant having the benefit of a properly conducted identification procedure.

Nor do I think the witnesses themselves can be ignored. They will now be required to be present at the convenience of counsel rather than their own. Many may be much less willing to participate if the identification stage is transformed into an adversary proceeding not under the control of a judge. Others may fear for their own safety if their identity is known at an early date, especially when there is no way of knowing until the lineup occurs whether or not the police really have the right man.

Finally, I think the Court's new rule is vulnerable in terms of its own unimpeachable purpose of increasing the reliability of identification testimony.

Law enforcement officers have the obligation to convict the guilty and to make sure they do not convict the innocent. They must be dedicated to making the criminal trial a procedure for the ascertainment of the true facts surrounding the commission of the crime. To this extent, our so-called adversary system is not adversary at all; nor should it be. But defense counsel has no comparable obligation to ascertain or present the truth. Our system assigns him a different mission. He must be and is interested in preventing the conviction of the innocent, but, absent a voluntary plea of guilty, we also insist that he defend his client whether he is innocent or guilty. The State has the obligation to present the evidence. Defense counsel need present nothing, even if he knows what the truth is. He need not furnish any witnesses to the police, or reveal any confidences of his client, or furnish any other information to help the prosecution's case. If he can confuse a witness, even a truthful one, or make him appear at a disadvantage, unsure or indecisive, that will be his normal course. Our interest in not convicting the innocent permits counsel to put the State to its proof, to put the State's case in the worst possible light, regardless of what he thinks or knows to be the truth. Undoubtedly there are some limits which defense counsel must observe but more often than not, defense counsel will cross-examine a prosecution witness, and impeach him if he can, even if he thinks the witness is telling the truth, just as he will attempt to destroy a witness who he thinks is lying. In this respect, as part of our modified adversary system and as part of the duty imposed on the most honorable defense counsel, we countenance or require conduct which in many instances has little, if any, relation to the search for truth.

I would not extend this system, at least as it presently operates, to police investigations and would not require counsel's presence at pretrial identification procedures. Counsel's interest is in not having his client placed at the scene of the crime, regardless of his whereabouts. Some counsel may advise their clients to refuse to make any movements or to speak any words in a lineup or even to appear in one. To that extent the impact on truthful factfinding is quite obvious. Others will not only observe what occurs and develop possibilities for later cross-examination but will hover over witnesses and begin their cross-examination then, menacing truthful factfinding as thoroughly as the Court fears the police now do. Certainly there is an implicit invitation to counsel to suggest rules for the lineup and to manage and produce it as best he can. I therefore doubt that the Court's new rule, at least absent some clearly defined limits on counsel's role, will measurably contribute to more reliable pretrial identifications. My fears are that it will have precisely the opposite result. It may well produce fewer convictions, but that is hardly a proper measure of its long-run acceptability. In my view, the State is entitled to investigate and develop its case outside the presence of defense counsel. This includes the right to have private conversations with identification witnesses, just as defense counsel may have his own consultations with these and other witnesses without having the prosecutor present.

Whether today's judgment would be an acceptable exercise of supervisory power over federal courts is another question. But as a constitutional matter, the judgment in this case is erroneous and although I concur in Parts I and III of the Court's opinion I respectfully register this dissent.

Mr. Justice Fortas, with whom The Chief Justice and Mr. Justice Douglas join, concurring in part and dissenting in part.

1. I agree with the Court that the exhibition of the person of the accused at a lineup is not itself a violation of the privilege against self-incrimination. In itself, it is no more subject to constitutional objection than the exhibition of the person of the accused in the courtroom for identification purposes. It is an incident of the State's power to arrest, and a reasonable and justifiable aspect of the State's custody resulting from arrest. It does not require that the accused take affirmative, volitional action, but only that, having been duly arrested he may be seen for identification purposes. It is, however, a "critical stage" in the prosecution, and I agree with the Court that the opportunity to have counsel present must be made available.

2. In my view, however, the accused may not be compelled in a lineup to speak the words uttered by the person who committed the crime. I am confident that it could not be compelled in court. It cannot be compelled in a lineup. It is more than passive, mute assistance to the eyes of the victim or of witnesses. It is the kind of volitional act—the kind of forced cooperation by the accused—which is within the historical perimeter of the privilege against compelled self-incrimination. * * *

An accused cannot be compelled to utter the words spoken by the criminal in the course of the crime. I thoroughly disagree with the Court's statement that such compulsion does not violate the Fifth Amendment. The Court relies upon Schmerber v. State of California to support this. I dissented in *Schmerber* but if it were controlling here, I should, of course, acknowledge its binding effect unless we were prepared to overrule it. But *Schmerber*, which authorized the forced extraction of blood from the veins of an unwilling human being, did not compel the person actively to cooperate—to accuse himself by a volitional act which differs only in degree from compelling him to act out the crime, which, I assume, would be rebuffed by the Court. It is the latter feature which places the compelled utterance by the accused squarely within the history and noble purpose of the Fifth Amendment's commandment.

To permit *Schmerber* to apply in any respect beyond its holding is, in my opinion, indefensible. To permit its insidious doctrine to extend beyond the invasion of the body, which it permits, to compulsion of the will of a man, is to deny and defy a precious part of our historical faith and to discard one of the most profoundly cherished instruments by which we have established the freedom and dignity of the individual. We should not so alter the balance between the rights of the individual and of the state, achieved over centuries of conflict.

NEIL v. BIGGERS

Supreme Court of the United States, 1972.
409 U.S. 188, 93 S.Ct. 375, 34 L.Ed.2d 401.

MR. JUSTICE POWELL delivered the opinion of the Court.

In 1965, after a jury trial in a Tennessee court, respondent was convicted of rape and was sentenced to 20 years' imprisonment. The State's evidence consisted in part of testimony concerning a stationhouse identification of respondent by the victim. The Tennessee Supreme Court affirmed. * * * Respondent then brought a federal habeas corpus action raising several claims. The District Court held in an unreported opinion that the station-house identification procedure was so suggestive as to violate due process. The Court of Appeals affirmed. * * *

We proceed, then, to consider respondent's due process claim.[3] As the claim turns upon the facts, we must first review the relevant testimony at the jury trial and at the habeas corpus hearing regarding the rape and the identification. The victim testified at trial that on the evening of January 22, 1965, a youth with a butcher knife grabbed her in the doorway to her kitchen:

3. The dissent would have us decline to address the merits because the District Court, after an evidentiary hearing, found due process to have been violated, and the Court of Appeals—after reviewing the entire record—found that "the conclusions of fact of the District Judge are [not] clearly erroneous." 448 F.2d 91, 95. It is said that we should not depart from "our long-established practice not to reverse findings of fact concurred in by two lower courts unless shown to be clearly erroneous." This rule of practice, under which the Court does not lightly overturn the concurrent findings of fact of two lower federal courts, is a salutary one to be followed where applicable. We think it inapplicable here where the dispute between the parties is not so much over the elemental facts as over the constitutional significance to be attached to them. Moreover, this is a habeas corpus case in which the facts are contained primarily in the state court record (equally available to us as to the federal courts below) and where the evidentiary hearing in the District Court purported to be "confined" to two specific issues which we deem not controlling. * * *

"A.   [H]e grabbed me from behind, and grappled—twisted me on the floor. Threw me down on the floor.

"Q.   And there was no light in that kitchen?

"A.   Not in the kitchen.

"Q.   So you couldn't have seen him then?

"A.   Yes, I could see him, when I looked up in his face.

"Q.   In the dark?

"A.   He was right in the doorway—it was enough light from the bedroom shining through. Yes, I could see who he was.

"Q.   You could see? No light? And you could see him and know him then?

"A.   Yes."

When the victim screamed, her 12–year-old daughter came out of her bedroom and also began to scream. The assailant directed the victim to "tell her [the daughter] to shut up, or I'll kill you both." She did so, and was then walked at knifepoint about two blocks along a railroad track, taken into a woods, and raped there. She testified that "the moon was shining brightly, full moon." After the rape, the assailant ran off, and she returned home, the whole incident having taken between 15 minutes and half an hour.

She then gave the police what the Federal District Court characterized as "only a very general description," describing him as "being fat and flabby with smooth skin, bushy hair and a youthful voice." Additionally, though not mentioned by the District Court, she testified at the habeas corpus hearing that she had described her assailant as being between 16 and 18 years old and between five feet ten inches and six feet tall, as weighing between 180 and 200 pounds, and as having a dark brown complexion. This testimony was substantially corroborated by that of a police officer who was testifying from his notes.

On several occasions over the course of the next seven months, she viewed suspects in her home or at the police station, some in lineups and others in showups, and was shown between 30 and 40 photographs. She told the police that a man pictured in one of the photographs had features similar to those of her assailant, but identified none of the suspects. On August 17, the police called her to the station to view respondent, who was being detained on another charge. In an effort to construct a suitable lineup, the police checked the city jail and the city juvenile home. Finding no one at either place fitting respondent's unusual physical description, they conducted a showup instead.

The showup itself consisted of two detectives walking respondent past the victim. At the victim's request, the police directed respondent to say "shut up or I'll kill you." The testimony at trial was not altogether clear as to whether the victim first identified him and then asked that he repeat the words or made her identification after he had spoken. In any event, the victim testified that she had "no doubt" about her identification. At the habeas corpus hearing, she elaborated in response to questioning.

> "A. That I have no doubt, I mean that I am sure that when I—see, when I first laid eyes on him, I knew that it was the individual, because his face—well, there was just something that I don't think I could ever forget. I believe—
>
> "Q. You say when you first laid eyes on him, which time are you referring to?
>
> "A. When I identified him—when I seen him in the courthouse when I was took up to view the suspect."

We must decide whether, as the courts below held, this identification and the circumstances surrounding it failed to comport with due process requirements.

III

We have considered on four occasions the scope of due process protection against the admission of evidence deriving from suggestive identification procedures. In Stovall v. Denno, 388 U.S. 293 (1967), the Court held that the defendant could claim that "the confrontation conducted * * * was so unnecessarily suggestive and conducive to irreparable mistaken identification that he was denied due process of law." This we held, must be determined "on the totality of the circumstances." We went on to find that on the facts of the case then before us, due process was not violated, emphasizing that the critical condition of the injured witness justified a showup in her hospital room. At trial, the witness, whose view of the suspect at the time of the crime was brief, testified to the out-of-court identification, as did several police officers present in her hospital room, and also made an in-court identification.

Subsequently, in a case where the witnesses made in-court identifications arguably stemming from previous exposure to a suggestive photographic array, the Court restated the governing test:

> "[W]e hold that each case must be considered on its own facts, and that convictions based on eye-witness identification at trial following a pretrial identification by photograph will be set aside on that ground only if the photographic identification procedure was so impermissibly suggestive as to give rise to a very substantial likelihood of irreparable misidentification." Simmons v. United States, 390 U.S. 377, 384 (1968).

Again we found the identification procedure to be supportable, relying both on the need for prompt utilization of other investigative leads and on the likelihood that the photographic identifications were reliable, the witnesses having viewed the bank robbers for periods of up to five minutes under good lighting conditions at the time of the robbery.

The only case to date in which this Court has found identification procedures to be violative of due process is Foster v. California, 394 U.S. 440 (1969). There, the witness failed to identify Foster the first time he confronted him, despite a suggestive lineup. The police then arranged a showup, at which the witness could make only a tentative identification. Ultimately, at yet another confrontation, this time a lineup, the witness was able to muster a definite identification. We held all of the identifications inadmissible, observing that the identifications were "all but inevitable" under the circumstances.

In the most recent case of Coleman v. Alabama, 399 U.S. 1 (1970), we held admissible an in-court identification by a witness who had a fleeting but "real good look" at his assailant in the headlights of a passing car. The witness testified at a pretrial suppression hearing that he identified one of the petitioners among the participants in the lineup before the police placed the participants in a formal line. Mr. Justice Brennan for four members of the Court stated that this evidence could support a finding that the in-court identification was "entirely based upon observations at the time of the assault and not at all induced by the conduct of the lineup."

Some general guidelines emerge from these cases as to the relationship between suggestiveness and misidentification. It is, first of all, apparent that the primary evil to be avoided is a very substantial likelihood of irreparable misidentification. * * * It is the likelihood of misidentification which violates a defendant's right to due process, and it is this which was the basis of the exclusion of evidence in *Foster*. Suggestive confrontations are disapproved because they increase the likelihood of misidentification, and unnecessarily suggestive ones are condemned for the further reason that the increased chance of misidentification is gratuitous. But as *Stovall* makes clear, the admission of evidence of a showup without more does not violate due process.

What is less clear from our cases is whether, as intimated by the District Court, unnecessary suggestiveness alone requires the exclusion of evidence.[4] While we are inclined to agree with the courts below that the police did not exhaust all possibilities in seeking persons physically comparable to respondent, we do not think that the evidence must therefore be excluded. The purpose of a strict rule barring evidence of unnecessarily suggestive confrontations would be to deter the police from using a less reliable procedure where a more reliable one may be available, and would not be based on the assumption that in every instance the admission of evidence of such a confrontation offends due process. Such a rule would have no place in the present case, since both the confrontation and the trial preceded Stovall v. Denno, *supra*, when we first gave notice that the suggestiveness of confrontation procedures was anything other than a matter to be argued to the jury.

We turn, then, to the central question, whether under the "totality of the circumstances" the identification was reliable even though the

---

4. The District Court stated:

"In this case it appears to the Court that a line-up, which both sides admit is generally more reliable than a show-up, could have been arranged. The fact that this was not done tended needlessly to decrease the fairness of the identification process to which petitioner was subjected."

confrontation procedure was suggestive. As indicated by our cases, the factors to be considered in evaluating the likelihood of misidentification include the opportunity of the witness to view the criminal at the time of the crime, the witness' degree of attention, the accuracy of the witness' prior description of the criminal, the level of certainty demonstrated by the witness at the confrontation, and the length of time between the crime and the confrontation. Applying these factors, we disagree with the District Court's conclusion.

In part, as discussed above, we think the District Court focused unduly on the relative reliability of a lineup as opposed to a showup, the issue on which expert testimony was taken at the evidentiary hearing. It must be kept in mind also that the trial was conducted before *Stovall* and that therefore the incentive was lacking for the parties to make a record at trial of facts corroborating or undermining the identification. The testimony was addressed to the jury, and the jury apparently found the identification reliable. Some of the State's testimony at the federal evidentiary hearing may well have been self-serving in that it too neatly fit the case law, but it surely does nothing to undermine the state record, which itself fully corroborated the identification.

We find that the District Court's conclusions on the critical facts are unsupported by the record and clearly erroneous. The victim spent a considerable period of time with her assailant, up to half an hour. She was with him under adequate artificial light in her house and under a full moon outdoors, and at least twice, once in the house and later in the woods, faced him directly and intimately. She was no casual observer, but rather the victim of one of the most personally humiliating of all crimes. Her description to the police, which included the assailant's approximate age, height, weight, complexion, skin texture, build, and voice, might not have satisfied Proust but was more than ordinarily thorough. She had "no doubt" that respondent was the person who raped her. In the nature of the crime, there are rarely witnesses to a rape other than the victim, who often has a limited opportunity of observation. The victim here, a practical nurse by profession, had an unusual opportunity to observe and identify her assailant. She testified at the habeas corpus hearing that there was something about his face "I don't think I could ever forget."

There was, to be sure, a lapse of seven months between the rape and the confrontation. This would be a seriously negative factor in most cases. Here, however, the testimony is undisputed that the victim made no previous identification at any of the showups, lineups, or photographic showings. Her record for reliability was thus a good one, as she had previously resisted whatever suggestiveness inheres in a showup. Weighing all the factors, we find no substantial likelihood of misidentification. The evidence was properly allowed to go to the jury.

Affirmed in part, reversed in part, and remanded.

[Dissenting opinion omitted. See footnote 3 in the majority opinion.]

PEOPLE v. WRIGHT

Supreme Court of California, 1987.
43 Cal.3d 399, 233 Cal.Rptr. 89, 729 P.2d 280.

MOSK, JUSTICE.

In *People v. McDonald* (1984) 690 P.2d 709, we held that in appropriate cases it is error to exclude expert testimony on psychological factors shown by the evidence that may affect the accuracy of an eyewitness identification of the defendant. We left open the question of the propriety of jury instructions on such factors. Addressing that question in the case at bar, we hold that the court erred in denying defendant's request for instructions cautioning the jurors on the dangers of mistaken identification and focusing their attention on such factors, and that on the record of this case the error is prejudicial.

At 11:30 a.m. on June 8, 1982, a gang of masked men entered the premises of a wholesale beverage company in San Francisco and robbed its 11 employees at gunpoint. Defendant and one Victor Wellington were jointly charged with being two of the robbers. The sole issue at trial was identity. No physical evidence linking defendant to the crime was introduced. All the robbers wore stocking masks, and throughout the events they took pains to prevent the employees from seeing their faces. In these circumstances it is not surprising that most of the victims were unable to identify anyone.[5] Three of the employees did identify defendant with varying degrees of certainty, but in the testimony of each there were factors that could have raised reasonable doubts in the minds of the jurors as to the accuracy of the identification. The defense also presented alibi witnesses who testified that defendant was in their company at the time of the crime. Because of these discrepancies and their bearing on the issue on this appeal, we set forth the relevant testimony in some detail.

Peter Marino testified he was in the warehouse with three other employees when a young Black man came in through the rear door and demanded their money at gunpoint. The man wore a stocking mask pulled down below his chin. After the four employees gave him their cash, he told each to lie on the floor and directed them not to look at him. When the witness nevertheless glanced up, a coat was thrown over his face. A second Black man came in, also wearing a stocking mask and carrying a gun, and the employees were compelled to give up their jewelry. A third armed and masked Black man then entered with another employee and forced him to lie down with the others. Two of the robbers then left and Marino heard the remaining man apparently talking to a fourth person outside the warehouse. Some 20 minutes after they arrived, the robbers departed.

---

5. Indeed, it was never even established how many robbers there were. The most that can be inferred from the record is that there might have been as few as three or as many as six.

That afternoon Inspector Cisneros showed Marino a group of photographs; he selected a photograph of defendant as resembling one of the robbers who had been in the warehouse, but testified that "I could not tell you which one he was." At the preliminary hearing he testified he could not positively identify defendant as one of the robbers, or indeed anyone else at the scene. Yet when asked at trial if any of the robbers was in the courtroom, the witness replied, "I believe Carl Wright [defendant here] was in the robbery that day."

On cross-examination Marino admitted that the robbers all wore tight-fitting stocking masks, and that because of such masks he was unable to make out the features—either eyes, nose, or mouth—of any of their faces. He conceded that at the preliminary hearing he was shown a group of photographs and asked to pick out the one he had selected on the day of the crime for Inspector Cisneros, but that the photograph he thereupon selected turned out to be of someone other than defendant. He further acknowledged that the first time he saw defendant in court was on July 22, 1982, at a preliminary hearing that was continued to July 29, and that on the latter date he testified he did not recall having seen defendant before their encounter in court a week earlier.

On redirect examination Marino testified when he first saw defendant in court he did not recognize him, and that his belief that defendant "was somewhere in that warehouse" was not based on viewing defendant in person but solely "On the picture that I saw."

Finally, the court itself inquired into the question of identification. In reply to a query about the effect of the stocking masks, Marino explained that they pressed tightly on the wearer's skin and "The face looked like it was drawn." When asked if he could see through the mask enough to give an opinion as to the identity of the wearer, the witness replied that he could not. But when the court asked whether it was nevertheless his opinion that defendant was one of the masked men, the witness answered: "I believe so, and how, I don't know. With three people in the room yelling and screaming somewhere I saw the face. How I saw it, where he was at, I can't tell you." He insisted he had seen defendant at the scene, even though in such circumstances he agreed "you don't get a full look at everybody and you're scared."

The other four employees who were in the warehouse with Marino all testified in turn, but none identified defendant or his codefendant as being among the robbers. * * *

The remaining five witnesses were all in the main office building of the company. Edward Derry, the general manager, testified that a masked Black man entered his office with a gun and demanded money. When asked if he got a good look at the man, Derry said no and explained, "I got a good look at the gun. It was in my face." After the robber took his money a second masked man appeared, but the witness saw very little of him either, "because the gun was still in my face." The first robber then asked where the company safe was, and Derry led him to its location in another room. In that room several women employees were already lying facedown on the floor, and Derry was compelled to join them. The robbers demanded the key to the safe, and Derry instructed one of the employees, Stephanie Sung, to get it. Every time Derry lifted his head, it was pushed back down by a man standing over him. Because of the stocking mask, the witness was unable to see any of the robbers' features or identify anyone in court.

Stephanie Sung testified that someone grabbed her from behind, pushed her to the floor, and sat on her back; she could not see the person restraining her. After a few minutes she heard Derry tell her to get the key to the safe. She was allowed to stand up, and someone pushed her into the next office where the key was kept; the person pushing her ordered her to keep her head down at all times. She retrieved the key and went to open the safe. In so doing she came face-to-face for the first time with one of the robbers, whom she described as a young Black man with a narrow face. She admitted that he was wearing a stocking mask and that she saw his face for only "a second or two," but testified she could see his features despite the mask. She became "very nervous" and had difficulty in opening the safe. Eventually she managed to do so, and as she left the area she saw another robber's face for "a second or two." She was then compelled to lie down again, and could observe no other faces.

At trial Sung identified defendant as the first robber she confronted at the safe. She testified that on the day of the robbery she was shown a group of photographs and picked out one of defendant as resembling that person because of the shape of his face. She also testified she recognized defendant at a lineup a week later. But she admitted she did not write his number on her lineup card (People's exhibit No. 20), as she had been told to do if she were able to make a positive identification; when asked why not, she explained that she was only 75 percent sure that defendant was one of the robbers—"I wasn't a hundred percent sure it was him." At a second lineup six weeks later, moreover, she made a positive identification of someone other than defendant as the robber.

Erica Albertsen, the receptionist, testified she was sitting at her desk facing the wall, talking on the telephone, when she heard someone shout. As she turned, an armed Black man ran around the desk and ordered her to drop the telephone and lie down on the floor. She started to crawl under her desk, but he grabbed her shoulder from behind and pushed her facedown on the floor with the others. At that point she "couldn't see anything but a lot of carpet." She subsequently heard voices demand her jewelry, but ultimately nothing was taken from her.

Albertsen identified defendant in court as the man who pushed her to the floor, saying she saw his face "very clearly" as he was running around her desk. She acknowledged that she was "really scared and startled," and that the man was wearing a black stocking mask that covered his face; contrary to other witnesses, however, she claimed the mask "didn't pull his features tight." She explained that she could not recognize anyone other than this man because "he had the gun on me," and she was able to describe the weapon in detail. The witness identified defendant at a lineup a week after the robbery; yet on the day of the crime she did not describe defendant to the investigating officers, and only two days later Inspector Cisneros showed her a photographic array containing a photograph of defendant but she failed to select that photograph. Indeed, she admitted that "I told him definitely they weren't the robbers."

None of the other three employees in the office identified defendant. * * *

The prosecution offered no other evidence to connect defendant with the robbery. The defense called two witnesses to establish that defendant was with them throughout the late morning hours of June 8, 1982. Pearl Wright, defendant's wife, testified that Sunday, June 6, 1982, was her birthday and also her mother's birthday. To celebrate the double event she and defendant attended a party on June 7 that went on past midnight. They awoke the next day at 11:15 a.m., dressed, and at 11:45 a.m. went to a neighborhood club to decorate it for a second birthday party to be held that evening. The witness testified that she and defendant remained at the club until late afternoon on June 8. The witness's sister also took the stand, and corroborated Pearl's testimony.

Defendant was convicted of nine counts of armed robbery and two counts of attempted armed robbery. He was denied probation, and was sentenced to 12 years in state prison. He was 19 years old at the time. As to his codefendant Wellington, however, the jury was unable to reach a verdict and a mistrial was declared. * * *

[The opinion observed that the trial court gave correct instructions about such general matters as the factors bearing on the credibility of witnesses, the prosecution's burden of proof, and the specific need for proof of identity to overcome the defense of alibi.]

A difficult issue is presented by the court's refusal to give an instruction focusing the jury's attention on certain psychological factors that could affect the accuracy of the eyewitness identifications in this case.[6] The proposal is based on a well-known model instruction originally

---

6. As requested by defendant, the instruction reads:

"Identification testimony is an expression of belief or impression by the witness. Its value depends on the opportunity the witness had to observe the offender at the time of the offense and to make a reliable identification later.

"In evaluating the identification testimony of a witness, you should consider the following:

"1. The circumstances under which the original observation was made, including: the witness's ability to observe when considering lighting and obstructions, if any; the length of time the witness had to make the original observation; whether or not the witness was under stress at the time of the observation; and any other circumstances which you find from the evidence;

"2. The circumstances of the subsequent identification, including whether or not the identification was the product of the witness's own independent recollection, and the strength of that identification; and

"3. Any occasions on which the witness failed to make an identification of the defendant or made an identification inconsistent with his or her identification at trial."

promulgated in *United States v. Telfaire* (D.C.Cir.1972) 469 F.2d 552, 558–559, for use in the federal district court for the District of Columbia. The *Telfaire* instruction has been adopted in most federal circuits, and in the states of New York, Massachusetts, Kansas, and West Virginia; in other states it has met with resistance on various grounds.[7]

* * *

Finally, as noted at the outset, this court recently addressed the subject of psychological factors that can affect the accuracy of eyewitness identifications in *People v. McDonald*, supra. Although the particular issue was the admissibility of expert testimony on such factors, much of our analysis is relevant here. We began by recognizing, together with distinguished federal courts, that eyewitness identifications are often unreliable, particularly when a witness identifies a stranger on the basis of a single brief observation made in fear or under stress.

Throughout our opinion we acknowledged, as numerous empirical studies have found, that certain psychological factors inherent in the observer or the event can adversely affect the accuracy of eyewitness identifications, and some of those factors "may be known only to some jurors, or may be imperfectly understood by many, or may be contrary to the intuitive beliefs of most." Such factors include "the effects or perception of an eyewitness' personal or cultural expectations or beliefs [citation], the effects on memory of the witness' exposure to subsequent information or suggestions [citation], and the effects on recall of bias or cues in identification procedures or methods of questioning." Others are "the pitfalls of cross-racial identification" and "the lack of correlation between the degree of confidence an eyewitness expresses in his identification and the accuracy of that identification."

We held that the exclusion of qualified expert testimony on the foregoing factors constituted, on the record in *McDonald*, a prejudicial abuse of discretion. First, the issue affected by the ruling—identity—was crucial because no evidence connected the defendant with the crime other than the testimony of the eyewitnesses. Second, that testimony contained elements that could have raised reasonable doubts as to the accuracy of the identification, including the suddenness and unexpectedness of the event, discontinuity and other difficulty of observation, fear and other stress at the time of perception, failure or uncertainty of several witnesses in identifying the defendant before trial, and the cross-racial nature of the identifications. We reasoned that the exclusion of expert testimony on such factors undercut the defense of mistaken

---

7. The out-of-state cases are analyzed in Note, *Eyewitness Identification Testimony and the Need for Cautionary Jury Instructions in Criminal Cases* (1983) 60 Wash. U.L.Q. 1387, 1402–1419. (See also Annot., 23 A.L.R.4th 1089 (1983).) The need for a *Telfaire* instruction in appropriate cases is discussed in the cited note at pages 1419–1435 and other recent scholarly writings. (Comment, *Helping the Jury Evaluate Eye-* *witness Testimony: The Need for Additional Safeguards* (1984) 12 Am.J.Crim.L. 189, 212–223; Comment, *Seeing is Believing? The Need for Cautionary Jury Instructions on the Unreliability of Eyewitness Identification Testimony* (1983) 11 U. San Fernando Val.L.Rev. 95, 114–122; see also Johnson, *Cross-Racial Identification Errors in Criminal Cases* (1984) 69 Cornell L.Rev. 934, 974–985.)

identity and deprived the jurors of information that could have assisted them in resolving that crucial issue. And we concluded that "An error that impairs the jury's determination of an issue that is both critical and closely balanced will rarely be harmless."

In light of these precedents it is apparent that the court, erred in refusing to give defendant's special instruction No. 3. It does not duplicate the general instruction on eyewitness identification which relates the standard of proof beyond a reasonable doubt to the issue of the identity of the defendant but does not tell the jury what factors it should consider in applying that standard. * * *

Indeed, if defendant's special instruction No. 3 sins at all, it sins by omission: it does not call the jury's attention, for example, to the cross-racial nature of the eyewitness identifications in this case. But even if this or any other shortcoming were deemed to excuse the court from giving the instruction as proposed, it would not relieve the court of the duty of tailoring the wording to fit the case by inserting any factors it believed missing. Defense counsel begged the court to make any changes it found necessary, but to no avail. * * *

[W]e emphasize that defendant's special instruction No. 3 is not, in its proposed form, a model instruction. We do not underestimate the difficulties of drafting such a charge. If, in an effort to be complete, the court lists every factor shown by the evidence that conceivably might bear on the accuracy of eyewitness identifications in the case, it risks telling the jurors the obvious and/or overwhelming them with detail. * * *

On the other hand, if the court merely lists factors—whether few or many—that the jurors "should consider," it fails to inform them what *effect* any such factor may have on the accuracy of the eyewitness identifications in the case; and as we stressed in *McDonald* the effect of certain factors may be known only to some jurors or be contrary to the intuitive beliefs of most. If the court goes too far in providing such information, however, it may be led to instruct on effects that arguably are still controversial; it would then stray into the domain of expert testimony and impair the prosecution's right to cross-examine.

Yet despite these pitfalls the effort must be made, for all the reasons we recognized in *McDonald*. It is true that some commentators doubt the effectiveness of an instruction on eyewitness identification and believe that a better solution is expert testimony on the subject; but while we approved of that solution in *McDonald*, we are aware it is not the answer in many cases. Few defendants can afford to retain such experts. Moreover, the admission of such testimony remains generally a matter of trial court discretion, but an instruction on the subject is mandatory on request in any case in which it is warranted by the evidence and the accuracy of the eyewitness identification is crucial to the issue of guilt. And even when expert testimony on eyewitness identification is introduced, an appropriate instruction will still be needed to assist the jury in appraising that testimony. * * *[8]

The judgment is reversed.

APPENDIX

EYEWITNESS TESTIMONY TO BE VIEWED WITH CAUTION

Eyewitness testimony has been received in this trial for the purpose of identifying the defendant as the person who committed the crime[s] charged. The law recognizes that eyewitness identification is not always reliable, and that cases of mistaken identity have been known to occur. You should therefore view eyewitness identification testimony with caution, and evaluate it carefully in light of the factors I shall discuss.

FACTORS TO CONSIDER IN DETERMINING IDENTITY BY EYEWITNESS TESTIMONY

Many factors can affect the accuracy of eyewitness identification. In determining the weight to be given the eyewitness identification testimony in this case, you should first consider the factors I have previously mentioned that may affect the testimony of all witnesses generally. But you should also consider other factors that may particularly affect eyewitness identification testimony. Some are known to you from your personal experiences, while others have been the subject of scientific study and proof. Among the more important factors to consider are the following:*

Did the witness have an adequate opportunity to observe the person who committed the crime? In answering this question, you should take into account such matters as the length of time the witness saw the offender, their positions and the distance between them, the lighting conditions, and the presence or absence of any circumstances that might focus or distract the witness's attention.

[Was the witness's capacity to observe the offender impaired by injury, alcohol or drugs?]

Was the witness already familiar with the offender, or were they strangers? In general, people are better at identifying persons they already know than persons with whom they have had no previous contact.

---

8. In oral argument the Attorney General stated that "the People have no objection" to a properly worded instruction on this topic. We suggest such an instruction in the appendix. It is not meant to be exhaustive, and lists only the factors most commonly affecting eyewitness identification testimony; in any particular case factors not shown by the evidence should be deleted, and omitted factors should be added. The instruction refrains from explaining the effects of some of the listed factors because they are likely to be known to all jurors (e.g., time, distance, and lighting). It explains the effects of others because they may well be misunderstood (e.g., the level of witness stress, the influence of postevent information), and still others because they are especially important (e.g., the circumstances surrounding pretrial identifications). Each explanation finds support in numerous studies reported in the professional literature; no effect that can fairly be deemed controversial is mentioned.

* The trial court should delete all references to factors not shown by the evidence.

[Were the witness and the offender of different races? Studies show that when the witness and the person he is identifying are of different races, and particularly when the witness is white and the offender is black, the identification tends to be less reliable than if both persons are of the same race.]

Did the witness give a description of the offender immediately after the alleged crime? If so, how well does the defendant fit that description?

Was the witness's memory affected by intervening time and events? Memory tends to fade over time. And studies show that a witness may subconsciously incorporate into his memory information from other sources, such as descriptions by other witnesses.

Did the witness identify the defendant before trial, either from photographs or in a lineup? If so, were the photographs or the lineup suggestive in any way? An identification made from a lineup tends to be more reliable than an identification from photographs. And an identification made when the witness views the defendant in a group of people of similar appearance tends to be more reliable than when he views the defendant alone.

[On any occasion before trial did the witness fail to identify the defendant, or did he identify someone else as the offender?]

I remind you that no single factor determines the reliability of an eyewitness identification. The presence of one or more factors in a particular case may offset the effect of others. In weighing the identification testimony of an eyewitness, you should therefore evaluate all the relevant evidence, both positive and negative, that may bear on the accuracy of that testimony.

[Dissenting opinion omitted. The dissent agreed that defendant's requested instruction (note 15, supra) should have been given, but thought the omission was not prejudicial because the factors relevant to evaluating the identification testimony were thoroughly brought out on cross-examination and in the arguments to the jury. The dissent objected to the majority's recommended instruction (see Appendix, supra) on the ground that it is one-sided and invades the domain of the jury. "Because of its wholesale adoption of expert opinion without room for jury weighing, the instruction usurps the jury's usual functions of considering the qualifications and credibility of an expert witness and ascribing to an expert's testimony such value as it deems appropriate."]

PEOPLE v. SIMAC (DAVID SOTOMAYOR, CONTEMNOR–APPELLANT)

Supreme Court of Illinois, 1994.
161 Ill.2d 297, 204 Ill.Dec. 192, 641 N.E.2d 416.

CHIEF JUSTICE BILANDIC delivered the opinion of the court:

The sole issue in this appeal is whether appellant, David Sotomayor, an attorney licensed to practice law in this State, was properly found in direct criminal contempt of court. * * *

The incident that gave rise to the contempt citation occurred during appellant's representation of defendant, Christopher Simac, for charges that arose from a car accident on March 20, 1990. Defendant was charged with driving with a revoked license and failure to yield while making a left-hand turn. After several delays, the case was called for trial on December 11, 1990. The State's only witness was Officer Ronald H. LaMorte. * * *

Before trial, appellant seated David P. Armanentos, a clerical worker employed at his law firm, next to him at counsel's table. Defendant was seated at another location in the courtroom. Armanentos and defendant shared similar physical characteristics, in that they were both tall, thin, dark blond-haired men who wore eyeglasses. On the date of trial, Armanentos wore a white shirt with blue stripes, while defendant was dressed in a white shirt with red stripes.

Appellant did not ask the court's permission, or notify the court that he had substituted Armanentos in the customary place for a defendant at counsel's table. The State's Attorney also was not notified of the substitution. The court ordered all witnesses who were going to testify to come forth and be sworn. The clerk asked appellant, "Is your defendant [going to be sworn]?" Appellant replied, "No."

In the State's case in chief Officer LaMorte testified regarding the automobile accident that he investigated on March 20, 1990, which resulted in injuries to a woman and her young child. He described the intersection where the accident occurred and the position of the cars. LaMorte testified that he asked defendant for identification; however, he believed that defendant was unable to produce his driver's license.

LaMorte identified Armanentos, who was seated next to appellant at counsel's table, as the person who was involved in the accident. The court noted LaMorte's identification of Armanentos as the defendant for the record. Appellant did not inform the court of the misidentification at this time or reveal that defendant was seated elsewhere in the courtroom.

After the State rested its case in chief appellant made a motion to exclude witnesses. The motion was granted, and LaMorte left the courtroom. Appellant then called Armanentos, the person whom LaMorte previously identified, as a witness. Armanentos was sworn at this time, as he did not come forward to be sworn when the court called for witnesses at the beginning of the trial. When Armanentos stated his name for the record, the court received the first indication that a misidentification had occurred.

On direct examination, Armanentos testified that he was not driving a motor vehicle at the intersection in question on March 20, 1990. The defense then rested. Under cross-examination, Armanentos testified that he had never met defendant. He stated that he temporarily worked as a clerical employee in the appellant's law firm. It was his understanding that he was brought to court by appellant and instructed to sit at counsel's table to see whether the testifying officer would identify him as the defendant. Armanentos testified that he was told that he resembled defendant. He further admitted that he looked similar to defendant, as they were both tall, thin, and Caucasian. In response to the court's inquiry, Armanentos admitted that he did not approach the clerk to be sworn in as a witness before the commencement of the trial.

Appellant stated for the record that Armanentos never approached the bench. He was not sworn in, and was seated in the corner of the courtroom until appellant directed him to sit in the chair next to him. Appellant argued that no fraud was perpetrated on the court, for defendant was in open court as required. He asked that a directed finding of not guilty be entered in the traffic case based on the misidentification.

After appellant said that he did not intend to call any further witnesses, the State called defendant to testify. After taking the stand and stating his name for the record, defendant invoked his fifth amendment privilege and was excused. The court refused the State's request to call appellant as a witness. The State then asked that defendant take his position next to his attorney. The court replied: "He can sit any place he wants to in the courtroom. He is here." Over appellant's objection, the court allowed the State to recall LaMorte. LaMorte again misidentified Armanentos as the defendant. The court granted appellant's request for a directed finding of not guilty based upon the misidentification. In addition, the court entered an order for contempt of court against the appellant for placing the witness in such a manner as to mislead the State's Attorney and the arresting officer. The court stated that the person seated next to appellant did not look like co-counsel or anyone employed in an attorney's office. The court stated that appellant had seated Armanentos next to him to purposely mislead the court. The order prepared by the court stated that "defense attorney is held in direct contempt of court for having a person bearing the likeness of [defendant] sit at the counsel table with him in the location usually occupied by defendant." The court imposed a $500 fine on appellant for direct criminal contempt.

The next day, the court made the following supplemental findings concerning this episode:

"The court finds that it was the totality of the conduct of [defense] attorney in court in connection with this case that is the basis for the court's finding of criminal contempt for misrepresentation by inference including the following findings:

1. That a person with the likeness of the defendant, a young, white male, was the only person with defense attorney at the counsel table when defense attorney came to the bench and said, 'Here is my jury waiver.'

2. That person was dressed in jeans and a shirt with no tie that is not the courtroom attire of an attorney or co-counsel, yet that person sat in the customary location of a defendant throughout the State's case.

3. That person was asked by the clerk to be sworn with other witnesses at the start of the trial, to which defense attorney said that said person was not going to testify. The obvious inference of this comment to the court and clerk was that the person was the defendant because witnesses were excluded except for defendant.

4. That person was identified as the defendant by the State witness police officer, and all of the foregoing resulted in the court's comment that the record could show that the defendant was identified for the record; there was no defense attorney response to this court's comment that advised of the court's impression and finding based on all that had occurred and that the court was misled as to the identity of the defendant.

5. That person's only apparent purpose in the courtroom, in a defendant's customary location with defense attorney, was to create an inference to the court that he was the defendant, and this was done with the knowledge of defense attorney.

6. That while there was no express misrepresentation by words, there was a misrepresentation by inference by the totality of the conduct of the defense attorney, and that was the basis of the criminal contempt of court finding."

On the same day that these supplemental findings were filed, appellant presented a motion to reconsider the order holding him in direct criminal contempt. In support of the motion, appellant stated that defendant was seated in the courtroom at the commencement of the trial. Appellant also stated that he made no representation to the court or State's Attorney concerning the identity of the person sitting next to him. Armanentos never approached the bench, nor did he take any affirmative action to falsely represent his identity. The motion to reconsider also described the six persons seated in the courtroom at the time of the misidentification. Appellant argued that his conduct did not embarrass, hinder or obstruct the court. He noted that the State was afforded every opportunity for the police officer to make an identification. The motion for reconsideration was denied. Appellant appealed the conviction of direct criminal contempt.

On appeal, a divided appellate court affirmed the judgment of direct criminal contempt, but reduced the fine from $500 to $100. * * *

It is well established law that all courts have the inherent power to punish contempt; such power is essential to the maintenance of their authority and the administration of judicial powers. This court has defined criminal contempt of court " 'as conduct which is calculated to embarrass, hinder or obstruct a court in its administration of justice or derogate from its authority or dignity, thereby bringing the administration of law into disrepute.' " [Citations]

Direct criminal contempt is contemptuous conduct occurring "in the very presence of the judge, making all of the elements of the offense matters within his own personal knowledge." [Citations] On appeal, the standard of review for direct criminal contempt is whether there is sufficient evidence to support the finding of contempt and whether the judge considered facts outside of the judge's personal knowledge.

I. INTENT

In contending that the appellate court's holding violates principles of direct criminal contempt, appellant argues that the intent necessary to support a conviction of direct criminal contempt was not within the circuit court's personal knowledge and, therefore, his conviction must be overturned. In this regard, appellant argues that he has an ethical obligation to vigorously represent his client. Appellant asserts that, by placing a substitute at counsel's table, he merely intended in good faith to fulfill his ethical duties of zealous advocacy by testing the veracity of the State's identification testimony. Appellant argues that he was operating in unchartered waters, and that his intent was to facilitate rather than impede the administration of justice by preventing the conviction of a potentially innocent defendant based on a tainted in-court identification. He asserts that there was no evidence known to the court to establish an intent to obstruct the administration of justice or to derogate from the court's dignity or authority. Therefore, appellant asserts that, by its holding, the appellate court has improperly eliminated from the offense of direct criminal contempt the intent to embarrass, hinder, derogate, or obstruct the court. * * *

We find that appellant's conduct clearly reveals that his intent was not merely to test the State's identification testimony. Rather, we find that appellant intended to cause a misidentification, thereby misleading not only the State and its witness but also the court itself. Appellant commissioned a clerical employee from his office to sit with him at the defendant's customary place at counsel's table. Appellant's employee resembled the defendant in important identification characteristics. Moreover, both the substitute and the defendant wore glasses and were similarly dressed. Under these circumstances, we find that appellant calculated to cause a misidentification.

Additionally, appellant's conduct before the court indicates appellant's intent to create a misapprehension and thereby cause a misidentification. It is evident to us that appellant's conduct was intended to deceive. For instance, appellant responded in the negative to the clerk's direct inquiry as to whether his defendant would be sworn. Appellant responded negatively even though, at the same time, he obviously anticipated that the substitute would eventually testify as a witness concerning the misidentification. Clearly, appellant was aware that the only inference the court could draw from the totality of these circumstances was that the person sitting next to appellant at counsel's table was the defendant and that the defendant was not going to testify at trial.

Most revealing of appellant's intent to deceive, however, was appellant's failure to correct the court and the record upon the court's erroneous statement for the record that the witness had identified the defendant. At this point, as an officer of the court, appellant had a responsibility to the court and the integrity of the proceedings to correct the court and the record. When the court made the erroneous statement for the record, appellant clearly knew that the court was laboring wider a misconception as to the identity of the defendant, yet he took no action to correct the court's mistaken impression. If appellant had not calculated to cause such a misconception, he would have taken some action to clarify the defendant's identity.

As this court has stated, "An attorney's zeal to serve his client should never be carried to the extent of * * * seeking to secure from a court an order or judgment without a full and frank disclosure of all matters and facts which the court ought to know." [Citation] The true identity of the defendant is clearly a fact "which the court ought to know" because it is the responsibility of the court to ensure the defendant's right to be present at all stages of the proceedings against him. Therefore, an attorney must not deceive the court as to the defendant's identity despite the attorney's obligation to vigorously represent his client. Such a deception prevents the court from fulfilling its obligation and derogates from the court's dignity and authority.

Furthermore, we reject appellant's claim that he merely intended in good faith to test the veracity of the State's identification testimony. Appellant could have easily achieved this purpose without resorting to deceptive and misleading practices. Many alternative methods are available to an attorney to test identification testimony. These available alternatives include conducting an in-court lineup, having defendant sit in the gallery without placing a substitute at counsel's table, or placing more than one person at counsel's table. It is readily apparent, therefore, that appellant could have achieved his goal as an advocate without misleading or deceiving the court, the State, and the witness and thereby remained within the bounds of his responsibilities as an officer of the court.

For the foregoing reasons, we conclude that there is sufficient evidence in the record to support appellant's conviction for direct criminal contempt. Appellant's actions derogated from the court's dignity and authority by causing the court to erroneously find for the record that the witness had identified the defendant, and his conduct delayed the proceedings. In view of appellant's actions and the surrounding circumstances, we find that appellant's conduct was calculated to and actually did embarrass, hinder, and obstruct the court and the proceedings.

II. PROFESSIONAL RESPONSIBILITY

Appellant raises an additional argument that we will briefly address. Before us, appellant argues that requiring a defense attorney to give the court prior notice and obtain its permission before placing a substitute at counsel's table would violate principles of professional responsibility. Appellant contends that, in a bench trial such as this where the court also functions as the trier of fact, prior disclosure to the court of his concern regarding an identification issue would somehow influence the court's ability to render a just verdict based solely on evidence presented during the proceedings. Additionally, appellant argues that, since he cannot engage in ex parte communications with the court, he would also have to reveal his concern and strategy to the prosecution in violation of ethical obligations. Further, appellant contends that the prosecutor would then be placed in the ethical dilemma of deciding whether to inform the State's identification witness what to expect, or to seek a just result by refraining from influencing the identification witness' testimony.

We reject appellant's arguments. It is well established that, in a bench trial, the court is presumed to consider only competent evidence in making a finding. In order to overcome this presumption, the record must affirmatively demonstrate that the court's finding rests on a private investigation of the evidence or other private knowledge about the facts in the case. Furthermore, the court and prosecution are frequently made aware of defense concerns and potential strategies in situations involving motions in limine. Such pretrial motions occur on a daily basis. Defense attorneys who utilize this pretrial procedure do not violate their ethical obligations to their clients. Nor has the State ever indicated that such motion practice places it in an ethical dilemma. Many times in cases where the defense attorney's motion in limine has been granted, the prosecution is aware of evidence which it cannot use or allude to at trial. Nevertheless, the prosecution has been able to proceed with its function without violating its professional responsibilities. We find the practice of giving the court prior notice and obtaining its permission to place a substitute at counsel's table to be analogous to the filing and arguing of motions in limine. Therefore, we dismiss appellant's argument.

Before closing, we note that our determination in this case is supported by cases decided in other jurisdictions. These decisions have refused to allow the practice of placing a substitute at counsel's table without notifying the court of the attorney's intent to do so. For instance, in United States v. Thoreen (9th Cir.1981), 653 F.2d 1332, an attorney representing a defendant accused of violating a preliminary injunction against salmon fishing decided to test the witness' identification by placing at counsel's table another person who resembled the defendant. The substitute was dressed in outdoor clothing, while the defendant was dressed in a business suit and sat behind the rail in a row normally reserved for the press. Defense counsel neither notified the prosecutor nor asked the court's permission to arrange this substitution. On defense counsel's motion at the start of the trial, the court ordered all witnesses excluded from the courtroom. However, the substitute remained seated next to defense counsel. Throughout the trial, defense counsel did not correct any mistaken representation of the court when it expressly referred to the substitute as the defendant for the record. Two government witnesses misidentified the substitute as the defendant. Following the prosecutor's case in chief, defense counsel called the substitute as a witness and disclosed the substitution. The prosecutor was allowed to reopen his case. Defendant was identified by an agent who had cited him for two of the violations, and was ultimately convicted.

Based upon defense counsel's substitution of another individual for defendant at counsel's table, the district court found him in criminal contempt. On review, the Ninth Circuit rejected defense counsel's argument that his conduct was a good-faith tactic to aid cross-examination. The court held that the substitution crossed over the line from zealous advocacy to actual obstruction because it delayed the proceedings in the time taken for the witnesses' misidentification of the defendant. (*Thoreen*, 653 F.2d at 1339.) In addition, it violated the custom practiced in Federal and State courts of general jurisdiction to allow only counsel, parties, and others having the court's permission to sit at counsel's table.

Most importantly, the defense counsel's subversive tactics impeded the court's ability to ascertain the truth. The *Thoreen* court noted that making misrepresentations to the court is inappropriate and unprofessional behavior. The guidelines promulgated in that State's code of professional responsibility to guide an attorney's conduct explicitly decree that an attorney's participation in the presentation or participation of false evidence is unprofessional and subjects him to discipline. In addition, the *Thoreen* court noted that substituting a person for the defendant in a criminal case without a court's knowledge has been noted as an example of unethical behavior by the American Bar Association Committee on Professional Ethics. (*Thoreen*, 653 F.2d at 1340 (citing Informal Opinion No. 914 (February 24, 1966)), decided under the former American Bar Association Code of Professional Responsibility).

Similarly, in Miskovsky v. State ex rel. Jones (Okla.Crim.App.1978), 586 P.2d 1104, the defense counsel was found in direct contempt of court after he substituted another person at counsel's table, and seated his own client in the gallery. The reviewing court found that counsel's conduct consisted of knowingly implementing a plan of deception that would affect the witnesses, the District Attorney, and the court. The defense counsel's actions were designed to create that mistaken assumption. By resorting to deception and misrepresentation to protect his client's interests, the defense counsel showed a disrespectful attitude for the judicial process. * * *

For the reasons stated, the judgment of the appellate court, which affirmed the judgment of the circuit court in finding appellant guilty of direct criminal contempt but reduced the fine imposed to $100, is affirmed.

JUSTICE NICKELS, dissenting:

I do not agree that placing an individual in the defendant's customary place at counsel's table, without more, is a sufficient basis from which to infer an intent to hinder or obstruct the administration of justice or impugn the integrity of the court. After a thorough review of the record, I believe that defense counsel was acting in good faith to protect his client from a suggestive in-court identification. * * *

Under different circumstances, I agree that placing someone other than the defendant at counsel's table could evidence the contemptuous intent necessary to support a contempt charge. The *Thoreen* case relied upon by the appellate court and the majority provides an example. *Thoreen* involved the trial of a salmon fisherman for violating an injunction against salmon fishing. First, the character of the defense attorney's conduct in *Thoreen* showed an intent to mislead the court. The defense attorney in *Thoreen* actually disguised the person seated in defendant's place at counsel's table by dressing him in outdoor clothing, including heavy shoes, a plaid shirt and a jacket-vest. Unlike the contemnor below, the defense attorney in *Thoreen* actually gestured to the imposter as though he were the defendant and conferred with him during the trial.

Second, there were no circumstances in *Thoreen* showing a need to test the reliability of the State's identification, as identification was not in issue. In using a disguise where identification was not in issue and gesturing to the defendant as his client, the attorney in *Thoreen* was not acting in good-faith representation of his client but was engaging in conduct calculated to obstruct the administration of justice.

I recognize that several jurisdictions which have considered the issue require counsel to inform the court before testing an in-court identification by placing someone other than defendant at counsel's table. (See, e.g., Thoreen, 653 F.2d 1332; Miskovsky v. State ex rel. Jones (Okla. Crim.App.1978), 586 P.2d 1104.) I agree with the majority that there are a variety of better ways to protect a defendant from such suggestive in-court identifications, including in-court lineups or other experiments done with the court's permission. The issue presented for review is not whether counsel made the best choice, but whether his specific conduct showed disregard for the court's authority and the administration of justice. A review of the record shows defense counsel was respectful at all times. Counsel did not misrepresent the identity of defendant in any way and attempted in good faith to test the veracity of the State's case. Under these facts, I believe counsel successfully charted a narrow pathway through a questionable course of conduct.

For the reasons stated, I would vacate the order finding defense counsel in direct criminal contempt of court. Therefore, I respectfully dissent.

JUSTICES HARRISON and McMORROW join in this dissent.

Commentary

The *Wade-Gilbert* rule is rarely litigated today, because the police usually do not employ post-indictment lineups or invite counsel if they do. There are exceptional cases, however. One was Tomlin v. Myers, 30 F.3d 1235 (9th Cir.1994), a federal *habeas* case involving a prisoner who had been convicted 15 years previously in a state court on the basis of a controverted eyewitness identification. The State conducted a post–indictment lineup without advising counsel. At trial the witness not only identified the defendant as the murderer in court, but even testified that she had identified the defendant at the (unconstitutional) lineup. These were clear violations of the *Wade–Gilbert* rule; the problem was that defense counsel did not object to either, and even was responsible for bringing up the lineup in the first place in his cross-examination of the eyewitness. The Ninth Circuit panel (2–1) voided the conviction on the ground that defense counsel was ineffective under the standard established in Strickland v. Washington, *supra*, p. 430.

Treating the reliability of identification testimony as a constitutional issue is at odds with the tradition that it is for the jury to weigh credibility of witnesses and decide whether the defendant committed the crime. Consequently, courts (especially appellate courts) are reluctant to find identification procedures unnecessarily suggestive, and still more reluctant to hold that testimony of a crime victim who made a positive identification was incurably tainted by some flaw in the way identification procedures were conducted. See e.g., United States v. Wong, 40 F.3d 1347 (2d Cir.1994), involving gang members who were convicted of brutal crimes on the basis of eyewitness identifications that were not above reproach.

For a rare instance of an appellate court voiding a conviction on the basis of flaws in the identification procedure, see State v. Rosette, 653 So.2d 80 (La.App.1995). In *Rosette* an undercover narcotics officer (Lewis) made four "buys" within an hour from different persons whom she had never seen before. She then identified defendant as one of the sellers in a photo lineup. The state appellate court describe the problem with the photo lineup:

> Officer Lewis testified she perceived the defendant as being a black male, about 5′6″ or 5′7″, and weighing about 135 pounds. Four (4) photographs were shown to Officer Lewis. All of the photographs display black males. Two of the photographs display black males in front of a height chart, with both their heights being approximately 6′5″. The defendant's photograph, the one selected by Officer Lewis, shows defendant in front of a height chart, with his height being about 5′6″. The remaining photograph is of a black male with no height chart shown. However, the male in the remaining photograph appears to be in his mid-thirties while Officer Lewis' report describes defendant as a black male in his late teens. We find that the presence of the height chart in three of the four photographs, coupled with the significant difference in age between the suspect and the man in the fourth photograph, unduly focused attention on Rosette as the only person in the line-up whose height and age fit Officer Lewis' description. Because the photographs improperly singled out the defendant, this line-up was unduly suggestive.

The Louisiana court went on to explain that

> Assuming a suggestive identification procedure, courts must look to several factors to determine, from the totality of the circumstances, whether the suggestive identification presents a substantial likelihood of misidentification. These factors were initially set out in Neil v. Biggers, 409 U.S. 188, 199–200 (1972), and approved in *Brathwaite*, [432 U.S. 98 (1977)]. They include: (1) the opportunity of the witness to view the criminal at the time of the crime; (2) the witness's degree of attention; (3) the accuracy of his prior description of the criminal; (4) the level of certainty demonstrated at the confrontation; and (5) the time between

the crime and the confrontation. (Citations omitted) "Against these factors is to be weighed the corrupting effect of the suggestive identification itself." (Citations omitted).

In other words, even where an identification is considered suggestive it is usually still necessary to evaluate the likelihood of misidentification. It is only where the identification violates both of these tests that a defendant's right to due process has been violated.

The court then found that the second part of the constitutional identification test was met and the conviction should be reversed because

Officer Lewis only had a brief opportunity to view the suspect. We further note that these transactions were occurring in rapid succession, lasting only minutes, and involving strangers. Even conceding that Officer Lewis' attention was focused on each dealer during each transaction, the possibility for an erroneous identification is great under these circumstances.

Such a decision may motivate the police to conduct these "drug buy" stings under circumstances which provide reliable identification of the identity of the drug seller.

PENNSYLVANIA v. MUNIZ

Supreme Court of the United States, 1990.
496 U.S. 582, 110 S.Ct. 2638, 110 L.Ed.2d 528.

JUSTICE BRENNAN delivered the opinion of the Court, except as to Part III–C.

I

[Respondent Muniz was arrested for drunk driving after he failed field sobriety tests, and was taken to the local jail booking center.] Following its routine practice for receiving persons suspected of driving while intoxicated, the Booking Center videotaped the ensuing proceedings. Muniz was informed that his actions and voice were being recorded, but he was not at this time (nor had he been previously) advised of his [*Miranda*] rights. Officer Hosterman first asked Muniz his name, address, height, weight, eye color, date of birth, and current age. He responded to each of these questions, stumbling over his address and age. The officer then asked Muniz, "Do you know what the date was of your sixth birthday?" After Muniz offered an inaudible reply, the officer repeated, "When you turned six years old, do you remember what the date was?" Muniz responded, "No, I don't." Hosterman next requested Muniz to perform each of the three sobriety tests that Muniz had been asked to perform earlier during the initial roadside stop. The videotape reveals that his eyes jerked noticeably during the gaze test, that he did not walk a very straight line, and that he could not balance himself on one leg for more than several seconds. During the latter two tests, he did not complete the requested verbal counts from one to nine and from one to thirty. Moreover, while performing these tests, Muniz attempted to explain his difficulties in performing the various tasks, and often requested further clarification of the tasks he was to perform.

Finally, Officer Deyo asked Muniz to submit to a breathalyzer test. Officer Deyo read to Muniz the Commonwealth's Implied Consent Law, and explained that under the law his refusal to take the test would result in automatic suspension of his drivers' license for one year. Muniz asked a number of questions about the law, commenting in the process about his state of inebriation. Muniz ultimately refused to take the breath test. At this point, Muniz was for the first time advised of his *Miranda* rights. Muniz then signed a statement waiving his rights and admitted in response to further questioning that he had been driving while intoxicated. Both the video and audio portions of the videotape were admitted into evidence at Muniz's bench trial, along with the arresting officer's testimony that Muniz failed the roadside sobriety tests and made incriminating remarks at that time. Muniz was convicted of driving under the influence of alcohol. * * *

[The state appellate court reversed the conviction, holding that Muniz' statements on the videotape were testimonial and communicative, and that therefore the audio portion of the videotape should have been suppressed as obtained in violation of *Miranda*.]

II

* * * Because Muniz was not advised of his *Miranda* rights until after the videotaped proceedings at the Booking Center were completed, any verbal statements that were both testimonial in nature and elicited during custodial interrogation should have been suppressed. We focus first on Muniz's responses to the initial informational questions, then on his questions and utterances while performing the physical dexterity and balancing tests, and finally on his questions and utterances surrounding the breathalyzer test.

III

In the initial phase of the recorded proceedings, Officer Hosterman asked Muniz his name, address, height, weight, eye color, date of birth, current age, and the date of his sixth birthday. Both the delivery and content of Muniz's answers were incriminating. * * * The Commonwealth argues, however, that admission of Muniz's answers to these questions does not contravene Fifth Amendment principles because Muniz's statement regarding his sixth birthday was not "testimonial" and his answers to the prior questions were not elicited by custodial interrogation. We consider these arguments in turn.

A

We agree with the Commonwealth's contention that Muniz's answers are not rendered inadmissible by *Miranda* merely because the slurred nature of his speech was incriminating. * * * Under *Schmerber* and its progeny, any slurring of speech and other evidence of lack of muscular coordination revealed by Muniz's responses to Officer Hosterman's direct questions constitute nontestimonial components of those responses. Requiring a suspect to reveal the physical manner in which he articulates words, like requiring him to reveal the physical properties of the sound produced by his voice does not, without more, compel him to provide a testimonial response for purposes of the privilege.

B

This does not end our inquiry, for Muniz's answer to the sixth birthday question was incriminating, not just because of his delivery, but also because of his answer's content: the trier of fact could infer from Muniz's answer (that he did not know the proper date) that his mental state was confused. The Commonwealth and United States as amicus curiae argue that this incriminating inference does not trigger the protections of the Fifth Amendment privilege because the inference concerns "the physiological functioning of Muniz's brain," which is asserted to be every bit as "real or physical" as the physiological makeup of his blood and the timbre of his voice.

But this characterization addresses the wrong question; that the "fact" to be inferred might be said to concern the physical status of Muniz's brain merely describes the way in which the inference is incriminating. The correct question for present purposes is whether the incriminating inference of mental confusion is drawn from a testimonial act or from physical evidence. * * *

We recently explained in Doe v. United States, 487 U.S. 201 (1988), that "in order to be testimonial, an accused's communication must itself, explicitly or implicitly, relate a factual assertion or disclose information." * * * At its core, the privilege reflects our fierce "unwillingness to subject those suspected of crime to the cruel trilemma of self-accusation, perjury or contempt," that defined the operation of the Star Chamber, wherein suspects were forced to choose between revealing incriminating private thoughts and forsaking their oath by committing perjury. * * * Whenever a suspect is asked for a response requiring him to communicate an express or implied assertion of fact or belief, the suspect confronts the "trilemma" of truth, falsity, or silence and hence the response (whether based on truth or falsity) contains a testimonial component.

* * * When Officer Hosterman asked Muniz if he knew the date of his sixth birthday and Muniz, for whatever reason, could not remember or calculate that date, he was confronted with the trilemma. By hypothesis the inherently coercive environment created by the custodial interrogation precluded the option of remaining silent. Muniz was left with the choice of incriminating himself by admitting that he did not then know the date of his sixth birthday, or answering untruthfully by reporting a date that he did not then believe to be accurate (an incorrect guess would be incriminating as well as untruthful). The content of his truthful answer supported an inference that his mental faculties were impaired, because his assertion (he did not know the date of his sixth birthday) was different from the assertion (he knew the date was [correct date]) that the trier of fact might reasonably have expected a

lucid person to provide. Hence, the incriminating inference of impaired mental faculties stemmed, not just from the fact that Muniz slurred his response, but also from a testimonial aspect of that response. * * *

C

The Commonwealth argues that the seven questions asked by Officer Hosterman just prior to the sixth birthday question—regarding Muniz's name, address, height, weight, eye color, date of birth, and current age—did not constitute custodial interrogation. * * * In Rhode Island v. Innis, 446 U.S. 291 (1980), [we said that the functional equivalent of express questioning includes] "any words or actions on the part of the police (other than those normally attendant to arrest and custody) that the police should know are reasonably likely to elicit an incriminating response from the suspect. The latter portion of this definition focuses primarily upon the perceptions of the suspect, rather than the intent of the police." * * * We disagree with the Commonwealth's contention that Officer Hosterman's first seven questions regarding Muniz's name, address, height, weight, eye color, date of birth, and current age do not qualify as custodial interrogation as we defined the term in *Innis* merely because the questions were not intended to elicit information for investigatory purposes. * * * We agree with amicus United States, however, that Muniz's answers to these first seven questions are nonetheless admissible because the questions fall within a "routine booking question" exception which exempts from *Miranda's* coverage questions to secure the biographical data necessary to complete booking or pretrial services. * * * In this context, therefore, the first seven questions asked at the Booking Center fall outside the protections of *Miranda* and the answers thereto need not be suppressed.

IV

During the second phase of the videotaped proceedings, Officer Hosterman asked Muniz to perform the same three sobriety tests that he had earlier performed at roadside prior to his arrest. While Muniz was attempting to comprehend the instructions and then perform the requested sobriety tests, he made several audible and incriminating statements. [The majority opinion held that these statements, and the statements Muniz volunteered after being asked to submit to a breathalyzer examination, were not in response to interrogation and were admissible.]

V

We agree with the state court's conclusion that Miranda requires suppression of Muniz's response to the question regarding the date of his sixth birthday, but we do not agree that the entire audio portion of the videotape must be suppressed. Accordingly, the court's judgment reversing Muniz's conviction is vacated, and the case is remanded for further proceedings not inconsistent with this opinion.

CHIEF JUSTICE REHNQUIST, with whom JUSTICE WHITE, JUSTICE BLACKMUN and JUSTICE STEVENS join, concurring in part, concurring in the result in part, and dissenting in part.

I join Parts I, II, III–A, and IV of the Court's opinion. In addition, although I agree with the conclusion in Part III–C that the seven "booking" questions should not be suppressed, I do so for a reason different from that of Justice Brennan. I dissent from the Court's conclusion that Muniz' response to the "sixth birthday question" should have been suppressed. * * *

The sixth birthday question here was an effort on the part of the police to check how well Muniz was able to do a simple mathematical exercise. Indeed, had the question related only to the date of his birth, it presumably would have come under the "booking exception" to which the Court refers elsewhere in its opinion. The Court holds in this very case that Muniz may be required to perform a "horizontal gaze nystagmus" test, and "the walk and turn" test, and the "one leg stand" test, all of which are designed to test a suspect's physical coordination. If the police may require Muniz to use his body in order to demonstrate the level of his physical coordination, there is no reason why they should not be able to require him to speak or write in order to determine his mental coordination. * * *

For substantially the same reasons, Muniz' responses to the video-taped "booking" questions were not testimonial and do not warrant application to the privilege. Thus, it is unnecessary to determine whether the questions fall within the "routine booking question" exception to *Miranda* Justice Brennan recognizes.

I would reverse in its entirety the judgment of the Superior Court of Pennsylvania. But given the fact the five members of the Court agree that Muniz' response to the sixth birthday question should have been suppressed, I agree that the judgment of the Superior Court should be vacated so that on remand, the court may consider whether admission of the response at trial was harmless error.

JUSTICE MARSHALL, concurring in part and dissenting in part.

I concur in Part III–B of the Court's opinion that the "sixth birthday question" required a testimonial response from respondent Muniz. Because the police did not apprise Muniz of his Miranda rights before asking the question, his response should have been suppressed.

I disagree, however, with the plurality's recognition in Part III–C of a "routine booking question" exception to *Miranda*. Moreover, even were such an exception warranted, it should not extend to booking questions that the police should know are reasonably likely to elicit incriminating responses. Because the police in this case should have known that the seven booking questions were reasonably likely to elicit incriminating responses and because those questions were not preceded by *Miranda* warnings, Muniz's testimonial responses should have been suppressed.

I dissent from the Court's holding in Part IV that Muniz's testimonial statements in connection with the three sobriety tests and the breathalyzer test were not the products of custodial interrogation. The police should have known that the circumstances in which they confronted Muniz, combined with the detailed instructions and questions concerning the tests and the State's Implied Consent Law, were reasonably likely to elicit an incriminating response, and therefore constituted the "functional equivalent" of express questioning. Rhode Island v. Innis, 446 U.S. 291, 301 (1980). Muniz's statements to the police in connection with these tests thus should have been suppressed because he was not first given the Miranda warnings. Finally, the officer's directions to Muniz to count aloud during two of the sobriety tests sought testimonial responses, and Muniz's responses were incriminating. Because Muniz was not informed of his Miranda rights prior to the tests, those responses also should have been suppressed. * * *

Commentary

The "lineup" cases have not turned out to be as important as first appeared, mainly because the Supreme Court has retreated from the broad principles that it at one time seemed to be promulgating. These decisions remain important, however, to an understanding of the way the Justices were thinking about the 5th and 6th Amendments during the period in which the Court was revolutionizing American criminal procedure under the leadership of Chief Justice Warren. The cases involve three kinds of issues: the scope of the 5th Amendment's privilege against self-incrimination; the scope of the 6th Amendment's right to counsel; and the application of the due process clause to potentially unreliable eyewitness identification testimony.

The 5th Amendment Privilege

For a number of years, the Supreme Court was closely divided over whether the 5th Amendment privilege protects the accused only from having to give testimony (i.e. be a *witness* against himself), or whether it also protects the accused from: (1) being required to perform any "volitional" act which assists the prosecution; (2) any invasion of the body for evidence, such as the taking of a blood sample to establish intoxication; and (3) the production by subpoena or search of private papers, business records, or other documentary evidence. [On the third point, see *Andresen v. Maryland, supra* p. 230, and *Guarino, infra* p. 688.]

The key decision on the scope of the 5th Amendment was Schmerber v. California, 384 U.S. 757 (1966), where Justice Brennan joined the more conservative Justices to form a 5–4 majority upholding the constitutionality of taking a blood sample from a person where there was probably cause to arrest for drunk driving. Chief Justice Warren and Justices Douglas, Black and Fortas dissented, with considerable emotion. None of the dissenting opinions discussed the practical implications of banning chemical evidence from drunk driving and vehicular manslaughter prosecutions; the dissenters simply drew back in horror from the very idea of extracting a person's blood in order to convict him of a crime.

Despite the narrow majority in *Schmerber* and the intensity of the dissenting opinions, the *Schmerber* doctrine is no longer controversial and has been substantially extended. See, for example, In re Special Federal

Grand Jury, 809 F.2d 1023 (3d Cir.1987), upholding a subpoena directing a suspect to furnish handwriting exemplars "in a backhand slant," although that was not the suspect's usual style of writing. The suspect argued that such a sample would "communicate the angle he would normally use if he were to disguise his writing by using a backward slant," and as such would be testimonial in nature. The majority of the Court of Appeals responded that "The minimal thought process involved in slanting one's handwriting is of no significance in transforming physical evidence into testimony."

6th Amendment

Although the 5th Amendment privilege did not protect Wade from being required to "exhibit his physical characteristics," the Court went on to hold that his 6th Amendment right to counsel was nonetheless applicable at this "post-indictment lineup" because of the assistance counsel might have provided in seeing that the lineup was properly conducted. But why the limitation to *post-indictment* lineups? The opinion also stated the more general principle that "the accused is guaranteed that he need not stand alone against the State at any stage of the prosecution, formal or informal, in court or out, where counsel's absence might derogate from the accused's right to a fair trial." [p. 482.] The *Massiah* case [p. 454] had said that the 6th Amendment right to counsel attaches at the commencement of formal adversary proceedings, with the filing of an indictment, but surely counsel is no less helpful when the lineup is held before the indictment.

Despite the compelling force of this logic, the Supreme Court decided in Kirby v. Illinois, 406 U.S. 682 (1972), that the *Wade-Gilbert*[a] rule did not apply to a police station show-up that took place after arrest but before the defendant had been indicted or otherwise formally charged with a criminal offense. This decision made the rule of relatively little value to defendants, because the prosecution can always delay asking for an indictment until it has had time to conduct a lineup or other identification procedure. *Kirby* is also important as a gloss on the *Miranda* rule, because it makes clear that *Miranda* (unlike *Massiah*) is based on the 5th Amendment privilege rather than the 6th Amendment right to counsel. Although *Miranda* requires that a suspect in custody be warned that he has a right to have counsel present at the interrogation, the right in question is not the 6th Amendment right to counsel but, as Justice White put it in his *Miranda* dissent, "a limited Fifth Amendment right to counsel." [See p. 516, supra]. If that sounds confusing it is because it *is* confusing, but the point is nonetheless important. Consider in this connection the argument of the Solicitor General, discussed in footnote 4 of Justice Steven's dissent in *Moran v. Burbine* [p. 399, *supra*], that *Miranda*'s warning of a "right to counsel" is a kind of harmless fiction, because what the accused really has is not a right to the presence of counsel but a right to cut off questioning. Perhaps what the accused should be told is not that he has a right to the assistance of counsel at interrogation, but rather that he has a right to put a stop to the questioning at any time.

The Supreme Court further limited the *Wade-Gilbert* doctrine in United States v. Ash, 413 U.S. 300 (1973), where the majority held the right to counsel inapplicable when the Government conducts a post-

a. Gilbert v. California, 388 U.S. 263 (1967) was a companion case to *Wade*.

indictment photographic display where the suspect is not present personally. The majority opinion likened the identification from photographs to other trial-preparation interviews between the prosecutor and witnesses, and refused to extend the right to counsel to such pretrial preparation.

Due Process

On the same date that it decided the *Wade* and *Gilbert* cases, the Supreme Court also decided Stovall v. Denno, 388 U.S. 293 (1967). *Stovall* first established that the right to counsel announced in *Wade* and *Gilbert* would apply only to lineups conducted after the announcement of the decisions in those cases. In other words, the Court for the first time established a "violation date" standard of retroactivity for newly-announced constitutional rights. The *Stovall* opinion added, however, that a lineup or other identification procedure would violate a fully retroactive due process doctrine if it "was so unnecessarily suggestive and conducive to irreparable mistaken identification that [the defendant] was denied due process of law." In *Stovall* a stabbing victim (Mrs. Behrendt), was hospitalized for surgery. The defendant, who had already been arraigned in court, was taken by police to the hospital room in handcuffs. (He was the only black person in the room.) The victim identified him from her hospital bed and testified at the trial to the identification in the hospital. Despite the potential for suggestion in the circumstances of the confrontation, the Supreme Court in an opinion by Justice Brennan held that the showup did not violate the due process doctrine because of the possibility that the victim might die before a more formal identification procedure could be held.

Because of the *Kirby* limitation, most of the cases charging suggestive identification procedures are litigated under the due process doctrine rather than the right to counsel. Since *Neil v. Biggers, supra*, p. 491, the due process doctrine has also had relatively little bite. Once the issue is put in terms of whether the identification evidence is on the whole reliable, rather than on whether some improper action occurred in the pretrial identification process, then it is not easy to see why the issue should not be left, like other disputed questions of fact, to the determination of the jury. See also, Manson v. Brathwaite, 432 U.S. 98 (1977). Both *Manson* and *Biggers* allowed the use of the pretrial identification itself, as well as the in-court identification, despite the unnecessarily suggestive confrontation procedure.

In summary, the Supreme Court has almost completely abandoned its attempt to formulate Sixth Amendment and Due Process doctrines to deal with the very real danger that an innocent person may be convicted on unreliable identification testimony. Whether the experiment might have been successful if the Court had not backed away from its revolutionary holding in *Wade* and *Gilbert* remains problematical. There is some force in Justice White's argument [p. 489] that defense lawyers in our system see their duty as being to frustrate the prosecution rather than to assure that reliable fact-finding procedures are followed. There is without question a need to address the problem of mistaken identifications, but there is reason to doubt whether opening up pretrial preparation to defense counsel is the best means of accomplishing this end. *People v. Wright, supra* p. 478, explores some other possibilities.

Chapter 13

THE POST-*MIRANDA* CONFESSION CASES

A. CUSTODIAL INTERROGATION

UNITED STATES v. MESA

United States Court of Appeals, Third Circuit, 1980.
638 F.2d 582.

SEITZ, CHIEF JUDGE.

This is an appeal by the government from an interlocutory order of the district court, granting the motion of the defendant, Rigoberto Mesa, to suppress a tape-recorded conversation between Mesa and an FBI agent.

I.

The facts are undisputed. On January 28, 1980, Karin Little, Mesa's "common-law" wife, and Sonia Mesa, his daughter, were shot and wounded. Later that day, the victims, both of whom survived, informed the FBI that Mesa had inflicted their injuries. The FBI was unable to locate Mesa on January 28 and obtained a warrant for his arrest from a United States Magistrate the next morning. At approximately 2:00 p.m. on January 29, three FBI agents went to the El Sombrero Motel in Brown Mills, New Jersey and inquired about Mesa. They learned that Mesa had barricaded himself in his room sometime before 10:00 a.m. that day. The agents evacuated the rooms on each side of Mesa's room and blocked off traffic in the vicinity.

The agents then called to Mesa through a bullhorn, informed him that they were FBI agents, that they had a warrant for his arrest, and that he should come out with his hands raised. Mesa did not respond. The agents repeated their statement between ten and twelve times over the course of approximately one hour, but Mesa still did not respond. During this period, additional law enforcement officials arrived at the scene. Eventually, between twenty-five and thirty officers surrounded the motel.

The agents believed that Mesa was armed, and they did not know whether he had hostages. Because they deemed it inadvisable to forcibly take Mesa into their custody, the agents requested the assistance of Special Agent Theodore Viater, the FBI's hostage negotiator for the area.

When Agent Viater arrived, the agents decided that because there was no commercial telephone in Mesa's room it would be necessary to use a mobile telephone to talk with Mesa. An FBI agent then used the bullhorn to ask Mesa if he would take a telephone receiver into the room to talk with Viater. Mesa indicated by hand signals that he would take the phone.

Viater and Mesa then conversed over the mobile phone for approximately three and one half hours. This conversation primarily involved long narrative monologues by Mesa, with Viater passively listening. Viater had been informed that Mesa had been under psychiatric care and that he might have suicidal tendencies. The comments Viater made during the conversation were supportive and seemed designed to keep Mesa talking in order to establish a relationship of trust. The following comment is representative:

> I'm concerned about you Rigoberto, I'm concerned about your welfare, and I'm concerned about your health and I want to make absolutely certain that you and I trust each other and we can bring this problem to a successful solution.

During this conversation, Mesa discussed his experiences in Vietnam, his relationship with his family during his childhood in Cuba, his relationship with his "common-law" wife and children, other events of his life, and the events surrounding the shooting on January 28. Viater generally limited his interjections into this narrative to comments such as "Umhum" and "I understand," with an occasional question concerning Mesa's most recent statement or a longer comment evidencing understanding for Mesa's situation. Viater hoped that by establishing this atmosphere of trust he could convince Mesa to surrender without harming himself or any of the officials in the area.

Mesa finally surrendered peacefully at approximately 6:30 p.m. At this point, the FBI agents gave Mesa the *Miranda* warnings. After he had surrendered, Mesa thanked Viater for listening to him and stated that he would have killed himself had it not been for Viater.

At no time during the taped conversation did Viater give Mesa *Miranda* warnings. Mesa argues that the contents of the conversation should be suppressed because of the failure to give these warnings. The district court conducted a hearing on Mesa's motion to suppress on April 3, 1980. It held that the taped conversation must be suppressed because Viater's conversation with Mesa constituted "custodial interrogation" within the meaning of *Miranda*. I now will consider whether the FBI's conduct was "custodial interrogation" as contemplated by the *Miranda* Court.

II.

* * *

The circumstances under which Mesa talked with Viater can be distinguished from the custodial setting that concerned the *Miranda* Court. Mesa successfully had barricaded himself in his motel room in such a way that he prevented the law enforcement officials from exercising immediate control over his actions. They could not compel Mesa even to listen to any questions they might want to ask, much less subject him to the interviewing techniques or "tricks" that concerned the *Miranda* Court. They had no power to handcuff him or use other reasonable means to confine him in such a manner that he had no choice but to listen to questioning.

The conversation between Mesa and Viater did not occur in a setting where Viater was alone in a room or other enclosed area with Mesa and thus had eliminated all possible distractions. Mesa was free to terminate the phone conversation at any time, either completely or temporarily whenever he was tired of talking. The tape transcript indicates that, although Viater wanted to keep the conversation going to ensure that Mesa would not harm himself, he was always agreeable when Mesa wanted to take a break and would interrupt those breaks only to determine that Mesa had not harmed himself. Mesa in fact took several breaks to smoke cigarettes and to rest.

The FBI agents not only were prevented from controlling the timing of the conversation with Mesa, they also could not control its substance. Mesa was not in a police-dominated atmosphere in which the police could dictate the subjects to be discussed. In this situation, Mesa himself controlled the direction of the conversation and he was free to discuss anything he wanted. There is no indication on the tape that Viater attempted to control the direction of Mesa's conversation[3]—in fact, the facts indicate that Viater could not have forced Mesa to even listen to, much less respond to, any particular line of questioning. * * * I therefore conclude that Mesa was not in "custody" within the meaning of *Miranda*.

I do not retreat from this conclusion because the presence of law enforcement officials surrounding the motel restricted Mesa's freedom to leave the motel. The defendant argues that this fact establishes "custody" because *Miranda* requires warnings when the suspect is taken into custody or "otherwise deprived of his freedom by the authorities in any significant way." * * *

3. The *only* place in the entire three and one half hour taped conversation that Viater possibly could be said to have directed the conversation toward the shooting of January 28, is where he said to Mesa: "Tell me what happened yesterday. What was the provocation?" This statement immediately followed Mesa's statement: "What happened yesterday was a provocation. It was a provocation because I am not a criminal. I am not a criminal. Because I didn't hurt anybody until I went to Viet Nam." Because Viater's reference to the previous day's event came in direct response to Mesa's reference to the same event, we do not think that Viater can fairly be said to have directed the conversation toward that event.

Supreme Court decisions after *Miranda* have relied on this broad language to determine whether the suspect was in "custody." *See Oregon v. Mathiason*, 429 U.S. 492 (1977) (per curiam); *Orozco v. Texas*, 394 U.S. 324 (1969). In these cases, the Court construed this language as focusing on the suspect's "freedom to come and go as he pleased." In *Orozco*, police officers interrogated the defendant in his bedroom at approximately 4:00 a.m. The Court held that, because the defendant "was not free to go where he pleased but was under arrest," this was "custodial interrogation" despite the fact that it occurred at the defendant's home and not at the police station. In *Mathiason*, the Court held that the defendant had not been subjected to "custodial interrogation" even though he had been questioned at the police station for approximately one half hour. Although the defendant was interrogated while he was alone in the police station, the presence of other factors convinced the Court that he was not in "custody." He had come to the station voluntarily upon the police's request; he was told that he was not under arrest, that he was free to leave, and he actually left after the questioning. Therefore statements he made during this interrogation were admissible despite the absence of *Miranda* warnings.

The Court's focus in these cases on the suspect's freedom to come and go as he pleases must be considered in conjunction with the concerns underlying the custody requirement detailed above. The *Miranda* Court's description of the custodial setting demonstrates that, at a minimum, the police must have immediate control over the suspect. *Mathiason* and *Orozco* stand for the proposition that when the police have a suspect within their immediate control, the proper inquiry to determine whether he is in "custody" is not to ask if he was at the police station, but to ask if he was free to leave. My decision in this case is not inconsistent with this analysis. * * *

However, I recognize that there may be situations in which it would be unfair to admit statements made by a suspect under the conditions present in this case. * * * If the police compel an armed, barricaded suspect to incriminate himself by psychological trickery or other police overreaching, the suspect can attack the admissibility of his statements on the ground that they were not voluntary, but compelled by the police in violation of his fifth amendment rights. * * *

When a suspect places himself in a situation like that of Mesa in this case, any statements he makes should be closely scrutinized for voluntariness, but *Miranda* warnings are not a necessary prerequisite to the admission of those statements. Mesa has not claimed on this appeal that his statements to Viater were involuntary. Consequently, I do not reach this question. * * *

The order of the district court suppressing the taped conversation will be reversed.

Adams, Circuit Judge, concurring.

I concur in the result reached by Chief Judge Seitz because, in my view, Mesa's statements were made in the course of a colloquy that is not an "interrogation," * * *

Several factors lead me to conclude that Agent Viater was not interrogating Mesa. Viater spoke with Mesa in an attempt to defuse an admittedly delicate and volatile situation, which presented a tangible danger of suicide or other violence. Mesa indicated that he wished to talk to the agent, because he was in need of a sympathetic listener to whom he could vent his confused and tortured mind. Viater acted not as a questioner, but primarily as a listener. The conversation between Viater and Mesa was nonadversarial and noninquisitive in nature, and Viater's empathetic tone conveyed little of the subtle compulsion that characterizes police interrogation. * * *

Admittedly, in light of the lower court's finding that Viater had a secondary purpose of gathering possible evidence, the question of whether Mesa was subjected to interrogation is an extremely close one. My conclusion that the statements are admissible is compelled by the realization that it would be impractical and counterproductive to require *Miranda* warnings to be given in such a sensitive situation fraught with a potential for tragedy. The success of a negotiating mission such as the one undertaken by Agent Viater is ultimately dependent on establishing an atmosphere of trust and understanding. It was crucial for Viater to convince Mesa that his aim was to provide help and a sympathetic ear. If the agent had been required to commence the conversation with the *Miranda* warnings, he would have created an adversarial atmosphere from the outset. * * *

WEINER, DISTRICT JUDGE, dissenting.

* * *

It is evident to me that the situation at the motel was replete with the very same dangers to Mesa's Fifth Amendment rights as are present in a station-house custody situation. Indeed, the need for the protection of a *Miranda* warning in order to safeguard Mesa's right against self-incrimination may even have been more acute here than it would have been in the more ordinary custodial setting of a police station. Mesa was in a particularly vulnerable position with respect to his Fifth Amendment rights because of his mental condition and the relationship of trust which Agent Viater was able to establish with him. Mesa was confused, frightened, and depressed, and repeatedly voiced concern for his safety. Throughout the conversation Agent Viater reassured Mesa that he was Mesa's friend, and that Mesa should trust him and speak freely to him.

Furthermore, Judge Seitz ascribes undue importance to what he considers to be Mesa's ability to control the conversation with the agent. While it is true that a person barricaded in a motel room with a gun retains some ability to "call the shots", the overall "balance of power" that existed at the motel scene was with the authorities surrounding the motel, who were clearly in command of the situation. In addition, any suspect being questioned in a police station or other custodial setting has a similar ability to terminate a conversation with law enforcement officers by simply refusing to speak to his interrogators. The purpose of the *Miranda* warning though is that unless apprised of his constitutional rights, a person being interrogated while in custody or "otherwise deprived of his freedom of action" may not be aware that he has such rights. The mere ability to terminate questioning by the authorities does not abrogate one's rights under the Fifth Amendment and the *Miranda* rule; rather it is the need to assure that those who in fact possess Fifth Amendment rights are actually informed of their right and ability to exercise them that gives rise to the required safeguards of the *Miranda* rule. * * *

I am unable to agree with Judge Adams' characterization of the conversation as nonadversarial and non-inquisitive * * * especially in light of the District Court's finding, with which I agree, that Viater had a secondary purpose of gathering information about Mesa's involvement in the previous day's shootings. To the contrary, it is precisely because Mesa's mind was confused and tortured and because Viater's empathetic tone did convey sympathy and understanding that Mesa was in a vulnerable position with respect to the interrogatory aspects of the conversation. Rather than evidencing an absence of interrogation, Agent Viater's tone contributed to the "unusual susceptibility" of Mesa to this "particular form of persuasion." It must be remembered that Viater's primary role was not merely one of sympathetic counselor, but rather that of a trained law enforcement officer. * * *

Officers engaged in the delicate art of negotiation with an armed, barricaded suspect are admittedly placed in a difficult position. No one can doubt that the officers' primary responsibility in such an event must be to defuse the situation as peacefully and safely as possible. Yet the Fifth Amendment compels a court to protect the precious rights guaranteed to an accused and to reject the government's attempt to introduce an accused's statements made during a custodial interrogation without the benefit of the required *Miranda* warning.

Accordingly, I would affirm the District Court's order suppressing the taped conversation.

GIBBONS, CIRCUIT JUDGE, dissenting from the denial of a petition for rehearing in banc. * * *

Like the three panel members, I agree that the agent's motives were primarily humanitarian. I also agree that the formality of giving *Miranda* warnings might in those circumstances be counterproductive of the psychological results sought to be achieved. But Chief Judge Seitz and Judge Adams both make the logical error of assuming that an affirmance would somehow require the police to give *Miranda* warnings in the situation described. There is another possibility, which in their discomfort with the *Miranda* rule they chose to ignore. The police, recognizing the humane concerns which suggest talking to a barricaded and unstable gunman in an effort to persuade him to surrender, could simply decide, as they probably did here, that it was better to withhold the *Miranda* warnings and do without the evidence obtained during the conversation. After all, they would not have had that evidence if they broke into the room and shot Mesa. Thus the opinions supporting the judgment on different theories both are predicated upon a false premise.

I would grant rehearing in banc, and would affirm the trial court's suppression motion.

NEW YORK v. QUARLES

Supreme Court of the United States, 1984.
467 U.S. 649, 104 S.Ct. 2626, 81 L.Ed.2d 550.

JUSTICE REHNQUIST delivered the opinion of the Court.

Respondent Benjamin Quarles was charged in the New York trial court with criminal possession of a weapon. The trial court suppressed the gun in question, and a statement made by respondent, because the statement was obtained by police before they read respondent his "*Miranda* rights." That ruling was affirmed on appeal through the New York Court of Appeals. We conclude that under the circumstances involved in this case, overriding considerations of public safety justify the officer's failure to provide *Miranda* warnings before he asked questions devoted to locating the abandoned weapon.

On September 11, 1980, at approximately 12:30 a.m., Officer Frank Kraft and Officer Sal Scarring were on road patrol in Queens, New York, when a young woman approached their car. She told them that she had just been raped by a black male, approximately six feet tall, who was wearing a black jacket with the name "Big Ben" printed in yellow letters on the back. She told the officers that the man had just entered an A & P supermarket located nearby and that the man was carrying a gun.

The officers drove the woman to the supermarket, and Officer Kraft entered the store while Officer Scarring radioed for assistance. Officer Kraft quickly spotted respondent, who matched the description given by the woman, approaching a check-out counter. Apparently upon seeing the officer, respondent turned and ran toward the rear of the store, and Officer Kraft pursued him with a drawn gun. When respondent turned the corner at the end of an aisle, Officer Kraft lost sight of him for several seconds, and upon regaining sight of respondent, ordered him to stop and put his hands over his head.

Although more than three other officers had arrived on the scene by that time, Officer Kraft was the first to reach respondent. He frisked him and discovered that he was wearing a shoulder holster which was then empty. After handcuffing him, Officer Kraft asked him where the gun was. Respondent nodded in the direction of some empty cartons and responded, "the gun is over there." Officer Kraft thereafter retrieved a loaded .38 caliber revolver from one of the cartons, formally placed respondent under arrest, and read him his *Miranda* rights from a printed card. Respondent indicated that he would be willing to answer questions without an attorney present. Officer Kraft then asked respondent if he owned the gun and where he had purchased it. Respondent answered that he did own it and that he had purchased it in Miami, Florida.

In the subsequent prosecution of respondent for criminal possession of a weapon, the judge excluded the statement, "the gun is over there," and the gun because the officer had not given respondent the warnings required by our decision in *Miranda* before asking him where the gun was located. The judge excluded the other statements about respondent's ownership of the gun and the place of purchase, as evidence tainted by the prior *Miranda* violation. [The state appellate courts affirmed this ruling.]

The New York Court of Appeals was undoubtedly correct in deciding that the facts of this case come within the ambit of the *Miranda* decision as we have subsequently interpreted it. * * * Here Quarles was surrounded by at least four police officers and was handcuffed when the questioning at issue took place. As the New York Court of Appeals observed, there was nothing to suggest that any of the officers were any longer concerned for their own physical safety. The New York Court of Appeals' majority declined to express an opinion as to whether there might be an exception to the *Miranda* rule if the police had been acting to protect the public, because the lower courts in New York had made no factual determination that the police had acted with that motive.

We hold that on these facts there is a "public safety" exception to the requirement that *Miranda* warnings be given before a suspect's answers may be admitted into evidence, and that the availability of that exception does not depend upon the motivation of the individual officers involved. In a kaleidoscopic situation such as the one confronting these officers, where spontaneity rather than adherence to a police manual is necessarily the order of the day, the application of the exception which we recognize today should not be made to depend on *post hoc* findings at a suppression hearing concerning the subjective motivation of the arresting officer. Undoubtedly most police officers, if placed in Officer Kraft's position, would act out of a host of different, instinctive, and largely unverifiable motives—their own safety, the safety of others, and perhaps as well the desire to obtain incriminating evidence from the suspect. * * *

In such a situation, if the police are required to recite the familiar *Miranda* warnings before asking the whereabouts of the gun, suspects in Quarles' position might well be deterred from responding. Procedural safeguards which deter a suspect from responding were deemed acceptable in *Miranda* in order to protect the Fifth Amendment privilege; when the primary social cost of those added protections is the possibility of fewer convictions, the *Miranda* majority was willing to bear that cost. Here, had *Miranda* warnings deterred Quarles from responding to Officer Kraft's question about the whereabouts of the gun, the cost would have been something more than merely the failure to obtain evidence useful in convicting Quarles. Officer Kraft needed an answer to his question not simply to make his case against Quarles but to insure that further danger to the public did not result from the concealment of the gun in a public area. * * *

In recognizing a narrow exception to the *Miranda* rule in this case, we acknowledge that to some degree we lessen the desirable clarity of that rule. * * *

As we have in other contexts, we recognize here the importance of a workable rule to guide police officers, who have only limited time and expertise to reflect on and balance the social and individual interests involved in the specific circumstances they confront. But as we have pointed out, we believe that the exception which we recognize today lessens the necessity of that on-the-scene balancing process. The exception will not be difficult for police officers to apply because in each case it will be circumscribed by the exigency which justifies it. We think police officers can and will distinguish almost instinctively between questions necessary to secure their own safety or the safety of the public and questions designed solely to elicit testimonial evidence from a suspect.

The facts of this case clearly demonstrate that distinction and an officer's ability to recognize it. Officer Kraft asked only the question necessary to locate the missing gun before advising respondent of his rights. It was only after securing the loaded revolver and giving the warnings that he continued with investigatory questions about the ownership and place of purchase of the gun. The exception which we recognize today, far from complicating the thought processes and the on-the-scene judgments of police officers, will simply free them to follow their legitimate instincts when confronting situations presenting a danger to the public safety.

We hold that the Court of Appeals in this case erred in excluding the statement, "the gun is over there," and the gun because of the officer's failure to read respondent his *Miranda* rights before attempting to locate the weapon. Accordingly we hold that it also erred in excluding the subsequent statements as illegal fruits of a *Miranda* violation. We therefore reverse and remand for further proceedings not inconsistent with this opinion.

It is so ordered.

JUSTICE O'CONNOR, concurring in part in the judgment and dissenting in part.

* * *

I

In my view, a "public safety" exception unnecessarily blurs the edges of the clear line heretofore established and makes *Miranda's* requirements more difficult to understand. In some cases, police will benefit because a reviewing court will find that an exigency excused their failure to administer the required warnings. But in other cases, police

will suffer because, though they thought an exigency excused their noncompliance, a reviewing court will view the "objective" circumstances differently and require exclusion of admissions thereby obtained. The end result will be a fine-spun new doctrine on public safety exigencies incident to custodial interrogation, complete with the hair-splitting distinctions that currently plague our Fourth Amendment jurisprudence.
* * *

Miranda has never been read to prohibit the police from asking questions to secure the public safety. Rather, the critical question *Miranda* addresses is who shall bear the cost of securing the public safety when such questions are asked and answered: the defendant or the State. *Miranda*, for better or worse, found the resolution of that question implicit in the prohibition against compulsory self-incrimination and placed the burden on the State. When police ask custodial questions without administering the required warnings, *Miranda* quite clearly requires that the answers received be presumed compelled and that they be excluded from evidence at trial.

The Court concedes, as it must, both that respondent was in "custody" and subject to "interrogation" and that his statement "the gun is over there" was compelled within the meaning of our precedent. In my view, since there is nothing about an exigency that makes custodial interrogation any less compelling, a principled application of *Miranda* requires that respondent's statement be suppressed.

II

The court below assumed, without discussion, that the privilege against self-incrimination required that the gun derived from respondent's statement also be suppressed, whether or not the State could independently link it to him. That conclusion was, in my view, incorrect.

* * *

[For Justice O'Connor's views on the applicability of the "fruit of the poisonous tree" doctrine to *Miranda* violations, see her opinion for the majority in Oregon v. Elstad, infra, p. 562.]

JUSTICE MARSHALL, with whom JUSTICE BRENNAN and JUSTICE STEVENS join, dissenting. * * *

The majority's entire analysis rests on the factual assumption that the public was at risk during Quarles' interrogation. This assumption is completely in conflict with the facts as found by New York's highest court. * * *

The irony of the majority's decision is that the public's safety can be perfectly well protected without abridging the Fifth Amendment. If a bomb is about to explode or the public is otherwise imminently imperiled, the police are free to interrogate suspects without advising them of their constitutional rights. Such unconsented questioning may take place not only when police officers act on instinct but also when higher faculties lead them to believe that advising a suspect of his constitutional rights might decrease the likelihood that the suspect would reveal life-saving information. If trickery is necessary to protect the public, then the police may trick a suspect into confessing. While the Fourteenth Amendment sets limits on such behavior, nothing in the Fifth Amendment or our decision in *Miranda v. Arizona* proscribes this sort of emergency questioning. All the Fifth Amendment forbids is the introduction of coerced statements at trial.

To a limited degree, the majority is correct that there is a cost associated with the Fifth Amendment's ban on introducing coerced self-incriminating statements at trial. Without a "public-safety" exception, there would be occasions when a defendant incriminated himself by revealing a threat to the public, and the State was unable to prosecute because the defendant retracted his statement after consulting with counsel and the police cannot find independent proof of guilt. Such occasions would not, however, be common. The prosecution does not always lose the use of incriminating information revealed in these situations. After consulting with counsel, a suspect may well volunteer to repeat his statement in hopes of gaining a favorable plea bargain or more lenient sentence. The majority thus overstates its case when it suggests that a police officer must necessarily choose between public safety and admissibility.

But however frequently or infrequently such cases arise, their regularity is irrelevant. The Fifth Amendment prohibits compelled self-incrimination.[4] As the Court has explained on numerous occasions, this prohibition is the mainstay of our adversarial system of criminal justice. Not only does it protect us against the inherent unreliability of compelled testimony, but it also ensures that criminal investigations will be conducted with integrity and that the judiciary will avoid the taint of official lawlessness. The policies underlying the Fifth Amendment's privilege against self-incrimination are not diminished simply because testimony is compelled to protect the public's safety. The majority should not be permitted to elude the Amendment's absolute prohibition simply by calculating special costs that arise when the public's safety is at issue. Indeed, were constitutional adjudication always conducted in such an *ad hoc* manner, the Bill of Rights would be a most unreliable protector of individual liberties.

Having determined that the Fifth Amendment renders inadmissible Quarles' response to Officer Kraft's questioning, I have no doubt that our precedents require that the gun discovered as a direct result of Quarles' statement must be presumed inadmissible as well. * * * [The dissent would have remanded to allow the state courts to determine whether the gun should be admitted under the "inevitable discovery" rule.]

---

4. In this sense, the Fifth Amendment differs fundamentally from the Fourth Amendment, which only prohibits unreasonable searches and seizures. Accordingly, the various exceptions to the Fourth Amendment permitting warrantless searches under various circumstances should have no analogy in the Fifth Amendment context.

Commentary

By defining "custodial interrogation" as the starting point after which the suspect is protected by the Fifth Amendment privilege and the warnings must be given, the Court departed from the "focus" test which it had seemed to favor in *Escobedo* [p. 458, *supra*]. If the Court had held that a person upon whom suspicion has focused is entitled to the protections of the Fifth Amendment privilege (and perhaps the Sixth Amendment right to counsel as well), then the effect on law enforcement might have been enormous. For example, the "wired informer" cases such as *United States v. White* [p. 94, *supra*], could be decided under the principle announced in *Massiah* [p. 454, *supra*], without regard to whether or not advance judicial authorization for the surveillance was obtained. The common technique of having an undercover narcotics officer purchase drugs from a dealer would become constitutionally suspect, because the agent would be obtaining incriminating statements from a person upon whom suspicion had already focused. Compare, Lewis v. United States, 385 U.S. 206 (1966), which held that it does not violate the Fourth Amendment for the Government to send a secret agent to a suspect's home to purchase narcotics. In this sense, the *Miranda* opinion can fairly be described as pulling back from the broad implications of *Escobedo*.

A suspect can be in custody in his own home. In Orozco v. Texas, 394 U.S. 324 (1969) several police officers entered the defendant's home at 4:00 a.m. and questioned him in his own bedroom. The Court found that the circumstances created a potential for compulsion equivalent to interrogation at the police station, and held that the warnings should have been given. The Court distinguished *Orozco* in Beckwith v. United States, 425 U.S. 341 (1976), where an agent from the division of the Internal Revenue Service which prepares cases for criminal prosecution "interviewed" the suspect at his home. Although suspicion had focused upon the accused, the Court did not consider the circumstances to be custodial or potentially coercive.

On two occasions the Supreme Court has held that a defendant was not in custody when he accepted an invitation to come to the police station for questioning, but was not under arrest. See Oregon v. Mathiason, 429 U.S. 492 (1977) (per curiam); California v. Beheler, 463 U.S. 1121 (1983) (per curiam). When the "invitation" appears to be the kind of offer that cannot be refused, then a finding of custody is likely. See *Dunaway v. New York* [p. 244, *supra*].

The Supreme Court addressed the problem of roadside questioning of a suspected drunk driver who was being detained following a traffic stop in Berkemer v. McCarty, 468 U.S. 420 (1984). The opinion by Justice Marshall held that such questioning does not constitute custodial interrogation for purposes of the *Miranda* doctrine and announced the broader principle that "*Terry* stops" for investigation of suspicious circumstances do not trigger the need to give warnings. The opinion rejected the argument, however, that the *Miranda* rules do not apply to misdemeanor arrests.

A New York court has held that the public safety exception is not limited to brief, on-the-scene questioning. In People v. Oquendo, 252 A.D.2d 312, 685 N.Y.S.2d 437 (1999) the Appellate Division upheld the admissibility of a statement where the police had questioned an unwarned defendant in custody intermittently over several hours about where he had concealed a gun. The court observed that "a missing and possibly loaded gun was left in a publicly accessible place, and could not be found readily without the suspect's cooperation. . . . The police should have flexibility to respond to true emergency circumstances, whether the danger is momentary or ongoing, and that purpose would not be served by setting artificial limits as to the time and location of questions that are objectively necessary for the immediate public safety. The police had no alternative to questioning defendant, since it would be impossible to secure several heavily snow-covered populated Manhattan blocks."

RHODE ISLAND v. INNIS

Supreme Court of the United States, 1980.
446 U.S. 291, 100 S.Ct. 1682, 64 L.Ed.2d 297.

MR. JUSTICE STEWART delivered the opinion of the Court.

* * * The issue in this case is whether the respondent was "interrogated" in violation of the standards promulgated in the *Miranda* opinion.

I

[Respondent Innis was identified from photographs as a suspect in a robbery murder that had been committed with a sawed-off shotgun.]

At approximately 4:30 a.m. on the same date, Patrolman Lovell, while cruising the streets of Mount Pleasant in a patrol car, spotted the respondent standing in the street facing him. When Patrolman Lovell stopped his car, the respondent walked towards it. Patrolman Lovell then arrested the respondent, who was unarmed, and advised him of his so-called *Miranda* rights. While the two men waited in the patrol car for other police officers to arrive, Patrolman Lovell did not converse with the respondent other than to respond to the latter's request for a cigarette.

Within minutes, Sergeant Sears arrived at the scene of the arrest, and he also gave the respondent the *Miranda* warnings. Immediately thereafter, Captain Leyden and other police officers arrived. Captain Leyden advised the respondent of his *Miranda* rights. The respondent stated that he understood those rights and wanted to speak with a lawyer. Captain Leyden then directed that the respondent be placed in a "caged wagon," a four-door police car with a wire screen mesh between the front and rear seats, and be driven to the central police station. Three officers, Patrolmen Gleckman, Williams, and McKenna, were assigned to accompany the respondent to the central station. They placed the respondent in the vehicle and shut the doors. Captain Leyden then instructed the officers not to question the respondent or intimidate or coerce him in any way. The three officers then entered the vehicle, and it departed.

While en route to the central station, Patrolman Gleckman initiated a conversation with Patrolman McKenna concerning the missing shotgun. As Patrolman Gleckman later testified:

"A.   At this point, I was talking back and forth with Patrolman McKenna stating that I frequent this area while on patrol and [that because a school for handicapped children is located nearby,] there's a lot of handicapped children running around in this area, and God forbid one of them might find a weapon with shells and they might hurt themselves."

Patrolman McKenna apparently shared his fellow officer's concern:

"A.   I more or less concurred with him [Gleckman] that it was a safety factor and that we should, you know, continue to search for the weapon and try to find it."

While Patrolman Williams said nothing, he overheard the conversation between the two officers:

"A.   He [Gleckman] said it would be too bad if the little—I believe he said a girl—would pick up the gun, maybe kill herself."

The respondent then interrupted the conversation, stating that the officers should turn the car around so he could show them where the gun was located. At this point, Patrolman McKenna radioed back to Captain Leyden that they were returning to the scene of the arrest and that the respondent would inform them of the location of the gun. At the time the respondent indicated that the officers should turn back, they had traveled no more than a mile, a trip encompassing only a few minutes.

The police vehicle then returned to the scene of the arrest where a search for the shotgun was in progress. There, Captain Leyden again advised the respondent of his *Miranda* rights. The respondent replied that he understood those rights but that he "wanted to get the gun out of the way because of the kids in the area in the school." The respondent then led the police to a nearby field, where he pointed out the shotgun under some rocks by the side of the road. * * *

[The] trial court sustained the admissibility of the shotgun and testimony related to its discovery. That evidence was later introduced at the respondent's trial, and the jury returned a verdict of guilty on all counts.

On appeal, the Rhode Island Supreme Court, in a 3–2 decision, set aside the respondent's conviction. * * * It was the view of the state appellate court that, even though the police officers may have been genuinely concerned about the public safety and even though the respondent had not been addressed personally by the police officers, the respondent nonetheless had been subjected to "subtle coercion" that was the equivalent of "interrogation" within the meaning of the *Miranda* opinion. Moreover, contrary to the holding of the trial court, the appellate court concluded that the evidence was insufficient to support a finding of waiver. Having concluded that both the shotgun and testimony relating to its discovery were obtained in violation of the *Miranda* standards and therefore should not have been admitted into evidence, the Rhode Island Supreme Court held that the respondent was entitled to a new trial. * * *

II

A

The starting point for defining "interrogation" in this context is, of course, the Court's *Miranda* opinion. There the Court observed that "[b]y custodial interrogation, we mean *questioning* initiated by law enforcement officers after a person has been taken into custody or otherwise deprived of his freedom of action in any significant way." This passage and other references throughout the opinion to "questioning" might suggest that the *Miranda* rules were to apply only to those police interrogation practices that involve express questioning of a defendant while in custody.

We do not, however, construe the *Miranda* opinion so narrowly. The concern of the Court in *Miranda* was that the "interrogation environment" created by the interplay of interrogation and custody would "subjugate the individual to the will of his examiner" and thereby undermine the privilege against compulsory self-incrimination. The police practices that evoked this concern included several that did not involve express questioning. For example, one of the practices discussed in *Miranda* was the use of line-ups in which a coached witness would pick the defendant as the perpetrator. This was designed to establish that the defendant was in fact guilty as a predicate for further interrogation. A variation on this theme discussed in *Miranda* was the so-called "reverse line-up" in which a defendant would be identified by coached witnesses as the perpetrator of a fictitious crime, with the object of inducing him to confess to the actual crime of which he was suspected in order to escape the false prosecution. The Court in *Miranda* also included in its survey of interrogation practices the use of psychological ploys, such as to "posi[t]" "the guilt of the subject," to "minimize the moral seriousness of the offense," and "to cast blame on the victim or on society." It is clear that these techniques of persuasion, no less than express questioning, were thought, in a custodial setting, to amount to interrogation.

* * *

We conclude that the *Miranda* safeguards come into play whenever a person in custody is subjected to either express questioning or its functional equivalent. That is to say, the term "interrogation" under *Miranda* refers not only to express questioning, but also to any words or actions on the part of the police (other than those normally attendant to arrest and custody) that the police should know are reasonably likely to elicit an incriminating response[5] from the suspect. The latter portion of this definition focuses primarily upon the perceptions of the suspect,

---

5. By "incriminating response" we refer to any response—whether inculpatory or exculpatory—that the *prosecution* may seek to introduce at trial.

rather than the intent of the police. This focus reflects the fact that the *Miranda* safeguards were designed to vest a suspect in custody with an added measure of protection against coercive police practices, without regard to objective proof of the underlying intent of the police. A practice that the police should know is reasonably likely to evoke an incriminating response from a suspect thus amounts to interrogation.[6] But, since the police surely cannot be held accountable for the unforeseeable results of their words or actions, the definition of interrogation can extend only to words or actions on the part of police officers that they *should have known* were reasonably likely to elicit an incriminating response.[7]

B

Turning to the facts of the present case, we conclude that the respondent was not "interrogated" within the meaning of *Miranda*. It is undisputed that the first prong of the definition of "interrogation" was not satisfied, for the conversation between Patrolmen Gleckman and McKenna included no express questioning of the respondent. Rather, that conversation was, at least in form, nothing more than a dialogue between the two officers to which no response from the respondent was invited.

Moreover, it cannot be fairly concluded that the respondent was subjected to the "functional equivalent" of questioning. It cannot be said, in short, that Patrolmen Gleckman and McKenna should have known that their conversation was reasonably likely to elicit an incriminating response from the respondent. There is nothing in the record to suggest that the officers were aware that the respondent was peculiarly susceptible to an appeal to his conscience concerning the safety of handicapped children. Nor is there anything in the record to suggest that the police knew that the respondent was unusually disoriented or upset at the time of his arrest.[8]

The case thus boils down to whether, in the context of a brief conversation, the officers should have known that the respondent would suddenly be moved to make a self-incriminating response. Given the fact that the entire conversation appears to have consisted of no more than a few off hand remarks, we cannot say that the officers should have known that it was reasonably likely that Innis would so respond. This is not a case where the police carried on a lengthy harangue in the presence of

---

6. This is not to say that the intent of the police is irrelevant, for it may well have a bearing on whether the police should have known that their words or actions were reasonably likely to evoke an incriminating response. In particular, where a police practice is designed to elicit an incriminating response from the accused, it is unlikely that the practice will not also be one which the police should have known was reasonably likely to have that effect.

7. Any knowledge the police may have had concerning the unusual susceptibility of a defendant to a particular form of persua-

sion might be an important factor in determining whether the police should have known that their words or actions were reasonably likely to elicit an incriminating response from the suspect.

8. The record in no way suggests that the officers' remarks were *designed* to elicit a response. See n. 7, *supra*. It is significant that the trial judge, after hearing the officers' testimony, concluded that it was "entirely understandable that [the officers] would voice their concern [for the safety of the handicapped children] to each other."

the suspect. Nor does the record support the respondent's contention that, under the circumstances, the officers' comments were particularly "evocative." It is our view, therefore, that the respondent was not subjected by the police to words or actions that the police should have known were reasonably likely to elicit an incriminating response from him.

The Rhode Island Supreme Court erred, in short, in equating "subtle compulsion" with interrogation. That the officers' comments struck a responsive chord is readily apparent. Thus, it may be said, as the Rhode Island Supreme Court did say, that the respondent was subjected to "subtle compulsion." But that is not the end of the inquiry. It must also be established that a suspect's incriminating response was the product of words or actions on the part of the police that they should have known were reasonably likely to elicit an incriminating response.[9] This was not established in the present case.

For the reasons stated, the judgment of the Supreme Court of Rhode Island is vacated, and the case is remanded to that court for further proceedings not inconsistent with this opinion.

MR. CHIEF JUSTICE BURGER, concurring in the judgment.

The meaning of *Miranda* has become reasonably clear and law enforcement practices have adjusted to its strictures; I would neither overrule *Miranda*, disparage it, nor extend it at this late date. I fear, however, that the rationale in Parts II–A and II–B, of the Court's opinion will not clarify the tension between this holding and *Brewer v. Williams*, [see p. 544] and our other cases. * * *

Trial judges have enough difficulty discerning the boundaries and nuances flowing from post-*Miranda* opinions, and we do not clarify that situation today.

[The dissenting opinion of Justice Brennan, joined by Justice Marshall, is omitted.]

MR. JUSTICE STEVENS, dissenting.

* * *

The difference between the approach required by a faithful adherence to *Miranda* and the stinted test applied by the Court today can be illustrated by comparing three different ways in which Officer Gleckman could have communicated his fears about the possible dangers posed by the shotgun to handicapped children. He could have:

(1) directly asked Innis:

9. By way of example, if the police had done no more than to drive past the site of the concealed weapon while taking the most direct route to the police station, and if the respondent, upon noticing for the first time the proximity of the school for handicapped children, had blurted out that he would show the officers where the gun was located, it could not seriously be argued that this "subtle compulsion" would have constituted "interrogation" within the meaning of the *Miranda* opinion.

Will you please tell me where the shotgun is so we can protect handicapped school children from danger?

(2) announced to the other officers in the wagon:

If the man sitting in the back seat with me should decide to tell us where the gun is, we can protect handicapped children from danger.

or (3) stated to the other officers:

It would be too bad if a little handicapped girl would pick up the gun that this man left in the area and maybe kill herself.

In my opinion, all three of these statements should be considered interrogation because all three appear to be designed to elicit a response from anyone who in fact knew where the gun was located. Under the Court's test, on the other hand, the form of the statements would be critical. The third statement would not be interrogation because in the Court's view there was no reason for Officer Gleckman to believe that Innis was susceptible to this type of an implied appeal; therefore, the statement would not be reasonably likely to elicit an incriminating response. Assuming that this is true, then it seems to me that the first two statements, which would be just as unlikely to elicit such a response, should also not be considered interrogation. But, because the first statement is clearly an express question, it *would* be considered interrogation under the Court's test. The second statement, although just as clearly a deliberate appeal to Innis to reveal the location of the gun, would presumably not be interrogation because (a) it was not in form a direct question and (b) it does not fit within the "reasonably likely to elicit an incriminating response" category that applies to indirect interrogation.

As this example illustrates, the Court's test creates an incentive for police to ignore a suspect's invocation of his rights in order to make continued attempts to extract information from him. If a suspect does not appear to be susceptible to a particular type of psychological pressure, the police are apparently free to exert that pressure on him despite his request for counsel, so long as they are careful not to punctuate their statements with question marks. And if, contrary to all reasonable expectations, the suspect makes an incriminating statement, that statement can be used against him at trial. The Court thus turns *Miranda's* unequivocal rule against any interrogation at all into a trap in which unwary suspects may be caught by police deception.

* * *

UNITED STATES v. HENRY

Supreme Court of the United States, 1980.
447 U.S. 264, 100 S.Ct. 2183, 65 L.Ed.2d 115.

Mr. Chief Justice Burger delivered the opinion of the Court. * * *

I

The Janaf Branch of the United Virginia Bank/Seaboard National in Norfolk, Va., was robbed in August 1972. Witnesses saw two men wearing masks and carrying guns enter the bank while a third man waited in the car. No witnesses were able to identify respondent Henry as one of the participants. About an hour after the robbery, the getaway car was discovered. Inside was found a rent receipt signed by one "Allen R. Norris" and a lease, also signed by Norris, for a house in Norfolk. Two men, who were subsequently convicted of participating in the robbery, were arrested at the rented house. Discovered with them were the proceeds of the robbery and the guns and masks used by the gunman.

Government agents traced the rent receipt to Henry; on the basis of this information, Henry was arrested in Atlanta, Ga., in November 1972. Two weeks later he was indicted for armed robbery under 18 U.S.C. §§ 2113(a) and (d). He was held pending trial in the Norfolk city jail. Counsel was appointed on November 27.

On November 21, 1972, shortly after Henry was incarcerated, Government agents working on the Janaf robbery contacted one Nichols, an inmate at the Norfolk city jail, who for some time prior to this meeting had been engaged to provide confidential information to the Federal Bureau of Investigation as a paid informant. Nichols was then serving a sentence on local forgery charges. The record does not disclose whether the agent contacted Nichols specifically to acquire information about Henry or the Janaf robbery.[10]

Nichols informed the agent that he was housed in the same cellblock with several federal prisoners awaiting trial, including Henry. The agent told him to be alert to any statements made by the federal prisoners, but not to initiate any conversation with or question Henry regarding the bank robbery. In early December, after Nichols had been released from jail, the agent again contacted Nichols, who reported that he and Henry had engaged in conversation and that Henry had told him about the robbery of the Janaf bank. Nichols was paid for furnishing the information.

When Henry was tried in March 1973, an agent of the Federal Bureau of Investigation testified concerning the events surrounding the discovery of the rental slip and the evidence uncovered at the rented house. Other witnesses also connected Henry to the rented house, including the rental agent who positively identified Henry as the "Allen R. Norris" who had rented the house and had taken the rental receipt described earlier. A neighbor testified that prior to the robbery she saw Henry at the rented house with John Luck, one of the two men who had by the time of Henry's trial been convicted for the robbery. In addition, palm prints found on the lease agreement matched those of Henry.

10. The record does disclose that on November 21, 1972, the same day the agent contacted Nichols, the agent's supervisor interrogated Henry at the jail. After denying participation in the robbery, Henry exercised his right to terminate the interview.

Nichols testified at trial that he had "an opportunity to have some conversations with Mr. Henry while he was in the jail," and that Henry told him that on several occasions he had gone to the Janaf Branch to see which employees opened the vault. Nichols also testified that Henry described to him the details of the robbery and stated that the only evidence connecting him to the robbery was the rental receipt. The jury was not informed that Nichols was a paid Government informant.

On the basis of this testimony,[11] Henry was convicted of bank robbery and sentenced to a term of imprisonment of 25 years. On appeal he raised no Sixth Amendment claims. His conviction was affirmed.

On August 28, 1975, Henry moved to vacate his sentence pursuant to 28 U.S.C. § 2255. At this stage, he stated that he had just learned that Nichols was a paid Government informant and alleged that he had been intentionally placed in the same cell with Nichols so that Nichols could secure information about the robbery. Thus, Henry contended that the introduction of Nichols' testimony violated his Sixth Amendment right to the assistance of counsel. The District Court denied the motion without a hearing. The Court of Appeals, however, reversed and remanded for an evidentiary inquiry into "whether the witness [Nichols] was acting as a government agent during his interviews with Henry."

On remand, the District Court requested affidavits from the Government agents. An affidavit was submitted describing the agent's relationship with Nichols and relating the following conversation:

> "I recall telling Nichols at this time to be alert to any statements made by these individuals [the federal prisoners] regarding the charges against them. I specifically recall telling Nichols that he was not to question Henry or these individuals about the charges against them, however, if they engaged him in conversation or talked in front of him, he was requested to pay attention to their statements. I recall telling Nichols not to initiate any conversations with Henry regarding the bank robbery charges against Henry, but that if Henry initiated the conversations with Nichols, I requested Nichols to pay attention to the information furnished by Henry."

The agent's affidavit also stated that he never requested anyone affiliated with the Norfolk city jail to place Nichols in the same cell with Henry.

The District Court again denied Henry's § 2255 motion, concluding that Nichols' testimony at trial did not violate Henry's Sixth Amendment right to counsel. The Court of Appeals reversed and remanded, holding that the actions of the Government impaired the Sixth Amendment rights of the defendant under *Massiah*.

11. Joseph Sadler, another of Henry's cellmates, also testified at trial. He stated that Henry had told him that Henry had robbed a bank with a man named "Lucky" or "Luck." Sadler testified that on advice of counsel he informed Government agents of the conversation with Henry. Sadler was not a paid informant and had no arrangement to monitor or report on conversations with Henry.

II

* * *

The question here is whether under the facts of this case a Government agent "deliberately elicited" incriminating statements from Henry within the meaning of *Massiah*. Three factors are important. First, Nichols was acting under instructions as a paid informant for the Government; second, Nichols was ostensibly no more than a fellow inmate of Henry; and third, Henry was in custody and under indictment at the time he was engaged in conversation by Nichols.

The Court of Appeals viewed the record as showing that Nichols deliberately used his position to secure incriminating information from Henry when counsel was not present and held that conduct attributable to the Government. Nichols had been a paid Government informant for more than a year; moreover, the FBI agent was aware that Nichols had access to Henry and would be able to engage him in conversations without arousing Henry's suspicion. The arrangement between Nichols and the agent was on a contingent-fee basis; Nichols was to be paid only if he produced useful information. This combination of circumstances is sufficient to support the Court of Appeals' determination. Even if the agent's statement that he did not intend that Nichols would take affirmative steps to secure incriminating information is accepted, he must have known that such propinquity likely would lead to that result.

The Government argues that the federal agents instructed Nichols not to question Henry about the robbery. Yet according to his own testimony, Nichols was not a passive listener; rather, he had "some conversations with Mr. Henry" while he was in jail and Henry's incriminatory statements were "the product of this conversation." * * *

It is undisputed that Henry was unaware of Nichols' role as a Government informant. The government argues that this Court should apply a less rigorous standard under the Sixth Amendment where the accused is prompted by an undisclosed undercover informant than where the accused is speaking in the hearing of persons he knows to be Government officers. That line of argument, however, seeks to infuse Fifth Amendment concerns against compelled self-incrimination into the Sixth Amendment protection of the right to the assistance of counsel. An accused speaking to a known Government agent is typically aware that his statements may be used against him. The adversary positions at that stage are well established; the parties are then "arms' length" adversaries.

When the accused is in the company of a fellow inmate who is acting by prearrangement as a Government agent, the same cannot be said. Conversation stimulated in such circumstances may elicit information that an accused would not intentionally reveal to persons known to be Government agents. * * * In that setting, Henry, being unaware that Nichols was a Government agent expressly commissioned to secure evidence, cannot be held to have waived his right to the assistance of counsel.

Finally Henry's incarceration at the time he was engaged in conversation by Nichols is also a relevant factor. [An accused person's confinement] may bring into play subtle influences that will make him particularly susceptible to the ploys of undercover Government agents. * * * By intentionally creating a situation likely to induce Henry to make incriminating statements without the assistance of counsel, the Government violated Henry's Sixth Amendment right to counsel. This is not a case where, in Justice Cardozo's words, the constable blundered; rather, it is one where the "constable" planned an impermissible interference with the right to the assistance of counsel.

The judgment of the Court of Appeals for the Fourth Circuit is affirmed.

[The concurring and dissenting opinions actually written in this case are omitted. Substituted for them is the following fictitious opinion.]

MR. JUSTICE FICTITIOUS, concurring.

I agree with the majority that the testimony of the informant Nichols should not have been admitted. I would exclude this testimony not only because it violated the defendant's Sixth Amendment right to counsel, but also because it was inherently unreliable. A jailhouse informant paid on a contingent fee basis to report any admissions by a cellmate awaiting trial is highly likely to invent a story that will satisfy his employers, or at least to exaggerate the significance of what he does hear. In this federal case we ought to exercise our supervisory power to protect the integrity of the fact-finding process by excluding testimony obtained by incentives that create such a high risk of perjury.

My main reason for writing separately, however, is to express my concern that the pattern of our decisions over the past 20 years does not adequately recognize that the Government has a legitimate interest in questioning accused persons in order to determine their guilt or innocence. The present case presents an excellent example. The evidence in the hands of the investigators at the time of Henry's arrest was sufficient to establish that he was probably involved in the robbery, but I doubt that it was sufficient to prove guilt beyond a reasonable doubt in the unanimous judgment of 12 reasonably skeptical jurors. Assuming that we will not allow the police to interrogate the accused in custody once he has invoked his rights, or to employ spies to obtain incriminating statements after he has been formally charged, should we permit the Government to question him in some manner that adequately protects his constitutional rights?

One possibility would be to allow the prosecuting attorney to call the defendant as a prosecution witness, after making a sufficient preliminary showing of guilt through the use of the circumstantial evidence. I realize that some will say that this procedure is unconstitutional on its face, because the Fifth Amendment permits specifically that the accused shall not "be compelled in any criminal case to be a witness against himself." I believe that this Amendment only protects the defendant from being required to *answer* questions, not from being *asked* them, in front of a jury or elsewhere. If Congress or a state legislature were to pass a statute authorizing such a procedure, I would therefore hold the statute constitutional.

This would of course require that we overrule our prior decisions in Griffin v. California, 380 U.S. 609 (1965), and Carter v. Kentucky, 450 U.S. 288 (1981). *Griffin* held that the prosecutor and the trial judge may not comment on the failure of the accused to take the stand, and *Carter* held that the trial judge upon request must instruct the jury that it may not use the defendant's refusal to testify to draw an inference of guilt or to prejudice him in any way. *Griffin* itself overruled a long line of precedent in reaching its holding that the Fifth Amendment forbids state rules permitting comment on the defendant's silence, and so I do not see why we should hesitate to reconsider *Griffin* after many years of experience in the changed circumstances created by the enforcement of the *Miranda* and *Massiah* rules. Of course the jury will draw an inference of guilt from the refusal of the accused to answer incriminating questions; that is precisely the idea. The innocent will answer truthfully, and the guilty will for the most part convict themselves. The only objection I can see to such a procedure is that it does not give guilty persons as good a chance of escaping conviction as our present system. That is its virtue in my eyes.

If calling the accused to the stand in front of the jury is too radical a step for serious consideration today, there is an alternative. As long ago as 1932, the eminent scholar Professor Paul Kauper wrote an article titled "Judicial examination of the accused—A Remedy for the Third Degree," the subject of which is adequately summarized by the title. (30 Mich.L.Rev. 1224) Building upon still older proposals by distinguished American legal scholars, Kauper proposed that a suspect be brought before a judicial officer immediately upon arrest, that he be allowed to answer questions or refuse to speak at this appearance, but that he be told that his silence could be the subject of inference and comment at trial. Kauper's proposal contemplated that defense counsel would not be present, but counsel could be provided if this is thought necessary to meet constitutional requirements. What is essential is that the accused should be interrogated as soon as possible after arrest by or under the supervision of a judicial officer, with an adequate record made of the proceedings and with the defendant understanding that the jury later will be allowed to draw the natural inference from his refusal to answer incriminating questions.* Allowing defense counsel to be present to protect the defendant's rights (but not to obstruct the questioning) would be all to the good.

---

* By the same reasoning, a defendant ought to be allowed to show, in support of his trial testimony, that he advanced the same story upon arrest when he had little opportunity to fabricate an account. At present such evidence is often excluded as hearsay.

As the title of his article indicates, Kauper advanced his proposal as an alternative to the "third degree" questioning that was all too common at that time. The article was, after all, written four years before the first due process "coerced confession" case, Brown v. Mississippi, 297 U.S. 278 (1936). In subsequent years, Kauper's proposal received favorable attention from such giants of the American judiciary as Roger Traynor, Walter Schaefer, and Henry Friendly.

Professor Yale Kamisar of the University of Michigan Law School wrote a very interesting article about the Kauper proposal and the favorable reaction of great judges to it in 1974. See Kamisar, "Kauper's 'Judicial Examination of the Accused' Forty Years Later—Some Comments on a Remarkable Article," reprinted in Kamisar, *Police Interrogation and Confessions* (1980). Kamisar's views are particularly important because he was an influential critic of police interrogation abuses in the period leading up to the *Miranda* decision in 1966, and because since then he has been one of the most prominent academic defenders of the *Miranda* and *Massiah* doctrines. I am therefore particularly impressed by the fact that Kamisar regards what he calls the "Kauper–Schaefer–Friendly plan" as a legitimate alternative for serious consideration, and that he believes that it might be upheld as constitutional today despite the provision for comment upon the defendant's silence, provided that the right to counsel is observed. See Id., at 90–91, note 12. For my part, I think it absurd that there should be any doubt about the constitutionality of a proposal which has been endorsed over many years by many of our most distinguished judges and scholars, not to mention organizations like the American Bar Association and the American Law Institute, and which has the additional virtue of reflecting common sense. "There is no war between the Constitution and common sense," as Justice Clark told us in Mapp v. Ohio, 367 U.S. 643, 657 (1961).

If a constitutional amendment is nonetheless necessary to permit orderly questioning of accused persons under judicial supervision, then one ought to be proposed and enacted. I am confident that it would have the support of the overwhelming majority of Americans. We ought to be proud of our record over the past 20 years in remedying long-standing police abuses that made a mockery of the protections granted by the Fourth and Fifth Amendments. We should be less proud of the tendency our decisions have had to reinforce the unfortunate impression that the American criminal trial is a sporting contest, rather than a serious effort aimed at separating the guilty from the innocent. Providing for orderly questioning of the accused person under judicial safeguards will help to make the point that we really do care about convicting the guilty, and at the same time reduce the temptation for investigators to try to "get around" the safeguards provided for the accused by the doctrines of the *Miranda* and *Massiah* cases.

Commentary

Direct and indirect questioning. As Chief Justice Burger commented [p. 549], there is an unclarified tension between the holding in *Innis* and the famous "Christian Burial Speech" case, Brewer v. Williams, 430 U.S. 387 (1977). The defendant Williams murdered a girl in Des Moines, fled across the state with the body, contacted a lawyer while still a fugitive, and eventually surrendered to the police in Davenport. He appeared in court there for arraignment on an arrest warrant, an event which, the Supreme Court assumed, made the *Massiah* doctrine applicable. A police officer, who had been instructed by the defense lawyer not to question Williams, drove to Davenport to take the prisoner back to Des Moines. The return trip over the snow-clogged roads of Iowa lasted several hours, and the officer seized the opportunity to urge "Reverend" Williams (an escaped mental patient with strong religious tendencies) to ponder the desirability of stopping en route to locate the body (before anticipated snowfall could conceal it) so that the girl's parents could give her a "good Christian burial."[a] The speech had its intended effect and the prisoner agreed to show the officer where he had hidden the body. The Supreme Court held that the speech constituted a "deliberately eliciting" of incriminating information in violation of the *Massiah* doctrine. The opinion did not say whether the same conduct would have violated the suspect's *Miranda* rights, if the fortuitous court appearance had not occurred.

In Arizona v. Mauro, 481 U.S. 520 (1987), the defendant spontaneously admitted having killed his own son. After being arrested and warned, he declined to make any further statement without having a lawyer present. All questioning ceased. The defendant's wife then asked to speak to her husband. After some reluctance the police agreed, but insisted that an officer must be present. The officer brought Mrs. Mauro into the room and seated himself at a desk, placing a tape recorder in plain sight. During the resulting conversation Mauro advised his wife not to answer any questions until she had the advice of a lawyer. At trial the defense was insanity, and the prosecutor played the tape to the jury to demonstrate Mauro's apparent sanity on the day of the killing. The jury returned a conviction of murder and a death sentence.

A narrow majority of the Supreme Court held that there was no interrogation and hence no violation of *Miranda*. Although the officers were aware that the defendant might make incriminating statements if allowed to talk to his wife, they acted reasonably and lawfully by allowing the conversation and were not required to "ignore legitimate security concerns by allowing spouses to meet in private." The dissent by Justice Stevens argued on the contrary that the police "employed a powerful psychological ploy" by taking "advantage of Mrs. Mauro's request to visit her husband, setting up a confrontation between them at a time when he manifestly desired to remain silent." The dissent would thus have affirmed the unanimous decision of the Supreme Court of Arizona, which had held that admission of the tape recording violated Mauro's privilege against self-incrimination.

a. For a fairly complete history of this fascinating case, see Johnson, "The Return of the *Christian Burial Speech Case*," 32 Emory L.J. 351 (1983). The case came to the Supreme Court a second time as Nix v. Williams, 467 U.S. 431 (1984), after Williams was reconvicted in a second trial. The Supreme Court upheld the state court determination that, although the statements of Williams and the fact that he led police to the body had to be suppressed, the body itself could be used as evidence because it would inevitably have been discovered by searching parties.

Neither the majority opinion nor the dissent attached any importance to the fact that the defendant made no confessions, admissions, or exculpatory statements regarding the crime on the tape. The tape was used only to show the apparent rationality of his thinking at the time. The Supreme Court opinions also did not discuss the possible relevance of Wainwright v. Greenfield, 474 U.S. 284 (1986), which held that it violates due process to use the defendant's invocation of *his own Miranda rights* as evidence that he was sane.

A Florida Court of Appeals found that an indirect interrogation had occurred under the *Innis* standard in Jones v. State, 497 So.2d 1268 (Fla.App.1986). After receiving the *Miranda* warnings, Jones indicated that he was unwilling to speak to the police in the absence of an attorney. He then was permitted to telephone his mother. While he was speaking to his mother, a detective picked up an extension phone, identified himself as a police officer, and informed the mother (with Jones listening) of the charges and the evidence against Jones. When the call ended, Jones signed a waiver of his right to counsel and confessed. The Florida court cited *Innis* for the general proposition that "interrogation" under *Miranda* includes not only express questions but also any words or actions that the police should know are reasonably likely to elicit an incriminating response. Without indicating any awareness that the Supreme Court had in fact upheld the admissibility of the statements obtained in *Innis*, the Florida court went on to describe *Innis* as having condemned "the type of police conduct employed here." The Florida court described the officer's accurate recital of the charges and evidence as an "intimidating message, ostensibly directed to his mother," which the officer knew would be likely to cause the mother to instruct her teenaged son to cooperate with the police. This conduct therefore violated the rule of *Edwards v. Arizona* [p. 547 *infra*], forbidding officers to continue interrogation after a suspect has invoked his right to counsel. The case provides a striking example of the fact that many state courts are far more enthusiastic about strictly enforcing the *Miranda* doctrine than is the Supreme Court itself.

Another interesting state case is People v. Ferro, 63 N.Y.2d 316, 482 N.Y.S.2d 237, 472 N.E.2d 13 (N.Y. 1984). The defendant was suspected of a felony murder involving the stealing of furs. He invoked his right to remain silent, but then asked to speak to a district attorney. He abandoned that attempt when told that he would first have to tell a detective what he wanted to talk about. The detective then left the police station and returned with the recovered stolen furs, placing them in front of defendant's jail cell. Ferro then made incriminating admissions. The New York Court of Appeals held that displaying the furs was reasonably likely to elicit an incriminating response, and that statements obtained thereby were inadmissible.

Custodial interrogation. Probably there is no "custodial interrogation" when the police ask a jailhouse informant to obtain evidence from a cellmate. The situation is inherently deceptive, but not inherently coercive. If the adversary process has begun and the *Massiah* doctrine is applicable, however, use of the informant is a deliberate elicitation of evidence from the accused in violation of the right to counsel. The Supreme Court distinguished United States v. Henry [p. 536, supra] in Kuhlmann v. Wilson, 477 U.S. 436 (1986). There the police asked the informer to "keep his ears open" for the names of the defendant's confederates, but the lower courts found that the informant did not question the defendant or seek to draw him out on the crime. The Supreme Court majority held that "a defendant does not make out a violation of [*Massiah*] simply by showing that an informant, either through prior arrangement or voluntarily, reported his incriminating statements to the police. Rather, the defendant must demonstrate that the police and their informant took some action, beyond merely listening, that was designed deliberately to elicit incriminating remarks." 477 U.S. at 459.

In Illinois v. Perkins, 496 U.S. 292 (1990), police learned from an informant (Charlton) that a prison inmate (Perkins) had admitted murdering a man named Stephenson. Perkins had revealed details of the Stephenson murder that were not generally known, and so the police took the report seriously. They arranged for Charlton and an undercover officer to pose as returned escapees and be placed in the cell block with Perkins. There they engaged Perkins in conversation and obtained a detailed confession to the Stephenson murder. The Supreme Court majority held that the *Massiah–Henry* rule was not applicable because "no charges had been filed on the subject of the indictment," and *Miranda* warnings were not required because there is no "police-dominated atmosphere" and potential for compulsion where an inmate speaks freely to a person whom he believes to be another inmate. Justice Brennan, concurring in the judgment, thought that the "deception and manipulation" involved in the rule might violate the Due Process Clause. Justice Marshall dissented.

A person who is not a suspect may be in custody. "Police officers investigating the rape-murder of a child learned that the victim had talked to two ice truck drivers. One was defendant Stansbury, but the police considered only the other driver to be a leading suspect. They asked Stansbury to come to the police station for questioning as a possible witness, and he accepted a ride in the front seat of a police car. After brief questioning Stansbury made significant admissions, and only then did police administer the *Miranda* warnings—after which Stansbury asked for an attorney, declined to answer further questions, and was placed under arrest. The California Supreme Court held that the admissions were admissible because the questioning was non-custodial, placing particular emphasis on the fact that the officers considered Stansbury a potential witness rather than a suspect. The Supreme Court reversed in Stansbury v. California, 511 U.S. 318 (1994), holding that an officer's subjective belief that individual being questioned was or was not a suspect was relevant only to the extent that this belief was communicated to the individual. The Supreme Court remanded for the California Supreme Court to determine whether "the objective facts in the record support a finding that Stansbury was not in custody until his arrest."

On remand, the California Supreme Court held that Stansbury was not in custody until after he made the crucial admissions. The Court explained that

> the record indicates that a reasonable person in defendant's shoes would not consider that he or she was in custody. A reasonable person who is asked if he or she would come to the police station to answer questions, and who is offered the choice of finding his or her own transportation or accepting a ride from the police, would not feel that he or she had been taken into custody. A police invitation to sit in the front of the car

(which was not a marked police car) could only add to the objective impression that no custody had been imposed. Further, it is relevant that when Officer Lee spoke to defendant at defendant's home, Lee asked defendant whether he would come to the police station to answer questions as a possible witness. Similarly, when Officer Johnston spoke to defendant in the interview room, the officer told defendant he desired to question him as a possible witness. It unlikely that a reasonable person who is told twice he or she is to be questioned as a witness would believe that he was in custody during such questioning. Finally, the nature of the interview in this case, which was brief and not accusatory, would not convey to the reasonable person the impression that he or she was in custody, despite the fact that the interview took place in an interview room in the jail area of the police station. People v. Stansbury, 9 Cal.4th 824, 38 Cal.Rptr.2d 394, 889 P.2d 588 (1995), *cert. denied*, 116 S.Ct. 320 (1995).

Compare, Loving v. State, 647 N.E.2d 1123 (Ind.1995). Defendant, who was found intoxicated at the scene of a fatal shooting, was not a suspect in the shooting but was handcuffed and taken to the police station for questioning. There an officer asked him for an account of what had happened. After defendant gave an initial explanation, the officer told him that his account was not consistent with the evidence officers had found at the crime scene, and defendant thereafter admitted firing his handgun. The officer then administered the warnings and defendant invoked his right to counsel. The Supreme Court of Indiana held that the preliminary admissions were inadmissible because defendant was in custody. Although the officers testified that they did not consider defendant a suspect, "their actions conveyed the opposite message." The Indiana court also held that the officer's comment about the inconsistency amounted to interrogation under the standard of Rhode Island v. Innis [casebook, p. 531], because it was tantamount to saying "I know you're lying. Why don't you tell me the truth?"

The presence of a lawyer may not always obviate the need for warnings. In United States v. Swint, 15 F.3d 286 (3d Cir.1994), a defendant (Swint) facing state drug charges was invited to come with his attorney to the state prosecutor's office for an "off-the record" conference to discuss the cooperation defendant might provide in connection with a possible plea bargain. Federal DEA agents were concurrently investigation Swint in connection with drug manufacturing activity he had engaged in after his arrest on the state charges. Without telling Swint the prosecutor arranged for the DEA agents to be on hand. When Swint denied post-arrest drug activity, the prosecutor brought the federal agents into the room, and they told Swint he was facing serious federal charges and might be taken into custody immediately. After conferring with his attorney, Swint agreed to make a statement and cooperate in the investigations. Believing that his "job was finished," the attorney then left because he did not want to be involved in the actual cooperation. Swint thereafter made incriminating statements; no *Miranda* warnings were ever administered. The Court of Appeals held that Swint's statements should be suppressed as involuntary. The swift transition from the "off-the record" conference with a state prosecutor to the interview with the DEA agents indicated that "the state and federal officers used a 'bait and switch' technique, first by leading Swint and his attorney to believe

Swint's statements would not be used against him, and then by depriving Swint of that protection without giving him *Miranda* warnings."

B. WAIVER

EDWARDS v. ARIZONA

Supreme Court of the United States, 1981.
451 U.S. 477, 101 S.Ct. 1880, 68 L.Ed.2d 378.

JUSTICE WHITE delivered the opinion of the Court. * * *

I

On January 19, 1976, a sworn complaint was filed against Edwards in Arizona state court charging him with robbery, burglary, and first-degree murder. An arrest warrant was issued pursuant to the complaint, and Edwards was arrested at his home later that same day. At the police station, he was informed of his rights as required by *Miranda v. Arizona*. Petitioner stated that he understood his rights, and was willing to submit to questioning. After being told that another suspect already in custody had implicated him in the crime, Edwards denied involvement and gave a taped statement presenting an alibi defense. He then sought to "make a deal." The interrogating officer told him that he wanted a statement, but that he did not have the authority to negotiate a deal. The officer provided Edwards with the telephone number of a county attorney. Petitioner made the call, but hung up after a few moments. Edwards then said: "I want an attorney before making a deal." At that point, questioning ceased and Edwards was taken to county jail.

At 9:15 the next morning, two detectives, colleagues of the officer who had interrogated Edwards the previous night, came to the jail and asked to see Edwards. When the detention officer informed Edwards that the detectives wished to speak with him, he replied that he did not want to talk to anyone. The guard told him that "he had" to talk and then took him to meet with the detectives. The officers identified themselves, stated they wanted to talk to him, and informed him of his *Miranda* rights. Edwards was willing to talk, but he first wanted to hear the taped statement of the alleged accomplice who had implicated him. After listening to the tape for several minutes, petitioner said that he would make a statement so long as it was not tape-recorded. The detectives informed him that the recording was irrelevant since they could testify in court concerning whatever he said. Edwards replied: "I'll tell you anything you want to know, but I don't want it on tape." He thereupon implicated himself in the crime.

Prior to trial, Edwards moved to suppress his confession on the ground that his *Miranda* rights had been violated when the officers returned to question him after he had invoked his right to counsel. The trial court initially granted the motion to suppress, but reversed its ruling when presented with a supposedly controlling decision of a higher Arizona court. The court stated without explanation that it found Edwards' statement to be voluntary. [The Arizona Supreme Court affirmed Edwards' conviction.] Contrary to the holdings of the state courts, Edwards insists that having exercised his right on the 19th to have counsel present during interrogation, he did not validly waive that right on the 20th. For the following reasons, we agree.

First, the Arizona Supreme Court applied an erroneous standard for determining waiver where the accused has specifically invoked his right to counsel. It is reasonably clear under our cases that waivers of counsel must not only be voluntary, but must also constitute a knowing and intelligent relinquishment or abandonment of a known right or privilege. * * *

In referring to the necessity to find Edwards' confession knowing and intelligent, the State Supreme Court cited *Schneckloth v. Busta-monte* [p. 103]. Yet, it is clear that *Schneckloth* does not control the issue presented in this case. The issue in *Schneckloth* was under what conditions an individual could be found to have consented to a search and thereby waived his Fourth Amendment rights. The Court declined to impose the "intentional relinquishment or abandonment of a known right or privilege" standard and required only that the consent be voluntary under the totality of the circumstances. The Court specifically noted that the right to counsel was a prime example of those rights requiring the special protection of the knowing and intelligent waiver standard, but held that "[t]he considerations that informed the Court's holding in *Miranda* are simply inapplicable in the present case." *Schneckloth* itself thus emphasized that the voluntariness of a consent or an admission on the one hand, and a knowing and intelligent waiver on the other, are discrete inquiries. Here, however sound the conclusion of the state courts as to the voluntariness of Edwards' admission may be, neither the trial court nor the Arizona Supreme Court undertook to focus on whether Edwards understood his right to counsel and intelligently and knowingly relinquished it. It is thus apparent that the decision below misunderstood the requirement for finding a valid waiver of the right to counsel, once invoked.

Second, although we have held that after initially being advised of his *Miranda* rights, the accused may himself validly waive his rights and respond to interrogation, the Court has strongly indicated that additional safeguards are necessary when the accused asks for counsel; and we now hold that when an accused has invoked his right to have counsel present during custodial interrogation, a valid waiver of that right cannot be established by showing only that he responded to further police-initiated custodial interrogation even if he has been advised of his rights. We further hold that an accused, such as Edwards, having expressed his desire to deal with the police only through counsel, is not subject to further interrogation by the authorities until counsel has been made available to him, unless the accused himself initiates further communication, exchanges, or conversations with the police. * * *

Accordingly, the holding of the Arizona Supreme Court that Edwards had waived his right to counsel was infirm, and the judgment of that court is reversed.

So ordered.

CHIEF JUSTICE BURGER, concurring in the judgment.

I concur only in the judgments because I do not agree that either any constitutional standard or the holding of *Miranda*—as distinguished from its dicta—calls for a special rule as to how an accused in custody may waive the right to be free from interrogation. The extraordinary protections afforded a person in custody suspected of criminal conduct are not without a valid basis, but as with all "good" things they can be carried too far. The notion that any "prompting" of a person in custody is somehow evil *per se* has been rejected. *Rhode Island v. Innis*, 446 U.S. 291 (1980). For me, the inquiry in this setting is whether resumption of interrogation is a result of a voluntary waiver, and that inquiry should be resolved under the traditional standards * * *. In this case, the Supreme Court of Arizona described the situation as follows:

> "When the detention officer told Edwards that the detectives were there to see him, he told the officer that he did not wish to speak to anyone. The officer told him *that he had to.*"

This is enough for me, and on this record the Supreme Court of Arizona erred in holding that the resumption of interrogation was the product of a voluntary waiver.

[The concurring opinion of Justice Powell, joined by Justice Rehnquist, is omitted.]

Commentary

The strict view of waiver which the Supreme Court took in *Edwards* surprised some observers, because *Edwards* was preceded by Michigan v. Mosley, 423 U.S. 96 (1975), which seemed to point in the other direction. Mosley was arrested in connection with certain robberies, and, after being warned, declined to answer questions. The interrogation ceased, but two hours later another detective arrived to question him about a separate murder charge. He was again given the *Miranda* warnings, agreed to talk, and made incriminating statements during a 15–minute interrogation. The Supreme Court majority held that Mosley's right to cut off questioning was fully respected when the first interrogation ceased, and it did not violate the right for the police to resume questioning after the passage of a significant period of time where the second interrogation was preceded by a fresh set of warnings and restricted to a crime that had not been the subject of the earlier interrogation.

In *Edwards*, the majority distinguished *Mosley* on the ground that Mosley had not explicitly invoked the right to counsel. It may be, therefore, that the defendant who asks for counsel is in a somewhat stronger position than the defendant who merely asserts a right to silence, if he later waives his rights in the course of further discussion with the police. On the other hand, the request for counsel must be clearly stated. In Davis v. United

States, 512 U.S. 452 (1994), defendant Davis (an enlisted man in the Navy) waived his *Miranda* rights after being taken into custody for murder. About an hour and a half into the interrogation, he said "Maybe I should talk to a lawyer." The Naval Investigative Service agents asked if he was requesting a lawyer or just making a comment, and he responded "No, I'm not asking for a lawyer," and then "No, I don't want a lawyer." The Supreme Court held that this ambiguous comment was not a request for a lawyer, and that "If the suspect's statement is not an unambiguous or unequivocal request for counsel, the officers have no obligation to stop questioning him."

The Supreme Court has continued to enforce the *Edwards* rule strictly where the defendant has not initiated further communication. For example, the defendant in Arizona v. Roberson, 486 U.S. 675 (1988), had stated that he wanted to talk to a lawyer before answering questions following his arrest for burglary. Three days later, a different police officer who was unaware of the request for counsel administered the standard *Miranda* warnings and questioned Roberson about a different burglary, obtaining an incriminating statement. The Supreme Court held that the *Edwards* rule required excluding this statement even though the second interrogation was by a different officer and for a different crime. The majority distinguished *Michigan v. Mosley* because "a suspect's decision to cut off questioning, unlike his request for counsel, does not raise the presumption that he is unable to proceed without a lawyer's advice."

Somewhat confusingly, invocation of the Sixth Amendment right to counsel under *Michigan v. Jackson,* 475 U.S. 625 (1986), does not prevent the police from questioning a defendant about unrelated crimes. The defendant in McNeil v. Wisconsin, 501 U.S. 171 (1991), appeared in court with an attorney at a bail hearing on robbery charges. Later, while he was still in custody on the robbery charge, the police approached him to ask questions about a murder. After receiving the *Miranda* warnings, McNeil agreed to answer questions and gave answers that were used against him on charges related to the murder. Under *Michigan v. Jackson,* the appearance with counsel at the robbery hearing was an invocation of the Sixth Amendment right, and it cut off any questioning on the robbery charge. The majority opinion by Justice Scalia held, however, that the Sixth Amendment right is "offense specific," and the defendant's appearance at a hearing with counsel was not equivalent to a request for the assistance of counsel in dealing with police interrogation. The dissenters (Stevens, Blackmun, Marshall) pointed out that defense attorneys could blunt the effect of the holding by advising their clients to invoke the *Miranda*-based right to counsel at preliminary judicial proceedings.

In Minnick v. Mississippi, 498 U.S. 146 (1990), the defendant was apprehended in San Diego, California, for murders committed in Mississippi. When questioned by FBI agents, he invoked his right to counsel. Subsequently, Minnick actually conferred with counsel two or three times. A deputy sheriff from Mississippi eventually arrived, and Minnick's jailers told him he would have to talk to the lawman. Minnick did so, and made incriminating statements. The Supreme Court majority opinion by Justice Kennedy held that once the right to counsel had been invoked, any further questioning not initiated by the accused could not be conducted except with counsel *present*. The dissenting opinion by Justice Scalia reasoned that the

Edwards rule was satisfied because the accused had actually consulted with counsel before the renewed interrogation.

The defendant in Patterson v. Illinois, 487 U.S. 285 (1988), was a street gang member suspected of involvement in the murder of a member of a rival gang. After arrest and *Miranda* warnings he agreed to answer questions and denied involvement in the death. Following his indictment for the murder, but before counsel was retained or appointed, officers again administered the warnings and interrogated, this time obtaining a full confession. On appeal the defense argued that the Sixth Amendment right attached upon indictment, and the *Miranda* warnings were not sufficient to support a finding that this more extensive right had been waived. The Supreme Court majority held that the warnings were adequate and the waiver valid, but implied strongly in a footnote that the outcome would have been different if counsel had been retained or appointed. "Once an accused has a lawyer, a distinct set of constitutional safeguards aimed at preserving the sanctity of the attorney-client relationship takes effect."

The defendant in *Patterson* was indicted, but not represented by counsel. The opposite situation was involved in United States v. Hammad, 846 F.2d 854 (2d Cir.1988), where the defendant retained counsel upon learning that he was the target of a federal grand jury investigation. Subsequently, the defendant made incriminating statements to a "false friend"—a co-conspirator who was by then cooperating with the government. Because no indictment had been filed the *Massiah* doctrine was not applicable, and in this situation the defense moved to suppress the recorded incriminating statements on the ground that the investigating prosecutor had violated Disciplinary Rule 7–104(A)(1) of the American Bar Association's Code of Professional Responsibility. This Rule prohibits a lawyer from communicating directly with a "party" he or she knows to be represented by counsel regarding the subject matter of that representation. The panel opinion of the Court of Appeals held that the Rule is applicable to the investigatory stages of a criminal prosecution where the prosecutor knows that the "target" has retained counsel with respect to the particular investigation, and that exclusion of evidence could be an appropriate remedy. The panel declined to order exclusion in the case before it, however, because "the government should not have its case prejudiced by suppression of its evidence when the law was previously unsettled in this area."

In an extreme case where prosecutors deliberately violate a defendant's Sixth Amendment right to counsel, the appropriate remedy may be dismissal of the charges. In People v. Frye, 897 S.W.2d 324 (Tex.Crim.App.1995), defendant was charged with theft of services and represented by counsel. On two occasions, employees of the prosecutor's office telephone defendant and engaged him in conversation about the case, surreptitiously taping the conversations. Defendant's statements were exculpatory and of no value to the state as evidence, but he argued that the prosecution had learned the theory of the defense, a harm that could be cured only by dismissing the charges. A closely divided Texas Court of Criminal Appeals upheld the trial court's order of dismissal.

For further discussion of the waiver issue in the light of the *Edwards* holding, see People v. Boyer, 48 Cal.3d 247, 256 Cal.Rptr. 96, 768 P.2d 610

(1989); Commonwealth v. Gibbs, 520 Pa. 151, 553 A.2d 409 (1989); Commonwealth v. Zook, 520 Pa. 210, 553 A.2d 920 (1989).

A statement obtained in violation of *Miranda* but otherwise voluntary may not be used in the prosecution's case-in-chief, but it may be used to impeach the defendant's testimony. See Harris v. New York, 401 U.S. 222 (1971); Oregon v. Hass, 420 U.S. 714 (1975). In Michigan v. Harvey, 494 U.S. 344 (1990), a closely divided Supreme Court held that this impeachment exception also applies to statements obtained in violation of the *Massiah–Henry* Sixth Amendment right to counsel.

The defendant in *Harvey* was taken into custody for rape, made a statement, and later was arraigned and had counsel appointed. More than two months later he told an officer that he wanted to make a second statement, but didn't know whether he should talk to his lawyer. The officer told him he did not need to speak with this attorney because "his lawyer was going to get a copy of the statement anyway." Harvey then signed a waiver form and made a statement, which was used to impeach his trial testimony on various details. The State conceded that the waiver was invalid under *Michigan v. Jackson*, supra, p. 528, because the colloquy between the defendant and the officer could not be characterized as a defendant-initiated interrogation. The 5–4 majority opinion by Chief Justice Rehnquist nonetheless held that the statement could be used for impeachment if Harvey's waiver was "knowing and voluntary."

The Supreme Court applied the *Edwards* rule to the Sixth Amendment right to counsel in Michigan v. Jackson, 475 U.S. 625 (1986). There the defendants had waived their rights and agreed to talk to the police without counsel. Before the interrogation occurred, however, they appeared in court for arraignment and asked the magistrate to appoint counsel for them because they were indigent. After the arraignment, but before the defendants had an opportunity to consult with counsel, the police advised them of their rights, obtained written waivers, and elicited confessions. The Supreme Court majority held that the written waivers were invalid under the *Edwards* rule.

Justice White's majority opinion in *Edwards* barred further interrogation following invocation of the right to counsel "unless the accused himself initiates further communication, exchanges, or conversations with the police." The Supreme Court applied this language in Oregon v. Bradshaw, 462 U.S. 1039 (1983), where the defendant, suspected of a vehicular manslaughter, invoked his right to counsel after answering a few questions. The officer immediately terminated the questioning. A few minutes later, either while still at the police station or en route to the jail, Bradshaw asked the officer: "Well, what is going to happen to me now?" The officer responded: "You do not have to talk to me. You have requested an attorney and I don't want you talking to me unless you so desire because anything you say—because—since you have requested an attorney, you know, it has to be at your own free will." Bradshaw said that he understood, conversation followed, and eventually Bradshaw agreed to take a lie detector test. He took the test the next day, after being given another set of warnings and signing a waiver, and gave a confession after failing the lie detector test. A closely divided Supreme Court held by a plurality opinion that there was no violation of the *Edwards* rule because the defendant initiated the conversation that led to the consent to take the test.

COLORADO v. CONNELLY

Supreme Court of the United States, 1986.
479 U.S. 157, 107 S.Ct. 515, 93 L.Ed.2d 473.

CHIEF JUSTICE REHNQUIST delivered the opinion of the Court. * * *

I

On August 18, 1983, Officer Patrick Anderson of the Denver Police Department was in uniform, working in an off-duty capacity in downtown Denver. Respondent Francis Connelly approached Officer Anderson and, without any prompting, stated that he had murdered someone and wanted to talk about it. Anderson immediately advised respondent that he had the right to remain silent, that anything he said could be used against him in court, and that he had the right to an attorney prior to any police questioning. Respondent stated that he understood these rights but he still wanted to talk about the murder. Understandably bewildered by this confession, Officer Anderson asked respondent several questions. Connelly denied that he had been drinking, denied that he had been taking any drugs, and stated that, in the past, he had been a patient in several mental hospitals. Officer Anderson again told Connelly that he was under no obligation to say anything. Connelly replied that it was "all right," and that he would talk to Officer Anderson because his conscience had been bothering him. To Officer Anderson, respondent appeared to understand fully the nature of his acts.

Shortly thereafter, Homicide Detective Stephen Antuna arrived. Respondent was again advised of his rights, and Detective Antuna asked him "what he had on his mind." Respondent answered that he had come all the way from Boston to confess to the murder of Mary Ann Junta, a young girl whom he had killed in Denver sometime during November 1982. Respondent was taken to police headquarters, and a search of police records revealed that the body of an unidentified female had been found in April 1983. Respondent openly detailed his story to Detective Antuna and Sergeant Thomas Haney, and readily agreed to take the officers to the scene of the killing. Under Connelly's sole direction, the two officers and respondent proceeded in a police vehicle to the location of the crime. Respondent pointed out the exact location of the murder. Throughout this episode, Detective Antuna perceived no indication whatsoever that respondent was suffering from any kind of mental illness.

Respondent was held overnight. During an interview with the public defender's office the following morning, he became visibly disoriented. He began giving confused answers to questions, and for the first time, stated that "voices" had told him to come to Denver and that he had followed the directions of these voices in confessing. Respondent was sent to a state hospital for evaluation. He was initially found incompetent to assist in his own defense. By March 1984, however, the doctors evaluating respondent determined that he was competent to proceed to trial.

At a preliminary hearing, respondent moved to suppress all of his statements. Doctor Jeffrey Metzner, a psychiatrist employed by the state hospital, testified that respondent was suffering from chronic schizophrenia and was in a psychotic state at least as of August 17, 1983, the day before he confessed. Metzner's interviews with respondent revealed that respondent was following the "voice of God." This voice instructed respondent to withdraw money from the bank, to buy an airplane ticket, and to fly from Boston to Denver. When respondent arrived from Boston, God's voice became stronger and told respondent either to confess to the killing or to commit suicide. Reluctantly following the command of the voices, respondent approached Officer Anderson and confessed.

Dr. Metzner testified that, in his expert opinion, respondent was experiencing "command hallucinations." This condition interfered with respondent's "volitional abilities; that is, his ability to make free and rational choices." Dr. Metzner further testified that Connelly's illness did not significantly impair his cognitive abilities. Thus, respondent understood the rights he had when Officer Anderson and Detective Antuna advised him that he need not speak. Dr. Metzner admitted that the "voices" could in reality be Connelly's interpretation of his own guilt, but explained that in his opinion, Connelly's psychosis motivated his confession.

On the basis of this evidence the Colorado trial court decided that respondent's statements must be suppressed because they were "involuntary." [The Colorado Supreme Court affirmed the suppression order, holding that the statements were involuntary and the *Miranda* waiver invalid.]

II

* * *

The difficulty with the approach of the Supreme Court of Colorado is that it fails to recognize the essential link between coercive activity of the State, on the one hand, and a resulting confession by a defendant, on the other. The flaw in respondent's constitutional argument is that it would expand our previous line of "voluntariness" cases into a far-ranging requirement that courts must divine a defendant's motivation for speaking or acting as he did even though there be no claim that governmental conduct coerced his decision.

The most outrageous behavior by a private party seeking to secure evidence against a defendant does not make that evidence inadmissible under the Due Process Clause. * * * Moreover, suppressing respondent's statements would serve absolutely no purpose in enforcing constitutional guarantees. The purpose of excluding evidence seized in violation of the Constitution is to substantially deter future violations of the Constitution. Only if we were to establish a brand new constitutional right—the right of a criminal defendant to confess to his crime only when totally rational and properly motivated—could respondent's present claim be sustained.

* * *

A statement rendered by one in the condition of respondent might be proved to be quite unreliable, but this is a matter to be governed by the evidentiary laws of the forum, see, *e.g.*, Fed.Rule Evid. 601, and not by the Due Process Clause of the Fourteenth Amendment. * * *

III

A

The Supreme Court of Colorado went on to affirm the trial court's ruling that respondent's later statements made while in custody should be suppressed because respondent had not waived his right to consult an attorney and his right to remain silent. That court held that the State must bear its burden of proving waiver of these *Miranda* rights by "clear and convincing evidence." * * *

[The majority opinion held that the State had the burden of proving waiver only by a preponderance of the evidence.]

B

We also think that the Supreme Court of Colorado was mistaken in its analysis of the question of whether respondent had waived his *Miranda* rights in this case. Of course, a waiver must at a minimum be "voluntary" to be effective against an accused. The Supreme Court of Colorado in addressing this question relied on the testimony of the court-appointed psychiatrist to the effect that respondent was not capable of making a "free decision with respect to his constitutional right of silence * * * and his constitutional right to confer with a lawyer before talking to the police."

We think that the Supreme Court of Colorado erred in importing into this area of constitutional law notions of "free will" that have no place there. There is obviously no reason to require more in the way of a "voluntariness" inquiry in the *Miranda* waiver context than in the Fourteenth Amendment confession context. The sole concern of the Fifth Amendment, on which *Miranda* was based, is governmental coercion. * * * Respondent's perception of coercion flowing from the "voice of God," however important or significant such a perception may be in other disciplines, is a matter to which the United States Constitution does not speak.

IV

The judgment of the Supreme Court of Colorado is accordingly reversed, and the cause remanded for further proceedings not inconsistent with this opinion.

JUSTICE STEVENS, concurring in the judgment in part and dissenting in part.

Respondent made incriminatory statements both before and after he was handcuffed and taken into custody. The only question presented by the Colorado district attorney in his certiorari petition concerned the admissibility of respondent's precustodial statements. I agree with the State of Colorado that the United States Constitution does not require suppression of those statements, but in reaching that conclusion, unlike the Court, I am perfectly willing to accept the state trial court's finding that the statements were involuntary.

The state trial court found that, in view of the "overwhelming evidence presented by the Defense," the prosecution did not meet its burden of demonstrating that respondent's initial statements to Officer Anderson were voluntary. Nevertheless, in my opinion, the use of these involuntary precustodial statements does not violate the Fifth Amendment because they were not the product of state compulsion. Although they may well be so unreliable that they could not support a conviction, at this stage of the proceeding I could not say that they have no probative force whatever. The fact that the statements were involuntary—just as the product of Lady Macbeth's nightmare was involuntary—does not mean that their use for whatever evidentiary value they may have is fundamentally unfair or a denial of due process.

The postcustodial statements raise an entirely distinct question. When the officer whom respondent approached elected to handcuff him and to take him into custody, the police assumed a fundamentally different relationship with him. Prior to that moment, the police had no duty to give respondent *Miranda* warnings and had every right to continue their exploratory conversation with him. Once the custodial relationship was established, however, the questioning assumed a presumptively coercive character. In my opinion the questioning could not thereafter go forward in the absence of a valid waiver of respondent's constitutional rights unless he was provided with counsel. Since it is undisputed that respondent was not then competent to stand trial, I would also conclude that he was not competent to waive his constitutional right to remain silent. * * *

JUSTICE BRENNAN, with whom JUSTICE MARSHALL joins, dissenting. * * *

Today's decision restricts the application of the term "involuntary" to those confessions obtained by police coercion. Confessions by mentally ill individuals or by persons coerced by parties other than police officers are now considered "voluntary." The Court's failure to recognize all forms of involuntariness or coercion as antithetical to due process reflects a refusal to acknowledge free will as a value of constitutional consequence. But due process derives much of its meaning from a conception of fundamental fairness that emphasizes the right to make vital choices voluntarily: "The Fourteenth Amendment secures against state invasion * * * the right of a person to remain silent unless he chooses to speak in the unfettered exercise of his own will * * *." *Malloy v. Hogan*, 378 U.S. 1, 8 (1964). This right requires vigilant protection if we are to safeguard the values of private conscience and human dignity.

This Court's assertion that we would be required "to establish a brand new constitutional right" to recognize the respondent's claim ignores 200 years of constitutional jurisprudence.[1] While it is true that police overreaching has been an element of every confession case to date, it is also true that in every case the Court has made clear that ensuring that a confession is a product of free will is an independent concern. * * *

Since the Court redefines voluntary confessions to include confessions by mentally ill individuals, the reliability of these confessions becomes a central concern. A concern for reliability is inherent in our criminal justice system, which relies upon accusatorial rather than inquisitorial practices. While an inquisitorial system prefers obtaining confessions from criminal defendants, an accusatorial system must place its faith in determinations of guilt by evidence independently and freely secured. * * *

The instant case starkly highlights the danger of admitting a confession by a person with a severe mental illness. The trial court made no findings concerning the reliability of Mr. Connelly's involuntary confession, since it believed that the confession was excludable on the basis of involuntariness. However, the overwhelming evidence in the record points to the unreliability of Mr. Connelly's delusional mind. Mr. Connelly was found incompetent to stand trial because he was unable to relate accurate information, and the court-appointed psychiatrist indicated that Mr. Connelly was actively hallucinating and exhibited delusional thinking at the time of his confession.

Moreover, the record is barren of any corroboration of the mentally ill defendant's confession. No physical evidence links the defendant to the alleged crime. Police did not identify the alleged victim's body as the woman named by the defendant. Mr. Connelly identified the alleged scene of the crime, but it has not been verified that the unidentified body was found there or that a crime actually occurred there. There is not a shred of competent evidence in this record linking the defendant to the charged homicide. There is only Mr. Connelly's confession.

Minimum standards of due process should require that the trial court find substantial indicia of reliability, on the basis of evidence extrinsic to the confession itself, before admitting the confession of a mentally ill person into evidence. I would require the trial court to make such a finding on remand. To hold otherwise allows the State to

---

1. Cf. *Bram v. United States*, 168 U.S. 532, 547–548 (1897) (reviewing the "rule [of law] in England at the time of the adoption of the Constitution and of the Fifth Amendment" and citing Hawkins' Pleas of the Crown (6th ed. 1787): "[a] confession, therefore, whether made upon an official examination or *in discourse with private persons*, which is obtained from a defendant, either by the flattery of hope, or by the impressions of fear, however slightly the emotions may be implanted, * * * is not admissible evidence; for the law will not suffer a prisoner to be made the deluded instrument of his own conviction") (emphasis added).

imprison and possibly to execute a mentally ill defendant based solely upon an inherently unreliable confession.

COLORADO v. SPRING

Supreme Court of the United States, 1987.
479 U.S. 564, 107 S.Ct. 851, 93 L.Ed.2d 954.

JUSTICE POWELL delivered the opinion of the Court. * * *

In February 1979, respondent John Leroy Spring and a companion shot and killed Donald Walker during a hunting trip in Colorado. Shortly thereafter, an informant told agents of the Bureau of Alcohol, Tobacco, and Firearms (ATF) that Spring was engaged in the interstate transportation of stolen firearms. The informant also told the agents that Spring had discussed his participation in the Colorado killing. At the time the ATF agents received this information, Walker's body had not been found and the police had received no report of his disappearance. Based on the information received from the informant relating to the firearms violations, the ATF agents set up an undercover operation to purchase firearms from Spring. On March 30, 1979, ATF agents arrested Spring in Kansas City, Missouri, during the undercover purchase.

An ATF agent on the scene of the arrest advised Spring of his *Miranda* rights. Spring was advised of his *Miranda* rights a second time after he was transported to the ATF office in Kansas City. At the ATF office, the agents also advised Spring that he had the right to stop the questioning at any time or to stop the questioning until the presence of an attorney could be secured. Spring then signed a written form stating that he understood and waived his rights, and that he was willing to make a statement and answer questions.

ATF agents first questioned Spring about the firearms transactions that led to his arrest. They then asked Spring if he had a criminal record. He admitted that he had a juvenile record for shooting his aunt when he was 10 years old. The agents asked if Spring had ever shot anyone else. Spring ducked his head and mumbled, "I shot another guy once." The agents asked Spring if he had ever been to Colorado. Spring said no. The agents asked Spring whether he had shot a man named Walker in Colorado and thrown his body into a snowbank. Spring paused and then ducked his head again and said no. The interview ended at this point.

On May 26, 1979, Colorado law enforcement officials visited Spring while he was in jail in Kansas City pursuant to his arrest on the firearms offenses. The officers gave Spring the *Miranda* warnings, and Spring again signed a written form indicating that he understood his rights and was willing to waive them. The officers informed Spring that they wanted to question him about the Colorado homicide. Spring indicated that he "wanted to get it off his chest." In an interview that lasted approximately 1½ hours, Spring confessed to the Colorado murder. During that time, Spring talked freely to the officers, did not indicate a desire to terminate the questioning, and never requested counsel. The officers prepared a written statement summarizing the interview. Spring read, edited, and signed the statement.

[Spring was convicted of first degree murder at a trial at which the May 26 statement was admitted. On appeal, the state courts held that the ATF agents should have advised him that he was a murder suspect before questioning him about that crime, and that the March 30 admission was therefore improperly obtained. Because the state had not met its burden of showing that the May 26 statement was not the product of the March 30 admission, the state appellate courts ordered a new trial.]

There is no dispute that the police obtained the May 26 confession after complete *Miranda* warnings and after informing Spring that he would be questioned about the Colorado homicide. The Colorado Supreme Court nevertheless held that the confession should have been suppressed because it was the illegal "fruit" of the March 30 statement. A confession cannot be "fruit of the poisonous tree" if the tree itself is not poisonous. Our inquiry, therefore, centers on the validity of the March 30 statement.* * * *

Spring relies on this Court's statement in *Miranda* that "any evidence that the accused was threatened, tricked, or cajoled into a waiver will * * * show that the defendant did not voluntarily waive his privilege." He contends that the failure to inform him of the potential subjects of interrogation constitutes the police trickery and deception condemned in *Miranda*, thus rendering his waiver of *Miranda* rights invalid. Spring, however, reads this statement in *Miranda* out of context and without due regard to the constitutional privilege the *Miranda* warnings were designed to protect.

We note first that the Colorado courts made no finding of official trickery. In fact, the trial court expressly found that "there was no element of duress or coercion used to induce Spring's statements." Spring nevertheless insists that the failure of the ATF agents to inform him that he would be questioned about the murder constituted official "trickery" sufficient to invalidate his waiver of his Fifth Amendment privilege, even if the official conduct did not amount to "coercion." Even assuming that Spring's proposed distinction has merit, we reject his conclusion. This Court has never held that mere silence by law enforcement officials as to the subject matter of an interrogation is "trickery" sufficient to invalidate a suspect's waiver of *Miranda* rights, and we expressly decline so to hold today. * * *

We have held that a valid waiver does not require that an individual be informed of all information "useful" in making his decision or all

---

* The State argued for the first time in its petition for rehearing to the Colorado Supreme Court that this Court's decision in *Oregon v. Elstad* [p. 539] (1985), renders the May 26 statement admissible without regard to the validity of the March 30 waiver. The Colorado Supreme Court noted that the State would be free to make this argument to the trial court on remand. The question whether our decision in *Oregon v. Elstad* provides an independent basis for admitting the May 26 statement therefore is not before us in this case.

information that "might * * * affec[t] his decision to confess." *Moran v. Burbine,* 106 S.Ct., at 1142. "[W]e have never read the Constitution to require that the police supply a suspect with a flow of information to help him calibrate his self-interest in deciding whether to speak or stand by his rights." Here, the additional information could affect only the wisdom of a *Miranda* waiver, not its essentially voluntary and knowing nature. Accordingly, the failure of the law enforcement officials to inform Spring of the subject matter of the interrogation could not affect Spring's decision to waive his Fifth Amendment privilege in a constitutionally significant manner.

This Court's holding in *Miranda* specifically required that the police inform a criminal suspect that he has the right to remain silent and that *anything* he says may be used against him. There is no qualification of this broad and explicit warning. The warning, as formulated in *Miranda,* conveys to a suspect the nature of his constitutional privilege and the consequences of abandoning it. Accordingly, we hold that a suspect's awareness of all the possible subjects of questioning in advance of interrogation is not relevant to determining whether the suspect voluntarily, knowingly, and intelligently waived his Fifth Amendment privilege.

The judgment of the Colorado Supreme Court is reversed, and the case is remanded for further proceedings not inconsistent with this opinion.

JUSTICE MARSHALL, with whom JUSTICE BRENNAN joins, dissenting. * * *

The interrogation tactics utilized in this case demonstrate the relevance of the information Spring did not receive. The agents evidently hoped to obtain from Spring a valid confession to the federal firearms charge for which he was arrested and then parlay this admission into an additional confession of first degree murder. Spring could not have expected questions about the latter, separate offense when he agreed to waive his rights, as it occurred in a different state and was a violation of state law outside the normal investigative focus of federal Alcohol, Tobacco and Firearms agents.

"Interrogators describe the point of the first admission as the 'breakthrough' and the 'beachhead,' R. Royal & S. Schutt, The Gentle Art of Interviewing and Interrogation: A Professional Manual and Guide 143 (1976), which once obtained will give them enormous 'tactical advantages,' F. Inbau & J. Reid, Criminal Interrogation and Confessions 82 (2d ed. 1967)." *Oregon v. Elstad,* 470 U.S. 298, 328 (1985) (Brennan, J., dissenting). The coercive aspects of the psychological ploy intended in this case, when combined with an element of surprise which may far too easily rise to a level of deception, cannot be justified in light of *Miranda's* strict requirements that the suspect's waiver and confession be voluntary, knowing, and intelligent. * * * It is reasonable to conclude that, had Spring known of the federal agents' intent to ask questions about a murder unrelated to the offense for which he was arrested, he would not have consented to interrogation without first consulting his attorney. In this case, I would therefore accept the determination of the Colorado Supreme Court that Spring did not voluntarily, knowingly, and intelligently waive his Fifth Amendment rights.

I dissent.

Commentary

How "knowing and intelligent" does a waiver have to be? If the standard is the same as that applied when an accused desires to represent himself at trial, then it is difficult to understand how a waiver can be valid when the authorities have deliberately concealed information which would have caused the accused to make a different decision. Trial courts routinely urge defendants to consult with a lawyer before making a decision about waiver, whereas police officers regard the opportunity for interrogation as lost once the accused has talked to counsel. (See *Moran v. Burbine, supra,* p. 388.) If a waiver were invalid because the accused did not know something that would have affected his decision had he known it, then few waivers would be valid.

Sometimes the suspect agrees to talk to police officers, but insists that nothing be put in writing or that the tape recorders be turned off. Conditioning the waiver in this way suggests that the suspect does not really understand that his statements can be used as evidence even if they are not recorded. Nonetheless, confessions obtained following such ambiguous waivers are ordinarily admitted. For example, see Connecticut v. Barrett, 479 U.S. 523 (1987). The Connecticut Supreme Court in that case held that Barrett's incriminating statements should have been suppressed under the *Edwards* rule, because, although he stated that he was willing to talk to the police, he also indicated that he would not make a written statement outside the presence of counsel. The Supreme Court reinstated the conviction, holding in an opinion by Justice Rehnquist that "The fact that officials took the opportunity provided by Barrett to obtain an oral confession is quite consistent with the Fifth Amendment." Dissenting Justice Stevens asked why Barrett's request for counsel was distinguishable from the request in *Edwards* itself, where the defendant said that he wanted an attorney "before making a deal." [See p. 549, *supra.*] Edwards had also said that he would talk to the police but did not want it on tape. According to Justice Stevens, "The police interrogation [in *Edwards*] complied with the everyday meaning of both of these conditions; it occurred before Edwards made any 'deal'— indeed, he never made a deal—and no tape recording of the session was made. The Court nevertheless found the interrogation objectionable." Justice Stevens reasoned that the invocation of the right to counsel by Barrett was in similar terms, and a similar result should have followed.

In People v. Jordan, 891 P.2d 1010 (Colo.1995), a psychiatrist testified that defendant's waiver of his *Miranda* rights was not intelligent due to lack of sleep, prior drug use, and a "serious difficulty with abstract concepts." The trial judge credited this testimony and suppressed the resulting statements. The Colorado Supreme Court reversed the suppression order, holding (4–3) that the record as a whole, including defendant's own testimony, showed that he understood his rights and hoped to talk his way out of trouble. The Colorado court contrasted two other cases where it had found waivers invalid: In People v. Jiminez, 863 P.2d 981 (Colo.1993), defendant was a Native American whose language was Kickapoo, but the police read him his rights in Spanish, a language he barely understood. Moreover, the testimony indicated that the Kickapoo language has no concept of a "right," and Jiminez did not understand such terms as "lawyer" or "jury." In People v. May, 859 P.2d 879 (Colo.1993), defendant was questioned by police in a hospital shortly after being involved in a serious automobile accident. He was "drifting in and out of consciousness," and mentally very confused.

In People v. Smith, 31 Cal.App.4th 1185, 37 Cal.Rptr.2d 524 (1995), a deaf man (Smith) was involved in a murder. After being advised of his rights through a sign language interpreter, Smith invoked his right to counsel. Due to the interpreter's misunderstanding there was some confusion about what Smith meant, however, and the officer asked further questions in the course of which Smith made statements that were used against him. The trial court found that Smith understood his rights and had invoked his right to counsel, but that the officer's further questions to clarify Smith's response were pursued in good faith and that, therefore, Smith's statements were admissible. The California Court of Appeals held statements given after the invocation of the right to counsel were inadmissible regardless of the good faith of the officer.

OREGON v. ELSTAD

Supreme Court of the United States, 1985.
470 U.S. 298, 105 S.Ct. 1285, 84 L.Ed.2d 222.

JUSTICE O'CONNOR delivered the opinion of the Court. * * *

In December, 1981, the home of Mr. and Mrs. Gilbert Gross, in the town of Salem, Polk County, Ore., was burglarized. Missing were art objects and furnishings valued at $150,000. A witness to the burglary contacted the Polk County Sheriff's office, implicating respondent Michael Elstad, an 18–year–old neighbor and friend of the Grosses' teenage son. Thereupon, Officers Burke and McAllister went to the home of respondent Elstad, with a warrant for his arrest. Elstad's mother answered the door. She led the officers to her son's room where he lay on his bed, clad in shorts and listening to his stereo. The officers asked him to get dressed and to accompany them into the living room. Officer McAllister asked respondent's mother to step into the kitchen, where he explained that they had a warrant for her son's arrest for the burglary of a neighbor's residence. Officer Burke remained with Elstad in the living room. He later testified:

> "I sat down with Mr. Elstad and I asked him if he was aware of why Detective McAllister and myself were there to talk with him. He stated no, he had no idea why we were there. I then asked him if he knew a person by the name of Gross, and he said yes, he did, and also added that he heard that there was a robbery at the Gross house. And at that point I told Mr. Elstad that I felt he was involved in that, and he looked at me and stated, 'Yes, I was there.' "

The officers then escorted Elstad to the back of the patrol car. As they were about to leave for the Polk County Sheriff's office, Elstad's father arrived home and came to the rear of the patrol car. The officers advised him that his son was a suspect in the burglary. Officer Burke testified that Mr. Elstad became quite agitated, opened the rear door of the car and admonished his son: "I told you that you were going to get into trouble. You wouldn't listen to me. You never learn."

Elstad was transported to the Sheriff's headquarters and approximately one hour later, Officers Burke and McAllister joined him in McAllister's office. McAllister then advised respondent for the first time of his *Miranda* rights, reading from a standard card. Respondent indicated he understood his rights, and, having these rights in mind, wished to speak with the officers. Elstad gave a full statement, explaining that he had known that the Gross family was out of town and had been paid to lead several acquaintances to the Gross residence and show them how to gain entry through a defective sliding glass door. The statement was typed, reviewed by respondent, read back to him for correction, initialed and signed by Elstad and both officers. As an afterthought, Elstad added and initialed the sentence, "After leaving the house Robby & I went back to [the] van & Robby handed me a small bag of grass." Respondent concedes that the officers made no threats or promises either at his residence or at the Sheriff's office.

Respondent was charged with first-degree burglary. He was represented at trial by retained counsel. Elstad waived his right to a jury and his case was tried by a Circuit Court Judge. Respondent moved at once to suppress his oral statement and signed confession. He contended that the statement he made in response to questioning at his house "let the cat out of the bag," and tainted the subsequent confession as "fruit of the poisonous tree," citing *Wong Sun v. United States*, 371 U.S. 471 (1963). The judge ruled that the statement, "I was there," had to be excluded because the defendant had not been advised of his *Miranda* rights. The written confession taken after Elstad's arrival at the Sheriff's office, however, was admitted in evidence. [The state Court of Appeals reversed the ensuing burglary Conviction on the ground that the written confession was tainted by the initial oral admission, which the state conceded was obtained in violation of the *Miranda* doctrine.]

Prior to *Miranda*, the admissibility of an accused's in custody statements was judged solely by whether they were "voluntary" within the meaning of the Due Process Clause. * * * The Court in *Miranda* required suppression of many statements that would have been admissible under traditional due process analysis by presuming that statements made while in custody and without adequate warnings were protected by the Fifth Amendment. * * * As the Court noted last Term in *New York v. Quarles*, [p. 505]:

> "The *Miranda* Court, however, presumed that interrogation in certain custodial circumstances is inherently coercive and * * * that statements made under those circumstances are inadmissible unless

the suspect is specifically informed of his *Miranda* rights and freely decides to forgo those rights. The prophylactic *Miranda* warnings therefore are 'not themselves rights protected by the Constitution but [are] instead measures to insure that the right against compulsory self-incrimination [is] protected.' *Michigan v. Tucker*, 417 U.S. 433, 444 (1974): * * *

Respondent's contention that his confession was tainted by the earlier failure of the police to provide *Miranda* warnings and must be excluded as "fruit of the poisonous tree" assumes the existence of a constitutional violation. This figure of speech is drawn from *Wong Sun*, supra, in which the Court held that evidence and witnesses discovered as a result of a search in violation of the Fourth Amendment must be excluded, from evidence. The *Wong Sun* doctrine applies as well when the fruit of the Fourth Amendment violation is a confession. It is settled law that "a confession obtained through custodial interrogation after an illegal arrest should be excluded unless intervening events break the causal connection between the illegal arrest and the confession so that the confession is 'sufficiently an act of free will to purge the primary taint.'" *Taylor v. Alabama*, 457 U.S. 687, 690 (1982) (quoting *Brown v. Illinois*, 422 U.S. 590, 602 (1975)).

But as we explained in *Quarles* and *Tucker*, a procedural *Miranda* violation differs in significant respects from violations of the Fourth Amendment, which have traditionally mandated a broad application of the "fruits" doctrine. * * * The *Miranda* exclusionary rule, however, serves the Fifth Amendment and sweeps more broadly than the Fifth Amendment itself. It may be triggered even in the absence of a Fifth Amendment violation. The Fifth Amendment prohibits use by the prosecution in its case in chief only of *compelled* testimony. Failure to administer *Miranda* warnings creates a presumption of compulsion. Consequently, unwarned statements that are otherwise voluntary within the meaning of the Fifth Amendment must nevertheless be excluded from evidence under *Miranda*. Thus, in the individual case, *Miranda's* preventive medicine provides a remedy even to the defendant who has suffered no identifiable constitutional harm.

But the *Miranda* presumption, though irrebuttable for purposes of the prosecution's case in chief, does not require that the statements and their fruits be discarded as inherently tainted. Despite the fact that patently *voluntary* statements taken in violation of *Miranda* must be excluded from the prosecution's case, the presumption of coercion does not bar their use for impeachment purposes on cross-examination. *Harris v. New York*, 401 U.S. 222 (1971). * * *

In *Michigan v. Tucker*, supra, the Court was asked to extend the *Wong Sun* fruits doctrine to suppress the testimony of a witness for the prosecution whose identity was discovered as the result of a statement taken from the accused without benefit of full *Miranda* warnings. As in respondent's case, the breach of the *Miranda* procedures in *Tucker* involved no actual compulsion. The Court concluded that the unwarned questioning "did not abridge respondent's constitutional privilege * * * but departed only from the prophylactic standards later laid down by this Court in *Miranda* to safeguard that privilege." Since there was no actual infringement of the suspect's constitutional rights, the case was not controlled by the doctrine expressed in *Wong Sun* that fruits of a constitutional violation must be suppressed. * * *

We believe that this reasoning applies with equal force when the alleged "fruit" of a noncoercive *Miranda* violation is neither a witness nor an article of evidence but the accused's own voluntary testimony. As in *Tucker*, the absence of any coercion or improper tactics undercuts the twin rationales—trustworthiness and deterrence—for a broader rule. Once warned, the suspect is free to exercise his own volition in deciding whether or not to make a statement to the authorities. * * * Because *Miranda* warnings may inhibit persons from giving information, this Court has determined that they need be administered only after the person is taken into "custody" or his freedom has otherwise been significantly restrained. Unfortunately, the task of defining "custody" is a slippery one, and policemen investigating serious crimes cannot realistically be expected to make no errors whatsoever. If errors are made by law enforcement officers in administering the prophylactic *Miranda* procedures, they should not breed the same irremediable consequences as police infringement of the Fifth Amendment itself. It is an unwarranted extension of *Miranda* to hold that a simple failure to administer the warnings, unaccompanied by any actual coercion or other circumstances calculated to undermine the suspect's ability to exercise his free will so taints the investigatory process that a subsequent voluntary and informed waiver is ineffective for some indeterminate period. Though *Miranda* requires that the unwarned admission must be suppressed, the admissibility of any subsequent statement should turn in these circumstances solely on whether it is knowingly and voluntarily made.

The Oregon court, however, believed that the unwarned remark compromised the voluntariness of respondent's later confession. It was the court's view that the prior *answer* and not the unwarned questioning impaired respondent's ability to give a valid waiver and that only lapse of time and change of place could dissipate what it termed the "coercive impact" of the inadmissible statement. When a prior statement is actually coerced, the time that passes between confessions, the change in place of interrogations, and the change in identity of the interrogators all bear on whether that coercion has carried over into the second confession. * * *

There is a vast difference between the direct consequences flowing from coercion of a confession by physical violence or other deliberate means calculated to break the suspect's will and the uncertain consequences of disclosure of a "guilty secret" freely given in response to an unwarned but noncoercive question, as in this case. * * * We must conclude that, absent deliberately coercive or improper tactics in obtaining the initial statement, the mere fact that a suspect has made an unwarned admission does not warrant a presumption of compulsion. A subsequent administration of *Miranda* warnings to a suspect who has given a voluntary but unwarned statement ordinarily should suffice to remove the conditions that precluded admission of the earlier statement. In such circumstances, the finder of fact may reasonably conclude that the suspect made a rational and intelligent choice whether to waive or invoke his rights.

The state has conceded the issue of custody and thus we must assume that Burke breached *Miranda* procedures in failing to administer *Miranda* warnings before initiating the discussion in the living room. This breach may have been the result of confusion as to whether the brief exchange qualified as "custodial interrogation" or it may simply have reflected Burke's reluctance to initiate an alarming police procedure before McAllister had spoken with respondent's mother. Whatever the reason for Burke's oversight, the incident had none of the earmarks of coercion. Nor did the officers exploit the unwarned admission to pressure respondent into waiving his right to remain silent. * * * We find that the dictates of *Miranda* and the goals of the Fifth Amendment proscription against use of compelled testimony are fully satisfied in the circumstances of this case by barring use of the unwarned statement in the case in chief. No further purpose is served by imputing "taint" to subsequent statements obtained pursuant to a voluntary and knowing waiver. We hold today that a suspect who has once responded to unwarned yet uncoercive questioning is not thereby disabled from waiving his rights and confessing after he has been given the requisite *Miranda* warnings.

The judgment of the Court of Appeals of Oregon is reversed, and the case is remanded for further proceedings not inconsistent with this opinion.

[The lengthy dissenting opinion of Justice Brennan, joined by Justice Marshall, is omitted.]

Justice Stevens, dissenting.

The Court concludes its opinion with a carefully phrased statement of its holding:

"We hold today that a suspect who has once responded to unwarned yet uncoercive questioning is not thereby disabled from waiving his rights and confessing after he has been given the requisite *Miranda* warnings."

I find nothing objectionable in such a holding. Moreover, because the Court expressly endorses the "bright line rule of *Miranda*," which conclusively presumes that incriminating statements obtained from a suspect in custody without administering the required warnings are the product of compulsion, and because the Court places so much emphasis on the special facts of this case, I am persuaded that the Court intends its holding to apply only to a narrow category of cases in which the initial questioning of the suspect was made in a totally uncoercive setting and in which the first confession obviously had no influence on the second. I nevertheless dissent because even such a narrowly confined exception is inconsistent with the Court's prior cases, because the attempt to identify its boundaries in future cases will breed confusion and uncertainty in the administration of criminal justice, and because it denigrates the importance of one of the core constitutional rights that protects every American citizen from the kind of tyranny that has flourished in other societies. * * *

In my opinion, the Court's attempt to fashion a distinction between actual coercion "by physical violence or other deliberate means calculated to break the suspect's will," and irrebuttably presumed coercion cannot succeed. The presumption is only legitimate if it is assumed that there is always a coercive aspect to custodial interrogation that is not preceded by adequate advice of the constitutional right to remain silent. Although I would not support it, I could understand a rule that refused to apply the presumption unless the interrogation took place in an especially coercive setting—perhaps only in the police station itself—but if the presumption arises whenever the accused has been taken into custody or his freedom has been restrained in any significant way, it will surely be futile to try to develop subcategories of custodial interrogation.* Indeed, a major purpose of treating the presumption of coercion as irrebuttable is to avoid the kind of fact-bound inquiry that today's decision will surely engender. * * *

For me, the most disturbing aspect of the Court's opinion is its somewhat opaque characterization of the police misconduct in this case. The Court appears ambivalent on the question whether there was any constitutional violation. This ambivalence is either disingenuous or completely lawless. This Court's power to require state courts to exclude probative self-incriminatory statements rests entirely on the premise that the use of such evidence violates the Federal Constitution. The same constitutional analysis applies whether the custodial interrogation is actually coercive or irrebuttably presumed to be coercive. If the Court does not accept that premise, it must regard the holding in the *Miranda* case itself, as well as all of the Federal jurisprudence that has evolved from that decision, as nothing more than an illegitimate exercise of raw judicial power. If the Court accepts the proposition that respondent's self-incriminatory statement was inadmissible, it must also acknowledge that the Federal Constitution protected him from custodial police interrogation without first being advised of his right to remain silent.

The source of respondent's constitutional protection is the Fifth Amendment's privilege against compelled self-incrimination that is secured against state invasion by the Due Process Clause of the Fourteenth Amendment. Like many other provisions of the Bill of Rights, that provision is merely a procedural safeguard. It is, however, the specific provision that protects all citizens from the kind of custodial interrogation that was once employed by the Star Chamber, by "the

---

* Of course, in *Orozco v. Texas*, 394 U.S. 324 (1969), this Court rejected the contention that *Miranda* warnings were inapplicable because a defendant "was interrogated on his own bed, in familiar surroundings."

Germans of the 1930's and early 1940's," and by some of our own police departments only a few decades ago. Custodial interrogation that violates that provision of the Bill of Rights is a classic example of a violation of a constitutional right.

I respectfully dissent.

Commentary

Justice O'Connor concluded her concurring opinion in *New York v. Quarles* (p. 525, *supra*) by observing that the Court in *Miranda* "looked to the experience of countries like England, India, Scotland, and Ceylon in developing its code to regulate custodial interrogations." It follows, she suggested, that the experience of these countries should be of equal importance in establishing the scope of the *Miranda* exclusionary rule today. In all these countries, nontestimonial evidence derived from confessions "not blatantly coerced" was and still is admitted. Moreover, "the trend in these other countries is to admit the improperly obtained statements themselves, if nontestimonial evidence later corroborates, in whole or in part, the admission." (1984).

For a vivid illustration of how tolerant the English courts are of police activities that would clearly violate American constitutional standards, see the description of the investigation and trial in *Regina v. David Fisher*, as reported by University of Illinois Law Professor Michael H. Graham in his book *Tightening the Reins of Justice in America* (1984):

Fisher took £3,800 from the Midland Bank in the Hockley district of Birmingham in a daylight robbery on February 25, 1980. A clerk and the bank manager were the only witnesses, but they gave highly inaccurate descriptions from which the police composed a composite photograph which did not resemble Fisher at all.

As part of a routine security check for suspected terrorists, police detained David Fisher when he arrived at the Birmingham Airport March on March 19 on a flight from Ireland, because he was in possession of £1,358.07 and was unemployed. When first questioned about the money, Fisher replied "I needn't tell you anything, in fact I am not going to tell you." Another officer (Sutcliffe) then arrived, and again demanded to know where the money had come from. This time, Fisher replied that he had won it gambling "here and there." Sutcliffe was dissatisfied with this vague explanation, and announced: "I am arresting you on suspicion of having stolen the money." He then "cautioned" Fisher by advising him that he was not obliged to say anything unless he wished to do so, but that whatever he did say could be put in writing and given in evidence.

The officers took Fisher to the Airport Police Station for further questioning. According to Sutcliffe's testimony, the following colloquy occurred:

A. I said, "Mr. Fisher you know why you have been arrested don't you?", and Fisher said, "Yes of course". I said, "Where has that money come from?", and I again cautioned him. Fisher said, "I told you I'm saying I got it gambling." I said, "Alright where; here in Birmingham, or over in Ireland?". Fisher said, "Here." I said, "Well now if you tell me where you won it, when and from whom, I can check your story from other people, can't I?". Fisher said, "Different blokes in pubs around, I can't say who." I said, "What were you gambling on; horses, dogs, cards?". Fisher said, "Just cards." I said, "I've seen a few card schools in pubs but never with the sort of money you're carrying. You have £1,358.07p. in your possession; are you seriously saying you won all that amount at cards?". Fisher said, "Yes that's what I'm saying." I said, "You are going to have to tell me the names of some of the people who you say you won this money from and the pubs you know", and Fisher said, "I'll have to think about it. I can't remember any names at the moment." I said, "Which area were the pubs in then?". Fisher said, "Oh around the town you know." I said, "Shall we carry on playing this silly game or do you think you could tell me the truth about all this?". Fisher said, "I want to see a solicitor and I am saying no more to you about anything until you let me see one." I said, "Yes you will be able to have a solicitor if that's what you want, and in the meantime I shall go and search your room at 155 Warwick Road, and also I've got to make some enquiries at other addresses found in your possession." Fisher said, "You bastard." I said, "What do you mean by that?". Fisher said, "I suppose you're going to turn over all my friends and make life difficult for them as well." I said, "David I am going to do what I consider to be my duty and that is to find out how you, a man out of work, is in possession of such a large amount of money." Fisher said, "You're not going to let go are you." I said, "No, not until you tell me the truth." Fisher said, "Don't do anything yet, let me think for a bit." I said, "Take as long as you like". A short time later * * *.

Q.   What sort of period elapsed?

A.   About 5 minutes sir. A short time later Fisher said, "O.K. I'll make your job easy for you, I'll tell you." I said, "What are you going to tell me now", and Fisher said, "How I got the money." I said, "Yes how?". Fisher said, "It was a bank job." I said, "Yes where, what did you do?". Fisher said, "The Midland Bank at Hockley, I held it up."

Fisher then dictated and signed a full confession, which began with an acknowledgment that he had been cautioned as to his rights. Until Fisher began making admissions, the officers had no knowledge of any robbery at the particular bank in question, and had arrested Fisher for theft solely because he was an unemployed person who possessed a large sum of money which he claimed he had won gambling.

Subsequently, officers searched Fisher's rented room without bothering to obtain a search warrant or consent, and recovered the blank starting pistol used in the robbery and other related items. A few hours later they confronted Fisher with the objects taken from his room, and he made a further written statement identifying items worn or used in the robbery, or purchased with the stolen money. Because of the seriousness of the charge (although the gun was loaded with blank cartridges) and Fisher's prior record of theft offenses, he was denied bail pending trial and remained in custody until his conviction several months later. All the statements obtained from him in custody and the evidence taken from his room was admitted at the trial.

C. THE VOLUNTARINESS DOCTRINE AFTER *MIRANDA*

ARIZONA v. FULMINANTE

Supreme Court of the United States, 1991.
499 U.S. 279, 111 S.Ct. 1246, 113 L.Ed.2d 302.

WHITE, J., delivered an opinion, Parts I, II, and IV of which are for the Court, and filed a dissenting opinion in Part III. MARSHALL, BLACKMUN, and STEVENS, JJ., joined Parts I, II, III, and IV of that opinion; SCALIA, J., joined Parts I and II; and KENNEDY, J., joined Parts I and IV. REHNQUIST, C.J., delivered an opinion, Part II of which is for the Court, and filed a dissenting opinion in Parts I and III. O'CONNOR, J., joined Parts I, II, and III of that opinion; KENNEDY and SOUTER, JJ., joined Parts I and II; and SCALIA, J., joined Parts II and III. KENNEDY, J., filed an opinion concurring in the judgment.

JUSTICE WHITE delivered the opinion of the Court.

The Arizona Supreme Court ruled in this case that respondent Oreste Fulminante's confession, received in evidence at his trial for murder, had been coerced and that its use against him was barred by the Fifth and Fourteenth Amendments to the United States Constitution. The court also held that the harmless-error rule could not be used to save the conviction. We affirm the judgment of the Arizona court, although for different reasons than those upon which that court relied.

I

Early in the morning of September 14, 1982, Fulminante called the Mesa, Arizona, Police Department to report that his 11–year–old step-daughter, Jeneane Michelle Hunt, was missing. He had been caring for Jeneane while his wife, Jeneane's mother, was in the hospital. Two days later, Jeneane's body was found in the desert east of Mesa. She had been shot twice in the head at close range with a large caliber weapon, and a ligature was around her neck. Because of the decomposed condition of the body, it was impossible to tell whether she had been sexually assaulted.

Fulminante's statements to police concerning Jeneane's disappearance and his relationship with her contained a number of inconsistencies, and he became a suspect in her killing. When no charges were filed against him, Fulminante left Arizona for New Jersey. He was later convicted in New Jersey on federal charges of possession of a firearm by a felon.

Fulminante was incarcerated in [a federal prison] in New York. There he became friends with another inmate, Sarivola, serving a 60–day sentence for extortion. The two men came to spend several hours a day together. Sarivola, a former police officer, had been involved in loan-sharking for organized crime but then became a paid informant for the FBI. After becoming friends with Fulminante, Sarivola heard a rumor that Fulminante was suspected of killing a child in Arizona. Sarivola then raised the subject with Fulminante in several conversations, but

Fulminante repeatedly denied any involvement in Jeneane's death. During one conversation, he told Sarivola that Jeneane had been killed by bikers looking for drugs; on another occasion, he said he did not know what had happened. Sarivola passed this information on to an FBI agent, who instructed him to find out more.

Sarivola learned more one evening in October 1983, as he and Fulminante walked together around the prison track. Sarivola said that he knew Fulminante was "starting to get some tough treatment and whatnot" from other inmates because of the rumor. Sarivola offered to protect Fulminante from his fellow inmates, but told him, "You have to tell me about it, you know. I mean, in other words, for me to give you any help." Fulminante then admitted to Sarivola that he had driven Jeneane to the desert on his motorcycle, where he choked her, sexually assaulted her, and made her beg for her life, before shooting her twice in the head.

Sarivola was released from prison in November 1983. Fulminante was released the following May, only to be arrested the next month for another weapons violation. In 1984, Fulminante was indicted in Arizona for the first-degree murder of Jeneane.

Prior to trial, Fulminante moved to suppress the statement he had given to Sarivola in prison, as well as a second confession he had given to Donna Sarivola, then Anthony Sarivola's fiancee and later his wife, following his May 1984 release from prison. He asserted that the confession to Sarivola was coerced, and that the second confession was the "fruit" of the first. [Both confessions were admitted. Fulminante was convicted of murder and sentenced to death. The Arizona Supreme Court at first held that the confession to Anthony Sarivola was coerced, but that the verdict could be upheld because the independent confession to Donna Sarivola was sufficient to prove the essential facts. On rehearing, the Arizona court held that the admission of a coerced confession required reversal regardless of the strength of the other evidence.]

* * * Because of differing views in the state and federal courts over whether the admission at trial of a coerced confession is subject to a harmless-error analysis, we granted the State's petition for certiorari. Although a majority of this Court finds that such a confession is subject to a harmless error analysis, for the reasons set forth below, we affirm the judgment of the Arizona court.

II

* * * Although the question is a close one, we agree with the Arizona Supreme Court's conclusion that Fulminante's confession was coerced. The Arizona Supreme Court found a credible threat of physical violence unless Fulminante confessed. Our cases have made clear that a finding of coercion need not depend upon actual violence by a government agent; a credible threat is sufficient. * * * As in Payne v. Arkansas, 356 U.S. 560 (1958), where the Court found that a confession was coerced because the interrogating police officer had promised that if the accused confessed, the officer would protect the accused from an angry mob outside the jailhouse door, so too here, the Arizona Supreme Court found that it was fear of physical violence, absent protection from his friend (and Government agent) Sarivola which motivated Fulminante to confess. Accepting the Arizona court's finding, permissible on this record, that there was a credible threat of physical violence, we agree with its conclusion that Fulminante's will was overborne in such a way as to render his confession the product of coercion.

III

Four of us, Justices Marshall, Blackmun, Stevens, and myself, would affirm the judgment of the Arizona Supreme Court on the ground that the harmless-error rule is inapplicable to erroneously admitted coerced confessions. We thus disagree with the Justices who have a contrary view. The majority today abandons what until now the Court has regarded as the axiomatic proposition that a defendant in a criminal case is deprived of due process of law if his conviction is founded, in whole or in part, upon an involuntary confession, without regard for the truth or falsity of the confession, and even though there is ample evidence aside from the confession to support the conviction. [Citations omitted] Today, a majority of the Court, without any justification, overrules this vast body of precedent without a word and in so doing dislodges one of the fundamental tenets of our criminal justice system. In extending to coerced confessions the harmless error rule of Chapman v. California, 386 U.S. 18 (1967), the majority declares that because the Court has applied that analysis to numerous other "trial errors," there is no reason that it should not apply to an error of this nature as well. The four of us remain convinced, however, that we should abide by our cases that have refused to apply the harmless error rule to coerced confessions, for a coerced confession is fundamentally different from other types of erroneously admitted evidence to which the rule has been applied. * * *

Chapman specifically noted three constitutional errors that could not be categorized as harmless error: using a coerced confession against a defendant in a criminal trial, depriving a defendant of counsel, and trying a defendant before a biased judge. The majority attempts to distinguish the use of a coerced confession from the other two errors listed in *Chapman* first by distorting the decision in *Payne,* and then by drawing a meaningless dichotomy between "trial errors" and "structural defects" in the trial process. Viewing *Payne* as merely rejecting a test whereby the admission of a coerced confession could stand if there were "sufficient evidence," other than the confession to support the conviction, the majority suggests that the Court in *Payne* might have reached a different result had it been considering a harmless error test. It is clear, though, that in *Payne* the Court recognized that regardless of the amount of other evidence, "the admission in evidence, over objection, of the coerced confession vitiates the judgment," because "where, as here, a coerced confession constitutes a part of the evidence before the jury and a general verdict is returned, no one can say what credit and weight the jury gave to the confession." The inability to assess its effect on a conviction causes the admission at trial of a coerced confession to defy analysis by harmless-error standards, just as certainly as do deprivation of counsel and trial before a biased judge.

The majority also attempts to distinguish "trial errors" which occur "during the presentation of the case to the jury," and which it deems susceptible to harmless error analysis, from "structural defects in the constitution of the trial mechanism," which the majority concedes cannot be so analyzed. This effort fails, for our jurisprudence on harmless error has not classified so neatly the errors at issue. For example, we have held susceptible to harmless error analysis the failure to instruct the jury on the presumption of innocence, Kentucky v. Whorton, 441 U.S. 786 (1979), while finding it impossible to analyze in terms of harmless error the failure to instruct a jury on the reasonable doubt standard, Jackson v. Virginia, 443 U.S. 307, 320, n. 14 (1979). These cases cannot be reconciled by labeling the former "trial error" and the latter not, for both concern the exact same stage in the trial proceedings. Rather, these cases can be reconciled only by considering the nature of the right at issue and the effect of an error upon the trial. A jury instruction on the presumption of innocence is not constitutionally required in every case to satisfy due process, because such an instruction merely offers an additional safeguard beyond that provided by the constitutionally required instruction on reasonable doubt. While it may be possible to analyze as harmless the omission of a presumption of innocence instruction when the required reasonable doubt instruction has been given, it is impossible to assess the effect on the jury of the omission of the more fundamental instruction on reasonable doubt. In addition, omission of a reasonable doubt instruction, though a "trial error," distorts the very structure of the trial because it creates the risk that the jury will convict the defendant even if the State has not met its required burden of proof.

These same concerns counsel against applying harmless error analysis to the admission of a coerced confession. A defendant's confession is "probably the most probative and damaging evidence that can be admitted against him," Cruz v. New York, 481 U.S. 186, 195 (1987) (WHITE, J., dissenting), so damaging that a jury should not be expected to ignore it even if told to do so, Bruton v. United States, 391 U.S. 123, 140 (1968) (WHITE, J., dissenting), and because in any event it is impossible to know what credit and weight the jury gave to the confession. Concededly, this reason is insufficient to justify a per se bar to the use of any confession. Thus, Milton v. Wainwright, 407 U.S. 371 (1972), applied harmless-error analysis to a confession obtained and introduced in circumstances that violated the defendant's Sixth Amendment right to counsel. Similarly, the Courts of Appeals have held that the introduction of incriminating statements taken from defendants in violation of Miranda v. Arizona, 384 U.S. 436 (1966), is subject to treatment as harmless error.

Nevertheless, in declaring that it is "impossible to create a meaningful distinction between confessions elicited in violation of the Sixth Amendment and those in violation of the Fourteenth Amendment," the majority overlooks the obvious. * * * First, some coerced confessions may be untrustworthy. Consequently, admission of coerced confessions may distort the truth-seeking function of the trial upon which the majority focuses. More importantly, however, the use of coerced confessions, "whether true or false," is forbidden "because the methods used to extract them offend an underlying principle in the enforcement of our criminal law: that ours is an accusatorial and not an inquisitorial system—a system in which the State must establish guilt by evidence independently and freely secured and may not by coercion prove its charge against an accused out of his own mouth," Rogers v. Richmond, 365 U.S., at 540–541. This reflects the "strongly felt attitude of our society that important human values are sacrificed where an agency of the government, in the course of securing a conviction, wrings a confession out of an accused against his will," Blackburn v. Alabama, 361 U.S., at 206–207, as well as "the deep-rooted feeling that the police must obey the law while enforcing the law; that in the end life and liberty can be as much endangered from illegal methods used to convict those thought to be criminals as from the actual criminals themselves," Spano, supra. Thus, permitting a coerced confession to be part of the evidence on which a jury is free to base its verdict of guilty is inconsistent with the thesis that ours is not an inquisitorial system of criminal justice.

As the majority concedes, there are other constitutional errors that invalidate a conviction even though there may be no reasonable doubt that the defendant is guilty and would be convicted absent the trial error. For example, a judge in a criminal trial is prohibited from entering a judgment of conviction or directing the jury to come forward with such a verdict, regardless of how overwhelmingly the evidence may point in that direction. A defendant is entitled to counsel at trial, and as *Chapman* recognized, violating this right can never be harmless error. See also White v. Maryland, 373 U.S. 59 (1963), where a conviction was set aside because the defendant had not had counsel at a preliminary hearing without regard to the showing of prejudice. In Vasquez v. Hillery, 474 U.S. 254 (1986), a defendant was found guilty beyond reasonable doubt, but the conviction had been set aside because of the unlawful exclusion of members of the defendant's race from the grand jury that indicted him, despite overwhelming evidence of his guilt. * * * *Vasquez*, like *Chapman*, also noted that rule of automatic reversal when a defendant is tried before a judge with a financial interest in the outcome, Tumey v. Ohio, 273 U.S. 510, 535 (1927), despite a lack of any indication that bias influenced the decision. Waller v. Georgia, 467 U.S. 39, 49 (1984), recognized that violation of the guarantee of a public trial required reversal without any showing of prejudice and even though the values of a public trial may be intangible and unprovable in any particular case. * * *

For the foregoing reasons the four of us would adhere to the consistent line of authority that has recognized as a basic tenet of our criminal justice system, before and after both *Miranda* and *Chapman*, the prohibition against using a defendant's coerced confession against him at his criminal trial. Stare decisis is of fundamental importance to the rule of law; the majority offers no convincing reason for overturning our long line of decisions requiring the exclusion of coerced confessions.

IV

Since five Justices have determined that harmless error analysis applies to coerced confessions, it becomes necessary to evaluate under that ruling the admissibility of Fulminante's confession to Sarivola. * * * While some statements by a defendant may concern isolated aspects of the crime or may be incriminating only when linked to other evidence, a full confession in which the defendant discloses the motive for and means of the crime may tempt the jury to rely upon that evidence alone in reaching its decision. In the case of a coerced confession such as that given by Fulminante to Sarivola, the risk that the confession is unreliable, coupled with the profound impact that the confession has upon the jury, requires a reviewing court to exercise extreme caution before determining that the admission of the confession at trial was harmless.

In the Arizona Supreme Court's initial opinion, in which it determined that harmless-error analysis could be applied to the confession, the court found that the admissible second confession to Donna Sarivola rendered the first confession to Anthony Sarivola cumulative. The court also noted that circumstantial physical evidence concerning the wounds, the ligature around Jeneane's neck, the location of the body, and the presence of motorcycle tracks at the scene corroborated the second confession. The court concluded that "due to the overwhelming evidence adduced from the second confession, if there had not been a first confession, the jury would still have had the same basic evidence to convict" Fulminante.

We have a quite different evaluation of the evidence. Our review of the record leads us to conclude that the State has failed to meet its burden of establishing, beyond a reasonable doubt, that the admission of Fulminante's confession to Anthony Sarivola was harmless error. Three considerations compel this result.

First, the transcript discloses that both the trial court and the State recognized that a successful prosecution depended on the jury believing the two confessions. Absent the confessions, it is unlikely that Fulminante would have been prosecuted at all, because the physical evidence from the scene and other circumstantial evidence would have been insufficient to convict. Indeed, no indictment was filed until nearly two years after the murder. Although the police had suspected Fulminante from the beginning, as the prosecutor acknowledged in his opening statement to the jury, "[W]hat brings us to Court, what makes this case fileable, and prosecutable and triable is that later, Mr. Fulminante confesses this crime to Anthony Sarivola and later, to Donna Sarivola, his wife." After trial began, during a renewed hearing on Fulminante's motion to suppress, the trial court opined, "You know, I think from what little I know about this trial, the character of this man [Sarivola] for truthfulness or untruthfulness and his credibility is the centerpiece of this case, is it not?," to which the prosecutor responded, "It's very important, there's no doubt." Finally, in his closing argument, the prosecutor prefaced his discussion of the two confessions by conceding, "We have a lot of circumstantial evidence that indicates that this is our suspect, this is the fellow that did it, but it's a little short as far as saying that it's proof that he actually put the gun to the girl's head and killed her. So it's a little short of that. We recognize that."

Second, the jury's assessment of the confession to Donna Sarivola could easily have depended in large part on the presence of the confession to Anthony Sarivola. Absent the admission at trial of the first confession, the jurors might have found Donna Sarivola's story unbelievable. Fulminante's confession to Donna Sarivola allegedly occurred in May 1984, on the day he was released from Ray Brook, as she and Anthony Sarivola drove Fulminante from New York to Pennsylvania.* Donna Sarivola testified that Fulminante, whom she had never before met, confessed in detail about Jeneane's brutal murder in response to her casual question concerning why he was going to visit friends in Pennsylvania instead of returning to his family in Arizona. Although she testified that she was "disgusted" by Fulminante's disclosures, she stated that she took no steps to notify authorities of what she had learned. In fact, she claimed that she barely discussed the matter with Anthony Sarivola, who was in the car and overheard Fulminante's entire conversation with Donna. Despite her disgust for Fulminante, Donna Sarivola later went on a second trip with him. Although Sarivola informed authorities that he had driven Fulminante to Pennsylvania, he did not mention Donna's presence in the car or her conversation with Fulminante. Only when questioned by authorities in June 1985 did Anthony Sarivola belatedly recall the confession to Donna more than a year before, and only then did he ask if she would be willing to discuss the matter with authorities. Although some of the details in the confession to Donna Sarivola were corroborated by circumstantial evidence, many, including details that Jeneane was choked and sexually assaulted, were not. As to other aspects of the second confession, including Fulminante's motive and state of mind, the only corroborating evidence was the first confession to Anthony Sarivola. Thus, contrary to what the Arizona Supreme Court found, it is clear that the jury might have believed that the two confessions reinforced and corroborated each other. For this reason, one confession was not merely cumulative of the other. While in some cases two confessions, delivered on different occasions to different listeners, might be viewed as being independent of each other, it strains credulity to think that the jury so viewed the two confessions in this case, especially given the close relationship between Donna and Anthony Sarivola.

* * * * The Arizona Supreme Court determined that the second confession, to Donna Sarivola was not the "fruit of the poisonous tree," because it was made six months after the confession to Sarivola; Fulminante's need for protection from Sarivola presumably had ended; and it took place in the course of a casual conversation with someone who was not an agent of the State. This aspect of the Arizona Supreme Court's decision is not challenged here.

The jurors could also have believed that Donna Sarivola had a motive to lie about the confession in order to assist her husband. Anthony Sarivola received significant benefits from federal authorities, including payment for information, immunity from prosecution, and eventual placement in the federal Witness Protection Program. In addition, the jury might have found Donna motivated by her own desire for favorable treatment, for she, too, was ultimately placed in the Witness Protection Program.

Third, the admission of the first confession led to the admission of other evidence prejudicial to Fulminante. For example, the State introduced evidence that Fulminante knew of Sarivola's connections with organized crime in an attempt to explain why Fulminante would have been motivated to confess to Sarivola in seeking protection. * * * Finally, although our concern here is with the effect of the erroneous admission of the confession on Fulminante's conviction, it is clear that the presence of the confession also influenced the sentencing phase of the trial. Under Arizona law, the trial judge is the sentencer. At the sentencing hearing, the admissibility of information regarding aggravating circumstances is governed by the rules of evidence applicable to criminal trials. In this case, "based upon admissible evidence produced at the trial," the judge found that only one aggravating circumstance existed beyond a reasonable doubt, i.e., that the murder was committed in "an especially heinous, cruel, and depraved manner." In reaching this conclusion, the judge relied heavily on evidence concerning the manner of the killing and Fulminante's motives and state of mind which could only be found in the two confessions. * * *

Because a majority of the Court has determined that Fulminante's confession to Anthony Sarivola was coerced and because a majority has determined that admitting this confession was not harmless beyond a reasonable doubt, we agree with the Arizona Supreme Court's conclusion that Fulminante is entitled to a new trial at which the confession is not admitted. Accordingly the judgment of the Arizona Supreme Court is

Affirmed.

JUSTICE KENNEDY, concurring in the judgment.

For the reasons stated by The Chief Justice, I agree that Fulminante's confession to Anthony Sarivola was not coerced. * * * Again for the reasons stated by The Chief Justice, I agree that harmless-error analysis should apply in the case of a coerced confession. That said, the court conducting a harmless-error inquiry must appreciate the indelible impact a full confession may have on the trier of fact, as distinguished, for instance, from the impact of an isolated statement that incriminates the defendant only when connected with other evidence. * * * For the reasons given by Justice White in Part IV of his opinion, I cannot with confidence find admission of Fulminante's confession to Anthony Sarivola to be harmless error.

The same majority of the Court does not agree on the three issues presented by the trial court's determination to admit Fulminante's first confession: whether the confession was inadmissible because coerced; whether harmless error analysis is appropriate; and if so whether any error was harmless here. My own view that the confession was not coerced does not command a majority. In the interests of providing a clear mandate to the Arizona Supreme Court in this capital case, I deem it proper to accept in the case now before us the holding of five Justices that the confession was coerced and inadmissible. I agree with a majority of the Court that admission of the confession could not be harmless error when viewed in light of all the other evidence; and so I concur in the judgment to affirm the ruling of the Arizona Supreme Court.

CHIEF JUSTICE REHNQUIST, with whom JUSTICE O'CONNOR joins, JUSTICE KENNEDY and JUSTICE SOUTER join as to Parts I and II, and JUSTICE SCALIA joins as to Parts II and III, delivering the opinion of the Court as to Part II, and dissenting as to Parts I and III.

The Court today properly concludes that the admission of an "involuntary" confession at trial is subject to harmless error analysis. Nonetheless, the independent review of the record which we are required to make shows that respondent Fulminante's confession was not in fact involuntary. And even if the confession were deemed to be involuntary, the evidence offered at trial, including a second, untainted confession by Fulminante, supports the conclusion that any error here was certainly harmless.

I

The question of whether Fulminante's confession was voluntary is one of federal law. * * * I am at a loss to see how the Supreme Court of Arizona reached the conclusion that it did. Fulminante offered no evidence that he believed that his life was in danger or that he confessed to Sarivola in order to obtain the proffered protection. * * * Since Fulminante was unaware that Sarivola was an FBI informant, there existed none of the danger of coercion resulting from the interaction of custody and official interrogation. * * * The conversations were not lengthy, and the defendant was free at all times to leave Sarivola's company. Sarivola at no time threatened him or demanded that he confess; he simply requested that he speak the truth about the matter. Fulminante was an experienced habitue of prisons, and presumably able to fend for himself. In concluding on these facts that Fulminante's confession was involuntary, the Court today embraces a more expansive definition of that term than is warranted by any of our decided cases.

II

Since this Court's landmark decision in Chapman v. California, 386 U.S. 18 (1967), in which we adopted the general rule that a constitutional error does not automatically require reversal of a conviction, the Court has applied harmless error analysis to a wide range of errors and has recognized that most constitutional errors can be harmless. [Citations] The common thread connecting these cases is that each involved "trial error"—error which occurred during the presentation of the case to the jury, and which may therefore be quantitatively assessed in the context of other evidence presented in order to determine whether its admission was harmless beyond a reasonable doubt. In applying harmless error analysis to these many different constitutional violations, the Court has been faithful to the belief that the harmless-error doctrine is essential to preserve the principle that the central purpose of a criminal trial is to decide the factual question of the defendant's guilt or innocence, and promotes public respect for the criminal process by focusing on the underlying fairness of the trial rather than on the virtually inevitable presence of immaterial error.

In *Chapman* the Court stated that "Although our prior cases have indicated that there are some constitutional rights so basic to a fair trial that their infraction can never be treated as harmless error, this statement in itself belies any belief that all trial errors which violate the Constitution automatically call for reversal." See, e.g., Payne v. Arkansas, 356 U.S. 560 (coerced confession); Gideon v. Wainwright, 372 U.S. 335 (right to counsel); Tumey v. Ohio, 273 U.S. 510 (impartial judge).

It is on the basis of this language in *Chapman* that Justice White in dissent concludes that the principle of stare decisis requires us to hold that an involuntary confession is not subject to harmless error analysis. I believe that there are several reasons which lead to a contrary conclusion. In the first place, the quoted language from *Chapman* does not by its terms adopt any such rule in that case. The language that "although our prior cases have indicated," coupled with the relegation of the cases themselves to a footnote, is more appropriately regarded as a historical reference to the holdings of these cases. This view is buttressed by an examination of the opinion in Payne v. Arkansas, 356 U.S. 560 (1958), which is the case referred to for the proposition that an involuntary confession may not be subject to harmless error analysis. There the Court said:

> "Respondent suggests that, apart from the confession, there was adequate evidence before the jury to sustain the verdict. But where, as here, an involuntary confession constitutes a part of the evidence before the jury and a general verdict is returned, no one can say what credit and weight the jury gave to the confession. And in these circumstances this Court has uniformly held that even though there may have been sufficient evidence, apart from the coerced confession, to support a judgment of conviction, the admission in evidence, over objection, of the coerced confession vitiates the judgment because it violates the Due Process Clause of the Fourteenth Amendment."

It is apparent that the State's argument which the Court rejected in *Payne* is not the harmless-error analysis later adopted in *Chapman,* but a much more lenient rule which would allow affirmance of a conviction if the evidence other than the involuntary confession was sufficient to sustain the verdict. This is confirmed by the dissent of Justice Clark in that case, which adopted the more lenient test. Such a test would, of course—unlike the harmless-error test—make the admission of an involuntary confession virtually risk-free for the state.

The admission of an involuntary confession—a classic "trial error"—is markedly different from the other two constitutional violations referred to in the *Chapman* footnote as not being subject to harmless-error analysis. One of those cases, Gideon v. Wainwright, 372 U.S. 335 (1963), involved the total deprivation of the right to counsel at trial. The other, Tumey v. Ohio, 273 U.S. 510 (1927), involved a judge who was not impartial. These are structural defects in the constitution of the trial mechanism, which defy analysis by "harmless-error" standards. The entire conduct of the trial from beginning to end is obviously affected by the absence of counsel for a criminal defendant, just as it is by the presence on the bench of a judge who is not impartial. Since our decision in *Chapman,* other cases have added to the category of constitutional errors which are not subject to harmless error the following: unlawful exclusion of members of the defendant's race from a grand jury, Vasquez v. Hillery, 474 U.S. 254 (1986); the right to self-representation at trial, McKaskle v. Wiggins, 465 U.S. 168 (1984); and the right to public trial, Waller v. Georgia, 467 U.S. 39 (1984). Each of these constitutional deprivations is a similar structural defect affecting the framework within which the trial proceeds, rather than simply an error in the trial process itself. * * *

The admission of an involuntary confession is a "trial error," similar in both degree and kind to the erroneous admission of other types of evidence. The evidentiary impact of an involuntary confession, and its effect upon the composition of the record, is indistinguishable from that of a confession obtained in violation of the Sixth Amendment, of evidence seized in violation of the Fourth Amendment, or of a prosecutor's improper comment on a defendant's silence at trial in violation of the Fifth Amendment. When reviewing the erroneous admission of an involuntary confession, the appellate court, as it does with the admission of other forms of improperly admitted evidence, simply reviews the remainder of the evidence against the defendant to determine whether the admission of the confession was harmless beyond a reasonable doubt. * * *

Of course an involuntary confession may have a more dramatic effect on the course of a trial than do other trial errors—in particular cases it may be devastating to a defendant—but this simply means that a reviewing court will conclude in such a case that its admission was not harmless error; it is not a reason for eschewing the harmless error test entirely. The Supreme Court of Arizona, in its first opinion in the present case, concluded that the admission of Fulminante's confession was harmless error. That court concluded that a second and more explicit confession of the crime made by Fulminante after he was released from prison was not tainted by the first confession, and that the second confession, together with physical evidence from the wounds (the victim had been shot twice in the head with a large calibre weapon at close range and a ligature was found around her neck) and other evidence introduced at trial rendered the admission of the first confession harmless beyond a reasonable doubt.

III

* * * This seems to me to be a classic case of harmless error: a second confession giving more details of the crime than the first was admitted in evidence and found to be free of any constitutional objection. Accordingly, I would affirm the holding of the Supreme Court of Arizona in its initial opinion, and reverse the judgment which it ultimately rendered in this case.

MILLER v. FENTON

United States Court of Appeals, Third Circuit, 1986.
796 F.2d 598, cert. denied, 479 U.S. 989, 107 S.Ct. 585, 93 L.Ed.2d 587 (1986).

BECKER, CIRCUIT JUDGE.

I. THE FACTUAL BACKGROUND

On August 13, 1973, seventeen-year-old Deborah Margolin was brutally murdered. According to her brothers, she was sitting on the porch of her home in rural East Amwell Township when a stranger approached in an automobile and informed her that a heifer was loose at the bottom of the driveway. Ms. Margolin drove alone in her brother's car to retrieve the heifer. She never returned. Later that day, her father found her mutilated body lying face down in a creek.

When the New Jersey State Police arrived at the scene, the victim's brothers gave them a description of the stranger who had driven up to the house and of the car he had driven, an old white car with the trunk tied shut and two dents in the side. One of the officers recalled that the petitioner, Miller, who lived nearby, drove a car that matched that description. Detective Boyce of the State Police confirmed the description of the car and also concluded that the description of the stranger fit Miller, who had been convicted in 1969 of carnal abuse and arrested in 1973 for statutory rape.

At about 10:50 p.m. that day, the state police questioned Miller at his place of employment, P.F.D. Plastics in Trenton. After a brief discussion, he agreed to accompany the officers to the police barracks for further questioning. At the barracks, Miller spent about seventy-five minutes waiting with Trooper Scott, during which time he was not questioned. He was then taken into an interrogation room by Detective Boyce and read his *Miranda* rights. Miller signed a *Miranda* card, thus waiving his *Miranda* rights, and Boyce's interrogation ensued. One hour into the interrogation, Miller confessed to the murder of Deborah Margolin, then passed out.

II. PROCEDURAL HISTORY

Miller was indicted for first-degree murder. Before his trial, he moved to suppress the confession as involuntary, but the state trial court denied the motion. After a trial at which the confession was received as evidence, Miller was convicted. On appeal of the conviction, a three-judge panel of the Appellate Division of the New Jersey Superior Court unanimously reversed, finding that Detective Boyce's technique in eliciting the confession had denied Miller due process of law. Characterizing Boyce's method of interrogation as "psychological pressure," the panel held that as a result of that pressure, Miller's confession had not been voluntary. In a 4–3 decision, the New Jersey Supreme Court reversed the Appellate Division and reinstated the conviction. Looking at the totality of the circumstances, the court held that Boyce's interrogation tactics had not over-borne Miller's will, and that the confession had indeed been voluntary and thus properly admissible into evidence.

Miller petitioned for a writ of habeas corpus in the United States District Court for the District of New Jersey. The petition was referred to a magistrate, who recommended that the writ be denied. The district court agreed, rejecting Miller's contention that Boyce's questioning created psychological pressure that rendered the confession involuntary. Miller thereupon appealed to this Court.

[We] held that under 28 U.S.C. § 2254(d), federal review of the state court's finding of voluntariness was deferential, limited to determining whether the state court had applied the proper legal test and whether the conclusion reached by the state court was supported by the record as a whole. Applying that standard, we upheld the determination that Miller's confession was voluntary. Although we noted in passing that even if our review on the question of voluntariness had been plenary, we would have reached the same result, we did not engage in any detailed analysis of the question of voluntariness under a plenary standard.

The United States Supreme Court granted *certiorari* and reversed. *Miller v. Fenton*, 106 S.Ct. 445 (1985). Stating that the issue of voluntariness is a legal, rather than a factual, question, the Court held that whether the challenged confession was voluntary is a matter for independent federal appellate determination. It remanded the case so that we might conduct a fuller analysis under the correct standard. We now engage in such an inquiry and conclude that Miller's confession was elicited in a manner compatible with the requirements of the Constitution.

III. THE INTERROGATION

At the outset of our analysis, it is essential that we review the salient features of the interrogation. Because the state police taped the interrogation, we have had an opportunity actually to hear Detective Boyce's questions and Miller's responses. A significant portion of the questioning was in the typical police interrogation mode, developing chronologically Miller's whereabouts on the day in question, confronting him with the identification of his car, asking him point-blank whether he committed the crime, challenging his answers, and attempting to discover the details of the crime. This element of the interrogation is unexceptionable and unchallenged. We shall therefore focus primarily on the features of the interrogation that are at issue.

It is clear that Boyce made no threats and engaged in no physical coercion of Miller. To the contrary, throughout the interview, Detective Boyce assumed a friendly, understanding manner and spoke in a soft tone of voice. He repeatedly assured Miller that he was sympathetic to him and wanted to help him unburden his mind. As the following excerpts demonstrate, the Detective's statements of sympathy at times approached the maudlin:

> Boyce: Now listen to me, Frank. This hurts me more than it hurts you, because I love people.

* * *

> Boyce: Let it come out, Frank. I'm here, I'm here with you now. I'm on your side, I'm on your side, Frank. I'm your brother, you and I are brothers, Frank. We are brothers, and I want to help my brother.

* * *

> Boyce: We have, we have a relationship, don't we? Have I been sincere with you, Frank?

Boyce also gave Miller certain factual information, some of which was untrue. At the beginning of the interrogation, for example, Boyce informed Miller that the victim was still alive; this was false. During the interview, Boyce told Miller that Ms. Margolin had just died, although in fact she had been found dead several hours earlier.

Detective Boyce's major theme throughout the interrogation was that whoever had committed such a heinous crime had mental problems and was desperately in need of psychological treatment. From early in the interview, Detective Boyce led Miller to understand that he believed that Miller had committed the crime and that Miller now needed a friend to whom he could unburden himself. The Detective stated several times that Miller was not a criminal who should be punished, but a sick individual who should receive help. He assured Miller that he (Detective Boyce) was sincerely understanding and that he wished to help him with his problem. The following excerpts from the transcript of the interrogation provide examples of the statements about Miller's having psychological problems, as well as of the assurances of help:

> Boyce: [L]et's forget this incident, [l]et's talk about your problem. This is what, this is what I'm concerned with, Frank, your problem.
>
> Miller: Right.
>
> Boyce: If I had a problem like your problem, I would want you to help me with my problem.
>
> Miller: Uh, huh.
>
> Boyce: Now, you know what I'm talking about.

Miller: Yeah.

Boyce: And I know, and I think that, uh, a lot of other people know. You know what I'm talking about. I don't think you're a criminal, Frank.

Miller: No, but you're trying to make me one.

Boyce: No I'm not, no I'm not, but I want you to talk to me so we can get this thing worked out.

* * *

Boyce: I want you to talk to me. I want you to tell me what you think. I want you to tell me how you think about this, what you think about this.

Miller: What I think about it?

Boyce: Yeah.

Miller: I think whoever did it really needs help.

Boyce: And that's what I think and that's what I know. They don't, they don't need punishment, right? Like you said, they need help.

Miller: Right.

Boyce: They don't need punishment. They need help, good medical help.

Miller: That's right.

Boyce: [T]o rectify their problem. Putting them in, in a prison isn't going to solve it, is it?

Miller: No, sir. I know, I was in there for three and a half years.

* * *

Boyce: You can see it Frank, you can feel it, you can feel it but you are not responsible. This is what I'm trying to tell you, but you've got to come forward and tell me. Don't, don't, don't let it eat you up, don't, don't fight it. You've got to rectify it, Frank. We've got to get together on this thing, or I, I mean really, you need help, you need proper help, and you know it, my God, you know, in God's name, you, you, you know it. You are not a criminal, you are not a criminal.

Boyce also appealed to Miller's conscience and described the importance of Miller's purging himself of the memories that must be haunting him. This aspect of the interrogation is exemplified in the preceding passage—"Don't, don't, don't let it eat you up, don't, don't fight it. You've got to rectify it, Frank." The following excerpts are representative of Boyce's arguments along this line:

Boyce: Frank, listen to me, honest to God, I'm, I'm telling you, Frank, (inaudible). I know, it's going to bother you, Frank, it's going to bother you. It's there, it's not going to go away, it's there. It's right in front of you, Frank. Am I right or wrong?

Miller: Yeah.

* * *

Boyce: Honest, Frank. It's got to come out. You can't leave it in. It's hard for you, I realize that, how hard it is, how difficult it is, I realize that, but you've got to help yourself before anybody else can help you.

* * *

Boyce: First thing we have to do is let it all come out. Don't fight it because it's worse, Frank, it's worse. It's hurting me because I feel it. I feel it wanting to come out, but it's hurting me, Frank.

* * *

Boyce: No, listen to me, Frank, please listen to me. The issue now is what happened. The issue now is truth. Truth is the issue now. You've got to believe this, and the truth prevails in the end, Frank. You have to believe that and I'm sincere when I'm saying it to you. You've got to be truthful with yourself.

* * *

Boyce: That's the most important thing, not, not what has happened, Frank. The fact that you were truthful, you came forward and you said, look I have a problem. I didn't mean to do what I did. I have a problem, this is what's important, Frank. This is very important, I got, I, I got to get closer to you, Frank, I got to make you believe this and I'm, and I'm sincere when I tell you this. You got to tell me exactly what happened, Frank. That's very important. I know how you feel inside, Frank, it's eating you up, am I right? It's eating you up, Frank. You've got to come forward. You've got to do it for yourself, for your family, for your father, this is what's important, the truth, Frank.

When Miller at last confessed, he collapsed in a state of shock. He slid off his chair and onto the floor with a blank stare on his face. The police officers sent for a first aid squad that took him to the hospital.

IV. THE VOLUNTARINESS OF THE CONFESSION

The sole question before this Court is whether Miller's confession was voluntary. Miller contends that Detective Boyce's method of interrogation constituted psychological manipulation of such magnitude that it rendered his confession involuntary. The government counters that Miller's confession was voluntary and hence properly admissible.

A. *The Legal Test of Voluntariness*

It is well established that an involuntary confession may result from psychological, as well as physical, coercion. * * *

We emphasize that the test for voluntariness is not a but-for test: we do not ask whether the confession would have been made in the absence of the interrogation. Few criminals feel impelled to confess to the police purely of their own accord, without any questioning at all. * * *

Moreover, it is generally recognized that the police may use some psychological tactics in eliciting a statement from a suspect. *See Haynes v. Washington*, 373 U.S. at 514–15. For example, the interrogator may play on the suspect's sympathies or explain that honesty might be the best policy for a criminal who hopes for leniency from the state, *see Rachlin v. United States, supra*, 723 F.2d at 1378 (agents may have told suspect that it was in his best interest to cooperate, but resulting confession was voluntary); *United States v. Vera*, 701 F.2d 1349, 1363–64 (11th Cir.1983) (agent told suspect that he could help himself by cooperating, but resulting confession was voluntary). These ploys may play a part in the suspect's decision to confess, but so long as that decision is a product of the suspect's own balancing of competing considerations, the confession is voluntary. The question we must answer, then, is not whether Detective Boyce's statements were the cause of Miller's confession—indeed, we assume that to be the case—but whether those statements were so manipulative or coercive that they deprived Miller of his ability to make an unconstrained, autonomous decision to confess. To that inquiry we now turn.

B. The Circumstances of the Miller Interrogation

A "totality of the circumstances" inquiry defies strictly analytic treatment. We cannot reach a conclusion simply by scrutinizing each circumstance separately, for the concept underlying the phrase "totality of the circumstances" is that the whole is somehow distinct from the sum of the parts. Nevertheless, we can understand the totality only after reviewing the constituent elements of the situation. We shall therefore discuss each relevant circumstance of the interrogation before addressing the question whether all of the circumstances, taken together, indicate that Miller's confession was voluntary.*

* Judge Gibbons argues in dissent that "the interrogation of Miller has no purpose other than obtaining admissions that could be used to charge Miller with felony murder," and that, apparently as a matter of law, "such an interrogation requires the closest scrutiny." The factual premise of this argument is stated at page 568:

Thus the police did not need to conduct an interrogation directed at investigating the murder—it was already solved so far as they were concerned.

Hence, the dissent concludes, there was a "complete absence of any legitimate investigative purpose for the interrogation."

This line of argument, never advanced by Miller's able counsel, is flawed. First, the evidence that the police already had—principally the description given by Ms. Margolin's brothers of an automobile just like Miller's and of a person generally fitting Miller's characteristics whom one of the brothers had seen shortly before the homicide—was *not* enough to solve the crime. Indeed, Judge Gibbons himself stresses the inconclusiveness of this evidence at a later point in the opinion. Neither a lineup nor the development of evidence undermining Miller's alibi would necessarily have filled the gap.

Second, the dissent implies that the interrogation would have been inappropriate as a matter of law even if it had been conducted according to Hoyle. We disagree. It is well settled that interrogation is a legitimate police investigative tool which the police have a right to pursue no matter how strong the other evidence of a suspect's guilt may be. It is obviously desirable for the police to get as much exact information as they can in any criminal case, and especially in a first-degree murder case, so as to

1. *Miller's Background*

Miller is a mature adult, thirty-two years of age. He is of normal intelligence and has some high school education. Such a person is more resistant to interrogation than a person who is very young, uneducated or weak-minded. * * *

Moreover, Miller had had previous experience with the criminal system; indeed, he had served a jail sentence. Thus, he was aware of the consequences of confessing. In addition to this experience, he received *Miranda* warnings. * * *

2. *The Length of the Interrogation*

Detective Boyce's interrogation of Miller lasted less than an hour. It was not "a process of interrogation * * * so prolonged and unremitting, especially when accompanied by deprivation of refreshment, rest or relief, as to accomplish extortion of an involuntary confession." *Stein v. New York*, 346 U.S. at 184. It is thus distinguishable from the lengthy interrogations during incommunicado detention that have been held to result in involuntary confessions. * * *

3. *Boyce's Friendly Approach*

Boyce's supportive, encouraging manner was an interrogation tactic aimed at winning Miller's trust and making him feel comfortable about confessing. Excessive friendliness on the part of an interrogator can be deceptive. In some instances, in combination with other tactics, it might create an atmosphere in which a suspect forgets that his questioner is in an adversarial role, and thereby prompt admissions that the suspect would ordinarily make only to a friend, not to the police.

Nevertheless, the "good guy" approach is recognized as a permissible interrogation tactic. Moreover, the Supreme Court has indicated that a sympathetic attitude on the part of the interrogator is not in itself enough to render a confession involuntary. * * * Only if other aspects of the interrogation strengthened the illusion that it was non-adversarial in character could Miller's confession have been involuntary because of psychological coercion.

4. *Boyce's Lie*

While a lie told to the detainee about an important aspect of the case may affect the voluntariness of the confession, the effect of the lie must be analyzed in the context of all the circumstances of the interrogation. *See e.g., Frazier v. Cupp*, 394 U.S. at 737, 739 (false statement by police officer that detainee's cousin had confessed, while relevant to issue of voluntariness, was insufficient to make otherwise voluntary confession inadmissible). We do not believe that the lie about the time of Ms. Margolin's death, by itself, constituted sufficient trickery to overcome Miller's will. Because Boyce never suggested that the time of Ms.

reduce to an absolute minimum the possibility that an innocent person will be convicted. Indeed we have found no support for the dissent's novel suggestion that even if the police have conclusive evidence of the identity of an offender, it is improper to interrogate him.

Margolin's death might be relevant in linking Miller to the crime, the only possible effect of Boyce's initial statement that she was alive, followed by his report that she had just died, would be an emotional response in Miller. The drama of the announcement of the victim's death might have prompted particularly acute feelings in Miller, which could have helped to induce his confession. However, the record suggests that this emotional reaction did not occur, for it appears that Miller was not affected at all by the news of the death. Indeed, he remained quite impassive. We therefore conclude that any pathos or remorse he might have felt was not particularly strong.

5. Boyce's Promises

Detective Boyce's statements that Miller was not a criminal, but rather a mentally ill individual not responsible for his actions, and Boyce's promises to help Miller raise a more serious question about the voluntariness of Miller's confession. By telling Miller that he was not responsible for anything he might have done, Boyce may have been understood to be making an implied promise to Miller that Miller would not be prosecuted, or that if he were prosecuted Boyce would aid him in presenting the insanity defense. Similarly, the promises of psychiatric help might have suggested to Miller that he would be treated, rather than prosecuted. If these promises, implicit and explicit, tricked Miller into confessing, his confession may have been involuntary. To determine whether Boyce's promises affected the voluntariness of Miller's confession, we must consider how manipulative these tactics in fact were.

a. The Rule Respecting Promises Made During Interrogation

In *Bram v. United States*, 168 U.S. 532 (1897), the Supreme Court endorsed the view that to be voluntary, a confession must not have been " 'extracted by any sort of threats or violence, *nor obtained by any direct or implied promises, however slight.* ' "Although the *Bram* test has been reaffirmed in *Hutto v. Ross*, 429 U.S. 28, 30 (1976) (per curiam), it has not been interpreted as a *per se* proscription against promises made during interrogation. Nor does the Supreme Court even use a but-for test when promises have been made during an interrogation, despite the seemingly plain meaning of the *Bram* rule. Rather, the Court had indicated that it does not matter that the accused confessed because of the promise, so long as the promise did not overbear his will. *See Hutto v. Ross, supra*, 429 U.S. at 30. Apparently, the words "obtained by * * * promises" in the *Bram* test have been read to mean "obtained because the suspect's will was overborne by * * * promises." In other words, promises do not trigger an analysis different from the totality of the circumstances test. * * *

b. The Promises Made to Miller

Detective Boyce's tone of voice and his frequent repetition of assurances may have lent credibility to his implied promise that Miller would not be prosecuted. However, Miller had been given *Miranda* warnings, which included the admonition that anything that Miller said could be used against him. Thus, when the interrogation began, Miller knew that if he confessed to the Margolin murder he could be prosecuted. * * * Indeed, Detective Boyce's statements that Miller was "not a criminal" need not be understood as assurances of leniency at all. Since the Detective's interrogation strategy was to present himself as a friend to whom Miller could unburden himself, he of course attempted throughout the interview to persuade Miller to trust him and confide in him. The statements at issue can be viewed as a means of convincing Miller that Boyce was sympathetic, no matter what the state's reaction might be. "You are not responsible" and "You are not a criminal" thus would mean "In my eyes, you are not responsible or a criminal and therefore you should relieve your conscience by talking to me, who understands you."

While such a statement might have made Miller feel more comfortable about speaking to Boyce, it would not render his confession the product of a mistaken belief that the state would grant him leniency. Detective Boyce never stated that anyone but he thought that Miller was "not a criminal," nor did he state that he had any authority to affect the charges brought against Miller. * * *

With regard to the psychiatric help, on the other hand, Boyce did make some outright promises. For example, he said, "[W]e're going to see to it that you get the proper help. This is our job, Frank." Such a promise could be quite compelling in itself and could also strengthen the implications that Miller might not be prosecuted at all.

A distinction can be drawn, however, between promises of leniency in the imminent criminal proceedings against the defendant and promises of help with some collateral problem. In *Bram, supra*, there was an implied promise that the defendant would not be prosecuted if he confessed.*

The promises of help to Miller fall somewhere between promises relating to purely collateral issues and promises of leniency in the immediate criminal proceedings against Miller, for help with the "problem" might be interpreted to mean commitment to a psychiatric hospital in lieu of imprisonment. Indeed, in combination with the statements that Miller was "not responsible," it could be interpreted to mean that there would be no prosecution of Miller. However, taking all these statements together, there is at most an implication that Miller will be treated leniently in the impending criminal proceedings. Boyce made no direct promise of such leniency; the only outright promise he made was to get Miller help with his psychological problem. As we have stated above, indirect promises do not have the potency of direct promises. * * *

Moreover, throughout the interview, Miller made remarks that indicate that he knew that this was an ordinary police interrogation, rather than an encounter with a compassionate friend, and that he was

---

* The detective informed the accused that another person had seen him commit the murder, and that he should tell the detective if he had an accomplice in order to avoid having "the blame of this horrible crime on your own shoulders." The Court interpreted the second statement as an offer of a benefit.

aware that a confession would result in criminal prosecution and possibly in conviction and sentence. Throughout the session, he appears to have retained a suspicious, guarded attitude. * * *

Indeed, from the tape of the interrogation, it clearly appears that the precipitating cause of Miller's confession was a desire to make a clean breast of it, rather than a reliance on any promises of leniency or psychiatric help. He expressed the reservation that "this is going to kill my father." Thereupon, Detective Boyce made a speech about the importance of truthfulness both for himself and his family. Miller capitulated immediately thereafter. Apparently, he took Boyce's words to heart and decided that it would be better for all concerned if he told the truth.** * * *

Detective Boyce's method of interrogation might have overborne the will of another detainee, for example, a young, inexperienced person of lower intelligence than Miller, or a person suffering from a painful physical ailment. It might have overcome the will of Miller himself if the interrogation had been longer or if Miller had been refused food, sleep, or contact with a person he wished to see. Moreover, if Miller had made remarks that indicated that he truly believed that the state would treat him leniently because he was "not responsible" for what he had done or that he believed that he would receive psychiatric help rather than punishment, we might not find the confession voluntary. We hold simply that, under the totality of the circumstances of this case, the confession was voluntarily given. * * *

The judgment of the district court will be affirmed.

GIBBONS, CIRCUIT JUDGE, dissenting:

* * *

[The dissent quoted Justice Frankfurter's famous lines from Watts v. Indiana, (footnote 1 on p. 393, supra) and took vigorous issue with the majority's statement (pp. 583–585) that questioning "in the typical police interrogation mode * * * is unexceptionable."]

I do not mean to suggest that an interrogation is never a legitimate tool of investigation. However, I do suggest, contrary to the majority, that an interrogation that has no investigative purpose and is used only as a means of obtaining a confession, is anything but unexceptional. In this case the interrogation of Miller had no purpose other than obtaining admissions that could be used to charge Miller with felony murder. Such an interrogation requires the closest scrutiny.

When Boyce commenced the second interrogation, the state police had in their possession his unique automobile, which had been sufficiently described by Ms. Margolin's brothers that it promptly led them to Miller. They had already determined the hours of Miller's factory shift

---

** The dissent states that we do not make much of Miller's collapse. However, we recognize the possibility that the human psyche, upon being released from the terrible burden of concealing such a heinous crime, might well react just as Miller's did after a confession.

and thus knew that he was not at work during the critical time period. They had already interrogated him about his whereabouts during the critical time period and learned about a claimed alibi at the Ringoes, New Jersey Post Office, which could easily be checked upon in the morning. They knew from his past record that he was a sexually disturbed person. They knew that one of Ms. Margolin's brothers had seen someone generally fitting Miller's description shortly before the homicide and could in all likelihood identify him. They could reasonably anticipate that an examination of Miller's automobile would produce evidence linking him to Ms. Margolin's death because the car contained fresh blood stains. They had no other suspects.

Thus the police did not need to conduct an interrogation directed at investigating the murder; it was already solved so far as they were concerned. The police could have, but did not, place Miller in a lineup so he could be identified as the person who spoke to Ms. Margolin. They could have, but did not, attempt to locate other witnesses who might have placed Miller near the scene of the crime. They could have, but did not, attempt to find witnesses who would undercut Miller's story about being at the Ringoes Post Office. Instead, the police conducted an interrogation directed at obtaining a confession from the sole suspect, and that interrogation was designed to assure Miller's prosecution for felony murder rather than a lesser offense.

For me, although obviously not for the majority, the most significant circumstance in this case supporting the conclusion that Miller's admission was obtained in a manner inconsistent with the Constitution is the complete absence of any legitimate investigative purpose for the interrogation. The circumstances of this case provide a classic illustration of the once common practice of obtaining guilty pleas in the back rooms of police stations rather than in open court. Moreover, the evidence of the method of interrogation must be examined in light of Officer Boyce's sole purpose—the obtaining of admissions of guilt, not the solution of a crime which Boyce believed to be solved already.

Keeping in mind that obtaining a confession, not investigating a crime, was Officer Boyce's sole purpose in conducting the interrogation, I turn to the methods he employed. The majority notes that Boyce "made no threats and engaged in no physical coercion of Miller." That statement is true only in the sense that Boyce did not physically beat Miller. It is intended, however, to divert attention from the fact that the setting was inherently coercive. Miller was apprehended at his place of work late at night, interrogated there for nearly an hour, and then taken to a police barracks. He was kept in isolation under guard until Boyce's interrogation began. Boyce could have postponed the interrogation until Miller, who had just finished a factory shift, obtained a night's sleep. Instead he commenced the interrogation at 1:47 A.M. for the obvious purpose of maximizing the impact of the inherently coercive environment in which Miller found himself.

The majority stresses that Boyce "repeatedly assured Miller that he was sympathetic to him and wanted to help him unburden his mind." Admittedly, Boyce did feign sympathy for Miller, but clearly unburdening Miller's mind was not Boyce's purpose. The repeated assurances, the friendly, understanding manner, and the soft tone of voice to which the majority makes reference were all directed to a single purpose—making an unwilling defendant admit his guilt. Referring to the detective's statement of sympathy as "maudlin" is deceptive. Every word, every nuance of expression, every change in tone of voice, was calculated toward one end, and one end only—obtaining an admission of guilt. From the tone of the majority opinion one might believe that its author actually credits these deceptive expressions of sympathy. But as the majority well knows the state police are not in the business of acting as religious or psychiatric counselors. Boyce was not sympathetic. He was no more interested in helping Miller "unburden his inner tensions," than he was in any other aspect of Miller's health. Instead Boyce was determined and ultimately successful in obtaining from an unwilling defendant the one thing that was his purpose—a confession.

Annexed to this opinion as an appendix is a transcript of Boyce's interrogation. Keeping Boyce's singular purpose in mind, that transcription conveys an entirely different effect than the majority attributes to the interrogation in its abridged account. The impression conveyed by the tape recording is even more compelling. * * *

[The dissent's thorough analysis of the transcript of the interrogation is greatly abridged here. The complete opinion is recommended reading, however.]

Once Miller made the blunder of placing himself in the victim's company, Boyce quickly pressed his advantage. Miller at first attempted to concoct a childishly implausible story about witnessing an attack by a stranger. Boyce continued with the psychological ploy of promising assistance, saying, "Let it come out, Frank, I'm here, I'm here with you now. I'm on your side, I'm on your side, Frank. I'm your brother, you and I are brothers Frank. We are brothers, and I want to help my brother." * * *

By the thirty-fifth minute of the interrogation Boyce had an admission from Miller that Ms. Margolin's body had been in his car, but Miller still persisted in his denial that he had killed her. At that point Boyce shifted to a new tactic, suggesting for the first time that the homicide may have been an accident, and thereby suggesting to Miller another way in which Boyce could help him. * * *

BOYCE: * * * You've got to do it for yourself, for your family, for your father, this is what's important the truth, Frank. Just tell me. You didn't mean to kill her did you?

* * *

BOYCE: What made you do this, please tell me. Please tell me now. What made you do this?

MILLER: I don't know.

Miller's response, "I don't know," forty-two minutes into the interrogation, was the first statement that could be construed as an admission that he had slashed Ms. Margolin's throat. At that point the tone of the interrogation immediately changed. Although Boyce twice more repeated that "you've got to get the proper help, Frank," and "I just want you to come out and tell me, so I can help you, that's all," the interrogation became quite crisp and specific. Once Miller was broken, Boyce's interrogation was carefully designed to elicit evidence that would support a charge that the homicide took place during an attempted rape; a charge that in New Jersey amounts to felony murder. The last eleven minutes of the interrogation is strikingly different from what went before. Miller, who until the critical admission thirty minutes into the interrogation had successfully resisted admitting being with Ms. Margolin, and who for the next twelve minutes continued to maintain he did not kill her, was led like an automaton through a series of admissions that totally incriminated him. The difference in the tone of the interrogation, during the last eleven minutes, of which the majority takes no notice, indicates that Miller's will to resist self-incrimination had been overborne. * * *

Incredibly, the only reference in the majority's opinion to Miller's collapse is the cryptic sentence at the end of Part I: "One hour into the interrogation, Miller confessed to the murder of Deborah Margolin, then passed out." The majority does not even recognize Miller's collapse into a catatonic state and his transportation to a hospital as relevant circumstances in its totality of the circumstances analysis! This most telling of all indications as to the effect on Miller of Boyce's tactics is simply ignored. Instead the majority opinion perversely reasons that Boyce's manner and statements may have stirred in Miller the urge to confess, "but, in our view, they did not produce psychological pressure strong enough to overbear the will of a mature, experienced man, who was suffering from no mental or physical illness. * * * " The reasoning is perverse because it ignores the fact that at the end of the interrogation Miller collapsed and was taken to a hospital. How can it be honestly represented that he was suffering from no mental or physical illness? And, unless the majority identifies some other reason for Miller's abrupt abandonment of his self-interested denials of guilt than the psychological coercion exercised by Boyce, what other cause is left?

* * *

It has long been established that confessions obtained by virtue of even implied promises of leniency are deemed to be inadmissible. *See Bram v. United States* [p. 451 of this book] (1897). The majority attempts to undercut the authority of the *Bram* rule by suggesting that it is no longer interpreted as a *per se* proscription against promises made during interrogations. The two Supreme Court cases cited in support of that proposition do not sustain it. Both cases state that promises made to a defendant in the presence of the defendant's attorney do not suffer from the same vice as promises made in the secrecy of police interrogation rooms. * * *

The majority emphasizes that the key issue is whether, in the totality of the circumstances, Miller's will was overborne. While I agree with the majority's general focus, I disagree with the majority's method of analysis. In ascertaining the effects of Boyce's interrogation tactics on Miller, the majority attempts to place itself in Miller's position and thereby evaluate the impact of Boyce's promises and lies. Unfortunately, we cannot know what effects those promises and lies had on Miller's will. Instead what we can know is that when, as in this case, the record reveals a series of repeated promises of psychological help and assurances that the suspect will not be punished, *Bram* requires as a matter of law that we hold the resulting confession to be coerced. Any other rule leads to the kind of subjective speculation that the majority engages in. Thus applying the *Bram* rule within the totality of the circumstances of Miller's interrogation, the confession used to commit Miller must be declared inadmissible as a violation of Miller's fifth amendment right to remain silent.

Note

Some state courts are more likely than the federal courts to find incriminating statements obtained by deception to be involuntary.

In State v. Ritter, 268 Ga. 108, 485 S.E.2d 492 (1997), the officer interrogating a murder suspect told him falsely that the victim (who had died) was recovering and would live. The Georgia Supreme Court treated the misrepresentation as equivalent to a false promise of leniency, and unanimously held that the resulting confession was coerced. In the court's words, "Detective Cox's representation regarding the victim's state of health constituted an implied promise that Ritter could not be charged with murder if he gave a statement to the police, but could only be charged with aggravated assault on a victim who was represented to be not only still alive but actively recovering and suffering from nothing more than a bad headache. Given Detective Cox's testimony that the representations were made to induce Ritter to speak based on the detective's assessment that Ritter would invoke his right to remain silent if he knew the full extent of the charges against him, the evidence supports the conclusion that Ritter was induced to talk to the police under the belief that he was incriminating himself only in regard to an aggravated assault charge and thus his confession was based upon the hope that he faced a lighter possible criminal penalty than he actually was facing."

In Voltaire v. State, 697 So.2d 1002 (Fla.App.1997) an undercover officer arrested the defendant for a drug sale, and then had himself placed in the same jail cell, as an apparent arrestee. (Why the defendant did not recognize the officer who had arrested him is not explained.) The officer then engaged the defendant in a brief conversation and obtained an incriminating statement. The Florida court held that this "gross deception" violated defendant's due process rights and that the statement was therefore involuntary.

PEOPLE v. ADAMS

California Court of Appeal, Fifth District, 1983.
143 Cal.App.3d 970, 192 Cal.Rptr. 290.

PAULINE DAVIS HANSON, ASSOCIATE JUSTICE.

Appellant, convicted by a jury of the first degree murder of her friend and lover, contends that crucial admissions were obtained from her through impermissibly coercive police tactics and that the use of these statements and their fruits was prejudicial.

[Appellant Nancy Adams was in a van with her friend and lover Jerry Pollock when Pollock was shot and killed. She initially claimed that she and Jerry were to be married the next day, and that they had been waiting to meet a woman who was going to show them a house when they were set upon by mysterious attackers who killed Jerry. During the investigation, she re-enacted the crime on videotape with police officers to demonstrate how it had happened. Because some of the physical evidence was inconsistent with her story and the video re-enactment, the investigating officers determined that she was a suspect and questioned her after advising her of her *Miranda* rights and obtaining a waiver. At this point, the county sheriff, who knew appellant personally and attended the same church that she did, decided to speak to her.]

MARCH 6TH STATEMENT

The interview with the sheriff was the subject of an extensive pretrial suppression hearing before Judge Rosson in Kings County. The sheriff testified that he first inquired whether appellant had in mind her *Miranda* rights; appellant indicated that she did. The sheriff then told appellant that he personally did not believe her story based upon his understanding of the physical evidence and appellant's behavior, specifically, her reluctance to look the sheriff in the eye and her failure to voice her innocence adamantly. Appellant again denied any responsibility for the shooting.

The sheriff suggested to appellant she was having a difficult time telling the truth because of their prior relationship through the church. The sheriff said he knew appellant professed to be a Christian and this might have caused her some embarrassment. He assured appellant that if she admitted the shooting of the victim, he would not be judgmental or think of her as less than a Christian or as "something ugly." He further stated that if she told the truth, he would have much respect for her courage. The sheriff told appellant that he was personally interested in being patient and listening to her tell the truth. He said there was accountability attached to her actions, that appellant knew this as a Christian, and should she continue to deny accountability for what he believed she had done, she would continue to have problems in experiencing more guilt. The sheriff knew that appellant was suffering from nervousness and was having difficulty sleeping.

The sheriff then referred specifically to the first chapter of Romans from the Bible, indicating that "God is a merciful God" and interested in people's lives, and accordingly has given man "a set of rules and regulations to guide us in our human government and personal living habits." He explained that the Bible states that if an individual chooses to disregard those rules by refusing to submit to them, God will cause that individual "to just go their own way." In other words, God would turn his back on that individual who would become a "reprobate who can no longer distinguish between right and wrong." In this connection, the sheriff referred to "living with somebody that wasn't your husband * * *." He suggested that if appellant continued to pursue her course of action by denying culpability for the homicide, she was capable of experiencing the moral isolation and abandonment described in the Book of Romans.

The sheriff further stated that people who stopped living according to God's law are bound to suffer some form of discipline. He referred to a book by Jay Adams, a minister, entitled Competent to Counsel, which includes a description of a young woman in a mental institution. Adams' thesis as explained by the sheriff is that the woman, diagnosed as a catatonic schizophrenic, was not mentally ill, but was suffering from a "sin factor" arising from guilt over an adulterous relationship. The woman was consumed by guilt because she was not living according to God's rules and God had begun to deal with her. The sheriff told appellant that he believed her situation correlated with the woman described in the book. He further advised appellant that he believed she was a candidate for a nervous breakdown because she was not telling the truth.

During the course of this discussion, the sheriff and detective sergeant told appellant that they did not believe the victim intended to marry her; that all indications were he had no intention of marrying her and that he used her to enjoy a physical relationship. The sheriff admitted that he suggested that Pollock might have attempted suicide, although there was no evidence whatsoever to support this theory.

> "I was looking for something that would cause her to start to tell the story that would go along with the evidence that we knew existed. * * * I simply suggested that, I guess, because there wasn't really much else to say that would encourage her to tell the truth."

At that point, appellant for the first time indicated that her story might not be true, but stated that she did not want to spend the rest of her life in jail. The sheriff responded that no one present in the room could tell her how much time she would spend in jail, only a judge could make that determination as a result of hearing the evidence. However, the sheriff did state that in some instances people spent as few as "four to seven years" in jail as a result of killing another person.

The detective sergeant testified that at one point he told appellant that "if it was hard for her to think that she had actually shot him, make it easier on herself by saying the gun had done the actual shooting rather than herself."

Appellant then admitted for the first time that she shot the victim and disposed of the gun. She said that the victim had become distraught over his divorce and the loss of his little girl and pulled the gun from under the seat of the van. Appellant said that the gun went off when she struggled with the victim to keep him from pointing it toward himself. When the victim got out of the van, appellant tried to empty the gun by shooting the bullets into the air. Appellant admitted that she concealed the gun in her purse and then in her bedroom, and threw it in a canal the next day. Appellant also admitted that the stranger-assailant story was a lie made up because appellant was "afraid you guys wouldn't believe me."

At approximately 4 p.m., appellant went with the officers to a canal on Java Avenue where the gun was recovered. They returned to the sheriff's office and a court-reported statement was taken beginning at 5:45 p.m. and ending at 6:15 p.m. This statement also was read into the record at trial over defense objection and contains the admissions noted above. Under this version of events, appellant maintained that the shooting was a complete accident and the gun was placed in the van by Pollock. Appellant then was asked if she would take a polygraph examination. Appellant agreed to do so and wished to take it immediately; however, because the officers were unable to locate a polygraphist that evening, appellant agreed to appear for the examination on Monday, March 10, 1980, in Fresno. The officers provided appellant with food which she was unable to eat; she was allowed to go home.

March 10 Statement

On March 10, 1980, appellant appeared at approximately 3:30 p.m. at the Fresno Police Department for the polygraph examination. An officer of the Fresno Police Department advised appellant of her constitutional rights and obtained oral and written waivers; he then administered the polygraph test, asking four questions based on appellant's most recent statement. The questions were: "Did Mrs. Dunlap tell you to meet her on 19th Avenue?" "Did you shoot Jerry on purpose?"; "Did you ever see that gun in Jerry's apartment?"; "Do you know how that gun got into the van?"

Appellant first repeated her story that she and the victim were at the intersection to meet Mrs. Dunlap, and denied shooting the victim intentionally, seeing the gun in his apartment, or knowing how it got into his van. After appellant repeated these responses several times, the officer confronted her with the results of the polygraph, which indicated that she was being deceptive. Eventually appellant said she was lying and changed her story. The officer testified that appellant then admitted that she shot the victim intentionally.

At that point, because the officer knew appellant was changing her story, he took her to an interrogation room containing a concealed recording device and continued the conversation. Appellant admitted that she met no woman at the mall, there was no rental house, and that she made up the story in order to get the victim into the country to talk with him. Appellant said that Pollock had asked her to marry him, but told her the day he was shot he was "having second thoughts." She admitted she took the gun from the victim's dresser, put it in her purse, and brought it with her when she and the victim met. She picked up the gun and tried to scare Pollock; it went off when he started shaking her. Appellant said she had both hands on the gun and squeezed the trigger; however, she insisted that she did not intend to shoot him, saying, "[I]t went off so easy."

The entire March 10 taped statement was played to the jury at trial. Defense counsel objected to the March 10 statement and all other statements made after March 6, 1980, as fruit of the poisonous tree. At the close of the March 10 statement, appellant was arrested for "suspicion of homicide."

Dr. Charles A. Davis, a physician and psychiatrist, interviewed appellant at the request of law enforcement at 7:15 a.m. on March 11, 1980; it was the morning after the taking of the damaging March 10 taped statement. Appellant was hospitalized for asthma and was receiving an intravenous drip and oxygen when Davis saw her; she had received medication the night before. Appellant appeared to be oriented and coherent and gave a statement about the killing similar to that of the previous evening.

The jury was instructed on excusable homicide committed by accident and misfortune, voluntary manslaughter committed upon a sudden quarrel or heat of passion, involuntary manslaughter, and both degrees of murder. After approximately three hours of deliberation, the jury returned its verdict finding appellant guilty of first degree murder.

DISCUSSION

* * *

Appellant testified that when she saw the sheriff on March 6, she was very glad because she regarded him as a friend. The sheriff told her about the woman in Jay Adams' book who was in a mental institution from guilt feelings because she had sinned by living with a man not her husband. The sheriff then said appellant's case was similar; appellant said she felt "very bad" about this and feared a similar fate. Appellant testified that she considered herself a sinner at that time because she had been living with Pollock; she changed her story because of fear of going to a mental institution and fear of "[e]ternal damnation." She did not believe the sheriff had the power to condemn her to eternal damnation, "but God certainly does." Appellant had not been threatened with physical harm at any time by any of the officers. The sheriff testified that "[Jay E. Adams] points out that people who are in mental institutions are not there because they are mentally ill, but because of the fact that they * * * have been unable to deal with the guilt that is associated with sin as described in the scriptures. I mentioned that to Nancy, because I knew she would understand that."

The trial judge characterized the sheriff's approach as "religious persuasion to tell the truth," and ruled that in the circumstances of this case, where *Miranda* warnings were given and appellant was not "close to being an imbecile," there was no improper coercion. Accordingly, the court found the statements voluntary and denied the motion to suppress.

Respondent reasons, as did the trial judge, that there was no improper inducement or coercion because the sheriff's remarks are in the nature of intellectual persuasion. Specifically, respondent contends that the "inducement" contained in the sheriff's comments was merely "philosophical or intellectual persuasion to tell the truth," and not the equivalent of coercion. However, accepting as true the sheriff's version of his remarks, the totality was not purely intellectual persuasion, but an overwhelming and calculated appeal to the emotions and beliefs, focusing appellant's fears in an area the sheriff knew appellant to be particularly vulnerable. * * *

The judge who conducted the pretrial suppression hearing in Kings County Superior Court recognized that there is something basically wrong about using religion as a means to induce a person to confess. "[R]eligious persuasion cannot be a part of police tactics. She should not be told that she is a sinner or that she can go to hell, and even possibly lose her mind for doing the things that she was alleged to have done (living with the victim without the benefit of marriage and not telling the truth as to what took place on the night of the killing)." In denying the motion to suppress the judge failed to recognize the obvious effect of this improper influence.

Respondent urges us to focus upon the *nature* of the benefit as represented by the police that appellant was to receive if she told the truth. In this case, says respondent, appellant's benefit exists only in the sphere of her own moral rehabilitation. Therefore, respondent contends no leniency or advantage was offered nor retribution threatened by the police. The argument is specious. The significant factor is the *tactic* of exciting the suspect's deep-seated fears, not the source or agency of the threatened harm. The sheriff purposely played on appellant's religious anxiety and specifically her fear of being incarcerated in a mental institution, because of the "sin factor." He suggested that she would be eaten up by guilt like the woman in Jay E. Adams' book, who was in a mental institution because "God had begun to deal with her" sin of having a sexual relationship with a man to whom she was not married.

* * *

Religious beliefs are not matters to be used by governmental authorities to manipulate a suspect to say things he or she otherwise would not say. The right to worship without fear is too precious a freedom for us to tolerate an invasion and manipulation by state officials of the religious beliefs of individuals, including those accused of crime.

Furthermore, the sheriff's speech in this case is analogous to conduct condemned in *Spano v. New York* (1959) 360 U.S. 315, and in *United States v. Tingle*, 658 F.2d 1332, because it displays a police tactic of delving into a suspect's psyche to find some area of special vulnerability and then concentrating on it to extract admissions. In *Spano*, the police exploited the defendant's friendship and concern for a particular rookie officer; in *Tingle*, the police purposely caused a mother to fear that if she failed to cooperate, she would not see her young child for a long time. The intrusion in this case, which focused on the suspect's religious anxieties, is no less offensive. The police must not be encouraged to probe into each suspect's personality to discover the means of psychological coercion.

Here the "reprobate mind" lecture was combined with the suggestion that failure to confess might well lead to mental illness, which together with other objectionable tactics, overwhelmingly establish impermissible coercion. The sheriff knew that appellant was ill and had guilt feelings concerning her relationship with the victim while unmarried. His warning appellant that her unexpiated guilt could lead to her commitment to a mental institution was not mere intellectual persuasion to tell the truth. Also present were elements of "softening-up" (see *People v. Honeycutt* (1977) 570 P.2d 1050), exploitation of friendship and deception. The sheriff admitted that he brought up the possibility of Pollock's suicide, without any evidence to support such a theory, and appellant immediately seized upon this suggestion. The detective sergeant's comment that "if it was hard for her to think that she had actually shot him, make it easier on herself by saying the gun had done the actual shooting rather than herself" adds to the improper persuasion.

We are not impressed with respondent's final argument that appellant's will was not overborne because her admissions appear calculated to meet the prosecution evidence which was irreconcilable with her earlier story. Under the law, the crucial question is whether appellant would have made *these* damaging admissions leading to still more incriminating statements, without the improper pressure. The record does not support such a conclusion. * * *

We next confront the question whether the gun and the March 10 statement, which contains the most damaging admissions, also must be suppressed. The record shows that they must be.

Accepting the evidence most favorable to the ruling below, the proceedings on March 10 were not *independently* coercive. However, appellant only argues that the seizure of the gun and the March 10 statement should have been suppressed as *fruit* of the poisonous tree. The record does not support respondent's assertion that the March 10 statement was given voluntarily by appellant independent of the prior illegality. * * *

Respondent's argument that the record shows the March 10 statement to be independent from any improper influences is unconvincing.

Appellant agreed to take a polygraph test *before* she left the sheriff's department on March 6; the appointment was set for March 10 only because a polygraphist was not available the evening of March 6. Appellant testified that she agreed to take a polygraph test at the sergeant's request because she felt she had no choice. The factors that appellant subsequently signed a written form agreeing to be examined of her free will without coercion, that she knew she could refuse to participate, and that she was aware of her *Miranda* rights, do not establish a break in causation. * * *

The gun and all subsequent statements, as well as the March 6 statement, should have been excluded. * * *

The judgment is reversed.

[Dissenting opinion omitted.]

Commentary

Compare, the Christian Burial Speech case noted on p. 545, supra. Would that speech have been coercive even if the *Massiah* or *Miranda* doctrines had not been involved?

Do you think that the sheriff's appeal to the religious beliefs and conscience of the defendant would be more likely to seem offensive to: (1) a judge who shares the religious beliefs of the sheriff and the defendant, and especially their belief that unrepented sin leads to consequences far more grave than imprisonment; or (2) a judge who regards such religious beliefs with a patronizing tolerance, and who suspects that most people professing such beliefs are either weak-minded (and therefore vulnerable), or hypocritical (and therefore manipulative)?

A federal court allowed admission of a confession obtained after an appeal to religious sensibilities in Barrera v. Young, 794 F.2d 1264 (7th Cir.1986) (Opinion of Easterbrook, J.). The opinion noted that "[The officer's] reminder to Barrera that if he believes in an afterlife he must consider the effect of his crimes and his failure to confess is * * * an appeal to Barrera's (very long run) self-interest. It is difficult to describe an appeal to religious beliefs as unacceptable in our society; such appeals are common parts of life and need not cease at the door of the jail."

The belief that "getting away with" murder is worse for the murderer than being caught and punished, because concealment of the crime involves spiritual torment and possibly mental illness, has impressive philosophical as well as religious support. In Plato's dialogue *Gorgias*, the revered sage Socrates undertakes to prove that "the wicked man and the doer of wicked acts is miserable in any case, but more miserable if he does not pay the penalty and suffer punishment for his crimes, and less miserable if he does pay the penalty and suffer punishment in this world and the next." Plato, *Gorgias*, p. 59 (Penguin Classics ed. 1960). A closely related argument is one of the major themes of what is probably the greatest philosophical work of all time, Plato's *Republic*. The argument seemed as contrary to worldly wisdom in ancient Athens as it does in modern America, and the other participants in the dialogues at times ridicule Socrates for holding this implausible opinion. Socrates' basic line of reasoning is that justice is like medicine, and the man who hires clever advocates to escape retribution for his crimes is like a sick man who conceals his symptoms from the doctor because he fears the pain of surgery. Socrates concludes:

> Such a man is presumably ignorant of the nature of health and physical well-being. And the agreement which we have now reached points to the conclusion that those who flee from justice are in a similar condition; they see the pain which punishment involves but are blind to its benefits and do not realize that to be chained to an unhealthy body is a far less miserable fate than the companionship of an unhealthy, rotten, wicked, impure soul. So they strain every nerve to escape punishment and to avoid being cured of the worst of all ailments; for this purpose they procure wealth and friends and make themselves as persuasive speakers as they can. [*Gorgias*, p. 71]

Suppose that Nancy Adams had been an idealistic philosophy graduate student, and had confessed after the sheriff read to her selections from the dialogues of Plato, detailing the spiritual isolation and psychological turmoil that awaits a criminal who succeeds in avoiding detection and punishment? Same result?

The view that punishment is in the interest of the offender as well as the community contrasts strongly with the "Hobbesian" theory that the social order is based upon an agreement between self-interested, competitive individuals. Although this theory was most systematically articulated by the seventeenth century philosopher Thomas Hobbes, it was anticipated in Book Two of Plato's *Republic*, where it is described as the "common opinion." According to this theory, people form a social contract to provide a compromise between what they most desire (the ability to pursue self-interest without hindrance), and what they most fear (having no protection against oppression by other people). Because the alternative to civilized society is a "war of all against all" where life is "nasty, brutish and short," the Hobbesian individual agrees to submit to a legal regime in the hope that his own vital interests will thereby be protected.

Because the basis of this social contract is self-preservation, however, the individual is not obligated to cooperate in his own destruction. The privilege against self-incrimination—and especially the very broad version of the privilege advanced in the opinions by Justices Black and Fortas in United *States v. Wade, supra* pp. 479–484 might be explained as a necessary proviso in a Hobbesian social contract.[a] The citizen assumes a general obligation to submit to legal processes, and in particular to answer questions in court, but this obligation is qualified by the proviso that no one consents

---

a. "It is manifest, that every Subject has Liberty in all those things, the right whereof cannot by Covenant be transferred. I have shewn before in the 14 Chapter, that Covenants, not to defend a mans own body, are voyd. Therefore,

If the Soveraign command a man (though justly condemned,) to kill, wound, or mayme himselfe; or not to resist those that assault him; or to abstain from the use of food, ayre, medicine, or any other thing, without which he cannot live; yet hath that man the Liberty to disobey.

If a man be interrogated by the Soveraign, or his Authority, concerning a crime done by himselfe, he is not bound (without assurance of Pardon) to confesse it; because no man (as I have shewn in the same Chapter) can be obliged by Covenant to accuse himself." Thomas Hobbes, *Leviathan* 269 [Penguin ed. 1968].

to assist the state in bringing about his own destruction. (The reasoning is particularly apt in a capital case.)

On this view, there is neither a moral nor a legal obligation to confess, and refusal to confess indicates a healthy sense of self-preservation. The role of an attorney at interrogation is thus not only to advise the accused of his legal rights, but also to protect him from any temporary impulse to confess that might be generated by feelings of remorse. If the accused does confess (or plead guilty), the attorney will see that he does so from motives of rational self-interest, to obtain leniency or other tangible benefit in the form of a plea bargain.

PEOPLE v. MEMRO

Supreme Court of California, 1985.
38 Cal.3d 658, 214 Cal.Rptr. 832, 700 P.2d 446.

BIRD, CHIEF JUSTICE.

This is an automatic appeal from a judgment imposing a sentence of death. * * *

I.

A. PROCEDURAL HISTORY

Appellant was accused by information of murdering Scott F. and Ralph C. on July 26, 1976, and Carl C., Jr. (Carl Jr.), on October 22, 1978. * * *

B. THE DISAPPEARANCE OF CARL JR. AND THE ARREST

About 8 p.m. on Sunday, October 22, 1978, the parents of seven-year-old Carl Jr. called the South Gate Police Department to report that their son had been missing since about 6 o'clock that evening. The police quickly began searching for the boy but were unable to locate him.

Detective William Sims of the South Gate Police Department was assigned to investigate the disappearance. In the course of his investigation, Sims contacted one Joan Julian, a psychic. Julian helped a police artist prepare a sketch of a person whom she visualized as having been with Carl Jr. at the time of his disappearance.

On Friday, October 27, 1978, Detective Sims went to the missing boy's parents' house and showed them the sketch. They said it resembled "Butch," a name commonly used for appellant. They told Sims that Carl Sr. (the missing boy's father) occasionally repaired cars for appellant and that appellant had dropped off his Volkswagen for repair about 11 p.m. on the night their son disappeared. Having no "good information" with regard to Carl Jr.'s disappearance and wanting to check out all possible leads, Detective Sims decided to talk with appellant "as a witness."

Sims and his partner Detective Louis Gluhak drove to appellant's apartment, which was located about one and one-half miles from Carl Jr.'s home. Sims knocked on the door, and appellant answered. The officers identified themselves and explained that they were investigating the disappearance of Carl Jr. Appellant invited them in. When the officers requested identification, appellant produced his driver's license. At some point, appellant said, "I knew you were coming sooner or later." Stating that the officers were "going to find out anyway," appellant indicated he had previously been in Atascadero State Hospital because he "went into a fit of rage and beat the shit out of a nine-year-old boy" in Huntington Park. Apparently, the officers did not inquire further into this topic.

Detective Sims asked appellant if he "had seen anything unusual in the area of [Carl Jr.'s home] the night he was dropping off his vehicle for Mr. [C.] to repair." Appellant said no.

While talking to appellant, the officers noticed on the walls and shelves "literally hundreds" of photographs of clothed and partially clad young boys. They also saw numerous "magazine type" pornographic books on the floor and the furniture. The officers testified these items were plainly visible from where they sat in the living room. They denied searching the apartment during this visit.[1]

The officers then departed. Although appellant had told the officers he was going to purchase the automobile part that Carl Sr. needed to repair his Volkswagen, he remained behind in the apartment.[2]

The officers drove back to Carl Jr.'s residence and spoke again with his parents, inquiring primarily about appellant. About 15 minutes later, appellant arrived with the part for the Volkswagen. He delivered it to Carl Sr., who said he would fix the car. As appellant started walking back toward his Plymouth, the officers followed.

When appellant and the officers arrived at the Plymouth, Sims asked him to explain what he had seen when he dropped off the Volkswagen on the night of Carl Jr.'s disappearance. Appellant replied,

---

1. Appellant admitted that photographs of nude boys were in his apartment, but denied they were in plain view. He claimed they were in the bedroom in a manila envelope that in turn was inside a blue document pouch.

The defense argued that it was unlikely that appellant would have had these items plainly visible in the apartment, especially if, as the officers contended, appellant knew they were coming. Instead, appellant claimed that this photographic material was discovered during a subsequent warrantless search of the apartment, conducted while appellant was being interrogated at the jail. The police denied that such a search occurred.

Appellant corroborated his claim with the testimony of three witnesses. They had visited the apartment, and had observed no pornographic photographs or magazines on the walls or otherwise in plain view.

2. Appellant's version of this encounter with Detectives Sims and Gluhak differed in several other respects.

According to appellant, the initial contact occurred on the street, as he was leaving in his Plymouth to purchase the part that Carl Sr. had told him was needed to repair the Volkswagen. Thereafter, Sims allegedly asked appellant if it was "all right" to search his apartment. Appellant queried if it would "do [him] any good to say no." Sims replied, "no," and started toward the apartment. Believing that the officers would break down the door if he did not open it, appellant let them in.

The officers conducted a relatively brief search of the apartment, but seized nothing. All three then left the apartment together, appellant intending to purchase the part for his Volkswagen. Sims then asked for permission to search the trunk of appellant's Plymouth. Appellant again acquiesced, and a search was conducted. Nothing was seized.

"Oh, yeah. I remember now." He then related that about 6 p.m. on Sunday he had gone to a restaurant located near the C.'s home. The line was too long, so he decided to stop by the house to talk to Carl Sr. about working on the car. When appellant got to the back door of the house, he met Carl Jr. and asked him if he wanted to have a Coke. Appellant then took the boy to a restaurant about three or four blocks away and bought him a soft drink. Appellant indicated that the last time he saw Carl Jr., the boy was walking down the street toward his home. He denied that he had harmed the boy.

After appellant made these remarks, Detective Sims arrested him for "investigation of 207," or "suspicion of kidnaping." Appellant was handcuffed and driven to the South Gate City jail.[1]

C.   THE INTERROGATIONS

The record contains sharply conflicting versions of what occurred between appellant's arrival at the South Gate City jail and his confessions some five hours later.

According to the officers involved, appellant was driven to the jail by Detectives Sims and Gluhak immediately after the arrest. He was placed in an eight-by-twelve-foot interrogation room where he was joined by the two officers. At approximately 5:15 p.m., appellant was advised of and voluntarily waived his constitutional rights. He essentially reiterated what he had told the officers just prior to his arrest.

Appellant returned to his cell. Thereafter, Sims directed two other officers—Detectives Lloyd Carter and Dennis Greene—to make some inquiries of people living in appellant's neighborhood.[1] These inquiries did not produce any new information. The officers did not search appellant's home or his Plymouth at that time.

At some point, Sims and Gluhak informed Carter that appellant "was not giving any information about the case." They requested Carter to assist them in the interrogation. About 10 p.m., after Carter and Greene had returned to the jail, appellant was brought into the interrogation room for a second time. Appellant and the four plainclothes officers (Sims, Gluhak, Carter, and Greene) were present. To "explain [Carter and Greene's] presence," Carter told appellant that he (Carter)

---

1. Appellant testified to a different version of the encounter at appellant's Plymouth. According to appellant, only Detective Sims followed him to the car. When Sims asked if appellant could talk, appellant agreed but said he was in a hurry because of a dinner date.

Sims asked appellant when he had last seen the missing boy. Appellant indicated the previous Saturday. Appellant denied telling Sims that he had taken the boy to the restaurant or that he had even seen him on the Sunday of his disappearance.

Shortly thereafter, Detective Gluhak joined the conversation. One of the officers asked if appellant would be willing to take a

polygraph test. After some discussion, appellant agreed. Because of his dinner date, he wanted to schedule the test for the following Monday, but Sims wanted it done that evening. Sims said that it would not take long and that appellant would be on his way quickly. Appellant then agreed, and he was driven—without handcuffs—to the police station.

1. Detective Carter apparently conversed with several young boys in the neighborhood. [Police subsequently found nude photographs of some of these boys in Memro's apartment.]

was "the boss" or "the boss man" and that "what [he] said went." Sims again advised appellant of his *Miranda* rights, and appellant again waived them. Carter conducted the subsequent interrogation.

Initially, appellant said he would not speak with Carter because he thought the interrogation room might be "bugged." Appellant asked Carter to have the other officers leave the room, and he requested that Carter prove there were no hidden tape recorders or listening devices. The three officers left, and Carter and appellant inspected the room. They found nothing. Appellant also wanted to know whether Carter was going to take notes of the interrogation. Carter indicated he would do what appellant desired, and appellant responded that he did not want any notes taken.

The other three officers then returned to the interrogation room, and appellant proceeded to confess to killing Carl Jr. In addition, when asked whether he was responsible for "other such incidents," he confessed to killing two other youths in Bell Gardens in 1976. The interrogation session ended about 12:30 a.m. Thereafter, while waiting to take the officers to Carl Jr.'s body, appellant agreed to repeat his confessions and to permit Carter to take notes. At no point during the interrogations did appellant request a lawyer, nor did the officers make any express or implied promises or threats during the second interrogation.

Later that night, according to the South Gate officer who transported appellant back to the jail from the area where Carl Jr.'s body was recovered, appellant remarked that Detective Carter had been "a very wonderful person" to him. Appellant further stated that the South Gate officers "had been very, very nice to him, and he couldn't understand how [they] could be so nice to him since he had done such a terrible thing." The following afternoon, appellant told officers from Bell Gardens that he was being treated "fine." He also "made some comment about his admiration for Detective Carter."

The defense version of these events was quite different. According to appellant, there were four separate interrogation sessions, none of them preceded by *Miranda* warnings. The first two interrogations were conducted by Detectives Sims and Gluhak. At the first session, appellant repeated the story he had told the officers prior to his arrest. (See *ante*, fn. 6.) At the second, Sims showed appellant some boys' clothing and asked why it had been in appellant's apartment. Appellant denied that the clothing belonged to the missing boy, but Sims appeared to disbelieve him.[1]

Appellant then asked about the delay in setting up the lie detector test. Sims said he was not going to give the test, because he had been informed by the Huntington Park police that appellant was a "sicko." Appellant replied that he still wanted to go home. Sims became angry

---

1. If appellant was shown such clothing, it clearly was not Carl Jr.'s, since his clothes were not found until after the inter-   rogation. [Memro led the officers to the body after confessing.]

and told appellant he was under arrest for kidnaping. Appellant was then taken to a small one-person jail cell.

Some time thereafter, appellant was brought to the interrogation room for a third time. Detectives Sims, Gluhak, Carter, and Greene were there. Carter stated that he was the "boss man" and that he was going to get some answers. Appellant repeated the story he had told Sims and Gluhak.

Carter was not satisfied with appellant's answers. Carter then made reference to Detective Greene, a large, muscular officer who was sitting on the floor at the interrogation room door, flexing his muscles. Carter noted that Greene was a "pretty big guy" and asked appellant if he thought he could beat Greene in a fight. Appellant said no. Carter indicated that Greene knew how to fight and how to get answers.[2]

Carter directed appellant's attention to a portion of the interrogation room wall where the plaster had been broken out. This four-or five-inch wide depression or "hole" was located to appellant's right, about shoulder level as he sat at the table. Carter asked appellant how he thought the hole had been created. Appellant understood that Carter was "either planning on enlarging it or making another one similar with [appellant's] head." Appellant changed the subject.

Appellant asked Carter why he had not been given his rights. Carter said that the police had "intentionally" done a number of things wrong. Carter indicated that he knew appellant was mentally ill and that he could help him return to Atascadero State Hospital if he cooperated. Appellant said he had cooperated when he agreed to take the polygraph test.

The officers then directed appellant to stand up, pull up his shirt, and drop his pants to his knees. One of the officers stated that they had found some pictures, and "were just comparing what they could see against the pictures." Appellant complied.

Appellant said he wanted to talk with a lawyer, but Carter became angry and asked appellant whether he wanted to talk or fight. Carter again asked appellant how he thought the hole in the wall had been created.

Appellant began to cry. Carter again said he would have appellant returned to Atascadero if he cooperated. Appellant asked permission to talk with Linda B., an acquaintance who was also a reserve deputy sheriff and lived nearby. Carter agreed, and appellant was allowed to make two telephone calls.

Shortly after completing the telephone calls, appellant was brought to the interrogation room for the fourth time. The four officers were present. Appellant asked Sims where Linda B. was, and Sims indicated

---

2. Appellant is 5 feet 10 inches tall and weighed 165 pounds. Detective Greene, a weightlifter, is 6 feet 2 inches tall and weighed between 220 and 225 pounds.

Greene testified that he spent most of the interrogation either standing or sitting directly against the interrogation room door.

she was out front. Appellant said he wanted to talk with her, but Sims refused, saying appellant should have talked with her on the telephone.

Detective Carter then began intensive questioning about the kidnaping. Appellant was afraid of the four officers in the room, especially Greene. He asked to speak to Carter alone, since he "figured if [he] was talking alone, [he] was less likely to get hurt." All the officers except Carter then left the room.

Appellant asked Carter if the room was "bugged." Carter said no and offered to help check it out. Appellant declined, saying it was not possible to "check it out physically that way." Appellant told Carter that "the reason [he] wanted to talk to him alone, other than being afraid of Greene, was that if [Carter] couldn't, wouldn't, or changed his mind about keeping his promise about sending [him] back to Atascadero, then [he] would deny everything that [Carter] claimed [he] said during that interrogation." Carter agreed to this plan.

Appellant then reiterated the story he had been telling throughout the evening. Carter "reminded" appellant that Greene was nearby and that "there were ways of finding out." He said "[m]aybe [appellant] would like [his] head to make a matching hole in the wall or something." Appellant began to cry and confessed to killing Carl Jr.

Carter said this was not enough to get appellant back to Atascadero and asked if there were other incidents. Appellant said there were none. Carter said appellant would not live long in a state prison and "wondered if Greene could uncover anything else." Appellant then confessed to the 1976 Bell Gardens killings.

The other officers then returned to the room and appellant repeated his confessions.

On many of the critical points, appellant's testimony was contradicted by that of the interrogating officers. In addition to testimony previously mentioned, Detective Carter denied telling appellant he would try to have him admitted to Atascadero State Hospital. Carter and Greene also denied that there was any discussion of a hole in the interrogation room wall or that they ever used such a hole as a threat or an "interrogation tool." Carter remembered that such a hole had existed, but he was unable to recall whether it was still there on the day of appellant's interrogation.

The defense sought to support appellant's testimony in several ways. For example, the defense attempted to photograph the hole in the interrogation room wall. On December 14, 1978, defense counsel sought an ex parte order authorizing his investigator to photograph the hole. In a supporting affidavit, counsel articulated his fear that "if [the police are] given sufficient warning, the hole, if it exists, may be repaired." The trial court declined to issue an ex parte order, but the following day the investigator was allowed to photograph the interrogation room. He found a fresh plaster patch, about 12 inches square, covering the area where appellant testified the hole had been.[1]

In addition, appellant moved the court for discovery of the records of complaints of excessive force and aggressive behavior on the part of the four interrogating officers, as well as twelve other South Gate officers who assertedly trained or supervised them. At the hearing on the discovery motion, defense counsel stated that despite "a limited ability to get witnesses in this regard," he had been able to find three or four persons who had assertedly confessed after being threatened or beaten by South Gate police officers.[2] One of these persons was a man who had allegedly confessed to a murder and led police officers to the victim's body, but whose case was dismissed when the prosecution discovered that the man had been in jail at the time of the killing. The court summarily denied the discovery motion.

Thereafter, on his own, defense counsel attempted to locate witnesses to other confessions assertedly coerced by threats or violence by South Gate officers.[3] In the 10 months he represented appellant prior to trial, counsel came across 17 such persons, none of whom knew of appellant at the time they made their allegations of mistreatment. Only two of these persons—Angelina N. and Michael B.—implicated any of the officers who had interrogated appellant. The trial court permitted them—but none of the remaining individuals—to testify at the hearings on appellant's motions.[1]

Both Angelina N. and Michael B. testified to having been beaten and threatened by Detective Greene. Angelina stated that during an interrogation on November 1, 1978, Greene pointed to a hole in the interrogation room wall and told her he "was going to push [her] head through that hole the same way he did to someone else's." Michael testified that Greene interrogated him on February 2, 1979. During the interrogation, Greene accused Bridges of lying, adding that "if [Michael] didn't tell him what he wanted to know that he would put [his] head through the [interrogation room] wall." Greene also mentioned "something about

---

1. A photograph of the wall showing the plaster patch was admitted as an exhibit at the hearing.

2. Counsel stated he also had "probably five or six other people" with "similar" experiences with South Gate police officers. In addition, the superior court judge sitting at the hearing on the discovery motion was apparently "in the middle of a hearing where somebody hung himself while being interrogated by the South Gate Police Department or during investigation by the South Gate Police Department."

Defense counsel did not specifically correlate any of the various incidents with the officers mentioned in the discovery motion.

3. The size of the South Gate Police Department is not made clear in the record.

Defense counsel suggested that the 16 officers mentioned in his discovery motion comprised the department's detective bureau. The prosecutor believed that the 16 officers were "almost the whole department."

1. Also not permitted to testify were the lawyers who had been in charge of the South Gate branch of the Los Angeles Public Defender's office during the previous two and one-half years. In his offer of proof, defense counsel represented that these witnesses would testify that during their tenure, "neither they nor to their knowledge anybody under them ever received a call from the South Gate Police Department requesting counsel to be present during questioning or prior to questioning of any individual that was in custody."

that they paint the room so often because they be knocking [*sic*] the paint off the wall."

At the hearing, Greene denied striking Angelina and said he did not interview her alone in the interrogation room as she had testified. Greene did not testify in response to Michael's claims.[2]

II.

Prior to trial, appellant moved to discover information regarding complaints against South Gate Police Department officers—including the four officers who had participated in appellant's postarrest interrogation. His motion requested the identity of individuals who had filed complaints "relating to unnecessary acts of aggressive behavior, * * * violence, and/or attempted violence, and * * * excessive force and/or attempted excessive force" against 16 officers in the department. Appellant also sought discovery of investigative reports based on these complaints, including statements of witnesses interviewed, information concerning the officers' use of excessive force or violence contained in personnel files, statements of psychiatrists, psychologists, or other officers contained in such files, and findings of disciplinary actions taken against any officers as a result of their use of force and violence. The purpose of such information, it was alleged, was to enable appellant to bolster his claim that his confession had been coerced.

At the hearing on the motion, defense counsel furnished additional information to the court. He revealed statements by four individuals who had asserted brutality and intimidation by South Gate officers during recent interrogations. In addition, counsel presented an affidavit in which the supervising public defender in South Gate indicated the absence of any "*Miranda* calls" during his tenure in that office.

Following argument by counsel and the prosecutor, the trial court denied the motion. Appellant claims error in this ruling.

[The Court reviewed the California law of discovery in criminal cases, which is unusually liberal in granting defendants access to police and prosecution files. The majority then held that the trial court committed prejudicial error in summarily denying the discovery motion, and that the error required reversal of the judgment. A separate opinion for three of the seven Justices dissented from the holding that statements by psychiatrists or psychologists contained in the officers' personnel files was discoverable, and argued that reversal of the conviction was inappropriate in view of the fact that it might turn out upon remand that the discoverable personnel files contained nothing materially supporting the claim of coercion.]

STEPHAN v. STATE
Supreme Court of Alaska, 1985.
711 P.2d 1156.

BURKE, JUSTICE.

More than five years ago, in *Mallott v. State*, 608 P.2d 737 (Alaska 1980), we informed Alaska law enforcement officials that "it is incum-

---

2. The trial court stated it did not believe the testimony of Angelina or Michael.

bent upon them to tape record, where feasible, any questioning [of criminal suspects,] and particularly that which occurs in a place of detention.'' * * * Today, we hold that an unexcused failure to electronically record a custodial interrogation conducted in a place of detention violates a suspect's right to due process, under the Alaska Constitution, and that any statement thus obtained is generally inadmissible.[1]

I. FACTS

The relevant facts in the two cases now before us are similar. Malcolm Scott Harris and Donald Stephan, petitioners, were arrested on unrelated criminal charges, taken to police stations and questioned by police officers. Harris was interrogated on two separate occasions; Stephan was interrogated only once. Both men made inculpatory statements. In each instance, a working audio or video recorder was in the room and was used during part, but not all, of the interrogation. The officers, in each case, offered no satisfactory excuse for their clear disregard of the *Mallott* rule.[1]

II. PROCEEDINGS BELOW

Prior to their respective trials, Harris and Stephan both moved to suppress confessions made during their interrogations. At the suppression hearings there was conflicting testimony about what occurred during the unrecorded portions of the interviews. Harris claimed that, in his first interrogation, he was not informed of his *Miranda* rights at the beginning of the session, that the questioning continued after he asserted his right to remain silent, and that the officer made threats and promises during the untaped portions. Stephan claimed that his ultimate confession was induced by promises of leniency and was obtained in the absence of an attorney, after he requested one. In both cases, the officers' testimony was to the contrary. Without a full recording to resolve the conflict, the superior court was required to evaluate the credibility of the witnesses and choose which version of the unrecorded events to believe. In each case, the court chose the police officers'

---

1. We are not alone in recognizing the importance of recording custodial interrogations. *See Hendricks v. Swenson,* 456 F.2d 503, 506–07 (8th Cir.1972) (suggesting that videotapes of interrogations protect a defendant's rights and are a step forward in the search for truth); *Ragan v. State,* 642 S.W.2d 489, 490 (Tex.Crim.App.1982) (Tex. Code Crim.Proc.Ann. art. 38.22, § 3 (Vernon 1979) requiring that oral statements of the accused during custodial interrogations must be recorded in order to be admissible); Model Code of Pre–Arraignment Procedure § 130.4 (Proposed Official Draft 1975) (requiring sound recordings of custodial inter-

views). *See generally* Kamisar, *Forward: Brewer v. Williams—A Hard Look at a Discomfitting Record,* 66 Geo.L.J. 209 (1977–78); Williams, *The Authentication of Statements to the Police,* Crim.L.Rev. 6 (Jan. 1979).

1. One officer stated that it was ''normal practice'' to get the suspect's statement ''laid out in the desired manner,'' and only then record the full, formal confession. Another officer explained that a suspect is more at ease and likely to talk without a tape recorder running.

recollections and determined that the confession was voluntary and, thus, admissible at trial. Harris and Stephan were ultimately found guilty and filed notices of appeal. * * *

III. RECORDING IS A REQUIREMENT OF STATE DUE PROCESS

* * *

It must be emphasized that *our holding is based entirely upon the requirements of article I, section 7, of the Alaska Constitution*, as interpreted by this court. *See Michigan v. Long*, 463 U.S. 1032 (1983) (a state court's reliance on federal authority will be presumed, unless its reliance on independent state grounds is clear from the face of the court's opinion). We accept the state's argument that custodial interrogations need not be recorded to satisfy the due process requirements of the United States Constitution, because a recording does not meet the standard of constitutional materiality recently enunciated by the United States Supreme Court in *California v. Trombetta*, 467 U.S. 479 (1984).[2] In interpreting the due process clause of the Alaska Constitution, however, we remain free to adopt more rigorous safeguards governing the admissibility of evidence than those imposed by the Federal Constitution. Thus, as we have done on previous occasions, we construe Alaska's constitutional provision, in this instance, as affording rights beyond those guaranteed by the United States Constitution. * * *

The contents of an interrogation are obviously material in determining the voluntariness of a confession. The state usually attempts to show voluntariness through the interrogating officer's testimony that the defendant's constitutional rights were protected. The defendant, on the other hand, often testifies to the contrary. The result, then, is a swearing match between the law enforcement official and the defendant, which the courts must resolve.[1] * * *

Although there are undoubtedly cases where the testimony on one side or the other is intentionally false, dishonesty is not our main concern. Human memory is often faulty—people forget specific facts, or reconstruct and interpret past events differently. * * *

In the absence of an accurate record, the accused may suffer an infringement upon his right to remain silent and to have counsel present

---

2. In *Trombetta* the Court held that federal due process does not require law enforcement agencies to preserve breath samples for the defendant's independent review, even though the process is technically feasible. The Court reasoned that the policy of non-preservation of breath samples was not prohibited under the United States Constitution because it did not meet the test of constitutional materiality. To meet this test, "evidence must both possess an exculpatory value that was apparent before the evidence was destroyed, and also be of such a nature that the defendant would be unable to obtain comparable evidence by other reasonably available means." *Compare Municipality of Anchorage v. Serrano*, 649 P.2d 256 (Alaska App. 1982) (Alaska due process clause requires preservation of breath samples in drunk driving cases).

1. In most confession cases that have reached the United States Supreme Court, the actual events that occurred in the interrogation room have been disputed. Grano, *Voluntariness, Free Will, and the Law of Confessions*, 65 Va.L.Rev. 859, 898 n.192 (1979). Such disputes are equally typical in the cases that have come before the appellate courts of this state.

during the interrogation. Also, his right to a fair trial may be violated, if an illegally obtained, and possibly false, confession is subsequently admitted. An electronic recording, thus, protects the defendant's constitutional rights, by providing an objective means for him to corroborate his testimony concerning the circumstances of the confession.

The recording of custodial interrogations is not, however, a measure intended to protect only the accused; a recording also protects the public's interest in honest and effective law enforcement, and the individual interests of those police officers wrongfully accused of improper tactics. A recording, in many cases, will aid law enforcement efforts, by confirming the content and the voluntariness of a confession, when a defendant changes his testimony or claims falsely that his constitutional rights were violated. In any case, a recording will help trial and appellate courts to ascertain the truth.

The concept of due process is not static; among other things, it must change to keep pace with new technological developments. For example, the gathering and preservation of breath samples was previously impractical. Now that this procedure is technologically feasible, many states require it, either as a matter of due process or by resort to reasoning akin to a due process analysis. The use of audio and video tapes is even more commonplace in today's society. The police already make use of recording devices in circumstances when it is to their advantage to do so. Examples would be the routine video recording of suspect behavior in drunk driving cases and, as was done in these cases, the recording of formal confessions. Furthermore, media reports indicate that many Alaska police officers have purchased their own recorders, carry them while on duty and regularly record conversations with suspects or witnesses, in order to protect themselves against false accusations. When a portable recorder has not been available, some officers have even used their patrol car radio to record conversations through the police dispatch center.

In both of the cases before us, the police were engaged in custodial interrogations of suspects in a place of detention. A working recording device was readily available, but was used to record only part of the questioning. Compliance with the recording rule is not unduly burdensome under these circumstances. Turning the recorder on a few minutes earlier entails minimal cost and effort. In return, less time, money and resources would have been consumed in resolving the disputes that arose over the events that occurred during the interrogations.

The only real reason advanced by police for their frequent failure to electronically record an entire interrogation is their claim that recordings tend to have a "chilling effect" on a suspect's willingness to talk. Given the fact that an accused has a constitutional right to remain silent, under both the state and federal constitutions, and that he must be clearly warned of that right prior to any custodial interrogation, this argument is not persuasive.[1]

1. Also relevant to this argument, perhaps, is the fact that, when the interroga-   tion occurs in a place of detention and the suspect knows or has reason to know he is

In summary, the rule that we adopt today requires that custodial interrogations in a place of detention, including the giving of the accused's *Miranda* rights, must be electronically recorded. To satisfy this due process requirement, the recording must clearly indicate that it recounts the entire interview. Thus, explanations should be given at the beginning, the end and before and after any interruptions in the recording, so that courts are not left to speculate about what took place.

Since its announcement, the *Mallott* rule has always included a proviso, "when feasible." The failure to electronically record an entire custodial interrogation will, therefore, be considered a violation of the rule, and subject to exclusion, *only if the failure is unexcused*. Acceptable excuses might include an unavoidable power or equipment failure, or a situation where the suspect refused to answer any questions if the conversation is being recorded.[1] We need not anticipate all such possible excuses here, for courts must carefully scrutinize each situation on a case-by-case basis. Any time a full recording is not made, however, the state must persuade the trial court, by a preponderance of the evidence, that recording was not feasible under the circumstances, and in such cases the failure to record should be viewed with distrust.[2] * * *

* * *

Reversed and Remanded for further proceedings, with orders that Harris' and Stephan's statements be suppressed.

ALLEN v. ILLINOIS

Supreme Court of the United States, 1986.
478 U.S. 364, 106 S.Ct. 2988, 92 L.Ed.2d 296.

JUSTICE REHNQUIST delivered the opinion of the Court.

The question presented by this case is whether the proceedings under the Illinois Sexually Dangerous Persons Act (Act), Ill.Rev.Stat., ch. 38, ¶ 105–1.01 *et seq.* (1985), are "criminal" within the meaning of the Fifth Amendment's guarantee against compulsory self-incrimination.

Petitioner Terry B. Allen was charged by information in the Circuit Court of Peoria County with committing the crimes of unlawful restraint and deviate sexual assault. Shortly thereafter the State filed a petition to

speaking to a police officer, there is no constitutional requirement that the suspect be informed that the interview is being recorded.

1. We hasten to add, however, that a suspect has no constitutional right *not* to have his interrogation recorded.

2. *Caveat:* We recognize that many custodial interrogations must take place in the field, where recording may not be feasible. Because of this, the rule that we announce today has limited application; it applies only to *custodial interrogations conducted in a place of detention*, such as a police station or jail, where it is reasonable to assume that recording equipment is available, or can be made available with little effort. In a future case, however, we may be persuaded to extend the application of this rule, *particularly if it appears that law enforcement officials are engaging in bad faith efforts to circumvent the recording requirement set forth in this opinion.*

have petitioner declared a sexually dangerous person within the meaning of the Act.[3] After a preliminary hearing on the information, the criminal charges were dismissed for lack of probable cause, and the petition was apparently dismissed as well.[*] Petitioner was then recharged by indictment, and the petition to declare him sexually dangerous was reinstated.

Pursuant to the Act, with petitioner and counsel present, the trial court ordered petitioner to submit to two psychiatric examinations; the court explained the procedure as well as petitioner's rights under the Act, and petitioner indicated that he understood the nature of the proceedings. At the bench trial on the petition, the State presented the testimony of the two examining psychiatrists, over petitioner's objection that they had elicited information from him in violation of his privilege against self-incrimination. The trial court ruled that petitioner's statements to the psychiatrists were not themselves admissible, but allowed each psychiatrist to give his opinion based upon his interview with petitioner. Both psychiatrists expressed the view that petitioner was mentally ill and had criminal propensities to commit sexual assaults. Petitioner did not testify or offer other evidence at the trial. Based upon the testimony of the psychiatrists, as well as that of the victim of the sexual assault for which petitioner had been indicted, the trial court found petitioner to be a sexually dangerous person under the Act. * * *

[The Illinois Supreme Court affirmed, holding that the evidence was sufficient and that no *Miranda* warnings were required because the self-incrimination privilege does not apply in civil commitment proceedings.][**]

The question whether a particular proceeding is criminal for the purposes of the Self–Incrimination Clause is first of all a question of statutory construction. * * * Here, Illinois has expressly provided that

3. The Act defines sexually dangerous persons as follows:

"All persons suffering from a mental disorder, which mental disorder has existed for a period of not less than one year, immediately prior to the filing of the petition hereinafter provided for, coupled with criminal propensities to the commission of sex offenses, and who have demonstrated propensities toward acts of sexual assault or acts of sexual molestation of children, are hereby declared sexually dangerous persons." ¶ 105–1.01.

[*] The reason for the dismissal of the initial criminal charges seems to have been the failure of the victim to resist the defendant's threatening sexual advances. She testified at the sex commitment hearing that she was afraid of the defendant and went along with his demands in the hope that this would induce him not to kill or injure her. The defendant did not actually use force or threaten her with a weapon. Despite the initial dismissal of the criminal

information, the Illinois courts found the victim's testimony sufficient to establish that the defendant had committed an act of sexual assault for the purpose of the commitment proceeding. See People v. Allen, 481 N.E.2d 690 (Ill.1985).—ed.

[**] The Illinois Supreme Court opinion indicates that the defendant was present with counsel when the trial court ordered him to submit to psychiatric examinations. The written order to this effect stated that the procedure and rights under the sexually dangerous persons statute were explained to the defendant and he indicated that he understood the nature of the proceedings. There is no indication that the defendant or defense counsel requested that counsel be present at the examinations or claimed any privilege. The prosecution argued in the state courts that the defendant had waived any privilege against self-incrimination that he might have had, but the Illinois Supreme Court did not reach this issue. See 481 N.E.2d at 696.—ed.

proceedings under the Act "shall be civil in nature," ¶ 105–3.01, indicating that when it files a petition against a person under the Act it intends to proceed in a nonpunitive, noncriminal manner, without regard to the procedural protections and restrictions available in criminal prosecutions. As petitioner correctly points out, however, the civil label is not always dispositive. Where a defendant has provided "the clearest proof" that "the statutory scheme [is] so punitive either in purpose or effect as to negate [the State's] intention" that the proceeding be civil, it must be considered criminal and the privilege against self-incrimination must be applied. United States v. Ward, 448 U.S. 242, 248–249 (1980). We think that petitioner has failed to provide such proof in this case.

The Illinois Supreme Court reviewed the Act and its own case law and concluded that these proceedings, while similar to criminal proceedings in that they are accompanied by strict procedural safeguards, are essentially civil in nature. We are unpersuaded by petitioner's efforts to challenge this conclusion. Under the Act, the State has a statutory obligation to provide "care and treatment for [persons adjudged sexually dangerous] designed to effect recovery," ¶ 105–8, in a facility set aside to provide psychiatric care, *ibid*. And "[i]f the patient is found to be no longer dangerous, the court shall order that he be discharged." ¶ 105–9. While the committed person has the burden of showing that he is no longer dangerous, he may apply for release at any time. *Ibid*. In short, the State has disavowed any interest in punishment, provided for the treatment of those it commits, and established a system under which committed persons may be released after the briefest time in confinement. The Act thus does not appear to promote either of the traditional aims of punishment—retribution and deterrence. Cf. *Addington v. Texas*, 441 U.S. 418, 428 (1979) (in Texas "civil commitment state power is not exercised in a punitive sense").

Petitioner offers several arguments in support of his claim that despite the apparently nonpunitive purposes of the Act, it should be considered criminal as far as the privilege against self-incrimination is concerned. He first notes that the State cannot file a sexually-dangerous-person petition unless it has already brought criminal charges against the person in question, ¶ 105–3. In addition, the State must prove that the person it seeks to commit perpetrated "at least one act of or attempt at sexual assault or sexual molestation." To petitioner, these factors serve to distinguish the Act from other civil commitment, which typically is not tied to any criminal charge and which petitioner apparently concedes is not "criminal" under the Self–Incrimination Clause. We disagree. That the State has chosen not to apply the Act to the larger class of mentally ill persons who might be found sexually dangerous does not somehow transform a civil proceeding into a criminal one. And as the State points out, it must prove more than just the commission of a sexual assault: the Illinois Supreme Court, as we noted above, has construed the Act to require proof of the existence of a mental disorder for more than one year and a propensity to commit sexual assaults, in addition to demonstration of that propensity through sexual assault.

In his attempt to distinguish this case from other civil commitment, petitioner places great reliance on the fact that proceedings under the Act are accompanied by procedural safeguards usually found in criminal trials. In particular, he observes that the Act provides an accused with the right to counsel, the right to demand a jury trial, and the right to confront and cross-examine witnesses. At the conclusion of the hearing, the trier of fact must determine whether the prosecution has proved the person's sexual dangerousness beyond a reasonable doubt. But as we noted above, the State has indicated quite clearly its intent that these commitment proceedings be civil in nature; its decision nevertheless to provide some of the safeguards applicable in criminal trials cannot itself turn these proceedings into criminal prosecutions requiring the full panoply of rights applicable there.

Relying chiefly on *In re Gault*, 387 U.S. 1 (1967), petitioner also urges that the proceedings in question are "criminal" because a person adjudged sexually dangerous under the Act is committed for an indeterminate period to the Menard Psychiatric Center, a maximum security institution that is run by the Illinois Department of Corrections and that houses convicts needing psychiatric care as well as sexually dangerous persons. Whatever its label and whatever the State's alleged purpose, petitioner argues, such commitment is the sort of punishment—total deprivation of liberty in a criminal setting—that *Gault* teaches cannot be imposed absent application of the privilege against self-incrimination. We believe that *Gault* is readily distinguishable.

First, *Gault's* sweeping statement that "our Constitution guarantees that no person shall be 'compelled' to be a witness against himself when he is threatened with deprivation of his liberty," *id.*, at 50, is plainly not good law. Although the fact that incarceration may result is relevant to the question whether the privilege against self-incrimination applies, *Addington* demonstrates that involuntary commitment does not itself trigger the entire range of criminal procedural protections. Indeed, petitioner apparently concedes that traditional civil commitment does not require application of the privilege. Only two Terms ago, in *Minnesota v. Murphy*, 465 U.S. at 435, n. 7, this Court stated that a person may not claim the privilege merely because his answer might result in revocation of his probationary status. * * *

The Court in *Gault* was obviously persuaded that the State intended to *punish* its juvenile offenders, observing that in many States juveniles may be placed in "adult penal institutions" for conduct that if committed by an adult would be a crime. 387 U.S., at 49–50. Here, by contrast, the State serves its purpose of *treating* rather than punishing sexually dangerous persons by committing them to an institution expressly designed to provide psychiatric care and treatment. That the Menard Psychiatric Center houses not only sexually dangerous persons but also prisoners from other institutions who are in need of psychiatric treatment does not transform the State's intent to treat into an intent to punish. * * *

Petitioner has not demonstrated, and the record does not suggest, that "sexually dangerous persons" in Illinois are confined under conditions incompatible with the State's asserted interest in treatment. Had petitioner shown, for example, that the confinement of such persons imposes on them a regimen which is essentially identical to that imposed upon felons with no need for psychiatric care, this might well be a different case. But the record here tells us little or nothing about the regimen at the psychiatric center, and it certainly does not show that there are no relevant differences between confinement there and confinement in the other parts of the maximum-security prison complex. Indeed, counsel for the State assures us that under Illinois law sexually dangerous persons must not be treated like ordinary prisoners. We therefore cannot say that the conditions of petitioner's confinement themselves amount to "punishment" and thus render "criminal" the proceedings which led to confinement. * * *

Affirmed.

JUSTICE STEVENS, with whom JUSTICE BRENNAN, JUSTICE MARSHALL, and JUSTICE BLACKMUN join, dissenting.

* * *

The Illinois "sexually dangerous person" proceeding may only be triggered by a criminal incident; may only be initiated by the sovereign State's prosecuting authorities; may only be established with the burden of proof applicable to the criminal law; may only proceed if a criminal offense is established; and has the consequence of incarceration in the State's prison system—in this case, Illinois' maximum security prison at Menard. It seems quite clear to me, in view of the consequences of conviction and the heavy reliance on the criminal justice system—for its definition of the prohibited conduct, for the discretion of the prosecutor, for the standard of proof, and for the Director of Corrections as custodian—that the proceeding must be considered "criminal" for purposes of the Fifth Amendment. * * *

In my opinion, permitting a State to create a shadow criminal law without the fundamental protection of the Fifth Amendment conflicts with the respect for liberty and individual dignity that has long characterized, and that continues to characterize, our free society.

I respectfully dissent.

D.   REQUIEM FOR MIRANDA?

18 U.S.C. § 3501 provides that "a confession . . . shall be admissible in evidence if it is voluntarily given." This statute was included in the pro-law enforcement Omnibus Crime Control Act of 1968, just two years after the *Miranda* decision, with the clear intent of overturning *Miranda* (for federal prosecutions) and returning to the voluntariness standard. At the time, this seemed like a futile political gesture, since *Miranda* was a constitutional decision and no one proposed to force a constitutional crisis over the matter. In consequence, the statute had no effect. The

Department of Justice decided to ignore it, and this tradition has persisted through subsequent Democratic and Republican administrations. For nearly 30 years, the statute appeared to be a dead letter, and was eventually omitted from casebooks such as this one.

There were, however, a few judicial rumblings. The constitutional underpinnings of *Miranda* were undermined by decisions such as Oregon v. Elstad (supra, p. 562), which seemed to imply a distinction between the constitutional standard of the Fifth Amendment and the mere "prophylactic rules" prescribed by the 5–4 majority in *Miranda*. In Davis v. United States, 512 U.S. 452 (1994), the Government declined to take a position on the applicability of § 3501 to a case involving suppression of a statement after an ambiguous request for counsel, Justice Scalia scolded the Department of Justice:

> The United States' repeated refusal to invoke § 3501, combined with the courts' traditional (albeit merely prudential) refusal to consider arguments not raised, has caused the federal judiciary to confront a host of "Miranda" issues that might be entirely irrelevant under federal law. Worse still, it may have produced—during an era of intense national concern about the problem of run-away crime—the acquittal and the nonprosecution of many dangerous felons, enabling them to continue their depredations upon our citizens. There is no excuse for this. 512 U.S. at 465.

In United States v. Dickerson, 166 F.3d 667 (4th Cir.1999), the federal Court of Appeals started with the sound premise that "Congress has the power to overrule judicially created rules of evidence and procedure that are not required by the Constitution." 166 F.3d at 672. The majority went on to hold that:

> whether Congress has the authority to enact § 3501 turns on whether the rule set forth by the Supreme Court in *Miranda* is required by the Constitution. Clearly it is not. At no point did the Supreme Court in Miranda refer to the warnings as constitutional rights. Indeed, the Court acknowledged that the Constitution did not require the warnings, *384 U.S. at 467,* disclaimed any intent to create a "constitutional straightjacket," id., referred to the warnings as "procedural safeguards," *id. 384 U.S. at 444,* and invited Congress and the States "to develop their own safeguards for [protecting] the privilege," *id. at 490.* Since deciding Miranda, the Supreme Court has consistently referred to the Miranda warnings as "prophylactic," *New York v. Quarles, 467 U.S. 649, 654 (1984),* and "not themselves rights protected by the Constitution," *Michigan v. Tucker, 417 U.S. 433, 444, (1974).* We have little difficulty concluding, therefore, that § 3501, enacted at the invitation of the Supreme Court and pursuant to Congress's unquestioned power to establish the rules of procedure and evidence in the federal courts, is constitutional. As a consequence, we hold that the admissibility of confessions in federal court is governed by § 3501, rather than the judicially created rule of *Miranda*.

The Supreme Court granted certiorari in *Dickerson* on December 6, 1999, but the case had not been argued when this casebook went to press. If Congress can overrule *Miranda*, the state courts and legislatures can presumably do the same. In the event that the Supreme Court affirms the holding of the Court of Appeals in *Dickerson*, perhaps Congress and/or some states will consider a statutory replacement for the *Miranda* rules. Here is one proposal, which the casebook author drafted long before the *Dickerson* decision and which provides a rationale for legislative revision of *Miranda*.

The Interrogation and Confession Act of 200X

Preamble

Whereas, the Supreme Court in the *Miranda* decision in 1966 imposed detailed regulations on the interrogation of criminal suspects in both state and federal criminal investigations; and

Whereas, the constitutional basis of the *Miranda* decision has been eroded by subsequent decisions of the Court; and

Whereas, the majority opinion in *Miranda* itself invited a legislative solution to the problem of protecting Fifth Amendment rights in the police interrogation process; and

Whereas, the *Miranda* majority opinion was internally inconsistent in describing custodial interrogation as inherently coercive while permitting uncounseled defendants to waive their rights in this setting; and

Whereas, the initial incoherence in the *Miranda* opinion has led to a body of case law which does not either satisfactorily curb abuse in the interrogation process or recognize the legitimate role of custodial interrogation in identifying the perpetrators of criminal acts;

Now therefore, the Congress of the United States makes the following Findings, and enacts the following statutory provisions:

Findings

1. Police interrogation of suspected persons is a necessary and legitimate practice in solving crimes and assuring that guilty persons are brought to justice.

2. Law enforcement officers have no authority to require any person, whether suspected of a crime or not, to answer their questions. The fact that persons may not be *compelled* to answer does not mean, however, that they may not be *encouraged* to do so. "Far from being prohibited by the Constitution, admissions of guilt by wrongdoers, if not coerced, are inherently desirable." United States v. Washington, 431 U.S. 181, 187 (1977).

3. The Sixth Amendment right to the assistance of counsel, applicable to the states through the Fourteenth Amendment, attaches at the initiation of adversary judicial proceedings, when the accused is in court for arraignment on a criminal charge. Prior to that time a suspect in custody is protected by the Fifth Amendment prohibition of compulsory

self-incrimination, and by the Due Process Clause, but not by the right to counsel. No warning of a right to counsel is necessary or appropriate before that right attaches at the initiation of adversary judicial proceedings.

4.   There is an inherent potential for coercion and inhumane treatment in the police interrogation process, particularly when the crime under investigation is one which arouses strong public revulsion. The law should prohibit interrogation techniques that are inhumane or that are likely to induce unreliable statements, while permitting reasonable methods of persuasion aimed at encouraging truthful admissions of guilt.

5.   It is highly desirable for interrogation sessions to be recorded, so that reviewing courts and other agencies can have complete and accurate information regarding the content of any statements and the circumstances under which statements were obtained.

6.   Constitutional principles require that coerced admissions not be used as evidence against the accused. Excessive reliance upon excluding evidence as the remedy for improper police conduct is costly to the public interest in accurate factual determinations in judicial proceedings, however. Excluding evidence is also often ineffective as a means of affecting police behavior. There is a need for clearer standards of conduct to guide police in questioning suspects, and there is also a need to employ remedies other than (or in addition to) exclusion of evidence.

7.   Federal legislation on this subject governing both state and federal investigations and judicial investigations is constitutionally appropriate. Congress has plenary power to legislate rules of investigative and judicial procedure for the federal system, and Congress has power under Section V of the Fourteenth Amendment to enforce by appropriate legislation the constitutional principle that no person shall be deprived of life, liberty or property without due process of law. The Supreme Court specifically invited legislatures to address the problem of custodial interrogation in the *Miranda* opinion itself, 384 U.S. at 490. Legislative action is still more appropriate now that we have the benefit of more than twenty years of experience under the rules promulgated in *Miranda*.

Statutory Provisions

On the basis of these Findings, the Congress of the United States enacts this legislation, which shall be called the Interrogation and Confession Act of 200X.

Section 1. Subject to constitutional principles and the provisions of this Act, officers may question persons, whether in custody or not, in the investigation of crimes and for the purpose of obtaining evidence.

Section 2. (a) Before questioning a suspect in custody, an officer shall advise the suspect that he (she) is not required to answer questions, and that any answers that are given may be used in evidence.

(b) An officer is not required to cease questioning merely because a suspect has initially refused to answer questions. When the suspect has communicated a firm and considered refusal to answer, however, the officers should respect that refusal and cease questioning.

Section 3. (a) In the custodial interrogation of a suspect, an officer shall not:

(1) Employ force or threats;

(2) Make any statement which is intended to imply or may reasonably be understood as implying that the suspect will not be prosecuted or punished;

(3) Intentionally misrepresent the amount of evidence available against the suspect, or the nature or seriousness of the anticipated charges; or

(4) Intentionally misrepresent his identity or employ any other deceptive stratagem not authorized by this Act which, in the circumstances, is fundamentally unfair; or

(5) Deny the suspect reasonable opportunity for food and rest.

(b) It does not violate this Act for an officer to:

(1) Express sympathy or compassion for the offender, whether real or feigned;

(2) Suggest that the crime may be morally understandable or excusable, whether or not the suggestion is sincere;

(3) Appeal to the suspect's conscience or values, religious or otherwise;

(4) Appeal to the suspect's sympathy for the victim or other affected persons;

(5) Inform the suspect honestly about the state of the evidence; or

(6) Inform the suspect that a voluntary admission of guilt and sincere repentance may be given favorable consideration at the time of sentence.

Section 4. (a) A suspect in custody shall be taken without unreasonable delay before a magistrate for arraignment, appointment of counsel, and consideration of pretrial release.

(b) Any period of delay shall be presumed to be reasonable if the suspect is brought before a magistrate on the next court day following arrest.

Section 5. When a suspect has appeared for arraignment in a court in the locality in which charges are to be filed, the adversary stage of the process commences and the Sixth Amendment right to counsel attaches. Thereafter, statements obtained in violation of the right to counsel are not admissible against the interrogated defendant on the pending charges.

Section 6. (a) A confession, admission or other statement shall be excluded from evidence on motion of the defendant if it was coerced by an officer, or if there is substantial doubt as to its reliability.

(b) A statement is presumed to have been coerced if it was obtained as a result of a violation of this Act.

(c) If any evidence of a violation of this Act is produced, the prosecution has the burden of establishing by clear and convincing evidence that the statement in question was not coerced.

(d) Evidence other than statements of the defendant shall be excluded only as required by the Constitution, or to the extent necessary to effectuate the purposes of this Act.

(e) Nothing in this Act prevents a State from enacting or maintaining additional grounds for excluding statements or other evidence from proceedings in its own courts.

Section 7. When a judicial officer excludes a statement pursuant to Section 6 on the ground that it was coerced, or admits the statement into evidence despite a substantial and willful violation of this Act, the judicial officer shall cause a report of the proceedings and the identities of the offending officer(s) to be transmitted to the appropriate United States Attorney for review for possible prosecution under 18 U.S.C. § 242,* or any other applicable provision of law.

Section 8. It is the intent of the Congress that, to the greatest extent feasible, interrogations of suspects in custody shall be recorded so as to provide a complete and accurate record of the content of any statements and the circumstances under which statements were obtained. The Attorney General is directed to prepare regulations implementing this Section and to report to Congress on or before June 30, 200_.

Section 9. It is the intent of Congress that the provisions of this Act shall be widely circulated to judicial officers and law enforcement officers throughout the nation, in order to obtain full compliance. Officers conducting interrogations should be trained or retrained in compliance with this Act. The Attorney General is directed to prepare regulations implementing this Section and to report to Congress on or before June 30, 200_.

Section 10. *Definitions.* As used in this Act:

(a) "Officer" means a federal, state or local law enforcement officer, or a person acting under the direction of such an officer;

(b) "Judicial Officer" means a judge or magistrate of a federal or state court or record;

(c) "Interrogation" and "Questioning" means saying or doing anything which is intended to elicit or reasonably calculated to elicit an

---

* 18 U.S.C. § 242 is the federal criminal statute which penalizes wilful violations of   civil rights.

incriminating statement from a suspect where the primary purpose is to obtain evidence for prosecution;

(d) "Custody" exists when a suspect is under the physical control of an officer under circumstances which objectively indicate that the suspect is not free to leave.

Committee Report

This report was prepared by the Joint Congressional Committee on Truth and Justice in order to explain the intent and purpose of the attached Act, which we drafted. Explaining our own statute may be a pointless activity. If we have drafted the statute competently, then its intent and purpose should be clear without the need for further explanation. If we have been unable to make ourselves clear in the statute, then probably we will only add to the confusion by attempting further explication. Nonetheless, it may be useful to provide some explanation of why we made the choices which we did make, in a manner more informal than would be suitable in the statute itself.[1]

By enacting this statute we do not mean to create a constitutional confrontation, to express disrespect for the Supreme Court, or even to show disapproval for the *Miranda* opinion itself. We are confident that Chief Justice Warren and the other Justices in the majority in that decision would have agreed that the particular set of rules that they prescribed ought to be reexamined periodically, and that comprehensive legislation on the subject would be in many respects superior to a solution dictated by a narrow majority of the Supreme Court acting within the limitations of the judicial process. The *Miranda* opinion itself invited a legislative solution, with the reservation that the legislation must be "fully as effective as [the *Miranda* rules] in informing accused persons of their right of silence and in affording a continuous opportunity to exercise it." We do not concede that we are bound by the quoted reservation,[2] but we believe that the legislation here provided meets that

---

1. It is of some importance that we have been able to obtain unanimous endorsement for this Report from the members of the Joint Committee. We felt that unanimity was important to demonstrate to the law enforcement community, as well as to the judiciary, that we mean business. Compare, Brown v. Board of Education, 347 U.S. 483 (1954) (unanimous opinion); Cooper v. Aaron, 358 U.S. 1 (1958) (opinion signed by all nine Justices); contrast, Miranda v. Arizona, 384 U.S. 436 (1966) (5–4 opinion). Of course, we have methods of promoting unity which are not available to the Court, as our press critics will point out when they see various pieces of legislation this year which provide generous subsidies for public works projects in the districts or states of representatives and senators whose support was otherwise difficult to obtain.

2. The Supreme Court itself has characterized the *Miranda* requirements as a set of "prophylactic rules" which are not themselves rights protected by the Constitution but are instead measures to ensure that the right against compulsory self-incrimination is protected. Oregon v. Elstad, 470 U.S. 298, 305 (1985) (quoting earlier post-*Miranda* decisions). Although we concede that the Supreme Court has authority to overturn an Act of Congress on the ground that it does not comply with the Constitution itself, we think it reasonably clear that the Court has no authority to overturn a statute on the ground that it is not in strict compliance with certain "prophylactic rules" enacted by the Court. See Grano, "Prophylactic Rules in Criminal Procedure: A Question of Article III Legitimacy," 80 NW.U.L.Rev. 100 (1985); Schrock, Welsh & Collins "Interrogation Rights: Reflections

standard. Although this Act rejects a number of the specific protections prescribed by the *Miranda* opinion, it provides others not found there, including a specification of interrogation techniques that may and may not be employed, a prompt arraignment provision, a provision for criminal prosecution of offending officers, and a provision for recording interrogations which should be invaluable in resolving factual disputes. We respect the *Miranda* decision as a milestone in the long struggle to reconcile the reality of police interrogation with the constitutional principles that protect suspects in the courtroom. We believe that a comprehensive statute can address the problem in a more satisfactory manner, however, and that a legislative solution is more likely to be respected by law enforcement officers and the general public, especially in view of the training programs which will be instituted pursuant to Section 9.

Our first task in drafting legislation was to resolve the contradiction inherent in the original *Miranda* opinion, a contradiction perceived by the dissenting Justices at the time and by numerous commentators thereafter. The majority opinion described police interrogation as inherently coercive in the absence of counsel, but then permitted the uncounseled suspect to waive his rights to counsel and to silence in this inherently coercive atmosphere.[1] Behind this contradiction was a basic uncertainty about whether the evil to be remedied was police interrogation itself, or a certain set of abuses in a basically legitimate interrogation process. If the interrogation room was to resemble the courtroom, with officers scrupulously respecting the suspect's right not even to be asked questions unless he chose to do so with the guidance of counsel, then interrogation was an impossibility. If the officers were to have full license to take advantage of the vulnerability of any suspect who was foolish enough to waive his rights, then it is difficult to understand what the *Miranda* rules were meant to accomplish.

We reject the view, frequently implied in the legal literature but seldom forthrightly stated, which holds that it is improper for investigating officers to seek to obtain confessions, or which identifies interrogation itself rather than specific abuses as the evil to be prevented. Like the majority in *Miranda* itself we have looked to the experience of other countries (especially England) for guidance, but the considerably more complete evidence available to us suggests that questioning of accused persons is regarded in other countries as a legitimate means of obtaining evidence for conviction. We see nothing in our Constitution to the contrary.

on Miranda v. Arizona," 52 So.Cal.L.Rev. 1 (1978); Monaghan, "Constitutional Common Law," 89 Harv.L.Rev. 1, 18–23, 30–34, 42 (1975).

1. See Kamisar Police Interrogation and Confessions 47–49, n. 11 (1980). Significantly, Professor Kamisar points out that the "amicus" brief of the American Civil Liberties Union, which the *Miranda* majority appeared to use as the basis for its own opinion, argued repeatedly that protection of the privilege requires the *presence* of counsel, not merely advice as to the immediate availability of counsel. Professor Kamisar considers it "surprising" that the court failed to deal explicitly with the ACLU conception even if only to reject it; we consider the omission as a tacit admission that the majority could not resolve the contradiction inherent in its own approach.

We also reject the argument that some principle of fairness or equal treatment requires that we not take advantage of the ignorance or vulnerability of particular criminal suspects. If rich, crafty and strong-willed persons are able to get away with murder, then we should remedy that situation and not compound the evil by extending similar advantages to everyone else. To deny this principle is to treat criminal investigation as a game, a tendency all too common in some circles of the legal profession.

One explanation for the internal contradiction in the *Miranda* opinion is that the Court was tempted by the notion of extending the Sixth Amendment right to counsel to the moment of arrest.[1] We accept the principle that, once the Sixth Amendment right has attached at the initiation of adversary judicial proceedings, the police may not attempt to circumvent that right.[2] We do not believe that the investigatory stage terminates until the police have had a reasonable opportunity to complete their investigation, however, including a reasonable opportunity to interrogate the suspect. Our formulation of this principle in Section 5 is designed to make this point clear, and to call into question the assumption made by the Supreme Court in Brewer v. Williams, 430 U.S. 387, 389 (1977), that the Sixth Amendment right attached when a defendant was briefly arraigned in a distant court on an arrest warrant. In our view, the initiation of adversary judicial proceedings in that case occurred at a later point, when the defendant appeared in court in the district having jurisdiction over the murder charge.

On the other hand, the police should not have an unlimited opportunity to postpone the initiation of judicial proceedings. The period of permissible interrogation should be measured in hours rather than days. Section 4 reflects this consideration by requiring reasonably prompt arraignment. The length of permissible interrogation is also limited by Section 3(5), which requires that the suspect be allowed reasonable opportunities for food and rest.

From what has been said, it should be clear why we have omitted any warning of a right to counsel from Section 2. Any such warning would be untrue, because the suspect has no right to counsel at this

1. "I was introduced for my accomplishments primarily as being of counsel in *Miranda*, and consistently I must disabuse everyone of the accomplishment * * *. When certiorari was granted and we were asked by the ACLU to prepare and file the brief, we had a meeting in our law office in which we agreed that the briefs should be written with the entire focus on the Sixth Amendment [right to counsel] because that is where the Court was headed after *Escobedo*, and, as you are all aware, in the very first paragraph [of the *Miranda* opinion] Chief Justice Warren said, 'It is the Fifth Amendment to the Constitution that is at issue today.' That was Miranda's effective use of counsel."—John J. Flynn, Panel Discussion on the Exclusionary Rule, 61 F.R.D. 259, 278 (1972) (Quoted in Kamisar, LaFave & Israel, Modern Criminal Procedure 541 (6th ed. 1986).

2. See Massiah v. United States, 377 U.S. 201 (1964); Kirby v. Illinois, 406 U.S. 682 (1972); United States v. Henry, 447 U.S. 264 (1980). By saying that we "accept the principle" of the *Massiah-Henry* doctrine, we do not mean to imply approval or disapproval. We mean only that the doctrine is firmly established in the case law as a constitutional principle (unlike the *Miranda* rules).

stage.[1] What the suspect has is a right not to be compelled to answer questions, which to our way of thinking is very different from a right not to be encouraged or persuaded. Some members of the Committee, following the suggestion of the wise and learned Justice Fictitious in his concurring opinion in *United States v. Henry* (*supra*, p. 536), proposed that the suspect should be told that refusals to answer as well as answers could be used at trial. After discussion, we concluded that this proposal would require a constitutional amendment.

Section 2(b) attempts to retain something of the spirit of the Supreme Court's decision in Edwards v. Arizona, 451 U.S. 477 (1981), without erecting an arbitrary technical barrier to legitimate interrogation.[2] The police are not required to cease interrogating merely because the suspect has expressed an initial reluctance to answer their questions. They may "make a pitch" aimed at encouraging him to cooperate. Once the suspect has heard what they have to say and expressed a considered and definite refusal to speak, however, he should not have to endure a prolonged campaign of wheedling, coaxing, and nagging aimed at overcoming his resistance. Naturally there will be borderline cases, as with any line-drawing rule, but we are confident that the police and the courts can understand the distinction we have expressed in Section 2(b).

Section 3 specifies what officers may and may not do in the course of interrogating suspects who have *not* made a firm and considered refusal to answer. Everyone agrees that the use of force or threats of force is an improper means of obtaining a confession, and other threats may also leave the suspect with no alternative but to comply with any demands that the officers make. For example, the officers in Lynumn v. Illinois, 372 U.S. 528 (1963), told a woman suspected of drug dealing that her welfare payments would be suspended and her children taken from her upon arrest, so that her only hope was to obtain favorable action from the police by confessing. We endorse the Supreme Court's holding that the confession in *Lynumn* was coerced. Similarly, "relay" questioning, or any other tactic which takes advantage of the exhaustion or hunger of the accused, is inhumane in itself and likely to induce unreliable statements.

Statements that promise leniency or imply that the suspect may not be prosecuted are similarly impermissible. Offers of leniency can be made later, in the plea bargaining process, where the accused is represented by counsel and can properly evaluate what is being offered. Promises of leniency from the police during interrogation are too likely to be deceptive, and too likely to give even an innocent suspect the impression that confession is the only way to escape conviction or mitigate the punishment. Section 3 also states a limit on these principles; officers may make the suspect aware of his situation by honestly explaining the state of the evidence, and by pointing out that confession

1. On this basis, we support the result in Moran v. Burbine, 475 U.S. 412 (1986).

2. The precise holding in *Edwards* has no place within our statutory scheme in any case, because it is based on the premise that the accused has a "right to counsel" at pre-indictment interrogation, and we have rejected that premise.

and sincere repentance may be given favorable consideration at sentencing. We believe that this last statement is true, and unlikely to overbear the will of a suspect or induce an unreliable confession.

Promises of leniency are forbidden, but expressions of sympathy and compassion are approved. A pose of sympathy is not overbearing or coercive, nor is it likely by itself to encourage an innocent person to provide a confession. A difficulty in this area is that the difference between expressions of compassionate understanding on the one hand, and implied promises of leniency on the other, is at the margin sometimes a matter of emphasis and nuance. As an example of what we have in mind, we think that the interrogating officer in Miller v. Fenton, 796 F.2d 598 (3d Cir.), cert. denied 479 U.S. 989 (1986), crossed the line from the permissible to the impermissible at several points, particularly when he emphasized that it is appropriate for mentally disturbed murderers to receive "good medical help" rather than punishment. That statement seemed to imply that, upon confession, the suspect would receive only a civil commitment. We do not mean to condemn the officer, because at that time there was no authoritative guidance from the courts or the legislatures to help a conscientious officer decide what to do and what not to do. Our aim is to provide that guidance, with the assistance of the administrators who will provide the training regulations specified in Section 9.

We do not regard it as an abuse for an officer to encourage a confession by appealing to the suspect's sense of moral guilt or feelings of sympathy for the victim and other injured persons. On the contrary, a sense of guilt is the most appropriate reason for confessing. Thus, we approve as a proper interrogation device the "Christian Burial Speech" employed in Brewer v. Williams, 430 U.S. 387 (1977), assuming that the Sixth Amendment right to counsel had not yet attached. We concede that reasonable persons differ on this question, and that there are those who think it unfair for the state to "take advantage of" a person's religious beliefs or guilt feelings. On balance we conclude that it is desirable that such considerations be brought forcibly to the mind of a person who has committed a serious crime, and that doing so is unlikely to induce an untrue statement from an innocent person. It is conceivable, of course, that a mentally disturbed individual might imagine himself guilty out of a desire to be punished or some similar motive, but we do not believe that general rules should be crafted to deal with such extraordinary exceptions. If the confession in the circumstances of the individual case is unreliable, a court should exclude it under Section 6.

Although there is no requirement that the police inform the suspect of all the information that might effect his decision to confess, we do not allow the police to practice outright deception as to the crime under investigation or the amount of evidence that they have. For example, the police may not put the accused in a staged line-up and have a "witness" pretend to identify him. Under Section 3(a)(4) it would also be forbidden for an officer to say, pose as a priest and invite the suspect to make confession, or to employ the outrageous "false friend" tactic condemned in Spano v. New York, 360 U.S. 315 (1959).

A few members of the Committee with backgrounds in law enforcement were inclined at first to defend the practice of leading a suspect to believe that the police have more evidence than they really do, because this technique has often been useful in inducing guilty persons to confess. On balance, however, the view prevailed that this type of misrepresentation might cause an innocent suspect to believe that the case was hopeless, or even that the police were prepared to "frame" him. Unanimity on Section 3 in its present form was eventually achieved when other members of the Committee, with backgrounds as criminal defense attorneys or law professors, threatened to withdraw their reluctant agreement to endorsement of the "sympathy ploy."

Section 6 provides a carefully limited exclusionary rule to enforce the provisions of this Act, and also to protect the possibly innocent suspect from conviction on the basis of an unreliable confession. Subsection (a) provides two independent bases for exclusion: that the confession was coerced, or that there is substantial doubt as to its reliability. For example, the confession by an insane person in Colorado v. Connelly, 479 U.S. 157 (1986), was not coerced (as we use the term). It may have been unreliable, however, if the dissenting opinion of Justice Brennan is correct in stating that it was not corroborated by any physical evidence. A confession by a severely mentally ill person, who may be fantasizing events which never occurred, should not be admitted if there is a substantial doubt as to its reliability.

Subsection (b) states a presumption which is intended to discourage police from violating the provisions of this Act. The presumption does not apply unless there was a causal relationship between the violation and the statement, and it may be rebutted by clear and convincing evidence. Our goal in these provisions is to avoid excluding reliable evidence needlessly, while also avoiding giving any encouragement to an officer who is tempted to cheat on the legal requirements in the hopes that the courts will be forgiving. Our purpose is further served by Section 7, which contemplates criminal prosecution of officers who substantially violate this Act, if the officer has had ample opportunity to learn to understand the statutory requirements and if the violation was wilful.

Section 6(d) deals with the vexing problem of whether to exclude the "fruits" of an unlawfully obtained confession, or rather declines to deal with it. For the time being, we believe that this problem should be left in the hands of the courts. A majority of the members of the Committee initially took the view that exclusion should stop with the statements themselves, and not extend to derivative evidence such as weapons, corpses, and witnesses. They were persuaded by a majority, however, who argued that, at least for the time being, we should retain the possibility of a wider exclusionary rule until we are satisfied that police evasion of the Act is not a serious problem. If federal, state and local law enforcement officers observe the provisions of this Act, as we expect that they will, then exclusionary orders of any type should be rare.

Subsection 6(e) makes clear that we are not "preempting the field." The states remain free to retain the *Miranda* rules, or even to exclude confessions altogether in state prosecutions. We are confident that our solution is a better one, however, and that the states will eventually come to agree with us.

Section 7 directs judicial officers to bring substantial and willful violations of this Act to the attention of the appropriate prosecuting officers, whether or not the violation results in exclusion of evidence under Section 6. The requirement that the violation be both substantial and willful adequately protects officers from the possibility of criminal prosecution in borderline situations where they acted in good faith, and we believe that prosecution is appropriate in cases of flagrant disregard of the protective provisions of this Act.

Section 8 expresses our conclusion that interrogations should be recorded by the means best suited to providing a complete and accurate record. Presumably, this requirement might be met by audio or video recording in some cases, and by stenographic transcript in others. We concluded that it would be premature to legislate a flat requirement of recording at this time, without further input from law enforcement agencies and other interested parties about the details. We also contemplate that recording requirements will be a major part of the training programs established pursuant to Section 9. Once there has been an adequate time for consideration of the details and for training programs, then it may be appropriate to amend Section 8 to state more definite requirements, and to provide explicitly for sanctions for willful non-recording.

Finally, the definition of "interrogation" and "questioning" in Section 10 makes clear that this Act governs questioning that occurs for the purpose of obtaining confessions or admissions. Its provisions do not necessarily apply to questioning which is primarily motivated by other concerns, as in New York v. Quarles, 467 U.S. 649 (1984), or United States v. Mesa, 638 F.2d 582 (3d Cir.1980). We can also imagine cases where, for example, officers question a kidnap suspect to determine the location of a child who is in mortal danger. In all these circumstances departures from what otherwise might be the requirements of this Act may be justified, and the resulting statements are admissible unless there is a substantial doubt as to their reliability. Lacking the ability to imagine all the circumstances which may arise, we leave the questions of application to the courts.

Chapter 14

THE PLEA BARGAINING SYSTEM

BRADY v. UNITED STATES

United States Supreme Court, 1970.
397 U.S. 742, 90 S.Ct. 1463, 25 L.Ed.2d 747.

MR. JUSTICE WHITE delivered the opinion of the Court.

In 1959, petitioner was charged with kidnaping in violation of [the Lindbergh Act], 18 U.S.C.A. § 1201(a). Since the indictment charged that the victim of the kidnaping was not liberated unharmed, petitioner faced a maximum penalty of death if the verdict of the jury should so recommend. Petitioner, represented by competent counsel throughout, first elected to plead not guilty. Apparently because the trial judge was unwilling to try the case without a jury, petition made no serious attempt to reduce the possibility of a death penalty by waiving a jury trial. Upon learning that his codefendant, who had confessed to the authorities, would plead guilty and be available to testify against him, petitioner changed his plea to guilty. His plea was accepted after the trial judge twice questioned him as to the voluntariness of his plea. Petitioner was sentenced to 50 years' imprisonment, later reduced to 30.

In 1967, petitioner sought relief under 28 U.S.C.A. § 2255,* claiming that his plea of guilty was not voluntarily given because § 1201(a) operated to coerce his plea, because his counsel exerted impermissible pressure upon him, and because his plea was induced by representations with respect to reduction of sentence and clemency. * * *

In United States v. Jackson, 390 U.S. 570 (1968) the defendants were indicted under § 1201(a). The District Court dismissed the § 1201(a) count of the indictment, holding the statute unconstitutional because it permitted imposition of the death sentence only upon a jury's recommendation and thereby made the risk of death the price of a jury trial. This Court held the statute valid, except for the death penalty provision; with respect to the latter, the Court agreed with the trial court "that the death penalty provision * * * imposes an impermissible

---

* This section permits a federal prisoner to file a motion in the court which sentenced him challenging the constitutionality or legality of his conviction or sentence.—ed.

burden upon the exercise of a constitutional right * * *." 390 U.S., at 572. The problem was to determine "whether the Constitution permits the establishment of such a death penalty, applicable only to those defendants who assert the right to contest their guilt before a jury." The inevitable effect of the provision was said to be to discourage assertion of the Fifth Amendment right not to plead guilty and to deter exercise of the Sixth Amendment right to demand a jury trial. Because the legitimate goal of limiting the death penalty to cases in which a jury recommends it could be achieved without penalizing those defendants who plead not guilty and elect a jury trial, the death penalty provision "needlessly penalize[d] the assertion of a constitutional right," and was therefore unconstitutional.

Since the "inevitable effect" of the death penalty provision of § 1201(a) was said by the Court to be the needless encouragement of pleas of guilty and waivers of jury trial, Brady contends that *Jackson* requires the invalidation of every plea of guilty entered under that section, at least when the fear of death is shown to have been a factor in the plea. Petitioner, however, has read far too much into the *Jackson* opinion.

The Court made it clear in *Jackson* that it was not holding § 1201(a) inherently coercive of guilty pleas: "the fact that the Federal Kidnaping Act tends to discourage defendants from insisting upon their innocence and demanding trial by jury hardly implies that every defendant who enters a guilty plea to a charge under the Act does so involuntarily." 390 U.S., at 583. * * *

It may be that Brady, faced with a strong case against him and recognizing that the chances for acquittal were slight, preferred to plead guilty and thus limit the penalty to life imprisonment rather than to elect a jury trial which could result in a death penalty. But even if we assume that Brady would not have pleaded guilty except for the death penalty provision of § 1201(a), this assumption merely identifies the penalty provision as a "but for" cause of his plea. That the statute caused the plea in this sense does not necessarily prove that the plea was coerced and invalid as an involuntary act.

The State to some degree encourages pleas of guilty at every important step in the criminal process. For some people, their breach of the State's law is alone sufficient reason for surrendering themselves and accepting punishment. For others, apprehension and charge, both threatening acts by the Government, jar them into admitting their guilt. In still other cases, the post-indictment accumulation of evidence may convince the defendant and his counsel that a trial is not worth the agony and expense to the defendant and his family. All these pleas of guilty are valid in spite of the State's responsibility for some of the factors motivating the pleas; the pleas are no more improperly compelled than is the decision by a defendant at the close of the State's evidence at trial that he must take the stand or face certain conviction.

Of course, the agents of the State may not produce a plea by actual or threatened physical harm or by mental coercion overbearing the will of the defendant. But nothing of the sort is claimed in this case; nor is there evidence that Brady was so gripped by fear of the death penalty or hope of leniency that he did not or could not, with the help of counsel, rationally weigh the advantages of going to trial against the advantages of pleading guilty. Brady's claim is of a different sort: that it violates the Fifth Amendment to influence or encourage a guilty plea by opportunity or promise of leniency and that a guilty plea is coerced and invalid if influenced by the fear of a possibly higher penalty for the crime charged if a conviction is obtained after the State is put to its proof.

Insofar as the voluntariness of his plea is concerned, there is little to differentiate Brady from (1) the defendant, in a jurisdiction where the judge and jury have the same range of sentencing power, who pleads guilty because his lawyer advises him that the judge will very probably be more lenient than the jury; (2) the defendant, in a jurisdiction where the judge alone has sentencing power, who is advised by counsel that the judge is normally more lenient with defendants who plead guilty than with those who go to trial; (3) the defendant who is permitted by prosecutor and judge to plead guilty to a lesser offense included in the offense charged; and (4) the defendant who pleads guilty to certain counts with the understanding that other charges will be dropped. In each of these situations,[1] as in Brady's case, the defendant might never plead guilty absent the possibility or certainty that the plea will result in a lesser penalty than the sentence that could be imposed after a trial and a verdict of guilty. We decline to hold, however, that a guilty plea is compelled and invalid under the Fifth Amendment whenever motivated by the defendant's desire to accept the certainty or probability of a lesser penalty rather than face a wider range of possibilities extending from acquittal to conviction and a higher penalty authorized by law for the crime charged.

The issue we deal with is inherent in the criminal law and its administration because guilty pleas are not constitutionally forbidden, because the criminal law characteristically extends to judge or jury a range of choice in setting the sentence in individual cases, and because both the State and the defendant often find it advantageous to preclude the possibility of the maximum penalty authorized by law. For a defendant who sees slight possibility of acquittal, the advantages of pleading guilty and limiting the probable penalty are obvious—his exposure is reduced, the correctional processes can begin immediately, and the practical burdens of a trial are eliminated. For the State there are also advantages—the more promptly imposed punishment after an admission of guilt may more effectively attain the objectives of punishment; and

---

1. We here make no reference to the situation where the prosecutor or judge, or both, deliberately employ their charging and sentencing powers to induce a particular defendant to tender a plea of guilty. In Brady's case there is no claim that the prosecutor threatened prosecution on a charge not justified by the evidence or that the trial judge threatened Brady with a harsher sentence if convicted after trial in order to induce him to plead guilty.

with the avoidance of trial, scarce judicial and prosecutorial resources are conserved for those cases in which there is a substantial issue of the defendant's guilt or in which there is substantial doubt that the State can sustain its burden of proof. It is this mutuality of advantage that perhaps explains the fact that at present well over three-fourths of the criminal convictions in this country rest on pleas of guilty,[2] a great many of them no doubt motivated at least in part by the hope or assurance of a lesser penalty than might be imposed if there were a guilty verdict after a trial to judge or jury.

Of course, that the prevalence of guilty pleas is explainable does not necessarily validate those pleas or the system which produces them. But we cannot hold that it is unconstitutional for the State to extend a benefit to a defendant who in turn extends a substantial benefit to the State and who demonstrates by his plea that he is ready and willing to admit his crime and to enter the correctional system in a frame of mind that affords hope for success in rehabilitation over a shorter period of time than might otherwise be necessary.

A contrary holding would require the States and Federal Government to forbid guilty pleas altogether, to provide a single invariable penalty for each crime defined by the statutes, or to place the sentencing function in a separate authority having no knowledge of the manner in which the conviction in each case was obtained. In any event, it would be necessary to forbid prosecutors and judges to accept guilty pleas to selected counts, to lesser included offenses or to reduced charges. The Fifth Amendment does not reach so far.

Bram v. United States, 168 U.S. 532 (1897), held that the admissibility of a confession depended upon whether it was compelled within the meaning of the Fifth Amendment. To be admissible, a confession must be " 'free and voluntary: that is, must not be extracted by any sort of threats or violence, nor obtained by any direct or implied promises, however slight, nor by the exertion of any improper influence.' " More recently, Malloy v. Hogan, [p. 453, supra] carried forward the *Bram* definition of compulsion in the course of holding applicable to the States the Fifth Amendment privilege against compelled self-incrimination.

Bram is not inconsistent with our holding that Brady's plea was not compelled even though the law promised him a lesser maximum penalty if he did not go to trial. *Bram* dealt with a confession given by a defendant in custody, alone and unrepresented by counsel. In such circumstances, even a mild promise of leniency was deemed sufficient to bar the confession, not because the promise was an illegal act as such, but because defendants at such times are too sensitive to inducement and the possible impact on them too great to ignore and too difficult to assess. But *Bram* and its progeny did not hold that the possibly coercive impact of a promise of leniency could not be dissipated by the presence

---

2. It has been estimated that about 90%, and perhaps 95%, of all criminal convictions are by pleas of guilty; between 70% and 85% of all felony convictions are estimated to be by guilty plea. D. Newman, Conviction, The Determination of Guilt or Innocence Without Trial 3 and n. 1 (1966).

and advice of counsel, any more than Miranda v. Arizona, held that the possibly coercive atmosphere of the police station could not be counteracted by the presence of counsel or other safeguards.

Brady's situation bears no resemblance to Bram's. Brady first pleaded not guilty; prior to changing his plea to guilty he was subjected to no threats or promises in face-to-face encounters with the authorities. He had competent counsel and full opportunity to assess the advantages and disadvantages of a trial as compared with those attending a plea of guilty; there was no hazard of an impulsive and improvident response to a seeming but unreal advantage. His plea of guilty was entered in open court and before a judge obviously sensitive to the requirements of the law with respect to guilty pleas. Brady's plea, unlike Bram's confession, was voluntary. * * *

It is true that Brady's counsel advised him that § 1201(a) empowered the jury to impose the death penalty and that nine years later in United States v. Jackson, the Court held that the jury had no such power as long as the judge could impose only a lesser penalty if trial was to the court or there was a plea of guilty. But these facts do not require us to set aside Brady's conviction.

Often the decision to plead guilty is heavily influenced by the defendant's appraisal of the prosecution's case against him and by the apparent likelihood of securing leniency should a guilty plea be offered and accepted. Considerations like these frequently present imponderable questions for which there are no certain answers; judgments may be made that in the light of later events seem improvident, although they were perfectly sensible at the time. The rule that a plea must be intelligently made to be valid does not require that a plea be vulnerable to later attack if the defendant did not correctly assess every relevant factor entering into his decision. A defendant is not entitled to withdraw his plea merely because he discovers long after the plea has been accepted that his calculus misapprehended the quality of the State's case or the likely penalties attached to alternative courses of action. More particularly, absent misrepresentation or other impermissible conduct by state agents, a voluntary plea of guilty intelligently made in the light of the then applicable law does not become vulnerable because later judicial decisions indicate that the plea rested on a faulty premise. A plea of guilty triggered by the expectations of a competently counseled defendant that the State will have a strong case against him is not subject to later attack because the defendant's lawyer correctly advised him with respect to the then existing law as to possible penalties but later pronouncements of the courts, as in this case, hold that the maximum penalty for the crime in question was less than was reasonably assumed at the time the plea was entered.

The fact that Brady did not anticipate United States v. Jackson does not impugn the truth or reliability of his plea. We find no requirement in the Constitution that a defendant must be permitted to disown his solemn admissions in open court that he committed the act with which he is charged simply because it later develops that the State would have had a weaker case than the defendant had thought or that the maximum penalty then assumed applicable has been held inapplicable in subsequent judicial decisions.

This is not to say that guilty plea convictions hold no hazards for the innocent or that the methods of taking guilty pleas presently employed in this country are necessarily valid in all respects. This mode of conviction is no more foolproof than full trials to the court or to the jury. Accordingly, we take great precautions against unsound results, and we should continue to do so, whether conviction is by plea or by trial. We would have serious doubts about this case if the encouragement of guilty pleas by offers of leniency substantially increased the likelihood that defendants, advised by competent counsel, would falsely condemn themselves. But our view is to the contrary and is based on our expectations that courts will satisfy themselves that pleas of guilty are voluntarily and intelligently made by competent defendants with adequate advice of counsel and that there is nothing to question the accuracy and reliability of the defendants' admissions that they committed the crimes with which they are charged. In the case before us, nothing in the record impeaches Brady's plea or suggests that his admissions in open court were anything but the truth.

Although Brady's plea of guilty may well have been motivated in part by a desire to avoid a possible death penalty, we are convinced that his plea was voluntarily and intelligently made and we have no reason to doubt that his solemn admission of guilt was truthful.

Affirmed.

Mr. Justice Brennan, with whom Mr. Justice Douglas and Mr. Justice Marshall join, concurring in the result.

* * *

The Court attempts to submerge the issue of voluntariness of a plea under an unconstitutional capital punishment scheme in a general discussion of the pressures upon defendants to plead guilty which are said to arise from, *inter alia*, the venerable institution of plea bargaining. The argument appears to reduce to this: because the accused cannot be insulated from *all* inducements to plead guilty, it follows that he should be shielded from *none*.

The principal flaw in the Court's discourse on plea bargaining, however, is that it is, at best, only marginally relevant to the precise issues before us. There are critical distinctions between plea bargaining as commonly practiced and the situation presently under consideration— distinctions which, in constitutional terms, make a difference. Thus, whatever the merit, if any, of the constitutional objections to plea bargaining generally, those issues are not presently before us.

We are dealing here with the legislative imposition of a markedly more severe penalty if a defendant asserts his right to a jury trial and a concomitant legislative promise of leniency if he pleads guilty. This is very different from the give-and-take negotiation common in plea bargaining between the prosecution and defense, which arguably possess relatively equal bargaining power. No such flexibility is built into the capital penalty scheme where the government's harsh terms with respect to punishment are stated in unalterable form.

Furthermore, the legislatively ordained penalty scheme may affect any defendant, even one with respect to whom plea bargaining is wholly inappropriate because his guilt is uncertain. Thus the penalty scheme presents a clear danger that the innocent, or those not clearly guilty, or those who insist upon their innocence, will be induced nevertheless to plead guilty. This hazard necessitates particularly sensitive scrutiny of the voluntariness of guilty pleas entered under this type of death penalty scheme.

The penalty scheme involved here [is] also distinguishable from most plea bargaining because [it] involves the imposition of death—the most severe and awesome penalty known to our law. * * *

An independent examination of the record in the instant case convinces me that the conclusions of the lower courts are not clearly erroneous. Although Brady was aware that he faced a possible death sentence, there is no evidence that this factor alone played a significant role in his decision to enter a guilty plea. Rather, there is considerable evidence, which the District Court credited, that Brady's plea was triggered by the confession and plea decision of his codefendant and not by any substantial fear of the death penalty. Moreover, Brady's position is dependent in large measure upon his own assertions, years after the fact, that his plea was motivated by fear of the death penalty and thus rests largely upon his own credibility. For example, there is no indication, contemporaneous with the entry of the guilty plea, that Brady thought he was innocent and was pleading guilty merely to avoid possible execution. Furthermore, Brady's plea was accepted by a trial judge who manifested some sensitivity to the seriousness of a guilty plea and questioned Brady at length concerning his guilt and the voluntariness of the plea before it was finally accepted.

In view of the foregoing, I concur in the result reached by the Court * * *.

NORTH CAROLINA v. ALFORD

Supreme Court of the United States, 1970.
400 U.S. 25, 91 S.Ct. 160, 27 L.Ed.2d 162.

MR. JUSTICE WHITE delivered the opinion of the Court.

On December 2, 1963, Alford was indicted for first-degree murder, a capital offense under North Carolina law. The court appointed an attorney to represent him, and this attorney questioned all but one of the various witnesses who appellee said would substantiate his claim of innocence. The witnesses, however, did not support Alford's story but gave statements that strongly indicated his guilt. Faced with strong evidence of guilt and no substantial evidentiary support for the claim of innocence, Alford's attorney recommended that he plead guilty, but left the ultimate decision to Alford himself. The prosecutor agreed to accept a plea of guilty to a charge of second-degree murder, and on December 10, 1963, Alford pleaded guilty to the reduced charge.

Before the plea was finally accepted by the trial court, the court heard the sworn testimony of a police officer who summarized the State's case. Two other witnesses besides Alford were also heard. Although there was no eyewitness to the crime, the testimony indicated that shortly before the killing Alford took his gun from his house, stated his intention to kill the victim, and returned home with the declaration that he had carried out the killing. After the summary presentation of the State's case, Alford took the stand and testified that he had not committed the murder but that he was pleading guilty because he faced the threat of the death penalty if he did not do so.[3] In response to the questions of his counsel, he acknowledged that his counsel had informed him of the difference between second-and first-degree murder and of his rights in case he chose to go to trial. The trial court then asked appellee if, in light of his denial of guilt, he still desired to plead guilty to second-degree murder and appellee answered, "Yes, sir. I plead guilty on—from the circumstances that he [Alford's attorney] told me." After eliciting information about Alford's prior criminal record, which was a long one, the trial court sentenced him to 30 years' imprisonment, the maximum penalty for second-degree murder. * * *

[After extensive proceedings in the state and federal courts, a federal Court of Appeals held that Alford's guilty plea was involuntary. The State obtained review in the Supreme Court.]

State and lower federal courts are divided upon whether a guilty plea can be accepted when it is accompanied by protestations of innocence and hence contains only a waiver of trial but no admission of guilt. * * *

The issue in Hudson v. United States, 272 U.S. 451 (1926), was whether a federal court has power to impose a prison sentence after accepting a plea of *nolo contendere*, a plea by which a defendant does not

---

3. After giving his version of the events of the night of the murder, Alford stated:

"I pleaded guilty on second degree murder because they said there is too much evidence, but I ain't shot no man, but I take the fault for the other man. We never had an argument in our life and I just pleaded guilty because they said if I didn't they would gas me for it, and that is all."

In response to questions from his attorney, Alford affirmed that he had consulted several times with his attorney and with members of his family and had been informed of his rights if he chose to plead not guilty.

Alford then reaffirmed his decision to plead guilty to second-degree murder:

"Q [by Alford's attorney]. And you authorized me to tender a plea of guilty to second degree murder before the court?

"A. Yes, sir.

"Q. And in doing that, that you have again affirmed your decision on that point?

"A. Well, I'm still pleading that you all got me to plead guilty. I plead the other way, circumstantial evidence; that the jury will prosecute me on—on the second. You told me to plead guilty, right. I don't—I'm not guilty but I plead guilty."

expressly admit his guilt, but nonetheless waives his right to a trial and authorizes the court for purposes of the case to treat him as if he were guilty. The Court held that a trial court does have such power, and except for the cases which were rejected in *Hudson*, the federal courts have uniformly followed this rule, even in cases involving moral turpitude. Implicit in the *nolo contendere* cases is a recognition that the Constitution does not bar imposition of a prison sentence upon an accused who is unwilling expressly to admit his guilt but who, faced with grim alternatives, is willing to waive his trial and accept the sentence.

These cases would be directly in point if Alford had simply insisted on his plea but refused to admit the crime. The fact that his plea was denominated a plea of guilty rather than a plea of *nolo contendere* is of no constitutional significance with respect to the issue now before us, for the Constitution is concerned with the practical consequences, not the formal categorizations, of state law. Thus, while most pleas of guilty consist of both a waiver of trial and an express admission of guilt, the latter element is not a constitutional requisite to the imposition of criminal penalty. An individual accused of crime may voluntarily, knowingly, and understandingly consent to the imposition of a prison sentence even if he is unwilling or unable to admit his participation in the acts constituting the crime.

Nor can we perceive any material difference between a plea that refuses to admit commission of the criminal act and a plea containing a protestation of innocence when, as in the instant case, a defendant intelligently concludes that his interests require entry of a guilty plea and the record before the judge contains strong evidence of actual guilt. Here the State had a strong case of first-degree murder against Alford. Whether he realized or disbelieved his guilt, he insisted on his plea because in his view he had absolutely nothing to gain by a trial and much to gain by pleading. Because of the overwhelming evidence against him, a trial was precisely what neither Alford nor his attorney desired. Confronted with the choice between a trial for first-degree murder, on the one hand, and a plea of guilty to second-degree murder, on the other, Alford quite reasonably chose the latter and thereby limited the maximum penalty to a 30–year term. When his plea is viewed in light of the evidence against him, which substantially negated his claim of innocence and which further provided a means by which the judge could test whether the plea was being intelligently entered, its validity cannot be seriously questioned. In view of the strong factual basis for the plea demonstrated by the State and Alford's clearly expressed desire to enter it despite his professed belief in his innocence, we hold that the trial judge did not commit constitutional error in accepting it.[4]

* * *

4. Our holding does not mean that a trial judge must accept every constitutionally valid guilty plea merely because a defendant wishes so to plead. A criminal defendant does not have an absolute right under the Constitution to have his guilty plea accepted by the court * * *

MR. JUSTICE BRENNAN, with whom MR. JUSTICE DOUGLAS and MR. JUSTICE MARSHALL join, dissenting. * * *

Without reaching the question whether due process permits the entry of judgment upon a plea of guilty accompanied by a contemporaneous denial of acts constituting the crime, I believe that at the very least such a denial of guilt is also a relevant factor in determining whether the plea was voluntarily and intelligently made. With these factors in mind, it is sufficient in my view to state that the facts set out in the majority opinion demonstrate that Alford was so gripped by fear of the death penalty that his decision to plead guilty was not voluntary but was the product of duress as much so as choice reflecting physical constraint. * * *

BORDENKIRCHER v. HAYES

Supreme Court of the United States, 1978.
434 U.S. 357, 98 S.Ct. 663, 54 L.Ed.2d 604.

MR. JUSTICE STEWART delivered the opinion of the Court.

* * *

The respondent, Paul Lewis Hayes, was indicted by a Fayette County, Ky., grand jury on a charge of uttering a forged instrument in the amount of $88.30, an offense then punishable by a term of two to 10 years in prison. After arraignment, Hayes, his retained counsel, and the Commonwealth's attorney met in the presence of the clerk of the court to discuss a possible plea agreement. During these conferences the prosecutor offered to recommend a sentence of five years in prison if Hayes would plead guilty to the indictment. He also said that if Hayes did not plead guilty and "save the court the inconvenience and necessity of a trial," he would return to the grand jury to seek an indictment under the Kentucky Habitual Criminal Act, (repealed 1975), which would subject Hayes to a mandatory sentence of life imprisonment by reason of his two prior felony convictions.[5] Hayes chose not to plead guilty, and the prosecutor did obtain an indictment charging him under the Habitual Criminal Act. It is not disputed that the recidivist charge was fully justified by the evidence, that the prosecutor was in possession of this evidence at the time of the original indictment, and that Hayes' refusal to plead guilty to the original charge was what led to his indictment under the habitual criminal statute.

---

5. At the time of Hayes' trial the statute provided that "[a]ny person convicted a * * * third time of felony * * * shall be confined in the penitentiary during his life." Ky.Rev.Stat. § 431.190 (repealed 1975). That statute has been replaced by Ky.Rev.Stat. § 532.080 (1977 Supp.) under which Hayes would have been sentenced to, at most, an indeterminate term of 10 to 20 years. In addition, under the new statute a previous conviction is a basis for enhanced sentencing only if a prison term of one year or more was imposed, the sentence or probation was completed within five years of the present offense, and the offender was over the age of 18 when the offense was committed. At least one of Hayes' prior convictions did not meet these conditions. See n. 3, infra.

A jury found Hayes guilty on the principal charge of uttering a forged instrument and, in a separate proceeding, further found that he had twice before been convicted of felonies. As required by the habitual offender statute, he was sentenced to a life term in the penitentiary. The Kentucky Court of Appeals rejected Hayes' constitutional objections to the enhanced sentence, holding in an unpublished opinion that imprisonment for life with the possibility of parole was constitutionally permissible in light of the previous felonies of which Hayes had been convicted,[6] and that the prosecutor's decision to indict him as an habitual offender was a legitimate use of available leverage in the plea bargaining process.

On Hayes' petition for a federal writ of habeas corpus, the United States District Court for the Eastern District of Kentucky agreed that there had been no constitutional violation in the sentence or the indictment procedure, and denied the writ. The Court of Appeals for the Sixth Circuit reversed the District Court's judgment. * * *

This Court held in North Carolina v. Pearce, 395 U.S. 711, 725, that the Due Process Clause of the Fourteenth Amendment "requires that vindictiveness against a defendant for having successfully attacked his first conviction must play no part in the sentence he receives after a new trial." The same principle was later applied to prohibit a prosecutor from reindicting a convicted misdemeanant on a felony charge after the defendant had invoked an appellate remedy, since in this situation there was also a "realistic likelihood of 'vindictiveness.'" Blackledge v. Perry, 417 U.S., at 27.

In those cases the Court was dealing with the State's unilateral imposition of a penalty upon a defendant who had chosen to exercise a legal right to attack his original conviction—a situation "very different from the give-and-take negotiation common in plea bargaining between the prosecution and the defense, which arguably possess relatively equal bargaining power."

The Court has emphasized that the due process violation in cases such as *Pearce* and *Perry* lay not in the possibility that a defendant might be deterred from the exercise of a legal right, but rather in the danger that the State might be retaliating against the accused for lawfully attacking his conviction.

To punish a person because he has done what the law plainly allows him to do is a due process violation of the most basic sort, and for an agent of the State to pursue a course of action whose objective is to penalize a person's reliance on his legal rights is patently unconstitutional. But in the "give-and-take" of plea bargaining, there is no such element of punishment or retaliation so long as the accused is free to accept or reject the prosecution's offer.

---

6. According to his own testimony, Hayes had pleaded guilty in 1961, when he was 17 years old, to a charge of detaining a female, a lesser included offense of rape, and as a result had served five years in the state reformatory. In 1970 he had been convicted of robbery and sentenced to five years imprisonment, but had been released on probation immediately.

Plea bargaining flows from "the mutuality of advantage" to defendants and prosecutors, each with his own reasons for wanting to avoid trial. Defendants advised by competent counsel and protected by other procedural safeguards are presumptively capable of intelligent choice in response to prosecutorial persuasion, and unlikely to be driven to false self-condemnation. Indeed, acceptance of the basic legitimacy of a plea bargaining necessarily implies rejection of any notion that a guilty plea is involuntary in a constitutional sense simply because it is the end result of the bargaining process. By hypothesis, the plea may have been induced by promises of a recommendation of a lenient sentence or a reduction of charges, and thus by fear of the possibility of a greater penalty upon conviction after a trial. * * * It follows that, by tolerating and encouraging the negotiation of pleas, this Court has necessarily accepted as constitutionally legitimate the simple reality that the prosecutor's interest at the bargaining table is to persuade the defendant to forego his right to plead not guilty.

It is not disputed here that Hayes was properly chargeable under the recidivist statute, since he had in fact been convicted of two previous felonies. In our system, so long as the prosecutor has probable cause to believe that the accused committed an offense defined by statute, the decision whether or not to prosecute, and what charge to file or bring before a grand jury, generally rests entirely in his discretion. Within the limits set by the legislature's constitutionally valid definition of chargeable offenses, "the conscious exercise of some selectivity in enforcement is not in itself a federal constitutional violation" so long as "the selection was [not] deliberately based upon an unjustifiable standard such as race, religion, or other arbitrary classification." Oyler v. Boles, 368 U.S. 448, 456. To hold that the prosecutor's desire to induce a guilty plea is an "unjustifiable standard," which, like race or religion, may play no part in his charging decision, would contradict the very premises that underlie the concept of plea bargaining itself. Moreover, a rigid constitutional rule that would prohibit a prosecutor from acting forthrightly in his dealings with the defense could only invite unhealthy subterfuge that would drive the practice of plea bargaining back into the shadows from which it has so recently emerged.

There is no doubt that the breadth of discretion that our country's legal system vests in prosecuting attorneys carries with it the potential for both individual and institutional abuse. And broad though that discretion may be, there are undoubtedly constitutional limits upon its exercise. We hold only that the course of conduct engaged in by the prosecutor in this case, which no more than openly presented the defendant with the unpleasant alternatives of foregoing trial or facing charges on which he was plainly subject to prosecution, did not violate the Due Process Clause of the Fourteenth Amendment.

Accordingly, the judgment of the Court of Appeals is

Reversed.

M<small>R</small>. J<small>USTICE</small> B<small>LACKMUN</small>, with whom M<small>R</small>. J<small>USTICE</small> B<small>RENNAN</small> and M<small>R</small>. J<small>USTICE</small> M<small>ARSHALL</small> join, dissenting. * * *

[In this case vindictiveness is present to the same extent as in North Carolina v. Pearce and Blackledge v. Perry.] The prosecutor here admitted that the sole reason for the new indictment was to discourage the respondent from exercising his right to a trial. Even had such an admission not been made, when plea negotiations, conducted in the face of the less serious charge under the first indictment, fail, charging by a second indictment a more serious crime for the same conduct creates a strong inference of vindictiveness. * * *

It might be argued that it really makes little difference how this case, now that it is here, is decided. The Court's holding gives plea bargaining full sway despite vindictiveness. A contrary result, however, merely would prompt the aggressive prosecutor to bring the greater charge initially in every case, and only thereafter to bargain. The consequences to the accused would still be adverse, for then he would bargain against a greater charge, face the likelihood of increased bail, and run the risk that the court would be less inclined to accept a bargained plea. Nonetheless, it is far preferable to hold the prosecution to the charge it was originally content to bring and to justify in the eyes of its public.[7]

[The separate dissent of Justice Powell is omitted.]

ALABAMA v. SMITH

Supreme Court of the United States, 1989.
490 U.S. 794, 109 S.Ct. 2201, 104 L.Ed.2d 865.

C<small>HIEF</small> J<small>USTICE</small> R<small>EHNQUIST</small> delivered the opinion of the Court.

* * * In 1985, an Alabama grand jury indicted Smith for burglary, rape, and sodomy. All the charges related to a single assault. Smith agreed to plead guilty to the burglary and rape charges in exchange for the State's agreement to dismiss the sodomy charge. The trial court granted the State's motion to dismiss the sodomy charge, accepted respondent's guilty pleas, and sentenced him to concurrent terms of 30–years' imprisonment on each conviction. Later, respondent moved to withdraw his guilty pleas, claiming that he had not entered them knowingly and voluntarily. The trial court denied this motion, but the Alabama Court of Criminal Appeals reversed, finding that respondent had not been properly informed of the penalties associated with the crimes to which he had pleaded guilty. 494 So.2d 182 (1986). The case

---

7. That prosecutors, without saying so, may sometimes bring charges more serious than they think appropriate for the ultimate disposition of a case, in order to gain bargaining leverage with a defendant, does not add support to today's decision, for this Court, in its approval of the advantages to be gained from plea negotiations, has never openly sanctioned such deliberate over-charging or taken such a cynical view of the bargaining process. See *North Carolina v. Alford*, 400 U.S. 25 (1970); *Santobello v. New York*, 404 U.S. 257 (1971). Normally, of course, it is impossible to show that this is what the prosecutor is doing, and the courts necessarily have deferred to the prosecutor's exercise of discretion in initial charging decisions.

was reassigned to the same trial judge. The State moved to reinstate the charge of first-degree sodomy; the trial court granted that motion, and respondent went to trial on all three original charges.

At trial, the victim testified that respondent had broken into her home in the middle of the night, clad only in his underwear and a ski mask and wielding a kitchen knife. Holding the knife to her chest, he had raped and sodomized her repeatedly and forced her to engage in oral sex with him. The attack, which lasted for more than an hour, occurred in the victim's own bedroom, just across the hall from the room in which her three young children lay sleeping. The State also offered respondent's postarrest statement, in which he admitted many of the details of the offenses. Respondent later took the stand and repudiated his postarrest statement, testifying instead that he had been in bed with his girlfriend at the time the attack took place.

The jury returned a verdict of guilty on all three counts. This time, the trial judge imposed a term of life imprisonment for the burglary conviction, plus a concurrent term of life imprisonment on the sodomy conviction and a consecutive term of 150 years' imprisonment on the rape conviction. The trial court explained that it was imposing a harsher sentence than it had imposed following respondent's guilty pleas because the evidence presented at trial, of which it had been unaware at the time it imposed sentence on the guilty pleas, convinced it that the original sentence had been too lenient. As the court explained, at the time it imposed sentence on the guilty pleas, it had heard only "[respondent's] side of the story"; whereas now, it "has had a trial and heard all of the evidence," including testimony that respondent had raped the victim at least five times, forced her to engage in oral sex with him, and threatened her life with a knife. The court stated that this new information about the nature of respondent's crimes and their impact on the victim, together with its observations of his "mental outlook on [the offenses] and [his] position during the trial," convinced it that it was "proper to increase the sentence beyond that which was given to [him] on the plea bargain."

The Alabama Court of Criminal Appeals affirmed respondent's convictions, as well as the life sentences imposed for burglary and sodomy, but remanded the rape conviction for resentencing. The Supreme Court of Alabama then granted respondent's request for review of the burglary sentence, and reversed and remanded by a divided vote. The majority held that under our decision in North Carolina v. Pearce, 395 U.S. 711 (1969), there can be no increase in sentence upon reconviction at a second trial after the first conviction has been overturned on appeal and remanded for a new trial, unless the increase is justified by events subsequent to the first trial. Because the majority thought the trial court had increased respondent's sentence for the burglary conviction based on new information about events occurring prior to the imposition of the original sentence—e.g., new information about the nature of the crime and its effect on the victim—the majority held that Pearce required it to set aside that sentence.

* * * While the *Pearce* opinion appeared on its face to announce a rule of sweeping dimension, our subsequent cases have made clear that its presumption of vindictiveness does not apply in every case where a convicted defendant receives a higher sentence on retrial. As we explained in Texas v. McCullough, 475 U.S. 134 (1986) [Casebook, p. 828], the evil *Pearce* sought to prevent was not the imposition of enlarged sentences after a new trial but vindictiveness of a sentencing judge. Because the *Pearce* presumption may operate in the absence of any proof of an improper motive and thus block a legitimate response to criminal conduct, we have limited its application, like that of other judicially created means of effectuating the rights secured by the Constitution, to circumstances where its objectives are thought most efficaciously served. * * *

In Colten v. Kentucky, 407 U.S. 104 (1972), for example, we refused to apply the presumption when the increased sentence was imposed by the second court in a two-tier system which gave a defendant convicted of a misdemeanor in an inferior court the right to trial de novo in a superior court. We observed that the trial de novo represented a completely fresh determination of guilt or innocence by a court that was not being "asked to do over what it thought it had already done correctly." * * * Consequently, we rejected the proposition that greater penalties on retrial were explained by vindictiveness with sufficient frequency to warrant the imposition of a prophylactic rule.[8] Similarly, in Chaffin v. Stynchcombe, 412 U.S. 17 (1973), we held that no presumption of vindictiveness arose when a second jury, on retrial following a successful appeal, imposed a higher sentence than a prior jury. We thought that a second jury was unlikely to have a "personal stake" in the prior conviction or to be "sensitive to the institutional interests that might occasion higher sentences."

We think the same reasoning leads to the conclusion that when a greater penalty is imposed after trial than was imposed after a prior guilty plea, the increase in sentence is not more likely than not attributable to the vindictiveness on the part of the sentencing judge. Even when the same judge imposes both sentences, the relevant sentencing information available to the judge after the plea will usually be considerably less than that available after a trial. * * * As this case demonstrates, in the course of the proof at trial the judge may gather a fuller appreciation of the nature and extent of the crimes charged. The defendant's conduct during trial may give the judge insights into his moral character and suitability for rehabilitation. See United States v. Grayson, 438 U.S. 41

---

8. We adopted a prophylactic rule to guard against vindictiveness by the prosecutor at the post-conviction stage in Blackledge v. Perry, 417 U.S. 21 (1974). There the prosecutor charged the defendant with a felony when the latter availed himself of de novo review of his initial conviction of a misdemeanor for the same conduct. He received a sentence of five to seven years for the felony compared to the 6-month sentence he had received for the misdemeanor. On these facts, we concluded that a presumption of vindictiveness arose analogous to that in *Pearce* because the prosecutor clearly has a considerable stake in discouraging convicted misdemeanants from appealing. * * *

(1978) (sentencing authority's perception of the truthfulness of a defendant testifying on his own behalf may be considered in sentencing). Finally, after trial, the factors that may have indicated leniency as consideration for the guilty plea are no longer present. * * *

Our conclusion here is not consistent with Simpson v. Rice, the companion case to North Carolina v. Pearce. In Simpson v. Rice, the complained of sentence followed trial after Rice had successfully attacked his previous guilty plea. We found that a presumption of vindictiveness arose when the State offered "no evidence attempting to justify the increase in Rice's original sentences * * *." With respect, it does not appear that the Court gave any consideration to a possible distinction between the *Pearce* case, in which differing sentences were imposed after two trials, and the *Rice* case, in which the first sentence was entered on a guilty plea.

The failure in Simpson v. Rice to note the distinction just described stems in part from that case having been decided before some important developments in the constitutional law of guilty pleas. [The majority opinion discussed the endorsement of plea bargaining provided in decisions such as Brady v. United States and Bordenkircher v. Hayes, pp. 607, 619, supra.] Part of the reason for now reaching a conclusion different from that reached in Simpson v. Rice, therefore, is the later development of this constitutional law relating to guilty pleas. Part is the Court's failure in *Simpson* to note the greater amount of sentencing information that a trial generally affords as compared to a guilty plea. Believing as we do that there is no basis for a presumption of vindictiveness where a second sentence imposed after a trial is heavier than a first sentence imposed after a guilty plea, we overrule Simpson v. Rice, supra, to that extent. Petitioner contends that there is evidence to support a finding of actual vindictiveness on the part of the sentencing judge in this case. This is not the question upon which we granted certiorari, and we decline to reach it here although it may be open to petitioner on our remand to the Supreme Court of Alabama.

The judgment of the Supreme Court of Alabama is reversed, and the cause remanded for further proceedings not inconsistent with this opinion.

JUSTICE MARSHALL, dissenting.

After successfully challenging the validity of his plea bargain on the grounds that the trial judge had misinformed him about the penalties he could face, respondent Smith went to trial. He was convicted and resentenced to a drastically longer sentence than the one he had initially received as a result of his plea bargain. The majority today finds no infirmity in this result. I, however, continue to believe that, "if for any reason a new trial is granted and there is a conviction a second time, the second penalty imposed cannot exceed the first penalty, if respect is had for the guarantee against double jeopardy." North Carolina v. Pearce, 395 U.S. 711, 727 (1969) (DOUGLAS, J., concurring, joined by MARSHALL, J.) I therefore dissent.

HILL v. LOCKHART

Supreme Court of the United States, 1985.
474 U.S. 52, 106 S.Ct. 366, 88 L.Ed.2d 203.

JUSTICE REHNQUIST delivered the opinion of the Court.

Petitioner William Lloyd Hill pleaded guilty in the Arkansas trial court to charges of first-degree murder and theft of property. More than two years later he sought federal habeas relief on the ground that his court-appointed attorney had failed to advise him that, as a second offender, he was required to serve one-half of his sentence before becoming eligible for parole.

* * *

Under Arkansas law, the murder charge to which petitioner pleaded guilty carried a potential sentence of 5 to 50 years or life in prison, along with a fine of up to $15,000. Petitioner's court-appointed attorney negotiated a plea agreement pursuant to which the State, in return for petitioner's plea of guilty to both the murder and theft charges, agreed to recommend that the trial judge impose concurrent prison sentences of 35 years for the murder and 10 years for the theft. Petitioner signed a written "plea statement" indicating that he understood the charges against him and the consequences of pleading guilty, that his plea had not been induced "by any force, threat, or promise" apart from the plea agreement itself, that he realized that the trial judge was not bound by the plea agreement and retained the sole "power of sentence," and that he had discussed the plea agreement with his attorney and was satisfied with his attorney's advice. The last two lines of the "plea statement," just above petitioner's signature, read: "I am aware of everything in this document. I fully understand what my rights are, and I voluntarily plead guilty because I am guilty as charged."

Petitioner appeared before the trial judge at the plea hearing, recounted the events that gave rise to the charges against him, affirmed that he had signed and understood the written "plea statement," reiterated that no "threats or promises" had been made to him other than the plea agreement itself, and entered a plea of guilty to both charges. The trial judge accepted the guilty plea and sentenced petitioner in accordance with the state's recommendations. The trial judge also granted petitioner credit for the time he had already served in prison, and told petitioner that "[y]ou will be required to serve at least one-third of your time before you are eligible for parole."

More than two years later petitioner filed a federal habeas corpus petition alleging, *inter alia*, that his guilty plea was involuntary by reason of ineffective assistance of counsel because his attorney had misinformed him as to his parole eligibility date. According to petitioner, his attorney had told him that if he pleaded guilty he would become eligible for parole after serving one-third of his prison sentence. In fact, because petitioner previously had been convicted of a felony in Florida, he was classified under Arkansas law as a "second offender" and was required to serve one-half of his sentence before becoming eligible for parole. Petitioner asked the United States District Court for the Eastern District of Arkansas to reduce his sentence to a term of years that would result in his becoming eligible for parole in conformance with his original expectations.

[The District Court denied relief, and the Court of Appeals affirmed by an evenly divided court.]

The long standing test for determining the validity of a guilty plea is "whether the plea represents a voluntary and intelligent choice among the alternative courses of action open to the defendant." [Citations] Here petitioner does not contend that his plea was "involuntary" or "unintelligent" simply because the State through its officials failed to supply him with information about his parole eligibility date. We have never held that the United States Constitution requires the State to furnish a defendant with information about parole eligibility in order for the defendant's plea of guilty to be voluntary, and indeed such a constitutional requirement would be inconsistent with the current rules of procedure governing the entry of guilty pleas in the federal courts. See Fed.Rule Crim.Proc. 11(c); Advisory Committee's Notes on 1974 Amendment to Fed.Rule Crim.Proc. 11, 18 U.S.C.App., p. 22 (federal courts generally are not required to inform defendant about parole eligibility before accepting guilty plea). Instead, petitioner relies entirely on the claim that his plea was "involuntary" as a result of ineffective assistance of counsel because his attorney supplied him with information about parole eligibility that was erroneous. Where, as here, a defendant is represented by counsel during the plea process and enters his plea upon the advice of counsel, the voluntariness of the plea depends on whether counsel's advice "was within the range of competence demanded of attorneys in criminal cases." *McMann v. Richardson*, 397 U.S. 759, 771 (1970). As we explained in *Tollett v. Henderson*, 411 U.S. 258 (1973), a defendant who pleads guilty upon the advice of counsel "may only attack the voluntary and intelligent character of the guilty plea by showing that the advice he received from counsel was not within the standards set forth in *McMann*."

Our concern in *McMann v. Richardson* with the quality of counsel's performance in advising a defendant whether to plead guilty stemmed from the more general principle that all defendants facing felony charges are entitled to the effective assistance of competent counsel. Two Terms ago, in *Strickland v. Washington* [p. 412 of this book], we adopted a two-part standard for evaluating claims of ineffective assistance of counsel. There, citing *McMann*, we reiterated that "[w]hen a convicted defendant complains of the ineffectiveness of counsel's assistance, the defendant must show that counsel's representation fell below an objective standard of reasonableness." We also held, however, that "[t]he defendant must show that there is a reasonable probability that, but for counsel's unprofessional errors, the result of the proceeding would have been different." This additional "prejudice" requirement was based on our conclusion that "[a]n error by counsel, even if professionally unreasonable, does not warrant setting aside the judgment of a criminal proceeding if the error had no effect on the judgment."

Although our decision in *Strickland v. Washington* dealt with a claim of ineffective assistance of counsel in a capital sentencing proceeding, and was premised in part on the similarity between such a proceeding and the usual criminal trial, the same two-part standard seems to us applicable to ineffective assistance claims arising out of the plea process. * * * In addition, we believe that requiring a showing of "prejudice" from defendants who seek to challenge the validity of their guilty pleas on the ground of ineffective assistance of counsel will serve the fundamental interest in the finality of guilty pleas we identified in *United States v. Timmreck*, 441 U.S. 780 (1979):

> " 'Every inroad on the concept of finality undermines confidence in the integrity of our procedures; and, by increasing the volume of judicial work, inevitably delays and impairs the orderly administration of justice. The impact is greatest when new grounds for setting aside guilty pleas are approved because the vast majority of criminal convictions result from such pleas. Moreover, the concern that unfair procedures may have resulted in the conviction of an innocent defendant is only rarely raised by a petition to set aside a guilty plea.' " *Id.*, at 784.

We hold, therefore, that the two-part *Strickland v. Washington* test applies to challenges to guilty pleas based on ineffective assistance of counsel. In the context of guilty pleas, the first half of the *Strickland v. Washington* test is nothing more than a restatement of the standard of attorney competence already set forth in *Tollett v. Henderson, supra*, and *McMann v. Richardson, supra*. The second, or "prejudice," requirement, on the other hand, focuses on whether counsel's constitutionally ineffective performance affected the outcome of the plea process. In other words, in order to satisfy the "prejudice" requirement, the defendant must show that there is a reasonable probability that, but for counsel's errors, he would not have pleaded guilty and would have insisted on going to trial.

In many guilty plea cases, the "prejudice" inquiry will closely resemble the inquiry engaged in by courts reviewing ineffective assistance challenges to convictions obtained through a trial. For example, where the alleged error of counsel is a failure to investigate or discover potentially exculpatory evidence, the determination whether the error "prejudiced" the defendant by causing him to plead guilty rather than go to trial will depend on the likelihood that discovery of the evidence would have led counsel to change his recommendation as to the plea. The assessment, in turn, will depend in large part on a prediction whether the evidence likely would have changed the outcome of a trial. Similarly, where the alleged error of counsel is a failure to advise the defendant of a potential affirmative defense to the crime charged, the resolution of the "prejudice" inquiry will depend largely on whether the affirmative defense likely would have succeeded at trial. * * *

In the present case the claimed error of counsel is erroneous advice as to eligibility for parole under the sentence agreed to in the plea bargain. We find it unnecessary to determine whether there may be circumstances under which erroneous advice by counsel as to parole eligibility may be deemed constitutionally ineffective assistance of counsel, because in the present case we conclude that petitioner's allegations are insufficient to satisfy the *Strickland v. Washington* requirement of "prejudice." Petitioner did not allege in his habeas petition that, had counsel correctly informed him about his parole eligibility date, he would have pleaded not guilty and insisted on going to trial. He alleged no special circumstances that might support the conclusion that he placed particular emphasis on his parole eligibility in deciding whether or not to plead guilty. Indeed, petitioner's mistaken belief that he would become eligible for parole after serving one-third of his sentence would seem to have affected not only his calculation of the time he likely would serve if sentenced pursuant to the proposed plea agreement, but also his calculation of the time he likely would serve if he went to trial and were convicted.

Because petitioner in this case failed to allege the kind of "prejudice" necessary to satisfy the second half of the *Strickland v. Washington* test, the District Court did not err in declining to hold a hearing on petitioner's ineffective assistance of counsel claim. The judgment of the Court of Appeals is therefore affirmed.

[Concurring opinion omitted.]

Note

Two 1995 decisions illustrate the kind of showing that must be made for a defendant to satisfy the standard of Hill v. Lockhart:

1. The defendant in Ostrander v. Green, 46 F.3d 347 (4th Cir.1995) was charged in state court with sexually molesting his 15–year-old sister in law. Ostrander's defense attorney (Joynes) told him he had worked out an agreement for Ostrander to plead guilty to four of six counts and receive a maximum sentence of 3–5 years. Moreover, the prosecutor had agreed not to oppose "work release." Joyce said he knew the people who ran the work release program, and assured Ostrander that his immediate release was guaranteed. Ostrander, though protesting his innocence, entered an *"Alford"* guilty plea on the advice of family and friends. He was then sentenced to 12 years, and thereafter learned that he was ineligible for work release due to the nature of his crimes. On federal *habeas*, the Court of Appeals held that the misadvice of the attorney as to defendant's eligibility for work release was central to his decision to plead guilty, that this misadvice fell "well below the range of competence we would expect from criminal defense lawyers," and that the misadvice was prejudicial because Ostrander would not have plead guilty if he had known the true situation.

2. In Esslinger v. Davis, 44 F.3d 1515 (11th Cir.1995), defendant entered a guilty plea to rape with an assurance that the prosecutor would

recommend the minimum sentence (10 years). Because the presentence report established that defendant had two prior felony convictions, the minimum sentence he actually received was 99 years. The federal Court of Appeals on *habeas* observed that counsel's failure to advise defendant about the effect of prior convictions was inexcusable, and that defendant (who had a triable defense) would probably have insisted on going to trial if he had understood that the sentence he actually received for the bargain (99 years) was effectively no different from the maximum sentence he could have received after trial (life).

BOYKIN v. ALABAMA

Supreme Court of the United States, 1969.
395 U.S. 238, 89 S.Ct. 1709, 23 L.Ed.2d 274.

Mr. Justice Douglas delivered the opinion of the Court.

In the spring of 1966, within the period of a fortnight, a series of armed robberies occurred in Mobile, Alabama. The victims, in each case, were local shopkeepers open at night who were forced by a gunman to hand over money. While robbing one grocery store, the assailant fired his gun once, sending a bullet through a door into the ceiling. A few days earlier in a drugstore, the robber had allowed his gun to discharge in such a way that the bullet, on ricochet from the floor, struck a customer in the leg. Shortly thereafter, a local grand jury returned five indictments against petitioner, a 27–year-old Negro, for common-law robbery—an offense punishable in Alabama by death.

Before the matter came to trial, the court determined that petitioner was indigent and appointed counsel to represent him. Three days later, at his arraignment, petitioner pleaded guilty to all five indictments. So far as the record shows, the judge asked no questions of petitioner concerning his plea, and petitioner did not address the court.

Trial strategy may of course make a plea of guilty seem the desirable course. But the record is wholly silent on that point and throws no light on it.

Alabama provides that when a defendant pleads guilty, "the court must cause the punishment to be determined by a jury" (except where it is required to be fixed by the court) and may "cause witnesses to be examined, to ascertain the character of the offense." Ala.Code, Tit. 15, § 277 (1958). In the present case a trial of that dimension was held, the prosecution presenting its case largely through eyewitness testimony. Although counsel for petitioner engaged in cursory cross-examination, petitioner neither testified himself nor presented testimony concerning his character and background. There was nothing to indicate that he had a prior criminal record.

In instructing the jury, the judge stressed that petitioner had pleaded guilty in five cases of robbery, defined as "the felonious taking of money * * * from another against his will * * * by violence or by putting him in fear * * * [carrying] from ten years minimum in the penitentiary to the supreme penalty of death by electrocution." The jury, upon deliberation, found petitioner guilty and sentenced him severally to die on each of the five indictments.

* * *

A plea of guilty is more than a confession which admits that the accused did various acts; it is itself a conviction; nothing remains but to give judgment and determine punishment. * * *

The requirement that the prosecution spread on the record the prerequisites of a valid waiver is no constitutional innovation. In Carnley v. Cochran, 369 U.S. 506, 516, we dealt with a problem of waiver of the right to counsel, a Sixth Amendment right. We held: "Presuming waiver from a silent record is impermissible. The record must show, or there must be an allegation and evidence which show, that an accused was offered counsel but intelligently and understandingly rejected the offer. Anything less is not waiver."

We think that the same standard must be applied to determining whether a guilty plea is voluntarily made. For, as we have said, a plea of guilty is more than an admission of conduct; it is a conviction. Ignorance, incomprehension, coercion, terror, inducements, subtle or blatant threats might be a perfect cover-up of unconstitutionality. The question of an effective waiver of a federal constitutional right in a proceeding is of course governed by federal standards.

Several federal constitutional rights are involved in a waiver that takes place when a plea of guilty is entered in a state criminal trial. First, is the privilege against compulsory self-incrimination guaranteed by the Fifth Amendment and applicable to the States by reason of the Fourteenth. Second, is the right to trial by jury. Third, is the right to confront one's accusers. We cannot presume a waiver of these three important federal rights from a silent record.

What is at stake for an accused facing death or imprisonment demands the utmost solicitude of which courts are capable in canvassing the matter with the accused to make sure he has a full understanding of what the plea connotes and of its consequence. When the judge discharges that function, he leaves a record adequate for any review that may be later sought, and forestalls the spin-off of collateral proceedings that seek to probe murky memories.

The three dissenting justices in the Alabama Supreme Court stated the law accurately when they concluded that there was reversible error "because the record does not disclose that the defendant voluntarily and understandingly entered his pleas of guilty."

Reversed.

[Dissenting opinion omitted.]

THE FEDERAL RULES OF CRIMINAL PROCEDURE

Rule 11. Pleas

(a) Alternatives.

(1) **In General.** A defendant may plead not guilty, guilty, or nolo contendere. If a defendant refuses to plead or if a defendant corporation fails to appear, the court shall enter a plea of not guilty.

(2) **Conditional Pleas.** With the approval of the court and the consent of the government, a defendant may enter a conditional plea of guilty or nolo contendere, reserving in writing the right, on appeal from the judgment, to review of the adverse determination of any specified pretrial motion. A defendant who prevails on appeal shall be allowed to withdraw the plea.

(b) Nolo Contendere. A defendant may plead nolo contendere only with the consent of the court. Such a plea shall be accepted by the court only after due consideration of the views of the parties and the interest of the public in the effective administration of justice.

(c) Advice to Defendant. Before accepting a plea of guilty or nolo contendere, the court must address the defendant personally in open court and inform the defendant of, and determine that the defendant understands, the following:

(1) the nature of the charge to which the plea is offered, the mandatory minimum penalty provided by law, if any, and the maximum possible penalty provided by law, including the effect of any special parole term and, when applicable, that the court may also order the defendant to make restitution to any victim of the offense; and

(2) if the defendant is not represented by an attorney, that the defendant has the right to be represented by an attorney at every stage of the proceeding against him and, if necessary, one will be appointed to represent the defendant; and

(3) that the defendant has the right to plead not guilty or to persist in that plea if it has already been made, the right to be tried by a jury and at that trial the right to the assistance of counsel, the right to confront and cross-examine adverse witnesses, and the right against compelled self-incrimination; and

(4) that if a plea of guilty or nolo contendere is accepted by the court there will not be a further trial of any kind, so that by pleading guilty or nolo contendere the defendant waives the right to a trial; and

(5) if the court intends to question the defendant under oath, on the record, and in the presence of counsel about the offense to which the defendant has pleaded, that the defendant's answers may

later be used against the defendant in a prosecution for perjury or false statement.

(d) Insuring That the Plea is Voluntary. The court shall not accept a plea of guilty or nolo contendere without first, by addressing the defendant personally in open court, determining that the plea is voluntary and not the result of force or threats or of promises apart from a plea agreement. The court shall also inquire as to whether the defendant's willingness to plead guilty or nolo contendere results from prior discussions between the attorney for the government and the defendant or the defendant's attorney.

(e) Plea Agreement Procedure.

(1) In General. The attorney for the government and the attorney for the defendant or the defendant when acting pro se may engage in discussions with a view toward reaching an agreement that, upon the entering of a plea of guilty or nolo contendere to a charged offense or to a lesser or related offense, the attorney for the government will do any of the following:

(A) move for dismissal of other charges; or

(B) make a recommendation, or agree not to oppose the defendant's request, for a particular sentence, with the understanding that such recommendation or request shall not be binding upon the court; or

(C) agree that a specific sentence is the appropriate disposition of the case.

The court shall not participate in any such discussions.

(2) Notice of Such Agreement. If a plea agreement has been reached by the parties, the court shall, on the record, require the disclosure of the agreement in open court or, on a showing of good cause, in camera, at the time the plea is offered. If the agreement is of the type specified in subdivision (e)(1)(A) or (C), the court may accept or reject the agreement, or may defer its decision as to the acceptance or rejection until there has been an opportunity to consider the presentence report. If the agreement is of the type specified in subdivision (e)(1)(B), the court shall advise the defendant that if the court does not accept the recommendation or request the defendant nevertheless has no right to withdraw the plea.

(3) Acceptance of a Plea Agreement. If the court accepts the plea agreement, the court shall inform the defendant that it will embody in the judgment and sentence the disposition provided for in the plea agreement.

(4) Rejection of a Plea Agreement. If the court rejects the plea agreement, the court shall, on the record, inform the parties of this fact, advise the defendant personally in open court or, on a showing of good cause, in camera, that the court is not bound by the plea agreement, afford the defendant the opportunity to then withdraw the plea, and advise the defendant that if the defendant persists in a guilty plea or plea of nolo contendere the disposition of the case may be less favorable to the defendant than that contemplated by the plea agreement.

(5) Time of Plea Agreement Procedure. Except for good cause shown, notification to the court of the existence of a plea agreement shall be given at the arraignment or at such other time, prior to trial, as may be fixed by the court.

(6) Inadmissibility of Pleas, Plea Discussions, and Related Statements. Except as otherwise provided in this paragraph, evidence of the following is not, in any civil or criminal proceeding, admissible against the defendant who made the plea or was a participant in the plea discussions:

(A) a plea of guilty which was later withdrawn;

(B) a plea of nolo contendere;

(C) any statement made in the course of any proceedings under this rule regarding either of the foregoing pleas; or

(D) any statement made in the course of plea discussions with an attorney for the government which do not result in a plea of guilty or which result in a plea of guilty later withdrawn.

However, such a statement is admissible (i) in any proceeding wherein another statement made in the course of the same plea or plea discussions has been introduced and the statement ought in fairness be considered contemporaneously with it, or (ii) in a criminal proceeding for perjury or false statement if the statement was made by the defendant under oath, on the record, and in the presence of counsel.

(f) Determining Accuracy of Plea. Notwithstanding the acceptance of a plea of guilty, the court should not enter a judgment upon such plea without making such inquiry as shall satisfy it that there is a factual basis for the plea.

(g) Record of Proceedings. A verbatim record of the proceedings at which the defendant enters a plea shall be made and, if there is a plea of guilty or nolo contendere, the record shall include, without limitation, the court's advice to the defendant, the inquiry into the voluntariness of the plea including any plea agreement, and the inquiry into the accuracy of a guilty plea.

(h) Harmless Error. Any variance from the procedures required by this rule which does not affect substantial rights shall be disregarded.

Note

Inadmissibility of Plea Discussions. Rule 11(e)(6) provides generally that a defendant's statements during plea discussion may not be used against him. In United States v. Mezzanatto, 513 U.S. 196 (1995), the Supreme Court held that a defendant can waive this protection. Charged with drug selling, defendant asked to meet with the prosecutor to discuss terms of cooperation. The prosecutor insisted as a precondition that defendant would have to be absolutely truthful, and would have to agree that statements he made in the discussions could be used to impeach any contradictory/ testimony he might give at trial if the case should go that far. Defendant agreed to proceed under those terms. In the discussions defendant admitted knowing that the package he had delivered to an undercover agent contained methamphetamine, but made other false statements that led the prosecutor to terminate the discussions. At his subsequent trial defendant denied knowing that the package contained methamphetamine, and the prosecutor used his admission to impeach his testimony. The Supreme Court held (7–2) that the waiver was valid and the statement admissible for impeachment. Three Justices in the majority noted in the concurrence that the waiver might not be valid if employed to admit statements made during plea bargaining in the Government's case-in-chief.

Withdrawing a Guilty Plea. A defendant has an absolute right to withdraw a guilty plea before the court accepts it. When a defendant enters a plea of guilty pursuant to a bargain with the prosecution, the judge will typically accept the plea but defer acceptance of the bargain for a few weeks so that a presentence report can be prepared and considered. What if the defendant seeks to withdraw the plea in the meantime? Federal Rule 32(e) says that the judge may allow a defendant to withdraw his plea for "any fair and just reason." The United States Court of Appeals for the Ninth Circuit held that, since the plea and the plea agreement "are inextricably bound together" the defendant retains his absolute right to withdraw the plea, "for any reason or for no reason," until the court accepts both the plea and the agreement.

This result would allow a defendant to plead guilty on the eve of trial, for example, and then withdraw the plea a few days or weeks later if it appeared that the prosecution's case had, for whatever reason, become weaker. If contract principles govern, prosecutors ready and willing to go to trial would presumably refuse to accept guilty pleas without some guarantee against subsequent withdrawal. In any case, the Supreme Court unanimously reversed the Ninth Circuit's decision in United States v. Hyde, 520 U.S. 670 (1997). The Supreme Court held that once the judge accepts the plea, and the defendant has stated in court that he is pleading guilty voluntarily and because he actually is guilty, the plea may be withdrawn only for good cause shown even though the judge has not yet decided whether to accept the plea agreement.

Commentary on Justifications for Plea Bargaining

The prevalence of plea bargaining is obviously not easy to justify in an "accusatorial" system of criminal justice that regards the Fifth Amendment privilege against self-incrimination as its "essential mainstay." [See *Malloy v. Hogan, supra,* p. 437.] The challenge of explaining, justifying, condemning, and administering this paradoxical institution has inspired some very interesting scholarship, a few outstanding examples of which will be summarized in this commentary.

A.   An Analogy to Torture

Professor John Langbein's article "Torture and Plea Bargaining," 46 U.Chi.L.Rev. 3 (1978), compared the role of plea bargaining in contemporary American criminal procedure with the use of torture against suspected criminals in Medieval Europe. Medieval courts had to resort to torture because the legal standards of the day required such a high degree of objective proof that it was impossible as a practical matter to enforce the criminal law. Convictions could not be based on circumstantial evidence, and often the testimony of two unimpeachable eyewitnesses was essential—unless the accused provided a voluntary confession. Because this system of proof could as a practical matter be effective only in cases involving overt crime or repentant criminals, the practice developed of obtaining a confession by torture when the proof was strong enough to indicate probable guilt, but not strong enough to convict. A confession obtained under torture was considered involuntary, and hence insufficient for conviction, unless the accused repeated it free from torture at a subsequent hearing. The accused generally did this, because he knew that he would be tortured again if he recanted his confession. Despite the well known and acknowledged defects in such a system of proof, the use of torture persisted for centuries because the unrealistic requirements for unimpeachable objective proof left European criminal procedure without a tolerable alternative.

Professor Langbein comments that "the parallels between the modern American plea bargaining system and the ancient system of judicial torture are many and chilling." Two centuries ago trials were summary proceedings that rarely lasted as long as a full day, but as a result of recent transformations they now last a minimum of several days and frequently weeks or even months.

> Both the medieval European law of proof and the modern Anglo–American law of jury trial set out to safeguard the accused by circumscribing the discretion of the trier in criminal adjudication. The medieval Europeans were trying to eliminate the discretion of the professional judge by requiring him to adhere to objective criteria of proof. The Anglo–American trial system has been caught up over the last two centuries in an effort to protect the accused against the dangers of the jury system, in which laymen ignorant of the law return a one-or two-word verdict that they do not explain or justify. Each system found itself unable to recant directly on the unrealistic level of safeguard to which it had committed itself, and each then concentrated on inducing the accused to tender a confession that would waive his right to the safeguards. Id. at 12.

Professor Langbein describes plea bargaining as simply a less gruesome means (compared to torture) of securing compelled confessions. A plea so coerced does not support an inference of guilt beyond a reasonable doubt. He goes on to describe the costs of this system:

> The factual unreliability of the negotiated plea has further consequences, quite apart from the increased danger of condemning an innocent man. In the plea bargaining that takes the form of charge bargaining (as opposed to sentence bargaining), the culprit is convicted not for what he did, but for something less opprobrious. When people

who have murdered are said to be convicted of wounding, or when those caught stealing are nominally convicted of attempt or possession, cynicism about the processes of criminal justice is inevitably reinforced. This wilful mislabelling plays havoc with our crime statistics, which explains in part why Americans—uniquely among Western peoples—attach so much importance to arrest records rather than to records of conviction. I think that the unreliability of the plea, the mislabelling of the offense, and the underlying want of adjudication all combine to weaken the moral force of the criminal law, and to increase the public's unease about the administration of criminal justice. Id. at 16–17.

Professor Langbein advocates moving to a more streamlined, non-adversarial system of criminal procedure with the system of West Germany as a model. See Langbein, *Comparative Criminal Procedure: Germany* (1977); Langbein, "Land Without Plea Bargaining: How the Germans Do It," 78 Mich.L.Rev. 204 (1979).

B. An Economic Analysis of Discretion and Bargaining

Professor (now United States Court of Appeals Judge) Frank Easterbrook takes a more benign view of plea bargaining in his article "Criminal Procedure as a Market System," 12 Journal of Legal Studies 289 (1983). Professor Easterbrook, a distinguished proponent of the use of economic methods of analysis on legal questions, begins his article by asserting that "The aspects of criminal procedure treated with the greatest skepticism by academics and the popular press—prosecutorial discretion, plea bargaining, and sentencing discretion—may be understood as elements of a well functioning market system. These three parts of the criminal justice system set the price of crime, and they set it in the traditional market fashion. Proposals to restrict the actors' discretion in criminal procedure produce effects similar to forms of command-and-control regulation of the economy." In short, Easterbrook's approval of plea bargaining reflects his approval of free market transactions generally:

> Criminal procedure is a method of allocating scarce resources. Police, judges, prosecutors, jails and jailers, and defense counsel are costly, and society gains by conserving their use. Crimes are even more costly. We would therefore like to do two things: first, to apportion more resources to the criminal justice system until the savings from preventing the marginal crime just equal the costs of doing so, and, second, to get the maximum deterrent punch out of whatever resources are committed to crime control. Id. at 290.

The way to achieve an efficient allocation of resources is to leave the interested parties free to strike deals that advance their interests:

> The defenders of plea bargaining are rarely enthusiastic; they are more likely to describe it as a necessary evil than as a desirable feature of criminal procedure. Yet plea bargaining is desirable, not just defensible, if the system attempts to maximize deterrence from a given commitment of resources. It serves the price-establishing function at low cost. Constant plea negotiations will lead to rapid adjustments in penalties as conditions change. The parties save the costs of trials. Defendants presumably prefer the lower sentences to the exercise of their trial

rights or they would not strike the deals. Prosecutors also prefer the agreements; they may put the released resources to use in other cases, thus increasing deterrence. If defendants and prosecutors (representing society) both gain, the process is desirable. Id. at 309.

Professor Easterbrook is unimpressed by the argument that bargaining pressures may cause innocent persons to plead guilty, because he thinks that incorrect verdicts are equally a risk at contested trials. Id. at 310. Bargaining allows the defendant to take into account the uncertainties of the trial process and obtain a more favorable outcome than he expects that a trial would produce.

> If plea bargains are honest compromises among the parties, in which defendants who might be acquitted surrender that possibility in exchange for a lower sentence, then there will be a sentence differential that is indistinguishable from the coercive threat of which the critics complain. If, for example, a defendant thinks that he has a 50 percent chance of being convicted and will receive a twenty-year sentence if convicted, and his discount rate is 10 percent, he will find attractive any offer of less than 5.82 years in jail.[a] Plea bargaining is "coercive" only if circumstances cause him to accept a higher sentence or if the risk of the twenty-year sentence would not exist but for the existence of plea bargaining. Because plea bargaining does exist, we cannot easily determine whether the twenty-year sentence would exist in its absence. Id. at 311.

Professor Easterbrook concludes that the existence of discretion in criminal procedure (including plea bargaining) produces not systematic arbitrariness but instead "the order of the market place, coordination of the acts of many thousands of people through a price system." Id. at 330. Attempting to eliminate this discretion and bargaining through regulation would have the same undesirable effects that price control regulation has in other areas: widespread evasion, and the forcing of the parties into a different disposition that all concerned regard as less advantageous.

C. Can We Do Away With Plea Bargaining?

Professor Stephen Schulhofer's article "Is Plea Bargaining Inevitable?," 97 Harv.L.Rev. 1037 (1984), reports an empirical study of non-jury trials in Philadelphia to refute the many observers who have argued that plea bargaining is inevitable because we cannot handle the huge felony caseloads that prevail today without bargaining, or because attorneys will find some way to circumvent any restrictions on bargaining that are enacted.

To test these assumptions Schulhofer and his researchers studied a sample of 340 cases in Philadelphia disposed of by plea or bench trial during June and July of 1982. Most of these were designated for what in Philadelphia is called the "List" program, which is to say that they were classified by the District Attorney's Office as routine felony cases that appeared to be headed for either a guilty plea or a bench trial. Relatively little serious plea

---

a. "Discounting means that the prospect of twenty years' imprisonment is not twice as onerous as the prospect of ten years' imprisonment. If the discount rate is 10 percent, the prospect of twenty years' imprisonment is twice as serious as the prospect of 5.82 years in jail. Id. at 295.

bargaining occurred in these cases, because the supervisor in the District Attorney's office rarely approved significant concessions in return for a guilty plea. The concessions that were normally given—such as dismissing a lesser charge when the defendant agreed to plead guilty to a more serious charge—were of the kind that rarely have a practical effect on the eventual sentence. In these circumstances only 42 percent of the defendants in the sample pleaded guilty, and the majority of these were utterly hopeless ("dead bang") cases where sentencing concessions could not be obtained but a trial was pointless.

Although Philadelphia judges do not appear to punish defendants for going to trial instead of pleading guilty, there does appear to be a substantial sentence differential for defendants who insist on their right to jury trial. Because of this disincentive, defendants frequently opt for a bench trial. The major focus of the study was to determine whether the resulting bench trials are, as previous observers had suggested, "slow pleas of guilty" rather than genuinely contested trials. In fact the observations of the researchers, which are reported in detail in the article, established that the trials were with rare exceptions genuine adversarial proceedings in which the defendants frequently prevailed at least to some extent. Somewhat more than 20 percent of the bench trials ended in acquittal, and (more importantly) many more bench trials ended in conviction only on charges significantly less serious than the principal counts.

> In the List program sample, significant charge reduction occurred in only 20% of the guilty plea cases but in 25% of the bench trial cases; moreover, significant charge reduction was present in 31% of the 128 bench trial *convictions*—55% more often than in guilty plea cases. Of course, the guilty plea and bench trial cases are not strictly comparable, because the former group presumably contains many more open-and-shut cases. But this is, in part, the point. When a case involves debatable issues, the defendant goes to trial and often wins significant charge reduction, a result normally unobtainable in Philadelphia plea bargaining. Thus, even the relatively simple criterion of case outcome suggests that a bench trial is not the functional equivalent of a guilty plea. Id. at 1076–78.

Observation of the behavior of the attorneys and judges in the bench trials reinforced the perception that these trials are genuine contested proceedings rather than "slow pleas of guilty." Despite this fact, the bench trials took surprisingly little court time, in comparison with the time required for taking a guilty plea. "Allowing for the waiting time attributable to each disposition, the total courtroom time consumed by the typical List program bench trial was approximately one hour and twenty minutes, compared to the fifty-five minutes of total courtroom time spent on a typical guilty plea." Id. at 1066. In short, there simply was no significant time or caseload pressure to decrease the number of bench trials by encouraging more guilty pleas.

Professor Schulhofer summed up the conclusions of his study as follows:

> [The present study] shows that in America's fourth-largest city, no concessions of any kind are offered for guilty pleas in the great majority of felony cases. In the absence of concessions, most felony defendants do

in fact demand a trial, and their cases are resolved in genuinely contested adversary proceedings. Many of these cases turn out to involve difficult, debatable questions of fact or law, and many defendants win acquittal or substantial charge reduction—results that in nearly all cases reflect not intuitive or off-the-cuff compromise, but the considered application of law to facts proved in open court.

Plea bargaining is not inevitable. In most American cities, judges and attorneys have *chosen* to process cases that way. The Supreme Court has chosen to tolerate, to legitimate, and finally to encourage the plea bargaining system. We can instead choose, if we wish, to afford criminal defendants a day in court. We can cease imposing a price, in months or years of incarceration, upon defendants who exercise that privilege, and can instead permit or even encourage defendants to ask for a hearing in which they may put the prosecution to its proof. We can make available a formal bench trial that permits the expeditious but fair and accurate resolution of criminal cases on the basis of public testimony, tested and challenged with the traditional tools of American adversary procedure. If we nevertheless continue to tolerate plea bargaining, that choice will not tell us that resources are too scarce or that *other* lawyers, those over there in court, are impatient with zealous advocacy and uncontrollably drawn to more comfortable modes of work. A choice to prefer plea bargaining to an inexpensive feasible adversary trial will instead tell us a great deal about ourselves. Id. at 1106–07.

Professor Schulhofer critiques the economic analysis of Professor Easterbrook in his article, "Discretion in the Criminal Justice System," forthcoming in vol. 17 of the Journal of Legal Studies (Jan. 1988).

D. *Alternatives to Plea Bargaining*

Professor Albert Alschuler has published a very thorough analysis of the changes we might make in our system of criminal procedure to make it possible and practical to do away with plea bargaining. The article is titled "Implementing the Criminal Defendant's Right to Trial: Alternatives to the Plea Bargaining System," 50 U.Chi.L.Rev. 931 (1983). The article is the latest in a series of stimulating papers which Alschuler has produced on plea bargaining; citations to the earlier papers are collected in footnote 4 of the "Alternatives" article, at page 931.

Alschuler begins by expressing doubt that any major alternatives are really necessary to accommodate the greater number of trials that would presumably result from a ban on plea bargaining. After pointing out that in fact we currently provide very limited resources for criminal trials, he concludes:

A doubling, a tripling, or even a quadrupling of the resources now devoted to felony prosecutions therefore might require one, two, or three additional judges in counties like Boulder; two, four or six additional judges in a city like Indianapolis; and five, ten, or fifteen additional judges in cities like Denver and San Francisco. Even when the necessary addition in physical plant, support personnel, jurors, prosecutors, and defense attorneys are considered, this sort of investment need not inspire panic. Indeed, in almost every American jurisdiction, a multiplication several times over of the resources devoted to the resolution of felony cases apparently would require no more than the building and staffing of one new courthouse. This task might be about as burdensome as the building and staffing of a new high school; it would be less burdensome than providing a new hospital. If the need were in medicine or education, however, responsible citizens would at least talk about meeting it. They would not insist that "practical necessity" required bargaining with patients to waive their operations or with students to waive their classes. Id. at 941.

Alschuler also reports evidence that a very considerable number of defendants would continue to plead guilty even in the absence of concessions. This is particularly true in misdemeanor cases, where the "process costs" of fighting the case (in terms of bail bondsman fees, lawyer fees, and especially repetitive court appearances) generally exceed any punishment which the court is likely to impose upon conviction. On this subject see generally, Malcolm Feeley, *The Process is the Punishment* (1979), a study of misdemeanor prosecutions whose thesis is reflected in the title.

Having supported the view that it is not really necessary to make major changes in our trial procedures to accommodate the additional caseload that would result from an abolition of plea bargaining, Professor Alschuler nonetheless carefully reviews the alternatives that are available. Like Professor Langbein, he cites European examples (particularly West Germany) to demonstrate the enormous efficiencies that can be achieved by eliminating the American-style common law jury:

> West German procedure promotes popular participation in the administration of criminal justice but does not employ what, despite its democratic virtues, has become the most cumbersome factfinding mechanism that humankind has devised, the twelve-person jury. All except the most trivial cases are heard by mixed tribunals of lay and professional judges, and although the size and composition of these tribunals varies with the seriousness of the offense charged, the lay judges always have sufficient voting power to force an acquittal. Because West German lay judges are subject to disqualification only on the same narrow grounds that justify the disqualification of professional judges, West German procedure is not burdened by the voir dire examinations of prospective jurors that prolong American jury trials. Also absent are our elaborate jury instructions ("If you find A, you must consider B, and if you find B * * * ")—instructions that also lengthen the trial and that, most studies indicate, jurors do not understand. Because the lay and professional judges deliberate together, the professional can explain points of law as they become relevant. An adversary check on the accuracy of the legal positions that they adopt is provided by a detailed written judgment that sets forth both the court's legal positions and its factual conclusions and that can (and often does) lead to wide ranging appellate review at the behest of either the prosecution or the defense. Id. at 991–92.

Alschuler goes on to explore reforms less drastic than replacing the common law jury trial with a system of mixed tribunals, such as simplification of jury selection and evidentiary procedures. Alschuler's critique of the criminal trial process is highly recommended not only because of its connection to the proposal to abolish plea bargaining, but because it makes a powerful argument that there are many wasteful absurdities in our criminal process that we ought to consider changing regardless of whether anything is done about plea bargaining.

Note on Giving incentives for Testimony

Prosecutors, especially federal prosecutors, frequently obtain the cooperation of witnesses by offering immunity or sentencing concessions in return for "truthful testimony." Where the incentive is sufficiently powerful, it may induce a defendant to give whatever testimony the prosecutors want. In U.S. v. Singleton, 165 F.3d 1297 (10th Cir.1999) (en banc), the defendant was convicted of drug-related money laundering on the testimony of her co-conspirator, who "entered into a plea agreement in which he agreed to testify truthfully in return for the government's promise not to prosecute him for related offenses, to advise the sentencing court of his cooperation, and to advise a state parole board of the "nature and extent" of his "cooperation." A federal statute, 18 U.S.C. § 201(c)(2) states that "Whoever . . . (2) directly or indirectly, gives, offers, or promises anything of value to any person, for or because of the testimony under oath or affirmation given or to be given by such person as a witness upon a trial . . . before any court . . . shall be fined under this title or imprisoned for not more than two years, or both."

Did the prosecutor in *Singleton*–and countless other cases–commit a felony by obtaining testimony by offering something of value? Of course the question was not whether the prosecutor should be sent to prison, but whether the defendant's conviction should be reversed.

A panel decision of the United States Court of Appeals for the 10th Circuit answered "yes." 144 F.3d 1343. Other Circuit courts disagreed, and the 10th Circuit en banc reversed the panel decision. The majority reasoned that the practice of granting immunity or sentence concessions in return for testimony is well established, and is approved implicitly in other statutes, such as those providing for new identities and relocation of witnesses who testify for the government. Hence the word "Whoever" does not include a federal prosecutor acting within customary boundaries. The dissenting opinion argued that the courts should enforce the statute as written, leaving it to Congress to change the statute if policy considerations require allowing prosecutors to offer incentives that defense lawyers and other persons would not be allowed to offer.

*

Part Three

TRIAL AND PRETRIAL PROCEDURE

Chapter 15

PROSECUTOR AND GRAND JURY

COSTELLO v. UNITED STATES

Supreme Court of the United States, 1956.
350 U.S. 359, 76 S.Ct. 406, 100 L.Ed. 397.

Mr. Justice Black delivered the opinion of the Court.

We granted certiorari in this case to consider a single question: " 'May a defendant be required to stand trial and a conviction be sustained where only hearsay evidence was presented to the grand jury which indicted him?' "

Petitioner, Frank Costello, was indicted for wilfully attempting to evade payment of income taxes due the United States for the years 1947, 1948, and 1949. The charge was that petitioner falsely and fraudulently reported less income than he and his wife actually received during the taxable years in question. Petitioner promptly filed a motion for inspection of the minutes of the grand jury and for a dismissal of the indictment. His motion was based on an affidavit stating that he was firmly convinced there could have been no legal or competent evidence before the grand jury which indicted him since he had reported all his income and paid all taxes due. The motion was denied. At the trial which followed the Government offered evidence designed to show increases in Costello's net worth in an attempt to prove that he had received more income during the years in question than he had reported. To establish its case the Government called and examined 144 witnesses and introduced 368 exhibits. All of the testimony and documents related to business transactions and expenditures by petitioner and his wife. The prosecution concluded its case by calling three government agents. Their investigations had produced the evidence used against petitioner at the trial. They were allowed to summarize the vast amount of evidence already heard and to introduce computations showing, if correct, that petitioner and his wife had received far greater income than they had reported. We have held such summarizations admissible in a "net worth" case like this.

Counsel for petitioner asked each government witness at the trial whether he had appeared before the grand jury which returned the

666

indictment. This cross-examination developed the fact that the three investigating officers had been the only witnesses before the grand jury. After the Government concluded its case, petitioner again moved to dismiss the indictment on the ground that the only evidence before the grand jury was "hearsay," since the three officers had no firsthand knowledge of the transactions upon which their computations were based. Nevertheless the trial court again refused to dismiss the indictment, and petitioner was convicted. The Court of Appeals affirmed, holding that the indictment was valid even though the sole evidence before the grand jury was hearsay. Petitioner here urges: (1) that an indictment based solely on hearsay evidence violates that part of the Fifth Amendment providing that "No person shall be held to answer for a capital, or otherwise infamous crime, unless on a presentment or indictment of a Grand Jury * * * " and (2) that if the Fifth Amendment does not invalidate an indictment based solely on hearsay we should now lay down such a rule for the guidance of federal courts.

The Fifth Amendment provides that federal prosecutions for capital or otherwise infamous crimes must be instituted by presentments or indictments of grand juries. But neither the Fifth Amendment nor any other constitutional provision prescribes the kind of evidence upon which grand juries must act. The grand jury is an English institution, brought to this country by the early colonists and incorporated in the Constitution by the Founders. There is every reason to believe that our constitutional grand jury was intended to operate substantially like its English progenitor. The basic purpose of the English grand jury was to provide a fair method for instituting criminal proceedings against persons believed to have committed crimes. Grand jurors were selected from the body of the people and their work was not hampered by rigid procedural or evidential rules. In fact, grand jurors could act on their own knowledge and were free to make their presentments or indictments on such information as they deemed satisfactory. Despite its broad power to institute criminal proceedings the grand jury grew in popular favor with the years. It acquired an independence in England free from control by the Crown or judges. Its adoption in our Constitution as the sole method for preferring charges in serious criminal cases shows the high place it held as an instrument of justice. And in this country as in England of old the grand jury has convened as a body of laymen, free from technical rules, acting in secret, pledged to indict no one because of prejudice and to free no one because of special favor. As late as 1927 an English historian could say that English grand juries were still free to act on their own knowledge if they pleased to do so. And in 1852 Mr. Justice Nelson on circuit could say "no case has been cited, nor have we been able to find any, furnishing an authority for looking into and revising the judgment of the grand jury upon the evidence, for the purpose of determining whether or not the finding was founded upon sufficient proof * * *." United States v. Reed, 27 Fed.Cas. pages 727, 738, No. 16,134.

* * * If indictments were to be held open to challenge on the ground that there was inadequate or incompetent evidence before the grand jury, the resulting delay would be great indeed. The result of such a rule would be that before trial on the merits a defendant could always insist on a kind of preliminary trial to determine the competency and adequacy of the evidence before the grand jury. This is not required by the Fifth Amendment. An indictment returned by a legally constituted and unbiased grand jury, like an information drawn by the prosecutor, if valid on its face, is enough to call for trial of the charge on the merits. The Fifth Amendment requires nothing more.

Petitioner urges that this Court should exercise its power to supervise the administration of justice in federal courts and establish a rule permitting defendants to challenge indictments on the ground that they are not supported by adequate or competent evidence. No persuasive reasons are advanced for establishing such a rule. It would run counter to the whole history of the grand jury institution, in which laymen conduct their inquiries unfettered by technical rules. Neither justice nor the concept of a fair trial requires such a change. In a trial on the merits, defendants are entitled to a strict observance of all the rules designed to bring about a fair verdict. Defendants are not entitled, however, to a rule which would result in interminable delay but add nothing to the assurance of a fair trial.

Affirmed.

UNITED STATES v. HOGAN

United States Court of Appeals, Second Circuit, 1983.
712 F.2d 757.

CARDAMONE, CIRCUIT JUDGE:

On this appeal our principal concern is directed not at the jury trial where the accused were found guilty, but at earlier events—those that transpired before the grand jury which indicted the appellants. * * *

I

On July 24, 1981 appellants, Lawrence A. Hogan and Leonard J. Patricelli, were indicted by a grand jury sitting in the District of Connecticut for conspiracy to possess with intent to distribute heroin, in violation of 21 U.S.C. § 846. Hogan was also charged with five counts of using a telephone to facilitate an attempt to possess with intent to distribute heroin, in violation of 21 U.S.C. § 843(b). One of the § 843(b) counts was dismissed prior to trial.

After a nine-day trial held before then Chief Judge T. Emmet Clarie and a jury in the United States District Court for the District of Connecticut, the jury returned guilty verdicts as to both appellants on the conspiracy count and as to Hogan alone on three of the telephone facilitation counts, acquitting him on the remaining one. Although the appellants had moved before trial to dismiss the indictment on the basis of prosecutorial misconduct before the grand jury, that motion was denied. Both appellants were sentenced to five-year terms for the conspiracy conviction. Hogan also received three one-year terms on the telephone facilitation convictions, all of his sentences to run concurrently.

This case arose from a Federal Drug Enforcement Administration (DEA) undercover investigation of Hogan, a retired Stamford Connecticut Police Lieutenant with 22 years service, who had formerly served as head of the Southwestern Connecticut Regional Narcotics Crime Squad, and Patricelli, an associate of Hogan's with alleged ties to organized crime. Playing a central role in this investigation was Martin "Yogi" Ruggieri, a businessman who had allegedly borrowed $20,000 from Hogan. The record discloses that in late January 1981 Yogi persuaded Hogan and Patricelli to travel to the Hilton Hotel in Rye, New York for the purpose of obtaining repayment of the debt. While the government contends that the contemplated medium of repayment was narcotics, appellants assert that it was cash. In any event, upon arriving at the Hilton, Hogan and Patricelli were stopped by Rye Police Detective John Carlucci who was acting upon a request he had received from the DEA. Carlucci told Hogan and Patricelli that DEA agents were investigating a narcotics transaction and requested appellants to accompany him to Rye police headquarters for questioning. When it became clear at police headquarters that there was no basis to hold appellants, they were permitted to leave. We will return to this incident later.

On February 4, 1981 Yogi informed DEA Agent Paul Salute that Patricelli wanted to meet Yogi that evening to discuss the Rye, New York incident and Yogi's loan. Agent Salute, posing as Yogi's cousin from New Jersey, called Patricelli and had that meeting postponed. In the ensuing weeks a series of four meetings were held. At the first meeting, on February 11, Yogi, Hogan and DEA Agent Alleva, posing as a business partner of Yogi's cousin, met to discuss the money Yogi owed Hogan. During this meeting Alleva offered to sell to Hogan heroin at a discount price in exchange for forgiveness of Yogi's debt. The other meetings, between Hogan, Alleva, and on two occasions Patricelli, occurred on February 19, March 2 and March 11 at various area bars and restaurants. A number of telephone calls (perhaps nine or ten) between Hogan and Alleva also were made during February and March. The subject of these meetings and telephone calls concerned the proposed drug deal.

Through February and early March plans to implement the deal were in the discussion stage. No drugs were ever actually obtained or distributed. Then on March 13, when Alleva called him, Hogan terminated his involvement in the scheme, stating that he did not believe in it. In response to this statement by the principal subject of the undercover investigation, Alleva threatened Hogan with bodily harm if he did not change his mind and go through with the deal. DEA agents equipped Yogi with a recording device and sent him to see Hogan on May 12 to find out what had happened. Hogan told Yogi that he could not get involved in distributing heroin because it was against everything he ever believed in and that he wanted nothing to do with Alleva. Shortly thereafter the government sought and obtained the indictments at issue in this case.

II

* * *

Interposing a grand jury between the individual and the government serves the intended purpose of limiting indictments for higher crimes to those offenses charged by a group of one's fellow citizens acting independently of the prosecution and the court. In this independent position, a grand jury performs two distinct roles. It serves as an accuser sworn to investigate and present for trial persons suspected of wrongdoing. At the same time—and equally important—it functions as a shield, standing between the accuser and the accused, protecting the individual citizen against oppressive and unfounded government prosecution. It is true of course that prosecutors, by virtue of their position, have gained such influence over grand juries that these bodies' historic independence has been eroded. After all, it is the prosecutor who draws up the indictment, calls and examines the grand jury witnesses, advises the grand jury as to the law, and is in constant attendance during its proceedings. Nonetheless, there remain certain limitations on the presentation that a prosecutor may make to the grand jury. *See, e.g., United States v. Ciambrone*, 601 F.2d 616, 623 (2d Cir.1979) (prosecutor may not mislead grand jury or engage in fundamentally unfair tactics before it). In fact the gain in prosecutors' influence over grand juries is all the more reason to insist that these limitations be observed strictly. Due process considerations prohibit the government from obtaining an indictment based on known perjured testimony. *See United States v. Basurto*, 497 F.2d 781, 785 (9th Cir.1974). Courts have also held that a prosecutor may not make statements or argue in a manner calculated to inflame the grand jury unfairly against an accused. *See, e.g., United States v. Serubo*, 604 F.2d 807, 818 (3d Cir.1979). Under the applicable guidelines prosecutors have an ethical obligation strictly to observe the status of the grand jury as an independent legal body. In short, a prosecutor as an officer of the court is sworn to ensure that justice is done, not simply to obtain an indictment.

III

Bearing in mind these general obligations, we turn to the specific instances of prosecutorial misconduct which occurred before the grand jury in this case. At one point during the proceedings, a grand juror, apparently troubled by the proposed prosecution, posed the following question to the Assistant United States Attorney (AUSA):

> What I don't understand is if this case fell through, in other words, if there was no deal made what is the purpose of us listening to this?

The AUSA's response, in pertinent part, was as follows:

> If the deal would have gone forward we would have had a real hoodlum trying to sell heroin. * * * I think even though in a general

case where somebody backs out and decides not to do the crime it probably shouldn't be prosecuted.

In a case like this I think is [sic] a matter of equity it should.

Having characterized Hogan as a real hoodlum, who should be indicted as "a matter of equity," the AUSA proceeded to present to the grand jury hearsay testimony to the effect that Connecticut police officials thought that Hogan had committed crimes wholly irrelevant to the alleged drug transaction then under federal investigation. Specifically, the prosecutor introduced testimony that Hogan was a "suspect" in the apparently unrelated murders of a drug dealer named David Avnayim and a Norwalk Connecticut policeman named Charles Dugan. The grand jury was never asked to consider returning indictments for any federal offenses relating to these two murders.

In addition to the testimony regarding the two murders, the AUSA suggested that Hogan was guilty of misconduct while he was a police officer. Making himself an unsworn witness, the prosecutor informed the grand jury that he had read various articles in a Stamford newspaper which accused "a high ranking officer" of receiving bribes from gamblers. Then the same AUSA went on to relate that Leo Tobin, a Stamford police officer, had told him that Stamford Police Chief Czankis had mentioned to Tobin that Hogan was "suspected of having been on the take from gambling establishments."

Further, the prosecutor, faced with explaining Hogan's refusal to go through with the drug deal, elicited the following testimony. In response to a question posed by the prosecutor, Agent Alleva testified that he had no direct knowledge of why Hogan had changed his mind, but that he had "heard why through other agents." The AUSA immediately followed up that question by asking Alleva whether "[t]he speculation is that Yogi told Hogan that this was an undercover deal?" To this Agent Alleva responded affirmatively. The identity of the persons so speculating and the basis for their conclusions were never explored. Moreover, evidence in the DEA's possession in the form of the recording of the May 12 conversation between Hogan and Yogi casts serious doubt on the accuracy of this speculation.

Concerned with the obvious possibility that the grand jury might not indict because no drugs were ever purchased, possessed or distributed, it was apparently the prosecution's view that it would be helpful to show appellants' predisposition to possess heroin; but much of the evidence it presented in this regard later proved to be false. This seems the only plausible explanation for the AUSA having elicited repeated testimony from Agents Salute and Alleva that in January 1981, prior to the proposed narcotics deal in question, Hogan and Patricelli had been caught in Rye, New York attempting to obtain heroin. Agent Salute categorically denied any DEA role in the Rye incident and Agent Alleva testified that he had thoroughly investigated the incident and that the stop of appellants by the Rye police was in no way caused by the DEA. But the facts in the record indicate just the opposite. Confronted with statements of the Rye police and writings made at the time of the stop, Agent Salute admitted in post trial proceedings that the DEA had in fact called the Rye police and *instigated* the detention of Hogan and Patricelli.

Additionally, Agent Salute told the grand jury that he had discussed heroin over the telephone with Patricelli prior to the first meeting with Hogan. This evidence, which tended to show that appellants were arranging a heroin deal even before the first meeting with DEA undercover agents, was later conceded by the government to be untrue. The subject of heroin was not mentioned until the first meeting in February. Similarly, Agent Alleva "mistakenly" testified before the grand jury that he had informed Hogan at the first meeting that Hogan would have to pay $50,000 prior to the heroin delivery. In fact, Hogan was initially offered nearly $2,000,000 worth of heroin for no cash down payment. This offer—one that Hogan admitted had tempted him—differed significantly from the offer Alleva described to the grand jury. At trial Agent Alleva conceded that on this particular point he had made an error. He testified that the $50,000 demand on Hogan was not made at the first meeting, but was in fact made several meetings later. His explanation was that he had "confused" the meetings during his grand jury testimony.

IV

The law of this Circuit is that dismissal of an indictment is justified to achieve either of two objectives: to eliminate prejudice to a defendant; or, pursuant to our supervisory power, to prevent prosecutorial impairment of the grand jury's independent role. Viewing the above-mentioned instances of conduct cumulatively, we believe that the latter function is implicated here.

Although there is no prohibition on the use of hearsay evidence before a grand jury, our decision in *United States v. Estepa*, 471 F.2d 1132 (2d Cir.1972), indicates that extensive reliance on hearsay testimony is disfavored. More particularly, the government prosecutor, in presenting hearsay evidence to the grand jury, must not deceive the jurors as to the quality of the testimony they hear. Heavy reliance on secondary evidence is disfavored precisely because it is not first-rate proof. It should not be used without cogent reason, and never be passed off to the grand jurors as quality proof when it is not. Here the prosecution presented extensive hearsay and double hearsay speculation regarding Hogan's involvement in two murders, corrupt activities as a policeman, and reason for terminating his participation in the proposed heroin deal. Such secondary evidence added a false aura of factual support to the government's case and may well have deceived the grand jurors.

Additionally, the impartiality and independent nature of the grand jury process was seriously impaired by the AUSA's argument that Hogan was a real hoodlum who should be indicted as a matter of equity. *See Serubo*, 604 F.2d at 818 (uncalled for references to accused's violent tendencies and purported Mafia associations impermissible). Added to this inflammatory rhetoric were the numerous speculative references to other crimes of which Hogan was "suspected." None of these other crimes, the two murders and Hogan's alleged taking of bribes while a policeman, was under investigation by the grand jury. In fact, there is no indication that Hogan has ever been charged with these offenses by any state or federal body. These government accusations and others appear to have been made, not to support additional charges, but in order to depict appellants as bad persons and thereby obtain an indictment for independent crimes. This tactic is fundamentally unfair.

Finally, the DEA agents' false testimony to the grand jury on the issues of predisposition and inducement is most disturbing. Although the government was not required to anticipate a defense of entrapment and introduce evidence of predisposition, having elected to do so it was duty bound not to introduce false and misleading testimony. While the factual misstatements in the agents' testimony may have been inadvertent, as the government now argues, the fact remains that the appellants were prejudiced by the misstatements of important facts and the grand jury's independent role was impaired. * * *

In summary, the incidents related are flagrant and unconscionable. Taking advantage of his special position of trust, the AUSA impaired the grand jury's integrity as an independent body. Thus, based on the particular facts of this case, we believe that the indictment below must be dismissed.

Because of the determination reached, we need not decide the numerous other issues raised on appeal. The judgments of conviction are reversed and the case remanded to the district court with instructions to dismiss the underlying indictment against appellants.

Note

The Supreme Court held 5–4 in United States v. Williams, 504 U.S. 36 (1992), that the supervisory power of the federal courts does not permit a judge to dismiss an indictment on the ground that the prosecutor failed to submit "substantial exculpatory evidence" to the grand jury. The defendant Williams was charged with obtaining loans from banks by submitting financial statements that vastly overstated the value of his assets. The District Court granted his motion for disclosure of all exculpatory portions of the grand jury transcript under Brady v. Maryland, 373 U.S. 83 (1963). (The *Brady* rule is discussed in Chapter 16.)

After reviewing this material, Williams moved to dismiss the indictment on the ground that the government had chosen not to show other financial records to the grand jury. These records would have shown that he consistently accounted for the same assets in a similar manner for other purposes, and thus that the apparent inflation in their value was due to his peculiar accounting methods rather than to any intent to deceive the banks. The District Court granted the motion on the authority of United States v. Page, 808 F.2d 723 (10th Cir.1987), finding that the evidence was relevant and created a reasonable doubt as to Williams' guilt. The Court of Appeals affirmed, holding that it was not an abuse of discretion under the circumstances for the District Court to require the Government to begin anew before the grand jury.

The Supreme Court majority opinion by Justice Scalia observed that "it is axiomatic that the grand jury sits not to determine guilt or innocence, but to assess whether there is adequate basis for bringing a criminal charge * * *. As a consequence, neither in this country nor in England has the suspect under investigation by the grand jury ever been thought to have a right to testify, or to have exculpatory evidence presented." 504 U.S. at 51. Moreover, the *Costello* rule (Casebook, p. 666) does not allow a judge to dismiss an indictment on the ground that the grand jury indicted on incompetent or inadequate evidence. The majority concluded that to impose upon the prosecutor a legal obligation to present exculpatory evidence would be incompatible with this system.

UNITED STATES v. COX

United States Court of Appeals, Fifth Circuit, 1965.
342 F.2d 167 (en banc).

[A federal grand jury impaneled in the Southern District of Mississippi wished to indict two persons for perjury, but Hauberg, the United States Attorney, refused to prepare the necessary indictments. District Judge Cox ordered Hauberg to prepare and sign such indictments as the grand jury required but Hauberg, under instructions from Acting Attorney General Katzenbach, refused. Judge Cox found Hauberg guilty of contempt of court and ordered Katzenbach to show cause why he should not also be found guilty of contempt. Hauberg, Katzenbach, and the Department of Justice appealed.]

JONES, CIRCUIT JUDGE: * * *

The constitutional requirement of an indictment or presentment as a predicate to a prosecution for capital or infamous crimes has for its primary purpose the protection of the individual from jeopardy except on a finding of probable cause by a group of his fellow citizens, and is designed to afford a safeguard against oppressive actions of the prosecutor or a court. The constitutional provision is not to be read as conferring on or preserving to the grand jury, as such, any rights or prerogatives. The constitutional provision is, as has been said, for the benefit of the accused. The constitutional provision is not to be read as precluding, as essential to the validity of an indictment, the inclusion of requisites which did not exist at common law.

Traditionally, the Attorney for the United States had the power to enter a nolle prosequi of a criminal charge at any time after indictment and before trial, and this he could have done without the approval of the court or the consent of the accused. It may be doubted whether, before the adoption of the Federal Rules of Criminal Procedure, he had any authority to prevent the return of an indictment by a grand jury. There would be no constitutional barrier to a requirement that the signature of a United States Attorney upon an indictment is essential to its validity.

It is now provided by the Federal Rules of Criminal Procedure that the Attorney General or the United States Attorney may by leave of court file a dismissal of an indictment. Rule 48(a) Fed.Rules Crim.Proc. 18 U.S.C.A. In the absence of the Rule, leave of court would not have been required. The purpose of the Rule is to prevent harassment of a defendant by charging, dismissing and recharging without placing a defendant in jeopardy. Rule 7 eliminates the necessity for the inclusion in an indictment of many of the technical and prolix averments which were required at common law, by providing that the indictment shall be a plain, concise and definite written statement of the essential facts constituting the offense charged. The Rule also provides that "It shall be signed by the attorney for the government." Rule 7(c) Fed.Rules Crim. Proc. 18 U.S.C.A.

The judicial power of the United States is vested in the federal courts, and extends to prosecutions for violations of the criminal laws of the United States. The executive power is vested in the President of the United States, who is required to take care that the laws be faithfully executed. The Attorney General is the hand of the President in taking care that the laws of the United States in legal proceedings and in the prosecution of offenses, be faithfully executed. The role of the grand jury is restricted to a finding as to whether or not there is probable cause to believe that an offense has been committed. The discretionary power of the attorney for the United States in determining whether a prosecution shall be commenced or maintained may well depend upon matters of policy wholly apart from any question of probable cause. Although as a member of the bar, the attorney for the United States is an officer of the court, he is nevertheless an executive official of the Government, and it is as an officer of the executive department that he exercises a discretion as to whether or not there shall be a prosecution in a particular case. It follows, as an incident of the constitutional separation of powers, that the courts are not to interfere with the free exercise of the discretionary powers of the attorneys of the United States in their control over criminal prosecutions. The provision of Rule 7, requiring the signing of the indictment by the attorney for the Government, is a recognition of the power of Government counsel to permit or not to permit the bringing of an indictment. If the attorney refuses to sign, as he has the discretionary power of doing, we conclude that there is no valid indictment. It is not to be supposed that the signature of counsel is merely an attestation of the act of the grand jury. The signature of the foreman performs that function. It is not to be supposed that the signature of counsel is a certificate that the indictment is in proper form to charge an offense. The sufficiency of the indictment may be tested before the court. Rather, we think, the requirement of the signature is for the purpose of evidencing the joinder of the attorney for the United States with the grand jury in instituting a criminal proceeding in the Court. Without the signature there can be no criminal proceeding brought upon an indictment. * * *

If it were not for the discretionary power given to the United States Attorney to prevent an indictment by withholding his signature, there might be doubt as to the constitutionality of the requirement of Rule 48 for leave of court for a dismissal of a pending prosecution.

Because, as we conclude, the signature of the Government attorney is necessary to the validity of the indictment and the affixing or withholding of the signature is a matter of executive discretion which cannot be coerced or reviewed by the courts, the contempt order must be reversed. It seems that, since the United States Attorney cannot be required to give validity to an indictment by affixing his signature, he should not be required to indulge in an exercise of futility by the preparation of the form of an indictment which he is unwilling to vitalize with his signature. Therefore he should not be required to prepare indictments which he is unwilling and under no duty to sign.

Judges Tuttle, Jones, Brown and Wisdom join in the conclusion that the signature of the United States Attorney is essential to the validity of an indictment. Judge Brown, as appears in his separate opinion, is of the view that the United States Attorney is required, upon the request of the grand jury, to draft forms of indictments in accordance with its desires. The order before us for review is in the conjunctive; it requires the United States Attorney to prepare and sign. A majority of the court, having decided that the direction to sign is erroneous, the order on appeal will be reversed. * * *

Rives, Gewin and Griffin B. Bell, Circuit Judges (concurring in part and dissenting in part):

* * * [T]he basic issue before this Court is whether the controlling discretion as to the institution of a felony prosecution rests with the Attorney General or with the grand jury. The majority opinion would ignore the broad inquisitorial powers of the grand jury, and limit the constitutional requirement of Amendment V to the benefit of the accused. * * *

The grand jury may be permitted to function in its traditional sphere, while at the same time enforcing the separation of powers doctrine as between the executive and judicial branches of the government. This can best be done, indeed, it is mandatory, by requiring the United States Attorney to assist the grand jury in preparing indictments which they wish to consider or return, and by requiring the United States Attorney to sign any indictment that is to be returned. Then, once the indictment is returned, the Attorney General or the United States Attorney can refuse to go forward. That refusal will, of course, be in open court and not in the secret confines of the grand jury room. To permit the district court to compel the United States Attorney to proceed beyond this point would invest prosecutorial power in the judiciary, power which under the Constitution is reserved to the executive branch of the government. It may be that the court, in the interest of justice, may require a showing of good faith, and a statement of some rational basis for dismissal. In the unlikely event of bad faith or irrational action, not here present, it may be that the court could appoint counsel to prosecute the case. In brief, the court may have the same inherent power to administer justice to the government as it does to the defendant. That question is not now before us and may never arise. Except for a very limited discretion, however, the court's power to withhold leave to dismiss an indictment is solely for the protection of the defendant. * * *

For the Attorney General to prevent the grand jury from returning an indictment would, in effect, be to confine the grand jury to returning a mere presentment. That derogates from the grand jury its alternative power to return either "a presentment or indictment." U.S. Const. amend. V. The power of the grand jury cannot be limited in any case to a presentment; it may return an indictment.

Looking beyond the present controversy, one can foresee the grave danger inherent in such a restriction of the powers of a grand jury. If a grand jury is prevented from returning an indictment no more effective than a presentment, the statute of limitations may permanently bar prosecution for the crime. When the presentment is made public, the accused may flee or witnesses may get beyond the jurisdiction of the court. For all practical purposes, the case could be dead and there would be no point in any future Attorney General causing the presentment to be followed by an indictment. Worse still, this could be accomplished in the shadows of secrecy, with the Attorney General not being required to disclose his reasons. How much better is the constitutional system by which the grand jury can find and return an effective indictment upon which a prosecution for crime is instituted. At that point the power of the grand jury ceases. It is effectively checked and overbalanced by the power of the Attorney General, recognized in Rule 48(a), to move for a dismissal of the indictment. The court may then require such a motion to be heard in open court. Instead of a prevention in the shadows of secrecy, there would be a dismissal in a formal, public judicial proceeding.

* * *

By way of precaution, let us state that nothing here said is intended to reflect upon the present Acting Attorney General, in whose integrity we have the utmost confidence. Memory goes back, however, to days when we had an Attorney General suspected of being corrupt. There is no assurance that that will never again happen. We are establishing a precedent for other cases; we are construing a Constitution; we should retain intact that great constitutional bulwark, the institution of the grand jury.

On the cases before the Court, we agree with Judge Brown that the United States Attorney is required, upon the request of the grand jury, to draft forms of indictment in accordance with its desires. There is thus a majority of the Court in favor of that holding. We go further, and think that the United States Attorney is required to sign any indictment that may be found by the grand jury. * * * We would * * * affirm the judgment of civil contempt against the United States Attorney. * * *

[The concurring opinion of Judge John R. Brown is omitted. He argued that the trial court could properly compel the United States Attorney to prepare the indictment, but not to sign it. He reasoned that this middle course would enable the grand jury to express its conclusions in proper legal form. The United States Attorney or Attorney General could still prevent further criminal proceedings by refusing to sign the indictment, but his refusal would be public and the issue would be clearly drawn.]

WISDOM, CIRCUIT JUDGE (concurring specially): * * *

The prosecution of offenses against the United States is an executive function within the exclusive prerogative of the Attorney General. * * *

This brings me to the facts. They demonstrate, better than abstract principles or legal dicta, the imperative necessity that the United States, through its Attorney General, have uncontrollable discretion to prosecute.

The crucial fact here is that Goff and Kendrick, two Negroes, testified in a suit by the United States against the Registrar of Clarke County, Mississippi, and the State of Mississippi, to enforce the voting rights of Negroes under the Fourteenth Amendment and the Civil Rights Act.

Goff and Kendrick testified that some seven years earlier at Stonewall, Mississippi, the registrar had refused to register them or give them application forms. They said that they had seen white persons registering, one of whom was a B. Floyd Jones. Ramsey, the registrar, testified that Jones had not registered at that time or place, but had registered the year before in Enterprise, Mississippi. He testified also that he had never discriminated against Negro applicants for registration.[20] Jones testified that he was near the registration table in Stonewall in 1955, had talked with the registrar, and had shaken hands with him. The presiding judge, Judge W. Harold Cox, stated from the bench that Goff and Kendrick should be "bound over to await the action of the grand jury for perjury".

In January 1963 attorneys of the Department of Justice requested the Federal Bureau of Investigation to investigate the possible perjury. The FBI completed a full investigation in March 1963 and referred the matter to the Department's Criminal Division. In June 1963, the Criminal Division advised the local United States Attorney, Mr. Hauberg, that the matter presented "no basis for a perjury prosecution". Mr. Hauberg

---

20. Judge Cox found "as a fact from the evidence that negro citizens have been discriminated against by the registrar", although he found also that there was "no pattern or practice of discrimination". In its original opinion in the Ramsey case this Court noted the "testimony which witness by witness convicts Ramsey of palpable discrimination." United States v. Ramsey, 5 Cir.1964, 331 F.2d 824, 826. In his opinion Judge Rives noted that "This case reveals gross and flagrant denials of the rights of Negro citizens to vote." 331 F.2d at 833. And on rehearing, this Court ruled that the finding that "there was no pattern or practice in the discrimination by the Registrar" was "clearly erroneous." 331 F.2d at 838. No one has suggested that Mr. Ramsey may have been guilty of perjury.

informed Judge Cox of the Department's decision. Judge Cox stated that in his view the matter was clearly one for the grand jury and that he would be inclined, if necessary, to appoint an outside attorney to present the matter to the grand jury. (I find no authority for a federal judge to displace the United States Attorney by appointing a special prosecutor.) On receiving this information, the Criminal Division again reviewed its files and concluded that the charge of perjury could not be sustained. General Katzenbach, then Deputy Attorney General, after reviewing the files, concurred in the Criminal Division's decision. In September 1963 General Katzenbach called on Judge Cox as a courtesy to explain why the Department had arrived at the conclusion that no perjury was involved. Judge Cox, unconvinced, requested the United States Attorney to present to the grand jury the Goff and Kendrick cases, which he regarded as cases of "palpable perjury".

[A Mississippi state grand jury indicted Goff and Kendrick for perjury for testifying falsely in the federal civil rights case, but the federal Department of Justice obtained an injunction against his prosecution. Judge Cox thereafter caused the federal grand jury to hear witnesses testify regarding the alleged perjury, and the grand jury decided to indict. Acting Attorney General Katzenbach directed the United States Attorney not to prepare or sign the indictments, and this contempt proceeding followed.]

Against the backdrop of Mississippi versus the Nation in the field of civil rights, we have a heated but bona fide difference of opinion between Judge Cox and the Attorney General as to whether two Negroes, Goff and Kendrick, should be prosecuted for perjury. Taking a narrow view of the case, we would be justified in holding that the Attorney General's implied powers, by analogy to the express powers of Rule 48(a), give him discretion to prosecute. Here there was a bona fide, reasonable exercise of discretion made after a full investigation and long consideration of the case—both sides of the case, not just the evidence tending to show guilt. If the grand jury is dissatisfied with that administrative decision, it may exercise its inquisitorial power and make a presentment in open court. It could be said, that is all there is to the case. But there is more to the case.

This Court, along with everyone else, knows that Goff and Kendrick, if prosecuted, run the risk of being tried in a climate of community hostility. They run the risk of a punishment that may not fit the crime. The Registrar, who provoked the original litigation, runs no risk, notwithstanding the fact that the district court, in effect, found that Ramsey did not tell the truth on the witness stand. In these circumstances, the very least demands of justice require that the discretion to prosecute be lodged with a person or agency insulated from local prejudices and parochial pressures. This is not the hard case that makes bad law. This is the type of case that comes up, in one way or another, whenever the customs, beliefs, or interests of a region collide with national policy as fixed by the Constitution or by Congress. It is not likely that the men who devised diversity jurisdiction expected to turn over to local juries the discretionary power to bring federal prosecutions. This case is unusual only for the clarity with which the facts, speaking for themselves, illuminate the imperative necessity in American Federalism that the discretion to prosecute be lodged in the Attorney General of United States.

My memory, too, goes back to the days, pointedly referred to by the dissenters, when we had "an Attorney General suspected of being corrupt." But I am not aware that we have had more lawless Attorneys General than lawless juries.

Commentary

In Inmates of Attica Correctional Facility v. Rockefeller, 477 F.2d 375 (2d Cir.1973) the plaintiffs sought to obtain a court order requiring federal and state officials to investigate and prosecute persons who allegedly had committed criminal acts in connection with the suppression of the uprising at the New York state prison. The Court of Appeals affirmed the dismissal of the action with the following comments:

> In the absence of statutorily defined standards governing reviewability, or regulatory or statutory policies of prosecution, the problems inherent in the task of supervising prosecutorial decisions do not lend themselves to resolution by the judiciary. The reviewing courts would be placed in the undesirable and injudicious posture of becoming "super-prosecutors." In the normal case of review of executive acts of discretion, the administrative record is open, public and reviewable on the basis of what it contains. The decision not to prosecute, on the other hand, may be based upon the insufficiency of the available evidence, in which event the secrecy of the grand jury and of the prosecutor's file may serve to protect the accused's reputation from public damage based upon insufficient, improper, or even malicious charges. *In camera* review would not be meaningful without access by the complaining party to the evidence before the grand jury or U.S. Attorney. Such interference with the normal operations of criminal investigations, in turn, based solely upon allegations of criminal conduct, raises serious questions of potential abuse by persons seeking to have other persons prosecuted. Any person, merely by filing a complaint containing allegations in general terms (permitted by the Federal Rules) of unlawful failure to prosecute, could gain access to the prosecutor's file and the grand jury's minutes, notwithstanding the secrecy normally attaching to the latter by law.

> Nor is it clear what the judiciary's role of supervision should be were it to undertake such a review. At what point would the prosecutor be entitled to call a halt to further investigation as unlikely to be productive? What evidentiary standard would be used to decide whether prosecution should be compelled? How much judgment would the United States Attorney be allowed? Would he be permitted to limit himself to a strong "test" case rather than pursue weaker cases? What collateral factors would be permissible bases for a decision not to prosecute, e.g., the pendency of another criminal proceeding elsewhere against the same parties? What sort of review should be available in cases like the present one where the conduct complained of allegedly violates state as well as

federal laws? With limited personnel and facilities at his disposal, what priority would the prosecutor be required to give to cases in which investigation or prosecution was directed by the court?

These difficult questions engender serious doubts as to the judiciary's capacity to review and as to the problem of arbitrariness inherent in any judicial decision to order prosecution. On balance, we believe that substitution of a court's decision to compel prosecution for the U.S. Attorney's decision not to prosecute, even upon an abuse of discretion standard of review and even if limited to directing that a prosecution be undertaken in good faith, would be unwise.

Id. at 380–81.

The laws of some states permit a court to appoint a private prosecutor in exceptional cases but in general a prosecutor's decision not to bring charges is controlled only by his own superiors and, in highly visible cases, by public opinion. Even where state law expressly or impliedly permits a private individual to initiate a criminal prosecution without the approval of the public prosecutor, the practice has tended to fall into disuse. In People v. Municipal Court, 27 Cal.App.3d 193, 103 Cal.Rptr. 645, 66 A.L.R.2d 717 (1972), the court refused to give a "literal" reading to a statute that appeared to allow private prosecution, explaining that it would violate the defendant's right to due process of law as well as the principle of separation of powers to permit a criminal prosecution to proceed without the approval of the District Attorney or Attorney General.

The absolute power of the Attorney General to refuse to bring a federal prosecution was limited to some degree by the Ethics in Government Act, 28 U.S.C.A. § 591. This statute, passed originally in response to the Watergate scandals of the Nixon administration, lapsed during the administration of President Bush. It was revived in strengthened form by President Clinton, who came to regret his decision. The statute requires the Attorney General to conduct an investigation whenever he "receives information sufficient to constitute grounds to investigate" an accusation that any high-ranking federal official has committed a serious violation of federal criminal law. If the Attorney General after preliminary investigation finds "reasonable grounds to believe that further investigation or prosecution is warranted," he must apply to a special federal court for the appointment of an independent counsel to investigate or prosecute the case. The special court has no authority to appoint an independent counsel if the Attorney General, after completion of the preliminary investigation, finds that there are no reasonable grounds for proceeding further. [28 U.S.C.A. § 592(b)(1).] Another subsection provides that "A majority of majority party members or a majority of all non-majority party members of the Committee on the Judiciary of either House of the Congress may request in writing that the Attorney General apply for the appointment of an independent counsel." [28 U.S.C.A. § 595(e).] The Attorney General must respond to such a request in writing, but he can still refuse to prosecute if he is willing to explain and defend that decision to the Congress.

Once appointed, the federal independent counsel is not subject to direction from the Attorney General or the President. This freedom from political interference is of course the whole point of the Act, but to some observers it seems that such counsel are altogether *too* independent. Appointed in the glare of partisan controversy and publicity, counsel may have an incentive to pursue minor or weakly supported charges that would be quickly abandoned in the exercise of prosecutorial discretion under the standards applied to ordinary cases by regular prosecutors.* Independent prosecutors who have no responsibility beyond their own cases may also take actions that affect other legitimate national interests, such as relations with foreign countries. All of these theoretical problems became concrete during the independent counsel investigations during the Clinton administration, with the result that by 1999 there was a bipartisan consensus that the independent counsel statute should permitted to expire according to its terms. Experience seems to have shown that it is better to leave prosecutorial discretion under the control of the Attorney General, and to rely on the normal political process to check any abuses of that discretionary power.

Prosecutions for criminal contempts of court involve special considerations, because the power to appoint a special prosecutor in such cases may be essential to preserve the power of the judiciary to enforce its own decrees. The Supreme Court has held that federal district courts have authority to appoint private attorneys in contempt cases, but that: (1) such appointments should ordinarily be made only after a request for prosecution by the appropriate prosecuting authority has been denied; and (2) private attorneys appointed to prosecute criminal contempt actions should be "disinterested." In other words, a court should not appoint an attorney who represents a client with an interest in the underlying court order giving rise to the contempt. See Young v. United States ex rel. Vuitton et Fils S.A., 481 U.S. 787 (1987).

PEOPLE v. SEARS

Supreme Court of Illinois, 1971.
49 Ill.2d 14, 273 N.E.2d 380.

In 1969, Chicago Police officers executed a warrant to search the headquarters of the Black Panther Party for illegal weapons. Two members of the Party were killed in the course of this "raid," and the incident became the subject of a national controversy. A federal grand jury was convened to investigate whether the police and local officials had violated the civil rights of the deceased persons and other Black Panther Party members. After extensive hearings, the federal grand jury voted no indictments, but it did issue a report on the incident which was highly critical of the local authorities.

Subsequently, a number of individuals and organizations filed petitions in the circuit court of Cook County asking that a special grand jury be called and a Special State's Attorney appointed to investigate the entire affair, including the possibility that the regular State's Attorney and subordinate officials had conspired to obstruct justice by covering up the facts. In response, Circuit Judge Power ordered that such a grand

---

* For example, independent counsel conducted a lengthy and expensive investigation of Hamilton Jordan, White House Chief of Staff in the Carter Administration, on the basis of unsubstantiated allegations of drug use.

jury be impanelled, and appointed Sears as Special State's Attorney to present the evidence. The grand jury convened, heard a number of witnesses, and received a copy of the federal grand jury report.

After the special grand jury had been at work for several months, a conflict developed between Sears and Judge Power for reasons not spelled out in the court's opinion. Judge Power ordered Sears to call every witness who had testified before the federal grand jury to testify before the special state grand jury. When Sears refused to comply, Judge Power found him in contempt and imposed a fine of $50 per hour "until such time as he complies with the order of this court," plus an additional $100 fine for making contemptuous statements outside the court room.

In addition, several police officers and assistant State's Attorneys who were under investigation filed petitions asking Judge Power to dismiss the special grand jury because its members had been exposed to massive prejudicial publicity concerning the case in the news media, and because newspapers had reported that Sears and his staff had exceeded their "common law duties of presenting evidence to the Special Grand Jury" and instead "engaged in exhortations, pleas and arguments to the Special Grand Jury that some or all of the petitioners should be indicted by the Special Grand Jury." Judge Power denied Sears' motion to dismiss these petitions, ordered Sears to provide the court with transcripts of the grand jury proceedings, and announced his intent to meet privately with individual members of the special grand jury who wished to talk to him.

The Illinois Supreme Court agreed to hear Sears' appeal from the two contempt orders, and consolidated it with the applications of Sears and various organizations supporting him for writs of *mandamus* and *prohibition* which would, in effect, forbid Judge Power to interfere with Sears' manner of conducting the grand jury proceedings. [The preceding summary of the facts was prepared by the casebook editor from the courts' opinion.]

PER CURIAM. * * *

We shall first consider the order of the circuit court adjudging Sears in contempt for refusing to subpoena the witnesses who testified before the Federal Grand Jury to appear and testify before the special grand jury. With respect to this order, Sears contends that the circuit court was without jurisdiction to order either him, or the grand jury, to subpoena these witnesses to appear before the special grand jury. He argues that the grand jury is independent of the court, beyond judicial control, and has the power to hear such evidence as it desires and indict whom it chooses. The People contend that the circuit court, vested with non-reviewable discretion in determining that a grand jury should be called, is empowered to order that all available testimony relevant to the subject of the grand jury's inquiry be presented to it.

* * *

It is clear that it is the duty of the grand jury to inquire into offenses which come to its knowledge whether from the court, the State's Attorney, its own members, or from any source. If from its own members, the following provision from section 19 of the Jurors Act is applicable: "No grand jury shall make presentments of their own knowledge, upon the information of a less number than 2 of their own body, unless the juror giving the information is previously sworn as a witness, in which case, if the evidence shall be deemed sufficient, an indictment may be found thereon in like manner as upon the evidence of any other witness who may not be of the jury." Clearly, People v. Parker holds that information from "any source" must come through the State's Attorney. The quaint concept of the English common law that a grand jury can, of itself, proceed with an investigation is not valid in this stage of our history. * * * As lawyers we know that a grand jury cannot proceed with an investigation without the investigatory staff of the State's Attorney, the police or the sheriff, and that it cannot prepare subpoenas or indictments without assistance of counsel. It is apparent, therefore, that to adopt the rule for which Sears contends would vest in the State's Attorney the nonreviewable discretion as to what evidence is to be presented to the grand jury. This in our opinion could lead to abuse of the process, purpose and function of the grand jury and is inconsistent with its historic place in our system of justice.

We hold, therefore, that there may be circumstances under which the circuit court will have jurisdiction to direct that witnesses be subpoenaed to appear before a grand jury. The preservation of the historic independence of the grand jury, however, requires that such supervisory power be exercised only when failure to do so will effect a deprivation of due process or result in a miscarriage of justice. It is the opinion of the majority of members of this court that the circumstances shown here do not furnish a sufficient basis for the action of the court and the order holding Sears in contempt for refusing to subpoena the witnesses is therefore reversed.

We turn now to the order of contempt based upon the court's finding that statements made by Sears outside the courtroom "were embarrassing to the court and tended to interfere with the administration of justice." * * *

[The court reversed this contempt order on the ground that it had been imposed without an adequate hearing.]

We consider now the petitions for issuance of writs of *mandamus* and prohibition. * * *

The substance of petitioners' argument in support of the issuance of the writs is that although admittedly Sears's conduct before the grand jury is not above judicial scrutiny, such scrutiny may be invoked only after indictment and "is justified only where by proper verified pleading a clear and positive showing is made of gross and prejudicial irregularity influencing the grand jury in returning indictments."

The respondents, who are Judge Power and the individuals who file the three petitions in the circuit court, contend that the circuit court has general supervisory power over the grand jury while it is in session, which supervisory power may be exercised prior to indictment, and has jurisdiction to conduct appropriate inquiries while the grand jury is still sitting. * * *

Much of petitioners' argument deals with the necessity for secrecy of the grand jury proceedings contending that a prosecutor can not fearlessly perform his duties if at any time the court "can intrude itself in these proceedings and exercise the powers claimed here." The short answer to that is that the grand jury is an integral part of the court and not the tool of the prosecutor and neither the prosecutor nor the grand jury is vested with power to proceed without regard to due process. * * *

It is the opinion of the majority of this court that the circuit court, in the exercise of its inherent supervisory powers over the grand jury has jurisdiction to order the transcript of the proceeding before the grand jury submitted to it for examination as provided in the order entered on May 17, 1971, and we so hold. The petition for a writ of *mandamus*, is, therefore, denied.

With respect to the circuit court's announcement of his availability to those jurors who wish to communicate with him privately, it is our opinion that such procedure is not desirable and presents the possibility of infringement upon the historic independence of the grand jury and its proceedings. We hold that the court has jurisdiction to meet *in camera* with the grand jury. Insofar as the petitioners seek a writ of prohibition to preclude *in camera* communication between the court and individual grand jurors, the writ of prohibition will issue, and in all other respects the petition for writ of prohibition is denied.

We need not further discuss the nature of the alleged improprieties in the proceedings before the grand jury nor the newspaper articles allegedly based upon information obtained in violation of the secrecy of the grand jury proceedings. At this stage these cases present no issue of whether there is a sufficient basis for action by the circuit court upon completion of its examination of the transcripts and its interviews, if any, with the grand jury. They present the question of whether the circuit court, upon learning of alleged improprieties, may examine the transcript and conduct *in camera* interviews with the grand jury, if so requested by it, to determine whether, in fact, there is a basis for action by the court.

Orders of the circuit court reversed in part and remanded. Petition for writ of mandamus denied and petition for writ of prohibition allowed in part and denied in part, and writ so awarded.

Commentary

The *Sears* case illustrates the grand jury in its role as an investigatory body, rather than in its role of reviewing the decision to prosecute where the evidence has already been obtained by law enforcement agencies. As a rule, citizens have no obligation to answer the questions of the police or prosecutors in a criminal investigation. A grand jury hearing is thus the prosecutor's customary method of compelling witnesses to give testimony before trial. The usefulness of a grand jury in uncovering concealed facts was spectacularly illustrated during the investigation of the Watergate scandal. The grand jurors themselves do not usually take an active role in an investigation, however, because it is the prosecutor who decides whom to subpoena and what evidence to present. In many cases it might make little difference to the investigation if the grand jurors were not present at all. In *Sears* it was clearly the independence of the special prosecutor which was at stake rather than the independence of the grand jury. Whatever may be the rule in the case of an elected district attorney, why should a special prosecutor such as Sears be protected from the close supervision of the judge who appointed him in the first place?

The answer to this question probably lies in facts which the court avoided stating. Contemporary newspaper accounts described Judge Power as a former law partner and friend of Chicago Mayor Richard Daley, and the State's Attorney, who was the prime subject of the investigation, as a "Daley protege." Many members of the public suspected, whether rightly or not, that the judge was acting to protect local officials from an investigation that was more aggressive than expected. After the special grand jury indicted the State's Attorney and others for conspiracy to obstruct justice, defense attorneys obtained statements from four grand jurors indicating possible misconduct by Sears, and they asked for a hearing on the charges in connection with a motion to quash the indictment. The Illinois Supreme Court held that state law did not permit such a hearing, and ruled that affidavits or testimony of grand jurors could not be used to establish prosecutorial misconduct. People ex rel. Sears v. Romiti, 50 Ill.2d 51, 277 N.E.2d 705 (Ill. 1971). The defendants were acquitted at trial.

MATTER OF GRAND JURY PROCEEDINGS OF GUARINO

Supreme Court of New Jersey, 1986.
104 N.J. 218, 516 A.2d 1063.

GARIBALDI, J.

* * *

Since 1959, respondent, Joseph Guarino, has been doing business as a sole proprietor under the name of Green Acres Estates, a real estate concern. In 1984, a state Grand Jury began an investigation of Green Acres Estates. During the course of that investigation, the Grand Jury served Guarino with a *subpoena duces tecum*. The subpoena directed him to produce [records of certain real estate transactions. He appeared before the Grand Jury but refused to produce the records, relying on the privilege against self-incrimination.]

We first examine whether, and to what extent, the Fifth Amendment privilege against self-incrimination applies to voluntarily-prepared business records of a sole proprietor. The constitutional privilege against self-incrimination is "essentially a personal one, applying only to natural individuals." *United States v. White*, 322 *U.S.* 694, 698 (1944). "[A]n individual cannot rely upon the privilege to avoid producing the records of a collective entity which are in his possession in a representative capacity, even if these records might incriminate him personally." *Bellis v. United States*, 417 *U.S.* 85, 88 (1974). Consequently, the privilege cannot be asserted by a collective group (such as a corporation or a union) or by a representative employee or agent of that collective group. [Citations]

Employing this principle, the Supreme Court in two recent cases, *Fisher v. United States*, 425 *U.S.* 391 (1976) and *United States v. Doe*, 465 *U.S.* 605 (1984), has substantially limited the application of the Fifth Amendment privilege to business records, including those possessed by sole proprietors. Since *Boyd v. United States*, 116 *U.S.* 616 (1886) but prior to *Fisher*, the Supreme Court in a series of opinions consistently had repeated the axiom that an individual's private papers were protected by the Fifth Amendment from compelled disclosure. The prevailing rule was that "the Fifth Amendment privilege against compulsory self-incrimination protects an individual from compelled production of his personal papers and effects as well as compelled oral testimony." The protection of personal privacy, the fear that private thoughts recorded on paper might become the object of criminal sanctions, was the most prevalent rationale for this rule. And the privilege was viewed quite expansively, applying to the business records of the sole proprietor or sole practitioner as well as to the personal documents containing more intimate information about an individual's private life. *Bellis*, 417 *U.S.* at 87; Note, "Organizational Papers and the Privilege Against Self–Incrimination," 99 *Harv.L.Rev.* 640 (1986).

In *Fisher* and then again in *Doe*, the Court departed from these precedents. In *Fisher*, the Court held that a sole proprietor's tax records in the possession of his accountant were not protected. Justice White, writing in *Fisher* for himself and five other Justices, noted that "[s]everal of [the old] express or implicit declarations have not stood the test of time." He stated that "the prohibition against forcing the production of private papers has long been a rule searching for a rationale consistent with the proscriptions of the Fifth Amendment against compelling a person to give 'testimony' that incriminates him."

No longer constrained by the old rule, the *Fisher* Court fashioned a new one. The Court focused on the precise words of the Fifth Amendment—"[n]o person * * * shall be *compelled* in any criminal case to be a *witness against himself*." Rather than existing to shield certain private writings from discovery by the Government, the Fifth Amendment "applies only when the accused is *compelled* to make a *testimonial* communication that is incriminating." In effect, the focus of the Court shifted from privacy to the process of compulsion.

Applying the new test to the facts of the *Fisher* case, the Court concluded that requiring a defendant-taxpayer to produce an accountant's workpapers in the taxpayer's possession would not violate the Fifth Amendment, regardless of how incriminating those papers might be to the taxpayer, because "the privilege protects a person only against being incriminated by his *own compelled testimonial communications.*" 425 *U.S.* at 409. * * *

The Court in *Fisher* recognized, however, that there were two situations where the act of producing evidence in response to a subpoena could have "communicative aspects of its own, wholly aside from the contents of the papers produced." First, the act of producing documents in some instances might amount to an admission of the existence of such documents and their possession or control by the taxpayer. Second, the act of production might resemble the act of testimonial self-incrimination if responding to a subpoena would in some sense "authenticate" the documents produced. Neither of these situations, however, was present in *Fisher*. Accordingly, the Court reiterated its conclusion that the Fifth Amendment did not prevent the Government from obtaining, through subpoena, an accountant's workpapers in the possession of a taxpayer or his attorney.

The Court subsequently employed the *Fisher* analysis in *U.S. v. Doe*, 465 *U.S.* 605 (1984), where the facts were virtually identical to those in this case. The respondent was a sole proprietor. He was served with five subpoenas during the course of a Grand Jury's investigation into corruption in the awarding of county and municipal contracts. The first two subpoenas demanded that he produce telephone records of several of his companies and all records pertaining to four of his banks. A third subpoena demanded the production of a list of virtually all the business records of one of his companies.

Respondent filed a motion in federal district court seeking to quash the subpoenas. The district court granted the motion, quashing all of the subpoenas except those that sought documents and records required by law to be kept or disclosed to a public agency. The Third Circuit affirmed.

In its opinion in *Doe*, the Supreme Court first stated that *Fisher's* rationale applied with equal force to a sole proprietor who prepared his own documents. As in *Fisher*, the Court found that a subpoena that demands the production of documents does not *compel* oral testimony. Doe did not contend, said the Court, that he prepared the documents involuntarily or that the subpoena would force him to restate, repeat, or affirm the truth of their contents. The fact that the records were in Doe's possession, as opposed to his accountant's, was irrelevant in determining whether the creation of the record was compelled. The Court, therefore reversed the Third Circuit in part and concluded that the *contents* of the records were not privileged.

The Court, however, continued to draw the distinction that it drew in *Fisher* between the *contents* of a document and the act of producing it. But in *Doe*, unlike in *Fisher*, the Court had the explicit findings of the District Court that the act of producing the documents would invoke testimonial self-incrimination. Declining to overturn that finding because it rested on a determination of factual issues that had some support in the record, it affirmed the lower courts insofar as they found the act of production to be privileged. The Court recognized that if the government wished to compel production of the documents, it could have sought a grant of use immunity with respect to the potentially incriminating evidence.

Following *Doe*, it is clear that the *contents* of business records, whether from a corporation, a partnership, or a sole proprietorship, are no longer privileged under the Fifth Amendment. The documents requested from the respondent in this case were far less extensive than those requested from Doe. The only request made of Guarino, doing business as Green Acres Estates, that was not made of Doe was for real estate contracts and documentation of real estate payments. Given the nature of Guarino's business, those contracts were clearly business, not personal, records, and they were related to the focus of the Grand Jury's investigation. Like Doe, Guarino does not contend that he prepared the requested records involuntarily or that the subpoena would force him to restate, repeat, or affirm the truth of the contents. Accordingly, under *Doe* the contents of respondent's business records are not protected by the Fifth Amendment privilege against self-incrimination. Furthermore, the prosecutors here, as the Supreme Court suggested in *Doe*, granted Guarino use immunity for *producing* the documents. Therefore, the production of the documents did not violate his Fifth Amendment privilege against self-incrimination.

III

We turn now to an examination of whether under independent principles of state law we might extend the privilege against self-incrimination to Guarino, doing business as Green Acres Estates. It is undisputed that State common law may provide greater protection to individual rights than afforded under the United States Constitution. * * *

We affirm our belief in the *Boyd* doctrine and hold that the New Jersey common law privilege against self-incrimination protects the individual's right "to a private enclave where he may lead a private life." *Murphy v. Waterfront Comm'n*, 378 U.S. 52, 55 (1964). To determine whether the evidence sought by the government lies within that sphere of personal privacy a court must look to the nature of the evidence. In the case of documents, therefore, a court must look to their contents, not to the testimonial compulsion involved in the act of producing them, as the Supreme Court has done in *Fisher* and *Doe*. Neither *Fisher* nor *Doe* recognize the fundamental privacy principles underlying the New Jersey common-law privilege against self-incrimination. Thus, in defining the scope of our common law privilege, we decline to follow the Court's rationale for its *Doe* decision.

IV

Nevertheless, as a matter of New Jersey common law, we agree with the result in *Fisher* and *Doe*. The subpoenaed documents in issue are the business records of Guarino, doing business as Green Acres Estates, a real estate concern. The business records of a sole proprietor do not lie within that special zone of privacy that forms the core of the documents protected by *Boyd* and its progeny, and that are protected by the New Jersey privilege against self-incrimination.[21]

* * *

The subpoenaed documents here illustrate that the business records of a sole proprietor are simply not private. They do not contain the requisite element of privacy or confidentiality essential to be privileged. The purpose of business records is frequently to record transactions with second and third parties. In today's highly computerized, commercialized and regulated world, there is little expectation of privacy for such records that touch so little on the intimate aspects of one's personal life. This is particularly true of the records requested here: contracts of sale, cash receipts, journals and general ledgers. They document payments made by purchasers of property from Guarino doing business as Green Acres Estates. Many of these documents of sale are presumably reviewed by the purchasers, their attorneys and their accountants, then used in preparing the purchaser's tax returns and possibly filed at county recording offices. Normally, such documents are disclosed to a significant number of individuals, to an extent totally inconsistent with any claim of privacy.

Moreover, we do not perceive any reason why the records of a sole proprietor kept in the ordinary course of business are entitled to any greater protection than the business records of a partnership or corporation. Sole proprietors may operate large, substantial business enterprises, in many instances more extensive than small one-person corporations or two-person partnership. * * *

[Order to produce documents upheld.]

HANDLER, J., dissenting.

* * *

Because of the unsoundness of [the Supreme Court's] new conceptualization of the Fifth Amendment, I am persuaded by Justice Brennan's reasoning that would keep the focus not solely upon the testimonial incidents that can be read into the act of producing personal records. Rather, the target should be the contents of documents, which are the

---

21. If Guarino had contended that any part of these records invoked concerns of personal privacy, e.g. personal comments, telephone numbers, or the like that would warrant protection, the result might be different. No such issue has been raised. Cf. *Klitzman, Klitzman & Gallagher v. Krut,* 744 F.2d 955 (3d Cir.1984) ("warrant authorizing virtually a wholesale search and seizure of business records" of a law firm in which one of its attorneys was the target of a criminal investigation was overbroad and constitutionally infirm).

heart of the Fifth Amendment's solicitude for privacy and the true object of the government's compulsory efforts. The Fifth Amendment's protection should attach to an individual's books and papers because their contents can be equated with an individual's mental notations.

> The common-law and constitutional extension of the privilege to testimonial materials, such as books and papers, was inevitable. An individual's books and papers are generally little more than an extension of his person. They reveal no less than he could reveal upon being questioned directly. Many of the matters within an individual's knowledge may as easily be retained within his head as set down on a scrap of paper. I perceive no principle which does not permit compelling one to disclose the contents of one's mind but does permit compelling the disclosure of the contents of that scrap of paper by compelling its production. Under a contrary view, the constitutional protection would turn on fortuity, and persons would, at their peril, record their thoughts and the events of their lives. The ability to think private thoughts, facilitated as it is by pen and paper, and the ability to preserve intimate memories would be curtailed through fear that those thoughts or the events of those memories would become the subject of criminal sanctions however invalidly imposed. Indeed, it was the very reality of those fears that helped provide the historical impetus for the privilege. [Citations] [*Fisher, supra*, 425 U.S. at 420 (Brennan., J., concurring).]

Assuming, moreover, that as a matter of logical analysis the contents of documents can be separated from their production, this analytical parsing should not serve to truncate or attenuate the substance of the privilege itself. There is nothing in the Fifth Amendment that insists that the contents of documents be created through compulsion in order to secure their protection—no more so than the thought which precedes the expression must itself be forced in order for the privilege to apply to a person's mental processes and verbalizations. As Justice Brennan observed, "it does not follow that the protection is necessarily unavailable if the papers were prepared voluntarily, for it is the compelled production of testimonial evidence, not just compelled creation of such evidence, against which the privilege protects." *Id.*, 425 U.S. at 423.[22]

---

22. Justice Marshall also recognized the infirmity of the Court's attempted distinction between the creation of documents and the production of documents. He predicted in *Fisher* that act-of-production immunity arising from self-incriminating existence testimony would derivatively protect the documents' contents.

Under the Court's theory, if the document is to be obtained the immunity grant must extend to the testimony that the document is presently in existence. Such a grant will effectively shield the contents of the document, for the contents are a direct fruit of the immunized testimony—that the document exists—and cannot usually be obtained without reliance on that testimony. Accordingly, the Court's theory offers substantially the same protection against procurement of documents under grant of immunity that our prior cases afford. [*Fisher v. United States, supra*, 425 U.S. at 433–34 (Marshall, J. concurring).]

It is obvious that this understanding is not shared by the Supreme Court. *See, e.g., United States v. Doe, supra*, 465 U.S. at 617, n. 17.

I am satisfied that the *Fisher-Doe* doctrine does not reflect a sound policy that can be commended as an interpretive source of the State's common-law privilege against self-incrimination. It is a doctrine that is problematic in its historical origins, contrary to constitutional tradition, a departure from long-standing constitutional philosophy, and productive of artificial and arbitrary applications. Our own common-law privilege against self-incrimination springs from a source that antedates *Fisher-Doe* and is nourished by constitutional principles alien to those that now dominate the Fifth Amendment. * * *

I am satisfied that the New Jersey common-law privilege against self-incrimination is fully protective of an individual's personal privacy interests, and would extend to the attempted prosecutorial use of any incriminating evidence that is of a testimonial nature. It would accord protection against the compelled production and resultant disclosure of the contents of an individual's personal business records. This common-law privilege is firmly grounded on sound principles of public policy that are solicitous of the personal privacy protected in the criminal law context. Further, these principles, which reflect a strong state tradition that respects individual privacy, have been consistently confirmed by decisional precedent. For these reasons I would hold that a subpoena may not be enforced to compel an individual to produce private and personal records relating to the conduct of his sole business.

* * *

JUSTICES CLIFFORD and POLLOCK join in this opinion.

Note

An additional Fifth Amendment issue arises when a grand jury subpoenas records in the custody of a foreign bank. Frequently the bank refuses to supply the records without the consent of its depositor, who is the subject of the grand jury investigation. May the prosecution obtain a court order directing the person who is the target of the investigation to sign a written consent to the production of the records? The Supreme Court held that such an order does not violate the suspect's Fifth Amendment rights, in Doe v. United States, 487 U.S. 201 (1988). The majority ruled that the consent directive was not testimonial in nature because executing it did not require the suspect to admit that any relevant records or accounts were in existence. Only Justice Stevens dissented, arguing that a suspect cannot "be compelled to use his mind to assist the Government in developing its case."

UNITED STATES v. ARMSTRONG

Supreme Court of the United States, 1996.
517 U.S. 456, 116 S.Ct. 1480, 134 L.Ed.2d 687.

CHIEF JUSTICE REHNQUIST delivered the opinion of the Court.

In this case, we consider the showing necessary for a defendant to be entitled to discovery on a claim that the prosecuting attorney singled him out for prosecution on the basis of his race. We conclude that respondents failed to satisfy the threshold showing: They failed to show that the Government declined to prosecute similarly situated suspects of other races.

In April 1992, respondents were indicted in the United States District Court for the Central District of California on charges of conspiring to possess with intent to distribute more than 50 grams of cocaine base (crack) and conspiring to distribute the same, in violation of 21 U.S.C. §§ 841 and 846 (1988 ed. and Supp. IV), and federal firearms offenses. For three months prior to the indictment, agents of the Federal Bureau of Alcohol, Tobacco, and Firearms and the Narcotics Division of the Inglewood, California, Police Department had infiltrated a suspected crack distribution ring by using three confidential informants. On seven separate occasions during this period, the informants had bought a total of 124.3 grams of crack from respondents and witnessed respondents carrying firearms during the sales. The agents searched the hotel room in which the sales were transacted, arrested respondents Armstrong and Hampton in the room, and found more crack and a loaded gun. The agents later arrested the other respondents as part of the ring.

In response to the indictment, respondents filed a motion for discovery or for dismissal of the indictment, alleging that they were selected for federal prosecution because they are black. In support of their motion, they offered only an affidavit by a "Paralegal Specialist," employed by the Office of the Federal Public Defender representing one of the respondents. The only allegation in the affidavit was that, in every one of the 24 §§ 841 or 846 cases closed by the office during 1991, the defendant was black. Accompanying the affidavit was a "study" listing the 24 defendants, their race, whether they were prosecuted for dealing cocaine as well as crack, and the status of each case.

The Government opposed the discovery motion, arguing, among other things, that there was no evidence or allegation "that the Government has acted unfairly or has prosecuted non-black defendants or failed to prosecute them." The District Court granted the motion. It ordered the Government (1) to provide a list of all cases from the last three years in which the Government charged both cocaine and firearms offenses, (2) to identify the race of the defendants in those cases, (3) to identify what levels of law enforcement were involved in the investigations of those cases, and (4) to explain its criteria for deciding to prosecute those defendants for federal cocaine offenses.

The Government moved for reconsideration of the District Court's discovery order. With this motion it submitted affidavits and other evidence to explain why it had chosen to prosecute respondents and why respondents' study did not support the inference that the Government was singling out blacks for cocaine prosecution. The federal and local agents participating in the case alleged in affidavits that race played no role in their investigation. An Assistant United States Attorney explained in an affidavit that the decision to prosecute met the general criteria for prosecution, because "there was over 100 grams of cocaine base involved, over twice the threshold necessary for a ten year mandatory minimum sentence; there were multiple sales involving multiple defendants, thereby indicating a fairly substantial crack cocaine ring; * * * there were multiple federal firearms violations intertwined with the narcotics trafficking; the overall evidence in the case was extremely strong, including audio and videotapes of defendants; * * * and several of the defendants had criminal histories including narcotics and firearms violations."

The Government also submitted sections of a published 1989 Drug Enforcement Administration report which concluded that "large-scale, interstate trafficking networks controlled by Jamaicans, Haitians and Black street gangs dominate the manufacture and distribution of crack." J. Featherly & E. Hill, Crack Cocaine Overview 1989; App. 103.

In response, one of respondents' attorneys submitted an affidavit alleging that an intake coordinator at a drug treatment center had told her that there are "an equal number of caucasian users and dealers to minority users and dealers." Respondents also submitted an affidavit from a criminal defense attorney alleging that in his experience many nonblacks are prosecuted in state court for crack offenses, and a newspaper article reporting that Federal "crack criminals * * * are being punished far more severely than if they had been caught with powder cocaine, and almost every single one of them is black," Newton, Harsher Crack Sentences Criticized as Racial Inequity, Los Angeles Times, Nov. 23, 1992, p. 1; App. 208–210.

The District Court denied the motion for reconsideration. When the Government indicated it would not comply with the court's discovery order, the court dismissed the case.[23] The Court of Appeals [en banc] * * * affirmed the District Court's order of dismissal, holding that "a defendant is not required to demonstrate that the government has failed to prosecute others who are similarly situated."

[The Supreme Court held that Federal Rule of Criminal Procedure 16 [infra, p. 774], which by its terms governs discovery in criminal cases, is not applicable to a claim of discriminatory prosecution.] * * *

A selective-prosecution claim is not a defense on the merits to the criminal charge itself, but an independent assertion that the prosecutor has brought the charge for reasons forbidden by the Constitution. Our cases delineating the necessary elements to prove a claim of selective prosecution have taken great pains to explain that the standard is a demanding one. These cases afford a "background presumption," that the showing necessary to obtain discovery should itself be a significant barrier to the litigation of insubstantial claims.

23. We have never determined whether dismissal of the indictment, or some other sanction, is the proper remedy if a court determines that a defendant has been the victim of prosecution on the basis of his race. Here, it was the government itself that suggested dismissal of the indictments to the district court so that an appeal might lie.

A selective-prosecution claim asks a court to exercise judicial power over a "special province" of the Executive. Heckler v. Chaney, 470 U.S. 821, 832 (1985). The Attorney General and United States Attorneys retain " 'broad discretion' " to enforce the Nation's criminal laws. Wayte v. United States, 470 U.S. 598, 607 (1985)(quoting United States v. Goodwin, 457 U.S. 368, 380, n. 11 (1982)). They have this latitude because they are designated by statute as the President's delegates to help him discharge his constitutional responsibility to "take Care that the Laws be faithfully executed." As a result, "the presumption of regularity supports" their prosecutorial decisions and "in the absence of clear evidence to the contrary, courts presume that they have properly discharged their official duties." United States v. Chemical Foundation, Inc., 272 U.S. 1, 14–15 (1926). In the ordinary case, "so long as the prosecutor has probable cause to believe that the accused committed an offense defined by statute, the decision whether or not to prosecute, and what charge to file or bring before a grand jury, generally rests entirely in his discretion." Bordenkircher v. Hayes, 434 U.S. 357, 364 (1978).

Of course, a prosecutor's discretion is "subject to constitutional constraints." United States v. Batchelder, 442 U.S. 114, 125 (1979). One of these constraints, imposed by the equal protection component of the Due Process Clause of the Fifth Amendment, is that the decision whether to prosecute may not be based on "an unjustifiable standard such as race, religion, or other arbitrary classification," Oyler v. Boles, 368 U.S. 448, 456 (1962). A defendant may demonstrate that the administration of a criminal law is "directed so exclusively against a particular class of persons * * * with a mind so unequal and oppressive" that the system of prosecution amounts to "a practical denial" of equal protection of the law. Yick Wo v. Hopkins, 118 U.S. 356, 373 (1886).

In order to dispel the presumption that a prosecutor has not violated equal protection, a criminal defendant must present "clear evidence to the contrary." Chemical Foundation, supra, at 14–15. We explained in *Wayte* why courts are "properly hesitant to examine the decision whether to prosecute." 470 U.S., at 608. Judicial deference to the decisions of these executive officers rests in part on an assessment of the relative competence of prosecutors and courts. "Such factors as the strength of the case, the prosecution's general deterrence value, the Government's enforcement priorities, and the case's relationship to the Government's overall enforcement plan are not readily susceptible to the kind of analysis the courts are competent to undertake." Id., at 607. It also stems from a concern not to unnecessarily impair the performance of a core executive constitutional function. "Examining the basis of a prosecution delays the criminal proceeding, threatens to chill law enforcement by subjecting the prosecutor's motives and decisionmaking to outside inquiry, and may undermine prosecutorial effectiveness by revealing the Government's enforcement policy." Ibid.

The requirements for a selective-prosecution claim draw on "ordinary equal protection standards." Id., at 608. The claimant must demonstrate that the federal prosecutorial policy "had a discriminatory effect and that it was motivated by a discriminatory purpose." Ibid.; accord, *Oyler,* supra, at 456. To establish a discriminatory effect in a race case, the claimant must show that similarly situated individuals of a different race were not prosecuted. This requirement has been established in our case law since Ah Sin v. Wittman, 198 U.S. 500 (1905). Ah Sin, a subject of China, petitioned a California state court for a writ of habeas corpus, seeking discharge from imprisonment under a San Francisco county ordinance prohibiting persons from setting up gambling tables in rooms barricaded to stop police from entering. He alleged in his habeas petition "that the ordinance is enforced 'solely and exclusively against persons of the Chinese race and not otherwise.' " We rejected his contention that this averment made out a claim under the Equal Protection Clause, because it did not allege "that the conditions and practices to which the ordinance was directed did not exist exclusively among the Chinese, or that there were other offenders against the ordinance than the Chinese as to whom it was not enforced." Id., at 507–508.

The similarly situated requirement does not make a selective-prosecution claim impossible to prove. Twenty years before *Ah Sin,* we invalidated an ordinance, also adopted by San Francisco, that prohibited the operation of laundries in wooden buildings. Yick Wo, 118 U.S., at 374. The plaintiff in error successfully demonstrated that the ordinance was applied against Chinese nationals but not against other laundry-shop operators. The authorities had denied the applications of 200 Chinese subjects for permits to operate shops in wooden buildings, but granted the applications of 80 individuals who were not Chinese subjects to operate laundries in wooden buildings "under similar conditions."
* * *

Having reviewed the requirements to prove a selective-prosecution claim, we turn to the showing necessary to obtain discovery in support of such a claim. If discovery is ordered, the Government must assemble from its own files documents which might corroborate or refute the defendant's claim. Discovery thus imposes many of the costs present when the Government must respond to a prima facie case of selective prosecution. It will divert prosecutors' resources and may disclose the Government's prosecutorial strategy. The justifications for a rigorous standard for the elements of a selective-prosecution claim thus require a correspondingly rigorous standard for discovery in aid of such a claim.

The parties, and the Courts of Appeals which have considered the requisite showing to establish entitlement to discovery, describe this showing with a variety of phrases, like "colorable basis," "substantial threshold showing," "substantial and concrete basis," or "reasonable likelihood." However, the many labels for this showing conceal the degree of consensus about the evidence necessary to meet it. The Courts of Appeals "require some evidence tending to show the existence of the essential elements of the defense," discriminatory effect and discriminatory intent. United States v. Berrios, 501 F.2d 1207, 1211 (C.A.2 1974).

In this case we consider what evidence constitutes "some evidence tending to show the existence" of the discriminatory effect element. The Court of Appeals held that a defendant may establish a colorable basis for discriminatory effect without evidence that the Government has failed to prosecute others who are similarly situated to the defendant. We think it was mistaken in this view. The vast majority of the Courts of Appeals require the defendant to produce some evidence that similarly situated defendants of other races could have been prosecuted, but were not, and this requirement is consistent with our equal protection case law. [Citations]

The Court of Appeals reached its decision in part because it started "with the presumption that people of all races commit all types of crimes—not with the premise that any type of crime is the exclusive province of any particular racial or ethnic group." It cited no authority for this proposition, which seems contradicted by the most recent statistics of the United States Sentencing Commission. Those statistics show that: More than 90% of the persons sentenced in 1994 for crack cocaine trafficking were black, United States Sentencing Comm'n, 1994 Annual Report 107 (Table 45); 93.4% of convicted LSD dealers were white; and 91% of those convicted for pornography or prostitution were white, id., at 41 (Table 13). Presumptions at war with presumably reliable statistics have no proper place in the analysis of this issue.

The Court of Appeals also expressed concern about the "evidentiary obstacles defendants face." But all of its sister Circuits that have confronted the issue have required that defendants produce some evidence of differential treatment of similarly situated members of other races or protected classes. In the present case, if the claim of selective prosecution were well founded, it should not have been an insuperable task to prove that persons of other races were being treated differently than respondents. For instance, respondents could have investigated whether similarly situated persons of other races were prosecuted by the State of California, were known to federal law enforcement officers, but were not prosecuted in federal court. We think the required threshold—a credible showing of different treatment of similarly situated persons—adequately balances the Government's interest in vigorous prosecution and the defendant's interest in avoiding selective prosecution.

In the case before us, respondents' "study" did not constitute "some evidence tending to show the existence of the essential elements of" a selective-prosecution claim. The study failed to identify individuals who were not black, could have been prosecuted for the offenses for which respondents were charged, but were not so prosecuted. This omission was not remedied by respondents' evidence in opposition to the Government's motion for reconsideration. The newspaper article, which discussed the discriminatory effect of federal drug sentencing laws, was not relevant to an allegation of discrimination in decisions to prosecute. Respondents' affidavits, which recounted one attorney's conversation with a drug treatment center employee and the experience of another attorney defending drug prosecutions in state court, recounted hearsay and reported personal conclusions based on anecdotal evidence. The judgment of the Court of Appeals is therefore reversed, and the case is remanded for proceedings consistent with this opinion.

[The concurring opinions of Justice Souter and Justice Ginsburg, joined by Justice Breyer, are omitted. They deal only with the scope of Federal Rule of Criminal Procedure 16.]

JUSTICE STEVENS, dissenting.

* * *

The Court correctly concludes that in this case the facts presented to the District Court in support of respondents' claim that they had been singled out for prosecution because of their race were not sufficient to prove that defense. Moreover, I agree with the Court that their showing was not strong enough to give them a right to discovery, either under Rule 16 or under the District Court's inherent power to order discovery in appropriate circumstances. Like Chief Judge Wallace of the Court of Appeals, however, I am persuaded that the District Judge did not abuse her discretion when she concluded that the factual showing was sufficiently disturbing to require some response from the United States Attorney's Office. Perhaps the discovery order was broader than necessary, but I cannot agree with the Court's apparent conclusion that no inquiry was permissible.

The District Judge's order should be evaluated in light of three circumstances that underscore the need for judicial vigilance over certain types of drug prosecutions. First, the Anti–Drug Abuse Act of 1986 and subsequent legislation established a regime of extremely high penalties for the possession and distribution of so-called "crack" cocaine. Those provisions treat one gram of crack as the equivalent of 100 grams of powder cocaine. The distribution of 50 grams of crack is thus punishable by the same mandatory minimum sentence of 10 years in prison that applies to the distribution of 5,000 grams of powder cocaine. The Sentencing Guidelines extend this ratio to penalty levels above the mandatory minimums: for any given quantity of crack, the guideline range is the same as if the offense had involved 100 times that amount in powder cocaine. These penalties result in sentences for crack offenders that average three to eight times longer than sentences for comparable powder offenders.

Second, the disparity between the treatment of crack cocaine and powder cocaine is matched by the disparity between the severity of the punishment imposed by federal law and that imposed by state law for the same conduct. For a variety of reasons, often including the absence of mandatory minimums, the existence of parole, and lower baseline penalties, terms of imprisonment for drug offenses tend to be substantially lower in state systems than in the federal system. The difference is especially marked in the case of crack offenses. The majority of States draw no distinction between types of cocaine in their penalty schemes; of those that do, none has established as stark a differential as the Federal

Government. For example, if respondent Hampton is found guilty, his federal sentence might be as long as a mandatory life term. Had he been tried in state court, his sentence could have been as short as 12 years, less worktime credits of half that amount.

Finally, it is undisputed that the brunt of the elevated federal penalties falls heavily on blacks. While 65% of the persons who have used crack are white, in 1993 they represented only 4% of the federal offenders convicted of trafficking in crack. Eighty-eight percent of such defendants were black. During the first 18 months of full guideline implementation, the sentencing disparity between black and white defendants grew from preguideline levels: blacks on average received sentences over 40% longer than whites. See Bureau of Justice Statistics, Sentencing in the Federal Courts: Does Race Matter? 6–7 (Dec. 1993). Those figures represent a major threat to the integrity of federal sentencing reform, whose main purpose was the elimination of disparity (especially racial) in sentencing. The Sentencing Commission acknowledges that the heightened crack penalties are a "primary cause of the growing disparity between sentences for Black and White federal defendants."

The extraordinary severity of the imposed penalties and the troubling racial patterns of enforcement give rise to a special concern about the fairness of charging practices for crack offenses. Evidence tending to prove that black defendants charged with distribution of crack in the Central District of California are prosecuted in federal court, whereas members of other races charged with similar offenses are prosecuted in state court, warrants close scrutiny by the federal judges in that District. In my view, the District Judge, who has sat on both the federal and the state benches in Los Angeles, acted well within her discretion to call for the development of facts that would demonstrate what standards, if any, governed the choice of forum where similarly situated offenders are prosecuted. * * *

Even if respondents failed to carry their burden of showing that there were individuals who were not black but who could have been prosecuted in federal court for the same offenses, it does not follow that the District Court abused its discretion in ordering discovery. There can be no doubt that such individuals exist, and indeed the Government has never denied the same. In those circumstances, I fail to see why the District Court was unable to take judicial notice of this obvious fact and demand information from the Government's files to support or refute respondents' evidence. The presumption that some whites are prosecuted in state court is not "contradicted" by the statistics the majority cites, which show only that high percentages of blacks are convicted of certain federal crimes, while high percentages of whites are convicted of other federal crimes. Those figures are entirely consistent with the allegation of selective prosecution. The relevant comparison, rather, would be with the percentages of blacks and whites who commit those crimes. But, as discussed above, in the case of crack far greater numbers of whites are believed guilty of using the substance. The District Court, therefore, was entitled to find the evidence before her significant and to require some explanation from the Government. * * * I therefore respectfully dissent.

Note

The defense of selective or discriminatory prosecution is well established in principle, but rarely successful in practice. Courts generally shrink from the difficult task of assessing a prosecutor's motives, and defendants rarely succeed in establishing that a prosecutorial policy is so rationally indefensible as to be arbitrary. For example, selective prosecution of suspected organized crime figures has long been common and has been upheld. United States v. Sacco, 428 F.2d 264 (9th Cir.1970). The government has a policy of vigorously prosecuting notorious tax resisters on criminal tax charges, and the courts have approved because the policy is rationally related to legitimate enforcement goals. United States v. Catlett, 584 F.2d 864 (8th Cir. 1978). The tax protestors have been singled out for *tax* prosecutions, however, and a different issue might be presented if the government selectively pursued them for non-tax offenses. For example, an Illinois appellate court held unconstitutional the arrest of a suspected prostitute for failing to have a bell on her bicycle, where the arresting officer was acting pursuant to a departmental policy of strictly enforcing all laws against suspected prostitutes. The court observed that "The purpose of requiring a bell on a bicycle clearly does not envision the eradication of prostitution." People v. Kail, 150 Ill.App.3d 75, 103 Ill.Dec. 662, 501 N.E.2d 979 (Ill.App. 1986).

Some cases hold that the defense of discriminatory prosecution is unavailable when the prosecution is under a statute which is generally enforced, even though the defendant asserts that the decision to prosecute in his case was based on some improper motive such as personal dislike. Determining motivation in such a situation is apt to be difficult, particularly where more than one person was involved in the charging decision. In rare cases, this difficulty may be overcome. In People v. Walker, 14 N.Y.2d 901, 252 N.Y.S.2d 96, 200 N.E.2d 779 (1964), the defendant was granted a hearing and eventually prevailed on her claim that she was charged with violating several building code provisions (that were generally enforced against other persons) after she exposed corrupt practices in the enforcing department.

In addition to the "equal protection" claim of discriminatory enforcement, there is a limited due process doctrine against prosecutorial "vindictiveness." The doctrine stems from the Supreme Court's decision in Blackledge v. Perry, 417 U.S. 21 (1974), where the defendant was convicted of misdemeanor assault, exercised his right to trial *de novo* in a higher court, and then was charged with felony assault for the same conduct. The Supreme Court held that a person should be entitled to pursue his statutory right to a trial *de novo* without the fear that the State may retaliate by charging a higher offense to punish him for exercising that right. The doctrine is similar to the rule that prohibits a judge from imposing a higher sentence on retrial and reconviction to punish a defendant for successfully appealing his original conviction. See *North Carolina v. Pearce*, described on page 953 of this book.

UNITED STATES v. BAGLEY

Supreme Court of the United States, 1985.
473 U.S. 667, 105 S.Ct. 3375, 87 L.Ed.2d 481.

JUSTICE BLACKMUN announced the judgment of the Court and delivered an opinion of the Court except as to Part III.

In *Brady v. Maryland*, 373 U.S. 83, 87 (1963), this Court held that "the suppression by the prosecution of evidence favorable to an accused upon request violates due process where the evidence is material either to guilt or punishment." The issue in the present case concerns the standard of materiality to be applied in determining whether a conviction should be reversed because the prosecutor failed to disclose requested evidence that could have been used to impeach Government witnesses.

I

In October 1977, respondent Hughes Anderson Bagley was indicted in the Western District of Washington on 15 charges of violating federal narcotics and firearms statutes. On November 18, 24 days before trial, respondent filed a discovery motion. The sixth paragraph of that motion requested:

> "The names and addresses of witnesses that the government intends to call at trial. Also the prior criminal records of witnesses, and any deals, promises or inducements made to witnesses in exchange for their testimony." App. 18.

The Government's two principal witnesses at the trial were James F. O'Connor and Donald E. Mitchell. O'Connor and Mitchell were state law-enforcement officers employed by the Milwaukee Railroad as private security guards. Between April and June 1977, they assisted the federal Bureau of Alcohol, Tobacco and Firearms (ATF) in conducting an undercover investigation of respondent.

The Government's response to the discovery motion did not disclose that any "deals, promises or inducements" had been made to O'Connor or Mitchell. In apparent reply to a request in the motion's ninth paragraph for "[c]opies of all Jencks Act material,"[24] the Government produced a series of affidavits that O'Connor and Mitchell had signed between April 12 and May 4, 1977, while the undercover investigation was in progress. These affidavits recounted in detail the undercover dealings that O'Connor and Mitchell were having at the time with respondent. Each affidavit concluded with the statement, "I made this statement freely and voluntarily without any threats or rewards, or promises of reward having been made to me in return for it."

---

24. The Jencks Act, 18 U.S.C. § 3500, requires the prosecutor to disclose, after direct examination of a Government witness and on the defendant's motion, any statement of the witness in the Government's possession that relates to the subject matter of the witness' testimony.

Respondent waived his right to a jury trial and was tried before the court in December 1977. At the trial, O'Connor and Mitchell testified about both the firearms and the narcotics charges. On December 23, the court found respondent guilty on the narcotics charges, but not guilty on the firearms charges.

In mid–1980, respondent filed requests for information pursuant to the Freedom of Information Act and to the Privacy Act of 1974, 5 U.S.C. §§ 552 and 552a. He received in response copies of ATF form contracts that O'Connor and Mitchell had signed on May 3, 1977. Each form was entitled "Contract for Purchase of Information and Payment of Lump Sum Therefor." The printed portion of the form stated that the vendor "will provide" information to ATF and that "upon receipt of such information by the Regional Director, Bureau of Alcohol, Tobacco and Firearms, or his representative, and upon the accomplishment of the objective sought to be obtained by the use of such information to the satisfaction of said Regional Director, the United States will pay to said vendor a sum commensurate with services and information rendered." Each form contained the following typewritten description of services:

> "That he will provide information regarding T–I and other violations committed by Hughes A. Bagley, Jr.; that he will purchase evidence for ATF; that he will cut [sic] in an undercover capacity for ATF; that he will assist ATF in gathering of evidence and testify against the violator in federal court." *Ibid.*

The figure "$300.00" was handwritten in each form on a line entitled "Sum to Be Paid to Vendor."

Because these contracts had not been disclosed to respondent in response to his pretrial discovery motion,[25] respondent moved under 28 U.S.C. § 2255 to vacate his sentence. He alleged that the Government's failure to disclose the contracts, which he could have used to impeach O'Connor and Mitchell, violated his right to due process under *Brady v. Maryland, supra.*

The motion came before the same District Judge who had presided at respondent's bench trial. An evidentiary hearing was held before a Magistrate. The Magistrate found that the printed form contracts were blank when O'Connor and Mitchell signed them and were not signed by an ATF representative until after the trial. He also found that on January 4, 1978, following the trial and decision in respondent's case, ATF made payments of $300 to both O'Connor and Mitchell pursuant to the contracts. Although the ATF case agent who dealt with O'Connor and Mitchell testified that these payments were compensation for expenses, the Magistrate found that this characterization was not borne out by the record. There was no documentation for expenses in these amounts; Mitchell testified that his payment was not for expenses, and the ATF forms authorizing the payments treated them as rewards.

---

25. The Assistant United States Attorney who prosecuted respondent stated in stipulated testimony that he had not known that the contracts existed and that he would have furnished them to respondent had he known of them.

The District Court adopted each of the Magistrate's findings except for the last one to the effect that "[n]either O'Connor nor Mitchell expected to receive the payment of $300 or any payment from the United States for their testimony." Instead, the court found that it was "probable" that O'Connor and Mitchell expected to receive compensation, in addition to their expenses, for their assistance, "though perhaps not for their testimony." The District Court also expressly rejected the Magistrate's conclusion that:

> Because neither witness was promised or expected payment for his testimony, the United States did not withhold, during pretrial discovery, information as to any 'deals, promises or inducements' to these witnesses. Nor did the United States suppress evidence favorable to the defendant, in violation of *Brady v. Maryland*.

The District Court found beyond a reasonable doubt, however, that had the existence of the agreements been disclosed to it during trial, the disclosure would have had no effect upon its finding that the Government had proved beyond a reasonable doubt that respondent was guilty of the offenses for which he had been convicted. The District Court reasoned: Almost all of the testimony of both witnesses was devoted to the firearms charges in the indictment. Respondent, however, was acquitted on those charges. The testimony of O'Connor and Mitchell concerning the narcotics charges was relatively very brief. On cross-examination, respondent's counsel did not seek to discredit their testimony as to the facts of distribution but rather sought to show that the controlled substances in question came from supplies that had been prescribed for respondent's personal use. The answers of O'Connor and Mitchell to this line of cross-examination tended to be favorable to respondent. Thus, the claimed impeachment evidence would not have been helpful to respondent and would not have affected the outcome of the trial. Accordingly, the District Court denied respondent's motion to vacate his sentence.

[The Court of Appeals for the Ninth Circuit reversed, stating that the failure to provide the requested impeachment evidence "requires an automatic reversal." The Supreme Court granted certiorari.]

II

The holding in *Brady v. Maryland* requires disclosure only of evidence that is both favorable to the accused and "material either to guilt or punishment." See also *Moore v. Illinois*, 408 U.S. 786, 794–795 (1972). The Court explained in *United States v. Agurs*, 427 U.S. 97, 104 (1976): "A fair analysis of the holding in *Brady* indicates that implicit in the requirement of materiality is a concern that the suppressed evidence might have affected the outcome of the trial." The evidence suppressed in *Brady* would have been admissible only on the issue of punishment and not on the issue of guilt, and therefore could have affected only Brady's sentence and not his conviction. Accordingly, the Court affirmed the lower court's restriction of Brady's new trial to the issue of punishment.

The *Brady* rule is based on the requirement of due process. Its purpose is not to displace the adversary system as the primary means by which truth is uncovered, but to ensure that a miscarriage of justice does not occur. Thus, the prosecutor is not required to deliver his entire file to defense counsel,[26] but only to disclose evidence favorable to the accused that, if suppressed, would deprive the defendant of a fair trial. * * *

The Court of Appeals treated impeachment evidence as constitutionally different from exculpatory evidence. According to that court, failure to disclose impeachment evidence is "even more egregious" than failure to disclose exculpatory evidence "because it threatens the defendant's right to confront adverse witnesses." Relying on *Davis v. Alaska*, 415 U.S. 308 (1974), the Court of Appeals held that the Government's failure to disclose requested impeachment evidence that the defense could use to conduct an effective cross-examination of important prosecution witnesses constitutes "constitutional error of the first magnitude" requiring automatic reversal.

This Court has rejected any such distinction between impeachment evidence and exculpatory evidence. * * *

Moreover, the court's reliance on *Davis v. Alaska* for its "automatic reversal" rule is misplaced. In *Davis*, the defense sought to cross-examine a crucial prosecution witness concerning his probationary status as a juvenile delinquent. The defense intended by this cross-examination to show that the witness might have made a faulty identification of the defendant in order to shift suspicion away from himself or because he feared that his probationary status would be jeopardized if he did not satisfactorily assist the police and prosecutor in obtaining a conviction. Pursuant to a state rule of procedure and a state statute making juvenile adjudications inadmissible, the trial judge prohibited the defense from conducting the cross-examination. This Court reversed the defendant's conviction, ruling that the direct restriction on the scope of cross-examination denied the defendant "the right of effective cross-examination which would be constitutional error of the first magnitude and no amount of showing of want of prejudice would cure it."

The present case, in contrast, does not involve any direct restriction on the scope of cross-examination. The defense was free to cross-examine the witnesses on any relevant subject, including possible bias or interest resulting from inducements made by the Government. The constitutional error, if any, in this case was the Government's failure to assist the defense by disclosing information that might have been helpful in conducting the cross-examination. As discussed above, such suppression

26. An interpretation of *Brady* to create a broad, constitutionally required right of discovery "would entirely alter the character and balance of our present systems of criminal justice." *Giles v. Maryland*, 386 U.S. 66, 117 (1967) (dissenting opinion). Furthermore, a rule that the prosecutor commits error by any failure to disclose evidence favorable to the accused, no matter how insignificant, would impose an impossible burden on the prosecutor and would undermine the interest in the finality of judgments.

of evidence amounts to a constitutional violation only if it deprives the defendant of a fair trial. Consistent with our overriding concern with the justice of the finding of guilt, a constitutional error occurs, and the conviction must be reversed, only if the evidence is material in the sense that its suppression undermines confidence in the outcome of the trial.

III

A

It remains to determine the standard of materiality applicable to the nondisclosed evidence at issue in this case. Our starting point is the framework for evaluating the materiality of *Brady* evidence established in *United States v. Agurs*. The Court in *Agurs* distinguished three situations involving the discovery, after trial, of information favorable to the accused that had been known to the prosecution but unknown to the defense. The first situation was the prosecutor's knowing use of perjured testimony or, equivalently, the prosecutor's knowing failure to disclose that testimony used to convict the defendant was false. The Court noted the well-established rule that "a conviction obtained by the knowing use of perjured testimony is fundamentally unfair, and must be set aside if there is any reasonable likelihood that the false testimony could have affected the judgment of the jury."[27] Although this rule is stated in terms that treat the knowing use of perjured testimony as error subject to harmless-error review, it may as easily be stated as a materiality standard under which the fact that testimony is perjured is considered material unless failure to disclose it would be harmless beyond a reasonable doubt. The Court in *Agurs* justified this standard of materiality on the ground that the knowing use of perjured testimony involves prosecutorial misconduct and, more importantly, involves "a corruption of the truth-seeking function of the trial process."

At the other extreme is the situation in *Agurs* itself, where the defendant does not make a *Brady* request and the prosecutor fails to disclose certain evidence favorable to the accused. The Court rejected a harmless-error rule in that situation, because under that rule every nondisclosure is treated as error, thus imposing on the prosecutor a constitutional duty to deliver his entire file to defense counsel. At the same time, the Court rejected a standard that would require the defendant to demonstrate that the evidence if disclosed probably would have resulted in acquittal. The Court reasoned: "If the standard applied to the usual motion for a new trial based on newly discovered evidence were the same when the evidence was in the State's possession as when it was found in a neutral source, there would be no special significance to the prosecutor's obligation to serve the cause of justice." The standard of

---

27. * * * [See especially] *Napue v. Illinois*, 360 U.S. 264 (1959). In *Napue*, the principal witness for the prosecution falsely testified that he had been promised no consideration for his testimony. The Court held that the knowing use of false testimony to obtain a conviction violates due process regardless of whether the prosecutor solicited the false testimony or merely allowed it to go uncorrected when it appeared. * * * The Court conducted its own independent examination of the record and concluded that the false testimony "may have had an effect on the outcome of the trial." Accordingly, the Court reversed the judgment of conviction.

materiality applicable in the absence of a specific *Brady* request is therefore stricter than the harmless-error standard but more lenient to the defense than the newly discovered evidence standard.

The third situation identified by the Court in *Agurs* is where the defense makes a specific request and the prosecutor fails to disclose responsive evidence. The Court did not define the standard of materiality applicable in this situation, but suggested that the standard might be more lenient to the defense than in the situation in which the defense makes no request or only a general request. The Court also noted:

> "When the prosecutor receives a specific and relevant request, the failure to make any response is seldom, if ever, excusable."

The Court has relied on and reformulated the *Agurs* standard for the materiality of undisclosed evidence in two subsequent cases arising outside the *Brady* context. In neither case did the Court's discussion of the *Agurs* standard distinguish among the three situations described in *Agurs*. In *United States v. Valenzuela–Bernal*, 458 U.S. 858, 874 (1982), the Court held that due process is violated when testimony is made unavailable to the defense by Government deportation of witnesses "only if there is a reasonable likelihood that the testimony could have affected the judgment of the trier of fact." And in *Strickland v. Washington* [p. 412 of this book] the Court held that a new trial must be granted when evidence is not introduced because of the incompetence of counsel only if "there is a reasonable probability that, but for counsel's unprofessional errors, the result of the proceeding would have been different." The *Strickland* Court defined a "reasonable probability" as "a probability sufficient to undermine confidence in the outcome."

We find the *Strickland* formulation of the *Agurs* test for materiality sufficiently flexible to cover the "no request," "general request," and "specific request" cases of prosecutorial failure to disclose evidence favorable to the accused: The evidence is material only if there is a reasonable probability that, had the evidence been disclosed to the defense, the result of the proceeding would have been different. A "reasonable probability" is a probability sufficient to undermine confidence in the outcome.

The Government suggests that a materiality standard more favorable to the defendant reasonably might be adopted in specific request cases. The Government notes that an incomplete response to a specific request not only deprives the defense of certain evidence, but has the effect of representing to the defense that the evidence does not exist. In reliance on this misleading representation, the defense might abandon lines of independent investigation, defenses, or trial strategies that it otherwise would have pursued. *Ibid.*

We agree that the prosecutor's failure to respond fully to a *Brady* request may impair the adversary process in this manner. And the more specifically the defense requests certain evidence, thus putting the prosecutor on notice of its value, the more reasonable it is for the defense to assume from the nondisclosure that the evidence does not exist, and to make pretrial and trial decisions on the basis of this assumption. This possibility of impairment does not necessitate a different standard of materiality, however, for under the *Strickland* formulation the reviewing court may consider directly any adverse effect that the prosecutor's failure to respond might have had on the preparation or presentation of the defendant's case. The reviewing court should assess the possibility that such effect might have occurred in light of the totality of the circumstances and with an awareness of the difficulty of reconstructing in a post-trial proceeding the course that the defense and the trial would have taken had the defense not been misled by the prosecutor's incomplete response.

B

In the present case, we think that there is a significant likelihood that the prosecutor's response to respondent's discovery motion misleadingly induced defense counsel to believe that O'Connor and Mitchell could not be impeached on the basis of bias or interest arising from inducements offered by the Government. * * *

The District Court, nonetheless, found beyond a reasonable doubt that, had the information that the Government held out the possibility of reward to its witnesses been disclosed, the result of the criminal prosecution would not have been different. If this finding were sustained by the Court of Appeals, the information would be immaterial even under the standard of materiality applicable to the prosecutor's knowing use of perjured testimony. Although the express holding of the Court of Appeals was that the nondisclosure in this case required automatic reversal, the Court of Appeals also stated that it "disagreed" with the District Court's finding of harmless error. In particular, the Court of Appeals appears to have disagreed with the factual premise on which this finding expressly was based. The District Court reasoned that O'Connor's and Mitchell's testimony was exculpatory on the narcotics charges. The Court of Appeals, however, concluded, after reviewing the record, that O'Connor's and Mitchell's testimony was in fact inculpatory on those charges. Accordingly, we reverse the judgment of the Court of Appeals and remand the case to that court for a determination whether there is a reasonable probability that, had the inducement offered by the Government to O'Connor and Mitchell been disclosed to the defense, the result of the trial would have been different.

It is so ordered.

JUSTICE POWELL took no part in the decision of this case.

JUSTICE WHITE, with whom THE CHIEF JUSTICE and JUSTICE REHNQUIST join, concurring in part and concurring in the judgment.

I agree with the Court that respondent is not entitled to have his conviction overturned unless he can show that the evidence withheld by the Government was "material," and I therefore join Parts I and II of the Court's opinion. I also agree with Justice Blackmun that for purposes of this inquiry, "evidence is material only if there is a reasonable probability that, had the evidence been disclosed to the defense, the result of the proceeding would have been different." As the Justice correctly observes, this standard is "sufficiently flexible" to cover all instances of prosecutorial failure to disclose evidence favorable to the accused. Given the flexibility of the standard and the inherently fact-bound nature of the cases to which it will be applied, however, I see no reason to attempt to elaborate on the relevance to the inquiry of the specificity of the defense's request for disclosure, either generally or with respect to this case. I would hold simply that the proper standard is one of reasonable probability and that the Court of Appeals' failure to apply this standard necessitates reversal. I therefore concur in the judgment.

JUSTICE MARSHALL, with whom JUSTICE BRENNAN joins, dissenting.

When the Government withholds from a defendant evidence that might impeach the prosecution's *only witnesses*, that failure to disclose cannot be deemed harmless error. Because that is precisely the nature of the undisclosed evidence in this case, I would affirm the judgment of the Court of Appeals and would not remand for further proceedings.

I

The federal grand jury indicted the respondent, Hughes Anderson Bagley, on charges involving possession of firearms and controlled substances with intent to distribute. Following a bench trial, Bagley was found not guilty of the firearms charges, guilty of two counts of knowingly and intentionally distributing Valium, and guilty of several counts of a lesser included offense of possession of controlled substances. He was sentenced to six months' imprisonment and a special parole term of five years on the first count of distribution, and to three years of imprisonment, which were suspended, and five years' probation, on the second distribution count. He received a suspended sentence and five years' probation for the possession convictions.

The record plainly demonstrates that on the two counts for which Bagley received sentences of imprisonment, the Government's entire case hinged on the testimony of two private security guards who aided the Bureau of Alcohol, Tobacco and Firearms (BATF) in its investigation of Bagley. In 1977 the two guards, O'Connor and Mitchell, worked for the Milwaukee Railroad; for about three years, they had been social acquaintances of Bagley, with whom they often shared coffee breaks. At trial, they testified that on two separate occasions they had visited Bagley at his home, where Bagley had responded to O'Connor's complaint that he was extremely anxious by giving him Valium pills. In total, Bagley received $8 from O'Connor, representing the cost of the pills. At trial, Bagley testified that he had a prescription for the Valium because he suffered from a bad back. No testimony to the contrary was introduced. O'Connor and Mitchell each testified that they had worn concealed transmitters and body recorders at these meetings, but the tape recordings were insufficiently clear to be admitted at trial and corroborate their testimony. * * *

Upon discovering [the impeaching information] through a Freedom of Information Act request, Bagley sought relief from his conviction. The District Court Judge denied Bagley's motion to vacate his sentence stating that because he was the same judge who had been the original trier of fact, he was able to determine the effect the contracts would have had on his decision, more than four years earlier, to convict Bagley. * * *

[The trial judge's explanation for denying the motion to vacate the sentence] is seriously flawed on its face. First, the testimony that the court describes was in fact the *only inculpatory testimony in the case* as to the two counts for which Bagley received a sentence of imprisonment. If, as the judge claimed, the testimony of the two information "vendors" was "very brief" and in part favorable to the defendant, that fact shows the weakness of the prosecutor's case, not the harmlessness of the error. If the testimony that might have been impeached is weak and also cumulative, corroborative or tangential, the failure to disclose the impeachment evidence could conceivably be held harmless. But when the testimony is the start and finish of the prosecution's case, and is weak nonetheless, quite a different conclusion must necessarily be drawn.

Second, the court's statement that Bagley did not attempt to discredit the witnesses' testimony, as if to suggest that impeachment evidence would not have been used by the defense, ignores the realities of trial preparation and strategy, and is factually erroneous as well. Initially, the Government's failure to disclose the existence of any inducements to its witnesses, coupled with its disclosure of affidavits stating that no promises had been made, would lead all but the most careless lawyer to step wide and clear of questions about promises or inducements. The combination of nondisclosure and disclosure would simply lead any reasonable attorney to believe that the witness could not be impeached on that basis. Thus, a firm avowal that no payment is being received in return for assistance and testimony, if offered at trial by a witness who is not even a Government employee, could be devastating to the defense. A wise attorney would, of necessity, seek an alternative defense strategy.

Moreover, counsel for Bagley in fact did attempt to discredit O'Connor, by asking him whether two BATF agents had pressured him or had threatened that his job might be in jeopardy, in order to get him to cooperate. But when O'Connor answered in the negative, counsel stopped this line of questioning. In addition, counsel for Bagley attempted to argue to the District Court, in his closing argument, that O'Connor and Mitchell had "fabricated" their accounts, but the court rejected the proposition:

> "Let me say this to you. I would find it hard to believe really that their testimony was fabricated. I think they might have been mistaken. You know, it is possible that they were mistaken. *I really did not get the impression at all that either one or both of those men*

were trying at least in court here to make a case against the defendant."

* * * It simply cannot be denied that the existence of a contract signed by those witnesses, promising a reward whose size would depend on the Government's satisfaction with the end result, might sway the trier of fact, or cast doubt on the truth of all that the witnesses allege. In such a case, the trier of fact is absolutely entitled to know of the contract, and the defense counsel is absolutely entitled to develop his case with an awareness of it. Whatever the applicable standard of materiality, in this instance it undoubtedly is well met. * * *

JUSTICE STEVENS, dissenting.

This case involves a straightforward application of the rule announced in *Brady v. Maryland*, a case involving nondisclosure of material evidence by the prosecution in response to a specific request from the defense. I agree that the Court of Appeals misdescribed that rule, but I respectfully dissent from the Court's unwarranted decision to rewrite the rule itself.

As the Court correctly notes at the outset of its opinion, the holding in *Brady* was that "the suppression by the prosecution of evidence favorable to an accused upon request violates due process where the evidence is material either to guilt or punishment." We noted in *United States v. Agurs*, that the rule of *Brady* arguably might apply in three different situations involving the discovery, after trial, of evidence that had been known prior to trial to the prosecution but not to the defense. Our holding in *Agurs* was that the *Brady* rule applies in two of the situations, but not in the third.

The two situations in which the rule applies are those demonstrating the prosecution's knowing use of perjured testimony, exemplified by *Mooney v. Holohan*, 294 U.S. 103 (1935), and the prosecution's suppression of favorable evidence specifically requested by the defendant, exemplified by *Brady* itself. In both situations, the prosecution's deliberate nondisclosure constitutes constitutional error—the conviction must be set aside if the suppressed or perjured evidence was "material" and there was "any reasonable likelihood" that it "could have affected" the outcome of the trial. * * *

The question in *Agurs* was whether the *Brady* rule should be *extended*, to cover a case in which there had been neither perjury nor a specific request—that is, whether the prosecution has some constitutional duty to search its files and disclose automatically, or in response to a general request, all evidence that "might have helped the defense, or might have affected the outcome." Such evidence would, of course, be covered by the *Brady* formulation if it were specifically requested. We noted in *Agurs*, however, that because there had been no specific defense request for the later-discovered evidence, there was no notice to the prosecution that the defense did not already have that evidence or that it considered the evidence to be of particular value. Consequently, we stated that in the absence of a request the prosecution has a constitutional duty to volunteer only "obviously exculpatory evidence." Because this constitutional duty to disclose is *different* from the duty described in *Brady*, it is not surprising that we developed a different standard of materiality in the *Agurs* context. Necessarily describing the "inevitably imprecise" standard in terms appropriate to posttrial review, we held that no constitutional violation occurs in the absence of a specific request unless "the omitted evidence creates a reasonable doubt that did not otherwise exist."

What the Court ignores with regard to *Agurs* is that its analysis was restricted entirely to the general or no-request context. * * *

But the *Brady* rule itself unquestionably applies to this case, because the Government failed to disclose favorable evidence that was clearly responsive to the defendant's specific request. Bagley's conviction therefore must be set aside if the suppressed evidence was "material"— and it obviously was—and if there is "any reasonable likelihood" that it could have affected the judgment of the trier of fact. Our choice, therefore, should be merely whether to affirm for the reasons stated in Part I of Justice Marshall's dissent, or to remand to the Court of Appeals for further review under the standard stated in *Brady*. I would follow the latter course, not because I disagree with Justice Marshall's analysis of the record, but because I do not believe this Court should perform the task of reviewing trial transcripts in the first instance. I am confident that the Court of Appeals would reach the appropriate result if it applied the proper standard.

The Court, however, today sets out a reformulation of the *Brady* rule in which I have no such confidence. * * * The Court's approach stretches the concept of "materiality" beyond any recognizable scope, transforming it from merely an evidentiary concept as used in *Brady* and *Agurs*, which required that material evidence be admissible and probative of guilt or innocence in the context of a specific request, into a result-focused standard that seems to include an independent weight in favor of affirming convictions despite evidentiary suppression. Evidence favorable to an accused and relevant to the dispositive issue of guilt apparently may still be found not "material," and hence suppressible by prosecutors prior to trial, unless there is a reasonable probability that its use would result in an acquittal. Justice Marshall rightly criticizes the incentives such a standard creates for prosecutors to gamble, to play the odds, and to take a chance that evidence will later turn out not to have been potentially dispositive.

Moreover, the Court's analysis reduces the significance of deliberate prosecutorial suppression of potentially exculpatory evidence to that merely of one of numerous factors that "may" be considered by a reviewing court. This is not faithful to our statement in *Agurs* that "[w]hen the prosecutor receives a specific and relevant request, the failure to make any response is seldom, if ever, excusable." Such suppression is far more serious than mere nondisclosure of evidence in which the defense has expressed no particular interest. A reviewing court should attach great significance to silence in the face of a specific request, when responsive evidence is later shown to have been in the Government's possession. Such silence actively misleads in the same way as would an affirmative representation that exculpatory evidence does not exist when, in fact, it does (*i.e.*, perjury)—indeed, the two situations are aptly described as "sides of a single coin." Babcock, Fair Play: Evidence Favorable to An Accused and Effective Assistance of Counsel, 34 Stan.L.Rev. 1133, 1151 (1982).

Accordingly, although I agree that the judgment of the Court of Appeals should be vacated and that the case should be remanded for further proceedings, I disagree with the Court's statement of the correct standard to be applied. I therefore respectfully dissent from the judgment that the case be remanded for determination under the Court's new standard.

Commentary

The Brady Doctrine

The defendant in Brady v. Maryland, 373 U.S. 83 (1963), was found guilty of a felony murder committed with an accomplice named Boblit and sentenced to death. Prior to Brady's separate trial, defense counsel asked the prosecutor to produce all the statements that Boblit had given to the police. The prosecutor turned over some statements, but did not include one statement in which Boblit admitted that he had committed the actual killing. At trial Brady admitted his participation in the crime but claimed that he did not personally commit the killing, and defense counsel urged the jury to show leniency and not to impose the death penalty because of this fact. After the conviction and death sentence defense counsel learned of the undisclosed statement and sought a new trial. The Supreme Court affirmed a state court ruling granting a new trial on the issue of punishment alone. The identity of the actual killer had no effect on Brady's liability for felony murder, but withholding that information deprived Brady of a fair trial on the death penalty issue.

The *Brady* doctrine has been applied, interpreted or distinguished in a number of subsequent cases, including the following:

1. Giles v. Maryland, 386 U.S. 66 (1967), involved two young black brothers who were convicted and sentenced to death (later commuted to life imprisonment) for raping a sixteen-year-old white girl, in circumstances which led some contemporary observers to suspect that at least one of the defendants might have been innocent. The evidence allegedly suppressed went to the character of the victim, and included: (1) a prior juvenile proceeding at which a caseworker had recommended probation for the girl because she was beyond parental control; (2) an incident five weeks after the alleged rape at which the girl had sexual relations with two men at a party, took an overdose of pills and was hospitalized as an attempted suicide; (3) the fact that after the suicide attempt the girl initially claimed that the two men had raped her, and later withdrew the charges and admitted having had sexual relations with numerous men and boys; and (4) a commitment to a state reformatory that followed her release from the suicide hospitalization. In short the material was relevant to the mental stability and sexual habits

of the victim, but did not in any direct way contradict the account she gave of the rape. The Supreme Court was unable to agree on a majority opinion or legal theory, but five Justices voted to remand the case to the state courts for further proceedings regarding the allegedly suppressed information.[a]

2.   The defendant in Giglio v. United States, 405 U.S. 150 (1972), was convicted of passing forged money orders on the testimony of an unindicted co-conspirator named Taliento. Defense counsel tried to discredit Taliento's testimony by suggesting that he had been promised that he would not be prosecuted if he agreed to incriminate Giglio, but Taliento repeatedly denied on the stand that he had received any promises. After conviction the defense made a motion for a new trial on the basis of newly discovered evidence, specifically an affidavit from the Assistant United States Attorney who had presented the case to the grand jury relating that he had promised Taliento that he would not be prosecuted if Taliento testified for the Government at Giglio's trial. The AUSA who took over the case for trial filed an affidavit stating that the former prosecutor had told him that Taliento had *not* been promised immunity but had not been prosecuted because he was very young at the time of the offense and "obviously had been overreached by the defendant Giglio."

The District Court did not try to resolve the conflict between the affidavits, but denied relief on the theory that disclosure of any promise that may have been made would not have affected the verdict. The Supreme Court reversed in a unanimous opinion by Chief Justice Burger, citing the "knowing use of false testimony" cases and holding that the prosecutor's office as an entity had an obligation to see that the jury was not misled as to the existence of a promise of non-prosecution. Because Taliento's testimony was the entire basis of the prosecution case, "evidence of any understanding or agreement as to a future prosecution would be relevant to his credibility and the jury was entitled to know of it." 405 U.S. at 155.

3.   The defendant in Moore v. Illinois, 408 U.S. 786 (1972), was convicted and sentenced to death for murdering a bartender with a shotgun. Two eyewitnesses testified that they saw Moore commit the murder, and another witness (Sanders) testified that a man he knew as "Slick," whom he identified as Moore, admitted the killing in a conversation in another bar. The facts of the case are too complex to report completely here, but the allegedly suppressed exculpatory evidence essentially consisted of: (1) A statement and accompanying diagram by another person who was in the bar at the time of the murder. The diagram indicated that one of the eyewitnesses was seated at a card table facing away from the door, and the defense could have used this information to cast doubt upon this witness's testimony that he saw Moore enter and commit the killing. (2) Certain evidence

---

a. Dissenting Justice Harlan described the Court's disposition of the case in the following terms: "The unarticulated basis of today's disposition, and of the disparate reasons which accompany it, is quite evidently nothing more than the Court's uneasiness with these convictions, engendered by post-trial indications of the promiscuity of this unfortunate girl. Unable to discover a constitutional infirmity and unwilling to affirm the convictions, the Court simply returns the case to the Maryland Court of Appeals, in hopes that, despite the plurality's repeated disclaimers, that court will share the Court's discomfort and discover a formula under which these convictions can be reversed." 386 U.S. at 119. For the state court's reaction, see 227 A.2d 745, 229 A.2d 97 (1967).

indicating that the witness Sanders might have been confused about the identity of "Slick," and that therefore it could have been another person rather than Moore who admitted killing the bartender. The defense had made a general motion for discovery of all written witness statements, and the prosecutor had turned over his entire file. The missing items either were not in the file, or were turned over and not noted by the defense at the time. The Supreme Court affirmed the conviction (but reversed the death sentence on other grounds) by a 5–4 vote. The majority concluded that there had been no deliberate suppression, and that the evidence which subsequently came to light did not sufficiently undermine the state's case so as to call for relief on due process principles.

4. The opinion in United States v. Agurs, 427 U.S. 97 (1976), is discussed at some length in *Bagley*. The facts of the case were as follows: The defendant Agurs, apparently a prostitute, went to a motel room with the victim, Sewell. Sewell was wearing a bowie knife in a sheath and carried another knife in his pocket. He probably also had $360 in cash on his person. The evidence indicated that, after the parties completed an act of intercourse, Sewell had gone to the bathroom down the hall. Upon his return a violent struggle occurred. Motel employees responding to Agurs' screams for help entered the room and found Sewell on top of her struggling for possession of the bowie knife. While police were being summoned Agurs managed to depart, and Sewell died shortly afterward of wounds received in the struggle. The contents of his pockets were in disarray on the dresser and no money was found, indicating that the stabbing may have occurred after Sewell caught Agurs in the act of stealing his money.

The next day Agurs surrendered to the police. She was given a physical examination which showed no cuts or bruises, except for needle marks on her arm. An autopsy of Sewell disclosed that he had several deep stab wounds in his chest and abdomen, and a number of slashes on his arms and hands, characterized by the pathologist as "defensive wounds." Agurs did not testify, but her attorney argued that Sewell initially attacked her with a knife and that the killing was therefore in self-defense.

Following the murder conviction, defense counsel filed a motion for a new trial. It asserted that the prosecution had failed to disclose that Sewell had previously been convicted of assault and carrying a deadly weapon. The Government responded that the prior record could have been obtained by discovery, that there was no duty to tender such information to the defense in the absence of an appropriate request, and that the evidence was not material in any case. The Supreme Court majority affirmed the denial of the new trial motion because the victim's prior record was not requested, and because, in the context of the rest of the evidence, the record of prior convictions was not sufficient to create a reasonable doubt of the defendant's guilt. *Agurs* thus establishes that, in the absence of a defense request, prosecutorial suppression will not be found unless the withheld evidence is powerful enough to create a reasonable doubt.

5. The Supreme Court held that the *Brady* doctrine was not violated where the police failed to preserve important physical evidence, in Arizona v. Youngblood, 488 U.S. 51 (1988). In *Youngblood* the victim, a ten-year-old boy was abducted and sodomized by a middle-aged man. After the assault the boy was taken to a hospital where a physician used a swab from a "sexual

assault kit" to collect semen samples from the victim's rectum. The police also collected the boy's clothing, which they failed to refrigerate. A police criminologist performed some tests on the rectal swab and the clothing, but he was unable to obtain information about the identity of the assailant. The boy later picked the defendant as the assailant from a photographic lineup; defendant was not arrested until several weeks after that. At trial the defense claimed mistaken identity, and experts testified that the defendant might have been completely exonerated by more thorough tests that could have been performed if the clothing had been refrigerated and the evidence preserved. The Supreme Court nonetheless held that the *Brady* doctrine was not violated where the failure to preserve evidence was at most negligent and there was no "bad faith on the part of the police." Three Justices dissented. Justice Stevens, concurring in the judgment, emphasized that defense counsel was allowed to argue the issue to the jury, and the judge instructed the jury that they could infer that any evidence lost or destroyed by the state would have been likely to be to the benefit of the defendant. Justice Stevens reasoned that "In declining defense counsel's and the court's invitations to draw the permissive inference, the jurors in effect indicated that, in their view, the other evidence at trial was so overwhelming that it was highly improbable that the lost evidence was exculpatory."

It is important to distinguish the *constitutional* issue (knowing use of perjured testimony or suppression of exculpatory evidence) from the *non-constitutional* question of when a defendant can obtain a new trial on the basis of newly discovered evidence. For example, Federal Rule of Criminal Procedure 33 provides that "A motion for a new trial based on the ground of newly discovered evidence may be made only before or within two years after final judgment, but if an appeal is pending the court may grant the motion only on remand of the case." The granting of such a motion is not dependent upon a finding that the prosecutor suppressed anything, and of course evidence may fail to come to light in time for trial without anyone being at fault. To obtain relief under Rule 33, however, the convicted defendant must "satisfy the severe burden of demonstrating that newly discovered evidence probably would have resulted in acquittal." United States v. Agurs, 427 U.S. at 111, with citations. Where the prosecutor (or the Government as an entity) was at fault, the burden of showing prejudice is not so severe.

When the time for making a new trial motion has passed, then a convicted person can obtain relief from a conviction or sentence only by showing a violation of the Constitution. In other words, it is not enough to establish that on the basis of current information there is a reasonable doubt as to guilt, if the trial was fairly conducted at the time. The defendant must show not only that new evidence casts doubt upon guilt, but also that the prosecution suppressed this evidence, or defense counsel was ineffective under the *Strickland* [p. 412, *supra*] standard in failing to discover and present it. Unless either the prosecution or defense counsel was to blame there probably was no constitutional error, and the only avenue of relief is Executive Clemency.

Some of the most difficult cases arise when a key prosecution witness subsequently recants and claims that the defendant was innocent. A nationally publicized case of this type occurred in 1985, when a young woman "victim" told an Illinois court that her story of rape and kidnapping, which had led to the conviction and incarceration of a defendant several years earlier, had been a complete fabrication. After holding a hearing on the change of story, the state court determined that she had been telling the truth the first time and denied the defendant's new trial motion. The defendant was released from prison, however, because the Illinois Governor commuted the sentence to time served. The case is described in Comment, "Rethinking the Standard for New Trial Motions Based Upon Recantations as Newly Discovered Evidence," 134 U.Pa.L.Rev. 1433 (1986). Courts generally tend to be highly suspicious of recantation testimony, fearing that it may be the product of duress, bribery, or misplaced sympathy. For this reason, it is fairly unusual for a witness recantation to cause the grant of a new trial.

Most cases have assumed that the *Brady* doctrine could be applied only where someone involved with the prosecutor's office was aware of the suppressed evidence or perjured testimony. In Sanders v. Sullivan, 863 F.2d 218 (2d Cir.1988), the federal Court of Appeals held that a person convicted in a state court on the basis of perjured testimony could obtain relief on due process grounds in federal court even though the state prosecutor was unaware of the perjury. Defendant Sanders was convicted in a New York State court of shooting a drug dealer, on the testimony of Perez and Semiday, who were common-law husband and wife. After the conviction Semiday died, and Perez met Sanders in prison. Perez thereafter recanted his trial testimony, and gave Sanders several affidavits recounting that he had given false testimony in order to protect Semiday.

The state court and the federal district court denied relief on the grounds that, whether the recantation was credible or not, the prosecutor had had no knowledge of any perjury and thus there was no violation of the *Brady* doctrine. The Court of Appeals held that a defendant convicted on perjured testimony was entitled to habeas corpus relief whether or not the prosecutor knew of the perjury, and remanded for a determination by the district court of the credibility of the recantation. The district court was directed to vacate the conviction if it found that Perez did indeed commit perjury at the state trial, and if the court was convinced that the defendant would most likely not have been convicted but for the perjured testimony.

In People v. Washington, 171 Ill.2d 475, 216 Ill.Dec. 773, 665 N.E.2d 1330 (1996), the Illinois Supreme Court faced the classic hard case. Newly discovered evidence indicated that a defendant convicted of murder was probably innocent, but it did not establish either than the prosecutor suppressed anything or that defense counsel was ineffective. The Illinois Post–Conviction Hearing Act allowed relief only in the case of constitutional claims. Could a constitutional basis be found for the defendant's persuasive claim of innocence?

The Illinois Court discussed the Supreme Court's opinion in Herrera v. Collins, 506 U.S. 390 (1993). There the defendant, sentenced to death for murder, submitted affidavits 10 years after conviction to support his claim that his brother, who had since died, had committed the murder. The claim was not particularly persuasive in the circumstances, and the Illinois Court characterized the Supreme Court as "conflicted" over whether a "free-standing claim of innocence" in a capital case might raise a constitutional issue. The Illinois court concluded, however, that "Conflicted or not, at least for noncapital cases, *Herrera* clearly states * * * that a free-standing claim of innocence is not cognizable as a fourteenth amendment due process claim."

The divided Illinois court then turned to the state constitution's Due Process Clause, and framed the issue not as whether the original conviction violated due process, but as whether "additional process [should] be afforded in Illinois when newly discovered evidence indicates that a convicted person is actually innocent." That way of putting the question led to the answer: "We therefore hold as a matter of Illinois constitutional jurisprudence that a claim of newly discovered evidence showing a defendant to be actually innocent of the crime for which he was convicted is cognizable as a matter of due process. That holding aligns Illinois with other jurisdictions likewise recognizing, primarily as a matter of state habeas corpus jurisprudence, a basis to raise such claims under the rubric of due process."

Perhaps the best way to state the law on free-standing claims of innocence is that such claims do not raise constitutional issues unless the court with final power to decide finds them so persuasive, and the consequences of upholding the sentence so appalling, that something just has to be done.

Chapter 16

PRETRIAL HEARINGS AND MOTIONS

CALIFORNIA v. SUPERIOR COURT OF CALIFORNIA, SAN BERNARDINO COUNTY (SMOLIN)

Supreme Court of the United States, 1987.
482 U.S. 400, 107 S.Ct. 2433, 96 L.Ed.2d 332.

[This extradition case grew out of a child custody battle between Richard and Judith Smolin. Following their 1978 divorce, a California trial court awarded custody of the two Smolin children to Judith, with visitation rights for Richard. In 1979 Judith married James Pope and moved with him and the children to Oregon without informing Richard. Richard alleged, and the California courts later found, that the Popes deliberately attempted to defeat his visitation rights in the course of their succeeding relocations from Oregon to Texas to Louisiana. In 1981 the Popes obtained a decree from a Texas court granting full faith and credit to the original California order awarding sole custody to Judith. Richard was served but did not appear in this Texas proceeding. Before the Texas decree was granted, however, Richard obtained an order in California modifying the original decree to award joint custody to himself and Judith. Although properly served, the Popes did not appear in the California proceedings and ignored the order. The California court then modified the original order again to grant sole custody to Richard, subject to visitation rights for Judith.

The Popes continued to ignore these California orders, apparently being advised by counsel that the California courts no longer had jurisdiction. When Richard finally located the Popes in Louisiana, they began an adoption proceeding, later described by the California courts as "verging on the fraudulent," to sever Richard's legal tie to the two children. After securing a California warrant to obtain custody of the children in 1984, Richard and his father went to Louisiana, picked up the children as they waited for a bus, and brought them back to California. The custody battle then continued in the California courts.

718

Meanwhile, the Popes persuaded a Louisiana prosecutor to file an information charging the Smolins with kidnapping, and the Governor of Louisiana formally demanded extradition from the Governor of California. The California Governor signed the extradition warrant, but a California trial court granted a writ of habeas corpus to block the extradition on the ground that there was no basis for the Louisiana criminal charge.

The California Supreme Court agreed with the trial court that there was no basis for extradition. The opinion reasoned that under the federal Parental Kidnaping Prevention Act of 1980 (which requires each state to grant full faith and credit to the custody decrees of other states), California had exclusive modification jurisdiction over the original custody decree. Therefore, Richard Smolin was the lawful custodian of the children at the time they were taken from Louisiana to California. The opinion further held that, under Louisiana criminal law, a person having lawful custody of children could not be guilty of kidnapping them. The United States Supreme Court granted certiorari to consider whether extradition could be denied on these grounds.]

Justice O'Connor delivered the opinion of the Court.

* * *

The Federal Constitution places certain limits on the sovereign powers of the States, limits that are an essential part of the Framers' conception of national identity and Union. One such limit is found in Art. IV, § 2, cl. 2, the Extradition Clause:

"A person charged in any State with Treason, Felony, or other Crime, who shall flee from Justice, and be found in another State, shall on Demand of the executive Authority of the State from which he fled, be delivered up, to be removed to the State having Jurisdiction of the Crime."

The obvious objective of the Extradition Clause is that no State should become a safe haven for the fugitives from a sister State's criminal justice system. * * *

The Extradition Clause, however, does not specifically establish a procedure by which interstate extradition is to take place, and, accordingly, has never been considered to be self-executing. Early in our history, the lack of an established procedure led to a bitter dispute between the States of Virginia and Pennsylvania. In 1791, Pennsylvania demanded the extradition of three men charged with kidnaping a free black man and selling him into slavery. Virginia refused to comply with Pennsylvania's demand. The controversy was finally submitted to President Washington who, relying upon the advice of Attorney General Randolph, personally appeared before the Congress to obtain the enactment of a law to regulate the extradition process. Congress responded by enacting the Extradition Act of 1793, which provides in its current form:

"Whenever the executive authority of any State or Territory demands any person as a fugitive from justice, of the executive authority of any State, District or Territory to which such person has fled, and produces a copy of an indictment found or an affidavit made before a magistrate of any State or Territory, charging the person demanded with having committed treason, felony or other crime, certified as authentic by the governor or chief magistrate of the State or Territory from whence the person so charged has fled, the executive authority of the State, District or Territory to which such person has fled shall cause him to be arrested and secured, and notify the executive authority making such demand, or the agent of such authority appointed to receive a fugitive, and shall cause the fugitive to be delivered to such agent when he shall appear." 18 U.S.C. § 3182. * * * The language, history, and subsequent construction of the Extradition Act make clear that Congress intended extradition to be a summary procedure. As we have repeatedly held, extradition proceedings are "to be kept within narrow bounds"; they are "emphatically" not the appropriate time or place for entertaining defenses or determining the guilt or innocence of the charged party. [Citations]. Those inquiries are left to the prosecutorial authorities and courts of the demanding State, whose duty it is to justly enforce the demanding State's criminal law—subject, of course, to the limitations imposed by the Constitution and laws of the United States. The courts of asylum States may do no more than ascertain whether the requisites of the Extradition Act have been met. As the Court held in *Michigan v. Doran,* 439 U.S. 282 (1978), the Act leaves only four issues open for consideration before the fugitive is delivered up:

"(a) whether the extradition documents on their face are in order; (b) whether the petitioner has been charged with a crime in the demanding state; (c) whether the petitioner is the person named in the request for extradition; and (d) whether the petitioner is a fugitive." 439 U.S., at 289.

The parties argue at length about the propriety of the California courts taking judicial notice of their prior child custody decrees in this extradition proceeding. But even if taking judicial notice of the decrees is otherwise proper, the question remains whether the decrees noticed were relevant to one of these four inquiries. The Smolins do not dispute that the extradition documents are in order, that they are the persons named in the documents and that they meet the technical definition of a "fugitive." Their sole contention is that, in light of the earlier California custody decrees and the federal Parental Kidnaping Prevention Act, 28 U.S.C. § 1738A, they have not been properly charged with a violation of Louisiana's kidnaping statute, La.Rev.Stat.Ann. § 14:45 (West 1986).

Section 14:45A(4) prohibits the

"intentional taking, enticing or decoying away and removing from the state, by any parent, of his or her child, from the custody of any person to whom custody has been awarded by any court of competent jurisdiction of any state, without the consent of the legal custodian, with intent to defeat the jurisdiction of the said court over the custody of the child."

A properly certified Louisiana information charges the Smolins with violating this statute by kidnaping Jennifer and Jamie Smolin. The information is based on the sworn affidavit of Judith Pope which asserts:

" 'On March 9, 1984, at approximately 7:20 a.m., Richard Smolin and Gerard Smolin, kidnapped Jennifer Smolin, aged 10, and James C. Smolin, aged 9, from the affiant's custody while said children were at a bus stop in St. Tammany Parish, Louisiana.

"The affiant has custody of the said children by virtue of a Texas court order dated February 5, 1981, a copy of said order attached hereto and made part hereof. The information regarding the actual kidnaping was told to the affiant by witnesses Mason Galatas and Cheryl Galatas of 2028 Mallard Street, Slidell, Louisiana, and Jimmie Huessler of 2015 Dridle Street, Slidell, Louisiana. Richard Smolin and Gerard Smolin were without authority to remove children from affiant's custody.' " The information is in proper form, and the Smolins do not dispute that the affidavit, and documents incorporated by reference therein, set forth facts that clearly satisfy each element of the crime of kidnaping as it is defined in [the Louisiana statute]. If we accept as true every fact alleged, the Smolins are properly charged with kidnaping under Louisiana law. In our view, this ends the inquiry into the issue of whether or not a crime is charged for purposes of the Extradition Act. * * *

This proceeding is neither the time nor place for the Smolins' arguments that Judith Pope's affidavit is fraudulent and that the California custody decrees establish Richard as the lawful custodian under the full faith and credit provision of the federal Parental Kidnaping Prevention Act of 1980. There is nothing in the record to suggest that the Smolins are not entirely correct in all of this: that California had exclusive modification jurisdiction over the custody of Jennifer and Jamie; that, under the California decrees, Richard Smolin had lawful custody of the children when he brought them to California; and, that, accordingly, the Smolins did not violate La.Rev.Stat.Ann. § 14:45A(4) (West 1986) as is charged. Of course, the Parental Kidnaping Prevention Act of 1980 creates a uniform federal rule governing custody determinations, a rule to which the courts of Louisiana must adhere when they consider the Smolins' case on the merits. We are not informed by the record why it is that the States of California and Louisiana are so eager to force the Smolins halfway across the continent to face criminal charges that, at least to a majority of the California Supreme Court, appear meritless. If the Smolins are correct, they are not only innocent of the charges made against them, but also victims of a possible abuse of the criminal process. But, under the Extradition Act, it is for the Louisiana courts to do justice in this case, not the California courts: "surrender is not to be interfered with by the summary process of *habeas corpus* upon speculations as to what ought to be the result of a

trial in the place where the Constitution provides for its taking place."
Drew v. Thaw, 235 U.S., at 440. The judgment of the California Supreme
Court is *Reversed*.

JUSTICE STEVENS, with whom JUSTICE BRENNAN joins, dissenting. * * *

The scope of the legal inquiry preceding extradition is extremely
restricted because the courts of the asylum State cannot be expected to
make "a critical examination of the laws of States with whose jurisprudence and criminal procedure they can have only a general acquaintance." *Pierce v. Creecy*, 210 U.S. 387, 405 (1908). Nevertheless, our
precedents make clear that if a critical allegation of fact in the indictment is "impossible in law," the asylum State must refuse the extradition demand because the person has not been substantially charged with
a crime. *Munsey v. Clough*, 196 U.S. 364, 373 (1905). In *Drew v. Thaw*,
235 U.S. 432 (1914), the habeas corpus petitioner was under a New York
indictment for conspiracy to obstruct the due administration of laws; he
was charged with plotting to effect his own escape from an insane
asylum to which he had been committed. Justice Holmes' opinion for the
Court held that the indictment charged a crime because New York courts
could decide that the conspiracy charged "did tend to obstruct the due
administration of the law." Even though the habeas court could not
inquire "upon the facts or the law of the matter to be tried," Justice
Holmes made it clear that there nevertheless must be a "reasonable
possibility" that the crime charged "may be such." * * *

The Smolins' conviction for this crime was an impossibility for three
reasons. First, a California court, the court of competent jurisdiction
under the Federal Parental Kidnaping Prevention Act, had awarded sole
custody of Jennifer and Jamie to Richard Smolin more than three years
before he took them to California; he plainly could not be convicted of
removing the children from his own custody. Second, regardless of
whether Richard or Judith Smolin had custody of the children, he clearly
believed that custody had been awarded to him by a California court
which retained jurisdiction. His act of taking the children to California
therefore could not have been accomplished with the intent to defeat the
jurisdiction of that court. Third, because he did not believe that a
Louisiana court had jurisdiction over the custody determination, he
could not logically be convicted under the kidnaping statute for departing from Louisiana with the intent to defeat the jurisdiction of the courts
of that State. There is, in short, no possibility—and certainly no "reasonable possibility"—that his conduct violated the Louisiana statute cited in
the extradition papers.[4] A sensible application of the requirement that a

---

4. The Louisiana assistant district attorney who filed the information against the
Smolins was aware of the California custody orders at the time he filed the information. He believed, however, that a crime had
been committed because " 'he viewed the
California judgment as being void, having
been obtained by fraudulent misrepresentations, and the valid order having been that

issued by Texas on February 13, 1981.' " In
my opinion that speculation on the part of
the assistant district attorney is inadequate
to overcome the fact that Richard Smolin,
as the holder of a custody determination
that was valid on its face, could not be
substantially charged with a crime for his
exercise of the parental rights conferred
upon him by that custody determination.

fugitive must be "substantially charged" with a crime, informed by the twin necessities of avoiding a trial-like inquiry into the law of sister States and preventing the injustice of extradition to face a legally impossible charge, leads me to conclude that the judgment of the California Supreme Court should be affirmed. * * *

Commentary

Smolin deals with the question of whether the courts of an asylum state may intervene to protect a fugitive from extradition when the Governor of that state has signed the extradition warrant. Sometimes the Governor of the asylum state is reluctant to extradite, and then the demanding state may request a federal court to compel extradition. This issue is historically a very sensitive one, because of our states-rights traditions and because some of the cases have involved fugitives from slavery, racial discrimination, or inhumane penal conditions. In Commonwealth of Kentucky v. Dennison, 65 U.S. (24 How.) 66 (1860), the Kentucky indictment charged Willis Lago, a "free man of color," with the crime of assisting the escape of a slave. The defendant was a resident of Ohio, and papers requesting his extradition were served upon Dennison, the Governor of that state. When Dennison refused to order the extradition, Kentucky sought a writ of mandamus in the Supreme Court.

The case was decided in March, 1861, on the eve of the Civil War. In the circumstances, it is understandable that the opinion by Chief Justice Taney tried to strike a compromise. On the one hand, the Court declared that it was no defense to extradition that the underlying conduct would be innocent under the laws of the asylum state, and held that the asylum Governor had the "merely ministerial" duty to deliver up the fugitive upon appropriate demand. On the other hand, the Court concluded that the duty was only a moral one, and that the principle of state sovereignty precluded allowing a federal court to enforce it. For over 125 years this doctrine remained in force. Despite the shaky logic and the damage done to the federal system by arbitrary refusals of extradition, there was apparently some reluctance to destroy a "loophole" that occasionally permitted a Governor to protect an individual from an oppressive prosecution.

The Supreme Court finally overruled *Dennison* in Puerto Rico v. Branstad, 483 U.S. 219 (1987). Respondent Calder, an Iowa resident employed as an air traffic controller in Puerto Rico, had a fight in a parking lot with a man named de Jesus Gonzalez. As he left the parking lot Calder's car struck de Jesus Gonzalez and his wife, killing the woman and her unborn child. De Jesus Gonzalez and another witness told the police that after striking the couple Calder backed his car two or three times over the prostrate body of the pregnant wife.

On the basis of these statements Calder was charged in Puerto Rico with first degree murder, and he subsequently jumped bail to return to his family home in Iowa. The Governor of Puerto Rico requested extradition, and a hearing on the supporting documents was held before the counsel for the Governor of Iowa. At this hearing Calder's counsel testified to his belief that "a white American man * * * could not receive a fair trial in the Commonwealth of Puerto Rico," and Calder himself testified to his understanding that on numerous occasions witnesses in Puerto Rican courts had been "bought." The Iowa Governor was reluctant to extradite unless Puerto Rico would agree to reduce the charges, and eventually refused extradition after negotiations failed. Puerto Rico brought a federal court action to compel extradition, and the lower federal courts reluctantly held that the *Dennison* precedent deprived them of the power to grant relief.

The Supreme Court granted review to consider the continuing validity of the doctrine that the courts may not order a reluctant Governor to extradite. The opinion by Justice O'Connor reaffirmed the first part of the *Dennison* holding, that the duty to grant extradition was mandatory and ministerial in nature. Such duties are usually judicially enforceable, and the opinion observed that the Supreme Court has ordered state officials to fulfill their constitutional duties on many occasions since 1861—most notably in the school desegregation cases. The doctrine that the federal courts have no power to order a Governor to extradite has survived only as a historical anomaly. Accordingly, the Court held that "there is no justification for distinguishing the duty to deliver fugitives from the many other species of constitutional duty enforceable in the federal courts."

GERSTEIN v. PUGH

Supreme Court of the United States, 1975.
420 U.S. 103, 95 S.Ct. 854, 43 L.Ed.2d 54.

Mr. Justice Powell delivered the opinion of the Court.

The issue in this case is whether a person arrested under a prosecutor's information is constitutionally entitled to a judicial determination of probable cause for pretrial restraint of liberty.

I

In March 1971 respondents Pugh and Henderson were arrested in Dade County, Florida. Each was charged with several offenses under a prosecutor's information.[5] Pugh was denied bail because one of the charges against him carried a potential life sentence, and Henderson remained in custody because he was unable to post a $4,500 bond.

In Florida, indictments are required only for prosecution of capital offenses. Prosecutors may charge all other crimes by information, without a prior preliminary hearing and without obtaining leave of court. At the time respondents were arrested, a Florida rule seemed to authorize adversary preliminary hearings to test probable cause for detention in all cases. But the Florida courts had held that the filing of an information foreclosed the suspect's right to a preliminary hearing. They had also held that habeas corpus could not be used, except perhaps in exceptional circumstances, to test the probable cause for detention under an infor-

---

5. Respondent Pugh was arrested on March 3, 1971. On March 16 an information was filed charging him with robbery, carrying a concealed weapon, and possession of a firearm during commission of a felony. Respondent Henderson was arrested on March 2, and charged by information on March 19 with the offenses of breaking and entering and assault and battery. The record does not indicate whether there was an arrest warrant in either case.

mation. The only possible methods for obtaining a judicial determination of probable cause were a special statute allowing a preliminary hearing after 30 days, and arraignment, which the District Court found was often delayed a month or more after arrest. As a result, a person charged by information could be detained for a substantial period solely on the decision of a prosecutor.

Respondents Pugh and Henderson filed a class action against Dade County officials in the Federal District Court, claiming a constitutional right to a judicial hearing on the issue of probable cause and requesting declaratory and injunctive relief. * * *

[The District Court granted the relief sought and the Court of Appeals affirmed. Gerstein, the prosecuting attorney of Dade County, petitioned for review in the Supreme Court.]

II

As framed by the proceedings below, this case presents two issues; whether a person arrested and held for trial on an information is entitled to a judicial determination of probable cause for detention, and if so, whether the adversary hearing ordered by the District Court and approved by the Court of Appeals is required by the Constitution.

A

Both the standards and procedures for arrest and detention have been derived from the Fourth Amendment and its common-law anteced- ents. The standard for arrest is probable cause, defined in terms of facts and circumstances "sufficient to warrant a prudent man in believing that the [suspect] had committed or was committing an offense." Beck v. Ohio, 379 U.S. 89, 91. This standard, like those for searches and seizures, represents a necessary accommodation between the individual's right to liberty and the State's duty to control crime. * * *

Maximum protection of individual rights could be assured by requir- ing a magistrate's review of the factual justification prior to any arrest but such a requirement would constitute an intolerable handicap for legitimate law enforcement. Thus, while the Court has expressed a preference for the use of arrest warrants when feasible, it has never invalidated an arrest supported by probable cause solely because the officers failed to secure a warrant.*

Under this practical compromise, a policeman's on-the-scene assess- ment of probable cause provides legal justification for arresting a person suspected of crime, and for a brief period of detention to take the administrative steps incident to arrest. Once the suspect is in custody, however, the reasons that justify dispensing with the magistrate's neu- tral judgment evaporate. There no longer is any danger that the suspect will escape or commit further crimes while the police submit their evidence to a magistrate. And, while the State's reasons for taking

---

* Subsequently, the Supreme Court held that entry into a home to make an arrest is unlawful in the absence of a warrant or exigent circumstances. See *Steagald v. United States, supra*, p. 126.

summary action subside, the suspect's need for a neutral determination of probable cause increases significantly. The consequences of prolonged detention may be more serious than the interference occasioned by arrest. Pretrial confinement may imperil the suspect's job, interrupt his source of income, and impair his family relationships. See R. Goldfarb, Ransom 32–91 (1965); L. Katz, Justice Is the Crime 51–62 (1972). Even pretrial release may be accompanied by burdensome conditions that effect a significant restraint on liberty. See, e.g., 18 U.S.C.A. § 3146(a)(2), (5). When the stakes are this high, the detached judgment of a neutral magistrate is essential if the Fourth Amendment is to furnish meaningful protection from unfounded interference with liberty. Accordingly, we hold that the Fourth Amendment requires a judicial determination of probable cause as a prerequisite to extended restraint on liberty following arrest. * * *

B

Under the Florida procedures challenged here, a person arrested without a warrant and charged by information may be jailed or subjected to other restraints pending trial without any opportunity for a probable cause determination. Petitioner defends this practice on the ground that the prosecutor's decision to file an information is itself a determination of probable cause that furnishes sufficient reason to detain a defendant pending trial. Although a conscientious decision that the evidence warrants prosecution affords a measure of protection against unfounded detention, we do not think prosecutorial judgment standing alone meets the requirements of the Fourth Amendment. Indeed, we think the Court's previous decisions compel disapproval of the Florida procedure. In Albrecht v. United States, 273 U.S. 1, 5 (1927), the Court held that an arrest warrant issued solely upon a United States Attorney's information was invalid because the accompanying affidavits were defective. Although the Court's opinion did not explicitly state that the prosecutor's official oath could not furnish probable cause, that conclusion was implicit in the judgment that the arrest was illegal under the Fourth Amendment.[6] * * *

In holding that the prosecutor's assessment of probable cause is not sufficient alone to justify restraint on liberty pending trial, we do not imply that the accused is entitled to judicial oversight or review of the decision to prosecute. Instead, we adhere to the Court's prior holding that a judicial hearing is not prerequisite to prosecution by information. [Citations.] Nor do we retreat from the established rule that illegal arrest or detention does not void a subsequent conviction. [Citations.] Thus, as the Court of Appeals noted below, although a suspect who is presently detained may challenge the probable cause for that confine-

---

6. By contrast, the Court has held that an indictment "fair upon its face," and returned by a "properly constituted grand jury" conclusively determines the existence of probable cause and requires issuance of an arrest warrant without further inquiry. The willingness to let a grand jury's judgment substitute for that of a neutral and detached magistrate is attributable to the grand jury's relationship to the courts and its historical role of protecting individuals from unjust prosecution.

ment, a conviction will not be vacated on the ground that the defendant was detained pending trial without a determination of probable cause.

III

Both the District Court and the Court of Appeals held that the determination of probable cause must be accompanied by the full panoply of adversary safeguards—counsel, confrontation, cross-examination, and compulsory process for witnesses. A full preliminary hearing of this sort is modeled after the procedure used in many States to determine whether the evidence justifies going to trial under an information or presenting the case to a grand jury. The standard of proof required of the prosecution is usually referred to as "probable cause," but in some jurisdictions it may approach a prima facie case of guilt. When the hearing takes this form, adversary procedures are customarily employed. The importance of the issue to both the State and the accused justifies the presentation of witnesses and full exploration of their testimony on cross-examination. This kind of hearing also requires appointment of counsel for indigent defendants. And, as the hearing assumes increased importance and the procedures become more complex, the likelihood that it can be held promptly after arrest diminishes.

These adversary safeguards are not essential for the probable cause determination required by the Fourth Amendment. The sole issue is whether there is probable cause for detaining the arrested person pending further proceedings. This issue can be determined reliably without an adversary hearing. The standard is the same as that for arrest. That standard—Probable cause to believe the suspect has committed a crime—Traditionally has been decided by a magistrate in a nonadversary proceeding on hearsay and written testimony, and the Court has approved these informal modes of proof.

* * *

The use of an informal procedure is justified not only by the lesser consequences of a probable cause determination but also by the nature of the determination itself. It does not require the fine resolution of conflicting evidence that a reasonable-doubt or even a preponderance standard demands, and credibility determinations are seldom crucial in deciding whether the evidence supports a reasonable belief in guilt. This is not to say that confrontation and cross-examination might not enhance the reliability of probable cause determinations in some cases. In most cases, however, their value would be too slight to justify holding, as a matter of constitutional principle, that these formalities and safeguards designed for trial must also be employed in making the Fourth Amendment determination of probable cause.

Because of its limited function and its nonadversary character, the probable cause determination is not a "critical stage" in the prosecution that would require appointed counsel. The Court has identified as "critical stages" those pretrial procedures that would impair defense on the merits if the accused is required to proceed without counsel. Coleman v. Alabama, 399 U.S. 1 (1970). In Coleman v. Alabama, where the Court held that a preliminary hearing was a critical stage of an Alabama prosecution, the majority and concurring opinions identified two critical factors that distinguish the Alabama preliminary hearing from the probable cause determination required by the Fourth Amendment. First, under Alabama law the function of the preliminary hearing was to determine whether the evidence justified charging the suspect with an offense. A finding of no probable cause could mean that he would not be tried at all. The Fourth Amendment probable cause determination is addressed only to pretrial custody. To be sure, pretrial custody may affect to some extent the defendant's ability to assist in preparation of his defense, but this does not present the high probability of substantial harm identified as controlling in *Coleman*. Second, Alabama allowed the suspect to confront and cross-examine prosecution witnesses at the preliminary hearing. The Court noted that the suspect's defense on the merits could be compromised if he had no legal assistance for exploring or preserving the witnesses' testimony. This consideration does not apply when the prosecution is not required to produce witnesses for cross-examination. * * *

IV

We agree with the Court of Appeals that the Fourth Amendment requires a timely* judicial determination of probable cause as a pre-requisite to detention, and we accordingly affirm that much of the judgment. As we do not agree that the Fourth Amendment requires the adversary hearing outlined in the District Court's decree, we reverse in part and remand to the Court of Appeals for further proceedings consistent with this opinion.

[Concurring opinion omitted.]

Commentary

According to the Supreme Court's opinion in *Gerstein v. Pugh*, the constitutionally indispensable function of the preliminary hearing is not the review of the decision to prosecute, but the more limited determination that sufficient probable cause exists to require the defendant to post bond or otherwise guarantee appearance at trial. Given that probable cause can be established by evidence that falls considerably short of the proof needed to establish guilt at trial, the Constitution does little to protect a defendant from having to stand trial on weakly supported charges. The Constitution also does little to guarantee defendants a right to remain at liberty before conviction.

---

* How soon after arrest must the probable cause hearing be held? In Riverside County, California v. McLaughlin, 111 S.Ct. 1661 (1991), the Supreme Court reversed a holding by the Ninth Circuit which had interpreted *Gerstein* to require that the hearing ordinarily occur within 36 hours after completion of the booking process. Justice O'Connor's opinion for the 5–4 majority held that a combined probable cause/arraignment hearing held within 48 hours of arrest is presumptively reasonable. If the hearing is delayed beyond 48 hours the burden shifts to the state to establish that the delay was necessitated by an emergency or other extraordinary circumstance. The majority held that intervening weekends and holidays do *not* constitute an excuse for delay beyond 48 hours.

It is of crucial importance to a defendant to obtain release from custody during the period of weeks or months that intervenes between the arrest and the end of the trial. Pretrial confinement is itself a punishment, especially given the deplorable conditions that prevail in city and county jails. Although the time spent in custody is credited against the eventual sentence, defendants are sometimes tempted to plead guilty just to get to the relatively more comfortable environment of the prison system. Defendants in custody normally lose their jobs; if free, they might be able to support their families and earn enough money to retain private counsel.

Most important, pretrial liberty increases the prospects for an ultimately successful defense. It permits the defendant to assist counsel by finding witnesses or persuading them to cooperate. The defendant in custody is under pressure to plead guilty to "get it over with," but the free defendant enters plea bargaining negotiations from a stronger position and can consider employing delaying tactics. Delay often works to the benefit of the defense, because the prosecution's witnesses may become unavailable or forgetful, and because old crimes sometimes seem less serious than recent ones. After conviction, the defendant who is at liberty has a better chance of staying out of jail than the defendant in custody. If the defendant has held a job all along and stayed out of trouble, the attorney can make a powerful argument for probation or a fine as the appropriate penalty rather than a jail sentence.

On the other hand, law enforcement authorities around the world claim that, if all defendants were released prior to trial, a significant number would flee, tamper with the prosecution's witnesses, or commit "other" crimes while at liberty. As a result, magistrates in nearly every country have the discretionary authority to order pretrial confinement of persons accused of serious crimes upon substantial evidence, if they feel that such confinement is necessary to prevent flight or to protect the safety of individuals or the community. (See e.g. the English case described on p. 545, supra.) In many countries, most particularly including those where the investigating authorities rely heavily on interrogation of the accused person, lengthy pretrial detention is extremely common.

Until recently American law was the exception, because the American legal tradition has theoretically granted defendants an absolute right to pretrial release, except when the prosecution is for a crime punishable by death, if they can post sufficient security with the court to assure that they will not flee. The security is usually in the form of money bail that will be forfeited in the event of non-appearance.* The system thus assumes that defendants will appear for trial if they have a sufficient financial incentive to do so. In the traditional view, the likelihood of non-appearance is the *only* proper consideration in setting the amount of bail to be required. Because so many criminal defendants are poor, and because even a defendant with substantial income may have difficulty in raising several thousand dollars in cash, many defendants cannot "make bail." The problem is compounded by the fact that bail is frequently set at an amount governed by the seriousness

---

* For traffic offenses the "bail" is usually exactly the amount of the standard fine, and the defendant may "forfeit bail" as a legitimate way of paying the fine without the inconvenience of going to court.

of the alleged offense, without much regard to the personal and financial circumstances of the offender.

Enter the bail bondsman. When the magistrate sets bail in the hundreds or thousands of dollars, few defendants have the resources or the inclination to post the entire amount in cash or equivalent security with the court. For a fee (usually a little more than 10% of the amount of the bail), the bondsman will post a surety bond with the court in the full amount of the bail and obtain the release of the client. The bondsman is in a sense betting that the accused will appear for trial, and of course the success of his business depends upon the accuracy of his judgment. As a practical matter, the accused will be at liberty before trial if he can afford to pay the bondsman's premium and if the bondsman trusts him not to flee.

But how does the money bail system operate to ensure the presence of the accused for trial if it is the bondsman who suffers the financial loss in the event of flight? The accused pays only the bondsman's fee, which is not refunded even if he does appear. Three factors explain how the bail system enforces the obligation to appear: (1) The bondsman would soon go out of business if many clients absconded, and so he refuses to post bond in doubtful cases. (2) The bondsman will often insist that the accused provide collateral to secure at least part of the risk, sometimes in the form of guarantees signed by solvent relatives or friends. Thus the accused himself or persons whose interests he presumably values will ultimately stand the financial loss in many cases. (3) The bondsman has a common law power to arrest a client and surrender him to the court at any time. Although the bond is forfeited when the defendant absconds, the forfeiture will normally be set aside if the bondsman brings him into court within a reasonable time. A bondsman who faces a substantial loss may exhibit great energy and employ resources not available to conventional law enforcement agencies to apprehend and return the fugitive.

The money bail system has been attacked on constitutional grounds, principally on the theory that setting a price for pretrial release invidiously discriminates between the rich and poor in violation of the Equal Protection Clause of the Fourteenth Amendment, or that bail in an amount higher than the accused can meet is "excessive" bail within the meaning of the Eighth Amendment. The constitutional case against the bail system was argued by Professor Caleb Foote in a much-admired article, "The Coming Constitutional Crisis in Bail," 113 U.Pa.L.Rev. 959 (1965). The prophesy in the title was mistaken, however, for the constitutional crisis never came. In Stack v. Boyle, 342 U.S. 1 (1951), the Supreme Court granted relief to certain Communist Party leaders whose bail had been set at an arbitrarily high figure, but the Court had no criticism for the money bail system itself. The reforms that have been made have come from legislative or administrative innovations, rather than from constitutional decisions by the courts. The reforms have been of three types:

(1) "O.R. release" programs. The laws of many jurisdictions now give magistrates discretionary authority to release an accused upon his "own recognizance," i.e. an unsecured written promise to appear. Willful violation of this promise is itself a criminal offense. Privately or publicly funded projects in many cities provide personnel who interview detainees at the jails to determine if they are good "O.R. risks." The "O.R. projects" have helped

many arrested persons to obtain pretrial freedom without paying a bondsman, but they can do little to help those who do not have steady employment, stable family ties, lengthy residence in the community or other indicia of reliability.

(2) "Citation release" provisions in many jurisdictions give either the arresting officer or the booking officer at the jail discretion to release minor offenders upon their written promise to appear. Where the officer has and uses this authority, the accused obtains what is in effect an O.R. release without staying in custody for the hours or days that may intervene between the arrest and the first appearance in court. Statutes in some jurisdictions also require officers to issue a citation or summons rather than to arrest for minor offenses where the defendant can produce adequate identification.

(3) The Federal Bail Reform Act of 1966, applicable only in the federal courts but imitated in some of the states, required the judge to order O.R. release in the absence of some indication that "such a release will not reasonably assure the appearance of the person as required." If O.R. release was not appropriate, the judge was directed to consider in order the following possibilities short of outright custody for guaranteeing appearance at trial: (1) placing the person in the custody of another person or organization; (2) placing restrictions on the defendant's travel, association or place of residence; (3) setting bail but allowing the defendant to meet it by making a refundable deposit of 10 percent of the amount in cash (thus depositing with the court the amount that would otherwise be paid to a bondsman); (4) requiring a traditional bail bond; or (5) requiring the person to be in custody during specified hours. Although the Bail Reform Act left the judges with discretion to set bail in an amount higher than the defendant could pay, its procedures encouraged serious consideration of O.R. release and other conditions that would allow the defendant to remain out of custody.

The Federal Bail Reform Act was substantially revised in 1984. As currently amended, the Act gives the magistrate a wide range of alternatives to ensure both appearance at trial and the safety of the public, but forbids the imposition of "a financial condition that results in the pretrial detention of the person."* On the other hand, the revised Act gives the magistrate substantial discretion in specified circumstances to impose pretrial detention where: (1) there is a serious risk that the person will flee; or (2) there is a serious risk that the person will attempt to influence a witness or juror; or (3) detention is necessary to protect the safety of other persons or the community.

Preventive Detention

As has previously been indicated, the tradition in the United States until recently was that assuring the appearance of the defendant at trial was the only legitimate purpose of bail, and judges had no authority to order pretrial confinement of defendants to protect the public from the crimes they might commit if released. The tradition was ambiguous, however, because it was an open secret that judges frequently imposed de facto detention by setting bail

---

* This provision does not require the magistrate to release a defendant who cannot meet a financial condition which the magistrate has determined to be essential to ensure the defendant's appearance in court, however. See United States v. Jessup, 757 F.2d 378 (1st Cir.1985).

in an amount higher than the defendant could afford. Moreover, the recognition of a right to bail in non-capital cases grew up during a period in which most serious crimes were punishable by death. Routine denial of bail in capital cases may have been based on a theory that a potential death sentence creates an enormous inducement to flight, rather than an assumption that capital offenders are inherently dangerous, but undoubtedly the exception for capital cases helped the courts to avoid the question of whether dangerousness could be an independent ground for detention.

Opponents of preventive pretrial detention have argued that the practice violates not only the Eighth Amendment's prohibition of "excessive bail," but also the "presumption of innocence," a phrase which is not found in the Constitution but is concededly part of our due process tradition. Supporters of detention have argued that the presumption is merely an aphoristic way of stating the rule that the prosecution has the burden *at trial* of proving the defendant's guilt, rather than the defendant of proving innocence, and that it has no application to pretrial matters such as bail and detention. This view finds support in the decision of the Supreme Court in Bell v. Wolfish, 441 U.S. 520 (1979), where the Court held that the presumption of innocence does not place any limitations on the conditions of confinement that may be imposed on a person who is detained before trial for failure to post bail. The opinion stated specifically that the presumption "has no application to a determination of the rights of a pretrial detainee during confinement before his trial has even begun."

The traditional ban on explicit preventive detention was challenged by the Nixon Administration, which persuaded Congress to authorize preventive pretrial detention for criminal prosecutions in the District of Columbia. This statute provoked a vigorous academic debate about constitutional principles, but its provisions were at first rarely employed. It seems that judges desiring to impose detention found it easier simply to set high bail.

For a thorough review of the constitutional and policy questions in the area of pretrial detention, see the article by Professor Albert Alschuler, "Preventive Pretrial Detention and the Failure of Interest–Balancing Approaches to Due Process," 85 Mich.L.Rev. 510 (1986). Alschuler argues that pretrial detention is justified in some cases, but that it should be based on certainty of guilt rather than predictions of dangerousness or interest-balancing.

The 1984 Bail Reform Act included a sweeping preventive detention statute applicable in the federal system as a whole, and the laws of many states now also provide for pretrial detention of categories of dangerous defendants. The federal statute, which is being applied with increasing frequency against drug dealers and organized crime figures, is the subject of the following case.

UNITED STATES v. SALERNO

Supreme Court of the United States, 1987.
481 U.S. 739, 107 S.Ct. 2095, 95 L.Ed.2d 697.

CHIEF JUSTICE REHNQUIST delivered the opinion of the Court. * * *

Responding to "the alarming problem of crimes committed by persons on release," Congress formulated the Bail Reform Act of 1984, 18

U.S.C. § 3141 *et seq.,* as the solution to a bail crisis in the federal courts. The Act represents the National Legislature's considered response to numerous perceived deficiencies in the federal bail process. By providing for sweeping changes in both the way federal courts consider bail applications and the circumstances under which bail is granted, Congress hoped to "give the courts adequate authority to make release decisions that give appropriate recognition to the danger a person may pose to others if released."

To this end, § 3141(a) of the Act requires a judicial officer to determine whether an arrestee shall be detained. Section 3142(e) provides that "[i]f, after a hearing pursuant to the provisions of subsection (f), the judicial officer finds that no condition or combination of conditions will reasonably assure the appearance of the person as required and the safety of any other person and the community, he shall order the detention of the person prior to trial." Section 3142(f) provides the arrestee with a number of procedural safeguards. He may request the presence of counsel at the detention hearing, he may testify and present witnesses in his behalf, as well as proffer evidence, and he may cross-examine other witnesses appearing at the hearing. If the judicial officer finds that no conditions of pretrial release can reasonably assure the safety of other persons and the community, he must state his findings of fact in writing, § 3142(i), and support his conclusion with "clear and convincing evidence," § 3142(f).

The judicial officer is not given unbridled discretion in making the detention determination. Congress has specified the considerations relevant to that decision. These factors include the nature and seriousness of the charges, the substantiality of the government's evidence against the arrestee, the arrestee's background and characteristics, and the nature and seriousness of the danger posed by the suspect's release. § 3142(g). Should a judicial officer order detention, the detainee is entitled to expedited appellate review of the detention order. §§ 3145(b), (c).

Respondents Anthony Salerno and Vincent Cafaro were arrested on March 21, 1986, after being charged in a 29–count indictment alleging various Racketeer Influenced and Corrupt Organizations Act (RICO) violations, mail and wire fraud offenses, extortion, and various criminal gambling violations. The RICO counts alleged 35 acts of racketeering activity, including fraud, extortion, gambling, and conspiracy to commit murder. At respondents' arraignment, the Government moved to have Salerno and Cafaro detained pursuant to § 3142(e), on the ground that no condition of release would assure the safety of the community or any person. The District Court held a hearing at which the Government made a detailed proffer of evidence. The Government's case showed that Salerno was the "boss" of the Genovese Crime Family of La Cosa Nostra and that Cafaro was a "captain" in the Genovese Family. According to the Government's proffer, based in large part on conversations intercepted by a court-ordered wiretap, the two respondents had participated in wide-ranging conspiracies to aid their illegitimate enterprises through violent means. The Government also offered the testimony of two of its trial witnesses, who would assert that Salerno personally participated in two murder conspiracies. Salerno opposed the motion for detention, challenging the credibility of the Government's witnesses. He offered the testimony of several character witnesses as well as a letter from his doctor stating that he was suffering from a serious medical condition. Cafaro presented no evidence at the hearing, but instead characterized the wiretap conversations as merely "tough talk."

The District Court granted the Government's detention motion, concluding that the Government had established by clear and convincing evidence that no condition or combination of conditions of release would ensure the safety of the community or any person:

> "The activities of a criminal organization such as the Genovese Family do not cease with the arrest of its principals and their release on even the most stringent of bail conditions. The illegal businesses, in place for many years, require constant attention and protection, or they will fail. Under these circumstances, this court recognizes a strong incentive on the part of its leadership to continue business as usual. When business as usual involves threats, beatings, and murder, the present danger such people pose in the community is self-evident." 631 F.Supp. 1364, 1375 (S.D.N.Y.1986).

[The Court of Appeals held that the Due Process Clause does not permit detention of accused persons simply as a means of preventing future crimes.] * * *

Respondents first argue that the Act violates substantive due process because the pretrial detention it authorizes constitutes impermissible punishment before trial. * * *

[The majority opinion held that the detention authorized by the Act is not "punishment" because it furthers the "regulatory" purpose of protecting the community from crime.]

We have repeatedly held that the government's regulatory interest in community safety can, in appropriate circumstances, outweigh an individual's liberty interest. For example, in times of war or insurrection, when society's interest is at its peak, the government may detain individuals whom the government believes to be dangerous. [Citations]. Even outside the exigencies of war, we have found that sufficiently compelling governmental interests can justify detention of dangerous persons. Thus, we have found no absolute constitutional barrier to detention of potentially dangerous resident aliens pending deportation proceedings. [Citations]. We have also held that the government may detain mentally unstable individuals who present a danger to the public, and dangerous defendants who become incompetent to stand trial. [Citations]. We have approved of postarrest regulatory detention of juveniles when they present a continuing danger to the community. *Schall v. Martin*, 467 U.S. 253 (1984). Even competent adults may face substantial liberty restrictions as a result of the operation of our criminal justice system. If the police suspect an individual of a crime, they may arrest and hold him until a neutral magistrate determines whether probable cause exists. *Gerstein v. Pugh*, [p. 694]. Finally, respondents concede and the Court of Appeals noted that an arrestee may be incarcerated until trial if he presents a risk of flight, or a danger to witnesses.

Respondents characterize all of these cases as exceptions to the "general rule" of substantive due process that the government may not detain a person prior to a judgment of guilt in a criminal trial. Such a "general rule" may freely be conceded, but we think that these cases show a sufficient number of exceptions to the rule that the congressional action challenged here can hardly be characterized as totally novel. Given the well-established authority of the government, in special circumstances, to restrain individuals' liberty prior to or even without criminal trial and conviction, we think that the present statute providing for pretrial detention on the basis of dangerousness must be evaluated in precisely the same manner that we evaluated the laws in the cases discussed above. * * *

Respondents also contend that the Bail Reform Act violates the Excessive Bail Clause of the Eighth Amendment. * * *

The Eighth Amendment addresses pretrial release by providing merely that "Excessive bail shall not be required." This Clause, of course, says nothing about whether bail shall be available at all. Respondents nevertheless contend that this Clause grants them a right to bail calculated solely upon considerations of flight. They rely on *Stack v. Boyle*, 342 U.S. 1, 5 (1951), in which the Court stated that "Bail set at a figure higher than an amount reasonably calculated [to ensure the defendant's presence at trial] is 'excessive' under the Eighth Amendment." In respondents' view, since the Bail Reform Act allows a court essentially to set bail at an infinite amount for reasons not related to the risk of flight, it violates the Excessive Bail Clause. Respondents concede that the right to bail they have discovered in the Eighth Amendment is not absolute. A court may, for example, refuse bail in capital cases. And, as the Court of Appeals noted and respondents admit, a court may refuse bail when the defendant presents a threat to the judicial process by intimidating witnesses. Respondents characterize these exceptions as consistent with what they claim to be the sole purpose of bail—to ensure integrity of the judicial process.

While we agree that a primary function of bail is to safeguard the courts' role in adjudicating the guilt or innocence of defendants, we reject the proposition that the Eighth Amendment categorically prohibits the government from pursuing other admittedly compelling interests through regulation of pretrial release. * * * Nothing in the text of the Bail Clause limits permissible government considerations solely to questions of flight. The only arguable substantive limitation of the Bail Clause is that the government's proposed conditions of release or detention not be "excessive" in light of the perceived evil. Of course, to determine whether the government's response is excessive, we must compare that response against the interest the government seeks to protect by means of that response. Thus, when the government has admitted that its only interest is in preventing flight, bail must be set by a court at a sum designed to ensure that goal, and no more. *Stack v. Boyle, supra*. We believe that when Congress has mandated detention on the basis of a compelling interest other than prevention of flight, as it has here, the Eighth Amendment does not require release on bail.

III

In our society liberty is the norm, and detention prior to trial or without trial is the carefully limited exception. We hold that the provisions for pretrial detention in the Bail Reform Act of 1984 fall within that carefully limited exception. The Act authorizes the detention prior to trial of arrestees charged with serious felonies who are found after an adversary hearing to pose a threat to the safety of individuals or to the community which no condition of release can dispel. The numerous procedural safeguards detailed above must attend this adversary hearing. We are unwilling to say that this congressional determination, based as it is upon that primary concern of every government—a concern for the safety and indeed the lives of its citizens—on its face violates either the Due Process Clause of the Fifth Amendment or the Excessive Bail Clause of the Eighth Amendment.

The judgment of the Court of Appeals is therefore *Reversed*.

————

JUSTICE MARSHALL, with whom JUSTICE BRENNAN joins, dissenting. * * *

[The dissent began by pointing out that, while this case was pending, Salerno was convicted on other charges in a separate prosecution and sentenced to 100 years in prison. The court which imposed that sentence nonetheless delayed its imposition, apparently with the Government's consent so that the preventive detention issue in this case would not become moot. Respondent Cafaro was actually released on bail in this case when he secretly agreed to become an informer for the Government. Thus, the issue in both cases could well have been moot.]

III

The essence of this case may be found, ironically enough, in a provision of the Act to which the majority does not refer. Title 18 U.S.C. § 3142(j) provides that "[n]othing in this section shall be construed as modifying or limiting the presumption of innocence." But the very pith and purpose of this statute is an abhorrent limitation of the presumption of innocence. The majority's untenable conclusion that the present Act is constitutional arises from a specious denial of the role of the Bail Clause and the Due Process Clause in protecting the invaluable guarantee afforded by the presumption of innocence. * * *

The statute now before us declares that persons who have been indicted may be detained if a judicial officer finds clear and convincing evidence that they pose a danger to individuals or to the community. The statute does not authorize the government to imprison anyone it has evidence is dangerous; indictment is necessary. But let us suppose that a defendant is indicted and the government shows by clear and convincing evidence that he is dangerous and should be detained pending a trial, at which trial the defendant is acquitted. May the government continue to hold the defendant in detention based upon its showing that he is dangerous? The answer cannot be yes, for that would allow the government to imprison someone for uncommitted crimes based upon "proof" not beyond a reasonable doubt. The result must therefore be that once the indictment has failed, detention cannot continue. But our fundamental principles of justice declare that the defendant is as innocent on the day before his trial as he is on the morning after his acquittal. Under this statute an untried indictment somehow acts to permit a detention, based on other charges, which after an acquittal would be unconstitutional. The conclusion is inescapable that the indictment has been turned into evidence, if not that the defendant is guilty of the crime charged, then that left to his own devices he will soon be guilty of something else.

To be sure, an indictment is not without legal consequences. It establishes that there is probable cause to believe that an offense was committed, and that the defendant committed it. Upon probable cause a warrant for the defendant's arrest may issue; a period of administrative detention may occur before the evidence of probable cause is presented to a neutral magistrate. Once a defendant has been committed for trial he may be detained in custody if the magistrate finds that no conditions of release will prevent him from becoming a fugitive. * * * The finding of probable cause conveys power to try, and the power to try imports of necessity the power to assure that the processes of justice will not be evaded or obstructed. The detention purportedly authorized by this statute bears no relation to the government's power to try charges supported by a finding of probable cause, and thus the interests it serves are outside the scope of interests which may be considered in weighing the excessiveness of bail under the Eighth Amendment. * * *

IV

There is a connection between the peculiar facts of this case and the evident constitutional defects in the statute which the Court upholds today. Respondent Cafaro was originally incarcerated for an indeterminate period at the request of the Government, which believed (or professed to believe) that his release imminently threatened the safety of the community. That threat apparently vanished, from the Government's point of view, when Cafaro agreed to act as a covert agent of the Government. There could be no more eloquent demonstration of the coercive power of authority to imprison upon prediction, or of the dangers which the almost inevitable abuses pose to the cherished liberties of a free society. * * *

I dissent.

————

JUSTICE STEVENS, dissenting.

There may be times when the government's interest in protecting the safety of the community will justify the brief detention of a person who has not committed any crime. To use Judge Feinberg's example, it is indeed difficult to accept the proposition that the government is without power to detain a person when it is a virtual certainty that he or she would otherwise kill a group of innocent people in the immediate future. *United States v. Salerno*, 794 F.2d 64, 77 (C.A.2 1986) (dissenting opinion). Similarly, I am unwilling to decide today that the police may never impose a limited curfew during a time of crisis. These questions are obviously not presented in this case, but they lurk in the background and preclude me from answering the question that is presented in as broad a manner as JUSTICE MARSHALL has. Nonetheless, I firmly agree with JUSTICE MARSHALL that the provision of the Bail Reform Act allowing pretrial detention on the basis of future dangerousness is unconstitutional. Whatever the answers are to the questions I have mentioned, it is clear to me that a pending indictment may not be given any weight in evaluating an individual's risk to the community or the need for immediate detention.

MYERS v. COMMONWEALTH

Supreme Judicial Court of Massachusetts, 1973.
363 Mass. 843, 298 N.E.2d 819.

TAURO, CHIEF JUSTICE.

This is a petition for a writ of certiorari and related relief * * * asking the court to exercise its supervisory power "to correct and prevent errors and abuses" in probable cause hearings conducted in the District Court of the Commonwealth. The petitioner asks us to vacate a finding of probable cause in the Municipal Court of the Roxbury District and remand the case to that court for a new probable cause hearing consistent with the requirements of G.L. c. 276, § 38, which he alleges were violated in his initial preliminary hearing.

* * *

The pertinent facts may be summarized briefly. On February 23, 1973, a preliminary examination was held * * * before a judge of the Municipal Court to determine whether there was probable cause to support the prosecution of the petitioner on charges of rape, assault by means of a dangerous weapon, breaking and entering at night, and breaking and entering at night and committing rape of a person lawfully therein. At that probable cause hearing, only the complaining witness was called to testify on behalf of the Commonwealth. At the end of direct examination the petitioner's counsel began his cross-examination of the witness. When the petitioner's counsel questioned the complaining witness about her alleged belief in witchcraft, the judge stated that he had heard enough testimony to find probable cause which made further cross-examination by the petitioner's counsel unnecessary. The petitioner's counsel stated to the court that he wished to complete his cross-examination of the complaining witness, and introduce further evidence,[7] in the defendant's behalf. The judge repeated his finding of probable cause and terminated the hearing. The question before us is whether the judge's finding of probable cause before the petitioner had an opportunity to complete cross-examination of the complaining witness and to present relevant testimony and witnesses in his own behalf violated the petitioner's "substantive rights."

1. The rules governing the conduct of preliminary hearings in the Commonwealth are summarily set forth in G.L. c. 276, § 38, "The court or justice before whom a person is taken upon a charge of crime shall, as soon as may be, examine on oath the complainant and the witnesses for the prosecution, in the presence of the defendant, relative to any material matter connected with such charge. * * * *[T]he witnesses for the prisoner, if any, shall be examined on oath, and he may be assisted by counsel in such examination and in the cross examination of the witnesses in support of the prosecution"* (emphasis supplied). The Commonwealth contends that this statute should not be interpreted as granting the defendant an absolute "inflexible" right to cross-examine prosecution witnesses and present testimony in his own behalf at the preliminary hearing because the examining magistrate has the discretion to find probable cause after listening only to the witnesses for the prosecution. The petitioner argues that c. 276, § 38, grants defendants at such hearings *mandatory* fundamental procedural rights to confront their accusers and present testimony in their own behalf. * * *

2. The judge's chief task at a preliminary hearing is to determine whether the defendant should be bound over for trial in the Superior Court. Defendants are held for trial only if the examining magistrate finds (1) "that a crime has been committed" *and* (2) "that there is probable cause to believe the prisoner guilty." G.L. c. 276, § 42 (and see G.L. c. 276, § 41). These two requirements are designed to establish an effective bind-over standard which distinguishes between groundless or unsupported charges and meritorious prosecutions. Thus, the preliminary hearing's primary function is to screen out at this early but critical stage of the criminal process those cases that should not go to trial thereby sparing individuals from being held for trial, and from being unjustifiably prosecuted * * *.

---

7. The petitioner's counsel told the court that he had a witness whom he wanted to present in behalf of the defendant's case, a medical report on the alleged victim which was made by the physician at the Boston City Hospital the morning of the alleged rape, and a psychiatric evaluation of the complaining witness which was conducted by a staff psychiatrist of the Roxbury Court Clinic after a motion requesting such an examination prior to the probable cause hearing had been granted by a judge of that court.

The United States Supreme Court recognized the importance of the preliminary hearing's screening function in Coleman v. Alabama, 399 U.S. 1 where the court held that Alabama's preliminary hearing is a "critical stage" of the State's criminal process at which the accused is entitled to the aid of counsel. "Plainly the guiding hand of counsel at the preliminary hearing is essential to protect the indigent accused against an erroneous or improper prosecution. First, the lawyer's skilled examination and cross-examination of witnesses may expose fatal weaknesses in the State's case that may lead the magistrate to refuse to bind the accused over. Second, in any event, the skilled interrogation of witnesses by an experienced lawyer can fashion a vital impeachment tool for use in cross-examination of the State's witnesses at the trial, or preserve testimony favorable to the accused of a witness who does not appear at the trial. Third, trained counsel [within the limitations of relevancy] can more effectively discover the case the State has against his client and make possible the preparation of a proper defense to meet that case at the trial. Fourth, counsel can also be influential at the preliminary hearing in making effective arguments for the accused on such matters as the necessity for an early psychiatric examination or bail." P. 9. * * *

Since the examining magistrate's chief task is to determine whether there is sufficient credible evidence to proceed to trial which justifies binding that defendant over, his determination of probable cause to bind over is somewhat analogous in function to the trial court's ruling on a motion for a directed verdict as to whether there is sufficient evidence to send the case to the jury. Unfortunately since this court has never defined the quantum of evidence needed to satisfy probable cause to bind over, some District Court judges have equated probable cause to bind over with probable cause for arrest (and search). * * * A judicial finding of probable cause to arrest validates only the initial decision to arrest the suspect, not the decision made later in the criminal process to hold the defendant for trial. Since many valid arrests are based on reliable hearsay information which could not be introduced at the defendant's trial, probable cause to arrest does not automatically mean that the Commonwealth has sufficient competent legal evidence to justify the costs both to the defendant and to the Commonwealth of a full trial. Therefore the standard of probable cause to bind over must require a greater quantum of legally competent[8] evidence than the probable cause to arrest finding to insure that the preliminary hearing's screening standard is defined in a way that effectuates its purpose.

Since the examining magistrate's determination of the minimum quantum of evidence required to find probable cause to bind over is

---

8. Since the primary objective of the probable cause hearing is to screen out those cases where the *legally admissible* evidence of the defendant's guilt would be insufficient to warrant submission of the case to a jury if it had gone to trial, the rules of evidence at the preliminary hearing should in general be the same rules that are applicable at the criminal trial. * * * Unlike a finding of probable cause for arrest which can be based solely on reliable hearsay testimony, probable cause to hold the defendant for trial must be based on competent testimony which would be admissible at trial. Compare Federal Rule 5.1 * * *

somewhat analogous in function to the court's ruling on a motion for a directed verdict at trial as to whether there is sufficient evidence to warrant submission of the case to the jury, we have decided to adopt a "directed verdict" rule in defining the minimum quantum of credible evidence necessary to support a bind-over determination. The examining magistrate should view the case as if it were a trial and he were required to rule on whether there is enough credible evidence to send the case to the jury. Thus, the magistrate should dismiss the complaint when, on the evidence presented, a trial court would be bound to acquit as a matter of law. * * *

3.   We must construe G.L. c. 276, § 38, in a manner which effectuates its primary purpose of screening out an erroneous or improper prosecution, promotes its ancillary functions and avoids any serious question of constitutional infirmities. The Commonwealth's interpretation of the statute fails in each of these three respects.

The Commonwealth argues that once a prima facie showing of probable cause has been made by prosecution testimony, the examining magistrate can end the hearing before the defendant's attorney has had an opportunity to make a complete cross-examination of the prosecution witness or to present an affirmative defence. We fail to see how such a limited procedure could possibly effectuate the hearing's primary function of screening out cases that should not go to trial. To require such minimal proof of probable cause would render the hearing, in many instances, an empty ritual with a foregone conclusion. If the examining magistrate could simply rest his finding of probable cause on the ipse dixit of the prosecution, there would be little need for defence counsel's presence, let alone the defendant's. * * *

The facts of the instant case provide an excellent illustration of this point. The only witness at the petitioner's probable cause hearing was the complaining witness who repeated her accusation that the petitioner had raped her. If the petitioner had been afforded his statutory rights, he would have introduced testimony challenging the complaining witness's credibility and supporting his defence of a consensual sexual relationship.[9] The examining magistrate could not have possibly made an informed judgment on the question of whether there was sufficient credible evidence of the defendant's guilt to support a bind over until he had considered all of this evidence.

In some cases, the evidence introduced in behalf of the defendant will do no more than raise a conflict which can best be resolved by a jury at the actual trial where the Commonwealth must prove the defendant's guilt beyond a reasonable doubt. But, in other cases, the evidence elicited

---

9. If permitted, the petitioner's counsel would have introduced in evidence a psychiatric evaluation of the prosecutrix which noted that she "has a hysterical neurosis, a condition in which people might make up stories and then half believe them themselves. I would question the veracity of her statements." Defence counsel also wished to introduce a "medical report on the prosecutrix which shows that she received no abdominal injury, no pelvic trauma and that a vaginal discharge test for spermatozoa performed by a physician at the Boston City Hospital the morning of the alleged rape indicated no spermatozoa."

by defence counsel on cross-examination or from the testimony of defence witnesses or from other evidence may lead the examining magistrate to disbelieve the prosecution's witnesses and discharge the defendant for lack of probable cause. * * *

5. The Commonwealth argues in its brief * * * that granting defendants inflexible statutory rights to cross-examine witnesses against them and to present testimony in their own behalf would transform the preliminary hearing into a full-blown trial with disastrous results to a criminal justice system that is already overburdened. However, past experience indicates that trial strategy usually prevents such a result as both the prosecution and the defence wish to withhold as much of their case as possible.

* * *

Since the summary manner in which the petitioner's probable cause hearing was conducted denied the petitioner his statutory right to cross-examine witnesses and present evidence before the issue of probable cause was determined, the petitioner must be given a new preliminary hearing to determine whether there is probable cause to hold him on the charges pending against him. * * *

So ordered.

PRESS–ENTERPRISE CO. v. SUPERIOR COURT

Supreme Court of the United States, 1986.
478 U.S. 1, 106 S.Ct. 2735, 92 L.Ed.2d 1.

CHIEF JUSTICE BURGER delivered the opinion of the Court.

We granted certiorari to decide whether petitioner has a First Amendment right of access to transcripts of a preliminary hearing growing out of a criminal prosecution.

On December 23, 1981, the State of California filed a complaint in the Riverside County Municipal Court, charging Robert Diaz with 12 counts of murder and seeking the death penalty. The complaint alleged that Diaz, a nurse, murdered 12 patients by administering massive doses of the heart drug lidocaine. The preliminary hearing on the complaint commenced on July 6, 1982. Diaz moved to exclude the public from the proceedings under California Penal Code Ann. § 868 (West 1985), which requires such proceedings to be open unless "exclusion of the public is necessary in order to protect the defendant's right to a fair and impartial trial."[10] The Magistrate granted the unopposed motion, finding that

10. * * *

Before 1982, the statute gave the defendant the unqualified right to close the proceedings. After the California Supreme Court rejected a First Amendment attack on the old statute in *San Jose Mercury–News v. Municipal Court*, 638 P.2d 655

(1982), the California Legislature amended the statute to include the present requirement that the hearing be closed only upon a finding by the Magistrate that closure is "necessary in order to protect the defendant's right to a fair trial."

closure was necessary because the case had attracted national publicity and "only one side may get reported in the media."

The preliminary hearing continued for 41 days. Most of the testimony and the evidence presented by the State was medical and scientific; the remainder consisted of testimony by personnel who worked with Diaz on the shifts when the 12 patients died. Diaz did not introduce any evidence, but his counsel subjected most of the witnesses to vigorous cross-examination. Diaz was held to answer on all charges. At the conclusion of the hearing, petitioner Press–Enterprise Company asked that the transcript of the proceedings be released. The Magistrate refused and sealed the record.

On January 21, 1983, the State moved in Superior Court to have the transcripts of the preliminary hearing released to the public; petitioner later joined in support of the motion. Diaz opposed the motion, contending that release of the transcripts would result in prejudicial pretrial publicity. The Superior Court found that the information in the transcript was "as factual as it could be," and that the facts were neither "inflammatory" nor "exciting" but there was, nonetheless, "a reasonable likelihood that release of all or any part of the transcript might prejudice defendant's right to a fair and impartial trial."

[After Diaz waived his right to jury trial the Superior Court released the transcript. Nonetheless the litigation continued and the California Supreme Court reviewed the merits of the order closing the preliminary hearing.]

The California Supreme Court thereafter denied petitioner's peremptory writ of mandate, holding that there is no general First Amendment right of access to preliminary hearings. The court reasoned that the right of access to criminal proceedings recognized in *Press-Enterprise Co. v. Superior Court*, 464 U.S. 501 (1984) (*Press-Enterprise I*), and *Globe Newspaper Co. v. Superior Court*, 457 U.S. 596 (1982), extended only to actual criminal trials. 691 P.2d 1026, 1028 (1984). Furthermore, the reasons that had been asserted for closing the proceedings in *Press–Enterprise I* and *Globe*—the interests of witnesses and other third parties—were not the same as the right asserted in this case—the defendant's right to a fair and impartial trial by a jury uninfluenced by news accounts.

Having found no general First Amendment right of access, the court then considered the circumstances in which the closure would be proper under the California access statute, Cal.Penal Code Ann. § 868 (West 1985). Under the statute, the court reasoned, if the defendant establishes a "reasonable likelihood of substantial prejudice" the burden shifts to the prosecution or the media to show by a preponderance of the evidence that there is no such reasonable probability of prejudice.

* * *

It is difficult to disagree in the abstract with that court's analysis balancing the defendant's right to a fair trial against the public right of access. It is also important to remember that these interests are not necessarily inconsistent. Plainly, the defendant has a right to a fair trial but, as we have repeatedly recognized, one of the important means of assuring a fair trial is that the process be open to neutral observers.

The right to an open public trial is a shared right of the accused and the public, the common concern being the assurance of fairness. Only recently, in *Waller v. Georgia*, 467 U.S. 39 (1984), for example, we considered whether the defendant's Sixth Amendment right to an open trial prevented the closure of a suppression hearing over the defendant's objection. We noted that the First Amendment right of access would in most instances attach to such proceedings and that "the explicit Sixth Amendment right of the accused is no less protective of a public trial than the implicit First Amendment right of the press and public." When the defendant objects to the closure of a suppression hearing, therefore, the hearing must be open unless the party seeking to close the hearing advances an overriding interest that is likely to be prejudiced.

Here, unlike *Waller*, the right asserted is not the defendant's Sixth Amendment right to a public trial since the defendant requested a *closed* preliminary hearing. Instead, the right asserted here is that of the public under the First Amendment. The California Supreme Court concluded that the First Amendment was not implicated because the proceeding was not a criminal trial, but a preliminary hearing. However, the First Amendment question cannot be resolved solely on the label we give the event, *i.e.*, "trial" or otherwise, particularly where the preliminary hearing functions much like a full scale trial.

In cases dealing with the claim of a First Amendment right of access to criminal proceedings, our decisions have emphasized two complementary considerations. First, because a " 'tradition of accessibility implies the favorable judgment of experience' " *Globe Newspaper*, 457 U.S., at 605, we have considered whether the place and process has historically been open to the press and general public. * * *

Second, in this setting the Court has traditionally considered whether public access plays a significant positive role in the functioning of the particular process in question. Although many governmental processes operate best under public scrutiny, it takes little imagination to recognize that there are some kinds of government operations that would be totally frustrated if conducted openly. A classic example is that "the proper functioning of our grand jury system depends upon the secrecy of grand jury proceedings." *Douglas Oil Co. v. Petrol Stops Northwest*, 441 U.S. 211, 218 (1979). Other proceedings plainly require public access. In *Press-Enterprise I*, we summarized the holdings of prior cases, noting that openness in criminal trials, including the selection of jurors, "enhances both the basic fairness of the criminal trial and the appearance of fairness so essential to public confidence in the system." 464 U.S., at 501.

These considerations of experience and logic are, of course, related, for history and experience shape the functioning of governmental processes. If the particular proceeding in question passes these tests of experience and logic, a qualified First Amendment right of public access attaches. But even when a right of access attaches, it is not absolute. While open criminal proceedings give assurances of fairness to both the public and the accused, there are some limited circumstances in which the right of the accused to a fair trial might be undermined by publicity.[11] In such cases, the trial court must determine whether the situation is such that the rights of the accused override the qualified First Amendment right of access. * * *

The considerations that led the Court to apply the First Amendment right of access to criminal trials in *Richmond Newspapers* and *Globe* and the selection of jurors in *Press–Enterprise I* lead us to conclude that the right of access applies to preliminary hearings as conducted in California.

First, there has been a tradition of accessibility to preliminary hearings of the type conducted in California. Although grand jury proceedings have traditionally been closed to the public and the accused, preliminary hearings conducted before neutral and detached magistrates have been open to the public. Long ago in the celebrated trial of Aaron Burr for treason, for example, with Chief Justice Marshall sitting as trial judge, the probable cause hearing was held in the Hall of the House of Delegates in Virginia, the court room being too small to accommodate the crush of interested citizens. From *Burr* until the present day, the near uniform practice of state and federal courts has been to conduct preliminary hearings in open court. As we noted in *Gannett*, several states following the original New York Field Code of Criminal Procedure published in 1850 have allowed preliminary hearings to be closed on the motion of the accused. But even in these states the proceedings are presumptively open to the public and are closed only for cause shown. Open preliminary hearings, therefore, have been accorded " 'the favorable judgment of experience.' "

The second question is whether public access to preliminary hearings as they are conducted in California plays a particularly significant positive role in the actual functioning of the process. We have already determined in *Richmond Newspapers, Globe*, and *Press–Enterprise I* that public access to criminal trials and the selection of jurors is essential to the proper functioning of the criminal justice system. California preliminary hearings are sufficiently like a trial to justify the same conclusion.

In California, to bring a felon to trial, the prosecutor has a choice of securing a grand jury indictment or a finding of probable cause following a preliminary hearing. Even when the accused has been indicted by a grand jury, however, he has an absolute right to an elaborate preliminary hearing before a neutral magistrate. *Hawkins v. Superior Court*, 586 P.2d 916, 918 (1978). The accused has the right to personally appear

---

11. Similarly, the interests of those other than the accused may be implicated. The protection of victims of sex crimes from the trauma and embarrassment of public scrutiny may justify closing certain aspects of a criminal proceeding. See *Globe Newspaper Co. v. Superior Court*, 457 U.S. 596, 607–610 (1982).

at the hearing, to be represented by counsel, to cross-examine hostile witnesses, to present exculpatory evidence, and to exclude illegally obtained evidence. Cal.Penal Code Ann. §§ 859–866 (West 1985), § 1538.5 (1982). If the magistrate determines that probable cause exists, the accused is bound over for trial; such a finding leads to a guilty plea in the majority of cases.

It is true that unlike a criminal trial, the California preliminary hearing cannot result in the conviction of the accused and the adjudication is before a magistrate or other judicial officer without a jury. But these features, standing alone, do not make public access any less essential to the proper functioning of the proceedings in the overall criminal justice process. Because of its extensive scope, the preliminary hearing is often the final and most important step in the criminal proceeding. * * *

Similarly, the absence of a jury, long recognized as an inestimable safeguard against the corrupt or overzealous prosecutor and against the compliant, biased, or eccentric judge, makes the importance of public access to a preliminary hearing even more significant. People in an open society do not demand infallibility from their institutions, but it is difficult for them to accept what they are prohibited from observing.

Denying the transcripts of a 41–day preliminary hearing would frustrate what we have characterized as the "community therapeutic value" of openness. Criminal acts, especially certain violent crimes, provoke public concern, outrage, and hostility. When the public is aware that the law is being enforced and the criminal justice system is functioning, an outlet is provided for these understandable reactions and emotions. In sum, "The value of openness lies in the fact that people not actually attending trials can have confidence that standards of fairness are being observed; the sure knowledge that *anyone* is free to attend gives assurance that established procedures are being followed and that deviations will become known. Openness thus enhances both the basic fairness of the criminal trial and the appearance of fairness so essential to public confidence in the system." *Press-Enterprise I*, 464 U.S., at 508.

Since a qualified First Amendment right of access attaches to preliminary hearings in California, the proceedings cannot be closed unless specific, on the record findings are made demonstrating that closure is essential to preserve higher values and is narrowly tailored to serve that interest. If the interest asserted is the right of the accused to a fair trial, the preliminary hearing shall be closed only if specific findings are made demonstrating that first, there is a substantial probability that the defendant's right to a fair trial will be prejudiced by publicity that closure would prevent and, second, reasonable alternatives to closure cannot adequately protect the defendant's free trial rights.

The California Supreme Court, interpreting its access statute, concluded "that the magistrate shall close the preliminary hearing upon finding a reasonable likelihood of substantial prejudice." As the court itself acknowledged, the "reasonable likelihood" test places a lesser burden on the defendant than the "substantial probability" test which we hold is called for by the First Amendment. Moreover, the court failed to consider whether alternatives short of complete closure would have protected the interests of the accused. * * *

The standard applied by the California Supreme Court failed to consider the First Amendment right of access to criminal proceedings. Accordingly, the judgment of the California Supreme Court is reversed.

[Dissenting opinion omitted.]

Commentary

The Fifth Amendment requires in federal cases that prosecutions for "infamous" crimes (i.e. felonies) be commenced by grand jury indictment. This is also the accepted practice in about one-third of the states. A majority of the states permit felony prosecutions to be brought by either information or indictment, and in these "information states" the use of the grand jury is exceptional. A few states permit the prosecutor to file an information directly in court without first going through a preliminary hearing, perhaps with supporting affidavits to establish probable cause, but the more common practice is to require that sufficient cause be established in a judicial proceeding prior to the filing of the information.

In California, for example, the prevailing practice is to begin the prosecution by filing a felony *complaint* in an inferior court, normally the court which handles misdemeanor trials and minor civil cases. If the magistrate in this court determines after a preliminary hearing that there is sufficient cause to believe that the defendant committed the crime, the defendant is held for trial in the superior court. The prosecutor may then file an *information* in the superior court: this document is the equivalent of a grand jury indictment. In misdemeanor cases the prosecutor may file a *complaint* directly in the inferior trial court and proceed to trial without any preliminary hearing or other review of the decision to prosecute. Once the complaint, information, or indictment has been filed, the defendant must be brought to court for arraignment on the charge. At arraignment the defendant appears with counsel or counsel is appointed, a plea is ordinarily entered, and the judge sets a date for the trial.

In some states, the preliminary hearing has developed into a full-fledged adversary proceeding, with the defense entitled to cross-examine prosecution witnesses and to put on witnesses for the defense. Occasionally, a defendant may be able to undermine the prosecution's case at this stage, and obtain dismissal of the charges without going through the greater ordeal of a jury trial. More often, the defense uses the preliminary hearing as an opportunity to discover the prosecution's evidence and cross-examine its witnesses for the purpose of "pinning them down" on matters of detail. In civil litigation, the parties may take the depositions of witnesses; in criminal litigation, the only comparable opportunity occurs at the preliminary hearing.

Defendants who exercise their right to subpoena witnesses rarely put on a complete defense at the preliminary hearing, since it is normally better tactics not to expose the defense case before trial. Instead, they subpoena and call to testify the prosecution witnesses whom the prosecutor had planned to save for the trial. The purpose usually is not so much to rebut probable cause as to find out what the witnesses will say and to build a record that may be useful in cross-examining them at trial. A thorough preliminary hearing also helps counsel to evaluate a case for purposes of plea bargaining.

A preliminary hearing may also be held in a felony case prosecuted in the federal courts or in one of the states which still requires a grand jury indictment, but it does not fulfil the same role. Where the grand jury has returned an indictment, no preliminary hearing is held because the grand jury has already determined that probable cause exists. The official purpose of the preliminary hearing in a jurisdiction that relies upon the grand jury for the ultimate decision on whether to prosecute is merely to decide whether the defendant should be held to answer (and thus required to remain in custody or give security for his appearance) until such time as the grand jury acts. Hence the prosecutor may avoid the preliminary hearing, and thus deprive the defendant of the discovery that the hearing would incidentally give him, by obtaining an indictment before the time of the hearing. The prosecutor may also be able to render moot any procedural errors occurring at the preliminary hearing by obtaining a supervening indictment. Compare Sciortino v. Zampano, 385 F.2d 132 (2d Cir.1967) and United States v. Coley, 441 F.2d 1299 (5th Cir.1971), with Coleman v. Burnett, 477 F.2d 1187 (D.C.Cir.1973). These cases contain useful discussions of the role of preliminary hearings in federal practice.

Lawyers in the information states have often argued that it is unfair to allow the prosecutor to avoid the preliminary hearing altogether by obtaining a grand jury indictment. Obviously, the grand jury procedure is far less favorable to the defense, and the prosecutor who wants to take a weak case to trial for some reason can probably do so by using the grand jury. Reacting against this denial of equal treatment, the Supreme Courts of California and Michigan have held that a defendant may have a preliminary hearing even if he has already been indicted by a grand jury. See, Hawkins v. Superior Court, 22 Cal.3d 584, 150 Cal.Rptr. 435, 586 P.2d 916 (1978); People v. Duncan, 388 Mich. 489, 201 N.W.2d 629 (Mich. 1972); contra, State v. Clark, 291 Or. 231, 630 P.2d 810 (Or. 1981); State v. Sisneros, 137 Ariz. 323, 670 P.2d 721 (Ariz. 1983).

Although most preliminary hearings are routine affairs even in California, the California-style preliminary hearing can easily become a very extended proceeding when the issues are complex or when the defense chooses to do battle at this stage in the proceedings. The longest preliminary hearing in California history, in a complex sexual abuse case with numerous child witnesses, lasted 18 months. This case was exceptional, but preliminary hearings that take several days of court time are not uncommon. From the defense point of view, having so extensive a hearing is justified by the desirability of protecting an innocent defendant from undergoing the burden of a jury trial, and the desirability of providing an alternative to the civil deposition procedure for effective pretrial preparation.

On the other hand, granting an adversary-type preliminary examination substantially increases the burdens on the witnesses and on the judicial system. Testifying in a criminal case may be an ordeal for a witness, particularly one who is the victim of a sexual crime or who fears retaliation from the defendant. Delays and continuances in adversary hearings are common, and witnesses may be subjected to great inconvenience and frustration as a result. From the viewpoint of the witness, the adversary preliminary hearing may appear to be merely another opportunity for harassment.

UNITED STATES v. LOUD HAWK

Supreme Court of the United States, 1986.
474 U.S. 302, 106 S.Ct. 648, 88 L.Ed.2d 640.

JUSTICE POWELL delivered the opinion of the Court.

In this case we must decide, first, whether the Speedy Trial Clause of the Sixth Amendment applies to time during which respondents were neither under indictment nor subjected to any official restraint, and, second, whether certain delays occasioned by interlocutory appeals were properly weighed in assessing respondents' right to a speedy trial. A divided panel of the Court of Appeals for the Ninth Circuit weighed most of the 90 months from the time of respondents' arrests and initial indictment in November 1975 until the District Court's dismissal of the indictment in May 1983 towards respondents' claims under the Speedy Trial Clause. We conclude that the time that no indictment was outstanding against respondents should not weigh towards respondents' speedy trial claims. We also find that in this case the delay attributable to interlocutory appeals by the Government and respondents do not establish a violation of the Speedy Trial Clause. Accordingly, we reverse the holding of the Court of Appeals that respondents were denied their right to a speedy trial.

I

In view of the nature of respondents' claim, we state the factual and procedural history of this case in some detail. On November 14, 1975, pursuant to a tip from the Federal Bureau of Investigation, Oregon State Troopers stopped two vehicles in search of several federal fugitives. After an exchange of gunfire and a motor chase, State Troopers captured all but one of the respondents, Dennis Banks. Both vehicles were locked and impounded while federal and state authorities obtained search warrants.

Searches of the vehicles over the next two days disclosed 350 pounds of dynamite, six partially assembled time bombs, 2,600 rounds of ammunition, 150 blasting caps, 9 empty hand grenades, and miscellaneous firearms. Oregon law enforcement officers, apparently unaware of the evidentiary consequences, adhered to their usual policy and destroyed the dynamite. A federal agent present at the destruction photographed the explosions. *United States v. Loud Hawk*, 628 F.2d 1139, 1142 (C.A.9 1979). State officials also preserved wrappers from the dynamite casings.

A federal grand jury indicted respondents on November 25, 1975, on charges of possessing firearms and explosives. Trial in the United States District Court for the District of Oregon was set for the week of February 9, 1976. On December 22, 1975, a grand jury returned a five-count superseding indictment. This indictment charged all respondents with three counts relating to possession and transportation in commerce of an unregistered destructive device (the dynamite counts) and two counts relating to unlawful possession of firearms (the firearms counts).

Two days later, respondents filed a motion to suppress all evidence concerning the dynamite, arguing that federal and state officials had intentionally and negligently destroyed the dynamite before the defense had the opportunity to examine it. After initially denying respondents' motion, and after two continuances at respondents' behest, the District Court granted respondents' motion to suppress on March 31, 1976. Three weeks later, the Government appealed the suppression order,[12] and moved that trial on all counts be continued pending the outcome of the appeal. The District Court denied the Government's request for a continuance, and when the case was called for trial, the Government answered not ready. Pursuant to Federal Rule of Criminal Procedure 48(b), the District Judge dismissed the indictment with prejudice. Six months had passed since the original indictment.

The Government immediately appealed the dismissal, and the two appeals were consolidated. The Court of Appeals heard argument on October 15, 1976, and a divided panel affirmed in an unreported opinion on July 26, 1977. On the Government's motion, the court voted on October 17, 1977, to hear the case en banc. On March 6, 1978, the Court of Appeals en banc remanded for findings of fact on whether federal officials participated in the destruction of the dynamite and whether respondents were prejudiced by its destruction. The court retained jurisdiction over the appeal pending the District Court's findings. The District Court issued its findings on August 23, 1978, and the case returned to the Court of Appeals.

On August 7, 1979, the Court of Appeals reversed the suppression order and directed that the dynamite counts be reinstated. *United States v. Loud Hawk*, 628 F.2d, at 1150. The court also held that although the Government could have gone to trial on the firearms counts pending the appeal, the District Court erred in dismissing those counts with prejudice. The Court of Appeals denied respondents' petition for rehearing on

---

12. The Government is permitted to pursue some interlocutory appeals under 18 U.S.C. § 3731. That section as then in effect read:

"In a criminal case an appeal by the United States shall lie to a court of appeals from a decision, judgment, or order of a district court dismissing an indictment or information as to any one or more counts, except that no appeal shall lie where the double jeopardy clause of the United States Constitution prohibits further prosecution.

"An appeal by the United States shall lie to a court of appeals from a decision or order of a district courts [*sic*] suppressing or excluding evidence or requiring the return of seized property in a criminal proceeding, not made after the defendant has been put in jeopardy and before the verdict or finding on an indictment or information, if the United States attorney certifies to the district court that the appeal is not taken for purpose of delay and that the evidence is a substantial proof of a fact material in the proceeding.

"The appeal in all such cases shall be taken within thirty days after the decision, judgment or order has been rendered and shall be diligently prosecuted.

"Pending the prosecution and determination of the appeal in the foregoing instances, the defendant shall be released in accordance with chapter 207 of this title.

"The provisions of this section shall be liberally construed to effectuate its purposes."

October 1, 1979. Respondents petitioned for certiorari; we denied the petition on March 3, 1980. The mandate of the Court of Appeals issued on March 12, 1980, 46 months after the Government filed its notice of appeal from the dismissal of the indictment. Respondents were unconditionally released during that time.

Following remand, the District Court ordered the Government to reindict on the firearms charges.[13] Respondents filed a number of motions during June and July of 1980 in response to the superseding indictment, including a motion to dismiss for vindictive prosecution. On August 8, 1980, the District Court granted the vindictive prosecution motion as to KaMook Banks and denied it as to respondents Dennis Banks, Render, and Loud Hawk. Both sides appealed. Respondents remained free on their own recognizance during this appeal.

The appeals were consolidated, and the Court of Appeals ordered expedited consideration. The court heard argument on January 7, 1981, but did not issue its decision until July 29, 1982. The court sustained the Government's position on all issues. Respondents' petitions for rehearing were denied on October 5, 1982. Respondents again petitioned for certiorari, and we denied the petition on January 10, 1983. The Court of Appeals' mandate issued on January 31, 1983, almost 29 months after the appeals were filed.

The District Court scheduled trial to begin on April 11, 1983. The Government sought and received a continuance until May 3, 1983, because of alleged difficulties in locating witnesses more than seven years after the arrests. Subsequently, the court on its own motion continued the trial date until May 23, 1983, and then again rescheduled the trial for June 13. The record in this Court does not reveal the reasons for these latter two continuances. Defendants objected to each continuance.

On May 20, 1983, the District Court again dismissed the indictment, this time on the ground that respondents' Sixth Amendment right to a speedy trial had been violated. The Government appealed, and unsuccessfully urged the District Court to request that the Court of Appeals expedite the appeal. On its own motion the court treated the appeal as expedited, and heard argument on January 4, 1984. A divided panel affirmed on August 30, 1984. We granted certiorari, and now reverse.

II

The Government argues that under *United States v. MacDonald*, 456 U.S. 1 (1982), the time during which defendants are neither under indictment nor subject to any restraint on their liberty should be excluded—weighed not at all—when considering a speedy trial claim.

---

13. The Government obtained a new indictment from the grand jury that recharged with the original firearms count (although it substituted "receiving" for "transporting") and two of the original three dynamite device counts. The new indictment also charged the defendants with two new destructive device counts relating to a slightly different type of destructive device. It also charged respondent KaMook Banks with a new count of receiving firearms while under indictment for a felony.

Respondents contend that even during the time the charges against them were dismissed, the Government was actively pursuing its case and they continued to be subjected to the possibility that bail might be imposed. This possibility, according to respondents, is sufficient to warrant counting the time towards a speedy trial claim.

The Court has found that when no indictment is outstanding, only the "*actual* restraints imposed by arrest and holding to answer a criminal charge * * * engage the particular protections of the speedy trial provision of the Sixth Amendment." *United States v. Marion*, 404 U.S. 307, 320 (1971). As we stated in *MacDonald:* "The speedy trial guarantee is designed to minimize the possibility of lengthy incarceration prior to trial, to reduce the lesser, but nevertheless substantial, impairment of liberty imposed on an accused while released on bail, and to shorten the disruption of life caused by arrest and the presence of unresolved criminal charges." 456 U.S., at 8.

During much of the litigation, respondents were neither under indictment nor subject to bail. Further judicial proceedings would have been necessary to subject the respondents to any actual restraints. * * *

Respondents argue that the speedy trial guarantee should apply to this period because the Government's desire to prosecute them was a matter of public record. Public suspicion, however, is not sufficient to justify the delay in favor of a defendant's speedy trial claim. We find that after the District Court dismissed the indictment against respondents and after respondents were freed without restraint, they were in the same position as any other subject of a criminal investigation. * * *

We therefore find that under the rule of *MacDonald*, when defendants are not incarcerated or subjected to other substantial restrictions on their liberty, a court should not weigh that time towards a claim under the Speedy Trial Clause.

III

The remaining issue is how to weigh the delay occasioned by an interlocutory appeal when the defendant is subject to indictment or restraint. As we have recognized, the Sixth Amendment's guarantee of a speedy trial is an important safeguard to prevent undue and oppressive incarceration prior to trial, to minimize anxiety and concern accompanying public accusation and to limit the possibilities that long delay will impair the ability of an accused to defend himself. These safeguards may be as important to the accused when the delay is occasioned by an unduly long appellate process as when the delay is caused by a lapse between the initial arrest and the drawing of a proper indictment, or by continuances in the date of trial, *Barker v. Wingo*, 407 U.S. 514, 517–518 (1972).

At the same time, there are important public interests in the process of appellate review. The assurance that motions to suppress evidence or to dismiss an indictment are correctly decided through orderly appellate review safeguards both the rights of defendants and the "rights of public justice." * * *

In *Barker*, we adopted a four-part balancing test to determine whether a series of continuances infringed upon the defendant's right to a speedy trial. 407 U.S., at 530. That test assessed the "[l]ength of delay, the reason for the delay, the defendant's assertion of his right, and prejudice to the defendant." The *Barker* test furnishes the flexibility to take account of the competing concerns of orderly appellate review on the one hand, and a speedy trial on the other. * * *

A

Barker's first, third, and fourth factors present no great difficulty in application. The first factor, the length of delay, defines a threshold in the inquiry: there must be a delay long enough to be "presumptively prejudicial." Here, a 90–month delay in the trial of these serious charges is presumptively prejudicial and serves to trigger application of *Barker*'s other factors.

The third factor—the extent to which respondents have asserted their speedy trial rights—does not support their position. Although the Court of Appeals found that respondents have repeatedly moved for dismissal on speedy trial grounds, that finding alone does not establish that respondents have appropriately asserted their rights. * * *

Here, respondents' speedy trial claims are reminiscent of Penelope's tapestry. At the same time respondents were making a record of claims in the District Court for speedy trial, they consumed six months by filing indisputably frivolous petitions for rehearing and for certiorari * * * They also filled the District Courts docket with repetitive and unsuccessful motions.

The Court of Appeals gave "little weight" to the fourth factor, prejudice to respondents. At most, the court recognized the possibility of "impairment of a fair trial that may well result from the absence or loss of memory of witnesses in this case." That possibility of prejudice is not sufficient to support respondents' position that their speedy trial rights were violated. In this case, moreover, delay is a two-edged sword. It is the Government that bears the burden of proving its case beyond a reasonable doubt. The passage of time may make it difficult or impossible for the Government to carry this burden.

B

The flag all litigants seek to capture is the second factor, the reason for delay. * * *

Under *Barker*, delays in bringing the case to trial caused by the Government's interlocutory appeal may be weighed in determining whether a defendant has suffered a violation of his rights to a speedy trial. It is clear in this case, however, that respondents have failed to show a reason for according these delays any effective weight towards their speedy trial claims. There is no showing of bad faith or dilatory purpose on the Government's part. The Government's position in each of the appeals was strong, and the reversals by the Court of Appeals are prima facie evidence of the reasonableness of the Government's action. Moreover, despite the seriousness of the charged offenses, the District Court chose not to subject respondents to any actual restraints pending the outcome of the appeals. * * *

IV

We cannot hold, on the facts before us, that the delays asserted by respondents weigh sufficiently in support of their speedy trial claim to violate the Speedy Trial Clause. They do not justify the severe remedy of dismissing the indictment. Accordingly, the judgment of the Court of Appeals for the Ninth Circuit is reversed.

JUSTICE MARSHALL, with whom JUSTICE BRENNAN, JUSTICE BLACKMUN, and JUSTICE STEVENS join, dissenting.

* * *

I

The majority concludes that when an appeal arises out of the district court's dismissal of an indictment, the lack of an outstanding indictment absolves the Government of its responsibility to provide a speedy trial. However, we have never conditioned Sixth Amendment rights solely on the presence of an outstanding indictment. Those rights attach to anyone who is "accused," and we have until now recognized that one may stand publicly accused without being under indictment. * * *

Unlike one who has not been arrested, or one who has had the charges against him dropped, respondents did not enjoy the protection of the statute of limitations while the Government prosecuted its appeal. That protection was an important aspect of our holding in *Marion* that pre-arrest delay is not cognizable under the Speedy Trial Clause. See 404 U.S., at 322–323. More importantly, in contrast to *MacDonald*, the Government has not "dropped" anything in this case. There has been at all relevant times a case on a court docket captioned *United States v. Loud Hawk*—I can think of no more formal indication that respondents stand accused by the Government.

The most telling difference between this case and *MacDonald*, however, is the fact that respondents' liberty could have been taken from them at any time during the Government's appeal. One of the primary purposes of the speedy trial right, of course, is to prevent prolonged restraints on liberty, and the absence of any possibility of such restraints was a vital part of our *MacDonald* holding. In contrast, Congress has declared explicitly, in 18 U.S.C. § 3731, that a person in respondents' position shall be subject to the same restraints as an arrested defendant awaiting trial. Thus the District Court had the undoubted authority to condition respondents' release on the posting of bail, or indeed to keep them in jail throughout the appeal, see 18 U.S.C.A. § 3142(e) (1985). Respondents' release could have been accompanied by restrictions on travel, association, employment, abode, and firearms possession, or conditioned on their reporting regularly to law enforcement officers and/or keeping a curfew. Considering all the circumstances, therefore, I believe that respondents' position is most closely analogous to that of a defendant who has been arrested but not yet indicted. * * *

II

The majority also declines to hold the Government accountable for delay attributable to appeals during which respondents were under indictment. In doing so the majority emphasizes the second *Barker* factor—the reason for the delay. Because it concludes that "[t]here is no showing of bad faith or dilatory purpose on the Government's part," the majority declines to accord any "effective weight" to this factor in the speedy trial balance. In reaching this conclusion, it virtually ignores the most obvious "reason for the delay" in this case—the fact that the Court of Appeals was unable to decide these appeals in a reasonably prompt manner. * * *

The Court of Appeals frankly admitted that "most of the delay must be attributed to the processes of this court," a conclusion that is difficult to escape. This case involves appeals from pretrial rulings. The Court of Appeals had every reason to know that these appeals should have been ruled upon as expeditiously as possible. See that court's Rule 20. Yet it took over five years for the Court of Appeals to decide two appeals, one of them "expedited." No complicated analysis is needed to identify the reason for the delay in this case.

I would hold, simply, that a nonfrivolous appeal by any party permits a *reasonable* delay in the proceedings. The number and complexity of the issues on appeal, or the number of parties, might permit a greater or lesser delay in a given case. The Government, not the defendant, must suffer the ultimate consequences of delays attributable to "overcrowded courts," *ibid.*, even at the appellate level. In the present case, the amount of time that the appeals consumed is patently unreasonable. I would therefore weigh the second *Barker* factor against the Government in this case. * * *

Note

In Doggett v. United States, 505 U.S. 647 (1992), the Supreme Court ordered dismissal of an indictment for violation of the Speedy Trial Clause even though the defendant could show no actual prejudice. Petitioner Doggett was indicted for conspiracy to smuggle and distribute cocaine. When DEA agents tried to arrest him at his parents' house, they found he had left the country. The agents later learned that he was in jail in Panama, and asked the Panamanian authorities to turn him over when their own proceedings were completed. Nonetheless, the Panamanians eventually released Doggett and allowed him to go to Colombia.

Doggett reentered the United States in 1982, settled in Virginia, married, earned a college degree, found a steady job as a computer operations manager, lived openly under his own name, and stayed within the law. The DEA made no serious effort to locate him, although doing so would not have been difficult. Doggett was apprehended in 1988, following a routine check by the U.S. Marshal's Service of the credit records of persons for whom there were outstanding arrest warrants. He was finally arrested more than 8½ years after the indictment, and nearly 6 years after his return to the United States.

Although the Government claimed that it had pursued Doggett diligently, the lower courts and the Supreme Court had little difficulty finding that it had been negligent. The Government also contended unsuccessfully that Doggett must have known about the indictment all along, and thus could have invoked his Speedy Trial right. There was no evidence of knowledge, however, and Doggett's mother (who had spoken to the DEA agents in 1980), testified that she had not told her son or anyone else about the charge.

The case thus turned on the question of prejudice. Doggett's liberty was not affected by the pending charge, and he suffered no anxiety from it if he knew nothing about it. He also could not show that the delay had impaired his ability to defend. Because of the absence of demonstrated prejudice, the district court denied the motion to dismiss and Doggett entered a conditional plea of guilty (which preserved his ability to appeal on the Speedy Trial claim). The judge imposed a sentence of probation and a $1000 fine—the leniency presumably reflecting the judge's appreciation that the defendant had the equities on his side if not the law.

The Supreme Court granted certiorari, and had so much difficulty deciding the prejudice issue that it asked the parties to brief an additional issue: "whether the history of the Speedy Trial Clause of the Sixth Amendment supports the view that the Clause protects a right of citizens to repose, free from the fear of secret or unknown indictments for past crimes, independent of any interest in preventing lengthy pretrial incarceration or prejudice to the case of a criminal defendant." When the Supreme Court decided the case, however, the opinion for the 5–4 majority by Justice Souter ignored this additional issue. The majority instead applied the four-part balancing test of *Barker v. Wingo*. The delay was very long, the Government was negligently to blame, and the defendant asserted his Speedy Trial right as soon as he had notice. With respect to the fourth part of the test— prejudice to the defense—the majority held that under the circumstances there was "presumptive prejudice." The dissent by Justice Thomas concluded that "By divorcing the Speedy Trial Clause from all considerations of prejudice to an accused, the Court positively invites the Nation's judges to indulge in ad hoc and result-driven second-guessing of the Government's investigatory efforts."

UNITED STATES v. NOBLES

Supreme Court of the United States, 1975.
422 U.S. 225, 95 S.Ct. 2160, 45 L.Ed.2d 141.

Mr. Justice Powell delivered the opinion of the Court.

* * *

Respondent was tried and convicted on charges arising from an armed robbery of a federally insured bank. The only significant evidence linking him to the crime was the identification testimony of two witnesses, a bank teller and a salesman who was in the bank during the robbery. Respondent offered an alibi but, as the Court of Appeals recognized his strongest defense centered around attempts to discredit these eyewitnesses. Defense efforts to impeach them gave rise to the events that led to this decision.

In the course of preparing respondent's defense, an investigator for the defense interviewed both witnesses and preserved the essence of those conversations in a written report. When the witnesses testified for the prosecution, respondent's counsel relied on the report in conducting their cross-examination. Counsel asked the bank teller whether he recalled having told the investigator that he had seen only the back of the man he identified as respondent. The witness replied that he did not remember making such a statement. He was allowed, despite defense counsel's initial objection, to refresh his recollection by referring to a portion of the investigator's report. The prosecutor also was allowed to see briefly the relevant portion of the report. The witness thereafter testified that although the report indicated that he told the investigator he had seen only respondent's back, he in fact had seen more than that and continued to insist that respondent was the bank robber.

The other witness acknowledged on cross-examination that he too had spoken to the defense investigator. Respondent's counsel twice inquired whether he told the investigator that "all blacks looked alike" to him, and in each instance the witness denied having made such a statement. The prosecution again sought inspection of the relevant portion of the investigator's report, and respondent's counsel again objected. The court declined to order disclosure at that time, but ruled that it would be required if the investigator testified as to the witnesses' alleged statements from the witness stand. The court further advised that it would examine the investigator's report *in camera* and would excise all reference to matters not relevant to the precise statements at issue.

After the prosecution completed its case, respondent called the investigator as a defense witness. The court reiterated that a copy of the report, inspected and edited *in camera*, would have to be submitted to Government counsel at the completion of the investigator's impeachment testimony. When respondent's counsel stated that he did not intend to produce the report, the court ruled that the investigator would not be allowed to testify about his interviews with the witnesses.

[The Court of Appeals reversed, holding that the trial court's ruling violated the 5th Amendment.]

In this instance disclosure of the relevant portions of the defense investigator's report would not impinge on the fundamental values protected by the Fifth Amendment. The court's order was limited to statements allegedly made by third parties who were available as witnesses to both the prosecution and the defense. Respondent did not prepare the report, and there is no suggestion that the portions subject to the disclosure order reflected any information that he conveyed to the investigator. The fact that these statements of third parties were elicited by a defense investigator on respondent's behalf does not convert them into respondent's personal communications. Requiring their production from the investigator therefore would not in any sense compel respondent to be a witness against himself or extort communications from him.

We thus conclude that the Fifth Amendment privilege against compulsory self-incrimination, being personal to the defendant, does not extend to the testimony or statements of third parties called as witnesses at trial. The Court of Appeals' reliance on this constitutional guarantee as a bar to the disclosure here ordered was misplaced. * * *

Respondent contends further that the work-product doctrine exempts the investigator's report from disclosure at trial. * * *

Although the work-product doctrine most frequently is asserted as a bar to discover in civil litigation, its role in assuring the proper functioning of the criminal justice system is even more vital. The interests of society and the accused in obtaining a fair and accurate resolution of the question of guilt or innocence demand that adequate safeguards assure the thorough preparation and presentation of each side of the case.

At its core, the work-product doctrine shelters the mental processes of the attorney, providing a privileged area within which he can analyze and prepare his client's case. But the doctrine is an intensely practical one, grounded in the realities of litigation in our adversary system. One of those realities is that attorneys often must rely on the assistance of investigators and other agents in the compilation of materials in preparation for trial. It is therefore necessary that the doctrine protect material prepared by agents for the attorney as well as those prepared by the attorney himself. Moreover, the concerns reflected in the work-product doctrine do not disappear once trial has begun. Disclosure of an attorney's efforts at trial, as surely as disclosure during pretrial discovery, could disrupt the orderly development and presentation of his case. We need not, however, undertake here to delineate the scope of the doctrine at trial, for in this instance it is clear that the defense waived such right as may have existed to invoke its protections.

The privilege derived from the work-product doctrine is not absolute. Like other qualified privileges, it may be waived. Here respondent sought to adduce the testimony of the investigator and contrast his recollection of the contested statements with that of the prosecution's witnesses. Respondent, by electing to present the investigator as a witness, waived the privilege with respect to matters covered in his testimony. Respondent can no more advance the work-product doctrine to sustain a unilateral testimonial use of work-product materials than he could elect to testify in his own behalf and thereafter assert his Fifth Amendment privilege to resist cross-examination on matters reasonably related to those brought out in direct examination.

Finally, our examination of the record persuades us that the District Court properly exercised its discretion in this instance. The court authorized no general "fishing expedition" into the defense files or indeed even into the defense investigator's report. Rather, its considered ruling was quite limited in scope, opening to prosecution scrutiny only the portion of the report that related to the testimony the investigator would offer to discredit the witnesses' identification testimony. The court further afforded respondent the maximum opportunity to assist in avoiding unwarranted disclosure or to exercise an informed choice to call for the investigator's testimony and thereby open his report to examination.

The court's preclusion sanction was an entirely proper method of assuring compliance with its order. Respondent's argument that this ruling deprived him of the Sixth Amendment rights to compulsory process and cross-examination misconceives the issue. The District Court did not bar the investigator's testimony. It merely prevented respondent from presenting to the jury a partial view of the credibility issue by adducing the investigator's testimony and thereafter refusing to disclose the contemporaneous report that might offer further critical insights. The Sixth Amendment does not confer the right to present testimony free from the legitimate demands of the adversarial system; one cannot invoke the Sixth Amendment as a justification for presenting what might have been a half-truth. * * *

The judgment of the Court of Appeals for the Ninth Circuit is therefore reversed.

[Concurring opinion omitted.]

Commentary

United States v. Nobles involves discovery at trial rather than pretrial discovery, and therefore the case technically belongs in the following chapter. It is included here because it illustrates the law of discovery, which is usually the subject of pretrial motions. The Federal Rules of Criminal Procedure relating to discovery are reprinted at the end of this chapter. Rule 26.2 codifies (for federal cases) the approach taken by the Supreme Court in *Nobles*. Pretrial statements of witnesses are not discoverable before trial, but must be produced for use in cross-examination after the witness has testified on direct examination.]*

In the previous chapter, we considered the scope of the prosecutor's constitutional duty to disclose *ex*culpatory evidence. The Constitution does not obligate the prosecutor to disclose *in*culpatory evidence in advance of trial to assist the defense in preparing for trial. Until fairly recently, discovery in criminal cases was rarely available. Judges commonly assumed that discovery against the defense would be barred by the privilege against self-incrimination, and they also tended to assume

---

* Federal Rule 26.2 is patterned after a statute (18 U.S.C.A. § 3500), commonly known as the "Jencks Act." The Act was named after a Supreme Court decision which had upheld an order requiring the prosecution to turn over witness statements, and it both confirmed and confined the principle that such orders are appropriate. The Act provided that witness statements were to be turned over, but only after the witness had testified on direct examination. Rule 26.2 extends this principle to discovery of statements by defense witnesses who testify.

that allowing discovery against the prosecution would simply permit guilty defendants to escape punishment. The leading opinion taking this view is State v. Tune, 13 N.J. 203, 98 A.2d 881 (N.J. 1953), where the trial judge had granted a murder defendant pretrial discovery of his own confession, but had denied discovery of the statements of witnesses. The majority opinion by Chief Justice Vanderbilt reversed the order granting discovery of the confession and affirmed the denial of all other discovery in the following language:

> In criminal proceedings long experience has taught the courts that often discovery will lead not to honest fact-finding, but on the contrary to perjury and the suppression of evidence. Thus the criminal who is aware of the whole case against him will often procure perjured testimony in order to set up a false defense. Another result of full discovery would be that the criminal defendant who is informed of the names of all of the State's witnesses may take steps to bribe or frighten them into giving perjured testimony or into absenting themselves so that they are unavailable to testify. Moreover, many witnesses, if they know that the defendant will have knowledge of their names prior to trial, will be reluctant to come forward with information during the investigation of the crime. * * * All these dangers are more inherent in criminal proceedings where the defendant has much more at stake, often his own life, than in civil proceedings.

* * *

> In considering the problem it must be remembered that in view of the defendant's constitutional and statutory protections against self-incrimination, the State has no right whatsoever to demand an inspection of any of his documents or to take his deposition, or to submit interrogatories to him. * * * Except for its right to demand particulars from the defendants as to any alibi on which he intends to rely, Rule 2:5–7, the State is completely at the mercy of the defendant who can produce surprise evidence at the trial, can take the stand or not as he wishes, and generally can introduce any sort of unforeseeable evidence he desires in his own defense. To allow him to discover the prosecutor's whole case against him would be to make the prosecutor's task almost insurmountable.

The dissenting opinion by Justice William Brennan (later appointed to the Supreme Court) would have affirmed the trial court order in its entirety. Brennan later elaborated his views in his article "The Criminal Prosecution: Sporting Event or Quest for Truth?", 1963 Wash.U.L.Q. 279 (1963). He argued that expanded discovery rights were necessary to allow defense counsel—often appointed to represent an indigent person with no resources for investigation—to prepare an effective defense. Extensive discovery might also benefit the prosecution, by encouraging guilty pleas. Responding to the above-quoted arguments from the majority opinion in *Tune*, Brennan argued that the danger of perjury is exaggerated, and that experience in civil cases suggests that "liberal discovery, far from abetting, actually deters perjury and fabrication." In any case it would be defense counsel rather than the defendant personally who would have access to discovered information, and Brennan thought that "the notion that [the defendant's] lawyer can't wait to conspire with him to [concoct a fraudulent defense] hardly comports with the foundation of trust and ethics which underlies our professional honor system." Brennan also doubted that the privilege against self-incrimination really bars all discovery against the defense, a doubt which is supported by the extensive two-way discovery permitted by the current Federal Rules.

The battle over the legitimacy of discovery in principle is a thing of the past. All of the states allow trial courts some discretion to order discovery for the benefit of the defense, either by statute, court rule, or common law decision. There is little controversy today over permitting a criminal defendant to obtain a copy of any confessions or other statements made to the police, as well as scientific reports, documentary evidence and the like. Actual practices vary from jurisdiction to jurisdiction, but in most localities prosecutors voluntarily provide considerable informal discovery of material in their files for defense attorneys without the need for formal motions or court orders.

There remains some controversy over whether defense counsel should have a general right to a list of prospective prosecution witnesses and copies of their recorded statements before trial (subject to protective orders or other limitations where the prosecutor can show a particularized likelihood of witness tampering or intimidation), or whether, as in the Federal Rules, witness lists should be omitted from the list of discoverable items and witness statements should be made available only after the witness has testified on direct. In California, for example, defense attorneys routinely obtain copies of police reports which list the names and addresses of witnesses and detail their statements to the police. They may also require the prosecutor to obtain and turn over material useful for cross examination which the prosecutor might otherwise not have on file, such as the prior criminal records of prosecution witnesses or the disciplinary records of police officers. [See e.g. *People v. Memro, supra,* p. 580.]

Whether criminal discovery should be a "two-way street" is a controversial subject. Federal Rule 16(b) [p. 776] provides that the court may order discovery against the defense when the defense "triggers" the prosecutor's right to discovery by requesting disclosure of information from the government. Assuming that the defense has no constitutional right to obtain discovery, it is arguably permissible to condition the allowance of discovery for the defense upon a waiver of whatever privileges might prevent discovery *against* the defense as an independent matter. Subsequent specific discovery provisions such as Federal Rules 12.1 and 12.2 do not take this conditional approach, reflecting a growing certainty that neither the privilege against self-incrimination nor any other constitutional doctrine protects the defense from discovery. The present situation is thoroughly reviewed in an article by Professor Robert P. Mosteller, "Discovery Against the Defense: Tilting the Adversarial Balance," 74 Calif.L.Rev. 1567 (1986). The article begins with the following summary (footnotes omitted):

> Beginning early in the 1970's, revolutionary expansion occurred in criminal discovery by the prosecution against the defense. Where the

defendant previously enjoyed apparently permanent constitutional protection from state incursions, extensive pretrial disclosures by the defendant are now routinely required. Discovery against the criminal defendant as a right of the prosecution, independent of any "triggering" request by the defendant for discovery, is both widespread—available in half the states—and wide-ranging in terms of the scope of information available through authorized disclosures. In several states, the prosecution may obtain:

1. A specification of all defenses that the defendant will raise;

2. The names and addresses of all witnesses that the defendant intends to call at trial; and

3. All statements of defense witnesses, including memoranda of unsigned oral statements.

In most of these states, neither the rules nor the case law explicitly prohibits the prosecutor from using the information so obtained in the state's case-in-chief. Two states even require the defense to create statements of defense witnesses for the purpose of discovery if the statements were not otherwise taken. Others require the defense to provide the prosecution with any statements obtained from government witnesses, whether or not the defense intends to use the statements for impeachment purposes.

Discovery of unsuccessful efforts to prepare a defense, even when that defense will not be presented at trial, is also widely available. Developments here have chiefly concerned discovery of the defense's expert witness; his identity and any report he may have prepared are often ruled discoverable. If the expert's report does not involve a communication from the defendant to the expert, courts frequently find it unprotected by any constitutional right or other privilege. When the expert has obtained statements from the defendant, they are generally recognized as protected at least by attorney-client privilege. Many courts, however, hold the privilege waived if the defense introduces any other evidence relating to the examination. One court has further held that when the defendant testifies in his own behalf he waives all protections; thus, the defendant's statement obtained by the expert may be used to impeach his testimony.

Professor Mosteller vigorously disputes the desirability of the developments just summarized, arguing that the move to extensive discovery against the defense violates the defendant's privilege against self-incrimination, the right to counsel, and the essential values of the adversary system. A negative view was also taken by the California Supreme Court in In re Misener, 38 Cal.3d 543, 213 Cal.Rptr. 569, 698 P.2d 637 (1985). A California statute similar to Federal Rule 26.2 permitted state prosecutors to discover prior statements made by defense witnesses, after the witnesses had testified on direct examination. The California Court held that the statute violates the state constitution's privilege against self-incrimination "by compelling the defendant to supply the prosecution with evidence that can impeach his defense witnesses and thereby tend to incriminate him." Ironically, the first important judicial endorsement of discovery on behalf of the prosecution was also an opinion by the California Supreme Court, by Justice Roger Traynor. Jones v. Superior Court, 58 Cal.2d 56, 22 Cal.Rptr. 879, 372 P.2d 919 (1962).

Assuming that discovery obligations may be imposed upon the defense, there is a further problem regarding the appropriate sanctions for noncompliance. In Taylor v. Illinois, 484 U.S. 400 (1988), the Supreme Court majority held that, although the Compulsory Process Clause of the Sixth Amendment confers on the accused the fundamental right to present defense witnesses, it is nevertheless permissible for a trial judge in appropriate circumstances to preclude a witness from testifying as a sanction for willful violation of a discovery order by defense counsel. The dissenters argued that, where it was the attorney rather than the defendant personally who was responsible for the discovery violation, punishing the conceivably innocent defendant by excluding a material defense witness was an inappropriate sanction. The trial court could have enforced the order by imposing a penalty directly on the attorney, and by permitting the prosecution to have a continuance to investigate the witness or even to comment on the violation in front of the jury.

MAINE v. SUPERIOR COURT

Supreme Court of California, 1968.
68 Cal.2d 375, 66 Cal.Rptr. 724, 438 P.2d 372.

MOSK, JUSTICE.

Petitioners, Leonard E. Maine and Thomas E. Braun, seek writs of mandate directed to the Superior Court of the County of Mendocino. By grand jury indictment they are each accused of murder, two counts of kidnaping, forcible rape, and assault with intent to commit murder. Petitioners each filed a timely motion under section 1033 of the Penal Code for a change of venue on the ground that a fair and impartial trial could not be had in Mendocino County. The trial court found there could be a fair and impartial trial and denied the motions.

In this proceeding petitioners request that we review the trial court's orders and direct that the venue be changed. The case at bench is one of first impression in this jurisdiction; this court has not heretofore entertained applications for mandamus relief before trial to compel a change of venue. As will appear, we conclude that mandate lies to test a nonappealable order denying a change of venue; we further conclude that petitioners' affidavits and exhibits persuasively demonstrate the need in this case for the mandamus relief requested.

* * *

I

The People, who are the real party in interest, insist that mandate should not lie "for very practical reasons": first, mandamus review will unduly prolong trial settings because most defendants will seek a writ of mandate if their motion for change of venue is denied; second, the present petitioners have an adequate remedy at law because the trial court denied their motion without prejudice to its renewal in the event that *voir dire* examination of prospective jurors indicates that it is impossible to empanel a fair and impartial jury. We find neither of these contentions persuasive.

Conceding that some defendants who unsuccessfully seek a change of venue at the trial level will apply for a writ of mandate in appellate courts, the delay in the commencement of their trials will not be significant. If the applications are frivolous or dilatory, the reviewing court may summarily deny relief. On the other hand, if the application has merit, the reviewing court must either grant the writ or issue a show cause order. Any delay that occurs pending appellate determination will be compensated in most cases, should the defendant be found guilty after a long and costly trial, by providing a substantial safeguard against subsequent reversal on appeal for failure to have changed the venue. We do not foresee, in short, that mandamus proceedings to compel a change of venue will deleteriously affect the administration of justice.

The People also contend that petitioners Maine and Braun have an adequate remedy at law in that the trial court denied their motion for a change of venue without prejudice to its renewal "if the facts should so warrant." * * *

Experience shows, however, that trial courts are often reluctant to order a venue change after a jury has been empaneled. Defense counsel, moreover, is placed in an unnecessarily awkward position: unless he exhausts all his peremptory challenges he cannot claim on appeal, in the absence of a specific showing of prejudice, that the jury was not impartial. Yet, convinced that he must go to trial because his motion for a venue change was at first denied and in all likelihood will not ultimately prevail, he may fail to use every peremptory challenge sensing that the jurors he has examined may be comparatively less biased than others who might be seated were his peremptory challenges exhausted. In an antagonistic atmosphere "there will remain the problem of obtaining accurate answers on *voir dire*—is the juror consciously or subconsciously harboring prejudice against the accused resulting from widespread news coverage in the community." We can only conclude that the naked right to renew the motion for change of venue is not an adequate remedy at law to require denial of a mandamus petition.

It would be inopportune, of course, to permit defendant to seek mandamus during or after empaneling the jury. Due regard for the orderly progress of a trial dictates that a defendant apply for a writ of mandate in advance of trial so that, if the application appears meritorious, the appellate court pending its own decision can stay the trial court proceeding. If the appellate court denies the application or if appellate review is not sought, defense counsel can continue, as under the previous practice, to renew his motion for a change of venue during or after the *voir dire* examination of prospective jurors, and the trial court should order a venue change if the situation so merits. * * *

II

Our next point of inquiry is the test to be applied in mandamus proceedings designed to compel a change of venue. Ordinarily we are reluctant to depart from the sound principle invariably pronounced that mandate lies not to control an exercise of discretion but only to correct an abuse of discretion. * * *

This traditional approach, however, is no longer adequate since Sheppard v. Maxwell, 384 U.S. 333 (1966). In extending the nature of the inquiry far beyond the validity of trial court discretion, the United States Supreme Court stated that "appellate tribunals have the duty to make an *independent evaluation* of the circumstances" (italics added), an unmistakable implication that appellate courts must, when their aid is properly invoked, satisfy themselves *de novo* on all the exhibits and affidavits that every defendant obtains a fair and impartial trial.

Although we have reversed judgments of conviction on but four occasions, many cases have presented serious constitutional issues arising out of prejudicial newspaper publicity which either caused or reflected widespread hostility to a defendant in the community. In such cases the offenses committed were often bestial and heinous, and the discovery of the crimes as well as the unfolding of subsequent events inevitably received abundant attention in the communications media. * * * In many cases that are the focus of unusual public attention, the effect of prejudicial pretrial disclosures or widespread community antagonism can be substantially overcome by a change of venue. This end can most readily be served by delineating with greater specificity the standard of reasonableness that should guide trial courts in the exercise of their discretion on a motion for a venue change and appellate courts, if pretrial review by mandamus is sought, in making their own independent review of the affidavits and exhibits.

After long study the American Bar Association has tendered proposals for judicial consideration which should contribute toward freeing criminal trials from the taint of partiality. The Reardon Report which embodies these proposals, details a comprehensive standard relating to motions for change of venue or continuance which we now consider authoritative. Section 3.2(c), entitled "Standards for granting the motion," provides: "A motion for change of venue or continuance shall be granted whenever it is determined that because of the dissemination of potentially prejudicial material, there is a reasonable likelihood that in the absence of such relief, a fair trial cannot be had. This determination may be based on such evidence as qualified public opinion surveys or opinion testimony offered by individuals, or on the court's own evaluation of the nature, frequency, and timing of the material involved. A showing of actual prejudice shall not be required."

The foregoing standard is fashioned on those suggested by the United States Supreme Court in Sheppard v. Maxwell supra. "[W]here there is a reasonable likelihood that prejudicial news prior to trial will prevent a fair trial," the Supreme Court wrote, "the judge should continue the case until the threat abates, or transfer it to another county not so permeated with publicity." While the Supreme Court explicitly declined to rest its reversal in *Sheppard* on the pretrial publicity, the court's noticeable sensitivity to potentially prejudicial pretrial publicity and disclosures has rendered imperative the implementation of the standard governing change of venue or continuance recommended in the Reardon Report. * * *

III

In the case at bench petitioners are accused of crimes of the gravest consequence. They are strangers to Ukiah, a small community where they have been held for trial. On the other hand, the two victims, a popular teen-age couple from respected families in the area, were assaulted under circumstances that would compel any community's shock and indignation. Since the case has not progressed beyond the pretrial stage it would be inappropriate for us to comment on the evidence that may unfold at the trial. We confine our discussion to a few uncontradicted illustrations which demonstrate a reasonable likelihood that petitioners cannot receive a fair trial in Mendocino County.

One of the victims, the girl, was discovered on a public road nearly unconscious with bullet wounds about her neck and head. Her condition was critical and several complicated operations were performed to save her life. Local citizens immediately organized a fund to help the girl's parents defray the medical expenses, and the Ukiah Daily Journal, the local newspaper, urged every citizen to contribute. It is no small measure of the community's laudable warmth and generosity that a substantial sum was quickly raised, mostly in modest contributions. We do not hold it to be an invariable rule that sympathy for a victim demonstrates antipathy to the alleged perpetrators of an offense. But such pervasive civic involvement in the fate of a victim, particularly when the events all transpire in a relatively small community,[14] is a strong indication that the venue should be changed.

We recognize that from the outset of the investigation the local law enforcement authorities scrupulously avoided divulging any details of the crime. Both the Ukiah Daily Journal and the Santa Rosa Press Democrat, which extensively reported the case to residents of Mendocino County and vicinity, noted that the sheriff and district attorney were "extremely close-mouthed on any details." Their commendable efforts in this regard, however, were frustrated by other authorities who talked freely with representatives of the press and other news media about the crime. Principally at fault appears to be an official of the State of Washington, where petitioners are also charged with murder, who revealed that one of the petitioners had confessed and placed full responsibility on the other for the crimes. This disclosure received substantial attention in the local newspaper, and it is undoubted that the existence

---

14. The 1960 population of Ukiah, the county seat of Mendocino County, was 9,900. The entire population of Mendocino County is 51,200; the county ranks 34th of California's 58 counties.

of a confession is now common knowledge in the community. The admissibility of the confession into evidence has not been tested in a judicial hearing, however and its premature release must be regarded as potentially prejudicial to petitioners. When such a disclosure occurs in a small community, the only effective remedy, if the defense so requests, is to change the venue. Indeed, failure to seek a change of venue may suggest to a reviewing court on appeal that no prejudice was suffered by the defendant. * * *

Finally, this case has to some extent become involved in county politics. The district attorney disqualified Judge Winslow, an experienced trial judge, whom he is opposing on the June 1968 election ballot. The People do not deny that political factors might have influenced the district attorney's decision, but contend that since a judge from outside the county has now been assigned to hear the case, petitioners' right to a fair trial will not be infringed. The People also note that counsel for one of the petitioners has announced his candidacy for the same judgeship, but assert their belief that the assigned trial judge can exercise effective control over both the district attorney and the defense counsel. Under these circumstances, nevertheless, we harbor a gnawing fear that the campaign competition between two election adversaries might inadvertently intrude during the course of a proceeding in which they are also trial adversaries. Political factors have no place in a criminal proceeding, and when they are likely to appear, as here, they constitute an independent reason for a venue change. * * *

The People insist that sufficient time has now elapsed since the date of petitioners' arrest that any prejudice they might have suffered has been dissipated. Under the circumstances of the case at bench this position is not persuasive. While a lengthy continuance might sufficiently protect the accused in some cases, it does not do so here. Delays may be an efficacious antidote to publicity in medium-size and large cities, but in small communities, where a major crime becomes embedded in the public consciousness, their effectiveness is greatly diminished. * * *

We hold that where, as here, the defendants are friendless in the community, the victims prominent, the occurrence of the crime probably fortuitous as to locale, community-wide interest and generosity are expressed on behalf of the victim, newspaper publicity includes accounts of a purported confession, and two opposing counsel are also election opponents, a change of venue is clearly necessary to assure a fair trial to the defendants.

It is now incumbent upon the parties to suggest a convenient site for a fair trial. In a case of this nature it would probably be prudent to transfer the cause to a metropolitan area where comparatively little difficulty will be encountered in empaneling a jury free from any kind of prejudgment. In the instant case, for example, it might not be inappropriate to select one of the cities in the San Francisco Bay area.

[Writ granted. All concur.]

Commentary

Maine v. Superior Court is unusual both in allowing pretrial appellate review of the denial of the motion for a change of venue, and in its holding that the motion should have been granted in the absence of more compelling evidence that it would be impossible to select an unbiased jury in the county in which the crime was committed. In most other states and the federal system, trial courts typically deny the motion until or unless it is demonstrated in the course of jury selection that a fair jury cannot be obtained. Ordinarily, it is possible to select an unbiased jury, or at least an apparently unbiased jury, even where the publicity has been pervasive. The mere fact that the jurors have been exposed to publicity does not make them ineligible, if they can convincingly assert that they are capable of judging the case fairly on the evidence presented at trial. For example, all the defendants in the notorious "Watergate" scandals of the Nixon Administration were tried in the District of Columbia, despite the enormous local interest in the crime and despite the fact that the Nixon Administration was locally unpopular.

Probably the decision in *Maine* was affected by the fact that the prosecution was asking for the death penalty. Presumably, local sentiment might make a Mendocino County jury less likely to show mercy on the issue of penalty than a jury from a distant community which might regard the crime more impersonally. The Santa Clara County jury that heard the case sentenced Braun but not Maine to death. See People v. Braun, 29 Cal.App.3d 949, 106 Cal.Rptr. 56 (1973). The death sentence was not carried out, because the California Supreme Court held the capital punishment statute unconstitutional.

Because the Sixth Amendment grants a federal defendant the right to trial in the state and district in which the crime occurred, the defendant's consent is essential to a change of venue. In some states, however, it is at least theoretically possible for the prosecution to obtain a change of venue on the ground that *it* cannot receive a fair trial in the locality where the crime occurred. Such motions are rarely granted, however. See e.g. Mast v. Superior Court, 102 Ariz. 225, 427 P.2d 917 (Ariz. 1967).

The effect of the liberal California rule on pretrial change of venue motions was dramatically illustrated in the prosecution of four white Los Angeles police officers for the beating of African–American Rodney King after an automobile chase. A state appellate court ordered a change of venue from Los Angeles County due to the massive publicity which the incident had engendered, which had included the repeated showing of a videotape of the beating on television. This required the Los Angeles trial judge to select another county for the trial, and he chose suburban Ventura County because the location was more convenient for counsel and witnesses than other, more distant possible sites. When the Ventura County jury returned verdicts of acquittal against three of the officers and failed to agree on a verdict against the fourth, riots erupted in Los Angeles. Many commentators attributed the verdicts to the fact that the case was tried in a relatively conservative county with a relatively small African–American population.

Subsequently, federal prosecutors charged the officers with criminal civil rights violations growing out of the same incident. (The double jeopardy clause does not prohibit successive state and federal prosecution for the same criminal acts.) In some respects the argument for a change of venue from Los Angeles was even stronger in the second trial, because local jurors might have feared that acquittals would set off further violence. Nonetheless, defense attorneys did not ask the federal court for a change of venue. One of the lawyers commented that such a motion "would not be well-received by the court." Another speculated that, if a change of venue were granted, "pressure from Washington" would prompt a transfer to the location in the United States most favorable to the prosecution. See Los Angeles Times, "Plea to move King case is unlikely," Sept. 5, 1992, p. 1, col. 4. On retrial the Los Angeles federal court jury convicted two of the officers.

The Los Angeles riots had an effect across the continent in Florida. Hispanic Miami policeman William Lozano had been convicted of the homicide of two African–American men in December, 1989, in a shooting that set off three days of rioting in Miami. A Florida Appellate Court reversed the conviction in 1991 on the ground that a change of venue from Miami should have been granted. State v. Lozano, 595 So.2d 558 (Fla.1992). A Miami trial judge named Spencer subsequently ordered the retrial to be held in Orlando. Immediately after the Los Angeles riots Judge Spencer changed his mind and, on his own motion, ordered the retrial to be held in Tallahassee because that county had a more substantial black population.*

The Florida appellate court reversed and ordered the retrial to be held in Orlando. The opinion commented that Judge Spencer's motive in changing the venue to Tallahassee was clearly to increase the likelihood that African–Americans would sit on the jury, but in so doing he had also virtually guaranteed the absence of Hispanic jurors. State v. Lozano, 616 So.2d 73 (Fla.App.1993).

FEDERAL RULES OF CRIMINAL PROCEDURE

Rule 12. Pleadings and Motions Before Trial; Defenses and Objections

(a) Pleadings and Motions. Pleadings in criminal proceedings shall be the indictment and the information, and the pleas of not guilty, guilty and nolo contendere. All other pleas, and demurrers and motions to quash are abolished, and defenses and objections raised before trial which heretofore could have been raised by one or more of them shall be raised only by motion to dismiss or to grant appropriate relief, as provided in these rules.

(b) Pretrial Motions. Any defense, objection, or request which is capable of determination without the trial of the general issue may be raised before trial by motion. Motions may be written or oral at the discretion of the judge. The following must be raised prior to trial:

> (1) Defenses and objections based on defects in the institution of the prosecution; or

---

* According to the opinion, the population of Dade County (Miami) was 19.8% black and 49.2% Hispanic; of Orange County (Orlando) 10.1% black and 9.6% Hispanic; and of Leon County (Tallahassee) 20.6% black and 2.4% Hispanic, with 0.7% Hispanic registered voters.

(2) Defenses and objections based on defects in the indictment or information (other than that it fails to show jurisdiction in the court or to charge an offense which objections shall be noticed by the court at any time during the pendency of the proceedings); or

(3) Motions to suppress evidence; or

(4) Requests for discovery under Rule 16; or

(5) Requests for a severance of charges or defendants under Rule 14.

(c) Motion Date. Unless otherwise provided by local rule, the court may, at the time of the arraignment or as soon thereafter as practicable, set a time for the making of pretrial motions or requests and, if required, a later date of hearing.

(d) Notice by the Government of the Intention to Use Evidence.

(1) At the Discretion of the Government. At the arraignment or as soon thereafter as is practicable, the government may give notice to the defendant of its intention to use specified evidence at trial in order to afford the defendant an opportunity to raise objections to such evidence prior to trial under subdivision (b)(3) of this rule.

(2) At the Request of the Defendant. At the arraignment or as soon thereafter as is practicable the defendant may, in order to afford an opportunity to move to suppress evidence under subdivision (b)(3) of this rule, request notice of the government's intention to use (in its evidence in chief at trial) any evidence which the defendant may be entitled to discover under Rule 16 subject to any relevant limitations prescribed in Rule 16.

(e) Ruling on Motion. A motion made before trial shall be determined before trial unless the court, for good cause, orders that it be deferred for determination at the trial of the general issue or until after verdict, but no such determination shall be deferred if a party's right to appeal is adversely affected. Where factual issues are involved in determining a motion, the court shall state its essential findings on the record.

(f) Effect of Failure to Raise Defenses or Objections. Failure by a party to raise defenses or objections or to make requests which must be made prior to trial, at the time set by the court pursuant to subdivision (c), or prior to any extension thereof made by the court, shall constitute waiver thereof, but the court for cause shown may grant relief from the waiver.

(g) Records. A verbatim record shall be made of all proceedings at the hearing, including such findings of fact and conclusions of law as are made orally.

(h) Effect of Determination. If the court grants a motion based on a defect in the institution of the prosecution or in the indictment or information, it may also order that the defendant be continued in custody or that bail be continued for a specified time pending the filing of a new indictment or information. Nothing in this rule shall be deemed to affect the provisions of any Act of Congress relating to periods of limitations.

(i) Production of Statements at Suppression Hearing. Except as herein provided, rule 26.2 shall apply at a hearing on a motion to suppress evidence under subdivision (b)(3) of this rule. For purposes of this subdivision, a law enforcement officer shall be deemed a witness called by the government, and upon a claim of privilege the court shall excise the portions of the statement containing privileged matter.

Rule 12.1. Notice of Alibi

(a) Notice by Defendant. Upon written demand of the attorney for the government stating the time, date, and place at which the alleged offense was committed, the defendant shall serve within ten days, or at such different time as the court may direct, upon the attorney for the government a written notice of the defendant's intention to offer a defense of alibi. Such notice by the defendant shall state the specific place or places at which the defendant claims to have been at the time of the alleged offense and the names and addresses of the witnesses upon whom the defendant intends to rely to establish such alibi.

(b) Disclosure of Information and Witness. Within ten days thereafter, but in no event less than ten days before trial, unless the court otherwise directs, the attorney for the government shall serve upon the defendant or his attorney a written notice stating the names and addresses of the witnesses upon whom the government intends to rely to establish the defendant's presence at the scene of the alleged offense and any other witnesses to be relied on to rebut testimony of any of the defendant's alibi witnesses.

(c) Continuing Duty to Disclose. If prior to or during trial, a party learns of an additional witness whose identity, if known, should have been included in the information furnished under subdivision (a) or (b), the party shall promptly notify the other party or the other party's attorney of the existence and identity of such additional witness.

(d) Failure to Comply. Upon the failure of either party to comply with the requirements of this rule, the court may exclude the testimony of any undisclosed witness offered by such party as to the defendant's absence from or presence at, the scene of the alleged offense. This rule shall not limit the right of the defendant to testify in his own behalf.

(e) Exceptions. For good cause shown, the court may grant an exception to any of the requirements of subdivisions (a) through (d) of this rule.

(f) Inadmissibility of Withdrawn Alibi. Evidence of an intention to rely upon an alibi defense, later withdrawn, or of statements made in connection with such intention, is not, in any civil or criminal proceeding, admissible against the person who gave notice of the intention.

Rule 12.2. Notice of Insanity Defense or Expert Testimony of Defendant's Mental Condition

(a) Defense of Insanity. If a defendant intends to rely upon the defense of insanity at the time of the alleged offense, the defendant shall, within the time provided for the filing of pretrial motions or at such later time as the court may direct, notify the attorney for the government in writing of such intention and file a copy of such notice with the clerk. If there is a failure to comply with the requirements of this subdivision, insanity may not be raised as a defense. The court may for cause shown allow late filing of the notice or grant additional time to the parties to prepare for trial or make such other order as may be appropriate.

(b) Expert Testimony of Defendant's Mental Condition. If a defendant intends to introduce expert testimony relating to a mental disease or defect or any other mental condition of the defendant bearing upon the issue of his guilt, the defendant shall, within the time provided for the filing of pretrial motions or at such later time as the court may direct, notify the attorney for the government in writing of such intention and file a copy of such notice with the clerk. The court may for cause shown allow late filing of the notice or grant additional time to the parties to prepare for trial or make such other order as may be appropriate.

(c) Mental Examination of Defendant. In an appropriate case the court may, upon motion of the attorney for the government, order the defendant to submit to an examination pursuant to 18 U.S.C. 4242. No statement made by the defendant in the course of any examination provided for by this rule, whether the examination be with or without the consent of the defendant, no testimony by the expert based upon such statement, and no other fruits of the statement shall be admitted in evidence against the defendant in any criminal proceeding except on an issue respecting mental condition on which the defendant has introduced testimony.

(d) Failure To Comply. If there is a failure to give notice when required by subdivision (b) of this rule or to submit to an examination when ordered under subdivision (c) of this rule, the court may exclude the testimony of any expert witness offered by the defendant on the issue of the defendant's guilt.

(e) Inadmissibility of Withdrawn Intention. Evidence of an intention as to which notice was given under subdivision (a) or (b), later withdrawn, is not, in any civil or criminal proceeding, admissible against the person who gave notice of the intention.

Rule 13. Trial Together of Indictments or Informations

The court may order two or more indictments or informations or both to be tried together if the offenses, and the defendants if there is more than one, could have been joined in a single indictment or information. The procedure shall be the same as if the prosecution were under such single indictment or information.

Rule 14.   Relief from Prejudicial Joinder

If it appears that a defendant or the government is prejudiced by a joinder of offenses or of defendants in an indictment or information or by such joinder for trial together, the court may order an election or separate trials of counts, grant a severance of defendants or provide whatever other relief justice requires. In ruling on a motion by a defendant for severance the court may order the attorney for the government to deliver to the court for inspection *in camera* any statements or confessions made by the defendants which the government intends to introduce in evidence at the trial.

Rule 15.   Depositions

(a) When Taken. Whenever due to exceptional circumstances of the case it is in the interest of justice that the testimony of a prospective witness of a party be taken and preserved for use at trial, the court may upon motion of such party and notice to the parties order that testimony of such witness be taken by deposition and that any designated book, paper, document, record, recording, or other material not privileged, be produced at the same time and place. If a witness is detained pursuant to section 3144 of title 18, United States Code, the court on written motion of the witness and upon notice to the parties may direct that the witness' deposition be taken. After the deposition has been subscribed the court may discharge the witness.

(b) Notice of Taking. The party at whose instance a deposition is to be taken shall give to every party reasonable written notice of the time and place for taking the deposition. The notice shall state the name and address of each person to be examined. On motion of a party upon whom the notice is served, the court for cause shown may extend or shorten the time or change the place for taking the deposition. The officer having custody of a defendant shall be notified of the time and place set for the examination and shall, unless the defendant waives in writing the right to be present, produce the defendant at the examination and keep the defendant in the presence of the witness during the examination, unless, after being warned by the court that disruptive conduct will cause the defendant's removal from the place of the taking of the deposition, the defendant persists in conduct which is such as to justify exclusion from that place. A defendant not in custody shall have the right to be present at the examination upon request subject to such terms as may be fixed by the court, but a failure, absent good cause shown, to appear after notice and tender of expenses in accordance with subdivision (c) of this rule shall constitute a waiver of that right and of any objection to the taking and use of the deposition based upon that right.

(c) Payment of Expenses. Whenever a deposition is taken at the instance of the government, or whenever a deposition is taken at the instance of a defendant who is unable to bear the expenses of the taking of the deposition, the court may direct that the expense of travel and subsistence of the defendant and the defendant's attorney for attendance at the examination and the cost of the transcript of the deposition shall be paid by the government.

(d) How Taken. Subject to such additional conditions as the court shall provide, a deposition shall be taken and filed in the manner provided in civil actions except as otherwise provided in these rules, provided that (1) in no event shall a deposition be taken of a party defendant without that defendant's consent, and (2) the scope and manner of examination and cross-examination shall be such as would be allowed in the trial itself. The government shall make available to the defendant or the defendant's counsel for examination and use at the taking of the deposition any statement of the witness being deposed which is in the possession of the government and to which the defendant would be entitled at the trial.

(e) Usc. At the trial or upon any hearing, a part or all of a deposition, so far as otherwise admissible under the rules of evidence, may be used as substantive evidence if the witness is unavailable, as unavailability is defined in Rule 804(a) of the Federal Rules of Evidence, or the witness gives testimony at the trial or hearing inconsistent with that witness' deposition. Any deposition may also be used by any party for the purpose of contradicting or impeaching the testimony of the deponent as a witness. If only a part of a deposition is offered in evidence by a party, an adverse party may require the offering of all of it which is relevant to the part offered and any party may offer other parts.

(f) Objections to Deposition Testimony. Objections to deposition testimony or evidence or parts thereof and the grounds for the objection shall be stated at the time of the taking of the deposition.

(g) Deposition by Agreement Not Precluded. Nothing in this rule shall preclude the taking of a deposition, orally or upon written questions, or the use of a deposition, by agreement of the parties with the consent of the court.

Rule 16. Discovery and Inspection

(a) Disclosure of Evidence by the Government.

(1) Information Subject to Disclosure.

(A) Statement of Defendant. Upon request of a defendant the government shall permit the defendant to inspect and copy or photograph: any relevant written or recorded statements made by the defendant, or copies thereof, within the possession, custody or control of the government, the existence of which is known, or by the exercise of due diligence may become known, to the attorney for the government; the substance of any oral statement which the government intends to offer in evidence at the trial made by the defendant whether before or after arrest in response to interrogation by any person then known to the defendant to be a government agent; and recorded testimony of the defendant before a grand jury which relates to the offense charged. Where the defendant is a corporation, partnership, association or labor union, the court may grant the defendant, upon its motion, discovery of relevant recorded testimony of any witness before a grand jury who (1) was, at the time of that testimony, so situated as an officer or employee as to have been able legally to bind the defendant in respect to conduct constituting the offense, or (2) was, at the time of the offense, personally involved in the alleged conduct constituting the offense and so situated as an officer or employee as to have been able legally to bind the defendant in respect to that alleged conduct in which the witness was involved.

(B) Defendant's Prior Record. Upon request of the defendant, the government shall furnish to the defendant such copy of the defendant's prior criminal record, if any, as is within the possession, custody, or control of the government, the existence of which is known, or by the exercise of due diligence may become known, to the attorney for the government.

(C) Documents and Tangible Objects. Upon request of the defendant the government shall permit the defendant to inspect and copy or photograph books, papers, documents, photographs, tangible objects, buildings or places, or copies or portions thereof, which are within the possession, custody or control of the government, and which are material to the preparation of the defendant's defense or are intended for use by the government as evidence in chief at the trial, or were obtained from or belong to the defendant.

(D) Reports of Examinations and Tests. Upon request of a defendant the government shall permit the defendant to inspect and copy or photograph any results or reports of physical or mental examinations, and of scientific tests or experiments, or copies thereof, which are within the possession, custody, or control of the government, the existence of which is known, or by the exercise of due diligence may become known, to the attorney for the government, and which are material to the preparation of the defense or are intended for use by the government as evidence in chief at the trial.

(2) Information Not Subject to Disclosure. Except as provided in paragraphs (A), (B), and (D) of subdivision (a)(1), this rule does not authorize the discovery or inspection of reports, memoranda, or other internal government documents made by the attorney for the government or other government agents in connection with the investigation or prosecution of the case, or of statements made by government witnesses or prospective government witnesses except as provided in 18 U.S.C. § 3500 [the "Jencks Act"].

(3) Grand Jury Transcripts. Except as provided in Rules 6, 12(i) and 26.2, and subdivision (a)(1)(A) of this rule, these rules do not relate to discovery or inspection of recorded proceedings of a grand jury.

(b) Disclosure of Evidence by the Defendant.

(1) Information Subject to Disclosure.

(A) Documents and Tangible Objects. If the defendant requests disclosure under subdivision (a)(1)(C) or (D) of this rule, upon compliance with such request by the government, the defendant, on request of the government, shall permit the government to inspect and copy or photograph books, papers, documents, photographs, tangible objects, or copies or portions thereof, which are within the possession, custody, or control of the defendant and which the defendant intends to introduce as evidence in chief at the trial.

(B) Reports of Examinations and Tests. If the defendant requests disclosure under subdivision (a)(1)(C) or (D) of this rule, upon compliance with such request by the government, the defendant, on request of the government, shall permit the government to inspect and copy or photograph any results or reports of physical or mental examinations and of scientific tests or experiments made in connection with the particular case, or copies thereof, within the possession or control of the defendant, which the defendant intends to introduce as evidence in chief at the trial or which were prepared by a witness whom the defendant intends to call at the trial when the results or reports relate to that witness' testimony.

(2) Information Not Subject to Disclosure. Except as to scientific or medical reports, this subdivision does not authorize the discovery or inspection of reports, memoranda, or other internal defense documents made by the defendant, or the defendant's attorneys or agents in connection with the investigation or defense of the case, or of statements made by the defendant, or by government or defense witnesses, or by prospective government or defense witnesses, to the defendant, the defendant's agents or attorneys.

(c) Continuing Duty to Disclose. If, prior to or during trial, a party discovers additional evidence or material previously requested or ordered, which is subject to discovery or inspection under this rule, such party shall promptly notify the other party or the other party's attorney or the court of the existence of the additional evidence or material.

(d) Regulation of Discovery.

(1) Protective and Modifying Orders. Upon a sufficient showing the court may at any time order that the discovery or inspection be denied, restricted, or deferred, or make such other order as is appropriate. Upon motion by a party, the court may permit the party to make such showing, in whole or in part, in the form of a written statement to be inspected by the judge alone. If the court enters an order granting relief following such an ex parte showing, the entire text of the party's statement shall be sealed and preserved in the records of the court to be made available to the appellate court in the event of an appeal.

(2) Failure To Comply With a Request. If at any time during the course of the proceedings it is brought to the attention of the court that a party has failed to comply with this rule, the court may order such party to permit the discovery or inspection, grant a continuance, or prohibit the party from introducing evidence not disclosed, or it may enter such other order as it deems just under the circumstances. The court may specify the time, place and manner of making the discovery and inspection and may prescribe such terms and conditions as are just.

(e) Alibi Witnesses. Discovery of alibi witnesses is governed by Rule 12.1.

Rule 26.2.   Production of Statements of Witnesses

(a) Motion for Production. After a witness other than the defendant has testified on direct examination, the court, on motion of a party who did not call the witness, shall order the attorney for the government or the defendant and the defendant's attorney, as the case may be, to produce, for the examination and use of the moving party, any statement of the witness that is in their possession and that relates to the subject matter concerning which the witness has testified.

(b) Production of Entire Statement. If the entire contents of the statement relate to the subject matter concerning which the witness has testified, the court shall order that the statement be delivered to the moving party.

(c) Production of Excised Statement. If the other party claims that the statement contains matter that does not relate to the subject matter concerning which the witness has testified, the court shall order that it be delivered to the court in camera. Upon inspection, the court shall excise the portions of the statement that do not relate to the subject matter concerning which the witness has testified, and shall order that the statement, with such material excised, be delivered to the moving party. Any portion of the statement that is withheld from the defendant over the defendant's objection shall be preserved by the attorney for the government, and, in the event of a conviction and an appeal by the defendant, shall be made available to the appellate court for the purpose of determining the correctness of the decision to excise the portion of the statement.

(d) Recess for Examination of Statement. Upon delivery of the statement to the moving party, the court, upon application of that party, may recess proceedings in the trial for the examination of such statement and for preparation for its use in the trial.

(e) Sanction for Failure to Produce Statement. If the other party elects not to comply with an order to deliver a statement to the moving party, the court shall order that the testimony of the witness be stricken from the record and that the trial proceed, or, if it is the attorney for the government who elects not to comply, shall declare a mistrial if required by the interest of justice.

(f) Definition. As used in this rule, a "statement" of a witness means:

    (1) a written statement made by the witness that is signed or otherwise adopted or approved by the witness;

    (2) a substantially verbatim recital of an oral statement made by the witness that is recorded contemporaneously with the making of the oral statement and that is contained in a stenographic, mechanical, electrical, or other recording or a transcription thereof; or

    (3) a statement, however taken or recorded, or a transcription thereof, made by the witness to a grand jury.

Chapter 17

JURY SELECTION AND TRIAL

A. THE RIGHT TO TRIAL BY JURY

DUNCAN v. LOUISIANA

Supreme Court of the United States, 1968.
391 U.S. 145, 88 S.Ct. 1444, 20 L.Ed.2d 491.

MR. JUSTICE WHITE delivered the opinion of the Court.

Appellant, Gary Duncan, was convicted of simple battery in the Twenty-fifth Judicial District Court of Louisiana. Under Louisiana law simple battery is a misdemeanor, punishable by a maximum of two years' imprisonment and a $300 fine. Appellant sought trial by jury, but because the Louisiana Constitution grants jury trials only in cases in which capital punishment or imprisonment at hard labor may be imposed,[1] the trial judge denied the request. Appellant was convicted and sentenced to serve 60 days in the parish prison and pay a fine of $150. * * *

[The state courts declined to hold that the denial of jury trial violated appellant's rights, and he appealed to the United States Supreme Court.]

Appellant was 19 years of age when tried. While driving on Highway 23 in Plaquemines Parish on October 18, 1966, he saw two younger cousins engaged in a conversation by the side of the road with four white boys. Knowing his cousins, Negroes who had recently transferred to a formerly all-white high school, had reported the occurrence of racial incidents at the school, Duncan stopped the car, got out, and approached

---

1. La.Const., Art. VII, § 41:

   "All cases in which the punishment may not be at hard labor shall * * * be tried by the judge without a jury. Cases, in which the punishment may be at hard labor, shall be tried by a jury of five, all of whom must concur to render a verdict; cases, in which the punishment is necessarily at hard labor, by a jury of twelve, nine of whom must concur to render a verdict; cases in which the punishment is necessarily at hard labor, by a jury of twelve, nine of whom must concur to render a verdict; cases in which the punishment may be capital, by a jury of twelve, all of whom must concur to render a verdict."

the six boys. At trial the white boys and a white onlooker testified, as did appellant and his cousins. The testimony was in dispute on many points, but the witnesses agreed that appellant and the white boys spoke to each other, that appellant encouraged his cousins to break off the encounter and enter his car, and that appellant was about to enter the car himself for the purpose of driving away with his cousins. The whites testified that just before getting in the car appellant slapped Herman Landry, one of the white boys, on the elbow. The Negroes testified that appellant had not slapped Landry, but had merely touched him. The trial judge concluded that the State had proved beyond a reasonable doubt that Duncan had committed simple battery, and found him guilty.

* * *

The guarantees of jury trial in the Federal and State Constitutions reflect a profound judgment about the way in which law should be enforced and justice administered. A right to jury trial is granted to criminal defendants in order to prevent oppression by the Government. Those who wrote our constitutions knew from history and experience that it was necessary to protect against unfounded criminal charges brought to eliminate enemies and against judges too responsive to the voice of higher authority. The framers of the constitutions strove to create an independent judiciary but insisted upon further protection against arbitrary action. Providing an accused with the right to be tried by a jury of his peers gave him an inestimable safeguard against the corrupt or overzealous prosecutor and against the compliant, biased, or eccentric judge. If the defendant preferred the common-sense judgment of a jury to the more tutored but perhaps less sympathetic reaction of the single judge, he was to have it. Beyond this, the jury trial provisions in the Federal and State Constitutions reflect a fundamental decision about the exercise of official power—a reluctance to entrust plenary powers over the life and liberty of the citizen to one judge or to a group of judges. Fear of unchecked power, so typical of our State and Federal Governments in other respects, found expression in the criminal law in this insistence upon community participation in the determination of guilt or innocence. The deep commitment of the Nation to the right of jury trial in serious criminal cases as a defense against arbitrary law enforcement qualifies for protection under the Due Process Clause of the Fourteenth Amendment, and must therefore be respected by the States.
* * *

Louisiana's final contention is that even if it must grant jury trials in serious criminal cases, the conviction before us is valid and constitutional because here the petitioner was tried for simple battery and was sentenced to only 60 days in the parish prison. We are not persuaded. It is doubtless true that there is a category of petty crimes or offenses which is not subject to the Sixth Amendment jury trial provision and should not be subject to the Fourteenth Amendment jury trial requirement here applied to the States. Crimes carrying possible penalties up to six months do not require a jury trial if they otherwise qualify as petty offenses, Cheff v. Schnackenberg, 384 U.S. 373 (1966). But the penalty authorized for a particular crime is of major relevance in determining whether it is serious or not and may in itself, if severe enough, subject the trial to the mandates of the Sixth Amendment. District of Columbia v. Clawans, 300 U.S. 617 (1937). The penalty authorized by the law of the locality may be taken as a gauge of its social and ethical judgments of the crime in question. In *Clawans* the defendant was jailed for 60 days, but it was the 90–day authorized punishment on which the Court focused in determining that the offense was not one for which the Constitution assured trial by jury. In the case before us the Legislature of Louisiana has made simple battery a criminal offense punishable by imprisonment for up to two years and a fine. The question, then, is whether a crime carrying such a penalty is an offense which Louisiana may insist on trying without a jury.

We think not. So-called petty offenses were tried without juries both in England and in the Colonies and have always been held to be exempt from the otherwise comprehensive language of the Sixth Amendment's jury trial provisions. There is no substantial evidence that the Framers intended to depart from this established common-law practice, and the possible consequences to defendants from convictions for petty offenses have been thought insufficient to outweigh the benefits to efficient law enforcement and simplified judicial administration resulting from the availability of speedy and inexpensive nonjury adjudications. These same considerations compel the same result under the Fourteenth Amendment. Of course the boundaries of the petty offense category have always been ill-defined, if not ambulatory. In the absence of an explicit constitutional provision, the definitional task necessarily falls on the courts, which must either pass upon the validity of legislative attempts to identify those petty offenses which are exempt from jury trial or, where the legislature has not addressed itself to the problem, themselves face the question in the first instance. In either case it is necessary to draw a line in the spectrum of crime, separating petty from serious infractions. This process, although essential, cannot be wholly satisfactory, for it requires attaching different consequences to events which, when they lie near the line, actually differ very little.

In determining whether the length of the authorized prison term or the seriousness of other punishment is enough in itself to require a jury trial, we are counseled by District of Columbia v. Clawans, supra, to refer to objective criteria, chiefly the existing laws and practices in the Nation. In the federal system, petty offenses are defined as those punishable by no more than six months in prison and a $500 fine. In 49 of the 50 States crimes subject to trial without a jury, which occasionally include simple battery, are punishable by no more than one year in jail. Moreover, in the late 18th century in America crimes triable without a jury were for the most part punishable by no more than a six-month prison term, although there appear to have been exceptions to this rule. We need not, however, settle in this case the exact location of the line between petty offenses and serious crimes. It is sufficient for our purposes to hold that a crime punishable by two years in prison is, based on past and contemporary standards in this country, a serious crime and not a petty offense. Consequently, appellant was entitled to a jury trial and it was error to deny it.

The judgment below is reversed and the case is remanded for proceedings not inconsistent with this opinion.

MR. JUSTICE HARLAN, whom MR. JUSTICE STEWART joins, dissenting.

Every American jurisdiction provides for trial by jury in criminal cases. The question before us is not whether jury trial is an ancient institution, which it is; nor whether it plays a significant role in the administration of criminal justice, which it does; nor whether it will endure, which it shall. The question in this case is whether the State of Louisiana, which provides trial by jury for all felonies, is prohibited by the Constitution from trying charges of simple battery to the court alone. In my view, the answer to that question, mandated alike by our constitutional history and by the longer history of trial by jury, is clearly "no." * * *

The jury is of course not without virtues. It affords ordinary citizens a valuable opportunity to participate in a process of government, an experience fostering, one hopes, a respect for law. It eases the burden on judges by enabling them to share a part of their sometimes awesome responsibility. A jury may, at times, afford a higher justice by refusing to enforce harsh laws (although it necessarily does so haphazardly, raising the questions whether arbitrary enforcement of harsh laws is better than total enforcement, and whether the jury system is to be defended on the ground that jurors sometimes disobey their oaths). And the jury may, or may not, contribute desirably to the willingness of the general public to accept criminal judgments as just.

It can hardly be gainsaid, however, that the principal original virtue of the jury trial—the limitations a jury imposes on a tyrannous judiciary—has largely disappeared. We no longer live in a medieval or colonial society. Judges enforce laws enacted by democratic decision, not by regal fiat. They are elected by the people or appointed by the people's elected officials, and are responsible not to a distant monarch alone but to reviewing courts, including this one.

The jury system can also be said to have some inherent defects, which are multiplied by the emergence of the criminal law from the relative simplicity that existed when the jury system was devised. It is a cumbersome process, not only imposing great cost in time and money on both the State and the jurors themselves, but also contributing to delay in the machinery of justice. Untrained jurors are presumably less adept at reaching accurate conclusions of fact than judges, particularly if the issues are many or complex. And it is argued by some that trial by jury, far from increasing public respect for law, impairs it: the average man, it is said, reacts favorably neither to the notion that matters he knows to be complex are being decided by other average men, nor to the way the jury system distorts the process of adjudication. * * *

Indeed, even if I were persuaded that trial by jury is a fundamental right in some criminal cases, I could see nothing fundamental in the rule, not yet formulated by the Court, that places the prosecution of appellant for simple battery within the category of "jury crimes" rather than "petty crimes." Trial by jury is ancient, it is true. Almost equally ancient, however, is the discovery that, because of it,

> the King's most loving Subjects are much travailed and otherwise encumbered in coming and keeping of the said six Weeks Sessions, to their Costs, Charges, Unquietness.

As a result, through the long course of British and American history, summary procedures have been used in a varying category of lesser crimes as a flexible response to the burden jury trial would otherwise impose. * * *

There is no obvious reason why a jury trial is a requisite of fundamental fairness when the charge is robbery, and not a requisite of fairness when the same defendant, for the same actions, is charged with assault and petty theft. The reason for the historic exception for relatively minor crimes is the obvious one: the burden of jury trial was thought to outweigh its marginal advantages. Exactly why the States should not be allowed to make continuing adjustments, based on the state of their criminal dockets and the difficulty of summoning jurors, simply escapes me. * * *

This Court, other courts, and the political process are available to correct any experiments in criminal procedure that prove fundamentally unfair to defendants. That is not what is being done today: instead, and quite without reason, the Court has chosen to impose upon every State one means of trying criminal cases; it is a good means, but it is not the only fair means, and it is not demonstrably better than the alternatives States might devise.

I would affirm the judgment of the Supreme Court of Louisiana.

Commentary

Duncan was a peculiar case to serve as a vehicle for imposing the Sixth Amendment right to jury trial on the states. Even if the defendant did "slap" one of the white boys on the elbow, only the explosive racial context can explain why this trivial incident led to a conviction for battery and a 60–day jail sentence. There ought to be some way to cure such an obvious injustice, of course, but there are some obvious defects in the idea that a right to jury trial is the best way to protect defendants from local prejudice. Even where reasonably nondiscriminatory standards of jury selection are enforced, the jury can be a conduit for community prejudice against an unpopular individual.

Following the decision in *Duncan*, the Supreme Court had to decide whether the states are obligated to follow all the common law rules pertaining to jury trials which had previously been incorporated into federal law. The common law criminal jury must be of exactly 12 persons, and it must agree unanimously to return a verdict of guilty or not guilty. If unanimous agreement cannot be reached, there is a "hung jury," and the case will ordinarily be set for a new trial. After two or more hung juries the court will usually dismiss the prosecution, especially if a substantial number of jurors voted for acquittal.

In Baldwin v. New York, 399 U.S. 66 (1970), the Supreme Court made explicit what was suggested in *Duncan*: a state must provide a right to trial by jury for any offense where imprisonment for more than six months is authorized. Note that the Sixth Amendment provides that the accused has a right to trial "by an impartial jury" and with "the Assistance of Counsel" in all "*criminal prosecutions*." Apparently, a petty offense punishable by imprisonment for six months or less is not a "criminal prosecution," for purposes of the jury trial right. Interpreting the same constitutional language, the Supreme Court has held that the defendant's right to counsel extends to any case in which the defendant is sentenced to jail for any time whatsoever. Argersinger v. Hamlin, 407 U.S. 25 (1972). The dividing line for *this* right depends upon the jail time actually imposed rather than the penalty provided in the statute. In other words, the defendant has a right to jury trial for an offense punishable by more than six months in jail regardless of whether any jail time is actually imposed, but the same defendant has no constitutional right to the assistance of counsel for an offense punishable by a year in jail if the judge actually imposes only a fine. By refusing to appoint counsel, the judge in effect converts the offense to one punishable only by fine.

In Lewis v. United States, 518 U.S. 322 (1996), the defendant was charged with two counts of obstructing the mail. Each count carried a maximum authorized prison sentence of six months, so his entitlement to a jury trial depended upon whether the possible penalties were to be aggregated or considered separately. The magistrate judge ordered a bench trial, announcing that she would not impose a sentence of more than six months imprisonment. The Supreme Court affirmed the resulting convictions, holding that a defendant has no more right to jury trial when charged with two petty offenses than when charged with one. Because the Court held that the defendant was not entitled to a jury trial in any case, it did not reach the question whether a judge's self-imposed limitation on sentencing might affect the right to jury trial.

A provision of the Louisiana Constitution (see the footnote on page 779 *supra*) provides that certain criminal cases shall be tried by a jury of 5, with a unanimous verdict, and others by a jury of 12, only 9 of whom must concur to render a verdict. Oregon also has a state constitutional provision permitting a jury to return a verdict if 10 of the 12 jurors concur. The other states require unanimous verdicts, but a number provide for six-person juries in certain types of cases. These variations created no constitutional issue as long as the Sixth Amendment right to trial by jury applied only to the federal government, but after *Duncan* their constitutionality became a close question.

In Apodaca v. Oregon, 406 U.S. 404 (1972) the Supreme Court held by a narrow vote that the Constitution requires unanimous jury verdicts in federal criminal cases but not in state cases. This decision came about because of a curious combination of votes. Eight of the nine Justices agreed that the standard for state and federal cases should be the same. Four of these eight Justices thought that the Sixth Amendment does not require unanimity in either case (although federal *statutory* law requires unanimous verdicts for federal cases), and the remaining four thought that the Sixth Amendment requires unanimous verdicts in *both* state and federal cases. Only Justice Powell thought that the constitutional requirement should be different for the federal government and for the states. His opinion argued that the Fourteenth Amendment, while requiring the states to provide jury trials for serious crimes, does not incorporate all the elements of a jury trial within the meaning of the Sixth Amendment, such as jury unanimity. There were thus five votes for imposing the unanimity requirement as a constitutional standard on the federal government, and five votes for not imposing such a requirement on the states, and so a position rejected by eight of the nine Justices became the majority position. Many persons who commented upon the *Apodaca* decision were under the impression that it heralded a major change in American jury procedure. In fact, however, it changed nothing; Oregon and Louisiana had allowed less-than unanimous jury verdicts for many years, and the other states did not choose to follow their example. England has permitted non-unanimous verdicts since 1967.

In other decisions the Supreme Court held that a jury in state cases may contain less than twelve persons but not less than six, and that a jury of six may not return a non-unanimous verdict. Ballew v. Georgia, 435 U.S. 223 (1978); Burch v. Louisiana, 441 U.S. 130 (1979).

The following excerpt, by a noted authority on comparative law, contrasts the Anglo–American jury trial with the continental mixed tribunal in which both professional and lay adjudicators deliberate together.

MIRJAN DAMASKA, EVIDENTIARY BARRIERS TO CONVICTION AND TWO MODELS OF CRIMINAL PROCEDURE

121 U.Pa.L.Rev. 506, 536–46 (1973).*

1. DIFFERENT RULES GOVERNING VOTING

The common law verdict of guilty was traditionally required to be unanimous. Of late this rule seems to be in eclipse, but is, despite some quite recent ominous signs, still retained in the majority of American jurisdictions. Continental systems never viewed the unanimity rule with favor. Even the French revolutionaries, who in 1791 were so enchanted by English institutions that they attempted a wholesale transplantation of English criminal procedure, never went so far as to require unanimous guilty verdicts from their juries. Continental adjudicators decide by a majority vote, often a bare majority. Rare indeed are voices claiming that the continental analogue of the requirement of proof of guilt beyond a reasonable doubt presupposes a voting *regime* whereby the prosecutor must overcome "reasonable doubts" of all adjudicators.

The implications of these different approaches to decisionmaking are obvious. The prosecutor will surely find it more difficult to obtain a conviction under the *regime* of unanimity than that of majority. For if only one juror refuses to convict, say, because of sympathy for the defendant, or because of very stringent views on sufficiency of the evidence presented, there will be no conviction. Consequently, where in the Anglo–American orbit the unanimity rule still prevails, the prosecutor can expect a less favorable "conviction-acquittal ratio."

2.   PROFESSIONAL AND LAY PROPENSITIES TO CONVICT

Since the common law unanimity rule seems to be diminishing in significance, another contrast between the two systems assumes greater importance. In a jury trial the determination of guilt is made solely by lay people, whereas in the continental mixed tribunal professional judges play an active role. If lay people tend to be on average more lenient in criminal adjudication than professional adjudicators, the jury will be more reluctant to convict than the mixed tribunal, and the prosecutor trying to persuade the jury of the defendant's guilt will have a somewhat harder task before him.

That lay adjudicators are, on the whole, more lenient, seems to be an impression so widely shared that it has almost become a truism. There is empirical evidence in support of these impressions, although perhaps not enough to remove the issue entirely from the realm of speculation. Disagreements between lay and professional judges have been studied, both in America and in Europe, and the results seem to indicate that in these disagreements lay judges seem on the average to favor the defendant. Moreover—and this is of particular importance to our subsequent discussion—there is some indication in these empirical studies that those disagreements may not be entirely accounted for by such reasons as sympathy for the defendant's plight, but also, to an extent, by "higher thresholds of reasonable doubt" on the part of laymen. Lay people seem often to require *more evidence* to convict than professional adjudicators, particularly in those cases where the decision turns on mere circumstantial evidence.

Why should lay adjudicators tend on average to be more lenient? I believe that we are presented here with only an instance of a larger phenomenon observable in other areas. Max Weber has analyzed it in talking about bureaucratization; sometimes it is discussed in connection with professionalization, but it is also an aspect of any routinization of activity. In all these processes what is acquired is an ever increasing measure of self-confidence, coupled with rational detachment and matter-of-factness. So, just as in other human activities, prolonged exposure to criminal litigation will result in a degree of case-hardening. Experienced professional judges will tell us about the agony they went through before convicting their first defendant on circumstantial evidence; *cognoscenti* might perhaps tell us that even jurors find it easier to convict toward the end of their term. The longer one is involved in the business of adjudicating criminal cases, the more these cases become depersonalized, more representatives of general classes. Gradually the morning freshness of perceiving each case as a unique human drama is gone, and one becomes adjusted to the efficient performance of a routine task. This, perhaps, is the unfortunate *"default de qualite"* of any professionalization.

Assume that there is truth in these widely shared observations. It can then be demonstrated that the civil law system exhibits counterpressures to neutralize, when necessary, the differential lay predispositions in the adjudication of guilt.

Whatever influence the common law judge has on the jury is limited mostly to instructions. The jury sits alone and decides independently. What evidentiary evaluation leads to a verdict remains unknown because the jurors are not required to justify factual findings. In addition, the absence of appeals from acquittals in the overwhelming majority of common law jurisdictions removes another means of professional supervision of the jury. By contrast, the lay element on the continental panel is much more effectively controlled by professionals. The professional judge or judges retire with the lay judges, participate in the deliberation process and preside over the debate. True, the lay assessors on the bench are more often than not in the majority. Further, in most jurisdictions lay judges do play an active role and are not members of the panel for mere cosmetic purposes. Yet, few would deny that the professional judge is a towering and influential figure in the eyes of his lay colleagues. There is typically also an appeal from factual findings, and the court must state in the judgment why it gave credence to one item of evidence rather than another. The prosecutor thus knows that even if he fails to obtain a conviction on strong evidence from the original adjudicator, he will have another chance with the appellate court.

Further reflection reveals that the two procedural systems face disparate problems in trying to attune lay factfinders to actual evidentiary standards in the practical activity of deciding criminal cases. As the continental judges sit together, there is no need for the professionals to instruct their lay colleagues about the quantum of proof in advance of actual deliberations. Nor is advance information needed on how to handle possible factual doubts. If such doubts arise, the professional judge will advise the lay judges in the debate over specific facts, during *in camera* deliberations. It is, then, not surprising that very few continental systems require formal instructions on proof sufficiency for conviction. The situation on the common law side of our comparison is quite different. There is no informal exchange of views and advice between the judge and the jurors at deliberations. Instead—anticipating that some doubts concerning evidence introduced are very likely to arise—the law requires the judge to instruct jurors on the necessary quantum of proof before they retire. The instruction is in the form of a rigid and abstract formula. * * *

3. TRIAL STRUCTURE AND EVIDENTIARY NEEDS

In talking about disparate difficulties faced by prosecutors in persuading the factfinder of the defendant's guilt, a number of additional factors must be considered. They are independent of the lay-professional dichotomy, but are intimately linked to the different structures of the continental and common law type of trial. On several occasions I have mentioned that the continental trial is typically conducted in such a manner that the presiding judge is required to study the file of the case in advance of the trial. The extent to which this practice creates a danger of bias varies from country to country. It is less pronounced in those continental jurisdictions where pre-trial investigations are less thorough, and the investigating officer is not required to voice his opinion on whether the case deserves to be transferred to the court for trial. But whether from a comparative perspective the trial amounts to a verification of the record prepared by the investigator or is genuinely "creative," the impact of the dossier on guilt deliberations of the mixed panel cannot in candor be denied. While it is open to conjecture whether or not lay judges will be less open-minded than jurors as a result of the knowledge that the case has been "objectively" investigated before trial, the fact remains that the professional judge will not approach the case as a *tabula rasa*. He will have an additional edge over lay assessors at deliberations as well: he will know more about the case than his lay colleagues.

Another factor, seldom discussed, is relevant here. It is well known to experimental psychologists that different people have disparate cognitive needs; they often require different information, or ways of presenting it, in order to be persuaded of, or simply to comprehend a point. The continental trial is in a sense more attuned to this psychological phenomenon. All continental decisionmakers, lay and professional, are entitled to address questions to witnesses and take an active part during the presentation of evidence. On the other hand, common law jurors are passive observers of the examination of evidence, although, somewhat paradoxically, it is they who will have to decide the case. Their immediate cognitive needs are often unpredictable to the parties presenting evidence. It is, of course, possible that their general predispositions and needs may be elicited through voir dire or anticipated through the familiarity attorneys sometimes acquire with a small and relatively stable venire. But, on balance, more uncertainties and doubts are likely to arise, *ceteris paribus*, among jurors than among members of the mixed panel.

One can only surmise that the adversary method of presenting evidence is somewhat more conducive to uncertainties and doubts than the more organized and detached continental method. It is a truism that the more points of view we take into consideration, the harder it is for us to make a decision. When we view reality "through eyes other than our own" and are presented each side of the story in the most favorable light, it will become somewhat harder for us to become absolutely certain that only one side to an argument is in the right. Thus, it is possible to argue that the prosecutor will have somewhat more difficulty in sustaining the burden of persuasion under the adversary than under the continental style of presenting evidence.

B. JURY SELECTION

CASTANEDA v. PARTIDA

Supreme Court of the United States, 1977.
430 U.S. 482, 97 S.Ct. 1272, 51 L.Ed.2d 498.

MR. JUSTICE BLACKMUN delivered the opinion of the Court.

The sole issue presented in this case is whether the State of Texas, in the person of petitioner, the Sheriff of Hidalgo County, successfully rebutted respondent prisoner's prima facie showing of discrimination against Mexican–Americans in the state grand jury selection process. In his brief, petitioner, in claiming effective rebuttal, asserts:

> "This list [of the grand jurors that indicted respondent] indicates that 50 percent of the names appearing thereon were Spanish. The record indicates that 3 of the 5 jury commissioners, 5 of the grand jurors who returned the indictment, 7 of the petit jurors, the judge presiding at the trial, and the Sheriff who served notice on the grand jurors to appear had Spanish surnames." Brief for Petitioner 6.

I

* * * Texas employs the "key man" system, which relies on jury commissioners to select prospective grand jurors from the community at large.[2] The procedure begins with the state district judge's appointment of from three to five persons to serve as jury commissioners. The commissioners then "shall select not less than 15 nor more than 20 persons from the citizens of different portions of the county" to compose the list from which the actual grand jury will be drawn. Art. 19.06 (Supp.1976–1977). When at least 12 of the persons on the list appear in court pursuant to summons, the district judge proceeds to "test their qualifications." Art. 19.21. The qualifications themselves are set out in Art. 19.08: A grand juror must be a citizen of Texas and of the county, be a qualified voter in the county, be "of sound mind and good moral character," be literate, have no prior felony conviction, and be under no pending indictment "or other legal accusation for theft or of any felony." Interrogation under oath is the method specified for testing the prospective juror's qualifications. * * * After the court finds 12 jurors who meet the statutory qualifications, they are impaneled as the grand jury. Art. 19.26.

II

Respondent, Rodrigo Partida, was indicted in March 1972 by the grand jury of the 92d District Court of Hidalgo County for the crime of burglary of a private residence at night with intent to rape. Hidalgo is one of the border counties of southern Texas. After a trial before a petit jury, respondent was convicted and sentenced to eight years in the custody of the Texas Department of Corrections. He first raised his claim

---

2. The other principal state mode of juror selection is a random method similar to that used in the federal system. See 28 U.S.C. § 1864.

of discrimination in the grand jury selection process on a motion for new trial in the State District Court. In support of his motion, respondent testified about the general existence of discrimination against Mexican–Americans in that area of Texas and introduced statistics from the 1970 census and the Hidalgo County grand jury records. The census figures show that in 1970, the population of Hidalgo County was 181,535. Persons of Spanish language or Spanish surname totaled 143,611. On the assumption that all the persons of Spanish language or Spanish surname were Mexican–Americans, these figures show that 79.1% of the county's population was Mexican–American.[3]

Respondent's data compiled from the Hidalgo County grand jury records from 1962 to 1972 showed that over that period, the average percentage of Spanish-surnamed grand jurors was 39%. In the 2½-year period during which the District Judge who impaneled the jury that indicted respondent was in charge, the average percentage was 45.5%. On the list from which the grand jury that indicted respondent was selected, 50% were Spanish surnamed. The last set of data that respondent introduced, again from the 1970 census, illustrated a number of ways in which Mexican–Americans tend to be underprivileged, including poverty-level incomes, less desirable jobs, substandard housing, and lower levels of education. The State offered no evidence at all either attacking respondent's allegations of discrimination or demonstrating that his statistics were unreliable in any way. The State District Court, nevertheless, denied the motion for a new trial.

On appeal, the Texas Court of Criminal Appeals affirmed the conviction. *Partida v. State*, 506 S.W.2d 209 (1974). Reaching the merits of the claim of grand jury discrimination, the court held that respondent had failed to make out a prima facie case. In the court's view, he should have shown how many of the females who served on the grand juries were Mexican–Americans married to men with Anglo–American surnames, how many Mexican–Americans were excused for reasons of age or health, or other legal reasons, and how many of those listed by the census would not have met the statutory qualifications of citizenship, literacy, sound mind, moral character, and lack of criminal record or accusation. Quite beyond the uncertainties in the statistics, the court found it impossible to believe that discrimination could have been directed against a Mexican–American, in light of the many elective positions held by Mexican–Americans in the county and the substantial representation of Mexican–Americans on recent grand juries. In essence, the court refused to presume that Mexican–Americans would discriminate against their own kind.

After exhausting his state remedies, respondent filed his petition for habeas corpus in the Federal District Court, alleging a denial of due

---

3. At oral argument, counsel for petitioner appears to have suggested that the presence of illegal aliens who have Spanish surnames might inflate the percentage of Mexican–Americans in the county's population. [The opinion concluded that, excluding a generously calculated estimate of the number of illegal aliens from the totals, Mexican–Americans would still constitute 76.1% of the county's population.]

process and equal protection, guaranteed by the Fourteenth Amendment, because of gross under-representation of Mexican–Americans on the Hidalgo County grand juries. At a hearing at which the state transcript was introduced, petitioner presented the testimony of the state judge who selected the jury commissioners who had compiled the list from which respondent's grand jury was taken. The judge first reviewed the State's grand jury selection process. In selecting the jury commissioners, the judge stated that he tried to appoint a greater number of Mexican–Americans than members of other ethnic groups. He testified that he instructed the commissioners about the qualifications of a grand juror and the exemptions provided by law. The record is silent, however, with regard to instructions dealing with the potential problem of discrimination directed against any identifiable group. The judge admitted that the actual results of the selection process had not produced grand jury lists that were "representative of the ethnic balance in the community." The jury commissioners themselves, who were the only ones in a position to explain the apparent substantial underrepresentation of Mexican–Americans and to provide information on the actual operation of the selection process, were never called.

On the basis of the evidence before it, the court concluded that respondent had made out a *"bare prima facie* case" of invidious discrimination with his proof of "a long continued disproportion in the composition of the grand juries in Hidalgo County." 384 F.Supp. 79, 90 (S.D.Tex. 1974) (emphasis in original). Based on an examination of the reliability of the statistics offered by respondent, however, despite the lack of evidence in the record justifying such an inquiry, the court stated that the prima facie case was weak. The court believed that the census statistics did not reflect the true situation accurately, because of recent changes in the Hidalgo County area and the court's own impression of the demographic characteristics of the Mexican–American community. On the other hand, the court recognized that the Texas key-man system of grand jury selection was highly subjective, and was "archaic and inefficient," and that this was a factor arguing for less tolerance in the percentage differences. On balance, the court's doubts about the reliability of the statistics, coupled with its opinion that Mexican–Americans constituted a "governing majority" in the county, caused it to conclude that the prima facie case was rebutted. The "governing majority" theory distinguished respondent's case from all preceding cases involving similar disparities. On the basis of those findings, the court dismissed the petition.[4]

4. The court suggested that the actual discrimination operating might be economic. The jury commissioners were from the higher socio-economic classes, and they tended to select prospective jurors from among their peers. Consequently, the number of Mexican–Americans was disproportionately low, since they were concentrated at the lower end of the economic scale. We find it unnecessary to decide whether a showing of simple economic discrimination would be enough to make out a prima facie case in the absence of other evidence, since that case is not before us. Cf. *Thiel v. Southern Pacific Co.*, 328 U.S. 217 (1946).

[The Court of Appeals reversed, and the Supreme Court granted certiorari.]

III

* * *

In order to show that an equal protection violation has occurred in the context of grand jury selection, the defendant must show that the procedure employed resulted in substantial underrepresentation of his race or of the identifiable group to which he belongs. The first step is to establish that the group is one that is a recognizable, distinct class, singled out for different treatment under the laws, as written or as applied. Next, the degree of underrepresentation must be proved, by comparing the proportion of the group in the total population to the proportion called to serve as grand jurors, over a significant period of time. This method of proof, sometimes called the "rule of exclusion," has been held to be available as a method of proving discrimination in jury selection against a delineated class. [Citations] Finally, as noted above, a selection procedure that is susceptible of abuse or is not racially neutral supports the presumption of discrimination raised by the statistical showing. *Washington v. Davis*, 426 U.S. 229, 241 (1976); *Alexander v. Louisiana*, 405 U.S., 625, 630 (1972). Once the defendant has shown substantial underrepresentation of his group, he has made out a prima facie case of discriminatory purpose, and the burden then shifts to the State to rebut that case.

B.   In this case, it is no longer open to dispute that Mexican–Americans are a clearly identifiable class. The statistics introduced by respondent from the 1970 census illustrate disadvantages to which the group has been subject. Additionally, as in *Alexander v. Louisiana*, the selection procedure is not racially neutral with respect to Mexican–Americans; Spanish surnames are just as easily identifiable as race was from the questionnaires in *Alexander* or the notations and card colors in *Whitus v. Georgia, infra*, and in *Avery v. Georgia*, 345 U.S. 559 (1953).

The disparity proved by the 1970 census statistics showed that the population of the county was 79.1% Mexican–American, but that, over an 11–year period, only 39% of the persons summoned for grand jury service were Mexican–American. This difference of 40% is greater than that found significant in *Turner v. Fouche*, 396 U.S. 346 (1970) (60% Negroes in the general population, 37% on the grand jury lists). Since the State presented no evidence showing why the 11–year period was not reliable, we take it as the relevant base for comparison. The mathematical disparities that have been accepted by this Court as adequate for a prima facie case have all been within the range presented here. For example, in *Whitus v. Georgia*, 385 U.S. 545 (1967), the number of Negroes listed on the tax digest amounted to 27.1% of the taxpayers, but only 9.1% of those on the grand jury venire. The disparity was held to be sufficient to make out a prima facie case of discrimination.[5] * * *

---

5.   If the jurors were drawn randomly from the general population, then the num-   ber of Mexican–Americans in the sample could be modeled by a binomial distribu-

Supporting this conclusion is the fact that the Texas system of selecting grand jurors is highly subjective. The facial constitutionality of the key-man system, of course, has been accepted by this Court. Nevertheless, the Court has noted that the system is susceptible of abuse as applied. Additionally, as noted, persons with Spanish surnames are readily identifiable.

The showing made by respondent therefore shifted the burden of proof to the State to dispel the inference of intentional discrimination. Inexplicably, the State introduced practically no evidence. The testimony of the State District Judge dealt principally with the selection of the jury commissioners and the instructions given to them. The commissioners themselves were not called to testify. * * * Without some testimony from the grand jury commissioners about the method by which they determined the other qualifications for grand jurors prior to the statutory time for testing qualifications, it is impossible to draw any inference about literacy, sound mind and moral character, and criminal record from the statistics about the population as a whole. These are questions of disputed fact that present problems not amenable to resolution by an appellate court. We emphasize, however, that we are not saying that the statistical disparities proved here could never be explained in another case; we are simply saying that the State did not do so in this case.

C.   In light of our holding that respondent proved a prima facie case of discrimination that was not rebutted by any of the evidence presently in the record, we have only to consider whether the District Court's "governing majority" theory filled the evidentiary gap. In our view, it did not dispel the presumption of purposeful discrimination in the circumstances of this case. Because of the many facets of human motivation, it would be unwise to presume as a matter of law that human beings of one definable group will not discriminate against other members of their group. * * * The problem is a complex one, about which widely differing views can be held, and, as such, it would be somewhat precipitate to take judicial notice of one view over another on the basis of a record as barren as this.[6]

Furthermore, the relevance of a governing majority of elected officials to the grand jury selection process is questionable. The fact that certain elected officials are Mexican–American demonstrates nothing about the motivations and methods of the grand jury commissioners who select persons for grand jury lists. The only arguably relevant fact in this record on the issue is that three of the five jury commissioners in respondent's case were Mexican–American. Knowing only this, we would

tion. [This footnote then explained at length how statistical analysis can be used to determine the likelihood that racial disparities are the product of discrimination (as opposed to chance) in a random selection system like the federal jury selection system.]

6.   This is not a case where a majority is practicing benevolent discrimination in favor of a traditionally disfavored minority, although that situation illustrates that motivations not immediately obvious might enter into discrimination against "one's own kind."

be forced to rely on the reasoning that we have rejected—that human beings would not discriminate against their own kind—in order to find that the presumption of purposeful discrimination was rebutted. Without the benefit of this simple behavioral presumption, discriminatory intent can be rebutted only with evidence in the record about the way in which the commissioners operated and their reasons for doing so. It was the State's burden to supply such evidence, once respondent established his prima facie case. The State's failure in this regard leaves unchallenged respondent's proof of purposeful discrimination.

Finally, even if a "governing majority" theory has general applicability in cases of this kind, the inadequacy of the record in this case does not permit such an approach. Among the evidentiary deficiencies are the lack of any indication of how long the Mexican–Americans have enjoyed "governing majority" status, the absence of information about the relative power inherent in the elective offices held by Mexican–Americans, and the uncertain relevance of the general political power to the specific issue in this case. Even for the most recent time period, when presumably the political power of Mexican–Americans was at its greatest, the discrepancy between the number of Mexican–Americans in the total population and the number on the grand jury lists was substantial. Thus, under the facts presented in this case, the "governing majority" theory is not developed fully enough to satisfy the State's burden of rebuttal.

Rather than relying on an approach to the jury discrimination question that is as faintly defined as the "governing majority" theory is on this record, we prefer to look at all the facts that bear on the issue, such as the statistical disparities, the method of selection, and any other relevant testimony as to the manner in which the selection process was implemented. Under this standard, the proof offered by respondent was sufficient to demonstrate a prima facie case of discrimination in grand jury selection. Since the State failed to rebut the presumption of purposeful discrimination by competent testimony, despite two opportunities to do so, we affirm the Court of Appeals' holding of a denial of equal protection of the law in the grand jury selection process in respondent's case.

It is so ordered.

Mr. Justice Marshall, concurring.

I join fully Mr. Justice Blackmun's sensitive opinion for the Court. I feel compelled to write separately, however, to express my profound disagreement with the views expressed by Mr. Justice Powell in his dissent. * * * Like the District Court, he appears to assume—without any basis in the record—that *all* Mexican–Americans, indeed *all* members of *all* minority groups have an "inclination to assure fairness" to other members of their group. Although he concedes the possibility that minority group members will violate this "inclination," he apparently regards this possibility as more theoretical than real. Thus he would reject the inference of purposeful discrimination here absent any alternative explanation for the disparate results. I emphatically disagree.

In the first place, Mr. Justice Powell's assumptions about human nature, plausible as they may sound, fly in the face of a great deal of social science theory and research. Social scientists agree that members of minority groups frequently respond to discrimination and prejudice by attempting to disassociate themselves from the group, even to the point of adopting the majority's negative attitudes towards the minority. Such behavior occurs with particular frequency among members of minority groups who have achieved some measure of economic or political success and thereby have gained some acceptability among the dominant group.

But even if my Brother Powell's behavioral assumptions were more valid, I still could not agree to making them the foundation for a constitutional ruling. It seems to me that especially in reviewing claims of intentional discrimination, this Court has a solemn responsibility to avoid basing its decisions on broad generalizations concerning minority groups. If history has taught us anything, it is the danger of relying on such stereotypes. The question for decision here is not how Mexican–Americans treat other Mexican–Americans, but how the particular grand jury commissioners in Hidalgo County acted. The only reliable way to answer that question, as we have said so many times, is for the State to produce testimony concerning the manner in which the selection process operated. Because the State failed to do so after respondent established a prima facie case of discrimination, I join the Court's opinion affirming the Court of Appeals.

MR. CHIEF JUSTICE BURGER, with whom MR. JUSTICE POWELL and MR. JUSTICE REHNQUIST join, dissenting.

In addition to the views expressed in Mr. Justice Powell's dissent, I identify one other flaw in the Court's opinion. What the majority characterizes as a prima facie case of discrimination simply will not "wash." The decisions of this Court suggest, and common sense demands, that *eligible* population statistics, not gross population figures, provide the relevant starting point.

The failure to produce evidence relating to the eligible population in Hidalgo County undermines respondent's claim that any statistical "disparity" existed in the first instance. Particularly where, as here, substantial numbers of members of the identifiable class actually served on grand jury panels, the burden rightly rests upon the challenger to show a meaningful statistical disparity. After all, the presumption of constitutionality attaching to all state procedures has even greater force under the circumstances presented here, where exactly one-half the members of the grand jury list now challenged by respondent were members of the allegedly excluded class of Mexican–Americans.

The Court has not previously been called upon to deal at length with the sort of statistics required of persons challenging a grand jury selection system. The reason is that in our prior cases there was little doubt that members of identifiable minority groups had been excluded in large numbers. * * * The case before us, in contrast, involves neither tokenism nor absolute exclusion; rather, the State has used a selection system resulting in the inclusion of large numbers of Spanish-surnamed citizens on grand jury lists. In this situation, it is particularly incumbent on respondent to adduce precise statistics demonstrating a significant disparity. To do that, respondent was obligated to demonstrate that disproportionately large numbers of eligible individuals were excluded systematically from grand jury service.

Respondent offered no evidence whatever in this respect. He therefore could not have established any meaningful case of discrimination, prima facie or otherwise. In contrast to respondent's approach, which the Court's opinion accepts without analysis, the Census Bureau's statistics for 1970 demonstrate that of the *adults* in Hidalgo County, 72%, not 79.1% as respondent implies, are Spanish surnamed. At the outset, therefore, respondent's gross population figures are manifestly overinclusive.

But that is only the beginning. Respondent offered no evidence whatever with respect to other basic qualifications for grand jury service.[7] The statistics relied on in the Court's opinion suggest that 22.9% of Spanish-surnamed persons over age 25 in Hidalgo County have had no schooling at all. Since one requirement of grand jurors in Texas is literacy in the English language, approximately 20% of adult-age Mexican–Americans are very likely disqualified on that ground alone.

The Court's reliance on respondent's overbroad statistics is not the sole defect. As previously noted, one-half of the members of respondent's grand jury list bore Mexican–American surnames. Other grand jury lists at about the same time as respondent's indictment in March 1972 were *predominantly Mexican–American*. Thus, with respect to the September 1971 grand jury list, 70% of the prospective grand jurors were Mexican–American. In the January 1972 Term, 55% were Mexican–American. Since respondent was indicted in 1972, by what appears to have been a truly representative grand jury, the mechanical use of Hidalgo County's practices some 10 years earlier seems to me entirely indefensible. We do not know, and on this record we cannot know, whether respondent's 1970 gross population figures, which served as the basis for establishing the "disparity" complained of in this case, had any applicability at all to the period prior to 1970. Accordingly, for all we know, the 1970 figures may be totally inaccurate as to prior year; if so, the apparent disparity alleged by respondent would be increased improperly.

Therefore, I disagree both with the Court's assumption that respondent established a prima facie case and with the Court's implicit approval of respondent's method for showing an allegedly disproportionate impact of Hidalgo County's selection system upon Mexican–Americans.

7. The burden of establishing a prima facie case obviously rested on respondent. It will not do to produce patently overinclusive figures and thereby seek to shift the burden to the State. Rather, a prima facie case is established only when the challenger shows a disparity between the percentage of minority persons in the eligible population and the percentage of minority individuals on the grand jury.

Mr. Justice Stewart, dissenting.

In my view, the findings of the District Court in this case cannot be said to be "clearly erroneous." Fed.Rule Civ.Proc. 52(a). Given those findings, there was no constitutional violation in the selection of the grand jury that indicted the respondent. Upon that basis I would reverse the judgment of the Court of Appeals. I add only that I am in substantial agreement with the dissenting opinions of The Chief Justice and Mr. Justice Powell.

Mr. Justice Powell, with whom The Chief Justice and Mr. Justice Rehnquist join, dissenting. * * *

In this case, the following critical facts are beyond dispute: the judge who appointed the jury commissioners and later presided over respondent's trial was Mexican–American; three of the five jury commissioners were Mexican–American; 10 of the 20 members of the grand jury array were Mexican–American; 5 of the 12 grand jurors who returned the indictment, including the foreman, were Mexican–American, and 7 of the 12 petit jurors who returned the verdict of guilt were Mexican–American. In the year in which respondent was indicted, 52.5% of the persons on the grand jury list were Mexican–American. In addition, a majority of the elected officials in Hidalgo County were Mexican–American, as were a majority of the judges. That these positions of power and influence were so held is not surprising in a community where 80% of the population is Mexican–American. As was emphasized by District Judge Garza, the able Mexican–American jurist who presided over the habeas proceedings in the District Court, this case *is* unique. Every other jury discrimination case reaching this Court has involved a situation where the governing majority, and the resulting power over the jury selection process, was held by a white electorate and white officials.

The most significant fact in this case, all but ignored in the Court's opinion, is that a majority of the jury commissioners were Mexican–American. The jury commission is the body vested by Texas law with the authority to select grand jurors. Under the Texas selection system, as noted by the Court, the jury commission has the opportunity to identify in advance those potential jurors who have Spanish surnames. In these circumstances, where Mexican–Americans control both the selection of jurors and the political process, rational inferences from the most basic facts in a democratic society render improbable respondent's claim of an intent to discriminate against him and other Mexican–Americans. As Judge Garza observed: "If people in charge can choose whom they want, it is unlikely they will discriminate against themselves." 384 F.Supp. 79, 90.

That individuals are more likely to discriminate in favor of, than against, those who share their own identifiable attributes is the premise that underlies the cases recognizing that the criminal defendant has a personal right under the Fourteenth Amendment not to have members of his own class excluded from jury service. Discriminatory exclusion of members of the defendant's class has been viewed as unfairly excluding persons who may be inclined to favor the defendant. Were it not for the perceived likelihood that jurors will favor defendants of their own class, there would be no reason to suppose that a jury selection process that systematically excluded persons of a certain race would be the basis of any legitimate complaint by criminal defendants of that race. Only the individuals excluded from jury service would have a personal right to complain.

* * * With all respect, I am compelled to say that the Court today *has* "lightly" concluded that the grand jury commissioners of this county have disregarded not only their sworn duty but also their likely inclination to assure fairness to Mexican–Americans.[8]

It matters little in this case whether such judicially noticeable facts as the composition of the grand jury commission are viewed as defeating respondent's prima facie case at the outset or as rebutting it after it was established by statistical evidence. The significance of the prima facie case is limited to its effect in shifting the burden of going forward to the State. Once the State has produced evidence—either by presenting proof or by calling attention to facts subject to judicial notice—the only question is whether the evidence in the record is sufficient to demonstrate deliberate and systematic discrimination in the jury selection process.

Here, respondent produced statistics showing that Mexican–Americans—while substantially represented on the grand jury lists—were not represented in numbers proportionate to their share of the total population. The State responded by presenting the testimony of the judge who appointed the grand jury commissioners. Other facts, such as the presence of Mexican–Americans in a majority of the elective positions of the county, entered the record through judicial notice. The testimony, together with the facts noted by the District Court, sufficed to satisfy the State's burden of production—even assuming that respondent's evidence was sufficient to give rise to such a burden. Accordingly, at the close of the evidence, the question for the District Court was whether respondent had demonstrated by a preponderance of the evidence that the State had "deliberately and systematically den[ied] to members of [respondent's class] the right to participate as jurors in the administration of justice." *Alexander*, 405 U.S., at 628–629. The District Court found that the judge and jury commissioners had not intentionally discriminated against Mexican–Americans. At the very least, that finding was not clearly erroneous.[9]

8. I agree with Mr. Justice Marshall that stereotypes concerning identifiable classes in our society have no place in the decisions of this Court. For that reason, I consider it inappropriate to characterize the Mexican–American majority in Hidalgo County as a "minority group" and on that basis to suggest that these Mexican–Americans may have "adopt[ed] the majority's negative attitudes towards the minority." This type of speculation illustrates the lengths to which one must go to buttress a holding of purposeful discrimination that otherwise is based solely on a lack of proportional representation.

9. In its preoccupation with the disparity of representation of Mexican–Americans in the total population and on the grand jury lists, the Court loses sight of the constitutional standard. Respondent has no

The Court labels it "inexplicable" that the State introduced only the testimony of the state trial judge. Perhaps the State fairly may be faulted for not presenting more evidence than it did. But until today's decision one may doubt whether many lawyers, familiar with our cases, would have thought that respondent's statistics, under the circumstances of this case and prevailing in Hidalgo County, were even arguably sufficient to establish deliberate and systematic discrimination.

There is for me a sense of unreality when Justices here in Washington decide solely on the basis of inferences from statistics that the Mexican–Americans who control the levers of power in this remote border county are manipulating them to discriminate "against themselves." In contrast, the judges on the scene, the state judge who appointed the jury commissioners and presided over respondent's trial and the United States District Judge—both Mexican–Americans and familiar with the community—perceived no basis for respondent's claim of invidious discrimination.

It seems to me that the Court today, in rejecting the District Court's finding that no such discrimination took place, has erred grievously. I would reinstate the judgment of the District Court.

DONALDSON v. CALIFORNIA

Supreme Court of the United States, 1971.
404 U.S. 968, 92 S.Ct. 332, 30 L.Ed.2d 288.

Petition for writ of certiorari to the Court of Appeal of California, Second Appellate District, denied.

MR. JUSTICE DOUGLAS, with whom MR. JUSTICE MARSHALL concurs, dissenting.

The Court today denies certiorari to a Black man who stands convicted by an all-White jury which had been selected through a process which petitioner alleges methodically excluded members of minority racial groups. The most pernicious of the practices used to exclude Black and Chicano jurors was what purported to be an intelligence test which, because of its cultural bias and its blatant unreliability, excluded nearly 50% of the otherwise qualified prospective jurors from minority groups. We would all agree that the brand of justice received in our courts should not depend upon the color of one's skin and that the selection of jury panels should not be tainted by the exclusion of racial groups. With all respect I fear precisely that result has obtained in the case.

Petitioner was convicted of the unlawful possession of marihuana. The State's evidence consisted of the testimony of two White police officers that they observed and smelled petitioner smoke a marihuana cigarette and that he dropped the cigarette on the ground before he was

right to "proportional representation" of Mexican–Americans, *Carter v. Jury Comm'n,* 396 U.S., at 339. He has only the right "to require that the State not deliber- ately and systematically deny to [Mexican–Americans] the right to participate as jurors in the administration of justice." *Alexander,* 405 U.S., at 628–629.

arrested. Petitioner steadfastly denied his guilt. He offered witnesses who "testified that, because of an obstruction, it was not possible to see" the area where petitioner was allegedly smoking marihuana, who supported his story "that no one was smoking marihuana," and who gave credence to the apparent theory of the defense that a Black man was being framed by White police officers.

The issue for the jury was the relative credibility of two White police officers and the four Black defense witnesses. That this question was close is indicated by the fact that after some 5¼ hours of deliberation the jury reported itself deadlocked eight-to-four and an Allen charge was then given. See Allen v. United States, 164 U.S. 492 (1896). It took an additional hour of deliberation before the jury resolved the credibility issue against petitioner and returned a verdict of guilty.

On appeal, the California Court of Appeal affirmed the conviction, holding that petitioner, as a Black, had no standing to challenge the exclusion of Chicanos from the jury panel,[a] that the exclusion of racial minorities was unintentional and that, in any event, it did not deny equal protection of the laws. The Supreme Court of California denied a petition for a hearing and petitioner now seeks a writ of certiorari.

The culturally-biased intelligence test used in this case excludes almost half of the otherwise qualified prospective jurors from minority groups. It is also argued that members of racial minority groups are effectively barred from jury service by (1) the selection of prospective jurors solely from voter registration lists despite the significantly lower incidence of registration by Blacks and Chicanos, (2) the absence of any follow-up procedures to correct for the high frequency with which Blacks and Chicanos fail to respond to jury service notices, and (3) the token $5 per diem paid jurors which precludes those in low economic strata from serving as jurors.[10]

Petitioner concludes that "[i]n the 1968 South District Jury Draw [from which his jury was selected], the cumulative effect of the * * * selection procedures * * * was such that the percentage selected from a white middle-class comparison area was *13 times* as great as the percentage selected from a low-income black comparison area, and the exclusion of low-income Mexican–Americans was *virtually total*."

---

10. Even if it were assumed that these exclusions were the unavoidable consequences of Los Angeles' method of jury selection, it does not follow that jury panels must be racially unrepresentative of the community. The names of prospective jurors are selected by a computer from voter registration lists. With modern sampling techniques, it would be a simple matter to program the computer so that its initial selection of names would—after the operation of these exclusions—yield a racially representative jury panel. Mills, *A Statistical Study of Occupations of Jurors in a* *United States District Court*, 22 Md.L.Rev. 205, 214 (1962).

"A selection system which is economically and racially unbalanced by the application of juror quality tests can produce representative panels if a larger percentage of those population segments which tend to fail the tests is considered for jury service so that a fair proportion of their members survive the selection process." Kuhn, *Jury Discrimination: The Next Phase*, 41 S.Cal.L.Rev. 235, 315 (1968).

The opinion of the Court of Appeal and the argument of the respondent do not, in my mind, sufficiently rebut the prima facie showing petitioner has made that he has been denied the equal protection of the law by his conviction by a jury selected through racially biased procedures.[11]

"If there has been discrimination, whether accomplished ingeniously or ingenuously, the conviction cannot stand." Smith v. Texas, 311 U.S. 128, 132 (1940). It would seem enough, therefore, to reverse this conviction out of hand because of the racial bias built into the jury selection and because of the improper legal standard applied by the court below.

The test in question was drafted in 1935 and it consists of some 33 questions designed to measure vocabulary and reading comprehension. The Jury Commissioner testified that it was administered "[t]o see if a prospective juror has sufficient knowledge of the English language," but expert scientific testimony indicated that the test was "not a good measure * * * of average verbal ability." The author of the examination, Psychology, Professor Dr. Neil Warren, testified that he validated the test and established the passing score by administering it to some 100 to 200 white middle-class college students. Over the years, the test questions themselves have remained unchanged despite changes in the common vocabulary. At some point, however, the test was divided into two parts and, for some inexplicable reason, the passing grade was changed. Dr. Warren testified that these changes would "reduce the reliability to the point where [he] would not want to condone the results." Another expert witness testified that the test was "completely arbitrary to use in its present form."

While the test may have been unreliable as a measure of juror competence, it effectively excluded minority group members from jury service. The rate of failure in minority group areas was almost four times that in a white, middle-class comparison area:

Area		*Failure Rate*
Long Beach (White, Middle–Class)	13%	(14/106)
Wilmington (48% Spanish Surname) and San Pedro		
(41% Mexican–American and 11% Black)	45%	(23/51)
Central Long Beach (55% Black)	48%	(12/25)
District–Wide	18%	(349/1937)

It would seem that this device is ill-suited to serve any legitimate state interest and does serve to exclude from jury panels significantly disproportionate numbers of minority groups. The Constitution does not of course require racially-balanced juries because, in our pluralistic society, a group of 12 men and women could not possibly represent all of

---

11. The Court of Appeal argues, for example, that "[t]he poor, the Black and Mexican–Americans have the power to register to vote, and voter registration is free and relatively uncomplicated." Be this as it may, this argument is unresponsive to petitioner's contention that jurors are selected from lists which are racially unbalanced.

the ethnic, racial and economic groups which comprise our diverse culture.

What the facts might show after oral argument, no one knows. I would hold constitutionally infirm a conviction returned by a jury from which a disproportionately large number of minority group members were excluded through the use of a culturally biased intelligence test is shown to be unreliable as a measure of jury competence. There is a prima facie showing that this test is vulnerable. Accordingly, I would grant the petition for a writ of certiorari.

Mr. Justice Brennan would also grant certiorari.

Note

In United States v. Ovalle, 136 F.3d 1092 (6th Cir.1998) the Court of Appeals dealt with a jury selection process which called for a "subtraction" method of balancing the jury wheel to ensure proportional representation of different cognizable groups in the community, whereby:

> the qualified jury wheel shall be composed of persons who represent a fair cross-section of the area of each place of holding court as set forth in Section III of this Plan. To this end, if the Court determines that a cognizable group of persons is substantially overrepresented in the qualified jury wheel, the Chief Judge shall order the Clerk to remove randomly a specific number of names so that the population of each cognizable group in the qualified wheel closely approximates the percentage of the population of each group in the area of each place of holding court, according to the most recently published national census report.

Several administrative orders were issued to implement the Jury Selection Plan, including the one in question in this case, filed on November 17, 1992.

Administrative Order 92–AO–080, signed by the chief judge of the district court, provided in pertinent part:

> IT APPEARING THAT the Black population, as reported in the 1990 census for the 21 counties for which the place of holding court is Bay City, is 4.2%, and
>
> IT FURTHER APPEARING THAT, as of November 4, 1992, the percentage of qualified Black jurors in the Bay City wheel created in 1992 is 3.45%,
>
> NOW, THEREFORE, IT IS ORDERED THAT, based on the information on the attached "Worksheet for the Removal of Jurors from the Qualified Bay City Jury Wheel," the Clerk of the Court shall remove by a random process the names of 877 White and Other Qualified Jurors from the 4,829 total qualified jurors in the 1992 wheel to bring it into compliance with the cognizable group requirements of Section VIII. B. of the Jury Selection Plan, approved on April 1, 1992, and the policy of the Court. As a result of this procedure, the 1992 qualified Bay City wheel shall be composed of 166 Black qualified jurors and 3,786 White and Other qualified jurors. A quotient of 5 and a starting number of 4 shall be used for the removal procedure.

The Court of Appeals noted that the Eastern District of Michigan was the only federal district which employed this "subtraction method." It also observed that the administrators of the plan gave no consideration to the under-representation of groups other than African–Americans. The Court concluded that defendants had standing to challenge this inherently biased jury selection procedure, even though their own group (Mexican–Americans) may not have been underrepresented, and ordered their convictions reversed.

BATSON v. KENTUCKY

Supreme Court of the United States, 1986.
476 U.S. 79, 106 S.Ct. 1712, 90 L.Ed.2d 69.

JUSTICE POWELL delivered the opinion of the Court.

This case requires us to reexamine that portion of *Swain v. Alabama*, 380 U.S. 202 (1965), concerning the evidentiary burden placed on a criminal defendant who claims that he has been denied equal protection through the State's use of peremptory challenges to exclude members of his race from the petit jury.

I

Petitioner, a black man, was indicted in Kentucky on charges of second-degree burglary and receipt of stolen goods. On the first day of trial in Jefferson Circuit Court, the judge conducted *voir dire* examination of the venire, excused certain jurors for cause, the permitted the parties to exercise peremptory challenges.[12] The prosecutor used his peremptory challenges to strike all four black persons on the venire, and a jury composed only of white persons was selected. Defense counsel moved to discharge the jury before it was sworn on the ground that the prosecutor's removal of the black veniremen violated petitioner's rights under the Sixth and Fourteenth Amendments to a jury drawn from a cross-section of the community, and under the Fourteenth Amendment to equal protection of the laws. Counsel requested a hearing on his motion. Without expressly ruling on the request for a hearing, the trial judge observed that the parties were entitled to use their peremptory challenges to "strike anybody they want to." The judge then denied petitioner's motion, reasoning that the cross-section requirement applies only to selection of the venire and not to selection of the petit jury itself.

The jury convicted petitioner on both counts. [The Kentucky Supreme Court affirmed the convictions and the Supreme Court granted certiorari.]

12. The Kentucky Rules of Criminal Procedure authorize the trial court to permit counsel to conduct *voir dire* examination or to conduct the examination itself. Ky.Rule Crim.Proc. 9.38. After jurors have been excused for cause, the parties exercise their peremptory challenges simultaneously by striking names from a list of qualified jurors equal to the number to be seated plus the number of allowable peremptory challenges. Rule 9.36. Since the offense charged in this case was a felony, and an alternate juror was called, the prosecutor was entitled to six peremptory challenges, and defense counsel to nine. Rule 9.40.

III

* * *

Swain required the Court to decide, among other issues, whether a black defendant was denied equal protection by the State's exercise of peremptory challenges to exclude members of his race from the petit jury. The record in *Swain* showed that the prosecutor had used the State's peremptory challenges to strike the six black persons included on the petit jury venire. While rejecting the defendant's claim for failure to prove purposeful discrimination, the Court nonetheless indicated that the Equal Protection Clause placed some limits on the State's exercise of peremptory challenges.

The Court sought to accommodate the prosecutor's historical privilege of peremptory challenge free of judicial control, and the constitutional prohibition on exclusion of persons from jury service on account of race. While the Constitution does not confer a right to peremptory challenges, those challenges traditionally have been viewed as one means of assuring the selection of a qualified and unbiased jury. To preserve the peremptory nature of the prosecutor's challenge, the Court in *Swain* declined to scrutinize his actions in a particular case by relying on a presumption that he properly exercised the State's challenges.

The Court went on to observe, however, that a state may not exercise its challenges in contravention of the Equal Protection Clause. It was impermissible for a prosecutor to use his challenges to exclude blacks from the jury "for reasons wholly unrelated to the outcome of the particular case on trial" or to deny to blacks "the same right and opportunity to participate in the administration of justice enjoyed by the white population." Accordingly, a black defendant could make out a prima facie case of purposeful discrimination on proof that the peremptory challenge system was "being perverted" in that manner. For example, an inference of purposeful discrimination would be raised on evidence that a prosecutor, "in case after case, whatever the circumstances, whatever the crime and whoever the defendant or the victim may be, is responsible for the removal of Negroes who have been selected as qualified jurors by the jury commissioners and who have survived challenges for cause, with the result that no Negroes ever serve on petit juries." Evidence offered by the defendant in *Swain* did not meet that standard. While the defendant showed that prosecutors in the jurisdiction had exercised their strikes to exclude blacks from the jury, he offered no proof of the circumstances under which prosecutors were responsible for striking black jurors beyond the facts of his own case.

A number of lower courts following the teaching of *Swain* reasoned that proof of repeated striking of blacks over a number of cases was necessary to establish a violation of the Equal Protection Clause. Since this interpretation of *Swain* has placed on defendants a crippling burden of proof, prosecutors' peremptory challenges are now largely immune from constitutional scrutiny. For reasons that follow, we reject this evidentiary formulation as inconsistent with standards that have been developed since *Swain* for assessing a prima facie case under the Equal Protection Clause. * * *

The standards for assessing a prima facie case in the context of discriminatory selection of the venire have been fully articulated since *Swain*. See *Castaneda v. Partida*, 430 U.S., at 494–495; *Washington v. Davis*, 426 U.S., at 241–242; *Alexander v. Louisiana*, 405 U.S., at 629–631. These principles support our conclusion that a defendant may establish a prima facie case of purposeful discrimination in selection of the petit jury solely on evidence concerning the prosecutor's exercise of peremptory challenges at the defendant's trial. To establish such a case, the defendant first must show that he is a member of a cognizable racial group, and that the prosecutor has exercised peremptory challenges to remove from the venire members of the defendant's race. Second, the defendant is entitled to rely on the fact, as to which there can be no dispute, that peremptory challenges constitute a jury selection practice that permits those to discriminate who are of a mind to discriminate. Finally, the defendant must show that these facts and any other relevant circumstances raise an inference that the prosecutor used that practice to exclude the veniremen from the petit jury on account of their race. This combination of factors in the empanelling of the petit jury, as in the selection of the venire, raises the necessary inference of purposeful discrimination.

In deciding whether the defendant has made the requisite showing, the trial court should consider all relevant circumstances. For example, a "pattern" of strikes against black jurors included in the particular venire might give rise to an inference of discrimination. Similarly, the prosecutor's questions and statements during *voir dire* examination and in exercising his challenges may support or refute an inference of discriminatory purpose. These examples are merely illustrative. We have confidence that trial judges, experienced in supervising *voir dire*, will be able to decide if the circumstances concerning the prosecutor's use of peremptory challenges creates a prima facie case of discrimination against black jurors.

Once the defendant makes a prima facie showing, the burden shifts to the State to come forward with a neutral explanation for challenging black jurors. Though this requirement imposes a limitation in some cases on the full peremptory character of the historic challenge, we emphasize that the prosecutor's explanation need not rise to the level justifying exercise of a challenge for cause. But the prosecutor may not rebut the defendant's prima facie case of discrimination by stating merely that he challenged jurors of the defendant's race on the assumption—or his intuitive judgment—that they would be partial to the defendant because of their shared race. Just as the Equal Protection Clause forbids the States to exclude black persons from the venire on the assumption that blacks as a group are unqualified to serve as jurors, so it forbids the States to strike black veniremen on the assumption that they will be biased in a particular case simply because the defendant is black. The core guarantee of equal protection, ensuring citizens that their State will not discriminate on account of race, would be meaningless were we to approve the exclusion of jurors on the basis of such assumptions, which arise solely from the jurors' race. Nor may the prosecutor rebut the defendant's case merely by denying that he had a discriminatory motive or affirming his good faith in individual selections. If these general assertions were accepted as rebutting a defendant's prima facie case, the Equal Protection Clause would be but a vain and illusory requirement. The prosecutor therefore must articulate a neutral explanation related to the particular case to be tried. The trial court then will have the duty to determine if the defendant has established purposeful discrimination.

* * *

V

In this case, petitioner made a timely objection to the prosecutor's removal of all black persons on the venire. Because the trial court flatly rejected the objection without requiring the prosecutor to give an explanation for his action, we remand this case for further proceedings. If the trial court decides that the facts establish, prima facie, purposeful discrimination and the prosecutor does not come forward with a neutral explanation for his action, our precedents require that petitioner's conviction be reversed.

It is so ordered.

JUSTICE MARSHALL, concurring. * * *

I wholeheartedly concur in the Court's conclusion that use of the peremptory challenge to remove blacks from juries, on the basis of their race, violates the Equal Protection Clause. I would go further, however, in fashioning a remedy adequate to eliminate that discrimination. Merely allowing defendants the opportunity to challenge the racially discriminatory use of peremptory challenges in individual cases will not end the illegitimate use of the peremptory challenge.

Evidentiary analysis similar to that set out by the Court, has been adopted as a matter of state law in States including Massachusetts and California. Cases from those jurisdictions illustrate the limitations of the approach. First, defendants cannot attack the discriminatory use of peremptory challenges at all unless the challenges are so flagrant as to establish a prima facie case. This means, in those States, that where only one or two black jurors survive the challenges for cause, the prosecutor need have no compunction about striking them from the jury because of their race. See *Commonwealth v. Robinson*, 415 N.E.2d 805, 809–810 (Mass.1981) (no prima facie case of discrimination where defendant is black, prospective jurors include three blacks and one Puerto Rican, and prosecutor excludes one for cause and strikes the remainder peremptorily, producing all-white jury); *People v. Rousseau*, 179 Cal.Rptr. 892, 897–898 (Cal.App.1982) (no prima facie case where prosecutor peremptorily strikes only two blacks on jury panel). Prosecutors are left free to discriminate against blacks in jury selection provided that they hold that discrimination to an "acceptable" level.

Second, when a defendant can establish a prima facie case, trial courts face the difficult burden of assessing prosecutors' motives. See *King v. County of Nassau*, 581 F.Supp. 493, 501–502 (E.D.N.Y.1984). Any prosecutor can easily assert facially neutral reasons for striking a juror, and trial courts are ill-equipped to second-guess those reasons. How is the court to treat a prosecutor's statement that he struck a juror because the juror had a son about the same age as defendant, see *People v. Hall*, 672 P.2d 854 (Cal.1983), or seemed "uncommunicative," *King, supra*, at 498, or "never cracked a smile" and, therefore "did not possess the sensitivities necessary to realistically look at the issues and decide the facts in this case," *Hall*, 672 P.2d, at 856? If such easily generated explanations are sufficient to discharge the prosecutor's obligation to justify his strikes on nonracial grounds, then the protection erected by the Court today may be illusory.

Nor is outright prevarication by prosecutors the only danger here. "[I]t is even possible that an attorney may lie to himself in an effort to convince himself that his motives are legal." *King, supra*, at 502. A prosecutor's own conscious or unconscious racism may lead him easily to the conclusion that a prospective black juror is "sullen," or "distant," a characterization that would not have come to his mind if a white juror had acted identically. A judge's own conscious or unconscious racism may lead him to accept such an explanation as well supported. As Justice Rehnquist concedes, prosecutors' peremptories are based on their "seat-of-the-pants instincts" as to how particular jurors will vote. Yet "seat-of-the-pants instincts" may often be just another term for racial prejudice. Even if all parties approach the Court's mandate with the best of conscious intentions, that mandate requires them to confront and overcome their own racism on all levels—a challenge I doubt all of them can meet. It is worth remembering that 114 years after the close of the War Between the States and nearly 100 years after *Strauder*, racial and other forms of discrimination still remain a fact of life, in the administration of justice as in our society as a whole. * * *

The inherent potential of peremptory challenges to distort the jury process by permitting the exclusion of jurors on racial grounds should ideally lead the Court to ban them entirely from the criminal justice system.

Some authors have suggested that the courts should ban prosecutors' peremptories entirely, but should zealously guard the defendant's peremptory as essential to the fairness of trial by jury. I would not find that an acceptable solution. Our criminal justice system requires not only freedom from any bias against the accused, but also from any prejudice against his prosecution. Between him and the state the scales are to be evenly held. We can maintain that balance, not by permitting both prosecutor and defendant to engage in racial discrimination in jury selection, but by banning the use of peremptory challenges by prosecutors and by allowing the States to eliminate the defendant's peremptory as well. * * *

CHIEF JUSTICE BURGER, joined by JUSTICE REHNQUIST, dissenting. * * * The peremptory challenge has been in use without scrutiny into its basis for nearly as long as juries have existed. It was in use amongst the Romans in criminal cases, and the *Lex Servilia* (B.C. 104) enacted that the accuser and the accused should severally propose one hundred *judices*, and that each might reject fifty from the list of the other, so that one hundred would remain to try the alleged crime.

In *Swain* Justice White traced the development of the peremptory challenge from the early days of the jury trial in England:

> "In all trials for felonies at common law, the defendant was allowed to challenge peremptorily 35 jurors, and the prosecutor originally had a right to challenge any number of jurors without cause, a right which was said to tend to 'infinite delays and danger.' Coke on Littleton 156 (14th ed. 1791). Thus The Ordinance for Inquests, 33 Edw. 1, Stat. 4 (1305), provided that if 'they that sue for the King will challenge any * * * Jurors, they shall assign * * * a Cause certain.' So persistent was the view that a proper jury trial required peremptories on both sides, however, that the statute was construed to allow the prosecution to direct any juror after examination to 'stand aside' until the entire panel was gone over and the defendant had exercised his challenges; only if there was a deficiency of jurors in the box at that point did the Crown have to show cause in respect to jurors recalled to make up the required number. Peremptories on both sides became the settled law of England, continuing in the above form until after the separation of the Colonies." 380 U.S., at 212–213.

Peremptory challenges have a venerable tradition in this country as well * * *

The Court's opinion, in addition to ignoring the teachings of history, also contrasts with *Swain* in its failure to even discuss the rationale of the peremptory challenge. *Swain* observed:

> "The function of the challenge is not only to eliminate extremes of partiality on both sides, but to assure the parties that the jurors before whom they try the case will decide on the basis of the evidence placed for them, and not otherwise. In this way the peremptory satisfies the rule that to perform its high function in the best way, justice must satisfy the appearance of justice." *Id.*, at 219.

Permitting unexplained peremptories has long been regarded as a means to strengthen our jury system in other ways as well. One commentator has recognized:

> "The peremptory, made without giving any reason, avoids trafficking in the core of truth in most common stereotypes. * * * Common human experience, common sense, psychosociological studies, and public opinion polls tell us that it is likely that certain classes of

people statistically have predispositions that would make them inappropriate jurors for particular kinds of cases. But to allow this knowledge to be expressed in the evaluative terms necessary for challenges for cause would undercut our desire for a society in which all people are judged as individuals and in which each is held reasonable and open to compromise. * * * [For example,] [a]lthough experience reveals that black males as a class can be biased against young alienated blacks who have not tried to join the middle class, to enunciate this in the concrete expression required of a challenge for cause is societally divisive. Instead we have evolved in the peremptory challenge a system that allows the covert expression of what we dare not say but know is true more often than not." Babcock, Voir Dire: Preserving "Its Wonderful Power," 27 Stan. L.Rev. 545, 553–554 (1975).

* * *

Instead of even considering the history or function of the peremptory challenge, the bulk of the Court's opinion is spent recounting the well-established principle that intentional exclusion of racial groups from jury venires is a violation of the Equal Protection Clause. I too reaffirm that principle, which has been a part of our constitutional tradition since at least *Strauder v. West Virginia*, 100 U.S. 303 (1880). But if today's decision is nothing more than mere "application" of the "principles announced in *Strauder*," as the Court maintains, some will consider it curious that the application went unrecognized for over a century. * * *

A moment's reflection quickly reveals the vast differences between the racial exclusions involved in *Strauder* and the allegations before us today:

"Exclusion from the venire summons process implies that the government (usually the legislative or judicial branch) * * * has made the general determination that those excluded are unfit to try *any* case. Exercise of the peremptory challenge, by contrast, represents the discrete decision, made by one of two or more opposed *litigants* in the trial phase of our adversary system of justice, that the challenged venireperson will likely be more unfavorable to that litigant in that *particular case* than others on the same venire.

"Thus, excluding a particular cognizable group from all venire pools is stigmatizing and discriminatory in several interrelated ways that the peremptory challenge is not. The former singles out the excluded group, while individuals of all grounds are equally subject to peremptory challenge on any basis, including their group affiliation. Further, venire-pool exclusion bespeaks *a priori* across-the-board total unfitness, while peremptory-strike exclusion merely suggests potential partiality in a particular isolated case. Exclusion from venires focuses on the inherent attributes of the excluded group and infers its *inferiority*, but the peremptory does not. To suggest that a particular race is unfit to judge in any case necessarily is racially insulting. To suggest that each race may have its own special concerns, or even may tend to favor its own, is not." *United States v. Leslie*, 783 F.2d 541, 554 (C.A.5 1986) (en banc).

Unwilling to rest solely on jury venire cases such as *Strauder*, the Court also invokes general equal protection principles in support of its holding. But peremptory challenges are often lodged, of necessity, for reasons "normally thought irrelevant to legal proceedings or official action, namely, the race, religion, nationality, occupation or affiliations of people summoned for jury duty." *Swain, supra*, 380 U.S., at 220. Moreover, in making peremptory challenges, both the prosecutor and defense attorney necessarily act on only limited information or hunch. The process can not be indicted on the sole basis that such decisions are made on the basis of "assumption" or "intuitive judgment." As a result, unadulterated equal protection analysis is simply inapplicable to peremptory challenges exercised in any particular case. A clause that requires a minimum "rationality" in government actions has no application to " 'an arbitrary and capricious right,' " *Swain, supra*, at 219, a constitutional principle that may invalidate state action on the basis of "stereotypic notions," does not explain the breadth of a procedure exercised on the " 'sudden impressions and unaccountable prejudices we are apt to conceive upon the bare looks and gestures of another.' " *Lewis v. United States*, 146 U.S., at 376 (quoting 4 W. Blackstone, Commentaries * 353).

That the Court is not applying conventional equal protection analysis is shown by its limitation of its new rule to allegations of impermissible challenge *on the basis of race;* the Court's opinion clearly contains such a limitation. * * * But if conventional equal protection principles apply, then presumably defendants could object to exclusions on the basis of not only race, but also sex, age, religious or political affiliation, mental capacity, number of children, living arrangements, and employment in a particular industry or profession. [Citations omitted.]

In short, it is quite probable that every peremptory challenge could be objected to on the basis that, because it excluded a venireman who had some characteristic not shared by the remaining members of the venire, it constituted a "classification" subject to equal protection scrutiny. * * *

The Court also purports to express "no views on whether the Constitution imposes any limit on the exercise of peremptory challenges by *defense* counsel." But the clear and inescapable import of this novel holding will inevitably be to limit the use of this valuable tool to both prosecutors and defense attorneys alike. Once the Court has held that *prosecutors* are limited in their use of peremptory challenges, could we rationally hold that defendants are not?[13] * * * Our system permits two types of challenges: challenges for cause and peremptory challenges. Challenges for cause obviously have to be explained; by definition, peremptory challenges do not. * * *

13. "[E]very jurisdiction which has spoken to the matter, and prohibited prosecution case-specific peremptory challenges on the basis of cognizable group affiliation, has held that the defense must likewise be so prohibited." *United States v. Leslie*, 783 F.2d 541, 565 (C.A.5 1986) (en banc).

Confronted with the dilemma it created, the Court today attempts to decree a middle ground. To rebut a prima facie case, the Court requires a "neutral explanation" for the challenge, but is at pains to "emphasize" that the "explanation need not rise to the level justifying exercise of a challenge for cause." I am at a loss to discern the governing principles here. A "clear and reasonably specific" explanation of "legitimate reasons" for exercising the challenge will be difficult to distinguish from a challenge for cause. Anything short of a challenge for cause may well be seen as an "arbitrary and capricious" challenge, to use Blackstone's characterization of the peremptory. Apparently the Court envisions permissible challenges short of a challenge for cause that are just a little bit arbitrary—but not too much. While our trial judges are "experienced in supervising *voir dire*," they have no experience in administering rules like this.

An example will quickly demonstrate how today's holding, while purporting to "further the ends of justice," will not have that effect. Assume an Asian defendant, on trial for the capital murder of a white victim, asks prospective jury members, most of whom are white, whether they harbor racial prejudice against Asians. See *Turner v. Murray*, [infra p. 796]. The basis for such a question is to flush out any "juror who believes that [Asians] are violence-prone or morally inferior. * * * " Assume further that all white jurors deny harboring racial prejudice but that the defendant, on trial for his life, remains unconvinced by these protestations. Instead, he continues to harbor a hunch, an "assumption" or "intuitive judgment," that these white jurors will be prejudiced against him, presumably based on part on race. The time honored rule before today was that peremptory challenges could be exercised on such a basis. * * * The effect of the Court's decision, however, will be to force the defendant to come forward and "articulate a neutral explanation," for his peremptory challenge, a burden he probably cannot meet. This example demonstrates that today's holding will produce juries that the parties do not believe are truly impartial. This will surely do more than "disconcert" litigants; it will diminish confidence in the jury system.

A further painful paradox of the Court's holding is that it is likely to interject racial matters back into the jury selection process, contrary to the general thrust of a long line of Court decisions and the notion of our country as a "melting pot." * * *

* * * Prosecutors and defense attorney's alike will build records in support of their claims that peremptory challenges have been exercised in a racially discriminatory fashion by asking jurors to state their racial background and national origin for the record, despite the fact that such questions may be offensive to some jurors and thus are not ordinarily asked on voir dire. * * *

Even after a "record" on this issue has been created, disputes will inevitably arise. In one case, for instance, a conviction was reversed based on the assumption that no blacks were on the jury that convicted a defendant. See *People v. Motton*, 704 P.2d 176, 180 (Cal.1985). However, after the court's decision was announced, Carolyn Pritchett, who had served on the jury, called the press to state that the court was in error and that she was black. 71 A.B.A.J. 22 (Nov. 1985). The California court nonetheless denied a rehearing petition. * * *

JUSTICE REHNQUIST, with whom THE CHIEF JUSTICE joins, dissenting. * * * In my view, there is simply nothing "unequal" about the State using its peremptory challenges to strike blacks from the jury in cases involving black defendants, so long as such challenges are also used to exclude whites in cases involving white defendants, Hispanics in cases involving Hispanic defendants, Asians in cases involving Asian defendants, and so on. This case-specific use of peremptory challenges by the State does not single out blacks, or members of any other race for that matter, for discriminatory treatment.[14] Such use of peremptories is at best based upon seat-of-the-pants instincts, which are undoubtedly crudely stereotypical and may in many cases be hopelessly mistaken. But as long as they are applied across the board to jurors of all races and nationalities, I do not see—and the Court most certainly has not explained—how their use violates the Equal Protection Clause. * * *

The use of group affiliations, such as age, race, or occupation, as a "proxy" for potential juror partiality, based on the assumption or belief that members of one group are more likely to favor defendants who belong to the same group, has long been accepted as a legitimate basis for the State's exercise of peremptory challenges. Indeed, given the need for reasonable limitations on the time devoted to *voir dire*, the use of such "proxies" by both the State and the defendant[15] may be extremely useful in eliminating from the jury persons who might be biased in one way or another. The Court today holds that the State may not use its peremptory challenges to strike black prospective jurors on this basis without violating the Constitution. But I do not believe there is anything in the Equal Protection Clause, or any other constitutional provision, that justifies such a departure from the substantive holding contained in Part II of *Swain*. Petitioner in the instant case failed to make a sufficient showing to overcome the presumption announced in *Swain* that the State's use of peremptory challenges was related to the context of the case. I would therefore affirm the judgment of the court below.

Commentary

In Allen v. Hardy, 478 U.S. 255 (1986), the Supreme Court held that the *Batson* rule would not be applied retroactively on collateral review to convictions that had become final before the date of the *Batson* decision. The majority reasoned that the rule against exercising peremptory challenge on a

---

14. I note that the Court does not rely on the argument that, because there are fewer "minorities" in a given population than there are "majorities," the equal use of peremptory challenges against members of "majority" and "minority" racial groups has an unequal impact. The flaws in this argument are demonstrated in Judge Garwood's thoughtful opinion for the en

banc Fifth Circuit in *United States v. Leslie*, 783 F.2d 541, 559 (C.A.5 1986).

15. See, *e.g., Commonwealth v. DiMatteo*, 427 N.E.2d 754 (Mass.1981) (under State constitution, trial judge properly rejected white defendant's attempted peremptory challenge of black prospective juror).

racial basis does not have "such a fundamental impact on the integrity of fact finding as to compel retroactive application," and that to apply the new doctrine to convictions which had already become final would seriously disrupt the administration of justice because of the difficulty of finding the facts years after conviction.

Does *Batson* stand for the narrow proposition that peremptory challenges may not be used systematically to exclude jurors on the basis of *race*, or the broader proposition that peremptory challenges may not be used systematically to exclude any category of jurors who could not be excused for cause? Supreme Court Justices Brennan and O'Connor debated this question when the Supreme Court denied certiorari in Brown v. North Carolina, 479 U.S. 940 (1986). *Brown* was a capital case in which the prosecution used peremptory challenges systematically to exclude any jurors who voiced scruples concerning the death penalty. Excluding such jurors for cause would be unconstitutional under the *"Witherspoon"* doctrine, described in the opinion in *Lockhart v. McCree, infra*, p. 800. Justice Brennan argued that the Supreme Court should have granted certiorari to review the State Supreme Court's affirmance of the conviction and death sentence, on the theory that the prosecutor's use of peremptory challenges to obtain a jury of death penalty supporters violated the *Batson* rule. In response, Justice O'Connor relied upon "the ordinary rule that a prosecutor may exercise his peremptory strikes for any reason at all, absent racial discrimination forbidden by the Equal Protection Clause." She concluded:

> That the Court will not tolerate prosecutors' racially discriminatory use of the peremptory challenge, in effect, is a special rule of relevance, a statement about what this Nation stands for, rather than a statement of fact. In my view, that special rule is a product of the unique history of racial discrimination in this country; it should not be divorced from that context. Outside the uniquely sensitive area of race the ordinary rule that a prosecutor may strike a juror without giving any reason applies. Because a juror's attitudes towards the death penalty may be relevant to how the juror judges, while, as a matter of law, his race is not, this case is not like *Batson*. 107 S.Ct. at 424.

The California Supreme Court invoked the impartial jury requirement rather than the Equal Protection Clause when it limited the exercise of peremptory challenges in its frequently cited opinion in People v. Wheeler, 22 Cal.3d 258, 148 Cal.Rptr. 890, 583 P.2d 748 (1978). The California Court reasoned that:

> When a party presumes that certain jurors are biased merely because they are members of an identifiable group distinguished on racial, religious, ethnic, or similar grounds—we may call this "group bias"— and peremptorily strikes all such persons for that reason alone, he not only upsets the demographic balance of the venire but frustrates the primary purpose of the representative cross-section requirement. That purpose, as we have seen, is to achieve an overall impartiality by allowing the interaction of the diverse beliefs and values the jurors bring from their group experiences. Manifestly if jurors are struck simply because they may hold those very beliefs, such interaction becomes impossible and the jury will be dominated by the conscious or unconscious prejudices of the majority. Seen in this light, the presumed group

bias that triggered the peremptory challenges against its members is indistinguishable from the group perspective we seek to encourage by the cross-section rule. 583 P.2d at 761.

The opinion indicated that this rule would bar discriminatory use of peremptory challenges by defense counsel, as well as the prosecutor, because "the People no less than individual defendants are entitled to a trial by an impartial jury drawn from a representative cross-section of the community." 583 P.2d at 765, n. 29.

In a companion case to *Wheeler*, the prosecutor frankly admitted that he intended to exclude all black jurors because of the peculiar facts of the case. The court stated the facts as follows:

> Defendant forced his way into the apartment of Janice Jared. After robbing and raping her, he tied her up and left. About that time Ray Wildt, who worked at a motorcycle shop across the street, looked up and saw a black man walk from Mrs. Jared's house, then down the street. Meanwhile Mrs. Jared freed herself, ran to a window, and screamed for help. As Wildt came towards her she shouted, "Ray, I have just been raped." Wildt called, "Was it the nigger?" and she answered that it was.

Wildt gave chase, and the defendant was subsequently apprehended and identified as the rapist. On these facts the prosecutor explained to the Court that "certain witnesses had made racially prejudicial statements that might be disclosed to the jury, which I would think would make it very difficult for any black person to be totally objective about [the case] either consciously or subconsciously." 583 P.2d at 775.

The California Supreme Court held this reasoning insufficient to justify use of peremptory challenges on a racial basis. The Court reasoned that the prosecutor could have attempted to determine by voir dire which individual black jurors were likely to be so affected, but he elected to avoid this effort and instead employ "decision-making by racial stereotype, a technique that should be anathema in our courts." The Court conceded that voir dire would not have identified "with a hundred percent accuracy" individual black jurors who would be so affected by the epithet that they would be unable to determine the defendant's guilt fairly on the evidence, but argued that use of the epithet would also have an "emotional impact" on white jurors, whose bias would go unchecked if the prosecutor were permitted to remove all black jurors from the case by peremptory challenges.

Suppose that the prosecutor had challenged all jurors, white or black, who said that they would be offended by racist language. Would that be less or more offensive than what he did?

Some of the difficulties in administering a broad ban on discriminatory use of peremptory challenges are illustrated by the California Supreme Court's decision in People v. Motton, 39 Cal.3d 596, 217 Cal.Rptr. 416, 704 P.2d 176 (1985), discussed briefly at the end of Justice Rehnquist's dissent in *Batson*. Defense counsel in that case claimed that the prosecutor was exercising peremptory challenges systematically against black jurors, but the trial judge rejected the contention without making an adequate record on whether a prima facie case of discrimination had been made out. Following conviction, the California Supreme Court reversed on the basis of *Wheeler*, stating in its opinion that no blacks were seated on the jury. One of the jurors, a black woman, read about this reversal in the newspapers and protested the error. On the state's motion for rehearing, the California Supreme Court modified its opinion but did not change its holding. The majority reasoned that the presence of one or more black persons on the jury would not necessarily acquit the prosecutor of discriminatory use of peremptory challenges:

> If the presence on the jury of members of the cognizable group in question is evidence of intent not to discriminate, then any attorney can avoid the appearance of systematic exclusion by simply passing the jury while a member of the cognizable group that he wants to exclude is still on the panel. This ignores the fact that other members of the group may have been excluded for improper, racially motivated reasons. In fact, the offending counsel who is familiar with basic selection and challenge techniques could easily accept a jury panel knowing that his or her opponent will exercise a challenge against a highly undesirable juror. If, for instance, three people on the panel exhibit a proprosecution bias, then the prosecutor could pass the jury with at least three members of the group which he ultimately wishes to exclude still remaining on the jury—knowing that he will have a later opportunity to strike them. By insisting that the presence of one or two black jurors on the panel is proof of an absence of intent to systematically exclude the several blacks that were excluded, the People exalt form over substance. 704 P.2d at 183.

When the defense has made a preliminary showing that the prosecutor is using peremptory challenges to excuse members of a particular minority group, how easy will it be for the prosecutor to justify those challenges by further explanation? The California Supreme Court dealt with this problem in People v. Turner, 42 Cal.3d 711, 230 Cal.Rptr. 656, 726 P.2d 102 (1986). The prosecutor in this capital case (a black defendant was on trial for murdering white victims) excused three blacks by peremptory challenge, and the jury that returned a death verdict was entirely white. Asked to explain, the prosecutor said that one of the three black jurors was "a truck driver * * * [who] had a great deal of difficulty in even understanding the questions that were being given [on voir dire]." The prosecutor vaguely justified the challenge of another black juror because "I think it was something in her work as to what she was doing that from our standpoint, that background was not—would not be good for the People's case." 726 P.2d at 108, 110. The Court indicated that discrimination against truck drivers as a class would also violate the *Wheeler* rule, and held that the justifications were too vague and unsupported by the record to sustain the prosecution's burden of showing that the challenged prospective jurors were not excluded because of group bias.

GEORGIA v. McCOLLUM

Supreme Court of the United States, 1992.
505 U.S. 42, 112 S.Ct. 2348, 120 L.Ed.2d 33.

JUSTICE BLACKMUN delivered the opinion of the Court.

For more than a century, this Court consistently and repeatedly has reaffirmed that racial discrimination by the State in jury selection offends the Equal Protection Clause. See, e.g., Strauder v. West Virginia, 100 U.S. 303 (1880). Last Term this Court held that racial discrimination in a civil litigant's exercise of peremptory challenges also violates the Equal Protection Clause. See Edmonson v. Leesville Concrete Co., 500 U.S. 614 (1991). Today, we are asked to decide whether the Constitution prohibits a criminal defendant from engaging in purposeful racial discrimination in the exercise of peremptory challenges.

I

[Respondents were charged with six counts of aggravated assault and simple battery.] Respondents are white; the alleged victims are African–Americans. Shortly after the events, a leaflet was widely distributed in the local African–American community reporting the assault and urging community residents not to patronize respondents' business. Before jury selection began, the prosecution moved to prohibit respondents from exercising peremptory challenges in a racially discriminatory manner. The State explained that it expected to show that the victims' race was a factor in the alleged assault. According to the State, counsel for respondents had indicated a clear intention to use peremptory strikes in a racially discriminatory manner, arguing that the circumstances of their case gave them the right to exclude African–American citizens from participating as jurors in the trial. Observing that 43 percent of the county's population is African–American, the State contended that, if a statistically representative panel is assembled for jury selection, 18 of the potential 42 jurors would be African–American. With 20 peremptory challenges, respondents therefore would be able to remove all the African–American potential jurors. Relying on Batson v. Kentucky, 476 U.S. 79 (1986), the Sixth Amendment, and the Georgia Constitution, the State sought an order providing that, if it succeeded in making out a prima facie case of racial discrimination by respondents, the latter would be required to articulate a racially neutral explanation for peremptory challenges. [The trial court denied the State's motion and the Georgia Supreme Court affirmed the order by a 4–3 vote.]

II

* * *

In Swain v. Alabama, 380 U.S. 202 (1965), the Court was confronted with the question whether an African–American defendant was denied equal protection by the State's exercise of peremptory challenges to exclude members of his race from the petit jury. Although the Court rejected the defendant's attempt to establish an equal protection claim premised solely on the pattern of jury strikes in his own case, it acknowledged that proof of systematic exclusion of African–Americans through the use of peremptories over a period of time might establish such a violation.

In Batson v. Kentucky, 476 U.S. 79 (1986), the Court discarded Swain's evidentiary formulation. The *Batson* Court held that a defendant may establish a prima facie case of purposeful discrimination in selection of the petit jury based solely on the prosecutor's exercise of peremptory challenges at the defendant's trial. "Once the defendant makes a prima facie showing, the burden shifts to the State to come forward with a neutral explanation for challenging black jurors." Id., at 97.

Last Term this Court applied the *Batson* framework in two other contexts. In Powers v. Ohio, 499 U.S. 400 (1991), it held that in the trial of a white criminal defendant, a prosecutor is prohibited from excluding African–American jurors on the basis of race. In Edmonson v. Leesville Concrete Co., 500 U.S. 614 (1991), the Court decided that in a civil case, private litigants cannot exercise their peremptory strikes in a racially discriminatory manner.

In deciding whether the Constitution prohibits criminal defendants from exercising racially discriminatory peremptory challenges, we must answer four questions. First, whether a criminal defendant's exercise of peremptory challenges in a racially discriminatory manner inflicts the harms addressed by *Batson*. Second, whether the exercise of peremptory challenges by a criminal defendant constitutes state action. Third, whether prosecutors have standing to raise this constitutional challenge. And fourth, whether the constitutional rights of a criminal defendant nonetheless preclude the extension of our precedents to this case.

III

A

The majority in *Powers* recognized that *Batson* was designed to serve multiple ends, only one of which was to protect individual defendants from discrimination in the selection of jurors * * *. As long ago as *Strauder*, this Court recognized that denying a person participation in jury service on account of his race unconstitutionally discriminates against the excluded juror. 100 U.S., at 308 * * *. One of the goals of our jury system is "to impress upon the criminal defendant and the community as a whole that a verdict of conviction or acquittal is given in accordance with the law by persons who are fair." *Powers,* 111 S.Ct., at 1372. Selection procedures that purposefully exclude African–Americans from juries undermine that public confidence—as well they should * * *.

The need for public confidence is especially high in cases involving race-related crimes. In such cases, emotions in the affected community will inevitably be heated and volatile. Public confidence in the integrity of the criminal justice system is essential for preserving community peace in trials involving race-related crimes. See Alschuler, "The Supreme Court and the Jury: Voir Dire, Peremptory Challenges, and the Review of Jury Verdicts," 56 U.Chi.L.Rev. 153, 195–196 (1989) (describing two trials in Miami, Fla., in which all African–American jurors were peremptorily struck by white defendants accused of racial beating, and the public outrage and riots that followed the defendants' acquittal).

Be it at the hands of the State or the defense, if a court allows jurors to be excluded because of group bias, it is a willing participant in a scheme that could only undermine the very foundation of our system of justice—our citizens' confidence in it. Just as public confidence in criminal justice is undermined by a conviction in a trial where racial discrimination has occurred in jury selection, so is public confidence undermined where a defendant, assisted by racially discriminatory peremptory strikes, obtains an acquittal.

B

The fact that a defendant's use of discriminatory peremptory challenges harms the jurors and the community does not end our equal protection inquiry. Racial discrimination, although repugnant in all contexts, violates the Constitution only when it is attributable to state action * * *.

The exercise of a peremptory challenge differs significantly from other actions taken in support of a defendant's defense. In exercising a peremptory challenge, a criminal defendant is wielding the power to choose a quintessential governmental body—indeed, the institution of government on which our judicial system depends. Thus, as we held in *Edmonson,* when "a government confers on a private body the power to choose the government's employees or officials, the private body will be bound by the constitutional mandate of race neutrality."

Lastly, the fact that a defendant exercises a peremptory challenge to further his interest in acquittal does not conflict with a finding of state action. Whenever a private actor's conduct is deemed fairly attributable to the government, it is likely that private motives will have animated the actor's decision. Indeed, in *Edmonson,* the Court recognized that the private party's exercise of peremptory challenges constituted state action, even though the motive underlying the exercise of the peremptory challenge may be to protect a private interest.

C

Having held that a defendant's discriminatory exercise of a peremptory challenge is a violation of equal protection, we move to the question whether the State has standing to challenge a defendant's discriminatory use of peremptory challenges. In *Powers,* this Court held that a white criminal defendant has standing to raise the equal protection rights of black jurors wrongfully excluded from jury service * * *. As the representative of all its citizens, the State is the logical and proper party to assert the invasion of the constitutional rights of the excluded jurors in a criminal trial. Indeed, the Fourteenth Amendment forbids the State from denying persons within its jurisdiction the equal protection of the laws * * *. Accordingly, we hold that the State has standing to assert the excluded jurors' rights.

D

The final question is whether the interests served by *Batson* must give way to the rights of a criminal defendant. As a preliminary matter, it is important to recall that peremptory challenges are not constitutionally protected fundamental rights; rather, they are but one state-created means to the constitutional end of an impartial jury and a fair trial. This Court repeatedly has stated that the right to a peremptory challenge may be withheld altogether without impairing the constitutional guarantee of an impartial jury and a fair trial. [Citations] * * *.

We do not believe that this decision will undermine the contribution of the peremptory challenge to the administration of justice. Nonetheless, "if race stereotypes are the price for acceptance of a jury panel as fair," we reaffirm today that such a "price is too high to meet the standard of the Constitution." Edmonson, 500 U.S., at 630. Defense counsel is limited to "legitimate, lawful conduct." Nix v. Whiteside, 475 U.S. 157, 166 (1986) (defense counsel does not render ineffective assistance when he informs his client that he would disclose the client's perjury to the court and move to withdraw from representation). It is an affront to justice to argue that a fair trial includes the right to discriminate against a group of citizens based upon their race * * *.

We recognize, of course, that a defendant has the right to an impartial jury that can view him without racial animus, which so long has distorted our system of criminal justice. We have, accordingly, held that there should be a mechanism for removing those on the venire whom the defendant has specific reason to believe would be incapable of confronting and suppressing their racism. See Ham v. South Carolina, 409 U.S. 524 (1973); Rosales–Lopez v. United States, 451 U.S. 182, 189–190 (1981) (plurality opinion of WHITE, J.). Cf. Morgan v. Illinois, 504 U.S. 719 (1992) (exclusion of juror in capital trial is permissible upon showing that juror is incapable of considering sentences other than death).

But there is a distinction between exercising a peremptory challenge to discriminate invidiously against jurors on account of race and exercising a peremptory challenge to remove an individual juror who harbors racial prejudice. This Court firmly has rejected the view that assumptions of partiality based on race provide a legitimate basis for disqualifying a person as an impartial juror * * *. We therefore reaffirm today that the exercise of a peremptory challenge must not be based on either the race of the juror or the racial stereotypes held by the party.

IV

We hold that the Constitution prohibits a criminal defendant from engaging in purposeful discrimination on the ground of race in the exercise of peremptory challenges. Accordingly, if the State demonstrates a prima facie case of racial discrimination by the defendants, the defendants must articulate a racially neutral explanation for peremptory challenges. The judgment of the Supreme Court of Georgia is reversed and the case is remanded for further proceedings not inconsistent with this opinion. It is so ordered.

CHIEF JUSTICE REHNQUIST, concurring.

I was in dissent in Edmonson v. Leesville Concrete Co., 500 U.S. 614 (1991), and continue to believe that case to have been wrongly decided.

But so long as it remains the law, I believe that it controls the disposition of this case on the issue of "state action" under the Fourteenth Amendment. I therefore join the opinion of the Court.

Justice Thomas, concurring in the judgment.

As a matter of first impression, I think that I would have shared the view of the dissenting opinions: A criminal defendant's use of peremptory strikes cannot violate the Fourteenth Amendment because it does not involve state action. Yet, I agree with the Court and The Chief Justice that our decision last term in Edmonson v. Leesville Concrete Co., 500 U.S. 614, governs this case and requires the opposite conclusion. Because the respondents do not question *Edmonson,* I believe that we must accept its consequences. I therefore concur in the judgment reversing the Georgia Supreme Court.

I write separately to express my general dissatisfaction with our continuing attempts to use the Constitution to regulate peremptory challenges. In my view, by restricting a criminal defendant's use of such challenges, this case takes us further from the reasoning and the result of Strauder v. West Virginia, 100 U.S. 303 (1880). I doubt that this departure will produce favorable consequences. On the contrary, I am certain that black criminal defendants will rue the day that this court ventured down this road that inexorably will lead to the elimination of peremptory strikes.

In *Strauder,* as the Court notes, we invalidated a state law that prohibited blacks from serving on juries. In the course of the decision, we observed that the racial composition of a jury may affect the outcome of a criminal case. We explained: "It is well known that prejudices often exist against particular classes in the community, which sway the judgment of jurors, and which, therefore, operate in some cases to deny to persons of those classes the full enjoyment of that protection which others enjoy." Id., 100 U.S. at 309. We thus recognized, over a century ago, the precise point that Justice O'Connor makes today. Simply stated, securing representation of the defendant's race on the jury may help to overcome racial bias and provide the defendant with a better chance of having a fair trial.

I do not think that this basic premise of *Strauder* has become obsolete. The public, in general, continues to believe that the makeup of juries can matter in certain instances. Consider, for example, how the press reports criminal trials. Major newspapers regularly note the number of whites and blacks that sit on juries in important cases.[16] Their editors and readers apparently recognize that conscious and unconscious prejudice persists in our society and that it may influence some juries. Common experience and common sense confirm this understanding.

In *Batson,* however, this Court began to depart from *Strauder* by holding that, without some actual showing, suppositions about the

---

16. A computer search, for instance, reveals that the phrase "all white jury" has appeared over two hundred times in the past five years in the New York Times, Chicago Tribune, and Los Angeles Times.

possibility that jurors may harbor prejudice have no legitimacy. We said, in particular, that a prosecutor could not justify peremptory strikes "by stating merely that he challenged jurors of the defendant's race on the assumption—or his intuitive judgment—that they would be partial to the defendant because of their shared race." 476 U.S., at 97. As noted, however, our decision in *Strauder* rested on precisely such an "assumption" or "intuition." We reasonably surmised, without direct evidence in any particular case, that all-white juries might judge black defendants unfairly. Our departure from Strauder has two negative consequences. First, it produces a serious misordering of our priorities. In *Strauder,* we put the rights of defendants foremost. Today's decision, while protecting jurors, leaves defendants with less means of protecting themselves. Unless jurors actually admit prejudice during voir dire, defendants generally must allow them to sit and run the risk that racial animus will affect the verdict. Cf. Fed.Rule Evid. 606(b) (generally excluding juror testimony after trial to impeach the verdict). In effect, we have exalted the right of citizens to sit on juries over the rights of the criminal defendant, even though it is the defendant, not the jurors, who faces imprisonment or even death. At a minimum, I think that this inversion of priorities should give us pause.

Second, our departure from *Strauder* has taken us down a slope of inquiry that had no clear stopping point. Today, we decide only that white defendants may not strike black veniremen on the basis of race. Eventually, we will have to decide whether black defendants may strike white veniremen.[17] See, e.g., State v. Carr, 261 Ga. 845, 413 S.E.2d 192 (1992). Next will come the question whether defendants may exercise peremptories on the basis of sex. See, e.g., United States v. De Gross, 960 F.2d 1433 (C.A.9 1992). The consequences for defendants of our decision and of these future cases remain to be seen. But whatever the benefits were that this Court perceived in a criminal defendant's having members of his class on the jury, they have evaporated.

[JUSTICE O'CONNOR's dissenting opinion argued that criminal defendants and their lawyers are not government actors when they perform traditional trial functions, because in all significant respects the relationship between the government and a criminal defendant is antagonistic. She distinguished *Edmonson* on the ground that the government does not have a similar adversarial relationship with private litigants.]

JUSTICE SCALIA, dissenting.

I agree with the Court that its judgment follows logically from Edmonson v. Leesville Concrete Co., Inc., 500 U.S. 614 (1991). For the reasons given in the *Edmonson* dissents, however, I think that case was wrongly decided. Barely a year later, we witness its reduction to the terminally absurd: A criminal defendant, in the process of defending

---

17. The NAACP has submitted a brief arguing, in all sincerity, that "whether white defendants can use peremptory challenges to purge minority jurors presents quite different issues from whether a mi-nority defendant can strike majority group jurors." Although I suppose that this issue technically remains open, it is difficult to see how the result could be different if the defendants here were black.

himself against the state, is held to be acting on behalf of the state. Justice O'Connor demonstrates the sheer inanity of this proposition (in case the mere statement of it does not suffice), and the contrived nature of the Court's justifications. I see no need to add to her discussion, and differ from her views only in that I do not consider *Edmonson* distinguishable in principle—except in the principle that a bad decision should not be followed logically to its illogical conclusion.

Today's decision gives the lie once again to the belief that an activist, "evolutionary" constitutional jurisprudence always evolves in the direction of greater individual rights. In the interest of promoting the supposedly greater good of race relations in the society as a whole (make no mistake that that is what underlies all of this), we use the Constitution to destroy the ages-old right of criminal defendants to exercise peremptory challenges as they wish, to secure a jury that they consider fair. I dissent.

UNITED STATES v. HUEY

United States Court of Appeals for the Fifth Circuit, 1996.
76 F.3d 638.

Wiener, Circuit Judge:

* * *

The convictions underlying this appeal arise from the drug-related activities of Defendants–Appellants Arthur S. Huey, IV, a Caucasian, and Antonio A. Garcia, an Hispanic–American. Over a period of a year and one-half, Huey and Garcia sold marijuana to Marshall Howell. The instant case concerns Huey's and Garcia's last sale to Howell. On this particular occasion, Howell paid Huey two-thirds of the purchase price for the marijuana, but did not have the remaining funds due for the drugs. Howell became fed up with defendants' efforts to collect the balance due, so he anonymously contacted the Federal Bureau of Investigation (FBI) and offered information. Subsequently, he met with an FBI agent and explained the series of events. Howell agreed to cooperate with the FBI and was provided a tape recording device to record telephone conversations. Howell taped several telephone conversations in which Huey and Garcia made demands for the money owed them. These tapes were later used by the government as evidence against Huey and Garcia [at their jury trial on charges of conspiring to distribute marijuana, making threats or using violence in order to collect an extension of credit, and using a firearm in relation to a crime of violence].

At the close of the voir dire of the venire, counsel for Huey moved to exclude six potential jurors. As noted on the record by Huey's counsel, these six jurors constituted all of the African–Americans and persons with Hispanic surnames in the jury pool. Huey's counsel explained that the government would be playing tapes and offering transcripts that contained harsh and offensive racial epithets. [Prior to trial, Huey's counsel had filed a Motion in Limine seeking to exclude these tape recordings from evidence because of, inter alia, the derogatory and offensive references to race, religion, ethnicity, and gender they contain. The district court ruled that the tapes would be played.] Accordingly, argued counsel for Huey, no minority juror would be able to make an unbiased decision regarding Huey's guilt or innocence after hearing these tapes.

The district court refused the request to exclude the prospective jurors who were African–American or had Hispanic surnames, but did state that it would voir dire the individuals with respect to whether any of them would be influenced by the tapes' racial slurs. The district court then advised the prospective jurors that the tapes contained racial slurs of significant proportion involving African–Americans and Hispanic–Americans and inquired whether such language would affect their ability to hear the case in a fair and impartial manner. None of the prospective jurors responded that the content of these tapes would influence their decision-making process with respect to determining the defendants' guilt or innocence.

Following this voir dire by the district court, jury selection began. The defendants' ten peremptory challenges were allocated equally, five to Huey and five to Garcia. Counsel for Huey began the selection process by striking three African–Americans from the jury pool. Both the government and counsel for Garcia made *Batson* objections, asserting that these strikes were improperly made on the basis of race. [See Batson v. Kentucky, 476 U.S. 79 (1986)]. The district court stated that Huey's counsel could respond to the objections if he wished, but that the court did not find it necessary for him to do so; and the record reflects no response from Huey's counsel.

The selection process continued, and the government and Garcia's counsel were given opportunities to exercise some of their peremptory challenges. When it was Huey's turn again, counsel used his two remaining peremptory challenges to strike two more African–Americans. Again, counsel for Garcia made a *Batson* objection. After noting this objection, the district court without further comment allowed Huey's five peremptory challenges—all of which had been used to strike African–Americans—to stand, and the trial proceeded.

The following day, the jury returned with a verdict of guilty on all counts as to both Huey and Garcia. Huey and Garcia now appeal, both arguing inter alia that the jury selection process violated Batson v. Kentucky and its progeny.

Garcia insists that the district court committed reversible error by failing to protect the equal protection rights of the five African–American prospective jurors who were peremptorily challenged. We agree.

In Batson v. Kentucky, supra, the Supreme Court held that equal protection principles prohibit a prospective juror from being peremptorily challenged on the basis of race. The protection of *Batson* from the harms of racial discrimination in jury selection is not extended solely to individual defendants, but also to the excluded jurors. "An individual juror does not have a right to sit on any particular petit jury, but he or she does possess the right not to be excluded from one on account of race." [*Batson*, 476 U.S. 79, 87.] Thus, discrimination in the form of excluding a prospective juror because of the juror's race—even a race that is different from that of the defendant—constitutes a violation of the excluded juror's equal protection rights. Whether the discriminatory challenge is made by the prosecution or a defendant makes no difference.

Under Powers v. Ohio [499 U.S. 400 (1991)], a defendant has standing to raise the prospective juror's claim of an equal protection violation by way of a *Batson* challenge. Although the instant case is atypical, in that one defendant is challenging the peremptory strikes of a co-defendant, the rationale articulated in *Powers* for holding that a defendant has standing to raise this claim on behalf of prospective jurors is equally cogent and applicable in this situation. Therefore, we conclude that Garcia has standing to challenge the juror selection process based on his co-defendant's improper racial use of peremptory challenges.

A three-step inquiry is made to determine whether a party has used peremptory challenges in a way that violates the Equal Protection Clause. First, the opponent of the strike must make a prima facie showing that the proponent of the strike exercised it on the basis of a juror's cognizable racial background. The burden then shifts to the proponent of the strike to articulate a race-neutral explanation for removing the juror in question. Finally, the trial court must determine whether the opponent of the strike has proved purposeful discrimination.

Huey's counsel used all five of his peremptory challenges to strike African–Americans from the venire. These strikes followed on the heels of the court's rejection of Huey's counsel's request that all of the African–Americans and persons with Hispanic surnames be excluded for cause. This request was based not on any particular characteristics of the individual prospective jurors but on counsel's belief that all members of these groups were incapable of being impartial in the face of the racially offensive content of the tape recordings that the jury would hear. We have no doubt, nor does the government contest, that Garcia met his first-step burden of making a prima facie case that Huey's counsel exercised these challenges on the basis of race.

The burden then shifted to Huey's counsel to offer a race-neutral explanation for these strikes. Although the district court stated that it did not find it necessary for Huey's counsel to respond to the *Batson* objections, it did provide an opportunity for Huey's counsel to make such a response. Yet no explanation—race-neutral or otherwise—was proffered in response to these objections.

The government argues that it may be that Huey's attorney simply did not believe the prospective jurors' responses to the court's voir dire and that this is a sufficient race-neutral explanation. The record, however, in no way supports this argument. The only reason articulated in the record for why these jurors—as a class and not individually—should not serve is that they would be biased after hearing the derogatory language and racial slurs contained on the tapes. This reason was premised only on the race of these jurors; no mention was ever made of any nonracial characteristic of any individual juror. Thus, the explanation in the record for these strikes is nothing more than an assumption of partiality based on race and a form of racial stereotyping, both of which have been repeatedly condemned by the courts. * * *

As the district court failed to discharge its clear duty either to elicit a race-neutral explanation for the peremptory challenges or deny the use of those challenges, it committed reversible error in determining implicitly that the equal protection rights of these jurors had not been violated. Such error requires a new trial as to both Garcia and Huey.

We are not unaware that there is some irony in reversing Huey's conviction given that it was his counsel who made the discriminatory strikes. We are convinced, however, that this result is consistent with the teachings of *Batson* and its progeny. In addition to harming individual defendants and prospective jurors, racial discrimination in the selection of jurors impugns the integrity of the judicial system and the community at large. * * *

The discriminatory jury selection process of this trial offends the Constitution and calls into question the integrity of our judicial system. We conclude that only by repudiating all results from such a trial can public confidence in the integrity of this system be preserved, even when it means reversing the conviction of the very defendant who exercised the discriminatory challenges. Although we recognize that some might fear that this resolution could become a source of mischief in the hands of some co-defendants, we believe that not only is this resolution mandated by *Batson* and its progeny, but that such mischief can be avoided with relative ease by the exercise of diligent oversight and sound judgment on the part of trial judges, and through their proper application of the well-known three-step inquiry for ensuring race-neutral use of peremptory challenges. * * *

We REVERSE and REMAND for a new trial consistent with this opinion. [Concurring opinion omitted.]

UNITED STATES v. ANNIGONI

United States Court of Appeals for the Ninth Circuit, 1996.
96 F.3d 1132 (en banc).

HAWKINS, CIRCUIT JUDGE:

This case asks us to reconsider the longstanding principle that automatic reversal of a conviction is the proper remedy where a trial court erroneously deprives a criminal defendant of the right of peremptory challenge. * * * Annigoni's conviction arises out of a series of fraudulent financial transactions that secured him a $2.85 million loan on which he and his associates later defaulted. * * *

II. JURY SELECTION

The rehearing of this appeal arises out of the district court's denial of one of Annigoni's peremptory challenges during jury selection. In the proposed voir dire questions Annigoni submitted to the district court, he included the following question: "Have you, or has anyone close to you, ever joined a limited partnership?" When the district court posed that question to the jury panel, potential juror Jue Hom raised his hand and the following colloquy ensued:

THE COURT: Tell me a little bit about that experience.

MR. HOM: I have a joint partnership with the brokerage house—Merrill Lynch.

THE COURT: All right. Was that in oil and gas or real estate, or what type of investment was it?

MR. HOM: Mostly it's properties.

THE COURT: And your investment in that is strictly as a passive investor?

MR. HOM: Yes, sir.

The district court next asked the jury pool whether any of them had been involved in litigation. Two potential jurors raised their hands, including Mr. Hom, who engaged the court in the following colloquy:

MR. HOM: Yes, on that investment through Merrill Lynch, I don't know if they have any allegation going on at this time which I don't know anything about—in the partnership.

THE COURT: All right. Do you suspect that there was any litigation regarding that investment? Have you received any notices about it?

MR. HOM: Not one in the past three months or so.

THE COURT: All right. How about in the past year?

MR. HOM: I have taken no action on that.

When the defense attempted to exercise a peremptory challenge against Mr. Hom, the government objected pursuant to Batson v. Kentucky, 476 U.S. 79 (1986), which prohibits the use of peremptory challenges in a racially discriminatory manner. During a sidebar conference, the following colloquy occurred:

THE COURT: All right, what's your reasons?

MR. ANDRES (Counsel for Fauria): He has conservative investments. He has—I think he has various limited partnerships and investments. Because of his investment background, I think that it would be in my client's best interest to have him excused from this jury.

THE COURT: He's Asian.

MR. ANDRES: I understand that, and I think the Prosecution has kicked off number three, who was an Asian lady first strike out of the box. I don't think we've struck any Asian prospective jurors.

MS. SUN (Counsel for Annigoni): Your Honor, can I just add to that? I believe the exchange between the Court and Mr. Hom was as follows—he indicated he hadn't received any notices about legal action within the last three months. The Court then said, "Within the last year?", and I think his answer was, "I didn't take any action about those", which suggests to me that he did get more information and, perhaps, just wasn't willing to share. That made him, to me—that gave me some concern about the extent of those kinds of activities that he's engaged in.

MS. LUM (the Prosecutor): Your Honor, I don't—I didn't interpret his answer that way. I don't think he's been involved in any litigation and there have been numerous minorities that have been on the panel and that have been struck by the Defendants. The fact that he is involved in limited partnerships—and it was in a very, very tangential way—he barely knew what it involved. I don't think that's sufficient reason to challenge.

THE COURT: I'm not going to allow the exercise of the peremptory challenge because I think it's racially motivated.

As a result of the district court's refusal to allow Annigoni to use one of his peremptory strikes, Mr. Hom was seated as a member of the jury that convicted Annigoni of bank fraud.

On appeal, the panel * * * concluded that it was error to deny Annigoni a peremptory strike based on "the bare fact of a male juror of Asian heritage." Although it acknowledged that a defendant may not use a peremptory challenge to discriminate on the basis of race, the panel invoked the Supreme Court's recent decision in Purkett v. Elem, 115 S. Ct. 1769 (1995), which established that unless a discriminatory intent is inherent in the explanation a litigant offers to defend a peremptory challenge, "the reason offered will be deemed race neutral." Applying *Purkett*, the panel concluded that Annigoni's defense attorney had offered an entirely plausible explanation for the proposed peremptory challenge: she wished to remove Mr. Hom because of his investment in a limited partnership that had been involved in litigation. Although that explanation did not, in the panel's view, rise to the level of "cause for challenge[,]" nonetheless it satisfactorily rebutted the government's Batson challenge, since it was "distinct ... from a manifestation of racial prejudice."

We have long followed a rule requiring automatic reversal for errors of this kind. * * *

Under harmless-error review, it is the government that bears the burden of persuasion with respect to prejudice. It is far from certain that this error was harmless here. Juror Hom took his place on the jury, over appellant's wishes, because the district court erroneously refused to allow appellant to exercise a peremptory strike against him. To apply a harmless-error analysis omits an important consideration: the potential harm of having Juror Hom sit in judgment of the appellant. In this case, Annigoni's attorney sought to excuse potential juror Jue Hom because she was concerned that his investments in Merrill Lynch limited partnerships and his possible involvement in litigation concerning those investments suggested he would be more inclined to convict Annigoni for his involvement in an allegedly fraudulent limited partnership. Such concerns appear well-founded. In recent years, numerous investors have filed class-action lawsuits over sales of risky limited partnerships, and Merrill Lynch is one of several major brokerage houses defending such suits. That Juror Hom was not challengeable for cause is irrelevant, since the harm alleged was denial of a peremptory strike, not denial of a challenge for cause. Based on Juror Hom's investment experience, one could plausibly infer that he might bear hostility toward purveyors of limited partnerships who undertake fraudulent transactions. The attempted application of harmless-error analysis in this case demonstrates the futility of evaluating the harm that flows from the denial of a defendant's right of peremptory challenge. * * *

For the reasons discussed above, we hold that the denial of a peremptory challenge was erroneous, and the error requires reversal of the conviction.

LEAVY, CIRCUIT JUDGE, with whom KOZINSKI and KLEINFELD, CIRCUIT JUDGES, join, dissenting:

* * * [w]hether Mr. Annigoni likes it or not, he was a state actor when he attempted to challenge Mr. Hom. He was free to act with no reason, or for implausible or fantastic or even superstitious reasons, so long as he was not motivated by race or gender. The government also took state action when it opposed the challenge to Mr. Hom, and even had the right to assert Mr. Hom's constitutional right to be free from race discrimination. In ruling on the challenge, the court was required to subject the challenge to scrutiny, because the erroneous grant of a racially or gender motivated peremptory challenge is per se reversible. The majority, in keeping with pre-*Batson* cases, now holds that the erroneous denial of a peremptory challenge, even when the denial is an effort to avoid unconstitutional race discrimination, is also per se reversible. * * *

In my view, to subject every trial court allowance or disallowance of a peremptory challenge to automatic reversal places the trial judge in an untenable position and endangers the continued existence of the statutory right. The erroneous disallowance of a peremptory challenge only deprives a party of a statutory right, and should be reviewed for harmless error. * * *

I would affirm Annigoni's conviction, based on the unanimous verdict of twelve impartial jurors in this case of clear guilt.

KOZINSKI, CIRCUIT JUDGE, dissenting.

I agree with much in Judge Hawkins's opinion and wish very much I could join it. In particular, I could not have expressed more clearly or eloquently the value of the peremptory challenge as a tool for ensuring not only that jurors be impartial, but that they appear so to the parties whose fates and fortunes they determine. I join Judge Leavy's dissent because it reflects more accurately the Supreme Court's teaching, and because I fear that the majority's ruling will undermine the viability of peremptory challenges. I elaborate briefly on these points.

1. What makes this case difficult for me is that the error is not amenable to normal harmless error analysis, as we can never figure out what would have happened if one member of the jury had been struck and replaced by some other, unknown, person. Thus, we are forced to choose from two all-or-nothing rules: the error is always harmless or it is never harmless. There is no practical middle ground.

Given this choice, I believe the Supreme Court would conclude that this kind of error is always harmless. The right to a certain number of peremptory strikes—or to any at all—is not guaranteed by the Constitution; it's not embodied in the concept of due process. See Georgia v. McCollum, 505 U.S. 42, 57 (1992). Since the Court has allowed for the possibility of harmless error even when important constitutional rights are violated, I find it hard to believe the Court would now conclude that it's always reversible error to deny a defendant a mere statutory right.

In Ross v. Oklahoma, 487 U.S. 81 (1988), the Court traveled too far in the other direction. Ross was forced to use a peremptory on a juror who should have been stricken for cause. It's not accurate to say, as does the majority, that "the court in Ross ... never deprived [defendant] of the right of peremptory challenge." [The majority's discussion of *Ross* is omitted from this severely edited version.—ed.] In fact, Ross was entitled to nine not-for-cause strikes but got only eight; he wasted one peremptory undoing the trial court's error. This was the fulcrum of Justice Marshall's dissent: "In this case, everyone concedes that the trial judge could not arbitrarily take away one of the defendant's peremptory challenges. Yet, that is in effect exactly what happened here." Id. at 91–92 (Marshall, J., dissenting). By our majority's logic, this should have resulted in automatic reversal, but did not. In language that speaks to our case, the *Ross* majority answered Justice Marshall: "We reject the notion that the loss of a peremptory challenge constitutes a violation of the constitutional right to an impartial jury." Annigoni, like Ross, didn't get to use a challenge to which he was entitled. But "so long as the jury that sits is impartial,"the defendant suffers no reversible error.

2. I also fear that the majority's ruling will make peremptory strikes too dear a luxury. *Batson* challenges have become commonplace in our courtrooms; rare is the trial where one side or the other does not rattle a Batson sabre. Today's opinion turns every erroneous ruling—either wrongfully sustaining or wrongfully rejecting a *Batson* challenge—into sudden death. Retrials are expensive, especially where the prosecutor, the defense lawyer and the judge are all on the government's payroll. A rule that turns every peremptory challenge error into a retrial gives a strong incentive to federal and state legislators to cut down the number of peremptories—or eliminate them altogether.

Unlike the majority, I do not take much comfort from Purkett v. Elem, 514 U.S. 765 (1995), because I do not read *Purkett* as reducing *Batson* to a formality. Under *Purkett*, trial courts must still decide whether a proffered explanation is a subterfuge, and this can be a basis for appeal and reversal. We do not help the noble cause of peremptory challenges by making every error in this delicate process fatal.

Commentary on the Batson Rule

The *Batson* rule has led to an enormous amount of appellate litigation. The principal issues have been how to determine whether challenges are based on a racial or other impermissible ground, and whether to extend the rule outside the core area of race and gender.

1. *Implausible race-neutral justifications.* In Purkett v. Elem, 514 U.S. 765 (1995), the Supreme Court narrowed the application of *Batson* in practice. The prosecutor in a robbery case in a Missouri state court used peremptories to strike two black men from the jury panel. After the (black) defendant invoked *Batson*, the prosecutor explained that he had struck on juror because of his shoulder length unkempt hair, and the other because of his mustache and goatee. "These are the only two people on the jury * * * with facial hair. * * * And I don't like the way they looked. * * *" The prosecutor also justified one of the strikes because the juror had had a sawed-off shotgun pointed at him in a robbery, and might believe that "to have a robbery you have to have a gun, and there is no gun in this case." The trial judge accepted the challenges. The Missouri Supreme Court affirmed the conviction, finding that the prosecutor's explanation constituted a legitimate "hunch" and that "the circumstances failed to raise the necessary inference of racial discrimination."

The federal Eighth Circuit on *habeas* held that the prosecutor's reliance upon the jurors' appearance was so implausible that it should be regarded as a pretext. The Supreme Court reversed *per curiam*, explaining in its opinion the three steps for determination of a *Batson* claim.

> "Under our *Batson* jurisprudence, once the opponent of a peremptory challenge has made out a prima facie case of racial discrimination (step 1), the burden of production shifts to the proponent of the strike to come forward with a race-neutral explanation (step 2). If a race-neutral explanation is tendered, the trial court must then decide (step 3) whether the opponent of the strike has proved purposeful racial discrimination. The second step of this process does not demand an explanation that is persuasive, or even plausible. * * * It is not until the third step that the persuasiveness of the justification becomes relevant—the step in which the trial court determines whether the opponent of the strike has carried his burden of proving purposeful discrimination. At that stage, implausible or fantastic justifications may (and probably will) be found to be pretexts for purposeful discrimination. But to say that a trial judge may choose to disbelieve a silly or superstitious reason at step 3 is quite different from saying that a trial judge must terminate the inquiry at step 2 when the race-neutral reason is silly or superstitious. The latter violates the principle that the ultimate burden of persuasion regarding racial motivation rests with, and never shifts from, the opponent of the strike."

The Supreme Court went on to hold that the prosecutor's explanation cited a race-neutral ground (facial hair) and that therefore "the inquiry properly proceeded to step 3, where the state court found that the prosecutor was not motivated by discriminatory intent." The Court of Appeals did not give any "proper basis for overturning the state court's finding of no racial motive, a finding which turned primarily on an assessment of credibility."

2. *Pattern of discrimination.* In Commonwealth v. Curtiss, 40 Mass. App.Ct. 350, 664 N.E.2d 461 (1996), the defendant was a white man charged with sexually assaulting a mentally handicapped black woman. The only black potential juror on the venire was married to a social worker who worked with sexually abused children. Defense counsel used a peremptory to strike this juror. The trial judge refused to allow the challenge, explaining:

> "Let me put it this way. I think the circumstances of this case and the fact that two panels, two arrays, and two separate days produced but one black potential juror, eliminate the need for establishing a pattern and require me to make a judgment as to whether your challenge has a nonracial basis. The fact that this man's wife works for a department of the State that investigates, among other things, children victims and family victims, is insufficient to take it out of the area of a potential challenge based on racial grounds. Now, I want to be careful. I'm not accusing counsel of doing something improper in the sense that he should be admonished, but I am sensitive to the need for there to be a racial balance."

The Massachusetts Court of Appeals held that this denial of defendant's challenge constituted reversible error even in the absence of a showing of prejudice. The court conceded that Massachusetts cases have held that "the challenge of even a single prospective juror within a protected class can, in certain instances, constitute a prima facie showing of impropriety." However, the defendant gave a specific and plausible race-neutral basis for the challenge, and the trial court could not reject the challenge merely on the basis of its policy preference for a jury with some black representation.

The Massachusetts decision illustrates the tension between "race-blind decision-making" and "diversity" (or "affirmative action") which pervades the entire field of civil rights law. Persons connected with a particular profession—law enforcement, for example—are routinely struck from juries, often for cause. Suppose the only black juror on the venire was a police sergeant, or a prison guard. Should the defendant be barred from exercising a challenge on that basis due to sensitivity to "the need for there to be racial balance?"

3. *Gender and age.* In J.E.B. v. Alabama ex rel. T.B., 511 U.S. 127 (1994)(a civil paternity suit), the Supreme Court held that "gender, like race, is an unconstitutional proxy for juror competence and impartiality." In Riley v. Commonwealth, 21 Va.App. 330, 464 S.E.2d 508 (1995), defendant was charged with raping a young woman jogger. The prosecutor used peremptories to strike 5 female jurors aged 58 to 66. Challenged for a (step 2) gender-neutral justification, the prosecutor replied

> What I have done, by removing the people I struck, I have removed women who are most unlike the victim, in terms of age. I have left on those who share the victim's characteristics as much as I can, in terms of their sex and their age. There is not a discriminatory basis. This is a basis based on the facts that I have a rape victim who is, (A) She's a working female. I don't know what attitude other individuals who are

older may take; and (B) I have a young lady who is out jogging, and I don't know what attitude older females may take, but I do know they're most unlike the victim, as far as I can determine from the scant evidence we have, their age and their lifestyle. I would point out to the Court that I have in the past, my experience, based on trying cases, and I am a veteran of seventeen years of trying cases, from Henrico County Circuit Court, is that in rape cases, feedback I have gotten from the jury afterwards, is that many times the elderly female jurors have difficulty accepting certain aspects of the cases, and they have a difficult time considering the evidence and reaching a verdict of guilt.

The Virginia appellate court reversed the resulting conviction because

the prosecutor's explanation clearly references his intention to strike only women—albeit older women—from the jury panel. The fact that the Commonwealth used age to identify which women to strike does not overcome the constitutional infirmity. The Commonwealth exercised its strikes based on the assumption that the women would hold particular views because of their gender. Such attempts to stereotype in the jury selection process are impermissible. Lying "at the very heart of the jury system" is the factual assumption that "jury competence is an individual rather than a group or class matter." J.E.B., 511 U.S. at 146.

4. *Religion*. In Casarez v. State, 913 S.W.2d 468 (Tex.Crim.App. 1994)(on rehearing), defendant was charged and convicted of aggravated sexual assault. He objected on *Batson* grounds to the prosecutor's peremptory challenge of two black venirepersons. The prosecutor's "step 2" explanation was that he had struck the jurors not because they were black but because they were Pentecostal Christians:

It's been my experience from a number of jury panels, in more than 70 felony jury trials and 27 misdemeanor jury trials, that people from that religion often have a problem in passing judgment on other persons, and that they often believe that that is a matter for God and not for man. And that they have trouble not so much, Your Honor, although some do, with the guilt phase of the trial, but especially the punishment phase of the trial, and they are want to—want probation rather than to be responsible, in their eyes, for sending someone to the penitentiary, thereby judging them. [Texas law gives major authority over sentencing to the jury.]

The divided Texas Court of Criminal Appeals originally held that challenges based upon religion violate the *Batson* rule. The court then granted the state's petition for rehearing, and concluded that

The treatment of religious creed as an inappropriate basis for peremptory exclusion cannot rationally be distinguished from a similar treatment of persons on account of their Libertarian politics, their advocacy of communal living, or their membership in the Flat Earth Society.

Construing the *Batson* rule that broadly would mean the abolition of the peremptory challenge altogether—an end-point that the Supreme Court has rejected explicitly—and so the Texas court decided that religion-based peremptories are permissible. It explained that

Attributing to women or African Americans as a group any specific moral, political, or social belief is overly broad because membership in the group does not depend upon subscription to the belief. It is invidious because individual members who do not share the belief are made to suffer the attribution anyway. But in the case of religion, the attribution is not overly broad, and therefore not invidious, when the belief is an article of faith. Because all members of the group share the same faith by definition, it is not unjust to attribute beliefs characteristic of the faith to all of them.

The dissenting opinion countered that:

It is illogical to attribute every belief held by a religion to its members. * * * For example, the United Methodist Church publishes The Book of Resolutions. The book is a collection of all current and official policies, and other resolutions adopted by the General Conference of The United Methodist Church. These policies and resolutions are subject to change and many are changed every four years. The Book of Resolutions was first published in 1968, and currently contains official policy statements on approximately two hundred subjects including: reduction of water usage by United Methodists, care-giving teams for persons with AIDS, organ and tissue donation, sexual violence and pornography, access of Hispanics to higher education, African–American family life, available and affordable housing, communications access for persons who have hearing and sight impairments, Native–American ministries, confronting the drug crisis, domestic violence and sexual abuse, equal rights of women, eradication of racism, health for all by the year 2000, school busing, suicide, bilingual education, gambling, rights of workers, gun control, grand jury abuse, unemployment, police firearms policies, concern for El Salvador, the U.S. military presence in Bolivia and recognition of Cuba. These categories represent just a sampling of policies adopted by one religion.

It is absurd to assume, as the majority does, that all Methodists are even aware of the Methodist Church's positions on housing, busing or gun control. And the majority fails to explain how the Methodist Church's formal position on pornography is necessarily reflective of its members beliefs on the same issue. Is it reasonable to assume that every Methodist has a view on El Salvador, Bolivia or Cuba? If so, is it reasonable to assume that those Methodists who have such views necessarily hold the same views as other Methodists with respect to gambling and suicide? But this is precisely the majority's holding: "Because all members of the [religious] group share the same faith by definition, it is not unjust to attribute beliefs characteristic of the faith to all of them."

Comment: If lying "at the very heart of the jury system" is the factual assumption that "jury competence is an individual rather than a group or class matter," then how does this principle apply to (say) sexual preference, or being a subscriber to a partisan magazine like The American Spectator or The Nation?

Limiting the Peremptory Challenge

The very existence of the peremptory challenge reflects the tension between the concept of the jury as representative of the entire community, and the concept of the jury as "impartial." The community may contain many persons who are biased in one direction or another, and the biases may be unconscious or concealed. Even profoundly biased people are likely to think of themselves as fair-minded, and persons whose thought processes are completely irrational are for that very reason often unaware of the fact. Challenges for cause are inadequate to reach cases of unconscious or concealed bias, and the process of articulating such a challenge may be offensive and socially divisive. Thus, in the well chosen words of Professor Babcock [see p. 778, supra], "we have evolved in the peremptory challenge a system that allows the covert expression of what we dare not say but know is true more often than not."

When both sides are allowed a great number of peremptory challenges, however, and especially when the lawyers are assisted by investigators and social science researchers, the peremptory challenge may be used not so much to exclude a few objectionable jurors as to shape the entire panel in the direction of a particular set of biases. Is there any way to limit the peremptory challenge so as to minimize its potential for *increasing* bias?

Much could be done simply by limiting the number of peremptory challenges allowed. For example, California Penal Code § 1070 allows each side to have 26 peremptory challenges in the trial of an offense punishable by death or life imprisonment, and ten peremptory challenges in the case of lesser felonies. Additional challenges are granted where there are multiple defendants, and the trial judge may grant additional challenges as a matter of discretion. Rule 24 of the Federal Rules of Criminal Procedure grants each side 20 peremptory challenges in a capital case, and for lesser felonies the government has six peremptories and the defendant or defendants jointly have ten. The Court may grant additional challenges if there are multiple defendants. In the case of misdemeanors, each side has three peremptory challenges. The ability of one side or the other to exclude an entire racial group or opinion group is considerably limited when only two or three challenges are allowed, as opposed to two or three dozen.

Another method of reducing the opportunity for manipulation in the use of peremptories is the "blind strike" method described in the following paragraph from United States v. Mosely, 810 F.2d 93 (6th Cir.1987):

> "Following voir dire of 50 potential jurors, which was conducted by the court with the allowance of follow-up questions submitted by counsel, peremptory challenges were exercised by the 'blind strike' method. Pursuant to the blind strike method, each side exhausted all of its peremptory challenges simultaneously (Mosely had 12 peremptories), without the benefit of knowing which venirepersons the adversary chose to strike. All venirepersons that were stricken by one or both parties were excused. The remaining panel members in the first 16 boxes then constituted the jury of 12 and four alternates."

Defendant Mosely argued that this procedure "deprived him of the ability to assess the potential jury incrementally as each peremptory was exercised," and it therefore frustrated his ability to exercise his peremptories intelligently. The court rejected this contention, noting that the method of exercising peremptories is within the discretion of the trial court, and that many federal decisions had specifically upheld the blind strike method.

Most discussions of the peremptory challenge proceed from the point of view of a defense attorney, but the challenge is of equal or greater importance to the prosecutor. Even when the evidence is overwhelming, a single holdout juror may prevent a verdict, sometimes for reasons that have nothing to do with the merits of the case. A single juror can also prevent a verdict of acquittal, but in general a hung jury is regarded as a favorable verdict for the defense. In capital cases in particular, prospects for a death verdict are increased if persons who oppose capital punishment in principal are excluded by peremptory challenge or by a challenge for cause. [See *Lockhart v. McCree, infra* p. 839.] Prosecutors also consider it important to excuse jurors who may have developed hostility to the police as a result of some unfortunate experience. Such a juror might vote for a not guilty verdict to retaliate for the earlier incident rather than because of any genuine doubt about the evidence. On the other hand, this type of juror might also bring valuable experience to the jury deliberations. Should we regard this kind of challenge as a troubling constitutional problem, or as a realistic method of obtaining a jury which is likely to be able to reach a unanimous verdict?

TURNER v. MURRAY

Supreme Court of the United States, 1986.
476 U.S. 28, 106 S.Ct. 1683, 90 L.Ed.2d 27.

JUSTICE WHITE announced the judgment of the Court and delivered the opinion of the Court with respect to Parts I and III, and an opinion with respect to Parts II and IV, in which JUSTICE BLACKMUN, JUSTICE STEVENS, and JUSTICE O'CONNOR join.

Petitioner is a black man sentenced to death for the murder of a white storekeeper. The question presented is whether the trial judge committed reversible error at *voir dire* by refusing petitioner's request to question prospective jurors on racial prejudice.

I

On July 12, 1978, petitioner entered a jewelry store in Franklin, Virginia, armed with a sawed-off shotgun. He demanded that the proprietor, W. Jack Smith, Jr., put jewelry and money from the cash register into some jewelry bags. Smith complied with petitioner's demand, but triggered a silent alarm, alerting the Police Department. When Alan Bain, a police officer, arrived to inquire about the alarm, petitioner surprised him and forced him to surrender his revolver.

Having learned that Smith had triggered a silent alarm, petitioner became agitated. He fired toward the rear wall of the store and stated that if he saw or heard any more police officers, he was going to start killing those in the store. When a police siren sounded, petitioner walked to where Smith was stationed behind a counter and without warning shot him in the head with Bain's pistol, wounding Smith and causing him to slump incapacitated to the floor.

Officer Bain attempted to calm petitioner, promising to take him anywhere he wanted to go and asking him not to shoot again. Petitioner angrily replied that he was going to kill Smith for "snitching," and fired two pistol shots into Smith's chest, fatally wounding him. As petitioner turned away from shooting Smith, Bain was able to disarm him and place him under arrest.

A Southampton County, Virginia, grand jury indicted petitioner on charges of capital murder, use of a firearm in the commission of a murder, and possession of a sawed-off shotgun in the commission of a robbery. Petitioner requested and was granted a change of venue to Northampton County, Virginia, a rural county some 80 miles from the location of the murder.

Prior to the commencement of *voir dire*, petitioner's counsel submitted to the trial judge a list of proposed questions, including the following:

"The defendant, Willie Lloyd Turner, is a member of the Negro race. The victim, W. Jack Smith, Jr., was a white Caucasian. Will these facts prejudice you against Willie Lloyd Turner or affect your ability to render a fair and impartial verdict based solely on the evidence?"

The judge declined to ask this question, stating that it "has been ruled on by the Supreme Court." The judge did ask the venire, who were questioned in groups of five in petitioner's presence, whether any person was aware of any reason why he could not render a fair and impartial verdict, to which all answered "no." At the time the question was asked, the prospective jurors had no way of knowing that the murder victim was white.

The jury that was empaneled, which consisted of eight whites and four blacks, convicted petitioner on all of the charges against him. After a separate sentencing hearing on the capital charge, the jury recommended that petitioner be sentenced to death, a recommendation the trial judge accepted.

Petitioner appealed his death sentence to the Virginia Supreme Court. Among other points, he argued that the trial judge deprived him of his constitutional right to a fair and impartial jury by refusing to question prospective jurors on racial prejudice. The Virginia Supreme Court rejected this argument. Relying on our decision in *Ristaino v. Ross*, 424 U.S. 589 (1976), the court stated that a trial judge's refusal to ask prospective jurors about their racial attitudes, while perhaps not the wisest decision as a matter of policy, is not constitutionally objectionable in the absence of factors akin to those in *Ham v. South Carolina*, 409 U.S. 524 (1973).[18] The court held that "[t]he mere fact that a defendant

---

18. In *Ham*, a young black man known in his small South Carolina hometown as a civil rights activist was arrested and charged with possession of marihuana. We held that the trial judge committed reversible error in refusing to honor Ham's request to question prospective jurors on racial prejudice. In *Ristaino, supra*, we specified the factors which mandated an inquiry into racial prejudice in *Ham:*

is black and that a victim is white does not constitutionally mandate * * * an inquiry [into racial prejudice]."

[Turner's petition for Federal habeas corpus was denied by the District Court, and the Court of Appeals for the Fourth Circuit affirmed.]

II

The Fourth Circuit's opinion correctly states the analytical framework for evaluating petitioner's argument: "The broad inquiry in each case must be whether under all of the circumstances presented there was a constitutionally significant likelihood that, absent questioning about racial prejudice, the jurors would not be indifferent as they stand unsworn." The Fourth Circuit was correct, too, in holding that under *Ristaino* the mere fact that petitioner is black and his victim white does not constitute a "special circumstance" of constitutional proportions. What sets this case apart from *Ristaino*, however, is that in addition to petitioner's being accused of a crime against a white victim, the crime charged was a capital offense.

In a capital sentencing proceeding before a jury, the jury is called upon to make a highly subjective, unique, individualized judgment regarding the punishment that a particular person deserves. The Virginia statute under which petitioner was sentenced is instructive of the kinds of judgments a capital sentencing jury must make. First, in order to consider the death penalty, a Virginia jury must find either that the defendant is likely to commit future violent crimes or that his crime was "outrageously or wantonly vile, horrible or inhuman in that it involved torture, depravity of mind or an aggravated battery to the victim." Second, the jury must consider any mitigating evidence offered by the defendant. Mitigating evidence may include, but is not limited to, facts tending to show that the defendant acted under the influence of extreme emotional or mental disturbance, or that at the time of the crime the defendant's capacity "to appreciate the criminality of his conduct or to conform his conduct to the requirements of law was significantly impaired." Finally, even if the jury has found an aggravating factor, and irrespective of whether mitigating evidence has been offered, the jury has discretion not to recommend the death sentence, in which case it may not be imposed.

* * *

Because of the range of discretion entrusted to a jury in a capital sentencing hearing, there is a unique opportunity for racial prejudice to operate but remain undetected. On the facts of this case, a juror who

---

"Ham's defense was that he had been framed because of his civil rights activities. His prominence in the community as a civil rights activist, if not already known to veniremen, inevitably would have been revealed to the members of the jury in the course of his presentation of that defense. Racial issues therefore were inextricably bound up with the conduct of the trial. Further, Ham's reputation as a civil rights activist and the defense he interposed were likely to intensify any prejudice that individual members of the jury might harbor." 424 U.S., at 596–597.

believes that blacks are violence-prone or morally inferior might well be influenced by the belief in deciding whether petitioner's crime involved the aggravating factors specified under Virginia law. Such a juror might also be less favorably inclined toward petitioner's evidence of mental disturbance as a mitigating circumstance. More subtle, less consciously held racial attitudes could also influence a juror's decision in this case. Fear of blacks, which could easily be stirred up by the violent facts of petitioner's crime, might incline a juror to favor the death penalty.

III

We hold that a capital defendant accused of an interracial crime is entitled to have prospective jurors informed of the race of the victim and questioned on the issue of racial bias. The rule we propose is minimally intrusive; as in other cases involving "special circumstances," the trial judge retains discretion as to the form and number of questions on the subject, including the decision whether to question the venire individually or collectively. Also, a defendant cannot complain of a judge's failure to question the venire on racial prejudice unless the defendant has specifically requested such an inquiry.

IV

The inadequacy of *voir dire* in this case requires that petitioner's death sentence be vacated. It is not necessary, however, that he be retried on the issue of guilt. Our judgment in this case is that there was an unacceptable risk of racial prejudice infecting the *capital sentencing proceeding*. This judgment is based on a conjunction of three factors: the fact that the crime charged involved interracial violence, the broad discretion given the jury at the death-penalty hearing, and the special seriousness of the risk of improper sentencing in a capital case." At the guilt phase of petitioner's trial, the jury had no greater discretion than it would have had if the crime charged had been noncapital murder. Thus, with respect to the guilt phase of petitioner's trial, we find this case to be indistinguishable from *Ristaino*, to which we continue to adhere.

The judgment of the Court of Appeals is reversed, and the case is remanded for further proceedings consistent with this opinion.

It is so ordered.

THE CHIEF JUSTICE concurs in the judgment.

JUSTICE BRENNAN, concurring in part and dissenting in part. * * *

A trial to determine guilt or innocence is, at bottom, nothing more than the sum total of a countless number of small discretionary decisions made by each individual who sits in the jury box. The difference between conviction and acquittal turns on whether key testimony is believed or rejected; on whether an alibi sounds plausible or dubious; on whether a character witness appears trustworthy or unsavory; and on whether the jury concludes that the defendant had a motive, the inclination, or the means available to commit the crime charged. A racially biased juror sits with blurred vision and impaired sensibilities and is incapable of fairly making the myriad decisions that each juror is called upon to make in the course of a trial. To put it simply, he cannot judge because he has prejudged. This is equally true at the trial on guilt as at the hearing on sentencing. * * * I would reverse the conviction as well as the sentence in this case to ensure compliance with the constitutional guarantee of an impartial jury.

[The separate dissent of Justice Marshall is omitted. The dissent by Justice Powell, joined by Justice Rehnquist, is also omitted. Powell would have affirmed both the conviction and the sentence.]

LOCKHART v. McCREE

Supreme Court of the United States, 1986.
476 U.S. 162, 106 S.Ct. 1758, 90 L.Ed.2d 137.

JUSTICE REHNQUIST delivered the opinion of the Court.

In this case we address the question left open by our decision nearly 18 years ago in *Witherspoon v. Illinois*, 391 U.S. 510 (1968): Does the Constitution prohibit the removal for cause, prior to the guilt phase of a bifurcated capital trial, of prospective jurors whose opposition to the death penalty is so strong that it would prevent or substantially impair the performance of their duties as jurors at the sentencing phase of the trial? We hold that it does not. * * *

[McCree was charged in an Arkansas state court with a robbery murder, a capital crime.] The trial judge at *voir dire* removed for cause, over McCree's objections, those prospective jurors who stated that they could not under any circumstances vote for the imposition of the death penalty. Eight prospective jurors were excluded for this reason. The jury convicted McCree of capital felony murder, but rejected the State's request for the death penalty, instead setting McCree's punishment at life imprisonment without parole. McCree's conviction was affirmed on direct appeal.

McCree then filed a federal habeas corpus petition raising *inter alia* the claim that "death qualification," or the removal for cause of the so-called "*Witherspoon*-excludable" prospective jurors,[19] violated his right under the Sixth and Fourteenth Amendments to have his guilt or innocence determined by an impartial jury selected from a representative cross-section of the community. [The District Court granted the writ.]

The Eighth Circuit found "substantial evidentiary support" for the District Court's conclusion that the removal for cause of "*Witherspoon*-excludables" resulted in "conviction-prone" juries, and affirmed the grant of habeas relief on the ground that such removal for cause violated

---

19. In *Wainwright v. Witt*, 105 S.Ct. 844 (1985), this Court emphasized that the Constitution does not require "ritualistic adherence" to the "talismanic" standard for juror exclusion set forth in footnote 21 of the *Witherspoon* opinion. Rather, the proper constitutional standard is simply whether a prospective juror's views would " 'prevent or substantially impair the performance of his duties as a juror in accordance with his instructions and his oath.' " *Id.*, at 852. Thus, the term "*Witherspoon*-excludable" is something of a misnomer. Nevertheless, because the parties and the courts below have used the term "*Witherspoon*-excludables" to identify the group of prospective jurors at issue in this case, we will use the same term in this opinion.

McCree's constitutional right to a jury selected from a fair cross-section of the community. * * *

Before turning to the legal issues in the case, we are constrained to point out what we believe to be several serious flaws in the evidence upon which the courts below reached the conclusion that "death qualification" produces "conviction-prone" juries. McCree introduced into evidence some fifteen social science studies in support of his constitutional claims, but only six of the studies even purported to measure the potential effects on the guilt-innocence determination of the removal from the jury of "*Witherspoon*-excludables." Eight of the remaining nine studies dealt solely with generalized attitudes and beliefs about the death penalty and other aspects of the criminal justice system, and were thus, at best, only marginally relevant to the constitutionality of McCree's conviction. The fifteenth and final study dealt with the effects on prospective jurors of *voir dire* questioning about their attitudes toward the death penalty, an issue McCree raised in his brief to this Court but that counsel for McCree admitted at oral argument would not, standing alone, give rise to a constitutional violation.

Of the six studies introduced by McCree that at least purported to deal with the central issue in this case, namely, the potential effects on the determination of guilt or innocence of excluding "*Witherspoon*-excludables" from the jury, three were also before this Court when it decided *Witherspoon, supra*. There, this Court reviewed the studies and concluded:

> "The data adduced by the petitioner * * * are too tentative and fragmentary to establish that jurors not opposed to the death penalty tend to favor the prosecution in the determination of guilt. We simply cannot conclude, either on the basis of the record now before us or as a matter of judicial notice, that the exclusion of jurors opposed to capital punishment results in an unrepresentative jury on the issue of guilt or substantially increases the risk of conviction. In light of the presently available information, we are not prepared to announce a *per se* constitutional rule requiring the reversal of every conviction returned by a jury selected as this one was." *Id.*, at 517–518.

It goes almost without saying that if these studies were "too tentative and fragmentary" to make out a claim of constitutional error in 1968, the same studies, unchanged but for having aged some eighteen years, are still insufficient to make out such a claim in this case.

Nor do the three post-*Witherspoon* studies introduced by McCree on the "death qualification" issue provide substantial support for the "*per se* constitutional rule*" McCree asks this Court to adopt. All three of the "new" studies were based on the responses of individuals randomly selected from some segment of the population, but who were not actual jurors sworn under oath to apply the law to the facts of an actual case involving the fate of an actual capital defendant. We have serious doubts about the value of these studies in predicting the behavior of actual jurors. In addition, two of the three "new" studies did not even attempt to simulate the process of jury deliberation, and none of the "new" studies was able to predict to what extent, if any, the presence of one or more "*Witherspoon*-excludables" on a guilt-phase jury would have altered the outcome of the guilt determination.

Finally, and most importantly, only one of the six "death qualification" studies introduced by McCree even attempted to identify and account for the presence of so-called "nullifiers," or individuals who, because of their deep-seated opposition to the death penalty, would be unable to decide a capital defendant's guilt or innocence fairly and impartially. McCree concedes, as he must, that "nullifiers" may properly be excluded from the guilt-phase jury, and studies that fail to take into account the presence of such "nullifiers" thus are fatally flawed. Surely a *"per se* constitutional rule" as far-reaching as the one McCree proposes should not be based on the results of the lone study that avoids this fundamental flaw.

Having identified some of the more serious problems with McCree's studies, however, we will assume for purposes of this opinion that the studies are both methodologically valid and adequate to establish that "death qualification" in fact produces juries somewhat more "conviction-prone" than "non-death-qualified" juries. We hold, nonetheless, that the Constitution does not prohibit the States from "death qualifying" juries in capital cases.

The Eighth Circuit ruled that "death qualification" violated McCree's right under the Sixth Amendment, as applied to the States via incorporation through the Fourteenth Amendment, to a jury selected from a representative cross-section of the community. But we do not believe that the fair cross-section requirement can, or should, be applied as broadly as that court attempted to apply it. We have never invoked the fair cross-section principle to invalidate the use of either for-cause or peremptory challenges to prospective jurors, or to require petit juries, as opposed to jury panels or venires, to reflect the composition of the community at large. See *Duren v. Missouri*, 439 U.S. 357, 363–364 (1979); *Taylor v. Louisiana*, 419 U.S. 522, 538 (1975) ("[W]e impose no requirement that petit juries actually chosen must mirror the community and reflect the various distinctive groups in the population"); cf. *Batson v. Kentucky*, 106 S.Ct. 1712, 1716, n. 4 (1986) (expressly declining to address "fair cross-section" challenge to discriminatory use of peremptory challenges). The limited scope of the fair cross-section requirement is a direct and inevitable consequence of the practical impossibility of providing each criminal defendant with a truly "representative" petit jury, a basic truth that the Court of Appeals itself acknowledged for many years prior to its decision in the instant case.

We remain convinced that an extension of the fair cross-section requirement to petit juries would be unworkable and unsound, and we decline McCree's invitation to adopt such an extension.

But even if we were willing to extend the fair cross-section requirement to petit juries, we would still reject the Eighth Circuit's conclusion that "death qualification" violates that requirement. The essence of a "fair cross-section" claim is the systematic exclusion of a distinctive group in the community. In our view, groups defined solely in terms of shared attitudes that would prevent or substantially impair members of the group from performing one of their duties as jurors, such as the "*Witherspoon*-excludables" at issue here, are not "distinctive groups" for fair cross-section purposes.

We have never attempted to precisely define the term "distinctive group," and we do not undertake to do so today. But we think it obvious that the concept of "distinctiveness" must be linked to the purposes of the fair cross-section requirement. In *Taylor, supra*, we identified those purposes as (1) "guard[ing] against the exercise of arbitrary power" and ensuring that the "commonsense judgment of the community" will act as "a hedge against the overzealous or mistaken prosecutor," (2) preserving "public confidence in the fairness of the criminal justice system," and (3) implementing our belief that "sharing in the administration of justice is a phase of civic responsibility."

Our prior jury-representativeness cases, whether based on the fair cross-section component of the Sixth Amendment or the Equal Protection Clause of the Fourteenth Amendment, have involved such groups as blacks, see *Peters v. Kiff*, 407 U.S. 493 (1972) (plurality opinion) (equal protection), women, see *Duren, supra* (fair cross-section); *Taylor, supra* (same), and Mexican–Americans, see *Castaneda v. Partida*, [p. 758 of this book] (equal protection). The wholesale exclusion of these large groups from jury service clearly contravened all three of the aforementioned purposes of the fair cross-section requirement. Because these groups were excluded for reasons completely unrelated to the ability of members of the group to serve as jurors in a particular case, the exclusion raised at least the possibility that the composition of juries would be arbitrarily skewed in such a way as to deny criminal defendants the benefit of the common-sense judgment of the community. In addition, the exclusion from jury service of large groups of individuals not on the basis of their inability to serve as jurors, but on the basis of some immutable characteristic such as race, gender, or ethnic background, undeniably gave rise to an "appearance of unfairness." Finally, such exclusion improperly deprived members of these often historically disadvantaged groups of their right as citizens to serve on juries in criminal cases.

The group of "*Witherspoon*-excludables" involved in the case at bar differs significantly from the groups we have previously recognized as "distinctive." "Death qualification," unlike the wholesale exclusion of blacks, women, or Mexican–Americans from jury service, is carefully designed to serve the State's concededly legitimate interest in obtaining a single jury that can properly and impartially apply the law to the facts of the case at both the guilt and sentencing phases of a capital trial. There is very little danger, therefore, and McCree does not even argue, that "death qualification" was instituted as a means for the State to arbitrarily skew the composition of capital-case juries.

Furthermore, unlike blacks, women, and Mexican–Americans, "*Witherspoon*-excludables" are singled out for exclusion in capital cases on the basis of an attribute that is within the individual's control. It is important to remember that not all who oppose the death penalty are subject to removal for cause in capital cases; those who firmly believe that the death penalty is unjust may nevertheless serve as jurors in capital cases so long as they state clearly that they are willing to temporarily set aside their own beliefs in deference to the rule of law. Because the group of "*Witherspoon*-excludables" includes only those who cannot and will not conscientiously obey the law with respect to one of the issues in a capital case, "death qualification" hardly can be said to create an "appearance of unfairness."

Finally, the removal for cause of "*Witherspoon*-excludables" in capital cases does not prevent them from serving as jurors in other criminal cases, and thus leads to no substantial deprivation of their basic rights of citizenship. They are treated no differently than any juror who expresses the view that he would be unable to follow the law in a particular case.

In sum, "*Witherspoon*-excludables," or for that matter any other group defined solely in terms of shared attitudes that render members of the group unable to serve as jurors in a particular case, may be excluded from jury service without contravening any of the basic objectives of the fair cross-section requirement. * * *

McCree argues that, even if we reject the Eighth Circuit's fair cross-section holding, we should affirm the judgment below on the alternative ground, adopted by the District Court, that "death qualification" violated his constitutional right to an impartial jury.

We do not agree. McCree's "impartiality" argument apparently is based on the theory that, because all individual jurors are to some extent predisposed towards one result or another, a constitutionally impartial *jury* can be constructed only by "balancing" the various predispositions of the individual *jurors*. Thus, according to McCree, when the State "tips the scales" by excluding prospective jurors with a particular viewpoint, an impermissibly partial jury results. * * *

The view of jury impartiality urged upon us by McCree is both illogical and hopelessly impractical. McCree characterizes the jury that convicted him as "slanted" by the process of "death qualification." But McCree admits that exactly the same twelve individuals could have ended up on his jury through the "luck of the draw," without in any way violating the constitutional guarantee of impartiality. Even accepting McCree's position that we should focus on the *jury* rather than the individual *jurors*, it is hard for us to understand the logic of the argument that a given jury is unconstitutionally partial when it results from a State-ordained process, yet impartial when exactly the same jury results from mere chance. On a more practical level, if it were true that the Constitution required a certain mix of individual viewpoints on the jury, then trial judges would be required to undertake the Sisyphean task of "balancing" juries, making sure that each contains the proper number of Democrats and Republicans, young persons and old persons, white-collar executives and blue-collar laborers, and so on. Adopting McCree's concept of jury impartiality would also likely require the elimination of peremptory challenges, which are commonly used by both the State and the defendant to attempt to produce a jury favorable to the challenger.

McCree argues, however, that this Court's decisions in *Witherspoon, supra*, and *Adams v. Texas*, 448 U.S. 38 (1980), stand for the proposition that a State violates the Constitution whenever it "slants" the jury by excluding a group of individuals more likely than the population at large to favor the criminal defendant. We think McCree overlooks two fundamental differences between *Witherspoon* and *Adams* and the instant case, and therefore misconceives the import and scope of those two decisions.

First, the Court in *Witherspoon* viewed the Illinois system as having been deliberately slanted for the purpose of making the imposition of the death penalty more likely. * * *

Here, on the other hand, the removal for cause of "*Witherspoon*-excludables" serves the State's entirely proper interest in obtaining a single jury that could impartially decide all of the issues in McCree's case. * * *

Second, and more importantly, both *Witherspoon* and *Adams* dealt with the special context of capital sentencing, where the range of jury discretion necessarily gave rise to far greater concern over the possible effects of an "imbalanced" jury.

In the case at bar, by contrast, we deal not with capital sentencing, but with the jury's more traditional role of finding the facts and determining the guilt or innocence of a criminal defendant, where jury discretion is more channeled. We reject McCree's suggestion that *Witherspoon* and *Adams* have broad applicability outside the special context of capital sentencing, and conclude that those two decisions do not support the result reached by the Eighth Circuit here.

In our view, it is simply not possible to define jury impartiality, for constitutional purposes, by reference to some hypothetical mix of individual viewpoints. Prospective jurors come from many different backgrounds, and have many different attitudes and predispositions. But the Constitution presupposes that a jury selected from a fair cross-section of the community is impartial, regardless of the mix of individual viewpoints actually represented on the jury, so long as the jurors can conscientiously and properly carry out their sworn duty to apply the law to the facts of the particular case. We hold that McCree's jury satisfied both aspects of this constitutional standard. The judgment of the Court of Appeals is therefore Reversed.

JUSTICE BLACKMUN concurs in the result.

JUSTICE MARSHALL, with whom JUSTICE BRENNAN and JUSTICE STEVENS join, dissenting. * * *

With a glib nonchalance ill-suited to the gravity of the issue presented and the power of respondent's claims, the Court upholds a practice that allows the State a special advantage in those prosecutions where the charges are the most serious and the possible punishments, the most severe. The State's mere announcement that it intends to seek the death penalty if the defendant is found guilty of a capital offense will, under today's decision, give the prosecution license to empanel a jury especially likely to return that very verdict. Because I believe that such a blatant disregard for the rights of a capital defendant offends logic, fairness, and the Constitution, I dissent. * * *

In the wake of *Witherspoon*, a number of researchers set out to supplement the data that the Court had found inadequate in that case. The results of these studies were exhaustively analyzed by the District Court in this case, see *Grigsby v. Mabry (Grigsby II)*, 569 F.Supp. 1273, 1291–1308 (E.D.Ark.1983), and can be only briefly summarized here. The data strongly suggest that death qualification excludes a significantly large subset—at least 11% to 17%—of potential jurors who could be impartial during the guilt phase of trial. Among the members of this excludable class are a disproportionate number of blacks and women.

The perspectives on the criminal justice system of jurors who survive death qualification are systematically different from those of the excluded jurors. Death-qualified jurors are, for example, more likely to believe that a defendant's failure to testify is indicative of his guilt, more hostile to the insanity defense, more mistrustful of defense attorneys, and less concerned about the danger of erroneous convictions. This pro-prosecution bias is reflected in the greater readiness of death-qualified jurors to convict or to convict on more serious charges. And, finally, the very process of death qualification—which focuses attention on the death penalty before the trial has even begun—has been found to predispose the jurors that survive it to believe that the defendant is guilty.

The evidence thus confirms, and is itself corroborated by, the more intuitive judgments of scholars and of so many of the participants in capital trials—judges, defense attorneys, and prosecutors.

Respondent's case would of course be even stronger were he able to produce data showing the prejudicial effects of death qualification upon actual trials. Yet until a State permits two separate juries to deliberate on the same capital case and return simultaneous verdicts, defendants claiming prejudice from death qualification should not be denied recourse to the only available means of proving their case, recreations of the *voir dire* and trial processes.

The evidence adduced by respondent is quite different from the "tentative and fragmentary" presentation that failed to move this Court in *Witherspoon*. Moreover, in contrast to *Witherspoon*, the record in this case shows respondent's case to have been subjected to the traditional testing mechanisms of the adversary process. At trial, respondent presented three expert witnesses and one lay witness in his case in chief, and two additional lay witnesses in his rebuttal. Testimony by these witnesses permitted the District Court, and allows this Court, better to understand the methodologies used here and their limitations. Further testing of respondent's empirical case came at the hands of the State's own expert witnesses. Yet even after considering the evidence adduced by the State, the Court of Appeals properly noted: "there are no studies which contradict the studies submitted [by respondent]; in other words, all of the documented studies support the district court's findings." * * *

Because it takes only one juror unwilling to find that the prosecution has met its burden for a trial to end in either a mistrial or a compromise verdict, it can be confidently asserted that, over time, some persons accused to capital crimes will be convicted of offenses—and to a higher degree—who would not be so convicted had all persons able to assess their guilt impartially been permitted to sit on their juries.

* * *

As the *Witherspoon* Court recognized, "the State's interest in submitting the penalty issue to a jury capable of imposing capital punishment" may be accommodated without infringing a capital defendant's interest in a fair determination of his guilt if the State uses "one jury to decide guilt and another to fix punishment." Any exclusion of death-penalty opponents, the Court reasoned, could await the penalty phase of a trial. The question here is thus whether the State has *other* interests that require the use of a single jury and demand the subordination of a capital defendant's Sixth and Fourteenth Amendment rights.

The only two reasons that the Court invokes to justify the State's use of a single jury are efficient trial management and concern that a defendant at his sentencing proceedings may be able to profit from "residual doubts" troubling jurors who have sat through the guilt phase of his trial. The first of these purported justifications is merely unconvincing. The second is offensive. * * *

In a system using separate juries for guilt and penalty phases, time and resources would be saved every time a capital case did not require a penalty phase. The *voir dire* needed to identify nullifiers before the guilt phase is less extensive than the questioning that under the current scheme conducted before *every* capital trial. The State could, of course, choose to empanel a death-qualified jury at the start of every trial, to be used only if a penalty stage is required. However, if it opted for the cheaper alternative of empanelling a death-qualified jury only in the event that a defendant were convicted of capital charges, the State frequently would be able to avoid retrying the entire guilt phase for the benefit of the penalty jury. Stipulated summaries of prior evidence might, for example, save considerable time. Thus, it cannot fairly be said that the costs of accommodating a defendant's constitutional rights under these circumstances are prohibitive, or even significant.

Even less convincing is the Court's concern that a defendant be able to appeal at sentencing to the "residual doubts" of the jurors who found him guilty. Any suggestion that the current system of death qualification may be in the defendant's best interests, seems specious unless the state is willing to grant the defendant the option to waive this paternalistic protection in exchange for better odds against conviction. Furthermore, this case will stand as one of the few times in which any legitimacy has been given to the power of a convicted capital defendant facing the possibility of a death sentence to argue as a mitigating factor the chance that he might be innocent. Where a defendant's sentence but not his conviction has been set aside on appeal, States have routinely empanelled juries whose only duty is to assess punishment, thereby depriving defendants of the chance to profit from the "residual doubts" that jurors who had already sat through a guilt phase might bring to the sentencing proceeding. * * *

But most importantly, it ill-behooves the majority to allude to a defendant's power to appeal to "residual doubts" at his sentencing when this Court has consistently refused to grant certiorari in state cases holding that these doubts cannot properly be considered during capital sentencing proceedings. Any suggestion that capital defendants will benefit from a single jury thus is more than disingenuous. It is cruel.

On occasion, this Court has declared what I believe should be obvious—that when a State seeks to convict a defendant of the most serious and severely punished offenses in its criminal code, any procedure that diminishes]the reliability of the guilt determination must be struck down. But in spite of such declarations, I cannot help thinking that respondent here would have stood a far better chance of prevailing on his constitutional claims had he not been challenging a procedure peculiar to the administration of the death penalty. For in no other context would a majority of this Court refuse to find any constitutional violation in a state practice that systematically operates to render juries more likely to convict, and to convict on the more serious charges. I dissent.

* * *

C. THE PROSECUTION'S BURDEN OF PROOF

MULLANEY v. WILBUR

Supreme Court of the United States, 1975.
421 U.S. 684, 95 S.Ct. 1881, 44 L.Ed.2d 508.

MR. JUSTICE POWELL delivered the opinion of the Court.

The State of Maine requires a defendant charged with murder to prove that he acted "in the heat of passion on sudden provocation" in order to reduce the homicide to manslaughter. We must decide whether this rule comports with the due process requirement, as defined in In re

Winship, 397 U.S. 358, 364 (1970),[a] that the prosecution prove beyond a reasonable doubt every fact necessary to constitute the crime charged.

In June 1966 a jury found respondent Stillman E. Wilbur, Jr., guilty of murder. The case against him rested on his own pretrial statement and on circumstantial evidence showing that he fatally assaulted Claude Hebert in the latter's hotel room. Respondent's statement, introduced by the prosecution, claimed that he had attacked Hebert in a frenzy provoked by Hebert's homosexual advance. The defense offered no evidence, but argued that the homicide was not unlawful since respondent lacked criminal intent. Alternatively, Wilbur's counsel asserted that at most the homicide was manslaughter rather than murder, since it occurred in the heat of passion provoked by the homosexual assault.

The trial court instructed the jury that Maine law recognizes only two kinds of homicide, murder and manslaughter, and that these offenses are not subdivided into different degrees. The common elements of both are that the homicide be unlawful—i.e., neither justifiable nor excusable—and that it be intentional. The prosecution is required to prove these elements by proof beyond a reasonable doubt, and only if they are so proved is the jury to consider the distinction between murder and manslaughter.

In view of the evidence the trial court drew particular attention to the difference between murder and manslaughter. After reading the statutory definitions of both offenses,[21] the court charged that "malice aforethought is an essential and indispensable element of the crime of murder," without which the homicide would be manslaughter. The jury was further instructed, however, that if the prosecution established that the homicide was both intentional and unlawful, malice aforethought was to be conclusively implied unless the defendant proved by a fair preponderance of the evidence that he acted in the heat of passion on sudden provocation. The court emphasized that "malice aforethought

a. The petitioner in the *Winship* case was a juvenile who was charged with larceny in the New York Family Court. The judge acknowledged that the proof might not establish guilt beyond a reasonable doubt, but concluded that in juvenile cases guilt need only be proved by a preponderance of the evidence. Applying that standard, he found the defendant to be a juvenile delinquent and committed him to a reformatory. The Supreme Court reversed the judgment, holding that the Due Process Clause of the Fourteenth Amendment requires proof beyond a reasonable doubt in criminal cases, and that this standard is applicable to juvenile criminal proceedings. In its opinion, the Supreme Court stated that "Lest there remain any doubt about the constitutional stature of the reasonable-doubt standard, we explicitly hold that the Due Process Clause protects the accused against conviction except upon proof be-

yond a reasonable doubt of *every fact necessary to constitute the crime* with which he is charged." 397 U.S. at 364.—ed. [Emphasis added]

21. The Maine murder statute, Me.Rev. Stat., Tit. 17, § 2651, provides:

"Whoever unlawfully kills a human being with malice aforethought, either express or implied, is guilty of murder and shall be punished by imprisonment for life."

The manslaughter statute, Tit. 17, § 2551, in relevant part provides:

"Whoever unlawfully kills a human being in the heat of passion, on sudden provocation, without express or implied malice aforethought * * * shall be punished by a fine of not more than $1,000 or by imprisonment for not more than 20 years * * *."

and heat of passion on sudden provocation are inconsistent things;" thus, by proving the latter the defendant would negate the former and reduce the homicide from murder to manslaughter. The court then concluded its charge with elaborate definitions of "heat of passion" and "sudden provocation."

After retiring to consider its verdict, the jury twice returned to request further instruction. It first sought reinstruction on the doctrine of implied malice aforethought, and later on the definition of "heat of passion." Shortly after the second reinstruction, the jury found respondent guilty of murder.

Respondent appealed to the Maine Supreme Judicial Court, arguing that he had been denied due process because he was required to negate the element of malice aforethought by proving that he had acted in the heat of passion on sudden provocation. He claimed that under Maine law malice aforethought was an essential element of the crime of murder—indeed that it was the sole element distinguishing murder from manslaughter. Respondent contended, therefore, that this Court's decision in *Winship* requires the prosecution to prove the existence of that element beyond a reasonable doubt.

The Maine Supreme Judicial Court rejected this contention, holding that in Maine murder and manslaughter are not distinct crimes but rather different degrees of the single generic offense of felonious homicide. State v. Wilbur, 278 A.2d 139 (1971). The court further stated that for more than a century it repeatedly had held that the prosecution could rest on a presumption of implied malice aforethought and require the defendant to prove that he had acted in the heat of passion on sudden provocation in order to reduce murder to manslaughter. With respect to *Winship*, which was decided after respondent's trial, the court noted that it did not anticipate the application of the *Winship* principle to a "reductive factor" such as the heat of passion on sudden provocation.

Respondent next successfully petitioned for a writ of habeas corpus in federal district court. * * * [On appeal from the district court's decision that the conviction was unconstitutional,] the Court of Appeals held that the principles enunciated in *Winship* control, and that to establish murder the prosecution must prove beyond a reasonable doubt that the defendant did not act in the heat of passion on sudden provocation.

Because of the importance of the issues presented, we again granted certiorari. We now affirm. * * *

Petitioners, the warden of the Maine Prison and the State of Maine, argue that *Winship* should not be extended to the present case. They note that as a formal matter the absence of the heat of passion on sudden provocation is not a "fact necessary to constitute the *crime*" of felonious homicide in Maine. This distinction is relevant, according to petitioners, because in *Winship* the facts at issue were essential to establish criminality in the first instance whereas the fact in question here does not come into play until the jury already has determined that the defendant is guilty and may be punished at least for manslaughter. In this situation, petitioners maintain, the defendant's critical interests in liberty and reputation are no longer of paramount concern since, irrespective of the presence or absence of the heat of passion on sudden provocation, he is likely to lose his liberty and certain to be stigmatized. In short, petitioners would limit *Winship* to those facts which, if not proved, would wholly exonerate the defendant.

This analysis fails to recognize that the criminal law of Maine, like that of other jurisdictions, is concerned not only with guilt or innocence in the abstract but also with the degree of criminal culpability. Maine has chosen to distinguish those who kill in the heat of passion from those who kill in the absence of this factor. Because the former are less "blameworth[y]," State v. Lafferty, 309 A.2d, at 671, 673 (concurring opinion), they are subject to substantially less severe penalties. By drawing this distinction, while refusing to require the prosecution to establish beyond a reasonable doubt the fact upon which it turns, Maine denigrates the interests found critical in *Winship*.

The safeguards of due process are not rendered unavailing simply because a determination may already have been reached that would stigmatize the defendant and that might lead to a significant impairment of personal liberty. The fact remains that the consequences resulting from a verdict of murder, as compared with a verdict of manslaughter, differ significantly. Indeed, when viewed in terms of the potential difference in restrictions of personal liberty attendant to each conviction, the distinction established by Maine between murder and manslaughter may be of greater importance than the difference between guilt or innocence for many lesser crimes.

Moreover, if *Winship* were limited to those facts that constitute a crime as defined by state law, a State could undermine many of the interests that decision sought to protect without effecting any substantive change in its law. It would only be necessary to redefine the elements that comprise different crimes, characterizing them as factors that bear solely on the extent of punishment. An extreme example of this approach can be fashioned from the law challenged in this case. Maine divides the single generic offense of felonious homicide into three distinct punishment categories—murder, voluntary manslaughter, and involuntary manslaughter. Only the first two of these categories require that the homicidal act either be intentional or the result of criminally reckless conduct. But under Maine law these facts of intent are not general elements of the crime of felonious homicide. Instead, they bear only on the appropriate punishment category. Thus, if petitioners' argument were accepted, Maine could impose a life sentence for any felonious homicide—even those that traditionally might be considered involuntary manslaughter—unless the *defendant* was able to prove that his act was neither intentional nor criminally reckless.[22]

22. Many States impose different statutory sentences on different degrees of as-   sault. If *Winship* were limited to a State's definition of the elements of a crime, these

Winship is concerned with substance rather than this kind of formalism. * * *

It has been suggested that because of the difficulties in negating an argument that the homicide was committed in the heat of passion the burden of proving this fact should rest on the defendant. No doubt this is often a heavy burden for the prosecution to satisfy. The same may be said of the requirement of proof beyond a reasonable doubt of many controverted facts in a criminal trial. But this is the traditional burden which our system of criminal justice deems essential.

Indeed, the Maine Supreme Judicial Court itself acknowledged that most States require the prosecution to prove the absence of passion beyond a reasonable doubt. State v. Wilbur, 278 A.2d, at 146.[23] Moreover, the difficulty of meeting such an exacting burden is mitigated in Maine where the fact at issue is largely an "objective, rather than a subjective, behavioral criterion." State v. Rollins, 295 A.2d, at 920. In this respect, proving that the defendant did not act in the heat of passion on sudden provocation is similar to proving any other element of intent; it may be established by adducing evidence of the factual circumstances surrounding the commission of the homicide. And although intent is typically considered a fact peculiarly within the knowledge of the defendant, this does not, as the Court has long recognized, justify shifting the burden to him. See Tot v. United States, 319 U.S. 463, 469 (1943); Leary v. United States, 395 U.S. 6, 45 (1969).

Nor is the requirement of proving a negative unique in our system of criminal jurisprudence. Maine itself requires the prosecution to prove the absence of self-defense beyond a reasonable doubt. See State v. Millett, 273 A.2d 504 (Me.1971).[24] Satisfying this burden imposes an obligation that, in all practical effect, is identical to the burden involved in negating the heat of passion on sudden provocation. Thus, we discern no unique hardship on the prosecution that would justify requiring the defendant to carry the burden of proving a fact so critical to criminal culpability. * * *

Affirmed.

MR. JUSTICE REHNQUIST, with whom THE CHIEF JUSTICE joins, concurring.

* * *

States could define all assaults as a single offense and then require the defendant to disprove the elements of aggravation—e.g., intent to kill or intent to rob. But see State v. Ferris, 249 A.2d 523 (Me.1969) (prosecution must prove elements of aggravation in criminal assault case by proof beyond a reasonable doubt).

23. Many States do require the defendant to show that there is "some evidence" indicating that he acted in the heat of passion before requiring the prosecution to negate this element by proving the absence of passion beyond a reasonable doubt. Nothing in this opinion is intended to affect that requirement.

24. In *Millett* the Maine Supreme Judicial Court adopted the "majority rule" regarding proof of self-defense. The burden of producing "some evidence" on this issue rests with the defendant, but the ultimate burden of persuasion by proof beyond a reasonable doubt remains on the prosecution.

I agree with the Court that In re Winship does require that the prosecution prove beyond a reasonable doubt every element which constitutes the crime charged against a defendant. I see no inconsistency between that holding and the holding of Leland v. Oregon, 343 U.S. 790 (1952). In the latter case this Court held that there was no constitutional requirement that the State shoulder the burden of proving the sanity of the defendant.

The Court noted in *Leland* that the issue of insanity as a defense to a criminal charge was considered by the jury only after it had found that all elements of the offense, including the *mens rea* if any required by state law, had been proven beyond a reasonable doubt. Although as the state court's instructions in *Leland* recognized, evidence relevant to insanity as defined by state law may also be relevant to whether the required *mens rea* was present, the existence or nonexistence of legal insanity bears no necessary relationship to the existence or nonexistence of the required mental elements of the crime. For this reason, Oregon's placement of the burden of proof on insanity on Leland, unlike Maine's redefinition of homicide in the instant case, did not effect an unconstitutional shift in the State's traditional burden of proof beyond a reasonable doubt of all necessary elements of the offense. Both the Court's opinion and the concurring opinion of Mr. Justice Harlan in In re Winship, supra, stress the importance of proof beyond a reasonable doubt in a criminal case as "bottomed on a fundamental value determination of our society that it is far worse to convict an innocent man than to let a guilty man go free." Having once met that rigorous burden of proof that, for example, in a case such as this, the defendant not only killed a fellow human being, but did it with malice aforethought, the State could quite consistently with such a constitutional principle conclude that a defendant who sought to establish the defense of insanity, and thereby escape any punishment whatever for a heinous crime, should bear the laboring oar on such an issue.

McMILLAN v. PENNSYLVANIA

Supreme Court of the United States, 1986.
477 U.S. 79, 106 S.Ct. 2411, 91 L.Ed.2d 67.

Justice Rehnquist delivered the opinion of the Court.

We granted certiorari to consider the constitutionality, under the Due Process Clause of the Fourteenth Amendment and the jury trial guarantee of the Sixth Amendment, of Pennsylvania's Mandatory Minimum Sentencing Act, 42 Pa.Const.Stat. § 9712 (1982) (the Act).

I

The Act was adopted in 1982. It provides that anyone convicted of certain enumerated felonies is subject to a mandatory minimum sentence of five years' imprisonment if the sentencing judge finds, by a preponderance of the evidence, that the person "visibly possessed a firearm" during the commission of the offense. At the sentencing hearing, the judge is directed to consider the evidence introduced at trial and any additional evidence offered by either the defendant or the Commonwealth. The Act operates to divest the judge of discretion to impose any sentence of less than five years for the underlying felony; it does not authorize a sentence in excess of that otherwise allowed for that offense.

Each petitioner was convicted of, among other things, one of § 9712's enumerated felonies. Petitioner McMillan, who shot his victim in the right buttock after an argument over a debt, was convicted by a jury of aggravated assault. Petitioner Peterson shot and killed her husband and, following a bench trial, was convicted of voluntary manslaughter. Petitioner Dennison shot and seriously wounded an acquaintance and was convicted of aggravated assault after a bench trial. Petitioner Smalls robbed a seafood store at gunpoint; following a bench trial he was convicted of robbery. In each case the Commonwealth gave notice that at sentencing it would seek to proceed under the Act. No § 9712 hearing was held, however, because each of the sentencing judges before whom petitioners appeared found the Act unconstitutional; each imposed a lesser sentence than that required by the Act.

The Commonwealth appealed all four cases to the Supreme Court of Pennsylvania. That Court consolidated the appeals and unanimously concluded that the Act is consistent with due process. * * *

II

Petitioners argue that under the Due Process Clause as interpreted in *Winship* and *Mullaney*, if a State wants to punish visible possession of a firearm it must undertake the burden of proving that fact beyond a reasonable doubt. We disagree. *Winship* held that "the Due Process Clause protects the accused against conviction except upon proof beyond a reasonable doubt of every fact necessary to constitute the crime with which he is charged." In *Mullaney v. Wilbur*, we held that the Due Process Clause "requires the prosecution to prove beyond a reasonable doubt the absence of the heat of passion on sudden provocation when the issue is properly presented in a homicide case." But in *Patterson v. New York*, 432 U.S. 197 (1977), we rejected the claim that whenever a State links the "severity of punishment" to "the presence or absence of an identified fact" the State must prove that fact beyond a reasonable doubt. In particular, we upheld against a due process challenge New York's law placing on defendants charged with murder the burden of proving the affirmative defense of extreme emotional disturbance.

Patterson stressed that in determining what facts must be proved beyond a reasonable doubt the state legislature's definition of the elements of the offense is usually dispositive: * * *

We believe that the present case is controlled by *Patterson*, our most recent pronouncement on this subject, rather than by *Mullaney*. As the Supreme Court of Pennsylvania observed, the Pennsylvania legislature has expressly provided that visible possession of a firearm is not an element of the crimes enumerated in the mandatory sentencing statute, § 9712(b), but instead is a sentencing factor that comes into play only after the defendant has been found guilty of one of those crimes beyond a reasonable doubt. Indeed, the elements of the enumerated offenses, like the maximum permissible penalties for those offenses, were established long before the Mandatory Minimum Sentencing Act was passed. While visible possession might well have been included as an element of the enumerated offenses, Pennsylvania chose not to redefine those offenses in order to so include it, and *Patterson* teaches that we should hesitate to conclude that due process bars the State from pursuing its chosen course in the area of defining crimes and prescribing penalties.

As *Patterson* recognized, of course, there are constitutional limits to the State's power in this regard; in certain limited circumstances *Winship*'s reasonable doubt requirement applies to facts not formally identified as elements of the offense charged. Petitioners argue that Pennsylvania has gone beyond those limits and that its formal provision that visible possession is not an element of the crime is therefore of no effect. We do not think so. While we have never attempted to define precisely the constitutional limits noted in *Patterson, i.e.*, the extent to which due process forbids the reallocation or reduction of burdens of proof in criminal cases, and do not do so today, we are persuaded by several factors that Pennsylvania's Mandatory Minimum Sentencing Act does not exceed those limits. * * *

The Court in *Mullaney* observed, with respect to the main criminal statute invalidated in that case, that once the State proved the elements which Maine required it to prove beyond a reasonable doubt the defendant faced "a differential in sentencing ranging from a nominal fine to a mandatory life sentence." In the present case the situation is quite different. * * * Section 9712 neither alters the maximum penalty for the crime committed nor creates a separate offense calling for a separate penalty; it operates solely to limit the sentencing court's discretion in selecting a penalty within the range already available to it without the special finding of visible possession of a firearm. * * *

Petitioners contend that this Court's decision in *Specht v. Patterson*, 386 U.S. 605 (1967), requires the invalidation of the Pennsylvania statute challenged here. Again, we think petitioners simply read too much into one of our previous decisions. Under the Colorado scheme at issue in *Specht*, conviction of a sexual offense otherwise carrying a maximum penalty of 10 years exposed a defendant to an indefinite term to and including life imprisonment if the sentencing judge made a post-trial finding that the defendant posed "a threat of bodily harm to members of the public, or is an habitual offender and mentally ill." This finding could be made, without notice or any "hearing in the normal sense," based solely on a presentence psychiatric report. This Court held that the Colorado scheme failed to satisfy the requirements of due process, and that the defendant had a right to be present with counsel, to be heard, to be confronted with and to cross-examine the witnesses against him, and to offer evidence of his own.

Petitioners suggest that had *Winship* already been decided at the time of *Specht*, the Court would have also required that the burden of proof as to the post-trial findings be beyond a reasonable doubt. But even if we accept petitioners' hypothesis, we do not think it avails them here. The Court in *Specht* observed that following trial the Colorado defendant was confronted with "a radically different situation" from the usual sentencing proceeding. The same simply is not true under the Pennsylvania statute. The finding of visible possession of a firearm of course "ups the ante" for a defendant, or it would not be challenged here; but it does so only in the way that we have previously mentioned, by raising the minimum sentence that may be imposed by the trial court.

Finally, we note that the specter raised by petitioners of States restructuring existing crimes in order to "evade" the commands of *Winship* just does not appear in this case.[25] The Pennsylvania legislature did not change the definition of any existing offense. It simply took one factor that has always been considered by sentencing courts to bear on punishment—the instrumentality used in committing a violent felony— and dictated the precise weight to be given that factor if the instrumentality is a firearm. Pennsylvania's decision to do so has not transformed against its will a sentencing factor into an "element" of some hypothetical "offense." * * *

We have noted a number of differences between this case and *Winship, Mullaney*, and *Specht*, and we find these differences controlling here. Our inability to lay down any "bright line" test may leave the constitutionality of statutes more like those in *Mullaney* and *Specht* than is the Pennsylvania statute to depend on differences of degree, but the law is full of situations in which differences of degree produce different results. We have no doubt that Pennsylvania's Mandatory Minimum Sentencing Act falls on the permissible side of the constitutional line.

III

Having concluded that States may treat "visible possession of a firearm" as a sentencing consideration rather than an element of a particular offense, we now turn to petitioners' subsidiary claim that due process nonetheless requires that visible possession be proved by at least clear and convincing evidence. Like the court below, we have little difficulty concluding that in this case the preponderance standard satisfies due process. Indeed, it would be extraordinary if the Due Process Clause as understood in *Patterson* plainly sanctioned Pennsylvania's scheme, while the same clause explained in some other line of less clearly relevant cases imposed more stringent requirements. There is, after all, only one Due Process Clause in the Fourteenth Amendment. Furthermore, petitioners do not and could not claim that a sentencing court may

---

25. We reject the view that anything in the Due Process Clause bars States from making changes in their criminal law that have the effect of making it easier for the prosecution to obtain convictions. "From the vantage point of the Constitution, a change in law favorable to defendants is not necessarily good, nor is an innovation favorable to the prosecution necessarily bad." Jeffries & Stephan, Defenses, Presumptions, and Burden of Proof in the Criminal Law, 88 Yale L.J. 1325, 1361 (1979).

never rely on a particular fact in passing sentence without finding that fact by "clear and convincing evidence." Sentencing courts have traditionally heard evidence and found facts without any prescribed burden of proof at all. See *Williams v. New York*, 337 U.S. 241 (1949). Pennsylvania has deemed a particular fact relevant and prescribed a particular burden of proof. We see nothing in Pennsylvania's scheme that would warrant constitutionalizing burdens of proof at sentencing.[26]

IV

In light of the foregoing, petitioners' final claim—that the Act denies them their Sixth Amendment right to a trial by jury—merits little discussion. Petitioners again argue that the jury must determine all ultimate facts concerning the offense committed. Having concluded that Pennsylvania may properly treat visible possession as a sentencing consideration and not an element of any offense, we need only note that there is no Sixth Amendment right to jury sentencing, even where the sentence turns on specific findings of fact.

For the foregoing reasons, the judgment of the Supreme Court of Pennsylvania is affirmed.

It is so ordered.

[The dissenting opinion of Justice Marshall, joined by Justices Brennan and Blackmun, is omitted.]

JUSTICE STEVENS, dissenting.

* * *

Once a State defines a criminal offense, the Due Process Clause requires it to prove any component of the prohibited transaction that gives rise to both a special stigma and a special punishment beyond a reasonable doubt. This much has been evident at least since *In re Winship*. * * *

Indeed, contrary to the supposition of the majority, *Patterson v. New York* is entirely in keeping with the limit on state definitional power implied in *Winship*. * * * *Patterson* clarified that the Due Process Clause requires proof beyond a reasonable doubt of conduct which exposes a criminal defendant to greater stigma or punishment, but does not likewise constrain state reductions of criminal penalties—even if such reductions are conditioned on a prosecutor's failure to prove a fact by a preponderance of the evidence or on proof supplied by the criminal defendant.

The distinction between aggravating and mitigating facts has been criticized as formalistic. But its ability to identify genuine constitutional threats depends on nothing more than the continued functioning of the

---

26. *Addington v. Texas*, 441 U.S. 418 (1979), and *Santosky v. Kramer*, 455 U.S. 745 (1982), which respectively applied the "clear and convincing evidence" standard where the State sought involuntary commitment to a mental institution and invol-untary termination of parental rights, are not to the contrary. Quite unlike the situation in those cases, criminal sentencing takes place only after a defendant has been adjudged guilty beyond a reasonable doubt. * * *

democratic process. To appreciate the difference between aggravating and mitigating circumstances, it is important to remember that although states may reach the same destination either by criminalizing conduct and allowing an affirmative defense, or by prohibiting lesser conduct and enhancing the penalty, legislation proceeding along these two paths is very different even if it might theoretically achieve the same result. Consider, for example, a statute making presence "in any private or public place" a "felony punishable by up to five years imprisonment" and yet allowing an affirmative defense for the defendant to prove, to a preponderance of the evidence, that he was not robbing a bank. No democratically-elected legislature would enact such a law, and if it did, a broad-based coalition of bankers and bank customers would soon see the legislation repealed. Nor is there a serious danger that a state will soon define murder to be the mere physical contact between the defendant and the victim leading to the victim's death, but then set up an affirmative defense leaving it to the defendant to prove that he acted without culpable *mens rea*. No legislator would be willing to expose himself to the severe opprobrium and punishment meted out to murderers for an accidental stumble on the subway. For similar reasons, it can safely be assumed that a State will not define all assaults as a single offense and then require the defendant to disprove the elements of aggravation. The very inconceivability of the hypothesized legislation—all of which has been sincerely offered to illustrate the dangers of permitting legislative mitigation of punishment in derogation of the requirement of proof beyond a reasonable doubt—is reason enough to feel secure that it will not command a majority of the electorate.

It is not at all inconceivable, however, to fear that a State might subject those individuals convicted of engaging in antisocial conduct to further punishment for aggravating conduct not proved beyond a reasonable doubt. As this case demonstrates, a State may seek to enhance the deterrent effect of its law forbidding the use of firearms in the course of felonies by mandating a minimum sentence of imprisonment upon proof by a preponderance against those already convicted of specified crimes. But *In re Winship* and *Patterson* teach that a State may not advance the objectives of its criminal laws at the expense of the accurate fact-finding owed to the criminally accused who suffer the risk of nonpersuasion.

Pennsylvania's Mandatory Minimum Sentencing Act reflects a legislative determination that a defendant who "visibly possessed a firearm" during the commission of an aggravated assault is more blameworthy than a defendant who did not. A judicial finding that the defendant used a firearm in an aggravated assault places a greater stigma on the defendant's name than a simple finding that he committed an aggravated assault. And not to be overlooked, such a finding with respect to petitioner Dennison automatically mandates a punishment that is more than twice as severe as the *maximum* punishment that the trial judge considered appropriate for his conduct.

It is true, as the Court points out, that the enhanced punishment is within the range that was authorized for any aggravated assault. That fact does not, however, minimize the significance of a finding of visible possession of a firearm whether attention is focused on the stigmatizing or punitive consequences of that finding. The finding identifies conduct that the legislature specifically intended to prohibit and to punish by a special sanction. In my opinion the constitutional significance of the special sanction cannot be avoided by the cavalier observation that it merely "ups the ante" for the defendant. No matter how culpable petitioner Dennison may be, the difference between 11½ months and five years of incarceration merits a more principled justification than the luck of the draw.

I respectfully dissent.

SANDSTROM v. MONTANA

Supreme Court of the United States, 1979.
442 U.S. 510, 99 S.Ct. 2450, 61 L.Ed.2d 39.

MR. JUSTICE BRENNAN delivered the opinion of the Court.

The question presented is whether, in a case in which intent is an element of the crime charged, the jury instruction, "the law presumes that a person intends the ordinary consequences of his voluntary acts," violates the Fourteenth Amendment's requirement that the State prove every element of a criminal offense beyond a reasonable doubt.

I

On November 22, 1976, 18-year-old David Sandstrom confessed to the slaying of Annie Jessen. Based upon the confession and corroborating evidence, petitioner was charged on December 2 with "deliberate homicide," Mont.Code Ann. § 45-5-102 (1978), in that he "purposely or knowingly caused the death of Annie Jessen." App. 3.[27] At trial, Sandstrom's attorney informed the jury that, although his client admitted killing Jessen, he did not do so "purposely or knowingly," and was therefore not guilty of "deliberate homicide" but of a lesser crime. The basic support for this contention was the testimony of two court-appointed mental health experts, each of whom described for the jury petitioner's mental state at the time of the incident. Sandstrom's attorney argued that this testimony demonstrated that petitioner, due to a personality disorder aggravated by alcohol consumption, did not kill Annie Jessen "purposely or knowingly."*

---

27. The statute provides:

"45-5-101. Criminal homicide. (1) A person commits the offense of criminal homicide if he purposely, knowingly, or negligently causes the death of another human being.

"(2) Criminal homicide is deliberate homicide, mitigated deliberate homicide, or negligent homicide.

"45-5-102. Deliberate homicide. (1) Except as provided in 45-5-103(1), crimi-

nal homicide constitutes deliberate homicide if:

"(a) it is committed purposely or knowingly * * *."

* According to the State Court opinion, the victim was an 89-year-old woman who was found dead in her home, the apparent victim of a brutal assault in which she received blows to her head from a shovel, and five stab wounds to her back from a kitchen knife. She had, in addition, been sexually assaulted and received a compound

The prosecution requested the trial judge to instruct the jury that "[t]he law presumes that a person intends the ordinary consequences of his voluntary acts." Petitioner's counsel objected, arguing that "the instruction has the effect of shifting the burden of proof on the issue of" purpose or knowledge to the defense, and that "that is impermissible under the Federal Constitution, due process of law." He offered to provide a number of federal decisions in support of the objection, including this Court's holding in Mullaney v. Wilbur, but was told by the judge: "You can give those to the Supreme Court. The objection is overruled." The instruction was delivered, the jury found petitioner guilty of deliberate homicide, and petitioner was sentenced to 100 years in prison.

Sandstrom appealed to the Supreme Court of Montana, again contending that the instruction shifted to the defendant the burden of disproving an element of the crime charged, in violation of Mullaney v. Wilbur, supra, In re Winship, and Patterson v. New York. The Montana court conceded that these cases did prohibit shifting the burden of proof to the defendant by means of a presumption, but held that the cases "do not prohibit allocation of *some* burden of proof to a defendant under certain circumstances." Since in the court's view, "[d]efendant's sole burden under instruction No. 5 was to produce some evidence that he did not intend the ordinary consequences of his voluntary acts, not to disprove that he acted 'purposely' or 'knowingly,' * * * the instruction does not violate due process standards as defined by the United States or Montana Constitution * * *."

Both federal and state courts have held, under a variety of rationales, that the giving of an instruction similar to that challenged here is fatal to the validity of a criminal conviction. We granted certiorari to decide the important question of the instruction's constitutionality. We reverse.

II

The threshold inquiry in ascertaining the constitutional analysis applicable to this kind of jury instruction is to determine the nature of the presumption it describes. See Ulster County Court v. Allen, 442 U.S. 140, 157–163 (1979). That determination requires careful attention to the words actually spoken to the jury, for whether a defendant has been accorded his constitutional rights depends upon the way in which a reasonable juror could have interpreted the instruction.

fracture to her leg, apparently inflicted after the slaying. Sandstrom confessed to the slaying after being arrested for an unrelated crime. The defense originally gave notice of an insanity defense, but abandoned this theory, apparently because the defense psychiatrists determined that Sandstrom was able to appreciate the consequences of his actions, despite his low intelligence level and aggressive/impulsive personality. The psychiatrists did testify that, while Sandstrom may not have had the specific intent to kill at the time of the offense, it was their opinion that he had the intent to "silence" the victim. State v. Sandstrom, 580 P.2d 106 (Montana 1978). Montana also punishes as "deliberate homicide" a killing committed during any violent felony, including rape. It is not clear why the prosecution did not invoke the felony murder theory.—ed.

Respondent argues, first, that the instruction merely described a permissive inference—that is, it allowed but did not require the jury to draw conclusions about defendant's intent from his actions—and that such inferences are constitutional. These arguments need not detain us long, for even respondent admits that "it's possible" that the jury believed they were required to apply the presumption. Tr. of Oral Arg. 28. Sandstrom's jurors were told that "[t]he law presumes that a person intends the ordinary consequences of his voluntary acts." They were not told that they had a choice, or that they might infer that conclusion; they were told only that the law presumed it. It is clear that a reasonable juror could easily have viewed such an instruction as mandatory.

In the alternative, respondent urges that, even if viewed as a mandatory presumption rather than as a permissive inference, the presumption did not conclusively establish intent but rather could be rebutted. On this view, the instruction required the jury, if satisfied as to the facts which trigger the presumption, to find intent *unless* the defendant offered evidence to the contrary. Moreover, according to the State, all the defendant had to do to rebut the presumption was produce "some" contrary evidence; he did not have to "prove" that he lacked the required mental state. Thus, "[a]t most, it placed a *burden of production* on the petitioner," but "did not shift to petitioner the *burden of persuasion* with respect to any element of the offense * * *." Brief for Respondent 3 (emphasis added). Again, respondent contends that presumptions with this limited effect pass constitutional muster.

We need not review respondent's constitutional argument on this point either, however, for we reject this characterization of the presumption as well. Respondent concedes there is a "risk" that the jury, once having found petitioner's act voluntary, would interpret the instruction as automatically directing a finding of intent. Moreover, the State also concedes that numerous courts "have differed as to the effect of the presumption when given as a jury instruction without further explanation as to its use by the jury," and that some have found it to shift more than the burden of production, and even to have conclusive effect. Brief for Respondent 17. Nonetheless, the State contends that the only authoritative reading of the effect of the presumption resides in the Supreme Court of Montana. * * *

The Supreme Court of Montana is, of course, the final authority on the legal weight to be given a presumption under Montana law, but it is not the final authority on the interpretation which a jury could have given the instruction. If Montana intended its presumption to have only the effect described by its Supreme Court, then we are convinced that a reasonable juror could well have been misled by the instruction given, and could have believed that the presumption was not limited to requiring the defendant to satisfy only a burden of production. Petitioner's jury was told that *"[t]he law presumes* that a person intends the ordinary consequences of his voluntary acts." They were not told that the presumption could be rebutted, as the Montana Supreme Court held, by the defendant's simple presentation of "some" evidence; nor even that it could be rebutted at all. Given the common definition of "presume" as "to suppose to be true without proof," Webster's New Collegiate Dictionary 911 (1974), and given the lack of qualifying instructions as to the legal effect of the presumption, we cannot discount the possibility that the jury may have interpreted the instruction in either of two more stringent ways.

First, a reasonable jury could well have interpreted the presumption as "conclusive," that is, not technically as a presumption at all, but rather as an irrebuttable direction by the court to find intent once convinced of the facts triggering the presumption. Alternatively, the jury may have interpreted the instruction as a direction to find intent upon proof of the defendant's voluntary actions (and their "ordinary" consequences), unless *the defendant* proved the contrary by some quantum of proof which may well have been considerably greater than "some" evidence—thus effectively shifting the burden of persuasion on the element of intent. Numerous federal and state courts have warned that instructions of the type given here can be interpreted in just these ways. * * *

We do not reject the possibility that some jurors may have interpreted the challenged instruction as permissive, or, if mandatory, as requiring only that the defendant come forward with "some" evidence in rebuttal. However, the fact that a reasonable juror could have given the presumption conclusive or persuasion-shifting effect means that we cannot discount the possibility that Sandstrom's jurors actually did proceed upon one or the other of these latter interpretations. And that means that unless these kinds of presumptions are constitutional, the instruction cannot be adjudged valid. * * *

[The Court held that the instruction unconstitutionally relieved the prosecution of its burden of proof.]

Respondent's final argument is that even if the jury did rely upon the unconstitutional instruction, this constituted harmless error under Chapman v. California, 386 U.S. 18 (1967), because both defendant's confession and the psychiatrist's testimony demonstrated that Sandstrom possessed the requisite mental state. In reply, it is said that petitioner confessed only to the slaying and not to his mental state, that the psychiatrist's testimony amply supported his defense, and that in any event an unconstitutional jury instruction on an element of the crime can never constitute harmless error. As none of these issues was considered by the Supreme Court of Montana, we decline to reach them as an initial matter here. The Montana court will, of course, be free to consider them on remand if it so desires. Accordingly, the judgment of the Supreme Court of Montana is reversed, and the case is remanded for further proceedings not inconsistent with this opinion.[a]

It is so ordered.

a. The Montana Supreme Court subsequently found that the error was not harmless and remanded for a new trial. State v. Sandstrom, 603 P.2d 244 (Mont.1979). See also, Rose v. Clark, this page.

MR. JUSTICE REHNQUIST, with whom THE CHIEF JUSTICE joins, concurring.

The Fourteenth Amendment to the United States Constitution prohibits any State from depriving a person of liberty without due process of law, and in Mullaney v. Wilbur, this Court held that the Fourteenth Amendment's guarantees prohibit a State from shifting to the defendant the burden of disproving an element of the crime charged. I am loath to see this Court go into the business of parsing jury instructions given by state trial courts, for as we have consistently recognized, "a single instruction to a jury may not be judged in artificial isolation, but must be viewed in the context of the overall charge." Cupp v. Naughten, 414 U.S. 141, 146–147 (1973). And surely if this charge had, in the words of the Court, "merely described a permissive inference," it could not conceivably have run afoul of the constitutional decisions cited by the Court in its opinion. But a majority of my Brethren conclude that "it is clear that a reasonable juror could easily have viewed such an instruction as mandatory," and counsel for the State admitted in oral argument "that 'it's possible' that the jury believed they were required to apply the presumption."

While I continue to have doubts as to whether this particular jury was so attentively attuned to the instructions of the trial court that it defined the difference recognized by lawyers between "infer" and "presume," I defer to the judgment of the majority of the Court that this difference in meaning may have been critical in its effect on the jury. I therefore concur in the Court's opinion and judgment.

ROSE v. CLARK

Supreme Court of the United States, 1986.
478 U.S. 570, 106 S.Ct. 3101, 92 L.Ed.2d 460.

JUSTICE POWELL delivered the opinion of the Court. * * *

I

On December 30, 1978, Charles Browning and Joy Faulk were shot to death while they sat in Browning's pickup truck in a remote area of Rutherford County, Tennessee. Respondent Stanley Clark, Faulk's former boyfriend, was charged with the murders.

The evidence introduced at trial showed that Browning, Faulk, and Faulk's two young children (ages 6 and 3) had been driving in Rutherford County on the night of the murders. According to the older child, another vehicle followed Browning's truck for about an hour. Browning pulled his truck into a private driveway, apparently to let the other vehicle pass. The driver of the second vehicle then pulled in behind Browning, thereby blocking any exit. The driver left his vehicle, walked up to the cab of Browning's truck, and fired four shots at point-blank range. One shot struck Browning in the head, two others struck Faulk in the head, and the fourth struck Faulk in the left shoulder. The killer left the scene in his vehicle. Both Browning and Faulk died.

Faulk's children, who had not been shot, went for help, telling a local resident that "Clicker" (the nickname by which the children knew respondent) had shot Browning and their mother. Earlier that night, police had seen respondent following Browning's truck. Police soon located respondent, but apprehended him only after a high-speed chase. Police found the murder weapon, a .25–caliber pistol that respondent had borrowed from a friend, near respondent's home. At trial, the State relied on the foregoing evidence, and on evidence showing that respondent and Joy Faulk had a stormy love affair that Faulk ended in the fall of 1978. Several times after their break-up, respondent threatened to kill Faulk if he ever found her with another man.

Respondent offered two lines of defense. First, he contended that Sam Faulk, Joy's ex-husband, killed the victims because of a dispute concerning custody of the two Faulk children. The State rebutted this contention by introducing evidence that no such dispute existed, and that Sam Faulk was elsewhere when the murders were committed. Second, respondent argued that he was either insane or incapable of forming the requisite criminal intent. To support this argument, respondent introduced evidence that he was suffering from amnesia and could not remember the events of the night of the murders. In addition, some testimony suggested that respondent had been drinking heavily the entire day before the murders. Finally, two defense psychiatrists testified that respondent was legally insane at the time the murders were committed because his depression concerning his recent break-up with Joy Faulk made it impossible for him to conform his conduct to the law.

At the close of trial, the court instructed the jury on the elements of both first-and second-degree murder. Under Tennessee law, first-degree murder requires proof of premeditation and deliberation, while second-degree murder requires proof of malice. The court's instructions defined malice as "an intent to do any injury to another, a design formed in the mind of doing mischief to another." Malice did not require proof of planning or premeditation; a killing "upon a sudden impulse of passion" sufficed if committed with intent to harm another. The court then charged the jury:

> "All homicides are presumed to be malicious in the absence of evidence which would rebut the implied presumption. Thus, if the State has proven beyond a reasonable * * * doubt that a killing has occurred, then it is presumed that the killing was done maliciously. But this presumption may be rebutted by either direct or circumstantial evidence, or by both, regardless of whether the same be offered by the Defendant, or exists in the evidence of the State."

The jury found respondent guilty of first-degree murder for killing Faulk and of second-degree murder for killing Browning.

The Tennessee Court of Criminal Appeals affirmed the convictions, rejecting respondent's argument that the jury instructions had impermissibly shifted the burden of proof as to malice.[28] Respondent then sought habeas corpus relief in the Middle District of Tennessee. The District Court held that the malice instruction had violated respondent's right to have his guilt proved beyond a reasonable doubt, as that right was defined in *Sandstrom v. Montana*.[29] The court went on to find that the error could not be deemed harmless because respondent had "relied upon a *mens rea* defense" in contesting his guilt. [The Court of Appeals for the Sixth Circuit affirmed.]

II

A

In *Chapman v. California*, 386 U.S. 18 (1967), this Court rejected the argument that errors of constitutional dimension necessarily require reversal of criminal convictions. And since *Chapman*, we have repeatedly reaffirmed the principle that an otherwise valid conviction should not be set aside if the reviewing court may confidently say, on the whole record, that the constitutional error was harmless beyond a reasonable doubt. * * * Our application of harmless-error analysis in these cases has not reflected a denigration of the constitutional rights involved. Instead, as we emphasized earlier this Term:

> "The harmless-error doctrine recognizes the principle that the central purpose of a criminal trial is to decide the factual question of the defendant's guilt or innocence, and promotes public respect for the criminal process by focusing on the underlying fairness of the trial rather than on the virtually inevitable presence of immaterial error. Cf. R. Traynor, The Riddle of Harmless Error 50 (1970) ('Reversal for error, regardless of its effect on the judgment, encourages litigants to abuse the judicial process and bestirs the public to ridicule it.')." *Delaware v. Van Arsdall*, 106 S.Ct., at 1436–37.

Despite the strong interests that support the harmless-error doctrine, the Court in *Chapman* recognized that some constitutional errors require reversal without regard to the evidence in the particular case. 386 U.S., at 23, n. 8, citing *Payne v. Arkansas*, 356 U.S. 560 (1958) (introduction of coerced confession); *Gideon v. Wainwright*, 372 U.S. 335 (1963) (complete denial of right to counsel); *Tumey v. Ohio*, 273 U.S. 510 (1927) (adjudication by biased judge). This limitation recognizes that some errors necessarily render a trial fundamentally unfair. * * *

28. The Tennessee Court of Criminal Appeals noted that, almost immediately following the "presumption" instruction, the judge charged:

> "The question of whether the alleged killing was done with malice is for you to determine from the entire case, and you should look to all of the facts and circumstances developed by the evidence to determine whether the State has * * * proven beyond a reasonable doubt the existence of malice. If you have a reason-

able doubt as to whether the alleged killing was done with malice, then the Defendant cannot be guilty of murder in the second degree and you must acquit him of that offense."

The Court of Criminal Appeals reasoned that this instruction adequately informed the jurors that the burden of proof on malice remained on the State at all times.

29. * * * *Sandstrom* was decided shortly before respondent's trial commenced.

Similarly, harmless-error analysis presumably would not apply if a court directed a verdict for the prosecution in a criminal trial by jury. We have stated that "a trial judge is prohibited from entering a judgment of conviction or directing the jury to come forward with such a verdict * * * regardless of how overwhelmingly the evidence may point in that direction." *United States v. Martin Linen Supply Co.*, 430 U.S. 564, 572–573 (1977) (citations omitted). This rule stems from the Sixth Amendment's clear command to afford jury trials in serious criminal cases. Where that right is altogether denied, the State cannot contend that the deprivation was harmless because the evidence established the defendant's guilt; the error in such a case is that the wrong entity judged the defendant guilty.

We have emphasized, however, that while there are some errors to which *Chapman* does not apply, they are the exception and not the rule. Accordingly, if the defendant had counsel and was tried by an impartial adjudicator, there is a strong presumption that any other errors that may have occurred are subject to harmless error analysis. The thrust of the many constitutional rules governing the conduct of criminal trials is to ensure that those trials lead to fair and correct judgments. Where a reviewing court can find that the record developed at trial establishes guilt beyond a reasonable doubt, the interest in fairness has been satisfied and the judgment should be affirmed. As we have repeatedly stated, the Constitution entitles a criminal defendant to a fair trial, not a perfect one.

B

Applying these principles to this case is not difficult. Respondent received a full opportunity to put on evidence and make argument to support his claim of innocence. He was tried by a fairly selected, impartial jury, supervised by an impartial judge. Apart from the challenged malice instruction, the jury in this case was clearly instructed that it had to find respondent guilty beyond a reasonable doubt as to every element of both first-and second-degree murder. Placed in context, the erroneous malice instruction does not compare with the kinds of errors that automatically require reversal of an otherwise valid conviction. We therefore find that the error at issue here—an instruction that impermissibly shifted the burden of proof on malice—is not "so basic to a fair trial" that it can never be harmless.

Nor is *Sandstrom* error equivalent to a directed verdict for the State. When a jury is instructed to presume malice from predicate facts, it still must find the existence of those facts beyond a reasonable doubt. * * *

No one doubts that the trial court properly could have instructed the jury that it could *infer* malice from respondent's conduct. Indeed, in the many cases where there is no direct evidence of intent, that is exactly how intent is established. For purposes of deciding this case, it is enough to recognize that in some cases that inference is overpowering. It would further neither justice nor the purposes of the *Sandstrom* rule to reverse a conviction in such a case. We accordingly hold that *Chapman*'s harmless-error standard applies in cases such as this one. * * *

The judgment of the Court of Appeals is vacated, and the case is remanded for further proceedings consistent with this opinion.

It is so ordered.

[The concurring opinion of Justice Stevens is omitted.]

JUSTICE BLACKMUN, with whom JUSTICE BRENNAN and JUSTICE MARSHALL join, dissenting.

Stanley Clark was deprived of two rights: the right guaranteed by the Due Process Clause of the Fourteenth Amendment to compel the State of Tennessee to prove beyond a reasonable doubt every element of the crimes with which he was charged, and the right guaranteed by the Sixth Amendment to have a jury of his peers determine whether the State had met that burden. Today, the Court focuses entirely on the former right and disregards totally the latter. A reviewing court's conclusion that the record would support a conviction by a properly instructed jury has no bearing on the question whether a defendant was denied the right to have the jury that actually tried him make that determination. A trial that was fundamentally unfair at the time it took place, because the jury was not compelled to perform its constitutionally required role, cannot be rendered fundamentally fair in retrospect by what amounts to nothing more than an appellate review of the sufficiency of the evidence. I therefore dissent from the Court's holding that harmless-error analysis should be applied. * * *

CAGE v. LOUISIANA

Supreme Court of the United States, 1990.
498 U.S. 39, 111 S.Ct. 328, 112 L.Ed.2d 339.

PER CURIAM.

The motion of petitioner for leave to proceed in forma pauperis and the petition for a writ of certiorari are granted.

In state criminal trials, the Due Process Clause of the Fourteenth Amendment "protects the accused against conviction except upon proof beyond a reasonable doubt of every fact necessary to constitute the crime with which he is charged." In re Winship, 397 U.S. 358, 364 (1970); see also Jackson v. Virginia, 443 U.S. 307, 315–316 (1979). This reasonable doubt standard "plays a vital role in the American scheme of criminal procedure." Winship, 397 U.S., at 363. Among other things, "it is a prime instrument for reducing the risk of convictions resting on factual error." Ibid. The issue before us is whether the reasonable doubt instruction in this case complied with Winship.

Petitioner was convicted in a Louisiana trial court of first-degree murder, and was sentenced to death. He appealed to the Supreme Court of Louisiana, arguing, inter alia, that the reasonable doubt instruction used in the guilt phase of his trial was constitutionally defective. The instruction provided in relevant part:

> "If you entertain a reasonable doubt as to any fact or element necessary to constitute the defendant's guilt, it is your duty to give him the benefit of that doubt and return a verdict of not guilty. Even where the evidence demonstrates a probability of guilt, if it does not establish such guilt beyond a reasonable doubt, you must acquit the accused. This doubt, however, must be a reasonable one; that is one that is founded upon a real tangible substantial basis and not upon mere caprice and conjecture. It must be such doubt as would give rise to a *grave* uncertainty, raised in your mind by reasons of the unsatisfactory character of the evidence or lack thereof. A reasonable doubt is not a mere possible doubt. It is an *actual substantial* doubt. It is a doubt that a reasonable man can seriously entertain. What is required is not an absolute or mathematical certainty, but a *moral certainty.*" State v. Cage, 554 So.2d 39, 41 (La.1989) (emphasis added).

The Supreme Court of Louisiana rejected petitioner's argument. The court first observed that the use of the phrases "grave certainty" and "moral certainty" in the instruction, "if taken out of context, might overstate the requisite degree of uncertainty and confuse the jury." But "taking the charge as a whole," the court concluded that "reasonable persons of ordinary intelligence would understand the definition of 'reasonable doubt.'" It is our view, however, that the instruction at issue was contrary to the "beyond a reasonable doubt" requirement articulated in Winship.

In construing the instruction, we consider how reasonable jurors could have understood the charge as a whole. Francis v. Franklin, 471 U.S. 307, 316 (1985). The charge did at one point instruct that to convict, guilt must be found beyond a reasonable doubt; but it then equated a reasonable doubt with a "grave uncertainty" and an "actual substantial doubt," and stated that what was required was a "moral certainty" that the defendant was guilty. It is plain to us that the words "substantial" and "grave," as they are commonly understood, suggest a higher degree of doubt than is required for acquittal under the reasonable doubt standard. When those statements are then considered with the reference to "moral certainty," rather than evidentiary certainty, it becomes clear that a reasonable juror could have interpreted the instruction to allow a finding of guilt based on a degree of proof below that required by the Due Process Clause.

Accordingly, the judgment of the Supreme Court of Louisiana is reversed, and the case is remanded for further proceedings not inconsistent with this opinion. It is so ordered.

SULLIVAN v. LOUISIANA

Supreme Court of the United States, 1993.
508 U.S. 275, 113 S.Ct. 2078, 124 L.Ed.2d 182.

JUSTICE SCALIA delivered the opinion of the Court.

The question presented is whether a constitutionally deficient reasonable-doubt instruction may be harmless error.

Petitioner was charged with first-degree murder in the course of committing an armed robbery at a New Orleans bar. His alleged accomplice in the crime, a convicted felon named Michael Hillhouse, testifying at the trial pursuant to a grant of immunity, identified petitioner as the murderer. Although several other people were in the bar at the time of the robbery, only one testified at trial. This witness, who had been unable to identify either Hillhouse or petitioner at a physical lineup, testified that they committed the robbery, and that she saw petitioner hold a gun to the victim's head. There was other circumstantial evidence supporting the conclusion that petitioner was the triggerman. 596 So.2d 177, 180–181 (La.1992). In closing argument, defense counsel argued that there was reasonable doubt as to both the identity of the murderer and his intent.

In his instructions to the jury, the trial judge gave a definition of "reasonable doubt" that was, as the State conceded below, essentially identical to the one held unconstitutional in Cage v. Louisiana, 498 U.S. 39 (1990) (per curiam). The jury found petitioner guilty of first-degree murder and subsequently recommended that he be sentenced to death. The trial court agreed. On direct appeal, the Supreme Court of Louisiana held, consistent with its opinion on remand from our decision in *Cage,* that the erroneous instruction was harmless beyond a reasonable doubt. 596 So.2d at 186. It therefore upheld the conviction, though remanding for a new sentencing hearing because of ineffectiveness of counsel in the sentencing phase. We granted certiorari. * * *

In Chapman v. California, 386 U.S. 18 (1967), we rejected the view that all federal constitutional errors in the course of a criminal trial require reversal. We held that the Fifth Amendment violation of prosecutorial comment upon the defendant's failure to testify would not require reversal of the conviction if the State could show "beyond a reasonable doubt that the error complained of did not contribute to the verdict obtained." The *Chapman* standard recognizes that "certain constitutional errors, no less than other errors, may have been 'harmless' in terms of their effect on the factfinding process at trial." Although most constitutional errors have been held amenable to harmless-error analysis, see Arizona v. Fulminante, [infra this casebook, p. 547] some will always invalidate the conviction. See, inter alia, Gideon v. Wainwright, 372 U.S. 335 (1963) (total deprivation of the right to counsel); Tumey v. Ohio, 273 U.S. 510 (1927) (trial by a biased judge); McKaskle v. Wiggins, 465 U.S.

168 (1984) (right to self-representation)). The question in the present case is to which category the present error belongs.

Chapman itself suggests the answer. Consistent with the jury-trial guarantee, the question it instructs the reviewing court to consider is not what effect the constitutional error might generally be expected to have upon a reasonable jury, but rather what effect it had upon the guilty verdict in the case at hand. The inquiry, in other words, is not whether, in a trial that occurred without the error, a guilty verdict would surely have been rendered, but whether the guilty verdict actually rendered in this trial was surely unattributable to the error. That must be so, because to hypothesize a guilty verdict that was never in fact rendered— no matter how inescapable the findings to support that verdict might be—would violate the jury-trial guarantee. See Rose v. Clark, 478 U.S. 570 (1986) (BLACKMUN, J., dissenting); Pope v. Illinois, 481 U.S. 497, 509– 510 (1987) (STEVENS, J., dissenting).

Once the proper role of an appellate court engaged in the *Chapman* inquiry is understood, the illogic of harmless-error review in the present case becomes evident. Since, for the reasons described above, there has been no jury verdict within the meaning of the Sixth Amendment, the entire premise of *Chapman* review is simply absent. There being no jury verdict of guilty-beyond-a-reasonable-doubt, the question whether the same verdict of guilty-beyond-a-reasonable-doubt would have been ren- dered absent the constitutional error is utterly meaningless. There is no object, so to speak, upon which harmless-error scrutiny can operate. The most an appellate court can conclude is that a jury would surely have found petitioner guilty beyond a reasonable doubt—not that the jury's actual finding of guilty beyond a reasonable doubt would surely not have been different absent the constitutional error. That is not enough. The Sixth Amendment requires more than appellate speculation about a hypothetical jury's action, or else directed verdicts for the State would be sustainable on appeal; it requires an actual jury finding of guilty.

Insofar as the possibility of harmless-error review is concerned, the jury-instruction error in this case is quite different from the jury- instruction error of erecting a presumption regarding an element of the offense. A mandatory presumption—for example, the presumption that a person intends the ordinary consequences of his voluntary acts—violates the Fourteenth Amendment, because it may relieve the State of its burden of proving all elements of the offense. Sandstrom v. Montana, 442 U.S. 510 (1979); Francis v. Franklin, 471 U.S. 307 (1985). But "when a jury is instructed to presume malice from predicate facts, it still must find the existence of those facts beyond a reasonable doubt." Rose v. Clark, 478 U.S. 570, 580 (1986). And when the latter facts "are so closely related to the ultimate fact to be presumed that no rational jury could find those facts without also finding that ultimate fact, making those findings is functionally equivalent to finding the element required to be presumed." Carella v. California, 491 U.S. 263, 271 (1989) (SCALIA, J., concurring in judgment). A reviewing court may thus be able to conclude that the presumption played no significant role in the finding of guilt beyond a reasonable doubt. But the essential connection to a "beyond-a-reasonable-doubt" factual finding cannot be made where the instructional error consists of a misdescription of the burden of proof, which vitiates all the jury's findings. A reviewing court can only engage in pure speculation—its view of what a reasonable jury would have done. And when it does that, "the wrong entity judges the defendant guilty."

Another mode of analysis leads to the same conclusion that harmless-error analysis does not apply: In *Fulminante,* we distinguished between, on the one hand, "structural defects in the constitution of the trial mechanism, which defy analysis by 'harmless-error' standards," and, on the other hand, trial errors which occur "during the presentation of the case to the jury, and which may therefore be quantitatively assessed in the context of other evidence presented." Denial of the right to a jury verdict of guilt beyond a reasonable doubt is certainly an error of the former sort, the jury guarantee being a "basic protection" whose precise effects are unmeasurable, but without which a criminal trial cannot reliably serve its function. The right to trial by jury reflects, we have said, "a profound judgment about the way in which law should be enforced and justice administered." Duncan v. Louisiana, 391 U.S., at 155. The deprivation of that right, with consequences that are necessarily unquantifiable and indeterminate, unquestionably qualifies as "structural error."

The judgment of the Supreme Court of Louisiana is reversed, and the case is remanded for proceedings not inconsistent with this opinion.

It is so ordered.

[The concurring opinion by Chief Justice Rehnquist is omitted.]

UNITED STATES v. HASTING

Supreme Court of the United States, 1983.
461 U.S. 499, 103 S.Ct. 1974, 76 L.Ed.2d 96.

CHIEF JUSTICE BURGER delivered the opinion of the Court.

We granted certiorari to review the reversal of respondents' convictions because of prosecutorial allusion to their failure to rebut the Government's evidence.

I

On October 11, 1979, in the vicinity of East St. Louis, Ill., three young women and a man, Randy Newcomb, were riding in an automobile when a turquoise Cadillac forced them off the road. The occupants of the Cadillac, later identified as Napoleon Stewart, Gregory Williams, Gable Gibson, Kevin Anderson, and Kelvin Hasting, respondents here, forcibly removed the women from the car in which they were riding with Newcomb; in Newcomb's presence, Stewart and Gibson immediately raped one of them and forced her to perform acts of sodomy. Newcomb was left behind while the three women were then taken in the Cadillac to a vacant garage in St. Louis, Mo.; there they were raped and forced to perform deviant sexual acts. Two of the women were then taken to Stewart's home where Stewart and Williams took turns raping and sodomizing them. The third victim was taken in a separate car to another garage where the other respondents repeatedly raped her and compelled her to perform acts of sodomy.

About 6 a.m., the three women were released and they immediately contacted the St. Louis police; they furnished descriptions of the five men, the turquoise Cadillac, and the locations of the sexual attacks. From these descriptions, the police immediately identified one of the places to which the women were taken—the home of respondent Napoleon Stewart. With the consent of Stewart's mother, police entered the home, arrested Stewart, and found various items of the victims' clothing and personal effects. The turquoise Cadillac was located, seized, and found to be registered to Williams. On the basis of the information gathered, the police arrested Williams, Gibson, Anderson, and Hasting, all of whom were later identified by the victims during police lineups.

Respondents were charged with kidnaping in violation of 18 U.S.C. § 1201(a)(1), transporting a woman across state lines for immoral purposes in violation of the Mann Act, 18 U.S.C. § 2421, and conspiracy to commit the foregoing offenses in violation of 18 U.S.C. § 371. They were tried before a jury. The defense relied on a theory of consent and—inconsistently—on the possibility that the victims' identification of the respondents was mistaken. None of the respondents testified.

At the close of the case, and during the summation of the prosecutor, the following interchange took place:

"[PROSECUTOR]: * * * Let's look at the evidence the defendant[s] put on here for you so that we can put that in perspective. I'm going to tell you what the defendant[s] did not do. Defendants on cross-examination and—

"[DEFENSE COUNSEL]: I'll object to that, Your Honor. You're going to instruct to the contrary on that and the defendants don't have to put on any evidence.

"[PROSECUTOR]: That's correct, Your Honor.

"[THE COURT]: That's right, they don't. They don't have to.

"[PROSECUTOR]: But if they do put on a case, the Government can comment on it. The defendants at no time ever challenged any of the rapes, whether or not that occurred, any of the sodomies. They didn't challenge the kidnapping, the fact that the girls were in East St. Louis and they were taken across to St. Louis. They never challenged the transportation of the victims from East St. Louis, Illinois to St. Louis, Missouri, and they never challenged the location or whereabouts of the defendants at all the relevant times. They want you to focus your attention on all of the events that were before all of the crucial events of that evening. They want to pull your focus away from the beginning of the incident in East St. Louis after they were bumped, and then the proceeding events. They want you to focus to the events prior to that. And you can use your common sense and still see what that tells you. * * * "

A motion for a mistrial was denied. The jury returned a verdict of guilty as to each respondent on all counts.

On appeal, various errors were alleged, including a claim that the prosecutor violated respondents' Fifth Amendment rights under *Griffin v. California*, 380 U.S. 609 (1965). In a terse opinion, the Court of Appeals reversed the convictions and remanded for retrial, 660 F.2d 301 (C.A.7 1981), citing its decision in *United States v. Buege*, 578 F.2d 187–188 (1978), for the proposition that *Griffin* error occurs even without a direct statement on the failure of a defendant to take the stand when the "prosecutor refers to testimony as uncontradicted where the defendant has elected not to testify and when he is the only person able to dispute the testimony." The Court of Appeals declined to rely on the harmless-error doctrine, however, stating that application of that doctrine "would impermissibly compromise the clear constitutional violation of the defendants' Fifth Amendment rights." * * *

II

The opinion of the Court of Appeals does not make entirely clear its basis for reversing the convictions in this gruesome case. Its cursory treatment of the harmless-error question and its focus on the failure generally of prosecutors within its jurisdiction to heed the court's prior admonitions about commenting on a defendant's failure to rebut the prosecution's case suggest that, notwithstanding the harmless nature of the error, the court acted in this case to discipline the prosecutor—and warn other prosecutors—for what it perceived to be continuing violations of *Griffin* and § 3481. The court pointedly emphasized its own decision in *United States v. Rodriguez*, 627 F.2d 110 (1980), where it characterized the problem of prosecutorial comments on a defendant's silence as one which "continues to arise with disturbing frequency throughout this circuit despite the admonition of trial judges and this court."

In *Rodriguez*, the court described its efforts to cure the problem by ordering circulation to all United States Attorneys of an unpublished order calling attention to the subject. In addition, the *Rodriguez* court discussed, without explicitly adopting, the rule announced by the First Circuit in *United States v. Flannery*, 451 F.2d 880, 882 (1971), that any prosecutorial reference to a defendant's failure to testify is *per se* grounds for reversal unless the judge immediately instructs the jury that the defendant had a constitutional right not to testify and advises the jury that the prosecutor's conduct was improper. Obviously the Court of Appeals is more familiar than we are with what appellate records show concerning prosecutorial indifference to the court's admonitions; the question we address is whether reversal of these convictions was an appropriate response. In view of this history of tension between what the Court of Appeals perceives as the requirements of *Griffin* and § 3481 and that court's view of the prosecutors' conduct, we proceed on the assumption that, without so stating, the court was exercising its supervisory powers to discipline the prosecutors of its jurisdiction. The question presented is whether, on this record, in a purported exercise of supervisory powers, a reviewing court may ignore the harmless-error analysis of *Chapman* v. California, 386 U.S. 18 (1967).

* * *

The goals that are implicated by supervisory powers are not, however, significant in the context of this case if, as the Court of Appeals plainly implied, the errors alleged are harmless. Supervisory power to reverse a conviction is not needed as a remedy when the error to which it is addressed is harmless since, by definition, the conviction would have been obtained notwithstanding the asserted error. Further, in this context, the integrity of the process carries less weight, for it is the essence of the harmless-error doctrine that a judgment may stand only when there is no reasonable possibility that the [practice] complained of might have contributed to the conviction. Finally, deterrence is an inappropriate basis for reversal where, as here, the prosecutor's remark is at most an attenuated violation of *Griffin*[30] and where means more narrowly tailored to deter objectionable prosecutorial conduct are available.[31]

To the extent that the values protected by supervisory authority are at issue here, these powers may not be exercised in a vacuum. Rather, reversals of convictions under the court's supervisory power must be approached "with some caution," *Payner*, 447 U.S., at 734, and with a view toward balancing the interests involved. As we shall see below, the Court of Appeals failed in this case to give appropriate—if, indeed, any—weight to these relevant interests. It did not consider the trauma the victims of these particularly heinous crimes would experience in a new trial, forcing them to relive harrowing experiences now long past, or the practical problems of retrying these sensitive issues more than four years after the events. See *Morris v. Slappy*, 461 U.S. 1, at 14–15 (1983). The conclusion is inescapable that the Court of Appeals focused exclusively on its concern that the prosecutors within its jurisdiction were indifferent to the frequent admonitions of the court. The court appears to have decided to deter future similar comments by the drastic step of reversal of these convictions. But the interests preserved by the doctrine of

30. Justice Stevens may well be correct that the prosecutor's argument was permissible comment. The question on which review was granted assumed that there was error and the question to be resolved was whether harmless error analysis should have applied.

31. Here, for example, the court could have dealt with the offending argument by directing the District Court to order the prosecutor to show cause why he should not be disciplined, see, *e.g.*, Southern District of Illinois Rule 33, or by asking the Department of Justice to initiate a disciplinary

proceeding against him, see, *e.g.*, 28 CFR § 0.39 *et seq.* (1982). The Government informs us that during the year 1980, the Department of Justice's Office of Professional Responsibility investigated 28 complaints of unethical conduct and that one Assistant United States Attorney resigned in the face of an investigation that he made improper arguments to a grand jury. The Court also could have publicly chastised the prosecutor by identifying him in its opinion. See also *United States v. Modica*, 663 F.2d 1173, 1183–1186 (C.A.2 1981).

harmless error cannot be so lightly and casually ignored in order to chastise what the court viewed as prosecutorial overreaching.

[The majority reviewed the evidence and concluded that it was satisfied beyond a reasonable doubt that the error was harmless.]

Reversed and remanded.

JUSTICE BLACKMUN would vacate the judgment of the Court of Appeals and remand the case for consideration by that court of the issue whether the Fifth Amendment violation it perceived to exist was harmless error.

JUSTICE STEVENS, concurring in the judgment.

In my opinion the prosecutor's closing argument was free of constitutional error. It is therefore unnecessary for this Court to consider the scope of the supervisory power of the federal appellate courts, and it is unjustifiable for the Court to decree that, upon examination of the record in this case, the error was harmless beyond a reasonable doubt.
* * *

The four young people involved in this case arrived at Millas' Steak House at about midnight on October 11, 1979, in a car driven by one of the young women, who had apparently borrowed the car from her boyfriend. The driver and another of the young women went into the bar-restaurant and stayed two or three hours, drinking Pina Coladas and dancing, while the third young woman sat in the back seat of the car drinking beer with the young man. When they left Millas' at approximately 3 a.m., the other young woman decided to drive. The car needed oil. Instead of turning right in the direction of their homes, along a highway that would bring them to at least one all-night gas station, they turned left. This route led them to a Clark station and then to the spot where they were forced off the road. Defense counsel emphasized these facts in an attempt to cast doubts on the victims' ability to identify all of the defendants accurately, and to suggest the implausibility of their accounts. The prosecutor argued, quite properly in my opinion, that the defense had tried to divert the jury's attention from the central question in the case—what happened after the car was forced off the road by defendants' Cadillac. That central question could have been addressed by defense witnesses and defense counsel even without testimony by the defendants themselves.

As I have written before, a defendant's election not to testify "is almost certain to prejudice the defense no matter what else happens in the courtroom." *United States v. Davis*, 437 F.2d 928, 933 (C.A.7 1971). Under *Griffin v. California*, it is improper for either the court or the prosecutor to ask the jury to draw an adverse inference from a defendant's silence. But I do not believe the protective shield of the Fifth Amendment should be converted into a sword that cuts back on the area of legitimate comment by the prosecutor on the weaknesses in the defense case. The comment in this record, is not remotely comparable to the error in either *Griffin*[32] or *Wilson v. United States*, 149 U.S. 60

32. " 'He would know that. He would know how she got down the alley. He would know how the blood got on the bottom of the concrete steps. He would know how

(1893).[33] In my opinion it did not violate either the Fifth Amendment or 18 U.S.C. § 3481 as construed in *Wilson.*

If I were persuaded that the prosecutor's comment was improper, I could not possibly join the Court's *sua sponte* harmless-error determination. * * *

This Court is far too busy to be spending countless hours reviewing trial transcripts in an effort to determine the likelihood that an error may have affected a jury's deliberations. In this case the parties did not provide us with a printed appendix containing any portion of the trial testimony or with any of the trial exhibits that are discussed at some length in the transcript. I have spent several hours reviewing the one copy of the trial transcript that has been filed with the Court. But I have not read all of its 1,013 pages, and I have read only a few of the 450 pages of the transcript of the suppression hearing. The task of organizing and digesting the testimony is a formidable one. * * * As a practical matter, it is impossible for any Member of this Court to make the kind of conscientious and detailed examination of the record that should precede a determination that there can be no reasonable doubt that the jury's deliberations as to each defendant were not affected by the alleged error. And it is an insult to the Court of Appeals to imply, as the Court does today, that it cannot be trusted with a task that would normally be conducted on remand. * * * I do not believe the prosecutor committed procedural error in this case; if he did, however, I feel strongly that this Court should not make a clumsy effort to avoid another trial by undertaking a function that can better be performed by other judges. We, of course, would not want any of the victims to go through the ordeal of testifying again unless reversible error has been committed. On the other hand, we surely would not want one of the defendants to spend 40 years in jail just because the evidence against the other four is overwhelming. * * *

JUSTICE BRENNAN, with whom JUSTICE MARSHALL joins, concurring in part and dissenting in part. * * *

---

long he was with her in that box. He would know how her wig got off. He would know whether he beat her or mistreated her. He would know whether he walked away from that place cool as a cucumber when he saw Mr. Villasenor because he was conscious of his own guilt and wanted to get away from that damaged or injured woman.

" 'These things he has not seen fit to take the stand and deny or explain.

" 'And in the whole world, if anybody would know, this defendant would know.

" 'Essie Mae is dead, she can't tell you her side of the story. The defendant won't.' " 380 U.S., at 611.

33. "When the District Attorney, referring to the fact that the defendant did not ask to be a witness, said to the jury, 'I want to say to you, that if I am ever charged with crime, I will not stop by putting witnesses on the stand to testify to my good character, but I will go upon the stand and hold up my hand before high Heaven and testify to my innocence of the crime,' he intimated to them as plainly as if he had said in so many words that it was a circumstance against the innocence of the defendant that he did not go on the stand and testify. Nothing could have been more effective with the jury to induce them to disregard entirely the presumption of innocence to which by the law he was entitled. * * * " 149 U.S., at 66.

These cases indicate that the policy considerations supporting the harmless-error rule and those supporting the existence of an appellate court's supervisory powers are not in irreconcilable conflict. Both the harmless-error rule and the exercise of supervisory powers advance the important judicial and public interest in the orderly and efficient administration of justice. Exercise of the supervisory powers also can further the strong public interest in the integrity of the judicial process. If Government prosecutors have engaged in a pattern and practice of intentionally violating defendants' constitutional rights, a court of appeals certainly might be justified in reversing a conviction, even if the error at issue is harmless, in an effort to deter future violations. If effective as a deterrent, the reversal could avert further damage to judicial integrity. Admittedly, using the supervisory powers to reverse a conviction under these circumstances appears to conflict with the public's interest in upholding otherwise valid convictions that are tainted only by harmless error. But it is certainly arguable that the public's interests in preserving judicial integrity and in insuring that Government prosecutors, as its agents, refrain from intentionally violating defendants' rights are stronger than its interest in upholding the conviction of a particular criminal defendant. Convictions are important, but they should not be protected at any cost.

I have no occasion now to define the precise contours of supervisory powers or to explore the circumstances in which using them to reverse a conviction based on harmless error might be appropriate. This much, however, is clear: A court of appeals should exercise its supervisory powers to reverse a conviction based on harmless error only in the most extreme circumstances and only after careful consideration, and balancing, of all the relevant interests.[34] The policies supporting the harmless-error rule announced in *Chapman* should be given considerable, but not controlling, weight in that balance. In my view, there is nothing in *Chapman* that requires us to adopt a *per se* rule against using the supervisory powers to reverse a conviction based on harmless error. In light of the importance of the interests potentially at stake, it would be surprising if there were.

D. THE RIGHT TO CONFRONT WITNESSES AND TO PRESENT A DEFENSE

POINTER v. TEXAS

Supreme Court of the United States, 1965.
380 U.S. 400, 85 S.Ct. 1065, 13 L.Ed.2d 923.

MR. JUSTICE BLACK delivered the opinion of the Court.

* * *

The petitioner Pointer and one Dillard were arrested in Texas and taken before a state judge for a preliminary hearing (in Texas called the

---

34. Although the interests of a victim in a particular case are not relevant to determining whether to enforce the established rights of a criminal defendant, the interests of a victim may be relevant to determining whether to invoke the supervisory powers to reverse a conviction in a particular case even though the error is harmless. Whether a continuing problem calls for the exercise of supervisory powers is a different question from whether a particular case is an appropriate context in which to exercise those powers.

"examining trial") on a charge of having robbed Kenneth W. Phillips of $375 "by assault, or violence, or by putting in fear of life or bodily injury," in violation of Texas Penal Code Art. 1408. At this hearing an Assistant District Attorney conducted the prosecution and examined witnesses, but neither of the defendants, both of whom were laymen, had a lawyer. Phillips as chief witness for the State gave his version of the alleged robbery in detail, identifying petitioner as the man who had robbed him at gunpoint. Apparently Dillard tried to cross-examine Phillips but Pointer did not, although Pointer was said to have tried to cross-examine some other witnesses at the hearing. Petitioner was subsequently indicted on a charge of having committed the robbery. Some time before the trial was held, Phillips moved to California. After putting in evidence to show that Phillips had moved and did not intend to return to Texas, the State at the trial offered the transcript of Phillips' testimony given at the preliminary hearing as evidence against petitioner. Petitioner's counsel immediately objected to introduction of the transcript, stating, "Your Honor, we will object to that, as it is a denial of the confrontment of the witnesses against the Defendant." Similar objections were repeatedly made by petitioner's counsel but were overruled by the trial judge, apparently in part because, as the judge viewed it, petitioner had been present at the preliminary hearing and therefore had been "accorded the opportunity of cross examining the witnesses there against him." The Texas Court of Criminal Appeals, the highest state court to which the case could be taken, affirmed petitioner's conviction, rejecting his contention that use of the transcript to convict him denied him rights guaranteed by the Sixth and Fourteenth Amendments. We granted certiorari to consider the important constitutional question the case involves.

In this Court we do not find it necessary to decide one aspect of the question petitioner raises, that is, whether failure to appoint counsel to represent him at the preliminary hearing unconstitutionally denied him the assistance of counsel.[a]

It cannot seriously be doubted at this late date that the right of cross-examination is included in the right of an accused in a criminal case to confront the witnesses against him. And probably no one, certainly no one experienced in the trial of lawsuits, would deny the value of cross-examination in exposing falsehood and bringing out the truth in the trial of a criminal case. The fact that this right appears in the Sixth Amendment of our Bill of Rights reflects the belief of the

a. In a subsequent case, the Court held that a criminal defendant has a constitutional right to the assistance of counsel at his preliminary hearing. Coleman v. Alabama, 399 U.S. 1 (1970).—ed.

Framers of those liberties and safeguards that confrontation was a fundamental right essential to a fair trial in a criminal prosecution. Moreover, the decisions of this Court and other courts throughout the years have constantly emphasized the necessity for cross-examination as a protection for defendants in criminal cases. * * *

We hold that petitioner was entitled to be tried in accordance with the protection of the confrontation guarantee of the Sixth Amendment, and that that guarantee, like the right against compelled self-incrimination, is "to be enforced against the States under the Fourteenth Amendment according to the same standards that protect those personal rights against federal encroachment." Malloy v. Hogan [supra, p. 453.].

Under this Court's prior decisions, the Sixth Amendment's guarantee of confrontation and cross-examination was unquestionably denied petitioner in this case. As has been pointed out, a major reason underlying the constitutional confrontation rule is to give a defendant charged with crime an opportunity to cross-examine the witnesses against him. This Court has recognized the admissibility against an accused of dying declarations, and of testimony of a deceased witness who has testified at a former trial. [Citations] Nothing we hold here is to the contrary. The case before us would be quite a different one had Phillips' statement been taken at a full-fledged hearing at which petitioner had been represented by counsel who had been given a complete and adequate opportunity to cross-examine. There are other analogous situations which might not fall within the scope of the constitutional rule requiring confrontation of witnesses. The case before us, however, does not present any situation like those mentioned above or others analogous to them. Because the transcript of Phillips' statement offered against petitioner at his trial had not been taken at a time and under circumstances affording petitioner through counsel an adequate opportunity to cross-examine Phillips, its introduction in a federal court in a criminal case against Pointer would have amounted to denial of the privilege of confrontation guaranteed by the Sixth Amendment. Since we hold that the right of an accused to be confronted with the witnesses against him must be determined by the same standards whether the right is denied in a federal or state proceeding, it follows that use of the transcript to convict petitioner denied him a constitutional right, and that his conviction must be reversed.

Reversed and remanded.

WHITE v. ILLINOIS

Supreme Court of the United States, 1992.
502 U.S. 346, 112 S.Ct. 736, 116 L.Ed.2d 848.

THE CHIEF JUSTICE delivered the opinion of the Court.

In this case we consider whether the Confrontation Clause of the Sixth Amendment requires that, before a trial court admits testimony under the "spontaneous declaration" and "medical examination" exceptions to the hearsay rule, the prosecution must either produce the declarant at trial or the trial court must find that the declarant is unavailable. The Illinois Appellate Court concluded that such procedures are not constitutionally required. We agree with that conclusion.

Petitioner was convicted by a jury of aggravated criminal sexual assault, residential burglary, and unlawful restraint. The events giving rise to the charges related to the sexual assault of S.G., then four years old. Testimony at the trial established that in the early morning hours of April 16, 1988, S.G.'s babysitter, Tony DeVore, was awakened by S.G.'s scream. DeVore went to S.G.'s bedroom and witnessed petitioner leaving the room and petitioner then left the house. DeVore knew petitioner because petitioner was a friend of S.G.'s mother, Tammy Grigsby. DeVore asked S.G. what had happened. According to DeVore's trial testimony, S.G. stated that petitioner had put his hand over her mouth, choked her, threatened to whip her if she screamed and had "touch[ed] her in the wrong places." Asked by DeVore to point to where she had been touched, S.G. identified the vaginal area.

Tammy Grigsby, S.G.'s mother, returned home about 30 minutes later. Grigsby testified that her daughter appeared "scared" and a "little hyper." Grigsby proceeded to question her daughter about what had happened. At trial, Grigsby testified that S.G. repeated her claims that petitioner choked and threatened her. Grigsby also testified that S.G. stated that petitioner "put his mouth on her front part." Grigsby also noticed that S.G. had bruises and red marks on her neck that had not been there previously. Grigsby called the police.

Officer Terry Lewis arrived a few minutes later, roughly 45 minutes after S.G.'s scream had first awakened DeVore. Lewis questioned S.G. alone in the kitchen. At trial, Lewis' summary of S.G.'s statement indicated that she had offered essentially the same story as she had first reported to DeVore and to Grigsby, including a statement that petitioner had "used his tongue on her in her private parts."

After Lewis concluded his investigation, and approximately four hours after DeVore first heard S.G.'s scream, S.G. was taken to the hospital. She was examined first by Cheryl Reents, an emergency room nurse, and then by Dr. Michael Meinzen. Each testified at trial and their testimony indicated that, in response to questioning, S.G. again provided an account of events that was essentially identical to the one she had given to DeVore, Grigsby, and Lewis. S.G. never testified at petitioner's trial. The State attempted on two occasions to call her as a witness but she apparently experienced emotional difficulty on being brought to the courtroom and in each instance left without testifying. The defense made no attempt to call S.G. as a witness and the trial court neither made, nor was it asked to make, a finding that S.G. was unavailable to testify.

Petitioner objected on hearsay grounds to DeVore, Grigsby, Lewis, Reents, and Meinzen being permitted to testify regarding S.G.'s statements describing the assault. The trial court overruled each objection. With respect to DeVore, Grigsby, and Lewis the trial court concluded that the testimony could be permitted pursuant to an Illinois hearsay exception for spontaneous declarations. Petitioner's objections to Reents' and Meinzen's testimony was similarly overruled, based on both the spontaneous declaration exception and an exception for statements made in the course of securing medical treatment. The trial court also denied petitioner's motion for a mistrial based on S.G.'s "presence [and] failure to testify."

Petitioner was found guilty by a jury, and the Illinois Appellate Court affirmed his conviction. * * *

We consider as a preliminary matter an argument not considered below but urged by the United States as amicus curiae in support of respondent. The United States contends that petitioner's Confrontation Clause claim should be rejected because the Confrontation Clause's limited purpose is to prevent a particular abuse common in 16th and 17th century England: prosecuting a defendant through the presentation of ex parte affidavits, without the affiants ever being produced at trial. Because S.G.'s out-of-court statements do not fit this description, the United States suggests that S.G. was not a "witness against" petitioner within the meaning of the Clause. The United States urges this position, apparently in order that we might further conclude that the Confrontation Clause generally does not apply to the introduction of out-of-court statements admitted under an accepted hearsay exception. The only situation in which the Confrontation Clause would apply to such an exception, it argues, would be those few cases where the statement sought to be admitted was in the character of an ex parte affidavit, i.e., where the circumstances surrounding the out-of-court statement's utterance suggest that the statement has been made for the principal purpose of accusing or incriminating the defendant.

Such a narrow reading of the Confrontation Clause, which would virtually eliminate its role in restricting the admission of hearsay testimony, is foreclosed by our prior cases. The discussions in these cases, going back at least as far as Mattox v. United States, 156 U.S. 237 (1895), have included historical examination of the origins of the Confrontation Clause, and of the state of the law of evidence existing at the time the Sixth Amendment was adopted and later. We have been careful "not to equate the Confrontation Clause's prohibitions with the general rule prohibiting the admission of hearsay statements," Idaho v. Wright, (1990) 110 S.Ct. 3139, 3146. Nonetheless we have consistently sought to "steer a middle course," that recognizes that "hearsay rules and the Confrontation Clause are generally designed to protect similar values," California v. Green, 399 U.S. 149, 155 (1970), and "stem from the same roots." Dutton v. Evans, 400 U.S. 74, 86 (1970). In Mattox itself, upon which the Government relies, the Court allowed the recorded testimony of a witness at a prior trial to be admitted. But, in the Court's view, the result was justified not because the hearsay testimony was unlike an ex parte affidavit, but because it came within an established exception to the hearsay rule. We think that the argument presented by the Government comes too late in the day to warrant reexamination of this approach.

We therefore now turn to petitioner's principal contention that our prior decision in [Ohio v.] Roberts[, 448 U.S. 56] (1980), requires that his conviction be vacated. In *Roberts* we considered a Confrontation Clause challenge to the introduction at trial of a transcript containing testimony from a probable-cause hearing, where the transcript included testimony from a witness not produced at trial but who had been subject to examination by defendant's counsel at the probable-cause hearing. In the course of rejecting the Confrontation Clause claim in that case, we used language that might suggest that the Confrontation Clause generally requires that a declarant either be produced at trial or be found unavailable before his out-of-court statement may be admitted into evidence. However, we think such an expansive reading of the Clause is negated by our subsequent decision in [United States v.] Inadi[, 475 U.S. 387 (1986)].

In *Inadi* we considered the admission of out-of-court statements made by a co-conspirator in the course of the conspiracy. As an initial matter, we rejected the proposition that *Roberts* established a rule that "no out-of-court statement would be admissible without a showing of unavailability." To the contrary, * * * *Roberts* stands for the proposition that unavailability analysis is a necessary part of the Confrontation Clause inquiry only when the challenged out-of-court statements were made in the course of a prior judicial proceeding. [The Court in *Inadi*] held that co-conspirator statements may be admitted even if the declarant is not unavailable to testify.]

These observations, although expressed in the context of evaluating co-conspirator statements, apply with full force to the case at hand. We note first that the evidentiary rationale for permitting hearsay testimony regarding spontaneous declarations and statements made in the course of receiving medical care is that such out-of-court declarations are made in contexts that provide substantial guarantees of their trustworthiness. But those same factors that contribute to the statements' reliability cannot be recaptured even by later in-court testimony. A statement that has been offered in a moment of excitement—without the opportunity to reflect on the consequences of one's exclamation—may justifiably carry more weight with a trier of fact than a similar statement offered in the relative calm of the courtroom. Similarly, a statement made in the course of procuring medical services, where the declarant knows that a false statement may cause misdiagnosis or mistreatment, carries special guarantees of credibility that a trier of fact may not think replicated by courtroom testimony. They are thus materially different from the statements at issue in *Roberts,* where the out-of-court statements sought to be introduced were themselves made in the course of a judicial proceeding, and where there was consequently no threat of lost evidentiary value if the out-of-court statements were replaced with live testimony.

The preference for live testimony in the case of statements like those offered in *Roberts* is because of the importance of cross examination, "the greatest legal engine ever invented for the discovery of truth." Thus courts have adopted the general rule prohibiting the receipt of hearsay evidence. But where proffered hearsay has sufficient guarantees of reliability to come within a firmly rooted exception to the hearsay rule, the Confrontation Clause is satisfied. * * *

As a second line of argument, petitioner presses upon us two recent decisions involving child-testimony in child-sexual assault cases, Coy v. Iowa [487 U.S. 1012 (1988)], and Maryland v. Craig, 110 S.Ct. 3157 (1990). Both *Coy* and *Craig* required us to consider the constitutionality of courtroom procedures designed to prevent a child witness from having to face across an open courtroom a defendant charged with sexually assaulting the child. In *Coy* we vacated a conviction that resulted from a trial in which a child witness testified from behind a screen, and in which there had been no particularized showing that such a procedure was necessary to avert a risk of harm to the child. In *Craig* we upheld a conviction that resulted from a trial in which a child witness testified via closed circuit television after such a showing of necessity. Petitioner draws from these two cases a general rule that hearsay testimony offered by a child should be permitted only upon a showing of necessity—i.e., in cases where necessary to protect the child's physical and psychological well-being. Petitioner's reliance is misplaced. *Coy* and *Craig* involved only the question of what in-court procedures are constitutionally required to guarantee a defendant's confrontation right once a witness is testifying. Such a question is quite separate from that of what requirements the Confrontation Clause imposes as a predicate for the introduction of out-of-court declarations. * * *

For the foregoing reasons, the judgment of the Illinois Appellate Court is Affirmed.

JUSTICE THOMAS, with whom JUSTICE SCALIA joins, concurring in part and concurring in the judgment.

The Court reaches the correct result under our precedents. I write separately only to suggest that our Confrontation Clause jurisprudence has evolved in a manner that is perhaps inconsistent with the text and history of the Clause itself. The Court unnecessarily rejects, in dicta, the United States' suggestion that the Confrontation Clause in general may not regulate the admission of hearsay evidence. The truth may be that this Court's cases unnecessarily have complicated and confused the relationship between the constitutional right of confrontation and the hearsay rules of evidence. * * * I respectfully suggest that, in an appropriate case, we reconsider how the phrase "witness against" in the Confrontation Clause pertains to the admission of hearsay. I join the Court's opinion except for its discussion of the narrow reading of this phrase proposed by the United States.

GRAY v. MARYLAND

Supreme Court of the United States, 1998.
523 U.S. 185, 118 S.Ct. 1151, 140 L.Ed.2d 294.

JUSTICE BREYER delivered the opinion of the Court.

The issue in this case concerns the application of Bruton v. United States, 391 U.S. 123 (1968). *Bruton* involved two defendants accused of participating in the same crime and tried jointly before the same jury. One of the defendants had confessed. His confession named and incriminated the other defendant. The trial judge issued a limiting instruction, telling the jury that it should consider the confession as evidence only against the codefendant who had confessed and not against the defendant named in the confession. *Bruton* held that, despite the limiting instruction, the Constitution forbids the use of such a confession in the joint trial.

The case before us differs from *Bruton* in that the prosecution here redacted the codefendant's confession by substituting for the defendant's name in the confession a blank space or the word "deleted." We must decide whether these substitutions make a significant legal difference. We hold that they do not and that *Bruton*'s protective rule applies.

I

In 1993, Stacy Williams died after a severe beating. Anthony Bell gave a confession, to the Baltimore City police, in which he said that he (Bell), Kevin Gray, and Jacquin "Tank" Vanlandingham had participated in the beating that resulted in Williams' death. Vanlandingham later died. A Maryland grand jury indicted Bell and Gray for murder. The State of Maryland tried them jointly.

The trial judge, after denying Gray's motion for a separate trial, permitted the State to introduce Bell's confession into evidence at trial. But the judge ordered the confession redacted. Consequently, the police detective who read the confession into evidence said the word "deleted" or "deletion" whenever Gray's name or Vanlandingham's name appeared. Immediately after the police detective read the redacted confession to the jury, the prosecutor asked, "after he gave you that information, you subsequently were able to arrest Mr. Kevin Gray; is that correct?" The officer responded, "That's correct." The State also introduced into evidence a written copy of the confession with those two names omitted, leaving in their place blank white spaces separated by commas. The State produced other witnesses, who said that six persons (including Bell, Gray, and Vanlandingham) participated in the beating. Gray testified and denied his participation. Bell did not testify.

When instructing the jury, the trial judge specified that the confession was evidence only against Bell; the instructions said that the jury should not use the confession as evidence against Gray. The jury convicted both Bell and Gray. Gray appealed [and the Maryland Supreme Court affirmed.]

II

In deciding whether *Bruton*'s protective rule applies to the redacted confession before us, we must consider both *Bruton*, and a later case, Richardson v. Marsh, 481 U.S. 200 which limited *Bruton*'s We shall briefly summarize each of these two cases.

Bruton, as we have said, involved two defendants—Evans and Bruton—tried jointly for robbery. Evans did not testify, but the Government introduced into evidence Evans' confession, which stated that both he (Evans) and Bruton together had committed the robbery. The trial judge told the jury it could consider the confession as evidence only against Evans, not against Bruton.

This Court held that, despite the limiting instruction, the introduction of Evans' out-of-court confession at Bruton's trial had violated Bruton's right, protected by the Sixth Amendment, to cross-examine witnesses. The Court recognized that in many circumstances a limiting instruction will adequately protect one defendant from the prejudicial effects of the introduction at a joint trial of evidence intended for use only against a different defendant. But it said that

"there are some contexts in which the risk that the jury will not, or cannot, follow instructions is so great, and the consequences of failure so vital to the defendant, that the practical and human limitations of the jury system cannot be ignored. Such a context is presented here, where the powerfully incriminating extrajudicial statements of a codefendant, who stands accused side-by-side with the defendant, are deliberately spread before the jury in a joint trial. Not only are the incriminations devastating to the defendant but their credibility is inevitably suspect.... The unreliability of such evidence is intolerably compounded when the alleged accomplice, as here, does not testify and cannot be tested by cross-examination." Id., at 135–136.

In Richardson v. Marsh, *supra*, the Court considered a redacted confession. The case involved a joint murder trial of Marsh and Williams. The State had redacted the confession of one defendant, Williams, so as to omit all reference to his codefendant, Marsh—"indeed, to omit all indication that *anyone* other than ... Williams" and a third person had "participated in the crime." Id., at 203 (emphasis in original). The trial court also instructed the jury not to consider the confession against Marsh. As redacted, the confession indicated that Williams and the third person had discussed the murder in the front seat of a car while they traveled to the victim's house. The redacted confession contained no indication that Marsh—or any other person—was in the car. Later in the trial, however, Marsh testified that she was in the back seat of the car. For that reason, in context, the confession still could have helped convince the jury that Marsh knew about the murder in advance and therefore had participated knowingly in the crime.

The Court held that this redacted confession fell outside *Bruton*'s scope and was admissible (with appropriate limiting instructions) at the joint trial. The Court distinguished Evans' confession in *Bruton* as a confession that was "incriminating on its face," and which had "expressly implicated" Bruton. By contrast, Williams' confession amounted to "evidence requiring linkage" in that it "became" incriminating in respect to Marsh "only when linked with evidence introduced later at trial." The Court held "that the Confrontation Clause is not violated by the admission of a nontestifying codefendant's confession with a proper limiting instruction when, as here, the confession is redacted to eliminate not only the defendant's name, but any reference to his or her existence." Id., at 211.

The Court added: "We express no opinion on the admissibility of a confession in which the defendant's name has been replaced with a symbol or neutral pronoun." Id., at 211, n. 5.

III

Originally, the codefendant's confession in the case before us, like that in *Bruton*, referred to, and directly implicated another defendant. The State, however, redacted that confession by removing the nonconfessing defendant's name. Nonetheless, unlike *Richardson*'s redacted confession, this confession refers directly to the "existence" of the nonconfessing defendant. The State has simply replaced the nonconfessing defendant's name with a kind of symbol, namely the word "deleted" or a blank space set off by commas. The redacted confession, for example, responded to the question "Who was in the group that beat Stacey," with the phrase, "Me, , and a few other guys." And when the police witness read the confession in court, he said the word "deleted" or "deletion" where the blank spaces appear. We therefore must decide a question that *Richardson* left open, namely whether redaction that replaces a defendant's name with an obvious indication of deletion, such as a blank space, the word "deleted," or a similar symbol, still falls within *Bruton's* protective rule. We hold that it does.

* * * Redactions that simply replace a name with an obvious blank space or a word such as "deleted" or a symbol or other similarly obvious indications of alteration, however, leave statements that, considered as a class, so closely resemble *Bruton*'s unredacted statements that, in our view, the law must require the same result. For one thing, a jury will often react similarly to an unredacted confession and a confession redacted in this way, for the jury will often realize that the confession refers specifically to the defendant. This is true even when the State does not blatantly link the defendant to the deleted name, as it did in this case by asking whether Gray was arrested on the basis of information in Bell's confession as soon as the officer had finished reading the redacted statement. Consider a simplified but typical example, a confession that reads "I, Bob Smith, along with Sam Jones, robbed the bank." To replace the words "Sam Jones" with an obvious blank will not likely fool anyone. A juror somewhat familiar with criminal law would know immediately that the blank, in the phrase "I, Bob Smith, along with , robbed the bank," refers to defendant Jones. A juror who does not know

the law and who therefore wonders to whom the blank might refer need only lift his eyes to Jones, sitting at counsel table, to find what will seem the obvious answer, at least if the juror hears the judge's instruction not to consider the confession as evidence against Jones, for that instruction will provide an obvious reason for the blank. A more sophisticated juror, wondering if the blank refers to someone else, might also wonder how, if it did, the prosecutor could argue the confession is reliable, for the prosecutor, after all, has been arguing that Jones, not someone else, helped Smith commit the crime.

For another thing, the obvious deletion may well call the jurors' attention specially to the removed name. By encouraging the jury to speculate about the reference, the redaction may overemphasize the importance of the confession's accusation—once the jurors work out the reference. * * * We concede certain differences between *Bruton* and this case. A confession that uses a blank or the word "delete" (or, for that matter, a first name or a nickname) less obviously refers to the defendant than a confession that uses the defendant's full and proper name. Moreover, in some instances the person to whom the blank refers may not be clear: Although the follow-up question asked by the State in this case eliminated all doubt, the reference might not be transparent in other cases in which a confession, like the present confession, uses two (or more) blanks, even though only one other defendant appears at trial, and in which the trial indicates that there are more participants than the confession has named. Nonetheless, as we have said, we believe that, considered as a class, redactions that replace a proper name with an obvious blank, the word "delete," a symbol, or similarly notify the jury that a name has been deleted are similar enough to *Bruton*'s unredacted confessions as to warrant the same legal results. * * *

Richardson expressed concern lest application of Bruton's rule apply where "redaction" of confessions, particularly "confessions incriminating by connection," would often not be possible, thereby forcing prosecutors too often to abandon use either of the confession or of a joint trial. Additional redaction of a confession that uses a blank space, the word "delete," or a symbol, however, normally is possible. Consider as an example a portion of the confession before us: The witness who read the confession told the jury that the confession (among other things) said,

"Question: Who was in the group that beat Stacey?

"Answer: Me, deleted, deleted, and a few other guys."

Why could the witness not, instead, have said:

"Question: Who was in the group that beat Stacey?

"Answer: Me and a few other guys."

The *Richardson* Court also feared that the inclusion, within *Bruton*'s protective rule, of confessions that incriminated "by connection" too often would provoke mistrials, or would unnecessarily lead prosecutors to abandon the confession or joint trial, because neither the prosecutors nor the judge could easily predict, until after the introduction of all the evidence, whether or not *Bruton* had barred use of the confession. To include the use of blanks, the word "delete," symbols, or other indications of redaction, within *Bruton's* protections, however, runs no such risk. Their use is easily identified prior to trial and does not depend, in any special way, upon the other evidence introduced in the case. We also note that several Circuits have interpreted Bruton similarly for many years [citations], yet no one has told us of any significant practical difficulties arising out of their administration of that rule.

For these reasons, we hold that the confession here at issue, which substituted blanks and the word "delete" for the respondent's proper name, falls within the class of statements to which Bruton's protections apply.

Justice SCALIA, with whom THE CHIEF JUSTICE, Justice KENNEDY, and Justice THOMAS join, dissenting.

* * * The almost invariable assumption of the law is that jurors follow their instructions. This rule "is a pragmatic one, rooted less in the absolute certitude that the presumption is true than in the belief that it represents a reasonable practical accommodation of the interests of the state and the defendant in the criminal justice process. * * * [The rule of the *Bruton* case is a narrow exception to this general rule.]

The Court's extension of *Bruton* to name-redacted confessions as a class will seriously compromise society's compelling interest in finding, convicting, and punishing those who violate the law. We explained in *Richardson* that forgoing use of codefendant confessions or joint trials was too high a price to insure that juries never disregard their instructions. The Court minimizes the damage that it does by suggesting that "additional redaction of a confession that uses a blank space, the word 'delete,' or a symbol ... normally is possible." In the present case, it asks, why could the police officer not have testified that Bell's answer was "Me and a few other guys"? The answer, it seems obvious to me, is because that is not what Bell said. Bell's answer was "Me, Tank, Kevin and a few other guys." Introducing the statement with full disclosure of deletions is one thing; introducing as the complete statement what was in fact only a part is something else. And of course even concealed deletions from the text will often not do the job that the Court demands. For inchoate offenses—conspiracy in particular—redaction to delete all reference to a confederate would often render the confession nonsensical. If the question was "Who agreed to beat Stacey?", and the answer was "Me and Kevin," we might redact the answer to "Me and [deleted]," or perhaps to "Me and somebody else," but surely not to just "Me"—for that would no longer be a confession to the conspiracy charge, but rather the foundation for an insanity defense. To my knowledge we have never before endorsed—and to my strong belief we ought not endorse—the redaction of a statement by some means other than the deletion of certain words, with the fact of the deletion shown. The risk to the integrity of our system (not to mention the increase in its complexity) posed by the approval of such free-lance editing seems to me infinitely greater than the risk posed by the entirely honest reproduction that the Court disapproves.* * * I would affirm the judgment.

CHAMBERS v. MISSISSIPPI

Supreme Court of the United States, 1973.
410 U.S. 284, 93 S.Ct. 1038, 35 L.Ed.2d 297.

Mr. Justice Powell delivered the opinion of the Court.

Petitioner, Leon Chambers, was tried by a jury in a Mississippi trial court and convicted of murdering a policeman. The jury assessed punishment at life imprisonment, and the Mississippi Supreme Court affirmed, one justice dissenting. * * *

I

The events that led to petitioner's prosecution for murder occurred in the small town of Woodville in southern Mississippi. On Saturday evening, June 14, 1969, two Woodville policemen, James Forman and Aaron "Sonny" Liberty, entered a local bar and pool hall to execute a warrant for the arrest of a youth named C. C. Jackson. Jackson resisted and a hostile crowd of some 50 or 60 persons gathered. The officers' first attempt to handcuff Jackson was frustrated when 20 or 25 men in the crowd intervened and wrestled him free. Forman then radioed for assistance and Liberty removed his riot gun, a 12–gauge sawed-off shotgun, from the car. Three deputy sheriffs arrived shortly thereafter and the officers again attempted to make their arrest. Once more, the officers were attacked by the onlookers and during the commotion five or six pistol shots were fired. Forman was looking in a different direction when the shooting began, but immediately saw that Liberty had been shot several times in the back. Before Liberty died, he turned around and fired both barrels of his riot gun into an alley in the area from which the shots appeared to have come. The first shot was wild and high and scattered the crowd standing at the face of the alley. Liberty appeared, however, to take more deliberate aim before the second shot and hit one of the men in the crowd in the back of the head and neck as he ran down the alley. That man was Leon Chambers.

Officer Forman could not see from his vantage point who shot Liberty or whether Liberty's shots hit anyone. One of the deputy sheriffs testified at trial that he was standing several feet from Liberty and that he saw Chambers shoot him. Another deputy sheriff stated that, although he could not see whether Chambers had a gun in his hand, he did see Chambers "break his arm down" shortly before the shots were fired. The officers who saw Chambers fall testified that they thought he was dead but they made no effort at that time either to examine him or to search for the murder weapon. Instead, they attended to Liberty, who was placed in the police car and taken to a hospital where he was declared dead on arrival. A subsequent autopsy showed that he had been hit with four bullets from a .22–caliber revolver.

Shortly after the shooting, three of Chambers' friends discovered that he was not yet dead. James Williams, Berkley Turner, and Gable McDonald loaded him into a car and transported him to the same hospital. Later that night, when the county sheriff discovered that Chambers was still alive, a guard was placed outside his room. Chambers was subsequently charged with Liberty's murder. He pleaded not guilty and has asserted his innocence throughout.

The story of Leon Chambers is intertwined with the story of another man, Gable McDonald. McDonald, a lifelong resident of Woodville, was in the crowd on the evening of Liberty's death. Sometime shortly after that day, he left his wife in Woodville and moved to Louisiana and found a job at a sugar mill. In November of that same year, he returned to Woodville when his wife informed him that an acquaintance of his, known as Reverend Stokes, wanted to see him. Stokes owned a gas station in Natchez, Mississippi, several miles north of Woodville, and upon his return McDonald went to see him. After talking to Stokes, McDonald agreed to make a statement to Chambers' attorneys, who maintained offices in Natchez. Two days later, he appeared at the attorneys' offices and gave a sworn confession that he shot Officer Liberty. He also stated that he had already told a friend of his, James Williams, that he shot Liberty. He said that he used his own pistol, a nine-shot .22–caliber revolver, which he had discarded shortly after the shooting. In response to questions from Chambers' attorneys, McDonald affirmed that his confession was voluntary and that no one had compelled him to come to them. Once the confession had been transcribed, signed, and witnessed, McDonald was turned over to the local police authorities and was placed in jail.

One month later, at a preliminary hearing, McDonald repudiated his prior sworn confession. He testified that Stokes had persuaded him to confess that he shot Liberty. He claimed that Stokes had promised that he would not go to jail and that he would share in the proceeds of a lawsuit that Chambers would bring against the town of Woodville. On examination by his own attorney and on cross-examination by the State, McDonald swore that he had not been at the scene when Liberty was shot but had been down the street drinking beer in a cafe with a friend, Berkley Turner. When he and Turner heard the shooting, he testified, they walked up the street and found Chambers lying in the alley. He, Turner, and Williams took Chambers to the hospital. McDonald further testified at the preliminary hearing that he did not know what had happened, that there was no discussion about the shooting either going to or coming back from the hospital, and that it was not until the next day that he learned that Chambers had been felled by a blast from Liberty's riot gun. In addition, McDonald stated that while he once owned a .22–caliber pistol he had lost it many months before the shooting and did not own or possess a weapon at that time. The local justice of the peace accepted McDonald's repudiation and released him from custody. The local authorities undertook no further investigation of his possible involvement.

Chambers' case came on for trial in October of the next year. At trial, he endeavored to develop two grounds of defense. He first attempted to show that he did not shoot Liberty. Only one officer testified that he actually saw Chambers fire the shots. Although three officers saw Liberty shoot Chambers and testified that they assumed he was shooting his attacker, none of them examined Chambers to see whether he was still alive or whether he possessed a gun. Indeed, no weapon was ever recovered from the scene and there was no proof that Chambers had ever owned a .22–caliber pistol. One witness testified that he was standing in the street near where Liberty was shot, that he was looking at Chambers when the shooting began, and that he was sure that Chambers did not fire the shots.

Petitioner's second defense was that Gable McDonald had shot Officer Liberty. He was only partially successful, however, in his efforts to bring before the jury the testimony supporting this defense. Sam Hardin, a lifelong friend of McDonald's, testified that he saw McDonald shoot Liberty. A second witness, one of Liberty's cousins, testified that he saw McDonald immediately after the shooting with a pistol in his hand. In addition to the testimony of these two witnesses, Chambers endeavored to show the jury that McDonald had repeatedly confessed to the crime. Chambers attempted to prove that McDonald had admitted responsibility for the murder on four separate occasions, once when he gave the sworn statement to Chambers' counsel and three other times prior to that occasion in private conversations with friends.

In large measure, he was thwarted in his attempt to present this portion of his defense by the strict application of certain Mississippi rules of evidence. Chambers asserts in this Court, as he did unsuccessfully in his motion for new trial and on appeal to the State Supreme Court, that the application of these evidentiary rules rendered his trial fundamentally unfair and deprived him of due process of law. It is necessary, therefore, to examine carefully the rulings made during the trial.

II

Chambers filed a pretrial motion requesting the court to order McDonald to appear. Chambers also sought a ruling at that time that, if the State itself chose not to call McDonald, he be allowed to call him as an adverse witness. Attached to the motion were copies of McDonald's sworn confession and of the transcript of his preliminary hearing at which he repudiated that confession. The trial court granted the motion requiring McDonald to appear but reserved ruling on the adverse-witness motion. At trial, after the State failed to put McDonald on the stand, Chambers called McDonald, laid a predicate for the introduction of his sworn out-of-court confession, had it admitted into evidence, and read it to the jury. The State, upon cross-examination, elicited from McDonald the fact that he had repudiated his prior confession. McDonald further testified, as he had at the preliminary hearing, that he did not shoot Liberty, and that he confessed to the crime only on the promise of Reverend Stokes that he would not go to jail and would share in a sizable tort recovery from the town. He also retold his own story of his actions on the evening of the shooting, including his visit to the cafe down the street, his absence from the scene during the critical period, and his subsequent trip to the hospital with Chambers.

At the conclusion of the State's cross-examination, Chambers renewed his motion to examine McDonald as an adverse witness. The trial court denied the motion, stating: "He may be hostile, but he is not adverse in the sense of the word, so your request will be overruled." On appeal, the State Supreme Court upheld the trial court's ruling, finding that "McDonald's testimony was not adverse to appellant" because "[n]owhere did he point the finger at Chambers."

Defeated in his attempt to challenge directly McDonald's renunciation of his prior confession, Chambers sought to introduce the testimony of the three witnesses to whom McDonald had admitted that he shot the officer. The first of these, Sam Hardin, would have testified that, on the night of the shooting, he spent the late evening hours with McDonald at a friend's house after their return from the hospital and that, while driving McDonald home later that night, McDonald stated that he shot Liberty. The State objected to the admission of this testimony on the ground that it was hearsay. The trial court sustained the objection.

Berkley Turner, the friend with whom McDonald said he was drinking beer when the shooting occurred, was then called to testify. In the jury's presence, and without objection, he testified that he had not been in the cafe that Saturday and had not had any beers with McDonald. The jury was then excused. In the absence of the jury, Turner recounted his conversations with McDonald while they were riding with James Williams to take Chambers to the hospital. When asked whether McDonald said anything regarding the shooting of Liberty, Turner testified that McDonald told him that he "shot him." Turner further stated that one week later, when he met McDonald at a friend's house, McDonald reminded him of their prior conversation and urged Turner not to "mess him up." Petitioner argued to the court that, especially where there was other proof in the case that was corroborative of these out-of-court statements, Turner's testimony as to McDonald's self-incriminating remarks should have been admitted as an exception to the hearsay rule. Again, the trial court sustained the State's objection.

The third witness, Albert Carter, was McDonald's neighbor. They had been friends for about 25 years. Although Carter had not been in Woodville on the evening of the shooting, he stated that he learned about it the next morning from McDonald. That same day, he and McDonald walked out to a well near McDonald's house and there McDonald told him that he was the one who shot Officer Liberty. Carter testified that McDonald also told him that he had disposed of the .22–caliber revolver later that night. He further testified that several weeks after the shooting, he accompanied McDonald to Natchez where McDonald purchased another .22 pistol to replace the one he had discarded.[35] The jury

---

35. A gun dealer from Natchez testified that McDonald had made two purchases. The witness' business records indicated that McDonald purchased a nine-shot .22–

was not allowed to hear Carter's testimony. Chambers urged that these statements were admissible, the State objected, and the court sustained the objection. On appeal, the State Supreme Court approved the lower court's exclusion of these witnesses' testimony on hearsay grounds.

In sum, then, this was Chambers' predicament. As a consequence of the combination of Mississippi's "party witness" or "voucher" rule and its hearsay rule, he was unable either to cross-examine McDonald or to present witnesses in his own behalf who would have discredited McDonald's repudiation and demonstrated his complicity. Chambers had, however, chipped away at the fringes of McDonald's story by introducing admissible testimony from other sources indicating that he had not been seen in the cafe where he said he was when the shooting started, that he had not been having beer with Turner, and that he possessed a .22 pistol at the time of the crime. But all that remained from McDonald's own testimony was a single written confession countered by an arguably acceptable renunciation. Chambers' defense was far less persuasive than it might have been had he been given an opportunity to subject McDonald's statements to cross-examination or had the other confessions been admitted.

III

The right of an accused in a criminal trial to due process is, in essence, the right to a fair opportunity to defend against the State's accusations. The rights to confront and cross-examine witnesses and to call witnesses in one's own behalf have long been recognized as essential to due process. * * *

In this case, petitioner's request to cross-examine McDonald was denied on the basis of a Mississippi common-law rule that a party may not impeach his own witness. The rule rests on the presumption—without regard to the circumstances of the particular case—that a party who calls a witness "vouches for his credibility." Although the historical origins of the "voucher" rule are uncertain, it appears to be a remnant of primitive English trial practice in which "oath-takers" or "compurgators" were called to stand behind a particular party's position in any controversy. Their assertions were strictly partisan and, quite unlike witnesses in criminal trials today, their role bore little relation to the impartial ascertainment of the facts. * * * The "voucher" rule, as applied in this case, plainly interfered with Chambers' right to defend against the State's charges.

We need not decide, however, whether this error alone would occasion reversal since Chambers' claimed denial of due process rests on the ultimate impact of that error when viewed in conjunction with the trial court's refusal to permit him to call other witnesses. The trial court refused to allow him to introduce the testimony of Hardin, Turner, and Carter. Each would have testified to the statements purportedly made by

caliber revolver about a year prior to the murder. He purchased a different style .22 three weeks after Liberty's death.

McDonald, on three separate occasions shortly after the crime, naming himself as the murderer. The State Supreme Court approved the exclusion of this evidence on the ground that it was hearsay.

The hearsay rule, which has long been recognized and respected by virtually every State, is based on experience and grounded in the notion that untrustworthy evidence should not be presented to the triers of fact. Out-of-court statements are traditionally excluded because they lack the conventional indicia of reliability: they are usually not made under oath or other circumstances that impress the speaker with the solemnity of his statements; the declarant's word is not subject to cross-examination; and he is not available in order that his demeanor and credibility may be assessed by the jury. California v. Green, 399 U.S. 149, 158 (1970). A number of exceptions have developed over the years to allow admission of hearsay statements made under circumstances that tend to assure reliability and thereby compensate for the absence of the oath and opportunity for cross-examination. Among the most prevalent of these exceptions is the one applicable to declarations against interest—an exception founded on the assumption that a person is unlikely to fabricate a statement against his own interest at the time it is made. Mississippi recognizes this exception but applies it only to declarations against pecuniary interest. It recognizes no such exception for declarations, like McDonald's in this case, that are against the penal interest of the declarant. Brown v. State, 99 Miss. 719, 55 So. 961 (1911).

This materialistic limitation on the declaration-against-interest hearsay exception appears to be accepted by most States in their criminal trial processes, although a number of States have discarded it. Declarations against penal interest have also been excluded in federal courts under the authority of Donnelly v. United States, 228 U.S. 243 (1913), although exclusion would not be required under the newly proposed Federal Rules of Evidence. Exclusion, where the limitation prevails, is usually premised on the view that admission would lead to the frequent presentation of perjured testimony to the jury. It is believed that confessions of criminal activity are often motivated by extraneous considerations and, therefore, are not as inherently reliable as statements against pecuniary or proprietary interest. While that rationale has been the subject of considerable scholarly criticism, we need not decide in this case whether, under other circumstances, it might serve some valid state purpose by excluding untrustworthy testimony.

The hearsay statements involved in this case were originally made and subsequently offered at trial under circumstances that provided considerable assurance of their reliability. First, each of McDonald's confessions was made spontaneously to a close acquaintance shortly after the murder had occurred. Second, each one was corroborated by some other evidence in the case—McDonald's sworn confession, the testimony of an eyewitness to the shooting, the testimony that McDonald was seen with a gun immediately after the shooting, and proof of his prior ownership of a .22–caliber revolver and subsequent purchase of a new weapon. The sheer number of independent confessions provided additional corroboration for each. Third, whatever may be the parameters of the penal-interest rationale, each confession here was in a very real sense self-incriminatory and unquestionably against interest. McDonald stood to benefit nothing by disclosing his role in the shooting to any of his three friends and he must have been aware of the possibility that disclosure would lead to criminal prosecution. Indeed, after telling Turner of his involvement, he subsequently urged Turner not to "mess him up." Finally, if there was any question about the truthfulness of the extrajudicial statements, McDonald was present in the courtroom and was under oath. He could have been cross-examined by the State, and his demeanor and responses weighed by the jury. * * *

We conclude that the exclusion of this critical evidence, coupled with the State's refusal to permit Chambers to cross-examine McDonald, denied him a trial in accord with traditional and fundamental standards of due process. * * *

Reversed and remanded.

[Concurring and dissenting opinions omitted.]

E. JURY DELIBERATIONS

PEOPLE v. DE LUCIA

New York Court of Appeals, 1967.
20 N.Y.2d 275, 282 N.Y.S.2d 526, 229 N.E.2d 211.

KEATING, JUDGE.

The issue on this appeal is the effect of an unauthorized visit by a jury to the scene of the alleged crime. Defendants De Lucia and Montella were convicted, after a jury trial, of attempted burglary in the third degree and of possession of burglar's instruments. The Appellate Division unanimously affirmed. By a closely divided court, we upheld the conviction, stating that "It has long been familiar law that jurors may not impeach their own duly rendered verdict by statements or testimony averring their own misconduct within or without the jury room." (People v. De Lucia, 206 N.E.2d 324.)

The United States Supreme Court denied certiorari. Subsequently, however, Parker v. Gladden, 385 U.S. 363 (1966), was decided. The case originated in Oregon, where a trial court found that a bailiff, assigned to shepherd a sequestered jury, had told them that the defendant (petitioner) was guilty and that, if there were any error in finding the petitioner guilty, the Supreme Court would correct it. The Oregon Supreme Court found that the bailiff's misconduct did not deprive the petitioner, Parker, of a fair trial.

In reversing, the United States Supreme Court found that the bailiff had, in a sense, become a witness against the defendant in contravention of his right to "be confronted with the witnesses against him". Referring to the bailiff's comments as an "outside influence", the court stated that it has "followed the 'undeviating rule,' that the rights of confrontation and cross-examination are among the fundamental requirements of a constitutionally fair trial."

Prior to the decision in Parker v. Gladden, the defendants, De Lucia and Montella, brought a petition for a writ of habeas corpus in the United States District Court for the Northern District of New York. The writ was dismissed. While the appeal was pending, Parker v. Gladden was decided. The United States Court of Appeals for the Second Circuit accordingly vacated the order of the District Court and dismissed the writ without prejudice in order to give the New York courts an opportunity to reconsider the petitioners' claims in light of the Supreme Court decision.

We are not unaware, nor was the Second Circuit, that there is a distinction between this case and Parker v. Gladden. In *Parker*, the Oregon court had not excluded the statements of the jurors as testimonially incompetent. Rather, it found that, despite this evidence of what the bailiff had said, the defendant had not been prejudiced. Our New York case law holds that statements by jurors impeaching their own verdicts are inadmissible. However, where the Supreme Court holds that a particular series of events, when proven, violates a defendant's constitutional rights, implicit in that determination is the right of the defendant to prove facts substantiating his claim.

The question which, therefore, presents itself in light of Parker v. Gladden is whether we should re-examine the applicability of the traditional common-law rule to circumstances such as those present in the case at bar or whether we should compel the defendants to seek the relief to which they are constitutionally entitled in the Federal courts. We believe that the undesirability of this latter alternative indicates that a re-examination of our common-law rule with respect to jurors in impeaching their own verdict is appropriate.

The policy reason for the present rule is, of course, that we do not wish to encourage the post-trial harassing of jurors for statements which might render their verdicts questionable. With regard to jury room deliberations, scarcely any verdict might remain unassailable, if such statements were admissible. Common experience indicates that at times articulate jurors may intimidate the inarticulate, the aggressive may unduly influence the docile. Some jurors may "throw in" when deliberations have reached an impasse. Others may attempt to compromise. Permitting jurors to testify regarding such occurrences would create chaos.

On the other hand, a defendant has a right to a trial by a fair and impartial jury. The public policy considerations must at all times be weighed against the defendant's fundamental rights.

We attempted to balance these opposing considerations in People v. Leonti, 262 N.Y. 256, 186 N.E. 693. The defendant in that case was a Sicilian, who had testified in his own behalf. After the verdict, one of the jurors swore in an affidavit that he would never believe a Sicilian under oath. We held that such an affidavit was admissible, reasoning that it did not operate so much to impeach the verdict as to prove that the juror, because of his prejudice never became eligible to *be* a juror and, therefore, his vote was a nullity.

Thus, where a patent injustice to a defendant was present, we distinguished the case on a philosophical ground, although the prohibited result, the impeachment of the verdict, remained. This was a recognition that the rule against jurors' impeachment of their verdicts should not operate in every case. Where, as in the case of statements regarding juryroom deliberations, every verdict might be rendered suspect, and jurors might become subjected to continuous posttrial harassment, the public policy reasons for holding such statements inadmissible must ordinarily override possible injustice to a defendant, for here our jury system itself is at stake.

Statements concerning outside influences on a jury, however, occurring less frequently and more susceptible to adequate proof, should be admissible to show that the defendant was prejudiced, for here the danger to our jury system is minimal compared with the more easily proven prejudice to the defendant.

In the instant case, it appears that several jurors not only went to the scene, but actually re-enacted the alleged crime.

To use the reasoning of the Supreme Court in Parker v. Gladden, these jurors became unsworn witnesses against the defendants in direct contravention of their right, under the Sixth Amendment, "to be confronted with the witnesses" against them.

Our re-evaluation of the common-law rule that jurors may not impeach their own verdicts reveals that in the case of such inherently prejudicial "outside influences" on a jury as were here present, the violation of the defendants' Sixth Amendment rights outweighs the policy reasons for the rule. * * *

In this type of case, proof of the fact of the unauthorized visit is sufficient to warrant a new trial without proof of how such visit may have influenced individual jurors in their juryroom deliberations. Such a visit, in and of itself, constitutes inherent prejudice to the defendants.

Since the District Attorney has never had an opportunity to examine the jurors regarding their statements, we remit this case to the trial court for a hearing in regard to the petitioners' allegations and, in the event the allegations of the petitioners are substantiated, the judgment of conviction should be vacated and a new trial ordered.

[Dissenting opinion omitted.]

STATE v. FAJARDO

Supreme Court of Hawaii, 1985.
67 Haw. 593, 699 P.2d 20.

HAYASHI, JUSTICE.

Eliseo Fuentes Fajardo (hereinafter "Appellant") was convicted of manslaughter in the death of Robert John Tavares. For the reasons stated below we reverse the conviction.

I.

On April 30, 1983, Appellant and Tavares got into a verbal altercation at the Atlantis discotheque in the Pacific Beach Hotel in Waikiki. They decided to settle the matter outside and walked out to the hallway by the entrance of the discotheque. A fight ensued. Appellant pulled out a knife and stabbed Tavares to death.

Appellant was charged with the murder of Tavares in violation of Hawaii Revised Statutes § 707–701 (1976). He claimed self-defense. The first trial ended in a mistrial on December 7, 1983. A second trial followed in the same courtroom on December 12–16, 19, 21–23 and 27, 1983. The trial court gave the jury its instructions on the law on Wednesday, December 21, 1983. The jury commenced deliberations that afternoon.

The jury could not reach a verdict by 3:55 p.m. on Friday, December 23, 1983. Appellant moved for a mistrial. The trial court denied the motion and released the jury for the long Christmas weekend.

The jury resumed deliberations at 8:30 a.m. on Tuesday, December 27, 1983. At 10:23 a.m. the jury sent a communication to the court:

Your Honor:

After a period of deliberation, self examination, contemplation and meditation, we the jury have arrived at decisions which are not unanimous. Each juror became more convinced in the decision they had reached on 12/21/83.

Our deliberations serve no purpose at this time and instruction is requested.

Record at 283.

A chambers conference was called to discuss this communication. The court indicated its intention to give the jury a supplemental instruction. Appellant objected that it was "improper to add another instruction in the middle of deliberations. * * * " Transcript, December 27, 1983, at 3. He asked for a mistrial. The motion was denied.

The trial court gave the following supplemental instruction to the jury:

Ladies and gentlemen, I am going to at this time give you another instruction. I am going to ask that you continue your deliberations in an effort to agree upon a verdict, and I have additional comments I would like you to consider as you do so.

If you cannot reach a verdict, this case must be tried again. Any future jury must be selected in a same manner and from the same source from which you were chosen. There is no reason to believe that this case could ever be submitted to twelve men and women more conscientious, more impartial, or more competent to decide it.

During your deliberations, you, as jurors, have a duty to consult with one another and to deliberate with the view to reaching an agreement if you can do so without violating your individual judgment. Although each juror must decide the case for himself, this should be done only after consideration of the evidence with his fellow jurors.

In the course of your deliberations, a juror should not hesitate to re-examine his own views and change his opinion if convinced it is erroneous. *Each juror who finds himself to be in the minority should reconsider his views in the light of the opinion of the jurors of the majority.* Conversely, each juror finding himself in the majority should give equal consideration to the views of the minority.

No juror should surrender his belief as to the weight or effect of the evidence for the mere purpose of returning a verdict.

Applying these additional comments together with all the instructions which I have previously given you, I will now ask that you retire once again and continue your deliberations and exercise your very best effort to reach a verdict.

Court was recessed at 1:40 p.m. (Transcript, December 27, 1983, at 5), and the jury communicated to the court at 2:40 p.m. that it had reached a verdict.

Appellant was convicted of the lesser-included offense of manslaughter. * * *

In *Allen v. United States*, 164 U.S. 492 (1896), the United States Supreme Court affirmed the murder conviction of a teenager after reviewing eighteen assignments of error raised in the record. Two of the assignments of error involved supplemental instructions given by the trial court to the jury.

After stating the standard admonition that each juror must come to his own conclusion while heeding other arguments with proper regard, the trial court gave further instructions which were summarized by the Supreme Court:

> that, if much the larger number were for conviction, a dissenting juror should consider whether his doubt was a reasonable one which made no impression upon the minds of so many men, equally honest, equally intelligent with himself. If, upon the other hand, the majority was for acquittal, the minority ought to ask themselves whether they might not reasonably doubt the correctness of a judgment which was not concurred in by the majority.

Allen, 164 U.S. at 501.

The Court gave a brief analysis of the legality of the instructions and concluded that there was no error in them. This case became the foundation of all modern law on instructions to deadlocked jurors.

Since *Allen*, such instructions to deadlocked jurors became increasingly popular apparently because of "its perceived efficiency as a means of 'blasting' a verdict out of a deadlocked jury in a manner which had the imprimatur of the highest court in the land." *People v. Gainer*, 566 P.2d 997, 1001 (Cal.1977) (footnote omitted).

Given the basic formulation in *Allen*, most judges add their own modifications to the instruction so there is no such thing as a standard *Allen* instruction.

It appears "the indisputable modern trend is to abandon *Allen*" instructions. *Gainer*, 566 P.2d at 1003 (citation omitted). Even confining our survey to states within the Ninth Circuit there seems to be sufficient authority to support the contention that *Allen* instructions are disfavored.

Allen instructions have been allowed if they were given *before* the jury began its deliberations. [Citations] But when they are given to a deadlocked jury some time after deliberations had been going on, courts have been more restrictive in approving them. [Citations]

Some states have totally banned the use of these instructions. [Citations]

Gainer, the California case, is particularly instructive because it discussed the two elements of the instruction that appear to be most problematical here—the admonition to minority jurors and the remark that the case must be decided or retried.

In *Gainer*, the trial court admonished the minority and said:

[I]f much the larger of your panel are for a conviction, a dissenting juror should consider whether a doubt in his or her own mind is a reasonable one, which makes no impression upon the minds of so many men or women equally honest, equally intelligent with himself or herself. * * *

This admonition was disapproved because "the trial judge pointedly directs the jurors to include an extraneous factor in their deliberations, i.e., the position of the majority of jurors at the moment. The one or more 'holdout' jurors are told that in reaching their independent conclusions as to whether or not a reasonable doubt of the defendant's guilt exists, they are to weigh not only the arguments and evidence but also their own status as dissenters—a consideration both rationally and legally irrelevant to the issue of guilt. They are thus deflected from their proper role as triers of fact, as effectively as if they had been instructed to consider their doubts as to guilt in light of their own prejudices or desire to go home." *Gainer*, 566 P.2d at 1004 (footnote omitted).

The California Supreme Court pointed out the correct law that has been well-settled in this and other jurisdictions that the jury is to decide the facts of the case based only on the evidence presented.

In *Gainer*, the trial court also instructed the jury that "[y]ou should consider that the case must at some time be decided." The California Supreme Court noted that a hung jury can and does result in the dismissal of a case. It found that the instruction misstated the law, and the trial court erred in giving the instruction.

Gainer proscribed the use of *Allen* instructions as a judicially declared rule of criminal procedure.

D. THE ALLEN INSTRUCTION HERE

As noted earlier, here, the trial court first indicated that if this jury could not reach a verdict, another jury would have to decide the case. As in *Gainer* this was clearly a misstatement of the law. A mistrial could certainly result in a retrial, but it could also lead to a dismissal of the case.

A mistrial from a hung jury is a safeguard built into the American system of jurisprudence. "In our system this is a desirable result. Despite the fact that each trial which ends in a hung jury may appear to be an exercise in futility and may create understandable judicial frustration, it should be remembered that a hung jury is only undesirable where the hanging jurors simply refuse to join in conscientious collective deliberation in an honest effort to reach a verdict. There simply is no evidence that any significant number of American jurors approach their task in such a manner. What evidence there is all points the other way." Note, *Due Process, Judicial Economy and the Hung Jury: A Reexamination of the Allen Charge*, 53 Va.L.Rev. 123, 146 (1967) (footnote omitted).

Whether or not a case must be retried is not something that a jury should consider in its deliberations. It is error for a trial court to comment on the possible effects of a hung jury.

The admonition to the minority jurors is also highly problematical. "The charge usually comes at a psychological low point in the proceedings when suggestions calculated to bring agreement are apt to be met with less than ordinary critical evaluation. A minority member might well take the charge as an invitation to allow the majority to rule. At least, there is a likelihood that he will be demoralized by this 'official' language urging him to heed the majority." Comment, *Deadlocked Juries and Dynamite: A Critical Look at the "Allen Charge,"* 31 U.Chi. L.Rev. 386, 388–389 (1964) (footnotes omitted).

Had the trial court simply repeated an instruction given earlier to the jury on how to go about its deliberations, we feel that no prejudicial effect would have befallen Appellant.[36] Repeating the deliberations instruction may have been a safer alternative had the trial court felt it necessary that the jury continue its deliberations.

---

36. For example, the trial court could have repeated Court's Instruction No. 15 which read:

A verdict must represent the considered judgment of each juror, and in order to return a verdict, it is necessary that each juror agree thereto. In other words your verdict must be unanimous.

Each of you must decide the case for yourself, but it is your duty to consult with one another and to deliberate with a view to reaching an agreement, if you can do so without violence to individual judgment. In the course of your deliberations, do not hesitate to reexamine your own views and change your opinion if convinced it is erroneous. But do not surrender your honest [sic] conviction as to the weight or effect of evidence for the mere purpose of returning a verdict.

It is clear from the record that the *Allen* instruction actually "blasted" the verdict from the jury. It had been deadlocked after deliberations covering parts of four days. Further deliberations were thought to be futile. Yet, just one hour after the *Allen* instruction was given, the jury reached a unanimous verdict. * * *

The *Allen* instruction given here was prejudicial and constituted reversible error.

Commentary

The Supreme Court discussed the problem of juror misconduct in *Tanner v. United States*, 483 U.S. 107 (1987). After the jury returned a verdict of guilty in that case and before the petitioners were sentenced, a defense lawyer asked for an evidentiary hearing on a motion for a new trial on the basis of an unsolicited telephone call he had received from a juror, Asbul. Juror Asbul had reported that other jurors had consumed alcohol during lunch breaks throughout the trial, causing them to sleep during the afternoons.

The District Court ruled that juror testimony on intoxication was inadmissible under Federal Rule of Evidence 606(b), which provided as follows:

> "Upon an inquiry into the validity of a verdict or indictment, a juror may not testify as to any matter or statement occurring during the course of the jury's deliberations or to the effect of anything upon his or any other juror's mind or emotions as influencing him to assent to or dissent from the verdict or indictment or concerning his mental processes in connection therewith, except that a juror may testify on the question whether extraneous prejudicial information was improperly brought to the jury's attention or whether any outside influence was improperly brought to bear upon any juror. Nor may his affidavit or evidence of any statement by him concerning a matter about which he would be precluded from testifying be received for these purposes."

Although the District Court refused to allow the petitioners to interview jurors or present any juror testimony, the Court invited them to call any nonjuror witnesses, such as courtroom personnel, who had observed any apparent intoxication. A defense lawyer testified that he had observed a juror "in a sort of giggly mood" during the trial.

The District Court noted that counsel had approached the bench during the trial to suggest the possibility that some jurors were falling asleep, and had been invited to call this problem to the Court's attention if inattentiveness were observed in the future. Despite this invitation the matter was not raised again. Against this background, and excluding from consideration the inadmissible statement by juror Asbul, the Court found that there was insufficient basis to conduct any further inquiry into jury misconduct and denied the motion for a new trial.

While the appeal from the conviction was pending, petitioners filed another new trial motion based on additional evidence of jury misconduct. The defense lawyer stated in a supporting affidavit that he had received another unsolicited communication from a juror, named Hardy. Hardy described a pattern of both alcohol and drug use by several jurors during recesses, to the extent that Hardy "felt like the jury was on one big party." The District Court once again refused to order a complete investigation of the facts and denied the motion for a new trial. The Court of Appeals affirmed.

The Supreme Court affirmed these rulings by a narrow majority. The majority opinion by Justice O'Connor reviewed the development of the doctrine that prohibits the admission of juror testimony to impeach a jury verdict, except in the case of "extraneous influence" over the jury. Allegations relating to the physical or mental incompetence of a juror are treated as "internal" rather than "external" influences and are thus inadmissible to impeach the verdict. The opinion explained the policy basis for this doctrine as follows:

"There is little doubt that post-verdict investigation into juror misconduct would in some instances lead to the invalidation of verdicts reached after irresponsible or improper juror behavior. It is not at all clear, however, that the jury system could survive such efforts to perfect it. Allegations of juror misconduct, incompetency, or inattentiveness, raised for the first time days, weeks, or months after the verdict seriously disrupt the finality of the process. * * * Moreover, full and frank discussion in the jury room, jurors' willingness to return an unpopular verdict, and the community's trust in a system that relies on the decisions of laypeople would all be undermined by a barrage of post verdict scrutiny of juror conduct."

The majority opinion then reviewed the legislative history of Federal Rule of Evidence 606(b). The opinion concluded that "the legislative history demonstrates with uncommon clarity that Congress specifically understood, considered, and rejected a version of Rule 606(b) that would have allowed jurors to testify on juror conduct during deliberations, including juror intoxication. This legislative history provides strong support for the most reasonable reading of the language of Rule 606(b)—that juror intoxication is not an 'outside influence' about which jurors may testify to impeach their verdict."

The dissent by Justice Marshall acknowledged "the important policy considerations supporting the common-law rule against admission of jury testimony to impeach a verdict, now embodied in Federal Rule of Evidence 606(b): freedom of deliberation, finality of verdicts, and protection of jurors against harassment by dissatisfied litigants." The dissent interpreted Rule 606(b) as prohibiting only testimony about what transpired during the course of jury deliberations. The privacy of jury deliberations would not be threatened by a post-verdict inquiry into juror consumption of alcohol and drugs during the trial, and in any case the use of drugs and alcohol could be considered an "outside influence" about which the rule permits a juror to testify.

When the existence of jury misconduct has been established by competent evidence, it must also be determined whether the misconduct prejudicially affected the verdict. In Wiser v. People, 732 P.2d 1139 (Colo.1987), the defendant was convicted of burglary based upon an incident in which he entered a woman's apartment and threatened her with a knife as a result of a disagreement about a debt she owed. Following the verdict, a juror told the bailiff that he had asked a friend who was a legal secretary "about the source of jury instructions." The friend had replied that the instructions usually have numbers on them indicating their source. Another juror told the bailiff that she had consulted a dictionary for a definition of burglary, and had been confused because the definition included a reference to theft. The Colorado Supreme Court characterized these incidents as involving "exposure to extraneous information" admissible under the Colorado version of Federal Rule 606(b). The inquiry about the source of jury instructions could not have prejudiced the verdict, however, and any confusion as to whether the definition of burglary requires an element of theft could only have benefited the defendant. Accordingly, there was no reasonable possibility that the extraneous information affected the verdict, and the Court therefore affirmed the conviction.

Chapter 18

DOUBLE JEOPARDY

ASHE v. SWENSON

Supreme Court of the United States, 1970.
397 U.S. 436, 90 S.Ct. 1189, 25 L.Ed.2d 469.

MR. JUSTICE STEWART delivered the opinion of the Court. * * *

Sometime in the early hours of the morning of January 10, 1960, six men were engaged in a poker game in the basement of the home of John Gladson at Lee's Summit, Missouri. Suddenly three or four masked men, armed with a shotgun and pistols, broke into the basement and robbed each of the poker players of money and various articles of personal property. The robbers—and it has never been clear whether there were three or four of them—then fled in a car belonging to one of the victims of the robbery. Shortly thereafter the stolen car was discovered in a field, and later that morning three men were arrested by a state trooper while they were walking on a highway not far from where the abandoned car had been found. The petitioner was arrested by another officer some distance away.

The four were subsequently charged with seven separate offenses—the armed robbery of each of the six poker players and the theft of the car. In May 1960 the petitioner went to trial on the charge of robbing Donald Knight, one of the participants in the poker game. At the trial the State called Knight and three of his fellow poker players as prosecution witnesses. Each of them described the circumstances of the holdup and itemized his own individual losses. The proof that an armed robbery had occurred and that personal property had been taken from Knight as well as from each of the others was unassailable. The testimony of the four victims in this regard was consistent both internally and with that of the others. But the State's evidence that the petitioner had been one of the robbers was weak. Two of the witnesses thought that there had been only three robbers altogether, and could not identify the petitioner as one of them. Another of the victims, who was the petitioner's uncle by marriage, said that at the "patrol station" he had positively identified each of the other three men accused of the holdup, but could say only that the petitioner's voice "sounded very much like" that of one of the robbers. The fourth participant in the poker game did identify the petitioner, but only by his "size and height, and his actions."

The cross-examination of these witnesses was brief, and it was aimed primarily at exposing the weakness of their identification testimony. Defense counsel made no attempt to question their testimony regarding the holdup itself or their claims as to their losses. Knight testified without contradiction that the robbers had stolen from him his watch, $250 in cash, and about $500 in checks. His billfold, which had been found by the police in the possession of one of the three other men accused of the robbery, was admitted in evidence. The defense offered no testimony and waived final argument.

The trial judge instructed the jury that if it found that the petitioner was one of the participants in the armed robbery, the theft of "any money" from Knight would sustain a conviction. He also instructed the jury that if the petitioner was one of the robbers, he was guilty under the law even if he had not personally robbed Knight. The jury—though not instructed to elaborate upon its verdict—found the petitioner "not guilty due to insufficient evidence."

Six weeks later the petitioner was brought to trial again, this time for the robbery of another participant in the poker game, a man named Roberts. The petitioner filed a motion to dismiss, based on his previous acquittal. The motion was overruled, and the second trial began. The witnesses were for the most part the same, though this time their testimony was substantially stronger on the issue of the petitioner's identity. For example, two witnesses who at the first trial had been wholly unable to identify the petitioner as one of the robbers, now testified that his features, size, and mannerisms matched those of one of their assailants. Another witness who before had identified the petitioner only by his size and actions now also remembered him by the unusual sound of his voice. The State further refined its case at the second trial by declining to call one of the participants in the poker game whose identification testimony at the first trial had been conspicuously negative. The case went to the jury on instructions virtually identical to those given at the first trial. This time the jury found the petitioner guilty, and he was sentenced to a 35–year term in the state penitentiary. * * *

[The State supreme court affirmed, and the lower federal courts denied habeas corpus relief on the authority of Hoag v. New Jersey, 356 U.S. 464 (1958). Justice Stewart's opinion conceded that "the operative facts here are virtually identical to those of *Hoag*," where the Supreme Court upheld the conviction. The authority of *Hoag* had been undermined, however, by the subsequent decision in Benton v. Maryland, 395 U.S. 784 (1969), holding that the Fifth Amendment guarantee against double jeopardy is enforceable against the States through the Fourteenth Amendment.]

The question is no longer whether collateral estoppel is a requirement of due process, but whether it is a part of the Fifth Amendment's guarantee against double jeopardy. And if collateral estoppel is embodied in that guarantee, then its applicability in a particular case is no longer a matter to be left for state court determination within the broad bounds of "fundamental fairness," but a matter of constitutional fact we must decide through an examination of the entire record.

"Collateral estoppel" is an awkward phrase, but it stands for an extremely important principle in our adversary system of justice. It means simply that when a issue of ultimate fact has once been determined by a valid and final judgment, that issue cannot again be litigated between the same parties in any future lawsuit. * * *

The federal decisions have made clear that the rule of collateral estoppel in criminal cases is not to be applied with the hypertechnical and archaic approach of a 19th century pleading book, but with realism and rationality. Where a previous judgment of acquittal was based upon a general verdict, as is usually the case, this approach requires a court to examine the record of a prior proceeding, taking into account the pleadings, evidence, charge, and other relevant matter, and conclude whether a rational jury could have grounded its verdict upon an issue other than that which the defendant seeks to foreclose from consideration. The inquiry must be set in a practical frame and viewed with an eye to all the circumstances of the proceedings. Any test more technically restrictive would, of course, simply amount to a rejection of the rule of collateral estoppel in criminal proceedings, at least in every case where the first judgment was based upon a general verdict of acquittal.

Straightforward application of the federal rule to the present case can lead to but one conclusion. For the record is utterly devoid of any indication that the first jury could rationally have found that an armed robbery had not occurred, or that Knight had not been a victim of that robbery. The single rationally conceivable issue in dispute before the jury was whether the petitioner had been one of the robbers. And the jury by its verdict found that he had not. The federal rule of law, therefore, would make a second prosecution for the robbery of Roberts wholly impermissible.

The ultimate question to be determined, then, in the light of Benton v. Maryland, *supra*, is whether this established rule of federal law is embodied in the Fifth Amendment guarantee against double jeopardy. We do not hesitate to hold that it is. For whatever else that constitutional guarantee may embrace, it surely protects a man who has been acquitted from having to "run the gantlet" a second time.

The question is not whether Missouri could validly charge the petitioner with six separate offenses for the robbery of the six poker players. It is not whether he could have received a total of six punishments if he had been convicted in a single trial of robbing the six victims. It is simply whether, after a jury determined by its verdict that the petitioner was not one of the robbers, the State could constitutionally hale him before a new jury to litigate that issue again.

* * *

Reversed and remanded.

[The separate concurring opinions of Justices Black and Harlan are omitted.]

MR. JUSTICE BRENNAN, whom MR. JUSTICE DOUGLAS and MR. JUSTICE MARSHALL join, concurring.

The Double Jeopardy Clause is a guarantee "that the State with all its resources and power [shall] not be allowed to make repeated attempts to convict an individual for an alleged offense, thereby subjecting him to embarrassment, expense and ordeal and compelling him to live in a continuing state of anxiety and insecurity * * *." Green v. United States, 355 U.S. 184, 187 (1957). This guarantee is expressed as a prohibition against multiple prosecutions for the "same offence." Although the phrase "same offence" appeared in most of the early common-law articulations of the double-jeopardy principle, questions of its precise meaning rarely arose prior to the 18th century, and by the time the Bill of Rights was adopted it had not been authoritatively defined.

When the common law did finally attempt a definition, it adopted the "same evidence" test, which provided little protection from multiple prosecution:

> "[U]nless the first indictment were such as the prisoner might have been convicted upon by proof of the facts contained in the second indictment, an acquittal on the first indictment can be no bar to the second."

The "same evidence" test of "same offence" was soon followed by a majority of American jurisdictions, but its deficiencies are obvious. It does not enforce but virtually annuls the constitutional guarantee. For example, where a single criminal episode involves several victims, under the "same evidence" test a separate prosecution may be brought as to each. The "same evidence" test permits multiple prosecutions where a single transaction is divisible into chronologically discrete crimes. *E.g.,* Johnson v. Commonwealth, 201 Ky. 314, 256 S.W. 388 (1923) (each of 75 poker hands a separate "offense"). Even a single criminal act may lead to multiple prosecutions if it is viewed from the perspectives of different statutes. Given the tendency of modern criminal legislation to divide the phrases of a criminal transaction into numerous separate crimes, the opportunities for multiple prosecutions for an essentially unitary criminal episode are frightening. And given our tradition of virtually unreviewable prosecutorial discretion concerning the initiation and scope of a criminal prosecution, the potentialities for abuse inherent in the "same evidence" test are simply intolerable. * * *

In my view, the Double Jeopardy Clause requires the prosecution, except in most limited circumstances, to join at one trial all the charges against a defendant that grow out of a single criminal act, occurrence, episode, or transaction. This "same transaction" test of "same offence" not only enforces the ancient prohibition against vexatious multiple prosecutions embodied in the Double Jeopardy Clause, but responds as well to the increasingly widespread recognition that the consolidation in one lawsuit of all issues arising out of a single transaction or occurrence best promotes justice, economy, and convenience. Modern rules of criminal and civil procedure reflect this recognition. * * *

The present case highlights the hazards of abuse of the criminal process inherent in the "same evidence" test and demonstrates the necessity for the "same transaction" test. The robbery of the poker game involved six players—Gladson, Knight, Freeman, Goodwin, McClendon, and Roberts. The robbers also stole a car. Seven separate informations were filed against the petitioner, one covering each of the robbery victims, and the seventh covering the theft of the car. Petitioner's first trial was under the information charging the robbery of Knight. Since Missouri has offered no justification for not trying the other informations at that trial, it is reasonable to infer that the other informations were held in reserve to be tried if the State failed to obtain a conviction on the charge of robbing Knight. Indeed, the State virtually concedes as much since it argues that the "same evidence" test is consistent with such an exercise of prosecutorial discretion. * * *

The prosecution plainly organized its case for the second trial to provide the links missing in the chain of identification evidence that was offered at the first trial. McClendon, who was an unhelpful witness at the first trial was not called at the second trial. The hesitant and uncertain evidence of Gladson and Roberts at the first trial became detailed, positive, and expansive at the second trial. One must experience a sense of uneasiness with any double-jeopardy standard that would allow the State this second chance to plug up the holes in its case. The constitutional protection against double jeopardy is empty of meaning if the State may make "repeated attempts" to touch up its case by forcing the accused to "run the gantlet" as many times as there are victims of a single episode.

Fortunately for petitioner, the conviction at the second trial can be reversed under the doctrine of collateral estoppel, since the jury at the first trial clearly resolved in his favor the only contested issue at that trial, which was the identification of him as one of the robbers. There is at least doubt whether collateral estoppel would have aided him had the jury been required to resolve additional contested issues on conflicting evidence. But correction of the abuse of criminal process should not in any event be made to depend on the availability of collateral estoppel. Abuse of the criminal process is foremost among the feared evils that led to the inclusion of the Double Jeopardy Clause in the Bill of Rights. That evil will be most effectively avoided, and the Clause can thus best serve its worthy ends, if "same offence" is construed to embody the "same transaction" standard. Then both federal and state prosecutors will be prohibited from mounting successive prosecutions for offenses growing out of the same criminal episode, at least in the absence of a showing of unavoidable necessity for successive prosecutions in the particular case.

[The dissenting opinion of Chief Justice Burger is omitted.]

UNITED STATES v. DIXON

Supreme Court of the United States, 1993.
509 U.S. 688, 113 S.Ct. 2849, 125 L.Ed.2d 556.

JUSTICE SCALIA announced the judgment of the Court and delivered the opinion of the Court with respect to Parts I, II, and IV, and an opinion with respect to Parts III and V, in which JUSTICE KENNEDY joins.

In both of these cases, respondents were tried for criminal contempt of court for violating court orders that prohibited them from engaging in conduct that was later the subject of a criminal prosecution. We consider whether the subsequent criminal prosecutions are barred by the Double Jeopardy Clause.

I

Respondent Alvin Dixon was arrested for second-degree murder and was released on bond. Consistent with the District of Columbia's bail law authorizing the judicial officer to impose any condition that "will reasonably assure the appearance of the person for trial or the safety of any other person or the community," Dixon's release form specified that he was not to commit "any criminal offense," and warned that any violation of the conditions of release would subject him "to revocation of release, an order of detention, and prosecution for contempt of court."

While awaiting trial, Dixon was arrested and indicted for possession of cocaine with intent to distribute. The court issued an order requiring Dixon to show cause why he should not be held in contempt or have the terms of his pretrial release modified. At the show-cause hearing, four police officers testified to facts surrounding the alleged drug offense; Dixon's counsel cross-examined these witnesses and introduced other evidence. The court concluded that the Government had established " 'beyond a reasonable doubt that [Dixon] was in possession of drugs and that those drugs were possessed with the intent to distribute.' " The court therefore found Dixon guilty of criminal contempt [and sentenced him to serve 180 days in jail]. Dixon later moved to dismiss the cocaine indictment on double jeopardy grounds; the trial court granted the motion.

Respondent Michael Foster's route to this Court is similar. Based on Foster's alleged physical attacks upon her in the past, Foster's estranged wife Ana obtained a civil protection order (CPO) in Superior Court of the District of Columbia. The order, to which Foster consented, required that he not " 'molest, assault, or in any manner threaten or physically abuse' " Ana Foster; a separate order, not implicated here, sought to protect her mother.

Over the course of eight months, Ana Foster filed three separate motions to have her husband held in contempt for numerous violations of the CPO. Of the 16 alleged episodes, the only charges relevant here are three separate instances of threats (on November 12, 1987, and March 26 and May 17, 1988) and two assaults (on November 6, 1987, and May 21, 1988), in the most serious of which Foster "threw [his wife] down basement stairs, kicking her body, * * * pushed her head into the floor causing head injuries, [and Ana Foster] lost consciousness."

After issuing a notice of hearing and ordering Foster to appear, the court held a 3–day bench trial. Counsel for Ana Foster and her mother prosecuted the action; the United States was not represented at trial, although the United States Attorney was apparently aware of the action, as was the court aware of a separate grand jury proceeding on some of the alleged criminal conduct. As to the assault charges, the court stated that Ana Foster would have "to prove as an element, first that there was a Civil Protection Order, and then that * * * the assault, as defined by the criminal code, in fact occurred." At the close of the plaintiffs' case, the court granted Foster's motion for acquittal on various counts, including the alleged threats on November 12 and May 17. Foster then took the stand and generally denied the allegations. The court found Foster guilty beyond a reasonable doubt of four counts of criminal contempt (three violations of Ana Foster's CPO, and one violation of the CPO obtained by her mother), including the November 6, 1987 and May 21, 1988 assaults, but acquitted him on other counts, including the March 26 alleged threats. He was sentenced to an aggregate 600 days' imprisonment.

The United States Attorney's Office later obtained an indictment charging Foster with simple assault on or about November 6, 1987 (Count I); threatening to injure another on or about November 12, 1987, and March 26 and May 17, 1988 (Counts II–IV); and assault with intent to kill on or about May 21, 1988 (Count V). App. 43–44. Ana Foster was the complainant in all counts; the first and last counts were based on the events for which Foster had been held in contempt, and the other three were based on the alleged events for which Foster was acquitted of contempt. Like Dixon, Foster filed a motion to dismiss, claiming a double jeopardy bar to all counts, and also collateral estoppel as to Counts II–IV. The trial court denied the double-jeopardy claim and did not rule on the collateral-estoppel assertion.

The Government appealed the double jeopardy ruling in *Dixon,* and Foster appealed the trial court's denial of his motion. The District of Columbia Court of Appeals consolidated the two cases, reheard them en banc, and, relying on our recent decision in Grady v. Corbin, 495 U.S. 508 (1990), ruled that both subsequent prosecutions were barred by the Double Jeopardy Clause. 598 A.2d, at 725. In its petition for certiorari, the Government presented the sole question "whether the Double Jeopardy Clause bars prosecution of a defendant on substantive criminal charges based upon the same conduct for which he previously has been held in criminal contempt of court." We granted certiorari.

II

To place these cases in context, one must understand that they are the consequence of an historically anomalous use of the contempt power. In both *Dixon* and *Foster,* a court issued an order directing a particular individual not to commit criminal offenses. (In Dixon's case, the court incorporated the entire criminal code; in Foster's case, the criminal offense of simple assault.) That could not have occurred at common law, or in the 19th–century American judicial system.

At common law, the criminal contempt power was confined to sanctions for conduct that interfered with the orderly administration of judicial proceedings. [There was also] a long common-law tradition against judicial orders prohibiting violation of the law. Injunctions, for example, would not issue to forbid infringement of criminal or civil laws, in the absence of some separate injury to private interest. The interest protected by the criminal or civil prohibition was to be vindicated at law—and though equity might enjoin harmful acts that happened to violate civil or criminal law, it would not enjoin violation of civil or criminal law as such. [Citations]

It is not surprising, therefore, that the double jeopardy issue presented here—whether prosecution for criminal contempt based on violation of a criminal law incorporated into a court order bars a subsequent prosecution for the criminal offense—did not arise at common law, or even until quite recently in American cases * * *

We have held that constitutional protections for criminal defendants other than the double jeopardy provision apply in nonsummary criminal contempt prosecutions just as they do in other criminal prosecutions. See, e.g., Gompers v. Buck's Stove & Range Co., 221 U.S. 418, 444 (1911) (presumption of innocence, proof beyond a reasonable doubt, and guarantee against self-incrimination); Cooke v. United States, 267 U.S. 517, 537 (1925) (notice of charges, assistance of counsel, and right to present a defense); In re Oliver, 333 U.S. 257, 278 (1948) (public trial). We think it obvious, and today hold, that the protection of the Double Jeopardy Clause likewise attaches.

In both the multiple punishment and multiple prosecution contexts, this Court has concluded that where the two offenses for which the defendant is punished or tried cannot survive the "same-elements" test, the double jeopardy bar applies. See, e.g., Brown v. Ohio, 432 U.S. 161, 168–169 (1977); Blockburger v. United States, 284 U.S. 299, 304 (1932) (multiple punishment); Gavieres v. United States, 220 U.S. 338, 342 (1911) (successive prosecutions). The same-elements test, sometimes referred to as the *"Blockburger"* test, inquires whether each offense contains an element not contained in the other; if not, they are the "same offence" and double jeopardy bars additional punishment and successive prosecution. In a case such as State v. Yancy, 4 N.C. 133 (1814), for example, in which the contempt prosecution was for disruption of judicial business, the same-elements test would not bar subsequent prosecution for the criminal assault that was part of the disruption, because the contempt offense did not require the element of criminal conduct, and the criminal offense did not require the element of disrupting judicial business.

We recently held in *Grady* that in addition to passing the *Blockburger* test, a subsequent prosecution must satisfy a "same-conduct" test to avoid the double jeopardy bar. The *Grady* test provides that, "if, to establish an essential element of an offense charged in that prosecution, the government will prove conduct that constitutes an offense for which the defendant has already been prosecuted," a second prosecution may not be had. 495 U.S., at 510.

III

A

The first question before us today is whether *Blockburger* analysis permits subsequent prosecution in this new criminal contempt context, where judicial order has prohibited criminal act. If it does, we must then proceed to consider whether *Grady* also permits it.

We begin with *Dixon* * * *. In this situation, in which the contempt sanction is imposed for violating the order through commission of the incorporated drug offense, the later attempt to prosecute Dixon for the drug offense resembles the situation that produced our judgment of double jeopardy in Harris v. Oklahoma, 433 U.S. 682 (1977) (per curiam). There we held that a subsequent prosecution for robbery with a firearm was barred by the Double Jeopardy Clause, because the defendant had already been tried for felony-murder based on the same underlying felony. We have described our terse per curiam in *Harris* as standing for the proposition that, for double jeopardy purposes, "the crime generally described as felony murder" is not "a separate offense distinct from its various elements." Illinois v. Vitale, 447 U.S. 410, 420–421 (1980). So too here, the "crime" of violating a condition of release cannot be abstracted from the "element" of the violated condition. The *Dixon* court order incorporated the entire governing criminal code in the same manner as the *Harris* felony-murder statute incorporated the several enumerated felonies. Here, as in *Harris,* the underlying substantive criminal offense is "a species of lesser-included offense."

To oppose this analysis, the Government can point only to dictum in In re Debs, 158 U.S. 564, 594, 599–600 (1895), which, to the extent it attempted to exclude certain nonsummary contempt prosecutions from various constitutional protections for criminal defendants, has been squarely rejected by cases such as Bloom v. Illinois, 391 U.S. 194 (1968). The Government also relies upon In re Chapman, 166 U.S. 661 (1897), and Jurney v. MacCracken, 294 U.S. 125 (1935), which recognize Congress' power to punish as contempt the refusal of a witness to testify before it. But to say that Congress can punish such a refusal is not to say that a criminal court can punish the same refusal yet again. Neither case dealt with that issue * * *.

Both the Government, and Justice Blackmun contend that the legal obligation in Dixon's case may serve "interests * * * fundamentally different" from the substantive criminal law, because it derives in part from the determination of a court rather than a determination of the legislature. That distinction seems questionable, since the court's power to establish conditions of release, and to punish their violation, was conferred by statute; the legislature was the ultimate source of both the criminal and the contempt prohibition. More importantly, however, the distinction is of no moment for purposes of the Double Jeopardy Clause, the text of which looks to whether the offenses are the same, not the interests that the offenses violate. And this Court stated long ago that criminal contempt, at least in its nonsummary form, "is a crime in every fundamental respect." *Bloom,* supra. Because Dixon's drug offense did not include any element not contained in his previous contempt offense, his subsequent prosecution violates the Double Jeopardy Clause.

The foregoing analysis obviously applies as well to Count I of the indictment against Foster, charging assault, based on the same event that was the subject of his prior contempt conviction for violating the provision of the CPO forbidding him to commit simple assault under [the same provision of the criminal code]. The subsequent prosecution for assault fails the *Blockburger* test, and is barred.

B

The remaining four counts in *Foster,* assault with intent to kill (Count V) and threats to injure or kidnap (Counts II–IV) are not barred under *Blockburger.* As to Count V: Foster's conduct on May 21, 1988 was found to violate the Family Division's order that he not "molest, assault, or in any manner threaten or physically abuse" his wife. At the contempt hearing, the court stated that Ana Foster's attorney, who prosecuted the contempt, would have to prove first, knowledge of a CPO, and second, a willful violation of one of its conditions, here simple assault as defined by the criminal code. On the basis of the same episode, Foster was then indicted for violation of D.C.Code § 22–501, which proscribes assault with intent to kill. Under governing law, that offense requires proof of specific intent to kill; simple assault does not. Similarly, the contempt offense required proof of knowledge of the CPO, which assault with intent to kill does not. Applying the *Blockburger* elements test, the result is clear: These crimes were different offenses and the subsequent prosecution did not violate the Double Jeopardy Clause.[7]

Counts II, III, and IV of Foster's indictment are likewise not barred. These charged Foster under D.C.Code § 22–2307 (forbidding anyone to "threaten * * * to kidnap any person or to injure the person of another or physically damage the property of any person") for his alleged threats on three separate dates. Foster's contempt prosecution included charges

---

7. Justice White's suggestion that if Foster received a lesser-included-offense instruction on assault at his trial for assault with intent to kill, we would uphold a conviction on that lesser count is simply wrong. Under basic *Blockburger* analysis, Foster may neither be tried a second time for assault nor again convicted for assault, as we have concluded as to Count I (charging simple assault). Thus, Foster certainly does receive the "full constitutional protection to which he is entitled": he may neither be tried nor convicted a second time for assault. That does not affect the conclusion that trial and conviction for assault with intent to kill are not barred. It merely illustrates the unremarkable fact that one offense (simple assault) may be an included offense of two offenses (violation of the CPO for assault, and assault with intent to kill) that are separate offenses under *Blockburger.*

that, on the same dates, he violated the CPO provision ordering that he not "in any manner threaten" Ana Foster. Conviction of the contempt required willful violation of the CPO—which conviction under § 22–2307 did not; and conviction under § 22–2307 required that the threat be a threat to kidnap, to inflict bodily injury, or to damage property—which conviction of the contempt (for violating the CPO provision that Foster not "in any manner threaten") did not. Each offense therefore contained a separate element, and the *Blockburger* test for double jeopardy was not met.

IV

Having found that at least some of the counts at issue here are not barred by the *Blockburger* test, we must consider whether they are barred by the new, additional double jeopardy test we announced three Terms ago in Grady v. Corbin. They undoubtedly are, since *Grady* prohibits "a subsequent prosecution if, to establish an essential element of an offense charged in that prosecution [here, assault as an element of assault with intent to kill, or threatening as an element of threatening bodily injury], the government will prove conduct that constitutes an offense for which the defendant has already been prosecuted [here, the assault and the threatening, which conduct constituted the offense of violating the CPO]." 495 U.S., at 510.

We have concluded, however, that *Grady* must be overruled. Unlike *Blockburger* analysis, whose definition of what prevents two crimes from being the "same offence," U.S. Const., Amdt. 5, has deep historical roots and has been accepted in numerous precedents of this Court, *Grady* lacks constitutional roots. The "same-conduct" rule it announced is wholly inconsistent with earlier Supreme Court precedent and with the clear common-law understanding of double jeopardy. See, e.g., Gavieres v. United States, 220 U.S., at 345 (in subsequent prosecution, "while it is true that the conduct of the accused was one and the same, two offenses resulted, each of which had an element not embraced in the other"). We need not discuss the many proofs of these statements, which were set forth at length in the *Grady* dissent. See 495 U.S., at 526 (Scalia, J., dissenting). We will respond, however, to the contrary contentions of today's pro-*Grady* dissents * * *. [Lengthy discussion of pre-*Grady* precedents omitted.]

Grady was not only wrong in principle; it has already proved unstable in application. Less than two years after it came down, in United States v. Felix, 112 S.Ct. 1377 (1992), we were forced to recognize a large exception to it. There we concluded that a subsequent prosecution for conspiracy to manufacture, possess, and distribute methamphetamine was not barred by a previous conviction for attempt to manufacture the same substance. We offered as a justification for avoiding a "literal" (i.e., faithful) reading of *Grady* "longstanding authority" to the effect that prosecution for conspiracy is not precluded by prior prosecution for the substantive offense. Of course the very existence of such a large and longstanding "exception" to the *Grady* rule gave cause for concern that the rule was not an accurate expression of the law. This "past practice" excuse is not available to support the ignoring of *Grady* in the present case, since there is no Supreme Court precedent even discussing this fairly new breed of successive prosecution (criminal contempt for violation of a court order prohibiting a crime, followed by prosecution for the crime itself).

A hypothetical based on the facts in *Harris* reinforces the conclusion that *Grady* is a continuing source of confusion and must be overruled. Suppose the State first tries the defendant for felony-murder, based on robbery, and then indicts the defendant for robbery with a firearm in the same incident. Absent *Grady,* our cases provide a clear answer to the double-jeopardy claim in this situation. Under *Blockburger,* the second prosecution is not barred—as it clearly was not barred at common law, as a famous case establishes. In King v. Vandercomb, 2 Leach. 708, 717, 168 Eng.Rep. 455, 460 (K.B.1796), the government abandoned, midtrial, prosecution of defendant for burglary by breaking and entering and stealing goods, because it turned out that no property had been removed on the date of the alleged burglary. The defendant was then prosecuted for burglary by breaking and entering with intent to steal. That second prosecution was allowed, because "these two offences are so distinct in their nature, that evidence of one of them will not support an indictment for the other." Ibid. Accord, English and American cases cited in *Grady,* 495 U.S., at 532–535 (Scalia, J., dissenting).[8]

Having encountered today yet another situation in which the pre-*Grady* understanding of the Double Jeopardy Clause allows a second trial, though the "same-conduct" test would not, we think it time to acknowledge what is now, three years after *Grady,* compellingly clear: the case was a mistake. We do not lightly reconsider a precedent, but, because *Grady* contradicted an "unbroken line of decisions," contained "less than accurate" historical analysis, and has produced "confusion," we do so here. Solorio v. United States, 483 U.S. 435, 439, 442, 450 (1987) * * *. We would mock stare decisis and only add chaos to our double jeopardy jurisprudence by pretending that *Grady* survives when it does not. We therefore accept the Government's invitation to overrule

8. Justice Souter dislikes this result because it violates "the principles behind the protection from successive prosecution included in the Fifth Amendment." The "principles behind" the Fifth Amendment are more likely to be honored by following longstanding practice than by following intuition. But in any case, Justice Souter's concern that prosecutors will bring separate prosecutions in order to perfect their case seems unjustified. They have little to gain and much to lose from such a strategy. Under Ashe v. Swenson, 397 U.S. 436 (1970), an acquittal in the first prosecution might well bar litigation of certain facts essential to the second one—though a conviction in the first prosecution would not excuse the Government from proving the same facts the second time. Surely, moreover, the Government must be deterred from abusive, repeated prosecutions of a single offender for similar offenses by the sheer press of other demands upon prosecutorial and judicial resources. Finally, even if Justice Souter's fear were well founded, no double-jeopardy bar short of a same-transaction analysis will eliminate this problem; but that interpretation of the Double Jeopardy Clause has been soundly rejected and would require overruling numerous precedents, the latest of which is barely a year old, United States v. Felix, 112 S.Ct. 1377 (1992).

Grady, and Counts II, III, IV, and V of Foster's subsequent prosecution are not barred.

V

Dixon's subsequent prosecution, as well as Count I of Foster's subsequent prosecution, violate the Double Jeopardy Clause.[9] For the reasons set forth in Part IV, the other Counts of Foster's subsequent prosecution do not violate the Double Jeopardy Clause.[10] The judgment of the District of Columbia Court of Appeals is affirmed in part and reversed in part, and the case is remanded for proceedings not inconsistent with this opinion.

CHIEF JUSTICE REHNQUIST, with whom JUSTICE O'CONNOR and JUSTICE THOMAS join, concurring in part and dissenting in part.

* * * The Court today concludes that the Double Jeopardy Clause prohibits the subsequent prosecutions of Foster for assault and Dixon for possession with intent to distribute cocaine, but does not prohibit the subsequent prosecutions of Foster for threatening to injure another or for assault with intent to kill. After finding that at least some of the charges here are not prohibited by the "same-elements" test set out in Blockburger v. United States, 284 U.S. 299, 304 (1932), the Court goes on to consider whether there is a double-jeopardy bar under the "same-conduct" test set out in Grady v. Corbin, 495 U.S. 508, 510 (1990), and determines that there is. However, because the same-conduct test is inconsistent with the text and history of the Double Jeopardy Clause, was a departure from our earlier precedents, and has proven difficult to apply, the Court concludes that Grady must be overruled. I do not join Part III of Justice Scalia's opinion because I think that none of the criminal prosecutions in this case were barred under *Blockburger.* I must then confront the expanded version of double jeopardy embodied in *Grady.* For the reasons set forth in the *Grady* dissent, and in Part IV of the Court's opinion, I, too, think that *Grady* must be overruled. I therefore join Parts I, II, and IV of the Court's opinion, and write separately to express my disagreement with Justice Scalia's application of *Blockburger* in Part III.

In my view, *Blockburger*'s same-elements test requires us to focus not on the terms of the particular court orders involved, but on the elements of contempt of court in the ordinary sense. Relying on Harris v. Oklahoma, 433 U.S. 682 (1977), a three-paragraph per curiam in an unargued case, Justice Scalia concludes otherwise today, and thus incorrectly finds in Part III–A of his opinion that the subsequent prosecutions of Dixon for drug distribution and of Foster for assault violated the Double Jeopardy Clause. In so doing, Justice Scalia rejects the traditional view—shared by every federal court of appeals and state supreme court that addressed the issue prior to *Grady*—that, as a general matter, double jeopardy does not bar a subsequent prosecution based on conduct for which a defendant has been held in criminal contempt. I cannot

9. Justices White, Stevens, and Souter concur in this portion of the judgment.

10. Justice Blackmun concurs only in the judgment with respect to this portion.

subscribe to a reading of *Harris* that upsets this previously well-settled principle of law. Because the generic crime of contempt of court has different elements than the substantive criminal charges in this case, I believe that they are separate offenses under *Blockburger.* I would therefore limit *Harris* to the context in which it arose: where the crimes in question are analogous to greater and lesser included offenses. The crimes at issue here bear no such resemblance * * *.

Our double jeopardy cases applying *Blockburger* have focused on the statutory elements of the offenses charged, not on the facts that must be proven under the particular indictment at issue—an indictment being the closest analogue to the court orders in this case * * *. By focusing on the facts needed to show a violation of the specific court orders involved in this case, and not on the generic elements of the crime of contempt of court, Justice Scalia's double-jeopardy analysis bears a striking resemblance to that found in *Grady*—not what one would expect in an opinion that overrules *Grady* * * *.

The following analogy, raised by the Government at oral argument, helps illustrate the absurd results that Justice Scalia's *Harris/Blockburger* analysis could in theory produce. Suppose that the offense in question is failure to comply with a lawful order of a police officer, and that the police officer's order was, "Don't shoot that man." Under Justice Scalia's flawed reading of *Harris,* the elements of the offense of failure to obey a police officer's lawful order would include, for purposes of *Blockburger*'s same-elements test, the elements of, perhaps, murder or manslaughter, in effect converting those felonies into a lesser included offense of the crime of failure to comply with a lawful order of a police officer.

In sum, I think that the substantive criminal prosecutions in this case, which followed convictions for criminal contempt, did not violate the Double Jeopardy Clause, at least before our decision in *Grady.* Under *Grady,* "the Double Jeopardy Clause bars a subsequent prosecution if, to establish an essential element of an offense charged in that prosecution, the government will prove conduct that constitutes an offense for which the defendant has already been prosecuted." As the Court points out, this case undoubtedly falls within that expansive formulation: To secure convictions on the substantive criminal charges in this case, the Government will have to prove conduct that was the basis for the contempt convictions. Forced, then, to confront *Grady,* I join the Court in overruling that decision.

JUSTICE WHITE, with whom JUSTICE STEVENS joins, and with whom JUSTICE SOUTER joins as to Part I, concurring in the judgment in part and dissenting in part.

I am convinced that the Double Jeopardy Clause bars prosecution for an offense if the defendant already has been held in contempt for its commission. Therefore, I agree with the Court's conclusion that both Dixon's prosecution for possession with intent to distribute cocaine and Foster's prosecution for simple assault were prohibited. In my view, however, Justice Scalia's opinion gives short shrift to the arguments raised by the United States. I also am uncomfortable with the reasoning underlying this holding, in particular the application of Blockburger v. United States, 284 U.S. 299 (1932), to the facts of this case, a reasoning that betrays an overly technical interpretation of the Constitution. As a result, I concur only in the judgment in Part III–A.

The mischief in Justice Scalia's approach is far more apparent in the second portion of today's decision. Constrained by his narrow reading of the Double Jeopardy Clause, he asserts that the fate of Foster's remaining counts depends on Grady v. Corbin, 495 U.S. 508 (1990), which the Court then chooses to overrule. I do not agree. Resolution of the question presented by Foster's case no more requires reliance on *Grady* than it points to reasons for reversing that decision. Rather, as I construe the Clause, double jeopardy principles compel equal treatment of all of Foster's counts. I dissent from the Court's holding to the contrary. Inasmuch as *Grady* has been dragged into this case, however, I agree with Justice Blackmun and Justice Souter that it should not be overruled. From this aspect of the Court's opinion as well, I dissent.

I

* * * Both the Government and amici submit that application of the Double Jeopardy Clause in this context carries grave practical consequences. It would, it is argued, cripple the power to enforce court orders or, alternatively, allow individuals to escape serious punishment for statutory criminal offenses. The argument, an offshoot of the principle of necessity familiar to the law of contempt, see, e.g., United States v. Wilson, 421 U.S. 309, 315–318 (1975), is that, just as we have relaxed certain procedural requirements in contempt proceedings where time is of the essence and an immediate remedy is needed to "prevent a breakdown of the proceedings," so too should we exclude double jeopardy protections from this setting lest we do damage to the courts' authority * * *.

Adherence to double jeopardy principles in this context, however, will not seriously deter the courts from taking appropriate steps to ensure that their authority is not flouted. Courts remain free to hold transgressors in contempt and punish them as they see fit. The government counters that this possibility will prove to be either illusory—if the prosecuting authority declines to initiate proceedings out of fear that they could jeopardize more substantial punishment for the underlying crime—or too costly—if the prosecuting authority, the risk notwithstanding, chooses to go forward. But it is not fanciful to imagine that judges and prosecutors will select a third option, which is to ensure, where necessary or advisable, that the contempt and the substantive charge be tried at the same time, in which case the double jeopardy issue would be limited to ensuring that the total punishment did not exceed that authorized by the legislature * * *.

Against this backdrop, the appeal of the principle of necessity loses much of its force. Ultimately, the urgency of punishing such contempt violations is no less, but by the same token no more, than that of punishing violations of criminal laws of general application—in which case, we simply do not question the defendant's right to the "protections worked out carefully over the years and deemed fundamental to our system of justice," Bloom v. Illinois, 391 U.S., at 208, including the protection of the Double Jeopardy Clause. "Perhaps to some extent we sacrifice efficiency, expedition, and economy, but the choice * * * has been made, and retained, in the Constitution. We see no sound reason in logic or policy not to apply it in the area of criminal contempt."

Dixon aptly illustrates these points. In that case, the motion requesting modification of the conditions of Dixon's release was filed by the government, the same entity responsible for prosecution of the drug offense. Indeed, in so doing it relied explicitly on the defendant's indictment on the cocaine charge. 598 A.2d 724, 728 (D.C.1991). Logically, any problem of coordination or of advance notice of the impending prosecution for the substantive offense was at most minimal. Nor, aside from the legitimate desire to punish all offenders swiftly, does there appear to have been any real need to hold Dixon in contempt immediately, without waiting for the second trial. By way of comparison, at the time of his drug offense Dixon was awaiting trial for second-degree murder, a charge that had been brought some 11 months earlier.

Besides, in the situation where a person has violated a condition of release, there generally exist a number of alternatives under which the defendant's right against being put twice in jeopardy for the same offense could be safeguarded, the while ensuring that disregard of the court's authority not go unsanctioned. To the extent that they are exercised with due regard for the Constitution, such options might include modification of release conditions or revocation of bail and detention. As respondents acknowledge, these solutions would raise no double jeopardy problem.

More difficult to deal with are the circumstances surrounding Foster's defiance of the court order. Realization of the scope of domestic violence—according to the American Medical Association (AMA), "the single largest cause of injury to women," AMA, Five Issues in American Health 5 (1991)—has come with difficulty, and it has come late.

There no doubt are time delays in the operation of the criminal justice system that are frustrating; they even can be perilous when an individual is left exposed to a defendant's potential violence. That is true in the domestic context; it is true elsewhere as well. Resort to more expedient methods therefore is appealing, and in many cases permissible. Under today's decision, for instance, police officers retain the power to arrest for violation of a civil protection order. Where the offense so warrants, judges can haul the assailant before the court, charge him with criminal contempt, and hold him without bail. Also, cooperation between the government and parties bringing contempt proceedings can be achieved. The various actors might not have thought such cooperation necessary in the past; after today's decision, I suspect they will.

Victims, understandably, would prefer to have access to a proceeding in which swift and expeditious punishment could be inflicted for that offense without prejudice to a subsequent full-blown criminal trial. The justification for such a system, however, has nothing to do with preventing disruption of a court's proceedings or even with vindicating its authority. While, under the principle of necessity, contempt proceedings have been exempted from some constitutional constraints, this was done strictly "to secure judicial authority from obstruction in the performance of its duties to the end that means appropriate for the preservation and enforcement of the Constitution may be secured." Ex parte Hudgings, 249 U.S. 378, 383 (1919). No such end being invoked here, the principle of necessity cannot be summoned for the sole purpose of letting contempt proceedings achieve what, under our Constitution, other criminal trials cannot.

II

If, as the Court agrees, the Double Jeopardy Clause cannot be ignored in this context, my view is that the subsequent prosecutions in both *Dixon* and *Foster* were impermissible as to all counts. I reach this conclusion because the offenses at issue in the contempt proceedings were either identical to, or lesser included offenses of, those charged in the subsequent prosecutions. Justice Scalia's contrary conclusion as to some of Foster's counts, which he reaches by exclusive focus on the formal elements of the relevant crimes, is divorced from the purposes of the constitutional provision he purports to apply. Moreover, the results to which this approach would lead are indefensible * * *.

Professing strict adherence to *Blockburger*'s so-called "same elements" test, Justice Scalia opts for a more circuitous approach. The elements of the crime of contempt, he reasons, in this instance are (1) the existence and knowledge of a court order, or CPO; and (2) commission of the underlying substantive offense. Where the criminal conduct that forms the basis of the contempt order is identical to that charged in the subsequent trial, Justice Scalia concludes, *Blockburger* forbids retrial. All elements of Foster's simple assault offense being included in his previous contempt offense, prosecution on that ground is precluded. The same is true of Dixon's drug offense. I agree with this conclusion, though would reach it rather differently: Because in a successive prosecution case the risk is that a person will have to defend himself more than once against the same charge, I would have put to the side the CPO (which, as it were, triggered the court's authority to punish the defendant for acts already punishable under the criminal laws) and compared the substantive offenses of which respondents stood accused in both prosecutions.

The significance of our disaccord is far more manifest where an element is added to the second prosecution. Under Justice Scalia's view, the double jeopardy barrier is then removed because each offense demands proof of an element the other does not: Foster's conviction for contempt requires proof of the existence and knowledge of a CPO, which conviction for assault with intent to kill does not; his conviction for assault with intent to kill requires proof of an intent to kill, which the contempt conviction did not. Finally, though he was acquitted in the contempt proceedings with respect to the alleged November 12, March 26, and May 17 threats, his conviction under the threat charge in the subsequent trial required the additional proof that the threat be to kidnap, to inflict bodily injury, or to damage property. As to these counts, and absent any collateral estoppel problem, Justice Scalia finds that the Constitution does not prohibit retrial.

The distinction drawn by Justice Scalia is predicated on a reading of the Double Jeopardy Clause that is abstracted from the purposes the constitutional provision is designed to promote. To focus on the statutory elements of a crime makes sense where cumulative punishment is at stake, for there the aim simply is to uncover legislative intent. The *Blockburger* inquiry, accordingly, serves as a means to determine this intent, as our cases have recognized. But, as Justice Souter shows, adherence to legislative will has very little to do with the important interests advanced by double jeopardy safeguards against successive prosecutions. The central purpose of the Double Jeopardy Clause being to protect against vexatious multiple prosecutions, these interests go well beyond the prevention of unauthorized punishment. The same-elements test is an inadequate safeguard, for it leaves the constitutional guarantee at the mercy of a legislature's decision to modify statutory definitions. Significantly, therefore, this Court has applied an inflexible version of the same-elements test only once, in 1911, in a successive prosecution case, see Gavieres v. United States, 220 U.S. 338 (1911), and has since noted that "the *Blockburger* test is not the only standard for determining whether successive prosecutions impermissibly involve the same offense." Brown, 432 U.S., at 166–167, n. 6. Rather, "even if two offenses are sufficiently different to permit the imposition of consecutive sentences, successive prosecutions will be barred in some circumstances where the second prosecution requires the relitigation of factual issues already resolved by the first." Ibid.

Take the example of Count V in Foster: For all intents and purposes, the offense for which he was convicted in the contempt proceeding was his assault against his wife. The majority, its eyes fixed on the rigid elements-test, would have his fate turn on whether his subsequent prosecution charges "simple assault" or "assault with intent to kill." Yet, because the crime of "simple assault" is included within the crime of "assault with intent to kill," the reasons that bar retrial under the first hypothesis are equally present under the second: These include principles of finality, protecting Foster from "embarrassment" and "expense," and preventing the government from gradually fine-tuning its strategy, thereby minimizing exposure to a mistaken conviction.

Analysis of the threat charges (Counts II–IV) makes the point more clearly still. In the contempt proceeding, it will be recalled, Foster was acquitted of the—arguably lesser-included—offense of threatening "in any manner." As we have stated, "the law attaches particular significance to an acquittal. To permit a second trial after an acquittal, however mistaken the acquittal might have been, would present an unacceptably high risk that the Government, with its vastly superior resources, might wear down the defendant so that 'even though innocent he may be found guilty.' " United States v. Scott, 437 U.S. 82, 91 (1978) (citation omitted).

To allow the government to proceed on the threat counts would present precisely the risk of erroneous conviction the Clause seeks to avoid. That the prosecution had to establish the existence of the CPO in the first trial, in short, does not in any way modify the prejudice potentially caused to a defendant by consecutive trials.

To respond, as the majority appears to do, that concerns relating to the defendant's interests against repeat trials are "unjustified" because prosecutors "have little to gain and much to lose" from bringing successive prosecutions and because "the Government must be deterred from abusive, repeated prosecutions of a single offender for similar offenses by the sheer press of other demands upon prosecutorial and judicial resources," is to get things exactly backwards. The majority's prophesies might be correct, and double jeopardy might be a problem that will simply take care of itself. Not so, however, according to the Constitution, whose firm prohibition against double jeopardy cannot be satisfied by wishful thinking.

C

Further consequences—at once illogical and harmful—flow from Justice Scalia's approach. I turn for illustration once more to Foster's assault case. In his second prosecution, the government brought charges of assault with intent to kill. In the District of Columbia, Superior Court Criminal Rule 31(c)—which faithfully mirrors its federal counterpart, Federal Rule of Criminal Procedure 31(c)—provides that a "defendant may be found guilty of an offense necessarily included in the offense charged or of an attempt to commit either the offense charged or an offense necessarily included therein if the attempt is an offense." This provision has been construed to require the jury to determine guilt of all lesser included offenses * * *.

Simple assault being a lesser included offense of assault with intent to kill, the jury in the second prosecution would in all likelihood receive instructions on the lesser offense and could find Foster guilty of simple assault. In short, while the government cannot, under the Constitution, bring charges of simple assault, it apparently can, under the majority's interpretation, secure a conviction for simple assault, so long as it prosecutes Foster for assault with intent to kill. As I see it, Foster will have been put in jeopardy twice for simple assault.[11] The result is as

---

11. Justice Scalia's dismissal of this concern is difficult to follow. As I understand it, he maintains that no double jeopardy problem exists because under *Block-* *burger* a conviction for assault would not be upheld. See ante, note 7. I suppose that the judge could upon request instruct the jury on the lesser included offense and await its

unjustifiable as it is pernicious. It stems, I believe, from a "hypertechnical and archaic approach," Ashe v. Swenson, 397 U.S. 436, 444 (1970) * * *.

III

Once it is agreed that the Double Jeopardy Clause applies in this context, the Clause, properly construed, both governs this case and disposes of the distinction between Foster's charges upon which Justice Scalia relies. I therefore see little need to draw Grady into this dispute. In any event, the United States itself has not attempted to distinguish between Dixon and Foster or between the charges of "assault" on the one hand and, on the other, "assault with intent to kill" and "threat to injure another." The issue was not raised before the Court of Appeals or considered by it, and it was neither presented in the petition for certiorari nor briefed by either party. Under these circumstances, it is injudicious to address this matter.

The majority nonetheless has chosen to consider *Grady* anew and to overrule it. I agree with Justice Blackmun and Justice Souter that such a course is both unwarranted and unwise. Hence I dissent from the judgment overruling *Grady* * * *.

JUSTICE BLACKMUN, concurring in the judgment in part and dissenting in part.

I cannot agree that contempt of court is the "same offence" under the Double Jeopardy Clause as either assault with intent to kill or possession of cocaine with intent to distribute it * * *.

If this were a case involving successive prosecutions under the substantive criminal law * * * I would agree that the Double Jeopardy Clause could bar the subsequent prosecution. But we are concerned here with contempt of court, a special situation * * *.

The purpose of contempt is not to punish an offense against the community at large but rather to punish the specific offense of disobeying a court order * * *.

Contempt is one of the very few mechanisms available to a trial court to vindicate the authority of its orders. I fear that the Court's willingness to overlook the unique interests served by contempt proceed-

---

verdict; if it were to find Foster guilty of simple assault, the court could then vacate the conviction as violative of the Double Jeopardy Clause—or, barring that, Foster could appeal his conviction on that basis. The sheer oddity of this scenario aside, it falls short of providing Foster with the full constitutional protection to which he is entitled. A double jeopardy violation occurs at the inception of trial, which is why an order denying a motion to dismiss on double jeopardy grounds is immediately appealable * * *. In light of the lesser included offense instructions, and the associated risk of conviction for that offense, Foster would have

to defend himself in his second trial once more against the charge of simple assault, thereby undergoing the "personal strain, public embarrassment, and expense of a criminal trial." Even if the conviction were set aside, he still would have been forced to endure a trial that the Double Jeopardy Clause was designed to prohibit * * *. This double jeopardy predicament, of course, could be avoided by Foster's attorney not requesting the lesser included offense instructions to which his client is entitled. But to place a defendant before such a choice hardly strikes me as a satisfactory resolution.

ings not only will jeopardize the ability of trial courts to control those defendants under their supervision but will undermine their ability to respond effectively to unmistakable threats to their own authority and to those who have sought the court's protection * * *.

JUSTICE SOUTER, with whom JUSTICE STEVENS joins, concurring in the judgment in part and dissenting in part.

While I agree with the Court as far as it goes in holding that a citation for criminal contempt and an indictment for violating a substantive criminal statute may amount to charges of the "same offence" for purposes of the Double Jeopardy Clause, U.S. Const., Amdt. 5, I cannot join the Court in restricting the Clause's reach and dismembering the protection against successive prosecution that the Constitution was meant to provide. The Court has read our precedents so narrowly as to leave them bereft of the principles animating that protection, and has chosen to overrule the most recent of the relevant cases, Grady v. Corbin, 495 U.S. 508 (1990), decided three years ago. Because I think that Grady was correctly decided, amounting merely to an expression of just those animating principles, and because, even if the decision had been wrong in the first instance, there is no warrant for overruling it now, I respectfully dissent. I join Part I of Justice White's opinion, and I would hold, as he would, both the prosecution of Dixon and the prosecution of Foster under all the counts of the indictment against him to be barred by the Double Jeopardy Clause * * *.

The interests at stake in avoiding successive prosecutions are different from those at stake in the prohibition against multiple punishments, and our cases reflect this reality * * *.

Consequently, while the government may punish a person separately for each conviction of at least as many different offenses as meet the *Blockburger* test, we have long held that it must sometimes bring its prosecutions for these offenses together. If a separate prosecution were permitted for every offense arising out of the same conduct, the government could manipulate the definitions of offenses, creating fine distinctions among them and permitting a zealous prosecutor to try a person again and again for essentially the same criminal conduct * * *. Thus, "the *Blockburger* test is not the only standard for determining whether successive prosecutions impermissibly involve the same offense. Even if two offenses are sufficiently different to permit the imposition of consecutive sentences, successive prosecutions will be barred in some circumstances where the second prosecution requires the relitigation of factual issues already resolved by the first." Brown, 432 U.S., at 166–167, n. 6.

An example will show why this should be so. Assume three crimes: robbery with a firearm, robbery in a dwelling and simple robbery. The elements of the three crimes are the same, except that robbery with a firearm has the element that a firearm be used in the commission of the robbery while the other two crimes do not, and robbery in a dwelling has the element that the robbery occur in a dwelling while the other two crimes do not.

If a person committed a robbery in a dwelling with a firearm and was prosecuted for simple robbery, all agree he could not be prosecuted subsequently for either of the greater offenses of robbery with a firearm or robbery in a dwelling. Under the lens of *Blockburger,* however, if that same person were prosecuted first for robbery with a firearm, he could be prosecuted subsequently for robbery in a dwelling, even though he could not subsequently be prosecuted on the basis of that same robbery for simple robbery. This is true simply because neither of the crimes, robbery with a firearm and robbery in a dwelling, is either identical to or a lesser-included offense of the other. But since the purpose of the Double Jeopardy Clause's protection against successive prosecutions is to prevent repeated trials in which a defendant will be forced to defend against the same charge again and again, and in which the government may perfect its presentation with dress rehearsal after dress rehearsal, it should be irrelevant that the second prosecution would require the defendant to defend himself not only from the charge that he committed the robbery, but also from the charge of some additional fact, in this case, that the scene of the crime was a dwelling * * *.

I would affirm the judgment of the Court of Appeals. I concur in the judgment of the Court in *Dixon* and with respect to Count I in *Foster,* but respectfully dissent from the disposition of the case with respect to Counts II–V in *Foster.*

ILLINOIS v. SOMERVILLE

Supreme Court of the United States, 1973.
410 U.S. 458, 93 S.Ct. 1066, 35 L.Ed.2d 425.

MR. JUSTICE REHNQUIST delivered the opinion of the Court. * * *

I

On March 19, 1964, respondent was indicted by an Illinois grand jury for the crime of theft. The case was called for trial and a jury impaneled and sworn on November 1, 1965. The following day, before any evidence had been presented, the prosecuting attorney realized that the indictment was fatally deficient under Illinois law because it did not allege that respondent intended to permanently deprive the owner of his property. Under the applicable Illinois criminal statute, such intent is a necessary element of the crime of theft, and failure to allege intent renders the indictment insufficient to charge a crime. But under the Illinois Constitution at that time, an indictment was the sole means by which a criminal proceeding such as this may be commenced against a defendant. Illinois further provides that only formal defects, of which this was not one, may be cured by amendment. The combined operation of these rules of Illinois procedure and substantive law meant that the defect in the indictment was "jurisdictional"; it could not be waived by the defendant's failure to object, and could be asserted on appeal or in a post-conviction proceeding to overturn a final judgment of conviction.

Faced with this situation, the Illinois trial court concluded that further proceedings under this defective indictment would be useless and granted the State's motion for a mistrial. On November 3, the grand jury handed down a second indictment alleging the requisite intent. Respondent was arraigned two weeks after the first trial was aborted, raised a claim of double jeopardy which was overruled, and the second trial commenced shortly thereafter. The jury returned a verdict of guilty, sentence was imposed, and the Illinois courts upheld the conviction. Respondent then sought federal habeas corpus, alleging that the conviction constituted double jeopardy contrary to the prohibition of the Fifth and Fourteenth Amendments. The Seventh Circuit affirmed the denial of habeas corpus prior to our decision in United States v. Jorn, 400 U.S. 470 (1971). The respondent's petition for certiorari was granted, and the case remanded for reconsideration in light of *Jorn* and Downum v. United States, 372 U.S. 734 (1963). On remand, the Seventh Circuit held that respondent's petition for habeas corpus should have been granted because, although he had not been tried and *acquitted* as in United States v. Ball, 163 U.S. 662 (1896), and Benton v. Maryland, 395 U.S. 784 (1969), jeopardy had attached when the jury was impaneled and sworn, and a declaration of mistrial over respondent's objection precluded a retrial under a valid indictment. For the reasons stated below, we reverse that judgment.

II

The fountainhead decision construing the Double Jeopardy Clause in the context of a declaration of a mistrial over a defendant's objection is United States v. Perez, 9 Wheat. 579 (1824). Mr. Justice Story, writing for a unanimous Court, set forth the standards for determining whether a retrial, following a declaration of a mistrial over a defendant's objection, constitutes double jeopardy within the meaning of the Fifth Amendment. In holding that the failure of the jury to agree on a verdict of either acquittal or conviction did not bar retrial of the defendant, Mr. Justice Story wrote:

> "We think, that in all cases of this nature, the law has invested Courts of justice with the authority to discharge a jury from giving any verdict, whenever, in their opinion, taking all the circumstances into consideration, there is a manifest necessity for the act, or the ends of public justice would otherwise be defeated. They are to exercise a sound discretion on the subject; and it is impossible to define all the circumstances, which would render it proper to interfere. To be sure, the power ought to be used with the greatest caution, under urgent circumstances, and for very plain and obvious causes; and, in capital cases especially, Courts should be extremely careful how they interfere with any of the chances of life, in favour of the prisoner. But, after all, they have the right to order the discharge; and the security which the public have for the faithful, sound, and conscientious exercise of this discretion, rests, in this, as in other cases, upon the responsibility of the Judges, under their oaths of office." *Id.*, at 580.

This formulation, consistently adhered to by this Court in subsequent decisions, abjures the application of any mechanical formula by which to judge the propriety of declaring a mistrial in the varying and often unique situations arising during the course of a criminal trial. * * *

While virtually all of the cases turn on the particular facts and thus escape meaningful categorization, it is possible to distill from them a general approach, premised on the "public justice" policy enunciated in United States v. Perez, to situations such as that presented by this case. A trial judge properly exercises his discretion to declare a mistrial if an impartial verdict cannot be reached, or if a verdict of conviction could be reached but would have to be reversed on appeal due to an obvious procedural error in the trial. If an error would make reversal on appeal a certainty, it would not serve "the ends of public justice" to require that the Government proceed with its proof when, if it succeeded before the jury, it would automatically be stripped of that success by an appellate court. * * * While the declaration of a mistrial on the basis of a rule or a defective procedure that would lend itself to prosecutorial manipulation would involve an entirely different question, such was not the situation in the above cases or in the instant case.

In Downum v. United States, the defendant was charged with six counts of mail theft, and forging and uttering stolen checks. A jury was selected and sworn in the morning, and instructed to return that afternoon. When the jury returned, the Government moved for the discharge of the jury on the ground that a key prosecution witness, for two of the six counts against defendant, was not present. The prosecution knew, prior to the selection and swearing of the jury, that this witness could not be found and had not been served with a subpoena. The trial judge discharged the jury over the defendant's motions to dismiss two counts for failure to prosecute and to continue the other four. This Court, in reversing the convictions on the ground of double jeopardy, emphasized that "[e]ach case must turn on its facts," 372 U.S., at 737, and held that the second prosecution constituted double jeopardy, because the absence of the witness and the reason therefor did not there justify, in terms of "manifest necessity," the declaration of a mistrial.

In United States v. Jorn, *supra*, the Government called a taxpayer witness in a prosecution for willfully assisting in the preparation of fraudulent income tax returns. Prior to his testimony, defense counsel suggested he be warned of his constitutional right against compulsory self-incrimination. The trial judge warned him of his rights, and the witness stated that he was willing to testify and that the Internal Revenue Service agent who first contacted him warned him of his rights. The trial judge, however, did not believe the witness' declaration that the IRS had so warned him, and refused to allow him to testify until after he had consulted with an attorney. After learning from the Government that the remaining four witnesses were "similarly situated," and after surmising that they, too, had not been properly informed of their rights, the trial judge declared a mistrial to give the witnesses the opportunity to consult with attorneys. In sustaining a plea in bar of double jeopardy to an attempted second trial of the defendant, the plurality opinion of the Court, emphasizing the importance to the defendant of proceeding before the first jury sworn, concluded:

> "It is apparent from the record that no consideration was given to the possibility of a trial continuance; indeed, the trial judge acted so abruptly in discharging the jury that, had the prosecutor been disposed to suggest a continuance, or the defendant to object to the discharge of the jury, there would have been no opportunity to do so. When one examines the circumstances surrounding the discharge of this jury, it seems abundantly apparent that the trial judge made no effort to exercise a sound discretion to assure that, taking all the circumstances into account, there was a manifest necessity for the *sua sponte* declaration of this mistrial. Therefore, we must conclude that in the circumstances of this case, appellee's reprosecution would violate the double jeopardy provision of the Fifth Amendment."

III

Respondent advances two arguments to support the conclusion that the Double Jeopardy Clause precluded the second trial in the instant case. The first is that since United States v. Ball, supra, held that jeopardy obtained even though the indictment upon which the defendant was first acquitted had been defective, and since Downum v. United States, *supra*, held that jeopardy "attaches" when a jury has been selected and sworn, the Double Jeopardy Clause precluded the State from instituting the second proceeding that resulted in respondent's conviction. Alternatively, respondent argues that our decision in United States v. Jorn, *supra*, which respondent interprets as narrowly limiting the circumstances in which a mistrial is manifestly necessary, requires affirmance. * * *

Respondent's first contention is precisely the type of rigid, mechanical rule which the Court had eschewed since the seminal decision in *Perez*. The major premise of the syllogism—that trial on a defective indictment precludes retrial—is not applicable to the instant case because it overlooks a crucial element of the Court's reasoning in United States v. Ball, *supra*. There, three men were indicted and tried for murder; two were convicted by a jury and one acquitted. This Court reversed the convictions on the ground that the indictment was fatally deficient in failing to allege that the victim died within a year and a day of the assault. A proper indictment was returned and the Government retried all three of the original defendants; that trial resulted in the conviction of all. This Court reversed the conviction of the one defendant who originally had been acquitted, sustaining his plea of double jeopardy. But the Court was obviously and properly influenced by the fact that the first trial had proceeded to verdict. * * *

In *Downum*, the Court held, as respondent argues, that jeopardy "attached" when the first jury was selected and sworn. But in cases in which a mistrial has been declared prior to verdict, the conclusion that jeopardy has attached begins, rather than ends, the inquiry as to whether the Double Jeopardy Clause bars retrial. That, indeed, was precisely the rationale of *Perez* and subsequent cases. Only if jeopardy has attached is a court called upon to determine whether the declaration of a mistrial was required by "manifest necessity" or the "ends of public justice." * * *

In the instant case, the trial judge terminated the proceeding because a defect was found to exist in the indictment that was, as a matter of Illinois law, not curable by amendment. The Illinois courts have held that even after a judgment of conviction has become final, the defendant may be released on habeas corpus, because the defect in the indictment deprives the trial court of "jurisdiction." The rule prohibiting the amendment of all but formal defects in indictments is designed to implement the State's policy of preserving the right of each defendant to insist that a criminal prosecution against him be commenced by the action of a grand jury. The trial judge was faced with a situation in which a procedural defect might or would preclude the public from either obtaining an impartial verdict or keeping a verdict of conviction if its evidence persuaded the jury. If a mistrial were constitutionally unavailable in situations such as this, the State's policy could only be implemented by conducting a second trial after verdict and reversal on appeal, thus wasting time, energy, and money for all concerned. Here, the trial judge's action was a rational determination designed to implement a legitimate state policy, with no suggestion that the implementation of that policy in this manner could be manipulated so as to prejudice the defendant. This situation is thus unlike *Downum*, where the mistrial entailed not only a delay for the defendant, but also operated as a post-jeopardy continuance to allow the prosecution an opportunity to strengthen its case. Here, the delay was minimal, and the mistrial was, under Illinois law, the only way in which a defect in the indictment could be corrected. Given the established standard of discretion, we cannot say that the declaration of a mistrial was not required by "manifest necessity" or the "ends of public justice." * * *

The determination by the trial court to abort a criminal proceeding where jeopardy has attached is not one to be lightly undertaken, since the interest of the defendant in having his fate determined by the jury first impaneled is itself a weighty one. Nor will the lack of demonstrable additional prejudice preclude the defendant's invocation of the double jeopardy bar in the absence of some important countervailing interest of proper judicial administration. But where the declaration of a mistrial implements a reasonable state policy and aborts a proceeding that at best would have produced a verdict that could have been upset at will by one of the parties, the defendant's interest in proceeding to verdict is outweighed by the competing and equally legitimate demand for public justice.

Reversed.

MR. JUSTICE WHITE, with whom MR. JUSTICE DOUGLAS and MR. JUSTICE BRENNAN join, dissenting. * * *

Somerville asserts a right to but one trial and to a verdict by the initial jury. A mistrial was directed at the instance of the State, over Somerville's objection, and was occasioned by official error in drafting the indictment—error unaccompanied by bad faith, overreaching, or specific prejudice to the defense at a later trial. The State may no more try the defendant a second time in these circumstances than could the United States in *Downum* and *Jorn*. Although the exact extent of the emotional and physical harm suffered by Somerville during the period between his first and second trial is open to debate, it cannot be gainsaid that Somerville lost "his option to go to the first jury and, perhaps, end the dispute then and there with an acquittal." United States v. Jorn, 400 U.S., at 484. *Downum* and *Jorn*, over serious dissent, rejected the view that the Double Jeopardy Clause protects only against those mistrials that lend themselves to prosecutorial manipulation and underwrote the independent right of a defendant in a criminal case to have the verdict of the initial jury. Both cases made it quite clear that the discretion of the trial court to declare mistrials is reviewable and that the defendant's right to a verdict by his first jury is not to be overridden except for "manifest necessity." There was not, in this case any more than in *Downum* and *Jorn*, "manifest necessity" for the loss of that right. * * *

Note

In United States v. Stevens, 177 F.3d 579 (6th Cir.1999) the prosecution's key witness suddenly announced during trial that he would not testify, threats having been made against him and his family. After three weeks in jail for contempt he still refused to testify, and the judge declared a mistrial. The trial judge found that there was no evidence linking the threats to the defendant, and that the threats might have come from other persons who stood to benefit from silencing the witness. The trial court also found that the prosecutor was not negligent in going to trial and describing the witness's anticipated testimony in his opening statement. In these circumstances, the Court of Appeals panel held (2–1) that the mistrial was not justified and there could be no retrial. The purpose of a mistrial would either be to allow the government to gather more evidence, or to make further efforts to coerce the witness to testify. Neither of these is sufficient to justify a new proceeding. The government had already had sufficient opportunity to make its case, and the defendant had already endured a lengthy trial without knowing until the end what the outcome would be. The dissenting judge argued that a manifest necessity for a mistrial is present when a government witness becomes unavailable after the jury has been sworn, the unavailability is not the fault of the government, and the witness's absence prejudices the government in the eyes of the jury. The majority observed that prejudice in the eyes of the jury was hardly the point, because without the reluctant witness the government's evidence was insufficient for conviction as a matter of law.

OREGON v. KENNEDY

Supreme Court of the United States, 1982.
456 U.S. 667, 102 S.Ct. 2083, 72 L.Ed.2d 416.

JUSTICE REHNQUIST delivered the opinion of the Court. * * *

I

Respondent was charged with the theft of an oriental rug. During his first trial, the State called an expert witness on the subject of Middle Eastern rugs to testify as to the value and the identity of the rug in question. On cross-examination, respondent's attorney apparently attempted to establish bias on the part of the expert witness by asking him whether he had filed a criminal complaint against respondent. The witness eventually acknowledged this fact, but explained that no action had been taken on his complaint. On redirect examination, the prosecutor sought to elicit the reasons why the witness had filed a complaint against respondent, but the trial court sustained a series of objections to this line of inquiry.[12] The following colloquy then ensued:

> "Prosecutor: Have you ever done business with the Kennedys?
>
> "Witness: No, I have not.
>
> "Prosecutor: Is that because he is a crook?"

The trial court then granted respondent's motion for a mistrial.

When the State later sought to retry respondent, he moved to dismiss the charges because of double jeopardy. After a hearing at which the prosecutor testified, the trial court[13] found as a fact that "it was not the intention of the prosecutor in this case to cause a mistrial." On the basis of this finding, the trial court held that double jeopardy principles did not bar retrial, and respondent was then tried and convicted.

Respondent then successfully appealed to the Oregon Court of Appeals, which sustained his double jeopardy claim. * * * The Court of Appeals accepted the trial court's finding that it was not the intent of the prosecutor to cause a mistrial. Nevertheless, the court held that retrial was barred because the prosecutor's conduct in this case constituted what it viewed as "overreaching." Although the prosecutor intended to rehabilitate the witness, the Court of Appeals expressed the view that the question was in fact "a direct personal attack on the general character of the defendant." This personal attack left respondent with a "Hobson's choice—either to accept a necessarily prejudiced jury, or to move for a mistrial and face the process of being retried at a later time."
* * *

II

The Double Jeopardy Clause of the Fifth Amendment protects a criminal defendant from repeated prosecutions for the same offense. As a

---

12. The [Oregon] Court of Appeals later explained that respondent's "objections were not well taken, and the judge's rulings were probably wrong."

13. These proceedings were not conducted by the same trial judge who presided over respondent's initial trial.

part of this protection against multiple prosecutions, the Double Jeopardy Clause affords a criminal defendant a "valued right to have his trial completed by a particular tribunal." *Wade v. Hunter*, 336 U.S. 684, 689 (1949). The Double Jeopardy Clause, however, does not offer a guarantee to the defendant that the State will vindicate its societal interest in the enforcement of the criminal laws in one proceeding. If the law were otherwise, the purpose of law to protect society from those guilty of crimes frequently would be frustrated by denying courts power to put the defendant to trial again.

Where the trial is terminated over the objection of the defendant, the classical test for lifting the double jeopardy bar to a second trial is the "manifest necessity" standard first enunciated in Justice Story's opinion for the Court in *United States v. Perez*, 9 Wheat. 579, 580, 6 L.Ed. 165 (1824). *Perez* dealt with the most common form of "manifest necessity": a mistrial declared by the judge following the jury's declaration that it was unable to reach a verdict. While other situations have been recognized by our cases as meeting the "manifest necessity" standard, the hung jury remains the prototypical example. See, *e.g., Arizona v. Washington*, 434 U.S. 497, 509 (1978); *Illinois v. Somerville*, 410 U.S. 458, 463 (1973). The "manifest necessity" standard provides sufficient protection to the defendant's interests in having his case finally decided by the jury first selected while at the same time maintaining the public's interest in fair trials designed to end in just judgments.

But in the case of a mistrial declared at the behest of the defendant, quite different principles come into play. Here the defendant himself has elected to terminate the proceedings against him, and the "manifest necessity" standard has no place in the application of the Double Jeopardy Clause.

Our cases, however, have indicated that even where the defendant moves for a mistrial, there is a narrow exception to the rule that the Double Jeopardy Clause is no bar to retrial. * * *

Since one of the principal threads making up the protection embodied in the Double Jeopardy Clause is the right of the defendant to have his trial completed before the first jury empaneled to try him, it may be wondered as a matter of original inquiry why the defendant's election to terminate the first trial by his own motion should not be deemed a renunciation of that right for all purposes. We have recognized, however, that there would be great difficulty in applying such a rule where the prosecutor's actions giving rise to the motion for mistrial were done "in order to goad the [defendant] into requesting a mistrial." *United States v. Dinitz*, 424 U.S. at 611. In such a case, the defendant's valued right to complete his trial before the first jury would be a hollow shell if the inevitable motion for mistrial were held to prevent a later invocation of the bar of double jeopardy in all circumstances. But the precise phrasing of the circumstances which *will* allow a defendant to interpose the defense of double jeopardy to a second prosecution where the first has terminated on his own motion for a mistrial have been stated with less than crystal clarity in our cases which deal with this area of the law. * * *

The difficulty with the more general standards which would permit a broader exception than one merely based on intent is that they offer virtually no standards for their application. Every act on the part of a rational prosecutor during a trial is designed to "prejudice" the defendant by placing before the judge or jury evidence leading to a finding of his guilt. Given the complexity of the rules of evidence, it will be a rare trial of any complexity in which some proffered evidence by the prosecutor or by the defendant's attorney will not be found objectionable by the trial court. Most such objections are undoubtedly curable by simply refusing to allow the proffered evidence to be admitted, or in the case of a particular line of inquiry taken by counsel with a witness, by an admonition to desist from a particular line of inquiry.

More serious infractions on the part of the prosecutor may provoke a motion for mistrial on the part of the defendant, and may in the view of the trial court warrant the granting of such a motion. The "overreaching" standard applied by the court below and urged today by Justice Stevens, however, would add another classification of prosecutorial error, one requiring dismissal of the indictment, but without supplying any standard by which to assess that error.

By contrast, a standard that examines the intent of the prosecutor, though certainly not entirely free from practical difficulties, is a manageable standard to apply. It merely calls for the court to make a finding of fact. Inferring the existence or nonexistence of intent from objective facts and circumstances is a familiar process in our criminal justice system. When it is remembered that resolution of double jeopardy questions by state trial courts are reviewable not only within the state court system, but in the federal court system on habeas corpus as well, the desirability of an easily applied principle is apparent.

Prosecutorial conduct that might be viewed as harassment or overreaching, even if sufficient to justify a mistrial on defendant's motion, therefore, does not bar retrial absent intent on the part of the prosecutor to subvert the protections afforded by the Double Jeopardy Clause. Only where the governmental conduct in question is intended to "goad" the defendant into moving for a mistrial may a defendant raise the bar of double jeopardy to a second trial after having succeeded in aborting the first on his own motion.

Were we to embrace the broad and somewhat amorphous standard adopted by the Oregon Court of Appeals, we are not sure that criminal defendants as a class would be aided. Knowing that the granting of the defendant's motion for mistrial would all but inevitably bring with it an attempt to bar a second trial on grounds of double jeopardy, the judge presiding over the first trial might well be more loath to grant a defendant's motion for mistrial. If a mistrial were in fact warranted under the applicable law, of course, the defendant could in many instances successfully appeal a judgment of conviction on the same grounds that he urged a mistrial, and the Double Jeopardy Clause would present no bar to retrial. But some of the advantages secured to him by the Double Jeopardy Clause—the freedom from extended anxiety, and the necessity to confront the government's case only once—would be to a large extent lost in the process of trial to verdict, reversal on appeal, and subsequent retrial. * * *

Since the Oregon trial court found, and the Oregon Court of Appeals accepted, that the prosecutorial conduct culminating in the termination of the first trial in this case was not so intended by the prosecutor, that is the end of the matter for purposes of the Double Jeopardy Clause of the Fifth Amendment to the United States Constitution. The judgment of the Oregon Court of Appeals is reversed, and the cause is remanded for further proceedings not inconsistent with this opinion.

It is so ordered.

JUSTICE BRENNAN, with whom JUSTICE MARSHALL joins, concurring in the judgment.

I concur in the judgment and join in the opinion of Justice Stevens. However, it should be noted that nothing in the holding of the Court today prevents the state courts, on remand, from concluding that respondent's retrial would violate the provision of the Oregon Constitution that prohibits double jeopardy, Ore.Const., Art. I, § 12, as that provision has been interpreted by the state courts. * * *

JUSTICE STEVENS, with whom JUSTICE BRENNAN, JUSTICE MARSHALL, and JUSTICE BLACKMUN join, concurring in the judgment. * * *

Even if I agreed that the balance of competing interests tipped in favor of a bar to reprosecution only in the situation in which the prosecutor intended to provoke a mistrial, I would not subscribe to a standard that conditioned such a bar on the determination that the prosecutor harbored such intent when he committed prejudicial error. It is almost inconceivable that a defendant could prove that the prosecutor's deliberate misconduct was motivated by an intent to provoke a mistrial instead of an intent simply to prejudice the defendant. The defendant must shoulder a strong burden to establish a bar to reprosecution when he has consented to the mistrial, but the Court's subjective intent standard would eviscerate the exception.

A broader objection to the Court's limitation of the exception is that the rationale for the exception extends beyond the situation in which the prosecutor intends to provoke a mistrial. There are other situations in which the defendant's double jeopardy interests outweigh society's interest in obtaining a judgment on the merits even though the defendant has moved for a mistrial. For example, a prosecutor may be interested in putting the defendant through the embarrassment, expense, and ordeal of criminal proceedings even if he cannot obtain a conviction. In such a case, with the purpose of harassing the defendant the prosecutor may commit repeated prejudicial errors and be indifferent between a mistrial or mistrials and an unsustainable conviction or convictions. Another example is when the prosecutor seeks to inject enough unfair prejudice into the trial to ensure a conviction but not so much as to cause a reversal of that conviction. This kind of overreaching would not be covered by the Court's standard because, by hypothesis, the prosecutor's intent is to obtain a conviction, not to provoke a mistrial. Yet the defendant's choice—to continue the tainted proceeding or to abort it and begin anew—can be just as "hollow" in this situation as when the prosecutor intends to provoke a mistrial.

To invoke the exception for overreaching, a court need not divine the exact motivation for the prosecutorial error. It is sufficient that the court is persuaded that egregious prosecutorial misconduct has rendered unmeaningful the defendant's choice to continue or to abort the proceeding. It is unnecessary and unwise to attempt to identify all the factors that might inform the court's judgment, but several considerations follow from the rationale for recognizing the exception. First, because the exception is justified by the intolerance of intentional manipulation of the defendant's double jeopardy interests, a finding of deliberate misconduct normally would be a prerequisite to a reprosecution bar. Second, because the defendant's option to abort the proceeding after prosecutorial misconduct would retain real meaning for the defendant in any case in which the trial was going badly for him, normally a required finding would be that the prosecutorial error virtually eliminated, or at least substantially reduced, the probability of acquittal in a proceeding that was going badly for the government. It should be apparent from these observations that only in a rare and compelling case will a mistrial declared at the request of the defendant or with his consent bar a retrial.[14] * * *

The petitioner, and the state court that denied the respondent's motion to dismiss, have correctly pointed out that it is unnecessary to cut back on the recognized exception, or even to disavow the most liberal construction given it by the federal courts, to conclude that the exception has not been established on the facts of this case. The isolated prosecutorial error occurred early in the trial, too early to determine whether the case was going badly for the prosecution. If anyone was being harassed at that time, it was the prosecutor, who was frustrated by improper defense objections in her attempt to rehabilitate her witness. The gist of the comment that the respondent was a "crook" could fairly have been elicited from the witness, since defense counsel injected the respondent's past alleged improprieties into the trial by questioning the witness about his bias towards the defendant. The comment therefore could not have injected the kind of prejudice that would render unmeaningful the defendant's option to proceed with the trial.

14. The petitioner and the United States as *amicus curiae* cite only a few cases in which the exception has been invoked to bar reprosecution. One commentator discovered only two cases in which a Federal Court of Appeals barred reprosecution. Note, Double Jeopardy: An Illusory Remedy for Governmental Overreaching at Trial, 29 Buffalo L.Rev. 759, 760, n. 16 (1980).

UNITED STATES v. SCOTT

Supreme Court of the United States, 1978.
437 U.S. 82, 98 S.Ct. 2187, 57 L.Ed.2d 65.

MR. JUSTICE REHNQUIST delivered the opinion of the Court.

On March 5, 1975, respondent, a member of the police force in Muskegon, Mich., was charged in a three-count indictment with distribution of various narcotics. Both before his trial in the United States District Court for the Western District of Michigan, and twice during the trial, respondent moved to dismiss the two counts of the indictment which concerned transactions that took place during the preceding September, on the ground that his defense had been prejudiced by preindictment delay. At the close of all the evidence, the court granted respondent's motion. Although the court did not explain its reasons for dismissing the second count, it explicitly concluded that respondent had "presented sufficient proof of prejudice with respect to Count I. The court submitted the third count to the jury, which returned a verdict of not guilty.

The Government sought to appeal the dismissals of the first two counts to the United States Court of Appeals for the Sixth Circuit. That court, relying on our opinion in *United States v. Jenkins*, 420 U.S. 358 (1975), concluded that any further prosecution of respondent was barred by the Double Jeopardy Clause of the Fifth Amendment, and therefore dismissed the appeal. The Government has sought review in this Court only with regard to the dismissal of the first count. We granted certiorari to give further consideration to the applicability of the Double Jeopardy Clause to Government appeals from orders granting defense motions to terminate a trial before verdict. We now reverse.

The problem presented by this case could not have arisen during the first century of this Court's existence. The Court has long taken the view that the United States has no right of appeal in a criminal case, absent explicit statutory authority. Such authority was not provided until the enactment of the Criminal Appeals Act of 1907, which permitted the United States to seek a writ of error in this Court from any decision dismissing an indictment on the basis of "the invalidity, or construction of the statute upon which the indictment is founded." Our consideration of Government appeals over the ensuing years ordinarily focused upon the intricacies of the Act and its amendments. In 1971, however, Congress adopted the current language of the Act, permitting Government appeals from any decision dismissing an indictment, "except that no appeal shall lie where the double jeopardy clause of the United States Constitution prohibits further prosecution." 18 U.S.C. § 3731 (1976 ed.).
* * *

In our first encounter with the new statute, we concluded that "Congress intended to remove all statutory barriers to Government appeals and to allow appeals whenever the Constitution would permit."

United States v. Wilson, 420 U.S. 332, 337 (1975). Since up to that point Government appeals had been subject to statutory restrictions independent of the Double Jeopardy Clause, our previous cases construing the statute proved to be of little assistance in determining when the Double Jeopardy Clause of the Fifth Amendment would prohibit further prosecution. A detailed canvass of the history of the double jeopardy principles in English and American law led us to conclude that the Double Jeopardy Clause was primarily "directed at the threat of multiple prosecutions," and posed no bar to Government appeals "where those appeals would not require a new trial." We accordingly held in *Jenkins, supra*, that, whether or not a dismissal of an indictment after jeopardy had attached amounted to an acquittal on the merits, the Government had no right to appeal, because "further proceedings of some sort, devoted to the resolution of factual issues going to the elements of the offense charged, would have been required upon reversal and remand."

If *Jenkins* is a correct statement of the law, the judgment of the Court of Appeals relying on that decision, as it was bound to do, would in all likelihood have to be affirmed. Yet, though our assessment of the history and meaning of the Double Jeopardy Clause in *Wilson, Jenkins*, and *Serfass v. United States*, 420 U.S. 377 (1975), occurred only three Terms ago, our vastly increased exposure to the various facets of the Double Jeopardy Clause has now convinced us that *Jenkins* was wrongly decided. It placed an unwarrantedly great emphasis on the defendant's right to have his guilt decided by the first jury empaneled to try him so as to include those cases where the defendant himself seeks to terminate the trial before verdict on grounds unrelated to factual guilt or innocence. We have therefore decided to overrule *Jenkins*, and thus to reverse the judgment of the Court of Appeals in this case. * * *

[The opinion reviewed the cases concerning retrial of a defendant after declaration of a mistrial.]

We turn now to the relationship between the Double Jeopardy Clause and reprosecution of a defendant who has successfully obtained not a mistrial but a termination of the trial in his favor before any determination of factual guilt or innocence. Unlike the typical mistrial, the granting of a motion such as this obviously contemplates that the proceedings will terminate then and there in favor of the defendant. The prosecution, if it wishes to reinstate the proceedings in the face of such a ruling, ordinarily must seek reversal of the decision of the trial court. * * *

In the present case, the District Court's dismissal of the first count of the indictment was based upon a claim of preindictment delay and not on the court's conclusion that the Government had not produced sufficient evidence to establish the guilt of the defendant. Respondent Scott points out quite correctly that he had moved to dismiss the indictment on this ground prior to trial, and that had the District Court chosen to grant it at that time the Government could have appealed the ruling under our holding in *Serfass v. United States*, 420 U.S. 377 (1975). He also quite correctly points out that jeopardy had undeniably "attached" at the time the District Court terminated the trial in his favor; since a successful Government appeal would require further proceedings in the District Court leading to a factual resolution of the issue of guilt or innocence, *Jenkins* bars the Government's appeal. However, our growing experience with Government appeals convinces us that we must reexamine the rationale of *Jenkins* * * *

[A] defendant once acquitted may not be again subjected to trial without violating the Double Jeopardy Clause. But that situation is obviously a far cry from the present case, where the Government was quite willing to continue with its production of evidence to show the defendant guilty before the jury first empaneled to try him, but the defendant elected to seek termination of the trial on grounds unrelated to guilt or innocence. This is scarcely a picture of an all-powerful state relentlessly pursuing a defendant who had either been found not guilty or who had at least insisted on having the issue of guilt submitted to the first trier of fact. It is instead a picture of a defendant who chooses to avoid conviction and imprisonment, not because of his assertion that the Government has failed to make out a case against him, but because of a legal claim that the Government's case against him must fail even though it might satisfy the trier of fact that he was guilty beyond a reasonable doubt.

We have previously noted that the trial judge's characterization of his own action cannot control the classification of the action.

Despite respondent's contentions, an appeal is not barred simply because a ruling in favor of a defendant is based upon facts outside the face of the indictment, or because it is granted on the ground that the defendant simply cannot be convicted of the offense charged. Rather, a defendant is acquitted only when the ruling of the judge, whatever its label, actually represents a resolution in the defendant's favor, correct or not, of some or all of the factual elements of the offense charged. Where the court, before the jury returns a verdict, enters a judgment of acquittal pursuant to Fed.Rule Crim.Proc. 29, appeal will be barred only when it is plain that the District Court evaluated the Government's evidence and determined that it was legally insufficient to sustain a conviction. * * *

We think that in a case such as this the defendant, by deliberately choosing to seek termination of the proceedings against him on a basis unrelated to factual guilt or innocence of the offense of which he is accused, suffers no injury cognizable under the Double Jeopardy Clause if the Government is permitted to appeal from such a ruling of the trial court in favor of the defendant. We do not thereby adopt the doctrine of "waiver" of double jeopardy rejected in *Green v. United States*, 355 U.S. 184 (1957).[15] Rather, we conclude that the Double Jeopardy Clause,

15. The original jury in that case had found the defendant guilty of second-degree murder, but did not find him guilty of first- degree murder. The Court held that his appeal did not waive his objection to a second prosecution for first-degree murder,

which guards against Government oppression, does not relieve a defendant from the consequences of his voluntary choice. In *Green* the question of the defendant's factual guilt or innocence of murder in the first degree was actually submitted to the jury as a trier of fact; in the present case, respondent successfully avoided such a submission of the first count of the indictment by persuading the trial court to dismiss it on a basis which did not depend on guilt or innocence. He was thus neither acquitted nor convicted, because he himself successfully undertook to persuade the trial court not to submit the issue of guilt or innocence to the jury which had been empaneled to try him.[16]

* * *

The judgment of the Court of Appeals is therefore reversed, and the cause is remanded for further proceedings.

Mr. Justice Brennan, with whom Mr. Justice White, Mr. Justice Marshall, and Mr. Justice Stevens join, dissenting.

In repeatedly holding that the Government may not appeal from an acquittal if a reversal would necessitate a retrial, the Court has, of course, recognized that this rule impairs to some degree the Government's interest in enforcing its criminal laws. Yet, while we have acknowledged that permitting review of acquittals would avoid release of guilty defendants who benefited from error, irrational behavior, or prejudice on the part of the trial judge, we nevertheless have consistently held that the Double Jeopardy Clause bars any appellate review in such circumstances. The reason is not that the first trial established the defendant's factual innocence, but rather that the second trial would present all the untoward consequences the Clause was designed to prevent. The Government would be allowed to seek to persuade a second trier of fact of the defendant's guilt, to strengthen any weaknesses in its first presentation, and to subject the defendant to the expense and anxiety of a second trial.

This basic principle of double jeopardy law has heretofore applied not only to acquittals based on the verdict of the fact-finder, but also to acquittals entered by the trial judge, following the presentation of evidence but before verdict, pursuant to Fed.Rule Crim.Proc. 29. For however egregious the error of the acquittal, the termination favorable

---

but it was careful to reaffirm the holding of *United States v. Ball*, 163 U.S. 662 (1896), that "a defendant can be tried a second time for an offense when his prior conviction for that same offense [has] been set aside on appeal."

16. We should point out that it is entirely possible for a trial court to reconcile the public interest in the Government's right to appeal from an erroneous conclusion of law, with the defendant's interest in avoiding a second prosecution. In *United States v. Wilson*, 420 U.S. 332 (1975), the court permitted the case to go to the jury, which returned a verdict of guilty, but it subsequently dismissed the indictment for preindictment delay on the basis of evidence adduced at trial. Most recently in *United States v. Ceccolini*, 435 U.S. 268 (1978), we described similar action with approval: "The District Court had sensibly first made its finding on the factual question of guilt or innocence, and then ruled on the motion to suppress; a reversal of these rulings would require no further proceedings in the District Court, but merely a reinstatement of the finding of guilt."

to the accused has been regarded as no different from a factfinder's acquittal that resulted from errors of the trial judge. These cases teach that the Government's means of protecting its vital interest in convicting the guilty is its participation as an adversary at the criminal trial where it has every opportunity to dissuade the trial court from committing erroneous rulings favorable to the accused.

Jenkins, was simply a necessary and logical extension of the rule that an acquittal bars any further trial proceedings. *Jenkins* recognized that an acquittal can never represent a determination that the criminal defendant is innocent in any absolute sense; the bar to a retrial following acquittal does not—and indeed could not—rest on any assumption that the finder of fact has applied the correct legal principles to all the admissible evidence and determined that the defendant was factually innocent of the offense charged. The reason further prosecution is barred following an acquittal, rather, is that the Government has been afforded one complete opportunity to prove a case of the criminal defendant's culpability and, when it has failed for any reason to persuade the court not to enter a final judgment favorable to the accused, the constitutional policies underlying the ban against multiple trials become compelling. Thus, *Jenkins* and *Lee* recognized that it mattered not whether the final judgment constituted a formal "acquittal." What is critical is whether the accused obtained, after jeopardy attached, a favorable termination of the charges against him.

The whole premise for today's retreat from *Jenkins* and *Lee*, of course, is the Court's new theory that a criminal defendant who seeks to avoid conviction on a "ground unrelated to factual innocence" somehow stands on a different constitutional footing from a defendant whose participation in his criminal trial creates a situation in which a judgment of acquittal has to be entered. This premise is simply untenable. The rule prohibiting retrials following acquittals does not and could not rest on a conclusion that the accused was factually innocent in any meaningful sense. If that were the basis for the rule, the decisions that have held that even egregiously erroneous acquittals preclude retrials were erroneous.

It is manifest that the reasons that bar a retrial following an acquittal are equally applicable to a final judgment entered on a ground "unrelated to factual innocence." The heavy personal strain of the second trial is the same in either case. So too is the risk that, though innocent, the defendant may be found guilty at a second trial. If the appeal is allowed in either situation, the Government will, following any reversal, not only obtain the benefit of the favorable appellate ruling but also be permitted to shore up any other weak points of its case and obtain all the other advantages at the second trial that the Double Jeopardy Clause was designed to forbid. * * *

Equally significant, the distinction between the two is at best purely formal. Many acquittals are the consequence of rulings of law made on the accused's motion that are not related to the question of his factual guilt or innocence: *e.g.*, a ruling on the law respecting the scope of the offense or excluding reliable evidence. * * *

The enormous practical problems that today's decision portends are very clear. A particularly appealing virtue of the *Jenkins* and *Lee* principle—in addition, of course, to its protection of constitutional values—was its simplicity. Any midtrial order contemplating an end to all prosecution of the accused would automatically erect a double jeopardy bar to a retrial. Under today's decision, the thousands of state and federal courts will be required to decide, with only minimal guidance from this Court, the question of the double jeopardy consequences of all favorable terminations of criminal proceedings on the basis of affirmative defenses. The only guidance the Court offers is its suggestion that defenses which provide legal justifications for otherwise criminal acts will erect double jeopardy bars whereas those defenses that arise from unlawful or unconstitutional Government acts will not. Consideration of the defense of entrapment illustrates how difficult the Court's decision will be to apply. To the extent the defense applies when there has been a showing the defendant was not "predisposed" to commit a criminal act, it perhaps does provide a "legal justification." But the defense of entrapment, in many jurisdictions is a device to deter police officials from engaging in reprehensible law enforcement techniques. Is the entrapment defense to erect a double jeopardy bar in such jurisdictions? Are the double jeopardy consequences to depend upon the appellate court's characterization of the operation of the defense in the particular case before it? And what of other traditional factual defenses, which are routinely submitted to the jury and which could be the basis for Rule 29 motions: *e.g.*, the statute of limitations? Ironically, it seems likely that, when all is said and done, there will be few instances indeed in which defenses can be deemed unrelated to factual innocence. If so, today's decision may be limited to disfavored doctrines like preaccusation delay.

It is regrettable that the Court should introduce such confusion in an area of the law that, until today, had been crystal clear. Its introduction might be tolerable if necessary to advance some important policy or to serve values protected by the Double Jeopardy Clause, but that manifestly is not the case. Rather, today's decision fashions an entirely arbitrary distinction that creates precisely the evils that the Double Jeopardy Clause was designed to prevent. I would affirm the judgment of the Court of Appeals.

SMALIS v. PENNSYLVANIA

Supreme Court of the United States, 1986.
476 U.S. 140, 106 S.Ct. 1745, 90 L.Ed.2d 116.

JUSTICE WHITE delivered the opinion of the Court.

At the close of the prosecution's case in chief, the trial court dismissed certain charges against petitioners on the ground that the evidence presented was legally insufficient to support a conviction. The question presented is whether the Double Jeopardy Clause bars the prosecution from appealing this ruling.

I

Petitioners, husband and wife, owned a building housing a restaurant and some apartments that burned under suspicious circumstances, killing two of the tenants. Petitioners were charged with various crimes in connection with this fire, including criminal homicide, reckless endangerment, and causing a catastrophe. They opted for a bench trial, and at the close of the prosecution's case in chief challenged the sufficiency of the evidence by filing a demurrer pursuant to Pennsylvania Rule of Criminal Procedure 1124(a)(1). The trial court sustained petitioners' demurrer to charges of murder, voluntary manslaughter, and causing a catastrophe, stating:

> "As the trier of fact and law, the court was not satisfied, after considering all of the facts together with all reasonable inferences which the Commonwealth's evidence tended to prove, that there was sufficient evidence from which it could be concluded that either of the defendants was guilty beyond a reasonable doubt of setting or causing to be set the fire in question."

The Commonwealth sought review of this ruling in the Superior Court of Pennsylvania, but a panel of that court quashed the appeal, holding it barred by the Double Jeopardy Clause. The Superior Court granted review en banc and affirmed. Citing a number of our decisions as controlling authority, the court set out two relevant principles of law. First, a judgment that the evidence is legally insufficient to sustain a guilty verdict constitutes an acquittal for purposes of the Double Jeopardy Clause. See, *e.g., United States v. Martin Linen Supply Co.*, 430 U.S. 564 (1977); *Burks v. United States*, 437 U.S. 1 (1978); *Sanabria v. United States*, 437 U.S. 54 (1978); *United States v. Scott*, 437 U.S. 82, 91 (1978) (dicta); *Hudson v. Louisiana*, 450 U.S. 40 (1981). Second, when a trial court enters such a judgment, the Double Jeopardy Clause bars an appeal by the prosecution not only when it might result in a second trial, but also if reversal would translate into further proceedings devoted to the resolution of factual issues going to the elements of the offense charged. The Superior Court concluded that because reversal of the trial court's granting of petitioners' demurrer would necessitate further trial proceedings, the Commonwealth's appeal was improper under *Martin Linen*.

The Commonwealth appealed to the Supreme Court of Pennsylvania, which reversed. The court relied heavily on the statement in *United States v. Scott, supra,* that a trial judge's ruling in a defendant's favor constitutes an acquittal "only when 'the ruling of the judge, whatever its label, actually represents a resolution [in the defendant's favor], correct or not, of some or all of the factual elements of the offense charged.'" *Id.,* 437 U.S., at 97. The court gave the following explanation of why the trial court's ruling on petitioners' demurrer is not within this definition of an acquittal:

> "In deciding whether to grant a demurrer, the court does not determine whether or not the defendant is guilty on such evidence,

but determines whether the evidence, if credited by the jury, is legally sufficient to warrant the conclusion that the defendant is guilty beyond a reasonable doubt. * * *

"Hence, by definition, a demurrer is not a factual determination. * * * [T]he question before the trial judge in ruling on a demurrer remains purely one of law.

"We conclude, therefore, that a demurrer is not the functional equivalent of an acquittal, and that the Commonwealth has the right to appeal from an order sustaining defendant's demurrer to its case-in-chief. In such a situation, the defendant himself elects to seek dismissal on grounds unrelated to his factual guilt or innocence."

Accordingly, the Pennsylvania Supreme Court remanded the case to the Superior Court for a determination on the merits of the appeal. We granted certiorari, and now reverse.

II

The Pennsylvania Supreme Court erred in holding that, for purposes of considering a plea of double jeopardy, a defendant who demurs at the close of the prosecution's case in chief "elects to seek dismissal on grounds unrelated to his factual guilt or innocence." What the demurring defendant seeks is a ruling that as a matter of law the State's evidence is insufficient to establish his factual guilt. Our past decisions, which we are not inclined to reconsider at this time, hold that such a ruling is an acquittal under the Double Jeopardy Clause. *United States v. Scott* does not overturn these precedents; indeed, it plainly indicates that the category of acquittals includes "judgment[s] * * * by the court that the evidence is insufficient to convict." 437 U.S., at 91.

The Commonwealth argues that its appeal is nonetheless permissible under *Justices of Boston Municipal Court v. Lydon*, 466 U.S. 294 (1984), because resumption of petitioners' bench trial following a reversal on appeal would simply constitute "continuing jeopardy." But *Lydon* teaches that "[a]cquittals, unlike convictions, terminate the initial jeopardy." 466 U.S., at 308, 104 S.Ct., at 1813. Thus, whether the trial is to a jury or to the bench, subjecting the defendant to postacquittal factfinding proceedings going to guilt or innocence violates the Double Jeopardy Clause. *Arizona v. Rumsey*, 467 U.S. 203, 211–212 (1984).[17]

When a successful post-acquittal appeal by the prosecution would lead to proceedings that violate the Double Jeopardy Clause, the appeal

---

17. In *Rumsey*, a trial judge sitting as a sentencer in a death-penalty proceeding entered an "acquittal," *i.e.*, a life sentence, based on an erroneous construction of the law governing a particular aggravating circumstance. The Court held that the Double Jeopardy Clause barred a second sentencing hearing. It distinguished *United States v. Wilson*, 420 U.S. 332 (1975), which holds that the prosecution may appeal when the trial court enters judgment n.o.v. following a jury verdict of guilty. *Rumsey* explains that "[n]o double jeopardy problem was presented in *Wilson* because the appellate court, upon reviewing asserted legal errors of the trial judge, could simply order the jury's guilty verdict reinstated; no new factfinding would be necessary, and the defendant therefore would not be twice placed in jeopardy."

itself has no proper purpose. Allowing such an appeal would frustrate the interest of the accused in having an end to the proceedings against him. The Superior Court was correct, therefore, in holding that the Double Jeopardy Clause bars a post-acquittal appeal by the prosecution not only when it might result in a second trial, but also if reversal would translate into "further proceedings of some sort, devoted to the resolution of factual issues going to the elements of the offense charged." *Martin Linen, supra*, 430 U.S., at 570.

We hold, therefore, that the trial judge's granting of petitioners' demurrer was an acquittal under the Double Jeopardy Clause, and that the Commonwealth's appeal was barred because reversal would have lead to further trial proceedings.

The judgment of the Pennsylvania Supreme Court is reversed.

TIBBS v. FLORIDA

Supreme Court of the United States, 1982.
457 U.S. 31, 102 S.Ct. 2211, 72 L.Ed.2d 652.

Justice O'Connor delivered the opinion of the Court.

We granted certiorari to decide whether the Double Jeopardy Clause bars retrial after a state appellate court sets aside a conviction on the ground that the verdict was against "the weight of the evidence." After examining the policies supporting the Double Jeopardy Clause, we hold that a reversal based on the weight, rather than the sufficiency, of the evidence permits the State to initiate a new prosecution.

I

In 1974, Florida indicted petitioner Delbert Tibbs for the first-degree murder of Terry Milroy, the felony murder of Milroy, and the rape of Cynthia Nadeau. Nadeau, the State's chief trial witness, testified that she and Milroy were hitchhiking from St. Petersburg to Marathon, Fla., on February 3, 1974. A man in a green truck picked them up near Fort Myers and, after driving a short way, turned off the highway into a field. He asked Milroy to help him siphon gas from some farm machinery, and Milroy agreed. When Nadeau stepped out of the truck a few minutes later, she discovered the driver holding a gun on Milroy. The driver told Milroy that he wished to have sex with Nadeau, and ordered her to strip. After forcing Nadeau to engage in sodomy, the driver agreed that Milroy could leave. As Milroy started to walk away, however, the assailant shot him in the shoulder. When Milroy fell to the ground, pleading for his life, the gunman walked over and taunted, "Does it hurt, boy? You in pain? Does it hurt, boy?" Then, with a shot to the head, he killed Milroy.

This deed finished, the killer raped Nadeau. Fearing for her life, she suggested that they should leave together and that she "would be his old lady." The killer seemed to agree and they returned to the highway in the truck. After driving a short distance, he stopped the truck and ordered Nadeau to walk directly in front of it. As soon as her feet hit the ground, however, she ran in the opposite direction. The killer fled with the truck, frightened perhaps by an approaching car. When Nadeau reached a nearby house, the occupants let her in and called the police.

That night, Nadeau gave the police a detailed description of the assailant and his truck. Several days later a patrolman stopped Tibbs, who was hitchhiking near Ocala, Fla., because his appearance matched Nadeau's description. The Ocala Police Department photographed Tibbs and relayed the pictures to the Fort Myers police. When Nadeau examined these photos, she identified Tibbs as the assailant.[18] Nadeau subsequently picked Tibbs out of a lineup and positively identified him at trial as the man who murdered Milroy and raped her.[19]

Tibbs' attorney attempted to show that Nadeau was an unreliable witness. She admitted during cross-examination that she had tried "just about all" types of drugs and that she had smoked marihuana shortly before the crimes occurred. *Id.*, at 526, 545–546. She also evidenced some confusion about the time of day that the assailant had offered her and Milroy a ride. Finally, counsel suggested through questions and closing argument that Nadeau's former boyfriend had killed Milroy and that Nadeau was lying to protect her boyfriend. Nadeau flatly denied these suggestions.[20]

In addition to these attempts to discredit Nadeau, Tibbs testified in his own defense. He explained that he was college educated, that he had published a story and a few poems, and that he was hitchhiking through Florida to learn more about how people live. He claimed that he was in

18. The State's witnesses conceded that, at the time of this identification, Nadeau saw only photographs of Tibbs; she did not have the opportunity to pick his picture out of a photographic array. An officer explained, however, that Nadeau had viewed photographs of single suspects on three or four other occasions and had not identified the killer on any of those occasions. Nadeau also had examined several books of photographs without making an identification. We do not pass upon any possible due process questions raised by the State's identification procedures, see generally *Neil v. Biggers*, 409 U.S. 188 (1972); *Simmons v. United States*, 390 U.S. 377 (1968), because Tibbs' challenge to retrial rests solely upon double jeopardy grounds.

19. The State's remaining witnesses included law enforcement agents, a man who had driven Milroy and Nadeau to Fort Myers, the houseowner who had called the police for Nadeau, acquaintances of Milroy, a doctor who had examined Nadeau shortly after the crimes, and the doctor who had performed the autopsy on Milroy. The doctors confirmed that Nadeau had had intercourse on the evening of February 3 and that Milroy had died that evening from a bullet wound in the head. The other wit-

nesses confirmed that Nadeau and Milroy had been hitchhiking through Fort Myers on February 3 and that Nadeau had arrived at a house, in a hysterical condition, that evening.

A Florida prisoner, sentenced to life imprisonment for rape, also testified for the State. This prisoner claimed that he had met Tibbs while Tibbs was in jail awaiting trial and that Tibbs had confessed the crime to him. The defense substantially discredited this witness on cross-examination, revealing inconsistencies in his testimony and suggesting that he had testified in the hope of obtaining leniency from the State.

20. The results of two polygraph examinations, described in a report read to the jury, indicated that Nadeau was "truthful as to the fact that a black male driving a green pickup truck had picked them up and that this black male had murdered Terry Milroy." The polygraphs also suggested that Nadeau was truthful when she identified Tibbs as the assailant. Tibbs challenged the admissibility of these polygraphs during his first appeal. The justices who voted to reverse Tibbs' conviction, however, did not reach the issue and we express no opinion on this matter of state law.

Daytona Beach, across the State from Fort Myers, from the evening of February 1, 1974, through the morning of February 6. He also testified that he did not own a green truck, and that he had not driven any vehicle while in Florida. Finally, he denied committing any of the crimes charged against him.

Two Salvation Army officers partially corroborated Tibbs' story. These officers produced a card signed by Tibbs, indicating that he had slept at the Daytona Beach Salvation Army Transit Lodge on the evening of February 1, 1974. Neither witness, however, had seen Tibbs after the morning of February 2. Tibbs' other witnesses testified to his good reputation as a law-abiding citizen and to his good reputation for veracity.

On rebuttal, the State produced a card, similar to the one introduced by Tibbs, showing that Tibbs had spent the night of February 4 at the Orlando Salvation Army Transit Lodge. This evidence contradicted Tibbs' claim that he had remained in Daytona Beach until February 6, as well as his sworn statements that he had been in Orlando only once, during the early part of January 1974, and that he had not stayed in any Salvation Army lodge after February 1. After the State presented this rebuttal evidence, Tibbs took the stand to deny both that he had been in Orlando on February 4 and that the signature on the Orlando Salvation Army card was his.

The jury convicted Tibbs of first-degree murder and rape. Pursuant to the jury's recommendation, the judge sentenced Tibbs to death. On appeal, the Florida Supreme Court reversed. *Tibbs v. State*, 337 So.2d 788 (1976) (*Tibbs I*). A plurality of three justices, while acknowledging that "the resolution of factual issues in a criminal trial is peculiarly within the province of a jury," identified six weaknesses in the State's case. First, except for Nadeau's testimony, the State introduced no evidence placing Tibbs in or near Fort Myers on the day of the crimes. Second, although Nadeau gave a detailed description of the assailant's truck, police never found the vehicle. Third, police discovered neither a gun nor car keys in Tibbs' possession. Fourth, Tibbs cooperated fully with the police when he was stopped and arrested. Fifth, the State introduced no evidence casting doubt on Tibbs' veracity. Tibbs, on the other hand, produced witnesses who attested to his good reputation. Finally, several factors undermined Nadeau's believability. Although she asserted at trial that the crimes occurred during daylight, other evidence suggested that the events occurred after nightfall when reliable identification would have been more difficult. Nadeau, furthermore, had smoked marihuana shortly before the crimes and had identified Tibbs during a suggestive photograph session. These weaknesses left the plurality in "considerable doubt that Delbert Tibbs [was] the man who committed the crimes for which he ha[d] been convicted." Therefore, the plurality concluded that the "interests of justice" required a new trial.

Justice Boyd concurred specially, noting that " '[t]he test to be applied in determining the adequacy of a verdict is whether a jury of reasonable men could have returned that verdict.' " Apparently applying that standard, Justice Boyd found the State's evidence deficient. He concluded that "the weakness of the evidence presented in the trial court might well require that [Tibbs] be released from incarceration without further litigation," but "reluctantly concur[red]" in the plurality's decision to order a new trial because he understood Florida law to permit retrial.

On remand, the trial court dismissed the indictment, concluding that retrial would violate the double jeopardy principles articulated in *Burks v. United States*, 437 U.S. 1 (1978), and *Greene v. Massey*, 437 U.S. 19 (1978). An intermediate appellate court disagreed and remanded the case for trial. The Florida Supreme Court affirmed the latter decision, carefully elaborating the difference between a reversal stemming from insufficient evidence and one prompted by the weight of the evidence. * * *

II

In 1896, this Court ruled that a criminal defendant who successfully appeals a judgment against him "may be tried anew * * * for the same offence of which he had been convicted." *United States v. Ball*, 163 U.S. 662, 672. This principle * * * has persevered to the present. Two considerations support the rule. First, the Court has recognized that society would pay too high a price were every accused granted immunity from punishment because of any defect sufficient to constitute reversible error in the proceedings leading to conviction. Second, the Court has concluded that retrial after reversal of a conviction is not the type of governmental oppression targeted by the Double Jeopardy Clause.

Burks v. United States and *Greene v. Massey* carved a narrow exception from the understanding that a defendant who successfully appeals a conviction is subject to retrial. In those cases, we held that the Double Jeopardy Clause precludes retrial once the reviewing court has found the evidence legally insufficient to support conviction. This standard, we explained, means that the government's case was so lacking that it should not have even been *submitted* to the jury. A conviction will survive review, we suggested, whenever the evidence and inferences therefrom most favorable to the prosecution would warrant the jury's finding the defendant guilty beyond a reasonable doubt. In sum, we noted that the rule barring retrial would be "confined to cases where the prosecution's failure is clear." *Burks, supra*, at 17.

So defined, the exception recognized in *Burks* and *Greene* rests upon two closely related policies. First, the Double Jeopardy Clause attaches special weight to judgments of acquittal. A verdict of not guilty, whether rendered by the jury or directed by the trial judge, absolutely shields the defendant from retrial. A reversal based on the insufficiency of the evidence has the same effect because it means that no rational factfinder could have voted to convict the defendant.

Second, *Burks* and *Greene* implement the principle that "[t]he Double Jeopardy Clause forbids a second trial for the purpose of affording the prosecution another opportunity to supply evidence which it failed to muster in the first proceeding." This prohibition, lying at the core of the Clause's protections, prevents the State from honing its trial strategies and perfecting its evidence through successive attempts at conviction. Repeated prosecutorial sallies would unfairly burden the defendant and create a risk of conviction through sheer governmental perseverance. For this reason, when a reversal rests upon the ground that the prosecution has failed to produce sufficient evidence to prove its case, the Double Jeopardy Clause bars the prosecutor from making a second attempt at conviction.

These policies do not have the same force when a judge disagrees with a jury's resolution of conflicting evidence and concludes that a guilty verdict is against the weight of the evidence. A reversal on this ground, unlike a reversal based on insufficient evidence, does not mean that acquittal was the only proper verdict. Instead, the appellate court sits as a "thirteenth juror" and disagrees with the jury's resolution of the conflicting testimony. This difference of opinion no more signifies acquittal than does a disagreement among the jurors themselves. A deadlocked jury, we consistently have recognized, does not result in an acquittal barring retrial under the Double Jeopardy Clause. Similarly, an appellate court's disagreement with the jurors' weighing of the evidence does not require the special deference accorded verdicts of acquittal.

A reversal based on the weight of the evidence, moreover, can occur only after the State both has presented sufficient evidence to support conviction and has persuaded the jury to convict. The reversal simply affords the defendant a second opportunity to seek a favorable judgment. An appellate court's decision to give the defendant this second chance does not create an unacceptably high risk that the Government, with its superior resources, will wear down the defendant and obtain conviction solely through its persistence.

While an appellate ruling based on the weight of the evidence thus fails to implicate the policies supporting *Burks* and *Greene*, it does involve the usual principles permitting retrial after a defendant's successful appeal. Just as the Double Jeopardy Clause does not require society to pay the high price of freeing every defendant whose first trial was tainted by prosecutorial error, it should not exact the price of immunity for every defendant who persuades an appellate panel to overturn an error-free conviction and give him a second chance at acquittal. * * *

Petitioner Tibbs resists these arguments on the grounds that a distinction between the weight and the sufficiency of the evidence is unworkable and that such a distinction will undermine the *Burks* rule by encouraging appellate judges to base reversals on the weight, rather than the sufficiency, of the evidence. We find these arguments unpersuasive for two reasons. First, trial and appellate judges commonly distinguish between the weight and the sufficiency of the evidence. We have no reason to believe that today's decision will erode the demonstrated ability of judges to distinguish legally insufficient evidence from evidence that rationally supports a verdict.

Second, our decision in *Jackson v. Virginia*, 443 U.S. 307 (1979), places some restraints on the power of appellate courts to mask reversals based on legally insufficient evidence as reversals grounded on the weight of the evidence. We held in *Jackson* that the Due Process Clause forbids any conviction based on evidence insufficient to persuade a rational factfinder of guilt beyond a reasonable doubt. The Due Process Clause, in other words, sets a lower limit on an appellate court's definition of evidentiary sufficiency.[21] This limit, together with our belief that state appellate judges faithfully honor their obligations to enforce applicable state and federal laws, persuades us that today's ruling will not undermine *Burks*. * * * Thus, we conclude that Tibbs' successful appeal of his conviction rested upon a finding that the conviction was against the weight of the evidence, not upon a holding that the evidence was legally insufficient to support the verdict. Under these circumstances, the Double Jeopardy Clause does not bar retrial. Accordingly, the judgment of the Florida Supreme Court is affirmed.

JUSTICE WHITE, with whom JUSTICE BRENNAN, JUSTICE MARSHALL, and JUSTICE BLACKMUN join, dissenting.

* * * The Florida Supreme Court found the verdict to be against the weight of the evidence, thus holding that as a matter of state law the prosecution failed to present evidence adequate to sustain the convictions. Were the State to present this same evidence again, we must assume that once again the state courts would reverse any conviction that was based upon it.* The State was not prevented from presenting its best case because of some incorrect procedural ruling by the trial court; rather, the State had a full opportunity to present its case, but that case was not adequate as a matter of state law. If the State presents no new evidence, the defendant has no new or additional burden to meet in successfully presenting a defense: He may stand on, *i.e.*, repeat, what he has already presented. Thus, the only point of any second trial on this case is to allow the State to present additional evidence to bolster its case. If it does not have such evidence, reprosecution can serve no purpose other than harassment. The majority holds that reprosecution

21. The evidence in this case clearly satisfied the due process test of *Jackson v. Virginia*. As we stressed in *Jackson*, the reviewing court must view "the evidence in the light most favorable to the prosecution." 443 U.S., at 319. The trier of fact, not the appellate court, holds "the responsibility * * * fairly to resolve conflicts in the testimony, to weigh the evidence, and to draw reasonable inferences from basic facts to ultimate facts." *Ibid.* In this case, Nadeau provided eyewitness testimony to the crimes. If the jury believed her story, the State's presentation was more than sufficient to satisfy due process.

* Two considerations cast doubt upon this statement in the dissenting opinion:

(1) The majority opinion responded in a footnote (18) that a trial or appellate court will not necessarily set aside a verdict a second time as against the weight of the evidence when two juries have found the evidence sufficient for conviction.

(2) The Florida Supreme Court announced in the second *Tibbs* decision that it would not in the future set aside a conviction as against the weight of the evidence. [Footnote by editor.]

under these circumstances does not offend the double jeopardy provision of the Constitution. I do not agree.

The majority concedes, as it must under *Burks, supra*, that if the State's evidence failed to meet the federal due process standard of evidentiary sufficiency, the Double Jeopardy Clause would bar reprosecution. The majority fails to explain why the State should be allowed another try where its proof has been held inadequate on state-law grounds, when it could not do so were it inadequate on federal-law grounds. In both cases the State has failed to present evidence adequate to sustain the conviction. The interests of the State in overcoming the evidentiary insufficiencies of its case would seem to be exactly the same in the two cases; the interests of the defendant in avoiding a second trial would also seem to be exactly the same in each case. Yet the majority holds that the Double Jeopardy Clause leads to different results in the two instances. Thus, the relevant distinction is between reversals based on evidentiary grounds and those based on procedural grounds: Only in the latter case can the State proceed to retrial without offending the deeply ingrained principle that the State with all its resources and power should not be allowed to make repeated attempts to convict an individual for an alleged offense.

It must also be noted that judges having doubts about the sufficiency of the evidence under the *Jackson* standard may prefer to reverse on the weight of the evidence, since retrial would not be barred. If done recurringly, this would undermine *Jackson, Burks*, and *Greene*. But under *Burks* and *Greene*, retrial is foreclosed by the Double Jeopardy Clause if the evidence fails to satisfy the *Jackson* standard. Hence, the *Jackson* issue cannot be avoided; if retrial is to be had, the evidence must be found to be legally sufficient, as a matter of federal law, to sustain the jury verdict. That finding must accompany any reversal based on the weight of the evidence if retrial is contemplated. The upshot may be that appellate judges will not be inclined to proclaim the evidence in a case to be legally sufficient, yet go on to disagree with the jury and the trial court by reversing on weight-of-the-evidence grounds. Indeed, in this case, the Florida Supreme Court declared that prospect to be an anomaly and a mistake and proclaimed that it would never again put itself in this position.

With all due respect, I dissent.

TEXAS v. McCULLOUGH

Supreme Court of the United States, 1986.
475 U.S. 134, 106 S.Ct. 976, 89 L.Ed.2d 104.

CHIEF JUSTICE BURGER delivered the opinion of the Court. * * *

I

In 1980, Sanford James McCullough was tried before a jury in the Randall County, Texas, District Court and convicted of murder. McCullough elected to be sentenced by the jury, as was his right under Texas law. The jury imposed a 20–year sentence. Judge Naomi Harney, the trial judge, then granted McCullough's motion for a new trial on the basis of prosecutorial misconduct.

Three months later, McCullough was retried before a jury, with Judge Harney again presiding. At this trial, the State presented testimony from two witnesses who had not testified at the first trial that McCullough rather than his accomplices had slashed the throat of the victim. McCullough was again found guilty by a jury. This time, he elected to have his sentence fixed by the trial judge. Judge Harney sentenced McCullough to 50 years in prison and, upon his motion, made findings of fact as to why the sentence was longer than that fixed by the jury in the first trial. She found that in fixing the sentence she relied on new evidence about the murder that was not presented at the first trial and hence never made known to the sentencing jury. The findings focused specifically on the testimony of two new witnesses, Carolyn Hollison McCullough and Willie Lee Brown, which "had a direct effect upon the strength of the State's case at both the guilt and punishment phases of the trial." In addition, Judge Harney explained that she learned for the first time on retrial McCullough had been released from prison only four months before the later crime had been committed. Finally, the judge candidly stated that, had she fixed the first sentence, she would have imposed more than twenty years.[22]

On appeal, the Texas Court of Appeals reversed and resentenced McCullough to 20 years' imprisonment. That court considered itself bound by this Court's decision in *North Carolina v. Pearce*, 395 U.S. 711 (1969), and held that a longer sentence upon retrial could be imposed only if it was based upon conduct of the defendant occurring after the original trial. * * *

II

In *North Carolina v. Pearce, supra*, the Court placed a limitation on the power of a sentencing authority to increase a sentence after reconviction following a new trial. It held that the Due Process Clause of the Fourteenth Amendment prevented increased sentences when that increase was motivated by vindictiveness on the part of the sentencing judge. The Court stated:

"Due process of law, then, requires that vindictiveness against a defendant for having successfully attacked his first conviction must play no part in the sentence he receives after a new trial. And since the fear of such vindictiveness may unconstitutionally deter a defendant's exercise of the right to appeal or collaterally attack his first conviction, due process also requires that a defendant be freed of apprehension of such a retaliatory motivation on the part of the sentencing judge.

22.　Later Judge Harney sentenced two other defendants for their role in the same murder. She gave both defendants 50 year sentences identical to McCullough's.

"In order to assure the absence of such a motivation, we have concluded that whenever a judge imposes a more severe sentence upon a defendant after a new trial, *the reasons for his doing so must affirmatively appear*."

Beyond doubt, vindictiveness of a sentencing judge is the evil the Court sought to prevent rather than simply enlarged sentences after a new trial. The *Pearce* requirements thus do not apply in every case where a convicted defendant receives a higher sentence on retrial. Like other judicially created means of effectuating the rights secured by the Constitution, we have restricted application of *Pearce* to areas where its objectives are thought most efficaciously served. Accordingly, in each case, we look to the need, under the circumstances, to "guard against vindictiveness in the resentencing process." *Chaffin v. Stynchcombe*, 412 U.S. 17, 25 (1973). For example, in *Moon v. Maryland*, 398 U.S. 319 (1970), we held that *Pearce* did not apply when the defendant conceded and it was clear that vindictiveness had played no part in the enlarged sentence. In *Colten v. Kentucky*, 407 U.S. 104 (1972), we saw no need for applying the presumption when the second court in a two-tier trial system imposed a longer sentence. In *Chaffin, supra*, we held *Pearce* not applicable where a *jury* imposed the increased sentence on retrial. Where the prophylactic rule of *Pearce* does not apply, the defendant may still obtain relief if he can show actual vindictiveness upon resentencing. *Wasman v. United States*, 468 U.S. 559 (1984).

The facts of this case provide no basis for a presumption of vindictiveness. In contrast to *Pearce*, McCullough's second trial came about because the trial judge herself concluded that the prosecutor's misconduct required it. Granting McCullough's motion for a new trial hardly suggests any vindictiveness on the part of the judge towards him. Unlike the judge who has been reversed, the trial judge here had no motivation to engage in self-vindication. *Chaffin*, 412 U.S., at 27. In such circumstances, there is also no justifiable concern about institutional interests that might occasion higher sentences by a judge desirous of discouraging what he regards as meritless appeals. In granting McCullough's new trial motion, Judge Harney went on record as agreeing that his "claims" had merit. Presuming vindictiveness on this basis alone would be tantamount to presuming that a judge will be vindictive towards a defendant merely because he seeks an acquittal. * * *

The presumption is also inapplicable because different sentencers assessed the varying sentences that McCullough received. In such circumstances, a sentence "increase" cannot truly be said to have taken place. * * *

III

Even if the *Pearce* presumption were to apply here, we hold that the findings of the trial judge overcome that presumption. Nothing in *Pearce* is to be read as precluding a rebuttal of intimations of vindictiveness. As we have explained, *Pearce* permits a sentencing authority to justify an increased sentence by affirmatively identifying relevant conduct or events that occurred subsequent to the original sentencing proceedings. This language, however, was never intended to describe exhaustively all of the possible circumstances in which a sentence increase could be justified. Restricting justifications for a sentence increase to *only* "events that occurred subsequent to the original sentencing proceedings" could in some circumstances lead to absurd results. The Solicitor General provides the following hypothetical example:

> "Suppose * * * that a defendant is convicted of burglary, a nonviolent, and apparently first, offense. He is sentenced to a short prison term or perhaps placed on probation. Following a successful appeal and a conviction on retrial, it is learned that the defendant has been using an alias and in fact has a long criminal record that includes other burglaries, several armed robbery convictions, and a conviction for murder committed in the course of a burglary. None of the reasons underlying *Pearce* in any way justifies the perverse result that the defendant receive no greater sentence in light of this information than he originally received when he was thought to be a first offender."

We agree with the Solicitor General and find nothing in *Pearce* that would require such a bizarre conclusion. * * *

To be sure, a defendant may be more reluctant to appeal if there is a risk that new, probative evidence supporting a longer sentence may be revealed on retrial. But this Court has never recognized this "chilling effect" as sufficient reason to create a constitutional prohibition against considering relevant information in assessing sentences. We explained in *Chaffin v. Stynchcombe*, 412 U.S., at 29, that "the Court [in *Pearce*] intimated no doubt about the constitutional validity of higher sentences in the absence of vindictiveness despite whatever incidental deterrent effect they might have on the right to appeal." We see no reason to depart from this conclusion. * * *

Reversed and remanded.

JUSTICE BRENNAN, concurring in the judgment.

After respondent was sentenced a twenty years imprisonment upon his conviction for murder, Judge Harney granted respondent's motion for a new trial based on prosecutorial misconduct. Under these circumstances, I believe that the possibility that an increased sentence upon retrial resulted from judicial vindictiveness is sufficiently remote that the presumption established in *North Carolina v. Pearce*, 395 U.S. 711 (1969), should not apply here. Because respondent has not shown that the fifty-year sentence imposed by Judge Harney after respondent's retrial resulted from actual vindictiveness for having successfully attacked his first conviction, I would reverse the judgment below.

I emphasize, however, that were I able to find that vindictiveness should be presumed here, I would agree with Justice Marshall that "the reasons offered by Judge Harney [were] far from adequate to rebut any presumption of vindictiveness." The Court's dictum to the contrary serves in my view only to distort the holding of *Pearce*.

JUSTICE MARSHALL, with whom JUSTICE BLACKMUN and JUSTICE STEVENS join, dissenting. * * *

I

After the jury in Sanford James McCullough's first trial imposed a sentence of 20 years' imprisonment, the Randall County Criminal District Attorney thought McCullough had been treated much too leniently. A local newspaper quoted the prosecutor as commenting: "A guy's life ought to be worth more than that." Luckily for the District Attorney, McCullough was not satisfied with the results of his first trial either. McCullough filed a motion with the trial court requesting a new trial and raising two challenges to Judge Harney's conduct of the first trial:

"I.

"The Trial Court erred in not granting Defendant's Motion for Mistrial subsequent to the prosecutor's improper jury argument concerning the fact that the jury, if they only gave the Defendant ten to fifteen years in the penitentiary, would look outside their window at the end of that period of time and wonder if the criminal out there was the Defendant.

"II.

"The Trial Court erred in overruling Defendant's Motion for Mistrial subsequent to the prosecutor's cross-examination of the witness, Dennis McCullough, as to a purported 'confession' given by a Co–Defendant, Kenneth McCullough. Such conduct constituted error in light of *Bruton v. United States* [, 391 U.S. 123 (1968)]."

When Judge Harney entertained this motion on October 6, 1980, there was no argument to be heard. The Assistant District Attorney noted the State's full agreement to a retrial. The next day's newspaper made the prosecutor's motives clear.

"In a rare occurrence, the Randall County Criminal District Attorney Randy Sherrod said yesterday he has joined a defense motion calling for a new trial in the case of Sanford James McCullough, who was found guilty Sept. 24 of the murder of George Preston Small and sentenced to 20 years in the penitentiary.

"Sherrod said it was the first time in his experience that he had been in agreement with a defense attorney in granting a new trial.

"He said one of the biggest factors influencing his decision to join the defense motion was the possibility of a [sic] getting a harsher sentence in a new trial." * * *

After McCullough was convicted a second time, Judge Harney heard argument on sentencing. Defense counsel urged that "there being no additional evidence on the part of the conduct or action of the Defendant subsequent to the prior conviction," the court was bound by *North Carolina v. Pearce, supra,* to impose a sentence of not more than 20 years. The prosecution replied that because defendant had elected to be sentenced by the trial judge, *North Carolina v. Pearce*, would not bar the court "from assessing a range of punishment greater than what was received by a jury." Judge Harney sentenced McCullough to 50 years' imprisonment. In response to defendant's motion, she later filed an order in which, while holding the rule of *North Carolina v. Pearce* inapplicable, she gave her reasons for imposing a heavier sentence in order to make remand unnecessary should the Court of Criminal Appeals hold the rule applicable. She found that the testimony of two new witnesses implicated defendant in the crime, added to the credibility of certain prosecution witnesses, and detracted from that of certain defense witnesses. The testimony also "shed new light upon the defendant's life, conduct, and his mental and moral propensities," especially his "propensity to commit brutal crimes against persons and to constitute a future threat to society." Judge Harney noted further that had defendant "elected to have the court set his punishment at the first trial, the court would have assessed more than the twenty (20) year sentence imposed by the jury." Finally, the court found:

> "Upon retrial after having been found guilty of murder for a second time by a jury and after having made known to the court that he had been involved in numerous criminal offenses and had served time in the penitentiary, the defendant never produced, or even attempted to produce, any evidence that he intended to change his life style, habits, or conduct, or that he had made any effort whatsoever toward rehabilitating himself. Again upon retrial, the [sic] failed to show this court any sign or indication of refraining from criminal conduct in the future, nor did he give any indication upon retrial that he no longer posed a violent and continuing threat to our society."

I believe the possibility of vindictiveness is even greater in this case than in the general run of cases in which a trial judge has granted a retrial. It is far from clear that Judge Harney's decision to grant a new trial was made out of either solicitude for McCullough or recognition of the merits of his claims. Defendant's motion was uncontested and, if the press coverage is any indication, the judge's decision to grant it was at least as much a boon to the prosecution as it was to defendant. Indeed, the most cynical might even harbor suspicions that the judge shared the District Attorney's hope that a retrial would permit the imposition of a sentence more commensurate with the prosecution's view of the heinousness of the crime for which McCullough had been brought to bar. At any rate, one can imagine that when it fell to Judge Harney to sentence McCullough after his second conviction, his decision to seek a retrial after receiving such a comparatively light sentence from his first jury was counted against him.

Whether any of these considerations actually played any part in Judge Harney's decision to give McCullough a harsher sentence after his retrial is not the issue here, just as it was not the issue in *Pearce*. The point is that the possibility they did play such a part is sufficiently real, and proving actual prejudice, sufficiently difficult, that a presumption of vindictiveness is as appropriate here as it was in *Pearce*. * * *

By finding the reasons given by Judge Harney adequate to rebut a presumption of vindictiveness, the majority not only disregards the clear rule in *Pearce*. It announces a new regime in which the "chill" that plagued defendants in the days before *Pearce* will once again be felt by those deciding whether to contest their convictions.

I do not doubt Judge Harney's assertions that the testimony of Carolyn Sue Hollison McCullough and Willie Lee Brown strengthened the prosecution's case against McCullough by corroborating evidence and testimony that had already been produced at his first trial and by adding a few brush strokes to the portrayal in the first proceeding of McCullough's role in the crime and of his character. However, in the natural course of events upon the retrial of a case, one might normally expect the Government to have available additional testimony and evidence of a defendant's guilt if for no other reason than that the Government has had additional time to prepare and refine its presentation. That such new evidence will be available to a trial judge sentencing a defendant after a retrial is thus inevitable. And if that judge wishes to punish defendant for having asserted his right to a fair trial, she will always be able to point to that new information as the basis for any increase in defendant's sentence the second time around. As one authority has noted: "If a court on retrial could justify an increased sentence on the ground that it now had additional knowledge concerning the defendant's participation in the offense, then the *Pearce* limitation could be evaded in almost every case." 3 W. LaFave & J. Israel, Criminal Procedure 176 (1984). This limitation would be even more easily avoided if a trial judge could rebut a presumption of vindictiveness merely by indicating that she would have given defendant a harsher sentence at his first trial had she been given the chance. That leaves, as the only "new" information to support 30 additional years' imprisonment, the fact that between his two trials, McCullough did not evince a desire to rehabilitate himself. Surely something more is required.

IV

A lot has happened since the final day of the October 1968 Term, the day *North Carolina v. Pearce* was handed down. But nothing has happened since then that casts any doubt on the need for the guarantee of fairness that this Court held out to defendants in *Pearce*. The majority today begins by denying respondent the promise of that guarantee even though his case clearly calls for its application. The Court then reaches out to render the guarantee of little value to all defendants, even to those whose plight was the explicit concern of the *Pearce* Court in 1969. To renege on the guarantee of *Pearce* is wrong. To do so while pretending not to is a shame. I dissent.

MORRIS v. MATHEWS

Supreme Court of the United States, 1986.
475 U.S. 237, 106 S.Ct. 1032, 89 L.Ed.2d 187.

JUSTICE WHITE delivered the opinion of the Court.

The question presented in this case is whether a state appellate court provided an adequate remedy for a violation of the Double Jeopardy Clause of the Fifth Amendment by modifying a jeopardy-barred conviction to that of a lesser-included offense that is not jeopardy-barred.

I

On February 17, 1978, respondent James Michael Mathews and Steven Daugherty robbed the Alexandria Bank in Alexandria, Ohio. After an automobile chase, the police finally surrounded the two men when they stopped at a farmhouse. Soon thereafter, the police heard shots fired inside the house, and respondent then emerged from the home and surrendered to police. When the officers entered the house, they found Daugherty dead, shot once in the head and once in the chest. The police also found the money stolen from the bank hidden in the pantry.

Once in custody, respondent gave a series of statements to law enforcement officials. In his first statement, given one hour after his surrender, respondent claimed that Daugherty and another man had forced him to aid in the bank robbery by threatening to kill both respondent and his girlfriend. Respondent denied shooting Daugherty. In the second statement, given the same day, respondent again denied shooting Daugherty, but admitted that no other man was involved with the robbery, and that he and Daugherty alone had planned and performed the crime.

Two days later, respondent gave a third statement to police in which he again confessed to robbing the bank. Respondent also related that after he and Daugherty arrived at the farmhouse, he had run back out to their van to retrieve the stolen money, and on his way back inside, he "heard a muffled shot from inside the house." App. 4. Upon investigation, respondent discovered that Daugherty had shot himself in the head. Respondent claimed that Daugherty was still conscious, and called to him by name.

The County Coroner initially ruled Daugherty's death to be a suicide. The Coroner made this determination, however, before receiving the results of an autopsy performed by a forensic pathologist. This report indicated that Daugherty had received two wounds from the same shotgun. The initial shot had been fired while Daugherty was standing, and entered the left side of his face. This shot fractured Daugherty's skull, and the mere force of the blast would have rendered him immediately unconscious. This wound was not fatal. The second shot was fired while Daugherty was lying on his back, and was fired directly into his heart from extremely close range. This shot was instantaneously fatal.

As a result of this evidence, the coroner issued a supplemental death certificate, listing "multiple gun shot wounds" as the cause of death. Record 295.

Based on the Coroner's first opinion that Daugherty took his own life, the State did not charge respondent with Daugherty's death. Instead, he was indicted on aggravated robbery charges. Respondent pleaded guilty on May 17 and was sentenced to a term of incarceration from 7 to 25 years.

Two days after entering his guilty plea, respondent made the first of two statements in which he admitted having shot Daugherty. Respondent maintained that Daugherty initially had shot himself in the head, and that he was still alive when respondent discovered him after returning to the farmhouse with the stolen money. Acting on the theory that, if Daugherty were dead, respondent could claim that he was kidnapped and had not voluntarily robbed the bank, respondent "put [the gun] an inch or two from [Daugherty's] chest and pulled the trigger." Respondent's second statement, given one week later, reiterated these same points.

On June 1, 1978, the State charged respondent with the aggravated murder of Steven Daugherty. Ohio Rev.Code § 2903.01 (1982) defines aggravated murder, in part, as "purposely caus[ing] the death of another * * * while fleeing immediately after committing * * * aggravated robbery." The aggravated robbery referred to in the indictment was the armed robbery of the Alexandria Bank to which respondent had previously pleaded guilty. The state trial court denied respondent's pretrial motion to dismiss the aggravated murder indictment as violative of the Double Jeopardy Clause of the Fifth Amendment.

At the conclusion of the evidence, the trial judge instructed the jury as to the elements of the offense of aggravated murder. The judge also instructed the jury on the lesser-included offense of murder as follows:

> "If you find that the State proved beyond a reasonable doubt all of the essential elements of aggravated murder, your verdict must be guilty of that crime and in that event you will not consider any lesser offense.

> "But if you find that the State failed to prove the killing was done while the defendant was committing or fleeing immediately after committing aggravated robbery, but that the killing was nonetheless purposely done, you will proceed with your deliberations and decide whether the State has proved beyond a reasonable doubt the elements of the lesser crime or murder.

> "The crime or murder is distinguished from aggravated murder by the State's failure to prove that the killing was done while the defendant was committing or fleeing immediately after committing the crime of aggravated robbery." App. 21.

The jury found respondent guilty of aggravated murder, and the court sentenced him to a term of life imprisonment.

Respondent appealed his conviction, claiming that his trial for aggravated murder following his conviction for aggravated robbery violated the Double Jeopardy Clause. [A state appellate court held that the Double Jeopardy Clause, as construed by the Supreme Court in Illinois v. Vitale, 447 U.S. 410 (1980), barred the conviction for aggravated murder. The state court modified the conviction one of simple murder. On Federal habeas, a divided panel of the Sixth Circuit ordered a new trial on the simple murder charge.]

II

As an initial matter, we note several issues that are not in dispute. First, the State concedes that under our cases the prosecution of respondent for aggravated murder violated the Double Jeopardy Clause. Similarly, respondent concedes that the Clause would not prevent the State from trying him for murder. Next, all of the courts that have reviewed this case have agreed that, in finding respondent guilty of aggravated murder, the jury necessarily found that he "purposely cause[d] the death of another," which is the definition of murder under Ohio Rev.Code Ann. § 2903.02 (1982). Finally, this is not a "harmless error" case: allowing respondent to be tried for aggravated murder was error, and it was not in any sense harmless. With these considerations aside, the only issue before us is whether reducing respondent's conviction for aggravated murder to a conviction for murder is an adequate remedy for the double jeopardy violation.

Respondent argues that, because the trial for aggravated murder should never have occurred, the Double Jeopardy Clause bars the State from taking advantage of the jeopardy-barred conviction by converting it into a conviction for the lesser crime of murder. He submits that a new trial must be granted whether or not there is a showing of prejudice.

Respondent relies heavily on *Price v. Georgia*, 398 U.S. 323 (1970), but his reliance is misplaced. Price was tried for murder and convicted of the lesser-included offense of manslaughter. After that conviction was reversed on appeal, there was another trial for murder and another conviction of the lesser crime of manslaughter. We held that the second conviction could not stand because Price had been impliedly acquitted of murder at the first trial and could not be tried again on that charge. Nor could we "determine whether or not the murder charge against petitioner induced the jury to find him guilty of the less serious offense of voluntary manslaughter rather than to continue to debate his innocence."

This holding in *Price* did not impose an automatic retrial rule whenever a defendant is tried for a jeopardy-barred crime and is convicted of a lesser-included offense. Rather, the Court relied on the likelihood that the conviction for manslaughter had been influenced by the trial on the murder charge—that the charge of the greater offense for which the jury was unwilling to convict also made the jury less willing to consider the defendant's innocence on the lesser charge. That basis for finding or presuming prejudice is not present here. The jury did not acquit Mathews of the greater offense of aggravated murder, but found him guilty of that charge and, *a fortiori*, of the lesser offense of murder as well.

Benton v. Maryland, 395 U.S. 784 (1969), also strongly indicates that to prevail here, Mathews must show that trying him on the jeopardy-barred charge tainted his conviction for the lesser-included offense. Benton was tried for both larceny and burglary. The jury acquitted him on the larceny count, but found him guilty of burglary. His conviction was later set aside because the jury had been improperly sworn. Benton again was tried for both burglary and larceny, and the second jury found him guilty of both offenses. The Maryland Court of Appeals held there had been no double jeopardy violation, but we disagreed, ruling that the Double Jeopardy Clause required setting aside the larceny conviction and sentence.

Benton urged that his burglary conviction must also fall because certain evidence admitted at his second trial would not have been admitted had he been tried for burglary alone. This evidence, he claimed, prejudiced the jury and influenced their decision to convict him of burglary. We rejected their argument, saying both that "[i]t [was] not obvious on the face of the record that the burglary conviction was affected by the double jeopardy violation," and that we should not make this kind of evidentiary determination "unaided by prior consideration by the state courts." We thus vacated the judgment of the Maryland court, and remanded for further proceedings.

Neither *Benton* nor *Price* suggest that a conviction for an unbarred offense is inherently tainted if tried with a jeopardy-barred charge. Instead, both cases suggest that a new trial is required only when the defendant shows a reliable inference of prejudice. We perceive no basis for departing from this approach here; for except that murder was a lesser offense included in the aggravated murder charge rather than a separate charge, there is no difference between this case and *Benton* for double jeopardy purposes.

Accordingly, we hold that when a jeopardy-barred conviction is reduced to a conviction for a lesser included offense which is not jeopardy barred, the burden shifts to the defendant to demonstrate a reasonable probability that he would not have been convicted of the non-jeopardy-barred offense absent the presence of the jeopardy-barred offense. In this situation, we believe that a "reasonable probability" is a probability sufficient to undermine confidence in the outcome. Cf. *Strickland v. Washington*, 466 U.S. 668, 695 (1984). After all, one of the purposes of the Double Jeopardy Clause is to prevent multiple prosecutions and to protect an individual from suffering the embarrassment, anxiety, and expense of another trial for the same offense. In cases like this, therefore, where it is clear that the jury necessarily found that the defendant's conduct satisfies the elements of the lesser included offense, it would be incongruous always to order yet another trial as a means of curing a violation of the Double Jeopardy Clause.

The Court of Appeals thus was correct in rejecting respondent's *per se* submission, but it was nevertheless too ready to find that Mathews had made the necessary showing of prejudice. First, the court's "reasonable possibility" standard, which could be satisfied by "an exceedingly small showing," was not sufficiently demanding. To prevail in a case like this, the defendant must show that, but for the improper inclusion of the jeopardy-barred charge, the result of the proceeding probably would have been different.

Second, the Court of Appeals appeared to agree with respondent that certain evidence admitted at his trial would not have been admitted in a separate trial for murder, but it did not expressly say so, nor did it refer to any Ohio authorities. The State submits that under Ohio law, conduct of a defendant tending to show either "his motive or intent," or his "scheme, plan or system," is admissible, "notwithstanding that such proof may show or tend to show the commission of another crime by the defendant." Ohio Rev.Code Ann. § 2945.59 (1982). We normally accept a Court of Appeals's view of state law, but if this case turns on the admissibility of the challenged evidence in a separate trial for murder, the issue deserves a more thorough consideration by the lower court.

Finally, the court's observation that the admission of questionable evidence "may have prejudiced the jury" falls far short of a considered conclusion that if the evidence at issue was not before the jury in a separate trial for murder, there is a reasonable probability that respondent would not have been convicted.

Because the Court of Appeals's legal and factual basis for ordering the writ of habeas corpus to issue was seriously flawed, its judgment is reversed and the case is remanded to the Court of Appeals for further proceedings consistent with this opinion.

It is so ordered.

Justice Blackmun, with whom Justice Powell joins, concurring in the judgment. * * *

The Court starts out on the wrong foot by asserting that "this is not a 'harmless error' case." Fundamentally, this *is* a "harmless error" case. Ohio concedes that it violated the Double Jeopardy Clause. To say that the remedy imposed by the state courts was constitutionally adequate is simply to say that the State's acknowledged transgression may be deemed harmless with respect to respondent's conviction for the lesser included offense. In *Chapman v. California*, 386 U.S. 18 (1967), this Court rejected the argument that no constitutional violation can ever be harmless. Some constitutional rights, of course, are "so basic to a fair trial" that their denial automatically requires reversal, but I agree with the Court that this category does not include double jeopardy violations of the sort involved here when the ultimate conviction is not for a jeopardy-barred offense. Under *Chapman*, therefore, respondent's conviction for simple murder may be sustained if the State shows "beyond a reasonable doubt" that its error did not contribute to the conviction. As was noted in *Chapman*, the "harmless beyond a reasonable doubt" standard is essentially the same as a requirement of reversal whenever there is a "reasonable possibility" that the error contributed to the conviction. * * *

The Court today offers virtually no explanation for departing from *Chapman* and *Fahy* in favor of a more lenient approach. It cites no support at all for the "reliable inference" and "probably would have been different" formulations of the new test it announces. In support of the "reasonable probability" formulation, the Court refers to *Strickland v. Washington*, 466 U.S. 668 (1984), which used the same words but did not concern the adequacy of a proffered remedy for an acknowledged constitutional violation. The question in *Strickland* was whether there had been a constitutional violation in the first place. We held that a professionally unreasonable mistake by defense counsel constitutes ineffective assistance of counsel under the Sixth Amendment only if in retrospect there is a "reasonable probability" that the mistake altered the verdict—that is, "a probability sufficient to undermine confidence in the outcome." In this case, however, it is common ground that respondent's rights under the Double Jeopardy Clause were violated when Ohio tried him for aggravated murder. The question is not whether Ohio has also violated the Sixth Amendment or the Due Process Clause. The question is whether the State has sufficiently contained the damage from its *acknowledged* violation of the Double Jeopardy Clause, or whether that transgression taints even the conviction for simple murder. At issue is the extent to which the law will tolerate a conviction that may have been obtained through abridgement of a defendant's constitutional rights. Once it is established that the State has violated the Constitution in the course of a prosecution, the proceedings lose whatever presumption of regularity they formerly enjoyed, and the State properly bears a heavy burden in arguing that the result should nonetheless be treated as valid. * * *

Given all this, respondent is obligated to spell out with some specificity how the trial might have gone better for him had the State charged only simple murder. He has not done so; instead, he has simply speculated that all sorts of things might have been different. That is not enough to prevent this Court from declaring a belief that the error was harmless beyond a reasonable doubt. If it were, the remand in *Benton v. Maryland* would have been inappropriate: the Court there simply would have vacated the burglary conviction, because there was no telling what would have happened had the defendant not been forced to defend himself against the larceny charge. Perhaps different trial tactics would have been tried; perhaps defense counsel would have prepared more fully on the burglary charge. Indeed, if abstract speculations of this sort sufficed to create a "reasonable doubt" that an error was harmless, it is difficult to see how any constitutional error ever would qualify.

I therefore concur in the Court's judgment, although I see no justification for departing from the traditional and established standards for deciding questions of this kind.

JUSTICE BRENNAN, dissenting.

Both the charge for aggravated robbery, to which respondent pleaded guilty, and the subsequent charge for aggravated murder arose from the same criminal transaction or episode. In those circumstances, Ohio's prosecution for aggravated murder, and the Ohio Court of Appeals' subsequent reduction of that conviction to simple murder, in my view, violated the [Double Jeopardy Clause]. I adhere to my view that the Double Jeopardy Clause requires that except in extremely limited circumstances not present here, "all the charges against a defendant that grow out of a single criminal act, occurrence, episode, or transaction" be prosecuted in one proceeding. Accordingly, I would affirm the judgment below reversing the District Court, with directions to the Court of Appeals to remand the case to the District Court with instructions to issue the writ. * * *

[The dissenting opinion of Justice Marshall is omitted.]

HEATH v. ALABAMA

Supreme Court of the United States, 1985.
474 U.S. 82, 106 S.Ct. 433, 88 L.Ed.2d 387.

JUSTICE O'CONNOR delivered the opinion of the Court. * * *

I

In August 1981, petitioner, Larry Gene Heath, hired Charles Owens and Gregory Lumpkin to kill his wife, Rebecca Heath, who was then nine months pregnant, for a sum of $2,000. On the morning of August 31, 1981, petitioner left the Heath residence in Russell County, Alabama, to meet with Owens and Lumpkin in Georgia, just over the Alabama border from the Heath home. Petitioner led them back to the Heath residence, gave them the keys to the Heaths' car and house, and left the premises in his girlfriend's truck. Owens and Lumpkin then kidnaped Rebecca Heath from her home. The Heath car, with Rebecca Heath's body inside, was later found on the side of a road in Troup County, Georgia. The cause of death was a gunshot wound in the head. The estimated time of death and the distance from the Heath residence to the spot where Rebecca Heath's body was found are consistent with the theory that the murder took place in Georgia, and respondent does not contend otherwise.

Georgia and Alabama authorities pursued dual investigations in which they cooperated to some extent. On September 4, 1981, petitioner was arrested by Georgia authorities. Petitioner waived his *Miranda* rights and gave a full confession admitting that he had arranged his wife's kidnaping and murder. In November 1981, the grand jury of Troup County, Georgia indicted petitioner for the offense of "malice" murder. Georgia then served petitioner with notice of its intention to seek the death penalty, citing as the aggravating circumstance the fact that the murder was "caused and directed" by petitioner. On February 10, 1982, petitioner pleaded guilty to the Georgia murder charge in exchange for a sentence of life imprisonment, which he understood could involve his serving as few as seven years in prison.

On May 5, 1982, the grand jury of Russell County, Alabama, returned an indictment against petitioner for the capital offense of murder during a kidnaping. Before trial on this indictment, petitioner entered pleas of *autrefois convict* and former jeopardy under the Alabama and United States Constitutions, arguing that his conviction and sentence in Georgia barred his prosecution in Alabama for the same conduct.

After a hearing, the trial court rejected petitioner's double jeopardy claims. It assumed, *arguendo*, that the two prosecutions could not have been brought in succession by one State but held that double jeopardy did not bar successive prosecutions by two different States for the same act. * * *

On January 12, 1983, the Alabama jury convicted petitioner of murder during a kidnaping in the first degree. After a sentencing hearing, the jury recommended the death penalty. Pursuant to Alabama law, a second sentencing hearing was held before the trial judge. The judge accepted the jury's recommendation, finding that the sole aggravating factor, that the capital offense was "committed while the defendant was engaged in the commission of a kidnapping," outweighed the sole mitigating factor, that the "defendant was convicted of the murder of Rebecca Heath in the Superior Court of Troup County, Georgia, * * * and received a sentence of life imprisonment in that court."

[The state appellate courts affirmed the conviction and sentence.]

II

Successive prosecutions are barred by the Fifth Amendment only if the two offenses for which the defendant is prosecuted are the "same" for double jeopardy purposes. Respondent does not contravene petitioner's contention that the offenses of "murder during a kidnaping" and "malice murder," as construed by the courts of Alabama and Georgia respectively, may be considered greater and lesser offenses and, thus, the "same" offense under Brown v. Ohio, 432 U.S. 161 (1977), absent operation of the dual sovereignty principle. We, therefore, assume *arguendo* that, had these offenses arisen under the laws of one State and had petitioner been separately prosecuted for both offenses in that State, the second conviction would have been barred by the Double Jeopardy Clause.

The sole remaining question upon which we granted certiorari is whether the dual sovereignty doctrine permits successive prosecutions under the laws of different States which otherwise would be held to "subject [the defendant] for the same offence to be twice put in jeopardy." Although we have not previously so held, we believe the answer to this query is inescapable. The dual sovereignty doctrine, as originally articulated and consistently applied by this Court, compels the conclusion that successive prosecutions by two States for the same conduct are not barred by the Double Jeopardy Clause.

The dual sovereignty doctrine is founded on the common law conception of crime as an offense against the sovereignty of the government. When a defendant in a single act violates the "peace and dignity" of two sovereigns by breaking the laws of each, he has committed two distinct "offences." * * *

In applying the dual sovereignty doctrine, then, the crucial determination is whether the two entities that seek successively to prosecute a defendant for the same course of conduct can be termed separate sovereigns. This determination turns on whether the two entities draw their authority to punish the offender from distinct sources of power. [Citations].

Thus, the Court has uniformly held that the States are separate sovereigns with respect to the Federal Government because each State's power to prosecute is derived from its own "inherent sovereignty," not from the Federal Government. * * *

The States are no less sovereign with respect to each other than they are with respect to the Federal Government. Their powers to undertake criminal prosecutions derive from separate and independent sources of power and authority originally belonging to them before admission to the Union and preserved to them by the Tenth Amendment. * * *

In those instances where the Court has found the dual sovereignty doctrine inapplicable, it has done so because the two prosecuting entities did not derive their powers to prosecute from independent sources of authority. Thus, the Court has held that successive prosecutions by federal and territorial courts are barred because such courts are "creations emanating from the same sovereignty." [Citations] Similarly, municipalities that derive their power to try a defendant from the same organic law that empowers the State to prosecute are not separate sovereigns with respect to the State. These cases confirm that it is the presence of independent sovereign authority to prosecute, not the relation between States and the Federal Government in our federalist system, that constitutes the basis for the dual sovereignty doctrine. * * *

III

Petitioner invites us to restrict the applicability of the dual sovereignty principle to cases in which two governmental entities, having concurrent jurisdiction and pursuing quite different interests, can demonstrate that allowing only one entity to exercise jurisdiction over the defendant will interfere with the unvindicated interests of the second entity and that multiple prosecutions therefore are necessary for the satisfaction of the legitimate interests of both entities. This balancing of interests approach, however, cannot be reconciled with the dual sovereignty principle. This Court has plainly and repeatedly stated that two identical offenses are *not* the "same offence" within the meaning of the Double Jeopardy Clause if they are prosecuted by different sovereigns. See, *e.g., United States v. Lanza,* 260 U.S. 377 (1922) (same conduct, indistinguishable statutes, same "interests"). If the States are separate sovereigns, as they must be under the definition of sovereignty which the Court consistently has employed, the circumstances of the case are irrelevant.

Petitioner, then, is asking the Court to discard its sovereignty analysis and to substitute in its stead his difficult and uncertain balancing of interests approach. The Court has refused a similar request on at least one previous occasion, see *Abbate v. United States,* 359 U.S. 187 (1959), and rightfully so. The Court's express rationale for the dual sovereignty doctrine is not simply a fiction that can be disregarded in difficult cases. It finds weighty support in the historical understanding and political realities of the States' role in the federal system and in the words of the Double Jeopardy Clause itself, "nor shall any person be subject for the same *offence* to be twice put in jeopardy of life or limb." * * *

The judgment of the Supreme Court of Alabama is affirmed.

It is so ordered.

JUSTICE MARSHALL, with whom JUSTICE BRENNAN joins, dissenting. * * *

Under the constitutional scheme, the Federal Government has been given the exclusive power to vindicate certain of our Nation's sovereign interests, leaving the States to exercise complementary authority over matters of more local concern. The respective spheres of the Federal Government and the States may overlap at times, and even where they do not, different interests may be implicated by a single act. See, *e.g., Abbate v. United States,* 359 U.S. 187 (1959) (conspiracy to dynamite telephone company facilities entails both destruction of property and disruption of federal communications network). Yet were a prosecution by a State, however zealously pursued, allowed to preclude further prosecution by the Federal Government for the same crime, an entire range of national interests could be frustrated. The importance of those federal interests has thus quite properly been permitted to trump a defendant's interest in avoiding successive prosecutions or multiple punishments for the same crime. Conversely, because the States under our federal system have the principal responsibility for defining and prosecuting crimes, it would be inappropriate—in the absence of a specific congressional intent to preempt state action pursuant to the Supremacy Clause—to allow a federal prosecution to preclude state authorities from vindicating the historic right and obligation of the States to maintain peace and order within their confines. * * *

Where two States seek to prosecute the same defendant for the same crime in two separate proceedings, the justifications found in the federal-state context for an exemption from double jeopardy constraints simply do not hold. Although the two States may have opted for different policies within their assigned territorial jurisdictions, the sovereign concerns with whose vindication each State has been charged are identical. Thus, in contrast to the federal-state context, barring the second prosecution would still permit one government to act upon the broad range of sovereign concerns that have been reserved to the States by the Constitution. The compelling need in the federal-state context to subordinate double jeopardy concerns is thus considerably diminished in cases involving successive prosecutions by different States. Moreover, from the defendant's perspective, the burden of successive prosecutions cannot be justified as the *quid pro quo* of dual citizenship.

To be sure, a refusal to extend the dual sovereignty rule to state-state prosecutions would preclude the State that has lost the "race to the courthouse" from vindicating legitimate policies distinct from those underlying its sister State's prosecution. But as yet, I am not persuaded that a State's desire to further a particular policy should be permitted to deprive a defendant of his constitutionally protected right not to be brought to bar more than once to answer essentially the same charges.
* * *

Even where the power of two sovereigns to pursue separate prosecutions for the same crime has been undisputed, this Court has barred both governments from combining to do together what each could not constitutionally do on its own. [Citations] And just as the Constitution bars one sovereign from facilitating another's prosecution by delivering testimony coerced under promise of immunity or evidence illegally seized, I believe that it prohibits two sovereigns from combining forces to ensure that a defendant receives only the trappings of criminal process as he is sped along to execution.

While no one can doubt the propriety of two States cooperating to bring a criminal to justice, the cooperation between Georgia and Alabama in this case went far beyond their initial joint investigation. Georgia's efforts to secure petitioner's execution did not end with its acceptance of his guilty plea. Its law enforcement officials went on to play leading roles as prosecution witnesses in the Alabama trial. Indeed, had the Alabama trial judge not restricted the State to one assisting officer at the prosecution's table during trial, a Georgia officer would have shared the honors with an Alabama officer. Although the record does not reveal the precise nature of the assurances made by Georgia authorities that induced petitioner to plead guilty in the first proceeding against him, I cannot believe he would have done so had he been aware that the officials whose forbearance he bought in Georgia with his plea would merely continue their efforts to secure his death in another jurisdiction.

Even before the Fourteenth Amendment was held to incorporate the protections of the Double Jeopardy Clause, four Members of this Court registered their outrage at "an instance of the prosecution being allowed to harass the accused with repeated trials and convictions on the same evidence, until it achieve[d] its desired result of a capital verdict." *Ciucci v. Illinois,* 356 U.S. 571, 573 (1958). Such "relentless prosecutions," they asserted, constituted "an unseemly and oppressive use of a criminal trial that violates the concept of due process contained in the Fourteenth Amendment, whatever its ultimate scope is taken to be." The only differences between the facts in *Ciucci* and those in this case are that here the relentless effort was a cooperative one between two States and that petitioner sought to avoid trial by pleading guilty. Whether viewed as a violation of the Double Jeopardy Clause or simply as an affront to the due process guarantee of fundamental fairness, Alabama's prosecution of petitioner cannot survive constitutional scrutiny. I therefore must dissent.

UNITED STATES v. DiFRANCESCO

Supreme Court of the United States, 1980.
449 U.S. 117, 101 S.Ct. 426, 66 L.Ed.2d 328.

JUSTICE BLACKMUN delivered the opinion of the Court.

The Organized Crime Control Act of 1970 contains, among other things, a definition of "dangerous special offender," 18 U.S.C. §§ 3575(e) and (f); authorizes the imposition of an increased sentence upon a convicted dangerous special offender, and grants the United States the right, under specified conditions, to take that sentence to the Court of Appeals for review. The issue presented by this case is whether § 3576, authorizing the United States so to appeal, violates the Double Jeopardy Clause of the Fifth Amendment of the Constitution.[23]

I

At a 1977 jury trial in the United States District Court for the Western District of New York, respondent Eugene DiFrancesco was convicted of conducting the affairs of an enterprise through a pattern of racketeering activity, and of conspiring to commit that offense, in violation of 18 U.S.C. §§ 1962(c) and (d). At another jury trial in 1978— before a different judge in the same District—based on an indictment

---

23. Academic and professional commentary on the general issue is divided. For conclusions that prosecution appeals of sentences do not violate the Double Jeopardy Clause, see Westen, The Three Faces of Double Jeopardy: Reflections on Government Appeals of Criminal Sentences, 78 Mich.L.Rev. 1001 (1980); Stern, Government Appeals of Sentences: A Constitutional Response to Arbitrary and Unreasonable Sentences, 18 Am.Crim.L.Rev. 51 (1980); Dunsky, The Constitutionality of Increasing Sentences on Appellate Review, 69 J.Crim.L. & Criminology 19 (1978). For conclusions that such appeals are unconstitutional, see Spence, The Federal Criminal Code Reform Act of 1977 and Prosecutorial Appeal of Sentences: Justice or Double Jeopardy?, 37 Md.L.Rev. 739 (1978); Free-

man & Earley, *United States v. DiFrancesco*: Government Appeal of Sentences, 18 Am.Crim.L.Rev. 91 (1980); Note, 63 Va. L.Rev. 325 (1977); Report on Government Appeal of Sentences, 35 Bus. Lawyer 617, 624–628 (1980). At least one commentator-witness some time ago regarded the answer to the constitutional issue as "simply unclear." Low, Special Offender Sentencing, 8 Am.Crim.L.Q. 70, 91 (1970) (reprint of statement submitted at Hearings on S. 30 et al. before the Subcommittee on Criminal Laws and Procedures of the Senate Committee on the Judiciary, 91st Cong., 1st Sess., 184, 197 (1969)).

See also ABA Standards for Criminal Justice 20–1.1(d), and appended commentary, pp. 20–7 through 20–13 (2d ed. 1980).

returned prior to the racketeering indictment, respondent was convicted of damaging federal property, in violation of 18 U.S.C. § 1361, of unlawfully storing explosive materials, in violation of 18 U.S.C. § 842(j), and of conspiring to commit those offenses, in violation of 18 U.S.C. § 371.

Respondent was first sentenced, in March 1978, on his convictions at the later trial. He received eight years on the charge for damaging federal property and five years on the conspiracy charge, these sentences to be served concurrently, and one year on the unlawful storage charge, to be served consecutively to the other sentences. This made a total of nine years' imprisonment. In April, respondent was sentenced as a dangerous special offender under § 3575 to two 10–year terms on the racketeering counts upon which he was convicted at the earlier trial; the court specified that these sentences were to be served concurrently with each other and with the sentences imposed in March. The dangerous special offender charge and sentences thus resulted in additional punishment of only about a year.

Respondent appealed the respective judgments of conviction to the Court of Appeals for the Second Circuit, and the United States sought review, under § 3576, of the sentences imposed upon respondent as a dangerous special offender. The Court of Appeals unanimously affirmed the judgments of conviction. By a divided vote, however, that court dismissed the Government's appeal on double jeopardy grounds. * * *

II

At the earlier racketeering trial, the evidence showed that respondent was involved in an arson-for-hire scheme in the Rochester, N.Y., area that was responsible for at least eight fires between 1970 and 1973; that the ring collaborated with property owners to set fire to buildings in return for shares of the insurance proceeds; and that insurers were defrauded of approximately $480,000 as a result of these fires. At the second trial, the evidence showed that respondent participated in the 1970 "Columbus Day bombings," including the bombing of the federal building at Rochester.

Prior to the first trial, the Government, in accordance with § 3575(a), filed with the trial court a notice alleging that respondent was a dangerous special offender. This notice recited the Government's intention to seek enhanced sentences on the racketeering counts in the event respondent was convicted at that trial. After respondent was found guilty, a dangerous special offender hearing, pursuant to § 3575(b), was held. At the hearing, the Government relied upon the testimony adduced at the trial and upon public documents that attested to other convictions of respondent for the Columbus Day bombings, for loansharking, and for murder. The defense offered no evidence. It conceded the validity of the public records, but objected to any consideration of the murder offense because that conviction had been vacated on appeal.

The District Court made findings of fact and ruled that respondent was a dangerous special offender within the meaning of the statute. The findings set forth respondent's criminal record and stated that that record revealed "virtually continuous criminal conduct over the past eight years, interrupted only by relatively brief periods of imprisonment in 1975, 1976 and 1977." The court found, in addition, that respondent's "criminal history, based upon proven facts, reveals a pattern of habitual and knowing criminal conduct of the most violent and dangerous nature against the lives and property of the citizens of this community. It further shows the defendant's complete and utter disregard for the public safety. The defendant, by virtue of his own criminal record, has shown himself to be a hardened habitual criminal from whom the public must be protected for as long a period as possible. Only in that way can the public be protected from further violent and dangerous criminal conduct by the defendant." The court thereupon sentenced respondent under § 3575(b) to the concurrent 10–year terms hereinabove described.

The United States then took its appeal under § 3576, claiming that the District Court abused its discretion in imposing sentences that amounted to additional imprisonment of respondent for only one year, in the face of the findings the court made after the dangerous special offender hearing. The dismissal of the Government's appeal by the Court of Appeals rested specifically upon its conclusion, which it described as "inescapable," that "to subject a defendant to the risk of substitution of a greater sentence, upon an appeal by the government is to place him a second time 'in jeopardy of life or limb.' " * * *

[Part III of the majority opinion, omitted here, provides a lengthy review of the Supreme Court's Double Jeopardy decisions, and the principles that can be derived from those decisions.]

IV

From these principles, certain propositions pertinent to the present controversy emerge:

A. The Double Jeopardy Clause is *not* a complete barrier to an appeal by the prosecution in a criminal case. * * *

B. The double jeopardy focus, thus, is not on the appeal but on the relief that is requested, and our task is to determine whether a criminal sentence, once pronounced, is to be accorded constitutional finality and conclusiveness similar to that which attaches to a jury's verdict of acquittal. * * * Appeal of a sentence, therefore, would seem to be a violation of double jeopardy only if the original sentence, as pronounced, is to be treated in the same way as an acquittal is treated, and the appeal is to be treated in the same way as a retrial. Put another way, the argument would be that, for double jeopardy finality purposes, the imposition of the sentence is an "implied acquittal" of any greater sentence.

We agree with the Government that this approach does not withstand analysis. * * *

Historically, the pronouncement of sentence has never carried the finality that attaches to an acquittal. The common-law writs of *autre fois acquit* and *autre fois convict* were protections against retrial. Although the distinction was not of great importance early in the English common law because nearly all felonies, to which double jeopardy principles originally were limited, were punishable by the critical sentences of death or deportation, it gained importance when sentences of imprisonment became common. The trial court's increase of a sentence, so long as it took place during the same term of court, was permitted. This practice was not thought to violate any double jeopardy principle. The common law is important in the present context, for our Double Jeopardy Clause was drafted with the common-law protections in mind. This accounts for the established practice in the federal courts that the sentencing judge may recall the defendant and increase his sentence, at least (and we venture no comment as to this limitation) so long as he has not yet begun to serve that sentence. Thus it may be said with certainty that history demonstrates that the common law never ascribed such finality to a sentence as would prevent a legislative body from authorizing its appeal by the prosecution. Indeed, countries that trace their legal systems to the English common law permit such appeals.

C. This Court's decisions in the sentencing area clearly establish that a sentence does not have the qualities of constitutional finality that attend an acquittal. In *Bozza v. United States*, 330 U.S. 160 (1947), the defendant was convicted of a crime carrying a mandatory minimum sentence of fine and imprisonment. The trial court, however, sentenced the defendant only to imprisonment. Later on the same day, the judge recalled the defendant and imposed both fine and imprisonment. This Court held that there was no double jeopardy. * * * And in *North Carolina v. Pearce*, 395 U.S. 711 (1969), the Court held that there was no absolute constitutional bar to the imposition of a more severe sentence on reconviction after the defendant's successful appeal of the original judgment of conviction. If any rule of finality had applied to the pronouncement of a sentence, the original sentence in *Pearce* would have served as a ceiling on the one imposed at retrial.

D. The double jeopardy considerations that bar reprosecution after an acquittal do not prohibit review of a sentence. We have noted above the basic design of the double jeopardy provision, that is, as a bar against repeated attempts to convict, with consequent subjection of the defendant to embarrassment, expense, anxiety, and insecurity, and the possibility that he may be found guilty even though innocent. These considerations, however, have no significant application to the prosecution's statutorily granted right to review a sentence. This limited appeal does not involve a retrial or approximate the ordeal of a trial on the basic issue of guilt or innocence. Under § 3576, the appeal is to be taken promptly and is essentially on the record of the sentencing court. The defendant, of course, is charged with knowledge of the statute and its appeal provisions, and has no expectation of finality in his sentence until the appeal is concluded or the time to appeal has expired. To be sure, the appeal may prolong the period of any anxiety that may exist, but it does so only for the finite period provided by the statute. The appeal is no more of an ordeal than any Government appeal under 18 U.S.C. § 3731 from the dismissal of an indictment or information. The defendant's primary concern and anxiety obviously relate to the determination of innocence or guilt, and that already is behind him. The defendant is subject to no risk of being harassed and then convicted, although innocent. Furthermore, a sentence is characteristically determined in large part on the basis of information, such as the presentence report, developed outside the courtroom. It is purely a judicial determination, and much that goes into it is the result of inquiry that is nonadversary in nature.

E. The Double Jeopardy Clause does not provide the defendant with the right to know at any specific moment in time what the exact limit of his punishment will turn out to be. Congress has established many types of criminal sanctions under which the defendant is unaware of the precise extent of his punishment for significant periods of time, or even for life, yet these sanctions have not been considered to be violative of the Clause. Thus, there is no double jeopardy protection against revocation of probation and the imposition of imprisonment. While these criminal sanctions do not involve the increase of a final sentence, and while the defendant is aware at the original sentencing that a term of imprisonment later may be imposed, the situation before us is different in no critical respect. Respondent was similarly aware that a dangerous special offender sentence is subject to increase on appeal. His legitimate expectations are not defeated if his sentence is increased on appeal any more than are the expectations of the defendant who is placed on parole or probation that is later revoked.

[Part V of the majority opinion held that increase of a sentence on appeal does not constitute multiple punishment for a single crime.]

It is perhaps worth noting in passing that § 3576 represents a considered legislative attempt to attack a specific problem in our criminal justice system, that is, the tendency on the part of some trial judges to mete out light sentences in cases involving organized crime management personnel. Section 3576 was Congress' response to that plea. The statute is limited in scope and is narrowly focused on the so identified. * * * It has been observed elsewhere that sentencing is one of the areas of the criminal justice system most in need of reform. See M. Frankel, Criminal Sentences: Law Without Order (1973). Judge Frankel himself has observed that the "basic problem" in the present system is "the unbridled power of the sentencers to be arbitrary and discriminatory." Appellate review creates a check upon this unlimited power, and should lead to a greater degree of consistency in sentencing.

We conclude that § 3576 withstands the constitutional challenge raised in the case before us. The judgment of the Court of Appeals is reversed, and the case is remanded for further proceedings consistent with this opinion.

JUSTICE BRENNAN, with whom JUSTICE WHITE, JUSTICE MARSHALL, and JUSTICE STEVENS join, dissenting.

Not only has the Court repeatedly said that sentences may not be increased after imposition without violating the double jeopardy prohibition against multiple punishments, but the analytic similarity of a verdict of acquittal and the imposition of sentence requires this conclusion. A verdict of acquittal represents the factfinder's conclusion that the evidence does not warrant a finding of guilty. Similarly, a guilty verdict of second-degree murder where the charge to the jury permitted it to find the defendant guilty of first-degree murder represents the factfinder's *implicit* finding that the facts do not warrant a first-degree murder conviction. Thus, a retrial on first-degree murder is constitutionally impermissible. See *Price v. Georgia*, 398 U.S. 323 (1970). The sentencing of a convicted criminal is sufficiently analogous to a determination of guilt or innocence that the Double Jeopardy Clause should preclude government appeals from sentencing decisions very much as it prevents appeals from judgments of acquittal. The sentencing proceeding involves the examination and evaluation of facts about the defendant, which may entail the taking of evidence, and the pronouncement of a sentence. Thus, imposition of a 10–year sentence where a 25–year sentence is permissible under the sentencing statute constitutes a finding that the facts justify only a 10–year sentence and that a higher sentence is unwarranted. In both acquittals and sentences, the trier of fact makes a factual adjudication that removes from the defendant's burden of risk the charges of which he was acquitted and the potential sentence which he did not receive. Unless there is a basis for according greater finality to acquittals, whether explicit or implicit, than to sentences, the Court's result is untenable.

* * * Although the Court acknowledges that the double jeopardy guarantee is at least in part directed at protecting the individual from government oppression and undue embarrassment, expense, anxiety, and insecurity, it reaches the startling conclusion that "[t]his limited appeal," exposes the defendant to minimal incremental embarrassment and anxiety because "the determination of innocence or guilt * * * is already behind him." I believe that the Court fundamentally misunderstands the import to the defendant of the sentencing proceeding.

I suggest that most defendants are more concerned with how much time they must spend in prison than with whether their record shows a conviction. This is not to say that the ordeal of trial is not important. And obviously it is the conviction itself which is the predicate for time in prison. But clearly, the defendant does not breathe a sigh of relief once he has been found guilty. Indeed, an overwhelming number of criminal defendants are willing to enter plea bargains in order to keep their time in prison as brief as possible. Surely, the Court cannot believe then that the sentencing phase is merely incidental and that defendants do not suffer acute anxiety. To the convicted defendant, the sentencing phase is certainly as critical as the guilt-innocence phase. To pretend otherwise as a reason for holding 18 U.S.C. § 3576 valid is to ignore reality.

The Court's contrary view rests on the circular notion that the defendant "has no expectation of finality in his sentence until the

[Government] appeal [pursuant to § 3576] is concluded or the time to appeal has expired." That is, the very statute which increases and prolongs the defendant's anxiety alleviates it by conditioning his expectations. Logically extended, the Court's reasoning could lead to the conclusion that the Double Jeopardy Clause permits Government appeals from verdicts of acquittal. If the purpose of insulating the verdict of acquittal from further proceedings is, at least in part, out of concern that defendants not be subjected to Government oppression, the Congress could dispose of this objection by a statute authorizing the Government to appeal from verdicts of acquittal. Under the Court's view, such a statute would "charge" the defendant "with knowledge" of its provisions and thus eradicate any expectation of finality in his acquittal. * * *

Because the Court has demonstrated no basis for differentiating between the finality of acquittals and the finality of sentences, I submit that a punishment enhanced by an appellate court is an unconstitutional multiple punishment. To conclude otherwise, as the Court does, is to create an exception to basic double jeopardy protection which, if carried to its logical conclusion, might not prevent Congress, on double jeopardy grounds, from authorizing the Government to appeal verdicts of acquittal. Such a result is plainly impermissible under the Double Jeopardy Clause.

I, therefore, dissent.

[The separate dissent of Justice Stevens is omitted.]

Commentary

The core meaning of the Double Jeopardy Clause seems to be that a defendant who has been acquitted after trial on criminal charges should not be forced to "run the gauntlet" a second time merely because the prosecutor disagrees with the verdict. By simple extension of this principle, a defendant who has been convicted and sentenced to a particular term should not be prosecuted again merely because the prosecutor is dissatisfied with the sentence. No one disputes these principles when they are stated that way, in the abstract, but in fact even the core principles of the Double Jeopardy Clause are sometimes honored in the letter but not in the spirit.

The most striking exception to the core principles just summarized is the "two sovereignties" doctrine, illustrated on particularly disturbing facts in *Heath v. Alabama* [p. 924]. Cases involving this doctrine are relatively rare, however, and the factual circumstances are frequently more appealing than in *Heath*. For example the federal government sometimes prosecutes on Civil Rights Act charges defendants who have been leniently treated by state courts following racially motivated assaults.

Even without resort to the myth of separate sovereigns, the federal government has ample leeway to force particularly disfavored defendants to run the gauntlet a second time through imaginative use of conspiracy concepts and particularly the RICO[a] statute. For example, consider what

a. The Racketeer Influenced and Corrupt Organizations Act, 18 U.S.C.A. § 1962,   punishes anyone who participates in the affairs of an "enterprise" through a "pat-

happened to James Licavoli, the reputed boss of organized crime in Cleveland. Licavoli was tried in state court for paying a professional killer to assassinate a business rival. The state jury convicted some defendants who were directly involved in the killing, but acquitted Licavoli and other persons who were accused of directing the crime from a distance. Federal prosecutors promptly charged the entire group of defendants with "conspiring to participate in the affairs of an enterprise through a pattern of racketeering activity." The enterprise was organized crime in Cleveland, and the two predicate offenses establishing a pattern of racketeering activity were the murder of the rival and the conspiracy to murder him. Despite the fact that the federal charge was in substance identical to the charge on which Licavoli was acquitted upon in state court, the federal Court of Appeals had little difficulty in disposing of the Double Jeopardy claim without invoking the dual sovereignty principle. Racketeering as defined in the RICO statute, the court explained patiently, is not at all the same crime as murder. United States v. Licavoli, 725 F.2d 1040 (6th Cir.1984).

A prosecutor can also obtain several chances for conviction, or for an adequate penalty, by dividing a single criminal episode into its component parts. Consider, for example, the vindictive tactics employed in Ciucci v. Illinois, 356 U.S. 571 (1958). The state charged Ciucci in four separate indictments with murdering his wife and three children in a single burst of murderous fury. In two successive trials, Ciucci was convicted of murdering his wife and one child, but the jury fixed the penalty at 20 years and 45 years imprisonment, respectively. Newspaper reports which were brought to the attention of the Supreme Court but which were not part of the official record indicated that the prosecutor had acknowledged that he intended to continue separate prosecutions until he obtained a death sentence. He succeeded in the third trial. The Supreme Court affirmed the conviction and death sentence in the third trial in a 5–4 per curiam opinion, but two members of the majority indicated that "the matters set forth in the aforementioned newspaper articles might, if established, require a ruling that fundamental unfairness existed here." State statutes or procedural rules would in many cases require the prosecutor to join in a single trial all criminal charges growing out of the same episode, but the Double Jeopardy Clause as construed by the Supreme Court does not require such joinder.

Brown v. Ohio, 432 U.S. 161 (1977) stated the uncontroversial principle that a defendant who has been convicted of one crime cannot subsequently be convicted of a lesser included offense, nor of a greater offense which includes the crime for which he was previously convicted. Thus, a defendant who is convicted of felony murder could not subsequently be tried for the robbery which supplied the underlying felony in the felony murder trial. Harris v. Oklahoma, 433 U.S. 682 (1977). Similarly, a defendant who was convicted and fined $15.00 for failing to reduce speed to avoid an accident could not subsequently be prosecuted for homicide in the deaths of two children killed in that accident if the state had to rely on his failure to reduce speed to prove the vehicular homicide charge. Illinois v. Vitale, 447 U.S. 410 (1980). Even if the Double Jeopardy Clause were not applicable, state statutes would in many jurisdictions prevent the prosecution from proceeding on a vehicular homicide charge after the defendant had pleaded

tern of racketeering activity," which must involve two or more "predicate offenses."

guilty to a minor driving offense based on the same conduct. Such situations occasionally develop when the policeman who files the traffic charge fails to coordinate his activities with the prosecutor who files the vehicular homicide charge. A reckless driver who has killed several people, and who discovers that he is charged with misdemeanor traffic offenses, is well advised to hurry into court and enter an immediate guilty plea before the prosecutor realizes what is going on.

The majority opinion in *Brown v. Ohio* stated that "The Double Jeopardy Clause is not such a fragile guaranty that prosecutors can avoid its limitations by the simple expedient of dividing a single crime into a series of temporal or spatial units." On other occasions, however, the Court has allowed highly technical exceptions to the principle that the prosecution may not pursue a defendant for the greater offense after he has been convicted of the lesser included offense. For example, the defendant in Garrett v. United States, 471 U.S. 773 (1985), pleaded guilty to a federal charge of importing marijuana off the coast of Washington. Subsequently, federal prosecutors obtained an indictment in a Florida federal court charging him with engaging in a "continuing criminal enterprise," which required proof of three or more successive similar violations within a specified period of time. One of the three included offenses was the Washington charge, and the defendant claimed that his conviction for engaging in a continuing criminal enterprise violated the holding in *Brown v. Ohio*, because the Washington importation charge was a lesser included offense. The Supreme Court affirmed the conviction for operating a continuing criminal enterprise, but without a majority opinion.

Consider now some Double Jeopardy doctrines which are rarely called into question, but which do not necessarily rest upon airtight logic:

1. A defendant who has obtained a reversal on appeal may be tried again (unless the reversal was for insufficiency of the evidence). Why is it so obvious that the successful appellant should be forced to run the gauntlet a second time, and endure all the continuing anxieties and expense of defending against criminal charges at a second trial? After all, the error at the first trial was the fault either of the prosecutor or of the judge, both of whom are officials of the Government. Why is it too much to ask of the Government that it conduct the trial properly the first time? Conceivably, our courts could follow the example of appellate courts in England, which ordinarily "quash" the conviction when an appeal is successful, allowing the defendant to go free. Of course, a legal system which has to set the defendant free when it acknowledges that prejudicial error occurred at the trial is correspondingly conservative about expanding the grounds for appeal.[a]

2. When the jury fails to agree on a verdict the defendant may be retried, even if the vote was 11–1 for acquittal. Again, why is this so obvious? If the prosecution cannot convince 12 jurors beyond a reasonable doubt that the defendant is guilty, then why should it have a second chance with another 12? As in the preceding example, barring a second trial would

---

a. For an amusingly written and insightful critique of the English practice, see Spencer, "Criminal Law and Criminal appeals: The Tail that Wags the Dog," 1982 Crim.L.Rev. 260. Spencer argues that the practice of quashing convictions without provision for retrial has led the appellate courts to "condone errors of law which should not be condoned."

probably have additional consequences, perhaps in creating pressure to dispense with the requirement of unanimity for conviction. It is easy to imagine a system in which the votes of 9 or 10 jurors would be sufficient for conviction, but in which the prosecutor would have only one chance to get the required majority.

3. The defendant who has been found not guilty by the judge or jury can never be tried again on the same charges, even if the verdict was based on outrageous legal error (such as the capricious exclusion of all the prosecutor's evidence), or even if it was downright corrupt. But why is *this* rule either logically required or desirable? As the revered Justice Cardozo once wrote in a Supreme Court majority opinion, it "is not cruelty at all, or even vexation in any immoderate degree," for a state statute to provide that criminal proceedings shall continue "until there shall be a trial free from the corrosion of substantial legal error." Palko v. Connecticut, 302 U.S. 319, 328 (1937). If we accepted that logic, we could say that the jeopardy was continuing rather than "double" following reversal of a defense verdict on appeal. History would not necessarily bar such an interpretation, because neither the prosecution nor the defense had a right to appeal in criminal cases at the time of the adoption of the Constitution.

4. The authorities all agree that the defendant has a right to complete his trial before the first jury. In particular, the prosecutor who sees that the case is going badly may not obtain a mistrial in order to shore up the case and try again before another 12 jurors. (In many jurisdictions the plaintiff in a civil case is sometimes allowed to take a "voluntary nonsuit" for just this purpose, and so a contrary rule is not exactly unthinkable.) The orthodox doctrine, therefore, is that a mistrial without the defendant's consent bars a retrial unless there was a "manifest necessity" for it, and the cases reprinted or summarized on pages 887–889, supra, illustrate the differing interpretations that have been given to the central requirements of manifest necessity and consent. Of particular interest is the decision in *United States v. Jorn*, discussed in the *Somerville* opinion at p. 888, where a hasty and unnecessary mistrial was declared by an eccentric federal judge who was carrying on a feud with the prosecutors. The upshot was that the defendant received an enormous windfall, and the prosecution bore the cost of the trial judge's capriciousness. Such situations occur only very rarely, because trial judges are usually careful to obtain the consent of the defendant or to make a record on manifest necessity before declaring a mistrial.

In summary, the field of Double Jeopardy law is characterized by noble abstract principles, evasion of those same principles by technical manipulation, and unquestioning acceptance of particular rules which could easily be made to seem doubtful if anyone seriously wished to do so.

*

0–314–24119–1